Multinational Business Finance

Sixteenth Edition

DAVID K. EITEMAN
University of California, Los Angeles

ARTHUR I. STONEHILL
Oregon State University and University of Hawaii at Manoa

MICHAEL H. MOFFETT
Thunderbird School of Global Management at Arizona State University

Please contact **https://support.pearson.com/getsupport/s/** with any queries to this content.
Cover Image by franckreporter/Getty images.

Library of Congress Cataloging-in-Publication Data
Names: Eiteman, David K., author. | Stonehill, Arthur I., author. | Moffett, Michael H., author.
Title: Multinational business finance / David K. Eiteman, University of California, Los Angeles, Arthur I. Stonehill, Oregon State University and University of Hawaii at Manoa, Michael H. Moffett, Thunderbird School of Global Management at Arizona State University.
Description: 16th Edition. | New York, NY : Pearson, 2022. | Revised edition of the authors's Multinational business finance, [2019] | Includes bibliographical references and index. |
Identifiers: LCCN 2021046409 (print) | LCCN 2021046410 (ebook) | ISBN 9780137496013 (hardback) | ISBN 9780137669202 (ebook)
Subjects: LCSH: International business enterprises—Finance.
Classification: LCC HG4027.5 .E36 2022 (print) | LCC HG4027.5 (ebook) | DDC 658.15/99—dc23/eng/20111105
LC record available at https://lccn.loc.gov/2021046409
LC ebook record available at https://lccn.loc.gov/2021046410

1 2022

ISBN 10: 0-13-749601-X
ISBN 13: 978-0-13-749601-3

For Art

Pearson's Commitment to Diversity, Equity, and Inclusion

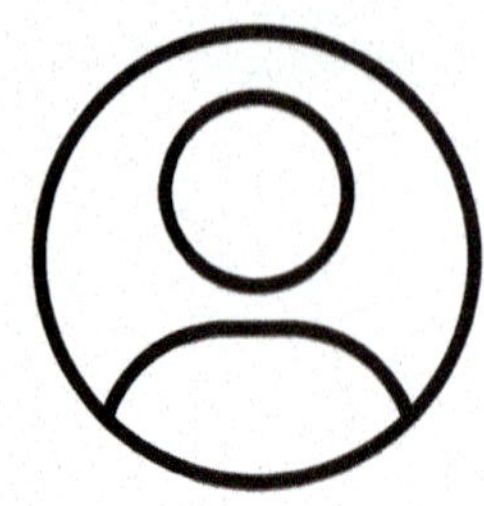

Pearson is dedicated to creating bias-free content that reflects the diversity, depth, and breadth of all learners' lived experiences.

We embrace the many dimensions of diversity, including but not limited to race, ethnicity, gender, sex, sexual orientation, socioeconomic status, ability, age, and religious or political beliefs.

Education is a powerful force for equity and change in our world. It has the potential to deliver opportunities that improve lives and enable economic mobility. As we work with authors to create content for every product and service, we acknowledge our responsibility to demonstrate inclusivity and incorporate diverse scholarship so that everyone can achieve their potential through learning. As the world's leading learning company, we have a duty to help drive change and live up to our purpose to help more people create a better life for themselves and to create a better world.

Our ambition is to purposefully contribute to a world where:

- Everyone has an equitable and lifelong opportunity to succeed through learning.
- Our educational content accurately reflects the histories and lived experiences of the learners we serve.
- Our educational products and services are inclusive and represent the rich diversity of learners.
- Our educational content prompts deeper discussions with students and motivates them to expand their own learning (and worldview).

Accessibility

We are also committed to providing products that are fully accessible to all learners. As per Pearson's guidelines for accessible educational Web media, we test and retest the capabilities of our products against the highest standards for every release, following the WCAG guidelines in developing new products for copyright year 2022 and beyond.

You can learn more about Pearson's commitment to accessibility at **https://www.pearson.com/us/accessibility.html**

Contact Us

While we work hard to present unbiased, fully accessible content, we want to hear from you about any concerns or needs with this Pearson product so that we can investigate and address them.

Please contact us with concerns about any potential bias at **https://www.pearson.com/report-bias.html**

For accessibility-related issues, such as using assistive technology with Pearson products, alternative text requests, or accessibility documentation, email the Pearson Disability Support team at **disability.support@pearson.com**

Preface

New to This Edition

Our continuing challenge is to strike a balance between being one of the very first textbooks in this field (and therefore in many ways defining the field) and introducing the many new concepts and components in global business today, from digital currencies to global fintech. We have hopefully found some balance between what is valued by continuing adopters and the valued insights of selected reviewers—the *innovator's dilemma*. Surveys of adopters were extremely useful in this revision, and a number of specific recommendations were included.

- **Corporate Governance, Activists, and Stakeholder Capitalism.** Chapter 4 on corporate governance, including elements of ownership, financial objectives, and the growing role of activist investors, has been revised and expanded. Of special note is the growth of stakeholder capitalism and its multiple objective framework as compared to stockholder wealth maximization.
- **The Impossible Trinity.** A core international financial principle, the *Impossible Trinity*'s use as a unifying theoretical link across multiple subjects—whether it be Iceland's financial crisis or choices made by the European Union on capital flows—is increasingly leveraged.
- **The Foreign Exchange Market and Digital Trade.** New material in this edition explores in depth how the changing structure of the global foreign exchange market—trading, communication, and settlement—is posing challenges for private players and public regulators and overseers.
- **Currency Manipulation.** This is a politically charged topic between the U.S. and China, and we explore in depth the motivations, methods, and metrics associated with currency manipulation. Included is a new mini-case that seeks to determine whether China is or is not a currency manipulator.
- **Emerging Market Regimes.** The sixteenth edition offers new insights into the currency and capital regime choices of many emerging market countries; many recognizing that they are trade-dependent economies in search of currency stability in lieu of attracting other capital account elements such as foreign direct investment.
- **International Taxation.** Integrally linked to a world of digital commerce, multinational tax management continues to rise in its significance in multinational financial management. We have expanded our coverage of this critical determinant of global finance, with emphasis on the constantly changing U.S. tax rates and rules.
- **Political Risk and Financial Losses.** The chapter on foreign direct investment and political risk has been revised to reflect the growing use of restrictions on convertibility, transferability, and the possibility of repudiation or expropriation.

Solving Teaching and Learning Challenges

Multinational Business Finance is the financial management of multinational enterprises (MNEs)—*multinational financial management*. MNEs are firms and organizations of all kinds and sizes—for-profit companies, family-owned businesses, sovereign states, and nongovernmental organizations (NGOs), among others—that have operations in more than one country and conduct their activities through a multitude of structures and contracts from wholly owned foreign subsidiaries to joint ventures with local or global partners to host governments.

Moreover, global business and finance, all the way down to the trading of currencies, has been revolutionized by digital platforms from electronic trading to the coming introduction of digital currencies, all adding to the complexity of international business.

Multinational Business Finance, Sixteenth Edition, is aimed at university-level courses in international financial management, international business finance, international finance, and similar titles. It can be used either at the graduate level or in executive education and corporate learning courses.

A prerequisite course or experience in corporate finance or financial management would be ideal. However, we review the basic finance concepts before we extend them to the multinational case. We also review the basic concepts of international economics and international business.

Over many years and many editions, as we ourselves have used the book in courses from Hyderabad to Helsinki to Honolulu, we have observed an ever-widening audience for this book. We continue to try to service this greater global audience with multicountry companies, markets, and challenges, whether in theoretical applications, practice boxes, mini-cases, or end-of-chapter problems.

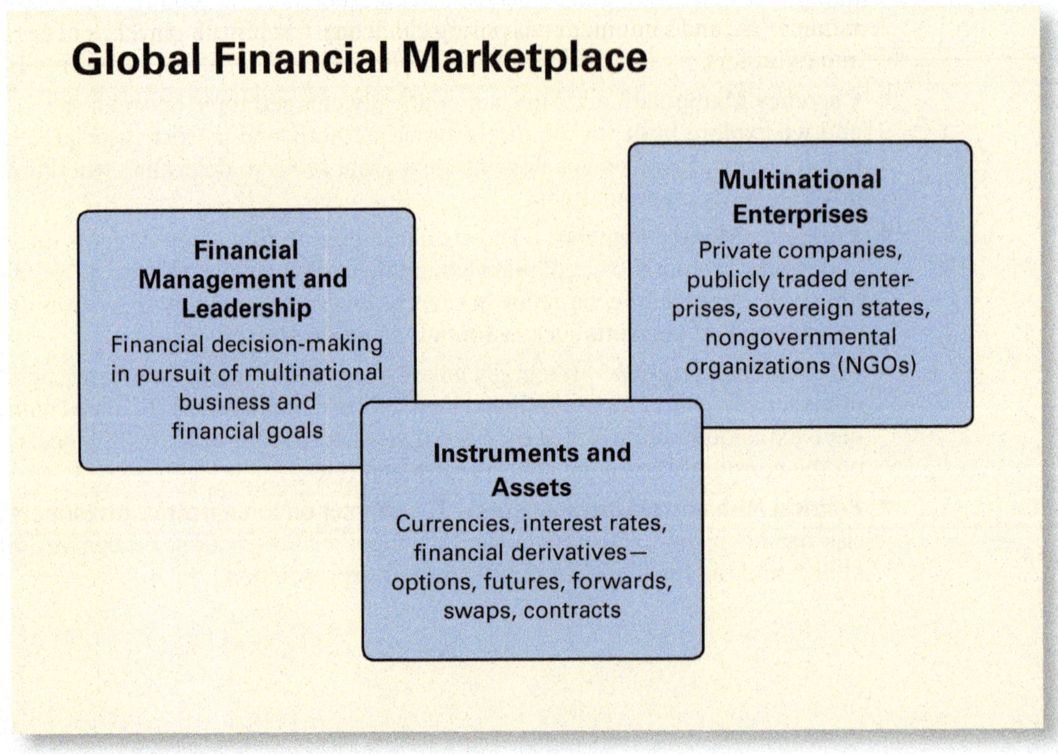

EXHIBIT 5.4 **The Foreign Exchange Market Today**

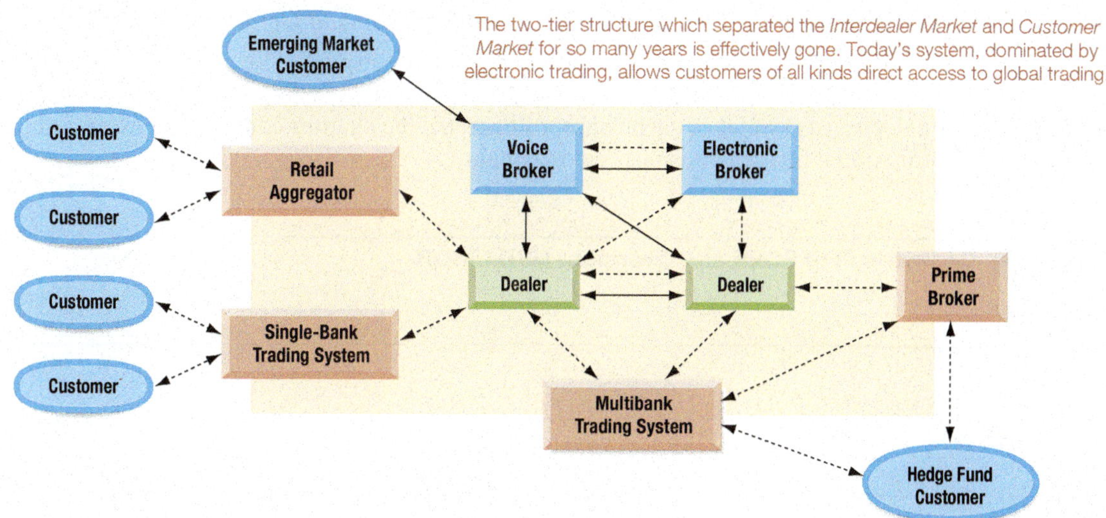

Constructed by authors based on a number of sources including "Foreign Exchange Market Structure, Players and Evolution," Michael R. King, Carol Osler and Dagfinn Rime, Norges Bank, Working Paper, Research Department, 2011, 10, p. 21, and "The anatomy of the global FX market through the lens of the 2013 Triennial Survey," by Dagfinn Rime and Andreas Schrimpf, *BIS Quarterly Review*, December 2013.

Organization

Multinational Business Finance has been redesigned and restructured for tightness—critical elements of the field but in a much shorter delivery framework. This has been accomplished by integrating a number of previous topics along financial management threads. The book is in five parts, the parts unified by the common thread of the globalization process by which a firm moves from a domestic to a multinational business orientation.

- Part 1 introduces the global financial environment.
- Part 2 explains foreign exchange theory and markets.
- Part 3 explores foreign exchange rate exposure.
- Part 4 details the financing of the global firm.
- Part 5 analyzes international investment decisions.

Pedagogical Tools

To make the book as comprehensible as possible, we use a large number of proven pedagogical tools. Again, our efforts have been informed by the detailed reviews and suggestions of a panel of professors who are recognized individually for excellence in the field of international finance, particularly at the undergraduate level. Among these pedagogical tools are the following:

- A student-friendly writing style combined with a structured presentation of material, beginning with *learning objectives* for each chapter and ending with a summarization of how those learning objectives were realized.

- A wealth of *illustrations and exhibits* to provide a visual parallel to the concepts and content presented.
- A running case on a hypothetical U.S.-based firm, *Ganado Corporation*, provides a cohesive framework for the multifaceted globalization process and is reinforced in several end-of-chapter problems.
- A *mini-case* at the end of each chapter illustrates the chapter content and extends it to the multinational financial business environment.

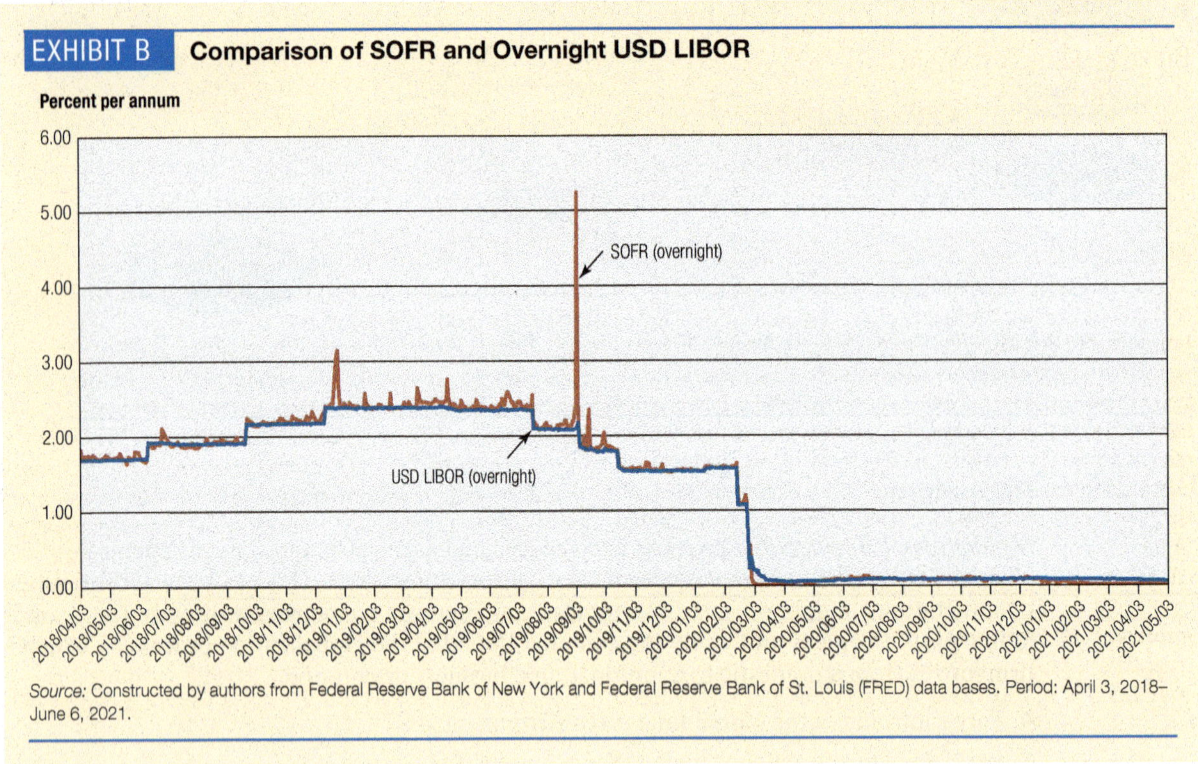

EXHIBIT B Comparison of SOFR and Overnight USD LIBOR

Source: Constructed by authors from Federal Reserve Bank of New York and Federal Reserve Bank of St. Louis (FRED) data bases. Period: April 3, 2018–June 6, 2021.

The continuing popularity of our mini-cases has prompted us to introduce 11 new mini-cases in the sixteenth edition. The new topics, among others, include the following:

- **Global fintech.** Global fintech's continuing role in opening the emerging world to global finance.
- **Digital currencies.** The rise of digital currencies like the Chinese eYuan.
- **Toshiba's corporate governance challenges.**
- **International remittances.** The role international remittances may play in alleviating global income inequality and opportunity.
- **Replacing LIBOR.** The rationale and complexity of replacing the global financial system's interest rate centerpiece—LIBOR.
- **Currency volatility.** The rise and fall of currency volatility during the year of COVID.
- **Google tax.** The U.S. development of what many term "the Google tax."
- **Saudi Aramco.** The initial public offering of the world's most profitable company, Saudi Aramco.

- **Hostile acquisitions.** A detailed exploration of one of the world's most hostile international acquisitions, Mittal's acquisition of Arcelor.
- *Global Finance in Practice* boxes in every chapter highlight how real firms and real managers deal with the never-ending complexity of executing global business deals in a changing marketplace, from the mundane accounts payable to the exceptional expropriation. These applications extend the concepts without adding to the length of the text itself.

GLOBAL FINANCE IN PRACTICE **13.1**

Brexit and the Cost of Capital

The decision for the United Kingdom to leave the European Union is resulting in more and more companies having a higher cost of capital on both sides of the Channel. A restructuring of the banking sectors in both regions involves direct costs as well as more segmented markets, all at a time when global interest rates—dollar, pound, and euro—are expected to start rising as the post-COVID stimulus programs fall further and further into the past.

Impacts on Banks. Banks in the UK are already incurring sizeable restructuring costs. A number of London banks have been moving quickly to move large portions of their operations and jobs to the Continent in an effort to retain clients and market share. London banks are estimating that restructuring costs alone may range between $200 million and $400 million. The costs of capital for banks themselves are expected to rise at least 4%, and many are looking to increase their capital bases by more than 30% as they establish European banks to retain Continental clients.

Impacts on Borrowers. One of the unintended results is a multitude of banks are reducing their lines of credit and increasing their fees to many of the small to medium-sized enterprises. Companies with annual revenue of up to €10 million are defined as *small businesses*, and firms with revenue between €10 and €50 million are *medium-sized* according to the European Union. This segment of borrowers is particularly sensitive to these changes as many of these firms use only one bank for the majority of their financial services. Without alternative banks, offering either alternative services or competitive rates, they are starting to feel the impacts of reduced services and increased costs. As a result of rising bank fees and fewer alternatives, borrowers have experienced rising costs of debt.

How this will ultimately impact business activity is hard to say, but early signs from these segments are not encouraging. Some experts, including Professor Aswath Damodaran of New York University's Stern School of Business, have been encouraging companies to focus on the three drivers of business valuation—cash flows, growth rates, and discount rates—and not fall victim to pessimism. He has characterized Brexit as a "garden variety crisis" that most businesses should endure. A number of firms, however, have cut back on new investment projects. Rising capital costs make fewer prospective investments financially viable. A number of borrowers have noted that their firms will intentionally now work to increase their cash balances—a form of precautionary source of funds—as they fear reduced access to affordable debt.

- A multitude of end-of-chapter questions and problems assess the students' understanding of the course material. All end-of-chapter problems are solved using spreadsheet solutions. Selected end-of-chapter problem answers are included at the back of this book.
- Numerous mathematical derivations, such as parity conditions, foreign currency option pricing, and complex option products, are placed in appendices. This allows selective use as the student or faculty member feels appropriate.

Acknowledgments

The authors are very thankful for the many detailed reviews of previous editions and suggestions from a number of colleagues.

Otto Adleberger
Essen University, Germany

Alan Alford
Northeastern University

Stephen Archer
Willamette University

Bala Arshanapalli
Indiana University Northwest

Hossein G. Askari
George Washington University

Robert T. Aubey
University of Wisconsin, Madison

David Babbel
University of Pennsylvania

James Baker
Kent State University

Morten Balling
Arhus School of Business, Denmark

Arindam Bandopadhyaya
University of Massachusetts, Boston

Ari Beenhakker
University of South Florida

Carl Beidleman
Lehigh University

Robert Boatler
Texas Christian University

Gordon M. Bodnar
Johns Hopkins University

Nancy Bord
University of Hartford

Finbarr Bradley
University of Dublin, Ireland

Tom Brewer
Georgetown University

Michael Brooke
University of Manchester, England

Robert Carlson
Assumption University, Thailand

Kam C. Chan
University of Dayton

Chun Chang
University of Minnesota

Sam Chee
Boston University Metropolitan College

Kevin Cheng
New York University

It-Keong Chew
University of Kentucky

Frederick D. S. Choi
New York University

Jay Choi
Temple University

Nikolai Chuvakhin
Pepperdine University

Mark Ciechon
University of California, Los Angeles

J. Markham Collins
University of Tulsa

Alan N. Cook
Baylor University

Kerry Cooper
Texas A&M University

Robert Cornu
Cranfield School of Management, UK

Roy Crum
University of Florida

Steven Dawson
University of Hawai'i at Mānoa

David Distad
University of California, Berkeley

Gunter Dufey
University of Michigan, Ann Arbor

Mark Eaker
Duke University

Rodney Eldridge
George Washington University

Imad A. Elhah
University of Louisville

Vihang Errunza
McGill University

Cheol S. Eun
Georgia Tech University

Mara Faccio
University of Notre Dame

Larry Fauver
University of Tennessee

Laura Field
University of Delaware

Joseph Finnerty
University of Illinois, Urbana-Champaign

William R. Folks, Jr.
University of South Carolina

Jennifer Foo
Stetson University

Lewis Freitas
University of Hawai'i at Mānoa

Anne Fremault
Boston University

Michael Fuerst
University of Miami

Fariborg Ghadar
George Washington University

Ian Giddy
New York University
Martin Glaum
Justus-Lievig-Universitat Giessen, Germany
John Gonzales
University of San Francisco
Joe Greco
Cal State Fullerton
Deborah Gregory
University of Georgia
Robert Grosse
Thunderbird
Christine Hekman
Georgia Tech University
Steven Heston
University of Maryland
James Hodder
University of Wisconsin, Madison
Alfred Hofflander
University of California, Los Angeles
Delroy M. Hunter
University of Southern Florida
Janice Jadlow
Oklahoma State University
Veikko Jaaskelainen
Helsinki School of Economics and Business Administration
Benjamas Jirasakuldech
University of the Pacific
Ronald A. Johnson
Northeastern University
Fred Kaen
University of New Hampshire
John Kallianiotis
University of Scranton
Charles Kane
Boston College
Robert Kemp
University of Virginia
W. Carl Kester
Harvard Business School
Jaemin Kim
San Diego State University
Seung Kim
St. Louis University
Yong Kim
University of Cincinnati
Yong-Cheol Kim
University of Wisconsin, Milwaukee
Gordon Klein
University of California, Los Angeles
Steven Kobrin
University of Pennsylvania
Paul Korsvold
Norwegian School of Management
Chris Korth
University of South Carolina
Chuck C. Y. Kwok
University of South Carolina
John P. Lajaunie
Nicholls State University
Sarah Lane
Boston University
Martin Laurence
William Patterson College
Eric Y. Lee
Fairleigh Dickinson University
Yen-Sheng Lee
Bellevue University
Donald Lessard
Massachusetts Institute of Technology
Ming Li
San Francisco State University
Sheen Liu
Washington State University
Arvind Mahajan
Texas A&M University
Rita Maldonado-Baer
New York University
Anthony Matias
Palm Beach Atlantic College
Charles Maxwell
Murray State University
Sam McCord
Auburn University
Jeanette Medewitz
University of Nebraska, Omaha
Robert Mefford
University of San Francisco
Paritash Mehta
Temple University
Antonio Mello
University of Wisconsin, Madison
Eloy Mestre
American University
Kenneth Moon
Suffolk University
Myra Moore
Terry College of Business, University of Georgia
Gregory Noronha
Arizona State University
Edmund Outslay
Michigan State University
Lars Oxelheim
Lund University, Sweden
Jacob Park
Green Mountain College
Yoon Shik Park
George Washington University
Richard L. Patterson
Indiana University, Bloomington
John Petersen
George Mason University
Harvey Poniachek
New York University

Yash Puri
University of Massachusetts, Lowell

Sergiy Rakhmayil
Ryerson University, Canada

R. Ravichandrarn
University of Colorado, Boulder

Scheherazade Rehman
George Washington University

Jeff Rosenlog
Emory University

David Rubinstein
University of Houston

Alan Rugman
Oxford University, UK

R. J. Rummel
University of Hawai'i at Mānoa

Sanjiv Sabherwal
University of Texas at Arlington

Mehdi Salehizadeh
San Diego State University

Michael Salt
San Jose State University

Mukunthan Santhanakrishnan
Southern Methodist University

Roland Schmidt
Erasmus University, the Netherlands

Lemma Senbet
University of Maryland

Alan Shapiro
University of Southern California

Hany Shawky
State University of New York, Albany

Hamid Shomali
Golden Gate University

Vijay Singal
Virginia Tech University

Sheryl Winston Smith
University of Minnesota

Luc Soenen
California Polytechnic State University

Marjorie Stanley
Texas Christian University

Joseph Stokes
University of Massachusetts–Amherst

Jahangir Sultan
Bentley College

Lawrence Tai
Loyola Marymount University

Kishore Tandon
CUNY—Bernard Baruch College

Russell Taussig
University of Hawai'i at Mānoa

Lee Tavis
University of Notre Dame

Sean Toohey
University of Western Sydney, Australia

Norman Toy
Columbia University

Niranjan Tripathy
University of North Texas

Joseph Ueng
University of St. Thomas

Gwinyai Utete
Auburn University

Tzveta Vateva
Kent State University

Rahul Verma
University of Houston-Downtown

Harald Vestergaard
Copenhagen Business School

K. G. Viswanathan
Hofstra University

Joseph D. Vu
University of Illinois, Chicago

Mahmoud Wahab
University of Hartford

Masahiro Watanabe
Rice University

Michael Williams
University of Texas at Austin

Brent Wilson
Brigham Young University

Bob Wood
Tennessee Technological University

J. Jimmy Yang
Oregon State University

Alexander Zamperion
Bentley College

Emilio Zarruk
Florida Atlantic University

Tom Zwirlein
University of Colorado, Colorado Springs

Industry (present or former affiliation)

Paul Adaire
Philadelphia Stock Exchange

Barbara Block
Tektronix, Inc.

Holly Bowman
Bankers Trust

Payson Cha
HKR International, Hong Kong

John A. Deuchler
Private Export Funding Corporation

Kåre Dullum
Gudme Raaschou Investment Bank, Denmark

Steven Ford
Hewlett Packard

David Heenan
Campbell Estate, Hawaii

Sharyn H. Hess
Foreign Credit Insurance Association

Aage Jacobsen
Gudme Raaschou Investment Bank, Denmark
Ira G. Kawaller
Chicago Mercantile Exchange
Kenneth Knox
Tektronix, Inc.
Arthur J. Obesler
Eximbank
I. Barry Thompson
Continental Bank
Gerald T. West
Overseas Private Investment Corporation
Willem Winter
First Interstate Bank of Oregon

A note of thanks is also extended to our accuracy reviewer, Michael Casey. We would like to thank all those with Pearson Education who have worked so diligently on this edition: Emily Biberger, Meredith Gertz, Miguel Leonarte, and Melissa Honig. We are also grateful to Gina Linko, our Project Manager at Integra.

We thank our wives, Megan and Kari, for their patience while we were preparing *Multinational Business Finance*.

Pacific Palisades, California D.K.E.
Honolulu, Hawaii A.I.S.
Glendale, Arizona M.H.M.

About the Authors

David K. Eiteman. David K. Eiteman is Professor Emeritus of Finance at the John E. Anderson Graduate School of Management at UCLA. He has also held teaching or research appointments at the Hong Kong University of Science & Technology, Showa Academy of Music (Japan), the National University of Singapore, Dalian University (China), the Helsinki School of Economics and Business Administration (Finland), University of Hawai'i at Mānoa, University of Bradford (U.K.), Cranfield School of Management (UK), and IDEA (Argentina). He is a former president of the International Trade and Finance Association, Society for Economics and Management in China, and Western Finance Association.

Professor Eiteman received a BBA (Business Administration) from the University of Michigan, Ann Arbor (1952); MA (Economics) from the University of California, Berkeley (1956); and a PhD (Finance) from Northwestern University (1959).

He has authored or coauthored four books and twenty-nine other publications. His articles have appeared in *The Journal of Finance, The International Trade Journal, Financial Analysts Journal, Journal of World Business, Management International, Business Horizons, MSU Business Topics, Public Utilities Fortnightly*, and others.

Arthur I. Stonehill. Arthur I. Stonehill was a Professor of Finance and International Business, Emeritus, at Oregon State University, where he taught for twenty-four years (1966–1990). During 1991–1997 he held a split appointment at the University of Hawai'i at Mānoa and Copenhagen Business School. From 1997 to 2001 he continued as a Visiting Professor at the University of Hawai'i at Mānoa. He has also held teaching or research appointments at the University of California, Berkeley; Cranfield School of Management (U.K.); and the North European Management Institute (Norway). He was a former president of the Academy of International Business and was a western director of the Financial Management Association.

Professor Stonehill received a BA (History) from Yale University (1953); an MBA from Harvard Business School (1957); and a PhD in Business Administration from the University of California, Berkeley (1965). He was awarded honorary doctorates from the Aarhus School of Business (Denmark, 1989), the Copenhagen Business School (Denmark, 1992), and Lund University (Sweden, 1998).

He authored or coauthored nine books and twenty-five other publications. His articles appeared in *Financial Management, Journal of International Business Studies, California Management Review, Journal of Financial and Quantitative Analysis, Journal of International Financial Management and Accounting, International Business Review, European Management Journal, The Investment Analyst* (U.K.), *Nationaløkonomisk Tidskrift* (Denmark), *Sosialøkonomen* (Norway), *Journal of Financial Education*, and others.

Michael H. Moffett. Michael H. Moffett is Continental Grain Professor in Finance at the Thunderbird School of Global Management at Arizona State University, where he has been since 1994. He also has held teaching or research appointments at Oregon State University (1985–1993); the University of Michigan, Ann Arbor (1991–1993); the Brookings Institution, Washington, D.C.; the University of Hawai'i at Mānoa; the Aarhus School of Business (Denmark); the Helsinki School of Economics and Business Administration (Finland), the International Centre for Public Enterprises (Yugoslavia); and the University of Colorado, Boulder.

Professor Moffett received a BA (Economics) from the University of Texas at Austin (1977), an MS (Resource Economics) from Colorado State University (1979), an MA (Economics) from the University of Colorado, Boulder (1983), and PhD (Economics) from the University of Colorado, Boulder (1985).

He has authored, coauthored, or contributed to a number of books, articles, case studies, and other publications. He has coauthored two books with Art Stonehill and David Eiteman, *Fundamentals of Multinational Finance*, and this book, *Multinational Business Finance*. His articles have appeared in the *Journal of Financial and Quantitative Analysis, Journal of Applied Corporate Finance, Journal of International Money and Finance, Journal of International Financial Management and Accounting, Contemporary Policy Issues, Brookings Discussion Papers in International Economics*, and others. He has contributed to a number of collected works including the *Handbook of Modern Finance*, the *International Accounting and Finance Handbook*, and the *Encyclopedia of International Business*. He is also coauthor of two books in multinational business with Michael Czinkota and Ilkka Ronkainen, *International Business* (7th edition) and *Global Business* (4th edition), and *The Global Oil and Gas Industry: Strategy, Finance, and Management*, with Andrew Inkpen.

Brief Contents

Contents

PART 1

Global Financial Environment

1

Multinational Financial Management: Opportunities and Challenges

The objects of a financier are, then, to secure an ample revenue; to impose it with judgment and equality; to employ it economically; and, when necessity obliges him to make use of credit, to secure its foundations in that instance, and forever, by the clearness and candor of his proceedings, the exactness of his calculations, and the solidity of his funds.

—Edmund Burke, *Reflections on the Revolution in France*, 1790, p. 467.

LEARNING OBJECTIVES

1.1 Explore the global financial marketplace—players and playing field

1.2 Consider how the theory of comparative advantage applies to multinational business

1.3 Examine how international financial management differs from domestic financial management

1.4 Discover the steps and stages of the globalization process

The subject of this book is the financial management of *multinational enterprises* (MNEs)—*multinational financial management*. MNEs are firms—both for-profit companies and not-for-profit organizations—that have operations in more than one country and conduct their business through branches, foreign subsidiaries, or joint ventures with host country firms.

It is a brave new world, a new world in which digital startups may become multinational enterprises in hours, where the number of publicly traded companies on earth is shrinking, where the most challenging competitors are arising from emerging markets, and where more and more value is being created by "idea firms." The global marketplace is seeing change—radical, disruptive, rapid, whatever terminology you prefer—from the growing role of the Chinese currency, the *yuan*; the continuing recuperative efforts to economies following the global pandemic; or the possible sea change likely to come from the introduction of digital currencies. In 2021 the world even saw the first country, El Salvador, adopt a cryptocurrency, Bitcoin, as legal tender. In the following chapters we will explore everything from how the international financial community is in the process of changing its global benchmark (LIBOR) of the past 50 years, to the changes in currency volatility during the global pandemic, to the entry of the world's most profitable company (Saudi Aramco) into the public security markets. Change is indeed the constant.

Multinational financial management requires managers and leaders all over the world to identify and navigate the prospective returns and risks of the global financial marketplace. These risks may all occur on the playing field of the global financial marketplace, but they are still a question of management—of navigating complexity in pursuit of the goals of the firm and all of its varied stakeholders.

This first chapter provides a brief overview of the global financial landscape including foreign currency markets and financial institutions—the ground rules and nomenclature of the game. We then explore the foundations of comparative advantage, those forces differentiating international from domestic finance. We conclude our introductory overview with the alternative paths firms may take in going global. The chapter concludes with a mini-case, *Global Fintech*, that examines how financial technology is changing all financial functions and services, how it offers the power to overcome barriers to access and inclusion across the globe, but also how its adoption faces many political and institutional barriers along the way.

1.1 The Global Financial Marketplace

Business—domestic, international, global—involves the interaction of individuals and individual organizations for the exchange of products, services, and capital across markets. The global *capital markets* and business marketplace is in many ways the field of play. This is the landscape upon which the daily activities of global business play out. Like all institutions created by humans, it is constantly changing, yet certain fundamental components rarely change. We begin by exploring the institutional and behavioral landscape of global business—specifically, the organizations and assets that make up the global financial marketplace.

Assets, Institutions, and Linkages

Exhibit 1.1 provides an overview of the global capital markets. One way to characterize the global financial marketplace is through its securities and institutions, all linked through the interbank market.

EXHIBIT 1.1 Global Capital Markets

The global capital market is a collection of institutions (central banks, commercial banks, investment banks, not-for-profit financial institutions like the IMF and World Bank) and securities (bonds, mortgages, derivatives, loans, etc.), which are all linked via a global network—the *Interbank Market*. This interbank market is the critical pipeline system for the movement of capital

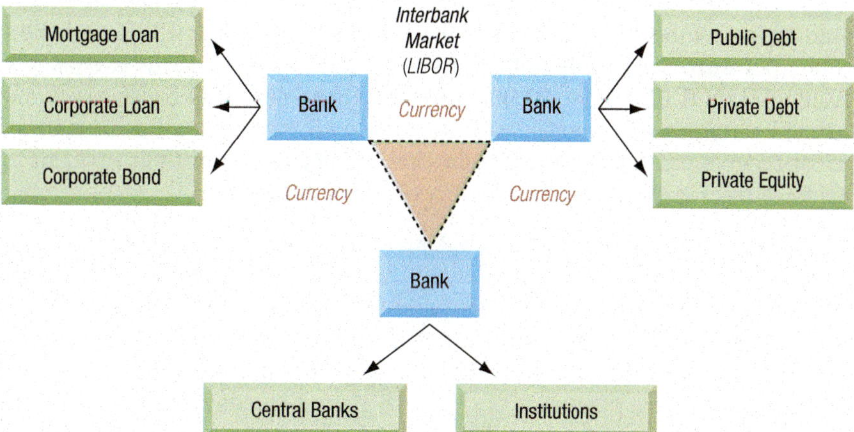

The exchange of securities, the movement of capital in the global financial system, must all take place through a vehicle—currency. The exchange of currencies is itself the largest of the financial markets. The interbank market, which must use currencies, bases its pricing through the single most widely quoted interest rate in the world—LIBOR (the London Interbank Offered Rate).

Securities. The securities—financial assets—at the heart of the global capital markets are the debt securities issued by highly industrialized country governments (e.g., U.S. Treasury Bonds, U.K. gilts). These low-risk or risk-free securities form the foundation for the creation, trading, and pricing of other financial securities like bank loans, corporate bonds, and equities (stock). In recent years, a number of additional securities—derivatives—have been created from existing securities, the value of which is based on market value changes of the underlying securities. The health and security of the global financial system rely on the quality of these securities.

Institutions. The institutions of global finance are the central banks, which create and control each country's money supply; the commercial banks, which take deposits and extend loans to businesses, both local and global; and the multitude of other financial institutions created to trade securities and derivatives. These institutions take many shapes and are subject to many different regulatory frameworks. The health and security of the global financial system rely on the stability of these financial institutions.

Linkages. The links between the financial institutions, the actual fluid or medium for exchange, are the interbank networks using currency. The ready exchange of currencies in the global marketplace is the first and foremost necessary element for the conduct of financial trading, and the global currency markets are the largest markets in the world. The exchange of currencies, and the subsequent exchange of all other securities globally via currency, is the international interbank market. This network, whose primary price is the London Interbank Offered Rate (LIBOR), is the core component of the global financial system. (In Chapter 8 we will examine the international effort to replace LIBOR and what it may mean for financial instruments and markets.)

The movement of capital across currencies and continents for the conduct of business has existed in many different forms for thousands of years. Yet it is only within the past 50 years that the velocity of these capital movements has increased to the pace of an electron in the digital marketplace. And it is only within the past 20 years that this market has been able to reach the most distant corners of the earth at any moment of the day. The result has been an explosion of innovative products and services—some for better and some for worse.

The Market for Currencies

The price of any one country's currency in terms of another country's currency is called a *foreign currency exchange rate*. For example, the exchange rate between the U.S. dollar (indicated by the symbols $ or USD) and the European euro (€ or EUR) may be stated as "1.1274 dollars per euro" or simply abbreviated as $1.1274 = €1.00. This exchange rate can also be stated as "USD1.1274 = EUR1.00" using the three-digit ISO codes. Since most international business activities require at least one of the two parties in a business transaction to either pay or receive payment in a currency that is different from their own, an understanding of exchange rates is critical to the conduct of global business.

Currency Symbols. As noted, USD and EUR are often used as the symbols for the U.S. dollar and the European Union's euro. These are the computer symbols (ISO-4217 codes) used today on the world's digital networks. The financial press, however, has a rich history of using a variety of different symbols, and a variety of different abbreviations are commonly used. For example, the British pound sterling may be indicated by £ (the pound symbol), GBP (Great Britain pound), STG (British pound sterling), ST£ (pound sterling), or UKL or UK£ (United Kingdom pound). This book uses both the simpler common symbols—the $ (dollar), the € (euro), the ¥ (yen), the £ (pound)—and the three-letter ISO codes.

Exchange Rate Quotations and Terminology. Exhibit 1.2 lists currency exchange rates for June 19, 2021, as would be quoted in New York or London. Each exchange rate listed is for a specific country's currency against the U.S. dollar, the euro, and the British pound. The

EXHIBIT 1.2 Selected Global Currency Exchange Rates for June 18, 2021

Country	Currency	Symbol	Code	Currency to equal 1 Dollar	Currency to equal 1 Euro	Currency to equal 1 Pound
Argentina	nuevo peso	Ps	ARS	95.3800	113.1875	131.8533
Australia	dollar	A$	AUD	1.3342	1.5833	1.8444
Brazil	real	R$	BRL	5.0522	5.9949	6.9800
Canada	dollar	C$	CAD	1.2406	1.4722	1.7150
Chile	peso	$	CLP	743.68	882.53	1,028.06
China	yuan	¥	CNY	6.4500	7.6542	8.9165
Czech Republic	koruna	Kc	CZK	21.5280	25.5470	29.7600
Denmark	krone	Dkr	DKK	6.2649	7.4346	8.6606
Eurozone	euro	€	EUR	0.8424	1.0000	1.1645
Hong Kong	dollar	HK$	HKD	7.7643	9.2116	10.7295
Hungary	forint	Ft	HUF	299.730	355.760	414.240
India	rupee	Rs	INR	74.083	87.914	102.412
Indonesia	rupiah	Rp	IDR	14,495.25	17,052.88	19,865.09
Israel	shekel	Shk	ILS	3.2795	3.8889	4.5266
Japan	yen	¥	JPY	110.38	130.99	152.59
Kuwait	dinar	KD	KWD	0.2971	0.3524	0.4104
Malaysia	ringgit	RM	MYR	4.1370	4.9123	5.7190
Mexico	new peso	$	MXN	20.6905	24.5534	28.6025
Morocco	dirham	DH	MAD	8.7967	10.4350	12.1501
New Zealand	dollar	NZ$	NZD	1.4397	1.7095	1.9905
Norway	krone	NKr	NOK	8.6678	10.2861	11.9824
Pakistan	rupee	Rs	PKR	153.1770	181.7477	211.5997
Philippines	peso	?	PHP	47.8400	56.7228	66.0317
Peru	new sol	SI	PEN	3.7814	4.4856	5.2229
Poland	zloty	zl	PLN	3.8335	4.5519	5.3002
Russia	ruble	R	RUB	72.4350	86.0093	100.1470
Saudi Arabia	riyal	—	SAR	3.7117	4.4009	5.1231
Singapore	dollar	S$	SGD	1.3441	1.5960	1.8584
South Africa	rand	R	ZAR	14.2702	16.9344	19.7271
South Korea	won	W	KRW	1,134.93	1,347.12	1,568.35
Sweden	krona	SKr	SEK	8.6176	10.2310	11.9147
Switzerland	franc	Fr.	CHF	0.9217	1.0938	1.2742
Taiwan	dollar	T$	TWD	27.8020	33.0121	38.4390
Thailand	baht	B	THB	31.4700	37.3675	43.5100
Turkey	lira	YTL	TRY	8.7136	10.3465	12.0474
United Arab Emirates	dirham	—	AED	3.6726	4.3583	5.0770
United Kingdom	pound	£	GBP	0.7236	0.8582	1.0000
United States	dollar	$	USD	1.0000	1.1867	1.3824
Vietnam	dong	d	VND	22,450.00	26,618.45	30,986.89

Note that a number of different currencies use the same symbol. (For example, both China and Japan have traditionally used the ¥ symbol, yen or yuan, meaning "round" or "circle.") All quotes are mid rates and are drawn from the *Financial Times*.

rate listed is termed a "midrate" because it is the middle or average of the rates at which currency traders buy currency (*bid rate*) and sell currency (*offer rate*).

The U.S. dollar has been the focal point of currency trading since the 1940s. As a result, most of the world's currencies are quoted against the dollar—Mexican pesos per dollar, Brazilian real per dollar, Hong Kong dollars per dollar, etc. They are also frequently quoted against other major world currencies like the euro and pound. For example, the Japanese yen is commonly quoted against the dollar, euro, and pound, as ¥110.38 = $1.00, ¥130.99 = €1.00, and ¥152.59 = £1.00, as illustrated in Exhibit 1.2.

Quotation Conventions. Several of the world's major currency exchange rates follow a specific quotation convention that is the result of tradition and history. The exchange rate between the U.S. dollar and the euro is always quoted as "dollars per euro" or $ = €1.00—for example, $1.1867 listed in Exhibit 1.2 for "United States." Similarly, the exchange rate between the U.S. dollar and the British pound is always quoted as "dollars per pound" or $ = £1.00—for example, $1.3824 listed for "United States" in Exhibit 1.2. In addition, countries that were formerly members of the British Commonwealth will often be quoted against the U.S. dollar, as in U.S. dollars per Australian dollar.

Global Finance in Practice 1.1 introduces the topic that is fundamental to this entire field of study, the quotation of currencies.

If exchange rates never changed, the global financial marketplace would be a much kinder, simpler place. But, alas, that is not the case. Exchange rates change, and when they do, they alter the business results and competitiveness of all players on the playing field. As illustrated in the following section, it requires a careful calculation of even the amount of the change—percentage change.

GLOBAL FINANCE IN PRACTICE 1.1

Exchange Rate Quotations

Exchange rate quotation would seemingly be a simple thing. It is not. For example, on the same day (April 24, 2021), these were the spot currency quotes across three major business and financial publications for the price of the euro in terms of the U.S. dollar:

Financial Times: EURUSD 1.2099
Bloomberg: EUR-USD 1.2096
Wall Street Journal: Euro (EUR/USD) 1.2098

To be clear, all three are saying nearly the same thing: that one dollar and 21 cents ($1.2099 or $1.2096 or $1.2098) is equivalent to one euro (€1.00). But there are obvious differences.

- First, they use the three-letter ISO-4217 code for each currency, EUR instead of € and USD instead of $. The ISO codes came into common use with increasing digital financial communications and trading roughly 25 years ago. Yet, in journalism, research articles, and business contracts, the $ and € remain in common use.
- Second, the order is always the same, EUR and then USD, but the "punctuation" differs. All three are different, one not using a separator, a second using a hyphen as a separator, and the third using a slash as a separator.
- Third, all of these are different from the way currencies were quoted for decades, when the common way to express these would have been $1.2099/€, spoken as "$1.2099 per euro."
- Fourth, to just state the obvious, all three are slightly different values.

Our objective in this book is to both educate and familiarize the reader with how international finance is both conducted and communicated today. That means we will use both forms of currency symbols, $ and USD, € and EUR, £ and GBP, etc. Everyone has their preferences, but both are used in business today. Most likely, older readers prefer the singular symbols ($, €, £), and younger readers are more comfortable with the three-letter codes (USD, EUR, GBP). We hope to bridge the gap across generations!

The issue of order in quotation is best solved by simply stating the exchange rate as USD1.2099 = EUR1.00 or using the singular currency symbols, $1.2099 = €1.00. This book will use this form whenever possible. But, and there's always a "but," in equations it can be extremely awkward to use this extended form. But we will try.

The final difference, the fact that all three numbers are slightly different although they are currency quotes for the same day, well, that is a big messy subject for Chapter 5. For now, let's just say that it depends on who you are, where you are, and at what time (Greenwich Mean Time [GMT]) you are. Now back to your previously scheduled program. . . .

Percentage Change in Spot Exchange Rates

Assume that the Mexican peso has recently changed in value from MXN 16.00 = USD 1.00 to MXN 20.00 = USD 1.00. If your home currency is the U.S. dollar (USD), what is the percent change in the value of the Mexican peso (MXN)? The calculation depends upon the designated home currency.

Foreign Currency Terms. When the foreign currency price (the price, MXN) of the home currency (the unit, USD) is used, Mexican pesos per U.S. dollar in this case, the formula for the percent change (%Δ) in the foreign currency becomes

$$\%\Delta = \frac{\text{Begin rate} - \text{End rate}}{\text{End rate}} \times 100 = \frac{\text{MXN}16.00 - \text{MXN}20.00}{\text{MXN}20.00} \times 100 = -20.00\%$$

The Mexican peso fell in value 20% against the dollar. Note that it takes more pesos per dollar, and the calculation resulted in a negative value, both characteristics of a fall in value.

Home Currency Terms. When the home currency price (the price, USD) for a foreign currency (the unit, MXN) is used—the reciprocals of the foreign exchange quotes above—the formula for the percent age change in the foreign currency is

$$\%\Delta = \frac{\text{End rate} - \text{Begin rate}}{\text{Begin rate}} \times 100 = \frac{\text{USD}0.05000 - \text{USD}0.06250}{\text{USD}0.06250} \times 100 = -20.00\%$$

The calculation yields the identical percentage change, a fall in the value of the peso by –20%. Many people find the home currency terms calculation to be the more intuitive because it reminds them of a general percentage change calculation (ending value less beginning value over beginning value); however, one must be careful to remember that these are exchanges of currency for currency, and the currency that is designated as the home currency is important.

The fall of the Argentine peso in 2015 serves as a clear example of percentage change. On December 16, 2015, the government of Argentina announced it would lift currency controls; it would no longer restrict the ability of its citizens to move money out of the country. Over the next 24 hours, as Argentinians took advantage of this new freedom, the value of the Argentine peso fell from ARG 9.7908 per U.S. dollar to 13.6160, as pesos poured out of Argentina into the foreign exchange markets.

$$\%\Delta = \frac{\text{Begin rate} - \text{End rate}}{\text{End rate}} \times 100 = \frac{\text{ARG}9.7908 - \text{ARG}13.6160}{\text{ARG}13.6160} \times 100 = -28\%$$

After the 28% drop in the value of the peso against the U.S. dollar, the peso stabilized. But a fall in its value of that magnitude, 28%, was both dramatic and devastating for some. The change in exchange rates is the first example of our next subject—*risk*.

Financial Globalization and Risk

> *Back in the halcyon pre-crisis days of the late 20th and early 21st centuries, it was taken as self evident that financial globalization was a good thing. But the subprime crisis and eurozone dramas are shaking that belief . . . what is the bigger risk now—particularly in the eurozone—is that financial globalization has created a system that is interconnected in some dangerous ways.*
>
> —"Crisis Fears Fuel Debate on Capital Controls," Gillian Tett, *Financial Times*, December 15, 2011.

Much of the discussion dominating global financial markets today is centered on the complexity of risks associated with *financial globalization*—the discussion goes far beyond whether such globalization is simply good or bad and encompasses ways to lead and manage multinational firms in the rapidly moving marketplace. The following is but a sampling of risks that must be explored, considered, and—ultimately—*managed*.

- The international monetary system, an eclectic mix of floating and managed fixed exchange rates, is under constant scrutiny. The rise of the Chinese renminbi is changing much of the world's outlook on currency exchange, reserve currencies, and the roles of the dollar and the euro (see Chapter 2).
- Large fiscal deficits, including the continuing eurozone crisis, plague most of the major trading countries of the world, complicating fiscal and monetary policies and, ultimately, leading to the use of negative interest rates in an attempt to stimulate economies and protect currencies (see Chapter 3).
- Many countries experience continuing balance of payments imbalances and, in some cases, dangerously large deficits and surpluses—whether it be the twin surpluses enjoyed by China, the current account surplus of Germany, or the continuing current account deficits of the United States and United Kingdom, all will inevitably move exchange rates (see Chapter 3).
- Ownership and governance vary dramatically across the world. The publicly traded company is not the dominant global business organization; the privately held firm or the state-owned enterprise dominates in many countries, changing corporate objectives and expectations for financial performance (see Chapter 4).
- Global capital markets that normally provide the means to lower a firm's cost of capital and, even more critically, increase the availability of capital, have in many ways shrunk in size and have become less open and accessible to many of the world's organizations (see Chapter 2).
- Today's emerging markets are confronted with a new dilemma: the problem of first being the recipients of capital inflows and then of experiencing rapid and massive capital outflows. Financial globalization has resulted in the ebb and flow of capital into and out of both industrial and emerging markets, greatly complicating financial management (Chapters 5 and 8).

Eurocurrencies and Eurocurrency Interest Rates

One of the major linkages of global money and capital markets is the eurocurrency market.

Eurocurrencies. *Eurocurrencies* are domestic currencies of one country on deposit in a second country. For example, a U.S. dollar deposit in a British bank, a eurodollar deposit, is one type of eurocurrency. Banks will pay interest on these deposits—eurocurrency interest—depending on the agreed-upon maturity—a period ranging from overnight to more than a year or longer. Eurocurrency deposits are digitally transferred between banks.

The eurocurrency market serves two valuable purposes: (1) eurocurrency deposits are an efficient and convenient money market device for holding excess corporate liquidity; and (2) the eurocurrency market is a major source of short-term bank loans to finance corporate working capital needs, including the financing of imports and exports.

Any *convertible currency* can exist in "euro" form. Note that this use of the "euro" prefix should not be confused with the European currency called the euro. The eurocurrency market includes eurosterling (British pounds deposited outside the United Kingdom), euroeuros (euros on deposit outside the eurozone), euroyen (Japanese yen deposited outside Japan), and *eurodollars* (U.S. dollars deposited outside the U.S.).

Banks in which eurocurrencies are deposited are called eurobanks. A eurobank is a financial intermediary that simultaneously bids for time deposits and makes loans in a currency other than that of its home currency. Eurobanks are major world banks that conduct a eurocurrency business in addition to all other banking functions. Thus, the eurocurrency operation that qualifies a bank for the name *eurobank* is, in fact, a department of a large commercial bank, and the name springs from the performance of this function.

The modern eurocurrency market was born shortly after World War II. Eastern European holders of dollars, including the various state trading banks of the Soviet Union, were afraid to deposit their dollar holdings in the United States because those deposits might be attached by U.S. residents with claims against communist governments. Therefore, Eastern Europeans deposited their dollars in Western Europe, particularly with two Soviet banks: the Moscow Narodny Bank in London and the Banque Commerciale pour l'Europe du Nord in Paris. These banks redeposited the funds in other Western banks, especially in London. Additional dollar deposits were received from various central banks in Western Europe, which elected to hold part of their dollar reserves in this form to obtain a higher yield. Commercial banks also placed their dollar balances in the market because specific maturities could be negotiated in the eurodollar market. Such companies found it financially advantageous to keep their dollar reserves in the higher-yielding eurodollar market. Various holders of international refugee funds also supplied funds.

Although the basic causes of the growth of the eurocurrency market are economic efficiencies, many unique institutional events during the 1950s and 1960s contributed to its growth.

- In 1957, British monetary authorities responded to a weakening of the pound by imposing tight controls on U.K. bank lending in sterling to nonresidents of the United Kingdom. Encouraged by the Bank of England, U.K. banks turned to dollar lending as the only alternative that would allow them to maintain their leading position in world finance. For this they needed dollar deposits.
- Although New York was "home base" for the dollar and had a large domestic money and capital market, international trading in the dollar centered in London because of that city's expertise in international monetary matters and its proximity in time and distance to major customers.
- Additional support for a European-based dollar market came from the balance of payments difficulties of the U.S. during the 1960s, which temporarily segmented the U.S. domestic capital market.

Ultimately, however, the eurocurrency market continues to thrive because it is a large international money market relatively free from governmental regulation and interference. The attitude of governments toward market intervention, such as the possible intentional undervaluation of one's own currency, is the subject of *Global Finance in Practice 1.2.*

Eurocurrency Interest Rates. The reference rate of interest in the eurocurrency market is the *London Interbank Offered Rate*, or LIBOR. LIBOR is the most widely accepted rate of interest used in standardized quotations, loan agreements, or financial derivatives valuations. The use of interbank offered rates, however, is not confined to London. Most major domestic financial centers construct their own interbank offered rates for local loan agreements. Examples of such rates include PIBOR (Paris Interbank Offered Rate), MIBOR (Madrid Interbank Offered Rate), SIBOR (Singapore Interbank Offered Rate), and FIBOR (Frankfurt Interbank Offered Rate), to name just a few. But as prevalent and central LIBOR is to the global financial system, it is now slated for replacement, the subject of our mini-case in Chapter 8.

GLOBAL FINANCE IN PRACTICE 1.2

Why Don't African Countries Undervalue Their Currencies?

One of the oldest strategies to promote a country's exports is to undervalue its currency, maintain its traded value against other currencies at a rate of exchange that makes it relatively cheap. And if the currency is cheap, products that are priced in that currency—the country's exports—will be relatively cheap. And, theoretically, cheaper prices mean greater sales. It is not a secret that many of the countries of south Asia maintained undervalued currencies for many years in pursuit of export-led growth. If it worked for them, why not Africa?

A representative of the International Monetary Fund (IMF) once encouraged the president of Tanzania to weaken its currency. The president, Julius Nyerere, responded, "I will devalue the shilling over my dead body." That perspective is commonly held across Africa. Countries like Nigeria use all possible ways to maintain their currency at a value that many in the world believe is either slightly overvalued or about equilibrium, but hardly ever will one find a currency significantly undervalued.

That's not to say that African currencies are famously solid. The Zimbabwe currency is infamous in its inability to maintain its value as a result of bouts of hyperinflation and rampant money printing by the government. And there are others. But the international markets keep a watchful eye on any African country's currency showing any sign of weakness and will pounce (or maybe *flee* is the more appropriate term) if they smell smoke. For much of Africa, however, maintaining the value of their currency is a matter of pride and demonstrated resilience and stability, and even if a weaker or cheaper home currency might help boost exports and therefore their economy, in their eyes, the "cost" is too much.

The key factor attracting both depositors and borrowers to the eurocurrency loan market is the narrow interest rate spread within that market. The difference between deposit and loan rates is often less than 1%. Interest spreads in the eurocurrency market are small for many reasons. Low lending rates exist because the eurocurrency market is a wholesale market where deposits and loans are made in amounts of $500,000 or more on an unsecured basis. Borrowers are usually large corporations or government entities that qualify for low rates because of their credit standing and because the transaction size is large. In addition, overhead assigned to the eurocurrency operation by participating banks is small.

Deposit rates are higher in the eurocurrency markets than in most domestic currency markets because the financial institutions offering eurocurrency activities are not subject to many of the regulations and reserve requirements imposed on traditional domestic banks and banking activities. With these costs removed, rates are subject to more competitive pressures, deposit rates are higher, and loan rates are lower. A second major area of cost savings associated with eurocurrency markets is that deposit insurance (such as the Federal Deposit Insurance Corporation [FDIC]) and other assessments paid on deposits in the United States, for example, are unnecessary.

1.2 The Theory of Comparative Advantage

The *theory of comparative advantage* provides a basis for explaining and justifying international trade in a model world assumed to enjoy free trade, perfect competition, no uncertainty, costless information, and no government interference. The theory's origins lie in the work of Adam Smith, and particularly his seminal book, *The Wealth of Nations*, published in 1776. Smith sought to explain why the division of labor in productive activities, and subsequently international trade of goods produced, increased the quality of life for all citizens. Smith based his work on the concept of *absolute advantage*, with every country specializing in the production of those goods for which it was uniquely suited. More would be produced for less. Thus, with each country specializing in products for which it possessed absolute advantage, countries could produce more in total and trade for goods that were cheaper in price than those produced at home.

In his work *On the Principles of Political Economy and Taxation*, published in 1817, David Ricardo sought to take the basic ideas set down by Smith a few logical steps further. Ricardo noted that even if a country possessed absolute advantage in the production of two goods, it might still be relatively more efficient than the other country in one good's production than the production of the other good. Ricardo termed this *comparative advantage*. Each country would then possess comparative advantage in the production of one of the two products, and both countries would benefit by specializing completely in one product and trading for the other.

Although international trade might have approached the comparative advantage model during the nineteenth century, it certainly does not today, for a variety of reasons. Countries do not appear to specialize only in those products that could be most efficiently produced by that country's particular factors of production. Instead, governments interfere with comparative advantage for a variety of economic and political reasons, such as to achieve full employment, economic development, national self-sufficiency in defense-related industries, and protection of an agricultural sector's way of life. Government interference takes the form of tariffs, quotas, and other non-tariff restrictions.

At least two of the factors of production—capital and technology—now flow directly and easily between countries, rather than only indirectly through traded goods and services. This direct flow occurs between related subsidiaries and affiliates of multinational firms, as well as between unrelated firms via loans and license and management contracts. Even labor can flow between countries to varying degrees, such as immigrants into the EU from North Africa and the Middle East and then in turn between states in the EU.

Modern factors of production are more numerous than in this simple model. Factors considered in the location of production facilities worldwide include managerial skills, a dependable legal structure for settling contract disputes, research and development competence, educational levels of available workers, energy resources, consumer demand for brand name goods, mineral and raw material availability, access to capital, tax differentials, supporting infrastructure (roads, ports, and communication facilities), and possibly others.

Although the *terms of trade* are ultimately determined by supply and demand, the process by which the terms are set is different from that visualized in traditional trade theory. They are determined partly by administered pricing in oligopolistic markets.

Comparative advantage shifts over time as less-developed countries become more developed and realize their latent opportunities. For example, over the past 150 years, comparative advantage in producing cotton textiles has shifted from the United Kingdom to the United States, to Japan, to Hong Kong, to Taiwan, and to China. The classical model of comparative advantage also does not address certain other issues such as the effect of uncertainty and information costs, the role of differentiated products in imperfectly competitive markets, and economies of scale.

Nevertheless, although the world is a long way from the pure theory of comparative advantage, the general principle of comparative advantage is still valid. The closer the world gets to true international specialization, the more world production and consumption can be increased, provided that the problem of equitable distribution of the benefits can be solved to the satisfaction of consumers, producers, and political leaders. Complete specialization, however, remains an unrealistic limiting case, just as perfect competition is a limiting case in microeconomic theory.

Comparative advantage is still a relevant theory to explain why particular countries are most suitable for exports of goods and services that support the global supply chain of both MNEs and domestic firms. The comparative advantage of the twenty-first century, however, is one that is based more on services and their cross-border facilitation by telecommunications and the Internet. The source of a nation's comparative advantage, however, is still the mixture of its own labor skills, access to capital, and technology.

The extent of global outsourcing is already reaching every corner of the globe. From financial back offices in Manila to information technology engineers in Hungary, modern telecommunications now bring business activities to labor rather than moving labor to the places of business.

1.3 What Is Different About International Financial Management?

Exhibit 1.3 details some of the main differences between international and domestic financial management. These component differences include institutions, corporate governance, foreign exchange, political risks, and the modifications required of financial theory and financial instruments.

Multinational financial management requires an understanding of cultural, historical, and institutional differences such as those affecting corporate governance. Although both domestic firms and MNEs are exposed to foreign exchange risks, MNEs alone face certain unique risks, such as political risks, that are not normally a threat to domestic operations. MNEs also face other risks that can be classified as extensions of domestic finance theory.

For example, the normal domestic approach to the cost of capital, sourcing debt and equity, capital budgeting, *working capital management*, taxation, and credit analysis needs to be modified to accommodate foreign complexities. Moreover, a number of financial instruments that are used in domestic financial management have been modified for use in international financial management. Examples are foreign currency options and futures, interest rate and currency swaps, and letters of credit.

The main theme of this book is to analyze how an MNE's financial management evolves as it pursues global strategic opportunities and as new constraints emerge. In this chapter, we introduce the challenges and risks associated with Ganado Corporation (Ganado), a company we use as an example throughout this book. Ganado is a company evolving from being domestic in scope to becoming truly multinational. The discussion includes constraints that a company will face in terms of managerial goals and governance as it becomes increasingly

EXHIBIT 1.3 What Is Different about International Financial Management?

Concept	International	Domestic
Culture, history, and institutions	Each foreign country is unique and not always understood by MNE management	Each country has a known base case
Corporate governance	Foreign countries' regulations and institutional practices are all uniquely different	Regulations and institutions are well known
Foreign exchange risk	MNEs face foreign exchange risks due to their subsidiaries, as well as import/export and foreign competitors	Foreign exchange risks from import/export and foreign competition (no subsidiaries)
Political risk	MNEs face political risk because of their foreign subsidiaries and high profile	Negligible political risks
Modification of domestic finance theories	MNEs must modify finance theories like capital budgeting and the cost of capital because of foreign complexities	Traditional financial theory applies
Modification of domestic financial instruments	MNEs utilize modified financial instruments such as options, forwards, swaps, and letters of credit	Limited use of financial instruments and derivatives because of few foreign exchange and political risks

involved in multinational operations. But first we need to clarify the unique value proposition and advantages that the MNE was created to exploit.

Market Imperfections: A Rationale for the Existence of the Multinational Firm

MNEs strive to take advantage of imperfections in national markets for products, factors of production, and financial assets. Imperfections in the market for products translate into market opportunities for MNEs. Large international firms are better able to exploit such competitive factors as economies of scale, managerial and technological expertise, product differentiation, and financial strength than are their local competitors. In fact, MNEs thrive best in markets characterized by international oligopolistic competition, where these factors are particularly critical. In addition, once MNEs have established a physical presence abroad, they are in a better position than purely domestic firms to identify and implement market opportunities through their own internal information network.

Why Do Firms Go Global?

Strategic motives drive the decision to invest abroad and become an MNE. These motives can be summarized under the following categories:

1. *Market seekers* produce in foreign markets either to satisfy local demand or to export to markets other than their home market. U.S. automobile firms manufacturing in Europe for local consumption are an example of market-seeking motivation.
2. *Raw material seekers* extract raw materials wherever they can be found, either for export or for further processing and sale in the country in which they are found—the host country. Firms in the oil, mining, plantation, and forest industries fall into this category.
3. *Production efficiency seekers* produce in countries where one or more of the factors of production are underpriced relative to their productivity. Labor-intensive production of electronic components in Taiwan, Malaysia, and Mexico is an example of this motivation.
4. *Knowledge seekers* operate in foreign countries to gain access to technology or managerial expertise. For example, German, Dutch, and Japanese firms have purchased U.S. electronics firms for their technology.
5. *Political safety seekers* acquire or establish new operations in countries that are considered unlikely to expropriate or interfere with private enterprise. For example, Hong Kong firms invested heavily in the United States, United Kingdom, Canada, and Australia in anticipation of the consequences of China's 1997 takeover of the British colony.

These five types of strategic considerations are not mutually exclusive. Forest products firms seeking wood fiber in Brazil, for example, may also find a large Brazilian market for a portion of their output.

In industries characterized by worldwide oligopolistic competition, each of the aforementioned strategic motives should be subdivided into proactive and defensive investments. Proactive investments are designed to enhance the growth and profitability of the firm itself. Defensive investments are designed to deny growth and profitability to the firm's competitors. Examples of the latter are investments that try to preempt a market before competitors can get established in it or capture raw material sources and deny them to competitors. But as highlighted by *Global Finance in Practice 1.3*, the objectives and responsibilities of the modern multinational enterprise have grown significantly more complex with these elements.

GLOBAL FINANCE IN PRACTICE 1.3

Corporate Responsibility and Corporate Sustainability

Sustainable development is development that meets the needs of the present without compromising the ability of future generations to meet their own needs.

—Brundtland Report, 1987, p. 54.

What is the purpose of the corporation? It is accepted that the purpose of the corporation is to certainly create profits and value for its stakeholders, but the responsibility of the corporation is to do so in a way that inflicts no costs on society, including the environment. As a result of globalization, this growing responsibility and role of the corporation in society have added a level of complexity to the leadership challenges faced by the multinational firm.

This developing controversy has been somewhat hampered to date by conflicting terms and labels—*corporate goodness, corporate responsibility, corporate social responsibility (CSR), corporate philanthropy*, and *corporate sustainability*, to list but a few. Confusion can be reduced by using a guiding principle—that sustainability is a goal, while responsibility is an obligation. It follows that the obligation of leadership in the modern multinational is to pursue profit, social development, and the environment, all along sustainable principles.

The term *sustainability* has evolved greatly within the context of global business in the past decade. A traditional primary objective of the family-owned business has been the "sustainability of the organization"—the long-term ability of the company to remain commercially viable and provide security and income for future generations. Although narrower in scope, the concept of environmental sustainability shares a common core thread—the ability of a company, a culture, or even the earth to survive and renew over time.

1.4 The Globalization Process

Ganado is a hypothetical U.S.-based firm that is used as an illustrative example throughout the book to demonstrate the phases of the globalization process—the structural and managerial changes and challenges experienced by a firm as it moves its operations from domestic to global.

Global Transition I: Domestic Phase to the International Trade Phase

Ganado is a young firm that manufactures and distributes an array of telecommunication devices. Its initial strategy is to develop a sustainable competitive advantage in the U.S. market. Like many other young firms, it is constrained by its small size, competitors, and lack of access to cheap and plentiful sources of capital. The top half of Exhibit 1.4 shows Ganado in its early domestic phase.

Ganado sells its products in U.S. dollars to U.S. customers and buys its manufacturing and service inputs from U.S. suppliers, paying U.S. dollars. The creditworthiness of all suppliers and buyers is established under domestic U.S. practices and procedures. A potential issue for Ganado at this time is that although Ganado is not international or global in its operations, some of its competitors, suppliers, or buyers may be. This is often the impetus to push a firm like Ganado into the first phase of the globalization process—into international trade. Ganado was founded in Los Angeles by James Winston in 1948 to make telecommunications equipment. The family-owned business expanded slowly but steadily over the following 40 years. The demands of continual technological investment in the 1980s, however, required that the firm raise additional equity capital in order to compete. This need for capital led to its initial public offering (IPO) in 1988. As a U.S.-based publicly traded company on the New York Stock Exchange, Ganado's management sought to create value for its shareholders.

As Ganado became a visible and viable competitor in the U.S. market, strategic opportunities arose to expand the firm's market reach by exporting products and services to one or more foreign markets. The North American Free Trade Agreement (NAFTA) made trade

EXHIBIT 1.4 **Ganado Corp: Initiation of the Globalization Process**

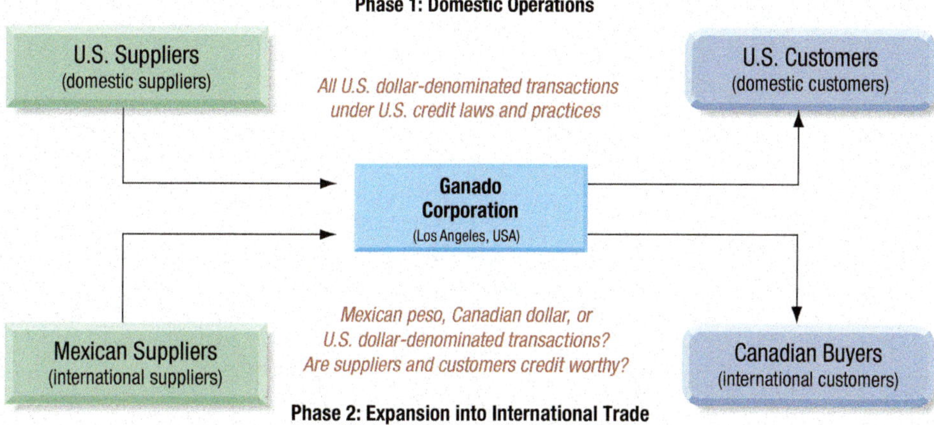

with Mexico and Canada attractive. This second phase of the globalization process is shown in the lower half of Exhibit 1.4.

Ganado responded to these globalization forces by importing inputs from Mexican suppliers and making export sales to Canadian buyers. We define this phase of the globalization process as the international trade phase. Exporting and importing products and services increase the demands of financial management over and above the traditional requirements of the domestic-only business in two ways. First, direct foreign exchange risks are now borne by the firm. Ganado may now need to quote prices in foreign currencies, accept payment in foreign currencies, or pay suppliers in foreign currencies. As the values of currencies change from minute to minute in the global marketplace, Ganado will increasingly experience significant risks from the changing values associated with these foreign currency payments and receipts.

Second, the evaluation of the credit quality of foreign buyers and sellers is now more important than ever. Reducing the possibility of non-payment for exports and non-delivery of imports becomes a key financial management task during the international trade phase. This credit risk management task is much more difficult in international business, as buyers and suppliers are new, subject to differing business practices and legal systems, and generally more challenging to assess.

Global Transition II: The International Trade Phase to the Multinational Phase

If Ganado is successful in its international trade activities, the time will come when the globalization process will progress to the next phase. Ganado will soon need to establish foreign sales and service affiliates. This step is often followed by establishing manufacturing operations abroad or by licensing foreign firms to produce and service Ganado's products. The multitude of issues and activities associated with this second, larger global transition is the real focus of this book.

Ganado's continued globalization will require it to identify the sources of its competitive advantage and, with that knowledge, expand its intellectual capital and physical presence globally. A variety of strategic alternatives are available to Ganado—the foreign

EXHIBIT 1.5 Ganado's Foreign Direct Investment Sequence

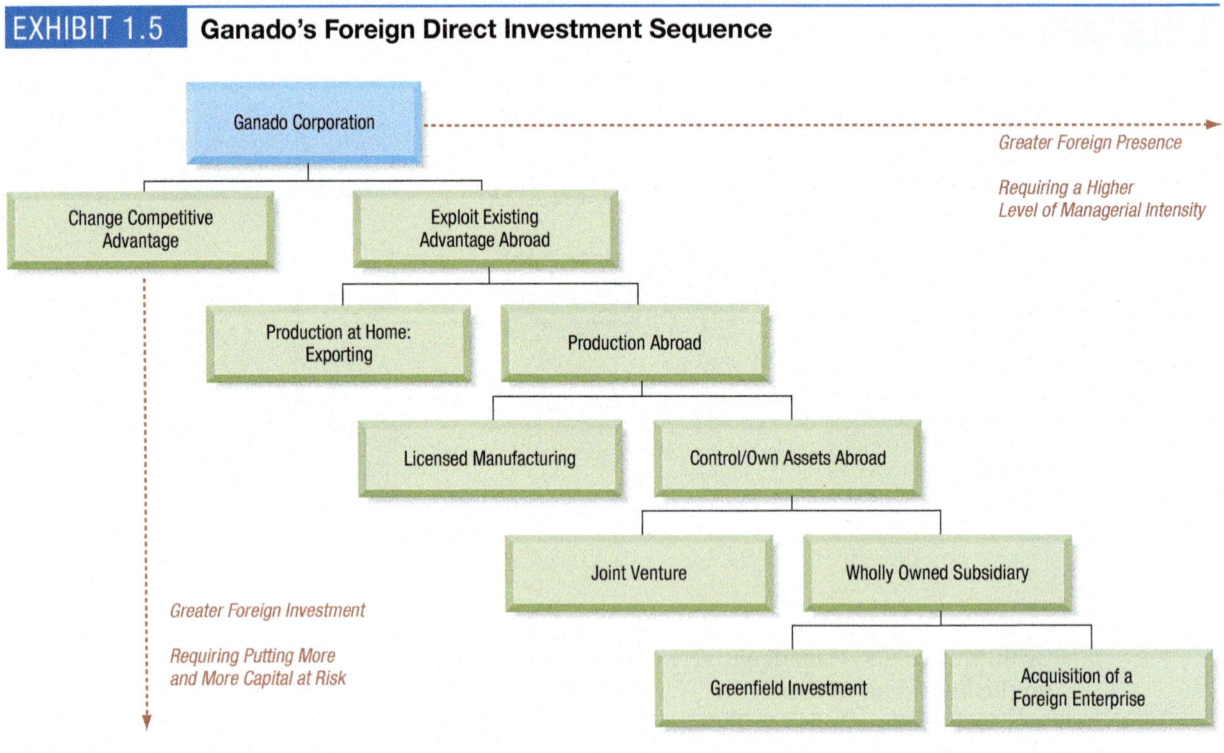

direct investment sequence—as shown in Exhibit 1.5. These alternatives include the creation of foreign sales offices, the licensing of the company name and everything associated with it, and the manufacturing and distribution of its products to other firms in foreign markets.

As Ganado moves further down and to the right in Exhibit 1.5, the extent of its physical presence in foreign markets increases. It may now own its own distribution and production facilities, and ultimately, it may want to acquire other companies. Once Ganado owns assets and enterprises in foreign countries it has entered the multinational phase of its globalization.

The Multinational Enterprise's Consolidated Financial Results

Ganado will create more and more foreign subsidiaries as it expands globally. Some MNEs may only have one foreign subsidiary, while others, like Johnson & Johnson (U.S.), have nearly 200. Each subsidiary will have its own set of financial statements and results (income statement, balance sheet, and statement of cash flow). Each subsidiary is also likely operating in a different currency, subject to differing tax rates, accounting practices such as depreciation, and a multitude of other financial parameters. The company, however, must periodically consolidate all those financial results and report them in the currency of its home country.

Exhibit 1.6 illustrates a simplified income statement consolidation for Ganado. Assuming that U.S.-based Ganado has two foreign subsidiaries, one in Europe and one in China, in addition to its U.S. operations, it converts the various income statement items to U.S. dollars from euros and Chinese renminbi at the average exchange rate for each currency pair for the period (in this case the year). As we will see in later chapters, this process results in a number of currency risks and exposures, as exchange rates may change in ways that increase or decrease consolidated results.

EXHIBIT 1.6 Selected Consolidated Income Results for Ganado (U.S.)

As a U.S.-based multinational company, Ganado must consolidate the financial results (in this case, sales and earnings from the income statements) of its foreign subsidiaries. This requires converting foreign currency values into U.S. dollars.

Country	Currency	Sales (millions)	Avg Exchange Rate for Year	Sales (millions US$)	Percent of Total
United States	U.S. dollar ($)	$300		$300.0	57%
Europe	European euro (€)	€120	$1.12 = €1.00	134.4	26%
China	Chinese renminbi (¥)	¥600	¥6.60 = $1.00	90.9	17%
				$525.3	100%

Country	Currency	Earnings (millions)	Avg Exchange Rate for Year	Earnings (millions US$)	Percent of Total
United States	U.S. dollar ($)	$28.6		$28.6	56%
Europe	European euro (€)	€10.50	$1.12 = €1.00	11.8	23%
China	Chinese renminbi (¥)	¥71.40	¥6.60 = $1.00	10.8	21%
				$51.2	100%

Ganado, for the year shown, generated 57% of its global sales in the United States, with those U.S. sales making up 56% of its consolidated profits. From quarter to quarter and year to year, both the financial performance of the individual subsidiaries will change in addition to exchange rates.

* This is a simplified consolidation. Actual consolidation accounting practices require a number of specific line item adjustments not shown here.

The Limits to Financial Globalization

The theories of international business and international finance introduced in this chapter have long argued that with an increasingly open and transparent global marketplace in which capital may flow freely, capital will increasingly flow and support countries and companies based on the theory of comparative advantage. Since the mid-twentieth century, this has indeed been the case as more and more countries have pursued more open and competitive markets. But the past decade has seen the growth of a new kind of limit or impediment to financial globalization: the increasing influence and self-enrichment of organizational insiders.

One possible representation of this process can be seen in Exhibit 1.7. If influential insiders in corporations and sovereign states continue to pursue the increase in firm value, there will be a definite and continuing growth in financial globalization. But if these same influential insiders pursue their own personal agendas, which may increase their personal power and influence or personal wealth, or both, then capital will not flow into these sovereign states and corporations. The result is the growth of financial inefficiency and the segmentation of globalization outcomes creating winners and losers. As we will see throughout this book, this barrier to international finance may indeed become increasingly troublesome. This growing dilemma is also something of a composite of what this book is about. The three fundamental elements—financial theory, global business, and management beliefs and actions—combine to present either the problem or the solution to the growing debate over the benefits of globalization to countries and cultures worldwide.

We close this chapter and open this book with the simple words of one of our colleagues on the outlook for global finance and global financial management:

> *Welcome to the future. This will be a constant struggle. We need leadership, citizenship, and dialogue.*
>
> —Donald Lessard, in *Global Risk, New Perspectives and Opportunities*, 2011, p. 33.

EXHIBIT 1.7 The Limits of Financial Globalization

There is a growing debate over whether many of the insiders and rulers of organizations with enterprises globally are taking actions consistent with creating firm value or consistent with increasing their own personal stakes and power.

If these influential insiders are building personal wealth over that of the firm, it will indeed result in preventing the flow of capital across borders, currencies, and institutions to create a more open and integrated global financial community.

Source: Constructed by authors based on "The Limits of Financial Globalization," Rene M. Stulz, *Journal of Applied Corporate Finance*, Vol. 19, No. 1, Winter 2007, pp. 8–15.

Summary Points

- The creation of value requires combining three critical elements: (1) an open marketplace, (2) high-quality strategic management, and (3) access to capital.
- The theory of comparative advantage provides a basis for explaining and justifying international trade in a model world of free and open competition.
- International financial management requires an understanding of cultural, historical, and institutional differences, such as those affecting corporate governance.
- Although both domestic firms and MNEs are exposed to foreign exchange risks, MNEs alone face certain unique risks, such as political risks, that are not normally a threat to domestic operations.
- MNEs strive to take advantage of imperfections in national markets for products, factors of production, and financial assets.
- The decision whether or not to invest abroad is driven by strategic motives and may require the MNE to enter into global licensing agreements, joint ventures, cross-border acquisitions, or greenfield investments.
- If influential insiders in corporations and sovereign states pursue their own personal agendas, which may increase their personal power, influence, or wealth, then capital will not flow into these sovereign states and corporations. This will, in turn, create limitations to globalization in finance.

MINI-CASE

Global Fintech[1]

Fintech—financial technology—will, in the eyes of some, revolutionize the world. To others, it is just the most recent evolutionary stage of the financial industry. It has, however, the power to overcome barriers of access and inclusion to people in many countries, altering the trajectory of economic betterment for many. Fintech could conceptually include any technology associated with the movement of or transactions involving money. The abacus, cash register, and automated teller machine (ATM) are all examples of financial technological developments. The term today is more commonly associated with online payments processing, such as AliPay, PayPal, or M-Pesa and cryptocurrencies like Bitcoin and Litecoin.[2]

But fintech is much more than just payments processing or cryptocurrencies.[3] Developments in financial technology associated with Internet access and mobile communications can potentially disrupt nearly every dimension of financial services. At present, across the globe, from Kenya to Kathmandu, new platforms and processes and products are advancing as rapidly as most nations will allow them to. The potential for fintech across countries will in many ways cross three different axes of national development: (1) level of economic development, (2) financial sector infrastructure, and (3) bank/financial services regulatory landscapes. But like all technologies, they are not inherently good or evil; the societal outcome depends on how they are applied.

Financial Landscape

> *Access to critical financial services, such as payments, savings and insurance, helps people improve their lives. But access is unequal and poor people and small firms typically have many fewer options. Fintech has shown its potential to close gaps in the delivery of financial services to households and firms in emerging markets and developing economies. Initially, such benefits were channeled via mobile money and digital payments solutions.*
>
> *Research conducted at country and regional level, and more recently at global level, has shown the effectiveness of such solutions for financial inclusion. Other types of fintech firms, such as lending and capital raising platforms, are showing their potential to improve access to finance for underserved groups, including SMEs, although these platform solutions are still at an early stage in the majority of emerging markets and developing economies. Finally, firms that provide supporting services such as credit scoring or digital ID solutions are helping to expand the benefits of fintech across the entire financial sector.* —"The Global Covid-19 FinTech Market Rapid Assessment Study," World Bank Group, 2020, p. 8.

What is fintech's real potential? Which societal financial functions are likely to be impacted? A basic overview of which financial functions and services society utilizes has been somewhat missing from the discussion. The World Economic Forum offered up a basic description of the financial landscape, what it called the *Wheel*, a number of years ago that is helpful in understanding the multitude of financial service sectors that could potentially be impacted by fintech. The Wheel identifies six sectors of potential impact.[4]

1. **Payments**. The execution of payment processing for both B2C and B2B transactions was the first and generally easiest financial service to be impacted by fintech. The movement toward digital payments is already quite advanced in a number of nations where the people are often ahead of the institutions, both banks and regulators.
2. **Market provisioning**. The development of technological data collection and analysis, some using artificial intelligence for rapid financial assessments, some using artificial intelligence, is expected to be a key area of impact. This sector is still considered in its infancy, as the artificial intelligence and big data necessary to support its use are still considered developing.
3. **Investment management**. The increased reach of fintech to previously ignored and underserved demographic and income sectors (e.g., Robinhood) has already proven both powerful and disruptive. The promise of the developing world is enormous in changing spending/saving-investment behaviors.
4. **Insurance**. Access to insurance services, particularly affordable services, is one of the key development barriers in emerging economies. Insurance is often one of the requirements for acquiring and utilizing assets for business and economic development. But new digital insurance providers are rapidly changing who and what is insured at what costs.
5. **Deposits and lending**. This is one of the core traditional banking functions that is already undergoing disruptive change. Financial institutions have been rapidly adopting fintech apps for deposit taking but have been slow to advance the lending functions. Fintech lending has some of the greatest potential but also some of the greatest risks—for example, the experience China has had with peer-to-peer (P2P) lending—for the global financial system.
6. **Capital raising**. Internet-based capital-raising channels such as crowdfunding have rapidly developed their own financial ecosystems. More innovation than disruption, fintech capital raising represents some of the greatest potential improvements in society through economic development.

This is just one taxonomy of societal financial functions. But regardless of how the financial service cake is sliced, it is clear that fintech's potential to alter the lives of people in all countries and markets is real and, in many cases, already here. The recent global pandemic provided a multitude of examples of how fintech could provide more

[2]Many of these developments and platforms use blockchain technology. Blockchain is an encrypted list of records, called blocks, that are linked together. Although fundamental to cryptocurrencies like Bitcoin, it is not a uniquely financial technology.

[3]El Salvador in 2021 became the first country to declare a cryptocurrency, Bitcoin, official legal tender, money.

[4]"The Future of Financial Services: How Disruptive Innovations Are Reshaping the Way Financial Services Are Structured, Provisioned and Consumed," World Economic Forum, Prepared in collaboration with Deloitte, Final Report, June 2015.

information and more financial services to people everywhere, partially in support of the world's struggle to ease human suffering from COVID.

> *Digital financial services are faster, more efficient, and typically cheaper than traditional financial services and, therefore, increasingly reaching lower-income households and small- and medium-sized enterprises (SMEs). During the COVID-19 health crisis, digital financial services can and are enabling contactless and cashless transactions. Where digital financial inclusion is advanced, they are helping facilitate the efficient and quick deployment of government support measures, including to people and firms affected by the pandemic.* —"The Promise of Fintech, Financial Inclusion in the Post COVID-19 Era," Ratna Sahay, Ulric Eriksson von Allmen, Amina Lahreche, Purva Khera, Sumiko Ogawa, Majid Bazarbash, and Kim Beaton, International Monetary Fund, No. 20/09, 2020.

Country Reach

One of the curious facets of fintech is that it may have the greatest impact on countries which are largely under-banked and, simultaneously, those that are over-banked.

Like mobile phones in countries without existing landline infrastructures, fintech can leapfrog the legacy physical infrastructure of traditional banking. It can potentially provide all of the basic financial services that the large marble-columned edifices have provided in older industrial markets for centuries at a fraction of the cost, both capital and operating. In these countries—for example, those in Sub-Saharan Africa—banking sectors are in some cases rudimentary, with a large part of the population not having access to traditional banking services. Here fintech can be fundamental, accessible at low cost, and powerful in reach. There is little to "disrupt"; here fintech can be seen in the role of a new financial infrastructure. And that can in turn act as a device for inclusion.

At the same time, fintech's potential may also be quite impactful and disruptive in the older highly banked industrialized markets. These are markets—for example, the United States or Mexico—where banks have operated profitably for more than two centuries. They are established within a societal structure of laws, regulations, and institutions that shelter and protect their activities and markets. And that long-term protection has in many cases resulted in low rates of innovation, most importantly in the under-investment in digital and cellular financial services that many customers now desire—now that people have discovered what those services may offer and cost. The traditional highly banked developed markets may be ripe for fintech disruption, as new digital financial services may be much cheaper and more efficient than the bureaucratic, stodgy banking empires of the past. But that will only happen if they can break down the political power and breach the turf of the established institutions.

The one sector of possibly the greatest potential benefit in global business is digital lending. A naive or simplistic view of the world might be to visualize that the rich, highly industrialized countries, that play host to most of the world's capital, could see massive opportunities in getting the capital to the business entrepreneurs, startups, and under-capitalized enterprises in the emerging world. This access, once again, has been somewhat denied as established banking industries in countries, not foreign investors or lenders, define the rules of access. Again, fintech innovations, like FairMoney in Nigeria or Goldman Sachs in Mexico, are finding their way through the forests of national regulatory barriers and data deficiencies to offer small enterprises access to capital.[5]

Cross-Border Potential

One example of the potential power of fintech for good is that of international money transfers. Migrant workers all over the world continue to suffer extremely high transfer costs, often ranging between 5% to 25%, to simply transfer the income they have generated in a host country back to their families and friends in their home countries.

International money transfers in many ways represent one of the biggest challenges of fintech: low-income populations, with no legal standing, political standing, or banking access, attempting to move small amounts of money across borders. Fintech firms have started building their own international correspondent relationships, some banking, allowing these transfers to bypass the legacy banking systems that exploited lower-income migrant populations. Unfortunately, that does not mean that the fintech providers do not similarly exploit low-income customers. M-Pesa, a payment processing platform founded in Kenya and then expanded to a multitude of countries across Africa, is considered by many one of the true success stories of fintech. But a multitude of studies have cited its monopoly status. With no real competitors, it has been able to charge high fees for its use. Once again technology does not assure healthy societal outcomes.

Promise and Peril

Probably no single case exemplifies the risks and rewards of fintech better than Alipay and China. China, all agree, is the leader in fintech development, in some ways because it is a nexus of both categories of markets described in the previous section—under-banked and over-banked. And China also offers a powerful device of expediting

[5]See for example "Why Goldman Sachs Is Interested in a Small Bike Shop in Mexico, Bank's Credit Line to Fintech Firm Credijusto Is Latest Example of Growing Market of Alternative Lenders to Local Business," by Robbie Whelan, *The Wall Street Journal*, March 14, 2019; and "FinTechs Find Lending's 'Atomic Data Points' in Emerging Markets," by *PYMNTS*, February 26, 2021.

fintech—those most capable of embracing digital transactions are also those with some of the greatest income/wealth-generating capabilities. Oh, to be young.

Home to an old, bureaucratic, and politically powerful banking industry, it has seen the advancement of two of the world's largest and most successful digital payments systems, WeChatPay (a unit of Tencent) and AliPay (a unit of Ant Group). These digital payments applications allow buying and selling of all things economic without the use of traditional cash, bank checks, or credit cards while operating outside the traditional banking system. AliPay, the largest, is a third-party mobile and online payment platform utilizing a Quick Response (QR) code on a personal phone to conduct electronically recorded transactions in an instant. As the world's largest online payment platform it grew in market share and reach with the most advanced of consumers in Shanghai (over-banked) to the poorest of farmers in the inland provinces (under-banked).

In November 2020, AliPay's parent company, the Ant Group, was 48 hours away from its initial public offering (IPO) when the Chinese government stepped in and stopped it. Expected to be the largest IPO in financial history, the Ant Group and its founder Jack Ma had purportedly grown so large and so powerful that Chinese authorities worried about its impact on their financial system's stability. One specific activity was Ant's role in originating loans, playing a middleman role in connecting borrowers with lenders (banks) through its digital interface. The fear was that it was starting to operate similar to bank lending seen in the U.S. leading up to the financial crisis of 2008, where a lack of prudent due diligence in lending led to subprime borrowing—and repayment delinquencies—at record rates.[6] In the months that followed, the Chinese government rolled out a series of additional regulations to ensure that most lending remained in the hands of the banks themselves, for now.

Fintech Themes

Fintech offers new and impactful opportunities for money and capital to flow outside the brick-and-mortar institutions of the past and present. Strangely, whether fintech will threaten the banks, partner with the banks, or both is dominating much of the discussion at present. Yet the banks or existing financial institutions are largely only distributors, the plumbing and plumber, moving the capital from those who have it to those who wish to use it. With greater capital freedom will come risks and failures that cause governments to take one step back with each two steps forward. Such is experience. The net result, that's positive.

MINI-CASE QUESTIONS

1. Why do you think fintech's relationship to banking systems is the focal point of such debate?
2. Why has China proven to be the leader in fintech?
3. In your opinion, is fintech revolutionary or evolutionary?

[6]Although Ant's lending activities was the common explanation for the regulatory crackdown, it is estimated that total Ant lending was less than 1% of total Chinese bank lending.

Questions

1.1 Globalization Risks in Business. What are some of the risks that come with the growing globalization of business?

1.2 Globalization and the Multinational Enterprise (MNE). The term *globalization* has become widely used in recent years. How would you define it?

1.3 Assets, Institutions, and Linkages. Which assets play the most critical role in linking the major institutions that make up the global financial marketplace?

1.4 Currencies and Symbols. What technological innovation is changing the symbols we use in the representation of different country currencies?

1.5 Eurocurrencies and LIBOR. Why have eurocurrencies and LIBOR remained the centerpiece of the global financial marketplace for so long?

1.6 Theory of Comparative Advantage. Define and explain the theory of comparative advantage.

1.7 Limitations of Comparative Advantage. The key to understanding most theories is found in what those theories say and what they do not have. Name four or five key limitations to the theory of comparative advantage.

1.8 International Financial Management. What is different about international financial management?

1.9 Ganado's Globalization. After reading the chapter's description of Ganado's globalization process, how would you explain the distinctions among international, multinational, and global companies?

1.10 Ganado, the MNE. At what point in the globalization process did Ganado become a multinational enterprise (MNE)?

1.11 Role of Market Imperfections. What is the role of market imperfections in the creation of opportunities for the multinational firm?

1.12 Why Go? Why do firms become multinational?

1.13 Multinational versus International. What is the difference between an international firm and a multinational firm?

1.14 Ganado's Phases. What are the main phases that Ganado passed through as it evolved into a truly global firm? What are the advantages and disadvantages of each?

1.15 Financial Globalization. How do the motivations of individuals, both inside and outside the organization or business, define the limits of financial globalization?

Problems

1.1 Chantal DuBois in Brussels. Chantal DuBois lives in Brussels. She can buy a U.S. dollar for €0.7600. Christopher Keller, living in New York City, can buy a euro for $1.3200. What is the foreign exchange rate between the dollar and the euro?

1.2 Mexico's Cada Seis Años. Mexico was famous—or infamous—or many years for having two things every six years (*cada seis años* in Spanish): a presidential election and a currency devaluation. This was the case in 1976, 1982, 1988, and 1994. In its last devaluation on December 20, 1994, the value of the Mexican peso (Ps) was officially changed from Ps3.30 = $1.00 to Ps5.50 = $1.00. What was the percentage devaluation?

1.3 Kyle's Competing Job Offers. Kyle, after an arduous post-graduation job search, has received an offer of the following three different country posts with a major multinational company. Each of the three countries—the United Kingdom, the Czech Republic, and France—offer different starting salaries and different signing bonuses, but in different currencies. Kyle wants to first compare all of the compensation packages in a common currency, the U.S. dollar. Use the data at the bottom of this page to determine which offer represents the greatest initial U.S. dollar compensation package.

1.4 Munich to Moscow. For your post-graduation celebratory trip you decide to travel from Munich, Germany, to Moscow, Russia. You leave Munich with 15,000 euros (EUR) in your wallet. Wanting to exchange all of them for Russian rubles (RUB), you obtain the following quotes:

Spot rate on the U.S. dollar to euro cross rate: USD1.0644 = EUR1.00

Spot rate on the Russian ruble to dollar cross rate: RUB59.468 = USD1.00

a. What is the Russian ruble-euro cross rate?
b. How many Russian rubles will you obtain for your euros?

1.5 Tokyo Olympic Games. Giselle Nolan had planned her trip to the Olympic Games in Tokyo, Japan, for many months. She had budgeted—saved—USD15,000 for expenses while in Tokyo. Giselle had waited till the last minute, however, to exchange the dollars for Japanese yen (JPY), doing it in the San Francisco airport in the United States on July 30 at JPY109.70 = 1.00USD. Given the following average exchange rates in the spring and summer of 2021, when should she have exchanged the dollars for yen to maximize her Tokyo spending money?

Month	JPY = 1.00 USD	Month	JPY = 1.00 USD
January	103.78	May	109.14
February	105.38	June	110.13
March	108.74	July	110.18
April	108.97		

1.6 Pokémon Go. Crystal Gomez, who lives in Mexico City, bought 100 Pokécoins for 17 Mexican pesos (Ps or MXN). Nintendo of Japan, one of the owners of Pokémon Go, will need to convert the Mexican pesos (Ps or MXN) into its home currency, the Japanese yen, in order to record the financial proceeds. The current spot exchange rate between the Mexican peso and the U.S. dollar is MXN18.00 = USD1.00, and the current spot rate between the dollar and the Japanese yen (¥ or JPY) is JPY100.00 = USD1.00. What are the yen proceeds of Crystal Gomez's purchase?

1.7 Isaac Díez of Brazil. Isaac Díez Peris lives in Rio de Janeiro, Brazil. While attending school in Spain he meets Juan Carlos Cordero from Guatemala. Over the summer holiday Isaac decides to visit Juan Carlos in Guatemala City for a couple of weeks. Isaac's parents give him some spending money, 4,500 Brazilian real (BRL). Isaac wants to exchange his Brazilian real for Guatemalan quetzals (GTQ). He collects the following rates:

Spot rate, Guatemalan quetzals per euro: GTQ10.5799 = EUR1.00

Spot rate, Euros per Brazilian real: EUR0.4462 = BRL1.00

a. What is the Brazilian reais/Guatemalan quetzal cross rate?

b. How many Guatemalan quetzals will Isaac get for his Brazilian reais?

Problem 1.3

Country	ISO	Currency	Salary	Signing Bonus	Currency = $1.00
United Kingdom	GBP	pounds (£)	73,000.00	20,000.00	0.700
Czech Republic	CZK	koruna (Kč)	1,850,000,00 Kč	325,000.00 Kč	24.35
France	EUR	euros (€)	€83,000.00	€17,000.00	0.9000

1.8 Moscow to Tokyo. After spending a week in Moscow you get an email from your friend in Japan. He can get you a very good deal on a plane ticket and wants you to meet him in Tokyo next week to continue your post-graduation celebratory trip. You have 450,000 Russian rubles (RUB) left in your money pouch. In preparation for the trip you want to exchange your Russian rubles for Japanese yen (JPY), so you get the following quotes:

Spot rate on the Russian ruble to U.S. dollar cross rate: RUB30.96 = USD1.00

Spot rate on the Japanese yen to U.S. dollar cross rate: JPY84.02 = USD1.00

a. What is the Russian ruble/yen cross rate?

b. How many Japanese yen will you obtain for your Russian rubles?

1.9 Comparing Cheap Dates around the World. Comparison of prices or costs across different country and currency environments requires translation of the local currency into a single common currency. This is most meaningful when the comparison is for the identical or near-identical product or service across countries. Deutsche Bank has recently started publishing a comparison of cheap dates—an evening on the town for two to eat at McDonald's, see a movie, and have a drink. Once all costs are converted to a common currency, the U.S. dollar in this case, the cost of the date can be compared across cities relative to the base case of a cheap date in USD in New York City. After completing the table below, answer the following questions.

a. Which city in the table truly offers the cheapest date?

b. Which city in the table offers the most expensive cheap date?

c. If the exchange rate in Moscow on the Russian ruble (RUB) was 0.04200, instead of 0.0283, what would be the USD price?

d. If the exchange rate in Shanghai was CNY 6.66 = 1 USD, what would be its cost in USD and relative to a cheap date in New York City?

Problem 1.9

Country	City	Cheap Date in Local Currency	Exchange Rate Quote	Exchange Rate	In USD	Relative to NYC
Australia	Sydney	AUD 111.96	USD = 1 AUD	0.9290	104.01	112%
Brazil	Rio de Janeiro	BRL 135.43	USD = 1 BRL	0.4363	_____	_____
Canada	Ottawa	CAD 78.33	USD = 1 CAD	0.9106	_____	_____
China	Shanghai	CNY 373.87	USD = 1 CNY	0.1619	_____	_____
France	Paris	EUR 75.57	USD = 1 EUR	1.3702	_____	_____
Germany	Berlin	EUR 76.49	USD = 1 EUR	1.3702	_____	_____
Hong Kong	Hong Kong	HKD 467.03	USD = 1 HKD	0.1289	_____	_____
India	Mumbai	INR 1,379.64	USD = 1 INR	0.0167	_____	_____
Indonesia	Jakarta	IDR 314,700	USD = 1 IDR	0.0001	_____	_____
Japan	Tokyo	JPY 10,269.07	USD = 1 JPY	0.0097	_____	_____
Malaysia	Kuala Lumpur	MYR 117.85	USD = 1 MYR	0.3048	_____	_____
Mexico	Mexico City	MXN 423.93	USD = 1 MXN	0.0769	_____	_____
New Zealand	Auckland	NZD 111.52	USD = 1 NZD	0.8595	_____	_____
Philippines	Manila	PHP 1,182.88	USD = 1 PHP	0.0222	_____	_____
Russia	Moscow	RUB 2,451.24	USD = 1 RUB	0.0283	_____	_____
Singapore	Singapore	SGD 77.89	USD = 1 SGD	0.7939	_____	_____
South Africa	Cape Town	ZAR 388.58	USD = 1 ZAR	0.0946	_____	_____
United Kingdom	London	GBP 73.29	USD = 1 GBP	1.6566	_____	_____
United States	New York City	USD 93.20	1 USD	1.0000	93.20	100%
United States	San Francisco	USD 88.72	1 USD	1.0000	_____	_____

Source: Data drawn from *The Random Walk, Mapping the World's Prices 2014*, Deutsche Bank Research, 09 May 2014, Figures 30 and 32, with author calculations.

Note: The *cheap date* combines the local currency cost of a cab ride for two, two McDonald's hamburgers, two soft drinks, two movie tickets, and two beers. In 2013 Deutsche Bank had included sending a bouquet of roses in the date, but did not include that in the 2014 index, making the two years not directly comparable.

1.10 Blundell Biotech. Blundell Biotech is a U.S.-based biotechnology company with operations and earnings in a number of foreign countries. The company's profits by subsidiary, in local currency (in millions), are shown in the following table for 2013 and 2014. The average exchange rate for each year, by currency pairs, was the following. Use this data to answer the following questions.

a. What were Blundell Biotech's consolidated profits in U.S. dollars in 2013 and 2014?

b. If the same exchange rates were used for both years—what is often called a "constant currency basis"—was the change in corporate earnings on a constant currency basis?

c. Using the results of the constant currency analysis in part b, is it possible to separate Blundell's growth in earnings between local currency earnings and foreign exchange rate impacts on a consolidated basis?

Net Income	Japanese Subsidiary	British Subsidiary	European Subsidiary	Chinese Subsidiary	Russian Subsidiary	U.S. Subsidiary
2013	JPY 1,500	GBP 100.00	EUR 204.00	CNY 168.00	RUB 124.00	USD 360.00
2014	JPY 1,460	GBP 106.40	EUR 208.00	CNY 194.00	RUB 116.00	USD 382.00

The average exchange rate for each year, by currency pairs, was the following. Use this data to answer the following questions.

Exchange Rate	JPY = 1 USD	USD = 1 GBP	USD = 1 EUR	CNY = 1 USD	RUB = 1 USD	USD
2013	97.57	1.5646	1.3286	6.1484	31.86	1.0000
2014	105.88	1.6473	1.3288	6.1612	38.62	1.0000

1.11 Peng Plasma Pricing. Peng Plasma is a privately held Chinese business. It specializes in the manufacture of plasma cutting torches. Over the past eight years it has held the Chinese renminbi price of the PT350 cutting torch fixed at Rmb 18,000 per unit. Over that same period it has worked to reduce costs per unit but has struggled of late due to higher input costs. Over that same period the renminbi has continued to be revalued against the U.S. dollar by the Chinese government. After completing the table—assuming the same price in renminbi for all years—answer the following questions.

a. What has been the impact of Peng's pricing strategy on the US$ price? How would you expect their U.S. dollar-based customers to have reacted to this?

b. What has been the impact on Peng's margins from this pricing strategy?

Fixed Rmb Pricing of the PT350 Plasma Cutting Torch

Year	Cost (Rmb)	Margin (Rmb)	Price (Rmb)	Margin (percent)	Average Rate (Rmb/US$)	Price (US$)	Percent Chg in US$ Price
2007	16,000	2,000	18,000	11.1%	7.61	2,365	—
2008	15,400	____	____	____	6.95	____	____
2009	14,800	____	____	____	6.83	____	____
2010	14,700	____	____	____	6.77	____	____
2011	14,200	____	____	____	6.46	____	____
2012	14,400	____	____	____	6.31	____	____
2013	14,600	____	____	____	6.15	____	____
2014	14,800	____	____	____	6.16	____	____
Cumulative							____

1.12 Santiago Pirolta's Compensation Agreement. Santiago Pirolta has accepted the Managing Director position for Vitro de Mexico's U.S. operations. Vitro is a Mexico-based manufacturer of flat and custom glass products. Much of its U.S. sales are based on a variety of bottle products, both mass market (e.g., glass bottles for soft drinks) as well as specialty products (high-end cosmetic bottles with rare metal coloring and quality).

Santiago will live and work in the United States (Dallas, Texas) and wishes to be paid in U.S. dollars. Vitro has agreed that his base salary of USD350,000 will be paid in U.S. dollars, but Vitro wishes to tie his annual performance bonus (potentially 10% to 30% above his base salary) to the Mexican peso value of U.S. sales since Vitro consolidates all final results for reporting to stockholders in Mexican pesos (MXN). Santiago, however, is a bit uncertain about having his bonus based on the Mexican peso values of U.S. sales. As a close friend and colleague, what advice would you give him based on your completion of the following table?

Year	(million USD)	Change	MXN=1 USD	(million MXN)	Change
2011	USD 820		12.80	MXN ____	
2012	USD 842	____%	13.30	MXN ____	____%
2013	USD 845	____%	12.70	MXN ____	____%
2014	USD 860	____%	13.40	MXN ____	____%

NexusTech Industries—2017. Problems 13–17 are based on NexusTech Industries. NexusTech is a U.S.-based multinational manufacturing firm with wholly owned subsidiaries in Brazil, Germany, and China, in addition to domestic operations in the United States. NexusTech is traded on the NASDAQ. NexusTech currently has 650,000 shares outstanding. The basic operating characteristics of the various business units is as follows:

Business Performance (000s)	U.S. Parent (US$)	Brazilian Subsidiary (reais, R$)	German Subsidiary (euros, €)	Chinese Subsidiary (yuan, ¥)
Earnings before taxes (EBT)	$4,500	R$6,250	€4,500	¥2,500
Corporate income tax rate	35%	25%	40%	30%
Average exchange rate for the period	—	R$1.80 = $1.00	€0.7018 = $1.00	¥7.750 = $1.00

1.13 NexusTech Industries' Consolidate Earnings. NexusTech must pay corporate income tax in each country in which it currently has operations.

a. After deducting taxes in each country, what are NexusTech's consolidated earnings and consolidated earnings per share in U.S. dollars?

b. What proportion of NexusTech's consolidated earnings arise from each individual country?

c. What proportion of NexusTech's consolidated earnings arise from outside the United States?

d. The U.S. cut its corporate income tax rate to 21% beginning in 2018. How would this change NexusTech's EPS?

1.14 NexusTech's EPS Sensitivity to Exchange Rates. Assume a major political crisis wracks Brazil, first affecting the value of the Brazilian reais and, subsequently, inducing an economic recession within the country. What would be the impact on NexusTech's consolidated EPS if the Brazilian reais were to fall in value to R$3.00/$, with all other earnings and exchange rates remaining the same?

1.15 NexusTech's EPS Sensitivity to Exchange Rates. Assume a major political crisis wracks Brazil, first affecting the value of the Brazilian reais and, subsequently, inducing an economic recession within the country. What would be the impact on NexusTech's consolidated EPS if, in addition to the fall in the value of the reais to R$3.00/$, earnings before taxes in Brazil fell as a result of the recession to R$5,800,000?

1.16 NexusTech's Earnings and the Fall of the Dollar. The dollar has experienced significant swings in value against most of the world's currencies in recent years.

a. What would be the impact on NexusTech's consolidated EPS if all foreign currencies were to appreciate 20% against the U.S. dollar?
b. What would be the impact on NexusTech's consolidated EPS if all foreign currencies were to depreciate 20% against the U.S. dollar?

1.17 NexusTech's Earnings and Global Taxation. All MNEs attempt to minimize their global tax liabilities. Return to the original set of baseline assumptions and answer the following questions regarding NexusTech's global tax liabilities:

a. What is the total amount—in U.S. dollars—that NexusTech is paying across its global business in corporate income taxes?
b. What is NexusTech's effective tax rate (total taxes paid as a proportion of pre-tax profit)?
c. What would be the impact on NexusTech's EPS and global effective tax rate if Germany instituted a corporate tax reduction to 28%, and NexusTech's earnings before tax in Germany rose to €5,000,000?

2

International Monetary System

The price of every thing rises and falls from time to time and place to place; and with every such change the purchasing power of money changes so far as that thing goes.

—Alfred Marshall, *Principles of Economics*, 8th ed. New York: Cosimo Inc., 2009

LEARNING OBJECTIVES

2.1 Explore how the international monetary system has evolved from the days of the gold standard to today's eclectic currency arrangement

2.2 Examine how the choice of fixed versus flexible exchange rate regimes is made by a country in the context of its desires for economic and social independence and openness

2.3 Describe the tradeoff a nation must make between a fixed exchange rate, monetary independence, and freedom of capital movements—the impossible trinity

2.4 Explain the dramatic choices the creation of a single currency for Europe—the euro—required of the European Union's member states

2.5 Study the complexity of exchange rate regime choices faced by many emerging market countries today including China

2.6 Evaluate trends in global reserve currencies and how the introduction of digital currencies may impact the future of the international monetary system

This chapter begins with a brief history of the international monetary system, from the days of the classical gold standard to the present time. The first section describes contemporary currency regimes and their construction and classification. The second section examines fixed versus flexible exchange rate principles. The third section, what we would consider the theoretical core of the chapter, describes the attributes of the ideal currency and the choices nations must make in establishing their currency regime. The fourth section describes the creation and development of the euro for European Union participating countries. The fifth section details the difficult currency regime choices faced by many emerging market countries today. We then conclude with both data and thoughts on global reserve currencies and what the future might hold. The chapter concludes with the mini-case *The Promise of the Digital Yuan*, which examines the rapid development of China's government-sponsored digital currency.

2.1 History of the International Monetary System

No world central bank issues a separate currency for commerce across national boundaries. Instead, a "system" of national monies works more or less well in providing a medium of exchange and unit of account for current international transactions, as well as a store of value and standard of deferred payment for longer-term borrowing and lending.

—Ronald I. McKinnon, The Rules of the Game: International Money in Historical Perspective, *Journal of Economic Literature*, Vol. 31, No. 1, March 1993, pp. 1–44

The system of international money, as noted by McKinnon above, is essentially a loose agreement between nations to exchange their currencies. Over the centuries, currencies have been defined in terms of gold, silver, and other items of value, all within a variety of different agreements between nations to recognize these varying definitions. A review of the evolution of these systems over the past two centuries, shown in Exhibit 2.1, provides one perspective against which to understand how we arrived at today's rather eclectic system of fixed rates, floating rates, crawling pegs, and others and helps us to evaluate weaknesses in and challenges for all enterprises conducting global business.

The Classical Gold Standard (1879–1913)

Since the days of the pharaohs (about 3000 B.C.), gold has served as a medium of exchange and a store of value. The Greeks and Romans used gold coins, and this tradition persisted through to the nineteenth century. The great increase in trade during the late nineteenth century led to a need for a more formalized system for settling international trade balances. One country after another set a par value for its currency in terms of gold or silver and then tried to adhere to the so-called *rules of the game*.[1]

EXHIBIT 2.1 The Evolution of the Global Monetary System

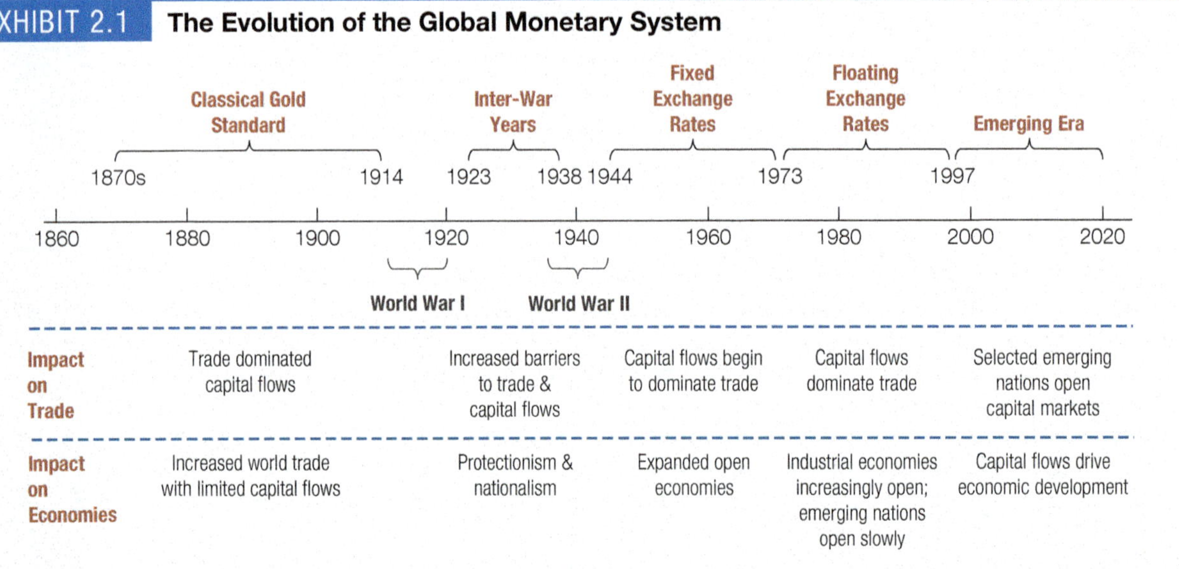

[1]Although the expression "rules of the game" is often attributed to John Maynard Keynes, he actually never listed what he thought those rules were. Keynes, in the "Economic Consequences of Mr. Churchill" (1925), described the Bank of England reducing credit as a result of the "rules of the gold standard game."

Some countries, like the U.S., first defined their currency in terms of both gold and silver (a bi-metallic standard), setting a ratio between the two (e.g., 1 unit of gold equaling 15 units of silver). If the market values of gold and silver diverged from this ratio, for example, if silver became relatively more valuable, then it (silver) would flow out of the nation leaving the other metal (gold) as the surviving metal backing the currency. The U.S. altered ratios and convertibility a number of times in the mid-1800s, even ending convertibility during the Civil War years of 1861–1865. In order to finance its war effort, the U.S. government suspended convertibility and printed paper money. The paper notes, printed in green on their back ("greenbacks"), had no intrinsic value and no exchange value in gold or silver and therefore were considered *fiat money*, money by decree. Following the Civil War the U.S. moved back to convertibility. As the rise of gold as the single metal (or *specie*) became prevalent across countries, the *classical gold standard* was born.

The gold standard as an international monetary system gained acceptance in Western Europe in the 1870s. France moved to gold alone in 1873, followed by Germany. Great Britain, far ahead of the other major powers of the time, had officially adopted a gold standard in 1844 under the Bank Charter Act, which made Bank of England notes fully convertible to gold. The U.S. was a bit of a latecomer to the system, not officially adopting the gold standard until 1879.

Under the gold standard, the rules of the game were clear and simple: Each country set the rate at which its currency unit (paper or coin) could be converted to a given weight of gold. For example, prior to the first world war the United States declared the U.S. dollar to be convertible to gold at a rate of \$20.67 per Troy ounce, while Great Britain pegged the British pound sterling at £4.2474 per Troy ounce of gold. As long as both currencies were freely convertible into gold within each nation, the rate of exchange between the two monies—the *parity*—was set:

$$\frac{\$20.67 = 1\,\text{ounce of gold}}{£4.2474 = 1\,\text{ounce of gold}} = \$4.8665/£1.0$$

Because the government of each country on the gold standard agreed to buy or sell gold on demand at its own fixed parity rate, *convertibility*, the value of each individual currency in terms of gold, and therefore exchange rates between currencies, was fixed. But the validity of each parity rate, whether the U.S. dollar, British pound, Russian rouble, or German mark, was based on the ability of an individual to exchange the currency for the metal—gold. Maintaining reserves of gold, gold ready to be exchanged for the currency on demand, was therefore critical in order for a government to maintain the faith of its citizens in its monetary system.

The system simultaneously implicitly limited the rate at which any individual government could expand its money supply. Growth in the money supply was limited to the rate at which official authorities (government treasuries or central banks) could acquire additional gold. This restriction was deemed essential to prevent governments from printing money and stoking inflationary forces. The gold standard worked adequately until the outbreak of World War I interrupted trade flows and the free movement of gold. This event caused the main trading nations to suspend operation of the gold standard. And as described in *Global Finance in Practice 2.1*, the gold standard allowed some governments to raise capital on the international markets by assuring investors of fixed rates of exchange.

The Interwar Years and World War II (1914–1944)

During World War I and through the early 1920s, currencies were allowed to fluctuate over fairly wide ranges in terms of gold and in relation to each other. Theoretically, supply and demand for a country's exports and imports caused moderate changes in an exchange rate

GLOBAL FINANCE IN PRACTICE 2.1

Czar Nicholas IV's Russian Gold Loan of 1894 (Bond)

Czar Nicholas IV of Russia issued a 100-year bearer bond in 1894. Each of the Gold Rouble bonds were 125 roubles in principal, paying 4% annual interest quarterly (e.g., 1% of principal paid on each quarterly coupon). A *bearer bond* is a security sold to an investor in which the *bearer* of the bond (the holder) is entitled to receive an interest payment at regularly scheduled dates as listed on the bond. No record is kept by any authority on who the owner of the bond is, allowing the investor to earn interest without tax authorities knowing the investor's identity. This allowed the bond issuer, in this case the czar, to raise capital at lower interest rates because investors would most likely be able to avoid paying taxes on the interest income they received. And that interest on the czar's bond could be collected in six different currencies: French francs, German marks, British pounds, Dutch florins, U.S. dollars, and its home currency, Russian (gold) roubles.

In order for the investor to receive their interest payments, the bond contained a sheet of coupons which were numbered and dated. In this case, 100 years of quarterly coupons (400 individual coupons), each individually numbered, dated, and amount payable in all six currencies detailed. Individual coupons were clipped from the sheet and taken to one of the listed banks globally in order to receive payment. The individual interest payments in six different currencies was only possible through the use (or assumption of validity) of fixed exchange rates under the international gold standard of the time.

BOND of one hundred and twenty-five Gold Roubles
= 500 Francs = 404 German Marks = 19 Pounds Sterling 15 shill. 6 pence = 239 Dutch Flor.
= 96.25 United States Gold Dollars

The currency of payment was at the choice of the bearer. The bond and all coupons listed the six different paying agents by city.

in St. Petersburg:	at the State Bank, in Gold Roubles or Credit Roubles, at the rate of exchange of the day;
in Paris:	at the Banque de Paris et des Pays-Bas, at the Crédit Lyonnais, at the Comptoir National d'Escompte de Paris, at the office of the Russian Bank for Foreign Trade and at Messrs Hottingeur & Co, in Francs;
in London:	at the Russian Bank for Foreign Trade (London-branch), in Pounds Sterling;
in Berlin:	at Messrs Mendelssohn & Co, in German Marks
in Amsterdam:	at Messrs Lippmann, Rosenthal & Co, in Dutch Florins;
in New York:	at Messrs Baring, Magoun & Co, in Gold Dollars.

The 118th coupon in the series, which the bearer could present for payment beginning June 18, 1923, is reproduced below.

RUSSIAN 4% GOLD LOAN, SIXTH ISSUE, 1894
Talon of the Bond of 187 Rouble 50 Cop.
(1/Rouble = 1/15 Imper.)
118th Coupon of the Bond, due 18 June/1 July 1923:
in Paris 5 Francs, in Berlin 4 Mark 4 Pf., in London 3 Schill. 11 ½ P., in Amsterdam 2 Flor. 39 C.,
In New York 96 1/4 Cents.

Valid for 10 years.

about a central equilibrium value. This was the same function that gold had performed under the previous gold standard. Unfortunately, such flexible exchange rates did not work in an equilibrating manner. On the contrary, international speculators sold the weak currencies short, causing them to fall further in value than warranted by real economic factors. Selling short is a speculation technique in which an individual speculator sells an asset, such as a currency, to another party for delivery at a future date. The speculator, however, does not yet own the asset and expects the price of the asset to fall before the date by which the speculator must purchase the asset in the open market for delivery.

The reverse happened with strong currencies. Fluctuations in currency values could not be offset by the relatively illiquid forward exchange market, except at exorbitant cost. The net result was that the volume of world trade did not grow in the 1920s in proportion to world gross domestic product. Instead, it declined to a very low level with the advent of the Great Depression in the 1930s.

GLOBAL FINANCE IN PRACTICE **2.2**

Britain Leaves the Gold Standard: Press Notice (Excerpts of September 19, 1931)

His Majesty's Government have decided after consultation with the Bank of England that it has become necessary to suspend for the time being the operation of Subsection (2) of Section 1 of the Gold Standard Act of 1925 which requires the Bank to sell gold at a fixed price. A Bill for this purpose will be introduced immediately and it is the intention of His Majesty's Government to ask Parliament to pass it through all its stages on Monday, 21st of September. In the meantime the Bank of England have been authorised to proceed accordingly in anticipation of the action of Parliament.

The reasons which have led to this decision are as follows. Since the middle of July funds amounting to more than £200 millions have been met partly from gold and foreign currency held by the Bank of England, partly from the proceeds of a credit of £50 millions which shortly matures secured by the Bank of England from New York and Paris and partly from the proceeds of the French and American credits amounting to £80 millions recently obtained by the Government. During the last few days the withdrawals of foreign balances have accelerated so sharply that His Majesty's Government have felt bound to take the decision mentioned above.

This decision will of course not affect obligations of His Majesty's Government or the Bank of England which are payable in foreign currencies.

The gold holding of the Bank of England amounts to some £130 millions and having regard to the contingencies which may have to be met it is inadvisable to allow the reserve to be further reduced.

His Majesty's Government are well aware that the present step is bound to have serious consequences both at home and abroad. But during the last few days the International financial markets have become demoralised and seem bent on liquidating their foreign assets in a spit of panic. In the circumstances there was no alternative but to protect the economy of this country the only means at our disposal.

Source: The National Archives. https://www.nationalarchives.gov.uk/wp-content/uploads/2014/03/t163-68-181.jpg

Britain had returned to the gold standard in 1925, but as a result of onset of the depression and the flight of gold out of Britain in 1931, it was forced to abandon the standard in September 1931. *Global Finance in Practice 2.2* presents excerpts of His Majesty's Government's decision.

The United States adopted a modified gold standard in 1934 when the U.S. dollar was devalued to $35 per ounce of gold from the $20.67 per ounce price in effect prior to World War I. Contrary to previous practice, the U.S. Treasury now traded gold only with foreign central banks, not private citizens. From 1934 to the end of World War II, exchange rates were theoretically determined by each currency's value in terms of gold. During World War II and its chaotic aftermath, however, many of the main trading currencies lost their convertibility into other currencies. The dollar was one of the few currencies that continued to be convertible.

Bretton Woods and the International Monetary Fund (1944)

As World War II drew to a close in 1944, the Allied Powers met at Bretton Woods, New Hampshire, to create a new postwar international monetary system. The Bretton Woods Agreement established a U.S. dollar-based international monetary system and provided for two new institutions: the International Monetary Fund and the World Bank. The International Monetary Fund (IMF) was created to aid countries with balance of payments and exchange rate problems. The International Bank for Reconstruction and Development (IBRD or as it is more commonly called, the World Bank) was formed to help fund postwar reconstruction and has since supported general economic development. *Global Finance in Practice 2.3* provides some insight into the debates at Bretton Woods.

The IMF was the key institution in the new international monetary system, and it has remained so to the present day. The IMF was established to render temporary assistance to

GLOBAL FINANCE IN PRACTICE 2.3

Hammering out an Agreement at Bretton Woods

The governments of the Allied powers knew that the devastating impacts of World War II would require swift and decisive policies. In the summer of 1944 (July 1–22), representatives of all 45 allied nations met at Bretton Woods, New Hampshire, for the United Nations Monetary and Financial Conference. Their purpose was to plan the postwar international monetary system. It was a difficult process, and the final synthesis was shaded by pragmatism.

The leading policymakers at Bretton Woods were the British and the Americans. The British delegation was led by Lord John Maynard Keynes, known as "Britain's economic heavy weight." The British argued for a postwar system that would be more flexible than the various gold standards used before the war. Keynes argued, as he had after World War I, that attempts to tie currency values to gold would create pressures for deflation in many of the war-ravaged economies.

The American delegation was led by the director of the U.S. Treasury's monetary research department, Harry D. White, and the U.S. Secretary of the Treasury, Henry Morgenthau, Jr. The Americans argued for stability (fixed exchange rates) but not a return to the gold standard itself. In fact, although the U.S. at that time held most of the gold of the Allied powers, the U.S. delegates argued that currencies should be fixed in parities* but that redemption of gold should occur only between official authorities like central banks.

On the more pragmatic side, all parties agreed that a postwar system would be stable and sustainable only if there was sufficient credit available for countries to defend their currencies in the event of payment imbalances, which they knew to be inevitable in a reconstructing world order. The conference divided into three commissions for weeks of negotiation. One commission, led by U.S. Treasury Secretary Morgenthau, was charged with the organization of a fund of capital to be used for exchange rate stabilization. A second commission, chaired by Lord Keynes, was charged with the organization of a second "bank" whose purpose would be for long-term reconstruction and development. A third commission was to hammer out details such as what role silver would have in any new system.

After weeks of meetings, the participants came to a three-part agreement—*the Bretton Woods Agreement*. The plan called for: (1) fixed exchange rates, termed an *adjustable peg*, among members; (2) a fund of gold and constituent currencies available to members for stabilization of their respective currencies, called the International Monetary Fund (IMF); and (3) a bank for financing long-term development projects (eventually known as the World Bank). One proposal resulting from the meetings, which was not ratified by the U.S., was the establishment of an international trade organization to promote free trade.

* *Fixed in parities* is an old expression in this field, which means that the value of currencies should be fixed at rates that equalize their value, typically measured by purchasing power.

member countries trying to defend their currencies against cyclical, seasonal, or random occurrences. It also assists countries having structural trade problems if they promise to take adequate steps to correct their problems. If persistent deficits occur, however, the IMF cannot save a country from eventual devaluation. In recent years, the IMF has attempted to help countries facing financial crises, providing massive loans as well as advice to Russia, Brazil, Greece, Indonesia, and South Korea, to name but a few.

Under the original provisions of Bretton Woods, all countries fixed the value of their currencies in terms of gold, but they were not required to exchange their currencies for gold. Only the dollar remained convertible into gold (at $35 per ounce). Each country established its exchange rate vis-à-vis the dollar and then calculated the gold par value of its currency to create the desired dollar exchange rate. Participating countries agreed to try to maintain the value of their currencies within 1% (later expanded to 2.25%) of par by buying or selling foreign exchange or gold as needed. Devaluation was not to be used as a competitive trade policy, but if a currency became too weak to defend, devaluation of up to 10% was allowed without formal approval by the IMF. Larger devaluations required IMF approval. This became known as the *gold-exchange standard*.

An additional innovation introduced by Bretton Woods was the creation of the Special Drawing Right (SDR). The SDR is an international reserve asset created by the IMF to supplement existing foreign exchange reserves. It serves as a unit of account for the IMF and other international and regional organizations. It is also the base against which some countries peg the exchange rate for their currencies. Initially defined in terms of a fixed quantity of gold, the SDR was for many years the weighted average of four major currencies: the U.S. dollar, the euro, the Japanese yen, and the British pound. On October 1, 2016, the Chinese yuan (or renminbi) was added as the fifth currency component.

The weight assigned to each SDR currency is updated every five years by the IMF. The 2015 weights, taking effect on October 1, 2016, are as follows:

Currency	2015 Weight	2010 Weight
U.S. dollar	41.73%	41.9%
Euro	30.93%	37.4%
Chinese renminbi	10.92%	—
Japanese yen	8.33%	9.4%
Pound sterling	8.09%	11.3%
Total	100.00%	100.0%

Individual countries hold SDRs in the form of deposits in the IMF. These holdings are part of each country's international monetary reserves, along with its official holdings of gold, its foreign exchange, and its reserve position at the IMF. Member countries may settle transactions among themselves with SDRs.

The SDR's use outside of reserve assets is extremely limited. Harvard economist Jeffrey Frankel has described the SDR as "basically the Esperanto, at best, of international currencies. It's not at all used." He is not quite correct, however, as the Suez Canal and the Universal Postal Union both use the SDR in the calculation of transit charges and postal fees, respectively. As a weighted index of five different currencies, it is mathematically less volatile than any single currency value and, therefore, has found specific uses in areas such as maritime contracts, securities in the eurobond market, and select international treaties. Most recently, in March 2021, the G7, the world's seven largest industrial economies, agreed to support the expansion of the IMF's reserves to help developing countries cope with the global pandemic.

Fixed Exchange Rates (1945–1973)

The currency arrangement negotiated at Bretton Woods and monitored by the IMF worked fairly well during the postwar period of reconstruction and rapid growth in world trade. However, widely diverging national monetary and fiscal policies, differential rates of inflation, and various unexpected external shocks eventually resulted in the system's demise. The U.S. dollar was the main reserve currency held by central banks and was the key to the web of exchange rate values. Unfortunately, the U.S. ran persistent and growing deficits in its balance of payments.

A heavy capital outflow of dollars was required to finance these deficits and to meet the growing demand for dollars from investors and businesses. Eventually, the heavy overhang of dollars held by foreigners resulted in a lack of confidence in the ability of the U.S. to meet its commitments in gold. This lack of confidence came to a head in the first half of 1971. In a little less than seven months, the U.S. suffered the loss of nearly one-third of its official gold reserves as global confidence in the value of the dollar plummeted. Exchange rates between most major currencies and the U.S. dollar began to float, and thus indirectly, so did their values relative to gold. A year and a half later, the U.S. dollar once again came under attack, thereby forcing a second devaluation in February 1973, this time by 10% to $42.22 per ounce of gold. By late February 1973, a fixed-rate system no longer appeared feasible given the speculative flows of currencies. The major foreign exchange markets were actually closed for several weeks in March 1973. When markets reopened, most currencies were allowed to float to levels determined by market forces.

Floating Exchange Rates, 1973–1997

Since 1973 exchange rates have become more volatile and less predictable than they were during the "fixed" exchange rate era, when changes occurred infrequently. Exhibit 2.2 illustrates the wide swings exhibited by the nominal exchange rate index of the U.S. dollar since 1964. Clearly, volatility has increased since 1973.

Exhibit 2.2 notes some of the most important shocks in recent history: the creation of the European Monetary System (EMS) in 1979, the run-up and peak of the dollar in 1985, the EMS crisis of 1992, the Asian crisis of 1997, the launch of the European euro in 1999, and the Brexit vote in 2016.

The Emerging Era, 1997–Present

The period following the Asian Crisis of 1997 has seen growth in both the breadth and depth of emerging market economies and currencies. We may end up being proven wrong on this count, but the final section of this chapter argues that the global monetary system has already begun embracing—for more than two decades now—a number of major emerging market currencies, beginning with the Chinese renminbi. Feel free to disagree.

EXHIBIT 2.2 Bank for International Settlements Index of the Dollar

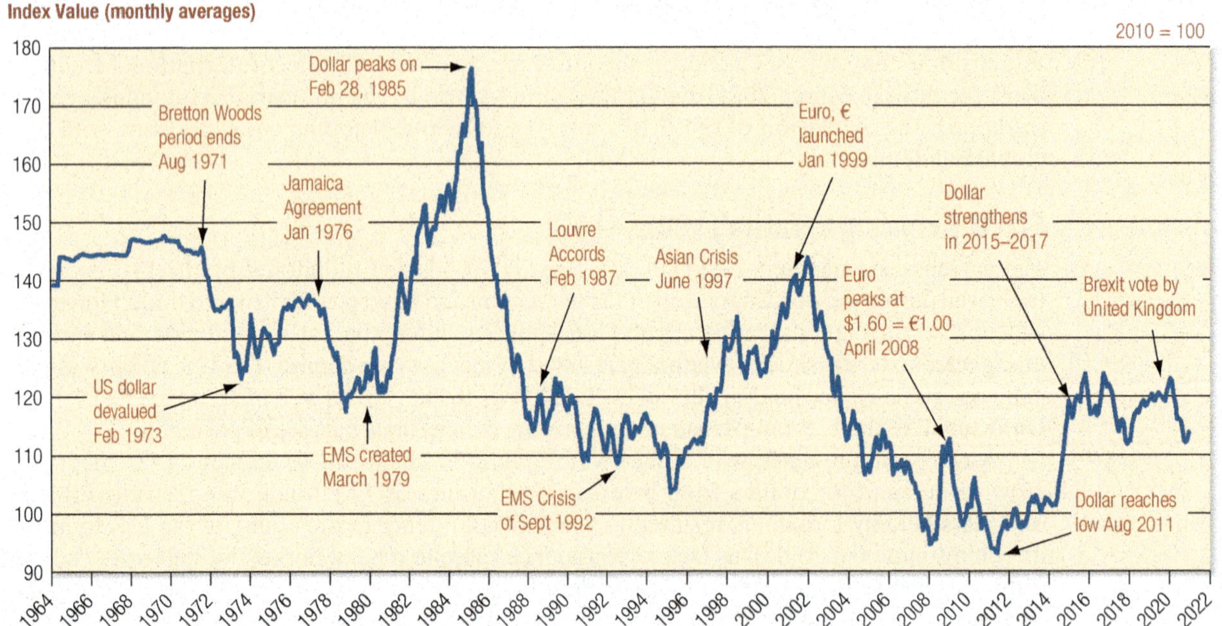

Source: BIS org Nominal exchange rate index (narrow definition), effective exchange rate (EER) for the U.S dollar (NNUS).

IMF Classification of Currency Regimes

The global monetary system—if there is indeed a singular "system"—is an eclectic combination of exchange rate regimes and arrangements. There is no single governing body or single official global policing authority for global exchange of currencies. The IMF, however, has at least played the role of "town crier" since World War II. As part of its self-appointed duties, it has created a classification system of currency regimes.

Brief Classification History

The IMF was for many years the central clearinghouse for exchange rate classifications. Member states submitted their exchange rate policies to the IMF, and those submissions were the basis for its categorization of exchange rate regimes. However, that all changed in 1997–1998 with the Asian Financial Crisis. During the crisis many countries began following very different exchange rate practices than those they had committed to with the IMF. Their actual practices—their de facto systems—were not what they had publicly and officially committed to—their de jure systems.

Beginning in 1998, the IMF changed its practice and stopped collecting regime classification submissions from member states. Instead, it confined its regime classifications and reports to analysis performed in-house. (This included the cessation of publishing its Annual Report on Exchange Arrangements and Exchange Restrictions, a document on which many of the world's financial institutions had relied for decades.) As a global institution, which is in principle apolitical, the IMF's analysis today is focused on classifying currencies on the basis of an ex post analysis of how the currency's value was based in the recent past. This analysis focuses on observed behavior, not on official government policy pronouncements.

The IMF's De Facto System

The IMF's methodology of classifying exchange rate regimes today, in effect since January 2009, is presented in Exhibit 2.3. It is based on actual observed behavior, de facto results, and not on the official policy statements of the respective governments, de jure classification. The classification process begins with the determination of whether the exchange rate of the country's currency is dominated by markets or by official action. Although the classification system is a bit challenging, there are four basic categories.

Category 1: Hard Pegs. These countries have given up their own sovereignty over monetary policy. This category includes countries that have adopted other countries' currencies (e.g., Zimbabwe's dollarization—its adoption of the U.S. dollar) and countries utilizing a currency board structure that limits monetary expansion to the accumulation of foreign exchange.

Category 2: Soft Pegs. This general category is colloquially referred to as fixed exchange rates. The five subcategories of soft peg regimes are differentiated on the basis of what the currency is fixed to, whether that fix is allowed to change (and if so under what conditions); what types, magnitudes, and frequencies of intervention are allowed/used; and the degree of variance about the fixed rate.

Category 3: Floating Arrangements. Currencies that are predominantly market-driven are further subdivided into free floating with values determined by open market forces without governmental influence or intervention and simple floating or floating with intervention, where government occasionally does intervene in the market in pursuit of some rate goals or objectives.

EXHIBIT 2.3 IMF Exchange Rate Classifications

Rate Classification	De Facto System	Description and Requirements
Hard Pegs	**Arrangement with no separate legal tender**	The currency of another country circulates as the sole legal tender (*formal dollarization*), as well as members of a monetary or currency union in which the same legal tender is shared by the members.
	Currency board arrangement	A monetary arrangement based on an explicit legislative commitment to exchange domestic currency for a specific foreign currency at a fixed exchange rate, combined with restrictions on the issuing authority. Restrictions imply that domestic currency will be issued only against foreign exchange and that it remains fully backed by foreign assets.
Soft Pegs	**Conventional pegged arrangement**	A country formally pegs its currency at a fixed rate to another currency or a basket of currencies of major financial or trading partners. Country authorities stand ready to maintain the fixed parity through direct or indirect intervention. The exchange rate may vary ±1% around a central rate or may vary no more than 2% for a six-month period.
	Stabilized arrangement	A spot market rate that remains within a margin of 2% for six months or more and is not floating. Margin stability can be met by either a single currency or basket of currencies (assuming statistical measurement). Exchange rate remains stable as a result of official action.
	Intermediate pegs: **Crawling peg**	Currency is adjusted in small amounts at a fixed rate or in response to changes in quantitative indicators (e.g., inflation differentials).
	Crawl-like arrangement	Exchange rate must remain with a narrow margin of 2% relative to a statistically defined trend for six months or more. Exchange rate cannot be considered floating. Minimum rate of change is greater than allowed under a stabilized arrangement.
	Pegged exchange rate within horizontal bands	Value of the currency is maintained within 1% of a fixed central rate or the margin between the maximum and minimum value of the exchange rate exceeds 2%. This includes countries which are today members of the ERM II system.
Floating Arrangements	**Floating**	Exchange rate is largely market determined without an ascertainable or predictable path. Market intervention may be direct or indirect and serves to moderate the rate of change (but not targeting). Rate may exhibit more or less volatility.
	Free floating	A floating rate is freely floating if intervention occurs only exceptionally and confirmation of intervention is limited to at most three instances in a six-month period, each lasting no more than three business days.
Residual	**Other managed arrangements**	This category is residual and is used when the exchange rate does not meet the criteria for any other category. Arrangements characterized by frequent shifts in policies fall into this category.

Source: "Revised System for the Classification of Exchange Rate Arrangements," by Karl Habermeier, Annamaria Kokenyne, Romain Veyrune, and Harald Anderson, IMF Working Paper WP/09/211, International Monetary Fund, November 17, 2009.

Category 4: Residual. As one would suspect, this category includes all exchange rate arrangements that do not meet the criteria of the previous three categories. Country systems demonstrating frequent shifts in policy typically make up the bulk of this category.

Exhibit 2.4 provides a glimpse into how these major regime categories translate in the global market—fixed or floating. The vertical dashed line, the crawling peg, is the zone some currencies move into and out of depending on their relative currency stability. Although the classification regimes appear clear and distinct, the distinctions are often more difficult to distinguish in practice in the market. For example, in January 2014, the Bank of Russia

EXHIBIT 2.4 **Taxonomy of Exchange Rate Regimes**

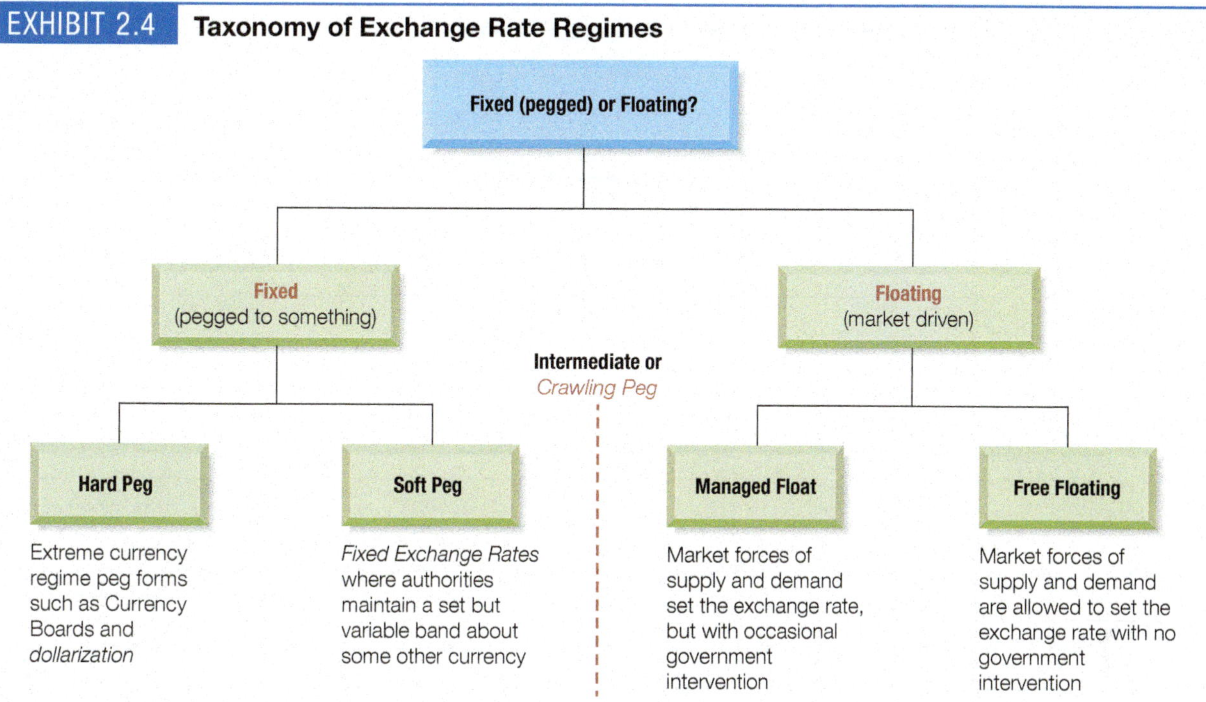

announced it would no longer conduct intervention activities with regard to the value of the ruble and that it planned to allow the ruble to trade freely with no intervention.

A Global Eclectic

Despite the IMF's attempt to apply rigor to regime classifications, the global monetary system today is indeed a global eclectic in every sense of the term. As Chapter 5 will describe in detail, the current global market in currency is dominated by two major currencies, the U.S. dollar and the European euro, and after that, a multitude of systems, arrangements, currency areas, and zones.

The IMF estimates that 20.3% of its member countries use the U.S. dollar as their *anchor currency*, with another 13% using the euro and 4.7% using a composite or other currency as anchor.[2] In addition to anchor currency systems, 12.5% of IMF members use some monetary aggregate (money supply measure) as their gauge to currency management, while another 20% pursue inflation rate targeting. A full 25% of IMF members use some other form of monetary policy framework or unstated exchange rate anchor.

The euro itself is an example of a rigidly fixed system, acting as a single currency for its member countries. However, the euro is also an independently floating currency against all other currencies. Other examples of rigidly fixed exchange regimes include Ecuador, Panama, and Zimbabwe, all of which use the U.S. dollar as their official currency; the Central African Franc (CFA) zone, in which countries such as Mali, Niger, Senegal, Cameroon, and Chad among others use a single common currency (the franc, which is tied to the euro); and the Eastern Caribbean Currency Union (ECCU), a set of countries that use the Eastern Caribbean dollar.

[2] *Annual Report on Exchange Arrangements and Exchange Restrictions, 2016*, International Monetary Fund, p. 10.

EXHIBIT 2.5 IMF Member Exchange Rate Regime Choices

Percentage of IMF membership by regime choice

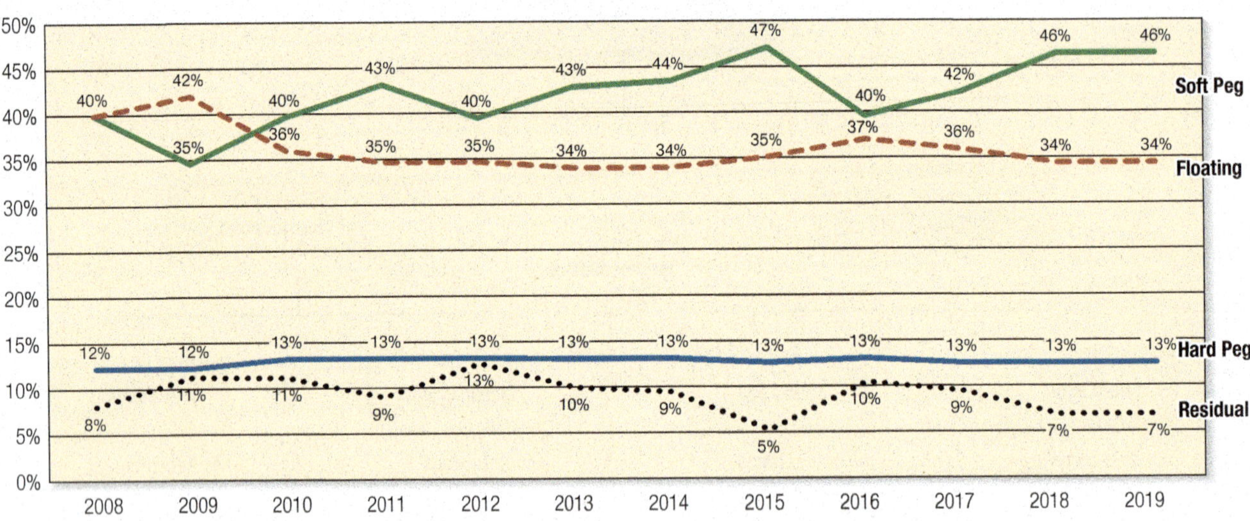

Source: Data drawn from ***Annual Report on Exchange Arrangements and Exchange Restrictions***, International Monetary Fund, Table 3, Exchange Rate Arrangements 2008–2019.

At the other extreme are countries with independently floating currencies. These include many of the most developed countries, such as Japan, the United States, the United Kingdom, Canada, Australia, New Zealand, Sweden, and Switzerland. However, this category also includes a number of unwilling participants—emerging market countries that tried to maintain fixed rates but were forced by the marketplace to let their currencies float. Among these are Korea, the Philippines, Brazil, Indonesia, Mexico, and Thailand.

As illustrated by Exhibit 2.5, the regime choices of IMF member countries have not changed dramatically over the past decade. Countries with floating regimes average 34% or 35% of member countries, while countries using soft peg regimes have increased from just under 40% to 46% in recent years. Although the contemporary international monetary system is typically referred to as a floating exchange rate system, that is clearly not the case for the majority of the world's nations.

2.2 Fixed versus Flexible Exchange Rates

A nation's choice as to which currency regime to follow reflects national priorities about all facets of the economy, including inflation, unemployment, interest rate levels, trade balances, and economic growth. The choice between fixed and flexible rates may change over time as priorities change. At the risk of overgeneralizing, the following points partly explain why countries pursue certain exchange rate regimes. Fixed exchange rates have a number of disadvantages—as we will show in the following section—and maintaining them can be difficult and costly. But they also offer some advantages as follows:

- Fixed rates provide stability in international prices for the conduct of trade. Stable prices aid in the growth of international trade and lessen risks for all businesses.

- Fixed exchange rates are inherently anti-inflationary, requiring the country to follow restrictive monetary and fiscal policies. This restrictiveness, however, can be a burden to a country wishing to pursue policies to alleviate internal economic problems such as high unemployment or slow economic growth.
- Fixed exchange rate regimes necessitate that central banks maintain large quantities of international reserves (hard currencies and gold) for use in the occasional defense of the fixed rate. As international currency markets have grown in size, increasing reserve holdings has become a growing burden.
- Fixed rates, once in place, may be maintained at levels that are inconsistent with economic fundamentals. As the structure of a nation's economy changes and as its trade relationships and balances evolve, the exchange rate itself should change. Flexible exchange rates allow this to happen gradually and efficiently, but fixed rates must be changed administratively—usually too late, with too much publicity, and at too large a one-time cost to the nation's economic health.

The terminology associated with changes in currency values is also technically specific. When a government officially declares its own currency to be worth less or more relative to other currencies, it is termed a *devaluation* or *revaluation*, respectively. This obviously applies to currencies whose value is controlled by government. When a currency's value is changed in the open currency market—not directly by government—it is called a *depreciation* (with a fall in value) or *appreciation* (with an increase in value).

2.3 The Impossible Trinity

If the ideal currency existed in today's world, it would possess the following three attributes, illustrated in Exhibit 2.6, often referred to as the *impossible trinity* or the *trilemma of international finance*:

EXHIBIT 2.6 The Impossible Trinity

Exchange Rate Stability:
A Managed or Pegged Exchange Rate

China & major industrial countries under Bretton Woods (give up free flow of capital)

A

B

Individual European Union Member States (give up independent monetary policy)

Monetary Independence: An Independent Monetary Policy

Full Financial Integration: Free Flow of Capital

C

United States, Japan (give up a fixed exchange rate)

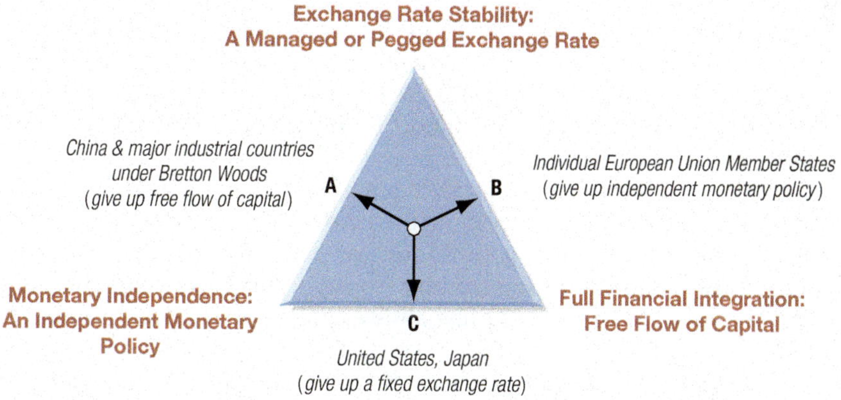

Nations must choose in which direction to move from the center—toward points A, B, or C. Their choice is a choice of what *to pursue* and what *to give up*—that of the opposite point of the pyramid. Marginal compromise is possible, but only marginal.

Source: Constructed by the authors based on *International Financial Integration*, Lar Oxelheim, Springer-Verlag, Berlin, 1990, p. 10.

1. **Exchange rate stability.** The value of the currency is fixed in relationship to other major currencies, so traders and investors could be relatively certain of the foreign exchange value of each currency in the present and into the near future.
2. **Full financial integration.** Complete freedom of monetary flows would be allowed, so traders and investors could easily move funds from one country and currency to another in response to perceived economic opportunities or risks.
3. **Monetary independence.** Domestic monetary and interest rate policies would be set by each individual country to pursue desired national economic policies, especially as they might relate to limiting inflation, combating recessions, and fostering prosperity and full employment.

Together, these qualities are termed the *impossible trinity* because the forces of economics do not allow a country to simultaneously achieve all three goals: monetary independence, exchange rate stability, and full financial integration. The impossible trinity makes it clear that each economy must choose its own medicine. Here is what many argue are the choices of three of the major global economic players:

Entity	Choice #1	Choice #2	Implied Condition #3
United States	Independent monetary policy	Free movement of capital	Currency value floats
China	Independent monetary policy	Fixed rate of exchange	Restricted movement of capital
Europe (EU)	Free movement of capital	Fixed rate of exchange	Integrated monetary policy

For example, a country like the U.S. has knowingly given up on having a fixed exchange rate—moving from the center of the pyramid toward point C—because it wishes to have an independent monetary policy, and it allows a high level of freedom in the movement of capital into and out of the country.

The choices made by the EU are clearly more complex. As a combination of different sovereign states, the EU has pursued integration of a common currency, the euro, and free movement of labor and capital. The result, according to the impossible trinity, is that EU member states had to give up independent monetary policy, replacing individual central banks with the European Central Bank (ECB). The recent fiscal deficits and near-collapses of government debt issuances in Greece, Portugal, and Ireland have raised questions over the efficacy of the arrangement.

China today is a clear example of a nation that has chosen to continue to control and manage the value of its currency and to conduct an independent monetary policy, moving from the center of the pyramid toward point A while continuing to restrict the flow of capital into and out of the country. To say it has "given up" the free flow of capital is probably inaccurate, as China has allowed no real freedom of capital flows in the past century.

The consensus of many experts is that the force of increased capital mobility has been pushing more and more countries toward full financial integration in an attempt to stimulate their domestic economies and to feed the capital appetites of their own MNEs. As a result, their currency regimes are being "cornered" into being either purely floating (like the U.S.) or integrated with other countries in monetary unions (like the European Union).

2.4 A Single Currency for Europe: The Euro

Beginning with the Treaty of Rome in 1957 and continuing with the Single European Act of 1987, the Maastricht Treaty of 1992, and the Treaty of Amsterdam of 1997, a core set of European countries worked steadily toward integrating their individual country markets into one larger, more efficient domestic market. However, even after the launch of the 1992 Single Europe program, a number of barriers to true openness remained, including the use of different currencies, which required both consumers and companies to treat the individual country markets separately. Currency risk of cross-border commerce still persisted. The creation of a single currency was seen as the way to move beyond these last vestiges of separated markets.

The original 15 members of the EU were also members of the European Monetary System (EMS). The EMS formed a system of fixed exchange rates among the member currencies, with deviations managed through bilateral responsibility to maintain rates at ±2.5% of an established central rate. This system of fixed rates, with adjustments along the way, remained in effect from 1979 to 1999. Its resiliency was seriously tested with exchange rate crises in 1992 and 1993, but it held.

The Maastricht Treaty and Monetary Union

In December 1991, the members of the EU met at Maastricht, the Netherlands, and concluded a treaty that changed Europe's currency future. The *Maastricht Treaty* specified a timetable and a plan to replace all individual EMS member currencies with a single currency—eventually named the euro. Other aspects of the treaty were also adopted that would lead to a full *European Economic and Monetary Union* (EMU). According to the EU, the EMU is a single-currency area within the singular EU market, now known informally as the eurozone, in which people, goods, services, and capital are allowed to move freely.

The integration of separate country monetary systems is not, however, a minor task. To prepare for the EMU, the Maastricht Treaty called for the integration and coordination of the member countries' monetary and fiscal policies. The EMU would be implemented by a process called *convergence*. Before becoming a full member of the EMU, each member country was expected to meet a set of convergence criteria in order to integrate systems that were at the same relative performance levels: (1) nominal inflation should be no more than 1.5% above the average for the three members of the EU that had the lowest inflation rates during the previous year, (2) long-term interest rates should be no more than 2% above the average of the three members with the lowest interest rates, (3) individual government budget deficits (fiscal deficits) should be no more than 3% of gross domestic product, and (4) government debt outstanding should be no more than 60% of gross domestic product. The convergence criteria were so tough that few, if any, of the members could satisfy them at that time, but 11 countries managed to do so just prior to 1999. (Greece was added two years later.)

The European Central Bank (ECB)

The cornerstone of any monetary system is a strong, disciplined central bank. The Maastricht Treaty established this single institution for the EMU, the European Central Bank (ECB), which was established in 1998. (The EU created the European Monetary Institute [EMI] in 1994 as a transitional step in establishing the European Central Bank.) The ECB's structure and functions were modeled after the German Bundesbank, which in turn had been modeled after the U.S. Federal Reserve System. The ECB is an independent central bank that dominates the activities of the individual countries' central banks. The individual central banks continue to regulate banks resident within their borders, but all financial market intervention and the issuance of the single currency are the sole responsibility of the ECB. The single most important mandate of the ECB is its charge to promote price stability within the European Union.

The Launch of the Euro

On January 4, 1999, 11 member states of the EU initiated the EMU. They established a single currency, the euro, which replaced the individual currencies of the participating member states. The 11 countries were Austria, Belgium, Finland, France, Germany, Ireland, Italy, Luxembourg, the Netherlands, Portugal, and Spain. Greece did not qualify for EMU participation at the time but joined the euro group later, in 2001. On December 31, 1998, the final fixed rates between the 11 participating currencies and the euro were put into place. On January 4, 1999, the euro was officially launched.

The United Kingdom, Sweden, and Denmark chose to maintain their individual currencies. The United Kingdom, skeptical of increasing EU infringement on its sovereignty, opted not to participate. Sweden, which has failed to see significant benefits from EU membership (although it is one of the newest members), has also been skeptical of EMU participation. Denmark, like the United Kingdom, Sweden, and Norway, has so far opted not to participate. (Denmark is, however, a member of ERM II, the Exchange Rate Mechanism II, which effectively allows Denmark to keep its own currency and monetary sovereignty but fixes the value of its currency, the krone, to the euro.)

The euro would generate a number of benefits for the participating states: (1) Countries within the eurozone enjoy cheaper transaction costs, (2) currency risks and costs related to exchange rate uncertainty are reduced, and (3) all consumers and businesses both inside and outside the eurozone enjoy price transparency and increased price-based competition. The primary cost of adopting the euro, the loss of monetary independence, would be a continuing challenge for the members for years to come.

On January 4, 1999, the euro began trading on world currency markets. Its introduction was a smooth one. The euro's value slid steadily following its introduction, however, primarily as a result of the robustness of the U.S. economy and U.S. dollar and sluggish economic sectors in the EMU countries. Beginning in 2002, the euro began appreciating versus the dollar, peaking in the summer of 2008. Since that time, as illustrated in Exhibit 2.7, it has trended, roughly downward against the dollar. It has, however, demonstrated significant volatility.

The use of the euro has continued to expand to more and more members of the European Union since its introduction. As of January 2018, the euro was the official currency for 19 of the 28 member countries in the European Union, as well as five other countries (Montenegro, Andorra, Monaco, San Marino, and Vatican City) that may eventually join the EU. The EU countries currently using the euro—the so-called eurozone—are detailed in Exhibit 2.8. Note that although the United Kingdom voted to exit the EU in June 2016 (Brexit), the UK had never adopted the euro. Both the UK and Denmark chose to remain outside the eurozone from the euro's inception. (Denmark does, however, continue to manage its currency against the euro as a participant in the ERM II mechanism offered by the EU.)

Exhibit 2.8 also highlights why the initial launch of the euro went so smoothly. With the exceptions of the UK and Denmark, all other initial euro adopters had pegged their currencies to the ECU for the previous 20 years. The exhibit also illustrates that as the EU itself has expanded, primarily to countries in Eastern Europe and the Baltic, individual members have followed an orderly transition to adopting the euro. Although all members of the EU are expected eventually to replace their currencies with the euro, recent years have seen some debate as to how far euro expansion can feasibly extend. Note that the United Kingdom has always been outside the euro. The Brexit vote in June 2016 did not alter that relationship.

EXHIBIT 2.7 The U.S. Dollar–European Euro Spot Exchange Rate

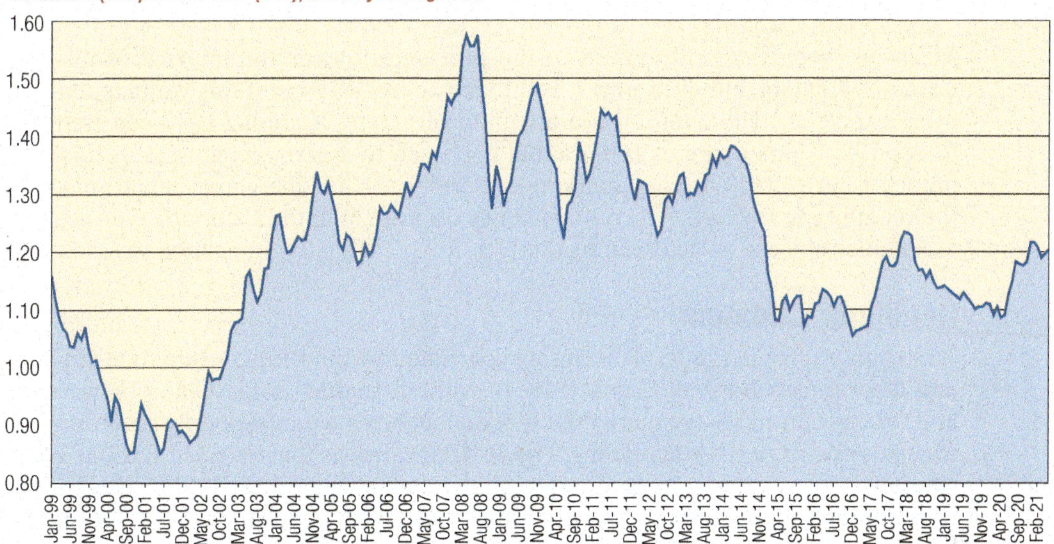

EXHIBIT 2.8 Exchange Rate Regimes of European Union Members

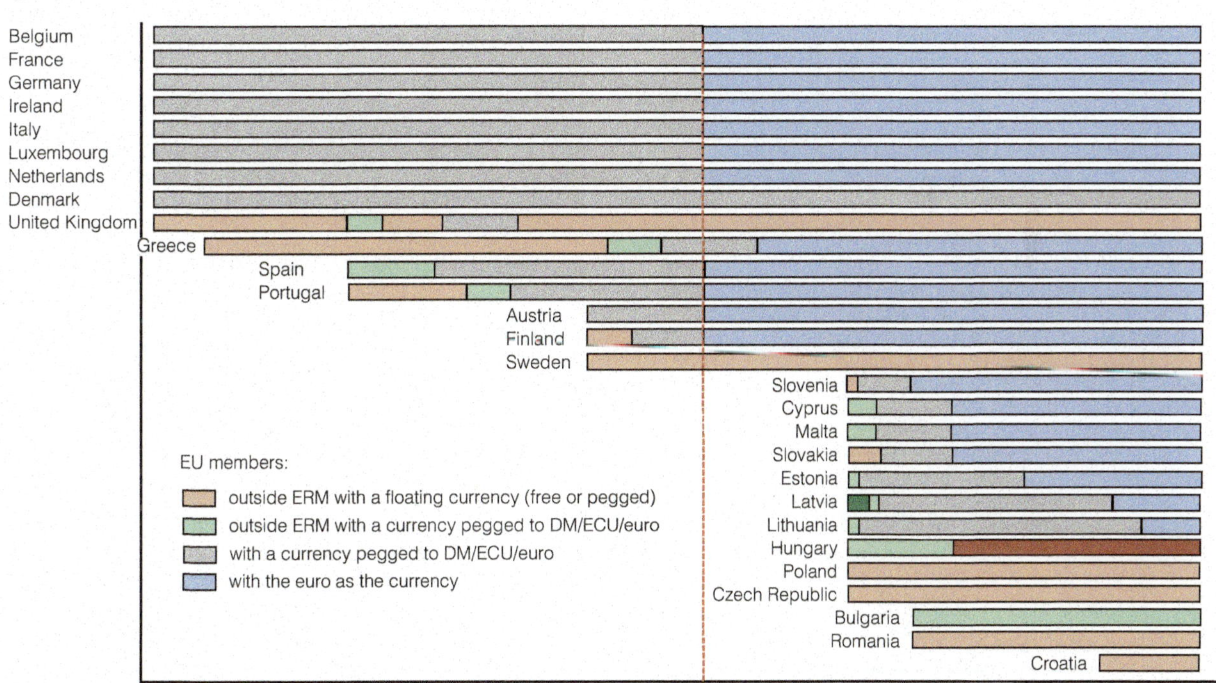

Source: Based on data from the European Union's Convergence Reports.
Notes: *ERM II participant; **Non-ERM participant; ERM = Exchange Rate Mechanism; ECU = European Currency Unit; DM = Deutsche mark.
In June 2016 the United Kingdom voted to leave the European Union.

2.5 Internationalization of the Chinese RMB

Crossing the stream by feeling the stones.

—attributed to former Chinese Premier Deng Xiaoping

Much has been said and written in the past decade over the internationalization of the Chinese renminbi, but even now it is difficult to say when or if this will happen at the level often expected.[3] The quote above attributed to Deng Xiaoping has been frequently used to describe China's careful and gradual approach to market economics. Is this gradual approach what global currency markets are seeing, or has the global marketplace relegated the renminbi to the backwaters of currency trading? Will the renminbi ever near the global acceptance and use as that seen by the U.S. dollar? What has happened to *renminbi-isation*?

Renminbi Valuation

Although trading in the RMB is closely controlled by the People's Republic of China (PRC) and the People's Bank of China (PBC)—with all trading inside China between the RMB and foreign currencies (primarily the U.S. dollar) being conducted only according to Chinese regulations—its reach is spreading. The RMB's value, as illustrated in Exhibit 2.9, has been carefully controlled but allowed to gradually revalue against the dollar over time—a lot of time. Despite the relative stability of China's currency over time, this is but one feature of how internationalized the currency may be.

EXHIBIT 2.9 Chinese Renminbi (CNY) to US Dollar (USD) Spot Rate (CNY = 1.00 USD)

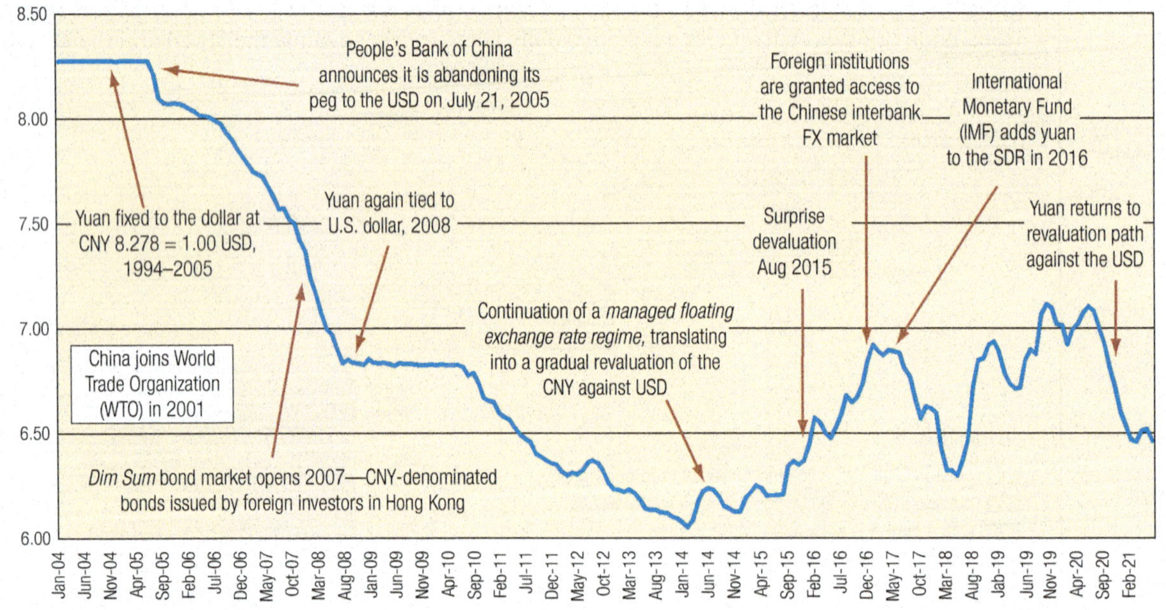

Source: Constructed by authors.

[3]The People's Republic of China officially recognizes the terms *renminbi* (RMB) and *yuan* (CNY) as names of its official currency. *Yuan* is used in reference to the unit of account (numerical values), while the physical currency is termed the *renminbi* (conceptual descriptions). This has resulted in common use of both RMB and CNY for currency codes. Officially, the ISO-4217 currency code used in all international digital trading of the Chinese currency is CNY.

Despite the changing valuation and regime choices associated with the RMB, it is still not a freely convertible currency. Nearly all foreign exchange transactions must still be conducted through a highly regulated and restrictive series of permits and processes. This restrictiveness, seen by some as part of China's legacy of financial repression, is at the forefront of the government's desire to maintain a balance between domestic financial control and stability while allowing a gradual introduction of market forces. What the Chinese government has made very clear, repeatedly, is that it will not allow either volatility or rapid and rising interest rates to affect domestic economic and business conditions.

Two-Market Currency Development

The RMB's development is driven by the Chinese economy. China makes up roughly 15% of the global economy. As such a large player in global trade and investment transactions—all requiring currency—there is a continuing and growing need for a more *liquid* and accessible currency. The PRC has clearly moved toward making the RMB an international currency since joining the World Trade Organization (WTO) in 2001. The method and timing of this internationalization process have, however, continued to frustrate many.

The RMB continues to develop along a segmented onshore/offshore two-market structure regulated by the PRC, as seen in Exhibit 2.10. The onshore market (carrying the official ISO code for the Chinese RMB, CNY) is a two-tier market, with retail exchange and an interbank wholesale exchange. The currency has, since mid-2005, been officially a managed float regime. Internally, the currency is traded through the China Foreign Exchange Trade System (CFETS), in which the People's Bank of China sets a daily central parity rate against the dollar (fixing). Actual trading is allowed to range within ±1% of the parity rate on a daily basis. This internal market continues to be gradually deregulated, with banks now being allowed to exchange negotiable certificates of deposit among themselves, with fewer and fewer interest rate restrictions. Nine different currencies are traded daily in the market against the RMB and themselves.

EXHIBIT 2.10 **Structure of the Chinese Renminbi Market**

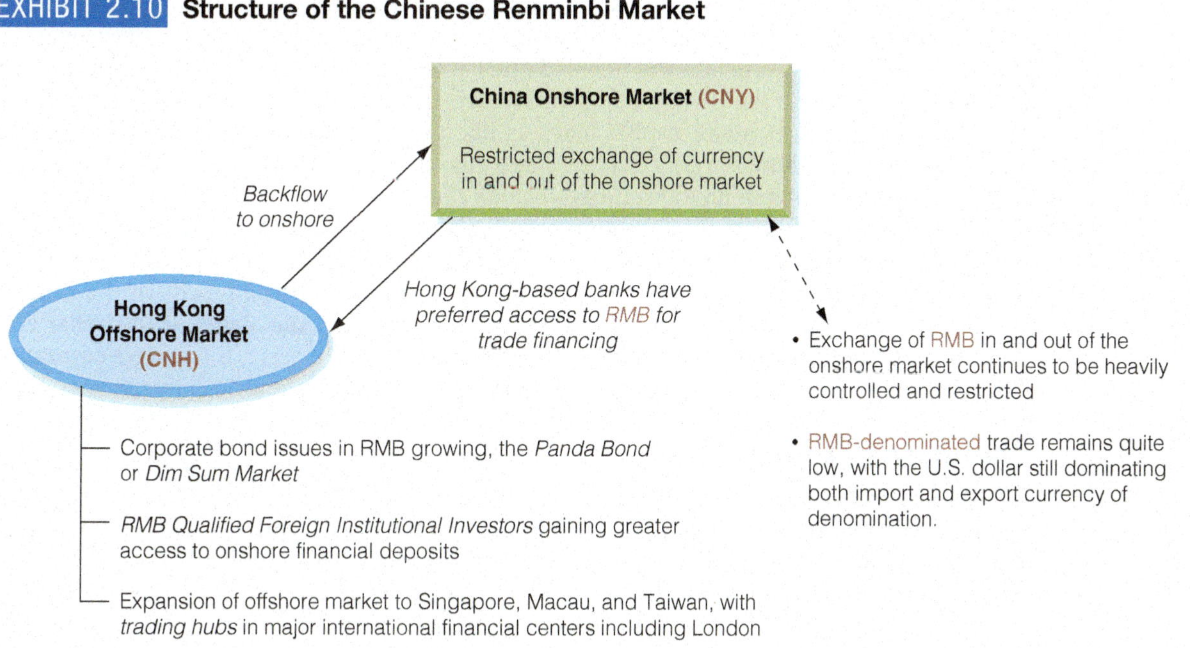

The offshore market for the RMB has grown out of a Hong Kong base (accounts labeled CNH, an unofficial symbol). This offshore market has enjoyed preferred access to the onshore market by government regulators, both in acquiring funds and reinjecting funds (termed *backflow*). Growth in this market has been fueled by the issuance of RMB-denominated debt, so-called *Panda Bonds*, by McDonald's Corporation, Caterpillar, and the World Bank, among others. Hong Kong-based institutional investors are now allowed access to onshore financial deposits (interest bearing), permitting a stronger use of these offshore deposits.

The PRC also continues to promote the expansion of the offshore market to other major regional and global financial centers like Singapore and London. One of the largest developments has been the establishment of currency trading *hubs* across the globe. These hubs, from London to Hong Kong to New York, are banks that the Chinese government has granted special status as clearing centers for renminbi currency trading.

Internationalization: Theoretical Principles and Practical Concerns

As the world's largest commercial trader and second-largest economy, it has been considered inevitable that China's currency would become an international currency. But the degree of internationalization varies.

A first degree of internationalization occurs when an international currency becomes readily accessible for trade. (This is technically described as current account use, to be described in detail in the next chapter.) As noted in Exhibit 2.10, the RMB, in the words of one publication, "punches far below its weight." A 2019 IMF study (using 2016 data) found that 93% of Chinese imports and 95% of exports were denominated in U.S. dollars. A Chinese exporter paid in U.S. dollars was not allowed to keep those dollar proceeds in any bank account. Exporters were required to exchange all foreign currencies for RMB at the official exchange rate set by the PRC and to turn them over to the Chinese government (resulting in a gross accumulation of foreign currency reserves). Times are changing. Importers and exporters are increasingly encouraged to use the RMB for trade denomination and settlement purposes.

A second degree of internationalization occurs with the use of the currency for international investment—capital account/market activity. This is an area of substantial concern and caution for the PRC at this time. The Chinese marketplace is the focus of many of the world's businesses, and if they were allowed free and open access to the market and its currency, there is fear that the value of the RMB could be driven up, decreasing Chinese export competitiveness. Simultaneously, as major capital markets like the dollar and euro head into stages of rising interest rates, there is a concern that large quantities of Chinese savings could flow out of the country in search of higher returns—*capital flight.*

A third degree of internationalization occurs when a currency takes on a role as a reserve currency (also termed an *anchor currency*), a currency to be held in the foreign exchange reserves of the world's central banks. The continued dilemma of fiscal deficits in the United States and the European Union has led to growing unease over the ability of the dollar and euro to maintain their value over time. Could, or should, the RMB serve as a reserve currency? Forecasts of the RMB's share of global reserves vary between 15% and 50% by the year 2024.

The Triffin Dilemma

One theoretical concern about becoming a reserve currency is the *Triffin Dilemma* (sometimes called the *Triffin Paradox*). The *Triffin Dilemma* is the potential conflict in objectives that may arise between domestic monetary and currency policy objectives and external or international policy objectives when a country's currency is used as a reserve currency. Domestic monetary and economic policies may on occasion require both contraction and the creation of a balance on trade surplus.

If a currency rises to the status of a global reserve currency, in which it is considered one of the two or three key stores of value on earth (possibly finding its way into the IMF's Special Drawing Right [SDR] definition), other countries will require the country to run current account deficits, essentially dumping growing quantities of the currency on global markets. This means that the country needs to become internationally indebted as part of its role as a reserve currency country. In short, when the world adopts a currency as a reserve currency, demands are placed on the use and availability of that currency, which many countries would prefer not to deal with. In fact, both Japan and Switzerland worked for decades to prevent their currencies from gaining wider international use, partially because of these complex issues. The Chinese RMB, however, may eventually find that it has no choice—the global market may choose.

2.6 Emerging Markets and Regime Choices

The 1997–2005 period specifically saw increasing pressures on emerging market countries to choose among more extreme types of exchange rate regimes. The increased capital mobility pressures noted in the previous section have driven a number of countries to choose between a free-floating exchange rate (as in Turkey in 2002) or, at the opposite extreme, a fixed-rate regime—such as a currency board (as in Argentina throughout the 1990s) or even dollarization (as in Ecuador in 2000). These systems deserve a bit more discussion.

Currency Boards

A currency board exists when a country's central bank commits to back its monetary base—its money supply—entirely with foreign reserves at all times. This commitment means that a unit of domestic currency cannot be introduced into the economy without an additional unit of foreign exchange reserves being obtained first. Eight countries, including Hong Kong, utilize currency boards as a means of fixing their exchange rates.

Argentina. In 1991, Argentina moved from its previous managed exchange rate of the Argentine peso to a currency board structure. The currency board structure pegged the Argentine peso's value to the U.S. dollar on a one-to-one basis. The Argentine government preserved the fixed rate of exchange by requiring that every peso issued through the Argentine banking system be backed by either gold or U.S. dollars held on account in banks in Argentina. This 100% reserve system made the monetary policy of Argentina dependent on the country's ability to obtain U.S. dollars through trade or investment. Only after Argentina had earned these dollars through trade could its money supply be expanded. This requirement eliminated the possibility of the nation's money supply growing too rapidly and causing inflation.

Argentina's system also allowed all Argentines and foreigners to hold dollar-denominated accounts in Argentine banks. These accounts were in actuality eurodollar accounts, dollar-denominated deposits in non-U.S. banks. These accounts provided savers with the ability to choose whether or not to hold pesos.

From the very beginning there was substantial doubt in the market that the Argentine government could maintain the fixed rate. Argentine banks regularly paid slightly higher interest rates on peso-denominated accounts than on dollar-denominated accounts. This interest differential represented the market's assessment of the risk inherent in the Argentine financial system. Depositors were rewarded for accepting risk—for keeping their money in peso-denominated accounts. In January 2002, after months of economic and political turmoil and nearly three years of economic recession, the Argentine currency board was ended. The peso was first devalued from Peso1.00/\$ to Peso1.40/\$; then it was floated completely. It fell in value dramatically within days. The Argentine decade-long experiment with a rigidly fixed exchange rate was over.

Dollarization

Several countries have suffered currency devaluation for many years, primarily as a result of inflation, and have taken steps toward dollarization. Dollarization is the use of the U.S. dollar as the official currency of the country. Panama has used the dollar as its official currency since 1907. Ecuador, after suffering a severe banking and inflationary crisis in 1998 and 1999, adopted the U.S. dollar as its official currency in January 2000. One of the primary attributes of dollarization was summarized well by *BusinessWeek* in a December 11, 2000, article titled "The Dollar Club":

> *One attraction of dollarization is that sound monetary and exchange rate policies no longer depend on the intelligence and discipline of domestic policymakers. Their monetary policy becomes essentially the one followed by the U.S., and the exchange rate is fixed forever.*

The arguments for dollarization follow logically from the previous discussion of the impossible trinity. A country that dollarizes removes any currency volatility (against the dollar) and would theoretically eliminate the possibility of future currency crises. Additional benefits are expectations of greater economic integration with other dollar-based markets, both product and financial. This last point has led many to argue in favor of regional dollarization, in which several countries that are highly economically integrated may benefit significantly from dollarizing together.

Three major arguments exist against dollarization. The first is the loss of sovereignty over monetary policy. This is, however, the point of dollarization. Second, the country loses the power of seigniorage, the ability to profit from its ability to print its own money. Third, the central bank of the country, because it no longer has the ability to create money within its economic and financial system, can no longer serve the role of lender of last resort. This role carries with it the ability to provide liquidity to save financial institutions that may be on the brink of failure during times of financial crisis.

Ecuador. Ecuador officially completed the replacement of the Ecuadorian sucre with the U.S. dollar as legal tender in September 2000. This step made Ecuador the largest national adopter of the U.S. dollar, and in many ways it made Ecuador a test case of dollarization for other emerging market countries to watch closely. Ecuador's dollarization came at the end of a massive two-year depreciation of the sucre.

During 1999, Ecuador suffered a rising rate of inflation and a falling level of economic output. In March 1999, the Ecuadorian banking sector was hit with a series of devastating "bank runs," financial panics in which all depositors attempted to withdraw all of their funds simultaneously. Although there were severe problems in the Ecuadorian banking system, even the healthiest financial institution would fail under the strain of this financial drain. Ecuador's president immediately froze all deposits. (This was termed a bank holiday in the U.S. in the 1930s when banks closed their doors.) The value of the Ecuadorian sucre plummeted in early March, inducing the country to default on more than $13 billion in foreign debt in 1999 alone. Ecuador's president moved quickly to propose dollarization to save the Ecuadorian economy.

By January 2000, when the next president took office (after a rather complicated military coup and subsequent withdrawal), the sucre had fallen in value to Sucre25,000 = $1.00. The new president continued the dollarization initiative. Although unsupported by the U.S. government and the IMF, Ecuador completed its replacement of its own currency with the dollar over the next nine months. Today, many years later, Ecuador continues to struggle to find both economic (a positive experience) and political balance (continuing concern over its lack of independent monetary policy) with its new currency regime.

El Salvador. El Salvador replaced its currency, the colón, in 2001 with the U.S. dollar. Like other dollarization adopters, El Salvador had suffered for years with hyperinflation and a dysfunctional monetary policy. Since dollarization it has enjoyed the lowest inflation rate in Central America, averaging just 2.0% per annum, and an extended period of relatively healthy economic growth.

In June 2021, El Salvador shocked the world when it would become the first country in the world to make a cryptocurrency, Bitcoin, legal tender. In the surprise announcement, the country's president announced that Bitcoin would not replace U.S. dollars as the currency of the realm but trade alongside them. It is obviously too easy to assess how this bi-currency monetary program will perform, but there is widespread concern that the volatility in Bitcoin's price is inconsistent with its use as money. The age-old description of what money should do—serve as a unit of account, a medium of exchange, and a store of value—did not necessarily fit Bitcoin. Bitcoin's volatile price made its use as a store of value unlikely.

Zimbabwe. Zimbabwe has long suffered from hyperinflation, most of which was driven by rapid increases in its money supply by printing money. The government of Zimbabwe repeatedly attempted to re-denominate the currency—2006, 2008, and 2009—by eliminating multiple 0s from its official rate, none of which worked to stabilize its value. In April 2009 the country officially abandoned the Zimbabwe dollar, adopting the use of multiple foreign currencies including the South African rand, Botswana pula, British pound sterling, Indian rupee, Japanese yen, Australian dollar, Chinese yuan, and U.S. dollar. The U.S. dollar, however, held the major share of exchange, frequently suffering from severe shortages.

The multiple foreign currency system by all accounts was more stable than the preceding Zimbabwe home currency but suffered from massive exchange costs and disruptions. In June 2019, the central bank of Zimbabwe, the Reserve Bank of Zimbabwe, officially ended the multiple-currency system and introduced the Real Time Gross Settlement Dollar (RTGS), commonly termed the *zimdollar* or *zollar*. In March 2020, official use of foreign currencies was once again initiated as inflation reignited. The rate of change in consumer prices was reportedly over 350% per annum by January 2021.

Currency Regime Choices for Emerging Markets

There is no doubt that for many emerging markets the choice of a currency regime may lie somewhere between the extremes of a hard peg (a currency board or dollarization) and free floating. However, many experts have argued for years that the global financial marketplace will drive more and more emerging market nations toward one of these extremes. As shown in Exhibit 2.11, there is a distinct lack of middle ground between rigidly fixed and free-floating extremes. But is the so-called bipolar choice inevitable?

There are three common features of emerging market economies that make any specific currency regime choice difficult: (1) weak fiscal, financial, and monetary institutions; (2) tendencies for commerce to allow currency substitution and the denomination of liabilities in dollars; and (3) the emerging market's vulnerability to sudden stoppages of outside capital flows. Calvo and Mishkin (2003) may have said it best:[4]

> *Indeed, we believe that the choice of exchange rate regime is likely to be one of second order importance to the development of good fiscal, financial and monetary institutions in producing macroeconomic success in emerging market countries. Rather than treating the exchange rate regime as a primary choice, we would encourage a greater focus on institutional reforms like improved bank and financial sector regulation, fiscal restraint, building consensus for a sustainable and predictable monetary policy and increasing openness to trade.*

[4]"The Mirage of Exchange Rate Regimes For Emerging Market Countries," Guillermo A. Calvo and Frederic S. Mishkin, *The Journal of Economic Perspectives*, Vol. 17, No. 4, Autumn 2003, pp. 99–118.

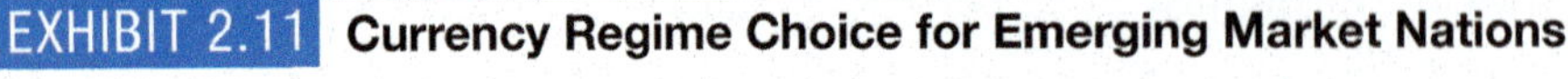

EXHIBIT 2.11 **Currency Regime Choice for Emerging Market Nations**

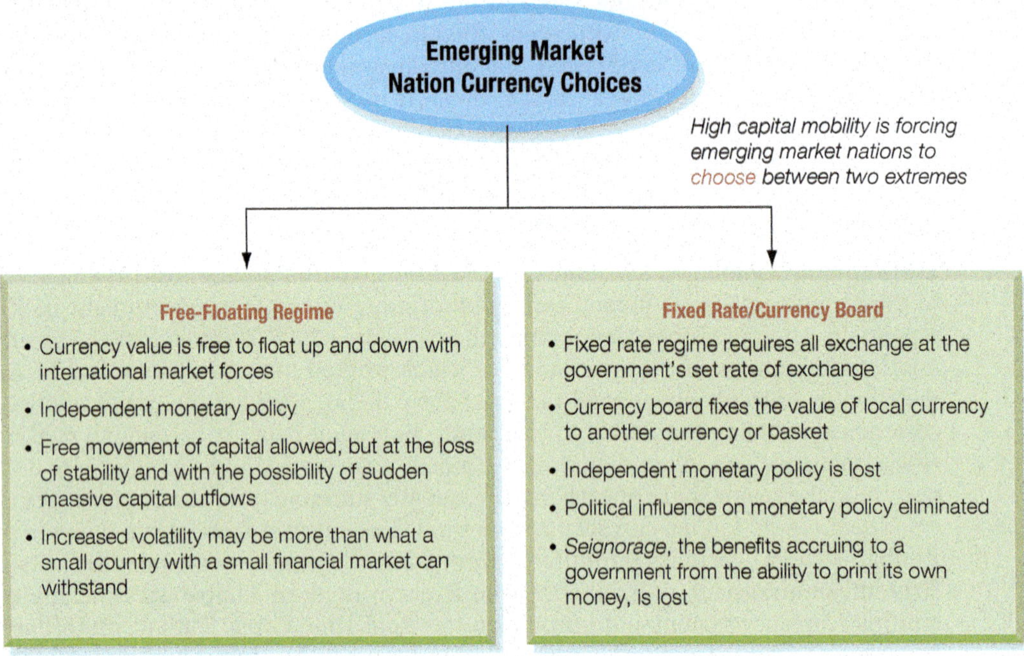

In anecdotal support of this argument, a poll of the general population in Mexico in 1999 indicated that 9 out of 10 people would prefer dollarization to a floating-rate peso. Clearly, many in the emerging markets have little faith in their leadership and institutions to implement an effective exchange rate policy. In the end, the currency regime choices of many emerging markets are under constant attack from innovation and digitization and even Internet startups, as illustrated by *Global Finance in Practice 2.4*.

Reserve Currencies and What Lies Ahead

Regime structures like the gold standard required no cooperative policies among countries, only the assurance that all would abide by the rules of the game. Under the gold standard, this assurance translated into the willingness of governments to buy or sell gold at parity rates on demand. The Bretton Woods Agreement, the system in place between 1944 and 1973, required more in the way of cooperation, in that gold was no longer the "rule," and countries were required to cooperate to a higher degree to maintain the dollar-based system. Exchange rate systems, like the European Monetary System's (EMS) fixed exchange rate band system used from 1979 to 1999, were hybrids of these cooperative and rule regimes.

The present international monetary system is characterized by no rules, with varying degrees of cooperation. Although there is no present solution to the continuing debate over what form a new international monetary system should take, many believe that it will succeed into the future only if it combines cooperation among nations with individual discretion to pursue domestic social, economic, and financial goals. Absent in new formal agreements internationally, trends in reserve currencies—currencies held by central banks and official exchange authorities—indicate the continuing dominance of the U.S. dollar and a growing role

GLOBAL FINANCE IN PRACTICE 2.4

Nigeria Fights Currency Exchange Innovation

The Central Bank of Nigeria (CBN) is the government body responsible for all currency-related exchange. The CBN maintained a fixed exchange rate of the currency, the Nigerian naira (NGN, ₦), versus the U.S. dollar until June 2016 when it allowed the naira to float. The fall in the global price of oil over the previous two years had resulted in significantly lower export earnings—and the ability to generate foreign exchange reserves of U.S. dollars. When Nigeria's export earnings fell, the CBN found itself short on dollars or other convertible currencies like the British pound for exchange. Anyone, including multinational companies, who wished to exchange Nigerian naira for foreign currency had to apply for the exchange with the CBN. CBN then determined some allocation, eventually.

British Airlines and the Nigerian Diaspora. A number of British airlines service the Nigerian market. Those airlines collect fares in local currency, naira, and then go to the CBN for exchange into either dollars or pounds. But with the growing shortage of hard currency, the airlines had to wait longer and longer periods of time. Following June 2016, this wait often meant getting fewer and fewer dollars or pounds with the declining value of the naira. But a solution arose from the large population of Nigerian nationals living and working in the UK. This diaspora earns British pounds and regularly exchanges it for Nigerian naira to be sent back to their families in Nigeria. Historically such a remittance process was quite costly, as remittance providers like Western Union or MoneyGram might charge a fee of 4% or higher. (A typical dollar exchange of $200 might cost $8.23 by Western Union from the UK to Nigeria in 2016.) A number of startup businesses began to consolidate the British pounds of Nigerians in the UK in a single large bank account and then do a "swap" of pounds for naira with the British airlines. The exchange was executed by simply drawing upon each other's accounts held in British and Nigerian banks. The consolidators paid money into a London bank (in pounds), and the airline in turn paid funds from its bank account in Nigeria to private accounts in Nigeria (in naira)—in effect, a modern version of a foreign exchange strategy long known as a back-to-back cross-currency swap.

Currency Apps. A number of startup companies—Xendpay and Azimo are two—have entered the London market in recent years with mobile apps lowering the cost of remittance dramatically for individual Nigerians, often to less than 1% of the transaction amount. Simply by transferring money between accounts in London banks and Nigerian banks, individuals could transfer funds at a fraction of the previous cost and often at a much more favorable exchange rate. Unfortunately, in July 2016, the CBN put a stop to both exchanges. Because the swaps and transfers exchanged Nigerian naira at exchange rates that did not go through the CBN, they were considered potentially harmful and "unwholesome." As one Nigerian journalist noted, just when you thought things couldn't get any worse, they did.

of the euro. (The euro's growth in use as a reserve and anchor currency in Africa has been dramatic.) But change may be in the wind as the increasing digitalization of global finance, including digital currencies like the digital yuan (eCNY), disrupt the international monetary system. A recent IMF study summarized the state of reserve currencies.[5]

> *Despite major structural shifts in the international monetary system over the past six decades, the US dollar remains the dominant international reserve currency. Using a newly compiled database of individual economies' reserve holdings by currency, this departmental paper finds that financial links have been an increasingly important driver of reserve currency configurations since the global financial crisis, particularly for emerging market and developing economies. The paper also finds a rise in inertial effects, implying that the US dollar dominance is likely to endure. But historical precedents of sudden changes suggest that new developments, such as the emergence of digital currencies and new payments ecosystems, could accelerate the transition to a new landscape of reserve currencies.*

[5] *Reserve Currencies in an Evolving International Monetary System*, Prepared by an IMF team led by Alina Iancu and comprising Gareth Anderson, Sakai Ando, Ethan Boswell, Andrea Gamba, Shushanik Hakobyan, Lusine Lusinyan, Neil Meads, and Yiqun Wu, Working Paper No. 20/02, Strategy, Policy & Review Department, Statistics Department, International Monetary Fund, 2020.

Summary Points

- Under the gold standard (1876–1913), the rules of the game were that each country set the rate at which its currency unit could be converted to a weight of gold.
- During the interwar years (1914–1944), currencies were allowed to fluctuate over fairly wide ranges in terms of gold and each other. Supply and demand forces determined exchange rate values.
- The Bretton Woods Agreement (1944) established a U.S. dollar-based international monetary system. Under the original provisions of the Bretton Woods Agreement, all countries fixed the value of their currencies in terms of gold but were not required to exchange their currencies for gold. Only the dollar remained convertible into gold (at $35 per ounce).
- A variety of economic forces led to the suspension of the convertibility of the dollar into gold in August 1971. Exchange rates of most of the leading trading countries were then allowed to float in relation to the dollar and thus indirectly in relation to gold.
- If the ideal currency regime existed in today's world, it would possess three attributes: a fixed value, convertibility, and independent monetary policy. However, in both theory and practice, it is impossible for all three attributes to be simultaneously maintained—the impossible trinity.
- Emerging market countries must often choose between two extreme exchange rate regimes: a free-floating regime or an extremely fixed regime, such as a currency board or dollarization.
- The members of the EU are also members of the European Monetary System (EMS). This group has tried to form an island of fixed exchange rates among themselves in a sea of major floating currencies. Members of the EMS rely heavily on trade with each other, so the day-to-day benefits of fixed exchange rates between them are perceived to be great.
- The euro affects markets in three ways: (1) Countries within the eurozone enjoy cheaper transaction costs, (2) currency risks and costs related to exchange rate uncertainty are reduced, and (3) all consumers and businesses both inside and outside the eurozone enjoy price transparency and increased price-based competition.
- Emerging market countries today often must make a currency regime choice between two extremes, freely floating and dollarization/currency board.
- China's currency, the yuan or renminbi, is rapidly moving toward taking a role as one of the top three or four currencies in the international monetary system.
- Although the U.S. dollar and European euro remain dominant reserve currencies, the introduction of digital currencies in the coming years, led by the Chinese digital yuan, may alter the global currency landscape dramatically.

MINI-CASE

The Promise of the Digital Yuan[6]

These "govcoins" are a new incarnation of money. They promise to make finance work better but also to shift power from individuals to the state, alter geopolitics and change how capital is allocated. They are to be treated with optimism, and humility.

—"The Digital Currencies That Matter," *The Economist*, May 8, 2021

China has long been a source of innovation in money, having been instrumental in the creation of the first coins, the first bank receipts (leading to the issuance of paper money), and now the development of digital currency, the *eYuan* (e-CNY) or digital yuan. A digital money backed by the central bank, a *central bank digital currency* (CBDC) or "govcoin" as the *Economist* termed it, would constitute a major change to the current financial ecosystem in any economy and in some ways coexist or compete with traditional bank-based financial accounts and payment processing, as well as contemporary innovations such as cryptocurrencies and private-sector digital wallets. Hundreds of questions surrounded these issues, but as China moved quickly toward the launch of its own CBDC, answers needed to come quickly.

Cryptocurrencies and Mobile Wallets

The role and development of a digital currency are best understood in the context of the rapid development of two potential threats or competitors to traditional money and payments transactions: cryptocurrencies and digital wallets (mobile wallets).

Cryptocurrencies have been called the anti-bank money or the anti-government money. A cryptocurrency is a virtual or digital currency that relies on some form of cryptography to protect it from being double-used or counterfeited. The first and foremost form of that cryptography, blockchain technology, allows a highly transparent and secure mechanism for its use in exchange. Led by the development of Bitcoin in 2009, a number of cryptocurrencies have gained widespread use globally. Whether they are true money or some form of investment or speculative vehicle remains a point of debate.[7]

Regardless, digital currency has sparked concern among government regulators and central banks everywhere, including China. The potential to be money used for exchange, particularly cross-border, without going through traditional financial institutions like banks while not being backed or issued by government was clearly disruptive. Would they constitute an uncontrollable dimension of money supply growth? Would they be used to move capital internationally out of the reach of official governance? Would they constitute a massive asset or security class beyond traditional securities and investment laws?[8] Despite official confusion by regulators, following Bitcoin's early success and popularity, other cryptocurrencies emerged—Ethereum, Ripple, Litecoin, NEO, IOTA—to name but a few.

At this same time, the growth of digital wallets—PayPal, AliPay, WeChat Pay—grew rapidly. These digital payments applications allow buying and selling of all things economic without the use of traditional cash, bank checks, or credit cards. And once again, they operated outside the traditional banking system. The largest in China, AliPay, was launched in China in 2004 by Alibaba, the Chinese e-commerce multinational. Led by its founder Jack Ma, AliPay is a third-party mobile and online payment platform utilizing a Quick Response (QR) code (a matrix barcode invented in 1994 by Denso Wave of Japan) on a personal phone to conduct electronically recorded transactions in an instant. Surpassing PayPal in 2013 as the world's largest online payment platform, it continues to grow in its market dominance position in China. In 2020, AliPay and WeChat Pay, a subsidiary of Tencent, combined made up more than 50% of all digital payments in China. This, combined with the growing monopoly power of Alibaba itself, concerned the Chinese government.

The Ant Group (formerly known as Alibaba), with AliPay's success, had grown extremely powerful in China by 2020. Its platform and apps allowed users to essentially bypass the existing Chinese financial system—and its regulations—mimicking the multitude of functions provided by commercial banks such as transaction processing and extending credit. The Ant Group's initial public offering (IPO), estimated at over $34 billion scheduled for October 2020, was stopped unceremoniously by the Chinese government. It seems that both it and its leader, Jack Ma, had transgressed too far into government-regulated territory. The following months saw Jack Ma go into seclusion, The Ant Group forced to undertake new regulatory restrictions including reduced lending activities, and the launch of the digital yuan accelerated.

Central Bank Digital Currencies (CBDC)

Central banks have been studying cryptocurrencies and digital wallets for more than a decade as they potentially threatened the abilities of central banks to effectively execute their public policy responsibilities. Those responsibilities, although different by country, always include controlling the size and growth of the money supply, ensuring a financial system's ability to provide credit and to process payments in the conduct of economic activity. Weighty responsibilities, to say the least.

Central bank interest at this stage of digital currency development follows two different lines of thought. The first is that the growing use of online payments could fail. As the lender of last resort in a national financial system, this would fall in the lap of the central bank. The second reason was related to current reality, the growing influence and power of private sector digital wallet providers. China was a prime example, with AliPay and WeChat Pay garnering more than 50% of the person-to-person payment market. With growing private sector power comes monopoly power, and with that comes fees and other forms of unregulated rent-taking.

In theory, CBDC could potentially restructure the entire financial ecosystem. The first example of this is why should an individual continue to hold CBDC in a commercial bank when they could hold it directly with the central bank? The commercial banks carry their own risks of failure; central banks cannot fail. And if there was no need to hold currency in the commercial banks, where would commercial banks acquire the deposits or capital to fund their lending? And if commercial banks were no longer based on fractional reserve banking, what would that mean for monetary policy within a national financial ecosystem? Obviously these were all questions far beyond peer-to-peer digital payments, but opening the door to direct central bank deposits by private entities beyond banks posed many challenges.

[7]In June 2021, El Salvador became the first country to make a cryptocurrency, Bitcoin, legal tender.

[8]Tesla, the electric vehicle creation of Elon Musk, announced in February 2021 that it had purchased $1.5 billion of Bitcoin as part of its investment holdings and that it would begin accepting payment for its various products in Bitcoin. That policy, as did the boom in Bitcoin prices, proved short-lived.

As central banks all over the world dove deeper in the digital abyss, structural guidance was clearly needed. A recent Bank for International Settlements study noted that there are three foundational principles that must be considered in the implementation of a digital currency:[9]

1. **Do No Harm.** Any new monetary innovations should not disrupt the central bank's ability to support monetary and financial stability. And it should not create new forms of money that constitute winners and losers for payments—so-called uniformity of a currency.
2. **Coexistence.** New forms of central bank–sponsored money should coexist with the currency organizations and systems for monetary policy and payments processing (think commercial banks).
3. **Innovation and Efficiency.** New monetary innovations introduced in the name of efficiency should not inadvertently reduce efficiency by creating winners and losers among organizations and monetary vehicles, specifically between public enterprises like regulators and central banks and their private industry partners, commercial banks and financial institutions.

Those principles could prove challenging to the current organizational landscape of the financial system.

Digital Yuan

The digital yuan resides in cyberspace, available on the owner's mobile phone—or on a card for the less tech-savvy—and spending it doesn't strictly require an online connection.[10]

The Chinese government began a series of tests of the government-backed digital currency in 2020 with significant success. In December, central bank authorities in the city of Suzhou awarded 20 million digital yuan ($3.1 million) through a lottery. Winners received 200 yuan in digital currency in a red envelope (the traditional way of gifting cash during Chinese holidays like the Chinese New Year) to be spent as they chose. Within months more than 100,000 people had downloaded the apps needed for e-CNY use.

The digital yuan (e-CNY) is part of an acknowledged initiative by the Chinese government to eventually replace physical currency. It would serve as a replacement for paper money, with each digital yuan effectively replacing a yuan circulating in paper form. The People's Bank of China would use the existing commercial banking system as the conduit for its introduction, distributing e-CNY to them and charging them with the task of expediting the exchange of hard currency, paper and coins, into digital currency.[11] But it would still mimic paper money as transactions are direct between buyer and seller and would not be processed through the banking system.

Unlike mobile payment systems, the digital yuan would not require or use Wi-Fi access. The digital yuan uses *near field communication* (NFC), a set of protocols for communication between two electronic devices a very short distance apart, roughly 4 centimeters or 11.5 inches. This allows increased user security without having to use a physical connection or link.

In early tests, private individuals and retailers alike showed a strong willingness to try it and use it. Retailers, including McDonald's and Starbucks, were quick to adopt it; payments required only a handheld phone or an electronic card. The currency has the look of paper money, with an image of Mao Zedong. Transactions did not incur charges or fees for either the customer or the vendor. This was particularly attractive to retailers who were charged by digital platforms for their use. Users simply had to sign up with the Chinese government and provide their personal identification code.

The digital yuan in some ways combined the best attributes of cryptocurrencies and mobile payment apps with none of the negatives: no fees, no Internet requirements, government backing. And the Chinese government gained as well. It could theoretically track all individual transactions in the economy, products and services, as well as the volume and nature of changing consumer tastes and trends. The government and People's Bank of China (PBC) would gain enormous information on money in the Chinese economy.

There are, however, a number of concerns about digital currency. For example, the money could have an expiration date; the government could set a calendar date that would cancel the currency if it had not been spent. This might prove useful for capital injection initiatives like those used by governments all over the world in an effort to jump-start economies after the COVID global pandemic.

A second concern, possibly of more weight, was that the Chinese government would now be able to track every single transaction made by every person. Although this would be a powerful tool in efforts to stop illegal business activities, it would also mean the average citizen giving

[9]*CBDC: Central Bank Digital Currencies: Foundational Principles and Core Features,* Report no 1, Bank for International Settlements, 2020, p. 10.

[10]"China Creates Its Own Digital Currency, a First for Major Economy: A Cyber Yuan Stands to Give Beijing Power to Track Spending in Real Time, Plus Money That Isn't Linked to the Dollar-Dominated Global Financial System," by James T. Areddy, *The Wall Street Journal*, April 5, 2021.

[11]The e-CNY is not the world's first official digital currency; that claim goes to the Bahamas, which launched its own official digital currency, the *sand dollar*, in October 2020.

up a great amount of privacy. Given the existing high degree of monitoring in China (e.g., the extremely high use of cameras in public places tracking people through facial recognition), this was for some not a great concern. The trade-off—"convenience for freedom," in the words of some—was worth it. The PBC had tried to calm such concerns by limiting the tracking of individuals, promoting a standard of "controllable anonymity."

International Reach

The Chinese government has continually reiterated its focus on launching digital yuan domestically, postponing any major expansion to international transactions. That said, in 2021 China entered into a number of joint projects with the Bank for International Settlements (BIS) and the central banks of Thailand, Hong Kong, and the United Arab Emirates to study the use of digital currency exchange and payments on a cross-border basis. Analysts, however, see China's stringent use of capital controls, capital's ability to move in and out of the Chinese economy, as a barrier to the growth of the yuan internationally, whether in physical or digital form.

China sees the launch of the digital yuan as the next step in securing what it terms *monetary sovereignty* to oppose dollar dominance. The digital yuan has raised concerns among Western nations that it might move to eventually replace the U.S. dollar as the world's premier reserve currency. If digital exchange agreements were established between selective governments on a bilateral basis, the international reach and resilience of the yuan could grow.

An expanding digital yuan would also have the potential to replace the U.S. government's political influence in some arenas (e.g., the U.S. ban on commercial transactions with Iran). Frequently referred to as *dollar weaponization*, the U.S. government has worked to maintain its ability to observe and in many cases manage who uses the currency globally, primarily by its power over the more than 20,000 commercial banks trading and processing currency payments globally. Dollar-based cross-border transactions must flow through the Society for Worldwide Interbank Financial Telecommunication (SWIFT) network, the global information system used for standardized and reliable financial transactions information, a network dominated by the U.S. dollar. The U.S. government has in the recent past used its influence to lock a number of countries out of the system, from North Korea to Myanmar.

Analysts believe there is no debate as to whether the digital yuan will be successful domestically by individuals; they take that as a given. But the world of cross-border payments, typically requiring an exchange of currencies, is one dominated not by individual personal transactions but by multinational businesses. Those business participants still value freedom from restrictions (capital controls) and selective degrees of privacy.

MINI-CASE QUESTIONS

1. Do you believe the digital yuan is meant to fight private enterprise, via cryptocurrencies and mobile apps, from capturing the market for monetary transactions?
2. What role will commercial banks and other traditional financial institutions have in the Chinese digital currency world? Banks employ hundreds of thousands of people in China. Do you believe the Chinese government would be willing to make many of those people obsolete?
3. If one tabulated the pros and cons of digital currency development, do the pros outweigh the cons? Is it possible to find "fixes" for the cons to allow an acceptable digital currency development in other major industrial markets like the United States or European Union?

Questions

2.1 **The Rules of the Game.** Under the gold standard, all national governments promised to follow the "rules of the game." What did this mean?

2.2 **Defending a Fixed Exchange Rate.** What did it mean under the gold standard to "defend a fixed exchange rate," and what did this imply about a country's money supply?

2.3 **Bretton Woods.** What was the foundation of the Bretton Woods international monetary system, and why did it eventually fail?

2.4 **Technical Float.** Speaking very specifically—technically, what does a floating rate of exchange mean? What is the role of government?

2.5 **Fixed versus Flexible.** What are the advantages and disadvantages of fixed exchange rates?

2.6 **De Facto and de Jure.** What do the terms *de facto* and *de jure* mean in reference to the International Monetary Fund's use of the terms?

2.7 **Crawling Peg.** How does a crawling peg fundamentally differ from a pegged exchange rate?

2.8 **Global Eclectic.** What does it mean to say the international monetary system today is a global eclectic?

2.9 The Impossible Trinity. Explain what is meant by the term *impossible trinity* and why it is in fact "impossible."

2.10 The Euro. Why are the formation and use of the euro considered to be such a great accomplishment? Was the euro really needed? Has it been successful?

2.11 Currency Board or Dollarization. Fixed exchange rate regimes are sometimes implemented through a currency board (Hong Kong) or dollarization (Ecuador). What is the difference between the two approaches?

2.12 Argentine Currency Board. How did the Argentine currency board function from 1991 to January 2002, and why did it collapse?

2.13 Special Drawing Rights. What are Special Drawing Rights?

2.14 The Ideal Currency. What are the attributes of the ideal currency?

2.15 Emerging Market Regimes. High capital mobility is forcing emerging market nations to choose between free-floating regimes and currency board or dollarization regimes. What are the main outcomes of each of these regimes from the perspective of emerging market nations?

2.16 Globalizing the Yuan. What are the major changes and developments that must occur for the Chinese yuan to be considered "globalized"?

2.17 Triffin Dilemma. What is the Triffin Dilemma? How does it apply to the development of the Chinese yuan as a true global currency?

2.18 China and the Impossible Trinity. What choices do you believe China will make in terms of the impossible trinity as it continues to develop global trading and use of the Chinese yuan?

2.19 Reserve Currencies. What do reserve currencies tell us about what the world's central banks think of what currencies will retain value over time?

2.20 Digital Currencies. What will be the likely impacts on the international monetary system of the introduction of digital currencies like the digital yuan? Will they replace physical currency—paper money? Or will they be relegated to the electronic payment systems in their home countries with limited cooperation across borders?

Problems

2.1 Sarah Shetty in Milan. Sarah Shetty lives in Milan, Italy. She can buy a U.S. dollar for EUR0.9000. Alex North, living in Chicago, can buy a euro for USD1.1000. What is the foreign exchange rate between the dollar and the euro?

2.2 Euro 2021 Ticket Prices. Tickets for the Euro 2020 Championship match between Germany and France, to be held in Munich on June 15, 2021 (Euro 2020 was canceled due to the global pandemic, so 2020 championships were held in 2021), were on sale for £349 per seat. If current spot exchange rates were $1.2127 = €1.00 and €1.1645 = £1.00, what was the U.S. dollar price of a seat for the match?

2.3 Gold Standard: French Franc. Before World War I, $20.67 was needed to buy one ounce of gold. If, at the same time, one ounce of gold could be purchased in France for FF410.00, what was the exchange rate between French francs and U.S. dollars?

2.4 Golden Ounce. Under the gold standard, the price of an ounce of gold in U.S. dollars was $20.67, while the price of that same ounce in British pounds was £3.7683. What would be the exchange rate between the dollar and the pound if the U.S. dollar price had been $42.00 per ounce of gold?

2.5 United Kingdom Imports. Toyota manufactures in Japan most of the vehicles it sells in the United Kingdom. The base platform for the Toyota Tundra truck line is JPY1,650,000. The spot rate of the Japanese yen against the British pound has recently moved from JPY197 = GBP1.00 to JPY190 = GBP1.00. How does this change the price of the Tundra to Toyota's British subsidiary in British pounds?

2.6 Mandarin Oriental. Cecilia Alvarez had always wanted to see Singapore. This was her chance. Round-trip airfare on Singapore Airlines (premium economy) from San Francisco where she lived was SNG1670. A three-night stay at the Mandarin Oriental, an excellent hotel overlooking the marina (which just so happens to have one of the best breakfasts in all of Singapore) was quoted to at SNG1050. If the current spot rate was SNG1.3257 = USD1.00, what would just air travel and hotel cost Cecilia in U.S. dollars?

2.7 Peso Changes. In December 1994, the government of Mexico officially changed the value of the Mexican peso from 3.2 pesos per dollar to 5.5 pesos per dollar. What was the percentage change in its value? Was this a *depreciation, devaluation, appreciation*, or *revaluation*? Explain.

2.8 Dollar Peg for Hong Kong. The Hong Kong dollar (HKD) has long been pegged to the U.S. dollar (USD) at HKD7.80 = USD1.00. When the Chinese yuan (CNY) was revalued in July 2005 against the U.S. dollar from

CNY8.28 = USD1.00 to CNY8.11 = USD1.00, how did the value of the Hong Kong dollar change against the yuan?

2.9 Renminbi Revaluation. Many experts believe that the Chinese currency should not only be revalued against the U.S. dollar as it was in July 2005 but also be revalued by 20% or 30%. What would be the new exchange rate value if the yuan was revalued an additional 20% or 30% from its initial post-revaluation rate of Yuan8.11 = $1.00?

2.10 Ranbaxy (India) in Brazil. Ranbaxy, an India-based pharmaceutical firm, has continuing problems with its cholesterol reduction product's price in one of its rapidly growing markets, Brazil. All product is produced in India, with costs and pricing initially stated in Indian rupees (Rps) but converted to Brazilian reais (R$) for distribution and sale in Brazil. In 2009, the unit volume was priced at Rps21,900, with a Brazilian reais price set at R$895. But in 2010, the reais appreciated in value versus the rupee, averaging Rps26.15 = R$1.00. In order to preserve the reais price and product profit margin in rupees, what should the new rupee price be set at?

2.11 Canadian Loonie. If the price of former Chairman of the U.S. Federal Reserve Alan Greenspan's memoir, *The Age of Turbulence*, is listed on Amazon.ca as C$26.33 but costs just US$23.10 on Amazon.com, what exchange rate does that imply between the two currencies?

2.12 Vietnamese Coffee Coyote. Many people were surprised when Vietnam became the second-largest coffee producing country in the world in recent years, second only to Brazil. The Vietnamese dong (VND or d) is managed against the U.S. dollar but is not widely traded. If you were a traveling coffee buyer for the wholesale market—a "coyote" by industry terminology—which of the following currency rates and exchange commission fees would be in your best interest if traveling to Vietnam on a buying trip?

Currency Exchange	Rate	Commission
Vietnamese bank rate	d19,800	2.50%
Saigon Airport exchange bureau rate	d19,500	2.00%
Hotel exchange bureau rate	d19,400	1.50%

2.13 Chunnel Choices. The Channel Tunnel or "Chunnel" passes underneath the English Channel between Great Britain and France, a land link between the European continent and the British Isles. One side is therefore an economy of British pounds (GBP), the other euros (EUR). If you were to check the Chunnel's rail ticket Internet rates, you would find that they would be denominated in U.S. dollars (USD). For example, a first-class round-trip fare for a single adult from London to Paris via the Chunnel through RailEurope may cost USD170.00. This currency neutrality, however, means that customers on both ends of the Chunnel pay differing rates in their home currencies from day to day. What are the British pound and euro-denominated prices for the USD170.00 round-trip fare in local currency if purchased on the following dates at the accompanying spot rates drawn from the *Financial Times*?

Date of Spot rate	British pound spot rate (GBP = USD1.00)	Euro spot rate (EUR = USD1.00)
Monday	0.5702	0.8304
Tuesday	0.5712	0.8293
Wednesday	0.5756	0.8340

2.14 SpeedFam of Las Cruces. SpeedFam Electronics of Las Cruces sells $12.5 million of computer circuits to Vectra of Monterey, Mexico, on January 1. The sale is invoiced in Mexican pesos (contract for settlement). The spot exchange rate on January 1, 2016, was MXN17.50 = USD1.00, so a sale of MXN 20 million is recorded on the U.S. financial statements as $1,142,857. If Vectra paid six weeks later on February 15, the spot rate is MXN18.75 = USD1.00. If Vectra did not pay until April 1 (90 days), the spot rate is MXN17.24 = USD1.00.

a. Complete the sale and settlement worksheet on top of the next page.
b. How would the gross margin on the sale change over the three different settlement dates?
c. If the total sale was settled on April 1, 2016, what would be the foreign exchange gain (loss) recorded on the sale?

2.15 Tsar Alexander's Gold Loan. The Russian government of Tsar Alexander III issued a 100-year bearer bond in 1894. (One of the coupon payments and the bond itself are reproduced on the following page.) A bearer bond is a security sold to an investor in which the bearer of the bond, the holder, is entitled to receive an interest payment (the coupon) at regularly scheduled dates as listed on the bond. There is no record kept by any authority of who owns the bond, the bearer is the implicit owner. There is also no record of who receives the coupon payments, if the coupons are redeemed at the recommended banks and cities of the time. This allowed the

Problem 2.14

	Booked January 1 2016	If settled on . . . Febuary 15 2016	If settled on . . . April 1 2016
Sale, in Mexican pesos	MXN 20,000,000	MXN 20,000,000	MXN 20,000,000
Mexican pesos per USD	17.50	18.75	17.24
Sales in USD	$1,142,857.14	______	______
Cost in USD (COGSI)	($850,000.00)	($850,000.00)	($850,000.00)
Expected Gross Margin (USD)	______	______	______
Expected Gross Margin (%)	______	______	______
Change from booked		______	______

investor to earn the interest without tax authorities knowing the investor's identity. These tax-free returns allowed the bond issuer, in this case the Tsar, to raise capital at lower interest rates.

This bond paid interest on a quarterly basis. As noted on the coupon and on the bond itself, there were explicit dates on each individual coupon as to when it could be redeemed. In order for the investor to redeem their coupons for cash payment, the bond contained a sheet of coupons that were numbered and dated. Individual coupons were clipped from the sheet and taken to one of the listed banks around the world to receive their interest payment. This bond listed the cities and the amount of the interest payment in local currency terms. The 118th coupon in the series is reproduced here.

This 118th coupon, which the bearer can present for payment beginning June 18, 1923, indicates what payment the bearer can receive depending on which currency the bearer is receiving payment. This obviously implies a set of fixed exchange rates in effect on the date of issuance (1894). Use the coupon reproduced below to answer the following questions.

a. What is the value of the total bond as originally issued in French francs, German marks, British pounds, Dutch florins, and U.S. dollars?
b. Create a chart that shows the fixed rate of exchange implied by the coupon for the six different currencies.

2.16 Quartzite. The spot rate for Mexican pesos is Ps12.42 = $1.00. If the U.S.-based company Quartzite Inc. buys Ps500,000 spot from its bank on Monday, how much must Quartzite pay and on what date?

2.17 Barcelona Machine Tools. Oriol D'ez Miguel S.R.L., a manufacturer of heavy-duty machine tools near Barcelona, ships an order to a buyer in Jordan. The purchase price is €425,000. Jordan imposes a 13% import duty on all products purchased from the European Union. The Jordanian importer then reexports the product to a Saudi Arabian importer, but only after imposing its own resale fee of 28%. Given the following spot exchange rates, what is the total cost to the Saudi Arabian importer in Saudi Arabian riyal, and what is the U.S. dollar equivalent of that price?

Currency Cross Rate	Spot Rate
Jordanian dinar (JD) per euro (€)	JD 0.96 = €1.00
Jordanian dinar (JD) per U.S. dollar ($)	JD 0.711 = $1.00
Saudi Arabian riyal (SRI) per U.S. dollar ($)	SRI 3.751 = $1.00

RUSSIAN 4% GOLD LOAN, SIXTH ISSUE, 1894

Talon of the Bond of 187 Rouble 50 Cop. (1/Rouble = 1/15 Imper.)

118th Coupon of the Bond, due 18 June/1 July 1923:
in Paris 5 Francs, in Berlin 4 Mark 4 Pf., in London 3 Schill. 11 ½ P.,
in Amsterdam 2 Flor. 39 C., in New York 96 1/4 Cents.

Valid for 10 years.

3

The Balance of Payments

The sort of dependence that results from exchange, i.e., from commercial transactions, is a reciprocal dependence. We cannot be dependent upon a foreigner without his being dependent on us. Now, this is what constitutes the very essence of society. To sever natural interrelations is not to make oneself independent, but to isolate oneself completely.

—Frederic Bastiat

LEARNING OBJECTIVES

3.1 Explore the fundamentals of balance of payments accounting, how nations measure their own levels of international economic activity and cross-border payments

3.2 Examine the two fundamental accounts of the balance of payments—the current account and financial account

3.3 Describe how changes in the balance of payments impact key macroeconomic rates—interest rates and exchange rates

3.4 Consider how international trade is altered by exchange rate changes

3.5 Explore the evolution of capital mobility and the conditions that sometimes lead to crisis

The measurement of all international economic transactions that take place between the residents of a country and foreign residents is called the *balance of payments* (BOP). This chapter provides a sort of navigational map to aid in interpreting the balance of payments and the multitude of economic, political, and business issues that it involves. But our emphasis is far from descriptive, as a deep understanding of trade and capital flows is integral to the management of multinational enterprises. In fact, the second half of the chapter emphasizes a more detailed analysis of how elements of the balance of payments affect trade volumes and prices, as well as how capital flows, capital controls, and capital flight alter the cost of and ability to do business internationally. The chapter concludes with the mini-case *Global Remittances: Contributions of the Invisibles*, which explores how the remittances of migrant workers impact their home countries, even in the year of a global pandemic.

Home-country and host-country BOP data, and their sub-accounts, are important to business managers, investors, consumers, and government officials because the data simultaneously influence and are influenced by other key macroeconomic variables, such as gross domestic product (GDP), employment levels, price levels, exchange rates, and interest rates. Monetary and fiscal policy must take the BOP into account at the national level. Business managers and investors need BOP data to anticipate changes in host-country economic policies that might be driven by BOP events. BOP data are also important for the following reasons:

- The BOP is an important indicator of pressure on a country's foreign exchange rate and thus of the potential for a firm trading with or investing in that country to experience foreign exchange gains or losses. Changes in the BOP may predict the imposition or removal of foreign exchange controls.
- Changes in a country's BOP may signal the imposition or removal of controls over payment of dividends and interest, license fees, royalty fees, or other cash disbursements to foreign firms or investors.
- The BOP helps to forecast a country's market potential, especially in the short run. A country experiencing a serious trade deficit is not as likely to expand imports, as it would be if running a surplus. It may, however, welcome investments that increase its exports.

3.1 Fundamentals of BOP Accounting

BOP accounting is saddled with terminology from corporate accounting, but this adopted terminology has different meanings within this context. The word *balance* creates a false image of a corporate balance sheet. A BOP statement is a statement of cash flows over an interval of time more in accord with a corporate income statement, but on a cash basis. BOP accounting also uses the terms debit and credit in its own unique way. A BOP credit is an event, such as the export of a good or service, that records foreign exchange earned—an inflow of foreign exchange to the country. A debit records foreign exchange spent, such as payments for imports or purchases of services—an outflow of foreign exchange. International transactions take many forms. Each of the following examples is an international economic transaction that is counted and captured in the U.S. balance of payments:

- A U.S.-based firm, Jacobs, manages the construction of a major water treatment facility in Bangkok, Thailand.
- The U.S. subsidiary of a French firm, Saint Gobain, pays profits back to its parent firm in Paris.
- An American tourist purchases a small Lapponia necklace in Finland.
- The U.S. government finances the purchase of military equipment for its military ally Norway.
- A Mexican lawyer purchases a U.S. corporate bond through an investment broker in Cleveland.

The BOP has three major sub-accounts: the *current account*, the *capital account*, and the *financial account*. And when these three sub-accounts are supplemented with errors and omissions, the BOP must balance. If it does not, something has not been counted or has been counted improperly. Therefore, it is incorrect to state that "the BOP is in disequilibrium." It cannot be. The supply and demand for a country's currency may be imbalanced, but that is not the same as the entire BOP. A sub-account of the BOP, such as the balance on goods and services (a sub-account of any country's current account), may be imbalanced (in surplus or deficit), but the entire BOP of a single country is always balanced.

Exhibit 3.1 illustrates that the BOP does indeed balance, in this case for the United States. The five balances listed in Exhibit 3.1—*current account, capital account, financial account, net errors and omissions*, and *reserves and related items*—do indeed sum to zero.

There are three main elements of the actual process of measuring international economic activity: (1) identifying what is and is not an international economic transaction; (2)

EXHIBIT 3.1 The U.S. Balance of Payments Accounts, Summary

Balance	2012	2013	2014	2015	2016	2017	2018	2019	2020
Current Account Balance	–418	–337	–368	–407	–395	–365	–450	–480	–647
Capital Account Balance	–1	7	7	8	7	–12	4	6	6
Financial Account Balance	452	397	293	327	366	332	425	400	753
Net Errors and Omissions	–29	–70	64	66	25	44	26	78	–102
Reserves and Related	–4	3	4	6	–2	2	–5	–5	–9
Sum or Total	0	0	0	0	0	0	0	0	0

Source: Data extracted by authors from *IMF Balance of Payments Statistics*.

understanding how the flow of goods, services, assets, and money creates debits and credits to the overall BOP; and (3) understanding the bookkeeping procedures for BOP accounting. The BOP provides a systematic method for classifying these transactions. But when all else fails, a rule of thumb always aids the understanding of BOP accounting: *Follow the cash flow.*

Defining International Economic Transactions

Identifying international transactions is ordinarily not difficult. The export of merchandise—goods such as trucks, machinery, computers, telecommunications equipment, and so forth—is obviously an international transaction. Imports, such as French wine, Japanese cameras, and German automobiles, are also clearly international transactions. But this merchandise trade is only a portion of the thousands of different international transactions that occur in the United States and other countries each year.

Many other international transactions are not so obvious. The purchase of a good like a glass figure in Venice, Italy, by a U.S. tourist is classified as a U.S. merchandise import. In fact, all expenditures made by U.S. tourists around the globe for services provided by, for example, restaurants and hotels are recorded in the U.S. balance of payments as imports of travel services in the current account.

The BOP as a Flow Statement

As noted above, the BOP is often misunderstood because many people infer from its name that it is a balance sheet. However, it is, in fact, a cash flow statement. By recording all international transactions over a period of time such as a year, the BOP tracks the continuing flows of purchases and payments between a country and all other countries. It does not add up the value of all assets and liabilities of a country on a specific date like a balance sheet does for an individual firm. (That is, in fact, the *net international investment position* [NIIP] of a country, described in a later section.) Two types of business transactions dominate the BOP:

1. **Exchange of real assets.** The exchange of goods (e.g., automobiles, computers, textiles) and services (e.g., banking, consulting, and travel services) for other goods and services (barter) or for money
2. **Exchange of financial assets.** The exchange of financial claims (e.g., stocks, bonds, loans, and purchases or sales of companies) for other financial claims or money.

Although assets can be identified as real or financial, it is often easier to think of all assets as goods that can be bought and sold. The purchase of a hand-woven area rug in a shop in Bangkok by a U.S. tourist is not all that different from a Wall Street banker buying a British government bond for investment purposes.

BOP Accounting

The measurement of all transactions in and out of a country is a daunting task. Mistakes, errors, and statistical discrepancies will occur. The primary problem is that double-entry bookkeeping is employed in theory but not in practice. Individual purchase and sale transactions should—in theory—result in financing entries in the balance of payments that match. In reality, current, capital, and financial account entries are recorded independently of one another, not together as double-entry bookkeeping would prescribe. Thus, there will be discrepancies (to use a polite term for it) between debits and credits.

3.2 The Accounts of the Balance of Payments

The balance of payments is composed of three major sub-accounts: the *current account*, the *capital account*, and the *financial account*. In addition, the *official reserves account* tracks government currency transactions, and a fifth statistical sub-account, the *net errors and omissions account*, is produced to preserve the balance in the BOP. The word "net" in account titles means that payments and receipts, i.e., debits and credits, are netted within that account.

The Current Account

The current account includes all international economic transactions with income or payment flows occurring within the year, the current period. The current account consists of four subcategories:

1. **Goods trade.** The export and import of goods is known as the goods trade. Merchandise trade is the oldest and most traditional form of international economic activity. Although many countries depend on both imports and exports of goods, most countries seek to preserve either a balance or surplus on goods trade.
2. **Services trade.** The export and import of services is known as the services trade. Common international services are financial services provided by banks to foreign importers and exporters, travel services of airlines, and construction services of domestic firms in other countries. For the major industrial countries, this sub-account has shown the fastest growth in the past decade.
3. **Income.** This is predominantly current income associated with investments made in previous periods. If a U.S. firm created a subsidiary in South Korea to produce metal parts in a previous year, the proportion of net income that is paid back to the parent company in the current year (the dividend) constitutes current investment income. Additionally, wages and salaries paid to nonresident workers are also included in this category.
4. **Current transfers.** Financial settlements associated with the change in ownership of real resources or financial items are called current transfers. Any transfer between countries that is one-way—a gift or grant—is termed a *current transfer*. For example, funds provided by the U.S. government to aid in the development of a less-developed nation are a current transfer. Transfer payments made by migrant or guest workers back to their home countries, *global remittances*, are an example of current transfers.

All countries possess some amount of trade, most of which is merchandise. Many less-developed countries have little in the way of service trade, or items that fall under the income or transfers sub-accounts. The current account is typically dominated by the first component described above, the export and import of merchandise. For this reason, the balance of trade

EXHIBIT 3.2 U.S. Trade Balances on Goods and Services, 1985–2020

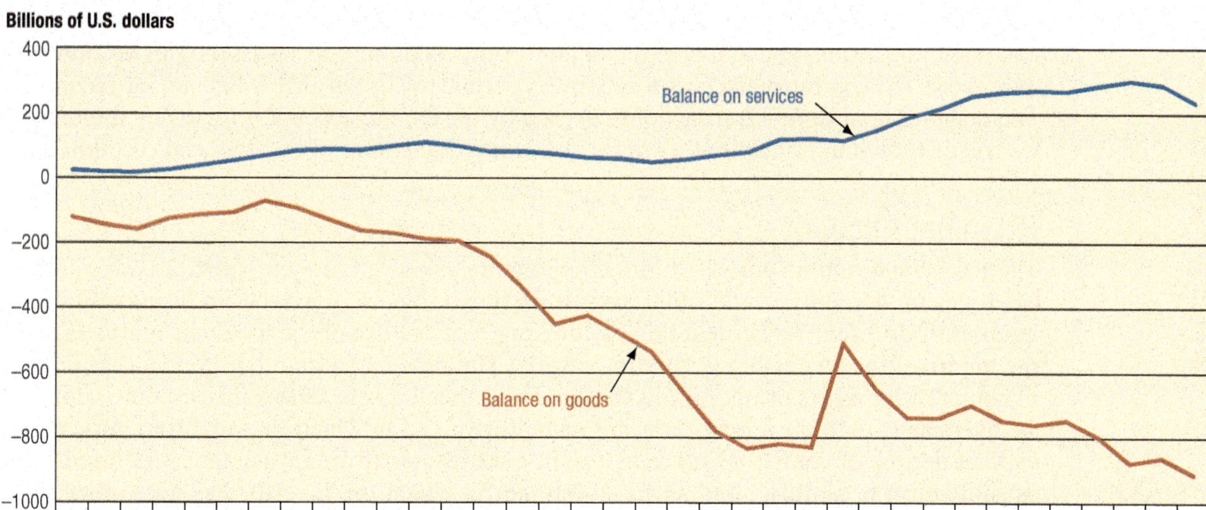

Source: Data abstracted by authors from the International Monetary Fund's Balance of Payments Statistics. https//data.inf.org.

(BOT) that is so widely quoted in the business press refers to the balance of exports and imports of goods trade only. If the country is a larger industrialized country, however, the BOT is somewhat misleading, in that service trade is not included.

Exhibit 3.2 presents the two major components of the U.S. current account for the 1985–2020 period: (1) goods trade and (2) services trade. The exhibit highlights the magnitude of the goods trade deficit. In contrast, the balance on services, although not large in comparison to net goods trade, has run a small but consistent surplus over the past two decades.

Merchandise trade is the original core of international trade. The manufacturing of goods was the basis of the industrial revolution and the focus of the theory of comparative advantage in international trade. Manufacturing is traditionally the sector of the economy that employs most of a country's workers. Declines in the U.S. BOT attributed to specific sectors, such as steel, automobiles, automotive parts, textiles, and shoe manufacturing, caused massive economic and social disruption.

Understanding merchandise import and export performance is much like understanding the market for any single product. The demand factors that drive both are income, the economic growth rate of the buyer, and price of the product in the eyes of the consumer after passing through an exchange rate. U.S. merchandise imports reflect the income level of U.S. consumers and growth of industry. As income rises, so does the demand for imports. Exports follow the same principles, but in reverse. U.S. manufacturing exports depend not on the incomes of U.S. residents, but on the incomes of buyers of U.S. products globally.

When those economies are growing, the demand for U.S. products is growing. As illustrated in Exhibit 3.2, the United States has consistently run a surplus in services trade income. The major categories of services include travel and passenger fares, transportation services, expenditures by U.S. students abroad and foreign students studying in the U.S., telecommunications services, and financial services.

The Capital and Financial Accounts

The capital and financial accounts of the balance of payments measure all international economic transactions of financial assets. The capital account is made up of transfers of financial assets and the acquisition and disposal of non-produced/nonfinancial assets. This account has only recently been introduced as a separate component in the IMF's balance of payments. The magnitude of capital transactions covered by the capital account is relatively minor, and we will include it in principle in all of the following discussions of the financial account.

Financial Account

The financial account consists of four components: direct investment, portfolio investment, net financial derivatives, and other asset investment. Financial assets can be classified in a number of different ways, including by the length of the life of the asset (its maturity) and the nature of the ownership (public or private). The financial account, however, uses degree of control over assets or operations to classify financial assets. Direct investment is defined as investment that has a long-term life or maturity and in which the investor exerts some explicit degree of control over the assets. In contrast, portfolio investment is defined both as short-term in maturity and as an investment in which the investor has no control over the assets.

Direct Investment. This investment measure is the net balance of capital dispersed from and into a country like the United States for the purpose of exerting control over assets. Control is defined as taking a minimum ownership interest of 10%. If a U.S. firm builds a new automotive parts facility in another country or purchases a company in another country, this is a direct investment in the U.S. balance of payments accounts. When the capital flows out of the U.S., it enters the balance of payments as a negative cash flow. If, however, a foreign firm purchases a U.S. firm, it is a capital inflow and enters the balance of payments positively.

Foreign resident purchases of assets in a country are always somewhat controversial. The focus of concern over foreign investment in any country, including the United States, is on two issues: control and profit. Some countries place restrictions on what foreigners may own in their country. This rule is based on the premise that domestic land, assets, and industry in general should be owned by citizens of the country. The U.S., however, has traditionally imposed few restrictions on what foreign residents or firms can own or control in the country (with the exception of national security concerns). Unlike the case in the traditional debates over whether international trade should be free, there is no consensus on international investment.

The second major focus of concern over foreign direct investment is who receives the profits from the enterprise. Foreign companies owning and operating firms in the U.S. will stimulate economic activity and provide jobs, regardless of who earns the profits—foreign or domestic investors. In spite of evidence that indicates foreign firms in the U.S. reinvest most of their profits in their U.S. businesses (in fact, at a higher rate than do domestic firms), the debate on possible profit drains has continued. Regardless of the actual choices made, the people of any nation feel that the profits of their work should remain at home.

The choice of words used to describe foreign investment can also influence public opinion. If these massive capital inflows are described as "capital investments from all over the world demonstrating faith in the future of U.S. industry," the net capital surplus is represented as decidedly positive. If, however, the net capital surplus is described as resulting in "the United States being the world's largest debtor nation," the negative connotation is obvious. Both are essentially spins on the same economic principles at work.

EXHIBIT 3.3 The U.S. Financial Accounts

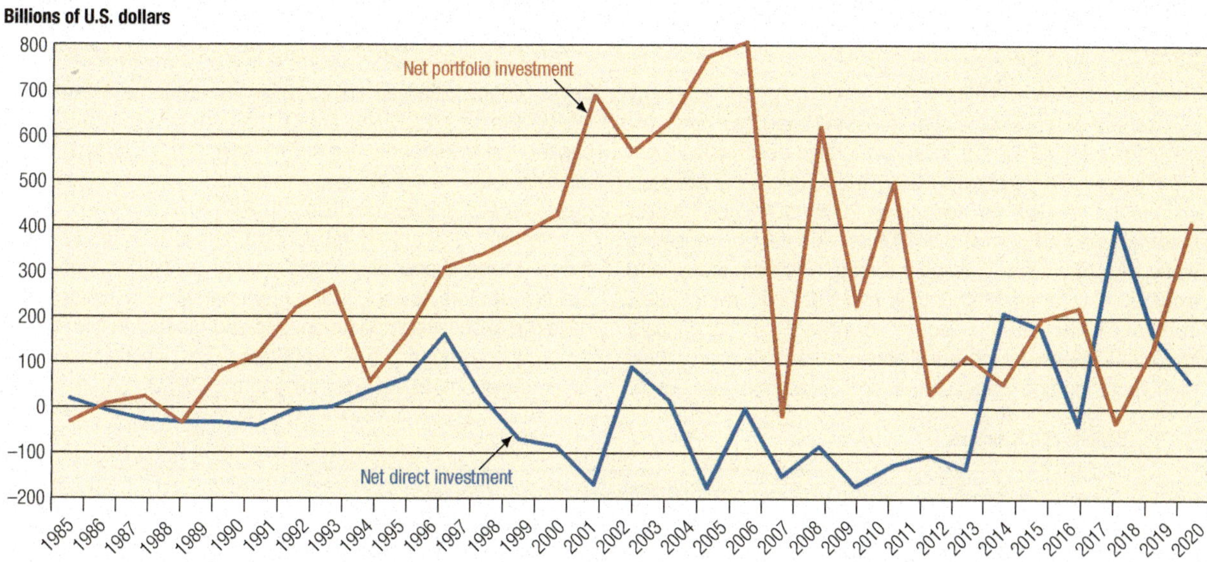

Source: Data abstracted by authors from the International Monetary Fund's Balance of Payments Statistics. https//data.inf.org.

Capital, whether short-term or long-term, flows to where the investor believes it can earn the greatest return for the level of risk. And although in an accounting sense this is "international debt," when the majority of the capital inflow occurs in the form of direct investment, a long-term commitment to jobs, production, services, technological, and other competitive investments, the impact on the competitiveness of industry located within a country is increased. Net direct investment cash flows for the U.S. for the 1990–2020 period are shown in Exhibit 3.3. *Global Finance in Practice 3.1* details the inward FDI to the U.S. and China over the past 15 years and how in the year of COVID (2020), China for the first time was the larger.

Portfolio Investment. This is the net balance of capital that flows into and out of a country but that does not reach the 10% ownership threshold of direct investment. If a U.S. resident purchases shares in a Japanese firm but does not attain the 10% threshold, we define the purchase as a portfolio investment (and an outflow of capital). The purchase or sale of debt securities (like U.S. Treasury bills) across borders is also classified as portfolio investment because debt securities by definition do not provide the buyer with ownership or control.

Portfolio investment is capital invested in activities that are purely profit-motivated (return) rather than activities to control or manage the investment. Purchases of debt securities, bonds, interest-bearing bank accounts, and the like are intended only to earn a return. They provide no vote or control over the party issuing the debt. Purchases of debt issued by the U.S. government (U.S. Treasury bills, notes, and bonds) by foreign investors constitute net portfolio investment in the United States. It is worth noting that most U.S. debt purchased by foreigners is U.S. dollar-denominated in the currency of the issuing country (dollars). Much of the foreign debt issued by nations such as Russia, Brazil, and Southeast Asian countries is also U.S. dollar-denominated and is therefore the currency of a foreign country. The foreign country must then earn dollars to repay its foreign-held debt, typically through exports.

As illustrated in Exhibit 3.3, portfolio investment has shown much more volatile behavior than net foreign direct investment over time, although that is not the case over the past

GLOBAL FINANCE IN PRACTICE 3.1

Inward Foreign Direct Investment in the Year of Covid

The global pandemic of 2020 shut down the global economy in a variety of ways. One area impacted that may have impacts for years to come is in inward foreign direct investment (FDI). Global FDI dropped by 38% in 2020 from the previous year, falling to a low not seen since 2005. COVID had a particularly devastating impact on FDI development because the world shut down travel. Without the ability to visit, study, and explore other physical countries and business landscapes, investors halted new project development. FDI is critically important to general industrial economic activity, particularly manufacturing and infrastructure, not for just one year but for years to follow. The fall in FDI in 2020 will have ripple effects for years to come.

Inward FDI is particularly the focus of many economic development initiatives. In 2020, a few countries—like the United States and China shown below—still attracted FDI capital, but in reduced levels. The year 2020 was also notable for being the first year on record in which China surpassed the U.S. in inward FDI.

In 2021 FDI activity rebounded, but in less productive forms. Mergers and acquisitions (M&A) activity was one of the first sectors to rebound. Unfortunately, M&A does not have the expansive impacts on jobs and other industry activity as new greenfield investment does. That sector may not fully recover until 2025, according to the OECD.

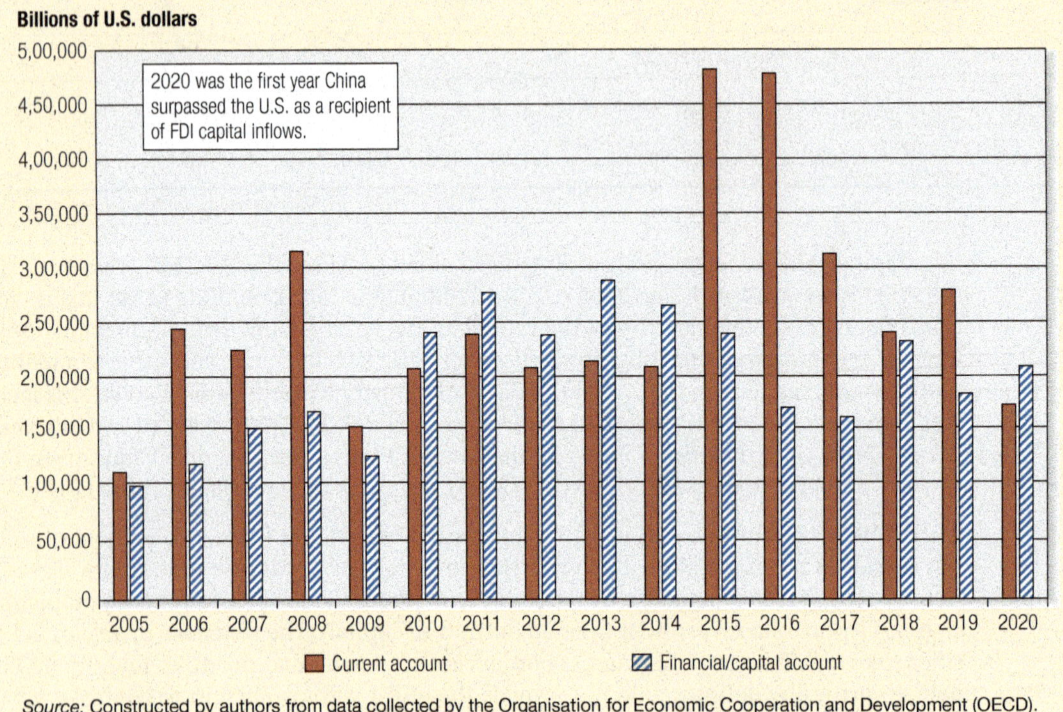

Source: Constructed by authors from data collected by the Organisation for Economic Cooperation and Development (OECD).

five years. Many U.S. debt securities, such as U.S. Treasury securities and corporate bonds, are consistently in high demand by foreign investors of all kinds. The motivating forces for portfolio investment flows are always the same: return and risk. But their net behavior can change dramatically and quickly, as seen in the net outflows during the financial crisis of 2008–2009. These same debt securities have also been influential in a different measure of international investment activity, as described in *Global Finance in Practice 3.2.*

Other Asset Investment. This final component of the financial account consists of various short-term and long-term trade credits, cross-border loans from all types of financial institutions, currency deposits and bank deposits, and other receivables and payables related to cross-border trade.

GLOBAL FINANCE IN PRACTICE 3.2

A Country's Net International Investment Position (NIIP)

The *net international investment position* (NIIP) of a country is an annual measure of the assets owned abroad by its citizens, its companies, and its government, less the assets owned by foreigners public and private in their country. Whereas a country's balance of payments is often described as a country's international *cash flow statement*, the NIIP may be interpreted as the country's international *balance sheet*. NIIP is a country's stock of foreign assets minus its stock of foreign liabilities.

The NIIP, in the same way company cash flows are related to a company's balance sheet, is based upon and categorized by the same capital and financial accounts used in the balance of payments: direct investment, portfolio investment, other investment and reserve assets. As international capital has found it easier and easier to move between currencies and cross borders in recent years, ownership of assets and securities has clearly boomed.

One common method of putting a country's NIIP into perspective is to measure it as a percentage of the total economic size of the nation—the gross domestic product (GDP) of the country. As illustrated here, the NIIP of the U.S. has clearly seen a dramatic increase in recent years, now averaging above 25% of U.S. GDP.

Although some observers have seen this growing percentage as a risk to the U.S. economy (for example, by calling the U.S. the world's largest debtor nation), these investments in assets of all kinds in many ways represent the faith foreign investors have in the future of the nation and its economy. A large part of this investment is the purchase of U.S. government securities, Treasury notes and bonds, issued in part to finance the U.S. government's growing deficits. These foreign purchasers have therefore aided in the financing of the U.S. government's budget deficit.

U.S Net International Investment Position (NIIP)

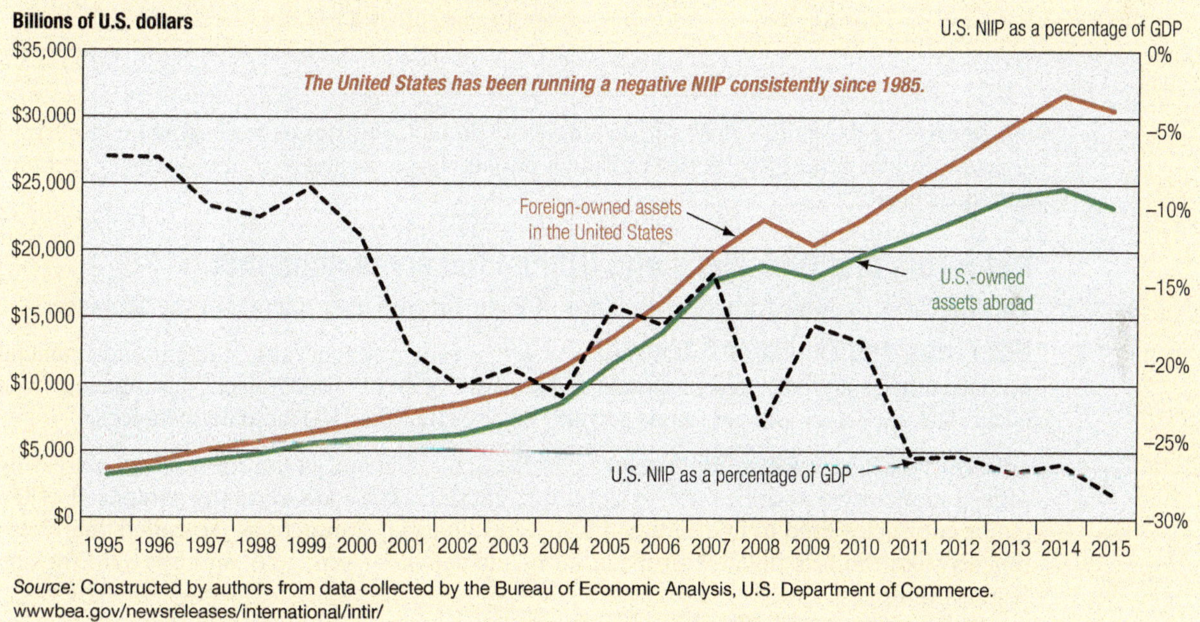

Source: Constructed by authors from data collected by the Bureau of Economic Analysis, U.S. Department of Commerce. wwwbea.gov/newsreleases/international/intir/

Exhibit 3.4 illustrates the current account balance and the capital/financial account balances for the United States for the 1992–2020 period. The exhibit shows one of the basic economic and accounting relationships of the balance of payments: the inverse relation between the current and financial accounts.

This inverse relationship is not accidental. The methodology of the balance of payments, double-entry bookkeeping, requires that the current and financial accounts be offsetting unless the country's exchange rate is being highly manipulated by governmental authorities. The upcoming section on China describes one high profile case in which government policy

EXHIBIT 3.4 **U.S. Current and Financial/Capital Account Balances**

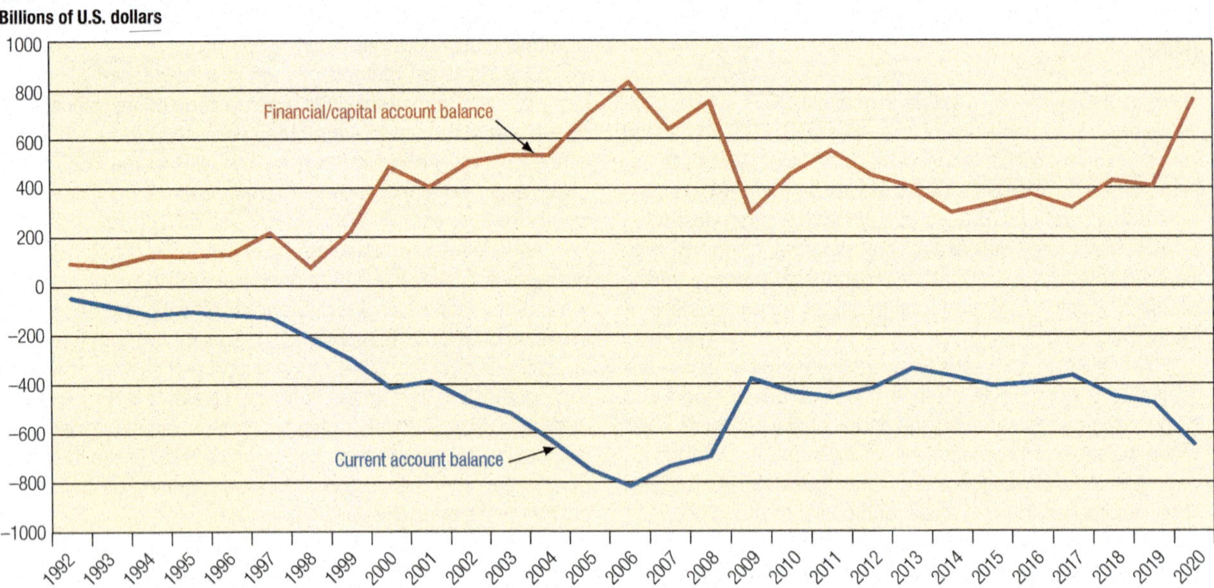

Source: Data abstracted by authors from the International Monetary Fund's Balance of Payments Statistics. http//data.inf.org.

has thwarted economics—the twin surpluses of China. Countries experiencing large current account deficits fund these deficits through equally large surpluses in the financial account, and vice versa.

Net Errors and Omissions and Official Reserves Accounts

The final two accounts within the Balance of Payments are instrumental in the "balance."

Net Errors and Omissions Account. As previously noted, because current and financial account entries are collected and recorded separately, errors or statistical discrepancies will occur. The net errors and omissions account ensures that the BOP actually balances.

Official Reserves Account. The Official Reserves Account is the total reserves held by official monetary authorities within a country. These reserves are normally composed of the major currencies used in international trade and financial transactions (so-called "hard currencies" like the U.S. dollar, European euro, and Japanese yen; gold; and Special Drawing Rights [SDRs]).

The significance of official reserves depends generally on whether a country is operating under a fixed exchange rate regime or a floating exchange rate system. If a country's currency is fixed, the government of the country officially declares that the currency is convertible into a fixed amount of some other currency. For example, the Chinese yuan was fixed to the U.S. dollar for many years. It was the Chinese government's responsibility to maintain this fixed rate, also called parity rate. If for some reason there was an excess supply of yuan on the currency market, to prevent the value of the yuan from falling, the Chinese government would have to support the yuan's value by purchasing yuan on the open market (by spending its hard currency reserves) until the excess supply was eliminated. Under a floating rate system, the Chinese government possesses no such responsibility and the role of official reserves is diminished. But as described in the following section, the Chinese government's foreign exchange reserves are now the largest in the world, and if need be, it probably possesses sufficient reserves to manage the yuan's value for years to come.

Breaking the Rules: China's Twin Surpluses

Exhibit 3.5 documents one of the more astounding BOP behaviors seen globally in many years—the twin surplus balances enjoyed by China for many years. China's surpluses in both the current and financial accounts—termed *the twin surplus* in the business press—are highly unusual. Ordinarily, for example, in the cases of the United States (recall Exhibit 3.4), Germany, and Great Britain, a country will demonstrate an inverse relationship between the two accounts. As noted previously, this inverse relationship is not accidental, and typically illustrates that most large, mature, industrial countries "finance" their current account deficits through equally large surpluses in the financial account. For some countries like Japan, it is the inverse; a current account surplus is matched against a financial account deficit.

China, however, has experienced a massive current account surplus and a sometimes sizable financial account surplus simultaneously. This is rare and an indicator of just how exceptional the growth of the Chinese economy has been. Although current account surpluses of this magnitude would ordinarily create a financial account deficit, the positive prospects of the Chinese economy have drawn such massive capital inflows into China that the financial account too is in surplus. It has also been perpetuated by rigid capital outflow restrictions, limiting the capital that may leave the country. Note that from 2014–2016 the net financial/capital account balance did indeed go negative, more in line with traditional theoretical

EXHIBIT 3.5 **China's Twin Surplus**

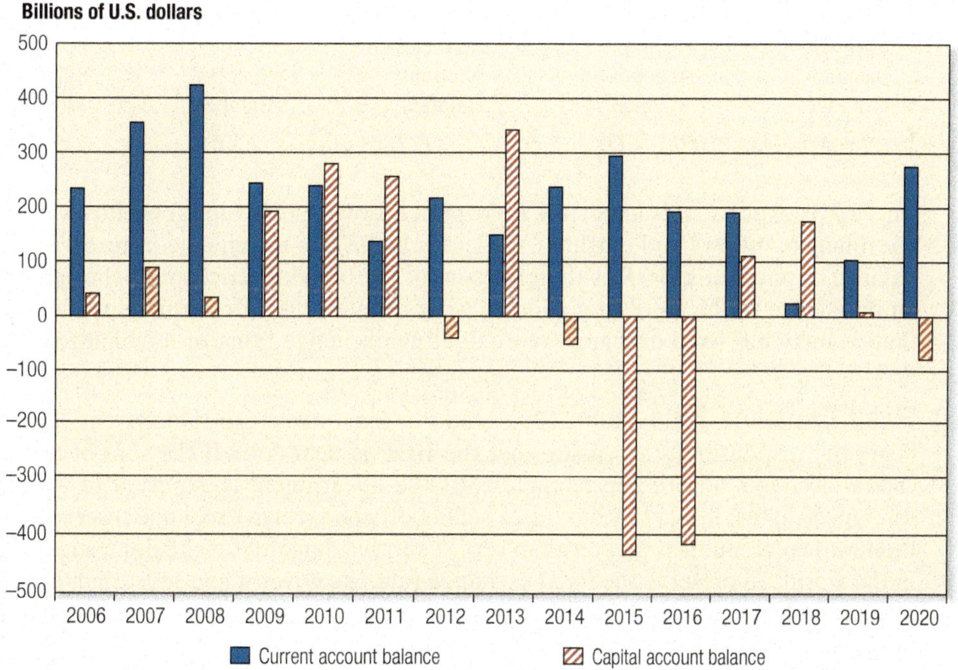

Source: Data abstracted by authors from the International Monetary Fund's Balance of Payments Statistics. http//data.inf.org.

expectations. This was partly a result of the continued deregulation of the Chinese financial sector combined with slowing economic growth. The financial/capital account balance returned to surplus in 2017–2019, partly the result of the reintroduction of capital controls and record inward investment.

The rise of the Chinese economy has been accompanied by a rise in its current account surplus, and subsequently, its accumulation of foreign exchange reserves, which increased by a factor of 16 between 2001 and 2013—rising from $200 billion to a peak level of nearly $3.7 trillion. Since that time, foreign exchange reserves have bounced upward and downward with accumulation and currency market intervention. As of January 2018 they stood at $3.0 trillion. There is no real precedent for this buildup in foreign exchange reserves in global financial history. These reserves allow the Chinese government to manage the value of the Chinese yuan and its impact on Chinese competitiveness in the world economy. The magnitude of these reserves will allow the Chinese government to maintain a relatively stable managed fixed rate of the yuan against other major currencies like the U.S. dollar as long as it chooses.

3.3 BOP Impacts on Key Macroeconomic Rates

A country's balance of payments both impacts and is impacted by the three macroeconomic rates of international finance: exchange rates, interest rates, and inflation rates.

The BOP and Exchange Rates

A country's BOP can have a significant impact on its exchange rate and vice versa, depending on that country's exchange rate regime. The relationship between the BOP and exchange rates can be illustrated by using a simplified equation that summarizes BOP data:

Current Account Balance		Capital Account Balance		Financial Account Balance		Reserve Balance		Balance of Payments
$(X - M)$	$+$	$(CI - CO)$	$+$	$(FI - FO)$	$+$	FXB	$=$	BOP

where X is exports, M is imports, CI is capital inflows, CO is capital outflows, and FI and FO are financial inflows and outflows, respectively. FXB is the change in reserves balance. The balance of payments, BOP, is then the sum of the individual account balances. The effect of an imbalance in the BOP of a country works somewhat differently depending on whether that country has fixed exchange rates, floating exchange rates, or a managed exchange rate system.

Fixed Exchange Rate Countries. Under a fixed exchange rate system, the government bears the responsibility to ensure that the BOP is near zero. If the sum of the current and capital accounts do not approximate zero, the government is expected to intervene in the foreign exchange market by buying or selling official foreign exchange reserves. If the sum of the first two accounts is greater than zero, a surplus demand for the domestic currency exists in the world. To preserve the fixed exchange rate, the government must then intervene in the foreign exchange market and sell domestic currency for foreign currencies or gold in order to bring back the BOP to near zero.

If the sum of the current and capital accounts is negative, an excess supply of the domestic currency exists in world markets. Then the government must intervene by buying the domestic currency with its reserves of foreign currencies and gold. It is obviously important for a government to maintain significant foreign exchange reserve balances, sufficient to allow it to intervene effectively. If the country runs out of foreign exchange reserves, it will be unable to buy back its domestic currency and will be forced to devalue its currency.

Floating Exchange Rate Countries. Under a floating exchange rate system, the government of a country has no responsibility to peg its foreign exchange rate. The fact that the current and capital account balances do not sum to zero will automatically—in theory—alter the exchange rate in the direction necessary to obtain a BOP near zero. For example, a country running a sizable current account deficit and a capital and financial accounts balance of zero will have a net BOP deficit. An excess supply of the domestic currency will appear on world markets. Like all goods in excess supply, the market will rid itself of the imbalance by lowering the price. Thus, the domestic currency will fall in value, and the BOP will move back toward zero.

Exchange rate markets do not always follow this theory, particularly in the short- to intermediate-term. This delay is known as the *J-curve* (detailed in an upcoming section). The deficit gets worse in the short run but moves back toward equilibrium in the long run.

Managed Floats. Although still relying on market conditions for day-to-day exchange rate determination, countries operating with managed floats often find it necessary to take action to maintain their desired exchange rate values. They often seek to alter the market's valuation of their currency by influencing the motivations of market activity, rather than through direct intervention in the foreign exchange markets.

The primary action taken by these governments is to change relative interest rates, thus influencing the economic fundamentals of exchange rate determination. In the context of the equation presented earlier, a change in domestic interest rates is an attempt to alter the capital account balance, $CI - CO$, especially the short-term portfolio component of these capital flows, in order to restore an imbalance caused by the deficit in the current account.

The power of interest rate changes on international capital and exchange rate movements can be substantial. A country with a managed float that wishes to defend its currency may choose to raise domestic interest rates to attract additional capital from abroad. This step will alter market forces and create additional market demand for the domestic currency. In this process, the government signals to the markets that it intends to take measures to preserve the currency's value within certain ranges. However, this process also raises the cost of local borrowing for businesses, so the policy is seldom without domestic critics.

The BOP and Interest Rates

Apart from the use of interest rates to intervene in the foreign exchange market, the overall level of a country's interest rates compared to other countries has an impact on the financial account of the balance of payments. Relatively low real interest rates should normally stimulate an outflow of capital seeking higher interest rates in other country currencies. However, in the case of the United States, the opposite effect has occurred. Despite relatively low real interest rates and large BOP deficits on the current account, the U.S. BOP financial account has experienced offsetting financial inflows due to relatively attractive U.S. growth rate prospects, high levels of productive innovation, and perceived political safety. Thus, the financial account inflows have helped the United States to maintain its lower interest rates and to finance its exceptionally large fiscal deficit. However, it is beginning to appear that the favorable inflow on the financial account is diminishing while the U.S. balance on the current account is worsening.

The BOP and Inflation Rates

Imports have the potential to lower a country's inflation rate. In particular, imports of lower-priced goods and services place a limit on what domestic competitors can charge for comparable goods and services. Thus, foreign competition substitutes for domestic competition to maintain a lower rate of inflation than might have been the case without imports.

On the other hand, to the extent that lower-priced imports substitute for domestic production and employment, gross domestic product will be lower as the balance on the current account falls with rising imports.

3.4 Trade Balances and Exchange Rates

A country's import and export of goods and services are affected by changes in exchange rates. The transmission mechanism is in principle quite simple: changes in exchange rates change relative prices of imports and exports, and changing prices in turn result in changes in quantities demanded through the price elasticity of demand. Although the theory seems straightforward, real global business is more complex.

Trade and Devaluation

Countries occasionally devalue their own currencies as a result of persistent and sizable trade deficits. Many countries in the not-so-distant past have intentionally devalued their currencies in an effort to make their exports more price-competitive on world markets. These competitive devaluations are often considered self-destructive, however, as they also make imports relatively more expensive. So what is the logic and likely result of intentionally devaluing the domestic currency to improve the trade balance?

The J-Curve Adjustment Path

International economic analysis characterizes the trade balance adjustment process as occurring in three stages: (1) the *currency contract period*, (2) the *pass-through period*, and (3) the *quantity adjustment period*. These three stages are illustrated in Exhibit 3.6. Assuming that the trade balance is already in deficit prior to the devaluation, a devaluation at time t_1 results initially in a further deterioration in the trade balance before an eventual improvement. The path of adjustment, as shown, takes on the shape of a flattened "j."

In the first period, the currency contract period, a sudden unexpected devaluation of the domestic currency has a somewhat uncertain impact, simply because all of the contracts for exports and imports are already in effect. Firms operating under these agreements are required to fulfill their obligations, regardless of whether they profit or suffer losses. Assume that the United States experienced a sudden fall in the value of the U.S. dollar. Most exports were priced in U.S. dollars but most imports were contracts denominated in foreign currency. The result of a sudden depreciation would be an increase in the size of the trade deficit at time t_2 because the cost to U.S. importers of paying their import bills would rise as they spent more dollars to buy the foreign currency they needed, while the revenues earned by U.S. exporters would remain unchanged. There is little reason, however, to believe that most U.S. imports are denominated in foreign currency and most exports in dollars.

The second period of the trade balance adjustment process is termed the pass-through period. As exchange rates change, importers and exporters eventually must pass these exchange rate changes through to their own product prices. For example, a foreign producer selling to the U.S. market after a major fall in the value of the U.S. dollar will have to cover its own domestic costs of production. This need will require the firm to charge higher dollar

EXHIBIT 3.6 **Trade Adjustment to Exchange Rates: The J-Curve**

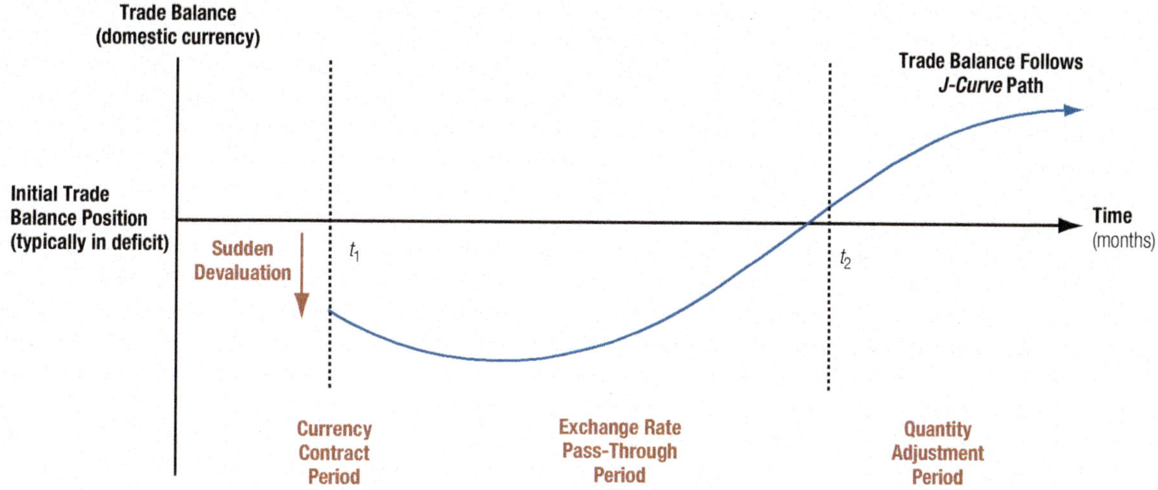

If export products are predominantly priced and invoiced in domestic currency and imports are predominantly priced and invoiced in foreign currency, a sudden devaluation of the domestic currency can possibly result—initially—in a deterioration of the balance on trade. After exchange rate changes are passed through to product prices, and markets have time to respond to price changes by altering market demands, the trade balance will improve. The currency contract period may last from three to six months, with pass-through and quantity adjustment following for an additional three to six months.

prices in order to earn its own local currency in large enough quantities. The firm must raise its prices in the U.S. market. U.S. import prices then rise, eventually passing the full exchange rate changes through to prices. Similarly, the U.S. export prices are now cheaper compared to foreign competitors' because the dollar is cheaper. Unfortunately for U.S. exporters, many of the inputs for their final products may actually be imported, dampening the positive impact of the fall of the dollar.

The third and final period, the quantity adjustment period, achieves the balance of trade adjustment that is expected from a domestic currency devaluation or depreciation. As the import and export prices change as a result of the pass-through period, consumers both in the United States and in the U.S. export markets adjust their demands to the new prices. Imports are relatively more expensive; therefore the quantity demanded decreases. Exports are relatively cheaper; therefore the quantity demanded increases. The balance of trade—the expenditures on exports less the expenditures on imports—improves.

Unfortunately, these three adjustment periods do not occur overnight. Countries like the U.S. that have experienced major exchange rate changes have also seen this adjustment take place over a prolonged period. Empirical studies have concluded that for industrial countries, the total time elapsing between time t_1 and t_2 can vary from 3 to 12 months. To complicate the process, new exchange rate changes often occur before the adjustment is completed.

Trade Balance Adjustment Path: The Equation

A country's trade balance is essentially the net of import and export revenues, where each is a multiple of price—$P_x^{\$}$ and P_m^{fc} —the prices of exports and imports, respectively. Export prices are assumed to be denominated in U.S. dollars, and import prices are denominated in foreign currency. The quantity of exports and the quantity of imports are denoted as Q_x and Q_m, respectively. Import expenditures are then expressed in U.S. dollars by

GLOBAL FINANCE IN PRACTICE 3.3

Do Trade Flows No Longer Follow the Theory?

Two major currency movements in recent years, the fall of the British pound after the June 2016 Brexit vote and the appreciation of the Swiss franc in the first six months of 2017, have led many market analysts to question the ability of exchange rates to alter trade flows. In both cases, a major change in the country's exchange rate on world markets should—at least eventually—alter imports and exports. In both cases, however, there has been little change that can be traced to exchange rate changes.

There are a number of possible explanations. In many cases, regardless of changes in effective price, demand for the specific product can be highly price inelastic. This inelasticity can arise from contractual conditions (as described in J-curve theory) or from the lack of appropriate and available substitutes. Clearly as global supply chains have grown in depth and breadth, many firms rely on very specialized suppliers, suppliers who have designed components and parts that are not replaceable in the open market.

Regardless of the specific case, it does appear that as economies have grown increasingly integrated across value chains, the ability of exchange rate changes to alter actual trade flows—imports and exports—has become increasingly moot.

multiplying the foreign currency denominated expenditures by the spot exchange rate $S^{\$=fc}$. The U.S. trade balance, expressed in U.S. dollars, is then expressed as follows:

$$\text{U.S. Trade Balance} = (P_x^{\$} \times Q_x) - (S^{\$=fc} \times P_M^{fc} \times Q_M)$$

The immediate impact of a devaluation of the domestic currency is to increase the value of the spot exchange rate $S^{\$=fc}$ resulting in an immediate deterioration in the trade balance (*currency contract period*). Only after a period in which the current contracts have matured, and new prices reflecting partial to full pass-through of the exchange rate change, will improvement in the trade balance be evident (*pass-through period*). In the final stage, in which the price elasticity of demand has time to take effect (*quantity adjustment period*), is the actual trade balance expected to rise above where it started in Exhibit 3.6. Regardless, trade adjustment takes time, an issue of some recent question, as discussed in *Global Finance in Practice 3.3.*

3.5 Capital Mobility

The degree to which capital moves freely cross-border is critically important to a country's balance of payments. We have already seen how the U.S. has suffered a deficit in its current account balance over the past 20 years while running a surplus in the financial account and how China has enjoyed a surplus in both the current and financial accounts over the last decade. But these are only two country cases and may not reflect the challenges for many countries, particularly smaller ones or emerging markets.

Current Account versus Financial Account Capital Flows

Capital inflows can contribute significantly to an economy's development. Capital inflows can increase the availability of capital for new projects, new infrastructure development, and productivity improvements. These, in turn, may stimulate general economic growth and job creation. For domestic holders of capital, the ability to invest outside the domestic economy may reap greater investment returns, portfolio diversification, and extend the commercial development of domestic enterprises.

That said, the free flow of capital into and out of an economy can potentially destabilize economic activity. Although the benefits of free capital flows have been known for centuries, so have the negatives. For this very reason, the creators of the Bretton Woods system were very careful to promote and require the free movement of capital for current account transactions—foreign exchange, bank deposits, money market instruments—but they did not require such free transit for capital account transactions—foreign direct investment and equity investments.

Experience has shown that current account-related capital flows can be more volatile, with capital flowing into and out of an economy and a currency on the basis of short-term interest rate differentials and exchange rate expectations. This volatility is somewhat compartmentalized, not directly impacting real asset investments, employment, or long-term economic growth. Longer-term capital flows reflect more fundamental economic expectations, including growth prospects and perceptions of political stability.

The complexity of issues, however, is apparent when you consider the plight of many emerging market countries. Recall the impossible trinity from Chapter 2—the theoretical structure that states that no country can simultaneously maintain a fixed exchange rate, allow complete capital mobility (both in and out of the country), and conduct independent monetary policy. Many emerging market countries have continued to develop by maintaining a near-fixed (soft peg) exchange rate regime—a strictly independent monetary policy—while restricting capital inflows and outflows. With the growth of current account business activity (exports and imports of goods and services), more current account-related capital flows are deregulated. If, however, the country experiences significant volatility in these short-term capital movements, capital flows potentially impacting either exchange rate pegs or monetary policy objectives, authorities are often quick to reinstitute capital controls.

The growth in capital openness over the past 30 years resulted in a significant increase in political pressures for more countries to open up more of their financial account sectors to international capital. But the devastation of the Asian Financial Crisis of 1997–1998 brought much of that to a halt. Smaller economies, no matter how successful their growth and development may have been under export-oriented trade strategies, found themselves still subject to sudden and destructive capital outflows in times of economic crisis and financial contagion.

Historical Patterns of Capital Mobility

Before leaving our discussion of the balance of payments, we need to gain additional insights into the history of capital mobility and the contribution of capital outflows—capital flight—to balance of payments crises. Has capital always been free to move in and out of a country? Definitely not. The ability of foreign investors to own property, buy businesses, or purchase stocks and bonds in other countries has been controversial.

Exhibit 3.7, first introduced in Chapter 2, provides a way of categorizing historical eras of capital mobility over the last 150 years. The exhibit divides economic history into five distinct exchange rate eras and their associated implications for capital mobility (or lack thereof). These exchange rate eras obviously reflect the exchange rate regimes we discussed and detailed in Chapter 2 but also reflect the evolution of political economy beliefs and policies of both industrialized and emerging market nations over this period.

Classical Gold Standard (1870–1914). Although an era of growing capital openness in which trade and capital began to flow more freely, it was an era dominated by industrialized nation economies that were dependent on gold convertibility to maintain confidence in the system.

EXHIBIT 3.7 The Evolution and Eras of the Global Monetary System

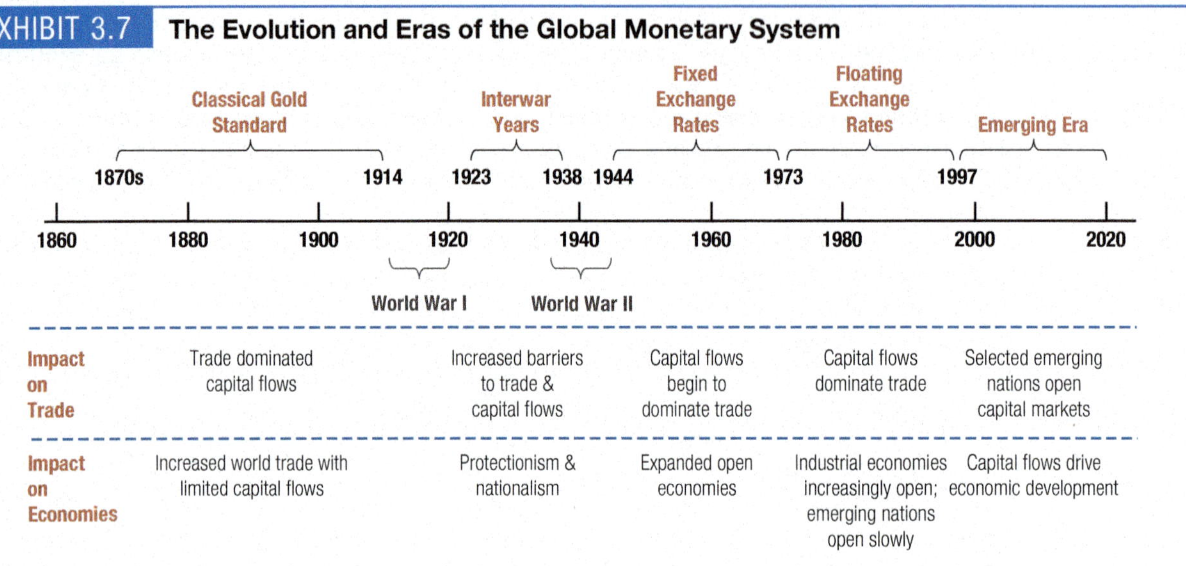

Interwar Years (1923–1938). This was an era of retrenchment in which major economic powers returned to policies of isolationism and protectionism, thereby restricting trade and nearly eliminating capital mobility. The devastating results included financial crisis, a global depression, and rising international political and economic disputes that drove nations into a second world war.

Fixed Exchange Rates (1944–1973). The dollar-based fixed exchange rate system under Bretton Woods gave rise to a long period of economic recovery and growing openness of both international trade and capital flows into and out of countries. Many believe it was the rapid growth in the speed and volume of capital flows that ultimately led to the failure of Bretton Woods—global capital could no longer be held in check.

Floating Exchange Rates (1973–1997). The Floating Era saw the rise of a growing schism between the industrialized and emerging market nations. The industrialized nations (primary currencies) moved to—or were driven to—floating exchange rates by capital mobility. The emerging markets (secondary currencies), in an attempt to both promote economic development and maintain control over their economies and currencies, opened trade but maintained restrictions on capital flows. Despite these restrictions, the era ended with the onslaught of the Asian Financial Crisis in 1997.

The Emerging Era (1997–Present). The emerging economies, led by China and India, attempt to gradually open their markets to global capital. But, as the impossible trinity taught the industrial nations in previous years, the increasing mobility of capital now requires that they give up either the ability to manage their currency values or to conduct independent monetary policies. The most challenging dimension in this current era is that a number of emerging market currencies are now being buffered by the magnitude of noncurrent account capital flows—termed *portfolio capital* or *"hot money" flows*—and their currencies now suffer larger swings in appreciation or depreciation as capital flows grow in magnitude.

The 2008–2014 period reinforced what some call the double-edged sword of global capital movements. The credit crisis of 2008–2009, beginning in the United States, quickly spread to the global economy, pulling down industrial and emerging market economies alike. But in the post credit crisis period, global capital now flowed toward the emerging markets. Although this capital both funded and fueled their rapid economic recoveries, it came—in the words of one journalist—"with luggage." The increasing pressure on emerging market currencies to appreciate is partially undermining their export competitiveness. But then, just as suddenly as the capital came, it went. In late 2013, the U.S. Federal Reserve announced that it would be slowing money supply growth and allowing U.S. interest rates to rise. Capital once again moved; this time out of the emerging markets and into the more traditional industrial countries like the U.S. and Europe.

Capital Controls

A capital control is any restriction that limits or alters the rate or direction of capital movement into or out of a country. Capital controls may take many forms, sometimes dictating which parties may undertake which types of capital transactions for which purposes—the who, what, when, where, and why of investment.

It is in many ways the bias of the journalistic and academic press that believes that capital has been able to move freely across boundaries. Free movement of capital into and out of a country is more the exception than the rule. The United States has been relatively open to capital inflows and outflows for many years, while China has been one of the most closed over that same period. When it comes to moving capital, the world is full of requirements, restrictions, taxes, and documentation approvals.

There is a spectrum of motivations for capital controls, with most associated with either insulating the domestic monetary and financial economy from outside markets or political motivations over ownership and access interests. As illustrated in Exhibit 3.8, capital controls are just as likely to occur over capital inflows as they are over capital outflows. Although there is a tendency for a negative connotation to accompany capital controls (possibly the word "control" itself), the impossible trinity requires that capital flows be controlled if a country wishes to maintain a fixed exchange rate and an independent monetary policy.

Capital controls may take a variety of forms that mirror restrictions on trade. They may simply be a tax on a specific transaction, they may limit the quantity or magnitude of specific capital transactions, or they may prohibit transactions altogether. The controls themselves have tended to follow the basic dichotomy of the balance of payments current account transactions versus financial account transactions.

In some cases capital controls are intended to stop or thwart capital outflows and currency devaluation or depreciation. The case of Malaysia during the Asian Crisis of 1997–1998 is one example. As the Malaysian currency came under attack and capital started to leave the Malaysian economy, the government imposed capital controls to stop short-term capital movements, in or out, but not hinder nor restrict long-term inward investment. All trade-related requests for access to foreign exchange were granted, allowing current account-related capital flows to continue. But access to foreign exchange for inward or outward money market or capital market investments was restricted. Foreign residents wishing to invest in Malaysian assets—real assets not financial assets—had open access.

Capital controls can be implemented in the opposite case, in which the primary fear is that large rapid capital inflows will both cause currency appreciation (and therefore harm export competitiveness) and complicate monetary policy (capital inflows flooding money markets and bank deposits). Chile in the 1990s provides an example. Newfound political and economic soundness started attracting international capital. The Chilean government responded with its *encaje* program, which imposed taxes and restrictions on short-term

EXHIBIT 3.8 Purposes of Capital Controls

Control Purpose	Method	Capital Flow Controlled	Example
General Revenue/ Finance War Effort	Controls on capital outflows permit a country to run higher inflation with a given fixed-exchange rate and also hold down domestic interest rates.	Outflows	Most belligerents in WWI and WWII
Financial Repression/Credit Allocation	Governments that use the financial system to reward favored industries or to raise revenue, may use capital controls to prevent capital from going abroad to seek higher returns.	Outflows	Common in developing countries
Correct a Balance of Payments Deficit	Controls on outflows reduce demand for foreign assets without contractionary monetary policy or devaluation. This allows a higher rate of inflation than otherwise would be possible.	Outflows	US. interest equalization tax 1963–1974
Correct a Balance of Payments Surplus	Controls on inflows reduce foreign demand for domestic assets without expansionary monetary policy or revaluation. This allows a lower rate of inflation than would otherwise be possible.	Inflows	German Bardepot Scheme 1972–1974
Prevent Potentially Volatile Inflows	Restricting inflows enhances macroeconomic stability by reducing the pool of capital that can leave a country during a crisis.	Inflows	Chilean *encaje* 1991–1998
Prevent Financial Destabilization	Capital controls can restrict or change the composition of international capital flows that can exacerbate distorted incentives in the domestic financial system.	Inflows	Chilean *encaje* 1991–1998
Prevent Real Appreciation	Restricting inflows prevents the necessity of monetary expansion and greater domestic inflation that would cause a real appreciation of the currency.	Inflows	Chilean *encaje* 1991–1998
Restrict Foreign Ownership of Domestic Assets	Foreign ownership of certain domestic assets—especially natural resources—can generate resentment.	Inflows	Article 27 of the Mexican Constitution
Preserve Savings for Domestic Use	The benefits of investing in the domestic economy may not fully accrue to savers so the economy as a whole can be made better off by restricting the outflow of capital.	Outflows	—
Protect Domestic Financial Firms	Controls that temporarily segregate domestic financial sectors from the rest of the world may permit domestic firms to attain economies of scale to compete in world markets.	Inflows and Outflows	—

Source: "An Introduction to Capital Controls," Christopher J. Neely, *Federal Reserve Bank of St. Louis Review,* November/December 1999, p. 16.

(less than one year) capital inflows, as well as restrictions on the ability of domestic financial institutions to extend credits or loans in foreign currency. Although credited with achieving its goals of maintaining domestic monetary policy and preventing a rapid appreciation in the Chilean peso, this program came at substantial cost to Chilean firms, particularly smaller ones.

A similar use of capital controls to prevent domestic currency appreciation is the so-called case of *Dutch Disease*. With the rapid growth of the natural gas industry in the Netherlands in the 1970s, there was growing fear that massive capital inflows would drive up the demand for the Dutch guilder and cause a substantial currency appreciation. A more expensive guilder would harm other Dutch manufacturing industries, causing them to decline relative to the natural resource industry. This is a challenge faced by a number of resource-rich economies of relatively modest size and with relatively small export sectors in recent years, including oil and gas development in Azerbaijan, Kazakhstan, and Nigeria, to name but a few.

An extreme problem that has arisen a number of times in international financial history is capital flight, one of the problems that capital controls are designed to counter. Although defining capital flight is a bit difficult, the most common definition is the rapid outflow of capital in opposition to or in fear of domestic political and economic conditions and policies. Although it is not limited to heavily indebted countries, the rapid and sometimes illegal transfer of convertible currencies out of a country poses significant economic and political problems. Many heavily indebted countries have suffered significant capital flight, compounding their problems of debt service.

A variety of mechanisms are used for moving money from one country to another, some legal, some not. Transfers via the usual international payments mechanisms (regular bank transfers) are obviously the easiest and lowest cost, and are legal. Most economically healthy countries allow free exchange of their currencies, but of course for such countries capital flight is not a problem. The opposite, transfer of physical currency by bearer (the proverbial smuggling out of cash in the false bottom of a suitcase) is more costly and, for transfers out of many countries, illegal. Such transfers may be deemed illegal for balance of payments reasons or to make difficult the movement of money from the drug trade or other illegal activities.

And there are other more creative solutions. One is to move cash via collectibles or precious metals, which are then transferred across borders. *Money laundering* is the cross-border purchase of assets that are managed in a way that hides the movement of money and ownership. And finally, *false invoicing* of international trade transactions occurs when capital is moved through the under-invoicing of exports or the over-invoicing of imports, where the difference between the invoiced amount and the actual agreed upon payment is deposited in banking institutions in a country of choice. Or as illustrated in *Global Finance in Practice 3.4*, sometimes the best barrier may be good old-fashioned bureaucracy.

GLOBAL FINANCE IN PRACTICE **3.4**

Chinese Regulatory Bureaucracy as a Capital Control

Chinese investment outside China—by private entities—has grown so rapidly in recent years that it has raised concerns within the Chinese government that the capital was not in pursuit of attractive foreign investments but rather fleeing the Chinese economy and its associated regulatory constraints.

A Chinese firm wishing to invest abroad must go through a series of regulatory filings. First, it must submit an application with the Ministry of Commerce, the state institution charged with formulating policy on trade flows and foreign direct investments. This is then followed by a second application with the National Development and Reform Commission, a state agency in charge of macroeconomic planning for China as a whole. If these applications are approved, a third application is then filed with the State Administration of Foreign Exchange, which must approve the exchange of Chinese renminbi for foreign exchange—typically U.S. dollars—to conduct the transaction.

Recently, as a result of growing concern of capital flight from the Chinese economy, many applications went into the system with no response. They were not denied, but they also were not approved. This "capital limbo" resulted in the failure of several planned acquisitions, from mining operations in Australia to movie studio purchases in Hollywood. In 2018 a new set of Chinese capital restrictions was applied to the increasing use of Bitcoin and other cryptocurrency investments to seemingly bypass Chinese capital controls.

Globalization of Capital Flows

Notwithstanding these benefits, many EMEs [emerging market economies] are concerned that the recent surge in capital inflows could cause problems for their economies. Many of the flows are perceived to be temporary, reflecting interest rate differentials, which may be at least partially reversed when policy interest rates in advanced economies return to more normal levels. Against this backdrop, capital controls are again in the news.

A concern has been that massive inflows can lead to exchange rate overshooting (or merely strong appreciations that significantly complicate economic management) or inflate asset price bubbles, which can amplify financial fragility and crisis risk. More broadly, following the crisis, policymakers are again reconsidering the view that unfettered capital flows are a fundamentally benign phenomenon and that all financial flows are the result of rational investing/borrowing/lending decisions. Concerns that foreign investors may be subject to herd behavior, and suffer from excessive optimism, have grown stronger; and even when flows are fundamentally sound, it is recognized that they may contribute to collateral damage, including bubbles and asset booms and busts.

—"Capital Inflows: The Role of Controls," Jonathan D. Ostry, Atish R. Ghosh, Karl Habermeier, Marcos Chamon, Mahvash S. Qureshi, and Dennis B.S. Reinhardt, IMF Staff Position Note, SPN/10/04, February 19, 2010, p. 3.

Traditionally, the primary concern over capital inflows is that they are short-term in duration, may flow out with short notice, and are characteristics of the politically and economically unstable emerging markets. But as described in the preceding quote, two of the largest capital flow crises in recent years have occurred within the largest, most highly developed, mature capital markets—the United States and Western Europe.

In both the 2008 global credit crisis, which had the United States as its core, and the ensuing European sovereign debt crisis, crisis befell markets that have long been considered some of the most mature, the most sophisticated, and the "safest." Much of the world is now waiting to see what capital will do in the years following the 2020 global pandemic.

Summary Points

- The BOP is the summary statement—a cash flow statement—of all international transactions between one country and all other countries over a period of time, typically a year.
- The two sub-accounts of the BOP that receive the most attention are the current account and the financial account. These accounts summarize the current trade and international capital flows of the country, respectively.
- The current account and financial account are typically inverse on balance, one in surplus and the other in deficit. Until very recently, though, China has been consistently enjoying a surplus of both.
- Monitoring the various sub-accounts of a country's BOP activity is helpful to decision makers and policymakers—in all levels of government and industry—in detecting the underlying trends and movements of fundamental economic forces driving a country's international economic activity.
- Changes in exchange rates affect relative prices of imports and exports, and changing prices in turn result in changes in quantities demanded through the price elasticity of demand.
- A devaluation results initially in a further deterioration of the trade balance before an eventual improvement—the path of adjustment taking on the shape of a flattened "j."
- The ability of capital to move instantaneously and massively cross-border has been one of the major factors in the severity of recent currency crises. In cases such as Malaysia in 1997

and Argentina in 2001, the national governments concluded that they had no choice but to impose drastic restrictions on the ability of capital to flow.

- Although not limited to heavily indebted countries, the rapid and sometimes illegal transfer of convertible currencies out of a country poses significant economic problems. Many heavily indebted countries have suffered significant capital flight, which has compounded their problems of debt service.

MINI-CASE

Global Remittances–Contributions of the Invisible[1]

> *Some 200m expatriate workers worldwide help four times as many relatives meet basic needs, set up businesses or pay school fees. These flows, on average, make up 60% of recipients' family income; in the eight largest receiving countries, they are the sole source of cash for about a fifth of households.* – "Trickles of Gold: Covid-19 Has Squeezed Migrants' Remittances to Their Families," *The Economist*, June 15, 2020.

Global remittances are one of the most invisible of international capital flows. In addition to providing critical income to recipients, estimated at one person in nine globally, they make up a growing proportion of GDP for many countries. COVID-19, however, posed a massive threat to this lifeblood cash flow.

According to the IMF, remittances are international transfers of funds sent by migrant workers from the country where they are working to people, typically family members, in the country from which they originated. A *migrant* is defined as a person who comes to a country and stays or intends to stay for a year or more. Because these workers are often transitory, employed in extremely low-wage industries, and not entitled to many public services in host countries, the workers themselves are often labeled "invisible." But the cash flow these migrants generate and remit to their home countries is large and in many cases critical to the health and well-being of the recipients. That income is largely channeled to critical human service needs like rent, food, utilities, and health care.

The U.S. Bureau of Economic Analysis (BEA), which is responsible for the compilation and reporting of U.S. balance of payments statistics, classifies migrant remittances as "current transfers" in the current account. Wider definitions of remittances may also include capital assets that migrants take with them to host countries and similar assets that migrants bring back with them to their home countries. These values, when compiled, are generally reported under the capital account of the balance of payments.

Determining exactly who is a migrant is also an area of some debate. For example, an expatriate (expat) working for a multinational organization but who is not considered a "resident" of that country may also be considered to be sending global remittances under current transfers in the current account.

Remittance Magnitudes

Remittance cash flows have been growing rapidly over the past two decades, reaching more than $700 billion globally in 2020. Remittances in 2020, after originally expected to drop by more than 20% as a result of the COVID-19-induced global recession, eventually recovered to near-2019 levels. Low-income and middle-income countries are the major recipients of remittances, averaging 75% of all inflows. And as illustrated also in Exhibit A, the two largest regions, East Asia/Pacific and South Asia, continue to grow. For countries in these regions, remittances follow historical patterns of migrant worker employment.

The scale of this capital contribution to these economies borders on unbelievable. Global remittances now surpass the capital inflows to low- and middle-income countries arising from foreign direct investment (FDI), portfolio investment, and official assistance. The contribution of remittances to economic development in many of these countries cannot be overstated. And it's not only about magnitude; they are also more stable from year to year than either FDI or portfolio capital. This resilience became apparent once again in 2020.

Exhibit B provides some insight into how important remittance inflows are to a multitude of countries. In 2020 remittances made up 37.7% of Tonga's GDP, followed by Somalia (35.3%), Lebanon (32.9%), South Sudan (29.5%) and the Kyrgyz Republic (29.4%), all proceeds from remittance of income earned by citizens of these countries laboring in other countries. The largest recipients on a dollar basis are India ($83 bn), China ($60 bn), Mexico ($43 bn), the Philippines ($35 bn), and Egypt ($35 bn), some of the world's largest contributors to the world's 250 million migrant workforce.

[1] This case was prepared from public sources for the purpose of classroom discussion only, and not to indicate effective or ineffective management.

EXHIBIT A Global Remittances (billions of U.S. dollars)

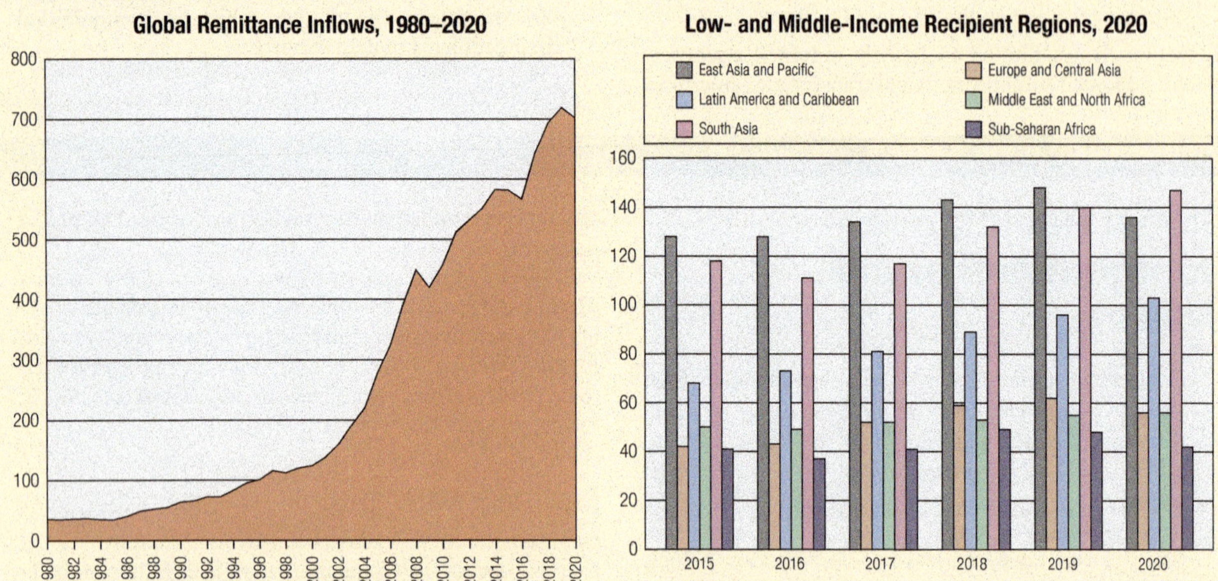

Source: Derived by author from "Resilience: Covid 19 through a Migration Lens," *Migration and Development Brief No. 34*, World Bank Group, May 2021. Value for 2020 is an estimate. Values for 2021 and 2022 are forecast.

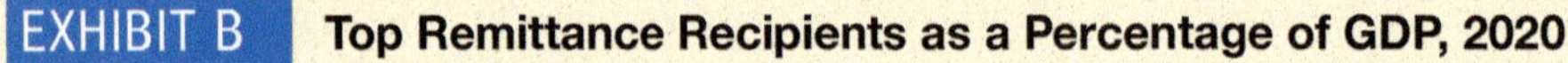

EXHIBIT B Top Remittance Recipients as a Percentage of GDP, 2020

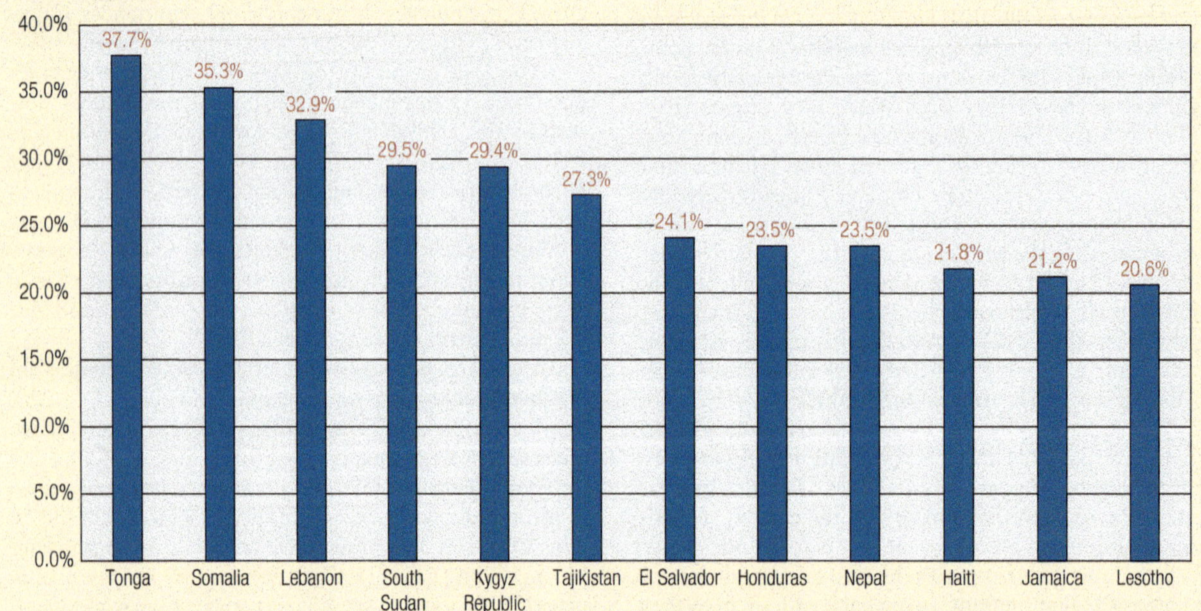

Source: Constructed by author from data drawn from the World Bank's Inward Remittance Flows, May 2021.

EXHIBIT C Top Remittance Corridors

Rank	From	To	Billion
1	United States	Mexico	$38
2	United States	China	$19
3	U.A.E.	India	$19
4	Hong Kong	China	$15
5	United States	India	$14
6	United States	Philippines	$14
7	Saudi Arabia	India	$13
8	United States	Guatemala	$10
9	United States	Vietnam	$9
10	Russia	Ukraine	$9

Source: Constructed by authors from 2019 World Bank data.

Remittances are analyzed by corridors, the bilateral links between sending and receiving country. Exhibit C lists the top 10 corridors for 2019. The United States is clearly the largest sending country (host), totaling nearly $104 billion for the year. The U.S.-Mexico corridor is, not surprisingly, the largest in the world by far. Other major corridors reflect long-standing guest worker institutional structures, such as the UAW-India and Saudi Arabia-India. Other major corridors reflect long-standing political linkages such as Hong Kong-China and Russia-Ukraine.

Remittance resilience has long been known, but the strength shown in 2020 was remarkable. Immediately following the onset of COVID-19, all authorities, from the World Bank to the United Nations, warned that remittances would likely drop more than 20% for the year.[2] With falling economic output, jobs, wages, combined with barriers to travel and migration, prospects were thought quite grim. COVID was immediately followed by the collapse of global oil prices, the driver of economic activity in a number of the countries playing host to so many migrant workers. The projected 20% fall appeared an underestimate. It proved to not be the case. Global remittances in 2020 dropped only to $702 billion from the previous year's $719 billion, a fall of only 2.4%. What analysts had not estimated was the ability of migrants to leverage unknown savings and resourceful income supplements to maintain their contributions to home-country recipients.

Means of Payment

Given the development impact of remittance flows, we will facilitate a more efficient transfer and improved use of remittances and enhance cooperation between national and international organizations, in order to implement the recommendations of the 2007 Berlin G8 Conference and of the Global Remittances Working Group established in 2009 and coordinated by the World Bank. We will aim to make financial services more accessible to migrants and to those who receive remittances in the developing world. We will work to achieve in particular the objective of a reduction of the global average costs of transferring remittances from the present 10% to 5% in five years through enhanced information, transparency, competition and cooperation with partners, generating a significant net increase in income for migrants and their families in the developing world. —The G8 Final Declaration on Responsible Leadership for a Sustainable Future, paragraph 134.

Reducing remittance payment costs has been the subject of major efforts by the World Bank, United Nations, and G8 for years. A typical remittance transaction takes place in three steps: (1) migrant earner pays the remittance to the sending agent using cash, check, money order, credit card, debit card, or a debit instruction sent by e-mail or phone; (2) sending agent instructs its corresponding agent in the recipient's country to deliver the funds; and (3) paying agent makes the payment to the final recipient. The problem is that despite all efforts, global payment costs averaged 6.75% in 2020, still relatively high.

The costs of a remittance transaction include a fee charged by the sending agent, typically paid by the sender, and a currency-conversion fee for delivery of local currency to the beneficiary in another country. Some smaller

[2]See "World Bank Predicts Sharpest Decline of Remittances in Recent History," press release, 4/22/2020, and "Trickles of Gold; Covid-19 Has Squeezed Migrants' Remittances to Their Families," *The Economist*, June 15, 2020.

EXHIBIT D The Cost to Send $200

Recipient Region	Percent	Dollars
South Asia	4.9%	$9.80
Latin American and Caribbean	5.6%	$11.20
Europe and Central Asia	6.4%	$12.80
East Asia and Pacific	6.9%	$13.80
Middle East and North Africa	6.6%	$13.20
Sub-Saharan Africa	8.2%	$16.40
Global	6.5%	$13.00

Source: Constructed by authors from World Bank data, Q4, 2020.

money transfer operators require the beneficiary to pay a fee to collect remittances, presumably to account for unexpected exchange-rate movements. In addition, remittance agents (especially banks) may earn an indirect fee in the form of interest (or "float") by investing funds before delivering them to the beneficiary. The float can be significant in countries where overnight interest rates are high.

The G8 countries launched an initiative in 2008 titled 5 × 5 to reduce transfer costs from a global average of 10% to 5% in five years. The World Bank supported this initiative by creating Remittance Prices Worldwide (RPW), a global database to monitor remittance price activity across geographic regions. It was hoped that, through greater transparency and access to transfer cost information, market forces would drive down these costs. The program fell significantly short of its goal of 5%.

Although fee structures differ, most transactions are charged a fixed fee per transaction and a fee calculated as a percentage of the value of the transaction. This latter component increases the returns to the transfer agents considerably. It should also be noted that these are charges imposed upon the sender, at the origin. Other fees or charges may occur to the receiver at the point of destination. It is also obvious from survey data that fees and charges may differ dramatically across institutions. Hence the objective of the program—to provide more information that is publicly available to people remitting funds thereby adding transparency to the process—is clear. Exhibit D provides an overview of cost estimates for the fourth quarter of 2020. It appears the 5% goal is still largely in the future.

Innovation and Digitalization

Remittances flow through a variety of service providers, including commercial banks, money transfer operators (MTOs), and post offices. According to the World Bank, commercial banks continue to be the most costly, with MTOs generally being the cheapest.

Financial technologies—fintech—theoretically should find this growth market segment promising. The problem, however, is the existing institutions already in place—primarily commercial banking systems. This poses two major barriers. First, many migrants do not have bank accounts in the countries in which they are working. This is a result of a variety of barriers including cost, government restrictions and regulations, and current business practices. Secondly, commercial banks have aggressively worked to protect their market segments, in some countries openly opposing online payment services like PayPal (e.g., India, the largest receiving country) as they cut into segments and profitability. Cryptocurrencies, once thought to offer promise in this arena, have proven unsuccessful for a variety of reasons including access, comfort by senders, and opposition by governments.

But COVID-19 and market economics are hard to defeat. A number of digital payments providers saw significant growth in their volume of transactions in 2020, as the needs of recipients were accentuated with the global pandemic. Most of this growth was in the major industrialized countries that are hosts to many migrant workers—the United Kingdom, Germany, and the United States—but also hosts to some of the more developed and established online payments providers.

In Mexico, for example, remittances now make up the second largest source of foreign exchange earnings, second only to oil exports. The Mexican government has increasingly viewed remittances as an integral component of its balance of payments and, in some ways, a "plug" to replace declining export competition and dropping foreign direct investment. But there is also growing evidence that remittances flow to those who need them most, the lowest-income component of the Mexican population, and therefore mitigate poverty and support consumer spending. Former Mexican President Vicente Fox was quoted as saying that Mexico's workers in other countries remitting income home to Mexico are "heroes." Mexico's own statistical agencies also disagree on the size of the funds remittances received as well as to whom the income is returning (family or non-family interests).

MINI-CASE QUESTIONS

1. Where are remittances across borders included within the balance of payments? Are they current or financial account components?
2. Under what conditions—for example, for which countries currently—are remittances significant contributors to the economy and overall balance of payments?
3. What are the basic costs involved in a remittance transaction?
4. Why is fintech finding it so difficult to successfully penetrate the remittance market and reduce the costs of remittances for senders and receivers?

Questions

3.1 **Balance of Payments Defined.** What is the balance of payments?

3.2 **BOP Data.** What institution provides the primary source of similar statistics for balance of payments and economic performance worldwide?

3.3 **Importance of BOP.** Business managers and investors need BOP data to anticipate changes in host-country economic policies that might be driven by BOP events. From the perspective of business managers and investors, list three specific signals that a country's BOP data can provide.

3.4 **Flow Statement.** What does it mean to describe the balance of payments as a flow statement?

3.5 **Economic Activity.** What are the two main types of economic activity measured by a country's BOP?

3.6 **Balance.** Why does the BOP always "balance"?

3.7 **BOP Accounting.** If the BOP were viewed as an accounting statement, would it be a balance sheet of the country's wealth, an income statement of the country's earnings, or a funds flow statement of money into and out of the country?

3.8 **Current Account.** What are the main component accounts of the current account? Give one debit and one credit example for each component account for the United States.

3.9 **Real versus Financial Assets.** What is the difference between a real asset and a financial asset?

3.10 **Direct versus Portfolio Investments.** What is the difference between a direct foreign investment and a portfolio foreign investment? Give an example of each. Which type of investment is a multinational industrial company more likely to make?

3.11 **Net International Investment Position.** What is a country's net international investment position and how does it differ from the balance of payments?

3.12 **The Financial Account.** What are the primary sub-components of the financial account? Analytically, what would cause net deficits or surpluses in these individual components?

3.13 **Classifying Transactions.** Classify each of the following as a transaction reported in a sub-component of the current account or of the capital and financial accounts of the two countries involved:

a. A U.S. food chain imports wine from Chile.
b. A U.S. resident purchases a euro-denominated bond from a German company.
c. Singaporean parents pay for their daughter to study at a U.S. university.
d. A U.S. university gives a tuition grant to a foreign student from Singapore.
e. A British company imports Spanish oranges, paying with eurodollars on deposit in London.
f. A Spanish orchard deposits half its proceeds in a eurodollar account in London.
g. A London-based insurance company buys U.S. corporate bonds for its investment portfolio.
h. An American multinational enterprise buys insurance from a London insurance broker.
i. A London insurance firm pays for losses incurred in the United States because of an international terrorist attack.
j. Cathay Pacific Airlines buys jet fuel at Los Angeles International Airport so it can fly the return segment of a flight back to Hong Kong.
k. A California-based mutual fund buys shares of stock on the Tokyo and London stock exchanges.
l. The U.S. Army buys food for its troops in South Asia from local vendors.
m. A Yale graduate gets a job with the International Committee of the Red Cross in Bosnia and is paid in Swiss francs.
n. The Russian government hires a Norwegian salvage firm to raise a sunken submarine.
o. A Colombian drug smuggler brings cocaine into the U.S., receives a suitcase of cash, and returns to Colombia with the cash.
p. The U.S. government pays the salary of a foreign service officer working in the U.S. embassy in Beirut.

q. A Norwegian shipping firm pays U.S. dollars to the Egyptian government for passage of a ship through the Suez Canal.

r. A German automobile firm pays the salary of its executive working for a subsidiary in Detroit.

s. An American tourist pays for a hotel in Paris with his American Express card.

t. A French tourist from the provinces pays for a hotel in Paris with his American Express card.

u. A U.S. professor goes abroad for a year on a Fulbright grant.

3.14 The Balance. What are the main summary statements of the balance of payments accounts and what do they measure?

3.15 Twin Surpluses. Why are China's twin surpluses—a surplus in both the current and financial accounts—considered unusual?

3.16 Capital Mobility—United States. The U.S. dollar has maintained or increased its value over the past 20 years despite running a gradually increasing current account deficit. Why has this phenomenon occurred?

3.17 Capital Mobility—Brazil. Brazil has experienced periodic depreciation of its currency over the past 20 years despite occasionally running a current account surplus. Why has this phenomenon occurred?

3.18 BOP Transactions. Identify the correct BOP account for each of the following transactions:

a. A German-based pension fund buys U.S. government 30-year bonds for its investment portfolio.

b. Scandinavian Airlines System (SAS) buys jet fuel at Newark Airport for its flight to Copenhagen.

c. Hong Kong students pay tuition to the University of California, Berkeley.

d. The U.S. Air Force buys food in South Korea to supply its air crews.

e. A Japanese auto company pays the salaries of its executives working for its U.S. subsidiaries.

f. A U.S. tourist pays for a restaurant meal in Bangkok.

g. A Colombian citizen smuggles cocaine into the United States, receives cash, and smuggles the dollars back into Colombia.

h. A U.K. corporation purchases a euro-denominated bond from an Italian MNE.

3.19 BOP and Exchange Rates. What is the relationship between the balance of payments and a fixed or floating exchange rate regime?

3.20 J-Curve Dynamics. What is the J-curve adjustment path?

3.21 Evolution of Capital Mobility. Has capital mobility improved steadily over the past 50 years?

3.22 Restrictions on Capital Mobility. What factors seem to play a role in a government's choice to restrict capital mobility?

3.23 Capital Controls. Which do most countries control, capital inflows or capital outflows? Why?

3.24 Globalization and Capital Mobility. How does capital mobility typically differ between industrialized countries and emerging market countries?

Problems

Australia's Current Account

Use the following balance of payments data from the International Monetary Fund to answer Problems 3.1–3.4.

Problem 3.1–3.4

Millions of U.S. dollars	2010	2011	2012	2013	2014	2015	2016	2017	2018	2019	2020
Goods: credit (exports)	213,782	271,719	257,950	254,180	240,704	188,212	192,907	231,566	257,849	271,441	250,660
Goods: debit (imports)	–196,303	–249,238	–270,136	–249,700	–240,252	207,225	198,703	221,064	236,906	223,427	210,721
Services: credit (exports)	46,968	51,653	53,034	53,550	54,240	54,894	58,024	65,174	69,470	70,990	48,382
Services: debit (imports)	–51,313	–61,897	–65,405	–67,977	–63,549	63,656	62,466	68,474	73,319	72,035	38,347
Primary income: credit	35,711	47,852	47,168	46,316	46,637	39,413	39,530	42,603	48,543	49,866	45,613
Primary income: debt	–84,646	–102,400	–88,255	–85,289	–79,805	67,763	69,556	84,511	94,786	88,067	60,852
Secondary income: credit	5,813	7,510	7,271	7,109	6,962	6,586	6,567	6,946	7,159	7,047	6,722
Secondary income: debt	–7,189	–9,723	9,635	–9,346	–8,996	7,419	7,339	8,192	7,796	7,782	7,629

3.1 What is Australia's balance on goods?

3.2 What is Australia's balance on services?

3.3 What is Australia's balance on goods and services?

3.4 What is Australia's current account balance?

India's Current Account

Use the following balance of payments data for India from the IMF (all items are for the current account) to answer Problems 3.5–3.9.

Problem 3.5–3.9

Millions of U.S. dollars	2010	2011	2012	2013	2014	2015	2016	2017	2018	2019	2020
Goods: credit (exports)	230,967	307,847	298,321	319,110	328,387	272,353	268,615	304,107	332,087	331,272	281,701
Goods: debit (imports)	–324,320	475,304	499,989	481,686	472,434	409,237	376,090	452,241	518,779	488,950	376,946
Services: credit (exports)	117,068	138,528	145,525	149,164	157,196	156,278	161,819	185,294	204,956	214,762	203,253
Services: debit (imports)	–114,739	77,758	79,920	78,722	81,119	82,643	95,922	109,371	124,182	130,535	116,230
Primary income: credit	9,961	10,147	9,899	11,230	12,637	14,533	15,485	18,547	21,381	23,348	22,783
Primary income: debt	–25,563	26,191	30,742	33,032	37,581	37,894	42,846	44,970	51,137	52,725	54,671
Secondary income: credit	54,380	62,735	68,611	69,441	69,906	67,806	61,545	67,068	76,763	80,742	79,973
Secondary income: debt	–2,270	2,523	3,176	4,626	4,306	3,653	4,718	6,601	6,688	7,675	6,856

3.5 What is India's balance on goods?

3.6 What is India's balance on services?

3.7 What is India's balance on goods and services?

3.8 What is India's balance on goods, services, and income?

3.9 What is India's current account balance?

China's (Mainland) Balance of Payments

Use the following balance of payments data for China (Mainland) from the IMF to answer Problems 3.10–3.14.

Problem 3.10–3.14

Assumptions (millions of U.S. dollars)	2010	2011	2012	2013	2014	2015	2016	2017	2018	2019	2020
A. Current account balance	237,810	136,097	215,392	148,204	236,047	293,022	191,337	188,676	24,131	102,910	273,980
B. Capital account balance	4,630	5,446	4,272	3,052	–33	316	–344	–91	–569	–327	–77
C. Financial account balance	282,234	260,024	–36,038	343,048	–51,361	–434,462	–416,070	109,537	172,682	7,308	–77,759
D. Net errors and omissions	–53,016	–13,768	–87,071	–62,922	–66,869	–201,817	–218,547	–206,595	–177,368	–129,178	–168,134
E. Reserves and related items	–471,658	–387,799	–96,555	–431,382	–117,783	342,941	443,625	–91,526	–18,877	19,288	–28,011

3.10 Is China experiencing a net capital inflow or outflow?

3.11 What is China's total for Groups A and B?

3.12 What is China's total for Groups A through C?

3.13 What is China's total for Groups A through D?

3.14 Does China's BOP balance?

Russia's Balance of Payments

Use the following balance of payments data for the Russian Federation from the IMF to answer Problems 3.15–3.19

Problem 3.15–3.19

Assumptions (millions of U.S. dollars)	**2010**	**2011**	**2012**	**2013**	**2014**	**2015**	**2016**	**2017**	**2018**	**2019**	**2020**
A. Current account balance	67,452	97,274	71,282	33,428	57,513	67,777	24,469	32,179	115,680	64,806	33,949
B. Capital account balance	–41	130	–5,218	–395	–42,005	–304	–764	–192	–1,104	–684	–522
C. Financial account balance	–21,526	–76,118	–25,675	–46,213	–130,992	–68,624	–10,063	–11,941	–78,489	3,868	–49,951
D. Net errors and omissions	–9,135	–8,647	–10,370	–8,898	7,939	2,858	–5,400	2,582	2,110	–1,506	2,770
E. Reserves and related items	–36,750	–12,638	–30,020	22,078	107,545	–1,702	–8,242	–22,628	–38,197	–66,484	13,754

3.15 Is Russia experiencing a net capital inflow?

3.16 What is Russia's total for Groups A and B?

3.17 What is Russia's total for Groups A through C?

3.18 What is Russia's total for Groups A through D?

3.19 Does Russia's BOP balance?

Iceland Balance of Payments

Use the following balance of payments data for Ice land from the IMF to answer Problems 3.20–3.24.

Problem 3.20–3.24

Assumptions (millions of U.S. dollars)	**2010**	**2011**	**2012**	**2013**	**2014**	**2015**	**2016**	**2017**	**2018**	**2019**	**2020**
A. Current account balance	–845	–716	–518	1,010	776	986	1,717	1,055	986	1,579	236
B. Capital account balance	–11	–13	–10	–11	–14	–11	–12	–13	–16	–16	–18
C. Financial account balance	–9,358	–5,865	–66	–957	2,894	70,325	582	–1,269	–1,419	–1,135	–1,429
D. Net errors and omissions	189	1,472	–397	90	–68	–123	138	–603	483	124	988
E. Reserves and related items	10,025	5,122	991	–132	–3,588	–71,177	–2,425	830	–34	–553	223

3.20 Is Iceland experiencing a net capital inflow?

3.21 What is Iceland's total for Groups A and B?

3.22 What is Iceland's total for Groups A through C?

3.23 What is Iceland's total for Groups A through D?

3.24 Does Iceland's BOP balance?

3.25 **Trade Deficits and J-Curve Adjustment Paths.** Assume the United States has the following import/export volumes and prices. It undertakes a major "devaluation" of the dollar, say 18% on average against all major trading partner currencies. What are the pre-devaluation and post-devaluation trade balance?

Initial spot exchange rate ($ = fc)	2.00
Price of exports, dollars ($)	20.0000
Price of imports, foreign currency (fc)	12.0000
Quantity of exports, units	100
Quantity of imports, units	120
Percentage devaluation of the dollar	18.00%
Price elasticity of demand, imports	–0.90

4

Financial Goals, Corporate Governance, and the Market for Corporate Control

A Corporation then, or a body politic, or body incorporate, is a collection of many individuals united into one body, under a special denomination, having perpetual succession under an artificial form, and vested, by policy of the law, with the capacity of acting, in several respects, as an individual, particularly of taking and granting property, of contracting obligations, and of suing and being sued, of enjoying privileges and immunities in common, and of exercising a variety of political rights, more or less extensive, according to the design of its institution, or the powers conferred upon it, either at the time of its creation, or at any subsequent period of its existence.

—Stewart Kyd, *A Treatise on the Law of Corporations*, 1793, p. 13.

LEARNING OBJECTIVES

4.1 Examine the different ownership structures for businesses globally and how this impacts the separation between ownership and management—the agency problem

4.2 Compare and contrast the two dominant theories of the corporate purpose, *shareholder capitalism* and *stakeholder capitalism*, in an era of growing concern over environmental, social and governance issues

4.3 Consider the differences in corporate governance regimes globally, including their ability to allow the market for corporate control to evaluate and discipline corporate performance

4.4 Explore the market for corporate control, the global marketplace for merging or acquiring control over corporate resources, and the multitude of strategies and tactics used to both effect and defend against hostile acquisitions.

Global business is conducted by many different types of organizations for many different purposes. Although it may appear at times that global business is dominated by the publicly traded corporation and for the sole purpose of profit, these are characteristic of only select companies, countries, and markets, and the global marketplace is much more diverse and complex.

This chapter explores the different forms of business organizations used today around the world, their governance and goals, and ultimately their ability to pursue sustainability. We begin our discussion by deepening our understanding of ownership, the legal construct so often associated with global business, the corporation, and then ultimately the roles and responsibilities of corporations by and for their major stakeholders. The chapter concludes with an examination of the 2021 turmoil surrounding Toshiba's failing corporate governance, a classic example of how difficult it is to change corporate governance practices in established corporate cultures.

4.1 Business Ownership

We begin our discussion of corporate financial goals by asking two basic questions: (1) Who owns the business? and (2) Do the owners of the business manage the business themselves? In global business today, the ownership and control of organizations vary dramatically across countries and cultures. To understand how and why those businesses operate, one must first understand the many different ownership structures.

Types of Ownership

The terminology associated with the ownership of a business can be confusing. A business owned by a government, the state, is frequently described as a *public enterprise* or a *state-owned enterprise* (SOE). A business that is owned by a private individual is a *private company* or *private enterprise*. If you were the owner of your own company, you would possess the full rights of ownership. You would set the strategic direction of the company, make all financial decisions, and ultimately receive any profits generated from the conduct of the business.

A second distinction on ownership clouds the terminology. A business owned by a private party, or a small group of private individuals, a private enterprise, is termed *privately held*. If those owners, however, wish to sell a portion of their ownership in the business in the capital markets—for example, by listing and trading the company's shares on a stock exchange—the firm's shares are then said to be *publicly traded*. And in the world today there are a multitude of hybrid ownership structures that could alter the financial objectives of the firms. Exhibit 4.1 provides a brief overview of these ownership distinctions.

Ownership can be held by a variety of different groups or organizations. A business may be owned by a single person (sole proprietorship), two or more people (partnership), a family

EXHIBIT 4.1 **Business Ownership**

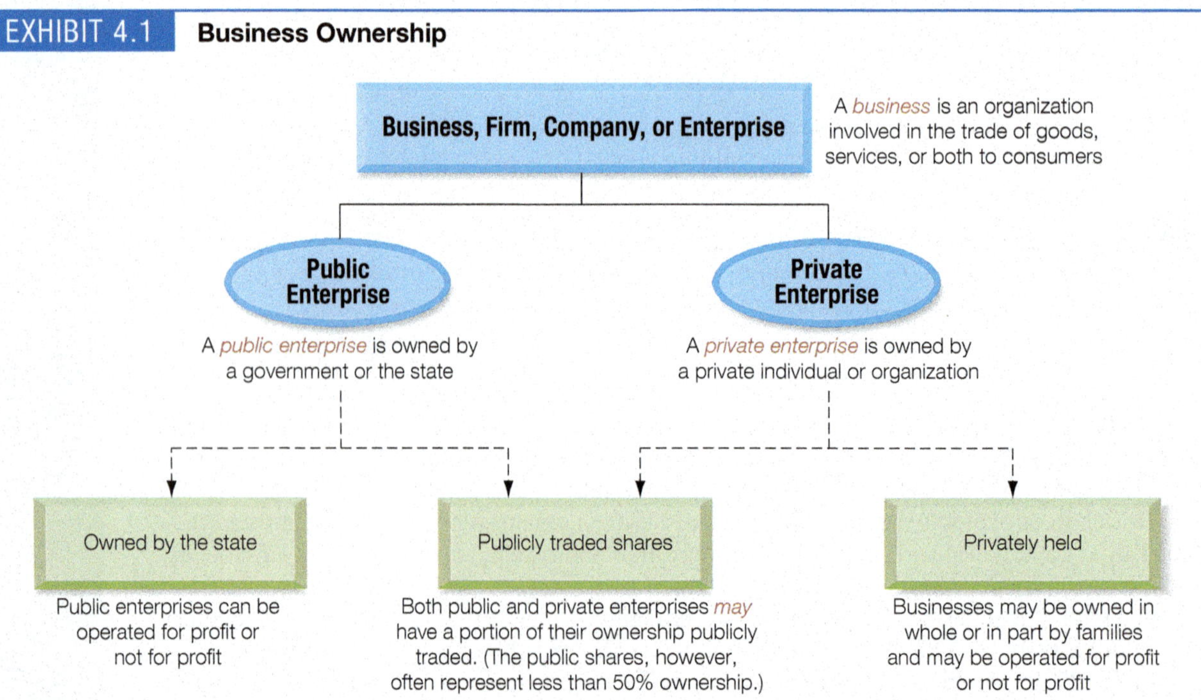

(family-owned business), two or more other companies (joint venture), thousands of individuals (publicly traded company), a government (state-owned enterprise), a foundation or trust (not-for-profit organization), or some combination.

The following three multinational enterprises are examples of how ownership differs in global business, as well as how it may evolve within any single enterprise over time.

- Petroleo Brasileiro S.A., or Petrobras, is the national oil company of Brazil. Founded in 1953, it was originally 100% owned by the Brazilian government—a state-owned enterprise. It eventually became publicly traded on the Sao Paulo stock exchange. Today the Brazilian government owns 64% of the shares of Petrobras, with 36% in the hands of private investors all over the world.
- Apple was founded in 1976 as a partnership of Steve Jobs, Steve Wozniak, and Ronald Wayne and incorporated in 1977, with Ronald Wayne selling his interest to his two partners. In 1980, Apple sold shares to the public for the first time in an initial public offering (IPO), with its shares listed (traded) on the NASDAQ Stock Market. Today Apple is considered *widely held*, with no single investor holding 5% of its shares. In recent years, Apple has periodically been the world's most valuable publicly traded company, as calculated by market capitalization (shares outstanding multiplied by the share price).
- Hermès International is a French multinational producer of luxury goods. Founded by Thierry Hermès in 1837, it has been owned and operated by the Hermès family for most of its history, making it a family-owned business. In 1993, in its initial public offering, the company sold 27% of its ownership to the general public. The family, however, retained 73% ownership and therefore control of the company.

Once the ownership of the business is established, it is then easier to understand where control lies, as ownership and control are separate concepts. Petrobras is a publicly traded Brazilian business that is controlled by the Brazilian government. Hermès International is a publicly traded family-controlled French-based business. Apple is a publicly traded and widely held business, so control rests with its board of directors and the senior leadership team hired by the board to run the company. Individual investors who hold shares in Apple may vote on issues presented to them on an annual basis, so they have some degree of influence, but the strategy, tactics, operations, and governance of Apple are under the control of the senior management team and the board.

Any business, whether initially owned by the state, a family, or a private individual or institution, may choose to have a portion of its ownership traded as shares in the public marketplace, as noted in Exhibit 4.1. (Note that we say a portion, as a 100% publicly traded firm can no longer be either state-owned or privately held by definition.) For example, many SOEs are publicly traded. China National Petroleum Corporation (CNPC), the state-owned parent company of PetroChina, is an example, with its shares being traded on stock exchanges in Shanghai, Hong Kong, and New York, yet majority ownership and control still rest with the government of China.

If a firm's owners decide to sell a portion of the company to the public, it conducts an *initial public offering*, or IPO. Typically only a small percentage of the company is initially sold to the public, anywhere from 10% to 20%, resulting in a company that may still be controlled by a small number of private investors, a family, or a government, but now with a portion of its shares traded publicly. Over time a company may gradually sell more of its equity interest into the public market, eventually becoming totally publicly traded.

Alternatively, a private owner or family may choose to retain a major share but may not retain control. It is also possible for the controlling interest in a firm to reverse its public share position, reducing the number of shares outstanding by repurchasing shares. The acquisition of one firm by another demonstrates yet another way ownership and control can change. For example, in 2005 a very large private firm, Koch Industries (U.S.), purchased all outstanding shares of Georgia-Pacific (U.S.), a very large publicly traded company. Koch took Georgia-Pacific private.

Even if a firm is publicly traded, it may still be controlled by a single investor or by a small group of investors, including major institutional investors. This means that the control of a publicly traded company is much like that of a privately held company, reflecting the interests and goals of the controlling individual investor or family. A continuing characteristic of many businesses operating in emerging markets is the dominance of family control, although many are simultaneously publicly traded.

As discussed later in this chapter, there is another significant implication of an initial sale of shares to the public: The firm becomes subject to many of the increased legal, regulatory, and reporting requirements related to the sale and trading of securities. In the U.S., for example, going public means the firm must disclose a sizable degree of financial and operational detail, publish this information at least quarterly, and comply with all the rules and regulations of the SEC and exchange on which its shares are traded. In most countries, firms which are privately held do not have to publish detailed financial and operating results.

The Corporation

A corporation is an organization, typically a group of people or companies, recognized legally by the state to act as a single entity. This is often described as a *legal person*. As a *legal person*, the corporation has many of the same rights and attributes of individuals, with some beneficial restrictions. The corporation can enter into contracts, take out loans, sue and be sued, and purchase or sell assets. Corporations are formed when individuals exchange some form of consideration, typically cash, in exchange for a financial interest—the interest entitling the shareholder to a portion of any profits. A very important benefit of the corporate form is that shareholders have limited liability, that is, they may only lose financially what they have invested. They do not, however, have personal liability. This feature is often seen as an incentive for shareholders to undertake greater risks. *Global Finance in Practice 4.1* traces some of the corporation's history.

The corporate form poses a number of complexities. First, shareholders are financial investors, not truly owners in the traditional sense of the word. Shareholders are not privy to the internal workings of the firm. They cannot sign contracts on behalf of the firm. They cannot purchase or sell assets on behalf of the firm. As financial investors and not operators, they are primarily interested in financial returns. The second complexity is one that is, well, more esoteric. The corporation is a legal person, an artificial person, not an actual person. This has led to a recurring debate over whether the corporation has social interests or a conscience or whether it is purely an organization for financial profit.

Separation of Ownership and Management

One of the most challenging issues in the financial management of the corporation or enterprise is the possible separation of ownership from management. Hired or professional management may be present under any ownership structure, though most common in SOEs and publicly traded companies. This separation of ownership from management raises the possibility that the two entities may have different business and financial objectives and—from a purely financial perspective—different risk tolerances or appetites. This is the so-called *principal agent problem* or simply *the agency problem*. Describing the problem in 1972, Jensen and Meckling used the words of Adam Smith to introduce it:[1]

[1] "Theory of the Firm: Managerial Behavior, Agency Costs, and Ownership Structure," by Michael C. Jensen and William H. Meckling, *Journal of Financial Economics* 3 (1976): 305–360.

GLOBAL FINANCE IN PRACTICE **4.1**

Historical Origins of the Modern Corporation

The corporate form has many historical antecedents. In the eleventh century, a system in Italy, the *commenda*, combined a financial partner (passive partner) with a merchant vessel (managing partner). When the vessel concluded its voyage with goods for sale, the partners divided up the profits by contract. The financial partner could lose no more than its investment; the managing partner—investing only their time and effort—assumed the majority of the nonfinancial risks. This was followed by groups of investors who combined or pooled their capital, spreading out the risks across multiple vessels and voyages—an early form of diversification.

The development of the joint stock company in Britain in the 1600s followed a similar structure. Groups of investors pooled their capital to undertake risky ventures, ventures requiring more capital and effort than individual investors could bear. The Crown reduced the risks with such efforts further by granting monopolies to these groups, such as the English East India Company; only the East India Company could conduct trade with India. This reduced the business risk associated with the organization's ventures, assuring higher rates of return. The company was originally formed as a combination of a guild (a member-based organization) and a joint stock company (a form of partnership). In its combination its shareholders were described as "members" and "owners" arising from their original organizations. Profits were distributed on the basis of capital invested.

Even the United States itself was somewhat the product of the early corporation. The Virginia Company, two distinct joint stock companies (Plymouth to the north, Virginia to the south) chartered by James I in 1606, was charged with establishing colonies on the North American coast. As Crown corporations, they were to govern themselves. This self-governance was later seen as one of the seeds of American democracy.

> *The directors of such [joint-stock] companies, however, being the managers rather of other people's money than of their own, it cannot well be expected, that they should watch over it with the same anxious vigilance with which the partners in a private copartnery frequently watch over their own. Like the stewards of a rich man, they are apt to consider attention to small matters as not for their master's honour, and very easily give themselves a dispensation from having it. Negligence and profusion, there- fore, must always prevail, more or less, in the management of the affairs of such a company.*
>
> —Adam Smith, *The Wealth of Nations*, 1776, Cannan Edition (Modern Library, New York, 1937) p. 700.

There are a multitude of examples of how this agency issue may be demonstrated. Management, for example, is hired as an agent of the shareholder to represent the shareholder's interests. Shareholders, benefiting from the corporate form, are interested in the firm, via its managers, taking significant risks in search of profits. Managers, however, dependent on the continuing operation of the corporation for their livelihood, may be reluctant to take excessive risk. This disconnect between shareholder and management-agent is at the core of the publicly traded firm. There are, however, several strategies available for aligning shareholder and management interests, the most common of which is for senior management to own shares or share options.

The United States and United Kingdom are two country markets characterized by widespread ownership of shares. Managers may own some small portion of stock in their firms, but largely management is a hired agent that is expected to represent the interests of shareholders. In contrast, many firms in many other global markets are characterized by controlling shareholders, such as government, institutions (e.g., banks in Germany), family (e.g., in France and Italy and throughout Asia and Latin America), and consortiums of interests (e.g., *keiretsus* in Japan and *chaebols* in South Korea). A business that is owned and managed by the same entity does not suffer the agency problem. In many of these cases, control is enhanced by ownership of shares with dual voting rights, interlocking directorates, staggered election of the board of directors, takeover safeguards, and other techniques that are not used in the Anglo-American markets.

Ownership in the publicly traded corporation differs dramatically across countries today. Substantial and sometimes controlling interests are held by private individuals or entities, government enterprises, a widely dispersed public ownership, or fund-based institutions. These ownership differences are explored in detail by global region in *Global Finance in Practice 4.2.*

GLOBAL FINANCE IN PRACTICE 4.2

Structural Ownership Differences Across the World

Ownership of any organization drives purpose and process. For example, a private owner—for example, a family—is typically interested in both financial returns and organizational longevity, whereas an individual private owner of a publicly traded share is focused on financial returns, both dividends and capital gains. A recent OECD study on global patterns revealed substantial differences across the world.

The OECD noted three areas of interest and concern over the data results.

- First, there is an obvious dominance of institutional ownership in both the United States and other advanced industrial economies. Institutional investors hold 41% of global market capitalization, a significant hold on the world's capital. If these large institutional investors act only passively in their ownership, they may pay little attention to the many risks and opportunities faced by individual corporations. As a result, they may not demand accountability for performance.
- Second, public sector ownership—government ownership—of shares in publicly listed companies is large and significant in China, other emerging Asia nations, and emerging markets in general. This ownership occurs through three primary channels: direct ownership, pension fund ownership and control, and sovereign wealth funds. Although government only controls 14% of global stock market capitalization, its ownership in these three key regional sectors is notable, as these owners have significant political as well as business interests, either through direct government ownership or through sovereign wealth funds, public pension funds, and state-owned enterprises.
- Third, strategic individuals—private individuals with significant ownership—are one of the most influential but "hidden" sources of control and influence. The OECD notes that in half of the world's publicly listed companies the top three strategic individuals control more than 50% of the capital. A topic for further study, this concentration of power may lead to a reduction in agency issues as these individuals exert influence on management but simultaneously potentially represent a tyranny of the minority in their control of the publicly traded company.

Source: "Owners of the World's Listed Companies," OECD Capital Market Series, OECD, Paris, 2019.

Ownership by Investor Category, Regions of the World

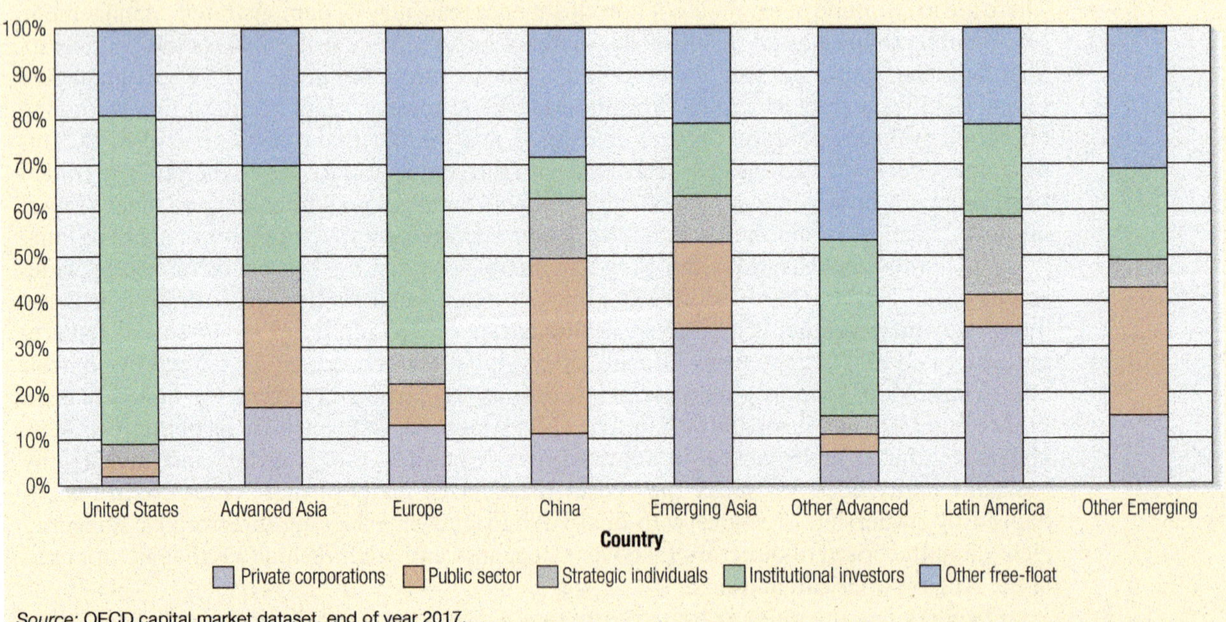

Source: OECD capital market dataset, end of year 2017.

4.2 The Corporate Objective?

What is the purpose of the corporation? The purpose of the corporation might be first defined as "to run a business." That business is in turn a system of mission, vision, and strategy. Depending on your field of study and perspective, the purpose of the corporation may be to enrich customers, provide jobs, generate wealth for shareholders, create value for stakeholders, or increase the welfare of society.[2] The financial objective of the firm, of specific interest to us in the field of financial management, might then be viewed as the metric of performance in the conduct of that business.

Companies today, whether domestic firms or multinational enterprises, are in the midst of a growing debate as to whom the corporation specifically serves. That is a question central to finance and financial metrics of performance. Assuming a market economy and a focus on for-profit organizations, the two most widely accepted forms of capitalism practiced in global business over the past 50 years are *shareholder capitalism* and *stakeholder capitalism*.[3] Exhibit 4.2 provides a stakeholder map of the corporation.

A *stakeholder* is any entity with an interest or right or concern with an organization and its activities. In the modern corporation, the firm in Exhibit 4.2, the *direct stakeholders* are those entities with a vested financial interest in the firm's success. Direct stakeholders can be subdivided into business stakeholders (suppliers and customers), internal stakeholders (employees and management), and financial stakeholders (equity investors and creditors). *Indirect stakeholders* are those which are impacted in some way by the firm's activities and include but are not limited to community, government, civil society, and the environment. Direct or indirect, each entity has its own interest or expectation of the firm's activities.

EXHIBIT 4.2 Stakeholders in the Firm

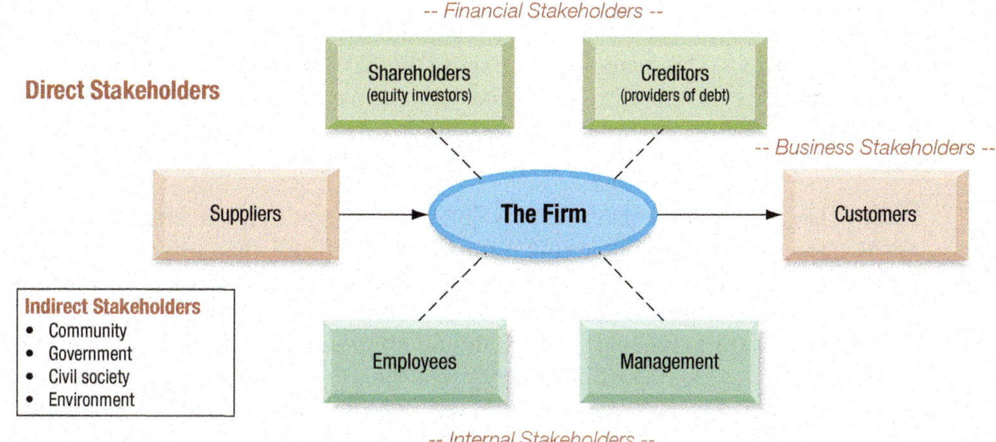

Differences in ownership, law, country of incorporation, activity, and culture lead to differences in interest and power among stakeholder groups (*business, financial, internal,* and *society*).

[2] See "The Nature of the Firm: Origin, Meaning, Influence," by Ronald Coase, *Journal of Law, Economics & Organization* 4, no. 1 (1988): 3–47; "The Pragmatic Theory of the Firm," by Bartley J. Madden, *Journal of Applied Corporate Finance* 33, no. 1 (Winter 2021): 98–110.

[3] Management of multinational not-for-profit organizations, issue-driven organizations (like benefit or B corps), and nongovernmental organizations (NGOs) follows many of these same fundamental business practices.

Every student today learns the concept of maximizing shareholder wealth sometime during their college education. This means that if a firm is pursuing shareholder capitalism, the firm's primary objective is to create value for shareholders in Exhibit 4.2. It does not mean that the other stakeholders are not important; it only directs the firm to consider shareholders first. If a firm is following stakeholder capitalism, it must find an operating balance among direct stakeholders and ultimately also consider indirect stakeholders as well. Balance is an exceedingly difficult concept to achieve, however, as we will explore in the practice of global financial management. Historically, an overly simplistic description of the world was the following: Anglo-American markets followed shareholder capitalism, the rest of the world pursuing some form of stakeholder capitalism. But as with so many aspects of life and business, it is a bit more complicated than that today!

Shareholder Capitalism

> *A business corporation is organized and carried on primarily for the profit of the stockholders. The powers of the directors are to be employed for that end. The discretion of directors is to be exercised in the choice of means to attain that end, and does not extend to a change in the end itself, to the reduction of profits, or to the non-distribution of profits among stockholders in order to devote them to other purposes.*
>
> —Michigan State Supreme Court, *Dodge v. Ford Motor Company*, 1991.

The Anglo-American markets have a philosophy that a firm's objective should follow *shareholder capitalism*, also frequently termed *shareholder wealth maximization* (SWM). More specifically, the firm should strive to maximize the financial returns to shareholders, as measured by the sum of capital gains and dividends, for a given level of risk. Alternatively, the firm should minimize the risk to shareholders for a given rate of return and do so in preference to the interests and returns to all other stakeholders of the firm.

Market Efficiency. The SWM theoretical model assumes, as a universal truth, that the stock market is efficient. This means that the share price is always correct because it captures all the expectations of return and risk as perceived by investors. It quickly incorporates new information into the share price. Share prices, in turn, are deemed the best allocators of capital in the macro economy.

Risk. The SWM model also treats its definition of risk as a universal truth. Risk is defined as the added probability of varying returns that the firm's shares bring to a diversified portfolio. The operational risk, the risk associated with the business line of the individual firm, can be eliminated through portfolio diversification by investors. Therefore, the unsystematic risk, the risk of the individual security, should not be a prime concern for management unless it increases the possibility of bankruptcy. On the other hand, systematic risk, the risk of the market in general, cannot be eliminated through portfolio diversification and is risk that the share price will be a function of the stock market.

Agency Theory. The field of agency theory is the study of how shareholders can motivate management to accept the prescriptions of the SWM model. For example, liberal use of stock options should encourage management to think like shareholders. Whether these inducements succeed is open to debate. However, if management deviates from the SWM objectives of working to maximize shareholder returns, then it is the responsibility of the board to replace management. In cases where the board is too weak or ingrown to take this action, the discipline of equity markets could do it through a takeover. This discipline is made possible by the one-share-one-vote rule that exists in most Anglo-American markets.

Long-Term versus Short-Term Value Maximization. During the 1990s, the economic boom and rising stock prices in most of the world's markets exposed a flaw in the SWM model, especially in the United States. Instead of seeking long-term value maximization, several large U.S. corporations sought short-term value maximization (e.g., the continuing debate about meeting the market's expected quarterly earnings). This strategy was partly motivated by the overly generous use of stock options to motivate top management.

This short-term focus sometimes created distorted managerial incentives. In order to maximize growth in short-term earnings and to meet inflated expectations by investors, firms such as Enron, Global Crossing, Health South, Adelphia, Tyco, Parmalat, and WorldCom undertook risky, deceptive, and sometimes dishonest practices for the recording of earnings and/or obfuscation of liabilities, which ultimately led to their demise. It also led to highly visible prosecutions of their CEOs, CFOs, accounting firms, and other related parties. This sometimes destructive short-term focus on the part of both management and investors has been labeled *impatient capitalism.*

This point of debate is also sometimes referred to as the firm's investment horizon in reference to how long it takes the firm's actions, its investments and operations, to result in earnings. In contrast to impatient capitalism is patient capitalism, which focuses on long-term shareholder wealth maximization. Legendary investor Warren Buffett, through his investment vehicle Berkshire Hathaway, represents one of the best of the patient capitalists. Buffett has become a billionaire by focusing his portfolio on mainstream firms that grow slowly but steadily with the economy, such as Coca-Cola.

Stakeholder Capitalism

> *The job of management is to maintain an equitable and working balance among the claims of the various directly interested groups . . . stockholders, employees, customers, and the public at large.*
>
> —Frank W. Abrams, Chairman, Standard Oil of New Jersey, 1951.

In the non-Anglo-American markets, controlling shareholders also strive to maximize long-term returns to equity. However, they are more constrained by other powerful stakeholders. In particular, outside the Anglo-American markets, labor unions are more powerful and governments interfere more in the marketplace to protect important stakeholder groups, such as local communities, the environment, and employment. In addition, banks and other financial institutions are more important creditors than securities markets. This model has been labeled the stakeholder capitalism (SCM).

Market Efficiency. Stakeholder capitalism does not assume that equity markets are either efficient or inefficient. In fact, it does not really matter because the firm's financial goals are not exclusively shareholder-oriented since they are constrained by the other stakeholders. In any case, the SCM model assumes that long-term "loyal" shareholders, typically controlling shareholders, should influence corporate strategy rather than the transient portfolio investor.

Risk. The SCM model assumes that total risk, that is, operating risk, does count. It is a specific corporate objective to generate growing earnings and dividends over the long run with as much certainty as possible, given the firm's mission statement and goals. Risk measurement is based more on product market variability than on short-term variation in earnings and share price.

Single versus Multiple Goals. Although the SCM model typically avoids a flaw of the SWM model—impatient capital that is short-run oriented—it has its own flaw. Trying to meet the desires of multiple stakeholders leaves management without a clear signal about the trade-offs. Instead, management tries to influence the trade-offs through written and oral disclosures and complex compensation systems.

The Scorecard. In contrast to the SCM model, the SWM model requires a single goal of value maximization with a well-defined scorecard. According to the theoretical model of SWM, the objective of management is to maximize the total market value of the firm. This means that corporate leadership should be willing to spend or invest more if each additional dollar creates more than one dollar in the market value of the company's equity, debt, or any other contingent claims on the firm.

Although both models have their strengths and weaknesses and in many ways they may not be too different in practice, a number of events and trends have renewed the debate.

- In the 1990s, as more of the non-Anglo-American markets privatized their industries, a shareholder wealth focus was seemingly needed to attract international capital from outside investors, many of which were from other countries.
- The global financial crisis, 2008–2010, demonstrated the major income and employment inequalities in market economies. Civil society called out for organizations, corporations, to facilitate societal change. Stakeholder capitalism appeared a more promising path.
- Since 2010, the world's focus has increasingly turned toward environmental (e.g., climate change) and social (e.g., the global income and employment inequities accentuated by the global pandemic of 2020) concerns, concerns seemingly more aligned with stakeholder capitalism.

Environmental, social, and governance (ESG) concerns are today an everyday topic in global business, one that has in some ways returned to its roots. Shareholder capitalists argue that the corporation is not a real human and has no specific conscience or social value judgments. Only the leaders of the publicly traded firm are humans, and many believe it is not appropriate for those leaders to impose their own values on the corporation itself. Their argument is that in the process of maximizing value for the shareholder, the entire pie is enlarged for all stakeholders. In the extreme, shareholder capitalists recite the words of Milton Friedman, a Nobel prize–winning champion of free markets:[4]

> *There is one and only one social responsibility of business—to use its resources and engage in activities designed to increase its profits so long as it stays within the rules of the game, which is to say, engages in open and free competition without deception or fraud.*

Stakeholder capitalists see these issues in a different way. They argue the corporation is a legal person and is obligated to benefit all of its stakeholders, including society, and not just shareholders. In recent years stakeholder capitalism has gained a number of victories in the debate, winning over a multitude of leaders in both government and industry. The investing

[4] "The Social Responsibility of Business Is to Increase Its Profits," by Milton Friedman, *The New York Times Magazine*, September 13, 1970.

GLOBAL FINANCE IN PRACTICE 4.3

Stakeholder Capitalism Metrics: The Four Ps

The World Economic Forum (WEF) believes that if businesses are to thrive, companies need to enhance their license to operate through greater commitment to long-term, sustainable value creation. The WEF believes there are four themes—the 4Ps—that make up good governance, each theme possessing core metrics in its reporting on performance against environmental, social, and governance (ESG) indicators.

1. **Principles of Governance:** Governing purpose, quality of governing, stakeholder engagement, ethical behavior, risk and opportunity oversights
2. **Planet:** Climate change, nature loss, freshwater availability
3. **People:** Dignity and equality, health and well-being, skills for the future
4. **Prosperity:** Employment and wealth generation, innovation of better products and services, community and social vitality

Source: Measuring Stakeholder Capitalism, Towards Common Metrics and Consistent Reporting of Sustainable Value Creation, White Paper, World Economic Forum, Prepared in collaboration with Deloitte, EY, KPMG, and PwC, September 2020, pp. 8–10.

public has played a major role in this resurgence, as green investing flowed toward firms considered ESG friendly. In 2020, the World Economic Forum came out in support of stakeholder capitalism, as described in *Global Finance in Practice 4.3.*

Operational Goals

The management objective of maximizing profit is not as simple as it sounds because the measure of profit used by ownership/management differs between the private firm and the publicly traded firm. In other words, is management attempting to maximize current income, capital appreciation as in a share price, or both?

Returns to Investors in Publicly Traded Firms. The return to a shareholder in a publicly traded firm combines current income in the form of dividends and capital gains from the appreciation of share price:

$$\textit{Shareholder return} = \frac{D_2}{P_1} + \frac{P_2 - P_1}{P_1}$$

where the initial price, P_1, is the beginning price, the initial investment by the shareholder; P_2, is the price of the share at the end of period, and D_2 is the dividend paid at the end of period.

Shareholders reap financial returns from both components. For example, in the United States in the 1990s, a diversified investor may have received an average annual return of 14%, 2% from dividends and 12% from capital gains. This "split" between dividend and capital gain returns, however, differs dramatically across the world's major markets over time.

Management generally believes it has the most direct influence over the first component—the dividend yield. Management makes strategic and operational decisions that grow sales and generate profits. Then it distributes those profits to ownership in the form of dividends. Capital gains—the change in the share price as traded in the equity markets—is much more complex and reflects many forces that are not under management control. Despite growing market share, profits, or any other traditional measure of business success, the market may not reward these actions directly with share price appreciation. In the end, leadership in the publicly traded firm typically concludes that it is its own growth—growth in top-line sales and bottom-line profits—that is its greatest hope for driving share price upward.

The Case of Apple. In March 2012, Apple announced it would end a 17-year period of no dividend payments. This was followed by a similarly shocking announcement in April 2013 that it would raise nearly $17 billion in debt, although the company had an enormous cash balance. Both financial policy changes were surprising to the market and uncommon in the tech sector. One way to understand the financial policy change is to consider whether Apple had grown and evolved from a *growth firm* to a *value firm*.

Growth firms are small to medium-sized firms in the early rapid growth stages of their businesses. Their value is growing rapidly in the public markets, their share prices rising, creating substantial capital gains for their shareholders. At the same time, since they are in such rapid growth stages, they need all the capital they can get their hands on, so, arguably, they need the dividend cash flow more than their shareholders. Although they could raise debt during this stage, debt is often viewed as an obligation that slows the ability of corporate leadership to respond quickly to changing customer and technology market demands.

Value firms are large, more mature businesses, which find it increasingly difficult to create material value changes in their business. Once an Alibaba or Amazon gets so large, major new business developments and successes rarely change the company's financial earnings and results significantly. Share price movements become slower and more subtle over time. Yet such companies continue to generate massive amounts of cash flow and earnings. For these firms, activist investors like Carl Icahn may pressure management to take on more and more debt and pay out greater and greater dividends. The debt requires corporate management to stay sharp in keeping up debt service obligations, while the dividend distributions provide added and sometimes significant returns to shareholders who are seeing capital appreciation slowing or stagnating.

In Apple's case, there is an additional issue driving its financial policy change: U.S. taxes. Although the company held massive cash balances, this cash was largely offshore—outside the United States—and would result in large tax obligations if the cash was returned to the U.S. Apple, not wishing to increase its tax liabilities, chose instead to issue debt in order to fund the newly declared cash dividends.

Returns to Owners of Privately Held Firms. A privately held firm has a much simpler shareholder return objective function: maximize current and sustainable financial income to its owners. The privately held firm does not have a share price. (It does have a value, but this is not a definitive market-determined value in the way in which we believe markets work.) It simply focuses on generating current financial income, dividend income (as well as salaries and other forms of income provided owners), to generate returns to its ownership.

If the privately held ownership is a family, the family may also place a great emphasis on the ability to sustain those earnings over time while maintaining a slower rate of growth, which can be managed by the family itself. Without a share price, "growth" is not of the same strategic importance in the privately held firm. It is therefore critical that ownership and ownership's specific financial interests be understood from the very start if we are to understand the strategic and financial goals and objectives of management.

The privately held firm may also be less aggressive (take fewer risks) than the publicly traded firm. Without a public share price, and therefore the ability of outside investors to speculate on the risks and returns associated with company business developments, the privately held firm—its owners and operators—may choose to take fewer risks. This may mean that it will not attempt to grow sales and profits as rapidly and therefore may not require the capital (equity and debt) needed for rapid growth. A recent study by McKinsey, one of the world's foremost consulting firms, found that privately held firms consistently used

EXHIBIT 4.3 Public versus Private Ownership

Organizational Characteristic	State-Owned	Publicly Traded	Privately Held
Entrepreneurial	No	No; stick to core competencies	Yes; do anything the owners wish
Long-term or short-term focus	Long-term focus; political cycles	Short-term focus on quarterly earnings	Long-term focus
Focused on profitable growth	No	Yes; growth in earnings is critical	No; needs defined by owner's earnings need
Adequately financed	Country-specific	Good access to capital and capital markets	Limited in the past but increasingly available
Quality of leadership	Highly variable	Professional; hiring from both inside and outside	Highly variable; family-run firms are lacking
Role of earnings (profits)	Earnings may constitute funding for government	Earnings to signal the equity markets	Earnings to support owners and family
Leaders are owners	Caretakers, not owners	Minimal interests; some have stock options	Yes; ownership and management often one and the same

significantly lower levels of debt (averaging 5% less debt to equity) than publicly traded firms. Interestingly, these same private firms also enjoyed a lower cost of debt, roughly 30 basis points lower based on corporate bond issuances. Exhibit 4.3 provides an overview of the variety of distinctive financial and managerial differences between state-owned, publicly traded, and privately held firms.

Operational Goals for MNEs. The MNE must be guided by operational goals suitable for various levels of the firm. Even if the firm's goal is to maximize shareholder value, the manner in which investors value the firm is not always obvious to the firm's top management. Therefore, most firms hope to receive a favorable investor response to the achievement of operational goals that can be controlled by the way in which the firm performs and then hope—if we can use that term—that the market will reward their results. The MNE must determine the proper balance between three common operational financial objectives:

1. Maximization of consolidated after-tax income
2. Minimization of the firm's effective global tax burden
3. Correct positioning of the firm's income, cash flows, and available funds as to country and currency

These goals are frequently incompatible, in that the pursuit of one may result in a less desirable outcome of another. Management must make decisions daily in business about the proper trade-offs between goals (which is why companies are managed by people and not computers).

Consolidated Profits. The primary operational goal of the MNE is to maximize consolidated profits after-tax. Consolidated profits are the profits of all the individual units of the firm, all of its foreign branches and subsidiaries. And all foreign subsidiaries have their own set of local currency financial statements needed for incorporation and tax obligations. The MNE must combine all of their financial results, originating in many different currencies, for reporting in the currency of the parent. This is not to say that management is not striving to maximize the present value of all future cash flows. It is simply the case that most of the day-to-day decision-making in global management is about current earnings. The leaders of the MNE, the management team who are implementing the firm's strategy, must think far beyond current earnings.

Public/Private Hybrids. The global business environment is, as one analyst termed it, "a messy place," and the ownership of companies of all kinds, including MNEs, is not necessarily purely public or purely private. One recent study of global business found that fully one-third of all companies in the S&P 500 are technically family businesses. And this is not just the case for the U.S.; roughly 40% of the largest firms in France and Germany are heavily influenced by family ownership and leadership. In other words, the firm may be publicly traded, but a family still wields substantial power over the strategic and operational decisions of the firm. This may prove to be a good thing.

Activist Investors

One of the most dramatic developments globally in the corporate governance of the publicly traded firm has been the development and activities of activist investors. Activist investors, when unhappy with the way the publicly traded company is being led, try to induce change in the strategy and financial management of the firm. This is a radical departure from the traditional passive investor who, if dissatisfied, simply sold their shares and exited. The activists themselves have become personalities of size in global media—Carl Icahn, Nelson Peltz, William Ackerman, Daniel Loeb, Paul Singer, among others—and they and their hedge fund capital firms have influenced publicly traded firms across the world including Apple (United States), AzkoNobel (Netherlands), Danone (France), ExxonMobil (United States), Google (United States), Nestlé (Switzerland), and ThyssenKrupp (Germany).

Activists are shareholders. As illustrated in Exhibit 4.4, activists accumulate anywhere between 3% and 10% of the public shares in a target firm. They then work to influence leadership through every means possible—phone calls, published letters and white papers, shareholder meetings, shareholder votes, board representation—any and all possible means of influence. What they want is for the firm to take actions, strategic and/or financial, which will increase the financial returns to shareholders.

EXHIBIT 4.4 The Activist's Playbook

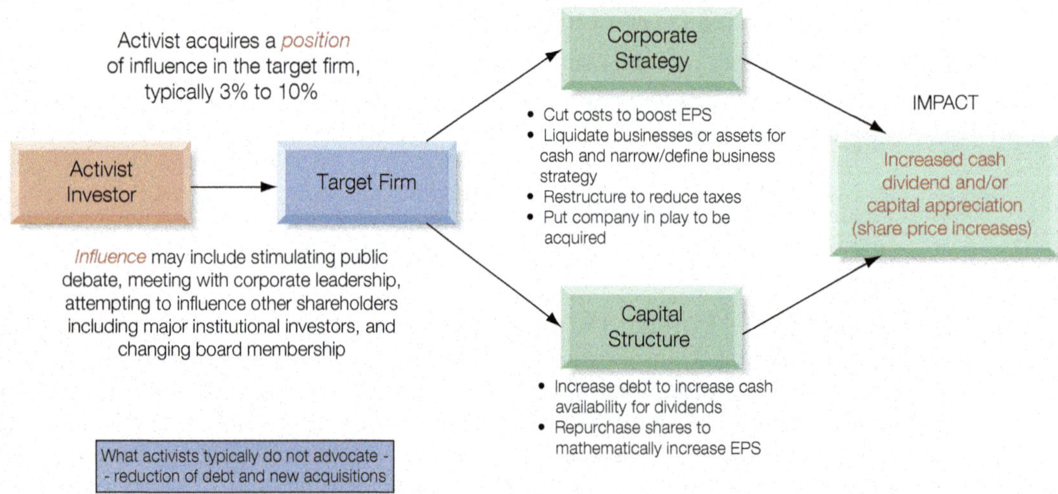

The activist's playbook is in most cases fairly standard. The strategic changes advocated include cutting costs (including executive compensation), selling off what they consider non-core businesses, actively restructuring to reduce global tax obligations, and increasing public (investor) debate on firm leadership and its direction. This last element, public debate, usually means putting the company "in play" in which share prices rise through investor speculation. The financial changes advocated usually include increasing the amount of debt in the firm's capital structure, reducing new investment (both capital expenditures and acquisitions), and returning more cash flow to investors through dividends and share repurchases.

The contributions of activists, the pros and cons, depend on where an individual sits. If you are a member of the leadership team in the target firm, activists are considered disruptive outsiders, interested in inducing short-term gains at the expense of long-term value creation. If you are an existing shareholder, activists are often welcomed as investors who are willing to step up and question established corporate leadership—an advocate for the small or passive investor. In the end, activists act as more engaged shareholders, taking on a role of a very engaged investor. Although they are often accused of promoting short-term thinking in their recommendations, they argue that they are advocating prudent policies that protect both corporate and investor interests. Activists in recent years have had a greater and greater impact in global markets in forcing change in structure (board membership) and strategy (e.g., oil and gas companies investing in renewable energy).

4.3 Corporate Governance

Corporate governance is the system of rules, practices, and processes by which an organization is directed and controlled. Although the governance structure of any company—domestic, international, or multinational—is fundamental to its very existence, this subject has become the lightning rod of political and business debate in the past few years as failures in governance in a variety of forms have led to corporate fraud and failure. Abuses and failures in corporate governance have dominated global business news in recent years. Beginning with the accounting fraud and questionable ethics of business conduct at Enron culminating in its bankruptcy in the fall of 2001, failures in corporate governance have raised issues about the ethics and culture of business conduct for the past 20 years.

The Structure of Governance

Our first challenge is to understand what people mean when they use the expression "corporate governance." Exhibit 4.5 provides an overview of the various parties and their responsibilities associated with the governance of a U.S. corporation. The various internal and external parties and organizations shown all exert some form of influence over the activities of the corporation, either by monitoring, reporting to the market or a regulator, active regulation, or simply valuation—buying and selling of any securities traded in the public market associated with the firm.

The internal forces, the officers of the corporation (CEO, CFO, etc.) and the board of directors of the corporation (including the chairman of the board), are directly responsible for determining both the strategic direction and the execution of the company's business. But they are not acting within a vacuum; the internal forces are subject to the constant prying eyes of the external forces in the marketplace that question the validity and soundness of the decisions and performance of internal forces. External forces include the equity market (stock exchanges) on which the company's shares are traded, the investment banking analysts who cover and critique the company shares, the company's creditors, the credit rating

EXHIBIT 4.5 **The Structure of Corporate Governance for a U.S. Firm**

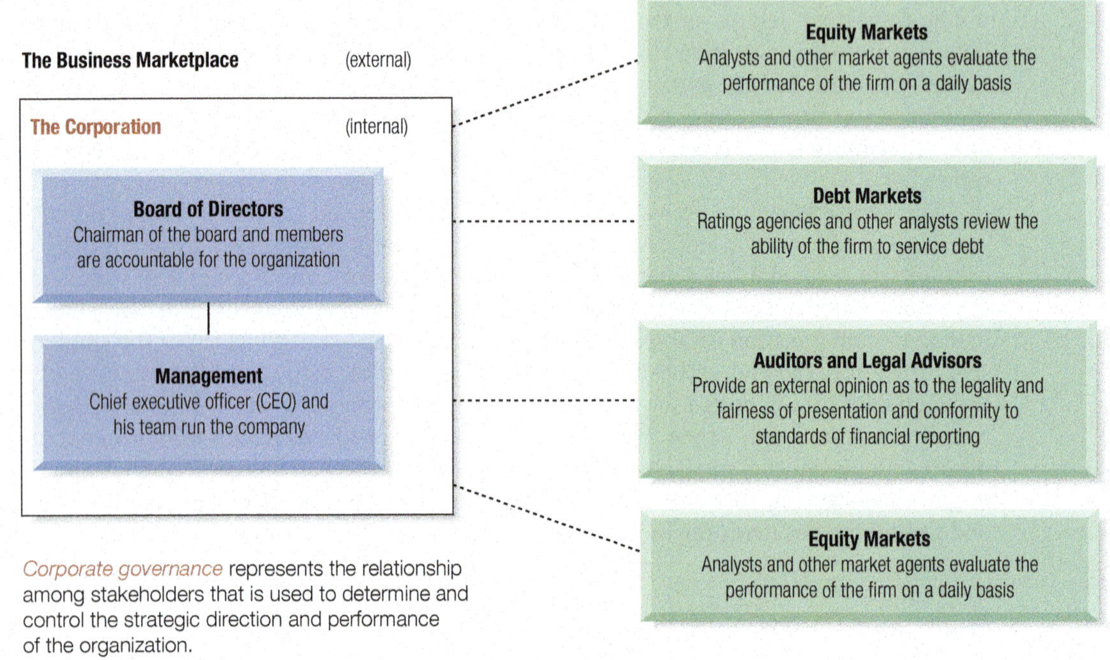

agencies that assign credit ratings to the company's debt or equity securities, the auditors and legal advisers who testify to the fairness and legality of the company's financial statements, and the multitude of regulators who oversee the company's actions—all in an attempt to assure the validity of information presented to investors.

This web of governance, where many different bodies and organizations constantly observe, monitor, and critique the U.S. corporation, is believed to not only provide a discipline to the firm but collectively work to protect the investor who places their hard-earned money in the securities of the firm. Most of the time it works as designed. In others, well, it does not so good.

Comparative Corporate Governance

The origins of the need for a corporate governance process arise from the separation of ownership from management and from the varying views by culture of who the stakeholders are and of their significance. This ensures that governance practices will differ across countries and cultures.

One method to categorize corporate governance regimes is by the evolution of ownership. Market-based regimes—like those of the United States, Canada, and the United Kingdom—are characterized by relatively efficient capital markets in which the ownership of publicly traded companies is widely dispersed. Family-based regimes, like those characterized in many of the emerging markets, Asian markets, and Latin American markets, not only started with strong concentrations of family ownership (as opposed to partnerships or small investment groups that are not family-based) but have also continued to be largely controlled by families even after going public. Bank-based and government-based regimes are those reflecting markets in which government ownership of property and industry has been a constant over time, resulting in only marginal public ownership of enterprise and, even then, subject to significant restrictions on business practices.

All exchange rate regimes are therefore a function of at least four major factors in the evolution of corporate governance principles and practices globally: (1) the financial market development, (2) the degree of separation between management and ownership, (3) the concept of disclosure and transparency, and (4) the historical development of the legal system.

Financial Market Development. The depth and breadth of capital markets are critical to the evolution of corporate governance practices. Country markets that have had relatively slow growth, as in the emerging markets, or have industrialized rapidly utilizing neighboring capital markets (for example, Western Europe) may not form large public equity market systems. Without significant public trading of ownership shares, high concentrations of ownership are preserved and few disciplined processes of governance are developed.

Separation of Management and Ownership. In countries and cultures where the ownership of the firm has continued to be an integral part of management, agency issues and failures have been less problematic. Family-based ownership maintains the owner–operator link. Family-based regimes are arguably more common and more important worldwide. For example, in a study of 5,232 corporations in 13 Western European countries, family-controlled firms represented 44% of the sample compared to 37% that were widely held. *Global Finance in Practice 4.4* describes the family cartel that controlled Italy for nearly 60 years. In countries like the United States, in which ownership has become largely separated from management (and widely dispersed), aligning the goals of management and ownership is much more difficult.

Disclosure and Transparency. The extent of disclosure regarding the operations and financial results of a company varies dramatically across countries. Disclosure practices reflect a wide range of cultural and social forces, including the degree to which ownership is public, the degree to which government feels the need to protect investor rights versus ownership rights, and the extent to which family-based and government-based business remains central to the culture. Transparency, a parallel concept to disclosure, reflects the visibility of decision-making processes within the business organization.

GLOBAL FINANCE IN PRACTICE 4.4

Italian Cross-Shareholding and the End of the *Salatto Buono*

Italy, in the years following World War II, was a country teetering on collapse. In an effort to stabilize industrial activity, the powerful families of the north—the Agnellis (of Fiat fame), the Pesentis, the Pirellis, the Ligrestis, and later the Benettons formed *salotto buono*—"the fine drawing room"—to control Italian finance, industry, and media through relatively small stakes. At the core of the relationship was that each family business held significant ownership and control in the other in an interlocking or cross-shareholding structure that assured that no outsiders could gain ownership or influence.

The creator of *salotto buono* was Enrico Cuccia, the founder of Mediobanca, the Milan-based investment bank. One man in particular, Cesare Geronzi, rose to the top of Italian finance. And every step of the way, he took three scarlet chairs with him. The chairs sat in his waiting room at Mediobanca and eventually Generali, Italy's largest financial group. Geronzi rose to the pinnacle of power despite twice being the target of major financial and accounting fraud cases, including Parmalat. Over the following half-century anyone wishing to gain influence had to pass through the "three chairs," the *salotto buono*.

But, alas, the global financial crisis of 2008–2009 broke down many of the world's last bastions of private power. One such casualty was the *salotto buono*, as more and more of its vested families fell further into debt and bankruptcy.

Historical Development of the Legal System. Investor protection is typically better in countries where English common law is the basis of the legal system, compared to the codified civil law that is typical in France and Germany (the so-called Code Napoleon). English common law is typically the basis of the legal systems in the United Kingdom and former colonies of the United Kingdom, including the United States and Canada. The Code Napoleon is typically the basis of the legal systems in former French colonies and the European countries that Napoleon once ruled, such as Belgium, Spain, and Italy. In countries with weak investor protection, controlling shareholder ownership is often a substitute for a lack of legal protection.

A second—simpler—way of categorizing governance regimes is on the basis of whether they are driven by forces from within, *insider regimes*, or by forces from without, *outsider* or *market-based regimes*. Exhibit 4.6 provides a detailed description of key components across representative countries.

Despite all of the rules, regulations, and regimes, corporate governance failures still occur. Although the Enron scandal in the U.S. is one of the most well known, it is in no way

EXHIBIT 4.6 Insider versus Outsider Corporate Governance

Dimension	Insider Regimes	Outsider Regimes
Example Countries	**Germany, Japan**	**United States, United Kingdom**
Share Ownership	**Concentrated.** Share ownership concentrated among insiders who often exert some control over corporate management.	**Widely distributed.** Significant separation of ownership and management, although among the larger firms management may hold sizeable shares.
Control	**Insider relationship-based control.** Strong family-based ownership or cross-shareholdings among companies, including banks in some cases, ensure a concentrated control of the organization.	**Management control (agency issues).** Public shareholders are so widely dispersed that few have significant influence, "ownership vacuum," giving management more power. This has created opportunities for activist investors to gain power and influence.
Market for Corporate Control	**Hostile takeovers are rare.** Hostile takeovers are rare as a result of legal barriers and cross-shareholding relationships with other companies and banking institutions. This prevents the equity market from acting as a disciplinarian of management.	**Hostile takeovers are common.** Hostile takeovers are common as a result of few institutional or legal barriers to market-based offerings. Financial institutions often back and fund hostile takeovers rather than opposing them. Equity markets act as managerial disciplinarians.
Government Role	**Participant role.** Government frequently holds shares and board seats, actively participating in the management and control of the firm.	**Non-participant role.** Government rarely owns or actively participates in the ownership or governance of the firm. Its role is typically regulatory only.
Board Structure	**Supervisory board overseeing Management board, separation of CEO and chairman.** Although the number of outside directors is growing, many are the results of corporate relationships and not true outsiders.	**Single board of directors, little separation of CEO and chairman.** Growing proportion of directors are outsiders. Outside directors commonly populate compensation committees.
Compensation Transparency	**Little transparency.** Little disclosure of board and management compensation.	**High degree of transparency.** Extensive disclosure of compensation systems, including amounts and performance objectives.
Minority Shareholder Protection	**High degree of protection.** Minority shareholder rights are often highly protected, much of which also secures power and control of major shareholder interests.	**Little minority shareholder protection.** Minority shareholders are not afforded significant protection. Unhappy shareholders exit, unless activists engage.

unique. In addition to Enron, other firms that have revealed major accounting and disclosure failures over time, as well as executive looting, are WorldCom, Parmalat, Tyco, Adelphia, and HealthSouth. In each case, prestigious auditing firms missed the violations or minimized them, possibly because of lucrative consulting relationships or other conflicts of interest. Moreover, security analysts and banks urged investors to buy the shares and debt issues of these and other firms that they knew to be highly risky or even close to bankruptcy. Even more egregious, most of the top executives who were responsible for the mismanagement that destroyed their firms often walked away with huge gains on shares sold before the downfall and overly generous severance packages.

The post-2000 period's experience with financial crisis (2008–2010) and global pandemic (2020) has driven more and more of the world's investors, governments, and societies to expect better governance. But change is slow, partially because it is steeped in law. Also note that we have not mentioned ethics. All of the principles and practices described so far have assumed that the individuals in roles of responsibility and leadership pursue them truly and fairly—a concept that was evidently not shared by someone, on some level, in Volkswagen, as described in *Global Finance in Practice 4.5*.

Good Governance and Corporate Reputation

Does good corporate governance matter? This is actually a difficult question, and the realistic answer has been largely dependent on outcomes historically. For example, as long as Enron's share price continued to rise, questions over transparency, accounting propriety, and even financial facts were largely overlooked by all of the stakeholders of the corporation. Yet, eventually, the fraud, deceit, and the failure of a multitude of corporate governance practices resulted in bankruptcy. It destroyed not only the wealth of investors but also the careers, incomes, and savings of many of its own employees. Ultimately, good governance should matter.

One way in which companies may signal good governance to the investor markets is to adopt and publicize a fundamental set of governance policies and practices. Nearly all publicly traded firms have adopted this approach, as becomes obvious when visiting corporate websites. This has also led to a standardized set of common principles, a consensus on good governance practices, led by the OECD.

1. **Shareholder rights**. Shareholders are the owners of the firm, and their interests should take precedence over other stakeholders.
2. **Board responsibilities**. The board of the company is recognized as the individual entity with final full legal responsibility for the firm, including proper oversight of management.
3. **Equitable treatment of shareholders**. Equitable treatment is specifically targeted toward domestic versus foreign residents as shareholders, as well as majority and minority interests.
4. **Stakeholder rights**. Governance practices should formally acknowledge the interests of other stakeholders—employees, creditors, community, and government.
5. **Transparency and disclosure**. Public and equitable reporting of firm operating and financial results and parameters should be done in a timely manner and should be made available to all interests equitably.

In principle, the idea is that good governance (at both the country and corporate levels) is linked to cost of capital (lower), returns to shareholders (higher), and corporate profitability (higher). An added dimension of interest is the role of country governance, as this influences the country in which international investors may choose to invest. Frustratingly, different governance rankings services often come up with very different rankings for the same firms, and

GLOBAL FINANCE IN PRACTICE 4.5

Volkswagen's Governance and Diesel Gate

Volkswagen AG is, periodically, the largest automobile company in the world. The company's organizational and governance structure is typical of large German firms. In September 2015 the company was discovered to have been utilizing software for years that tricked or "defeated" emissions testing technology worldwide. The market value of the firm fell by more than 30% within months. Like every corporate governance failure in history, the same question begged an answer: How did this happen?

The answer is complicated, combining unethical management and a governance structure which failed. VW's management culture, called the *VW System*, functioned via a network of deep relationships between management, workers, local politicians, and a frequently torrid family ownership structure. Although a global organization, its deep roots in Lower Saxony assured corporate longevity by protecting the jobs and industrial structure of its constituents.

VW had a dual-class ownership structure of common and preferred shares. Preferred shares would receive their guaranteed dividend in full before common shares were paid. In return for that guarantee, they gave up all voting rights. Common shares held all voting rights. The company's ownership was dominated by two families, the Porsche and Piëch families, who held 31.5% of the equity via common shares, the dual-class structure increasing their interest to 50.7%. One family member, Ferdinand Piëch, had long dominated the power structure of VW. He was known to seek power, control, and market dominance, not necessarily profit.

Common to German companies, VW had a two-tiered board structure, a supervisory board and a management board, as shown in the exhibit. The management board (led by the CEO as chairman) operated the company on a daily basis. The supervisory board's job was oversight of the management board, with 20 board seats split evenly between shareholder interests and the works council (worker union). Under German law, the Law of Codetermination (*mitbestimmungesetz* in German), any firm employing more than 2,000 workers had to have representatives of both employees and shareholders.

A final element, the government of Lower Saxony's board seats, added to governance complexity. VW had been a state-owned enterprise until privatized with the 1960 Volkswagen Law. The law required that VW's supervisory board always retain two government board seats (an extremely unusual element by Western standards).

The final result was a supervisory board structure ripe with conflicts. Workers wanted higher wages and job security, not necessarily profitability. Government interests were inherently political and often focused on increasing and sustaining employment. Ownership, represented by the two families and a single dominant personality, many of which did not agree on goals and interests, had pursued market dominance over profitability. Stir in a strong seasoning of what was considered a corporate culture of arrogance, and VW's governance was truly a witches' brew.

Volkswagen's Governance Structure

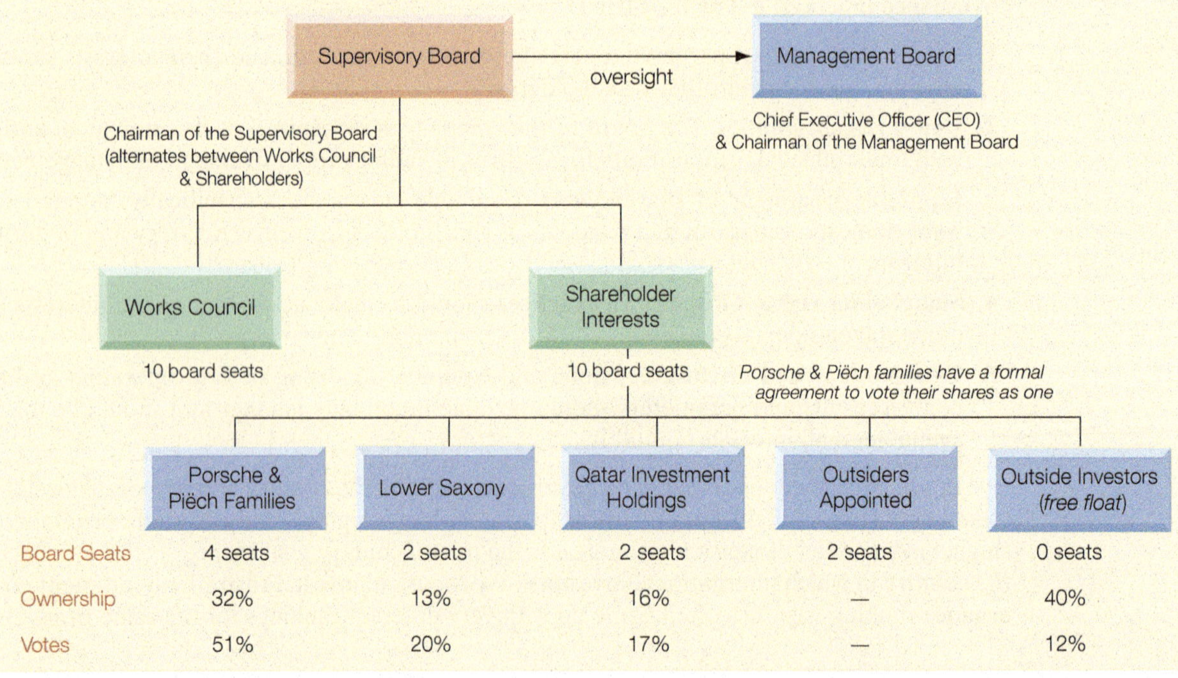

to compound the confusion, these governance rankings seem to have little predictive ability of good or poor governance—measured by firms' future likelihood of restating earnings, shareholder lawsuits, return on assets, and a variety of measures of stock price performance.

4.4 The Market for Corporate Control

> *... the market for corporate control is best viewed as an arena in which managerial teams compete for the rights to manage corporate resources.*
>
> —"The Market for Corporate Control: The Scientific Evidence," by Michael C. Jensen and Richard S. Ruback, *Journal of Financial Economics* 11 (1983), pp. 5–50.

Theoretically, a management team that is underperforming in its direction of a company could potentially be replaced by a competitive team under the expectation of superior performance. Or, as in the case of an acquisition—friendly or hostile—the combining of the two firms could create value that neither could obtain on its own. These synergies—cost, revenue, financial, tax—are the drivers for combining businesses. The process as a whole is called *the market for corporate control.*

This competition is about control, and the control of a publicly traded company could be obtained through a takeover or acquisition. Takeovers can be *friendly* or *hostile*. A *friendly takeover* is when a bidder works with the leadership of the target firm to arrive at a mutually agreed-upon price per share. In principle, both parties would benefit from cooperative negotiations in which detailed information regarding the target firm's operations was shared, leading to a more accurate valuation of the target and potentially a higher bid price. The target firm's leadership would then recommend to its shareholders that they support and approve the sale. If, however, the target firm's leadership was not interested in being acquired by the bidder, it might not cooperate in information-sharing. If the bidder wished to continue, the bidder could announce a public tender offer to shareholders, going around management of the target firm—a *hostile* offer.

Control of the publicly traded corporation may be acquired a variety of ways, and the global market for corporate control never ceases to innovate new ones. Regardless of method, the objective is the same: to gain control of a sufficient number of votes to dictate corporate actions. Exhibit 4.7 provides an overview of various key thresholds in the process of a change in corporate control.

Disclosure Threshold. Most countries regulate the purchase and accumulation of shares in public equity markets. The most common regulatory requirement is the *disclosure threshold.* An acquiring firm crossing this threshold is required to publicly disclose, often via a formal filing with a regulatory authority, that it has gained a specific level of voting rights in the target firm. This disclosure is powerful, as most investors do not have either access to or interest in actively monitoring share interests. This public announcement often results in a rise in the target firm's share price as an acquirer's growing ownership interest may be indicative of an effort to gain control. The most common threshold across countries is 5%, although there are exceptions (e.g., Canada, 10%; the United Kingdom, 3%). A small number of countries—Spain, Turkey, Vietnam—have no threshold and allow accumulation of shares without public disclosure.[5]

[5] For example, in the U.S., an acquirer surpassing 5% ownership in a publicly traded security has 10 days in which to file a Form 13D with the U.S. Securities and Exchange Commission. In this filing, which is a public record, the acquirer must state its shareholdings in the target. Additionally, it must also disclose its *intentions* behind its share acquisition—for a proxy fight, for potential acquisition or merger, or simply as an investment because the target is undervalued.

EXHIBIT 4.7 **Corporate Takeover Thresholds**

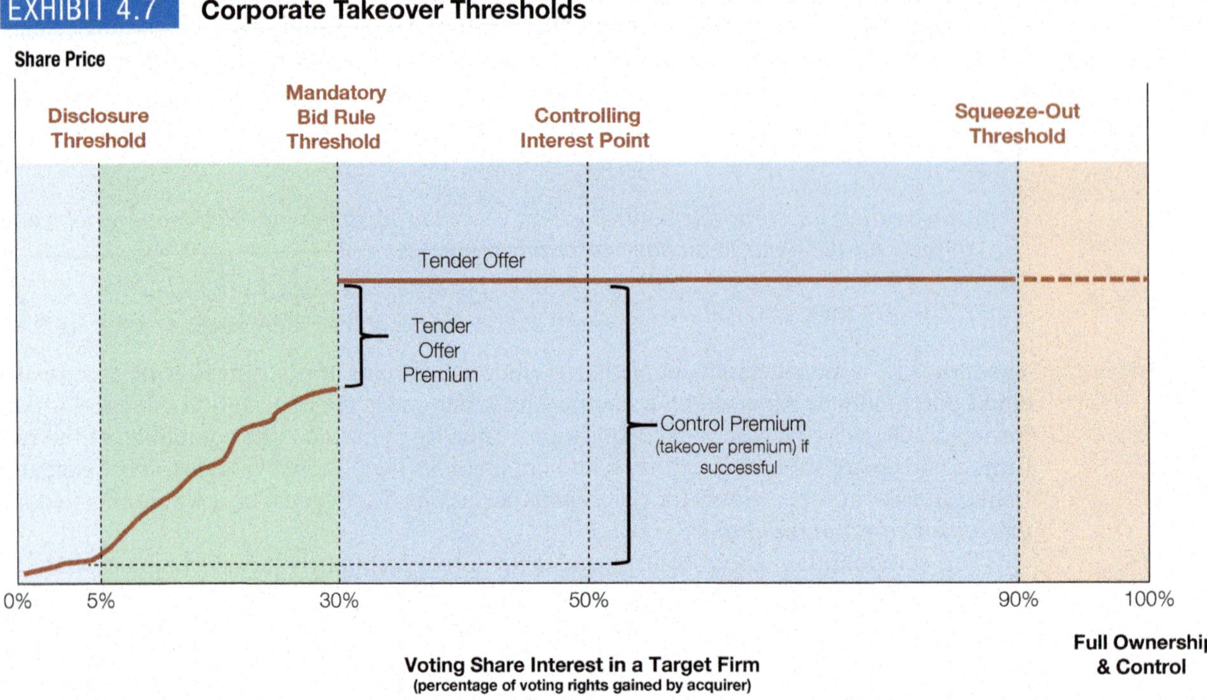

These thresholds represent no specific country.

Mandatory Bid Rule. The second common share accumulation restriction is the *mandatory bid rule threshold.* In many countries an acquirer is required to stop accumulating target firm shares at 30% or 33%. This rule requires the acquirer to make a *tender offer* for all or nearly all remaining shares of the target company if it wishes to proceed. The tender must also be open to shareholders for a specific period of time or at least until the desired number of shares are tendered. This serves as a major barrier to corporate takeovers, protecting holders of control, including management, as well as minority shareholders. This rule also prevents *creeping takeovers*, in which the acquirer continually accumulates shares purchased on the open market until gaining full control of the target firm, a possibility in the United States.

An acquirer faced with making a mandatory bid for control may also face a *minimum price rule*, sometimes referred to as a *fair price bid.* This is a rule that the tender price made by the acquirer is at least some minimum price based on the share price of the target firm in the period prior to the attempted takeover. Although this appears to be restrictive, it rarely proves effective. Most tender offers are made at a premium to the share price of the target firm at the point of mandatory bid threshold, itself often a peak share price.

Squeeze-Out/Sell-Out Rights. A *squeeze-out right* requires that remaining residual shareholders tender their shares to an acquirer once the acquirer has reached a specific ownership threshold, typically 90%. This is to prevent a few remaining holdout investors from imposing undue costs on acquirers completing a takeover.[6] *Sell-out rights,* the dual

[6] The case of Vodafone's (UK) acquisition of Mannesmann (Germany) in 2000 was one example. A few holdout shareholders of Mannesmann refused to sell. This required Vodafone to continue to generate Mannesmann management and financial documents, as well as hold an annual shareholders meeting, for the few—a costly outcome.

consideration to squeeze-out rights, ensure that residual minority shareholders are offered a fair price once control has changed. For example, an acquirer reaching the 90% threshold of voting rights could choose not to purchase the remaining shares outstanding of the target, allowing their trading to continue. Sell-out rights guarantee these shareholders a fair exit price.

Cross-Border Takeovers and Defenses

Takeovers, whether domestic or cross-border, are regulated by national law, primarily the laws of the country of the target firm. Most major industrial countries only established laws governing corporate acquisitions over the past 30 years. These legal structures all possessed a common objective—to strike a balance between creating an open and efficient marketplace for corporate control and the efficient deployment of capital. This was meant to ensure the fair treatment of all shareholders, including minority shareholders.

But what of the rights or abilities of management of a target company to defend itself against a takeover? The management of a target company normally takes a side—it is rarely neutral. If an acquisition or merger is described as benefiting from significant cost synergies (reduction of redundant activities between the two companies), managers of the target company will likely be out of a job. The management team of the target may take actions to defend itself against takeover—so-called *anti-takeover provisions* (ATPs).

ATPs generally either change the shares outstanding of the target firm (voting power) or change the target firm's value and risk (financial and business structure). Voting power ATPs include multiple classes of stock with varying voting rights or the issuance of new shares for intentional dilution. Firm value ATPs include divestment of assets, taking on debt, increased dividends and share repurchases, and merging with a third party, to name a few. All are intended to make acquiring the target firm more costly and more difficult.

Dual Class Stock. A *dual class stock* is when a company issues differing classes of shares. A dual class stock structure can consist of Class A and Class B shares, for example, where one class may be entitled to different dividends than the other, different numbers of voting rights than the other, or both. A family-based firm may restrict B-shares to family members while A-shares are sold to the public. In such a case the B-shares often carry significantly higher voting rights than the B-shares, ensuring continued family control.

Poison Pills. Named after the Cold War era's use of spies and their ability to take a poison pill to avoid interrogation, the concept is to make the target in some way too costly, too difficult, or too unattractive for the acquirer. A frequent form is a *shareholder rights plan*, in which the target firm's bylaws allow the issuance of additional shares to existing shareholders in an effort to dilute the voting shares of the acquirer.[7]

Staggered Boards. Although a corporate board does not own the firm, a change in board members might change a hostile takeover into a friendly one. To prevent an acquirer from gaining new influence via newly elected board members (typically via a proxy fight), a company can ensure that its board member terms are staggered. This means that no newly elected controlling board composition is attainable at any one time.

[7] The shares are often sold to existing shareholder groups at a discount to expedite successful issuance, termed a *flip-in poison pill.* A less common form is the *flip-over poison pill*, in which target firm shareholders gain rights to acquire shares in the target firm if the takeover is successful; these rights are supported and subsidized by the target firm.

White Knights. If a target firm's leadership believes that it may not be able to prevent a hostile takeover, a more extreme defense is to merge with another firm, a so-called *white knight*, that it prefers. The white knight will still need to out-bid the hostile acquirer. The target helps to support that higher bid price by working cooperatively with the white knight, particularly in information sharing. In some cases the cooperation of the target firm's leadership is in return for business and employment assurances post-acquisition.

Pac-Man Defense. Named after the game, the target firm may itself become the acquirer and the acquirer the target. In the earliest stages of a potential hostile takeover, the target firm may start buying shares in the bidder company in an effort to start gaining power and influence. Often in the process of funding these growing share accumulations, the target firm's debt levels begin to rise, making it less desirable as well.

Asset Divestment and Debt. Other defense mechanisms focus on making the target firm less desirable. This may include selling off key business lines or assets that are the focus of acquirer interest—selling off the most valued assets in the eyes of the acquirer. Similarly, a target firm may take on large additional debt obligations to make its acquisition more costly and more of a financial burden to the hostile acquirer.

Corporate takeover law differs across countries, including within integrated regional structures like the European Union. National laws and interests will ultimately determine which of the previously described bidding and defense tactics can legally be employed.

Corporate Responsibility and Sustainability

> *Sustainable development is development that meets the needs of the present without compromising the ability of future generations to meet their own needs.*
>
> —Brundtland Report, 1987, p. 54.

What is the purpose of the corporation? It is increasingly accepted that the purpose of the corporation is to certainly create profits and value for its stakeholders, but the responsibility of the corporation is to do so in a way that inflicts no costs on the environment and society. As a result of globalization, this growing role of the corporation in society has added an additional level of complexity not seen before.

The discussion has been somewhat hampered to date by a lot of conflicting terms and labels—corporate goodness, corporate responsibility, corporate social responsibility (CSR), corporate philanthropy, and corporate sustainability, to list but a few. To simplify, sustainability is often described as a goal, while responsibility is an obligation of the corporation. The obligation is to pursue profit, social development, and the environment—but to do so along sustainable principles.

Nearly two decades ago a number of large corporations began to refine their publicly acknowledged corporate objective as "the pursuit of the triple bottom line." This triple bottom line—profitability, social responsibility, and environmental sustainability—was considered an enlightened development of modern capitalism. What some critics termed a "softer and gentler" form of market capitalism was a growing desire on the part of the corporation to do something more than simply generate a financial profit. To better understand this development of an expanding view of corporate responsibilities, one can divide the arguments along two channels: the economic channel and the moral channel.

The economic channel argues that by pursuing corporate sustainability objectives, the corporation is actually still pursuing profitability, but it is doing so with a more intelligent longer-term perspective—"enlightened self-interest." It has realized that a responsible organization must ensure that its actions over time, whether or not required by law or markets, do not reduce future choices. Alternatively, the moral channel argues that the corporation has the rights and responsibilities of a citizen, including the moral responsibility to act in the best interests of society, regardless of its impacts on profitability. And you thought the management of a company was simple!

Summary Points

- Most commercial enterprises have their origins with either entrepreneurs (private enterprise) or governments (public enterprise). Regardless of origin, if they remain commercial in focus, they may over time choose to go public (in whole or in part) via an initial public offering (IPO).
- When a firm becomes widely owned, it is typically managed by hired professionals. Professional managers' interests may not be aligned with the interests of owners, thus creating an agency problem.
- The Anglo-American markets subscribe to a philosophy that a firm's objective should follow the shareholder wealth maximization (SWM) model. More specifically, the firm should strive to maximize the return to shareholders, the sum of capital gains and dividends, for a given level of risk.
- As do shareholders in Anglo-American markets, controlling shareholders in non-Anglo-American markets strive to maximize long-term returns to equity. However, they also consider the interests of other stakeholders, including employees, customers, suppliers, creditors, government, and community. This is known as stakeholder capitalism.
- The return to a shareholder in a publicly traded firm combines current income in the form of dividends and capital gains from the appreciation of share price. A privately held firm tries to maximize current and sustainable income since it has no share price.
- The MNE must determine for itself the proper balance between three common operational objectives: maximization of consolidated after-tax income; minimization of the firm's effective global tax burden; and correct positioning of the firm's income, cash flows, and available funds as to country and currency.
- The relationship between stakeholders that is used to determine the strategic direction and performance of an organization is termed *corporate governance*. Dimensions of corporate governance include agency theory; composition and control of boards of directors; and cultural, historical and institutional variables.
- The market-based contest for mergers, acquisitions, and other forms of combination is called the market for corporate control. And depending on which countries are involved and what governing law, mergers and acquisitions may be either friendly or hostile.
- A number of initiatives in corporate governance practices in the U.S., the UK, and the European Union—including board structure and compensation, transparency, auditing, and minority shareholder rights—are spreading to many other countries today including major emerging market countries.
- A variety of defensive strategies and tactics are employed by firms in the market for corporate control to entice or repel potential corporate acquirers. Defensive tactics may include acquisition, divestment, changing levels of debt, or changes to the firm's financial policies.
- Society's growing interest and concern over issues related to environment, societal impact, and open and fair governance have led to a growing debate and exploration of corporate responsibility and sustainability.

MINI-CASE

Toshiba's Failing Corporate Governance[8]

General Principle 1

Companies should take appropriate measures to fully secure shareholder rights and develop an environment in which shareholders can exercise their rights appropriately and effectively. In addition, companies should secure effective equal treatment of shareholders. Given their particular sensitivities, adequate consideration should be given to the issues and concerns of minority shareholders and foreign shareholders for the effective exercise of shareholder rights and effective equal treatment of shareholders.

—"Japan's Corporate Governance Code, Seeking Sustainable Corporate Growth and Increased Corporate Value over the Mid- to Long-Term," Tokyo Stock Exchange, Inc., June 1, 2018 edition, p. 2.

Toshiba Corporation, *Kabushiki gaisha Toshiba*, the once mighty Japanese industrial conglomerate, a symbol of Japanese technological excellence, had fallen on bad times. Still Japan's largest semiconductor manufacturer and its second largest industrial conglomerate, it could not seem to steer clear of a series of scandals that had plagued the company and its share price for nearly a decade. In 2015, the company was rocked by an accounting scandal when it was discovered that senior management in the company had pressured managers to falsify accounting results. In 2017, Westinghouse Electric Company, which Toshiba had acquired in 2006 at what many considered an inflated price of $5.4 billion, slid into bankruptcy. Now in 2021, the company was once more confronting a corporate governance failure, as leadership was charged with working against its largest shareholders—foreign shareholders.

The assorted series of scandals and failures were seen by some as partly the result of Japan's insular corporate governance, where senior management worked closely with government in opposition to competition (particularly foreign firms) and employees were guaranteed lifetime employment in exchange for unwavering support of leadership. That older club-like atmosphere, or "shared purpose," was thought to now be changing as a series of corporate governance reforms, including the adoption of a new corporate governance code, came about. A core element in Japan's new corporate governance code was General Principle 1, emphasizing equal treatment of all shareholders and their rights, including both minority and foreign shareholders. Toshiba was now charged with breaking General Principle 1.

Leadership and Investor Change

Japan has long been evolving a "hybrid form of governance" that seeks to balance shareholders' focus on performance and management's concern for stakeholders.[9]

Corporate governance in Japan had historically been seen as bank-based and government-aligned. Power and control of public companies in Japan were highly concentrated and held by the company's bankers, with complex networks of cross-shareholding among firms to protect management's power from shareholders. Even when banks did not directly own shares, they still exerted significant influence over firms by controlling their access to capital. But decades of anemic economic growth and declining corporate value had led the country to champion change in corporate governance practices to attract international capital. The new corporate governance code was symbolic of that change, championing the recognition of all shareholder rights, big and small, domestic and foreign.

Toshiba was emblematic of that change, as it had successfully attracted foreign capital. Following the Westinghouse subsidiary bankruptcy in 2017, in an effort to recapitalize the company, Toshiba had issued 600 billion yen in new shares, mostly to foreign investors. The percentage of shares held by foreign corporations increased overnight from 38% to 72%, foreign investors now holding the majority. But with that capital came expectations—expectations of financial performance and shareholder engagement. Exhibit A provides a summary of Toshiba's major foreign investors as of 2021.

At this same time, Toshiba moved to secure new leadership, taking the revolutionary step of choosing a new CEO from outside its own ranks in 2018, appointing Nobuaki Kurumatani. Kurumatani was recruited from CVC Capital Partners, a European private equity firm. He immediately committed to turning Toshiba's businesses around and adopting more open corporate governance practices.

[8] This case was prepared by Professor Michael H. Moffett for the purpose of classroom discussion only.

[9] "Analects and Abacus: How Japan's Stakeholder Capitalism Is Changing Slowly, with Stubborn Resistance to Change," *The Economist*, March 20, 2021.

EXHIBIT A Largest Foreign Investors in Toshiba

Rank	Foreign Investors	Nationality	Voting Rights	Percent of Total Voting Rights
1	Effissimo Capital Management Pte Ltd	Singaporean*	698,685	15.46%
2	Farallon Capital Management LLC	United States	292,395	6.47%
3	Harvard Management Company, Inc.	United States	200,000	4.43%
4	3D Investment Partners Pte Ltd	Singaporean	186,582	4.13%
5	King Street Capital Management LP	United States	145,102	3.21%
6	Argyle Street Management Ltd	Hong Kong	302	0.01%

Source: The Investigator Report, June 10, 2021. *The report specifically noted that the Singaporean citizens making up the core of Effissimo were Japanese in heritage.

Kurumatani, however, had only been on board two years when the global pandemic of 2020 pummeled the company's profits. He moved quickly to slash costs and divest a number of businesses and assets. But by the summer of 2020's Annual General Meeting of Shareholders (AGM), investors had grown frustrated. Toshiba's largest shareholder, a Singapore-based activist firm, Effissimo Capital Management, pushed for change, proposing its own slate of new board members. But at the July 31, 2020, AGM, Toshiba's shareholders rejected Effissimo's nominees and reelected Kurumatani CEO. It appeared that Toshiba's leadership team had survived the activist challenge.

But in the months that followed, new information surfaced regarding the conduct of the previous summer's shareholder vote that called the process into question. A number of Toshiba's major investors, including Effissimo, wished to convene a special shareholders' meeting to consider possible irregularities and commission an independent investigation. At an extraordinary shareholder meeting held on March 18, 2021, the Proposal for Appointment of Investigators was approved by shareholders. The vote was seen as a watershed moment in Japanese corporate governance. Historically, there had been only a handful of cases when a shareholder-sponsored initiative had gained shareholder support over the opposition of management.

Meanwhile CEO Kurumatani opened negotiations with his former employer, CVC Partners, on CVC's possible acquisition of Toshiba. Such a transaction would take one of Japan's premier industrial conglomerates private. Rumors of the possible sale riled many inside Toshiba, as the potential buyout was seen as a way for Kurumatani to fend off activist investors clamoring for greater movement and openness by corporate leadership. The offer shepherded by Kurumatani was purported to be around $20 billion, quite low in the eyes of most analysts and investors. On April 14, after it was announced that CVC was withdrawing from discussions, Kurumatani resigned. His replacement was his predecessor, Satoshi Tsunakawa, who had been CEO before and was currently chairman of the board.

The Investigator Report

The conclusion at this point is that we let METI beat them for a while.

—Excerpt from internal Toshiba e-mail.

The investigation team approved by shareholders was made up of three lawyers from outside Toshiba. That team saw their charge as the exploration of two basic concerns regarding the July 2020 shareholder vote:[10]

1. *Vote counting issue:* More than 1,139 voting forms delivered to the independent agent (Sumitomo Mitsui Trust Bank, administrator of the shareholder vote) for counting were excluded.
2. *Pressure issue:* Many shareholders had not voted as a result of pressures by a number of organizations, including Japan's Ministry of Economy, Trade, and Industry (METI), supporting Toshiba's leadership team.

The investigators undertook a large-scale exploration of the issues, including hundreds of personal interviews and

[10] *Investigation Report*, Investigators of Toshiba Corporation, June 10, 2021, p. 3.

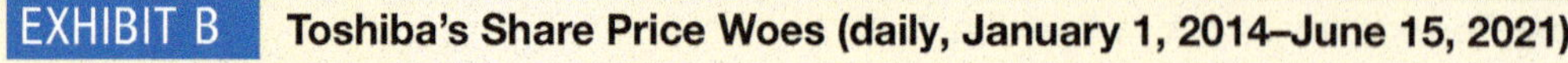

EXHIBIT B Toshiba's Share Price Woes (daily, January 1, 2014–June 15, 2021)

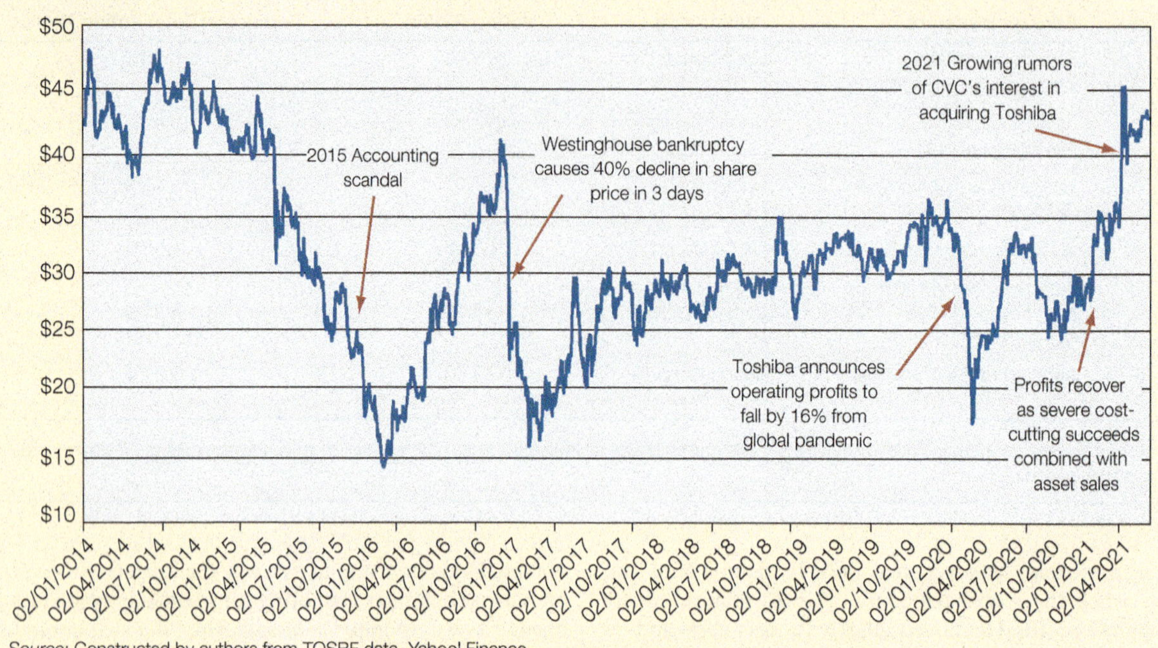

Source: Constructed by authors from TOSBF data, Yahoo! Finance.

detailed digital forensics. At the center of much of the exploration was the communication between Toshiba and its major foreign investors and select government agencies.

Shareholder Communications

A number of the communications between major shareholder groups and Toshiba highlighted not only Toshiba's failure to respond to shareholder questions but in some cases also its work to exclude their participation in shared governance.

On March 3, Harvard Management Company (HMC), the manager of Harvard University's endowment, sent a letter to Toshiba detailing its concerns over the board's failure to respond to the decline in the company's share price (see Exhibit B). HMC wished to see the company undertake asset sales to support a large-scale share buyback program. Toshiba reportedly took more than three months to reply to HMC and then only offered to take it under consideration.[11] Effissimo, Toshiba's single largest shareholder, repeatedly requested meetings with Toshiba directors to discuss a variety of concerns. One major concern was a series of fictitious and circular transactions at a subsidiary, Toshiba IT Services. Effissimo was concerned that the internal investigation of the transactions had been totally inadequate and that the root causes of risk management in Toshiba had not been addressed. Toshiba's CEO did respond by conducting a series of conference calls with Effissimo but limited the company's interaction with other board members.

A third investor group, 3D, sent a letter to Toshiba on April 16 detailing financial performance concerns. 3D argued that Toshiba's total shareholder return (TSR) and share price had been "stagnant" since Mr. Kurumatani took control. 3D considered the performance of the current management team "extremely poor," going on to explain that it thought Toshiba's biggest problem was the conglomerate discount, a reduced share value caused by a return on invested capital (ROIC) below the company's cost of capital.[12] 3D believed Toshiba should divest non-core businesses to reduce the conglomerate discount. Instead, Toshiba had moved to pursue inclusion of more non-core businesses.

[11] Share buybacks (share repurchases) are viewed as one of two ways money is returned to shareholders, the other being dividends. The objective of share buybacks is to reduce the number of shares outstanding, increasing earnings per share and, hopefully, increasing the share price.

[12] Many investment experts today believe that capital markets discount conglomerates, assigning them a value that is less than the sum of their various parts. The prescription for such discounts is to divest non-core businesses, focusing on core businesses that reflect the company's true expertise and competence.

Government Communications

One of the most powerful governmental organizations in Japan is METI. Created in 2001, the organization combines the previously powerful postwar organization credited with Japan's economic revitalization, the Ministry of International Trade and Industry (MITI), with other government agencies. The investigators found a series of communications between Toshiba and representatives of METI discussing the issues posed by a number of foreign investors, specifically Effissimo, and what actions might be taken to thwart their activities.

One e-mail discussion was found to be particularly troubling. On April 11, Toshiba had asked two director generals of METI "whether it is legally possible to eliminate or control undesirable organizations and institutions," and if so, "what measures are being prepared?" Toshiba implied in these discussions that it was a company of national security interest, and foreign investors could be seen as working against national security and taking advantage of the current more open governance system.

METI then asked Toshiba for a written request to open an investigation into the activities of Effissimo, Farallon, HMC, and 3D, among others. Toshiba sent a "draft" written request. Toshiba's draft to METI noted that the actions of the foreign investors were not explicitly a violation of the law but that if an investigation was opened, the "tone of the letter should be that there was a suspicion of violation [and] if it continued in the future, and that urgent action was required." HMC, after receiving notice from METI that it might be subject to investigation, had abstained from voting at the July 31 AGM. Toshiba and METI then purportedly devised a pressure scheme, the so-called 'let METI beat them for a while.'"[13]

Investigator Conclusions

The investigator's conclusions on the two concerns were clear. On the first, although they noted that there were some irregularities by the vote counting authorities ("unlawful and unfair"), they found that Toshiba's management had no knowledge or role in that process. On the second—the pressure issue—the investigators concluded that Toshiba had acted with METI to prevent shareholders from exercising their shareholder rights at the AGM and in some cases sought to have METI try to convince shareholders to change voting behavior.[14]

According to the above, Toshiba is found to have devised a plan to effectively prevent shareholders from exercising their shareholder proposal right and voting rights at the AGM by giving undue influence to shareholders Effissimo, 3D and HMC. Considering the importance of shareholders' right to make proposals and exercise their voting rights, and the fact that the Corporate Governance Code stipulates that "Given the importance of shareholder rights, companies should ensure that the exercise of shareholder rights is not impeded." . . . The Investigators believe that this AGM was not fairly managed.

June Reactions

Following the publication of the investigator report, two board members and two other senior executives resigned. Toshiba committed to continuing to study the investigator report and to improve its communication with shareholders. Despite the turmoil, Toshiba's Chairman Osamu Nagayama announced that he had no intention of resigning. He remained committed to correcting the company's ills. On this same day, Japan's trade minister reiterated to the press that he would not be launching any investigation into the purported influence by METI in opposing foreign investor interests. Similarly, the director of METI, in a separate statement, explained that METI saw no improper activity in its involvement, as it was part of METI's responsibility to protect Japan's national security and industrial concerns. "We merely implemented policies that were natural for METI."[15]

MINI-CASE QUESTIONS

1. What specific actions by Toshiba's leadership were considered inappropriate corporate governance practices?
2. What did the activist investors want Toshiba to do?
3. Do you believe it was inappropriate for METI to become involved in discussions of Toshiba's future and shareholder interests?
4. Does it appear that Japan and Toshiba's movement toward improved corporate governance will be successful?

[13] *Investigation Report*, Investigators of Toshiba Corporation, June 10, 2021, p. 76.
[14] *Investigation Report*, Investigators of Toshiba Corporation, June 10, 2021, p. 139.
[15] "Japan's Trade Minister Unapologetic about Ministry's Dealings with Toshiba," *Reuters*, June 15, 2021.

Questions

4.1 **Business Ownership.** What are the predominant ownership forms in global business?

4.2 **Business Control.** How does ownership alter the control of a business organization? Is the control of a private firm that different from a publicly traded company?

4.3 **Separation of Ownership and Management.** Why is the separation of ownership from management so critical to the understanding of how businesses are structured and led?

4.4 **Corporate Goals: Shareholder Wealth Maximization.** Explain the assumptions and objectives of the shareholder wealth maximization model.

4.5 **Corporate Goals: Stakeholder Capitalism Model (SCM).** Explain the assumptions and objectives of the stakeholder capitalization model.

4.6 **Management's Time Horizon.** Do shareholder wealth maximization and stakeholder capitalism have the same time-horizon for the strategic, managerial, and financial objectives of the firm? How do they differ?

4.7 **Operational Goals.** What should be the primary operational goal or goals of an MNE?

4.8 **Financial Returns.** How do shareholders in a publicly traded firm actually reap cash flow returns from their ownership? Who has control over which of these returns?

4.9 **Dividend Returns.** Are dividends really all that important to investors in publicly traded companies? Aren't capital gains really the point or objective of the investor?

4.10 **Ownership Hybrids.** What is a hybrid? How may it be managed differently?

4.11 **Corporate Governance.** Define corporate governance and the various stakeholders involved in corporate governance. What is the difference between internal and external governance?

4.12 **Governance Regimes.** What are the four major types of governance regimes, and how do they differ?

4.13 **Governance Development Drivers.** What are the primary drivers of corporate governance across the globe? Is the relative weight or importance of some drivers increasing over others?

4.14 **Good Governance Value.** Does good governance have a "value" in the marketplace? Do investors really reward good governance, or does good governance just attract a specific segment of investors?

4.15 **Shareholder Dissatisfaction.** If shareholders are unhappy with the current leadership of a firm—its actual management and control—what are their choices?

4.16 **Emerging Markets Corporate Governance Failures.** It has been claimed that failures in corporate governance have hampered the growth and profitability of some prominent firms located in emerging markets. What are some typical causes of these failures in corporate governance?

4.17 **Emerging Markets Corporate Governance Improvements.** In recent years, emerging market MNEs have improved their corporate governance policies and become more shareholder-friendly. What do you think is driving this phenomenon?

Problems

Use the following formula to answer problems on shareholder returns, where P_t is the share price at time, t, and D_t is the dividend paid at time t.

$$\text{Shareholder return} = \frac{D_2}{P_1} + \frac{P_2 - P_1}{P_1}$$

4.1 **Biloxi Shipping.** If the share price of Emaline, a Biloxi, Mississippi-based shipping firm, rises from \$12 to \$15 over a one-year period, what is the rate of return to the shareholder given each of the following:

a. The company paid no dividends.
b. The company paid a dividend of \$1 per share.
c. The company paid the dividend and the total return to the shareholder is separated into the dividend yield and the capital gain.

4.2 **Carty's Choices.** Brian Carty, a prominent investor, is evaluating investment alternatives. If he believes an individual equity will rise in price from \$59 to \$71 in the coming one-year period, and the share is expected to pay a dividend of \$1.75 per share, and he expects at least a 15% rate of return on an investment of this type, should he invest in this particular equity?

4.3 **Hercule Poirot and Vaniteux (A).** Hercule Poirot is a New York-based investor. He has been closely following his investment in 100 shares of Vaniteux, a French firm that went public in February 2010. When he purchased his 100 shares at €17.25 per share, the euro was trading at \$1.3600 = €1.00. Currently, one share is trading at €28.33 per share, and the dollar has fallen to \$1.4170 = €1.00.

a. If Hercule sells his shares today, what percentage change in the share price would he receive?

b. What is the percentage change in the value of the euro versus the dollar over this same period?
c. What would be the total return Hercule would earn on his shares if he sold them at these rates?

4.4 Hercule Poirot and Vaniteux (B). Hercule Poirot chooses not to sell his shares at the time described in Problem 4.3. He waits, expecting the share price to rise further after the announcement of quarterly earnings. His expectations are correct, and the share price rises to €31.14 per share after the announcement. He now wishes to recalculate his returns. The current spot exchange rate is $1.3110 = €1.00.

4.5 Vaniteux's Returns. Using the same prices and exchange rates as in Problem 4.4, Hercule Poirot and Vaniteux (B), what would be the total return on the Vaniteux investment by Laurent Vuagnoux, a Paris-based investor?

4.6 Microsoft's Dividend Yield. In January 2003, Microsoft announced that it would begin paying a dividend of $0.16 per share. Given the following share prices for Microsoft stock in the recent past, how would a constant dividend of $0.16 per share per year have changed the company's return to its shareholders over this period?

First Trading Day	Closing Share Price	First Trading Day	Closing Share Price
1998 (Jan 2)	$131.13	2001 (Jan 2)	$43.38
1999 (Jan 4)	$141.00	2002 (Jan 2)	$67.04
2000 (Jan 3)	$116.56	2003 (Jan 2)	$53.72

4.7 Yehti Manufacturing (A). Dual classes of common stock are common in a number of countries. Assume that Yehti Manufacturing has the following capital structure at book value. The A-shares have ten votes per share and the B-shares have one vote per share.

Yehti Manufacturing	Local Currency (millions)
Long-term debt	200
Retained earnings	300
Paid-in common stock:	
1 million A-shares	100
Paid-in common stock:	
4 million B-shares	400
Total long-term capital	1,000

a. What proportion of the total long-term capital has been raised by A-shares?
b. What proportion of voting rights is represented by A-shares?
c. What proportion of the dividends should the A-shares receive?

4.8 Yehti Manufacturing (B). Assume all of the same debt and equity values for Yehti Manufacturing in Problem 4.7, with the sole exception that both A-shares and B-shares have the same voting rights—one vote per share.
a. What proportion of the total long-term capital has been raised by A-shares?
b. What proportion of voting rights is represented by A-shares?
c. What proportion of the dividends should the A-shares receive?

4.9 Modo Unico Acquisition. During the 1960s, many conglomerates were created by firms that were enjoying a high price/earnings ratio (P/E). These firms then used their highly valued stock to acquire other firms that had lower P/E ratios, usually in unrelated domestic industries. Conglomerates went out of fashion during the 1980s when they lost their high P/E ratios, thus making it more difficult to find other firms with lower P/E ratios to acquire. During the 1990s, the same acquisition strategy was possible for firms located in countries where high P/E ratios were common compared to firms in other countries where low P/E ratios were common. Consider the hypothetical firms in the pharmaceutical industry shown in the table on the next page.

Modern American wants to acquire ModoUnico. It offers 5,500,000 shares of Modern American, with a current market value of $220,000,000 and a 10% premium on ModoUnico's shares, for all of ModoUnico's shares.
a. How many shares would Modern American have outstanding after the acquisition of ModoUnico?
b. What would be the consolidated earnings of the combined Modern American and ModoUnico?
c. Assuming the market continues to capitalize Modern American's earnings at a P/E ratio of 40, what would be the new market value of Modern American?
d. What would be the new earnings per share of Modern American?
e. What would be the new market value of a share of Modern American?
f. How much would Modern American's stock price increase?
g. Assume that the market takes a negative view of the acquisition and lowers Modern American's P/E ratio to 30. What would be the new market price per share of stock? What would be its percentage loss?

Problem 4.9

Company	P/E Ratio	Number of Shares	Market Value per Share	Earnings	EPS	Total Market Value
ModoUnico	20	10,000,000	$20.00	$10,000,000	$1.00	$200,000,000
Modern American	40	10,000,000	$40.00	$10,000,000	$1.00	$400,000,000

4.10 ModoUnico: Overstating Earnings. A number of firms, especially in the United States, have had to lower their previously reported earnings due to accounting errors or fraud. Assume that Modern American (Problem 4.7) had to lower its earnings to $5,000,000 from the previously reported $10,000,000. What might be its new market value prior to the acquisition? Could it still do the acquisition?

4.11 Lantau Beer (A): European Sales. Lantau Beer is a Hong Kong-based brewery and files all of its financial statements in Hong Kong dollars (HKD). The company's European sales director, Phillipp Bosse, has been criticized for his performance. He disagrees, arguing that sales in Europe have grown steadily in recent years. Who is correct?

	2018	2019	2020
Total net sales, HKD	171,275	187,500	244,900
Percent of total sales from Europe	48%	44%	39%
Total European sales, HKD	_____	_____	_____
Growth rate of European sales (based on HKD)	_____	_____	_____
Average exchange rate, HKD=EUR1.00	9.26	8.77	8.85
Total European sales, euros	_____	_____	_____
Growth rate of European sales (based on EUR)	_____	_____	_____

4.12 Lantau Beer (B): Japanese Yen Debt. Lantau Beer of Hong Kong borrowed Japanese yen (JPY) under a long-term loan agreement several years ago. The company's new CFO believes, however, that what was originally thought to have been relatively "cheap debt" is no longer true. What do you think?

	2018	2019	2020
Annual yen payments on debt agreement (JPY)	12,000,000	12,000,000	12,000,000
Average exchange rate, JPY=HKD1.00	14.09	13.92	13.76
Annual yen debt service, HKD	_____	_____	_____

4.13 Mattel's Global Performance. Mattel (U.S.) achieved significant sales growth in its major international regions between 2001 and 2004. In its filings with the United States Security and Exchange Commission (SEC), it reported both the amount of regional sales and the percentage change in those sales resulting from exchange rate changes.

a. What was the percentage change in sales, in U.S. dollars, by region?

b. What were the percentage changes in sales by region net of currency change impacts?

c. What impact did currency changes have on the level and growth of consolidated sales between 2001 and 2004?

4.14 Harrison Hydraulics and the Yuan. Harrison Equipment of Denver, Colorado, purchases all of its hydraulic tubing from manufacturers in mainland China. The company has recently completed a corporate-wide initiative in six sigma/lean manufacturing. Completed oil field hydraulic system costs were reduced 4% over a one-year period, from $880,000 to $844,800. The company is now worried that all of the hydraulic tubing that goes into the systems (making up 20% of their total costs) will be hit by the potential revaluation of the Chinese yuan—if some in Washington get their way. If the current spot rate is Yuan 8.28 per one U.S. dollar, how would a 12% revaluation of the yuan against the dollar impact total system costs?

Problem 4.13

Mattel's Global Sales

(thousands of US$)	2001 Sales ($)	2002 Sales ($)	2003 Sales ($)	2004 Sales ($)
Europe	$ 933, 450	$1,126,177	$1,356,131	$1,410,525
Latin America	471,301	466,349	462,167	524,481
Canada	155,791	161,469	185,831	197,655
Asia Pacific	119,749	136,944	171,580	203,575
Total International	$1,680,291	$1,890,939	$2,175,709	$2,336,236
United States	3,392,284	3,422,405	3,203,814	3,209,862
Sales Adjustments	(384,651)	(428,004)	(419,423)	(443,312)
Total Net Sales	$4,687,924	$4,885,340	$4,960,100	$5,102,786

Impact of Change in Currency Rates

Region	2001–2002	2002–2003	2003–2004
Europe	7.0%	15.0%	8.0%
Latin America	–9.0%	–6.0%	–2.0%
Canada	0.0%	11.0%	5.0%
Asia Pacific	3.0%	13.0%	6.0%

Source: Mattel, Annual Report, 2002, 2003, 2004.

4.15 S&P Equity Returns. The U.S. equity markets have delivered very different returns over the past 90 years. Use the data from the table below arranged by decade to answer the following questions about these U.S. equity investment returns.

a. Which period shown had the highest total returns? The lowest?
b. Which decade had the highest dividend returns? When were dividends clearly not a priority for publicly traded companies?
c. The 1990s was a boom period for U.S. equity returns. How did firms react in terms of their dividend distributions?
d. How has the 2000s period fared? How do you think publicly traded companies have started changing their dividend distribution habits as a result?

Problem 4.15
S&P 500 Equity Returns, 1930–2020 (average annual return, percent)

Period	1930s	1940s	1950s	1960s	1970s	1980s	1990s	2000s	2010s	1950 to 2020
Capital appreciation	–5.3%	3.0%	13.6%	4.4%	1.6%	12.6%	15.3%	–2.7%	14.2%	7.9%
Dividend yield	5.4%	6.0%	5.1%	3.3%	4.2%	4.4%	2.5%	1.8%	2.7%	3.3%
Total return	0.1%	9.0%	18.7%	7.7%	5.8%	17.0%	17.8%	–0.9%	16.9%	11.2%

PART

2

Foreign Exchange Theory and Markets

CHAPTER 5

The Foreign Exchange Market

CHAPTER 6

International Parity Conditions

CHAPTER 7

Foreign Currency Derivatives: Futures and Options

CHAPTER 8

Interest Rate Risk and Swaps

CHAPTER 9

Foreign Exchange Rate Determination and Intervention

5 The Foreign Exchange Market

The best way to destroy the capitalist system is to debauch the currency. By a continuing process of inflation, governments can confiscate, secretly and unobserved, an important part of the wealth of their citizens.

—John Maynard Keynes.

LEARNING OBJECTIVES

5.1 Explore the multitude of functions of the foreign exchange market

5.2 Detail how the structure of the global foreign exchange market has evolved

5.3 Describe the financial and operational transactions conducted in the foreign exchange market

5.4 Examine the forms of currency quotations used by currency dealers, financial institutions, and agents of all kinds when conducting foreign exchange transactions

The *foreign exchange market* provides the physical and institutional structure through which the money of one country is exchanged for that of another country. Through this market, the rate of exchange between currencies is determined and foreign exchange transactions are physically completed. *Foreign exchange* means the money of a foreign country; that is, foreign currency bank balances, banknotes, checks, and drafts. A *foreign exchange transaction* is an agreement between a buyer and seller that a fixed amount of one currency will be delivered for some other currency at a specified rate.

This chapter describes the foreign exchange marketplace—its functions, participants, daily trading life, transactions and transaction volumes, and changing quotation practices. The chapter concludes with the mini-case *Iceland: A Small Country in a Global Crisis*, which describes how Iceland's highly developed industrialized status and open capital markets led to the near destruction of its entire economy and currency.

5.1 Functions of the Foreign Exchange Market

The foreign exchange market is perhaps the largest, most globally integrated, and most active financial market in the world. The transactions that take place there are the lifeblood of a global economy that comprises many different national currencies. By enabling the transfer of funds and purchasing power from one currency to another, the foreign exchange market offers an important means for price discovery that facilitates international trade and investment activity.

—Simon Potter, Executive Vice President of the Markets Group of the Federal Reserve Bank of New York, at the 2015 FX Week Conference, New York City, July 14, 2015.

Money is an instrument that is accepted as payment for goods, services, and, in some cases, past debt. As all economics students learn, there are typically three functions of money: as *a unit of account*, as *a store of value*, and as *a medium of exchange*. The foreign exchange market is the mechanism by which participants transfer purchasing power between countries by exchanging money, obtaining or providing credit for international trade transactions, and minimizing exposure to the risks of exchange rate changes.

The transfer of purchasing power is necessary because international trade and capital transactions normally involve parties living in countries with different currencies. Usually each party wants to deal in its own currency, but the trade or capital transaction can be invoiced in only one currency. Hence, one party must deal in a foreign currency. Because the movement of goods between countries takes time, inventory in transit must be financed. The foreign exchange market therefore provides a source of credit in addition to the specialized instruments used, such as bankers' acceptances and letters of credit. The foreign exchange market also provides "hedging" facilities for transferring foreign exchange risk from one party to another.

5.2 Structure of the Foreign Exchange Market

The foreign exchange market has, like all markets, evolved dramatically over time. Beginning with money changing hands in stalls on the streets of Florence and Venice, to the trading rooms in London and New York, to a handheld computer anywhere in the world today, the market is based on supply and demand, market information and expectations, and negotiating strength.

The Global Trading Day

The foreign exchange market spans the globe, with prices moving and currencies trading—somewhere—every hour of every business day. But people—traders—do eventually sleep. This translates into four trading sessions per day, illustrated in Exhibit 5.1. The world's trading day begins each morning in Sydney and Tokyo, moving on to Hong Kong and Singapore, passing on to the Middle East and on to the European markets of Frankfurt, Zurich, and London, then making the final jump across the Atlantic to New York and Chicago, ending in San Francisco and Los Angeles. Many large international banks operate foreign exchange trading rooms in each major geographic trading center in order to serve both their customers and themselves—so-called *proprietary trading*—on a 24-hour-a-day basis.

Although global currency trading is indeed a 24-hour-a-day activity, there are segments of the 24-hour day that are busier than others. Historically, the major financial centers of the nineteenth and twentieth centuries dominated—London and New York. But as is the case with much of global commerce today, the Far East, represented by Hong Kong, Tokyo, and Singapore, is now threatening that dominance. As the Chinese renminbi continues to grow in volume and depth, the growing influence of Shanghai is likely inevitable. When the two largest city-based trading centers overlap, London and New York, the currency market exhibits the greatest depth and liquidity. Differences in time zones, however, have been the driver of much of the institutional structure of the global currency market, determining how it works and how it occasionally doesn't work—as illustrated by *Global Finance in Practice 5.1*.

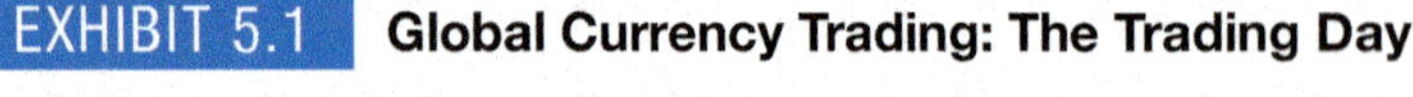

EXHIBIT 5.1 Global Currency Trading: The Trading Day

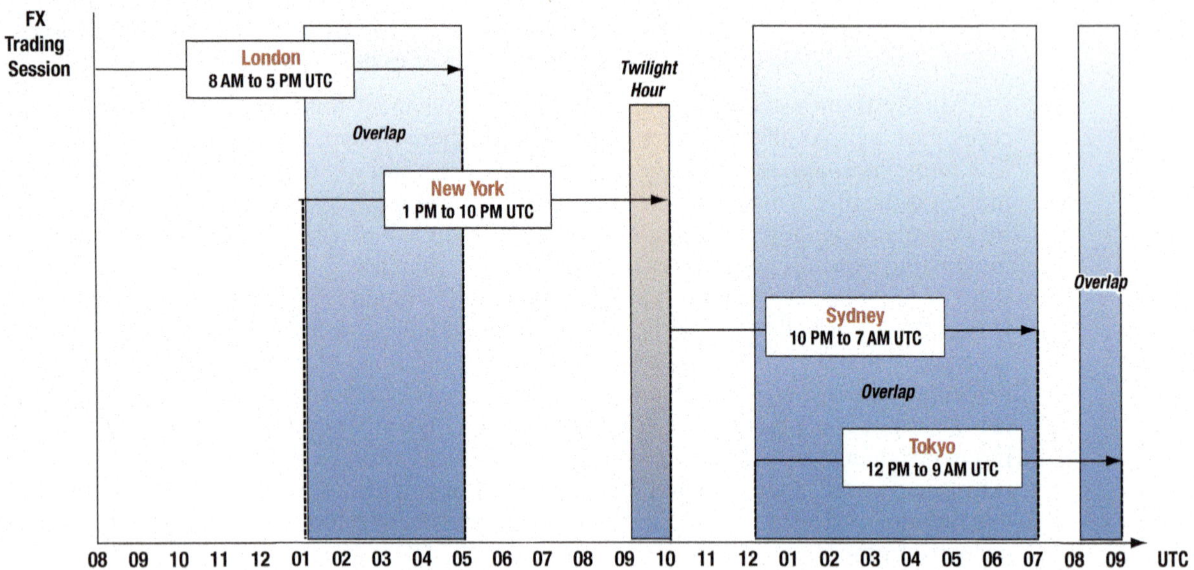

Note: Coordinated Universal Time (UTC) specifies the precise hour in the day. Greenwich Mean Time (GMT) is a time zone, not a time reference point.

GLOBAL FINANCE IN PRACTICE 5.1

The Twilight Hour in Global FX Trading

The exchange of currencies is indeed a 24-hour market. That said, there are peak and trough periods. The daily peak occurs between 9 and 10 a.m. New York time (GMT –5 during winter). This is the overlap period with London late trading. The daily trough occurs as New York closes and traders are heading home, roughly 5 to 7 p.m. And that is when twilight trading creeps in. Theoretically, this is when Sydney and Hong Kong are opening. But between 5 and 6 a.m., Hong Kong traders and trading are starting up slowly, and much of the world is doing the same.

But this is also when typically stable currencies can occasionally suffer some "instability." If a single trade or two of size occurs in a thin market or, alternatively, a piece of new information about one of the subject currencies or economies hits the airwaves during this usually placid period, a surge or jolt is possible. For example, on Thursday January 3, 2019, the Japanese yen suddenly surged by 3% against the U.S. dollar. This triggered losses against the Australian dollar and even Turkish lira—all in minutes between 5 and 5:30 p.m. New York and 6 and 6:30 a.m. Hong Kong. This jolt was the result of an Apple Inc. press release of weak sales in China for the previous quarter, prompting the dollar sell-off.

The twilight hour trades have a bit of history. For example, on October 7, 2016, in the days following the Brexit vote, the British pound fell 6% against the dollar to a 31-year low within the twilight hour in a quiet and thin market. The cause of the fall was linked to a senior British official's speculation in a press release that it would be a "hard exit" for the UK.

How significant these shocks are is unclear. In most cases the currencies return to their traditional trading ranges and values within hours or days. But that does not stop them from happening again. A month after the January 2019 fall of the dollar, another twilight hour hit occurred. The Swiss franc plummeted against both the euro and the dollar during a placid trading period. The quiet market was later attributed to the National Foundation Day holiday in Japan. The probable lesson to be learned is that it is a bad idea to release information to the market or the press during the the twilight hour, whether you are a private individual, a government, or a multinational enterprise.

Market Participants—The Players

Participants in the foreign exchange market can be simplistically divided into two major groups: those trading currency for commercial purposes, *liquidity seekers*, and those trading for profit, *profit seekers*. Although the foreign exchange market began as a market for liquidity purposes, facilitating the exchange of currency for the conduct of commercial trade and investment purposes, the exceptional growth in the market has been largely based on the expansion of profit-seeking agents. As might be expected, the *profit seekers* are typically much better informed about the market, looking to profit from its future movements, while *liquidity seekers* simply wish to secure currency for transactions. As might be predicted, the profit seekers generally profit from the liquidity seekers.

Five broad categories of institutional participants operate in the market: (1) bank and nonbank foreign dealers, (2) private individuals and firms conducting commercial or investment transactions, (3) speculators and arbitragers, (4) central banks and treasuries, and (5) foreign exchange brokers.

Bank and Nonbank Dealers. Bank and nonbank traders and dealers profit from buying foreign exchange at a bid price and reselling it at a slightly higher ask (also called an offer) price. Competition among dealers worldwide narrows the spread between bids and offers and so contributes to making the foreign exchange market "efficient" in the same sense as are securities markets.

Dealers in the foreign exchange departments of large international banks often function as "market makers." Such dealers stand willing at all times to buy and sell those currencies in which they specialize and thus maintain an "inventory" position in those currencies. They trade with other banks in their own monetary centers and with other centers around the world in order to maintain inventories within the trading limits set by bank policy. Trading limits are important because foreign exchange departments of many banks operate as profit centers and individual dealers are compensated on a profit incentive basis.

Currency trading is quite profitable for many institutions. Many of the world's major currency-trading banks average between 10% and 20% of their annual net income from currency trading. Currency trading is also very profitable for the bank's traders, who typically earn a bonus based on the profitability to the bank of their individual trading activities. Small to medium-sized banks and institutions are likely to participate but not to be market makers in the interbank market. Instead of maintaining significant inventory positions, they often buy from and sell to larger institutions in order to offset retail transactions with their own customers or to seek short-term profits for their own accounts.

Commercial and Investment Transactors. Importers and exporters, international portfolio investors, multinational corporations, tourists, and others use the foreign exchange market to facilitate execution of commercial or investment transactions. Their use of the foreign exchange market is necessary but incidental to their underlying commercial or investment purpose. Some of these participants use the market to hedge foreign exchange risk as well.

Speculators and Arbitragers. Speculators and arbitragers seek to profit from trading within the market itself. True profit seekers, they operate in their own interest, without a need or obligation to serve clients or to ensure a continuous market. Whereas dealers seek profit from the spread between bids and offers in addition to what they might gain from changes in exchange rates, speculators seek their profit from exchange rate changes. Arbitragers try to profit from simultaneous exchange rate differences in different markets.

Central Banks and Treasuries. Central banks and treasuries use the market to acquire or spend their country's foreign exchange reserves as well as to influence the price at which their own currency is traded, a practice known as *foreign exchange intervention*. They may act to support the value of their own currency because of national policies or because of commitments to other countries under exchange rate currency agreements. Consequently, the motive is not to earn a profit as such, but rather to influence the foreign exchange value of their currency in a manner that will benefit domestic interests. In many instances, central banks do their job best when they willingly take a loss on their foreign exchange transactions. As willing loss takers, central banks and treasuries differ in motive and behavior from other market participants.

Foreign Exchange Brokers. Foreign exchange brokers are agents who facilitate trading between dealers without themselves becoming principals in the transaction. They charge a small commission for this service. They maintain instant access to hundreds of dealers worldwide.

Evolution of the Market

The modern foreign exchange marketplace arose from the ashes of the Bretton Woods System. Under Bretton Woods, exchange rates were fixed, and trading of currencies was confined to commercial and investment purposes—the needs of the liquidity seekers. But with the collapse of Bretton Woods and the flotation of currencies, profit seekers entered the market in volume and, in the case of Herstatt—the subject of *Global Finance in Practice 5.2*—with impact.

The evolution of foreign exchange trading institutions is described in Exhibit 5.2. It serves as something of a microcosm of institutional change of global society, from the telephone to the computer to the Internet. How currency rates are quoted, prices posted, and trades consummated, confirmed, and settled—across borders, time zones, and oceans—has all changed very quickly.

GLOBAL FINANCE IN PRACTICE 5.2

Bankhaus Herstatt and Herstatt Risk

Bankhaus Herstatt was a relatively small Cologne bank, the eightieth largest in Germany. But Herstatt was a major player (speculator) in foreign exchange trading. In a three-year period, 1971–1973, foreign exchange trading had moved from 3% of total bank income to 57%. But for more than two years Herstatt had been the object of constant rumor, debate, and even regulator concern over the size and aggressiveness of its foreign currency positions. On June 26, 1974, at 15:30 (3:30 p.m.) Central European Time, German bank regulators shut it down.

Herstatt's large currency trading business meant that it was settling very large international currency transactions daily through its international correspondent banks. On June 26 a number of Herstatt's major counterparties—banks with which it had executed currency trades—had made large payments in deutsche marks to the bank, but they had not yet received their payments from Herstatt in U.S. dollars before it was closed by regulators. Chase Manhattan Bank of New York, Herstatt's primary correspondent bank in the U.S., had $620 million in accounts due from Herstatt to customer banks in the U.S., Germany, Switzerland, and Sweden.

The simple reason for Herstatt's delay in making the payments was time zone differences. At that hour in the afternoon in Cologne, Chase Manhattan in New York was just opening. Herstatt had only started to initiate counterparty payments when its doors were closed (as were its telex lines for transfers).

This settlement failure set off a chain reaction in the international currency markets. All major currency trading banks now froze in fear of the risk of settlement. Banks in New York specifically refused to make payments on trades until receiving confirmation that their countervalue had been received. The fall in currency trading in the New York market alone in the days following Herstatt's closure was estimated at more than 75%. This newly perceived risk, *settlement risk*, now became known as *Herstatt Risk*.

EXHIBIT 5.2 Evolution of the Modern Currency Trading Marketplace

All foreign currency transactions require some combination of three elements: 1) trading, 2) messaging, and 3) settlement. The modern history of currency trading involves the evolution of these elements from voice-based and paper-based communication to the use of computers for trading, financial messaging, and multilateral netting settlement.

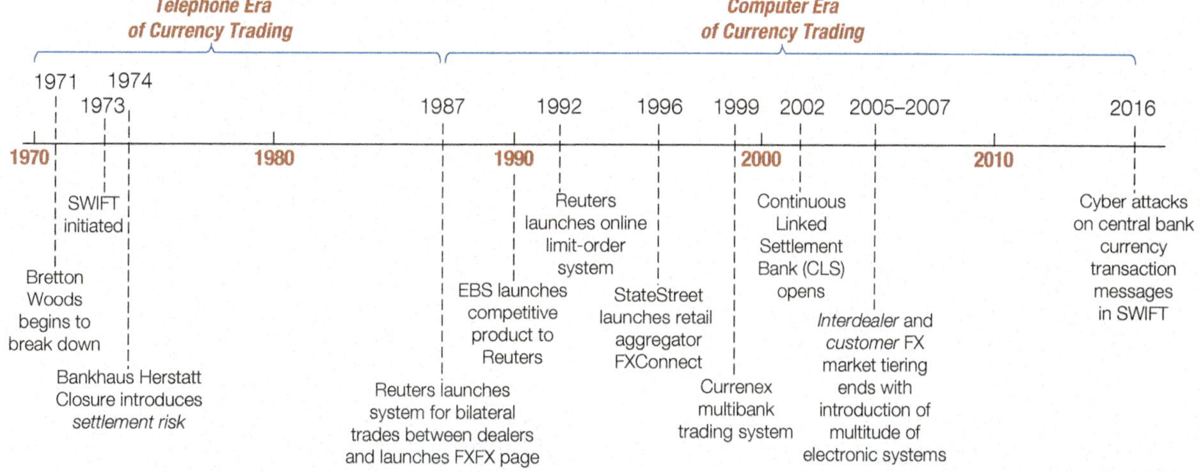

The foreign exchange market is the world's largest financial market. It is, however, an informal market—a market without a single dealer, a single exchange, a single global regulator, or even a single price. That said, the foreign exchange market is considered to be one of the world's most competitive markets.

The Evolution of FX Trading

To understand how the foreign exchange market has evolved over the past 30 years, consider the mechanics and content of a basic foreign currency trade undertaken by two voice traders, first in 1985, then in the 1990s, and again in 2010. Keep in mind that currency trading at this time is conducted between hundreds of banks around the world, much of it simultaneously, and all bilaterally.

1985. Two *foreign exchange dealers*, one in London and one in New York, are talking on the phone. Both work for major banks, and both are rewarded handsomely for making profits for their banks on foreign exchange trading. Each knows the other bank and the other trader. When one asks for an *indication*—a currency quote containing a bid-ask spread—on a foreign currency pair like the GBP/USD (the dollar–pound exchange rate, the U.S. dollars to equal one British pound, also termed *cable*)—the other knows who is quoting the rate and that the rate is valid for a trade (and not just a representative price, but one for which a contractual trade can be made). If they agree to a trade, each writes the key elements of the transaction on a piece of paper which is then carried by hand to the back-office staff for documentation, verification, and eventually settlement. This basic trading structure is illustrated in the left-hand panel of Exhibit 5.3.

Now consider what the two traders don't know. They don't know the rates at which other banks and other dealers have traded the currency pair in recent minutes or hours, unless they have called others or exchanged information with their colleagues sitting in the same trading room. They do not know what other dealers are quoting the same currency pair for at this same moment, so they don't have explicit data on how competitive the quote they are receiving or providing is—they have limited price discovery capability. If they complete a trade, one or the other may make an error in recording the transaction on paper, or the back-office itself

EXHIBIT 5.3 **Foreign Exchange Trading in the 1980s and 1990s**

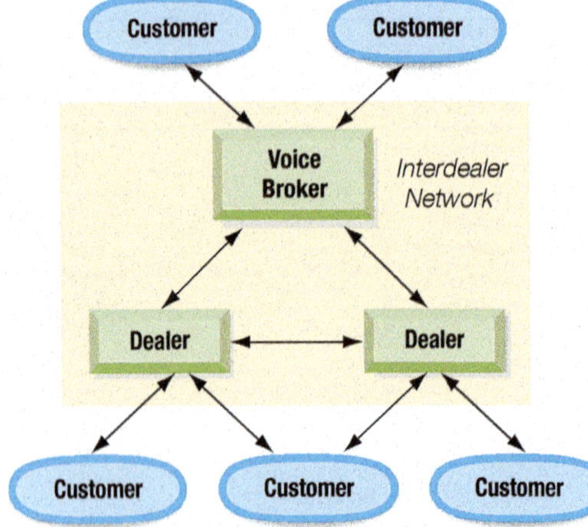

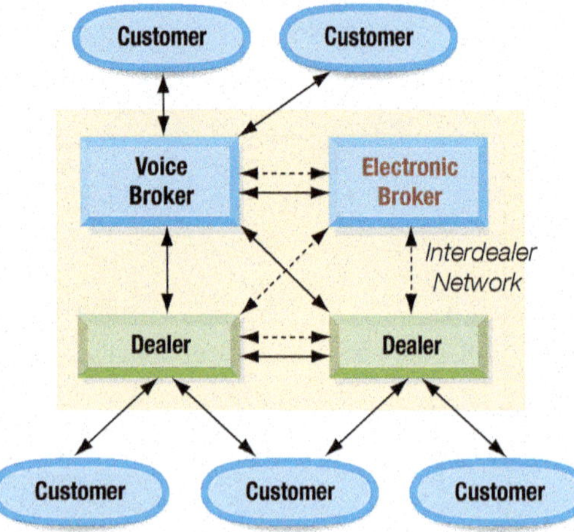

may introduce transcription errors of their own in trade documentation. The two banks are in different time zones, so settlement will be at risk in terms of each providing their currency balances for exchange.

1990s. Now move forward in time to the 1990s foreign exchange market, as seen on the right-hand side of Exhibit 5.3. The same two traders are considering a trade again, but now they are conversing using computers and the Internet. They still know the bank and trader on the other end of the link. But now they can look at a Reuters screen as they exchange the quote to track what other recent transactions have been completed at and possibly what other banks are at this moment giving as representative trade quotes. If they complete the trade, there is an instantaneous digital record of the trade, and the record is simultaneously passed to the back-office for verification and settlement. The introduction of an electronic broker changes things.

The computer-based process in the 1990s is obviously more efficient from a variety of operational perspectives, and more importantly, it is conducted in a market where individual agents have instantaneous access to much more relevant market data. But there are still constraints and limitations. The market is still accessible only by the intermarket dealers, typically big banks, and smaller banks and private customers like investment funds are outsiders and must still deal with the dealer to access this large and liquid market. For these smaller players, access comes at a higher cost and a higher spread. (Customers may also not have access to real-time price data.) And although there is now electronic messaging confirmation to expedite the trade verification and instructions for settlement, the banks are still in different countries and different time zones, so settlement risk (Herstatt Risk) still exists.

2010 - Today. Now move forward in time to 2010 to the present. The same two dealers are now looking at large digital screens of competing quotes and transaction records. Trades are conducted electronically, with no need for telephone or any specific direct trader contact. Trading is now fragmented, transactions occurring across a multitude of different venues.

EXHIBIT 5.4 The Foreign Exchange Market Today

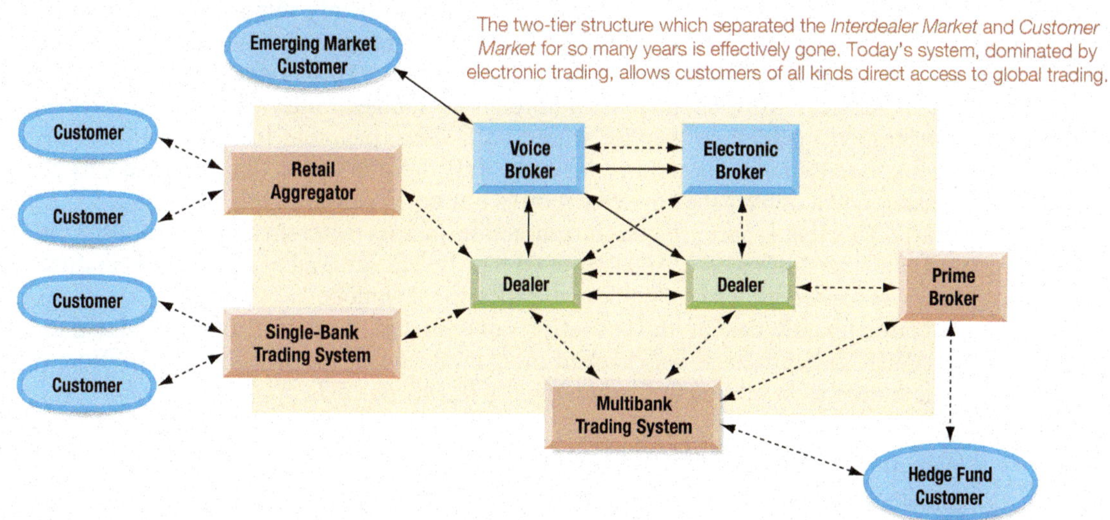

Constructed by authors based on a number of sources including "Foreign Exchange Market Structure, Players and Evolution," Michael R. King, Carol Osler and Dagfinn Rime, Norges Bank, Working Paper, Research Department, 2011, 10, p. 21, and "The anatomy of the global FX market through the lens of the 2013 Triennial Survey," by Dagfinn Rime and Andreas Schrimpf, BIS *Quarterly Review*, December 2013.

The separation of the *interdealer* and *customer markets* has effectively broken down, as seen in Exhibit 5.4, with the introduction of *multibank trading systems* (MBT), *single-bank trading systems* (SMT), and *prime brokerage* (PB). Prime brokerage is a dealer–customer structure that allows customers such as hedge funds to deal directly in the interdealer market. Small customers, those exchanging small notional amounts that in previous years would pay higher transaction costs and have access only to much wider spreads, now gain access to the global currency market through a variety of structures including *retail aggregators. Retail aggregators* collect and consolidate a multitude of small orders for large order execution.

Two types of trades or traders remain outside the core foreign exchange market today, emerging market currencies and small banks. The majority of the dealer and brokerage markets require large amounts of capital investment and volume trading, neither of which the small bank can support. Small banks therefore use one of the trading systems for access, often specializing in peripheral or emerging market currencies. Emerging market currencies, due to their relatively small volume and low liquidity, may still utilize voice brokers for trading.

The Three Components of FX Trades

The exchange of a foreign exchange trade today actually involves three different components: (1) the foreign exchange trade transaction agreement—the interaction of dealers, brokers, and aggregators as just described; (2) electronic communication and notification for payment and settlement; and (3) final settlement of the currency trade.

Foreign exchange trades today are recorded electronically, utilizing financial instructions for payment and settlement. These instructions are executed—hopefully securely—through the Society for Worldwide Interbank Financial Telecommunication (SWIFT). The SWIFT system, initiated in 1973, is a network that allows financial institutions all over the world to send and receive information about financial transactions in a secure, standardized, and reliable manner. The SWIFT network sends payment orders, but it does not facilitate the actual transfer of funds—*settlement. Settlement* of a foreign exchange trade is made by correspondent accounts that the banks and institutions have with each other. Nearly all cross-border foreign exchange transactions are executed via SWIFT today.

Final settlement of the currency trade is the critically important and topical issue of Herstatt Risk. Herstatt or settlement risk has been largely eliminated by *continuous linked settlement* (CLS), which was introduced in 2002. In a CLS, a specialist bank provides settlement services to its members for foreign exchange trades. CLS uses a *payment versus payment* (PvP) settlement service where both sides' payment instructions for an FX transaction are settled simultaneously. Without PvP, there is a risk that one party to a currency transaction will deliver the currency it owes but not receive the other currency from its counterparty. This risk is accentuated in transactions across different time zones, as in the case of Bankhaus Herstatt in 1974. As of 2015, CLS provided settlement services for 18 different currencies and more than 9,000 bank and institutional traders.

Unfortunately, despite the best efforts of man and machine, fraud and failure still persist. The SWIFT system itself was hacked in 2016 in one of the world's largest attempted electronic frauds, as described in *Global Finance in Practice 5.3*.

FX Market Manipulation: Fixing the Fix

Following the turmoil surrounding the setting of LIBOR rates in the interbank market during the 2007–2009 period (described in detail in Chapter 8), similar allegations arose over the possible manipulation of benchmarks in the foreign exchange markets in 2013 and 2014.

Much of the focus was on the London fix, the 4 p.m. daily benchmark rate used by a multitude of institutions and indices for marking value. Market analysts had noted steep spikes in trading just prior to the 4 p.m. fix, spikes that were not sustained in the hours and days that followed. Traders were alleged to be exchanging e-mails and using social networking sites and even phone calls to collaborate on market movements and price quotes at key times. After hours, personal trading by currency traders, an area of only marginal concern before, was also under review. Moving from voice trading (telephone) to electronic trading was thought to be one possible long-term fix, but traders still communicated with other traders using a variety of electronic mediums and social networks.

By 2014, nearly 75% of all currency trades were executed electronically. The growth of electronic execution was expected to be something of a *market fix* for the 4 p.m. market spikes seen previously, thought to be caused by collusion among traders. With more and more of the market's transactions executed electronically, computer algorithms were believed to be less likely to pursue fraudulent trading for fixing given the speed and frequency of transactions. Research has also shown strong evidence that electronic trading is more stabilizing than voice trading, as most of the algorithmic codes are based on *reversion to the mean*—to the market averages—over time.

But, as is the case with many technological fixes, the fix did not eliminate the problem—it had possibly just changed it. Electronic trading might still facilitate market manipulation, just of a more sophisticated kind. For example, there was a rumor of software in development that could detect mouse movements by other currency traders on some of the largest electronic platforms, allowing a computer (human attached) to detect another trader's mouse hovering over the bid or ask button prior to execution. Alas, it appears there will always be the human element in trading, for better or for worse.

The FX Global Code of Conduct 2016

Following the discovery of significant market manipulation and coordinated malfeasance in 2013 and 2014 in the foreign exchange market, the Bank for International Settlements (BIS) proposed a set of global principles of good practice in the foreign exchange market. The BIS's

GLOBAL FINANCE IN PRACTICE 5.3

Malware, Bangladesh Bank, and Bankers' Hours

On February 4, 2016, computer hackers—possibly involving insiders in Bangladesh—used a form of *malware* to send 35 separate fund transfer requests from the Bangladesh Bank, the central bank of Bangladesh, to move nearly $1 billion from the Bangladesh Bank's account at the Federal Reserve Bank of New York to other central banks. The fund transfer requests were correctly transmitted through the SWIFT global financial transaction messaging system.

Although the fund transfer requests were correctly coded, they were still considered unusual and questionable in the eyes of the New York Fed. The Fed did approve five of the total 35 requests, totaling $20 million to Sri Lanka and $81 million to the Central Bank of the Philippines, putting holds on the remaining requests until further verification could be received. The $81 million transferred to the Philippines Central Bank was then routed to personal accounts in Manila and used to purchase gambling chips—and never recovered.

Ironically, human error and "bankers' hours" seem to have played a large part in the scandal. The New York Fed sent repeated requests on Thursday, February 4, and Friday, February 5, to the Bangladesh Bank requesting verification. The messages went unanswered because of technical problems with the Bangladesh Bank's computer system. Once the Bangladesh Bank corrected the computer problem on Saturday, they found the New York Fed's multiple requests for verification. Realizing the bank's SWIFT account had been hacked at their local terminal, they immediately sent stop payment requests to the New York Fed (several e-mails and one fax). But their requests went unheeded because they were received on Saturday, February 6, and Sunday, February 7—when the New York Fed was closed.

The Bangladesh Bank Heist—from Dhaka to New York to Manila

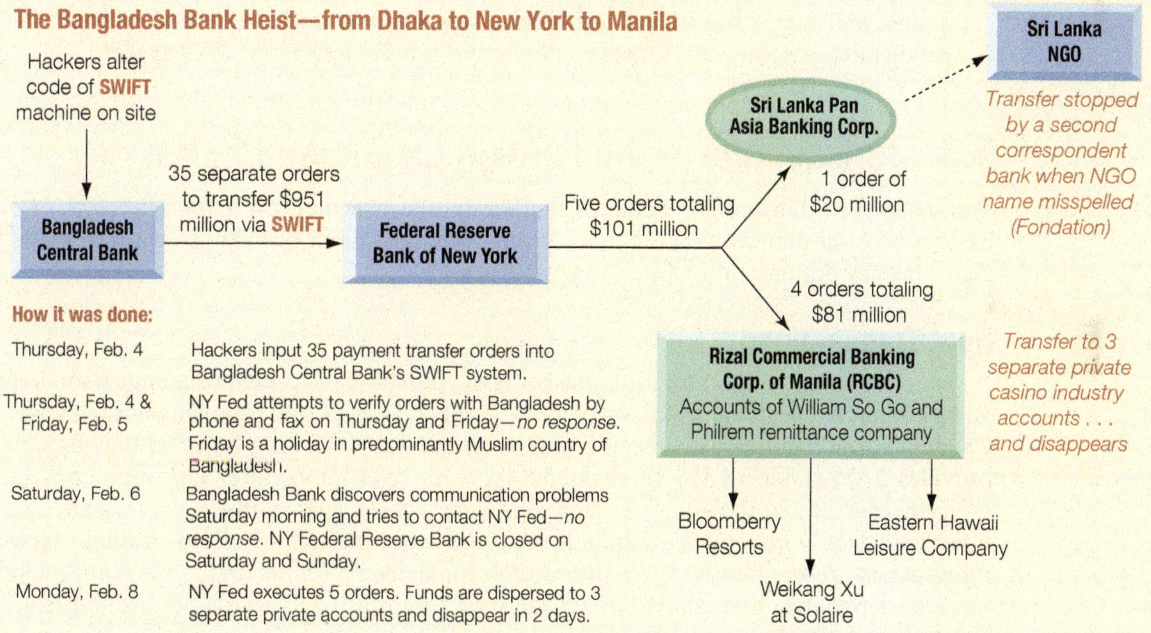

Global Code is intended to provide a common set of guidelines to promote the integrity and effective functioning of the foreign exchange market. As stated by the BIS, "It is intended to promote a robust, fair, liquid, open, and appropriately transparent market in which a diverse set of Market Participants, supported by resilient infrastructure, are able to confidently and effectively transact at competitive prices that reflect available market information and in a manner that conforms to acceptable standards of behaviour."[1] As with most codes of conduct, it does not impose legal or regulatory obligations; it only promotes global best practices and processes.

The Global Code is made up of six leading principles.

1. **Ethics:** Market Participants are expected to behave in an ethical and professional manner to promote the fairness and integrity of the FX Market.
2. **Governance:** Market Participants are expected to have robust and clear policies, procedures, and organizational structure in place to promote responsible engagement in the FX Market.
3. **Information Sharing:** Market Participants are expected to be clear and accurate in their communications and to protect confidential information to promote effective communication that supports a robust, fair, open, liquid, and appropriately transparent FX Market.
4. **Execution:** Market Participants are expected to exercise care when negotiating and executing transactions in order to promote a robust, fair, open, liquid, and appropriately transparent FX Market.
5. **Risk Management and Compliance:** Market Participants are expected to promote and maintain a robust control and compliance environment to effectively identify, measure, monitor, manage, and report on the risks associated with their engagement in the FX Market.
6. **Confirmation and Settlement Processes:** Market Participants are expected to put in place robust, efficient, transparent, and risk-mitigating post-trade processes to promote the predictable, smooth, and timely settlement of transactions in the FX Market.

5.3 Transactions in the Foreign Exchange Market

Transactions in the foreign exchange market can be executed on a *spot, forward*, or *swap* basis. A broader definition of the market, one including major derivatives, would include foreign currency options, futures, and swaps.

Spot Transactions

A *spot transaction* in the interbank market is the purchase of foreign exchange with delivery and payment between banks taking place normally on the second following business day. The Canadian dollar settles with the U.S. dollar on the first following business day. Exhibit 5.5 provides a timetable of the three major types of over-the-counter currency transactions typically executed in the global foreign exchange market: *spot transactions, forward transactions*, and *swap transactions*. Although there are a number of variations on these types, all transactions are defined by their future date for delivery. (Note that we are not including futures transactions here; they parallel the time footprint of forwards but are not executed over-the-counter.)

The date of settlement is referred to as the *value date*. On the value date, most dollar transactions in the world are settled through the computerized Clearing House Interbank Payments System (CHIPS) in New York, which calculates net balances owed by any one bank to another and which facilitates payment of those balances by 6:00 p.m. that same day in Federal Reserve Bank of New York funds. Other central banks and settlement services providers operate similarly in other currencies around the world.

[1] Bank for International Settlements, *FX Global Code: May 2016 Update*, p. 3.

EXHIBIT 5.5 **Foreign Exchange Transactions and Settlement**

Foreign exchange operations are defined by the timing—*the future date*—set for delivery. There are in principle three major categories of over-the-counter transactions categorized by future delivery: *spot* (which may be *overnight*), *forward* (including *outright forward*), and *swap transactions*.

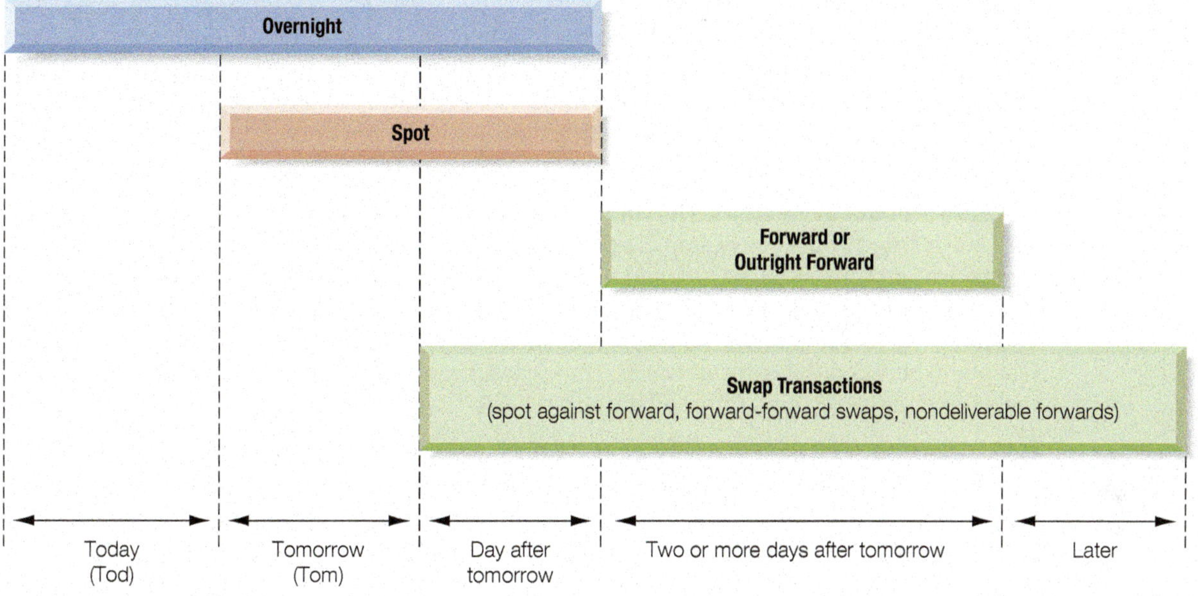

A typical spot transaction in the interbank market might involve a U.S. bank contracting on a Monday for the transfer of £10,000,000 to the account of a London bank. If the spot exchange rate were $1.8420 to each British pound (£), the U.S. bank would transfer £10 million to the London bank on Wednesday, and the London bank would transfer $18.42 million to the U.S. bank at the same time. A spot transaction between a bank and its commercial customer would not necessarily involve a wait of two days for settlement.

Forward Transactions

A *forward transaction* (or more formally, an *outright forward transaction*) requires delivery at a future value date of a specified amount of one currency for a specified amount of another currency. The exchange rate is established at the time of the agreement, but payment and delivery are not required until maturity. Forward exchange rates are normally quoted for value dates of one, two, three, six, and twelve months. Although the heaviest demand is for maturities of one year or less, forwards today are often quoted as far as 20 years into the future. According to the IMF, in 2014 there were 127 countries with forward markets.

Payment on forward contracts occurs on the second business day after the even-month anniversary of the trade. Thus, a two-month forward transaction entered into on March 18 will be for a value date of May 20, or the next business day if May 20 falls on a weekend or holiday. Note that as a matter of terminology we can speak of "buying forward" or "selling forward" to describe the same transaction. A contract to deliver dollars for euros in six months is both "buying euros forward for dollars" and "selling dollars forward for euros."

Swap Transactions

A *swap transaction* in the interbank market is the simultaneous purchase and sale of a given amount of foreign exchange for two different value dates. Both purchase and sale are conducted with the same counterparty. There are several types of swap transactions.

Spot Against Forward. The most common type of swap is a spot against forward. The dealer buys a currency in the spot market (at the spot rate) and simultaneously sells the same amount back to the same bank in the forward market (at the forward exchange rate). Since this is executed as a single transaction with just one counterparty, the dealer incurs no unexpected foreign exchange risk. Swap transactions and outright forwards combined made up more than half of all foreign exchange market activity in recent years.

Forward-Forward Swaps. A more sophisticated swap transaction is called a *forward-forward swap*. For example, a dealer sells £20,000,000 forward for dollars for delivery in, say, two months at $1.8420/£ and simultaneously buys £20,000,000 forward for delivery in three months at $1.8400/£. The difference between the buying price and the selling price is equivalent to the interest rate differential, which is the interest rate parity described in Chapter 6 between the two currencies. Thus, a swap can be viewed as a technique for borrowing another currency on a fully collateralized basis.

Nondeliverable Forwards (NDFs). Created in the early 1990s, the *nondeliverable forward (NDF)* is now a relatively common derivative offered by the largest providers of foreign exchange derivatives. NDFs possess the same characteristics and documentation requirements as traditional forward contracts, except that they are settled only in U.S. dollars; the foreign currency being sold forward or bought forward is not delivered. The dollar settlement feature reflects the fact that NDFs are contracted offshore, for example in New York for a Mexican investor, and so are beyond the reach and regulatory frameworks of the home country governments (Mexico in this case). NDFs are traded internationally using standards set by the International Swaps and Derivatives Association (ISDA). Although originally envisioned to be a method of currency hedging, it is now estimated that more than 70% of all NDF trading is for speculation purposes.

NDFs are used primarily for emerging market currencies or currencies subject to significant exchange controls, like Venezuela. Emerging market currencies often do not have open spot market currency trading, liquid money markets, or quoted Eurocurrency interest rates. Although most NDF trading focused on Latin America in the 1990s, many Asian currencies—including the Chinese renminbi—have been very widely traded in recent years. In general, NDF markets normally develop for country currencies having large cross-border capital movements, but which are still subject to convertibility restrictions.

Pricing of NDFs reflects basic interest differentials, as with regular forwards (described in detail in Chapter 6), plus some additional premium charged by the bank for dollar settlement. If, however, there is no accessible or developed money market for interest rate setting, the pricing of the NDF takes on a much more speculative element. Without true interest rates, traders may price NDFs based on what they believe spot rates may be in the future.

NDFs are traded and settled outside the country of the subject currency, and therefore are beyond the control of the country's government. In the past, this has created a difficult situation, in which the NDF market serves as something of a *gray market* in the trading of that currency. For example, in late 2001, Argentina was under increasing pressure to abandon its fixed exchange rate regime of one peso equaling one U.S. dollar. The NDF market, however, quoted much weaker rates of pesos per dollar, leading to increasing speculative pressure against the peso (to the ire of the Argentine government).

NDFs, however, have proven to be something of an imperfect replacement for traditional forward contracts. The problems with the NDF typically involve its "fixing of spot rate on the fixing date," the spot rate at the end of the contract used to calculate the settlement. In times of financial crisis, for example with the Venezuelan bolivar in 2003, the government of the subject currency may suspend foreign exchange trading in the spot market for an extended period. Without an official fixing rate, the NDF cannot be settled. In the case of Venezuela, the problem was compounded when a new official "devalued bolivar" was announced but was still not traded.

Size of the Foreign Exchange Market

The BIS, in conjunction with central banks around the world, conducts a survey of currency trading activity every three years. The most recent survey, conducted in April 2019, estimated daily global net turnover in the foreign exchange market to be $6.6 trillion, a 30% increase from 2016. The BIS data for surveys between 1989 and 2019 are shown in Exhibit 5.6.

Global foreign exchange turnover in Exhibit 5.6 is divided into the three categories of currency instruments discussed previously—*spot transactions, forward transactions*, and *swap transactions*—plus a fourth category of *options and other variable-value foreign exchange derivatives*. Growth has been dramatic: since 1989, daily foreign exchange market turnover has increased by more than 1,000%.

As of 2019 (daily trading in April), trading in the foreign exchange market was $6.6 trillion per day, with $2.0 trillion in spot trading, $1.0 trillion in outright forwards, $3.2 trillion in foreign exchange swaps, and $0.4 trillion in options and other foreign exchange derivatives. Although the global recession in 2000–2001 clearly dampened market activity, the global

EXHIBIT 5.6 Global Foreign Exchange Market Turnover, 1989–2019

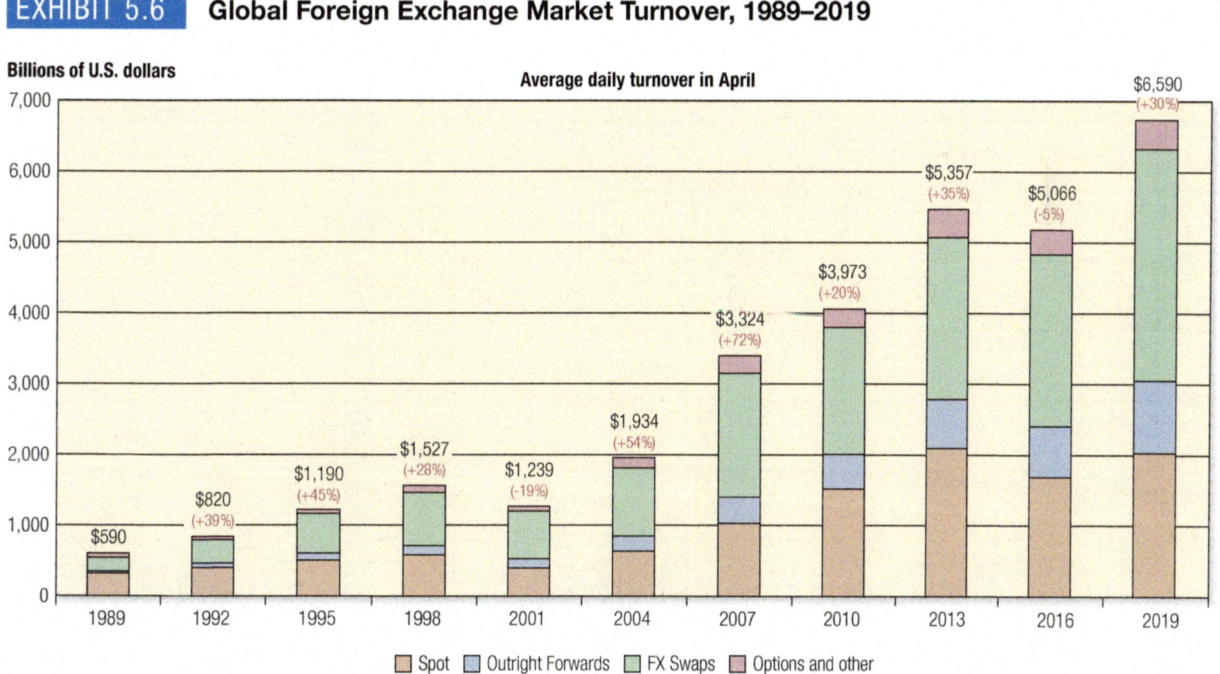

Source: Bank for International Settlements, "Triennial Central Bank Survey: Foreign Exchange Turnover in April 2019," Table 1, p.10, September 16, 2019.

financial crisis of 2008–2009 seemingly did not. Interestingly, the 2016 survey indicated a decline in spot trading for the first time since 2001. Trading, however, returned to its growth path in 2019, up 30% from 2016. The BIS and others believe that it is the growth in electronic trading, more investors in search of profit, and different distributors of big data that are driving this growth.

Geographical Distribution

Exhibit 5.7 shows the proportionate share of foreign exchange trading for the top 10 national markets in the world between 2013 and 2019. (Note that although the data are collected and reported on a national basis, the "U.S." and "UK" should largely be interpreted as "New York" and "London," respectively. The majority of foreign exchange trading takes place in each country's major financial city.) These 10 markets made up 91% of all trading in 2019.

The United Kingdom (London) continues to be the hub of global foreign exchange trading with 53% of the market, followed by the U.S. (New York) with 20%. Although those two markets alone make up 73% of all global trading, it does appear that Asian trading (Singapore, Hong Kong, and China) is growing appreciably in market share.

Older traditional centers like Japan are showing no real growth in trading, hence declining market share. Switzerland, however, one of the oldest in foreign exchange trading, saw a resurgence in 2019. The relative growth of currency trading in Asia versus Europe over the past 15 years is not surprising given the growth of the Asian economies, markets, and currencies, combined with the introduction and expansion of the euro (decreasing the need

EXHIBIT 5.7 Top 10 Geographic Trading Centers in the FX Market

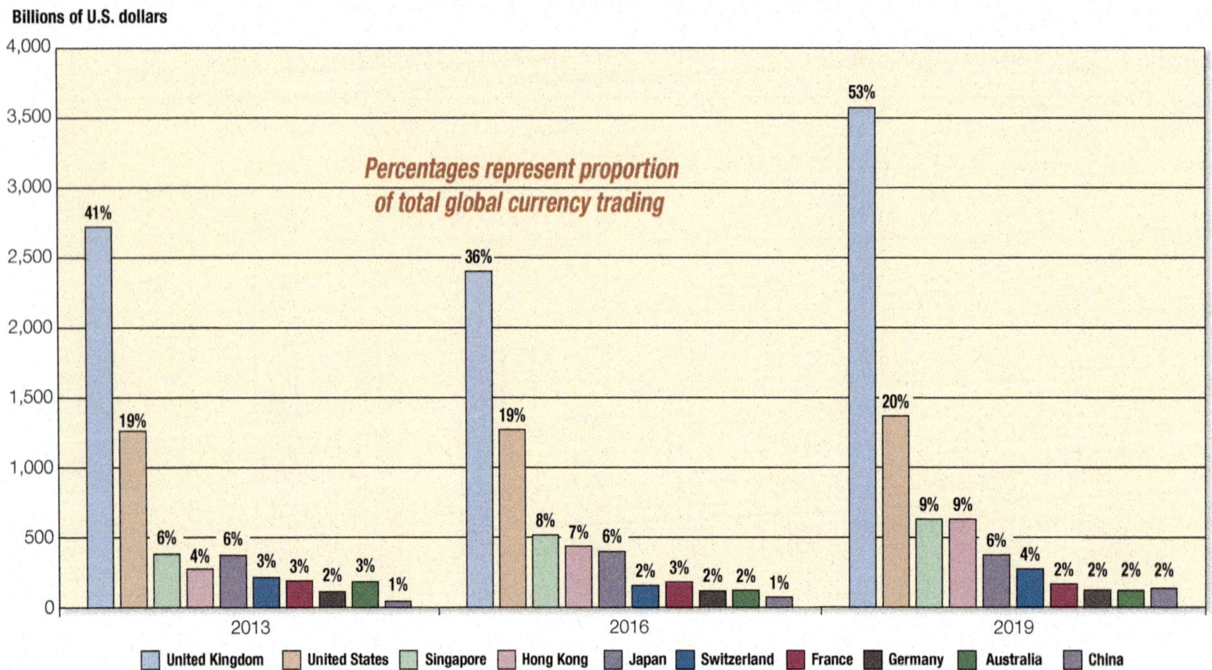

Source: Bank for International Settlements, "Triennial Central Bank Survey: Foreign Exchange Turnover in April 2019," Table 6, p.14, September 16, 2019. Values are on a net-gross basis, average daily turnover in April.

for intra-European currency trading with the elimination of individual country currencies) to shift currency exchange activity. The two biggest questions about the locus of future foreign exchange trading are how fast Chinese trading will grow and what Brexit (the United Kingdom's decision to exit the European Union) will mean for London-based trading.

Currency Composition

The currency composition of trading, as detailed in Exhibit 5.8, also indicates a number of global shifts. The U.S. dollar continues to maintain its share of global currency trades (being one of the currencies involved in individual trades) yet increasing ever so slightly in recent years to 88%. The Japanese yen and the European euro both showed minor declines in trade share, their roles as two of the world's three most frequently traded currencies appearing to be under siege by the Chinese renminbi (4.1%, nearly doubling since 2013) and a number of other emerging market currencies. Because all currencies are traded against other currencies—in pairs—all percentages shown in Exhibit 5.8 are for that currency versus another.

5.4 Foreign Exchange Rates and Quotations

A *foreign exchange rate* is the price of one currency expressed in terms of another currency. A foreign exchange quotation (or quote) is a statement of willingness to buy or sell at an announced rate. As we delve into the grammar of currency trading, keep in mind basic pricing, as in, say, the pricing of an orange. If the price of an orange is $1.20, the "price" is $1.20, and the "unit" is the orange.

Currency Symbols

Quotations may be designated by traditional currency symbols or by ISO codes. The International Organization for Standardization (ISO) is the world's largest developer of voluntary standards. ISO 4217 is the International Standard for currency codes, most recently updated in ISO 4217:2008. The ISO codes were developed for use in electronic communications. Both traditional symbols and currency codes are given in full at the end of this book, but the major ones used throughout this chapter are the following:

Currency	Traditional Symbol	ISO 4217 Code
U.S. dollar	$	USD
European euro	€	EUR
Great Britain pound	£	GBP
Japanese yen	¥	JPY
Mexican peso	Ps	MXN

Today, all electronic trading of currencies between institutions in the global marketplace uses the three-letter ISO codes. Although there are no hard-and-fast rules in the retail markets and in business periodicals, European and American periodicals have a tendency to use the traditional currency symbols, while many publications in Asia and the Middle East have embraced the use of ISO codes. Most countries, however, continue to use traditional currency symbols on paper currency (banknotes).

EXHIBIT 5.8 Daily FX Trading by Currency Pair (percent of total)

Currency Pair	Versus Dollar	2001	2004	2007	2010	2013	2016	2019
USD/EUR	Euro	30.0	28.0	26.8	27.7	24.1	23.1	24.0
USD/JPY	Japanese yen	20.2	17.0	13.2	14.3	18.3	17.8	13.2
USD/GBP	British pound	10.4	13.4	11.6	9.1	8.8	9.3	9.6
USD/AUD	Australian dollar	4.1	5.5	5.6	6.3	6.8	5.2	5.4
USD/CAD	Canadian dollar	4.3	4.0	3.8	4.6	3.7	4.3	4.4
USD/CNY	Chinese yuan	–	–	–	0.8	2.1	3.8	4.1
USD/CHF	Swiss franc	4.8	4.3	4.5	4.2	3.4	3.6	3.5
USD/HKD	Hong Kong dollar	–	–	–	2.1	1.3	1.5	3.3
USD/KRW	Korean won	–	–	–	1.5	1.1	1.5	1.9
USD/INR	Indian rupee	–	–	–	0.9	0.9	1.1	1.7
USD/SGD	Singapore dollar	–	–	–	–	1.2	1.6	1.7
USD/NZD	New Zealand dollar	–	–	–	–	1.5	1.5	1.6
USD/MXN	Mexican peso	–	–	–	–	2.4	1.8	1.6
USD/SEK	Swedish krona	–	–	1.7	1.1	1.0	1.3	1.3
USD/NOK	Norwegian krone	–	–	–	–	0.9	0.9	1.1
USD/BRL	Brazilian real	–	–	–	0.6	0.9	0.9	1.0
USD/RUB	Russian rouble	–	–	–	–	1.5	1.1	1.0
USD/ZAR	South African rand	–	–	–	0.6	1.0	0.8	0.9
USD/TRY	Turkish lira	–	–	–	–	1.2	1.3	0.9
USD/TWD	Taiwan dollar	–	–	–	–	0.4	0.6	0.9
USD/PLN	Polish zloty	–	–	–	–	0.4	0.4	0.4
USD/Other	USD versus others	16.0	15.9	18.4	11.2	4.0	4.2	4.9
	Dollar total	89.8	88.1	85.6	85.0	86.9	87.6	88.4
Currency Pair	**Versus Euro**							
EUR/GBP	British pound	2.1	2.4	2.1	2.7	1.9	2.0	2.0
EUR/JPY	Japanese yen	2.9	3.2	2.6	2.8	2.8	1.6	1.7
EUR/CHF	Swiss franc	1.1	1.6	1.9	1.8	1.3	0.9	1.1
EUR/SEK	Swedish krona	–	–	0.7	0.9	0.5	0.7	0.5
EUR/NOK	Norwegian krone	–	–	–	–	0.4	0.6	0.5
EUR/AUD	Australian dollar	0.1	0.2	0.3	0.3	0.4	0.3	0.3
EUR/CAD	Canadian dollar	0.1	0.1	0.2	0.3	0.3	0.3	0.2
EUR/PLN	Polish zloty	–	–	–	–	0.3	0.3	0.2
EUR/DKK	Danish krone	–	–	–	–	0.2	0.2	0.2
EUR/HUF	Hungarian forint	–	–	–	–	0.2	0.1	0.2
EUR/CNY	Chinese yuan	–	–	–	–	0.0	0.0	0.1
EUR/TRY	Turkish lira	–	–	–	–	0.1	0.1	0.0
EUR/Other	Other versus euro	1.6	1.9	2.5	2.6	0.9	1.3	1.3
	Euro total	7.9	9.4	10.3	11.4	9.3	8.4	8.3
Currency Pair	**Versus Japanese yen**							
JPY/AUD	Australian dollar	–	–	–	0.6	0.9	0.6	0.5
JPY/CAD	Canadian dollar	–	–	–	–	0.1	0.1	0.1
JPY/NZD	New Zealand dollar	–	–	–	0.1	0.1	0.1	0.1
JPY/TRY	Turkish lira	–	–	–	–	0.0	0.1	0.1
JPY/ZAR	South African rand	–	–	–	–	0.1	0.1	0.1
JPY/BRL	Brazilian real	–	–	–	–	0.1	0.0	0.0
JPY/Other	Other versus yen	1.2	0.7	1.5	1.2	0.8	1.3	1.0
	Yen total	1.2	0.7	1.5	1.9	2.1	2.3	1.9
Other currency pairs	all others	1.1	1.9	2.7	1.8	1.7	1.9	1.6
Global Total		100.0	100.0	100.0	100.0	100.0	100.0	100.0

Source: Constructed by authors based on data presented in Table 3, p. 11, of "Triennial Central Bank Survey: Foreign Exchange Turnover in April 2019," Bank for International Settlements, September 2019.

Exchange Rate Quotes

Foreign exchange quotations follow a number of principles, which at first may seem a bit confusing or non-intuitive. Every currency exchange involves two currencies, currency 1 (CUR1) and currency 2 (CUR2):

CUR1/CUR2

The currency on the left of the slash is called the *base currency* or the *unit currency*. The currency on the right of the slash is called the *price currency* or *quote currency*. The quotation always indicates the number of units of the price currency, CUR2, required in exchange for receiving one unit of the base currency, CUR1.

For example, the most commonly quoted currency exchange is that between the U.S. dollar and the European euro. For example, a quotation of *EUR/USD 1.2174* designates the euro (EUR) as the *base currency*, the dollar (USD) as the *price currency*, and the *exchange rate* is USD 1.2174 = EUR 1.00. If you can remember that the currency quoted on the left of the slash is always the base currency and always a single unit, you can avoid confusion. Exhibit 5.9 provides a brief overview of the multitude of terms used globally to quote currencies using the European euro and U.S. dollar.

Market Conventions

The international currency market, although the largest financial market in the world, is steeped in history and convention.

European Terms. *European terms*, the quoting of the quantity of a specific currency per one U.S. dollar, has been market practice for most of the past 60 years or more. Globally, the base currency used to quote a currency's value has typically been the U.S. dollar. Labeled *European terms*, this means that whenever a currency's value is quoted, it is quoted in terms of number of units of currency to equal one U.S. dollar.

For example, if a trader in Zurich, whose home currency is the Swiss franc (CHF), were to request a quote from an Oslo-based trader on the Norwegian krone (NOK), the Norwegian trader would quote the value of the NOK against the USD, not the CHF. The result is that most currencies are quoted per U.S. dollar—Japanese yen per U.S. dollar, Norwegian krone per U.S. dollar, Mexican pesos per U.S. dollar, Brazilian real per U.S. dollar, Malaysian ringgit per U.S. dollar, Chinese renminbi per U.S. dollar, and so on.

EXHIBIT 5.9 Foreign Currency Quotations

European terms Foreign currency price of one dollar (USD)	*American terms* U.S. dollar price of one euro (EUR)
USD/EUR 0.8214 **or** **USD 1.00 = EUR 0.8214**	**EUR/USD 1.2174** **or** **EUR 1.00 = USD 1.2174**
USD is the *base* or *unit currency* EUR is the *quote* or *price currency*	EUR is the *base* or *unit currency* USD is the *quote* or *price currency*

$$\frac{1}{\text{EUR } 0.8214 = \text{USD } 1.00} = \text{USD } 1.2714 = \text{EUR } 1.00$$

American Terms. There are two major exceptions to this rule of using European terms: the euro and the U.K. pound sterling (the pound sterling for historical tradition). Both are normally quoted in *American terms*—the U.S. dollar price of one euro and the U.S. dollar price of one pound sterling. Additionally, Australian dollars and New Zealand dollars are normally quoted on American terms.

For centuries, the British pound sterling consisted of 20 shillings, each of which equaled 12 pence. Multiplication and division with the non-decimal currency were difficult. The custom evolved for foreign exchange prices in London, then the undisputed financial capital of the world, to be stated in foreign currency units per pound. This practice remained even after sterling changed to decimals in 1971.

The euro was first introduced as a substitute or replacement for domestic currencies like the deutsche mark and French franc. To make the transition simple for residents and users of these historical currencies, all quotes were made on a "domestic currency per euro" basis. This held true for its quotation against the U.S. dollar; hence, "U.S. dollars per euro" is the common quotation used today.

American terms are also used in quoting rates for most foreign currency options and futures, as well as in retail markets that deal with tourists and personal remittances. Again, this is largely a result of established practices that have been perpetuated over time, rather than some basic law of finance.

Currency Nicknames. Foreign exchange traders may also use nicknames for major currencies. "Cable" means the exchange rate between U.S. dollars and U.K. pounds sterling, the name dating from the time when transactions in dollars and pounds were carried out over the transatlantic telegraph cable. A Canadian dollar is a "loonie," named after the water fowl on Canada's one dollar coin. "Kiwi" stands for the New Zealand dollar, "Aussie" for the Australian dollar, "Swissie" for Swiss francs, and "Sing dollar" for the Singapore dollar.

Direct and Indirect Quotations. A *direct quote* is the price of a foreign currency in domestic currency units. An *indirect quote* is the price of the domestic currency in foreign currency units. In retail exchange in many countries (such as currency exchanged in hotels or airports), it is common practice to quote the home currency as the price and the foreign currency as the unit. A woman walking down the Avenue des Champs-Élysées in Paris might see the following quote:

$$\text{EUR}\,0.8214 = \text{USD}\,1.00$$

Since in France the *home currency* is the euro (the price) and the *foreign currency* is the dollar (the unit), in Paris this quotation is a direct quote on the dollar or a price quote on the dollar. She might say to herself, "0.8214 euros per dollar," or "It will cost me 0.8214 euros to get one dollar." These are European terms.

At the same time a man walking down Broadway in New York City may see the following quote in a bank window:

$$\text{USD}\,1.2174 = \text{EUR}\,1.00$$

Since in the U.S. the *home currency* is the U.S. dollar (the price) and the *foreign currency* is the euro (the unit), in New York this would be a direct quote on the euro (the home currency price of one unit of foreign currency) and an indirect quote on the dollar (the foreign currency price of one unit of home currency). The man might say to himself, "I will pay

\$1.2174 dollars per euro." These are American terms. The two quotes are obviously equivalent (at least to four decimal places), one being the reciprocal of the other:

$$\frac{1}{\text{EUR}\,0.8214 \text{ per USD } 1.00} = \text{USD}\,1.2174 \text{ per EUR } 1.00$$

Bid and Ask Rates. Although a newspaper or magazine article will state an exchange rate as a single value, the market for buying and selling currencies, whether it be retail or wholesale, uses two different rates, one for buying and one for selling. Exhibit 5.10 provides a sample of how these quotations may be seen in the market for the dollar/euro.

A *bid* is the price (i.e., exchange rate) in one currency at which a dealer will buy another currency. An *ask* is the price (i.e., exchange rate) at which a dealer will sell the other currency. Dealers bid (buy) at one price and ask (sell) at a slightly higher price, making their profit from the spread between the prices. The bid-ask spread may be quite large for currencies that are traded infrequently, in small volumes, or both.

Bid and ask quotations in the foreign exchange markets are superficially complicated by the fact that the bid for one currency is also the offer for the opposite currency. A trader seeking to buy dollars with euros is simultaneously offering to sell euros for dollars. Closing rates for selected currencies as quoted by *The Wall Street Journal* are presented in Exhibit 5.11.

EXHIBIT 5.10 Bid, Ask, and Mid-Point Quotation

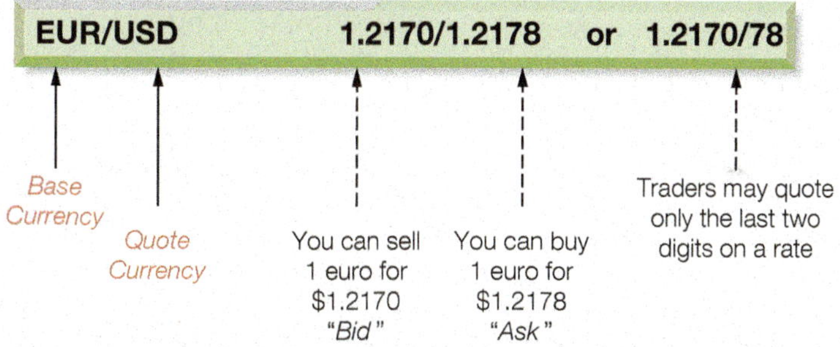

In text documents of any kind, the exchange rate may be started as *mid-point quote*, the average of the *bid* and *ask* quotes, or, in this case, \$1.2174/€.

For example, the *Wall Street Journal* would quote the following currencies as follows:

	Last Bid		***Last Bid***
euro (EUR/USD)	1.2170	Brazilian real (USD/BRL)	1.6827
Japanese yen (USD/JPY)	83.16	Canadian dollar (USD/CAD)	0.9930
UK pound (GBP/USD)	1.5552	Mexican peso (USD/MXN)	12.2365

EXHIBIT 5.11 Exchange Rates: New York Closing Snapshot

May 10, 2021

Country	Currency	Symbol	Code	USD Equivalent	Currency per USD
Americas					
Argentina	peso	Ps	ARS	0.0107	93.8528
Brazil	real	R$	BRL	0.1913	5.2287
Canada	dollar	C$	CAD	0.8261	1.2105
Chile	peso	$	CLP	0.001435	697
Mexico	new peso	$	MXN	0.0502	19.9392
Asia					
Australia	dollar	A$	AUD	0.7829	1.2773
China	yuan	¥	CNY	0.1558	6.4166
Hong Kong	dollar	HK$	HKG	0.1288	7.7656
India	rupee	Rs	INR	0.01361	73.48555
Indonesia	rupiah	Rp	IDR	0.0000704	14198
Japan	yen	¥	JPY	0.00919	108.84
Singapore	dollar	S$	SGD	0.7543	1.3257
South Korea	won	W	KRW	0.0008954	1116.83
Thailand	baht	B	THB	0.03213	31.12
Vietnam	dong	d	VND	0.00004336	23062
Europe					
Czech Republic	koruna	Kc	CZK	0.04744	21.08
Denmark	krone	Dkr	DKK	0.1631	6.1307
Euro area	euro	€	EUR	1.213	0.8244
Norway	krone	NKr	NOK	0.1209	8.2727
Russia	ruble	R	RUB	0.01345	74.327
Sweden	krona	SKr	SEK	0.1198	8.3452
Switzerland	franc	Fr.	CHF	1.1098	0.9011
Middle East/Africa					
Egypt	pound	£	EGP	0.0638	15.6713
Israel	shekel	Shk	ILS	0.3068	3.2593
Saudi Arabia	riyal	SR	SAR	0.2667	3.7502
South Africa	rand	R	ZAR	0.0712	14.0492

Note: Quotes based on trading among banks of $1 million and more, as quoted at 4 p.m. ET by Reuters. Rates are drawn from *The Wall Street Journal* online on May 11, 2021.

The *Wall Street Journal* gives American terms quotes under the heading "USD equivalent" and European terms quotes under the heading "Currency per USD." Quotes are given on an outright basis for spot, with forwards of one, three, and six months provided for a few select currencies. Quotes are for trading among banks in amounts of $1 million or more, as quoted at 4 p.m. EST by Reuters. The *Wall Street Journal* does not state whether these are bid, ask, or *midrate* (an average of the bid and ask) quotations.

The order of currencies in quotations used by traders can be confusing (at least the authors of this book think so). As noted by one major international banking publication: *The notation EUR/USD is the system used by traders, although mathematically it would be more correct to express the exchange rate the other way around, as it shows how many USD have to be paid to obtain EUR 1.* This is why the currency quotes shown previously in Exhibit 5.10—like EUR/USD, USD/JPY, or GBP/USD—are quoted and used in business and the rest of this text as $1.2170/€, ¥83.16/$, and $1.5552/£. International finance is not for the weak of heart!

Cross Rates

Many currency pairs are only inactively traded, so their exchange rate is determined through their relationship to a widely traded third currency. For example, a Mexican importer needs Japanese yen to pay for purchases in Tokyo. Both the Mexican peso (MXN or the old peso symbol, Ps) and the Japanese yen (JPY or ¥) are commonly quoted against the U.S. dollar (USD or $). Using the following quotes from Exhibit 5.11,

		Currency per USD
Japanese yen	USD/JPY	108.84
Mexican peso	USD/MXN	19.9392

the Mexican importer can buy one U.S. dollar for MXN19.9392, and with that dollar can buy JPY108.84. The *cross rate calculation* would be as follows:

$$\frac{\text{Japanese yen} = 1\,\text{U.S. dollar}}{\text{Mexican pesos} = 1\,\text{U.S. dollar}} = \frac{¥108.84 = \$1.00}{\text{Ps}\,19.9392 = \$1.00} = ¥5.4586\,\text{per peso}$$

The cross rate could also be calculated as the reciprocal, with the USD/MXN rate divided by the USD/JPY rate, yielding Ps0.1832 = ¥1.00. Cross rates often appear in various financial publications in the form of a matrix to simplify the math.

Intermarket Arbitrage

Cross rates can be used to check on opportunities for intermarket arbitrage. Suppose the following exchange rates are quoted:

Citibank quotes U.S. dollars per euro	USD1.3297 = 1 EUR
Barclays Bank quotes U.S. dollars per pound sterling	USD1.5585 = 1 GBP
Dresdner Bank quotes euros per pound sterling	EUR1.1722 = 1 GBP

The euro-pound sterling cross rate, derived from the Citibank and Barclays Bank quotes, is

$$\frac{\text{USD } 1.5585 = \text{GBP } 1.00}{\text{USD } 1.3297 = \text{EUR } 1.00} = \text{EUR } 1.1721 \text{ per GBP}$$

Note that the calculated cross rate of EUR 1.1721 per GBP is not the same as Dresdner Bank's quotation of EUR1.1722 = GBP1.00, so an opportunity exists to profit from arbitrage between the three markets. Exhibit 5.12 shows the steps in what is called triangular arbitrage.

A market trader at Citibank New York, with USD1,000,000, can sell that sum spot to Barclays Bank for British pounds sterling, and then in turn, sell these pounds to Dresdner Bank for euros. In the third and final simultaneous sale, the trader can sell the euros to Citibank for USD1,000,112.

EXHIBIT 5.12 **Triangular Arbitrage by a Market Trader**

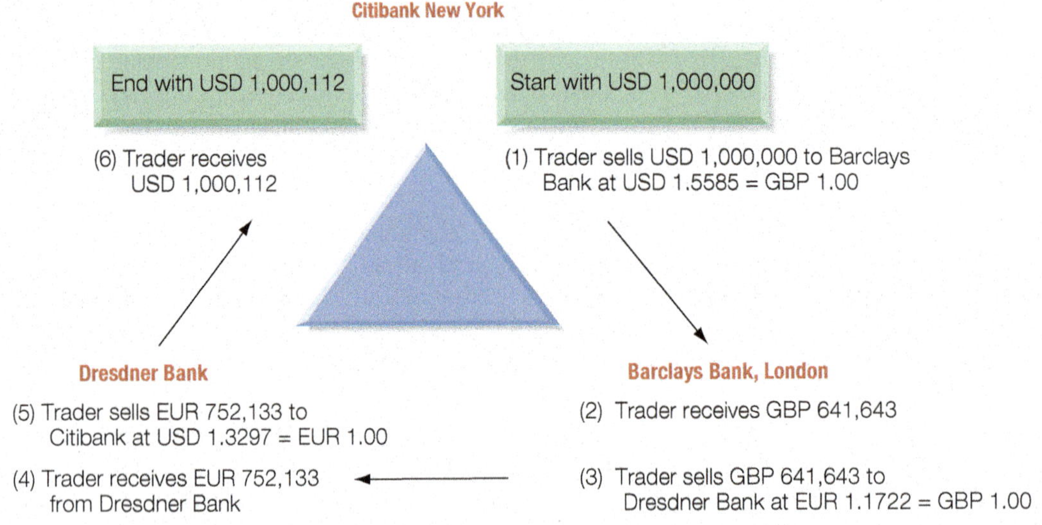

The profit on one such *turn* is a risk-free USD112: USD1,000,112 - USD1,000,000. We know that's not much, but it's digital! Such triangular arbitrage can continue until exchange rate equilibrium is *reestablished. Reestablished* in this case means when the calculated cross rate equals the actual quotation, less any tiny margin for transaction costs. This all appears mechanically sound and rather straightforward, but that assumes the market is not hit with major surprises. *Global Finance in Practice 5.4* describes one case in which one of the most conservative governments on earth proved to be not so predictable.

Forward Quotations

Although spot rates are typically quoted on an outright basis (meaning all digits expressed), forward rates are, depending on the currency, typically quoted in terms of *points* or *pips*, the last digits of a currency quotation. Forward rates of one year or less maturity are termed *cash rates*; for longer than one-year they are called *swap rates*. A forward quotation expressed in points is not a foreign exchange rate as such. Rather it is the difference between the forward rate and the spot rate. Consequently, the spot rate itself can never be given on a points basis.

Consider the spot and forward point quotes in Exhibit 5.13. The bid and ask spot quotes are outright quotes, but the forwards are stated as points from the spot rate. The three-month points quotations for the Japanese yen in Exhibit 5.13 are bid and ask. The first number refers to points away from the spot bid, and the second number refers to points away from the spot ask. Given the outright quotes of 118.27 bid and 118.37 ask, the outright three-month forward rates are calculated as follows:

	Bid	Ask
Outright spot	JPY118.27	JPY118.37
Plus points (3 months)	1.43	1.40
Outright forward	JPY116.84	JPY116.97

GLOBAL FINANCE IN PRACTICE 5.4

The Rocketing Swiss Franc

The Swiss franc has been fighting its appreciation against the euro for years. Not a member of the European Union and possessing one of the world's most stable currencies for over a century, Switzerland is however an economy and a currency completely encased within the Eurozone.

In 2011, in an attempt stop the Swiss franc from continuing to grow in value against the euro (stop its *appreciation*), the Swiss Central Bank announced a "floor" on its value against the euro of 1.20 Swiss francs to one euro. To preserve this value, the bank would intervene in the market by buying euros with Swiss francs anytime the market exchange rate threatened to hit the floor.

In early 2015 the markets continued to try to push the Swiss franc's value up against the euro (which means pushing its exchange value to lower than 1.20 Swiss francs per euro). The Swiss Central Bank continued to intervene, buying euros with Swiss francs and accumulating more and more euros in its reserves of foreign currency. The bank had also set central bank interest rates at negative levels. This meant that the bank charged depositors to hold Swiss franc deposits, an effort to dissuade investors from exchanging any currency, including the euro, for Swiss francs.

But the European Union's economies continued to struggle in 2014, and early reports of economic activity in 2015 were showing further slowing. Investors wished to exit the euro, fearing its future fall in value. The European Central Bank (ECB) had added to their anxiety as it had announced that it would be undertaking expansionary government debt purchases—*quantitative easing* (expansionary monetary policy)—to kick-start the sluggish EU economy.

On the morning of January 15, 2015, the Swiss Central Bank shocked the markets by announcing that it was abandoning the 1.20 floor and cutting interest rates further (more negative). It had concluded that with the forthcoming monetary expansion from the ECB, there was no longer any way to keep the flood gates closed. The Swiss franc appreciated versus the euro in minutes. For two of the world's major currencies, it was a very eventful day.

Swiss Franc's Appreciation by the Minute, January 2015

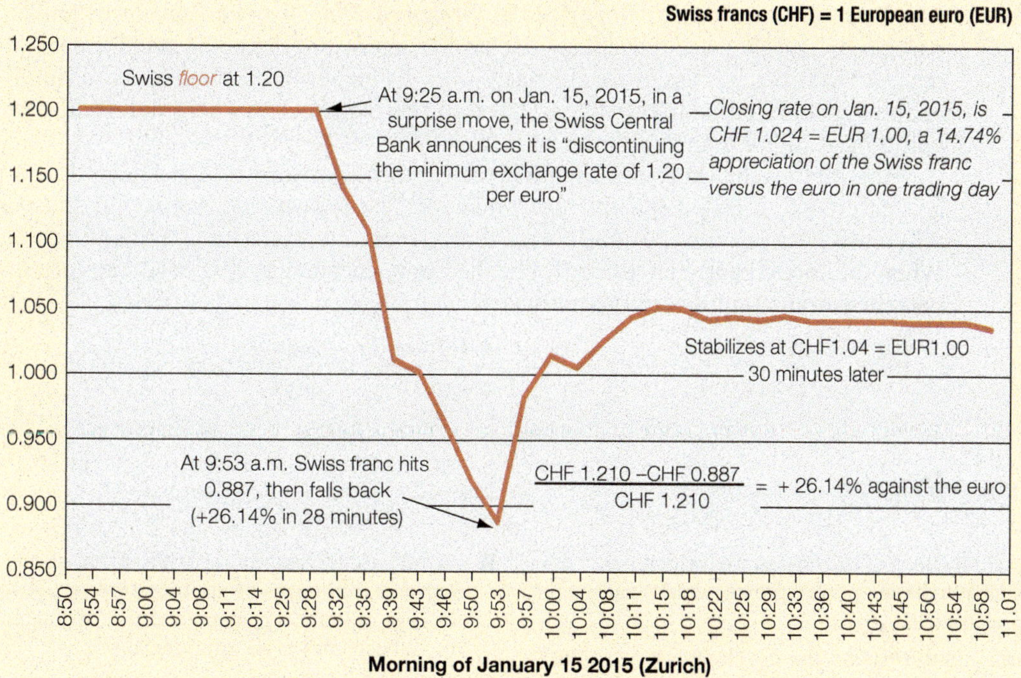

The forward bid and ask quotations of two years and longer are called swap rates. As mentioned earlier, many forward exchange transactions in the interbank market involve a simultaneous purchase for one date and sale (reversing the transaction) for another date. This "swap" is a way to borrow one currency for a limited time while giving up the use of another currency for the same time. In other words, it is a short-term borrowing of one currency

EXHIBIT 5.13 Spot and Forward Quotations for the Euro and Japanese yen

		Euro: Spot and Forward ($=€1.00)				Japanese yen: Spot and Forward (¥=$1.00)			
		Bid		Ask		Bid		Ask	
	Term	Points	Rate	Points	Rate	Points	Rate	Points	Rate
	Spot		1.0897		1.0901		118.27		118.37
Cash rates	1 week	3	1.0900	4	1.0905	−10	118.17	−9	118.28
	1 month	17	1.0914	19	1.0920	−51	117.76	−50	117.87
	2 months	35	1.0932	36	1.0937	−95	117.32	−93	117.44
	3 months	53	1.0950	54	1.0955	−143	116.84	−140	116.97
	4 months	72	1.0969	76	1.0977	−195	116.32	−190	116.47
	5 months	90	1.0987	95	1.0996	−240	115.87	−237	116.00
	6 months	112	1.1009	113	1.1014	−288	115.39	−287	115.50
	9 months	175	1.1072	177	1.1078	−435	113.92	−429	114.08
	1 year	242	1.1139	245	1.1146	−584	112.43	−581	112.56
Swap rates	2 years	481	1.1378	522	1.1423	−1150	106.77	−1129	107.08
	3 years	750	1.1647	810	1.1711	−1748	100.79	−1698	101.39
	4 years	960	1.1857	1039	1.1940	−2185	96.42	−2115	97.22
	5 years	1129	1.2026	1276	1.2177	−2592	92.35	−2490	93.47

combined with a short-term loan of an equivalent amount of another currency. This is in fact why forward contracts are categorized as *foreign currency loan agreements* by banks. The two parties could, if they wanted, charge each other interest at the going rate for each of the currencies. However, it is easier for the party with the higher-interest currency to simply pay the net interest differential to the other. The swap rate expresses this net interest differential on a points basis rather than as an interest rate.

The relationship between the spot rate and the forward rate, calculated as a percentage difference, is called the *forward premium*. The *forward premium*, *f*, is the percentage difference between the spot and forward exchange rate, stated in annual percentage terms. When the foreign currency price (fc) of the home currency (hc) is used, the formula for the percent-per-annum forward premium is:

$$f^{fc=hc} = \frac{\text{Spot} - \text{Forward}}{\text{Forward}} \times \frac{360}{\text{days}} \times 100$$

We will explore forward rates and forward premiums in further detail in chapter 6.

Summary Points

- The three functions of the foreign exchange market are to transfer purchasing power, provide credit, and minimize foreign exchange risk.
- Electronic platforms and the development of sophisticated trading algorithms have facilitated market access by traders of all kinds and sizes.
- Geographically the foreign exchange market spans the globe, with prices moving and currencies traded somewhere every hour of every business day.
- A foreign exchange rate is the price of one currency expressed in terms of another currency. A foreign exchange quotation is a statement of willingness to buy or sell currency at an announced price.
- European terms quotations are the foreign currency price of a U.S. dollar. American terms quotations are the dollar price of a foreign currency.
- Quotations can also be direct or indirect. A direct quote is the home currency price of a unit of foreign currency, while an indirect quote is the foreign currency price of a unit of home currency.

- Direct and indirect are not synonyms for American and European terms, because the home currency will change depending on who is doing the calculation, while European terms are always the foreign currency price of a dollar.
- A cross rate is an exchange rate between two currencies, calculated from their common relationships with a third currency. When cross rates differ from the direct rates between two currencies, intermarket arbitrage is possible.

MINI-CASE

Iceland: A Small Country in a Global Crisis[2]

There were the short story and the longer, more complex story. Iceland had seen both. And what was the moral of the story? Was the moral that it's better to be a big fish in a little pond, or was it once burned, twice shy or something else?

Iceland was a country of only 300,000 people. It was relatively geographically isolated, but its culture and economy were heavily intertwined with those of Europe. A former property of Denmark, it considered itself both independent and yet Danish. Iceland's economy was historically driven by fishing and natural resource development. Although not flashy by any sense of the word, they had proven to be solid and lasting industries and, in recent years, increasingly profitable. At least that was until Iceland discovered "banking."

The Icelandic Crisis: The Short Story

Iceland's economy had grown rapidly, so rapidly in the 2000–2008 period that inflation—an ill of the past in most of the economic world—was a growing problem. As a small, industrialized, and open economy, capital was allowed to flow into and out of Iceland freely. As inflationary pressures rose, the Central Bank of Iceland had tightened monetary policy, and interest rates rose. Higher interest rates attracted capital from outside Iceland, primarily European capital, and the banking system was flooded with capital. The banks in turn invested heavily in everything from real estate to Land Rovers (or *Game Overs*, as they became known).

Then September 2008 happened. The global financial crisis, largely originating in the U.S. and its real estate-securitized-mortgage-debt-credit-default-swap crisis, brought much of the international financial system and major industrial economies to a halt. Investments failed—in the U.S., in

EXHIBIT A The Icelandic Short Story—Fall of the Krona

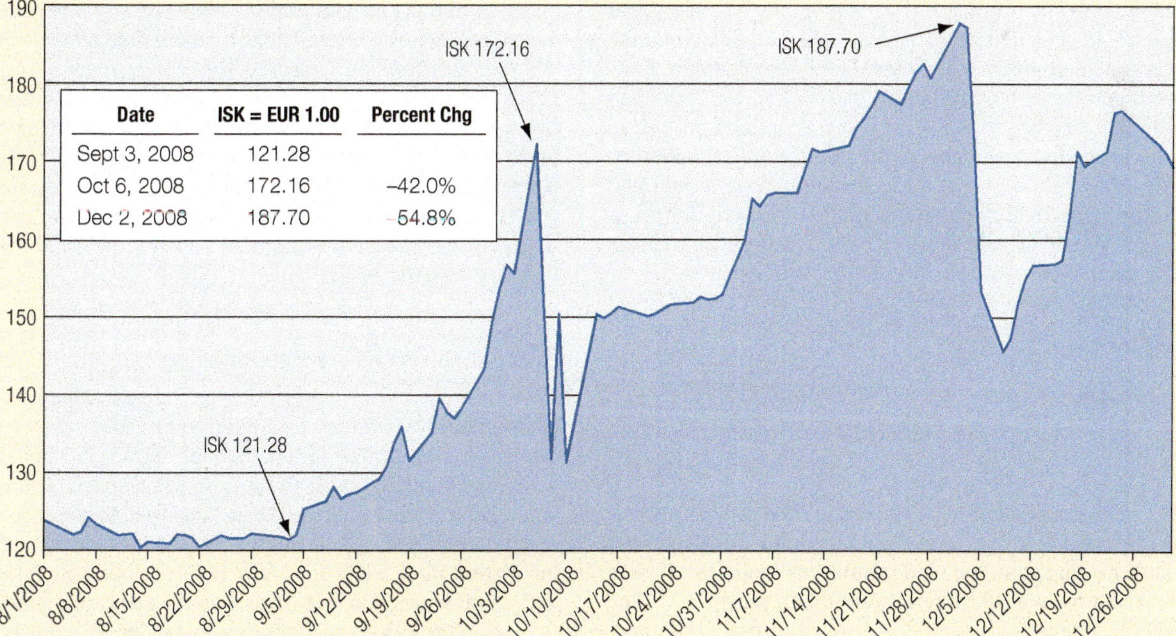

Date	ISK = EUR 1.00	Percent Chg
Sept 3, 2008	121.28	
Oct 6, 2008	172.16	−42.0%
Dec 2, 2008	187.70	−54.8%

[2] Copyright © 2015 Thunderbird School of Global Management, Arizona State University. All rights reserved. This case was prepared by Professor Michael H. Moffett for the purpose of classroom discussion only.

Europe, in Iceland. Loans to finance those bad investments fell delinquent. The Icelandic economy and its currency—the krona—collapsed. As illustrated in Exhibit A, the krona fell more than 40% against the euro in roughly 30 days and more than 50% in 90 days. Companies failed, banks failed, unemployment grew, and inflation boomed.

The Icelandic Crisis: The Longer Story

The longer story of Iceland's crisis has its roots in the mid-1990s, when Iceland, like many other major industrial economies, embraced privatization and deregulation. The financial sector, once completely owned and operated by government, was privatized and largely deregulated by 2003. Home mortgages were deregulated in 2003; new mortgages required only a 10% down payment. Investment—foreign direct investment (FDI)—flowed into Iceland rapidly. A large part of the new investment was in aluminum production, an energy-intensive process that could utilize much of Iceland's natural (after massive damn construction) hydroelectric power. But FDI of all kinds also flowed into the country, including household and business capital.

The new Icelandic financial sector was dominated by three banks: Glitnir, Kaupthing, and Landsbanki Islands. Their opportunities for growth and profitability seemed unlimited, both domestically and internationally. Iceland's membership in the European Economic Area (EEA) provided the Icelandic banks a financial passport to expand their reach throughout the greater European marketplace. As capital flowed into Iceland rapidly in 2003–2006, the krona rose, increasing the purchasing power of Icelanders but raising concerns with investors and government. Gross domestic product (GDP) had grown at 8% in 2004 and 6% in 2005 and was still above 4% by 2006. While the average unemployment rate of the major economic powers was roughly 6%, Iceland's overheating economy had only 3% unemployment. But rapid economic growth in a small economy, as happens frequently in economic history, stoked inflation. And the Icelandic government and central bank then applied the standard prescription: slow money supply growth to try to control inflationary forces. The result—as expected—was higher interest rates.

Lessons Not Learned

Brennt barn forðast eldinn.
(A burnt child keeps away from fire.)
—Icelandic proverb.

The mini-shock suffered by Iceland in 2006 was short-lived, and investors and markets quickly shook off its effects. Bank lending returned, and within two years the Icelandic economy was in more trouble than ever. In 2007 and 2008 Iceland's interest rates continued to rise—both market rates (like bank overnight rates) and central bank policy rates. Global credit agencies rated the major Icelandic banks AAA. Capital flowed into Icelandic banks, and the banks in turn funneled that capital into all possible investments (and loans) domestically and internationally. Iceland's banks created *Ice-save*, an Internet banking system to reach out to depositors in Great Britain and the Netherlands. It worked. Iceland's bank balance sheets grew 100% of GDP in 2003 to just below 1,000% of GDP by 2008.

Iceland's banks were now more international than Icelandic. (By the end of 2007 their total deposits were 45% in British pounds, 22% Icelandic krona, 16% euro, 3% dollar, and 14% other.) Icelandic real estate and equity prices boomed. Increased consumer and business spending resulted in growth in merchandise and service imports, while the rising krona depressed exports. The merchandise service and income balances in the current account all went into deficit. Behaving like an emerging market country that had just discovered oil, Icelanders dropped their fishing hooks, abandoned their boats, and became bankers. Everyone wanted a piece of the pie, and the pie appeared to be growing at an infinite rate. Everyone could become rich.

Then, without notice, the economic and banking boom stopped. What caused the sudden crash, whether it was the failure of Lehman Brothers in New York or something else, we may never know. But beginning in September 2008 the krona started falling and capital started fleeing. Interest rates were increased even further to try to entice (or "bribe") money to stay in Iceland and in krona. None of it worked. As illustrated by Exhibit B, the krona's fall was large, dramatic, and somewhat permanent. In retrospect, the 2006 crisis had been only a ripple; 2008 proved to be a tsunami.

Now those same interest rates, which had been driven up by both markets and policy, prevented any form of renewal; mortgage loans were either impossible to get or impossible to afford, and business loans were too expensive given the new limited business outlook. The international interbank market, which had largely frozen up during the midst of the crisis in September and October 2008, now treated the Icelandic financial sector like a leper. As illustrated by Exhibit C, interest rates had a long way to fall to reach earth. (The Central Bank of Iceland's overnight rate rose to well over 20%.)

Aftermath: The Policy Response

There is a common precept observed by governments and central banks when they fall victim to financial crises: save the banks. Regardless of whether the banks and bankers were considered the cause of the crisis or complicit (one Icelandic central banker termed them "the usual suspects"), it is common belief that all economies need a functioning banking system in order to have any hope for business rebirth and employment recovery. This was the same rule used in the U.S. in the 1930s and across South Asia in 1997 and 1998.

But the Icelandic people did not prescribe to the usual medicinal solutions. Their preference: let the banks fail.

EXHIBIT B The Icelandic Krona–European Euro Spot Exchange Rate

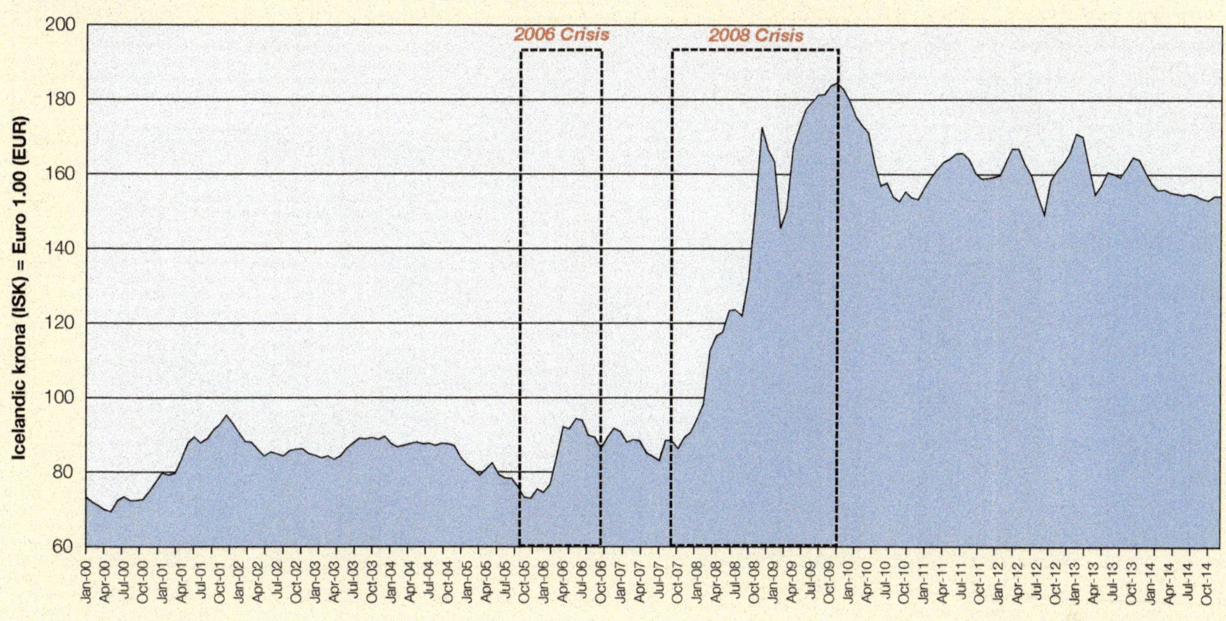

EXHIBIT C Icelandic Central Bank Interest Rate

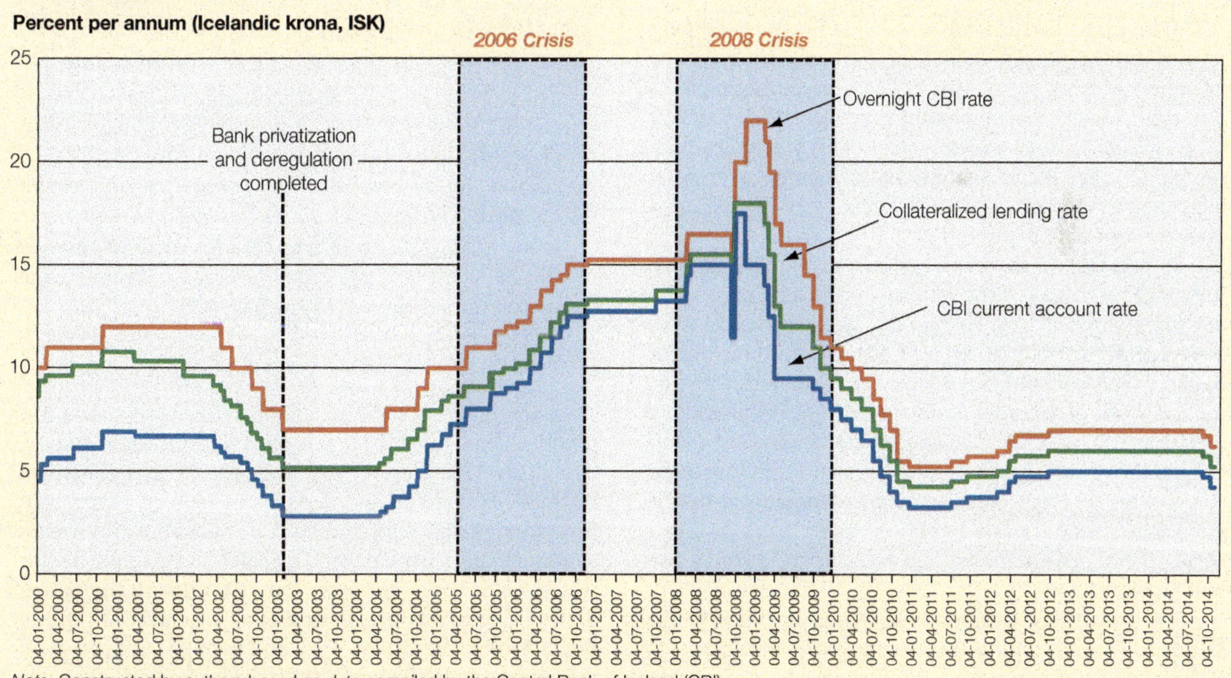

Note: Constructed by authors based on data compiled by the Central Bank of Iceland (CBI).

EXHIBIT D **Icelandic Banks Compared to Others in Potential Crisis**

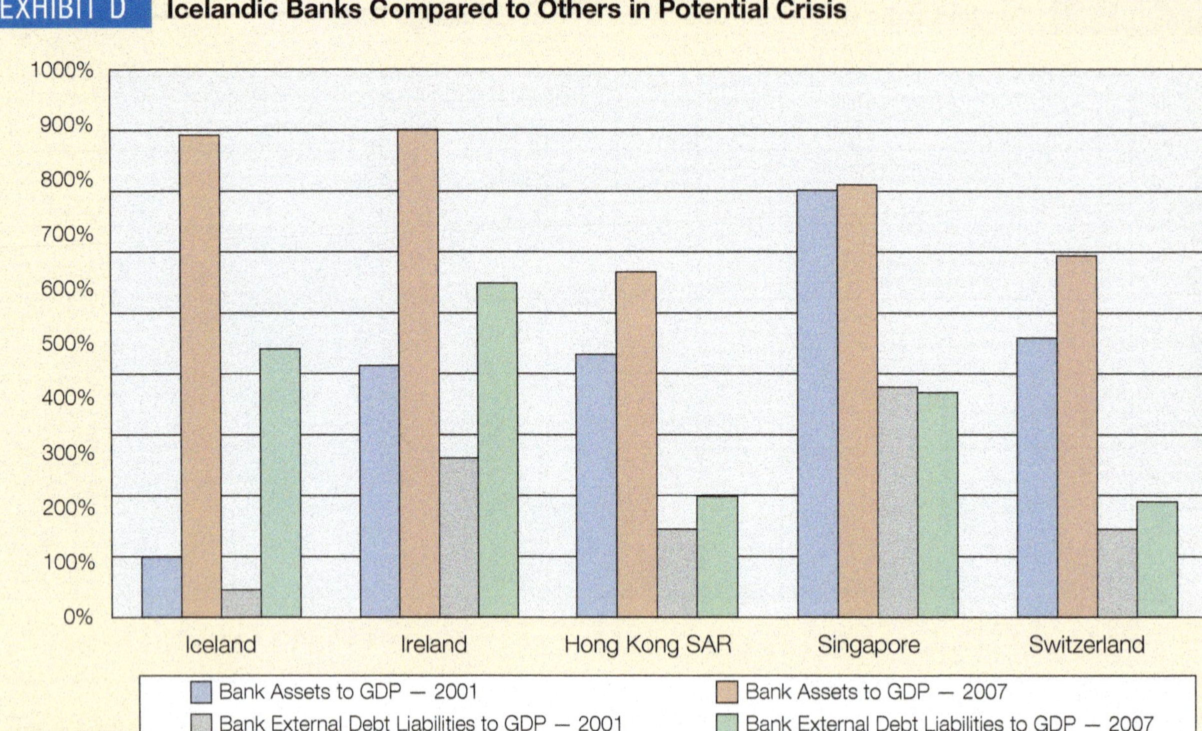

Source: IMF and Iceland Central Bank

Taking to the streets in what was called the pots and pans revolution, the people wanted no part of the banks, the bankers, the bank regulators, or even the prime minister. The logic was some combination of "allow free markets to work" and "I want some revenge." This is actually quite similar to what many analysts have debated over what happened in the U.S. at the same time when the U.S. government let Lehman go.

In contrast to the bank bailouts in the U.S. in 2008 following the onset of the financial crisis undertaken under the mantra of "too big to fail," Iceland's banks were considered "too big to save." Each of the three major banks, which had all been effectively nationalized by the second week of October 2008, was closed. As illustrated in Exhibit D, although Iceland's bank assets and external liabilities were large and had grown rapidly, Iceland was not alone. Each failed bank was reorganized by the government into a good bank and a bad bank in terms of assets but not combined into singular good banks and bad banks.

The governing authorities surviving in office in the fall of 2008 undertook a three-point emergency plan: (1) stabilize the exchange rate, (2) regain fiscal sustainability, and (3) rebuild the financial sector. The primary tool was capital controls. Iceland shut down the borders and the Internet lines for moving capital into or out of the country. The most immediate problem was the exchange rate. The falling krona had decimated purchasing power, and the rising prices of imported goods were adding even more inflationary pressure.

> *Given the substantial macroeconomic risks, capital controls were an unfortunate but indispensable ingredient in the policy mix that was adopted to stabilise the króna when the interbank foreign-exchange market was restarted in early December 2008.*
>
> —Capital Control Liberalisation, Central Bank of Iceland, August 5, 2009, p. 2.

The bank failures (without bailout) raised serious and contentious discussions between Iceland and other authorities in the UK, the EU, the Netherlands, and elsewhere. Because so many of the deposits in Iceland banks were from foreign depositors, home-country authorities wanted assurance that their citizens' financial assets would be protected. In Iceland, although the government guaranteed domestic residents that their money was insured (up to a limit), foreign depositors were not. Foreign residents holding accounts with Icelandic financial institutions were prohibited from pulling the money out of Iceland and out of the krona.

Capital controls were introduced in October—upon the recommendation of the IMF—and then altered and magnified in revisions in November and December 2008 and again in March 2009.

> *Payments linked to current account transactions and inward FDI were released after a short period of time. Thus, transactions involving actual imports and exports of goods and services are allowed and so are interest payments, if exchanged within a specified time limit. Most capital transactions are controlled both for residents and non-residents; that is, their ability to shift between ISK and FX is restricted. Króna-denominated bonds and other like instruments cannot be converted to foreign currency upon maturity. The proceeds must be reinvested in other ISK instruments. Furthermore, the Rules require residents to repatriate all foreign currency that they acquire.*
>
> —Capital Control Liberalisation, Central Bank of Iceland, August 5, 2009, p. 23.

It also turned out that the crisis itself was not such a big surprise. The Central Bank of Iceland had approached the European Central Bank (ECB), the Bank of England, and the U.S. Federal Reserve in the spring of 2008 (months before the crisis erupted), hoping to arrange foreign exchange swap agreements in case its foreign exchange reserves proved inadequate. The answer was no, basically summarized as "talk to the International Monetary Fund (IMF)." In the end, the IMF did indeed help, providing a Stand-By Arrangement to provide favorable access to foreign capital.

The krona's value was stabilized, as seen previously in Exhibit B, but has stayed weaker, which has helped return the merchandise trade account to surplus in subsequent years. Inflation took a bit longer to get under control but was successfully cut to near 2% by the end of 2010. Iceland remains a heavily indebted Lilliputian country (according to the *Financial Times*), in both public debt and private debt as a percentage of GDP.

20/20 Hindsight

Interestingly, in the years since the crisis, there has been a reversal (or, as one writer described it, 20/20/20/20 hindsight) in the assessment of Iceland's response to the crisis. In the first few years, it was believed that Iceland's recovery would be shorter and stronger than other European countries falling into crisis in 2009 and 2010, like Ireland, Estonia, and others. But then, after a few more years of experience, revised hindsight concluded that Iceland's recovery has been slower, weaker, and less successful than that of others, partly a result of allowing the banks to fail, partly a result of the country's "addiction" to capital controls.

What are the lessons to be taken from the Icelandic saga? Deregulation of the financial system is risky? Banks and bankers are not to be trusted? Cross-border banking is risky? Inadequate cross-border banking regulations allow banks to borrow too much where they shouldn't and invest too much where they shouldn't? Bank loan books and bank capital need to be regulated? Small countries cannot conduct independent monetary policy? Small fish should not swim in big ponds? Or . . .

> *The paper concludes that, to prevent future crises of similar proportions, it is impossible for a small country to have a large international banking sector, its own currency and an independent monetary policy.*
>
> —"Iceland's Economic and Financial Crisis: Causes, Consequences and Implications," Rob Spruk, European Enterprise Institute, February 23, 2010.

MINI-CASE QUESTIONS

1. Do you think a country the size of Iceland—a Lilliputian—is more or less sensitive to the potential impacts of global capital movements?
2. Many countries have used interest rate increases to protect their currencies for many years. What are the pros and cons of using this strategy?
3. How does the Iceland story fit with our understanding of the impossible trinity? In your opinion, which of the three elements of the trinity should Iceland have taken steps to control more?
4. In the case of Iceland, the country was able to sustain a large current account deficit for several years and at the same time have ever-rising interest rates and a stronger and stronger currency. Then one day, it all changed. How does that happen?

Questions

5.1 Definitions. Define the following terms:

a. Foreign exchange market
b. Foreign exchange transaction
c. Foreign exchange

5.2 Functions of the Foreign Exchange Market. What are the three major functions of the foreign exchange market?

5.3 Structure of the FX Market. How is the global foreign exchange market structured? Is digital telecommunication replacing people?

5.4 Market Participants. For each of the foreign exchange market participants, identify their motive for buying or selling foreign exchange.

5.5 Foreign Exchange Transaction. Define each of the following types of foreign exchange transactions:
a. Spot
b. Outright forward
c. Forward-forward swaps

5.6 Swap Transactions. Define and differentiate the different types of swap transactions in the foreign exchange markets.

5.7 Nondeliverable Forward. What is a nondeliverable forward, and why does it exist?

5.8 Foreign Exchange Market Characteristics. With reference to foreign exchange turnover in 2013:
a. Rank by volume the relative size of spot, forwards, and swaps.
b. List the five most important geographic locations for foreign exchange turnover in descending order.
c. List the three most important currencies of denomination in descending order.

5.9 Foreign Exchange Rate Quotations. Define and give an example of each of the following:
a. Bid rate quote
b. Ask rate quote

5.10 Reciprocals. Convert the following indirect quotes to direct quotes and direct quotes to indirect quotes:
a. Euro: €1.22/$ (indirect quote)
b. Russia: Rbl30/$ (indirect quote)
c. Denmark: $0.1644/DKr (direct quote)

5.11 Geography and the Foreign Exchange Market. Answer the following:
a. What is the geographical location of the foreign exchange market?
b. What are the two main types of trading systems for foreign exchange?
c. How are foreign exchange markets connected for trading activities?

5.12 American and European Terms. With reference to interbank quotations, what is the difference between American terms and European terms?

5.13 Direct and Indirect Quotes. Define and give an example of the following:
a. Direct quote between the U.S. dollar and the Mexican peso, where the United States is designated as the home country.
b. Indirect quote between the Japanese yen and the Chinese renminbi (yuan), where China is designated as the home country.

5.14 Base and Price Currency. Define base currency, unit currency, price currency, and quote currency.

5.15 Cross Rates and Intermarket Arbitrage. Why are cross currency rates of special interest when discussing intermarket arbitrage?

Problems

5.1 Study Abroad: Paris to Moscow. On your summer study abroad program in Europe you stay an extra two weeks to travel from Paris to Moscow. You leave Paris with 2,000 euros (EUR) in your belt pack. Wanting to exchange all of these for Russian rubles (RUB), you obtain the following quotes:

Spot rate: USD1.1280 = EUR1.00

Spot rate: RUB62.40 = USD1.00

a. What is the Russian ruble to euro cross rate?
b. How many Russian rubles will you obtain for your euros?

5.2 Summer Abroad: Moscow to Mumbai. After spending a week in Moscow you get an e-mail from your friend in India. She can get you a really good deal on a plane ticket and wants you to meet her in Mumbai next week to continue your global studies. You have 450,000 Russian rubles (RUB) left in your money pouch. In preparation for the trip you want to exchange your Russian rubles for Indian rupee (INR) at the Moscow airport:

Spot rate: RUB64.60 = USD1.00

Spot rate: INR66.80 = USD1.00

a. What is the Russian ruble to Indian rupee cross rate?
b. How many Indian rupee will you obtain for your rubles?
c. What is this amount in U.S. dollars?

5.3 Anne Dietz at Changi #3 (Singapore). Anne Dietz lives in Singapore but is making her first business trip to Sydney, Australia. Standing in Singapore's new terminal #3 at Changi Airport, she looks at the foreign exchange quotes posted over the FX trader's booth. She wishes to exchange 1,000 Singapore dollars (S$ or SGD) for Australian dollars (A$ or AUD). What Anne sees:

Spot rate: SGD1.34 = USD1.00USD

Spot rate: USD0.7640 = AUD1.00

a. What is the Singapore dollar to Australian dollar cross rate?
b. How many Australian dollars will Anne get for her Singapore dollars?

5.4 James Bay Exports. A Canadian exporter, James Bay Exports, will be receiving six payments of €12,000, ranging from now to 12 months in the future. Since the company keeps cash balances in both Canadian dollars and U.S. dollars, it can choose which currency to exchange the euros for at the end of the various periods. Which currency appears to offer the better rates in the forward market?

Period Days Forward	C$ = €1.00	US$ = €1.00
spot	1.3360	1.3221
1 month 30	1.3368	1.3230
2 months 60	1.3376	1.3228
3 months 90	1.3382	1.3224
6 months 180	1.3406	1.3215
12 months 360	1.3462	1.3194

5.5 Japanese Yen Forward. Use the following spot and forward bid-ask rates for the Japanese yen/U.S. dollar (¥/$) exchange rate from September 16, 2010, to answer the following questions:

Period	¥=$1.00 Bid Rate	¥=$1.00 Ask Rate
spot	85.41	85.46
1 month	85.02	85.05
2 months	84.86	84.90
3 months	84.37	84.42
6 months	83.17	83.20
12 months	82.87	82.91
24 months	81.79	81.82

a. What is the mid-rate for each maturity?
b. What is the annual forward premium for all maturities?
c. Which maturities have the smallest and largest forward premiums?

5.6 Andreas Broszio (Geneva). Andreas Broszio just started as an analyst for Credit Suisse in Geneva, Switzerland. He receives the following quotes for Swiss francs (CHF) against the dollar (USD) for spot, 1 month forward, 3 months forward, and 6 months forward.

Spot exchange rate:

Bid rate CHF1.2575 = USD1.00

Ask rate CHF1.2585 = USD1.00

1 month forward 10 to 15

3 months forward 14 to 22

6 months forward 20 to 30

a. Calculate outright quotes for bid and ask and the number of points spread between each.
b. What do you notice about the spread as quotes evolve from spot toward 6 months?
c. What is the 6-month Swiss bill rate?

5.7 Swissie Triangular Arbitrage. The following exchange rates are available to you. (You can buy or sell at the stated rates.) Assume you have an initial SF12,000,000. Can you make a profit via triangular arbitrage? If so, show the steps and calculate the amount of profit in Swiss francs (Swissies).

Mt. Fuji Bank	¥92.00 = $1.00
Mt. Rushmore Bank	SF1.02 = $1.00
Mt. Blanc Bank	¥90.00 = SF1.00

5.8 Asian Pacific Crisis (1997). The Asian financial crisis that began in July 1997 wreaked havoc throughout the currency markets of East Asia.

Country and Currency	*July 1997 (currency per USD)*	*November 1997 (currency per USD)*
China yuan	8.40	8.40
Hong Kong dollar	7.75	7.73
Indonesia rupiah	2,400	3,600
Korea won	900	1,100
Malaysia ringgit	2.50	3.50
Philippine peso	27	34
Singapore dollar	1.43	1.60
Taiwan dollar	27.80	32.70
Thailand baht	25.0	40.0

a. Which of the currencies in the table had the largest depreciations or devaluations during the July to November period?
b. Which seemingly survived the first five months of the crisis with the least impact on their currencies?

5.9 Vienna Corporate Treasury. A corporate treasury working out of Vienna with operations in New York simultaneously calls Citibank in New York City and Barclays in London. The banks give the following quotes on the euro simultaneously.

Citibank NYC	Barclays London
Bid: USD0.7551 = EUR1.00	Bid: USD0.7545 = EUR1.00
Ask: USD0.7561 = EUR1.00	Ask: USD0.7575 = EUR1.00

Using USD5.5 million or its euro equivalent, show how the corporate treasury could make geographic arbitrage profit with the two different exchange rate quotes.

5.10 Bloomberg Cross Rates. Use the following table from Bloomberg to calculate each of the following:
a. Japanese yen per U.S. dollar?
b. U.S. dollars per Japanese yen?
c. U.S. dollars per euro?

Problem 5.10

Currency	USD	EUR	JPY	GBP	CHF	CAD	AUD	HKD
HKD	7.7736	10.2976	0.0928	12.2853	7.9165	7.6987	7.6584	
AUD	1.015	1.3446	0.0121	1.6042	1.0337	1.0053		0.1306
CAD	1.0097	1.3376	0.0121	1.5958	1.0283		0.9948	0.1299
CHF	0.9819	1.3008	0.0117	1.5519		0.9725	0.9674	0.1263
GBP	0.6328	0.8382	0.0076		0.6444	0.6267	0.6234	0.0814
JPY	83.735	110.9238		132.3348	85.2751	82.9281	82.4949	10.7718
EUR	0.7549		0.009	1.193	0.7688	0.7476	0.7437	0.0971
USD		1.3247	0.0119	1.5804	1.0184	0.9904	0.9852	0.1286

d. Euros per U.S. dollar?
e. Japanese yen per euro?
f. Euros per Japanese yen?
g. Canadian dollars per U.S. dollar?
h. U.S. dollars per Canadian dollar?
i. Australian dollars per U.S. dollar?
j. U.S. dollars per Australian dollar?
k. British pounds per U.S. dollar?
l. U.S. dollars per British pound?
m. U.S. dollars per Swiss franc?
n. Swiss francs per U.S. dollar?

5.11 Bid/Ask on U.S. Dollar to Euro Forwards. Use the following spot and forward bid-ask rates for the U.S. dollar/euro (USD = EUR1.00) from December 10, 2010, to answer the following questions:
a. What is the mid-rate for each maturity?
b. What is the annual forward premium for all maturities?
c. Which maturities have the smallest and largest forward premiums?

Period	Bid Rate	Ask Rate
spot	1.3231	1.3232
1 month	1.3230	1.3231
2 months	1.3228	1.3229
3 months	1.3224	1.3227
6 months	1.3215	1.3218
12 months	1.3194	1.3198
24 months	1.3147	1.3176

5.12 Bid/Ask **on Aussie Dollar Forward.** Use the following spot and forward bid-ask rates for the U.S. dollar to Australian dollar (USD = AUD1.00) exchange rate to answer the following questions:
a. What is the midrate for each maturity?
b. What is the annual forward premium for all maturities?
c. Which maturities have the smallest and largest forward premiums?

Period	Bid Rate	Ask Rate
spot	0.98510	0.98540
1 month	0.98131	0.98165
2 months	0.97745	0.97786
3 months	0.97397	0.97441
6 months	0.96241	0.96295
12 months	0.93960	0.94045
24 months	0.89770	0.89900

5.13 Venezuelan Bolivar (A). The Venezuelan government officially floated the Venezuelan bolivar (Bs) in February 2002. Within weeks, its value had moved from the pre-float fix of Bs778 = \$1.00 to Bs1,025 = \$1.00.
a. Is this a devaluation or a depreciation?
b. By what percentage did the value change?

5.14 Venezuelan Bolivar (B). The Venezuelan political and economic crisis deepened in late 2002 and early 2003. On January 1, 2003, the bolivar was trading at Bs1400 = \$1.00. By February 1, its value had fallen to Bs1950 = \$1.00. Many currency analysts and forecasters were predicting that the bolivar would fall an additional 40% from its February 1 value by early summer 2003.
a. What was the percentage change in January?
b. What is the forecast value for June 2003?

5.15 Indirect Forward Premium on the Dollar. Calculate the forward premium on the dollar (the dollar is the home currency) if the spot rate is €1.3300 = \$1.00 and the 3-month forward rate is €1.3400 = \$1.00.

5.16 Direct Forward Discount on the Dollar. Calculate the forward discount on the dollar (the dollar is the home currency) if the spot rate is \$1.5800 = £1.00 and the 6-month forward rate is \$1.5550 = £1.00.

5.17 Great Pyramids. Inspired by his recent trip to the Great Pyramids, Citibank trader Ruminder Dhillon wonders if he can make an intermarket arbitrage profit using Libyan dinars (LYD) and Saudi riyals (SAR). He has USD1,000,000 to work with so he gathers the following quotes. Is there an opportunity for an arbitrage profit?

Citibank quotes U.S. dollar per Libyan dinar	USD1.9324 = LYD1.00
National Bank of Kuwait quotes Saudi riyal per Libyan dinar	SAR1.9405 = LYD1.00
Barclay quotes U.S. dollar per Saudi riyal	USD0.2667 = SAR1.00

5.18 Mexican Peso–European Euro Cross Rate. Calculate the cross rate between the Mexican peso (Ps) and the euro (€) from the following spot rates: Ps12.45 = $1.00 and €0.7550 = $1.00.

5.19 Pura Vida. Calculate the cross rate between the Costa Rican colón (CRC) and the Canadian dollar (CAD) from the following spot rates: CRC500.29 = USD1.00 and CAD1.02 = USD1.00.

5.20 Around the Horn. Assuming the following quotes, calculate how a market trader at Citibank with $1,000,000 can make an intermarket arbitrage profit.

Citibank quotes U.S. dollar per pound	$1.5900 = £1.00
National Westminster quotes euros per pound	€1.2000 = £1.00
Deutschebank quotes U.S. dollar per euro	$0.7550 = €1.00

5.21 Bangkok Obligation. The Siam Cement Group of Bangkok borrowed EUR12.5 million for one year on February 14, 2020, short-term financing provided by a European customer. The interest rate was a low 6.500%. The problem, however, was that the exchange rate between the Thai baht (THB) and the euro (EUR) changed from THB33.860 = EUR1.00 on February 14, 2020 to THB36.327 = EUR1.00 on February 16, 2021, when the loan repayment was due. In the end, what was the interest rate paid by Siam Cement in its own currency, Thai baht?

6

International Parity Conditions

... if capital freely flowed towards those countries where it could be most profitably employed, there could be no difference in the rate of profit, and no other difference in the real or labour price of commodities, than the additional quantity of labour required to convey them to the various markets where they were to be sold.

—David Ricardo, *On the Principles of Political Economy and Taxation*, 1817, Chapter 7.

LEARNING OBJECTIVES

6.1 Examine how price levels and price level changes (inflation) in countries determine the exchange rates at which their currencies are traded

6.2 Show how interest rates reflect inflationary forces within each country and drive currency exchange rates

6.3 Explain how forward markets for currencies reflect expectations held by market participants about the future spot exchange rate

6.4 Analyze how, in equilibrium, the spot and forward currency markets are aligned with interest differentials and differentials in expected inflation

What are the determinants of exchange rates? Are changes in exchange rates predictable? Managers of MNEs, international portfolio investors, importers and exporters, and government officials must deal with these fundamental questions every day. This chapter describes the core financial theories surrounding the determination of exchange rates. Chapter 7 will demonstrate how these core elements are combined to create foreign currency derivatives, while Chapter 8 will introduce two other major theoretical schools of thought regarding currency valuation and then demonstrate how the three different theories are combined in a variety of real-world applications.

The economic theories that link exchange rates, price levels, and interest rates are called international parity conditions. In the eyes of many, international parity conditions form the core of the financial theory that is considered unique to the field of international finance. These theories do not always work out to be "true" when compared to what students and practitioners observe in the real world, but they are central to any understanding of how multinational business is conducted and funded in the world today. And, as is often the case, the mistake is not always in the theory itself, but in the way it is interpreted or applied in practice. This chapter concludes with the mini-case *Mrs. Watanabe and the Japanese Yen Carry Trade*, which demonstrates how both the theory and practice of international parity conditions sometimes combine to form unusual opportunities for profit—for those who are willing to bear the risk!

6.1 Prices and Exchange Rates

If identical products or services can be sold in two different markets and no restrictions exist on the sale or transportation of product between markets, the price should be the same in both markets. This is called the *law of one price*.

A primary principle of competitive markets is that prices will equalize across markets if frictions or costs of moving the products or services between markets do not exist. If a product is sold in two markets in two different countries, that product's price may be stated in different currency terms, but the price of the product should still be the same. Comparing prices would require only a conversion from one currency to the other. For example,

$$P^{\$} \times S^{¥=\$1.00} = P^{¥}$$

where the price of the product in U.S. dollars, $P^{\$}$, is multiplied by the spot exchange rate, $S^{¥=\$1.00}$ (yen per U.S. dollar), equals the price of the product in Japanese yen, $P^{¥}$. Conversely, if the prices of the two products were stated in local currencies and markets were efficient at competing away a higher price in one market relative to the other, the exchange rate could be deduced from the relative local product prices:

$$S^{¥=\$1.00} = \frac{P^{¥}}{P^{\$}}$$

Purchasing Power Parity and the Law of One Price

If the law of one price were true for all goods and services, the purchasing power parity (PPP) exchange rate could be found from any individual set of prices. By comparing the prices of identical products denominated in different currencies, one could determine the "real" or PPP exchange rate that should exist if markets were efficient. This is the absolute version of purchasing power parity. Absolute purchasing power parity states that the spot exchange rate is determined by the relative prices of similar baskets of goods.

The "Big Mac Index," as it has been christened by *The Economist* (see Exhibit 6.1) and calculated regularly since 1986, is a prime example of the law of one price. Assuming that the Big Mac is indeed identical in all countries listed, it serves as one form of comparison of whether currencies are currently trading at market rates that are close to the exchange rate implied by Big Macs in local currencies.

For example, using Exhibit 6.1, in China a Big Mac costs Yuan22.4 (local currency), while in the United States the same Big Mac costs \$5.66. The actual spot exchange rate was Yuan6.4751 = \$1.00 at this time. The price of a Big Mac in China in U.S. dollar terms was therefore:

$$\frac{\text{Price of Big Mac in China in Yuan}}{\text{Yuan} = \text{US\$1.00 spot rate}} = \frac{\text{Yuan 22.4}}{\text{Yuan 6.4751} = \text{US\$1.00}} = \text{US\$3.46}$$

This is the value in column 3 of Exhibit 6.1 for China. We then calculate the implied purchasing power parity rate of exchange using the actual price of the Big Mac in China (Yuan22.4) over the price of the Big Mac in the United States in U.S. dollars (US\$5.66):

$$\frac{\text{Price of Big Mac in China in Yuan}}{\text{Price of Big Mac in US in \$}} = \frac{\text{Yuan22.4}}{\text{US\$ 5.66}} = \text{or Yuan3.9576} = \text{US\$1.00}$$

This is the value in column 4 of Exhibit 6.1 for China. In principle, this is what the Big Mac Index is saying the exchange rate between the Yuan and the dollar should be according to the theory.

EXHIBIT 6.1 Selected Rates from the Bic Mac Index

Country	Currency	(1) Big Mac Price in Local Currency	(2) Actual Dollar Exchange Rate January 2021	(3) Big Mac Price in Dollars	(4) Implied PPP of the Dollar	(5) Under/ overvaluation against Dollar
United States	$	5.66	---------	5.66	---------	---------
Britain	£	3.29	1.3489*	4.44	1.7204*	−21.6%
Canada	C$	6.77	1.2803	5.29	1.1961	−6.6%
China	Yuan	22.4	6.4751*	3.46	3.9576*	−38.9%
Denmark	DK	30.0	6.1207	4.90	5.3004	−13.4%
Euro area	€	4.25	1.2151	5.16	1.3318	−8.8%
India	Rupee	190.0	73.390	2.59	33.569	−54.3%
Japan	¥	390	104.295	3.74	68.905	−33.9%
Mexico	Peso	54.0	20.1148	2.68	9.5406	−52.6%
Norway	kr	52.0	8.5439	6.09	9.1873	7.5%
Peru	Sol	11.9	3.6207	3.29	2.1025	−41.9%
Russia	Rouble	135.0	74.63	1.81	23.852	−68.0%
Singapore	S$	5.90	1.3308	4.43	1.0424	−21.7%
Thailand	Baht	128.0	30.1300	4.25	22.6148	−24.9%

Source: Data for columns (1) and (2) drawn from "The Big Mac Index Tells You about Currency Wars," *The Economist*, January 12, 2021.

Note:* These exchange rates are stated in US$ per unit of local currency, $ = £1.00 and $ = €1.00.

** Percentage under/overvaluation against the dollar is calculated as (Implied − Actual)/(Actual), except for the Britain and Euro area calculations, which are (Actual − Implied)/(Implied).

Now comparing this implied PPP rate of exchange, Yuan3.9576 = US$1.00, with the actual market rate of exchange at that time, Yuan6.4751 = US$1.00, the degree to which the yuan is either *undervalued* (−%) or *overvalued* (+%) versus the U.S. dollar is calculated as follows:

$$\frac{\text{Implied Rate} - \text{Actual Rate}}{\text{Actual Rate}} = \frac{\text{Yuan}3.9576 - \text{Yuan}6.4751}{\text{Yuan}6.4751} \approx -38.9\%$$

In this case, the Big Mac Index indicates that the Chinese yuan is undervalued by 38.9% versus the U.S. dollar as indicated in column 5 for China in Exhibit 6.1. *The Economist* is also quick to note that although this indicates a sizable undervaluation of the managed value of the Chinese yuan versus the dollar, the theory of purchasing power parity is supposed to indicate where the value of currencies should go over the long term and not necessarily its value today.

It is important to understand why the Big Mac may be a good candidate for the application of the law of one price and for the measurement of under- or overvaluation. First, the product itself is nearly identical in each market. This is the result of product consistency, process excellence, and McDonald's brand image and pride. Second, and just as important, the product is a result of predominantly local materials and input costs. This means that its price in each country is representative of domestic costs and prices and not imported ones, which would be influenced by exchange rates themselves.

The index, however, still possesses limitations. Big Macs cannot be traded across borders, and costs and prices are influenced by a variety of other factors in each country market, such as real estate rental rates and taxes. That said, the prominence and weight the Big Mac Index has had globally is undeniable, as illustrated by *Global Finance in Practice 6.1.*

A less extreme form of this principle asserts that in relatively efficient markets, the price of a basket of goods—rather than a single product—would be the same in each market. Replacing the price of a single product with a price index allows the PPP exchange rate between two countries to be stated as

$$S = \frac{PI^{¥}}{PI^{\$}}$$

where $PI^{¥}$ and $PI^{\$}$ are price indices expressed in local currency for Japan and the United States, respectively. For example, if the identical basket of goods cost ¥1,000 in Japan and $10 in the United States, the PPP exchange rate would be

$$\frac{¥100}{\$10} \text{ or } ¥100 = \text{US}\$1.00$$

Relative Purchasing Power Parity

If the assumptions of the absolute version of PPP theory are relaxed a bit, we observe what is termed *relative purchasing power parity. Relative PPP* holds that PPP is not particularly helpful in determining what the spot rate is today, but that the relative change in prices between two countries over a period of time determines the change in the exchange rate over that period. More specifically:

> *If the spot exchange rate between two countries starts in equilibrium, any change in the differential rate of inflation between them tends to be offset over the long run by an equal but opposite change in the spot exchange rate.*

GLOBAL FINANCE IN PRACTICE 6.1

Lies, Damn Lies, and Statistics: Big Mac Prices in Argentina

Many countries have struggled with high rates of inflation over history. Once inflation has become imbedded in the expectations of society, and possibly institutionalized through automatic price index-based price increases, it is very hard to stop. One of the most common anti-inflation measures used by governments is price controls, where a government agency sets prices for most products in order to prevent (hopefully) prices from rising. The United States used price controls in the 1970s when it was struggling with high rates of inflation. The detail of price controls in the U.S. reached new depths, with the U.S. government setting the price of everything, all the way down to the price of pickles (dill, gherkin, etc.).

The Argentine government led by President Cristina Fernández de Kirchner in 2012 was another such government struggling with inflation. The government had taken a number of steps to both try and control the rate of inflation (for example by setting price controls and limiting wage rate increases), to pressuring businesses to restrict the prices of products and services. One such product price restriction was placed on the Big Mac.

Unofficially—at least no one in the Argentine government or in McDonald's restaurants in Argentina would admit it—the government had seemingly influenced the restaurant chain to restrict the price of the Big Mac. The Big Mac was singled out among all menu offerings because it is included in the *Economist* magazine's semi-annual calculation of the *Big Mac Index*, the popularized measure of purchasing power parity (PPP) and relative prices across the world. When an Angus Tasty was 35 pesos ($8.24 at the official exchange rate of ARG4.245 = 1 USD), a Doble Cuarto de Libra con Queso was 33 pesos ($7.77), and the Big Mac, often only listed at the very bottom of the restaurant menu, was 20 pesos ($4.71). The Big Mac was still on the menu, but with a much lower price, and was not a menu item pushed by the restaurant chain.

The logic behind the application of PPP to changes in the spot exchange rate is that if a country experiences inflation rates higher than those of its main trading partners, and its exchange rate does not change, its exports of goods and services become less competitive with comparable products produced elsewhere. Imports from abroad become more price-competitive with higher-priced domestic products. These price changes lead to a deficit on the current account in the balance of payments unless offset by capital and financial flows.

Empirical Tests of Purchasing Power Parity

There has been extensive testing of both the absolute and relative versions of purchasing power parity and the law of one price. These tests have, for the most part, not proved PPP to be accurate in predicting future exchange rates. Goods and services do not in reality move at zero cost between countries, and in fact many services are not "tradable," for example, for haircuts. Many goods and services are not of the same quality across countries, reflecting differences in the tastes and resources of the countries of their manufacture and consumption.

Two general conclusions can be made from these tests: (1) PPP holds up well over the very long run but poorly for shorter time periods, and (2) the theory holds better for countries with relatively high rates of inflation and underdeveloped capital markets.

Exchange Rate Indices: Real and Nominal

Because any single country trades with numerous partners, we need to track and evaluate its individual currency value against all other currency values in order to determine relative purchasing power. The objective is to discover whether a country's exchange rate is "overvalued" or "undervalued" in terms of PPP. One of the primary methods of dealing with this problem is the calculation of *exchange rate indices*. These indices are formed through trade—by weighting the bilateral exchange rates between the home country and its trading partners.

The *nominal effective exchange rate index* uses actual exchange rates to create an index, on a weighted average basis, of the value of the subject currency over time. It does not really indicate anything about the "true value" of the currency or anything related to PPP. The nominal index simply calculates how the currency value relates to some arbitrarily chosen base period, but it is used in the formation of the *real effective exchange rate index*. The *real effective exchange rate index* indicates how the weighted average purchasing power of the currency has changed relative to some arbitrarily selected base period. Exhibit 6.2 plots the real effective exchange rate indexes for Japan, the euro area, and the U.S. for the 1980–2021 period.

The real effective exchange rate index for the U.S. dollar, $E_R^{\$}$, is found by multiplying the nominal effective exchange rate index, $E_N^{\$}$, by the ratio of U.S. dollar costs, $C^{\$}$, over foreign currency costs, C^{FC}, both in index form:

$$E_R^{\$} = E_N^{\$} \times \frac{C^{\$}}{C^{FC}}$$

If changes in exchange rates just offset differential inflation rates—if purchasing power parity *holds*—all the real effective exchange rate indices would stay at 100. If an exchange rate strengthened more than was justified by differential inflation, its index would rise above 100. If the real effective exchange rate index were above 100, the currency would be considered "overvalued" from a competitive perspective, and vice versa.

Exhibit 6.2 shows how the real effective exchange rate of the U.S. dollar, Japanese yen, and the European euro have changed over the past 40 years. The dollar's index value was substantially above 100 in the early 1980s (overvalued), falling below 100 during the 1988–1996 period (undervalued), then rising far above 100 since 2014. While the euro has not strayed far from "proper valuation" since 2009, the Japanese yen has bounced from undervalued to

EXHIBIT 6.2 Real Effective Exchange Rate Indexes (base year 2010 = 100)

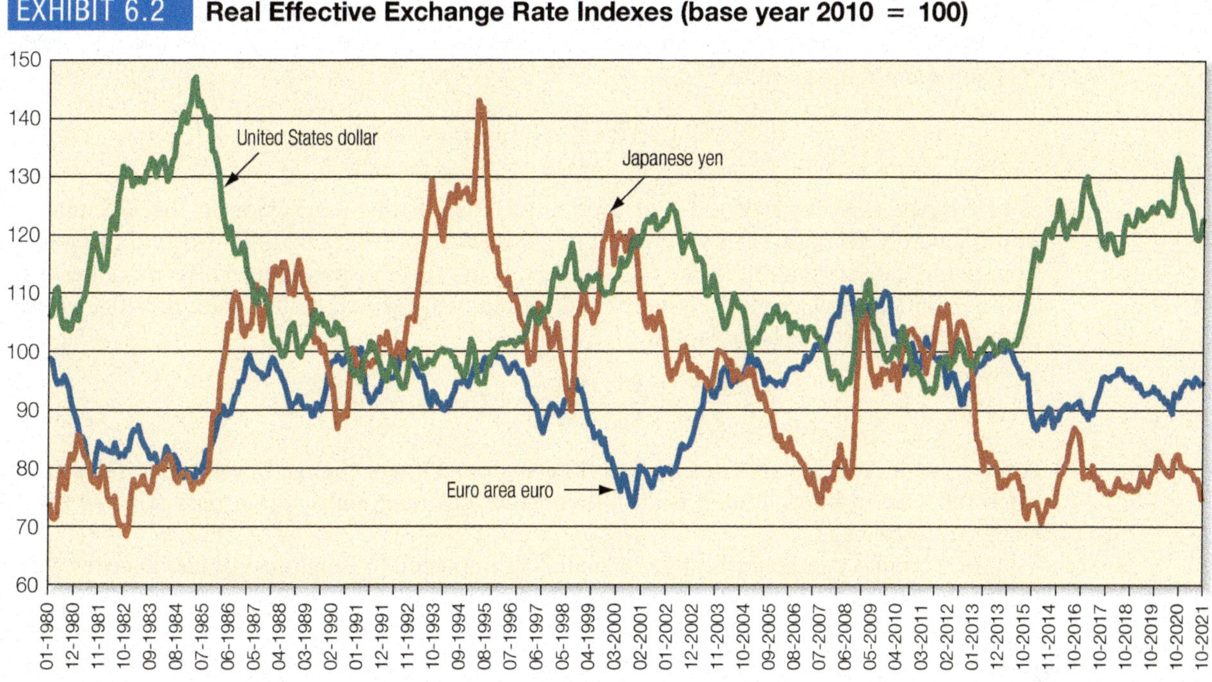

Source: Bank International Settlements, www.bis.orgistatistics/eer/. BIS effective exchange rate (EER), real (CPI-based), narrow indices, monthly averages, January 1980–March 2021.

overvalued to undervalued again over the past decade. Apart from measuring deviations from PPP, a country's real effective exchange rate is an important tool for management when predicting upward or downward pressure on a country's balance of payments and exchange rate, as well as an indicator of whether producing for export in that country could be competitive.

Exchange Rate Pass-Through

Exchange rate pass-through is a measure of the response of imported and exported product prices to changes in exchange rates. When that pass-through is partial, meaning the full percentage change in the exchange rate is not reflected in prices, a country's real effective exchange rate index can deviate from its PPP equilibrium level of 100. Although PPP implies that all exchange rate changes are passed through by equivalent changes in prices to trading partners, empirical research in the years following the growth in floating-rate currencies questioned this long-held assumption.

Complete versus Partial Pass-Through. To illustrate exchange rate pass-through, assume that Volvo produces an automobile in Belgium and pays all production expenses in euros. The price of this specific model is €50,000. When the firm exports the auto to the United States, the price of the Volvo in the U.S. market should simply be the euro value converted to U.S. dollars at the spot exchange rate:

$$P^{\$}_{\text{Volvo}} = P^{€}_{\text{Volvo}} \times S^{\$=€1.00}$$

where $P_{\text{Volvo}^{\$}}$ is the Volvo price in dollars, $P_{\text{Volvo}^{€}}$ is the Volvo price in euros, and $S^{\$=€1.00}$ is the spot exchange rate in number of dollars per euro. If the euro were to appreciate 20% versus the U.S. dollar—from \$1.00 = €1.00 to \$1.20 = €1.00 the price of the Volvo in the U.S.

market should theoretically rise to $60,000. If the price in dollars increases by the same percentage change as the exchange rate, then there has been complete pass-through (or 100%) of changes in exchange rates.

$$\frac{P^{\$}_{\text{Volvo},2}}{P^{\$}_{\text{Volvo},1}} = \frac{\$60{,}000}{\$50{,}000} = 1.20 \text{ or a } 20\% \text{ increase}$$

However, if Volvo worried that a price increase of this magnitude in the U.S. market would severely decrease sales volumes, it might work to prevent the dollar price of this model from rising the full amount in the U.S. market. If the price of this same Volvo model rose to only $58,000 in the U.S. market, the percentage increase would be less than the 20% appreciation of the euro versus the dollar.

$$\frac{P^{\$}_{\text{Volvo},2}}{P^{\$}_{\text{Volvo},1}} = \frac{\$58{,}000}{\$50{,}000} = 1.16 \text{ or a } 16\% \text{ increase}$$

If the price in U.S. dollars rises by less than the percentage change in exchange rates (as is often the case in international trade), then there has been only *partial pass-through* of exchange rate changes.

For example, components and raw materials imported to Belgium cost less in euros when the euro appreciates versus the currency of foreign suppliers. It is also likely that some time may pass before all exchange rate changes are finally reflected in the prices of traded goods, including the period over which previously signed contracts are delivered upon. It is obviously in the interest of Volvo to do what it can to prevent appreciation of the euro from raising the price of its automobiles in major export markets.

Price Elasticity of Demand. The concept of price elasticity of demand is useful when determining the desired degree of pass-through. Recall that the *price elasticity of demand* for any good is the percentage change in quantity of the good demanded as a result of the percentage change in the good's price:

$$\text{Price elasticity of demand} = \varepsilon_p = \frac{\%\Delta Q_d}{\%\Delta P}$$

where Q_d is quantity demanded and P is product price. If the absolute value of ε_p is less than 1.0, then the good is relatively "inelastic." If ε_p is greater than 1.0, the good is relatively "elastic."

A Belgian product that is relatively *price-inelastic*—meaning that the quantity demanded is relatively unresponsive to price changes—may often demonstrate a high degree of passthrough. This is because a higher dollar price in the United States market would have little noticeable effect on the quantity of the product demanded by consumers. Dollar revenue would increase, but euro revenue would remain the same. However, products that are relatively price-elastic would respond in the opposite way. If the 20% euro appreciation resulted in 20% higher dollar prices, U.S. consumers would decrease the number of Volvos purchased. If the price elasticity of demand for Volvos in the United States were greater than one, total dollar sales revenue of Volvos would decline.

Pass-Through and Emerging Market Currencies. A number of emerging market countries have chosen in recent years to change their objectives and choices, as described in the impossible trinity (introduced and detailed previously in Chapter 2). These countries have shifted from choosing a pegged exchange rate and independent monetary policy over the free flow of capital (point A in Exhibit 6.3) to policies allowing more capital flows at the expense of a pegged or fixed exchange rate (toward point C in Exhibit 6.3).

EXHIBIT 6.3 **Pass-Through, the Impossible Trinity, and Emerging Markets**

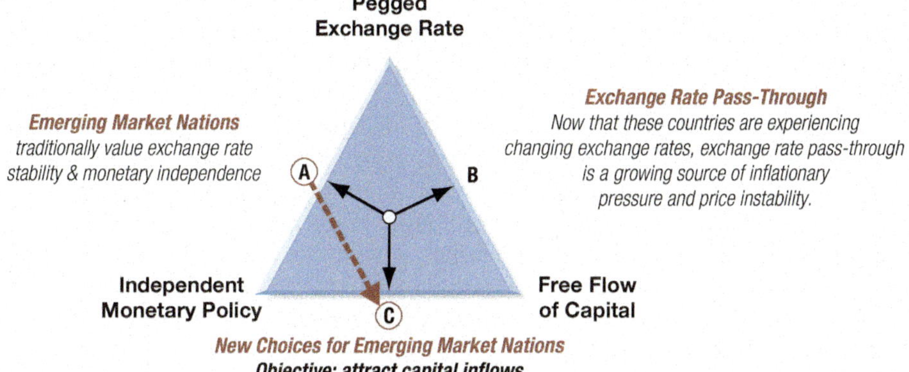

Many emerging market countries have chosen to move from Point A to Point C, exchanging fixed exchange rates for the chance of attracting capital inflows. The result is that these countries are now the subject to varying levels of exchange rate pass-through.

This change in focus has also now introduced exchange rate pass-through as an issue in these same emerging markets. With changing exchange rates and increased trade and financial product movements in and out of these countries, prices are changing. Although price volatility alone is a source of growing concern, price changes contributing to inflationary pressure is even more unsettling. The root cause of these problems lies not with choices made by the emerging market nations but rather with the interest rate choices made by the major industrial countries with which they trade.

Since 2009, all the major industrial country currency markets—the dollar, the euro, the yen—have been characterized by extremely low interest rates, as concerns over economic growth and employment have dominated. Select emerging market countries have then experienced appreciating currencies in some cases (because their interest rates are higher than industrial country currencies). Those exchange rate changes have led to exchange rate pass-through of imported products—rising prices—contributing to inflationary pressures.

6.2 Interest Rates and Exchange Rates

We have already seen how prices of goods in different countries should be related through exchange rates. We now consider how interest rates are linked to exchange rates.

The Fisher Effect

The *Fisher effect*, named after economist Irving Fisher, states that nominal interest rates in each country are equal to the required real rate of return plus compensation for expected inflation. More formally, this is derived from $(1 + r)(1 + \pi) - 1$ as

$$i = r + \pi + r\pi$$

where i is the nominal rate of interest, r is the real rate of interest, and π is the expected rate of inflation over the period of time for which funds are to be lent. The final compound term, $r\pi$ is frequently dropped from consideration due to its relatively minor value. The Fisher effect then reduces to (approximate form):

$$i = r + \pi$$

The Fisher effect applied to the United States and Japan would be as follows:

$$i^{\$} = r^{\$} + \pi^{\$}; i^{¥} = r^{¥} + \pi^{¥}$$

where the superscripts \$ and ¥ pertain to the respective nominal (i), real (r), and expected inflation (π) components of financial instruments denominated in dollars and yen, respectively.

We need to forecast the future rate of inflation, not what inflation has been. Predicting the future is, well, difficult. Empirical tests using ex post national inflation rates have shown that the Fisher effect usually exists for short-maturity government securities, such as Treasury bills and notes. Comparisons based on longer maturities suffer from the increased financial risk inherent in fluctuations of the market value of the bonds prior to maturity. Comparisons of private sector securities are influenced by unequal creditworthiness of the issuers. All the tests are inconclusive to the extent that recent past rates of inflation are not a correct measure of future expected inflation.

The International Fisher Effect

The relationship between the percentage change in the spot exchange rate over time and the differential between comparable interest rates in different national capital markets is known as the *international Fisher effect*. *Fisher-open*, as it is often termed, states that the spot exchange rate should change in an equal amount but in the opposite direction to the difference in interest rates between two countries. More formally,

$$\frac{S_1 - S_2}{S_2} \times 100 = i^{\$} - i^{¥}$$

where $i^{\$}$ and $i^{¥}$ are the respective national interest rates, and S is the spot exchange rate using indirect quotes (an indirect quote on the dollar is, for example, ¥ = \$1.00) at the beginning of the period (S_1) and the end of the period (S_2). This is the approximation form commonly used in industry. The precise formulation is as follows:

$$\frac{S_1 - S_2}{S_2} = \frac{i^{\$} - i^{¥}}{1 + i^{¥}}$$

Justification for the international Fisher effect is that investors must be rewarded or penalized to offset the expected change in exchange rates. For example, if a dollar-based investor buys a 10-year yen bond earning 4% interest, instead of a 10-year dollar bond earning 6% interest, the investor must be expecting the yen to appreciate vis-à-vis the dollar by at least 2% per year during the 10 years. If not, the dollar-based investor would be better off remaining in dollars. If the yen appreciates 3% during the 10-year period, the dollar-based investor would earn a bonus of 1% higher return. However, the international Fisher effect predicts that, with unrestricted capital flows, an investor should be indifferent to whether his bond is in dollars or yen, because investors worldwide would see the same opportunity and compete it away.

Empirical tests lend some support to the relationship postulated by the international Fisher effect, although considerable short-run deviations occur. A more serious criticism has been posed, however, by recent studies that suggest the existence of a foreign exchange risk premium for some major currencies. Also, speculation in uncovered interest arbitrage creates distortions in currency markets. Thus, the expected change in exchange rates might consistently be greater than the difference in interest rates. *Global Finance in Practice 6.2* explores a key dimension of international Fisher, the distinction between high inflation and high real rates of interest in attracting capital.

GLOBAL FINANCE IN PRACTICE 6.2

When Do Higher Interest Rates Attract or Not Attract Capital?

One of the biggest challenges faced by governments and central banks historically is how to balance economic growth, inflationary forces and expectations, and the "right" value of their currency. And one of the biggest challenges for students of international finance is to understand when high interest rates attract capital—and when they do not.

For example, the United States in the late 1970s suffered from very high rates of inflation. Inflation had persisted for much of the decade and had embedded itself in the minds and expectations of all. (The U.S. government had even tried price controls.) Those inflationary expectations were also embedded in interest rates, and interest rates were high as a result, the expected inflation component of the Fisher equation, $i = r + \pi$.

Appointed chairman of the Federal Reserve in 1979, Paul Volker immediately undertook a drastic program to rid the U.S. of its inflation habit once and for all. (Volker had written his undergraduate senior thesis at Princeton on how U.S. monetary policy in the post–World War II era had led to overly high rates of inflation and what needed to be done—restrict money supply growth.) Under his leadership, the Fed restricted the growth of the U.S. money supply, driving interest rates up even further.

The policy did indeed squeeze inflationary forces out of the U.S. economy but also drove the U.S. economy into a short but severe recession in 1981–1982 (the unemployment rate reaching a high of 10.8% at one point in 1982). But for the first time in many years, inflationary fires were extinguished. U.S. interest rates remained high for an extended period, but it was the real rate of interest, r, not π, that was holding them up. And those high real rates of interest attracted capital inflows for years, driving the value of the dollar up on world markets. It was the r that attracted capital, not the π. The stronger dollar and renewed economic growth also initiated a trade deficit beginning in 1982, something the U.S. had not historically possessed.

Many countries over time have faced similar challenges. The problem, however, is that the removal of inflation from the economy has to come at a cost. That cost, slow or negative economic growth, unemployment, and their commensurate lower levels of civil income, is often too large for an elected government to bear. Few central banks are as truly independent as the U.S. Federal Reserve, allowing them to have the political independence needed to implement such a difficult and painful treatment for inflation.

The Forward Rate

A forward rate (or outright forward as described in Chapter 5) is an exchange rate quoted today for settlement at some future date. A forward exchange agreement between currencies states the rate of exchange at which a foreign currency will be "bought forward" or "sold forward" at a specific date in the future (typically after 30, 60, 90, 180, 270, or 360 days).

The forward rate is calculated for any specific maturity by adjusting the current spot exchange rate by the ratio of euro currency interest rates of the same maturity for the two subject currencies. For example, the 90-day forward rate for the Swiss franc/U.S. dollar exchange rate ($F^{S=/\$}{}_{90}$) is found by multiplying the current spot rate ($S^{SF=\$}$) by the ratio of the 90-day euro-Swiss franc deposit rate (i^{SF}) over the 90-day eurodollar deposit rate:

$$F_{90}^{SF=\$} = S^{SF=\$} \times \frac{\left[1 + \left(i^{SF} \times \frac{90}{360}\right)\right]}{\left[1 + \left(i^{\$} \times \frac{90}{360}\right)\right]}$$

Assuming a spot rate of SF1.4800 = \$1.00, a 90-day euro Swiss franc deposit rate of 4.00% per annum, and a 90-day eurodollar deposit rate of 8.00% per annum, the 90-day forward rate is SF1.4655 = \$1.00:

$$F_{90}^{SF=\$} = \text{SF}1.4800 \times \frac{\left[1 + \left(.0400 \times \frac{90}{360}\right)\right]}{\left[1 + \left(.0800 \times \frac{90}{360}\right)\right]} = \text{SF}1.4800 \times \frac{1.01}{1.02} = \text{SF}1.4655$$

The *forward premium* or discount, *f*, is the percentage difference between the spot and forward exchange rate, stated in annual percentage terms. When the foreign currency price of the home currency is used, as in this case of SF = \$, the formula for the percent-per-annum forward premium or discount on the Swiss franc, f^{SF}, becomes:

$$f^{SF} = \frac{\text{Spot} - \text{Forward}}{\text{Forward}} \times \frac{360}{\text{days}} \times 100$$

Substituting the SF = \$ spot and forward rates, as well as the number of days forward (90),

$$f^{SF} = \frac{\text{SF}1.4800 - \text{SF}1.4655}{\text{SF}1.4655} \times \frac{360}{90} \times 100 = +3.96\%\,\text{per annum}$$

The sign is positive, indicating that the Swiss franc is selling forward at a 3.96% per annum premium over the dollar. (It takes 3.96% more dollars to get a franc at the 90-day forward rate.)

As illustrated in Exhibit 6.4, the forward premium on the eurodollar forward arises from the differential between eurodollar and Swiss franc interest rates. Because the forward rate for any particular maturity utilizes the specific interest rates for that term, the forward premium or discount on a currency is visually obvious—the currency with the higher interest rate (in this case the U.S. dollar)—will sell forward at a discount, and the currency with the lower interest rate (here the Swiss franc) will sell forward at a premium.

The forward rate is calculated from three observable data items—the spot rate, the foreign currency deposit rate, and the home currency deposit rate—and is not a forecast of the future spot exchange. However, the forward rate is frequently used as a forecast by managers, yielding mixed results, as the following section describes.

Calculation of Forward Premiums

The percent per annum deviation of the forward from the spot rate is termed the *forward premium*. However, as with the calculation of percentage changes in spot rates, the forward premium—which may be either a positive (a premium) or negative value (a discount)—depends

EXHIBIT 6.4 Currency Yield Curves and the Forward Premium

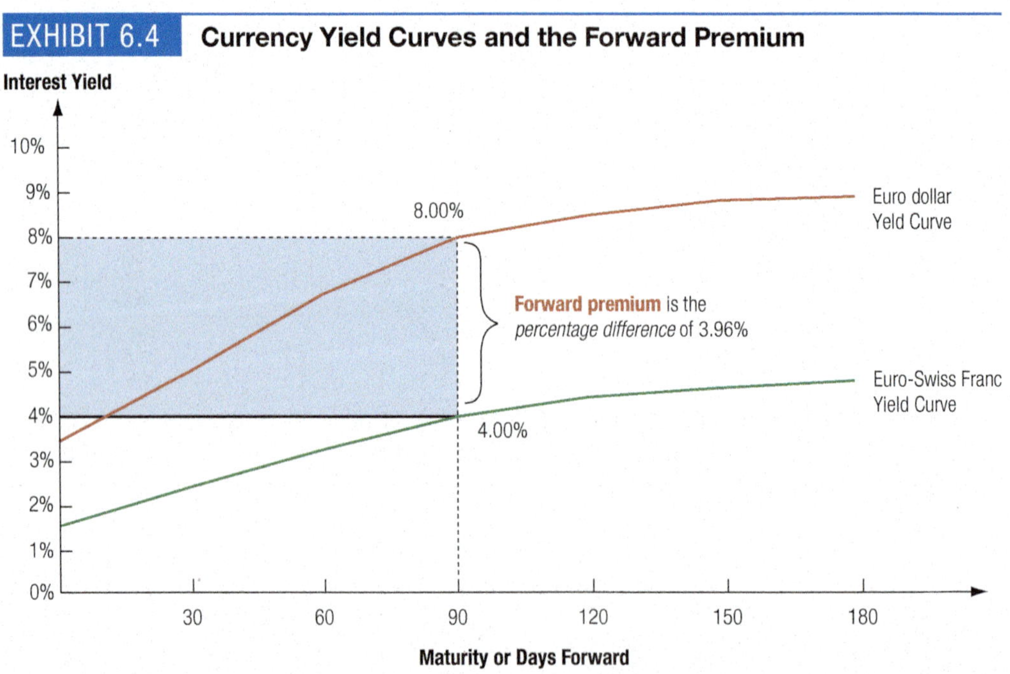

upon the designated home (or base) currency. Assume the following spot rate for our discussion of foreign currency terms and home currency terms.

	Foreign currency (price)/ home currency (unit)	Home currency (price)/ foreign currency (unit)
Spot rate	¥118.27 = $1.00	$0.0084552 = ¥1.00
3-month forward	¥116.84 = $1.00	$0.0085587 = ¥1.00

Foreign Currency Terms. Using the foreign currency as the price of the home currency (the unit), JPY/USD spot and forward rates, and 90 days forward, the forward premium on the yen, f^{JPY}, is calculated as follows:

$$f^{\text{JPY}} = \frac{\text{Spot} - \text{Forward}}{\text{Forward}} \times \frac{360}{90} \times 100 = \frac{118.27 - 116.84}{116.84} \times \frac{360}{90} \times 100 = +4.90\%$$

The sign is positive indicating that the Japanese yen is selling forward at a premium of 4.90% against the U.S. dollar.

Forward rates have been a pillar of multinational financial management for 50 years. Their rates or values, however, have structurally changed—fallen—as short-term money market interest rates have trended downward over time. That trend, described in *Global Finance in Practice 6.3*, continues.

Interest Rate Parity (IRP)

The theory of interest rate parity (IRP) provides the link between the foreign exchange markets and the international money markets. The theory states:

> *The difference in the national interest rates for securities of similar risk and maturity should be equal to, but opposite in sign to, the forward rate discount or premium for the foreign currency, except for transaction costs.*

Exhibit 6.5 shows how the theory of IRP works. Assume that an investor has $1,000,000 and several alternative but comparable Swiss franc (SF) monetary investments. If the investor

EXHIBIT 6.5 **Interest Rate Parity (IRP)**

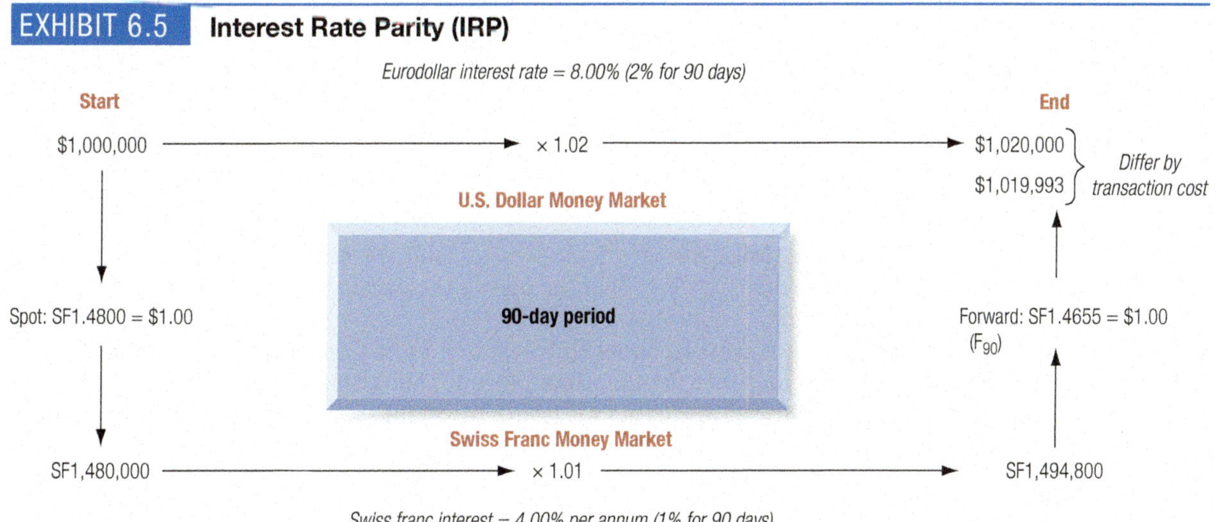

GLOBAL FINANCE IN PRACTICE 6.3

Global Money Market Interest Rates, 1986–2021

The price of money has clearly gotten cheaper over the past four decades. The most commonly used reference rate of interest for bank loans and financial derivatives, the 3-month London Interbank Offered Rate or LIBOR, has clearly trended down for three of the world's largest business-based currencies, the U.S. dollar, British pound sterling, and Japanese yen.

The drivers of change in the levels of these three major currency money rates lie with the Fisher effect ($i = r + \pi$). First, major economies like those of the United Kingdom and United States suffered and then rid themselves of inflationary forces, the π. The source of that inflation was primarily that of political economy—economic stimulus in the pursuit of full employment. Those same concerns gave birth to the next downward drive in interest rates, the fall to near-zero in the real return to capital, r, in the aftermath of the global financial crisis of 2008–2010. And just when interest rates started to claw their way up from zero, the global pandemic of 2020 forced governments to open up the monetary spigots once more.

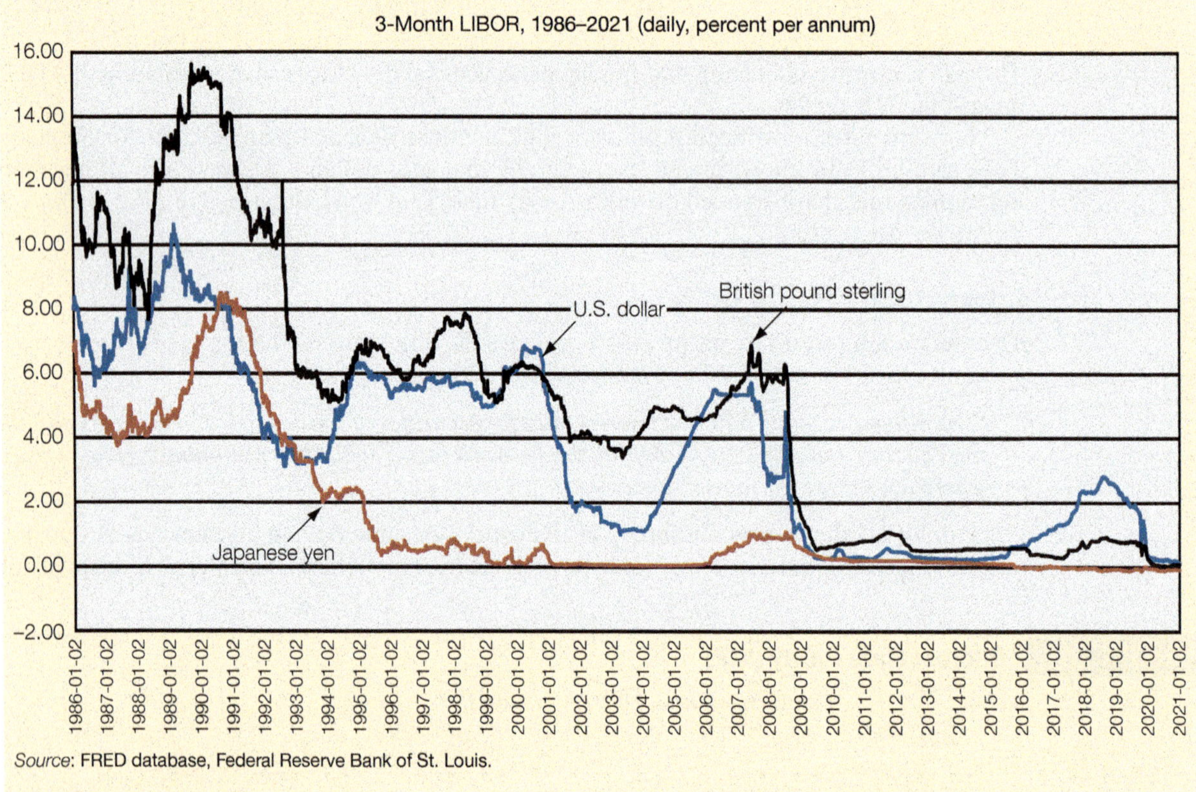

Source: FRED database, Federal Reserve Bank of St. Louis.

chooses to invest in a dollar money market instrument, the investor would earn the dollar rate of interest. This results in $(1 + i^{\$})$ at the end of the period, where $i^{\$}$ is the dollar rate of interest in decimal form.

The investor may, however, choose to invest in a Swiss franc money market instrument of identical risk and maturity for the same period. This action would require that the investor exchange the dollars for francs at the spot rate, invest the francs in a money market instrument, sell the francs forward (in order to avoid any risk that the exchange rate would change), and at the end of the period convert the resulting proceeds back to dollars. A dollar-based investor would evaluate the relative returns of starting in the top-left corner and investing in the dollar market (straight across the top of the box) compared to corner. The comparison of returns would be as follows:

$$(1 + i^{\$}) = S^{SF=\$} \times (1 + i^{SF}) \times \frac{1}{F^{SF=\$}}$$

where S is the spot rate of exchange and F is the forward rate. Substituting in the spot rate (SF1.4800 = \$1.00) and forward rate (SF1.4655 = \$1.00) and respective interest rates from Exhibit 6.5, the *interest rate parity condition* is

$$(1 + .02) = 1.4800 \times (1 + .01) \times \frac{1}{1.4655}$$

The left-hand side of the equation is the gross return the investor would earn by investing in dollars. The right-hand side is the gross return the investor would earn by exchanging dollars for Swiss francs at the spot rate, investing the franc proceeds in the Swiss franc money market, and simultaneously selling the principal plus interest in Swiss francs forward for dollars at the current 90-day forward rate.

Ignoring transaction costs, if the returns in dollars are equal between the two alternative money market investments, the spot and forward rates are considered to be at IRP. The transaction is covered, because the exchange rate back to dollars is guaranteed at the end of the 90-day period. Therefore, as shown in Exhibit 6.6, in order for the two alternatives to be equal, any differences in interest rates must be offset by the difference between the spot and forward exchange rates (in approximate form):

$$\frac{F}{S} = \frac{(1 + i^{SF})}{(1 + i^{\$})}, \text{ or } \frac{\text{SF}1.4655}{\text{SF}1.4800} = \frac{1.01}{1.02} = 0.9902 \approx 1\%$$

Covered Interest Arbitrage (CIA)

The spot and forward exchange markets are not constantly in the state of equilibrium described by interest rate parity. When the market is not in equilibrium, the potential for "riskless" or arbitrage profit exists. The arbitrager who recognizes such an imbalance will move to take advantage of the disequilibrium by investing in the currency offering the higher return on a covered basis. This is called *covered interest arbitrage* (CIA).

Exhibit 6.6 describes the steps that a currency trader, most likely working in the arbitrage division of a large international bank, would implement to perform a CIA transaction. The currency trader, Fye Hong, may utilize any of a number of major eurocurrencies that his bank holds to conduct arbitrage investments. The morning conditions indicate to Fye Hong that a CIA transaction that exchanges U.S.\$1 million for Japanese yen, invested in a six-month euroyen account and sold forward back to dollars, will yield a profit of \$4,638 (\$1,044,638 – \$1,040,000) over and above the profit available from a euro dollar investment. Conditions in the exchange markets and euromarkets change rapidly however, so if Fye Hong waits even a few minutes, the profit opportunity may disappear.

Fye Hong now executes the following transaction:

EXHIBIT 6.6 **Covered Interest Arbitrage (CIA)**

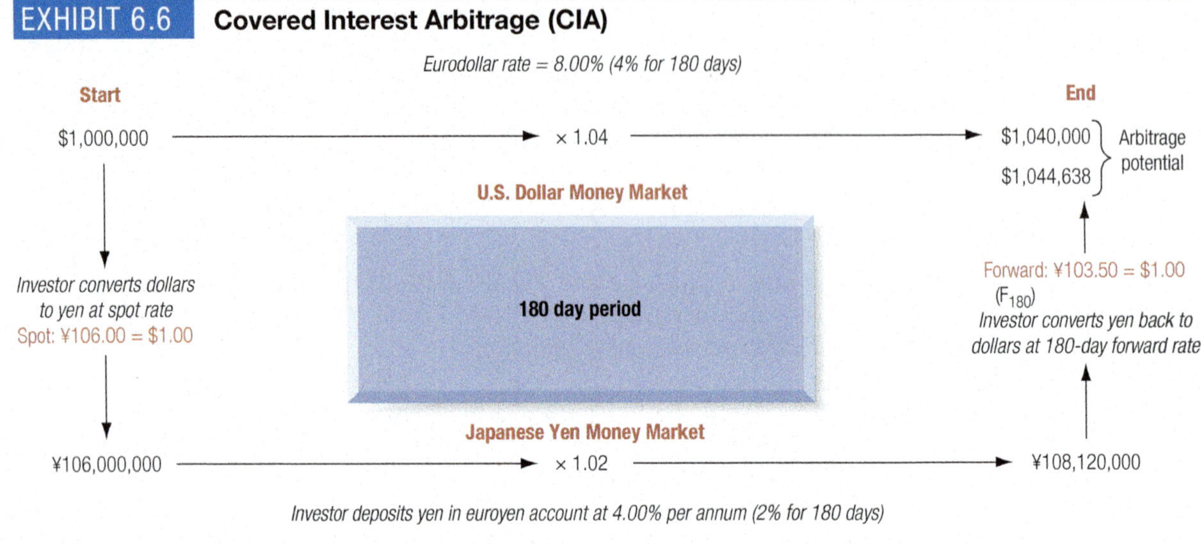

Step 1: Convert $1,000,000 at the spot rate of ¥106.00 = $1.00 to ¥106,000,000 (see "Start" in Exhibit 6.6).

Step 2: Invest the proceeds, ¥106,000,000, in a euroyen account for six months, earning 4.00% per annum, or 2% for 180 days.

Step 3: Simultaneously sell the future yen proceeds (¥108,120,000) forward for dollars at the 180-day forward rate of ¥103.50 = $1.00. This action "locks in" gross dollar revenues of $1,044,638 (see "End" in Exhibit 6.6).

Step 4: Calculate the cost (opportunity cost) of funds used at the eurodollar rate of 8.00% per annum, or 4% for 180 days, with principal and interest then totaling $1,040,000. Profit on CIA ("End") is $4,638 ($1,044,638 − $1,040,000).

Note that all profits are stated in terms of the currency in which the transaction was initialized, but that a trader may conduct investments denominated in U.S. dollars, Japanese yen, or any other major currency. All that is required to make a covered interest arbitrage profit is for interest rate parity not to hold. Depending on the relative interest rates and forward premium, Fye Hong would have started in Japanese yen, invested in U.S. dollars, and sold the dollars forward for yen. The profit would then end up denominated in yen. But how would Fye Hong decide in which direction to go around the box in Exhibit 6.6?

Rule of Thumb. The key to determining whether to start in dollars or yen is to compare the differences in interest rates to the forward premium on the yen (the "cost of cover"). For example, in Exhibit 6.6, the difference in 180-day interest rates is 2.00% (dollar interest rates are higher by 2.00%). The premium on the yen for 180 days forward is as follows:

$$f^{¥} = \frac{\text{Spot} - \text{Forward}}{\text{Forward}} \times \frac{360}{180} \times 100 = \frac{¥106.00 - ¥103.50}{¥103.50} \times 200 = 4.8309\%$$

In other words, by investing in yen and selling the yen proceeds forward at the forward rate, Fye Hong earns more on the combined interest rate arbitrage and forward premium than if he continues to invest in dollars.

Arbitrage Rule of Thumb: *If the difference in interest rates is greater than the forward premium (or expected change in the spot rate), invest in the higher interest yielding currency. If the difference in interest rates is less than the forward premium (or expected change in the spot rate), invest in the lower interest yielding currency.*

Using this rule of thumb should enable Fye Hong to choose in which direction to go around the box in Exhibit 6.6. It also guarantees that he will always make a profit if he goes in the right direction. This rule assumes that the profit is greater than any transaction costs incurred. This process of CIA drives the international currency and money markets toward the equilibrium described by interest rate parity. Slight deviations from equilibrium provide opportunities for arbitragers to make small riskless profits. Such deviations provide the supply and demand forces that will move the market back toward parity (equilibrium).

Covered interest arbitrage opportunities continue until interest rate parity is reestablished, because the arbitragers are able to earn risk-free profits by repeating the cycle as often as possible. Their actions, however, nudge the foreign exchange and money markets back toward equilibrium for the following reasons:

1. The purchase of yen in the spot market and the sale of yen in the forward market narrows the premium on the forward yen. This is because the spot yen strengthens from the extra demand and the forward yen weakens because of the extra sales. A narrower premium on the forward yen reduces the foreign exchange gain previously captured by investing in yen.
2. The demand for yen-denominated securities causes yen interest rates to fall, and the higher level of borrowing in the U.S. causes dollar interest rates to rise. The net result is a wider interest differential in favor of investing in the dollar.

Uncovered Interest Arbitrage (UIA)

A deviation from covered interest arbitrage is *uncovered interest arbitrage* (UIA), wherein investors borrow in countries and currencies exhibiting relatively low interest rates and convert the proceeds into currencies that offer much higher interest rates. The transaction is "uncovered," because the investor does not sell the higher yielding currency proceeds forward, choosing to remain uncovered and accept the currency risk of exchanging the higher yield currency into the lower yielding currency at the end of the period. Exhibit 6.7 demonstrates the steps an uncovered interest arbitrager takes when undertaking what is called the "yen carry trade."

The "yen carry trade" is an age-old application of UIA. Investors, from both inside and outside Japan, take advantage of extremely low interest rates in Japanese yen (0.40% per annum) to raise capital. Investors exchange the capital they raise for other currencies like U.S. dollars or euros. Then they reinvest these dollar or euro proceeds in dollar or euro money markets where the funds earn substantially higher rates of return (5.00% per annum in Exhibit 6.7). At the end of the period—a year, in this case—they convert the dollar proceeds back into yen in the spot market. The result is a tidy profit over what it costs to repay the loan.

The trick, however, is that the spot exchange rate at the end of the year must not change significantly from what it was at the beginning of the year. If the yen were to appreciate significantly against the dollar, as it did in late 1999, moving from ¥120 = $1.00 to ¥105 = $1.00, these "uncovered" investors would suffer sizable losses when they convert their dollars into yen to repay the yen they borrowed. Higher return at higher risk. The mini-case at the end of this chapter details one of the most frequent carry trade structures, the Australian dollar/Japanese yen cross rate.

EXHIBIT 6.7 **Uncovered Interest Arbitrage (UIA): The Yen Carry Trade**

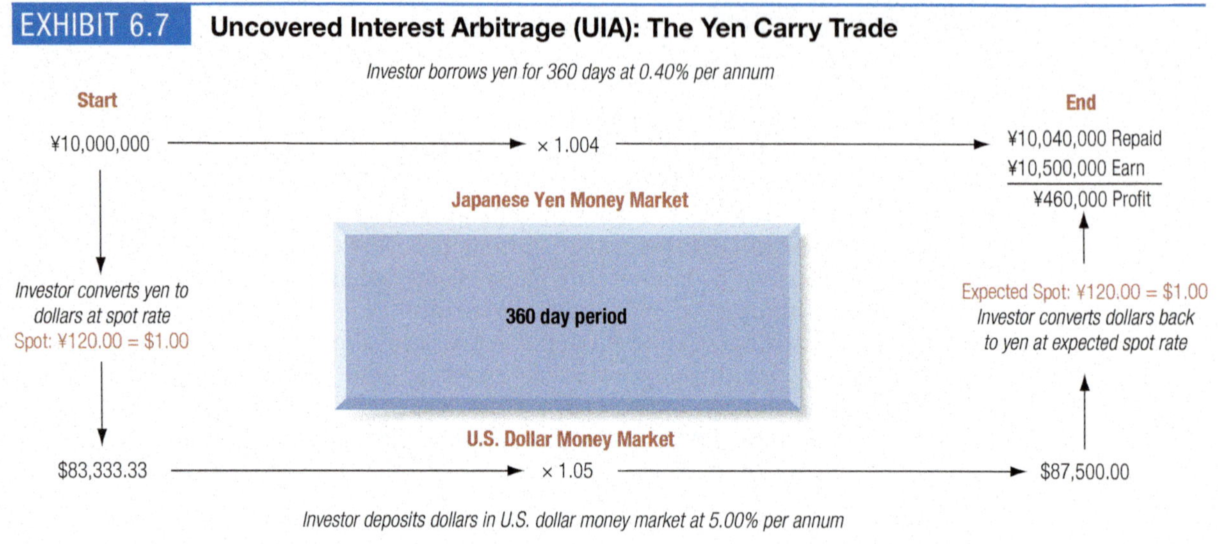

Equilibrium between Interest Rates and Exchange Rates

Exhibit 6.8 illustrates the conditions necessary for equilibrium between interest rates and exchange rates. The vertical axis shows the difference in interest rates in favor of the foreign currency, and the horizontal axis shows the forward premium or discount on that currency. The interest rate parity line shows the equilibrium state, but transaction costs cause the line to be a band rather than a thin line.

Since 2009, all the major industrial country currency markets—the dollar, the euro, the yen—have been characterized by extremely low interest rates, as concerns over economic growth and employment have dominated. Select emerging market countries have then experienced appreciating currencies in some cases (because their interest rates are higher than industrial country currencies). Those exchange rate changes have led to exchange rate passthrough of imported products—rising prices—contributing to inflationary pressures.

Transaction costs arise from foreign exchange and investment brokerage costs on buying and selling securities. Typical transaction costs in recent years have been in the range of 0.18% to 0.25% on an annual basis. For individual transactions, like Fye Hong's covered interest arbitrage (CIA) activities illustrated in Exhibit 6.7, there is no explicit transaction cost per trade; rather, the costs of the bank in supporting Fye Hong's activities are the transaction costs. Point X in Exhibit 6.8 shows one possible equilibrium position, where a 4% lower rate of interest on yen securities would be offset by a 4% premium on the forward yen.

The disequilibrium situation, which encouraged the interest rate arbitrage in the previous CIA example of Exhibit 6.6, is illustrated in Exhibit 6.8 by point U. Point U is located off the interest rate parity line because the lower interest on the yen is 4% (annual basis), whereas the premium on the forward yen is slightly over 4.8% (annual basis). Using the formula for forward premium presented earlier, we calculate the forward premium on the Japanese yen as follows:

$$\frac{¥106.00 - ¥103.50}{¥103.50} \times \frac{360\,\text{days}}{180\,\text{days}} \times 100 = 4.83\%$$

The situation depicted by point U is unstable, because all investors have an incentive to execute the same covered interest arbitrage. Except for a bank failure, the arbitrage gain is virtually risk-free.

EXHIBIT 6.8 Interest Rate Parity and Equilibrium

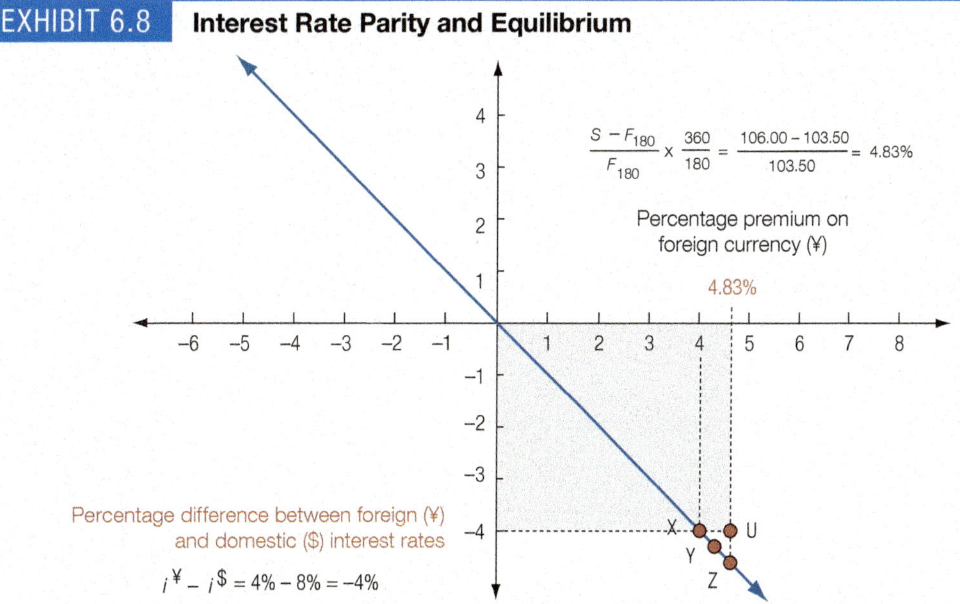

If market interest rates were at point U, covered interest arbitrage profits are available and would be undertaken until the market drove interest rate differences back to point X, Y, or Z.

Some observers have suggested that political risk does exist, because one of the governments might apply capital controls that would prevent execution of the forward contract. This risk is fairly remote for covered interest arbitrage between major financial centers of the world, especially because a large portion of funds used for CIA is in eurodollars. The concern may be valid for pairings with countries not noted for political and fiscal stability.

The net result of the disequilibrium is that fund flows will narrow the gap in interest rates and/or decrease the premium on the forward yen. In other words, market pressures will cause point U in Exhibit 6.8 to move toward the interest rate parity band. Equilibrium might be reached at point Y or at any other locus between X and Z, depending on whether forward market premiums are more or less easily shifted than interest rate differentials.

Uncovered interest arbitrage takes many forms in global financial markets today, and opportunities do exist for those who are willing to bear the risk (and potentially pay the price). *Global Finance in Practice 6.4* describes one such speculation, foreign-currency home mortgages in Hungary, which, as described, can turn an innocent homeowner into a foreign currency speculator.

6.3 Forward Rate as an Unbiased Predictor of the Future Spot Rate

Some forecasters believe that foreign exchange markets for the major floating currencies are "efficient" and forward exchange rates are unbiased predictors of future spot exchange rates.

Exhibit 6.9 demonstrates the meaning of "unbiased prediction" in terms of how the forward rate performs in estimating future spot exchange rates. If the forward rate is an unbiased predictor of the future spot rate, the expected value of the future spot rate at time 2 equals the present forward rate for time 2 delivery, available now, $E_1(S_2) = F_{1,2}$.

GLOBAL FINANCE IN PRACTICE 6.4

Hungarian Mortgage

No one has learned the linkage between interest rates and currencies better than Hungarian homeowners. Given the choice of taking mortgages in local currency (Hungarian forint) or foreign currency (Swiss francs for example), many chose francs because the interest rates were lower. Regardless of the actual interest rate itself, the fall in the value of the forint against the franc by more than 40% resulted in radically increasing mortgage debt service payments. These borrowers are now trying to have their own mortgages declared "unconstitutional" in order to get out from under their rising debt burdens.

Hungarian Forint (HUF) = Swiss Francs (CHF) 1.00 (monthly, January 2000–January 2014)

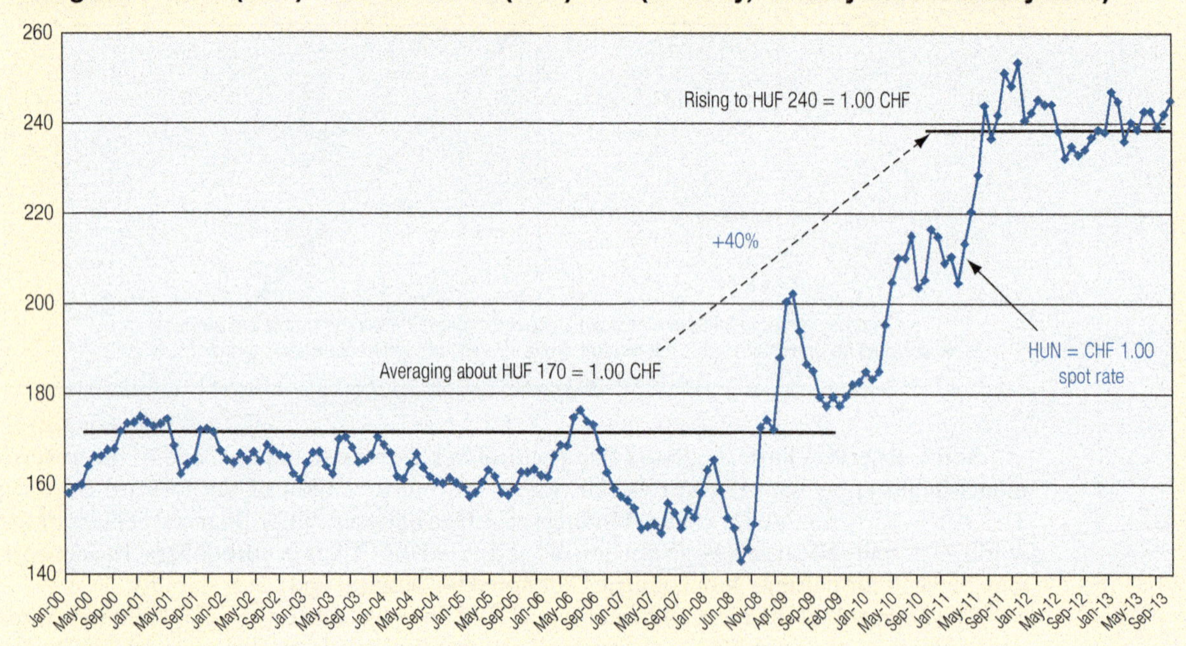

EXHIBIT 6.9 Forward Rate as an Unbiased Predictor of Future Spot

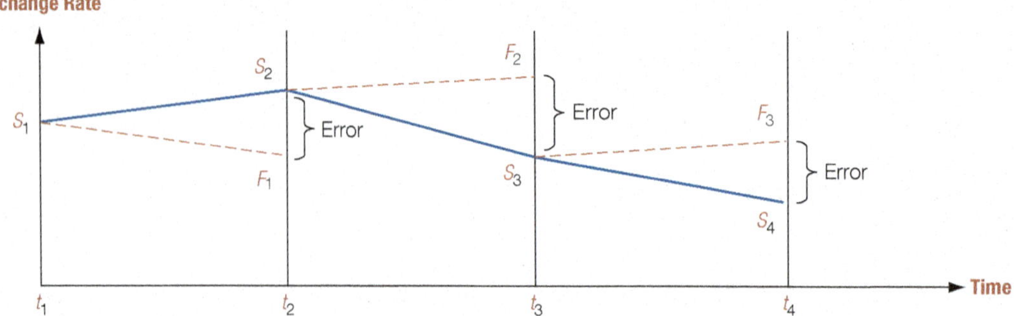

The forward rate available "today" (F_t) for delivery at a future time ($t + 1$) is used as a forecast or *predictor* of the spot rate at time $t + 1$. The difference between the spot rate which then occurs and the forward rate is the forecast error. When the forward rate is termed an "unbiased predictor of the future spot rate," it means that the errors are normally distributed around the mean future spot rate (the sum of the errors equals zero).

Intuitively, this means that the distribution of possible actual spot rates in the future is centered on the forward rate. The fact that it is an unbiased predictor, however, does not mean that the future spot rate will actually be equal to what the forward rate predicts. Unbiased prediction simply means that the forward rate will, on average, overestimate and underestimate the actual future spot rate in equal frequency and degree. The forward rate may, in fact, never actually equal the future spot rate. The rationale for this relationship is based on the hypothesis that the foreign exchange market is reasonably efficient. Market efficiency assumes that (1) all relevant information is quickly reflected in both the spot and forward exchange markets, (2) transaction costs are low, and (3) instruments denominated in different currencies are perfect substitutes for one another.

Empirical studies of the efficient foreign exchange market hypothesis have yielded conflicting results. Nevertheless, a consensus is developing that rejects the efficient market hypothesis. It appears that the forward rate is not an unbiased predictor of the future spot rate and that it does pay to use resources to attempt to forecast exchange rates.

If the efficient market hypothesis is correct, a financial executive cannot expect to profit in any consistent manner from forecasting future exchange rates, because current quotations in the forward market reflect all that is presently known about likely future rates. Although future exchange rates may well differ from the expectation implicit in the present forward market quotation, we cannot know today in which way actual future quotations will differ from today's forward rate. The expected mean value of deviations is zero. The forward rate is therefore an "unbiased" estimator of the future spot rate.

Tests of foreign exchange market efficiency, using longer time periods of analysis, conclude that either exchange market efficiency is untestable or, if it is testable, that the market is not efficient. Furthermore, the existence and success of foreign exchange forecasting services suggest that managers are willing to pay a price for forecast information even though they can use the forward rate as a forecast at no cost. The "cost" of buying this information is, in many circumstances, an "insurance premium" for financial managers who might get fired for using their own forecast, including forward rates, when that forecast proves incorrect. If they "bought" professional advice that turned out wrong, the fault was not in their forecast!

If the exchange market is not efficient, it is sensible for a firm to spend resources on forecasting exchange rates. This is the opposite conclusion to the one in which exchange markets are deemed efficient.

6.4 Prices, Interest Rates, and Exchange Rates in Equilibrium

Exhibit 6.10 illustrates all of the fundamental parity relations simultaneously, in equilibrium, using the U.S. dollar and the Japanese yen. The forecasted inflation rates for Japan and the United States are 1% and 5%, respectively—a 4% differential. The nominal interest rate in the U.S. dollar market (1-year government security) is 8%—a differential of 4% over the Japanese nominal interest rate of 4%. The spot rate is ¥104 = $1.00, and the 1-year forward rate is ¥100 = $1.00.

Relation A: Purchasing Power Parity (PPP). According to the relative version of purchasing power parity, the spot exchange rate one year from now, S_2, is expected to be ¥100 = $1.00:

$$S_2 = S_1 \times \frac{1 + \pi^{¥}}{1 + \pi^{\$}} = ¥104 \times \frac{1.01}{1.05} = ¥100$$

This is a 4% change and equal but opposite in sign to the difference in expected rates of inflation (1% – 5%, or 4%).

EXHIBIT 6.10 **International Parity Conditions in Equilibrium**

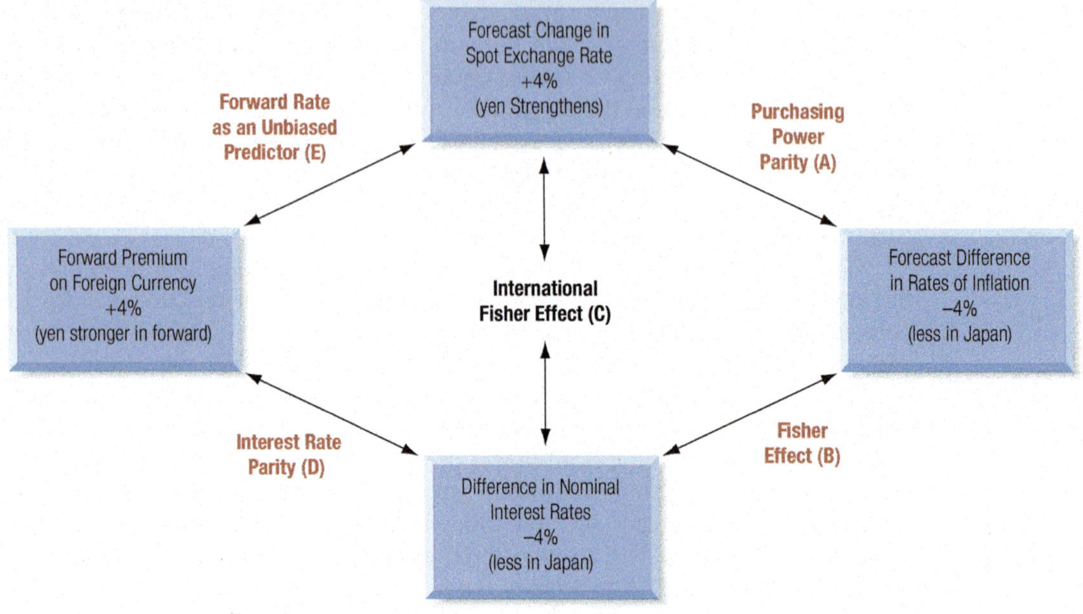

Note: The presentation is in the approximate form.

Relation B: The Fisher Effect. The real rate of return is the nominal rate of interest less the expected rate of inflation. Assuming efficient and open markets, the real rates of return should be equal across currencies.

Here, the real rate is 3% in U.S. dollar markets ($r = i - \pi = 8\% - 5\%$) and in Japanese yen markets ($4\% - 1\%$). Note that the 3% real rate of return is not in Exhibit 6.10, but rather the Fisher effect's relationship—that nominal interest rate differentials equal the difference in expected rates of inflation, −4%.

Relation C: International Fisher Effect. The forecast change in the spot exchange rate, in this case 4%, is equal to but opposite in sign to the differential between nominal interest rates:

$$\frac{S_1 - S_2}{S_2} \times 100 = i^{¥} - i^{\$} = -4\%$$

Relation D: Interest Rate Parity (IRP). According to the theory of IRP the difference in nominal interest rates is equal to, but opposite in sign to, the forward premium. For this numerical example, the nominal yen interest rate (4%) is 4% less than the nominal dollar interest rate (8%):

$$i^{¥} - i^{\$} = 4\% - 8\% = -4\%$$

and the forward premium, $f^{¥}$, is a positive 4%:

$$f^{¥} = \frac{S_1 - F}{F} \times 100 = \frac{¥104 - ¥100}{¥100} \times 100 = 4\%$$

Relation E: Forward Rate as an Unbiased Predictor. Finally, the 1-year forward rate on the Japanese yen, F, if assumed to be an unbiased predictor of the future spot rate, also forecasts ¥100 = \$1.00.

Summary Points

- Parity conditions have traditionally been used by economists to help explain the long-run trend in an exchange rate.
- Under conditions of freely floating rates, the expected rate of change in the spot exchange rate, differential rates of national inflation and interest, and the forward discount or premium are all directly proportional to each other and mutually determined. A change in one of these variables has a tendency to change all of them with a feedback on the variable that changes first.
- If the identical product or service can be sold in two different markets, and there are no restrictions on its sale or transportation costs of moving the product between markets, the product's price should be the same in both markets. This is called the law of one price.
- The absolute version of purchasing power parity states that the spot exchange rate is determined by the relative prices of similar baskets of goods.
- The relative version of purchasing power parity states that if the spot exchange rate between two countries starts in equilibrium, any change in the differential rate of inflation between them tends to be offset over the long run by an equal but opposite change in the spot exchange rate.
- The Fisher effect, named after economist Irving Fisher, states that nominal interest rates in each country are equal to the required real rate of return plus compensation for expected inflation.
- The international Fisher effect, "Fisher-open" as it is often termed, states that the spot exchange rate should change in an equal amount, but in the opposite direction, as the difference in interest rates between two countries.
- The theory of interest rate parity (IRP) states that the difference in the national interest rates for securities of similar risk and maturity should be equal to, but opposite in sign to, the forward rate discount or premium for the foreign currency, except for transaction costs.
- When the spot and forward exchange markets are not in equilibrium, as described by interest rate parity, the potential for riskless or arbitrage profit exists. This is called covered interest arbitrage (CIA).
- Some forecasters believe that for the major floating currencies, foreign exchange markets are "efficient" and forward exchange rates are unbiased predictors of future spot exchange rates.

MINI-CASE

Mrs. Watanabe and the Japanese Yen Carry Trade[1]

> *At more than ¥1,500,000bn (some $16,800bn), these savings are considered the world's biggest pool of investable wealth. Most of it is stashed in ordinary Japanese bank accounts; a surprisingly large amount is kept at home in cash, in tansu savings, named for the traditional wooden cupboards in which people store their possessions. But from the early 2000s, the housewives—often referred to collectively as "Mrs. Watanabe," a common Japanese surname—began to hunt for higher returns.* —"Shopping, Cooking, Cleaning, Playing the Yen Carry Trade," *Financial Times*, February 21, 2009.

Over the past 20 years, Japanese yen interest rates have remained extremely low by global standards. For years the monetary authorities at the Bank of Japan have worked tirelessly fighting equity market collapses and deflationary forces, keeping yen-denominated interests rates hovering at around 1% per annum or lower. Combined with a sophisticated financial industry of size and depth, these low interest rates have spawned an international financial speculation termed the yen carry trade.

In the textbooks, this trading strategy is categorized more formally, as uncovered interest arbitrage (UIA). It is a fairly simple speculative position: borrow money where it is cheap and invest it in a different currency market with higher interest returns. The only real trick is to time the market correctly so that when the currency in the high-yield market is converted back to the original currency, the exchange rate has either stayed the same or moved in favor of the speculator. "In favor of" means that the high-yielding currency has strengthened against the borrowed currency. But as Shakespeare noted, "Ay, there's the rub."

[1] This case was prepared by Professor Michael Moffett for the purpose of classroom discussion only, and not to indicate either effective or ineffective management.

Yen Availability

But why the focus on Japan? Aren't there other major currency markets in which interest rates are periodically low? Japan and the Japanese yen turn out to have a number of uniquely attractive characteristics to investors and speculators pursuing carry trade activities.

First, Japan has consistently demonstrated for decades one of the world's highest savings rates. This means that an enormous pool of funds has accumulated in the hands of private savers, savers who are traditionally very conservative. Those funds, whether stuffed in the mattress or placed in savings accounts, earn little in return. (In fact, given the extremely low interest rates offered, there is little effective difference between the mattress and the bank.)

A second factor facilitating the yen carry trade is the sheer size and sophistication of the Japanese financial sector. Not only is the Japanese economy one of the largest industrial economies in the world, it is one that has grown and developed with a strong international component. One only has to consider the size and global reach of Toyota or Sony to understand the established and developed infrastructure surrounding business and international finance in Japan. Japanese banking, however, has been continuously in search of new and diverse investments with which to balance the often despondent domestic economy. It therefore sought out foreign investors and foreign borrowers who are attractive customers. MNEs have found ready access to yen-denominated debt for years—debt, which is, once again, available at extremely low interest.

A third expediter of the yen carry trade is the value of the Japanese yen itself. The yen has long been considered the most international of Asian currencies, and is widely traded. It has, however, also been exceedingly volatile over time. But it is not volatility alone, as volatility itself could undermine interest arbitrage overnight. The key has been in the relatively long trends in value change of the yen against other major currencies like the U.S. dollar, or as in the following example, the Australian dollar.

Australian Dollar/Japanese Yen Exchange Rate

Exhibit A illustrates the movement of the Japanese yen/Australian dollar exchange rate over a 13-year period, from 2000 through 2013. This spot rate movement and long-running periodic trends have offered a number of extended periods in which interest arbitrage was highly profitable. The two periods of Aussie dollar appreciation are clear after the fact. During those periods, an investor who was short yen and long Aussie dollars (and enjoying relatively higher Aussie dollar interest) could and did enjoy substantial returns.

But what about shorter holding periods—say, a year—in which the speculator does not have a crystal ball

EXHIBIT A The Trending JPY and AUD Spot Rate

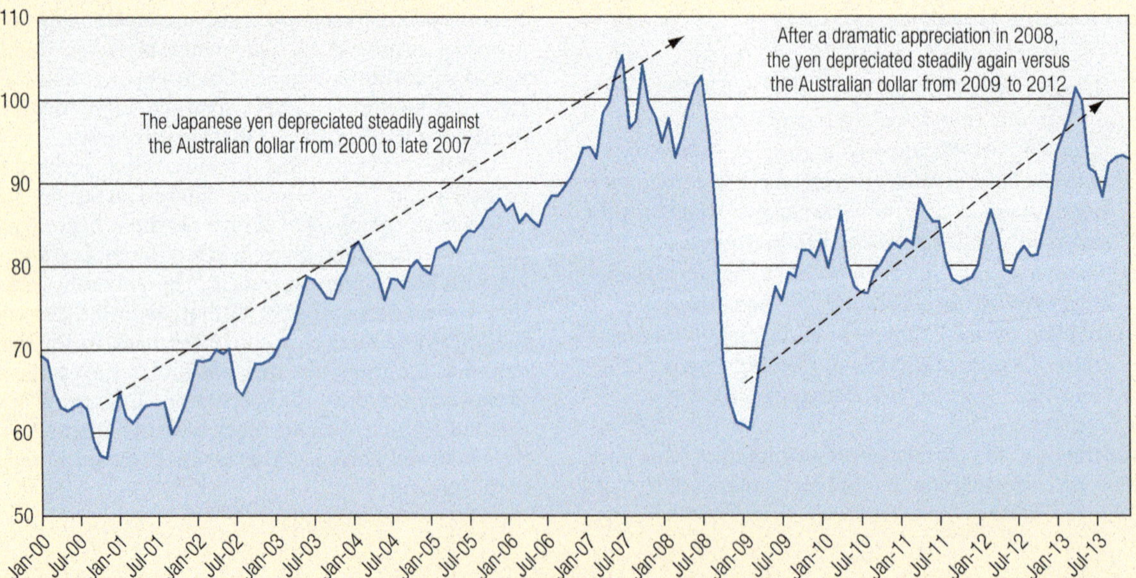

over the long-term trend of the spot rate but only a guess? Consider the one-year speculation detailed in Exhibit B. An investor looking at the exchange rate in January 2009 (Exhibit A) would see a yen that had reached a recent historical "low"—a strong position against the Aussie dollar. Betting that the yen would likely bounce, weakening once again against the Aussie dollar, she could borrow JPY50 million at 1.00% interest per annum for one year. She could then exchange the JPY50 million for Australian dollars at JPY60.91 = AUD1.00, and then deposit the AUD820,883 proceeds for one year at the Australian interest rate of 4.50% per annum. The investor could also have rationalized that even if the exchange rate did not change, she would earn a 3.50% per annum interest differential.

As it turned out, the spot exchange rate one year later, in January 2010, saw a much weaker yen against the Aussie dollar, JPY83.19 = AUD1.00. The one-year Aussie-Yen carry trade position would then have earned a very healthy profit of JPY20,862,296.83 on a one-year investment of JPY50,000,000, a 41.7% rate of return.

Post 2009 Financial Crisis. The global financial crisis of 2008–2009 has left a marketplace in which the U.S. Federal Reserve and the European Central Bank (ECB) have pursued easy money policies. Both central banks, in an effort to maintain high levels of liquidity and to support fragile commercial banking systems, have kept interest rates at near-zero levels. Now global investors who see opportunities for profit in an anemic global economy are using those same low-cost funds in the U.S. and Europe to fund uncovered interest arbitrage activities. But what is making this "emerging market carry trade" so unique is not the interest rates, but the fact that investors are shorting two of the world's core currencies: the dollar and the euro.

Consider the strategy outlined in Exhibit C—a Euro-Indian rupee carry trade. An investor borrows EUR20 million at an incredibly low rate (again, because of ECB strategy to stimulate the sluggish European economy), say 1.00% per annum or 0.50% for 180 days. The EUR20 million are then exchanged for Indian rupees (INR), the current spot rate at the start of 2012 being a dramatic low of of INR67.4 = EUR1.00. The resulting INR1,348,000,000 are put into an interest-bearing deposit with any of a number of Indian banks attempting to attract capital. The rate of interest offered, 2.50% (1.25% for 180 days), is not particularly high, but is greater than that available in the dollar, euro, or even yen markets. The account value at the end of 180 days, INR1,364,850,000, is then returned to euros at the spot rate of INR68.00 = EUR1.00, but at a loss. Although the rupee had not moved much, it had moved enough to eliminate the arbitrage profits.

Carry trade activity is often described in the global press as if it is easy or riskless profit. It is not. As in the case of the euro-rupee just described, the combination of interest rates and exchange rates is subject to a volatile global marketplace which does indeed have a lot of moving parts. An accurate crystal ball will always prove quite useful.

EXHIBIT B The Aussie–Yen Carry Trade

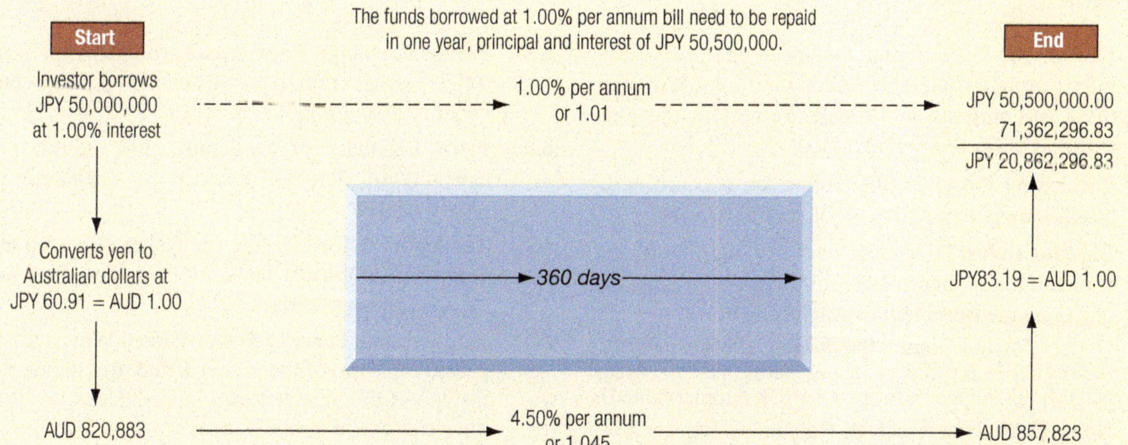

The Australian dollars are then invested at the higher Australian dollar interest rate of 4.50% per annum for one year. The result, principal, and interest of AUD 857,823, are then converted back to Japanese yen at the current spot rate. With luck, talent, or both, the result is profitable.

EXHIBIT C **The Euro–Rupee Carry Trade**

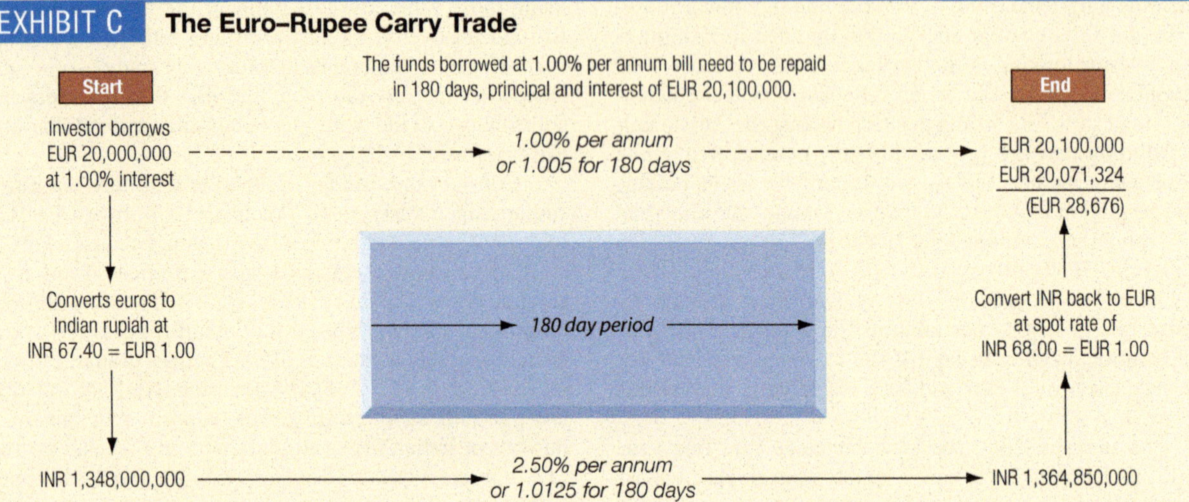

The Indian rupees are invested at 2.50% per annum, 1.25% for 180 days. The result, principal, and interest of INR1,364,850,000, are converted back to euros at the spot rate in the market in 180 days of INR68.00 = EUR1.00. Unfortunately, the small movement in the spot rate has eliminated the interest arbitrage profits.

MINI-CASE QUESTIONS

1. Why are interest rates so low in the traditional core markets of USD and EUR?
2. What makes this "emerging market carry trade" so different from traditional forms of uncovered interest arbitrage?
3. Why are many investors shorting the dollar and the euro?

Questions

6.1 Law of One Price. Define the law of one price carefully, noting its fundamental assumptions. Why are these assumptions so difficult to apply in the real world in order to apply the theory?

6.2 Purchasing Power Parity. Define the two forms of purchasing power parity, absolute and relative.

6.3 Big Mac Index. How close does the Big Mac Index conform to the theoretical requirements for a law of one price measurement of purchasing power parity?

6.4 Undervaluation and Purchasing Power Parity. According to the theory of purchasing power parity, what should happen to a currency that is undervalued?

6.5 Nominal Effective Exchange Rate Index. Explain how a nominal effective exchange rate index is constructed.

6.6 Real Effective Exchange Rate Index. What formula is used to convert a nominal effective exchange rate index into a real effective exchange rate index?

6.7 Exchange Rate Pass-Through. What is exchange rate pass-through?

6.8 Partial Exchange Rate Pass-Through. What is partial exchange rate pass-through, and how can it occur in efficient global markets?

6.9 Price Elasticity of Demand. How is the price elasticity of demand relevant to exchange rate pass-through?

6.10 The Fisher Effect. Define the Fisher effect. To what extent do empirical tests confirm that the Fisher effect exists in practice?

6.11 Approximate Form of Fisher Effect. Why is the approximate form of the Fisher Effect frequently used instead of the precise formulation? Does this introduce significant analysis error?

6.12 The International Fisher Effect. Define the international Fisher effect. To what extent do empirical tests confirm that the international Fisher effect exists in practice?

6.13 Interest Rate Parity. Define interest rate parity. What is the relationship between interest rate parity and forward rates?

6.14 Covered Interest Arbitrage. Define the terms covered interest arbitrage and uncovered interest arbitrage. What is the difference between these two transactions?

6.15 Uncovered Interest Arbitrage. Explain what expectations an investor or speculator would need to undertake an uncovered interest arbitrage investment?

6.16 Forward Rate Calculation. If someone you were working with argued that the current forward rate quoted on a currency pair is the market's expectation of where the future spot rate will end up, what would you say?

6.17 Forward Rate as an Unbiased Predictor. Some forecasters believe that foreign exchange markets for the major floating currencies are "efficient," and forward exchange rates are unbiased predictors of future spot exchange rates. What is meant by "unbiased predictor" in terms of the reliability of the forward rate in estimating future spot exchange rates?

6.18 Transaction Costs. If transaction costs for undertaking covered or uncovered interest arbitrage were large, how do you think it would influence arbitrage activity?

6.19 Carry Trade. The term *carry trade* is used quite frequently in the business press. What does it mean, and what conditions and expectations do investors need to hold to undertake carry trade transactions?

6.20 Market Efficiency. Many academics and professionals have tested the foreign exchange and interest rate markets to determine their efficiency. What have they concluded?

Problems

6.1 Grupo Bimbo (Mexico). Grupo Bimbo, headquartered in Mexico City, is one of the largest bakery companies in the world. On January 1, when the spot exchange rate is MXN10.80 = USD1.00, the company borrows USD25.0 million from a New York bank for one year at 6.80% interest. (Mexican banks had quoted 9.60% for an equivalent loan in Mexican pesos.) During the year, U.S. inflation is 2% and Mexican inflation is 4%. At the end of the year, the firm repays the dollar loan.

a. If Bimbo expected the spot rate at the end of one year to be that equal to purchasing power parity, what would be the cost to Bimbo of its dollar loan in peso-denominated interest?

b. What is the real interest cost (adjusted for inflation) to Bimbo, in peso-denominated terms, of borrowing the dollars for one year, again assuming purchasing power parity?

c. If the actual spot rate at the end of the year turned out to be MXN9.60 = USD1.00, what was the actual peso-denominated interest cost of the loan?

6.2 Dalin's Luggage: Sydney to Denver. Dalin Chen owns homes in Sydney, Australia, and Denver, United States. She travels between the two cities at least twice a year. Because of her frequent trips, she wants to buy some new high-quality luggage. She has done her research and has decided to purchase a Briggs and Riley three-piece luggage set. There are retail stores in Denver and Sydney. Dalin was a finance major and wants to use purchasing power parity to determine if she is paying the same price regardless of where she makes her purchase.

a. If the price of the three-piece luggage set in Denver is USD850 and the price of the same three-piece set in Sydney is AUD930, using purchasing power parity, is the price of the luggage truly equal if the spot rate is AUD1.0941 = USD1.00?

b. If the price of the luggage remains the same in Denver one year from now, determine the price of the luggage in Sydney in one year's time if PPP holds true. The U.S. inflation rate is 1.15%, and the Australian inflation rate is 3.13%.

6.3 Toyota's Pass-Through. Assume that the export price of a Toyota Corolla from Osaka, Japan, is ¥2,150,000. The exchange rate is ¥87.60 = $1.00. The forecast rate of inflation in the United States is 2.2% per year, and in Japan it is 0.0% per year. Use this data to answer the following questions on exchange rate pass-through.

a. What was the export price for the Corolla at the beginning of the year expressed in U.S. dollars?

b. Assuming purchasing power parity holds, what should be the exchange rate at the end of the year?

c. Assuming 100% exchange rate pass-through, what will be the dollar price of a Corolla at the end of the year?

d. Assuming 75% exchange rate pass-through, what will be the dollar price of a Corolla at the end of the year?

6.4 Pulau Penang, Malaysia. Theresa Nunn is planning a 30-day vacation on Pulau Penang, Malaysia, one year from now. The present charge for a luxury suite plus meals in Malaysian ringgit (RM) is RM1,045/day. The Malaysian ringgit presently trades at RM3.1350 = $1.00. She determines that the dollar cost today for a 30-day stay would be $10,000. The hotel informs her that any increase in its room charges will be limited to any increase in the Malaysian cost of living. Malaysian inflation is expected to be 2.75% per annum, while U.S. inflation is expected to be 1.25%.

a. How many dollars might Theresa expect to need one year hence to pay for her 30-day vacation?
b. By what percent will the dollar cost have gone up? Why?

6.5 Argentine Float. The Argentine peso was fixed through a currency board at Ps1.00 = $1.00 throughout the 1990s. In January 2002, the Argentine peso was floated. On January 29, 2003, it was trading at Ps3.20 = $1.00. During that one-year period, Argentina's inflation rate was 20% on an annualized basis. Inflation in the United States during that same period was 2.2% annualized.

a. What should have been the exchange rate in January 2003 if PPP held?
b. By what percentage was the Argentine peso undervalued on an annualized basis?
c. What were the probable causes of undervaluation?

6.6 Caleb Fajardo and Yen–Dollar Parity. Caleb Fajardo is attempting to determine whether U.S./Japanese financial conditions are at parity. The current spot rate is a flat ¥89.00 = $1.00, while the 360-day forward rate is ¥84.90 = $1.00. Forecast inflation is 1.100% for Japan and 5.900% for the United States. The 360-day euroyen deposit rate is 4.700%, and the 360-day eurodollar deposit rate is 9.500%.

a. Diagram and calculate whether international parity conditions hold between Japan and the United States.
b. Find the forecasted change in the Japanese yen to U.S. dollar (¥ = $1.00) exchange rate one year from now.

6.7 Trans-Atlantic Quotes. Separated by more than 3,000 nautical miles and five time zones, money and foreign exchange markets in both London and New York are very efficient. The following information has been collected from the respective areas:

Assumptions	London	New York
Spot exchange rate (USD = EUR1.00)	1.3264	1.3264
1-year Treasury bill rate	3.900%	4.500%
Expected inflation rate	Unknown	1.250%

a. What do the financial markets suggest for inflation in Europe next year?
b. Estimate today's 1-year forward exchange rate between the dollar and the euro.

6.8 Starbucks (Croatia). Starbucks opened its first store in Zagreb, Croatia, in October 2010. In Zagreb, the price of a tall vanilla latte is 25.70 Croatian *kuna* (kn). In New York City, the price of a tall vanilla latte is $2.65. The exchange rate between the Croatian kuna and U.S. dollar is kn5.6288 = $1.00. According to purchasing power parity, is the Croatian kuna overvalued or undervalued?

6.9 Kamada: CIA Japan (A). Takeshi Kamada, a foreign exchange trader at Credit Suisse (Tokyo), is exploring covered interest arbitrage possibilities. He wants to invest $5,000,000 or its yen equivalent, in a covered interest arbitrage between U.S. dollars and Japanese yen. He faced the following exchange rate and interest rate quotes. Is CIA profit possible? If so, how?

Arbitrage funds available	$5,000,000
Spot rate (¥ = $1.00)	118.60
180-day forward rate (¥ = $1.00)	117.80
180-day U.S. dollar interest rate	4.800%
180-day Japanese yen interest rat	3.400%

6.10 Kamada: UIA Japan (B). Takeshi Kamada, Credit Suisse (Tokyo), observes that the yen–dollar spot rate has been holding steady, and that both dollar and yen interest rates have remained relatively fixed over the past week. Takeshi wonders if he should try an uncovered interest arbitrage (UIA) and thereby save the cost of forward cover. Many of Takeshi's research associates—and their computer models—are predicting the spot rate to remain close to ¥118.00 = $1.00 for the coming 180 days. Using the same data as in Problem 6.9, analyze the UIA potential.

6.11 Chamonix Rentals. You are planning a ski vacation to Mt. Blanc in Chamonix, France, one year from now. You are negotiating the rental of a chateau. The chateau's owner wishes to preserve his real income against both inflation and exchange rate changes, and so the present weekly rent of €9,800 (Christmas season) will be adjusted upward or downward for any change in the French cost of living between now and then. You are basing your budgeting on purchasing power parity (PPP). French inflation is expected to average 3.5% for the coming year, while U.S. dollar inflation is expected to be 2.5%. The current spot rate is $1.3620 = €1.00. What should you budget as the U.S. dollar cost of the 1-week rental?

Spot exchange rate $ = €1.00	1.3620
Expected U.S. inflation for coming year	2.500%
Expected French inflation for coming year	3.500%
Current chateau nominal weekly rent (€)	9,800.00

6.12 Copenhagen Covered (A). Heidi Høi Jensen, a foreign exchange trader at JPMorgan Chase, can invest $5 million or the Danish kroner (kr) equivalent of the bank's short-term funds in a covered interest arbitrage with Denmark. Using the following quotes, can Heidi make a covered interest arbitrage (CIA) profit?

Arbitrage funds available	$5,000,000
Spot exchange rate (kr = $1.00)	6.1720
3-month forward rate (kr = $1.00)	6.1980
U.S. dollar 3-month interest rate	3.000%
Danish kroner 3-month interest rate	5.000%

6.13 Copenhagen Covered (B). Heidi Høi Jensen is now evaluating the arbitrage profit potential in the same market after interest rates change. (Note that any time the difference in interest rates does not exactly equal the forward premium, it must be possible to make a CIA profit one way or another.)

Arbitrage funds available	$5,000,000
Spot exchange rate (kr = $1.00)	6.1720
3-month forward rate (kr = $1.00)	6.1980
U.S. dollar 3-month interest rate	4.000%
Danish kroner 3-month interest rate	5.000%

6.14 Copenhagen Covered (C). Heidi Høi Jensen is again evaluating the arbitrage profit potential in the same market after another change in interest rates. (Remember that any time the difference in interest rates does not exactly equal the forward premium, it must be possible to make a CIA profit one way or another.)

Arbitrage funds available	$5,000,000
Spot exchange rate (kr = $1.00)	6.1720
3-month forward rate (kr = $1.00)	6.1980
U.S. dollar 3-month interest rate	3.000%
Danish kroner 3-month interest rate	6.000%

6.15 East Asiatic—Thailand. The East Asiatic Company (EAC), a Danish company with subsidiaries throughout Asia, has been funding its Bangkok subsidiary primarily with U.S. dollar debt because of the cost and availability of dollar capital as opposed to Thai baht–denominated (THB) debt. The treasurer of EAC-Thailand is considering a 1-year bank loan for USD250,000. The current spot rate is THB32.06 = USD1.00, and the dollar-based interest is 6.75% for the 1-year period. One-year loans are 12.00% in baht.

a. Assuming expected inflation rates for the coming year of 4.3% and 1.25% in Thailand and the United States, respectively, according to purchase power parity, what would be the effective cost of funds in Thai baht terms?
b. If EAC's foreign exchange advisers believe strongly that the Thai government wants to push the value of the baht down against the dollar by 5% over the coming year (to promote its export competitiveness in dollar markets), what might be the effective cost of funds in baht terms?
c. If EAC could borrow Thai baht at 13% per annum, would this be cheaper than either part (a) or part (b)?

6.16 Peder Mueller—CIA (A). Peder Mueller is a foreign exchange trader for a bank in New York. He has USD1 million (or its Swiss franc equivalent) for a short-term money market investment and wonders whether he should invest in U.S. dollars for three months or make a CIA investment in the Swiss franc (CHF). He faces the following quotes:

Arbitrage funds available	USD1,000,000
Spot exchange rate (CHF = USD1.00)	1.2810
3-month forward rate (CHF = USD1.00)	1.2740
U.S. dollar 3-month interest rate	4.800%
Swiss franc 3-month interest rate	3.200%

6.17 Peder Mueller—UIA (B). Peder Mueller, using the same values and assumptions as in Problem 6.16, decides to seek the full 4.800% return available in U.S. dollars by not covering his forward dollar receipts—an uncovered interest arbitrage (UIA) transaction. Assess this decision.

6.18 Peder Mueller—Thirty Days Later. One month after the events described in Problems 6.16 and 6.17, Peder Mueller once again has USD1 million (or its Swiss franc equivalent) to invest for three months. He now faces the following rates. Should he again enter into a covered interest arbitrage (CIA) investment?

Arbitrage funds available	USD 1,000,000
Spot exchange rate (CHF = USD1.00)	1.3392
3-month forward rate (CHF = USD1.00)	1.3286
U.S. dollar 3-month interest rate	4.750%
Swiss franc 3-month interest rate	3.625%

6.19 Equinor's Corporate Arbitrage. Equinor, the national oil company of Norway, is a large, sophisticated, and active participant in both the currency and petrochemical markets. Although it is a Norwegian company, because it operates within the global oil market, it considers the U.S. dollar, rather than the Norwegian krone (Nok), as its functional currency. Ari Karlsen is a currency trader for Equinor and has immediate use of either $3 million or the Norwegian krone equivalent. He is faced with the following market rates and wonders whether he can make some arbitrage profits in the coming 90 days.

Arbitrage funds available	$3,000,000
Spot exchange rate (Nok = $1.00)	6.0312
3-month forward rate (Nok = $1.00)	6.0186
U.S. dollar 3-month interest rate	5.000%
Norwegian krone 3-month interest rate	4.450%

6.20 Maltese Falcon: The Black Bird. Imagine that the mythical solid gold falcon, initially intended as a tribute by the Knights of Malta to the King of Spain in appreciation for his gift of the island of Malta to the order in 1530, has recently been recovered. The falcon is 14 inches high and solid gold, weighing approximately 48 pounds. Assume that gold prices have risen to $440/ounce, primarily as a result of increasing political tensions. The falcon is currently held by a private investor in Istanbul, who is actively negotiating with the Maltese government on its purchase and prospective return to its island home. The sale and payment are to take place one year from now, and the parties are negotiating over the price and currency of payment. The investor has decided, in a show of goodwill, to base the sales price only on the falcon's specie value—its gold value. The current spot exchange rate is 0.39 Maltese lira (ML) per 1.00 U.S. dollar. Maltese inflation is expected to be about 8.5% for the coming year, while U.S. inflation, on the heels of a double-dip recession, is expected to come in at only 1.5%. If the investor bases value in the U.S. dollar, would he be better off receiving Maltese lira in one year (assuming purchasing power parity) or receiving a guaranteed dollar payment (assuming a gold price of $420 per ounce one year from now).

6.21 African Beer Standard. Years ago *The Economist* reported the creation of an index, or standard, for the evaluation of African currency values using the local prices of beer. Beer, instead of Big Macs, was chosen as the product for comparison because McDonald's had not penetrated the African continent beyond South Africa and beer met most of the same product and market characteristics required for the construction of a proper currency index. Investec, a South African investment banking firm, has replicated the process of creating a measure of purchasing power parity (PPP) like that of the Big Mac Index of *The Economist* for Africa. The index compares the cost of a 375-milliliter bottle of clear lager beer across Sub-Saharan Africa. As a measure of PPP, the beer needs to be relatively homogeneous in quality across countries and must possess substantial elements of local manufacturing, inputs, distribution, and service in order to actually provide a measure of relative purchasing power. The beer is first priced in local currency (purchased in the taverns of the locals, and not in the high-priced tourist centers). The price is then converted to South African rand and the rand-price compared to the local currency price as one measure of whether the local currency is undervalued or overvalued versus the South African rand. Use the data in the table and complete the calculation of whether the individual currencies are undervalued or overvalued.

Problem 6.21

Country	Beer	Local Currency	Beer Prices: Price in Currency	Beer Prices: Price in Rand	Implied PPP Rate	Spot Rate
South Africa	Castle	Rand	2.30	–	–	–
Botswana	Castle	Pula	2.20	2.94	0.96	0.75
Ghana	Star	Cedi	1,200.00	3.17	521.74	379.10
Kenya	Tusker	Shilling	41.25	4.02	17.93	10.27
Malawi	Carlsberg	Kwacha	18.50	2.66	8.04	6.96
Mauritius	Phoenix	Rupee	15.00	3.72	6.52	4.03
Namibia	Windhoek	N$	2.50	2.50	1.09	1.00
Zambia	Castle	Kwacha	1,200.00	3.52	521.74	340.68
Zimbabwe	Castle	Z$	9.00	1.46	3.91	6.15

6.22 AvtoVAZ of Russia's Kalina Export Pricing Analysis. AvtoVAZ OAO, a leading auto manufacturer in Russia, was launching a new automobile model in 2001, and was in the midst of generating a complete pricing analysis of the car for sales in Russia and export. The new car, the Kalina, would be initially priced in Russian rubles at RUB260,000 in Russia and, if exported, USD8,666.67 in U.S. dollars at the current spot rate of RUB30.00 = USD1.00. AvtoVAZ intends to raise the price domestically with the rate of Russian inflation over time, but is worried about how that compares to the export price given U.S. dollar inflation and the future exchange rate. Use the following data table to answer the pricing analysis questions.

a. If the domestic price of the Kalina increases with the rate of inflation, what would its price be over the 2002–2006 period?
b. Assuming that the forecasts of U.S. and Russian inflation prove accurate, what would the value of the ruble be over the coming years if its value versus the dollar followed purchasing power parity?
c. If the export price of the Kalina were set using the purchasing power parity forecast of the ruble-dollar exchange rate, what would the export price be over the 2002–2006 period?

Calendar Year	2001	2002	2003	2004	2005	2006
Kalina price (Russian rubles)	260,000					
Russian inflation (forecast)		14.0%	12.0%	11.0%	8.0%	8.0%
U.S. inflation (forecast)		2.5%	3.0%	3.0%	3.0%	3.0%
Exchange rate (RUB = USD1.00)	30.00					

d. How would the Kalina's export price evolve over time if it followed Russian inflation and the exchange rate of the ruble versus the dollar remained relatively constant over this period of time?
e. Vlad, one of the newly hired pricing strategists, believes that prices of automobiles in both domestic and export markets will both increase with the rate of inflation, and that the ruble/dollar exchange rate will remain fixed. What would this imply or forecast for the future export price of the Kalina?
f. If you were AvtoVAZ, what would you hope would happen to the ruble's value versus the dollar over time given your desire to export the Kalina? Now if you combined that "hope" with some assumptions about the competition—other automobile sales prices in dollar markets over time—how might your strategy evolve?
g. What did the Russian ruble end up doing over the 2001–2006 period?

6.23 Clayton Moore's Money Fund. Clayton Moore is the manager of an international money market fund managed out of London. Unlike many money funds that guarantee their investors a near risk-free investment with variable interest earnings, Clayton Moore's fund is a very aggressive fund that searches out relatively high interest earnings around the globe, but at some risk. The fund is pound-denominated. Clayton is currently evaluating a rather interesting opportunity in Malaysia. Since the Asian Crisis of 1997, the Malaysian government enforced a number of currency and capital restrictions to protect and preserve the value of the Malaysian ringgit. The ringgit was fixed to the U.S. dollar at RM3.80 = \$1.00 for seven years. In 2005, the Malaysian government allowed the currency to float against several major currencies. The current spot rate today is RM3.1345 = \$1.00. Local currency time deposits of 180-day maturities are earning 8.900% per annum. The London eurocurrency market for pounds is yielding 4.200% per annum on similar 180-day maturities. The current spot rate on the British pound is \$1.5820 = −£1.00, and the 180-day forward rate is \$1.5561 = £1.00. What would you recommend Clayton do?

CHAPTER 6 APPENDIX

An Algebraic Primer to International Parity Conditions

The following is a purely algebraic presentation of the parity conditions explained in this chapter. It is offered to provide those who wish additional theoretical detail and definition ready access to the step-by-step derivation of the various conditions.

The Law of One Price

The *law of one price* refers to the state in which, in the presence of free trade, perfect substitutability of goods, and costless transactions, the equilibrium exchange rate between two currencies is determined by the ratio of the price of any commodity *i* denominated in two different currencies. For example,

$$S_t = \frac{P^{\$}_{i,t}}{P^{SF}_{i,t}}$$

where $P^{\$}_i$ and P^{SF}_i refer to the prices of the same commodity *i*, at time *t*, denominated in U.S. dollars and Swiss francs, respectively. The spot exchange rate, S_t, is simply the ratio of the two currency prices.

Purchasing Power Parity

The more general form in which the exchange rate is determined by the ratio of two price indexes is termed the absolute version of *purchasing power parity* (PPP). Each price index reflects the currency cost of the identical "basket" of goods across countries. The exchange rate that equates purchasing power for the identical collection of goods is then stated as follows:

$$S_t = \frac{P^{\$}_t}{P^{SF}_t}$$

where $P^{\$}_t$ and P^{SF}_t are the price index values in U.S. dollars and Swiss francs at time *t*, respectively. If $\pi^{\$}$ and π^{SF} represents the rate of inflation in each country, the spot exchange rate at time $t + 1$ would be

$$S_{t+1} = \frac{P^{\$}_t(1 + \pi^{\$})}{P^{SF}_t(1 + \pi^{SF})} = S_t\left[\frac{(1 + \pi^{\$})}{(1 + \pi^{SF})}\right]$$

The change from period t to $t + 1$ is then

$$\frac{S_{t+1}}{S_t} = \frac{\dfrac{P^{\$}_t(1 + \pi^{\$})}{P^{SF}_t(1 + \pi^{SF})}}{\dfrac{P^{\$}_t}{P^{SF}_t}} = \frac{S_t\left[\dfrac{(1 + \pi^{\$})}{(1 + \pi^{SF})}\right]}{S_t} = \frac{(1 + \pi^{\$})}{(1 + \pi^{SF})}$$

Isolating the percentage change in the spot exchange rate between periods t and $t + 1$ is then

$$\frac{S_{t+1} - S_t}{S_t} = \frac{S_t\left[\dfrac{(1 + \pi^{\$})}{(1 + \pi^{SF})}\right] - S_t}{S_t} = \frac{(1 + \pi^{\$}) - (1 + \pi^{SF})}{(1 + \pi^{SF})}$$

This equation is often approximated by dropping the denominator of the right-hand side if it is considered to be relatively small. It is then stated as

$$\frac{S_{t+1} - S_t}{S_t} = (1 + \pi^{\$}) - (1 + \pi^{SF}) = \pi^{\$} - \pi^{SF}$$

Forward Rates

The *forward exchange rate* is that contractual rate which is available to private agents through banking institutions and other financial intermediaries who deal in foreign currencies and debt instruments. The annualized percentage difference between the forward rate and the spot rate is termed the *forward premium*,

$$f^{SF} = \left[\frac{F_{t,t+1} - S_t}{S_t}\right] \times \left[\frac{360}{n_{t,t+1}}\right]$$

where f^{SF} is the forward premium on the Swiss franc, $F_{t,t+1}$is the forward rate contracted at time t for delivery at time $t + 1$, S_t is the current spot rate, and $n_{t,t+1}$ is the number of days between the contract date (t) and the delivery date ($t + 1$).

Covered Interest Arbitrage (CIA) and Interest Rate Parity (IRP)

The process of *covered interest arbitrage* is when an investor exchanges domestic currency for foreign currency in the spot market, invests that currency in an interest-bearing instrument, and signs a forward contract to "lock in" a future exchange rate at which to convert the foreign currency proceeds (gross) back to domestic currency. The net return on CIA is

$$\text{Net Return} = \left[\frac{(1 + i^{SF})F_{t,t+1}}{S_t}\right] - (1 + i^{\$})$$

where S_2 and $F_{t,t+1}$ are the spot and forward rates $(\$/SF)$, i^{SF} is the nominal interest rate (or yield) on a Swiss franc-denominated monetary instrument, and $i^{\$}$ is the nominal return on a similar dollar-denominated instrument.

If they possess exactly equal rates of return—that is, if CIA results in zero riskless profit—*interest rate parity* (IRP) holds and appears as

$$(1 + i^{\$}) = \left[\frac{(1 + i^{SF})F_{t,t+1}}{S_t}\right]$$

or alternatively as

$$\frac{(1 + i^{\$})}{(1 + i^{SF})} = \frac{F_{t,t+1}}{S_t}$$

If the percent age difference of both sides of this equation is found (the percentage difference between the spot and forward rate is the *forward premium*), then the relationship between the forward premium and relative interest rate differentials is

$$\frac{F_{t,t+1} - S_t}{S_t} = f^{SF} = \frac{i^{\$} - i^{SF}}{1 + i^{SF}}$$

If these values are not equal (thus, the markets are not in equilibrium), there exists a potential for riskless profit. The market will then be driven back to equilibrium through CIA by agents attempting to exploit such arbitrage potential, until CIA yields no positive return.

Fisher Effect

The *Fisher effect* states that all nominal interest rates can be decomposed into an implied real rate of interest (return) and an expected rate of inflation:

$$i^{\$} = [(1 + r^{\$})(1 + \pi^{\$})] - 1$$

where $r^{\$}$ is the real rate of return and $\pi^{\$}$ is the expected rate of inflation for dollar-denominated assets. The subcomponents are then identifiable:

$$i^{\$} = [(1 + r^{\$})(1 + \pi^{\$})] - 1$$

As with PPP, there is an approximation of this function that has gained wide acceptance. The cross-product term of $r^{\$}\pi^{\$}$ is often very small and therefore dropped altogether:

$$i^{\$} = r^{\$} + \pi^{\$}$$

International Fisher Effect

The *international Fisher effect* is the extension of this domestic interest rate relationship to the international currency markets. If capital, by way of covered interest arbitrage (CIA), attempts to find higher rates of return internationally resulting from current interest rate differentials, the real rates of return between currencies are equalized (e.g., $r^{\$} = r^{SF}$):

$$\frac{S_{t+1} - S_t}{S_t} = \frac{(1 + i^{\$}) - (1 + i^{SF})}{(1 + i^{SF})} = \frac{i^{\$} - i^{SF}}{(1 + i^{SF})}$$

If the nominal interest rates are then decomposed into their respective real and expected inflation components, the percentage change in the spot exchange rate is

$$\frac{S_{t+1} - S_t}{S_t} = \frac{(r^{\$} + \pi^{\$} + r^{\$}\pi^{\$}) - (r^{SF} + \pi^{SF} + r^{SF}\pi^{SF})}{1 + r^{SF} + \pi^{SF} + r^{SF}\pi^{SF}}.$$

The international Fisher effect has a number of additional implications, if the following requirements are met: (1) capital markets can be freely entered and exited, (2) capital markets possess investment opportunities that are acceptable substitutes, and (3) market agents have complete and equal information regarding these possibilities.

Given these conditions, international arbitragers are capable of exploiting all potential riskless profit opportunities, until real rates of return between markets are equalized $(r^{\$} = r^{SF})$. Thus, the expected rate of change in the spot exchange rate reduces to the differential in the expected rates of inflation:

$$\frac{S_{t+1} - S_t}{S_t} = \frac{\pi^{\$} + r^{\$}\pi^{\$} - \pi^{SF} - r^{SF}\pi^{SF}}{1 + r^{SF} + \pi^{SF} + r^{SF}\pi^{SF}}.$$

If the approximation forms are combined (through the elimination of the denominator and the elimination of the interactive terms of r and π), the change in the spot rate is simply

$$\frac{S_{t+1} - S_t}{S_t} = \pi^{\$} - \pi^{SF}$$

Note the similarity (identical in equation form) of the approximate form of the international Fisher effect to purchasing power parity, discussed previously. The only potential difference is that between *ex post* and *ex ante*, (expected) inflation.

7

Foreign Currency Derivatives: Futures and Options

Unless derivatives contracts are collateralized or guaranteed, their ultimate value also depends on the creditworthiness of the counterparties to them. In the meantime, though, before a contract is settled, the counterparties record profits and losses—often huge in amount—in their current earnings statements without so much as a penny changing hands. The range of derivatives contracts is limited only by the imagination of man (or sometimes, so it seems, madmen).

—Warren Buffett, *Berkshire Hathaway Annual Report*, 2002.

LEARNING OBJECTIVES

7.1 Explain how foreign currency futures are quoted, valued, and used for speculation purposes

7.2 Explore the buying and writing of foreign currency options in terms of risk and return

7.3 Describe how option values are composed of intrinsic and time-based value elements

7.4 Examine how foreign currency option values change with exchange rate movements, interest rate movements, and other option pricing components over time

Financial management of the multinational enterprise in the twenty-first century will certainly include the use of financial derivatives. These derivatives, so named because their values are derived from an underlying asset like a stock or a currency, are powerful tools used in business today for two very distinct management objectives: speculation and hedging. The financial manager of an MNE may purchase financial derivatives in order to take positions in the expectation of profit—*speculation*—or may use these instruments to reduce the risks associated with the everyday management of corporate cash flow—*hedging*. Before these financial instruments can be used effectively, however, the financial manager must understand certain basics about their structure and pricing.

In this chapter, we cover the primary foreign currency financial derivatives used today in multinational finance. Here we focus on the fundamentals of their valuation and use for speculative purposes; Chapter 9 will describe how these foreign currency derivatives can be used to hedge commercial transactions. The mini-case at the end of this chapter, *The Ups and Downs of Volatility*, explores currency volatility through times of crisis like the global financial crisis of 2008–2009 and the global pandemic of 2020, as well as times of record calm as in 2019, and ultimately whether these bouts of volatility are predictable.

A word of caution before proceeding: Financial derivatives are powerful tools in the hands of careful and competent financial managers. They can also be destructive devices when used recklessly and carelessly. The history of finance is littered with cases in which financial managers, either intentionally or unintentionally, took huge positions resulting in significant losses for their companies. In the right hands and with proper controls, however, derivatives may provide management with opportunities to enhance and protect corporate value.

7.1 Foreign Currency Futures

A *foreign currency futures contract* is an alternative to a forward contract that calls for future delivery of a standard amount of foreign exchange at a fixed time, place, and price. It is similar to futures contracts that exist for commodities (hogs, cattle, lumber, etc.), interest-bearing deposits, and gold. Most world money centers have established foreign currency futures markets. In the United States, the most important market for foreign currency futures is the International Monetary Market of the Chicago Mercantile Exchange.

Contract Specifications

Contract specifications are established by the exchange on which futures are traded. Using the Chicago IMM as an example, the major features of standardized futures trading can be illustrated by the Mexican peso futures traded on the Chicago Mercantile Exchange (CME), as shown in Exhibit 7.1.

Each futures contract is for 500,000 Mexican pesos. This is the notional principal. Trading in each currency must be done in an even multiple of currency units. The method of stating exchange rates is in American terms, the U.S. dollar cost (price) of a foreign currency (unit), where the CME is mixing the old dollar symbol with the ISO 4217 code for the peso, MXN. In Exhibit 7.1 this is U.S. dollars per Mexican peso. Contracts mature on the third Wednesday of January, March, April, June, July, September, October, or December. Contracts may be traded through the second business day prior to the Wednesday on which they mature. Unless holidays interfere, the last trading day is the Monday preceding the maturity date.

One of the defining characteristics of futures is the requirement that the purchaser deposit a sum as an initial margin or collateral. This requirement is similar to requiring a performance bond, and it can be met by a letter of credit from a bank, Treasury bills, or cash. In addition, a maintenance margin is required. The value of the contract is marked to market daily, and all changes in value are paid in cash daily. *Marked-to-market* means that the value of the contract is revalued using the closing price for the day. The amount to be paid is called the *variation margin*.

EXHIBIT 7.1 Mexican Peso (CMM)-MXN 500,000; USD per MXN

						Lifetime		
Maturity	**Open**	**High**	**Low**	**Settle**	**Change**	**High**	**Low**	**Open Interest**
Mar	0.10953	0.10988	0.10930	0.10958	. . .	0.11000	0.09770	34,481.00
June	0.10790	0.10795	0.10778	0.10773	. . .	0.10800	0.09730	3,405.00
Sept	0.10615	0.10615	0.10610	0.10573	. . .	0.10615	0.09930	1,481.00

All contracts are for 500,000 Mexican pesos. "Open" means the opening price on the day. "High" means the high price on the day. "Low" indicates the lowest price on the day. "Settle" is the closing price on the day. "Change" indicates the change in the settle price from the previous day's close. "High" and "Low" to the right of "Change" indicate the highest and lowest prices this specific contract (as defined by its maturity) has experienced over its trading history. "Open Interest" indicates the number of contracts outstanding.

Only about 5% of all futures contracts are settled by the physical delivery of foreign exchange between buyer and seller. More often, buyers and sellers offset their original position prior to delivery date by taking an opposite position. That is, an investor will normally close out a futures position by selling a futures contract for the same delivery date. The complete buy/sell or sell/buy is called a "round turn."

Customers pay a commission to a broker to execute a round turn and a single price is quoted. This practice differs from that of the interbank market, where dealers quote a bid and an offer and do not charge a commission. All contracts are agreements between the client and the exchange clearinghouse, rather than between the two clients involved. Consequently, clients need not worry that a specific counterparty in the market will fail to honor an agreement, termed counterparty risk. The clearinghouse is owned and guaranteed by all members of the exchange.

Using Foreign Currency Futures

The principle of a futures contract is as follows: A speculator who buys a futures contract is locking in the price at which she must buy that currency on the specified future date. A speculator who sells a futures contract is locking in the price at which she must sell that currency on that future date. Any investor wishing to speculate on the movement of the Mexican peso versus the U.S. dollar could pursue one of the following futures strategies.

Short Positions. If Laura Cervantes, a speculator working for International Currency Traders, believes that the Mexican peso will fall in value versus the U.S. dollar (USD) by March, she could sell a March futures contract, taking a *short position*. By selling a March contract, Laura locks in the right to sell 500,000 Mexican pesos (MXN) at a set price. If the price of the peso falls by the maturity date as she expects, Laura has a contract to sell pesos at a price above their current price on the spot market. Hence, she makes a profit.

Using the quotes on Mexican peso futures in Exhibit 7.1, Laura sells one March futures contract for MXN500,000 at the closing price, termed the settle price, of USD0.10958=MXN1.00. The value of her position at maturity—at the expiration of the futures contract in March—is then

$$\text{Value at maturity (Short position)} = -\text{Notional principal} \times (\text{Spot} - \text{Futures})$$

Note that the short position is entered into the valuation as a negative notional principal. If the spot exchange rate at maturity is USD0.09500 = MXN1.00, the value of her position on settlement is

$$\begin{aligned}\text{Value} &= -\text{MXN }500{,}000 \times (\text{USD}0.09500 \text{ per MXN} - \text{USD}0.10958 \text{ per MXN})\\ &= \text{USD}7{,}290\end{aligned}$$

Laura's expectation proved correct; the Mexican peso fell in value versus the U.S. dollar. We could say, "Laura buys at USD0.09500 and sells at USD0.10958 per peso."

All that was really required of Laura to speculate on the Mexican peso's value was for her to have a *directional view*—an opinion on the Mexican peso's future exchange value versus the U.S. dollar. In this case, she opined that the Mexican peso would fall in value against the U.S. dollar by the March maturity date of the futures contract.

Long Positions. If Laura Cervantes expected the peso to rise in value versus the dollar in the near term, she could take a *long position* by buying a March future on the Mexican peso. Buying a March future means that Laura is locking in the price at which she must buy Mexican pesos at the future's maturity date. Laura's futures contract at maturity would have the following value:

$$\text{Value at maturity (Long position)} = \text{Notional principal} \times (\text{Spot} - \text{Futures})$$

Again using the March settle price on Mexican peso futures in Exhibit 7.1, USD0.10958 = MXN1.00, if the spot exchange rate at maturity is USD0.1100 = MXN1.00, then Laura has indeed correctly predicted the movement of the peso. The value of her position on settlement is then

$$\begin{aligned} \text{Value} &= \text{MXN } 500{,}000 \times (\text{USD}0.11000 \text{ per MXN} - \text{USD}0.10958 \text{ per MXN}) \\ &= \text{USD}210 \end{aligned}$$

In this case, Laura makes a profit in a matter of months of $210 on the single futures contract. We could say, "Laura buys at USD0.10958 and sells at USD0.11000 per peso."

But what happens if Laura's expectation about the future value of the Mexican peso proves wrong? For example, if the Mexican government announces that the rate of inflation in Mexico has suddenly risen dramatically, and the peso falls to USD0.08000 = MXN1.00 by the March maturity date, the value of Laura's futures contract on settlement is

$$\begin{aligned} \text{Value} &= \text{MXN } 500{,}000 \times (\text{USD}0.08000 \text{ per MXN} - \text{USD}0.10958 \text{ per MXN}) \\ &= -\text{USD}14{,}790 \end{aligned}$$

In this case, Laura Cervantes suffers a speculative loss. Futures contracts could obviously be used in combinations to form a variety of more complex positions. When we combine contracts, valuation is fairly straightforward and additive in character.

Foreign Currency Futures versus Forward Contracts

Foreign currency futures contracts differ from forward contracts in a number of important ways. Individual investors find futures contracts useful for speculation because they usually do not have access to forward contracts. For businesses, futures contracts are often considered inefficient and burdensome because the futures position is marked to market on a daily basis over the life of the contract. Although this does not require the business to pay or receive cash daily, it does result in more frequent margin calls from its financial service providers than the business typically wants.

7.2 Foreign Currency Options

A *foreign currency option* is a contract that gives the option purchaser (the buyer) the right, but not the obligation, to buy or sell a given amount of foreign exchange at a fixed price per unit for a specified time period (until the maturity date). A key phrase in this definition is "but not the obligation," which means that the owner of an option possesses a valuable choice.

In many ways, buying an option is like buying a ticket to a benefit concert. The buyer has the right to attend the concert but is not obliged to. The buyer of the concert ticket risks nothing more than what she pays for the ticket. Similarly, the buyer of an option cannot lose more than what he pays for the option. If the buyer of the ticket decides later not to attend the concert, prior to the day of the concert, the ticket can be sold to someone else who wishes to go.

Option Fundamentals

There are two basic types of options, *calls* and *puts*. A *call* is an option to buy foreign currency, and a *put* is an option to sell foreign currency. The buyer of an option is termed the holder, while the seller of an option is referred to as the writer or grantor.

Every option has three different price elements: (1) the *exercise price* or *strike price*—also commonly referred to as the *strike rate*—is the exchange rate at which the foreign currency can be purchased (call) or sold (put); (2) the *premium*, which is the cost, price, or value of the option itself; and (3) the underlying or actual spot exchange rate in the market.

An *American option* gives the buyer the right to exercise the option at any time between the date of writing and the expiration or maturity date. A *European option* can be exercised only on its expiration date, not before. Nevertheless, American and European options are priced almost the same because the option holder would normally sell the option itself before maturity. The option would then still have some "time value" above its "intrinsic value" if exercised (explained later in this chapter).

The *premium* or option price is the cost of the option, and is usually paid in advance by the buyer to the seller. In the over-the-counter (OTC) market—options offered by banks—premiums are quoted as a percentage of the transaction amount. Premiums on exchange-traded options are quoted as a domestic currency amount per unit of foreign currency.

An option that has an exercise price equal to the spot price of the underlying currency is said to be *at-the-money* (ATM). An option that would be profitable, excluding the cost of the premium, if exercised immediately is said to be *in-the-money* (ITM). An option that would not be profitable, again excluding the cost of the premium, if exercised immediately is referred to as *out-of-the-money* (OTM).

Foreign Currency Options Markets

In the past three decades, the use of foreign currency options as a hedging tool and for speculative purposes has blossomed into a major foreign exchange activity. A number of banks in the United States and other capital markets offer flexible foreign currency options on transactions of $1 million or more. The bank market, or over-the-counter market as it is called, offers custom-tailored options on all major trading currencies for any period up to one year and, in some cases, two to three years.

The Philadelphia Stock Exchange introduced trading in standardized foreign currency option contracts in the United States in 1982. The Chicago Mercantile Exchange and other exchanges in the U.S. and abroad have followed suit. Exchange-traded contracts are particularly appealing to speculators and individuals who do not normally have access to the over-the-counter market. Banks also trade on the exchanges because it is one of several ways they can offset the risk of options they may have transacted with clients or other banks. Increased use of foreign currency options is a reflection of the explosive growth in the use of other kinds of options and the resulting improvements in option pricing models. The original option-pricing model developed by Fischer Black and Myron Scholes in 1973 has been expanded, adapted, and commercialized in hundreds of forms since that time.

Options on the Over-the-Counter Market. Over-the-counter (OTC) options are most frequently written by banks for U.S. dollars against British pounds sterling, Canadian dollars, Japanese yen, Swiss francs, or the euro but are becoming increasingly available for nearly every major traded currency.

The main advantage of OTC options is that they are tailored to the specific needs of the firm. Financial institutions are willing to write or buy options that vary by amount (the notional principal), strike price, and maturity. Although the OTC markets were relatively illiquid in the early years, these markets have grown to such proportions that liquidity is now quite good. On the other hand, the buyer must assess the writing bank's ability to fulfill the option contract. The financial risk associated with the counterparty—*counterparty risk*—is an ever-present issue in international markets as a result of the increasing use of financial contracts like options and swaps. Exchange-traded options are more the territory of individuals and financial institutions than of business firms.

If an investor wishes to purchase an option in the OTC market, the investor will normally place a call to the currency option desk of a major money center bank; specify the currencies, maturity, and strike rate(s); and ask for an indication, a bid-offer quote. The bank will normally take a few minutes to a few hours to price the option and respond to the request.

Options on Organized Exchanges. Options on the physical (underlying) currency are traded on a number of organized exchanges worldwide, including the Philadelphia Stock Exchange (PHLOX) and the Chicago Mercantile Exchange. Exchange-traded options are settled through a clearinghouse, which means that buyers do not deal directly with sellers. The clearinghouse is the counterparty to every option contract and it guarantees fulfillment. Clearinghouse obligations are in turn the obligation of all members of the exchange, including a large number of banks. For the Philadelphia Stock Exchange, clearinghouse services are provided by the Options Clearing Corporation.

Digital Trading. Digital trading of currency options is thought to combine the best of OTC and exchange traded options. Theoretically, they can be customized to the needs of the buyer but simultaneously be accessed and priced through a digital interface (described as "straight-through processing"). FXall, a foreign exchange and currency option trading house for banks and brokers owned by the Blackstone Group, has seen rapid growth in sales of digital foreign currency option trades in recent years.

Currency Option Quotations and Prices

Typical quotes for options on Swiss francs are shown in Exhibit 7.2. These quotes are for transactions completed on the Philadelphia Stock Exchange on the previous day. Although a multitude of strike prices and expiration dates are quoted (shown in the exhibit), not all were actually traded the previous trading day, and in that case no premium price is shown. Currency option strike prices and premiums on the U.S. dollar are typically quoted as direct quotations on the U.S. dollar and indirect quotations on the foreign currency, as in US$ per Swiss franc (SF) or US$ per Japanese yen (¥).

EXHIBIT 7.2 Swiss Franc Option Quotations (U.S. cents/SF)

		Calls – Last			Puts – Last		
Option & Underlying	**Strike Price**	**Aug**	**Sep**	**Dec**	**Aug**	**Sep**	**Dec**
58.51	56.0	–	–	2.76	0.04	0.22	1.16
58.51	56.5	–	–	–	0.06	0.30	–
58.51	57.0	1.13	–	1.74	0.10	0.38	1.27
58.51	57.5	0.75	–	–	0.17	0.55	–
58.51	58.0	0.71	1.05	1.28	0.27	0.89	1.81
58.51	58.5	0.50	–	–	0.50	0.99	–
58.51	59.0	0.30	0.66	1.21	0.90	1.36	–
58.51	59.5	0.15	0.40	–	2.32	–	–
58.51	60.0	–	0.31	–	2.32	2.62	3.30

Each option = 62,500 Swiss francs. The August, September, and December listings are the option maturities or expiration dates. Table constructed by authors to illustrate how option quotations are often presented in *The Wall Street Journal*.

Buyer of a Call

Options differ from other types of financial instruments in the patterns of risk they produce. The holder of an option has the choice to exercise the option or to allow it to expire unused. The owner will exercise the option only when doing so is profitable, which means only when the option is in the money. In the case of a call option, as the spot price of the underlying currency moves up, the holder has the possibility of unlimited profit. On the down side, however, the holder can abandon the option and walk away, losing only the premium paid.

Exhibit 7.2 illustrates the three different prices that characterize any foreign currency option. In the exhibit, the highlighted option is referred to using the month and strike price as an "August 58.5 call option." The three prices that characterize an "August 58.5 call option" are as follows:

1. **Spot rate.** "Option and Underlying" in the exhibit means that 58.51 cents, or $0.5851, was the spot dollar price of one Swiss franc at the close of trading on the preceding day.
2. **Exercise price.** The exercise price, or "Strike Price" in the exhibit, is the price per franc that must be paid if the option is exercised. The August call option on francs of 58.5 indicates $0.5850 = SF1.00. Exhibit 7.2 lists nine different strike prices, ranging from $0.5600 to $0.6000, although more were available on that date than are listed.
3. **Premium.** The premium is the cost or price of the option. The price of the August 58.5 call option on Swiss francs was 0.50 U.S. cents per franc, or $0.0050=SF1.00. The premium is the market value of the option, and therefore, the terms premium, cost, price, and value are all interchangeable for options.

The August 58.5 call option premium is 0.50 cents per franc, and in this case, the August 58.5 put's premium is also 0.50 cents per franc. Since one option contract on the Philadelphia Stock Exchange consists of 62,500 francs, the total cost of one option contract for the call (or put in this case) is SF62,500 × $0.0050 per SF = $312.50.

Hans Schmidt is a currency speculator in Zurich. The position of Hans as a buyer of a call is illustrated in Exhibit 7.3. Assume he purchases the August call option on Swiss francs described previously, the one with a strike price of $0.585 and a premium of $0.005 per SF. The vertical axis measures profit or loss for the option buyer at each of several different spot prices for the franc up to the time of maturity.

At all spot rates below the strike price of $0.585, Hans would choose not to exercise his option. This is obvious because at a spot rate of $0.580, for example, he would prefer to buy a Swiss franc for $0.580 on the spot market rather than exercising his option to buy a franc at $0.585. If the spot rate were to remain at $0.580 or below until August when the option expired, Hans would not exercise the option. His total loss would be limited to only what he paid for the option, the $0.005 = SF1.00 purchase price. Regardless of how far the spot rate was to fall, his loss would be limited to the original $0.005 per SF cost.

Alternatively, at all spot rates above the strike price of $0.585, Hans would exercise the option, paying only the strike price for each Swiss franc. For example, if the spot rate were $0.595 per franc at maturity, he would exercise his call option, buying Swiss francs for $0.585 each instead of purchasing them on the spot market at $0.595 each. He could sell the Swiss francs immediately in the spot market for $0.595 each, pocketing a gross profit of $0.010 per SF, or a net profit of $0.005 per SF after deducting the original cost of the option of $0.005. Hans's profit, if the spot rate is greater than the strike price, with strike price $0.585, a premium of $0.005, and a spot rate of $0.595, is

$$\begin{aligned}\text{Profit} &= \text{Spot Rate} - (\text{Strike Price} + \text{Premium})\\ &= \$0.595 - (\$0.585 + \$0.005)\\ &= \$0.005 \text{ per SF}\end{aligned}$$

EXHIBIT 7.3 **Profit and Loss for the Buyer of a Call Option**

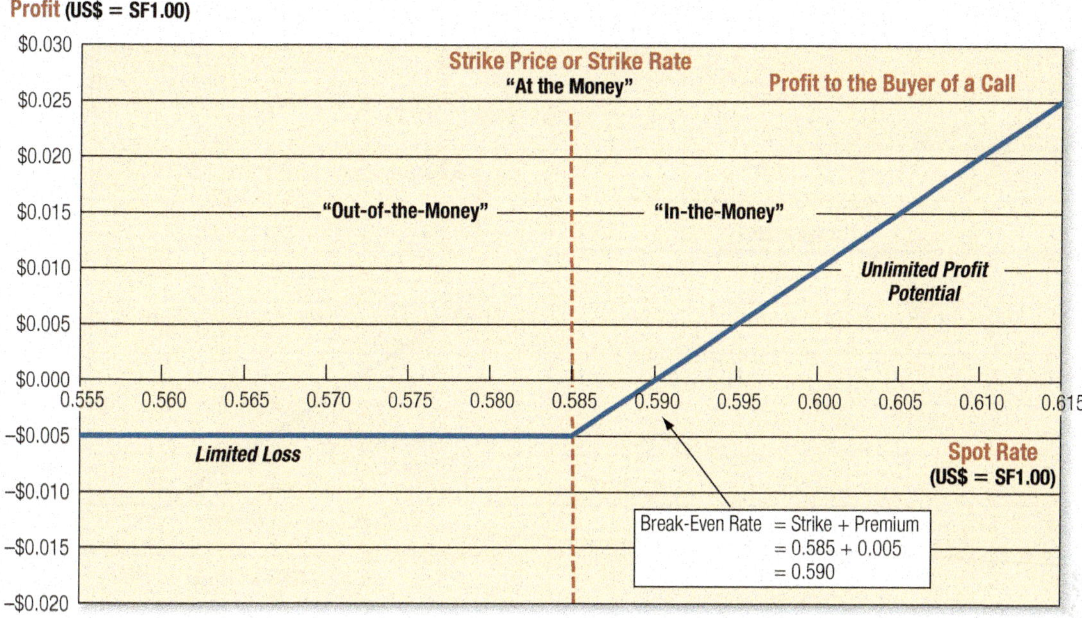

The buyer of a call option has unlimited profit potential (*in the money*) and limited loss potential, the amount of the premium (*out of the money*).

More likely, Hans would realize the profit through executing an offsetting contract on the options exchange rather than taking delivery of the currency. Because the dollar price of a franc could rise to an infinite level (off the upper right-hand side of Exhibit 7.3), maximum profit is unlimited. The buyer of a call option thus possesses an attractive combination of outcomes: limited loss and unlimited profit potential.

Note that the break-even price of $0.590 is the price at which Hans neither gains nor loses on exercising the option. The premium cost of $0.005, combined with the cost of exercising the option of $0.585, is exactly equal to the proceeds from selling the francs in the spot market at $0.590. Hans will still exercise the call option at the break-even price. This is because by exercising it, he at least recoups the premium paid for the option. At any spot price above the exercise price but below the break-even price, the gross profit earned on exercising the option and selling the underlying currency covers part (but not all) of the premium cost.

Writer of a Call

The position of the writer (seller) of the same call option is illustrated in Exhibit 7.4. If the option expires when the spot price of the underlying currency is below the exercise price of $0.585, the option holder does not exercise it. What the holder loses, the writer gains. The writer keeps as profit the entire premium paid of $0.005 per SF. If the option is exercised when the spot price of the underlying currency is above the exercise price of 58.5, the writer of the call must deliver the underlying currency for $0.585 per SF at a time when the value of the franc is above $0.585. If the writer wrote the option naked, that is, without owning the currency, then the writer will need to buy the currency at spot and, in this scenario, take the loss. The amount of such a loss is unlimited and increases as the price of the underlying currency rises.

EXHIBIT 7.4 **Profit and Loss for the Writer of a Call Option**

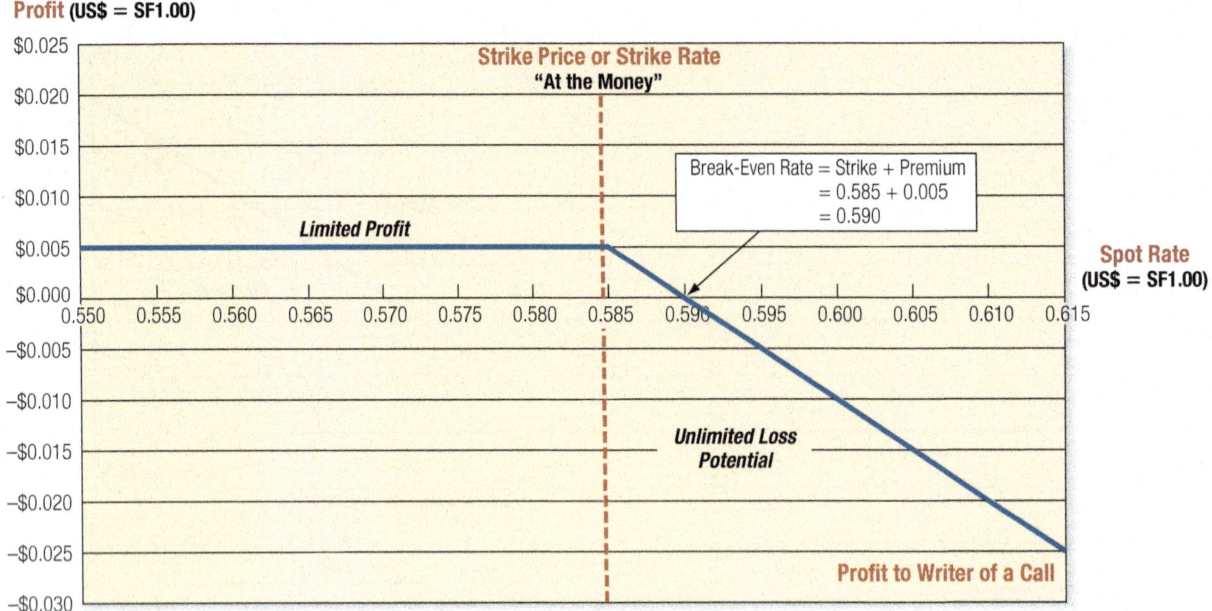

The writer of a call option has unlimited loss potential and limited profit potential, the amount of the premium.

Once again, what the holder gains, the writer loses, and vice versa. Even if the writer already owns the currency, the writer will experience an opportunity loss, surrendering against the option the same currency that could have been sold for more in the open market. For example, the profit to the writer of a call option of strike price \$0.585, premium \$0.005, and a spot rate of \$0.595 is

$$\begin{aligned} \text{Profit} &= \text{Premium} + (\text{Spot Rate} - \text{Strike Price}) \\ &= \$0.005 - (\$0.595 + \$0.585) \\ &= -\$0.005 \text{ per SF} \end{aligned}$$

but only if the spot rate is greater than or equal to the strike rate. At spot rates less than the strike price, the option will expire worthless and the writer of the call option will keep the premium earned. The maximum profit that the writer of the call option can make is limited to the premium. The writer of a call option has a rather unattractive combination of potential outcomes—limited profit potential and unlimited loss potential—but there are ways to limit such losses through other offsetting techniques that we will discuss later in this chapter.

It's not always easy to know when to buy a call or write a call, but as *Global Finance in Practice 7.1* explains, there are times in history when it would certainly have been a good idea.

Buyer of a Put

Hans's position as buyer of a put is illustrated in Exhibit 7.5. The basic terms of this put are similar to those we just used to illustrate a call. The buyer of a put option, however, wants to be able to sell the underlying currency at the exercise price when the market price of that currency drops (rather than when it rises as in the case of a call option). If the spot price of a

GLOBAL FINANCE IN PRACTICE 7.1

Currency Options and Lufthansa

The Philadelphia Stock Exchange (PSE) launched foreign currency options trading in 1982. Several years later, Lufthansa, the national flag carrier for Germany, became the subject of a promotional add for currency options for many years.

In January 1985, Lufthansa, under the chairmanship of Herr Heinz Ruhnau, signed a contract with Boeing (US) for the purchase of 20 Boeing 737 jets. A single payment of $500 million was due on delivery in January 1986, or 1.6 billion Deutschemarks (DM, Germany's currency at the time) at the current spot rate of DM3.20 = $1.00. All major currency analysts, as well as Herr Ruhnau himself, believed that the DM would appreciate versus the dollar over the coming year. The dollar had been rising nearly nonstop for five years and was at a peak that even most major governments thought too high.

But Ruhnau was cautious. He did not want to leave his short-dollar position uncovered (unhedged). So he chose to "split the difference" and purchased a forward contract to buy dollars for Deutschemarks on one-half of the exposure ($250 million) and leave the other half ($250 million) unhedged. As it turned out, Ruhnau was right. The dollar did fall against the Deutschemark. By January 1985 it was trading at DM2.3 = $1.00. Unfortunately, that meant the $250 million that was uncovered could be attained at DM2.3, while the other $250 million, locked in with a forward contract, cost DM3.2 for each dollar. Ruhnau was heavily criticized for the forward contract, was accused of speculating on currency exposures of the company, and eventually stepped down from being chairman.

The PSE—after the fact—used this as a golden example of when using foreign currency options would have been the perfect strategy. Since Ruhnau believed the spot exchange rate was going to move in his favor but still needed protection if it didn't, according to the PSE he should have purchased a call option on U.S. dollars at a strike rate near the current spot rate (forward-at-the-money). In hindsight, yes, it would have been a very good strategy. In hindsight.

EXHIBIT 7.5 Profit and Loss for the Buyer of a Put Option

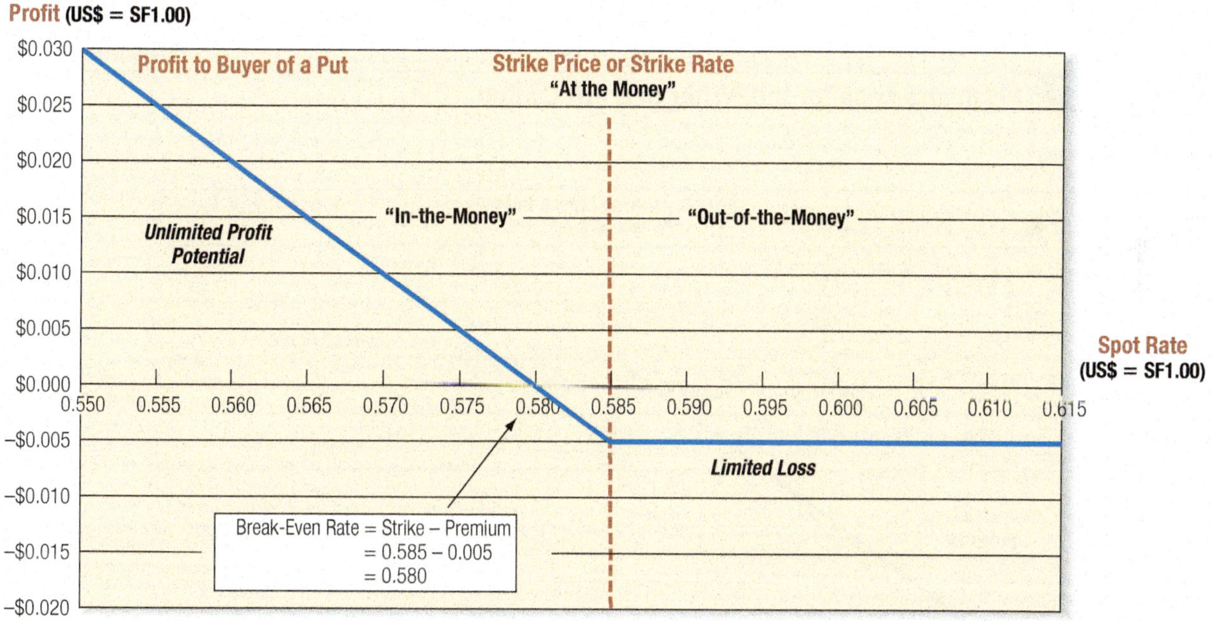

Profit (US$ = SF1.00)
$0.030
$0.025
$0.020
$0.015
$0.010
$0.005
$0.000
−$0.005
−$0.010
−$0.015
−$0.020
Profit to Buyer of a Put
Strike Price or Strike Rate
"At the Money"
"In-the-Money"
"Out-of-the-Money"
Unlimited Profit Potential
Spot Rate (US$ = SF1.00)
0.550 0.555 0.560 0.565 0.570 0.575 0.580 0.585 0.590 0.595 0.600 0.605 0.610 0.615
Limited Loss
Break-Even Rate = Strike − Premium
= 0.585 − 0.005
= 0.580

The buyer of a put option has nearly unlimited profit potential (*in the money*), and limited loss potential, the amount of the premium (*out of the money*).

franc drops to, say, $0.575 = SF1.00, Hans will deliver francs to the writer and receive $0.585 per SF. The francs can now be purchased on the spot market for $0.575 each. Because the cost of the option was $0.005 per SF, he will have a net gain of $0.005 per SF.

Explicitly, the profit to the holder of a put option if the spot rate is less than the strike price, with a strike price \$0.585, a premium of \$0.005, and a spot rate of \$0.575, is

$$\begin{aligned} \text{Profit} &= \text{Strike Price} - (\text{Spot Rate} + \text{Premium}) \\ &= \$0.585 - (\$0.575 + \$0.005) \\ &= \$0.005 \text{ per SF} \end{aligned}$$

The break-even price for the put option is the strike price less the premium, or \$0.580 in this case. As the spot rate falls further and further below the strike price, the profit potential continues to increase, and Hans' profit could be up to a maximum of \$0.580, when the price of a franc would be zero. At any exchange rate above the strike price of 58.5, Hans would not exercise the option, and so would lose only the \$0.005 premium paid per SF for the put option. The buyer of a put option has an almost unlimited profit potential with a limited loss potential. Like the buyer of a call, the buyer of a put can never lose more than the premium paid up front.

Writer of a Put

The position of the writer who sold the put option to Hans is shown in Exhibit 7.6. Note the symmetry of profit/loss, strike price, and break-even prices between the buyer and the writer of the put. If the spot price of francs drops below \$0.585 per franc, Hans will exercise the option. Below a price of \$0.585 per franc—below breakeven—the writer will lose more than the premium received from writing the option (\$0.005 per SF). Between \$0.580 and \$0.585 the writer will lose part, but not all, of the premium received. If the spot price is above \$0.585, Hans will not exercise the option, and the option writer will pocket the entire premium of \$0.005.

EXHIBIT 7.6 Profit and Loss for the Writer of a Put Option

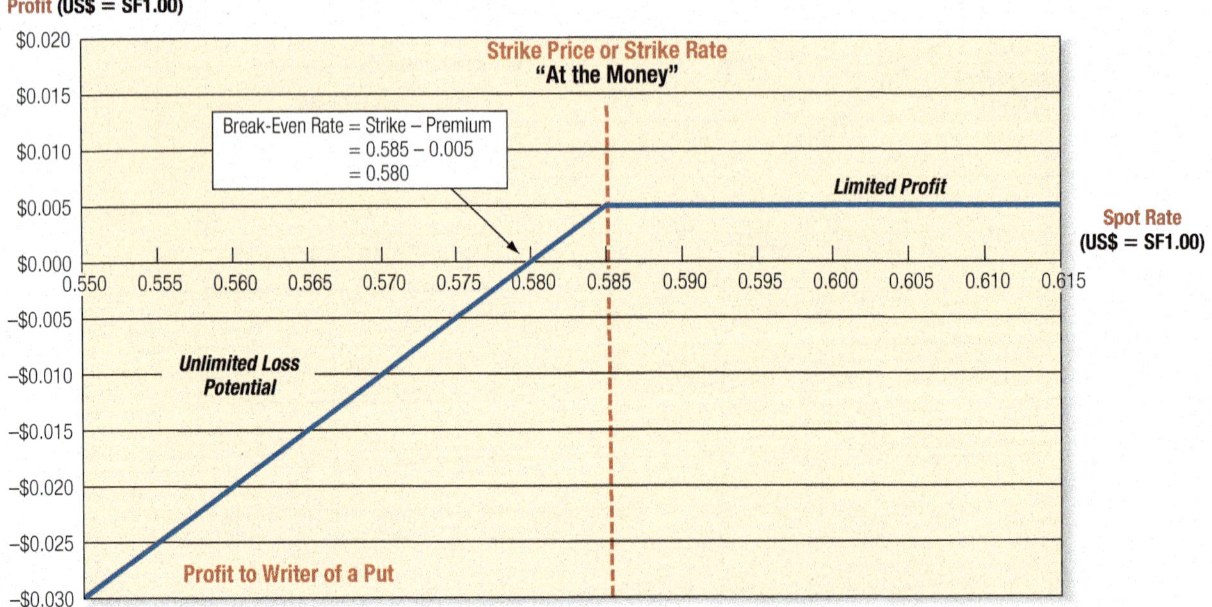

The writer of a put option has limited profit potential, the premium, and an unlimited loss potential.

The profit (or loss) earned by the writer of a $0.585 strike price put, premium $0.005, at a spot rate of $0.575, is

$$\begin{aligned}\text{Profit} &= \text{Premium} - (\text{Strike Price} - \text{Spot Rate}) \\ &= \$0.005 - (\$0.585 - \$0.575) \\ &= -\$0.005 \text{ per SF}\end{aligned}$$

but only for spot rates that are less than or equal to the strike price. At spot rates greater than the strike price, the option expires out-of-the-money and the writer keeps the premium. The writer of the put option has the same combination of outcomes available to the writer of a call: limited profit potential and loss potential.

Currency options can be combined in a variety of ways to produce even more complex and powerful structures. Unfortunately, they do not always turn out for the best, as described in *Global Finance in Practice 7.2*.

GLOBAL FINANCE IN PRACTICE 7.2

Exotic Options: *Caveat Emptor*

Banks have acquired a bit of a shady reputation over the years when it comes to their marketing of exotic financial derivatives. The sale by South Korean banks of KiKos—knock-in knock-out option agreements—is a prime example. Between 2006 and 2008, Korean banks sold these complex option agreements to major Korean exporters who feared that the Korean won's (KRW) recent appreciation—although only marginal in size—against their major trading partner, the U.S., would continue. If the won did continue to rise in value against the dollar (USD), their competitiveness, sales, and ultimately, profitability was in danger.

The KiKos were a complex option agreement that basically bet that the won would continue to trade in a relatively narrow range against the dollar. It combined the sale of call options on the KRW, the knock-in component, with the purchase of put options on the dollar, the knock-out component. Selling calls earned a premium, while purchasing puts required paying a premium. The problem was that the puts possessed strike rates which were very close to the current spot rate, making their purchase very expensive. In order to construct a net-zero premium position (or close to it for salability to the Korean exporters), the call options sold were for multiples of the notional principal of the puts. This last part was called the "turbo feature."

An added feature intensified the complexity—the feature related to the "knock" term. If the spot exchange rate at any time during the contract fell below the put option strike rate, the put options automatically canceled, or knocked out. If the spot exchange rate at any time during the contract rose above (meaning more and more KRW to get a USD), the call option strike rate knocked in, requiring the Korean companies to deliver on the call options they had sold.

In early 2008, the KRW started falling against the USD, rapidly. The spot rate quickly blew through the knock-in rate, and the calls were exercised against the buyers of the KiKo products. The Korean companies that had purchased the KiKo options from the Korean banks suffered massive financial losses because of the multiple notional principles.

The losses resulted in the filing of hundreds of lawsuits in Korean courts. Korean manufacturers that had purchased the KiKos sued the Korean banks to avoid the payment of losses that would in many cases bankrupt the companies.

Exporters argued that the Korean banks had sold them complex products which they did not understand. The lack of understanding was on at least two different levels. First, many of the KiKo contracts were only in English, and many buyers did not understand English. (The KiKos had actually been created by a number of major Western hedge funds that then sold the products through the Korean banks.) Secondly, exporters argued that the risks associated with the KiKos were not adequately explained to them. The exporters argued that the Korean banks had a duty to adequately explain to them the risks and—even more importantly—only sell them products that were suitable for their needs. (Under U.S. law this would be termed a "fiduciary responsibility.") The Korean banks responded they had no such specific duty, and regardless, they had explained the risks sufficiently. The banks argued that this was not a case of an unsophisticated buyer not understanding a complex product; both buyer and seller were sufficiently sophisticated to understand the intricate workings and risks of these structures.

In the end the Korean courts found in favor of the exporters in some cases and in favor of the banks in others. One principle that the courts followed was that the exporters found themselves in "changed circumstances" in which the change in the spot exchange rate was unforeseeable and the losses resulting too great. But some firms—for example, GM Daewoo—the losses were enormous, almost $1 billion.

7.3 Option Pricing and Valuation

Exhibit 7.7 illustrates the profit/loss profile of a European-style call option on British pounds. The call option allows the holder to buy British pounds at a strike price of $1.70/£. It has a 90-day maturity. The value of this call option is actually the sum of two components:

$$\text{Total Value (premium)} = \text{Intrinsic Value} + \text{Time Value}$$

The pricing of any currency option combines six elements. For example, this European-style call option on British pounds has a premium of $0.033/£ (3.3 cents per pound) at a spot rate of $1.70=£1.00. This premium is calculated using the following assumptions: a spot rate of $1.70=£1.00, a 90-day maturity, a $1.70=£1.00 forward rate, both U.S. dollar and British pound interest rates of 8.00% per annum, and an option volatility for the 90-day period of 10.00% per annum.

Intrinsic value is the financial gain if the option is exercised immediately. It is shown by the solid line in Exhibit 7.7, which is zero until it reaches the strike price, then rises linearly (1 cent for each 1-cent increase in the spot rate). Intrinsic value will be zero when the option is *out-of-the-money*—that is, when the strike price is above the market price—as no gain can be derived from exercising the option. When the spot rate rises above the strike price, the intrinsic value becomes positive because the option is always worth at least this value if exercised. On the date of maturity, an option will have a value equal to its intrinsic value (zero time remaining means zero time value).

Exhibit 7.7 (graphically) and Exhibit 7.8 (table) illustrate all three value elements of the $1.70 strike 90-day call option on British pounds across a spectrum of spot rates. When the

EXHIBIT 7.7 Option Intrinsic Value, Time Value, and Total Value

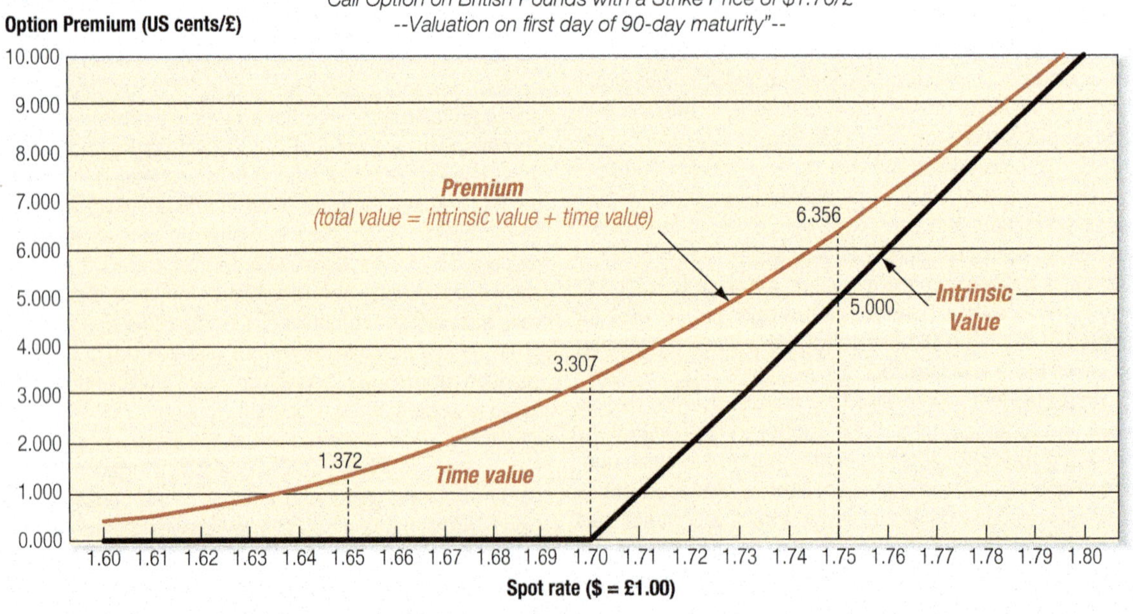

EXHIBIT 7.8 Call Option Premiums: Intrinsic Value and Time Value Components

Strike Rate ($ = £1.00)	Spot Rate ($ = £1.00)	Money	Call Premium (U.S. cents per £)	=	Intrinsic Value (U.S. cents per £)	+	Time Value (U.S. cents per £)
1.70	1.75	In-the-money (ITM)	6.37	=	5.00	+	1.37
1.70	1.70	At-the-money (ATM)	3.30	=	0.00	+	3.30
1.70	1.65	Out-of-the-money (OTM)	1.37	=	0.00	+	1.37

spot rate is $1.75/£, the option is *in-the-money* and has positive time (¢1.356 per £) and intrinsic values (¢5.000 per £). When the spot rate is $1.70 = £1.00—the same as the option strike rate—the option is *at-the-money,* has no intrinsic value, but does have time value (¢3.302 per £). When the spot rate is $1.65 = £1.00, the option is *out-of-the-money*, has no intrinsic value, but does have a time value (¢1.372 per £).

The *time value* of an option exists because the price of the underlying currency, the spot rate, can potentially move further and further into the money before the option's expiration. Time value is shown in Exhibit 7.7 as the area between the total value of the option and its intrinsic value. An investor will pay something today for an out-of-the-money option (i.e., zero intrinsic value) on the chance that the spot rate will move far enough before maturity to move the option in-the-money. Consequently, the price of an option is always somewhat greater than its intrinsic value, since there is always some chance—some might say "hope everlasting"—that the intrinsic value will rise by the expiration date. *Global Finance in Practice 7.3* describes one of the largest and most successful currency option speculations ever made, that by Andrew Krieger against the New Zealand kiwi. We should all be so good.

GLOBAL FINANCE IN PRACTICE 7.3

The New Zealand Kiwi and Andrew Krieger

In 1987 Andrew Krieger was a 31-year-old currency trader for Bankers Trust of New York (BT). Following the U.S. stock market crash in October 1987, the world's currency markets moved rapidly to exit the dollar. Many of the world's other currencies—including small ones that were in stable, open, industrialized markets, like that of New Zealand—became the subject of interest. As the world dumped dollars and bought kiwis, the value of the kiwi rose.

Krieger believed that the markets were overreacting. He took a short position on the kiwi, betting on its eventual fall, in a big way, combining spot, forward, and options positions. (Krieger supposedly had approval for positions rising to nearly $700 million in size, while all other BT traders were restricted to $50 million.) Krieger is purported to have shorted 200 million kiwi, more than the entire New Zealand money supply at the time. His view proved correct. The kiwi fell, and Krieger was able to earn millions in currency gains for BT. Months later, Krieger resigned when bonuses were announced and he was reportedly awarded only $3 million on the $300 million profit.

Eventually, the New Zealand central bank lodged complaints with BT, in which the CEO at the time, Charles S. Sanford Jr., seemingly added insult to injury when he reportedly remarked, "We didn't take too big a position for Bankers Trust, but we may have taken too big a position for that market."

7.4 Currency Option Pricing Sensitivity

If currency options are to be used effectively, either for the purposes of speculation or risk management (covered in the coming chapters), the individual trader needs to know how option values—premiums—react to their various components. The following section will analyze these six basic sensitivities:

1. The impact of changing forward rates
2. The impact of changing spot rates
3. The impact of time to maturity
4. The impact of changing volatility
5. The impact of changing interest differentials
6. The impact of alternative option strike prices

Forward Rate Sensitivity

Although rarely noted, standard foreign currency options are priced around the forward rate because the current spot rate and both the domestic and foreign interest rates (home currency and foreign currency rates) are included in the option premium calculation.

Recall from Chapter 4 that the forward rate is calculated from the current spot rate and the two subject currency interest rates for the desired maturity. For example, the 90-day forward rate for the call option on British pounds described above, a spot rate of \$1.70 = £1.00, with both interest rates at 8.0% per annum, is calculated as follows:

$$F_{90} = \$1.70 \times \frac{\left[1 + \left(.08 \times \frac{90}{360}\right)\right]}{\left[1 + \left(.08 \times \frac{90}{360}\right)\right]} = \$1.70$$

Regardless of the specific strike rate chosen and priced, the forward rate is central to valuation. The option-pricing formula calculates a subjective probability distribution centered on the forward rate. This approach does not mean that the market expects the forward rate to be equal to the future spot rate, it is simply a result of the arbitrage-pricing structure of options.

The forward rate focus also provides helpful information for the trader managing a position. When the market prices a foreign currency option, it does so without any bullish or bearish sentiment on the direction of the foreign currency's value relative to the domestic currency. If the trader has specific expectations about the future spot rate's direction, those expectations can be put to work. A trader will not be inherently betting against the market. In a following section we will also describe how a change in the interest differential between currencies, the theoretical foundation of forward rates, also alters the value of the option.

Spot Rate Sensitivity (*delta*)

The call option on British pounds depicted in Exhibit 5.8 possesses a premium that exceeds the intrinsic value of the option over the entire range of spot rates surrounding the strike rate. As long as the option has time remaining before expiration, the option will possess this time value element. This characteristic is one of the primary reasons why an American-style option, which can be exercised on any day up to and including the expiration date, is seldom actually exercised prior to expiration. If the option holder wishes to liquidate it for its value, it would normally be sold, not exercised, so any remaining time value can also be captured by the holder. If the current spot rate falls on the side of the option's strike price which would induce the option holder to exercise the option upon expiration, the option also has an intrinsic value. The call option illustrated in Exhibit 7.7 is *in-the-money* at spot rates to the right of the strike rate of \$1.70, *at-the-money* at \$1.70, and *out-of-the-money* at spot rates less than \$1.70=£1.00.

The vertical distance between the market value and the intrinsic value of a call option on pounds is greatest at a spot rate of \$1.70 = £1.00. At \$1.70 the spot rate equals the strike price (at-the-money). This premium of 3.30 cents per pound consists entirely of time value. In fact, the value of any option which is currently out-of-the-money (OTM) is made up entirely of time value. The further the option's strike price is out-of-the-money, the lower the value or premium of the option. This is because the market believes the probability of this option actually moving into the exercise range prior to expiration is significantly less than one which is already at-the-money. If the spot rate were to fall to \$1.68 = £1.00, the option premium falls to 2.39 cents/£—again, entirely time value. If the spot rate were to rise above the strike rate to \$1.72, the premium rises to 4.39 cents/£. In this case, the premium represents an intrinsic value of 2.00 cents (\$1.72 – \$1.70) plus a time value element of 2.39 cents. Note the symmetry of time value premiums (2.39 cents) to the left and to the right of the strike rate.

The symmetry of option valuation about the strike rate is seen by decomposing the option premiums into their respective intrinsic and time values. Exhibit 7.8 illustrates how varying the current spot rate by ± \$0.05 about the strike rate of \$1.70 alters each option's intrinsic and time values.

The sensitivity of the option premium to a small change in the spot exchange rate is called the *delta*. For example, the delta of the \$1.70 call option, when the spot rate changes from \$1.70 to \$1.71, is simply the change in the premium divided by the change in the spot rate:

$$\text{Delta} = \frac{\Delta \text{ premium}}{\Delta \text{ spot rate}} = \frac{\$0.038 - \$0.033}{\$1.71 - \$1.70} = 0.5$$

If the delta of the specific option is known, it is easy to determine how the option's value will change as the spot rate changes. If the spot rate changes by one cent (\$0.01 per £), given a delta of 0.5, the option premium would change by 0.5 × \$0.01, or \$0.005. If the initial premium was \$0.033 per £, and the spot rate increased by 1 cent (from \$1.70 to \$1.71), the new option premium would be \$0.033 + \$0.005 = \$0.038. Delta varies between +1 and 0 for a call option and -1 and 0 for a put option.

Traders in options categorize individual options by their delta rather than in-the-money, at-the-money, or out-of-the-money. As an option moves further in-the-money, like the in-the-money option in Exhibit 5.10, delta rises toward 1.0 (in this case to .71). As an option moves further out-of-the-money, delta falls toward zero. Note that the out-of-the-money option in Exhibit 5.10 has a delta of only .28.[1]

Rule of Thumb: *The higher the delta (deltas of .7 or .8 and up are considered high) the greater the probability of the option expiring in-the-money.*

Time to Maturity: Value and Deterioration (*theta*)

Option values increase with the length of time to maturity. The expected change in the option premium from a small change in the time to expiration is termed *theta*. Theta is calculated as the change in the option premium over the change in time. If the \$1.70 = £1.00 call option were to age 1 day from its initial 90-day maturity, the theta of the call option would be the

[1] The expected change in the option's delta resulting from a small change in the spot rate is termed *gamma*. It is often used as a measure of the stability of a specific option's *delta*. *Gamma* is utilized in the construction of more sophisticated hedging strategies which focus on *deltas* (delta-neutral strategies).

difference in the two premiums, 3.30 cents per £ and 3.28 cents per £ (assuming a spot rate of $1.70 = £1.00):

$$\text{Theta} = \frac{\Delta \text{ premium}}{\Delta \text{ time}} = \frac{¢3.30 - ¢3.28}{90 - 89} = 0.02$$

Theta is based not on a linear relationship with time, but rather the square root of time. Option premiums deteriorate at an increasing rate as they approach expiration. In fact, the majority of the option premium—depending on the individual option—is lost in the final 30 days prior to expiration.

This exponential relationship between option premium and time is seen in the ratio of option values between the three-month and the one-month at-the-money maturities. The ratio for the at-the-money call option is not 3 to 1 (holding all other components constant), but rather 1.73 times the price.

$$\frac{\text{Premium of 3 month}}{\text{Premium of 1 month}} = \frac{\sqrt{3}}{\sqrt{1}} = \frac{1.73}{1.00} = 1.73$$

The rapid deterioration of option values in the last days prior to expiration is seen by once again calculating the theta of the $1.70 = £1.00 call option, but now as its remaining maturity moves from 15 days to 14 days:

$$\text{Theta} = \frac{\Delta \text{ premium}}{\Delta \text{ time}} = \frac{¢1.37 - ¢1.32}{15 - 14} = .05$$

A decrease of one day in the time to maturity now reduces the option premium by .05 cents per £, rather than only .02 cents per £ as it did when the maturity was 90 days.

The implications of time value deterioration for traders are quite significant. A trader purchasing an option with only one or two months until expiration will see the option's value deteriorate rapidly. If the trader were to then sell the option, it would have a significantly smaller market value in the periods immediately following its purchase. At the same time, however, a trader who is buying options of longer maturities will pay more, but not proportionately more, for the longer maturity option. A six-month option's premium is approximately 2.45 times more expensive than the one-month, while the 12-month option would be only 3.46 times more expensive than the one-month. This implies that two three-month options do not equal one six-month option.

Rule of Thumb: *A trader will normally find longer-maturity options better values, giving the trader the ability to alter an option position without suffering significant time value deterioration.*

Sensitivity to Volatility (*lambda*)

There are few words in the financial field more used and abused than *volatility*. Option *volatility* is defined as the standard deviation of daily percentage changes in the underlying exchange rate. Volatility is important to option value because of an exchange rate's perceived likelihood to move either into or out of the range in which the option would be exercised. If the exchange rate's volatility is rising, and therefore the risk of the option being exercised is increasing, the option premium would be increasing.

Volatility is stated in percent per annum. For example, an option may be described as having a 12.6% annual volatility. The percentage change for a single day can be found as follows:

$$\frac{12.6\%}{\sqrt{365}} = \frac{12.6\%}{19.105} = 0.66\% \text{ daily volatility}$$

For our $1.70 strike call option, an increase in annual volatility of 1 percentage point—for example, from 10.0% to 11.0%—will increase the option premium from $0.033 per £ to $0.036 per £. The marginal change in the option premium is equal to the change in the option premium itself divided by the change in volatility:

$$\frac{\Delta \text{ premium}}{\Delta \text{ volatility}} = \frac{\$0.036 - \$0.033}{.11 - .10} = 0.30$$

The primary problem with volatility is that it is unobservable; it is the only input into the option pricing formula that is determined subjectively by the trader pricing the option. No single correct method for its calculation exists. The problem is one of forecasting; historical volatility is not necessarily an accurate predictor of the future volatility of the exchange rate's movement, yet there is little to go on except history.

Volatility is viewed three ways: historic, where the volatility is drawn from a recent period of time; forward-looking, where the historic volatility is altered to reflect expectations about the future period over which the option will exist; and implied, where the volatility is backed out of the market price of the option.

Historic Volatility. Historic volatility is normally measured as the percentage movement in the spot rate on a daily, 6-, or 12-hour basis over the previous 10, 30, or even 90 days.

Forward-Looking Volatility. Alternatively, an option trader may adjust recent historic volatilities for expected market swings or events, either upward or downward. If option traders believe that the immediate future will be the same as the recent past, the historic volatility will equal the forward-looking volatility. If, however, the future period is expected to experience greater or lesser volatility, the historic measure must be altered for option pricing.

Implied Volatility. Implied volatility is equivalent to having the answers to the test; implied volatilities are calculated by being backed out of the market option premium values traded. Since volatility is the only unobservable element of the option premium price, after all other components are accounted for, the residual value of volatility implied by the price is found.

Sample implied volatilities for a number of currency pairs are listed in Exhibit 7.9. The exhibit clearly illustrates that option volatilities vary considerably across currencies, and that the relationship between volatility and maturity (time to expiration) does not move just one direction. For example, the first exchange rate quoted, the US$/euro cross-rate, initially falls from 8.1% volatility at one week to 7.4% for the 1-month and 2-month maturities and then rises to 9.3% for the 3-year maturity.

Because volatilities are the only judgmental component that the option writer contributes, they play a critical role in the pricing of options. All currency pairs have historical series that contribute to the formation of the expectations of option writers. But in the end, the truly talented option writers are those with the intuition and insight to price the future effectively.

Like all futures markets, option volatilities react instantaneously and negatively to unsettling economic and political events (see the mini-case at the end of this chapter for a look at currency volatility over the past decade, including the global pandemic). A doubling of volatility for an at-the-money option will result in an equivalent doubling of the option's price. Most currency option traders focus their activities on predicting movements of currency volatility in the short run, because short-run movements move price the most. For example, option

EXHIBIT 7.9 Foreign Currency Implied Volatilities (percent)

Currency (cross)	Symbol	1 week	1 month	2 month	3 month	6 month	1 year	2 year	3 year
European euro	EUR	8.1	7.4	7.4	7.4	7.8	8.5	9.0	9.3
Japanese yen	JPY	12.3	11.4	11.1	11.0	11.0	11.2	11.8	12.7
Swiss franc	CHF	8.9	8.4	8.4	8.4	8.9	9.5	9.8	9.9
British pound	GBP	7.7	7.3	7.2	7.1	7.3	7.5	7.9	8.2
Canadian dollar	CAD	6.4	6.4	6.3	6.4	6.7	7.1	7.4	7.6
Australian dollar	AUD	11.2	10.7	10.5	10.3	10.4	10.6	10.8	11.0
British pound/euro	GBPEUR	6.7	6.4	6.5	6.4	6.8	7.3	7.6	7.8
Euro/Japanese yen	EURJPY	11.6	11.1	11.2	11.3	11.8	12.6	13.4	14.1

Note: These implied volatility rates are averages of mid-level rates for bid and ask "at-money quotations" on selected currencies at 11 a.m. on the last business day of the month, September 30, 2013.

Source: Federal Reserve Bank of New York.

volatilities rose significantly in the months preceding the Persian Gulf War, in September 1992 when the European Monetary System was in crisis, in 1997 after the onset of the Asian financial crisis, in the days following the terrorist attacks on the U.S. in September 2001, and in the months following the onset of the global financial crisis in September 2008. In all instances, option volatilities for major cross-currency combinations rose to nearly 20% for extended periods. As a result, premium costs rose by corresponding amounts.

Rule of Thumb: *Traders who believe volatilities will fall significantly in the near-term will sell (write) options now, hoping to buy them back for a profit immediately after volatilities fall causing option premiums to fall.*

Sensitivity to Changing Interest Rate Differentials (*rho* and *phi*)

At the start of this section we pointed out that currency option prices and values are focused on the forward rate. The forward rate is in turn based on the theory of interest rate parity discussed previously in Chapter 6. Interest rate changes in either currency will alter the forward rate, which in turn will alter the option's premium or value. The expected change in the option premium from a small change in the domestic interest rate (home currency) is term *rho*. The expected change in the option premium from a small change in the foreign interest rate (foreign currency) is termed *phi*.

Continuing with our numerical example, an increase in the U.S. dollar interest rate from 8.0% to 9.0% *increases* the ATM call option premium on British pounds from \$0.033 per £ to \$0.035 per £. This is a *rho* value of positive 0.2

$$\text{Rho} = \frac{\Delta \text{ Premium}}{\Delta \text{ US dollar interest rate}} = \frac{\$0.035 - \$0.033}{9.0\% - 8.0\%} = 0.2$$

A similar 1% increase in the foreign interest rate, the pound sterling rate in this case, *reduces* the option value (premium) from \$0.033 per £ to \$0.031 per £. The *phi* for this call option premium is therefore a negative 0.2.

$$\text{Phi} = \frac{\Delta \text{ Premium}}{\Delta \text{ foreign interest rate}} = \frac{\$0.031 - \$0.033}{9.0\% - 8.0\%} = -0.2$$

For example, throughout the 1990s U.S. dollar (domestic currency) interest rates were substantially lower than pound sterling (foreign currency) interest rates. This meant that the pound consistently sold forward at a discount versus the U.S. dollar. If this interest differential were to widen (from either U.S. interest rates falling or foreign currency interest rates rising or some combination of both), the pound would sell forward at a larger discount. An increase in the forward discount is the same as a decrease in the forward rate (in U.S. dollars per unit of foreign currency). The option premium condition above states that the premium must increase as interest rate differentials increase (assuming spot rates remain unchanged).

For the option trader, an expectation on the differential between interest rates can obviously help in the evaluation of where the option value is headed. For example, when foreign interest rates are higher than domestic interest rates, the foreign currency sells forward at a discount. This results in relatively lower call option premiums (and lower put option premiums).

Rule of Thumb: *A trader who is purchasing a call option on foreign currency should do so before the domestic interest rate rises. This will allow the trader to purchase the option before its price increases.*

Alternative Strike Prices and Option Premiums

The sixth and final element that is important in option valuation (but, thankfully, has no Greek alias) is the selection of the actual strike price. Although we have conducted all of our sensitivity analysis using the strike price of \$1.70 = £1.00 (a forward-at-the-money strike rate), a firm purchasing an option in the OTC market may choose its own strike rate. Options with strike rates that are already in-the-money will have both intrinsic and time value elements. Options with strike rates which are out-of-the-money will have only a time value component.

Exhibit 7.10 summarizes the various "Greek" elements and impacts discussed in the previous sections. The option premium is one of the most complex concepts in financial theory, and the application of option pricing to exchange rates does not make it any simpler. Only

EXHIBIT 7.10 Summary of Option Premium Components

Greek	Definition	Interpretation
Delta	Expected change in the option premium for a small change in the spot rate	The higher the delta, the more likely the option will move in-the-money
Theta	Expected change in the option premium for a small change in time to expiration	Premiums are relatively insensitive until the final 30 or so days
Lambda	Expected change in the option premium for a small change in volatility	Premiums rise with increases in volatility
Rho	Expected change in the option premium for a small change in the domestic interest rate	Increases in domestic interest rates cause increasing call option premiums
Phi	Expected change in the option premium for a small change in the foreign interest rate	Increases in foreign interest rates cause decreasing call option premiums

GLOBAL FINANCE IN PRACTICE 7.4

GM and Fiat's Put Option

Option theory has long been utilized in corporate strategy. In the late 1990s the global automobile industry went through a period of consolidation. Companies like Daimler Benz (Germany) and Chrysler (U.S.) combined as the industry tried to deal with increasing costs and overcapacity. General Motors (GM, U.S.) appeared to have been left out in the cold, but GM had shown no real sense of urgency in pursing any deals.

In early 2000, however, DaimlerChrysler offered to buy Fiat Auto (Italy) out. This threatened GM in terms of markets and opportunities. GM quickly signed an alliance agreement with Fiat. The agreement involved an exchange of shares, GM taking a 20% interest in Fiat Auto and Fiat taking a 5.1% interest in GM, in addition to creating a number of joint ventures for engineering development and procurement.

The agreement also included a put option. The put gave Fiat the right to sell its remaining shares (the remaining 80% interest not held by GM) to GM, beginning 3.5 years following the agreement and expiring 9 years after the agreement. Although it is not clear that either party ever wished for GM to ever actually acquire Fiat, the put option was seen by leadership at Fiat as a type of insurance against an unprofitable future (a financial out), but both parties agreed there was little likelihood of the put ever being exercised.

In the fall of 2004 Fiat's fortunes were reaching rock-bottom prospects; bankruptcy loomed. Fiat began to publicly discuss the fact that it believed it had the right to sell itself (the put option) to GM. GM responded by making noises that it did not believe the clause was enforceable (it did not want to buy Fiat) and also threatened that if it *did* have to acquire Fiat, it would most likely shut it down. This did not sit well with Italian autoworkers. The Italian autoworkers went on strike in December 2004 in opposition to any closure and any sale to GM.

On February 13, 2005, in what has become known as the Valentine's Day Annulment, GM and Fiat announced they had agreed to terminate the agreement, including canceling the put option and unwinding of the joint ventures between the two companies. The price of annulment, however, was all GM's. GM paid Fiat $2.3 billion to cancel the agreement.

with a considerable amount of time and effort can the individual be expected to attain a "second-sense" in the management of currency option positions.

Prudence in Practice

In the following chapters we will illustrate how derivatives can be used to reduce the risks associated with the conduct of multinational financial management. It is critical, however, that the user of any financial tool or technique—including financial derivatives—follow sound principles and practices. Many a firm has been ruined as a result of the misuse of derivatives. A word to the wise: Do not fall victim to what many refer to as the gambler's dilemma—confusing luck with talent. Major corporate financial disasters related to financial derivatives continue to be a problem in global business. As is the case with so many issues in modern society, technology is not the problem, the problem is user error—human users. *Global Finance in Practice 7.4* describes how one use of options did indeed include human error.

Summary Points

- Foreign currency futures contracts are standardized forward contracts. Unlike forward contracts, however, trading occurs on the floor of an organized exchange rather than between banks and customers.
- Futures also require collateral and are normally settled through the purchase of an offsetting position.
- Corporate financial managers typically prefer foreign currency forwards over futures out of simplicity of use and position maintenance. Financial speculators typically prefer foreign currency futures over forwards because of the liquidity of the futures markets.
- Foreign currency options are financial contracts that give the holder the right, but not the obligation, to buy (in the case of calls) or sell (in the case of puts) a specified amount of foreign exchange at a predetermined price on or before a specified maturity date.
- The use of a currency option as a speculative device for the buyer of an option arises from the fact that an option gains in value as the underlying currency rises (for calls) or falls (for puts). The amount of loss to the buyer of an option when the underlying currency moves opposite to the desired direction is limited to the option premium.

- The use of a currency option as a speculative device for the writer (seller) of an option arises from the option premium. If the option—either a put or call—expires out-of-the-money (valueless), the writer of the option has earned and retains the entire premium.
- Speculation is an attempt to profit by trading on expectations about prices in the future. In the foreign exchange market, one speculates by taking a position in a foreign currency and then closing that position afterward; a profit results only if the rate moves in the direction that the speculator expected.
- Currency option valuation, the determination of the option's premium, is a complex combination of the current spot rate, the specific strike rate, the forward rate (which itself is dependent on the current spot rate and interest differentials), currency volatility, and time to maturity.
- The total value of an option is the sum of its intrinsic value and time value. Intrinsic value depends on the relationship between the option's strike price and the current spot rate at any single point in time, whereas time value estimates how intrinsic value may change—for the better—prior to maturity.

MINI-CASE

The Ups and Downs of Volatility[2]

Global currency volatility reached its lowest level in more than 40 years in January 2020. It would prove to be the true bottom before the bounce.

In January 2020 the United States and China signed a trade agreement ending a long-standing spat in which the U.S. accused China of manipulating the value of the Chinese renminbi. The agreement was considered enormously important—calming the relationship between the world's two largest trading partners. In the days that followed, JP Morgan's Global FX Volatility Index, a measure of currency volatility, hit a record low of 5.18, a value approached but never reached over the previous 20 years. This of course made currency options extremely cheap. As illustrated in Exhibit A, each of the previous record lows was followed by short and significant increases in volatility. Fundamentalists would of course look to find economic drivers of these changes, while technical chartists would see trend and barriers driving change. Regardless, in January 2020 currency volatility globally was a sea of glass.

Global Pandemic (COVID)

Investors are scrambling to adjust their portfolios to a surge of volatility in foreign exchange markets, as the coronavirus outbreak and massive swings in oil prices roil currencies around the globe.

—"Explosion in Forex Volatility Cheers Some, Bruises Others as Virus Fears Drive Swings," Reuters, March 11, 2020.

Every global currency trader wishes that, in the early spring of 2020, they could have possessed that most mystical of capabilities—*the third eye*. Having an organ with which the individual investor or currency trader could see the future would have been quite an advantage. With March 2020 came COVID—the global pandemic. And to add insult to injury, a nearly instantaneous drop in global oil prices sent markets spiraling downward even further. Currency volatilities soared. The volatilities associated with the world's three most widely traded currencies—the U.S. dollar, the euro, and the Japanese yen—all spiked upward. Exhibit B illustrates how implied volatilities on at-the-money (ATM) strike rate calls on both the yen and the euro skyrocketed to 16% and 13%, respectively.

Everyone knows what followed—2020, the year of lemons: Global pandemic, quarantine, isolation, unemployment, and economic crisis. Eventually, in 2021, through social distancing, a multitude of anti-pandemic practices, and the development of vaccines, much of the world returned to some form of new normal.

The world's currency markets, however, recovered much more rapidly. For global currencies like the dollar, euro, and yen, recovery took only two to three months to return to moderate volatilities. For country currencies that always seemed to suffer more debilitating times like the Brazilian real and Mexican peso, the recovery in option volatilities was slower and more muted, as illustrated in Exhibit C. Currencies like the peso and real are, unfortunately, a bit more used to suffering such high volatilities, induced by political uncertainties or periodic bouts of inflation or currency uncertainty. But the global stalwarts—the dollar, euro, and yen—rarely have experienced such volatility, such as that of the global financial crisis in 2008–2009.

EXHIBIT A **JP Morgan Global FX Volatility Index**

Source: Constructed by authors. JPMVXYGL, daily, January 1, 2000–February 27, 2020.

EXHIBIT B **Option Volatilities on the Japanese Yen and Euro against the Dollar**

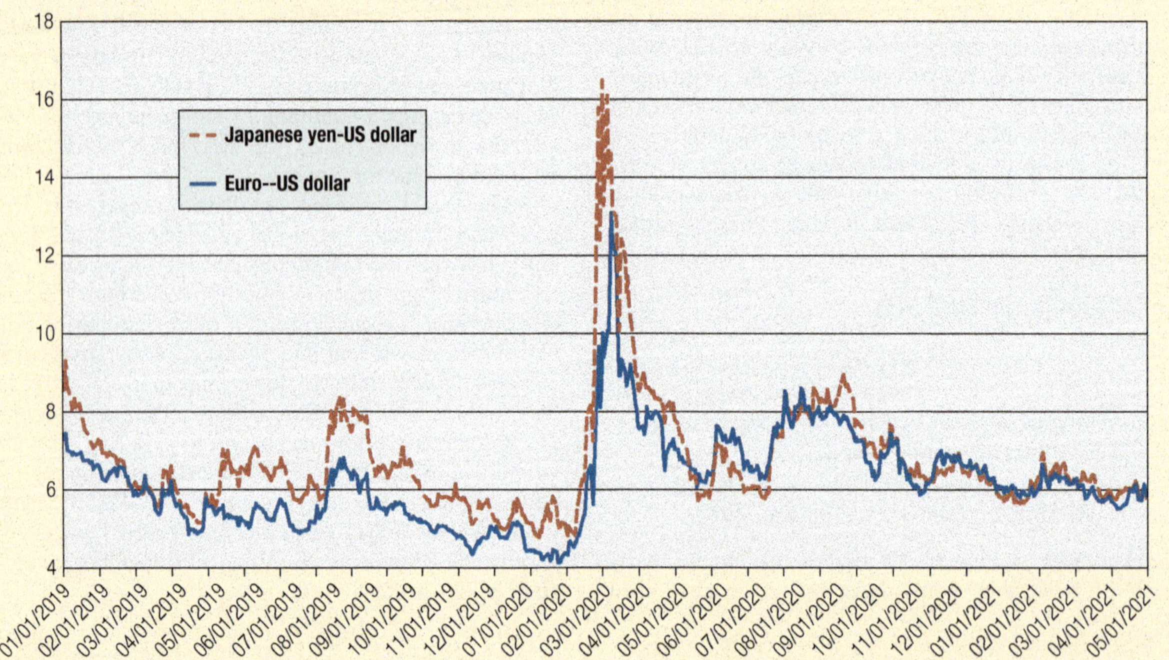

Source: Constructed by authors. Volatilities are implied volatilities on 3-month call option on at-the-money strike rate options.

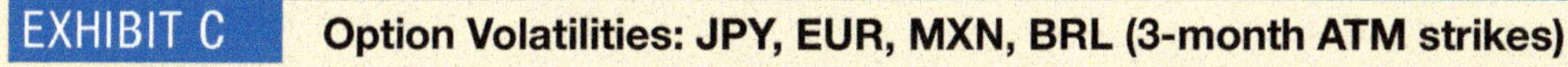

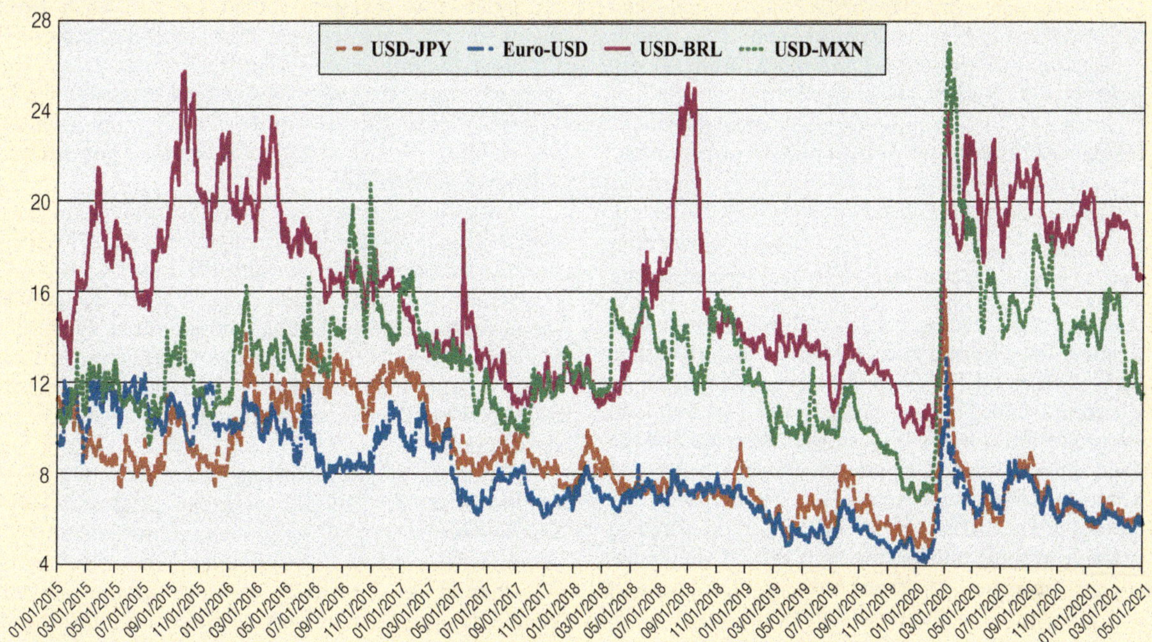

Source: Constructed by authors. Volatilities are Implied volatilities on 3-month call options on at-the-money strike rate options.

Option Trading

> *The more violently prices fluctuate, the more chance there is that an out-of-the-money option . . . becomes a winning lottery ticket at some point before it matures.*
>
> —"When You Have Options, Volatility Is Your Friend," *The Economist*, May 11, 2019.

Fear, anxiety, uncertainty, volatility—one and the same. When selling currency options, or holding currency options, volatility is said to be your friend.[3] The logic is simple. Increases in volatility drive increases in the value of options.

There are hundreds of different option trading strategies, and the unpredictability of volatility is at the core of many. Currency option pricing is based on *choices*—the currency pair, the strike rate, the time to maturity, *observables*—the appropriate term interest rates associated with the two currencies, and one *unknowable*—what the volatility will be for the coming term. As is fundamental to economics and finance, when we do not know the future, we analyze the past. Most option volatility assumptions for pricing are based on extrapolation of what similar volatilities have been for the most recent past.

This is not a surprising problem. No one knows the future. Even Fischer Black, the Nobel Prize–winning co-developer of modern option pricing theory with Myron Scholes, noted, "The Black-Scholes formula is still around, even though it depends on 10 unrealistic assumptions."[4] A major flaw was that the pricing formulas for assets of any kind—stocks, bonds, and currencies among others—assumed the assets' volatilities were known and fixed. They are not. He also noted that volatility differences would have profound impacts on far-out-of-the-money strike rates. He then offered some advice. "You should 'buy volatility' if you think volatility will rise, and 'sell volatility' if you think it will fall." He also noted that far out-of-the-money options were extremely sensitive to changes in volatility. This proved a fruitful line of thought for some.

[3] A fellow student of the author's in graduate school once asked the professor what he thought about the future direction of the U.S. dollar. The academic, after pause, said the following: "I don't know, that is why I am teaching. And, theoretically, if I did know, and could profit from knowing, why would I tell you?"

[4] "How to Use the Holes in Black-Scholes," by Fischer Black, *Journal of Applied Corporate Finance*, Winter 1989, Vol. 1.4.

Tail Risk (Fat Tails)

Put another way, investors are more volatile than investments. Economic reality governs the returns earned by our businesses, and Black Swans are unlikely. But emotions and perceptions—the swings of hope, greed, and fear among the participants in our financial system—govern the returns earned in our markets. Emotional factors magnify or minimize this central core of economic reality, and Black Swans can appear at any time.

—John C. Bogle, Founder of The Vanguard Group.[5]

One man has spent much of his career developing theories along similar lines: Nassim Nicholas Taleb. Taleb published a book in 2001 titled *Fooled by Randomness* in which he introduced the analogy of the black swan.[6] The argument is quite simple: Prior to the discovery of Australia and the existence of black swans, all swans were thought to be white. Black swans did not exist because no one had ever seen one. But that did not mean they did not exist. Taleb then applied this premise to financial markets, arguing that simply because a specific event had never occurred did not mean it couldn't. He concluded that most statistically based analyses, whether it be portfolios or options, regularly underestimated the probabilities associated with extreme events.

Taleb argued that a black swan event is characterized by three fundamentals, in order:

1. *Rarity*: The event is a shock or surprise to the observer.
2. *Extremeness*: The event has a major impact.
3. *Retrospective predictability*: After the event has occurred, the event is rationalized by hindsight and found to have been predictable.

Although the third argument is a characteristic of human intellectual nature, it is the first element which is fundamental to the debate. If an event has not been recorded, does that mean it cannot occur? Option theory is a mathematical analysis of inputs and assumptions. Its outcomes are no better than its inputs. The theory itself does not predict price movements. It simply prices rights on the basis of current market conditions and assumptions about the future based on the recent past—a past that has occurred.

Taleb does not argue that he has some secret ability to predict the future when historical data cannot. Rather, he argues that investors should structure their investments to either protect against or embrace the extremes. Leverage the *improbable events* rather than the *probable* ones. He argues for what many call "investment humility," to acknowledge that the world we live in is not always the one we think we live in and to understand how much we will never understand.

For example, traditional Black-Scholes option pricing assumes that volatility is normally distributed. This means that the model assumes that there is a 99.7% probability of volatility occurring within three standard deviations of the mean (or 0.3% of it falling outside three standard deviations). But what if this is underestimating the probability of volatility falling outside? This is what is referred to as *tail-risk* or alternatively relatively *fat tails* of the normal distribution.

Taleb developed investing strategies based on this inappropriate distribution of probabilities in his opinion. The *barbel strategy* combines safe investments with opportunities. An investor should create a strategy that was shaped like a barbel. Most of the capital, say 90%, should be invested in very low-risk investments, like Treasury bonds. These investments are likely to yield the traditional results seen in normal distributions. But, cognizant of the bias or inadequacies of traditional statistics, the investor should also invest some small portion, say 10%, of their capital in the extremes—the ends of the barbel. These extremes, the potential fat tails of the unknowable distribution, performed like lottery tickets. They generally never occur and therefore expire worthless. But, but, in rare cases, they prove true and extremely valuable.

Currency option pricing in the marketplace must follow rational thought and statistical methods. They need predictions of what may come, even if it is generally based on the past, a past which may not include the so-called "outliers." Kenneth Arrow, a famed economist and Nobel Prize winner himself, relayed the following story about statistics, forecasting, and humans recognizing what they don't know. During the World War II a group of statisticians were tasked with forecasting weather patterns over the English Channel.

[5] "Black Monday and Black Swans," Remarks by John C. Bogle, Founder and Former Chief Executive, The Vanguard Group, before the Risk Management Association, Boca Raton, Florida, October 11, 2007, p.6.

[6] Nassim Nicholas Taleb, *Fooled by Randomness: The Hidden Role of Chance in Life and in the Markets*, Random House, 2001. He later extended his premise to many other fields beyond finance in *The Black Swan: The Impact of the Highly Improbable*, Random House, 2007.

> *The statisticians subjected these forecasts to verification and found they differed in no way from chance. The forecasters themselves were convinced and requested that the forecasts be discontinued. The reply read approximately like this: "The Commanding General is well aware that the forecasts are no good. However, he needs them for planning purposes."*[7]

Taleb, in a revised edition of *Black Swan Theory*, noted that "the event," whatever it may be, is a surprise to the specific observer and that "what is a surprise to the turkey is not a surprise to the butcher." The challenge of course is to avoid being the turkey.

MINI-CASE QUESTIONS

1. Should the options market have predicted the events of March 2020?
2. Does the global pandemic of March 2020 fulfill the criteria for a black swan event?
3. What should a black swan investor have done in January 2020 when they observed the record low global currency volatility in the market?

[7] "I Know a Hawk from a Handsaw," *Eminent Economists: Their Life Philosophies*, edited by Michael Szenberg, Cambridge University Press, 1992, p. 47.

Questions

7.1 Foreign Currency Futures. What is a foreign currency future?

7.2 Futures Terminology. Explain the meaning and probable significance for international business of the following contract specifications:

a. notional principal
b. margin
c. marked-to-market

7.3 Long and a Short. How can foreign currency futures be used to speculate on the exchange rate movements, and what role do long and short positions play in that speculation?

7.4 Futures and Forwards. How do foreign currency futures and foreign currency forwards compare?

7.5 Puts and Calls. Define a put and call on the British pound sterling.

7.6 Options versus Futures. Explain the difference between foreign currency options and futures and when either might be most appropriately used.

7.7 Call Option Contract. Suppose that exchange-traded American call options on pounds sterling with a strike price of 1.460 and a maturity of next March are now quoted at 3.67. What does this mean to a potential buyer?

7.8 Premiums, Prices, and Costs. What is the difference between the price of an option, the value of an option, the premium on an option, and the cost of a foreign currency option?

7.9 Three Prices. What are the three different prices or "rates" integral to every foreign currency option contract?

7.10 Writing Options. Why would anyone write an option, knowing that the gain from receiving the option premium is fixed but the loss, if the underlying price goes in the wrong direction, can be extremely large?

7.11 Decision Prices. Once an option has been purchased, only two prices or rates are part of the holder's decision-making process. Which two and why?

7.12 Option Cash Flows and Time. The cash flows associated with a call option on euros by a U.S. dollar-based investor occur at different points in time. What are they and how much does the time element matter?

7.13 Option Valuation. The value of an option is stated to be the sum of its intrinsic value and its time value. Explain what is meant by these terms.

7.14 Time Value Deterioration. An option's value declines over time, but it does not do so evenly. Explain what that means for option valuation.

7.15 Option Values and Money. Options are often described as in-the-money, at-the-money, or out-of-the-money. What does that mean and how is it determined?

7.16 Option Pricing and the Forward Rate. What is the relationship or link between the forward rate and the foreign currency option premium?

7.17 Option Deltas. What is an option delta? How does it change when the option is in-the-money, at-the-money, or out-of-the-money?

7.18 Historic versus Implied Volatility. What is the difference between a historic volatility and an implied volatility?

Problems

7.1 Yize Shen at Sumatra Funds. Yize Chen trades currencies for Sumatra Funds in Jakarta. She focuses nearly all of her time and attention on the U.S. dollar (USD) to Singapore dollar (SGD) cross-rate. The current spot rate is USD0.6000 = SGD1.00. After considerable study, she has concluded that the Singapore dollar will appreciate versus the U.S. dollar in the coming 90 days, probably to about USD0.7000 = SGD1.00. She has the following options on the Singapore dollar to choose from:

Option	Strike Price	Premium
Put on SGD	USD0.6500 = SGD1.00	USD0.00003 per SGD
Call on SGD	USD0.6500 = SGD1.00	USD0.00046 per SGD

a. Should Yize buy a put on Singapore dollars or a call on Singapore dollars?
b. What is Yize's break-even price on the option purchased in part (a)?
c. Using your answer from part (a), what are Yize's gross profit and net profit (including premium) if the spot rate at the end of 90 days is indeed USD0.7000?
d. Using your answer from part (a), what are Yize's gross profit and net profit (including premium) if the spot rate at the end of 90 days is USD0.8000?

7.2 RiverRock Capital Geneva (A). Christoph Hoffeman trades currency for RiverRock Capital of Geneva. Christoph has USD10 million to begin with, and he must state all profits at the end of any speculation while the 30-day forward rate is USD1.3350 = EUR1.00.

a. If Christoph believes the euro will continue to rise in value against the U.S. dollar and expects the spot rate to be USD1.3600=EUR1.00 at the end of 30 days, what should he do?
b. If Christoph believes the euro will depreciate in value against the U.S. dollar and expects the spot rate to be USD1.2800 = EUR1.00 at the end of 30 days, what should he do?

7.3 RiverRock Capital Geneva (B). Christoph Hoffeman of RiverRock Capital now believes the Swiss franc (CHF) will appreciate versus the U.S. dollar in the coming 3-month period. He has USD100,000 to invest. The current spot rate is USD0.5820 = CHF1.00, the 3-month forward rate is USD0.5640=CHF1.00, and he expects the spot rates to reach USD0.6250 = CHF1.00 in three months.

a. Calculate Christoph's expected profit assuming a pure spot market speculation strategy.
b. Calculate Christoph's expected profit assuming he buys or sells CHG three months forward.

7.4 Tony Begay at Saguaro Funds. Tony Begay, a currency trader for Chicago-based Saguaro Funds, uses the following futures quotes on the British pound (£) to speculate on the value of the pound.

a. If Tony buys 5 June pound futures and the spot rate at maturity is $1.3980 = £1.00, what is the value of his position?
b. If Tony sells 12 March pound futures and the spot rate at maturity is $1.4560 = £1.00, what is the value of his position?
c. If Tony buys 3 March pound futures and the spot rate at maturity is $1.4560 = £1.00, what is the value of his position?
d. If Tony sells 12 June pound futures and the spot rate at maturity is $1.3980 = £1.00, what is the value of his position?

7.5 Laura Cervantes. Laura Cervantes, the currency speculator we met in the chapter, sells eight June futures contracts for 500,000 pesos (Ps) at the closing price quoted in Exhibit 7.1.

a. What is the value of her position at maturity if the ending spot rate is $0.12000 = Ps1.00?
b. What is the value of her position at maturity if the ending spot rate is $0.09800 = Ps1.00?
c. What is the value of her position at maturity if the ending spot rate is $0.11000 = Ps1.00?

7.6 Kiko Peleh. Kiko Peleh writes a put option on Japanese yen with a strike price of $0.008000 = ¥1.00 (¥125.00 = $1.00) at a premium of 0.0080¢ per yen and with an expiration date six months from now. The option is for ¥12,500,000. What is Kiko's profit or loss at maturity if the ending spot rates are ¥110, ¥115, ¥120, ¥125, ¥130, ¥135, and ¥140 per dollar?

Problem 7.4

British Pound Futures, $=£1.00 (CME) **Contract = £62,500**

Maturity	Open	High	Low	Settle	Change	High	Open_Interest
March	1.4246	1.4268	1.4214	1.4228	0.0032	1.4700	25,605
June	1.4164	1.4188	1.4146	1.4162	0.0030	1.4550	809

7.7 Alcasa of Caracas. Alcasa, a Venezuelan company, wishes to borrow $8,000,000 for eight weeks. A rate of 6.250% per annum is quoted by potential lenders in New York, Great Britain, and Switzerland using, respectively, international, British, and the Swiss-eurobond definitions of interest (day count conventions). Although all three currency markets assume a 360-day year for interest rate calculations, the U.S. and British markets use the exact number of days in the period in question, 56 days in this case, while the Swiss market assumes a standardized 30-day month. From which source should Alcasa borrow?

7.8 Cachita Haynes. Cachita Haynes works as a currency speculator for Vatic Capital of Los Angeles. Her latest speculative position is to profit from her expectation that the U.S. dollar will rise significantly against the Japanese yen. The current spot rate is ¥120.00 = $1.00. She must choose between the following 90-day options on the Japanese yen:

Option	Strike Price	Premium
Put on yen	¥125 = $1.00	$0.00003 per $
Cal on yen	¥120 = $1.00	$0.00046 per $

a. Should Cachita buy a put on yen or a call on yen?
b. What is Cachita's break-even price on the option purchased in part (a)?
c. Using your answer from part (a), what are Cachita's gross profit and net profit (including premium) if the spot rate at the end of 90 days is ¥140 = $1.00?

7.9 Henrik's Options. Assume Henrik writes a call option on euros with a strike price of $1.2500=€1.00 at a premium of 3.80 cents per euro ($0.0380 per €) and with an expiration date three months from now. The option is for 100,000 euros. Calculate Henrik's profit or loss should he exercise before maturity at a time when the euro is traded spot at strike prices beginning at $1.10 = €1.00, rising to $1.40 = €1.00 in increments of $0.05.

7.10 Baker Street. Arthur Doyle is a currency trader for Baker Street, a private investment house in London. Baker Street's clients are a collection of wealthy private investors who, with a minimum stake of £250,000 each, wish to speculate on the movement of currencies. The investors expect annual returns in excess of 25%. Although officed in London, all accounts and expectations are based in U.S. dollars. Arthur is convinced that the British pound will slide significantly—possibly to $1.3200 = £1.00—in the coming 30 to 60 days. The current spot rate is $1.4260 = £1.00. Arthur wishes to buy a put on pounds, which will yield the 25% return expected by his investors. Which of the following put options would you recommend he purchase? Prove your choice is the preferable combination of strike price, maturity, and up-front premium expense.

Strike Price	Maturity	Premium
$1.36 = £1.00	30 days	$0.00081 per £
$1.34 = £1.00	30 days	$0.00021 per £
$1.32 = £1.00	30 days	$0.00004 per £
$1.36 = £1.00	60 days	$0.00333 per £
$1.34 = £1.00	60 days	$0.00150 per £
$1.32 = £1.00	60 days	$0.00060 per £

7.11 Calandra Panagakos at CIBC. Calandra Panagakos works for CIBC Currency Funds in Toronto. Calandra is something of a contrarian; as opposed to most of the forecasts, she believes the Canadian dollar (CAD) will appreciate versus the U.S. dollar (USD) over the coming 90 days. The current spot rate is USD0.6750 = CAD1.00. Calandra may choose between the following options on the Canadian dollar.

Option	Strike Price	Premium
Put on CAD	USD0.7000 = CAD1.00	USD0.00003 per CAD
Call on CAD	USD0.7000 = CAD1.00	USD0.00049 per CAD

a. Should Calandra buy a put on Canadian dollars or a call on Canadian dollars?
b. What is Calandra's break-even price on the option purchased in part (a)?
c. Using your answer from part (a), what are Calandra's gross profit and net profit (including premium) if the spot rate at the end of 90 days is indeed USD0.7600?
d. Using your answer from part (a), what are Calandra's gross profit and net profit (including premium) if the spot rate at the end of 90 days is USD0.8250?

Pricing Your Own Options

An Excel workbook titled FX Option Pricing is downloadable from this book's website. The workbook has five spreadsheets constructed for pricing currency options for the following five currency pairs (the U.S. dollar/euro spreadsheet from the workbook is shown below): U.S. dollar-euro, U.S. dollar-Japanese yen, euro-Japanese yen, U.S. dollar-British pound, and euro-British pound. Use the appropriate spreadsheet from the workbook to answer Problems 7.12–7.16.

7.12 U.S. Dollar–Euro. The following table indicates that a 1-year call option on euros at a strike rate of \$1.25 = €1.00 will cost the buyer \$0.0632 per €, or 4.99%. But that assumed a volatility of 12.000% when the spot rate was \$1.2674 = €1.00. What would that same call option cost if the volatility was reduced to 10.500% when the spot rate fell to \$1.2480 = €1.00?

7.13 U.S. Dollar–Japanese Yen. What would be the premium expense, in home currency, for a Japanese firm to purchase an option to sell 750,000 U.S. dollars, assuming the initial values listed in the FX Option Pricing workbook?

7.14 Euro–Japanese Yen. A French firm is expecting to receive ¥10.4 million in 90 days as a result of an export sale to a Japanese semiconductor firm. What will it cost, in total, to purchase an option to sell the yen at €0.0072=¥1.00?

7.15 U.S. Dollar–British Pound. Assuming the same initial values for the U.S. dollar–British pound cross-rate in the FX Option Pricing workbook, how much more would a call option on pounds be if the maturity was doubled from 90 to 180 days? What percentage increase is this for twice the length of maturity?

7.16 Euro–British Pound. How would the call option premium change on the right to buy pounds with euros if the euro interest rate changed to 4.000% from the initial values listed in the FX Option Pricing workbook?

Problem 7.12–7.16

Pricing Currency Options on the Euro

	A U.S.-based firm wishing to buy or sell euros (the foreign currency)		*A European firm wishing to buy or sell dollars (the foreign currency)*	
	Variable	**Value**	**Variable**	**Value**
Spot rate (domestic/foreign)	S_0	\$1.2480	S_0	€0.8013
Strike rate (domestic/foreign)	X	\$1.2500	X	€0.8000
Domestic interest rate (% p.a.)	r_d	1.453%	r_d	2.187%
Foreign interest rate (% p.a.)	R_f	2.187%	R_f	1.453%
Time (years, 365 days)	T	1.000	T	1.000
Days Equivalent		365		365
Volatility (% p.a.)	s	10.500%	s	10.500%
Call option premium (per unit fc)	c	\$0.0461	c	€0. 0366
Put option premium (per unit fc)	p	\$0.0570	p	€0.0295
(European Pricing)				
Call option premium (%)	c	3.69%	c	4.56%
Put option premium (%)	p	4.57%	P	3.68%

CHAPTER 7 APPENDIX

Currency Option Pricing Theory

The foreign currency option model presented here, the European style option, is the result of the work of Black and Scholes (1972), Cox and Ross (1976), Cox, Ross, and Rubinstein (1979), Garman and Kohlhagen (1983), and Bodurtha and Courtadon (1987). Although we do not explain the theoretical derivation of the following option-pricing model, the original model derived by Black and Scholes is based on the formation of a riskless hedged portfolio composed of a long position in the security, asset, or currency and a European call option. The solution to this model's expected return yields the option *premium*.

The basic theoretical model for the pricing of a European call option is:

$$C = e^{-r_f T} SN(d_1) - Ee^{-r_d T} N(d_2)$$

where

C = premium on a European call
e = continuous time discounting
S = spot exchange rate (\$/foreign currency)
E = exercise or strike rate
T = time to expiration
N = cumulative normal distribution function
r_f = foreign interest rate
r_d = domestic interest rate
σ = standard deviation of asset price (volatility)
ln = natural logarithm

The two density functions, d_1 and d_2, are defined:

$$d_1 = \frac{\ln\left(\frac{S}{E}\right) + \left(r_d - r_f + \frac{\sigma^2}{2}\right)T}{\sigma\sqrt{T}}$$

and

$$d_2 = d_1 - \sigma\sqrt{T}$$

This expression can be rearranged so the premium on a European call option is written in terms of the forward rate:

$$C = e^{-r_f T} FN(d_1) - e^{-r_d T} EN(d_2)$$

where the spot rate and foreign interest rate have been replaced with the forward rate, F, and both the first and second terms are discounted over continuous time, e. If we now slightly simplify, we find that the option premium is the present value of the difference between two cumulative normal density functions.

$$C = [FN(d_1) - EN(d_2)]e^{-r_d T}$$

The two density functions are now defined:

$$d_1 = \frac{\ln\left(\frac{F}{E}\right) + \left(\frac{\sigma^2}{2}\right)T}{\sigma\sqrt{T}}$$

and

$$d_2 = d_1 - \sigma\sqrt{T}$$

Solving each of these equations for d_1 and d_2 allows the determination of the European call option premium. The premium for a European put option, P, is similarly derived:

$$P = [F(N(d_1) - 1) - E(N(d_2) - 1)]\, e^{-r_d T}$$

The European Call Option: Numerical Example

The actual calculation of the option premium is not as complex as it appears from the preceding set of equations. Assuming the following basic exchange rate and interest rate values, computation of the option premium is relatively straightforward.

Spot rate	= \$1.7000/£
90-day forward	= \$1.7000/£
Strike rate	= \$1.7000/£
U.S. dollar interest rate	= 8.00 % (per annum)
Pound sterling interest rate	= 8.00 % (per annum)
Time (days)	= 90
Std. dev. (volatility)	= 10.00 %
e (infinite discounting)	= 2.71828

The value of the two density functions is first derived:

$$d_1 = \frac{\ln\left(\frac{F}{E}\right) + \left(\frac{\sigma^2}{2}\right)T}{\sigma\sqrt{\mathrm{T}}} = \frac{\ln\left(\frac{1.7000}{1.700}\right) + \left(\frac{.1000^2}{2}\right)\frac{90}{365}}{.1000\sqrt{\frac{90}{365}}} = .025$$

and

$$d_2 = 0.025 - 0.1000\sqrt{\frac{90}{365}} = -.025$$

The values of d_1 and d_2 are then found in a cumulative normal probability table,

$$N(d_1) = N(.025) = 0.51; \quad N(d_2) = N(-.025) = .49$$

The premium of the European call with a "forward-at-the-money" strike rate is

$$C = [(1.7000)(.51) - (1.7000)(.49)]\, 2.71828^{-.08(90/365)} = \$0.033/£$$

This is the call option *premium, price, value,* or *cost.*

8

Interest Rate Risk and Swaps

Confidence in markets and institutions, it's a lot like oxygen. When you have it, you don't even think about it. Indispensable. You can go years without thinking about it. When it's gone for five minutes, it's the only thing you think about. The confidence has been sucked out of the credit markets and institutions.

—Warren Buffett, October 1, 2008

LEARNING OBJECTIVES

8.1 Explain interest rate foundations, including interest rate calculations and reference rates

8.2 Define the cost of debt for both governments (sovereign borrowers) and corporate borrowers

8.3 Analyze interest rate risk and examine a variety of methods for its management

8.4 Explore the use of interest rate futures and forward rate agreements in managing interest rate risk

8.5 Examine the use of interest rate swaps to manage the interest rate risks of multinational firms

All firms—domestic or multinational, small or large, leveraged or unleveraged—are sensitive to changes in interest rates. Although a variety of interest rate risks exist, this book focuses on the financial management of the nonfinancial (nonbank) multinational firm. The international financial marketplace in which these multinational firms operate is largely defined by both interest rates and exchange rates, and those theoretical linkages were established in Chapter 6 on parity relationships. We now turn to the interest rate structures and the challenges facing firms operating in a multi-currency interest rate world.

The first section of this chapter on interest rate foundations details the various reference rates and floating rates that all multinationals deal in. The chapter then turns to the government—corporate interest rate relationships that define the costs and availability of capital. The third section focuses on the various forms of interest rate risk confronting multinational firms. The fourth and fifth sections detail how a variety of financial derivatives, including interest rate swaps, can be used to manage these interest rate risks. The mini-case at the end of the chapter, *Replacing LIBOR*, explores the complex multinational effort to move the world's financial structure to a new benchmark interest rate, replacing LIBOR, which has been used for the past 50 years.

8.1 Interest Rate Foundations

We begin our discussion of interest rates with some definitions, namely, interest rate calculation practices internationally and the use of reference interest rates.

Interest Rate Calculations

International interest rate calculations are the first major concern of any firm borrowing or investing globally. Interest rate calculations differ by the number of days used in the period's calculation and in the definition of how many days there are in a year (for financial purposes). Exhibit 8.1 illustrates three examples of how different calculation methodologies result in different 1 month payments of interest on a $10 million loan, 5.500% per annum interest, for an exact period of 28 days.

The first example shown, *International Practice*, uses a 28-day month in a 360-day financial year. The result is an interest payment of $42,777.78:

$$0.055 \times \$10{,}000{,}000 \times (28/360) = \$42{,}777.78$$

If, however, the interest rate calculation had utilized the Swiss Practice (Eurobond) of a standard 30-day calculation, the interest cost for the same one-month period would have been $45,833.33, a substantial $3,055.56 higher. Clearly, calculation methods matter.

The Reference Rate: LIBOR

A *reference rate*—for example, U.S. dollar LIBOR—is the rate of interest used in a standardized quotation, loan agreement, or financial derivative valuation. Most reference rates used are widely quoted interbank rates, the rate of interest for lending between major financial institutions on an overnight, daily, or multiple day basis. LIBOR, or ICE LIBOR as it is sometimes referred to today, is the *London Interbank Offered Rate*, the most widely used and quoted benchmark rate. A second source of reference rates is government borrowing rates. The U.S. Treasury bill, note, and bond rate is one such common reference rate.

LIBOR is administered by the ICE Benchmark Administration (IBA) and is calculated for five different currencies: U.S. dollar (USD), euro (EUR), British pound sterling (GBP), Japanese yen (JPY), and the Swiss franc (CHF). It is quoted for seven different maturities: overnight; one week; and 1, 2, 3, 6, and 12 months. LIBOR was for decades calculated and published by the British Bankers Association. These different maturities terms are one of the most important characteristics of LIBOR, as they offer the ability of a borrower and lender to enter into a loan agreement for a specific maturity and have a market-based rate for that

EXHIBIT 8.1 International Interest Rate Calculations

International interest rate calculations differ by the number of days used in the period's calculation and their definition of how many days there are in a year (for financial purposes). The following example highlights how the different methods result in different one-month payments of interest on a $10 million loan, 5.500% per annum interest, for an exact period of 28 days.

			$10 million @ 5.500% per annum	
Practice	**Day Count in Period**	**Days/Year**	**Days Used**	**Interest Payment**
International	Exact number of days	360	28	$42,777.78
British	Exact number of days	365	28	$42,191.78
Swiss (Eurobond)	Assumed 30 days/month	360	30	$45,833.33

coming period known to both parties. This forward-looking feature is fundamental to borrowers particularly.

As detailed in the mini-case at the end of this chapter, LIBOR is now being replaced by a variety of different reference rates by country. As is common globally in interest rate quotations, all ICE LIBOR rates are quoted on an annualized basis. For example, using the practices described in Exhibit 8.1, an overnight British pound sterling interest rate quote of 2.00000% would indicate that a bank would expect to pay 2% divided by 365 on the principal of the loan.

The interbank interest rate market is not, however, confined to London. There are a total of 35 different LIBOR rates quoted globally each business day. The most commonly utilized rate is the three-month U.S. dollar rate. It is the most common reference rate for business loans of all kinds and many different forms of financial derivatives. Most major regional financial centers construct their own interbank offered rates for local loan agreement purposes. These rates include PIBOR (Paris Interbank Offered Rate), MIBOR (Madrid Interbank Offered Rate), and SIBOR (Singapore Interbank Offered Rate), to name but a few.

Exhibit 8.2 shows 3-month USD LIBOR over the past 30 years. It has obviously moved over large ranges, from over 10% in the late 1980s to near zero percent in the post-2008 financial crisis years. The single most dramatic interest rate characteristic is how LIBOR has dropped leading up to and into major recessions. This is key in understanding corporate loan needs and practices. As economic conditions slow and prospects for new investments decline, the demand for debt of all forms declines, as do interest rates. At the same time, central banks—in this case, the U.S. Federal Reserve—typically undertake expansionary monetary policy to try to lower interest rates even further and hopefully kick-start new borrowing and investment. The most extreme examples of this is the Fed's use of quantitative easing (QE), the pumping of liquidity into the financial system, following the

EXHIBIT 8.2 U.S. Dollar 3-Month LIBOR (monthly, January 1986–June 2021)

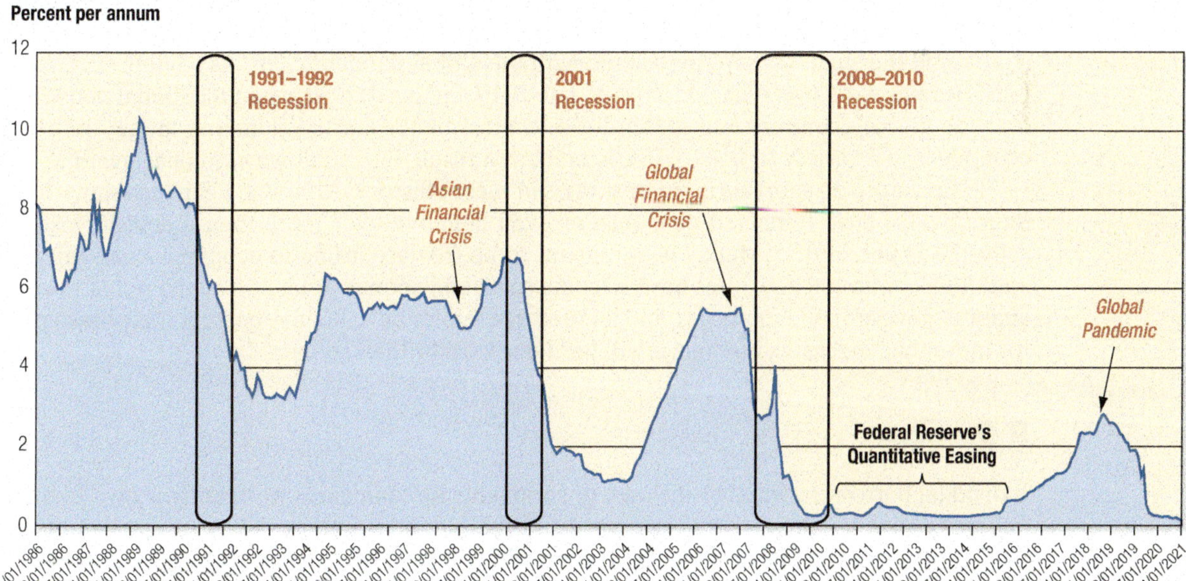

Source: LIBOR data from the Federal Reserve Economic Data (FRED), Federal Reserve Bank of St. Louis.

EXHIBIT 8.3 **Three-Month LIBOR for Select Currencies (daily, January 1999–June 2021)**

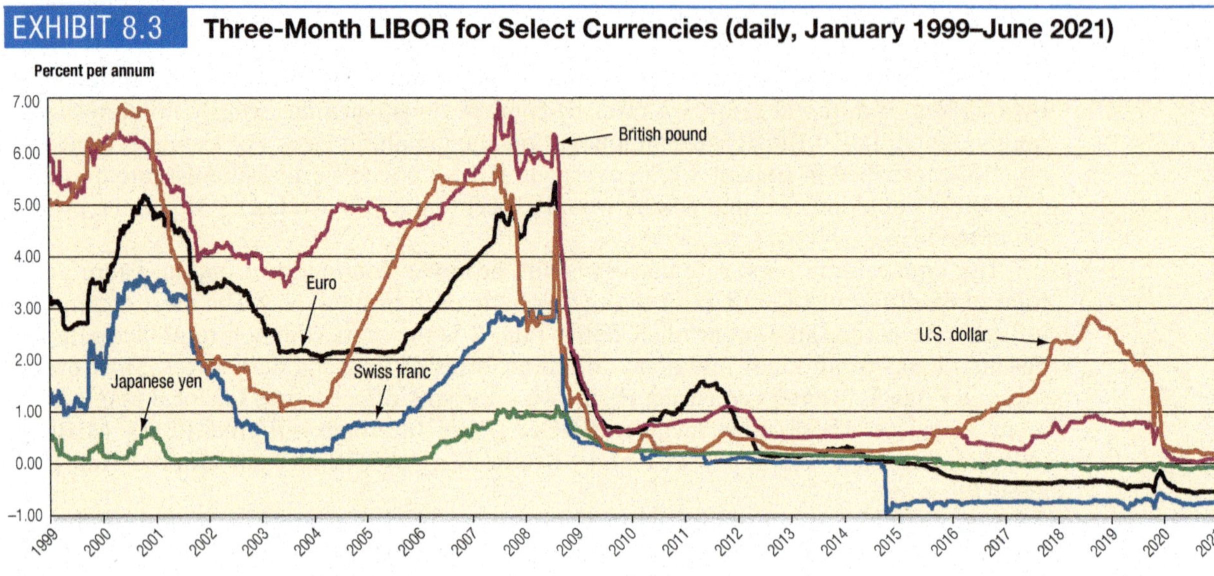

Source: LIBOR data from the Federal Reserve Economic Data (FRED), Federal Reserve Bank of St. Louis.

2008–2010 financial crisis. A similar massive injection of money into the economy is seen with the onset of the global pandemic in 2020.

But, as we noted in Chapter 6 on international parity conditions, interest rates are currency specific. Exhibit 8.3 makes that very apparent as it presents three-month LIBOR rates for the five world currency markets for which LIBOR is officially calculated—the U.S. dollar, euro, Swiss franc, British pound, and Japanese yen. The true volatility of short-term interest rates is clear here, in that in just the past 15 years these major loan rate foundations have bounced from near 7.00% to near or—in some cases recently—below zero percent. Note again the slight "bump" associated with the global pandemic. Just as a number of these LIBOR rates were just starting to rise in late 2019 and early 2020, when the global pandemic sent the global economy into a shutdown, central banks started pumping money into the economies in a variety of ways. LIBOR rates, as a result, moved downward once again.

A final note on short-term interest rates in recent history: Although near-zero short-term interest rates have remained near-zero or even negative over more than a decade, historically, this is unheard of. Money is not meant to be free according to economics and finance, and these continuing low rates have to come to an end sooner or later. But given that market analysts, government dignitaries, and learned academics have been repeating this phrase now for more than a decade, it seems it will be "later" rather than sooner!

8.2 The Cost of Debt

Individual borrowers, whether they are governments or companies, possess their own individual credit quality—the market's assessment of their ability to repay debt in a timely manner. These credit assessments result in the assignments of designations of differences in the cost and access to capital. This means individual organizational borrowers not only pay different rates to borrow (different interest rates) but have access to different amounts of capital or debt.

The cost of debt for any individual borrower will therefore possess two components, the base rate (a reference rate like LIBOR or a risk-free rate of interest like U.S. Treasury bills), $k_{US}^{\$}$, plus a *credit risk premium* reflecting the assessed credit quality of the individual borrower, $RPM^{\$}_{Rating}$. For an individual borrower in the United States, acquiring dollar-denominated debt, the cost of debt ($k_{Debt}^{\$}$) would be:

$$k_{Debt}^{\$} = k_{US}^{\$} + RPM^{\$}_{Rating}$$

The *credit risk premium* represents the credit risk of the individual borrower. In credit markets, this assignment is typically based on the borrower's credit rating as designated by one of the major credit rating agencies: Moody's, Standard & Poor's, and Fitch. An overview of those credit ratings is presented in Exhibit 8.4. Although each agency utilizes different methodologies, they all consider a standard set of common characteristics including the industry in which the firm operates, the diversity and sustainability of its revenues, its current level of indebtedness, and its past, present, and prospective operating performance.

EXHIBIT 8.4 Credit Ratings and Cost of Funds

Investment Grade	**Moody's**	**S&P**	**Fitch**	**5-Year Avg Rate**	**Spread over Treasury**
Prime	Aaa	AAA	AAA	1.92%	0.18%
High grade	Aa1	AA+	AA+		
	Aa2	AA	AA	2.24%	0.50%
	Aa3	AA–	AA–		
Upper medium grade	A1	A+	A+		
	A2	A	A	2.35%	0.61%
	A3	A–	A–		
Lower medium grade	Baa1	BBB+	BBB+		
	Baa2	BBB	BBB	2.81%	1.07%
	Baa3	BBB–	BBB–		
Speculative Grade					
Speculative grade	Ba1	BB+	BB+		
	Ba2	BB	BB	4.69%	2.95%
	Ba3	BB–	BB–		
Highly speculative	B1	B+	B+		
	B2	B	B	7.01%	5.27%
	B3	B–	B–		
Substantial risks	Caa1	CCC+	CCC	8.56%	6.82%
Extremely speculative	Caa2	CCC			
Default imminent	Caa3	CCC–			
In default	C	C, D	DDD, DD, D		

*These are long-term credit ratings. Rates quoted are for October 28, 2014, all for 5-year maturities. The 5-year U.S. Treasury rate was 1.74%.

Credit Ratings and Cost of Funds

Although there is obviously a wide spectrum of credit ratings, the designation of *investment grade* versus *speculative grade* is extremely important. An *investment grade* borrower (Baa3, BBB-, and above) is considered a high-quality borrower that is expected to be able to repay a new debt obligation in a timely manner regardless of market events or business performance. A *speculative grade* borrower (Ba1 or BB+ and below) is believed to be a riskier borrower and, depending on the nature of a market downturn or business shock, may have difficulty servicing new debt.

Exhibit 8.4 also illustrates how the cost of debt changes with credit quality. At this time, the U.S. Treasury was paying 1.74% for funds for a 5-year period. The average single-A borrower ("A") paid 2.35% per annum for funds for a 5-year period at this time, 0.61% above the U.S. Treasury. Note that the costs of credit quality—credit spreads—are quite minor for borrowers of investment grade. Speculative grade borrowers, however, are charged a hefty premium in the market. For example, the average single-B borrower paid a full 5.27% above U.S. Treasuries.

The cost of debt for corporate borrowers also changes over maturity. Exhibit 8.5 graphically presents the full range of maturities of the same credit ratings and costs presented in the previous exhibit. Once again, it is the U.S. Treasury yield curve, the U.S. government's cost of funds over varying maturities that establishes the base rates at which all corporate credits are then priced. Note that AAA-rated firms (currently there are only two remaining—Microsoft and Johnson & Johnson—ExxonMobil having lost its AAA-rating in the spring of 2016) pay very little more than the U.S. government to borrow money. The bulk of the larger S&P500 firms operating in the U.S. today are either A, BBB, or BB in rating. The U.S. Treasury yield curve is quite flat but still upward sloping, indicating that short-term funds are cheaper than

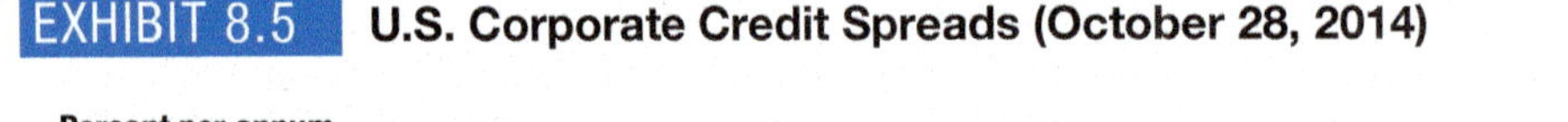

EXHIBIT 8.5 U.S. Corporate Credit Spreads (October 28, 2014)

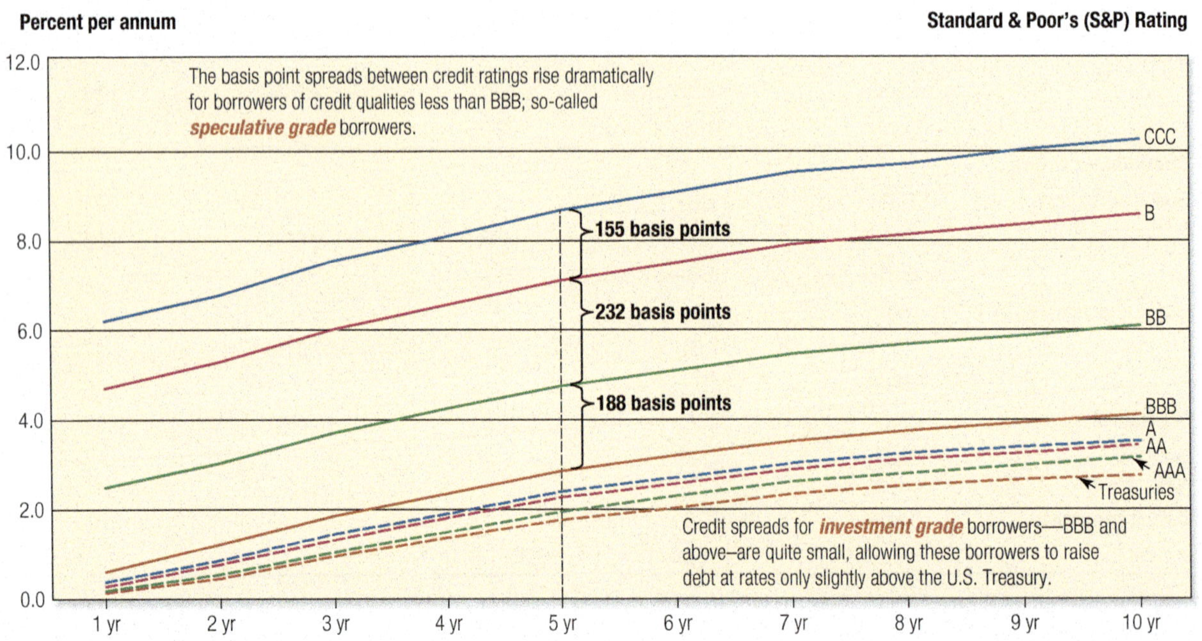

long-term funds. (We have limited the graphic to 10 years in maturity. U.S. Treasuries actually extend out to 30 years.)

Every country with an established financial system will have some version of this same spread structure—government yield curve plus corporate borrowing. In addition to the U.S., the largest such systems in the world would be those of the European Union, the United Kingdom, and Japan. As we will see later in this chapter, however, different countries—and currencies—possess very different costs of funds.

Credit Risk and Repricing Risk

For a corporate borrower, it is especially important to distinguish between *credit risk* and *repricing risk*. *Credit risk*, sometimes termed *roll-over risk*, is the possibility that a borrower's creditworthiness at the time of renewing a credit—its credit rating—is reclassified by the lender. This can result in changing fees, changing interest rates, altered credit line commitments, or even denial. *Repricing risk* is the risk of changes in interest rates charged (earned) at the time a financial contract's rate is reset. A borrower that is renewing a credit will face current market conditions on the base rate used for financing, a true floating rate.

In the past some countries have struggled so mightily with inflation, and how it destroys the ability of all entities, people and companies alike, to borrow, that they have created new forms of indexed interest rates. *Global Finance in Practice 8.1* describes one such well-established system.

Sovereign Debt

Debt issued by governments—*sovereign debt*—is historically considered debt of the highest quality, higher than that of nongovernment borrowers within that same country. This quality preference stems from the ability of a government to tax its people and, if need be, print more money. Although the former may cause significant economic harm in the form

GLOBAL FINANCE IN PRACTICE 8.1

The Chilean Alternative Unit of Account: The *Unidad De Fomento*

The *unidad de fomento* (unit of promotion)—the UF—was created by the Central Bank of Chile in 1967 during a period of hyperinflation. Conceptually, it was an indexed value of the Chilean peso (CLP) that would adjust regularly (daily) to inflation. The Central Bank of Chile updates the exchange rate between the Chilean peso and the UF daily. It is always quoted as Chilean pesos = 1.00 UF. For example, on March 14, 2019, the Central Bank of Chile quoted CLP 25, 565.76 = 1.00 UF.

Chilean Mortgages

The UF has become the predominant unit of account for real estate and mortgage loans in Chile. The borrower will acquire a loan denominated in UF with a set interest rate. That loan principal, interest rate, and loan maturity are then used to calculate the monthly principal and interest payments on the mortgage (assuming an amortizing loan). Monthly payments on the UF loan have to be made in Chilean pesos (CLP). The actual peso payment is made at that rate published by the Central Bank of Chile, the authority responsible for the UF.

A mortgage loan in Chilean pesos, assuming a fixed term of say 15 years and a fixed interest rate of 8.000%, would have a set monthly mortgage payment for the life of the loan. That is the standard mortgage structure used in most countries today. A mortgage loan in UF, assuming a fixed term of 15 years and a fixed interest rate of 4.000%, would have a set of UF payments for the life of the loan, which have to be paid in Chilean pesos. Since the UF rate to Chilean pesos changes every day, a borrower would not have any real certainty over the payments to be made over the life of the loan.

Although it appears relatively more risky from a financial perspective, the UF has gained such popularity in Chile that it is the predominant mortgage structure used today. The hyperinflation is gone, but the UF has lived on.

of unemployment and the latter may result in significant financial harm in the form of inflation, they are both tools available to the sovereign. The government, therefore, has the ability to service its own debt—one way or another—when that debt is denominated in its own currency.

A government, typically through its central banking authority, also conducts its own monetary policy. That policy will, in combination with economic conditions of growth and inflation, determine the entire structure of its own interest rates of all maturities. Depending on the depth and breadth of domestic financial markets—the sophistication of the domestic financial marketplace—those maturities may be very short or very long. A large industrial country like the U.S. or Japan may issue its own debt instruments (borrow money) at maturities as long as 30 years or longer. These debt instruments would typically be denominated in the issuer's own currency and openly saleable on global markets to both domestic and foreign investors. The U.S., for example, has financed a large portion of its government debt by selling U.S. Treasuries to a variety of investors all over the world—private individuals, organizations, and governments.

Domestic interest rates are in domestic currency, and as discussed in Chapter 6 on international parity conditions, interest rates are themselves currency specific. A direct comparison of interest rates across countries is only truly economically possible if the rates have all been converted to one currency (as is the case when looking at various opportunities for uncovered interest arbitrage), when different countries raise debt in a common currency (say the U.S. dollar), or if exchange rates never change.

Sovereign Spreads

Many developing country governments raise debt capital in the international markets, and they do so typically in one of the world's most widely traded currencies like the U.S. dollar, European euro, or Japanese yen. Exhibit 8.6 provides a comparison of what several sovereign borrowers have had to pay for U.S. dollar funds over and above that of the U.S. Treasury—the U.S. dollar sovereign spread—over the past two decades.

What Exhibit 8.6 details is the global financial market's assessment of *sovereign credit risk* —the ability of these sovereign borrowers to repay foreign currency denominated debt—U.S. dollar debt in this case—in a timely manner. For example, the cost of Brazilian sovereign dollar debt ($k_{\text{Brazil}}{}^{\$}$), the cost for the government of Brazil to raise U.S. dollar debt on global markets, can be decomposed into two basic components: (1) the U.S. government's own cost of dollar debt ($k_{\text{US}}{}^{\$}$) and (2) the Brazilian sovereign spread, a risk premium for a dollar borrower who must earn U.S. dollars in order to service the debt ($RPM^{\$}{}_{\text{Brazil}}$):

$$k^{\$}_{\text{Brazil}} = \text{U.S. Treasury Dollar rate} + \text{Brazilian sovereign spread} = k_{\text{US}}{}^{\$} + RPM^{\$}_{\text{Brazil}}$$

As illustrated in Exhibit 8.6, for some of these country borrowers like Russia or Pakistan, the sovereign spread has periodically been extremely high. This serves as a clear indicator by the international financial markets that these sovereign borrowers—at these specific points in time—were believed to present significant risks as borrowers. For example, in early 2015 Russia was downgraded to "speculative" status by the major credit rating agencies. This downgrade, a result of economic deterioration associated with sanctions by Western nations (related to Ukraine) and the fall in the price of oil (that provides more than 50% of Russian government revenues), reduced Russia's access to capital. The mini-case in Chapter 13, however, describes a very different situation, when the issuer (Saudi Aramco, the most profitable company in the world) was considered such a low risk that it borrowed at rates approaching those of the U.S. Treasury!

EXHIBIT 8.6 Selected Sovereign Spreads over U.S. Treasuries

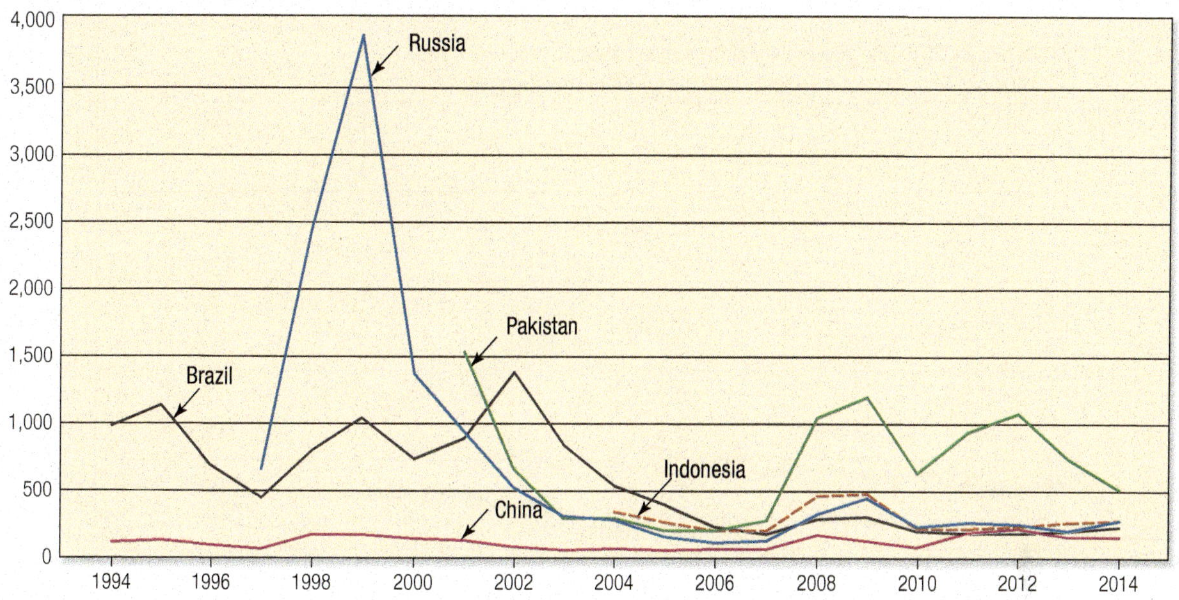

European Sovereign Debt

The European Union is a complex organism compared to the customary structure of fiscal and monetary policy institutions described in the typical Economics 101 course. With the adoption of a common currency, the EU members participating in the euro gave up exclusive rights over the ability to print money (to service debt). Because it is a common currency, no one EU member has the right to simply print more euros—that is the policy realm of the European Central Bank (ECB). The members of the EU do have relative freedom to set their own fiscal policies—government spending, taxation, and the creation of government surpluses or deficits. This structure sets up one of the more unique sovereign debt situations seen globally.

Each EU sovereign borrower has the ability to raise debt in the international marketplace but do so in its home currency, the euro. The financial markets, however, have the ability to differentiate borrowers by assessed credit quality. This has led to very different costs of sovereign debt across the EU. A number of member countries of the European Union—particularly Greece, Portugal, and Ireland—have themselves struggled with recessionary economies and rising costs of debt in recent years.

Following the onslaught of the global financial crisis in 2008–2009, a number of EU member countries suffered significant economic crises. Part of their economic woes included growing fears over their ability to service their outstanding sovereign debt. As seen in Exhibit 8.7, these market fears and concerns drove the cost of their funds on the international marketplace very high, showing a dramatic separation of sovereign debt costs. The widest separation is that between the highest-quality EU borrower, Germany, and the lowest-quality borrower for the period in question, Greece.

EXHIBIT 8.7 **Selected EU Sovereign Spreads**

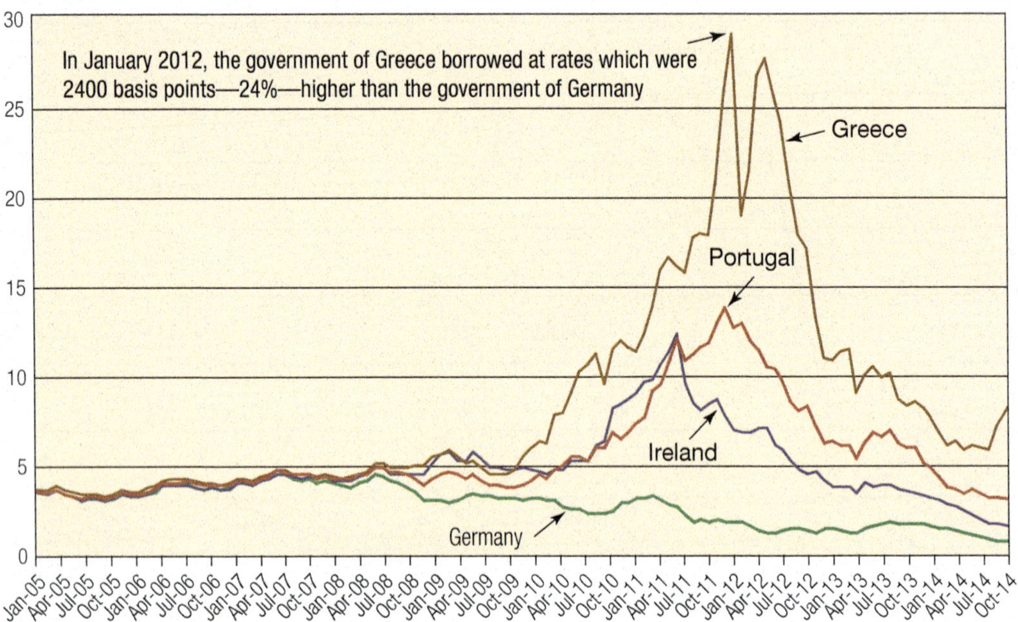

Source: Long-term interest rate statistics for EU member states, European Central Bank, www.ecb.int/stats/money/long. 10-year maturities.

8.3 Interest Rate Risk

The single largest interest rate risk of the nonfinancial firm is debt service. The debt structure of the MNE will possess differing maturities of debt, different interest rate structures (such as fixed versus floating-rate), and different currencies of denomination. Therefore the management of this debt portfolio can be quite complex and, in all cases, important. The second most prevalent source of interest rate risk for the MNE lies in its holdings of interest-sensitive securities. Unlike debt, which is recorded on the right-hand side of the firm's balance sheet (a liability), the marketable securities portfolio of the firm appears on the left-hand side (an asset). Marketable securities represent potential earnings or interest inflows to the firm. Ever-increasing competitive pressures have pushed financial managers to tighten their management of interest rates on both the left and right sides of the firm's balance sheet.

Debt Structures and Strategies

Consider the three different bank loan structures being considered by U.S. medical equipment manufacturer MedStat. Each is intended to provide $1 million in financing for a 3-year period.

Strategy 1: Borrow $1 million for three years at a fixed rate of interest.

Strategy 2: Borrow $1 million for three years at a floating rate, LIBOR + 2% (LIBOR to be reset annually).

Strategy 3: Borrow $1 million for one year at a fixed rate and then renew the credit annually.

Although the lowest cost of funds is always a major selection criterion, it is not the only one. If MedStat chooses Strategy 1, it assures itself of the funds for the full three years at a known interest rate. It has maximized the predictability of cash flows for the debt obligation. What it has sacrificed to some degree is the ability to enjoy a lower interest rate in the event that interest rates fall over the period. Of course, it has also eliminated the risk that it would face higher rates if interest rates rose over the period.

Strategy 2 offers what Strategy 1 did not—flexibility. It too assures MedStat of full funding for the three-year period. This eliminates *credit risk*. *Repricing risk* is, however, alive and well in Strategy 2. If LIBOR changes dramatically by the second or third year, the LIBOR rate change is passed through completely to the borrower. The spread, however, remains fixed (reflecting the credit standing that has been locked in for the full three years). Flexibility comes at a cost—in this case, the risk that interest rates may go up as well as down.

Strategy 3 offers MedStat more flexibility and more risk. First, the firm is borrowing at the shorter end of the yield curve. If the yield curve is positively sloped, as is commonly the case in major industrial markets, the base interest rate should be lower. But the short end of the yield curve is also the more volatile. It responds to short-term events in a much more pronounced fashion than do longer-term rates. The strategy also exposes the firm to the possibility that its credit rating may be different when it is time for credit renewal, for better or worse. Noting that credit ratings in general attempt to establish whether a firm can meet its debt-service obligations under worsening economic conditions, firms that are highly creditworthy (investment-rated grades) may view Strategy 3 as a more relevant alternative than do firms of lower quality (speculative grades).

Although the previous example gives only a partial picture of the complexity of funding decisions and choices within the firm, it demonstrates the many ways credit risks and repricing risks are inextricably intertwined. The expression "interest rate exposure" is a complex concept, and the proper measurement of exposure prior to the management of this risk is critical. We now proceed to describe the interest rate risk of the most common form of corporate debt, floating-rate loans.

An Illustration: MedStat's Floating-Rate Loans

Floating-rate loans are a widely used source of debt for firms worldwide. They are also the source of the single largest and most frequently observed corporate interest rate exposure. Exhibit 8.8 shows the costs and cash flows for a 3-year floating rate loan taken out by MedStat. The loan of US$10 million will be serviced with annual interest payments and total principal repayment at the end of the 3-year period.

The loan is priced at U.S. dollar LIBOR + 1.250% (note that the cost of money—interest—is often referred to as price). The LIBOR base will be reset each year on an agreed-upon date (say two days prior to payment). Whereas the LIBOR component is truly floating, the spread of 1.250% is actually a fixed component of the interest payment, which is known with certainty for the life of the loan.

MedStat will not know the actual interest cost of the loan until the loan has been completely repaid. Caitlin Kelly, the CFO of MedStat, may forecast what LIBOR will be for the life of the loan, but she will not know with certainty until all payments have been completed. This uncertainty is not only an interest rate risk, but it is also an actual cash flow risk associated with the interest payment. While a fixed interest rate loan also has interest rate risk in the form of opportunity cost, the exact size of the cash flows promised by the borrower in repayment is known.

Exhibit 8.8 illustrates the cash flows and *all-in costs* (AIC) of the floating-rate loan. The AIC is found by calculating the internal rate of return (IRR) of the total cash flow stream, including proceeds up-front and repayment over time. This baseline analysis assumes that

EXHIBIT 8.8 MedStat's Floating-Rate Loan

The expected interest rates and cash flows associated with a 3-year $10 million floating-rate loan with annual payments. MedStat pays an initiation (origination) fee of 1.500% of principal up front.

Loan Interest		**Year 0**	**Year 1**	**Year 2**	**Year 3**
LIBOR (floating)			5.000%	5.000%	5.000%
Credit spread (fixed)			1.250%	1.250%	1.250%
Total interest payable			6.250%	6.250%	6.250%
Principal Payments					
Loan principal		$10,000,000			
Origination fees	1.50%	(150,000)			
Loan proceeds		$9,850,000			
Principal repayment					($10,000,000)
Interest Cash Flows					
LIBOR (floating)			($500,000)	($500,000)	($500,000)
Credit spread (fixed)			(125,000)	(125,000)	(125,000)
Total interest payable			($625,000)	($625,000)	($625,000)
Total loan cash flows		$9,850,000	($625,000)	($625,000)	($10,625,000)
All-in-Cost (AIC) or IRR		**6.820%**			

Note: The effective cost of funds (before-tax) for MedStat—the *all-in-cost* (AIC)—is calculated by finding the *internal rate of return* (IRR) of the total cash flows associated with the loan and its repayment. The AIC of the original loan agreement, without fees, would be 6.250%.

LIBOR remains at 5.000% for the life of the loan. Including the up-front loan origination fees of 1.50%, the AIC to MedStat is 6.820% (or 6.250% without fees). But this is only hypothetical, as MedStat and its bank both assume that over time LIBOR will change. Which direction it will change and by how much per year is, of course, unknown. The loan's LIBOR component, but not the credit spread, creates a debt-service cash flow risk over time for MedStat.

If MedStat Corporation decided, after it had taken out the loan, that it wished to manage the interest rate risk associated with the loan agreement, it would have a number of management alternatives:

- **Refinancing.** MedStat could go back to its lender and restructure and refinance the entire agreement. This is not always possible, and it is often expensive.
- **Interest rate futures.** Interest rate futures have gained substantial acceptance in the corporate sector. MedStat could lock in the future interest rate payments by taking an interest rate futures position.
- **Forward rate agreements (FRAs).** MedStat could lock in the future interest rate payments with forward rate agreements (FRAs), interest rate contracts similar to foreign exchange forward contracts.
- **Interest rate swaps.** MedStat could enter into an additional agreement with a bank or swap dealer in which it exchanged—swapped—future cash flows in such a way that the interest rate payments on the floating-rate loan would become fixed.

The following two sections detail the latter three interest rate derivative management solutions described previously—how they work and how they might be utilized by a corporate borrower.

8.4 Interest Rate Futures and Forward Rate Agreements

Like foreign currency, there are many interest rate-based financial derivatives. We first describe *interest rate futures* and *forward rate agreements* (FRAs) before moving on to the *interest rate swap*.

Interest Rate Futures

Unlike foreign currency futures, *interest rate futures* are relatively widely used by financial managers and treasurers of nonfinancial companies. Their popularity stems from the high liquidity of the interest rate futures markets, their simplicity in use, and the rather standardized interest rate exposures most firms possess. The two most widely used futures contracts are the eurodollar futures traded on the Chicago Mercantile Exchange (CME) and the U.S. Treasury Bond Futures of the Chicago Board of Trade (CBOT). To illustrate the use of futures for managing interest rate risks, we will focus on the 3-month eurodollar futures contracts. Exhibit 8.9 presents eurodollar futures for two years. (They actually trade 10 years into the future.)

The yield of a futures contract is calculated from the settlement price, which is the closing price for that trading day. For example, a financial manager examining the eurodollar quotes in Exhibit 8.9 for a March 2011 contract would see that the settlement price on the previous day was 94.76, an annual yield of 5.24%:

$$\text{Yield} = (100.00 - 94.76) = 5.24\%$$

Since each contract is for a 3-month period (one quarter) and has a notional principal of \$1 million, each basis point is actually worth \$2,500 (0.01 × \$1,000,000 × 90/360).

If a financial manager were interested in *hedging*—managing the risk of—a floating-rate interest payment due in March 2011, she would need to sell a future—to take a short position. This strategy is referred to as a *short position* because the manager is selling something she does not own (as in shorting common stock or short currency futures described in Chapter 7). If interest rates rise by March, as the manager predicts, the futures price will fall and she will be able to close the position at a profit. This profit will roughly offset the losses associated with rising interest payments on her debt. If the manager is wrong, however, and interest rates actually fall by the maturity date, causing the futures price to rise, she will suffer a loss that will wipe out the "savings" derived from making a lower floating-rate interest payment than she expected. So by selling the March 2011 futures contract, the manager locks in an interest rate of 5.24%.

EXHIBIT 8.9 Eurodollar Futures Prices

Maturity	Open	High	Low	Settle	Yield	Open Interest
June 10	94.99	95.01	94.98	95.01	4.99	455,763
Sept	94.87	94.97	94.87	94.96	5.04	535,932
Dec	94.60	94.70	94.60	94.68	5.32	367,036
March 11	94.67	94.77	94.66	94.76	5.24	299,993
June	94.55	94.68	94.54	94.63	5.37	208,949
Sept	94.43	94.54	94.43	94.53	5.47	168,961
Dec	94.27	94.38	94.27	94.36	5.64	130,824

Typical presentation by *The Wall Street Journal*. Only regular quarterly maturities shown. All contracts are for \$1 million; points of 100%. Open interest is number of contracts outstanding.

EXHIBIT 8.10 Interest Rate Futures Strategies for Common Exposures

Exposure or Position	Futures Action	Interest Rates	Position Outcome
Paying interest on future date	Sell a Futures (short position)	If rates go up	Futures price falls; short earns a profit
		If rates go down	Futures price rises; short earns a loss
Earning interest on future date	Buy a Futures (long position)	If rates go up	Futures price falls; long earns a loss
		If rates go down	Futures price rises; long earns a profit

Obviously, interest rate futures positions could be, and are on a regular basis, purchased purely for speculative purposes. Although that is not the focus of the managerial context here, the example shows how any speculator with a directional view on interest rates could take positions with expectations of profit. As mentioned previously, the most common interest rate exposure of the nonfinancial firm is interest payable on debt. Such exposure is not, however, the only interest rate risk. As more and more firms manage their entire balance sheet, the interest earnings from the left-hand side are under increasing scrutiny. If financial managers are expected to earn higher interest on interest-bearing securities (marketable securities), they may well find a second use for the interest rate futures market—to lock in future interest earnings. Exhibit 8.10 provides an overview of these two basic interest rate exposures and management strategies.

Forward Rate Agreements

A forward rate agreement (FRA) is an interbank-traded contract to buy or sell interest rate payments on a notional principal. These contracts are settled in cash. The buyer of an FRA obtains the right to lock in an interest rate for a desired term that begins at a future date. The contract specifies that the seller of the FRA will pay the buyer the increased interest expense on a nominal sum (the notional principal) of money if interest rates rise above the agreed rate, but the buyer will pay the seller the differential interest expense if interest rates fall below the agreed rate. Maturities available are typically 1, 3, 6, 9, and 12 months.

Like foreign currency forward contracts, FRAs are useful on individual exposures. They are contractual commitments by the firm that allow little flexibility to take advantage of favorable movements, such as when LIBOR is falling as described in the previous section. Firms also use FRAs if they plan to invest in securities at future dates but worry that interest rates might fall prior to the investment date. Because of the limited maturities and currencies available, however, FRAs are not widely used outside the largest industrial economies and currencies.

8.5 Interest Rate Swaps

Swaps are contractual agreements to exchange or swap a series of cash flows. These cash flows are most commonly the interest payments associated with debt service—the payments associated with fixed-rate and floating-rate debt obligations.

Swap Structures

There are two main types of swaps, interest rate and currency, and a single swap may combine elements of both types. For example, a swap agreement may swap fixed-rate dollar payments for floating-rate euro payments.

- **Interest rate swap.** If the agreement is for one party to swap its fixed interest rate payment for the floating interest rate payments of another, it is termed an interest rate swap, sometimes referred to as a plain-vanilla swap.
- **Currency swap.** If the agreement is to swap currencies of debt service—for example, Swiss franc interest payments in exchange for U.S. dollar interest payments—it is termed a currency swap or cross-currency swap.

In all cases, the swap serves to alter the firm's cash flow obligations, as in changing floating-rate payments into fixed-rate payments associated with an existing debt obligation. The swap itself is not a source of capital, but rather an alteration of the cash flows associated with payment.

The two parties may have various motivations for entering into the agreement. For example, a very common position is as follows: A corporate borrower of good credit standing has existing floating-rate debt service payments. The borrower, after reviewing current market conditions and forming expectations about the future, may conclude that interest rates are about to rise. In order to protect the firm against rising debt-service payments, the company's treasury may enter into a swap agreement to pay fixed/receive floating. This means the firm will now make fixed interest rate payments and receive from the swap counterparty floating interest rate payments. The floating-rate payments that the firm receives are used to service the debt obligation of the firm, so the firm on a net basis is now making fixed interest rate payments. Using derivatives, it has synthetically changed floating-rate debt into fixed-rate debt. It has done so without going through the costs and intricacies of refinancing existing debt obligations.

The cash flows of an interest rate swap are interest rates applied to a set amount of capital (notional principal). For this reason, these cash flows are also referred to as coupon swaps. Firms entering into interest rate swaps set the notional principal so that the cash flows resulting from the interest rate swap cover their interest rate management needs. Interest rate swaps are contractual commitments between a firm and a swap dealer and are completely independent of the interest rate exposure of the firm. That is, the firm may enter into a swap for any reason it sees fit and then swap a notional principal that is less than, equal to, or even greater than the total position being managed. For example, a firm with a variety of floating-rate loans on its books may, if it wishes, enter into interest rate swaps for only 70% of the existing principal. The size of the swap notional principal is a choice purely in the hands of corporate management and is not confined to the size of existing floating-rate loan obligations.

It should also be noted that the interest rate swap market is filling a gap in market efficiency. If all firms had free and equal access to capital markets, regardless of interest rate structure or currency of denomination, the swap market would most likely not exist. The fact that the swap market not only exists but also flourishes and provides benefits to all parties is in some ways the proverbial "free lunch."

Illustrative Case: MedStat's Floating-Rate Debt

MedStat is a U.S.-based firm with a $40 million floating-rate bank loan. The company is finishing the first two years of the loan agreement (it is the end of the third quarter of 2017), with three years remaining. The loan is priced at the 3-month LIBOR rate plus a 1.250% credit risk premium. The recent movements of LIBOR and MedStat's floating-rate debt are depicted in Exhibit 8.11.

As shown in Exhibit 8.11, LIBOR has started moving upward in the past year. MedStat's management is now worried that interest rates will continue to rise and that the company's

EXHIBIT 8.11 MedStat Considers a Plain-Vanilla Interest Rate Swap

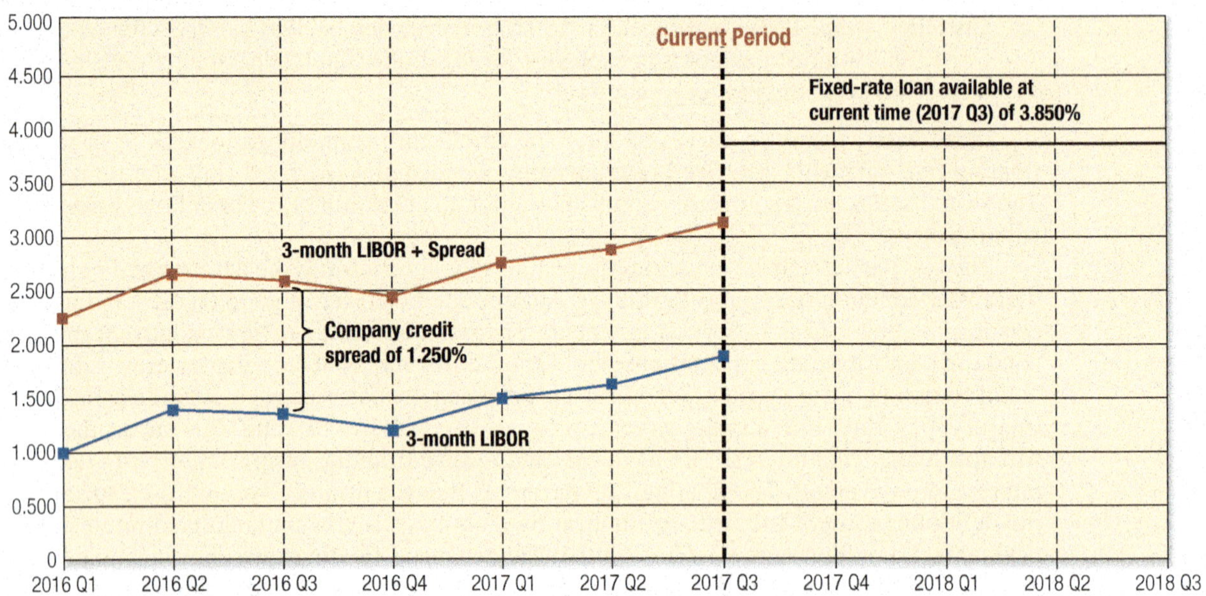

MedStat has $40 million in floating rate loans, paying a floating interest rate of LIBOR + 1.250%. Over the past year, LIBOR has been trending upward. Company management is now considering swapping its floating-rate debt for fixed-rate payments—a pay-fixed receive-floating plain-vanilla interest rate swap. If it swaps now, it can lock in a fixed rate payment of 3.850% (pay fixed component) in exchange for LIBOR (received floating component).

interest costs will rise with them. Management is considering entering into a pay-fixed receive-floating plain-vanilla interest rate swap. MedStat's New York bank has quoted a fixed-rate payment of 3.850% in exchange for LIBOR. The notional principal of the swap, the base amount for calculating the interest cash flows, is something MedStat must choose. In this case, they decide to enter into a notional principal equal to the full amount of the floating-rate loan—$40 million. The interest rates of the proposed swap, when combined with MedStat's current floating-rate debt obligations, would appear as follows:

Debt/Swap Component	Floating	Fixed
Floating-rate loan	(LIBOR)	(1.250%)
Swap (pay fixed, receive floating)	LIBOR	(3.850%)
Floating-rate loan after swap	—	(5.100%)

MedStat will now receive a floating-rate payment from the bank of LIBOR, which is then used to pay the LIBOR component on its floating-rate loan. What then remains is for MedStat to pay the fixed-rate spread on the loan—the 1.250% spread—plus the fixed-rate payment of the swap of 3.850%, for a total of 5.100%. The fixed rate quoted to MedStat is based on a corporate issuer of AA quality for a 3-year maturity, which is the length of time the swap needs in order to cover the floating-rate loan. The fixed rates available in the swap market will therefore always reflect the current government and corporate yield curves in the appropriate currency market, in this case the U.S. dollar.

Note that the swap agreement swaps only the floating-rate component, LIBOR, and does not swap or deal with the credit spread in any way. This is because of two principles: (1) the swap market does not wish to deal with the credit risk of any individual borrower, only the core fixed and floating-rate foundations; and (2) the fixed-rate credit spread is indeed a fixed-rate component, and it does not change over the life of the loan. The swap market is intended only for the true floating-rate component, and therefore the final combined fixed-rate obligation of MedStat after the swap is purely a fixed-rate payment at a combined rate of 5.100%. The plain-vanilla interest rate swap is a very cheap and effective method of altering the cash flows associated with debt. It allows a firm to alter the interest rate associated with any debt obligation without suffering the costs (time and money) of repayment and refinancing.

Whether MedStat's swap to pay fixed (entering an interest rate swap agreement to pay a fixed rate of interest in exchange for receiving a floating rate of interest) proves to be the right strategy depends on what happens in the coming series of quarters. If LIBOR increases over the coming two or three quarters but only marginally, then the decision to swap may not turn out to be the best one. If, however, LIBOR rises significantly, the swap may save MedStat sizable interest expenses.

It is also important to consider what might have happened if MedStat had decided not to execute the swap. Exhibit 8.12 provides one potential future: LIBOR continues to rise and MedStat's interest cost management options worsen. Both floating rates and fixed rates available are now higher. This is because as short-term interest rates rise, so do the fixed rates in the marketplace. In this case, as 3-month LIBOR rose from 1.885% to 2.250%, the fixed rate offered in the plain-vanilla swap rose from 3.850% to 4.200%. The company could still enter into a swap, but all interest rates, fixed and floating, are now higher.

EXHIBIT 8.12 MedStat's Deteriorating Choices as LIBOR Rises

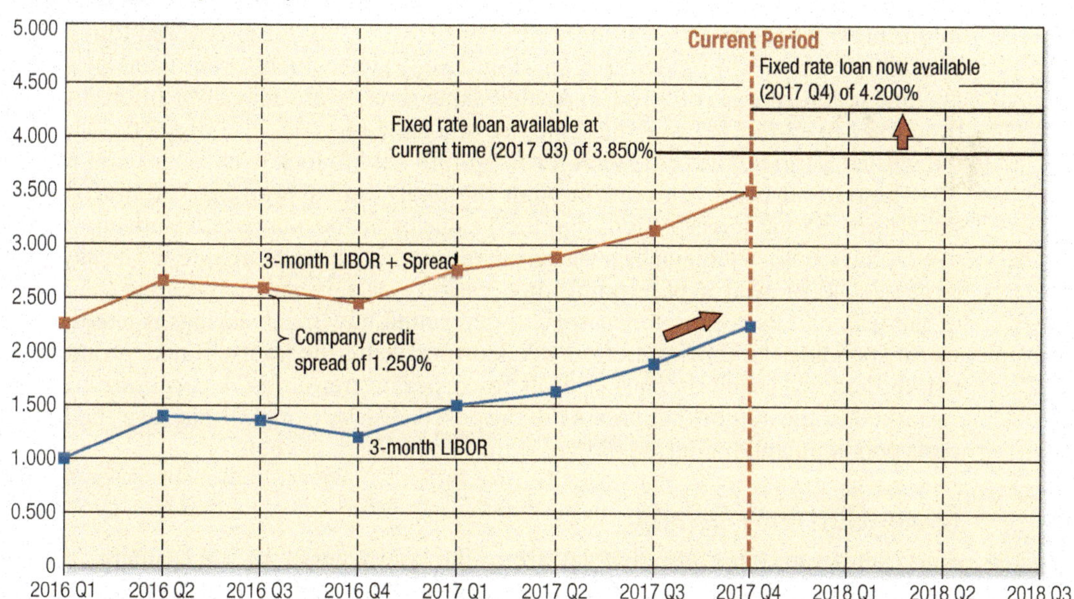

If MedStat had decided not to execute the swap, and LIBOR continued to rise, MedStat would be left with increasingly poor choices. If MedStat decided that it would now enter into the pay fixed receive floating swap, the fixed rate available to the company is now higher, 4.200%, rather than the previous quote of 3.850%. This is because as short-term floating rates of interest like LIBOR rise, so do the fixed rates of interest in the marketplace.

Plain-Vanilla Swap Strategies

The use of the plain-vanilla swap market by firms can be divided into two basic categories, *debt structure* and *debt cost.*

Debt Structure. All companies will pursue a target debt structure that combines maturity, currency of composition, and fixed/floating pricing. The fixed/floating objective is one of the most difficult for many companies to determine with any confidence, and they often simply try to replicate industry averages.

Companies that have very high credit quality and therefore advantaged access to the fixed-rate debt markets, A or AA companies like Walmart or IBM, often raise large amounts of debt in long maturities at fixed rates. They then use the plain-vanilla swap market to alter selective amounts of their fixed-rate debt into floating-rate debt to achieve their desired objective. Swaps allow them to alter the fixed/floating composition quickly and easily without the origination and registration fees of the direct debt markets.

Companies of lower credit quality, sometimes those of less than investment grade, often find the fixed-rate debt market not open to them. For them, getting fixed-rate debt may be either impossible or too costly. Such firms will generally raise debt at floating rates and then periodically evaluate whether the plain-vanilla swap market offers any attractive alternatives to swap from paying-floating to paying-fixed. The plain-vanilla swap market is also frequently used by firms to adjust their fixed/floating debt structure. This was the case of MedStat described previously. Expectations of rising interest rates led the company to use plain-vanilla swaps to swap out of floating-rate payments into fixed-rate payments. During the 2009–2014 period, with interest rates often hitting historical lows in U.S. dollar and European euro debt markets, many firms used the swap market frequently to swap increasingly into fixed-rate obligations.

Debt Cost. All firms are always interested in opportunities to lower the cost of their debt. The plain-vanilla swap market is one highly accessible and low-cost method of doing so.

Assume that MedStat regularly explored opportunities in the debt and swap markets. In our previous example, in the third quarter of 2017, MedStat discovered that it could swap $40 million of its existing debt for an all-in fixed-rate cost (the swap fixed-rate plus the remaining credit spread) of 5.100%. At that same time, banks may have offered the company three-year fixed-rate loans of the same size at a fixed rate of 5.20% or 5.30%. MedStat could, if it wished, swap floating-rate debt for fixed-rate debt to lock in cheaper fixed-rate debt.

These lower costs, achieved through the plain-vanilla swap market, may simply reflect short-term market imperfections and inefficiencies or the comparative advantage some borrowers have in selected markets via selective financial service providers. The savings may be large—30, 40, or even 50 basis points on occasion—or quite small. It is up to the management of the firm and its corporate treasury to determine how much savings is needed to make it worth spending the time and effort needed to execute the swaps. Banks promote the swap market and will regularly market deals to corporate treasuries. A corporate treasurer once remarked to the author that unless the proposed structure or deal can save the firm 15 or 20 basis points, at a minimum, he did not want to hear from the banker.

Cross-Currency Swaps

Since all swap rates are derived from the yield curve in each major currency, the fixed-to-floating interest rate swap existing in each currency allows firms to swap across currencies. Exhibit 8.13 lists typical swap rates for the euro, the U.S. dollar, the Japanese yen, and the Swiss franc. These swap rates are based on the government security yields in each of the individual currency markets, plus a credit spread applicable to investment grade borrowers in the respective markets.

EXHIBIT 8.13 Interest Rate Swap Quotes

	Euro €		£ Sterling		Swiss franc		U.S. dollar		Japanese yen	
Years	**Bid**	**Ask**	**Bid**	**Ask**	**Bid**	**Ask**	**Bid**	**Ask**	**Bid**	**Ask**
1	0.14	0.18	0.63	0.66	−0.14	−0.08	0.42	0.45	0.11	0.17
2	0.16	0.20	0.91	0.95	−0.18	−0.10	0.86	0.89	0.11	0.17
3	0.20	0.24	1.11	1.15	−0.14	−0.06	1.26	1.29	0.13	0.19
4	0.26	0.30	1.28	1.33	−0.07	0.01	1.55	1.58	0.15	0.21
5	0.34	0.38	1.42	1.47	0.02	0.10	1.75	1.78	0.19	0.25
6	0.42	0.46	1.53	1.58	0.11	0.19	1.90	1.93	0.24	0.30
7	0.51	0.55	1.62	1.67	0.21	0.29	2.02	2.05	0.30	0.36
8	0.60	0.64	1.69	1.74	0.30	0.38	2.11	2.10	0.36	0.42
9	0.70	0.74	1.76	1.81	0.39	0.47	2.19	2.22	0.42	0.48
10	0.79	0.83	1.82	1.87	0.47	0.55	2.26	2.29	0.49	0.55
12	0.95	0.99	1.91	1.98	0.59	0.69	2.37	2.40	0.61	0.69
15	1.12	1.16	2.02	2.11	0.75	0.85	2.48	2.51	0.82	0.90
20	1.30	1.34	2.12	2.25	0.95	1.05	2.59	2.62	1.09	1.17
25	1.39	1.43	2.15	2.28	1.06	1.16	2.64	2.67	1.22	1.30
30	1.44	1.48	2.17	2.30	1.11	1.21	2.67	2.70	1.29	1.37
LIBOR										

Typical presentation by the *Financial Times*. Bid and ask spreads as of close of London business. US$ is quoted against 3-month LIBOR; Japanese yen against 6-month LIBOR; Euro and Swiss franc against 6-month LIBOR. Rates are for December 31, 2014.

Note that the swap rates in Exhibit 8.13 are not rated or categorized by credit ratings. This is because the swap market itself does not carry the credit risk associated with individual borrowers. Individual borrowers with obligations priced at LIBOR plus a spread will keep the spread. The fixed spread, a credit risk premium, is still borne by the firm itself. For example, lower-rated firms may pay spreads of 3% or 4% over LIBOR, while some of the world's largest and most financially sound MNEs may raise capital at LIBOR rates. The swap market does not differentiate the rate by the participant; all swap at fixed rates versus LIBOR.

The usual motivation for a currency swap is to replace cash flows scheduled in an undesired currency with flows in a desired currency. The desired currency is probably the currency in which the firm's future operating revenues will be generated. Firms often raise capital in currencies in which they do not possess significant revenues or other natural cash flows. The reason they do so is cost; specific firms may find capital costs in specific currencies attractively priced to them under special conditions. Having raised the capital, however, the firm may wish to swap its repayment into a different currency—one in which it will have future operating revenues (cash inflows).

The utility of the currency swap market to an MNE is significant. An MNE wishing to swap a 10-year fixed 2.29% U.S. dollar cash flow stream could swap to 0.83% fixed in euros, 1.87% fixed in British pounds, 0.55% fixed in Swiss francs, or 0.55% fixed in Japanese yen. In addition to swapping to fixed rates, it could also swap from fixed dollars to floating LIBOR rates in the various currencies. Any of these swaps could be arranged with the swap dealer/bank in a matter of just hours and at a fraction of the transaction costs and fees of actually borrowing in those currencies.

Illustrative Case: MedStat Uses a Cross-Currency Swap

We return to MedStat Corporation to demonstrate how to use a cross-currency swap. After raising $10 million in floating-rate financing and subsequently swapping into fixed-rate payments, MedStat decides that it would prefer to make its debt service payments in British pounds. MedStat had recently signed a sales contract with a British buyer that will be paying pounds to MedStat over the next 3-year period. This would be a natural inflow of British pounds for the coming three years, and MedStat wishes to match the currency of denomination of the cash flows through a cross-currency swap.

MedStat enters into a 3-year pay-British-pounds and receive-U.S.-dollars cross-currency swap. Both interest rates are fixed. MedStat will pay 1.15% (the ask rate) fixed British pound interest and receive 1.26% (the bid rate) fixed U.S. dollars (swap rates are taken from Exhibit 8.13). As seen in Exhibit 8.14, the 3-year currency swap MedStat selected is different from the plain-vanilla interest rate swap in two important ways:

1. The spot exchange rate in effect on the date of the agreement establishes the notional principal in the target currency. The target currency is the currency MedStat is swapping into, in this case the British pound. The $10,000,000 notional principal converts to a £6,410,256 notional principal. This is the principal used to establish the actual cash flows MedStat is committing to making.
2. The notional principal itself is part of the swap agreement. In plain-vanilla interest rate swaps, both interest payment cash flows are based on the same notional principal (in the same currency). Hence, there is no need to include the principal in the agreement. In a cross-currency swap, however, because the notional principals are denominated in two different currencies and the exchange rate between those two currencies may change over time, the notional principals are part of the swap agreement.

At the time of the swap's inception, both positions have the same net present value. MedStat's swap commits it to three future cash payments in British pounds in return for

EXHIBIT 8.14 MedStat's Cross-Currency Swap

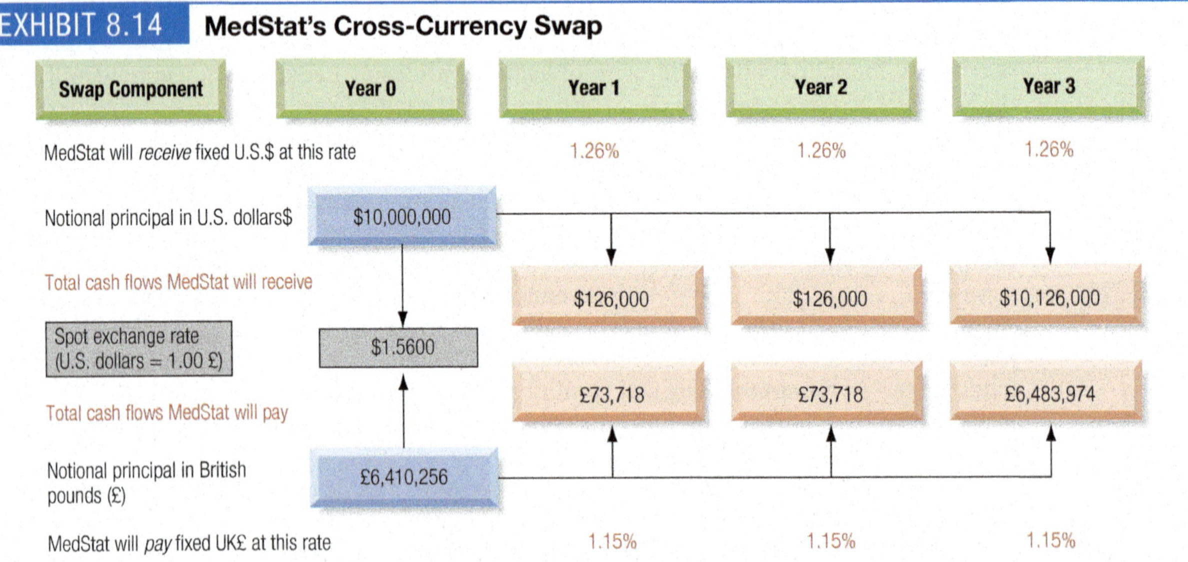

Note: The U.S. $ receive fixed rate is the three-year bid rate in Exhibit 8.12. The British pound pay fixed rate is the three-year ask rate in Exhibit 8.12.

receiving three payments in U.S. dollars. The payments are set. Accounting practices will require MedStat to regularly track and value its position—*mark-to-market* the swap—on the basis of current exchange rates and interest rates. If after the swap is initiated, the British pound appreciates versus the dollar, and MedStat is paying pounds, MedStat will record a loss on the swap for accounting purposes. (Similarly, the swap dealer's side of the transaction will record a gain.) At the same time, if interest rates in British pound markets rise, and MedStat's swap commits it to a fixed rate of 1.15%, then a gain will result from the interest component of the swap's value. In short, gains and losses on the swap, at least for accounting purposes, will persist throughout the swap's life. The currency swaps described here are non-amortizing swaps, where the swap parties pay the entire principal at maturity, rather than over the life of the swap agreement, standard practice in the market.

Illustrative Case: MedStat Unwinds a Currency Swap

As with all original loan agreements, it may happen that at some future date the partners to a swap may wish to terminate the agreement before it matures. If, for example, after one year, MedStat Corporation's British sales contract is terminated, MedStat will no longer need the swap as part of its hedging program. MedStat could terminate or unwind the swap with the swap dealer.

Unwinding a currency swap requires the discounting of the remaining cash flows under the swap agreement at current interest rates, then converting the target currency (British pounds in this case) back to the home currency of the firm (U.S. dollars for MedStat). If MedStat has two payments remaining on the swap agreement (an interest-only payment, and a principal and interest payment), and the 2-year fixed rate of interest for pounds is now 1.50%, the present value of MedStat's commitment in British pounds is:

$$PV(£) = \frac{£73{,}717.95}{(1.015)^1} + \frac{£6{,}483{,}974.36}{(1.015)^2} = £6{,}366{,}374.41$$

At the same time, the present value of the remaining cash flows on the dollar side of the swap is determined using the current 2-year fixed dollar interest rate, which is now 1.40%:

$$PV(\$) = \frac{\$126{,}000.00}{(1.014)^1} + \frac{\$10{,}126{,}000.00}{(1.014)^2} = \$9{,}972{,}577.21$$

MedStat's currency swap, if unwound at this time, would yield a present value of net inflows (what it receives under the swap) of $9,972,577.21 and a present value of outflows (what it pays under the swap) of £6,366,374.41. If the exchange rate is now $1.65=£1.00, the net settlement of this currency swap will be:

$$\text{Settlement} = \$9{,}972{,}577.21 - (£6{,}366{,}374.41 \times \$1.65) = -\$531{,}940.57$$

MedStat must therefore make a cash payment to the swap dealer of $531,941 to unwind the swap. MedStat's cash loss on this swap would result largely from the appreciation of the British pound against the U.S. dollar (the interest rates both rose marginally). Since MedStat had promised to pay in the currency that is now stronger in value—the pound—unwinding the swap will be costly. (If for example the exchange rate was still $1.56=£1.00, MedStat would have closed out the position with a gain of $41,033.) It is important to remember, however, that the swap was entered into as a hedge of MedStat's long British pound position; it was not meant as a financial investment. But unwinding swaps can sometimes be much more complex, like that of the swaps Procter & Gamble purchased from Bankers Trust, as described in *Global Finance in Practice 8.2.*

GLOBAL FINANCE IN PRACTICE 8.2

Procter & Gamble and Bankers Trust

In 1994, Procter & Gamble (P&G) announced that it had incurred a $157 million pre-tax loss from closing out an interest rate swap transaction it had entered into with Bankers Trust. The loss would result in a $102 million after-tax charge to third-quarter earnings. According to P&G, this swap was a highly complex and speculative transaction that was counter to P&G's policy of conservatively managing their debt portfolio.

> *Derivatives like these are dangerous and we were badly burned. We won't let this happen again. We are seriously considering our legal options relative to Bankers Trust, the financial institution that designed these swaps and brought them to us.*
>
> —Edwin L. Artzt, chairman of Procter & Gamble, as quoted in "Procter & Gamble's Tale of Derivative Woe," by Lawrence Malkin, The New York Times, April 14, 1994.

P&G wanted to continue to make floating-rate payments in return for receiving fixed-rate payments in order to maintain a balance between its fixed and floating-rate debt obligations. The swap would essentially transform existing fixed-rate debt obligations held by P&G into floating-rate obligations at a quite attractive rate. According to Bankers Trust, P&G was confident that interest rates would not rise significantly over the next year (although interest rates were at that time at historically low levels). P&G wanted to achieve the same favorable floating-rate as under another swap which had just matured, CP minus 40 basis points. But it did not want to incur significant risk.

Bankers Trust sold P&G a "5/30 Year Linked Swap," a 5-year swap structure with a notional principal of $200 million. Bankers Trust would pay P&G a fixed rate of 5.30% on a semi-annual basis. P&G in turn would pay Bankers Trust commercial paper (CP) less 75 basis points for the first six months of the swap agreement, and thereafter, CP less 75 basis points plus an additional spread (the "Spread") which could never be less than zero, and which would be fixed at the end of the first six months. The Spread was calculated as follows:

$$\text{Spread} = \frac{98.5 \times \dfrac{\text{(5-year-Treasury -Note Yield)}}{5.78\%} - \text{30-year 6.25\% Treasury price}}{100}$$

The Spread formula was actually a speculative play on the entire U.S. Treasury yield curve. If 5-year Treasuries remained fairly constant at their current level, the spread stayed near zero. However, because the Spread could increase geometrically with interest rate increases, rather than the customary arithmetic increases of standard interest rate movements, the instrument was considered highly leveraged.

The Spread formula was also extraordinarily sensitive to rising 5-year Treasury note yields. Each 1% increase in 5-year yields would increase P&G's payments under the leveraged swap by more than 17% of notional principal per year (CP + 1,700 basis points), while each 1% decline in long bond prices would cost P&G 1% of notional principal. P&G had interpreted the Spread as 0.17%, not 17%. A number of analysts noted the rather peculiar way in which the Spread was expressed. The division by 100 gave a number less than one, which appeared as a fraction of 1%. In the end, what P&G and other firms observing P&G's travails learned was that one should not agree to something they do not understand. Or as it is oft-quoted in Latin, *caveat emptor*—buyer beware.

Counterparty Risk

Counterparty risk is the potential exposure any individual firm bears that the second party to any financial contract will be unable to fulfill its obligations under the contract's specifications. Concern over counterparty risk periodically rises, usually associated with large and well-publicized derivative and swap defaults. The rapid growth in the currency and interest rate financial derivatives markets has actually been accompanied by a surprisingly low default rate to date, particularly in a global market that is unregulated in principle.

Counterparty risk has long been one of the major factors that favor the use of exchange-traded rather than over-the-counter derivatives. Most exchanges, like the Philadelphia Stock Exchange for currency options or the Chicago Mercantile Exchange for Eurodollar futures, are themselves the counterparty to all transactions. This allows all firms a high degree of confidence in being able to buy or sell exchange-traded products quickly and with little concern over the credit quality of the exchange itself. Financial exchanges typically require a small fee from all traders on the exchanges to pay for insurance funds created expressly for the purpose of protecting all parties. Over-the-counter products, however, are direct credit exposures to the firm because the contract is generally between the buying firm and the selling financial institution. Most financial derivatives in today's world financial centers are sold or brokered only by the largest and soundest financial institutions. This structure does not mean, however, that firms can enter continuing agreements with these institutions without some degree of real financial risk and concern.

A firm entering into a currency or interest rate swap agreement retains ultimate responsibility for the timely servicing of its own debt obligations. Although a swap agreement may constitute a contract to exchange U.S. dollar payments for euro payments, the firm that actually holds the dollar debt is still legally responsible for payment. The original debt remains on the borrower's books. In the event that a counterparty to a swap does not make the payment as agreed, the firm legally holding the debt is still responsible for debt service. In the event of such a failure, the payments would cease by the right of offset, and the losses associated with the failed swap would be mitigated.

The real exposure of an interest or currency swap is not the total notional principal, but the mark-to-market values of differentials in interest or currency interest payments (replacement cost) since the inception of the swap agreement. The real exposure is similar to the change in swap value discovered by unwinding a swap described previously. This amount is typically only 2% to 3% of the notional principal.

Summary Points

- The single largest interest rate risk of the nonfinancial firm is debt service. The debt structure of the MNE will possess differing maturities of debt, different interest rate structures (such as fixed versus floating rate), and different currencies of denomination.
- The increasing volatility of world interest rates, combined with the increasing use of short-term and variable-rate debt by firms worldwide, has led many firms to actively manage their interest rate risks.
- The primary sources of interest rate risk to a multinational nonfinancial firm are short-term borrowing, short-term investing, and long-term debt service.
- The techniques and instruments used in interest rate risk management in many ways resemble those used in currency risk management. The primary instruments used for interest rate risk management include refinancing, forward rate agreements (FRAs), interest rate futures, and interest rate swaps.
- The interest rate and currency swap markets allow firms that have limited access to specific currencies and interest rate structures to gain access at relatively low costs. This in turn allows these firms to manage their currency and interest rate risks more effectively.
- A cross-currency interest rate swap allows a firm to alter both the currency of denomination of cash flows in debt service and the fixed-to-floating or floating-to-fixed interest rate structure.

MINI-CASE

Replacing LIBOR[1]

Transitioning from LIBOR is like having to figure out how to re-lay the tracks of the global financial system.

—Timothy Bowler, president of ICE Benchmark Administration, "This Man Wants to Mend, Not End, Libor," by Daniel Kruger, *Wall Street Journal*, May 5, 2019.

It has often been described as "the world's most important number." No single interest rate is more fundamental to the operation of the global financial markets than the London Interbank Offered Rate, or LIBOR. But it was now being replaced. LIBOR has been the world's most widely used reference interest rate for more than 50 years. It is used daily in hundreds of thousands of different

[1] This case was prepared by Professor Michael H. Moffett for the purpose of classroom discussion only.

financial contracts, derivatives, mortgages, bank loans, and insurance agreements. But LIBOR had failed in a number of ways beginning with the multitude of crises in the United States and United Kingdom as far back as 2007, and the world's financial leaders were now moving to replace it. That replacement process, *LIBOR cessation*, was actively underway. But replacing a global benchmark used in more than $350 trillion of financial contracts worldwide, essentially a global institution, was a massive undertaking.

LIBOR Defined

LIBOR is administered by the ICE Benchmark Administration (IBA) and is calculated for five different currencies: U.S. dollar (USD), Euro (EUR), British pound sterling (GBP), Japanese yen (JPY), and the Swiss franc (CHF). It is quoted for seven different maturities: overnight; one week; and 1, 2, 3, 6, and 12 months, a daily matrix of 35 different interest rate references. Prior to the IBA taking over its publication, LIBOR was for decades calculated and published by the British Bankers Association (BBA).

Each day, a panel of 16 major multinational banks was requested to submit estimated borrowing rates in the unsecured interbank market, which were then collected, massaged, and published in three steps. In the first step, the banks on the LIBOR panels would submit their estimated borrowing rates by 11:10 a.m. London time. The submissions were made directly to Thomson Reuters, which executed the process on behalf of the BBA. In the second step, Thomson Reuters discarded the lowest 25% and highest 25% of interest rates submitted. It then calculated an average rate by maturity and currency using the remaining 50% of borrowing rate quotes. In the third and final step, the BBA published the day's LIBOR rates 20 minutes later, by 11:30 a.m. London time. The same process was used to publish LIBOR for the five currencies and seven maturities. The 3-month and 6-month maturities are the most significant maturities due to their widespread use in various loan and derivative agreements, with the dollar and the euro being the most widely used currencies.

At its core LIBOR represents interbank borrowing. Each bank surveyed daily is asked to base its LIBOR submissions on the following question:

> *At what rate could you borrow funds, were you to do so by asking for and then accepting interbank offers in a reasonable market size just prior to 11 a.m. London time?*

This would require the reporting of the lowest perceived rate at which a bank could actually receive funds for a specific maturity and currency. The phrase *reasonable market size* is intentionally vague, as typical trading transaction sizes change frequently and the value of those transactions would vary dramatically depending upon currency.

In theory this produced a daily sample of the cost of funds for the largest and most active commercial banks in the world. The values submitted by the banks surveyed by the IBA were not, however, actual transactions. They were in fact nothing other than "indications" or perceptions and were limited to the relatively small sample of banks. And they could not be termed risk-free; the rates submitted represented the cost of funds for commercial enterprises, enterprises that still possessed a core—but likely extremely small—credit risk component. The market had in fact for decades considered a core set of banks to be inherently risk-free and "on the run," so much so that their rates were quoted as the base benchmarks reflecting little credit risk premium.

LIBOR's Decline

> *The idea that my word is my LIBOR is dead.*
>
> —Mervyn King, Bank of England Governor, Press conference on Central Bank's Financial Stability Report, 2012.

LIBOR and the interbank market had always been prone to freeze up during times of financial crisis. During the financial crisis of September 2008, for example, for weeks the market showed so little trading that banks no longer saw it as a source of overnight funds—the exact role it was supposed to play. If trading occurred at all, it was at extremely low volumes. Low volumes in turn resulted in relatively high volatility as fewer quotes and traders provided poor price discovery.

The funding structure of financial institutions had been changing dramatically over an extended period. Commercial banking institutions, depository institutions, were required to hold more reserves, in turn requiring less overnight lending and borrowing activity, to support their balance sheets. And as many of the distinctions and regulations separating commercial banking and investment banking disappeared, investment banking firms played a greater role in markets. One such role change was that investment banks and similar financial institutions looked to the *repo market* for short-term funds. A repo or repurchase agreement combines the simultaneous sale and repurchase of a security (typically a government security such as a Treasury bill) as a form of short-term borrowing. The seller sells the underlying security to a buyer and by agreement buys that security back shortly afterward, usually the following day, at a slightly higher price. This difference in price is the cost of short-term funds.

Beginning in 2012 another series of troubling events eroded much of the faith in LIBOR. A series of scandals uncovered manipulation in rate quotes to the BBA. On a number of occasions, it was discovered that banks—including Barclays, one of the oldest and most esteemed banking houses in the world—were submitting interbank quotes to the BBA working cooperatively with other banks to push LIBOR rates quoted in one direction or another, sometimes by 30 or 40 basis points, for both personal and institutional gain. Quotes did not realistically represent the cost of funds for the banks in the market.

LIBOR also suffered from certain behavioral risks, particularly during crisis. One example can be found in the concerns of banks in the interbank market in September 2008 when the credit crisis was in full bloom. When a bank reported that it was being charged a higher rate by other banks, it was effectively self-reporting the market's assessment that it was increasingly risky. In the words of one analyst, it was akin "to hanging a sign around one's neck that I am carrying a contagious disease."

Following the discovery of the fraudulent activity, LIBOR was placed under the direct regulation of the British government by the Financial Securities Act 2012, and its administration was transferred to the Intercontinental Exchange (ICE). One of the primary changes to LIBOR required by its new administrators was that it reflect actual transactions. But this proved challenging as fewer and fewer financial institutions were using interbank borrowing on a daily basis. The financial sector regulators across countries jointly began to search for a new alternative.

LIBOR Cessation

The Financial Stability Board (FSB) and Financial Stability Oversight Council (FSOC) have both publicly recognized for some time that the secular decline in wholesale unsecured term money market funding by banks poses serious structural risks for unsecured benchmarks such as ICE LIBOR (LIBOR). Although significant progress has been made in strengthening the governance and processes underlying LIBOR, the scarcity of underlying transactions poses a continuing risk of a permanent cessation of its production.

Because U.S. dollar (USD) LIBOR is used in such a large volume and broad range of financial products and contracts, the risks surrounding it pose a potential threat to the safety and soundness of individual financial institutions and to financial stability. Without advanced preparation, a sudden cessation of such a heavily used reference rate would cause considerable disruptions to and uncertainties around the large gross flows of USD LIBOR–related payments and receipts between many firms. It would also impair the normal functioning of a variety of markets, including business and consumer lending.

—"Second Report," The Alternative Reference Rates Committee, March 2018.

LIBOR replacement efforts have been led by the Financial Stability Board (FSB), an international body of the G20 countries responsible for the oversight of the global financial system.[2] In turn, each of the individual countries has led its own domestic development. In the United Kingdom, efforts have been led by the Financial Conduct Authority (FCA), a nongovernmental authority, working alongside the Prudential Regulation Authority and the Financial Policy Committee.

In the U.S. the LIBOR transition is being led by the U.S. Federal Reserve and its Alternative Reference Rates Committee (ARRC). ARRC is a group of private-industry participants convened by the Federal Reserve Board and the New York Fed to help ensure a successful transition to a new, hopefully more dependable rate. Other transitions have largely been the responsibility of central banks—the Bank of Japan, the Swiss Central Bank, and the European Central Bank (ECB).

LIBOR cessation faces challenges financially and legally. For example, the United Kingdom, in an effort to avoid endless litigation involving the changeover, gave its regulator, the Financial Conduct Authority (FCA), the legal right to maintain a "LIBOR-like" reference rate, a "zombie-type" rate, that could be used for the most difficult of legacy contracts. Although the original time line announced was to end the publication of all LIBOR rates by December 31, 2021, this schedule was revised to allow more time.

On March 5, 2021, the final time line for LIBOR phaseout was announced.[3]

(i) the overnight and 1, 3, 6, and 12 months USD LIBOR settings immediately following the LIBOR publication on Friday, June 30, 2023, and

(ii) all other LIBOR settings, including the 1 week and 2 months USD LIBOR settings, immediately following the LIBOR publication on Friday, December 31, 2021.

LIBOR Replacements

Exhibit A lists the replacements for LIBOR for the five currencies. Although not all of the individual new reference rates are secured (do not have an explicit security

[2] The FSB was founded in 2009 and has on occasion been described as the "fourth pillar" of global economic governance, joining the International Monetary Fund, the World Bank, and the World Trade Organization. The FSB, however, has no legal power or form, only working as an informal group of cooperation.

[3] "FCA Announcement on Future Cessation and Loss of Representativeness of the LIBOR Benchmarks," Financial Conduct Authority, March 5, 2021.

EXHIBIT A LIBOR Replacements by Currency

Currency	RFR	Reference Rate	Secured?	Administrator
U.S. dollar	SOFR	Secured overnight financing rate	Secured	Federal Reserve Bank of New York
British pound sterling	SONIA	Sterling overnight interest average	Unsecured	Bank of England
Japanese yen	TONA	Tokyo overnight average rate	Unsecured	SIX Swiss Exchange
European euro	€STER	Euro short-term rate	Unsecured	European Central Bank
Swiss franc	SARON	Swiss average overnight rate	Secured	Bank of Japan

Source: Progress Report on Reforming Major Interest Rate Benchmarks, October 2017, and ARRC FAQ. RFR is risk-free rate.

or asset as collateral as part of the transaction), they are all considered risk-free rates by national authorities as they reflect actual transactions conducted in the regulated national bank markets. Each of the risk-free rate choices of the five nations is different in its calculation and structure, a major departure from the traditional LIBOR system.

SOFR (Secured Overnight Financing Rate) is a broad measure of the cost of borrowing cash overnight collateralized by Treasury securities. The SOFR includes all trades in the Broad General Collateral Rate plus bilateral Treasury repurchase agreement (repo) transactions cleared through the Delivery-versus-Payment (DVP) service offered by the Fixed Income Clearing Corporation (FICC).

SONIA (Sterling Overnight Index Average) is a risk-free rate for British pounds sterling. SONIA is based on actual transactions and reflects the average of the interest rates that banks pay to borrow sterling overnight from other financial institutions and other institutional investors. Financial businesses and institutions use SONIA in a variety of ways including the interest paid on sterling floating-rate notes.

TONA or TONAR (Tokyo Overnight Average Rate) is an unsecured interbank overnight interest rate and reference rate for Japanese yen. Since 2016, the Bank of Japan has recommended TONAR as the preferred risk-free reference rate.

€STR (Euro Short-Term Rate) is a reference rate for the currency euro. The €STR is calculated by the European Central Bank and is based on the money market statistical reporting of the Eurosystem. The working group on euro risk-free rates has recommended €STR as a replacement for the EMMI Euro Overnight Index Average (EONIA) as the euro risk-free rate for all products and contracts.

SARON (Swiss Average Rate Overnight) represents the overnight interest rate of the secured funding market for the Swiss franc. It is based on transactions and quotes posted in the Swiss repo market.

The advantages of moving to these benchmarks are substantial. SOFR is superior to LIBOR in a number of ways. SOFR is calculated on actual documented transactions, whereas LIBOR is based on surveys of possible transactions. SOFR is based on secured transactions of government securities, truly risk-free. LIBOR is based on the unsecured borrowing costs of a firm possessing credit risk. (That credit risk for the majority of the banks surveyed daily is exceedingly small but still positive.) SOFR is calculated from transactions in the single largest overnight financial market reflecting the opinions of thousands of different buyers and sellers, including all forms of financial institutions and investors. LIBOR is based only on the perceived borrowing and lending costs between select commercial banks, a weak measure of market activity. As illustrated by Exhibit B, SOFR and USD LIBOR (overnight) track extremely closely over time, with a few exceptional divergences.[4]

Yet there remain a number of major challenges. The three challenges of most immediate concern are fallback language, spreads, and the term challenge. The first is legal in nature, the second transitional behavior in character, and the third—well, the third is complicated.

Fallback Language. Fallback language refers to the legal practices and provisions in a financial contract that apply if the underlying reference rate (LIBOR) is discontinued or unavailable. For example, when USD LIBOR

[4] Exhibit B shows SOFR spiking in mid-September 2019. SOFR rose from 2.43% on September 16 to 5.25% on September 17. The cause is believed to have been the simultaneous settlement of bank tax payments due on September 16 with more than $54 billion in settlement of U.S. Treasury debt.

EXHIBIT B Comparison of SOFR and Overnight USD LIBOR

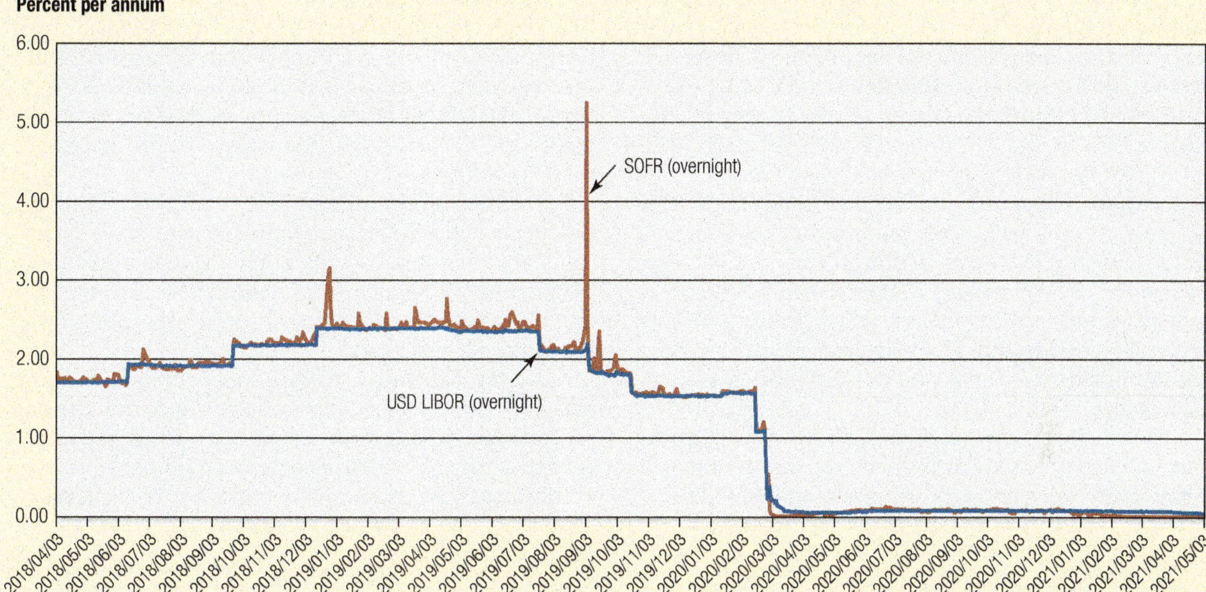

Source: Constructed by authors from Federal Reserve Bank of New York and Federal Reserve Bank of St. Louis (FRED) data bases. Period: April 3, 2018–June 6, 2021.

ceases, contracts that contain fallback provisions will switch to a "fallback rate"—a rate to be used if the base rate is not available. Many contracts over time have used fallback language calling for the use of the "last quoted rate" in case of unavailability. That would obviously prove an unattractive solution if contracts continued for months or even years after LIBOR stopped being quoted. Hence, national authorities have worked through legal channels in their own countries to "fix" this language and collectively to provide both advice and even samples of language to be used in financial contracts moving forward.

Spread Adjustment. Spread adjustment is the concern on how to make the transition from LIBOR to the new reference rates fair and reasonable for both borrowers and lenders. For example, the USD replacement, SOFR, is historically lower than USD LIBOR. ARRC has called for a one-year transition period as part of its recommended spread adjustments for consumer products. The ARRC specified that the starting point for the transition period would be based on a 2-week average of the relevant LIBOR-SOFR spread prior to the time of the benchmark replacement date.

Term Challenge. The replacement rates are largely overnight rates and do not have the multitude (seven) terms LIBOR offers. These terms allowed interest rates in contracts to be "forward-looking," where contract participants would know the rate of interest for the term at the start of the time period of the contract. Many standard structures like floating-rate bank loans need a term measure, such as a loan priced on 3-month LIBOR. But there is no 3-month SOFR. ARRC has recommended that financial institutions use an average rate calculation in new contracts, either simple averaging or compound interest. For example, a business loan with interest rate resets every 3 months could use the average of the SOFR rate for that 3-month period. Critics of this replacement point out that although the math can provide a 90-day moving average, SOFR itself is only an overnight rate and does not implicitly contain expectations for returns, both real and nominal, for any future period more than a day.

Associated with this averaging requirement is whether these will be *in advance* or *in arrears. In arrears* means that the interest rate used in a contract would be the average for a period that has ended, historical and factual. But interest rate reference rates like LIBOR have effectively been *in advance* markets, a forward-looking rate for the coming period of time based on both history and expectations. This is a particularly troublesome dimension for business loans. Borrowers are certainly used to knowing the interest rate for the coming debt-service period at the beginning of the period, not the end.

Exhibit C illustrates the differences between USD 3-month LIBOR and SOFR since SOFR's launch in 2018. SOFR itself is obviously more volatile than LIBOR. Even excluding the September 2019 one-day spike, SOFR is seen to vary on a daily basis much more than 3-month LIBOR. When a direct comparison of 3-month LIBOR is made with a 90-day moving average for SOFR, the recommended replacement for 3-month LIBOR, SOFR is seen to be considerably less volatile than LIBOR. This is not surprising; it is simply the result of moving average mathematics.

The extended time taken for LIBOR cessation is a function of its use. Exhibit D shows the latest estimates of how many assets by class are subject to USD LIBOR replacement. (These estimates have continued to be revised upward as more and more assets have been found to have residual LIBOR languages and price-setting.) The good news for USD LIBOR is that the majority of instruments are relatively short-term in remaining life, the two years between March 2021 and June 2023 retiring $150 trillion of the balance. This is not surprising given that LIBOR rates, regardless of term, are money market interest rates.

The bulk of assets in the USD LIBOR footprint are over-the-counter (OTC) derivatives. And of these, the majority are interest rate swaps. Given the longer maturities of swaps, some extending out to more than 20 years, it is understandable that they are not necessarily rapidly aging out of the exposed assets.

As the five major LIBOR-based economies move into LIBOR cessation, other countries and their city and regionally based interbank markets are also moving to new reference rates (e.g., Singapore from SIBOR, Paris from PIBOR, etc.). For them it may prove less of challenge as

EXHIBIT C Comparison of SOFR and 3-Month USD LIBOR

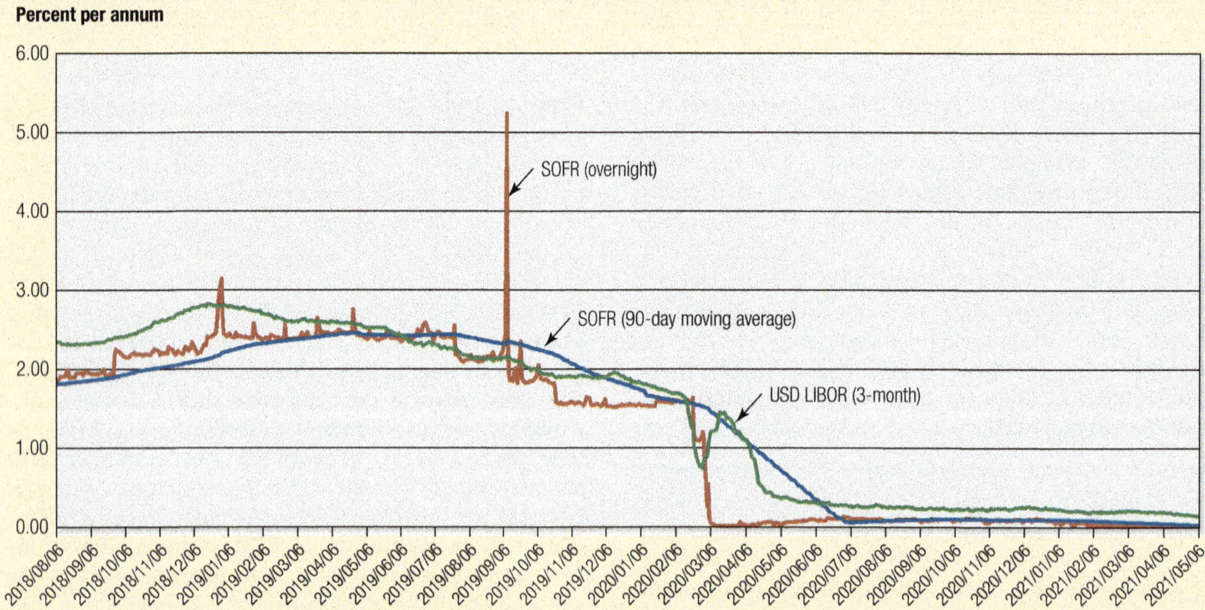

Source: Constructed by authors from Federal Reserve Bank of New York and Federal Reserve Bank of St. Louis (FRED) data bases. Period: Aug 6, 2018–May 21, 2021.

EXHIBIT D USD LIBOR Market Asset Footprint

Trillion U.S. dollars	March 2021	After June 2023
Over-the-Counter Derivatives		
Interest rate swaps	81.0	46.0
Forward rate agreements	47.0	0.0
Interest rate options	20.0	12.0
Cross-currency swaps	23.0	8.0
Exchange-Traded Derivatives		
Interest rate options	32.0	0.0
Interest rate futures	11.0	2.0
Business Loans		
Syndicated loans	2.0	1.1
Non-syndicated business loans	1.3	0.4
Non-syndicated commercial mortgages	1.5	0.8
Consumer Loans		
Retail mortgages	1.3	0.8
Other consumer loans	0.1	0.1
Bonds Floating/variable rate notes	1.1	0.3
Securitizations		
Mortgage-back securities & CMOs	0.8	0.8
Collateralized loans obligations	0.5	0.5
Asset-backed securities	0.2	0.2
Collateralized debt obligations	0.1	0.1
Total asset footprint	222.9	73.1

Source: "Progress Report: The Transition from U.S. Dollar LIBOR," The Alternative Reference Rates Committee, March 2021 (Updated as of March 31, 2021), p. 3.

the road is paved ahead of them. But critics and concerns remain about the replacements, particularly that new reference rates like SOFR are "too LIBIOR-like." That is, they react to overnight events as SOFR did in September 2019. Such events, even in larger markets like the secured repo market, can be subject to lack of liquidity and its result, interest rate spikes. To others, these are just the expected downsides—the risks—of basing the cost of money on markets.

MINI-CASE QUESTIONS

1. Has LIBOR served successfully as a benchmark interest rate?
2. Why is LIBOR being replaced? Do you believe its weaknesses or failures justify its replacement?
3. Will LIBOR's replacements across countries really serve the same purposes as LIBOR has for the past 50 years?

Questions

8.1 Reference Rates. What is an interest "reference rate," and how is it used to set rates for individual borrowers?

8.2 My Word Is My LIBOR. Why has LIBOR played such a central role in international business and financial contracts? Why has this been questioned in recent debates over its value reported?

8.3 Credit Risk Premium. What is a credit risk premium?

8.4 Credit and Repricing Risk. From the point of view of a borrowing corporation, what are credit and repricing risks? Explain steps a company might take to minimize both.

8.5 Credit Spreads. What is a credit spread? What credit rating changes have the most profound impact on the credit spread paid by corporate borrowers?

8.6 Investment Grade versus Speculative Grade. What do the general categories of investment grade and speculative grade represent?

8.7 Sovereign Debt. What is sovereign debt? What specific characteristic of sovereign debt constitutes the greatest risk to a sovereign issuer?

8.8 Floating-Rate Loan Risk. Why do borrowers of lower credit quality often find their access limited to floating-rate loans?

8.9 Interest Rate Futures. What is an interest rate future? How can it be used to reduce interest rate risk by a borrower?

8.10 Interest Rate Futures Strategies. What would be the preferred strategy for a borrower paying interest on a future date if they expected interest rates to rise?

8.11 Forward Rate Agreement. How can a firm that has borrowed on a floating-rate basis use a forward rate agreement to reduce interest rate risk?

8.12 Plain Vanilla. What is a plain-vanilla interest rate swap? Are swaps a significant source of capital for multinational firms?

8.13 Swaps and Credit Quality. If interest rate swaps are not the cost of government borrowing, what credit quality do they represent?

8.14 LIBOR Flat. Why do fixed-for-floating interest rate swaps never swap the credit spread component on a floating-rate loan?

8.15 Debt Structure Swap Strategies. How can interest rate swaps be used by a multinational firm to manage its debt structure?

8.16 Cost-Based Swap Strategies. How do corporate borrowers use interest rate or cross-currency swaps to reduce the costs of their debt?

8.17 Cross-Currency Swaps. Why would one company with interest payments due in pounds sterling want to swap those payments for interest payments due in U.S. dollars?

8.18 Value Swings in Cross-Currency Swaps. Why are there significantly larger swings in the value of a cross-currency swap than in a plain-vanilla interest rate swap?

8.19 Unwinding a Swap. How does a company cancel or unwind a swap?

8.20 Counterparty Risk. How does organized exchange trading in swaps remove any risk that the counterparty in a swap agreement will not complete the agreement?

Problems

8.1 Botany Bay Corporation. Botany Bay Corporation (BBC) of Australia seeks to borrow US$30,000,000 in the eurodollar market. Funding is needed for two years. Investigation leads to three possibilities. Compare the alternatives and make a recommendation.

1. Botany Bay could borrow the US$30,000,000 for two years at a fixed 5% rate of interest.
2. Botany Bay could borrow the US$30,000,000 at LIBOR + 1.5%. LIBOR is currently 3.5%, and the rate would be reset every six months.
3. Botany Bay could borrow the US$30,000,000 for one year only at 4.5%. At the end of the first year, Botany Bay Corporation would have to negotiate for a new 1-year loan.

8.2 CB Solutions. Heather O'Reilly, the treasurer of CB Solutions, believes interest rates are going to rise, so she wants to swap her future floating-rate interest payments for fixed rates. Presently, she is paying per annum on $5,000,000 of debt for the next two years, with payments due semiannually. LIBOR is currently 4.00% per annum. Heather has just made an interest payment today, so the next payment is due six months from today. Heather finds that she can swap her current floating rate payments for fixed payments of 7.00% per annum. (CB Solution's weighted average cost of capital is 12%, which Heather calculates to be 6% per 6-month period, compounded semiannually.)

a. If LIBOR rises at the rate of 50 basis points per 6-month period, starting tomorrow, how much does Heather save or cost her company by making this swap?

b. If LIBOR falls at the rate of 25 basis points per 6-month period, starting tomorrow, how much does Heather save or cost her company by making this swap?

8.3 **T-Bill Yields.** The interest yields on U.S. Treasury securities in early 2009 fell to very low levels as a result of the combined events surrounding the global financial crisis. Calculate the simple and annualized yields for the 3-month and 6-month Treasury bills auctioned on March 9, 2009, listed here.

3-Month T-Bill	**6-Month T-Bill**	
Treasury bill, face value	$10,000.00	$10,000.00
Price at sale	$9,993.93	$9,976.74
Discount	$6.07	$23.26

8.4 **TED Spread in the Global Credit Crisis.** During financial crises, short-term interest rates will often change quickly (typically up) as indications that markets are under severe stress. The interest rates shown in the table below are for selected dates in September–October 2008. Different publications define the TED Spread, the Treasury-Eurodollar spread, in different ways. One measure is the differential between the overnight LIBOR interest rate and the 3-month U.S. Treasury bill rate.

a. Calculate the TED spread—the difference between the two market rates shown in the table—in September and October 2008.

b. On what date is the spread the narrowest? The widest?

c. When the spread widens dramatically, presumably demonstrating some form of financial anxiety or crisis, which of the rates moves the most and why?

8.5 **Bernie's Mortgage.** Bernie Madeoff pays $240,000 for a new four-bedroom 2,400-square-foot home outside Tonopah, Nevada. He plans to make a 20% down payment but is having trouble deciding whether he wants a 15-year fixed rate (6.400%) or a 30-year fixed rate (6.875%) mortgage.

a. What is the monthly payment for both the 15- and 30-year mortgages, assuming a fully amortizing loan of equal payments for the life of the mortgage? Use a spreadsheet calculator for the payments.

b. Assume that instead of making a 20% down payment, he makes a 10% down payment and finances the remainder at 7.125% fixed interest for 15 years. What is his monthly payment?

c. Assume that the home's total value falls by 25%. If Bernie sells the house at the new market value, what will be his gain or loss on the home and mortgage assuming all of the mortgage principal remains? Use the same assumptions as in part a.

Date	**Overnight USD LIBOR**	**3-Month US Treasury**	**TED spread**	**Date**	**Overnight USD LIBOR**	**3-Month US Treasury**	**TED spread**
9/8/2008	2.15%	1.70%	_____	9/29/2008	2.57%	0.41%	_____
9/9/2008	2.14%	1.65%	_____	9/30/2008	6.88%	0.89%	_____
9/10/2008	2.13%	1.65%	_____	10/1/2008	3.79%	0.81%	_____
9/11/2008	2.14%	1.60%	_____	10/2/2008	2.68%	0.60%	_____
9/12/2008	2.15%	1.49%	_____	10/3/2008	2.00%	0.48%	_____
9/15/2008	3.11%	0.83%	_____	10/6/2008	2.37%	0.48%	_____
9/16/2008	6.44%	0.79%	_____	10/7/2008	3.94%	0.79%	_____
9/17/2008	5.03%	0.04%	_____	10/8/2008	5.38%	0.65%	_____
9/18/2008	3.84%	0.07%	_____	10/9/2008	5.09%	0.55%	_____
9/19/2008	3.25%	0.97%	_____	10/10/2008	2.47%	0.18%	_____
9/22/2008	2.97%	0.85%	_____	10/13/2008	2.47%	0.18%	_____
9/23/2008	2.95%	0.81%	_____	10/14/2008	2.18%	0.27%	_____
9/24/2008	2.69%	0.45%	_____	10/15/2008	2.14%	0.20%	_____
9/25/2008	2.56%	0.72%	_____	10/16/2008	1.94%	0.44%	_____
9/26/2008	2.31%	0.85%	_____	10/17/2008	1.67%	0.79%	_____

Problem 8.7

Loan		Payments	1	2	3	4
Principal	$100	Interest	(10.00)	(7.85)	(5.48)	(2.87)
Interest rate	0.10	Principal	(21.55)	(23.70)	(26.07)	(28.68)
Maturity(years)	4.0	Total	(31.55)	(31.55)	(31.55)	(31.55)

8.6 DaimlerChrysler Debt. Chrysler LLC, the now privately held company sold off by DaimlerChrysler, must pay floating-rate interest three months from now. It wants to lock in these interest payments by buying an interest rate futures contract. Interest rate futures for three months from now settled at 93.07, for a yield of 6.93% per annum.

a. If the floating interest rate three months from now is 6.00%, what did Chrysler gain or lose?
b. If the floating interest rate three months from now is 8.00%, what did Chrysler gain or lose?

8.7 Sovereign Debt Negotiations. A sovereign borrower is considering a $100 million loan for a four-year maturity. It will be an amortizing loan, meaning that the interest and principal payments will total, annually, to a constant amount over the maturity of the loan. There is, however, a debate over the appropriate interest rate. The borrower believes the appropriate rate for its current credit standing in the market today is 10%, but a number of the international banks with which it is negotiating are arguing that it is most likely 12% and at the minimum 10%. What impact do these different interest rates have on the prospective annual payments?

8.8 Saharan Debt Negotiations. The country of Sahara is negotiating a new loan agreement with a consortium of international banks. Both sides have a tentative agreement on the principal—$220 million. But there are still wide differences of opinion on the final interest rate and maturity. The banks would like a shorter loan, four years in length, while Sahara would prefer a long maturity of six years. The banks also believe the interest rate will need to be 12.250% per annum, but Sahara believes that is too high, arguing instead for 11.750%.

a. What would the annual amortizing loan payments be for the bank consortium's proposal?
b. What would the annual amortizing loan payments be for Sahara's loan preferences?
c. How much would annual payments drop on the bank consortium's proposal if the same loan was stretched from four to six years?

8.9 Raid Gauloises. Raid Gauloises is a rapidly growing French sporting goods and adventure racing outfitter. The company has decided to borrow €20,000,000 via a euro-euro floating rate loan for four years. Raid must decide between two competing loan offers from two of its banks.

Banque de Paris has offered the four-year debt with an up-front initiation fee of 1.8%. Banque de Sorbonne, however, has offered a higher spread, but with no loan initiation fees up front, for the same term and principal. Both banks reset the interest rate at the end of each year. Euro-LIBOR is currently 4.00%. Raid's economist forecasts that LIBOR will rise by 0.5 percentage points each year. Banque de Sorbonne, however, officially forecasts euro-LIBOR to begin trending upward at the rate of 0.25 percentage points per year. Raid Gauloises's cost of capital is 11%. Which loan proposal do you recommend for Raid Gauloises?

8.10 Delos Debt Renegotiations (A). Delos borrowed €80 million two years ago. The loan agreement, an amortizing loan, was for six years at 8.625% interest per annum. Delos has successfully completed two years of debt service but now wishes to renegotiate the terms of the loan with the lender to reduce its annual payments.

a. What were Delos's annual principal and interest payments under the original loan agreement?
b. After two years debt service, how much of the principal is still outstanding?
c. If the loan was restructured to extend another two years, what would the annual payments—principal and interest—be? Is this a significant reduction from the original agreement's annual payments?

Problem 8.8

Loan	0	Payments	1	2	3	4	5	6
Principal	$220	Interest	(26.950)	(23.650)	(19.946)	(15.788)	(11.210)	(5.881)
Interest rate	12.250%	Principal	(26.939)	(30.239)	(33.943)	(38.101)	(42.769)	(48.008)
Maturity(years)	6.0	Total	(53.889)	(53.889)	(53.889)	(53.889)	(53.889)	(53.889)

8.11 Delos Debt Renegotiations (B). Delos is continuing to renegotiate its prior loan agreement (€80 million for six years at 8.625% per annum) two years into the agreement. Delos is now facing serious tax revenue shortfalls and fears for its ability to service its debt obligations, so it has decided to get more aggressive and has gone back to its lenders with a request for a haircut, a reduction in the remaining loan amount. The banks have, so far, only agreed to restructure the loan agreement for another two years (a new loan of six years on the remaining principal balance) but at an interest rate a full 200 basis points higher, 10.625%.

a. If Delos accepts the current bank proposal of the remaining principal for six years (extending the loan an additional two years since two of the original six years have already passed) but at the new interest rate, what are its annual payments going to be? How much relief does this provide Delos on annual debt service?

b. Delos's demands for a haircut are based on getting the new annual debt service payments down. If Delos does agree to the new loan terms, what size of haircut should it try to get from its lenders to get its payments down to €10 million per year?

8.12 MedStat Unwinds Its Cross-Currency Swap. In Exhibit 8.13, MedStat had entered into a 3-year cross-currency swap to pay British pounds at a fixed rate of interest and receive U.S. dollars at a fixed rate of interest. Using that same swap principal and contractual payments, calculate the cost of unwinding the swap after one year has passed (with two years remaining) if the two-year fixed rate of interest on British pounds is now 1.40%, the two-year fixed rate of interest on U.S. dollars is now 1.75%, and the current spot exchange rate is \$1.55 = £1.00.

8.13 Firenza Motors (Italy). Firenza Motors of Italy recently took out a 4-year, €5 million loan on a floating rate basis. It is now worried, however, about rising interest costs. Although it had initially believed interest rates in the eurozone would be trending downward when taking out the loan, recent economic indicators show growing inflationary pressures. Analysts are predicting that the European Central Bank will slow monetary growth, driving interest rates up.

a. Firenza is now considering whether to seek some protection against a rise in euro-LIBOR and is considering a forward rate agreement (FRA) with an insurance company. According to the agreement, Firenza would pay to the insurance company at the end of each year the difference between its initial interest cost at LIBOR + 2.50% (6.50%) and any fall in interest cost due to a fall in LIBOR. Conversely, the insurance company would pay to Firenza 70% of the difference between Firenza's initial interest cost and any increase in interest costs caused by a rise in LIBOR. LIBOR is currently 4.00%.

b. Purchase of the floating rate agreement will cost €100,000, paid at the time of the initial loan. What are Firenza's annual financing costs now if LIBOR rises and if LIBOR falls in increments of 0.5%? Firenza uses 12% as its weighted average cost of capital. Do you recommend that Firenza purchase the FRA?

8.14 Lluvia and Paraguas. Lluvia Manufacturing and Paraguas Products both seek funding at the lowest possible cost. Lluvia would prefer the flexibility of floating rate borrowing, while Paraguas wants the security of fixed rate borrowing. Lluvia is the more creditworthy company. They face the following rate structure. Lluvia, with the better credit rating, has lower borrowing costs in both types of borrowing. Lluvia wants floating rate debt, so it could borrow at LIBOR +1%. However, it could borrow fixed at 8% and swap for floating rate debt. Paraguas wants fixed rate debt, so it could borrow fixed at 12%. However, it could borrow floating at LIBOR +2% and swap for fixed rate debt. What should they do?

8.15 Ganado's Cross-Currency Swap: SFr for US\$. Ganado Corporation entered into a three-year cross-currency interest rate swap to receive U.S. dollars and pay Swiss francs. Ganado, however, decided to unwind the swap after one year—thereby having two years left on the settlement costs of unwinding the swap after one year. Repeat the calculations for unwinding swaps as demonstrated in the chapter using the following assumptions.

Problem 8.15

Assumptions	Values	Swap Rates	3-Year Bid	3-Year Ask
Notional principal	\$10,000,000	Original: US dollar	5.56%	5.59%
Original spot rate (SFr = \$1.00)	1.5000			
New (1-year later) spot (SFr = \$1.00)	1.5560	Original: Swiss franc	1.93%	2.01%
New fixed US\$ interest	5.20%			
New fixed Swiss franc interest	2.20%			

8.16 LaFarge Swaps Euros for Pounds. LaFarge, a major French multinational, has signed a number of new international sales agreements which will result in it receiving payments in British pounds for at least four years. It has decided to use some of those cash inflows in pounds to service debt obligations. It wishes to enter into a four-year cross-currency swap to pay British pounds and receive euros. The notional principal of the swap is €12 million, and the current spot rate is £0.80 = €1.00.

a. Use the swap rates presented in Exhibit 8.12 to lay out the contractual cash flows for all four years for the cross-currency swap.
b. Unfortunately, one year later LaFarge's business contracts have been canceled as a result of the Brexit vote. (The force majeure clauses allow contract cancellation.) The company decides to unwind its swap agreement with three years remaining on the swap. The spot exchange rate has changed and is now £0.8240 = €1.00. Euro interest rates have risen dramatically; a two-year rate is 1.20%, and a three-year rate is 1.40%. British pound interest rates have risen on a small amount; the two-year rate is now 1.44%, and the three-year rate is now 1.48%.

8.17 UAE Small Business Loan. Mohammad tried one last time to explain the loan structure offered by the company's Emirates bank. His boss just stared at him. Mo explained the detailed calculation of annual interest and principal payments, step-by-step, as detailed by the bank.

The loan was for USD5 million, for five years, with an 8.200% interest rate.

Step 1: Calculate simple interest on loan principal for one year.

Step 2: Multiply that interest by the number of years of the loan. The bank labeled this "total interest."

Step 3: Add the calculated total interest to the loan principal.

Step 4: Divide this calculated total by the number of years of the loan. This is the annual payment due on the loan (principal and interest).

Step 5: Using the calculated annual payment from step 4, structure the repayments to make all interest payments (totaling to total interest from step 2) up front. Once all interest has been paid, the remaining cash flows associated with the annual payment are considered repayment of principal.

a. Complete the full calculation of the proposed loan, including all five years of principal, interest, and total payments.
b. Estimate the all-in cost of this financing.
c. Recalculate all principal and interest payments for the same 5-year USD5 million dollar loan using traditional Western financial calculations. Include the all-in cost of funds in your calculations.
d. Compare the two loan structures. Why do you think the Emirates bank prefers this structure?

9

Foreign Exchange Rate Determination and Intervention

The herd instinct among forecasters makes sheep look like independent thinkers.

—Edgar R. Fiedler

LEARNING OBJECTIVES

9.1 Explore the three major theoretical approaches to exchange rate determination

9.2 Detail how and why direct and indirect foreign exchange market intervention is conducted by central banks

9.3 Analyze the primary causes of exchange rate disequilibrium in emerging market currencies

9.4 Observe how forecasters combine technical analysis with the three major theoretical approaches to forecasting exchange rates

What determines the exchange rate between currencies? This question has proven to be very difficult to answer. Companies and agents need foreign currency for buying imports, and they may earn foreign currency by exporting. Investors need foreign currency to invest in interest-bearing instruments in foreign markets, such as fixed-income securities (bonds), shares in publicly traded companies, or other new types of hybrid instruments. Tourists, migrant workers, speculators on currency movements—all of these economic agents buy and sell foreign currencies every day. This chapter offers a basic theoretical framework with which to organize these elements, forces, and principles.

Chapter 6 described the international parity conditions that integrate exchange rates with inflation and interest rates and provided a theoretical framework for both the global financial markets and the management of international financial business. Chapter 3 provided a detailed analysis of how an individual country's international economic activity, its balance of payments, can impact exchange rates. In the first section of this chapter, we build on those discussions of the schools of thought on exchange rate determination and look at another school of thought—the *asset market approach*. The chapter then turns to government intervention in the foreign exchange market. In the third and final section, we discuss a number of approaches to foreign exchange forecasting in practice. The chapter concludes with the mini-case *Is China a Currency Manipulator?*, an exploration of the U.S. labeling China as an official currency manipulator under U.S. trade law in 2019.

9.1 Exchange Rate Determination: The Theoretical Thread

There are basically three views of the exchange rate. The first takes the exchange rate as the relative price of monies (the monetary approach); the second, as the relative price of goods (the purchasing-power-parity approach); and the third, the relative price of bonds.

—Rudiger Dornbusch, "Exchange Rate Economics: Where Do We Stand?," *Brookings Papers on Economic Activity* 1, 1980, pp. 143–194.

Professor Dornbusch's three views of exchange rate theory are a good starting point but in some ways not sufficiently robust—in our humble opinion—to capture the multitude of theories and approaches. So, in the spirit of both tradition and completeness, we have amended Dornbusch's three views with several additional streams of thought in the following discussion.

Exhibit 9.1 provides an overview of the major schools of thought—theoretical determinants—of exchange rates. The exhibit is organized both by the three major schools of thought—*parity conditions approach, balance of payments approach, monetary and asset market approaches*—and by the individual drivers within each of those approaches. At first glance, the idea that there are three different theories may appear daunting, but it is important to remember that these are not competing theories, but rather complementary theories.

Without the depth and breadth of the various approaches combined, our ability to capture the complexity of the global market for currencies is lost. In addition to the three schools of thought described in Exhibit 9.1, note that two other institutional dimensions are considered—whether the country possesses the capital markets and banking systems needed to drive and discover value. Finally, note that most determinants of the spot exchange rate are also affected by changes in the spot rate. In other words, they are not only linked but also mutually determined.

EXHIBIT 9.1 The Theoretical Determinants of Exchange Rates

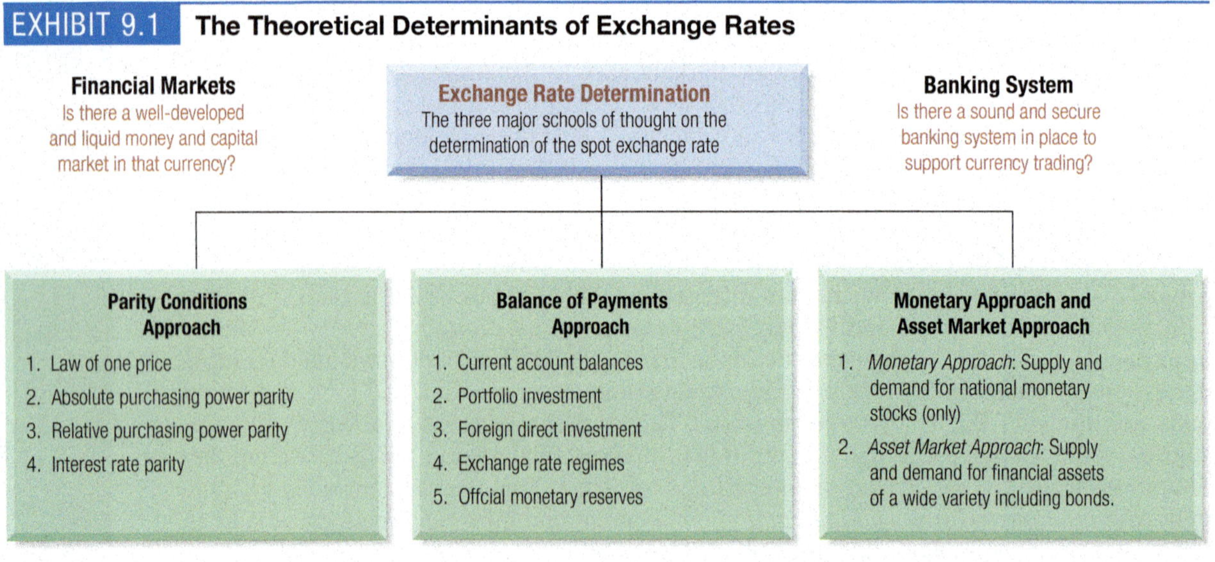

Parity Conditions Approach

Under the skin of an international economist lies a deep-seated belief in some variant of the PPP theory of the exchange rate.

—"Flexible Exchange Rates in the Short Run," Rudiger Dornbusch and Paul Krugman, *Brookings Papers on Economic Activity*, Vol. 1976, No. 3 (1976), pp. 537–584.

There are a number of different theories that make up the parity conditions approach: the *law of one price*, *absolute purchasing power parity*, *relative purchasing power parity*, and *interest rate parity*. All were discussed in detail in Chapter 6. The most widely accepted—the *theory of purchasing power parity* (PPP, both absolute and relative versions)—states that the long-run equilibrium exchange rate is determined by the ratio of domestic prices relative to foreign prices. PPP is both the oldest and most widely followed of the exchange rate theories described in Exhibit 9.1, and most theories of exchange rate determination have PPP elements embedded within their frameworks. The latter of the three theories, relative PPP is thought to be the most consistently relevant to possibly explaining what drives exchange rate values. In essence, it states that changes in relative prices between countries drive the change in exchange rates over time.

If, for example, the current spot exchange rate between the Japanese yen and U.S. dollar was ¥90.00 = $1.00 and Japanese and U.S. prices were to change at 2% and 1% over the coming period, respectively, the spot exchange rate next period would be ¥90.89 = $1.00.

$$S_{t+1} = S_t \times \frac{1 + \Delta \text{ in Japanese prices}}{1 + \Delta \text{ in US prices}} = ¥90.00 \times \frac{1.02}{1.01} = ¥90.89$$

Although PPP seems to possess a core element of common sense, it has proven to be quite poor at forecasting exchange rates (at least in the short to medium term). The problems are both theoretical and empirical. The theoretical problems lie primarily with its basic assumption that the only thing that matters is relative price changes. Yet many currency supply and demand forces are driven by other forces, including investment incentives, economic growth, and political change. The empirical issues lie primarily in deciding which measures or indexes of prices to use across countries, in addition to providing a "predicted change in prices" with the chosen indexes.

Balance of Payments Approach

After PPP, the most frequently used theoretical approach to exchange rate determination is probably the *balance of payments approach*, involving the supply and demand for currencies in the foreign exchange market. These exchange rate flows reflect current account and financial account transactions recorded in a nation's balance of payments, as described in Chapter 3. The basic balance of payments approach argues that the equilibrium exchange rate is found when the net inflow (or outflow) of foreign exchange arising from current account activities matches the net outflow (or inflow) of foreign exchange arising from financial account activities.

The balance of payments approach continues to enjoy widespread appeal, as balance of payments transactions are among the most frequently captured and reported of international economic activity. Trade surpluses and deficits, current account growth in service activity, and recently, the growth and significance of international capital flows continue to fuel this theoretical fire.

Criticisms of the balance of payments approach arise from the theory's emphasis on flows of currency and capital rather than on stocks of money or financial assets. Relative stocks of money or financial assets play no role in exchange rate determination in this theory, a weakness explored in the following discussion of monetary and asset market approaches. Curiously, while the balance of payments approach is largely dismissed by the academic community, market participants, including currency traders themselves, still rely on variations of this theory for much of their decision making.

Monetary Approach and Asset Market Approach

The third general approach to exchange rate determination, the *monetary approach* and *asset market approach*, is composed of two variations on the same theme—that the exchange rate is determined by the supply and demand for money (monetary approach) or the supply and demand for financial assets (asset market approach).

Monetary Approach. The monetary approach, in its simplest form, states that the exchange rate is determined by the supply and demand for national monetary stocks, as well as the expected future levels and rates of growth of monetary stocks. Other financial assets, such as bonds, are not considered relevant for exchange rate determination, as both domestic and foreign bonds are viewed as perfect substitutes. It is all about money stocks.

The monetary approach focuses on changes in the supply and demand for money as the primary determinant of inflation. Changes in relative inflation rates in turn are expected to alter exchange rates through a purchasing power parity effect. (Once again, PPP is embedded within another theory of exchange rate determination.) The monetary approach then assumes that prices are flexible in the short run as well as the long run, so that the transmission mechanism of inflationary pressure is immediate in impact.

A weakness of monetary models of exchange rate determination is that real economic activity is relegated to a role in which it only influences exchange rates through changes in the demand for money. The monetary approach is also criticized for its omission of a number of factors that are generally agreed upon by area experts as important to exchange rate determination, including (1) the failure of PPP to hold in the short to medium term; (2) money demand appears to be relatively unstable over time; and (3) the level of economic activity and the money supply appear to be interdependent, not independent.

Asset Market Approach. The *asset market approach*, sometimes called *the relative price of bonds* or *portfolio balance approach*, argues that exchange rates are determined by the supply and demand for financial assets of a wide variety, including bonds. Shifts in the supply and demand for widely varied financial assets alter exchange rates. Changes in monetary and fiscal policy alter expected returns and perceived relative risks of financial assets, which in turn alter rates.

Many of the macroeconomic theoretical developments in recent years focused on how monetary and fiscal policy changes altered the relative perceptions of return and risk to the stocks of financial assets driving exchange rate changes. Theories of currency substitution, the ability of individual and commercial investors to alter the composition of their portfolios, follow the same basic premises of the portfolio balance and re-balance framework.

Unfortunately, for all of the good work and research over the past 50 years, the ability to forecast exchange rate values in the short term to long term is—as noted by Frankel and Rose—sorry. Although academics and practitioners alike agree that in the long run fundamental principles such as purchasing power and external balances drive currency values, none of the fundamental theories have proven to be very useful in the short to medium term.

> *... the case for macroeconomic determinants of exchange rates is in a sorry state. [The] results indicate that no model based on such standard fundamentals like money supplies, real income, interest rates, inflation rates and current account balances will ever succeed in explaining or predicting a high percentage of the variation in the exchange rate, at least at short- or medium-term frequencies.*
>
> —Jeffrey A. Frankel and Andrew K. Rose, "A Survey of Empirical Research on Nominal Exchange Rates," NBER Working Paper No. 4865, 1994.

The forecasting inadequacies of these major theoretical schools of thought (the three approaches) has led to the increased popularity of technical analysis. *Technical analysis* is the study of past price behavior (for example, trends and formations of price movements) in an effort to gain insights into future price movements. The primary feature of technical analysis is the assumption that exchange rates—or, for that matter, all market-driven prices—follow trends. And those trends may be analyzed and projected to provide insights into short-term and medium-term price movements in the future. *Global Finance in Practice 9.1* illustrates one example of a simplified technical analysis of the Japanese yen–U.S. dollar cross rate.

Most theories of technical analysis differentiate fair value from market value. Fair value is the true long-term value that the price will eventually retain. The market value is subject to a multitude of changes and behaviors arising from widespread market participant perceptions and beliefs at the time.

The Asset Market Approach to Forecasting. Foreign investors are willing to hold securities and undertake foreign direct investment in highly developed countries based primarily on relative real interest rates (again, a form of parity condition) and the prospects for economic growth and profitability.

GLOBAL FINANCE IN PRACTICE **9.1**

Technical Analysis of the Japanese Yen-U.S. Dollar Exchange Rate (January 2011–February 2014)

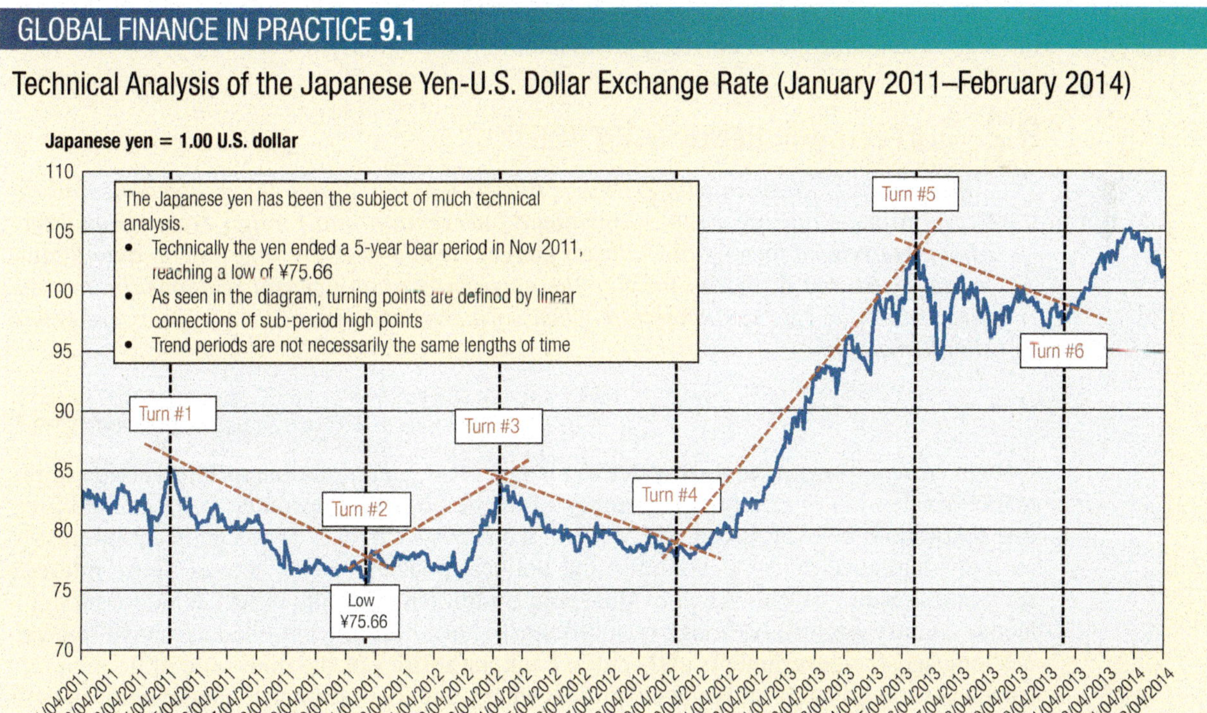

For example, the U.S. dollar strengthened in the period between 1990 and 2000 despite continued worsening balances on the current account. The dollar's strength, in both nominal and real terms, was due to foreign capital inflow motivated by rising stock and real estate prices, a low rate of inflation, high real interest returns, and a seemingly endless "irrational exuberance" about future economic prospects. This "bubble" burst following the September 11, 2001, terrorist attacks on the United States. The attacks and their aftermath caused a negative reassessment of long-term growth and profitability prospects in the U.S. (as well as a newly formed level of political risk for the United States itself). This negative outlook was reinforced by a sharp drop in the U.S. stock markets and a series of revelations about failures in corporate governance by several large corporations (the Enron era). As would be predicted by both the balance of payments and asset market approaches, the U.S. dollar depreciated.

The experience of the United States, as well as other highly developed countries, illustrates why some forecasters believe that exchange rates are more heavily influenced by economic prospects than by the current account. Consider the case of another asset price.

Assume oil prices have been down for several years (e.g., as was the case in 2020–2021), resulting in significantly lower earnings for oil and gas companies. As a result, their share prices fell. But that was the past. The price of the company's share now—today—should reflect what the market expects about future earnings, the future price of oil and the company's subsequent earnings in the future, not the past. This same logic can be applied to the relative value of a currency, the exchange rate. Only expectations about future events, future flows of capital across borders, will be reflected in the exchange value. All other past and present events and contemporaneous capital flows are already reflected in the current exchange rate.

The asset market approach to forecasting is also applicable to emerging markets. In this case, however, a number of additional variables contribute to exchange rate determination. A sampling of these variables includes illiquid capital markets, weak economic and social infrastructure, political instability, weak corporate governance laws and practices, susceptibility to contagion effects, and widespread speculation. These and other variables are illustrated in the section detailing major currency crises later in this chapter.

9.2 Currency Market Intervention

A fundamental problem with exchange rates is that no commonly accepted method exists to estimate the effectiveness of official intervention into foreign exchange markets. Many interrelated factors affect the exchange rate at any given time, and no quantitative model exists that is able to provide the magnitude of any causal relationship between intervention and an exchange rate when so many interdependent variables are acting simultaneously.

—Dick K. Nanto, "Japan's Currency Intervention: Policy Issues," CRS Report to Congress (United States), July 13, 2007, CRS-7.

Foreign currency intervention—the active management, manipulation, or intervention in the market's valuation of a country's currency—is a component of currency valuation and forecast that cannot be overlooked. The value of a country's currency is of significant interest to an individual government's economic and political policies and objectives. Those interests sometimes extend beyond the individual country but may actually reflect some form of collective country interest. Although many countries have moved from fixed exchange rate values long ago, the governments and central bank authorities of the multitude of floating rate currencies still privately and publicly profess what value their currency "should hold" in their eyes, regardless of whether the market for that currency agrees at that time.

Motivations for Currency Market Intervention

There is a long-standing saying that "what worries bankers is inflation, but what worries elected officials is unemployment." This idea is actually quite useful in understanding the various motives for currency market intervention. Depending upon whether a country's central bank is an independent institution (e.g., the U.S. Federal Reserve) or a subsidiary of its elected government (as was the Bank of England for many years), the bank's policies may either fight inflation or fight slow economic growth but rarely can they do both.

Traditionally, many countries have pursued policies of pushing the value of their currencies down in an effort to maintain the price competitiveness of their exports. This policy objective, long referred to as "beggar thy neighbor," has given rise to numerous competitive devaluations over the years. It has not, however, fallen out of fashion. The slow economic growth and continuing employment problems in many countries in 2012, 2013, and 2014 led some governments, the United States and the European Union being prime examples, to strive to hold their currency values down.

Alternatively, the fall in the value of the domestic currency will sharply reduce the purchasing power of its people. If the economy is forced, for a variety of reasons, to continue to purchase imported products (e.g., petroleum imports because of no domestic substitute), a currency devaluation or depreciation may prove highly inflationary and, in the extreme, impoverish the country's people (as in the case of Venezuela).

It is frequently noted that most countries would like to see stable exchange rates and to avoid the entanglements associated with manipulating currency values. Unfortunately, that would also imply that they are also happy with the current exchange rate's impact on country-level competitiveness. One must look no further than the continuing highly public debate between the U.S. and China over the value of the yuan. The U.S. believes the yuan is undervalued, making Chinese exports to the U.S. overly cheap, which in turn results in a growing current account deficit for the United States and current account surplus for China.

The International Monetary Fund, as one of its basic principles (Article IV), encourages members to avoid pursuing "currency manipulation" to gain competitive advantage over other members. The IMF defines manipulation as "protracted large-scale intervention in one direction in the exchange market." It seems, however, that many governments often choose to ignore the IMF's advice.

Intervention Methods

There are many ways in which an individual government or collective of governments and central banks can alter the value of their currencies. It should be noted, however, that the methods used for market intervention are very much determined by the size of the country's economy, the magnitude of global trading in its currency, and the depth and breadth of development in its domestic financial markets. A short list of the intervention methods would include *direct intervention, indirect intervention*, and *capital controls*.

Direct Intervention. This is the active buying and selling of the domestic currency against foreign currencies. This traditionally required a central bank to act like any other trader in the currency market—albeit a big one. If the goal were to increase the value of the domestic currency, the central bank would purchase its own currency using its foreign exchange reserves, at least to the limits that it could endure depleting its reserves. If the goal were to decrease the value of its currency—to fight an appreciation of its currency's value on the foreign exchange market—it would sell its own currency in exchange for foreign currency, typically a major hard currency like the dollar and euro. Although there are no physical limits to the ability of central banks to sell their own currency (they could theoretically continue to "print money" endlessly), central banks are cautious in the degree to which they may potentially change their monetary supplies through intervention.

There is debate among economists over the efficacy of intervention if central banks "sterilize" them by buying or selling domestic securities. If a central bank is attempting to support its currency value, it theoretically must allow the foreign exchange sales (intervention) to reduce the domestic money supply. Empirical studies of intervention, however, have not proven that theoretical concern to hold.

Direct intervention was the primary method used for many years, but beginning in the 1970s, the world's currency markets grew so large in size that any individual player, even a central bank, might not have the resources—foreign currency reserves—to move the market. One solution to this market size challenge has been the occasional use of coordinated intervention, in which several major countries, or a collective such as the G8 of industrialized countries, agree that a specific currency's value is out of alignment with their collective interests. In that situation, the countries may work collectively to intervene and push a currency's value in a desired direction. *Global Finance in Practice 9.2* describes the most famous of such collusive interventions. If getting agreements between nations was only so easy.

Indirect Intervention. *Indirect intervention* is the alteration of economic or financial fundamentals that are drivers of capital to flow into and out of specific currencies. This was a logical development for market manipulation given the growth in size of the global currency markets relative to the financial resources of central banks.

The most obvious and widely used factor here is interest rates. Following the financial principles outlined in the previous discussion of parity conditions, higher real rates of interest attract capital. If a central bank wishes to "defend its currency," for example, it might follow a restrictive monetary policy, which would drive real rates of interest up. The method is therefore no longer limited to the quantity of foreign exchange reserves held by the country. Instead, it is limited only by the country's willingness to suffer the domestic impacts of higher real interest rates in order to attract capital inflows and therefore drive up the demand for its currency. Alternatively, in a country wishing for its currency to fall in value, particularly when confronted with a continual appreciation of its value against major trading partner currencies, the central bank may work to lower real interest rates, reducing the returns to capital.

Because indirect intervention uses tools of monetary policy, a fundamental dimension of economic policy, the magnitude and extent of impacts may reach far beyond currency value. Overly stimulating economic activity, or increasing money supply growth beyond real economic activity, may prove inflationary. The use of such broad-based tools like interest rates to manipulate currency values requires a determination of importance, which in some cases may involve a choice to pursue international economic goals at the expense of domestic economic policy goals.

Capital Controls. This is the restriction of access to foreign currency by the government. This involves limiting the ability to exchange domestic currency for foreign currency. When access and exchange is permitted, trading takes place only with official designees of the government or central bank and only at dictated exchange rates.

Often, governments will limit access to foreign currencies to commercial trade—for example, allowing access to hard currency for the purchase of imports only. Access for investment purposes—particularly for short-term portfolios where investors are moving into and out of interest-bearing accounts and purchasing or selling securities or other funds—is often

GLOBAL FINANCE IN PRACTICE 9.2

Coordinated Intervention: The Plaza and Louvre Accords

The U.S. suffered extremely high rates of inflation throughout the 1970s. Beginning in 1979, the U.S. Federal Reserve undertook a stringent program to squeeze inflationary expectations out of the U.S. economy by restricting money supply growth. The result was rising—and record-high—interest rates. In the early 1980s, these high-dollar interest rates drove the value of the U.S. dollar up. By mid-1985, the dollar's value had risen by more than 50% since 1980. And an expensive dollar added to ever-growing U.S. trade deficits.

In September 1985, the G7 countries—the U.S., Canada, U.K., France, Germany, Italy, and Japan—met at the Plaza Hotel in New York City to discuss the extreme appreciation of the U.S. dollar. The G7 agreed, in what was known

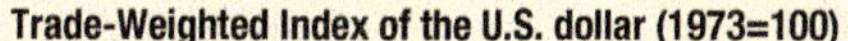

Trade-Weighted Index of the U.S. dollar (1973=100) **Japanese yen spot exchange rate (¥ = $1.00)**

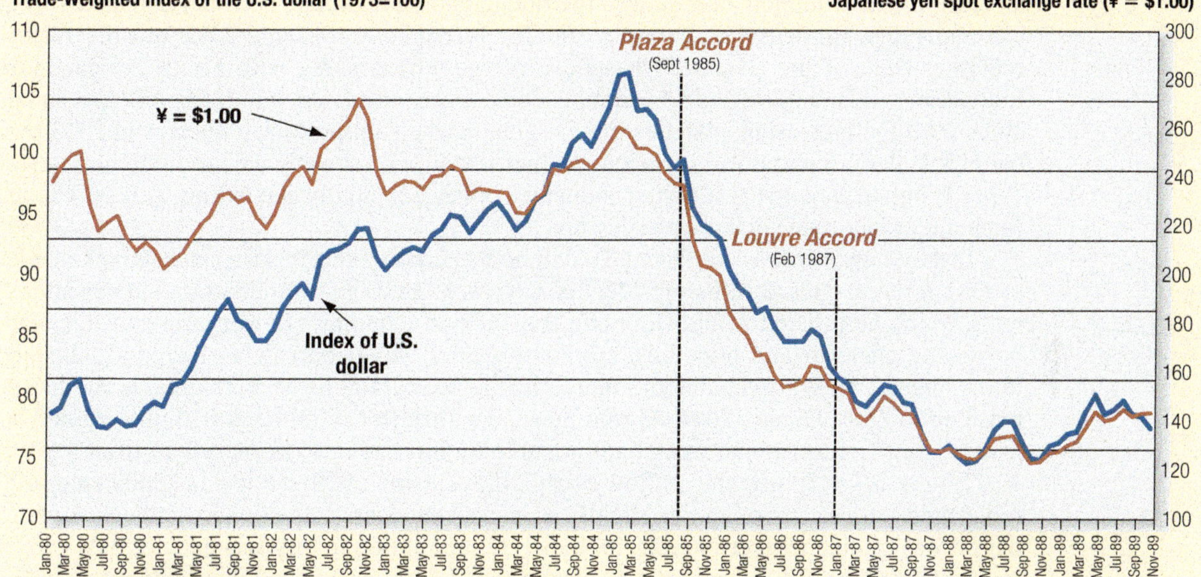

Source: Trade-weighted exchange rate of the U.S. dollar (TWEXMMTH), Federal Reserve Bank of St. Louis, 1973=100, monthly, Spot exchange rate of USD/JPY, monthly.

as the Plaza Accord, to push the value of the dollar down against two major global currencies, the German mark and the Japanese yen. (Note that the dollar was already declining in value when the accord was made.) This coordinated intervention was unprecedented, as the combined G7 central banks spent $10 billion in a coordinated "sale of dollars." As illustrated in the graph, the intervention was highly successful. The value of the dollar declined against both an index of its trading partners and, specifically, the Japanese yen.

In February 1987, less than two years later, the same G7 countries met once again, this time in Paris. (Officially, it was a G6 agreement as Italy abstained.) The new agreement, the Louvre Accord, was an official acknowledgment that the dollar had fallen far enough, and the G6 central banks agreed to act again in unison to stabilize its value. The dollar's value, however, continued to slide in the period following the accord.

The original motivation for the Plaza Accord in 1985 was to curtail the massive trade deficit the U.S. was running with its European trading partners and with Japan. The decline in the dollar's value following the accord did indeed rectify trade balances with Europe, but not Japan. The U.S. continued in deficit versus Japan.

The Plaza Accord may have, however, undermined the Japanese economy for years to come. As the Japanese yen appreciated (doubling in value against the dollar), the Japanese economy stagnated. In response, Japan undertook an expansionary monetary policy which fueled rapidly rising asset prices—share prices on the Tokyo Stock Exchange, real estate values throughout Japan—creating an asset price bubble. When those asset prices crashed in 1990 and 1991, Japan entered a decade-long slump of slow growth and deflation known today as the Lost Decade.

prohibited or limited. The Chinese regulation of access and trading of the Chinese yuan is a prime example of the use of capital controls over currency value. In addition to the government's setting the daily rate of exchange, access to the exchange is limited by a difficult and timely bureaucratic process for approval and limited to commercial trade transactions.

When Foreign Currency Intervention Fails

It is important to remember that intervention may—and often does—fail. Interventions by authorities in Turkey and Japan in recent years serve as classic examples.

Turkey 2014. The Turkish currency crisis of 2014 is a classic example of a drastic indirect intervention that ultimately only slowed the rate of capital flight and currency collapse. Turkey had enjoyed some degree of currency stability throughout 2012 and 2013, but the Turkish economy (one of the so-called "Fragile Five" countries, along with South Africa, India, Indonesia, and Brazil) suffered a widening current account deficit and rising inflation in late 2013. With the increasing anxieties in emerging markets in the fourth quarter of 2013 over the U.S. Federal Reserve's announcement that it would be slowing its bond purchasing (the Taper Program, essentially a tighter monetary policy), capital began exiting Turkey. The lira came under increasing downward pressure.

Turkey, however, was conflicted. To defend its currency, the Turkish central bank needed to raise interest rates. But the president of Turkey wanted the central bank to lower interest rates, which he insisted would stimulate the Turkish economy. (Lower interest rates made borrowing cheaper, and hopefully, more companies would borrow and expand.) Instead, lower interest rates provided additional incentive for capital flight. Pressures on the lira intensified in early January 2014. At that point, the Turkish central bank had little choice but to increase the Turkish one-week bank repurchase interest rate (or *repo rate*) from 4.5% to 10.0% in an effort to stop the outflow of capital. Although the first few hours indicated some relief, with the lira returning to a slightly stronger value versus the dollar (and euro), within days it was trading weaker once again. Indirect intervention in this case had not only proven to be a failure, but the attempted cure may in the end have worsened the economy.

Understanding the motivations and methods for currency market intervention is critical to any analysis of the determination of future exchange rates. And although it is often impossible to determine, in the end, whether intervention is successful—be it direct or indirect—it is a pervasive and persistent feature of currency markets. Governments will always try to protect their currencies during periods of weakness and on occasion protect weakness in pursuit of trade competitiveness. In the end, the success or failure of attempts at intervention may depend on both luck and talent. *Global Finance in Practice 9.3* provides a short list of possible best practices for effective intervention.

Japan 2010. In September 2010, the Bank of Japan intervened in the foreign exchange markets for the first time in nearly six years. In an attempt to slow the appreciating yen, Japan reportedly bought nearly 20 billion U.S. dollars in exchange. Finance Ministry officials had stated publicly that 82 yen per dollar was probably the limit of their tolerance for yen appreciation—and their tolerance was being tested.

As illustrated in Exhibit 9.2, the Bank of Japan intervened on September 13 as the yen approached 82 yen per dollar. (The Bank of Japan is independent in its ability to conduct Japanese monetary policy, but as the organizational subsidiary of the Japanese Ministry of Finance, it must conduct foreign exchange operations on behalf of the Japanese government.) Japanese officials reportedly notified authorities in both the United States and the European Union of their activity but noted that they had not asked for permission or support. The intervention resulted in public outcry from Beijing to Washington to London over the "new era of currency intervention."

GLOBAL FINANCE IN PRACTICE 9.3

Rules of Thumb for Effective Intervention

A variety of factors, features, and tactics, according to many currency traders, influence the effectiveness of an intervention effort.

Don't Lean into the Wind. Markets that are moving significantly in one direction, like the strengthening of the Japanese yen in the fall of 2010, are very tough to turn. Termed "leaning into the wind," intervention during a strong market movement will most likely result in a very expensive failure. Currency traders argue that central banks should time their intervention very carefully, choosing moments when trading volumes are light and the direction is nearly flat.

Coordinate Timing and Activity. The markets are much more likely to be influenced if they believe the intervention activity is reflecting a grassroots movement and not the activity of a single trading entity or bank. For this reason, using traders or associates in a variety of geographic markets and trading centers, possibly other central banks, may increase effectiveness.

Use Good News. Particularly when trying to quell a currency fall, timing the intervention to coincide with positive economic, financial, or business news closely associated with a country's currency market can be helpful. Traders often argue that "markets wish to celebrate good news," and currencies may be no different.

Don't Be Cheap; Overwhelm Them. Traders fear missing the moment, and a large, coordinated, well-timed intervention can make them fear they are leaning in the wrong direction. A successful intervention is in many ways a battle of psychology and can be used to leverage the insecurities of traders. If it appears the intervention is gradually having the desired impact, throw ever-increasing assets into the battle. Don't get cheap.

EXHIBIT 9.2 Intervention and the Japanese Yen, 2010

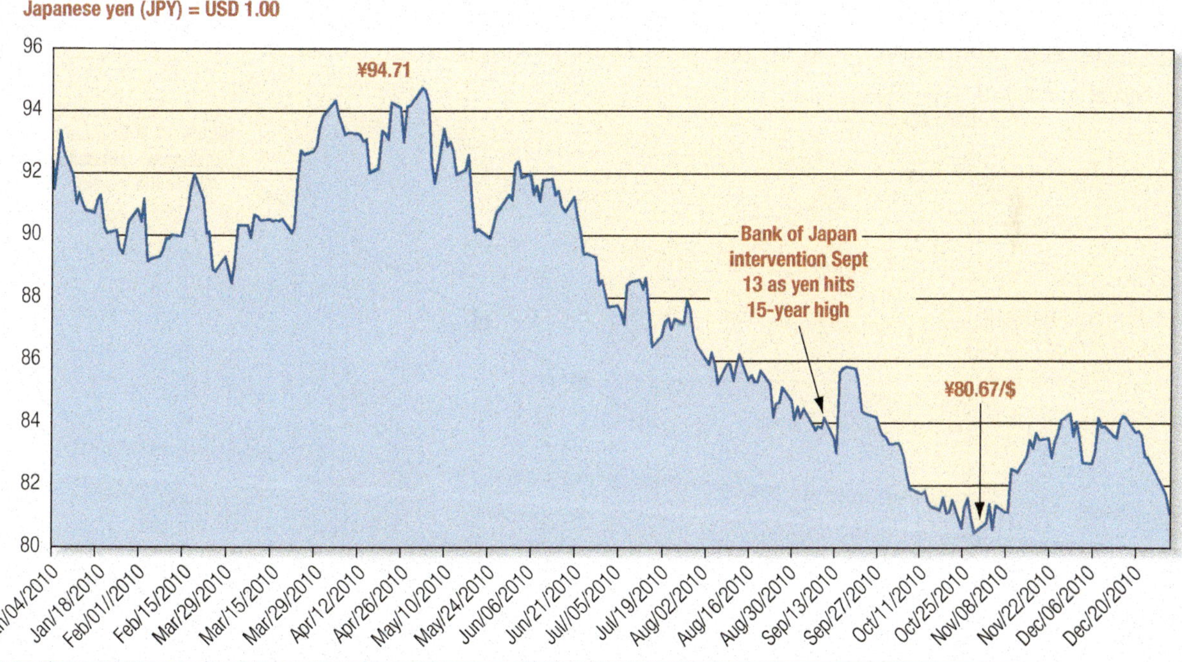

Although market intervention is always looked down upon by free market proponents, the move by Japan was seen as particularly frustrating as it came at a time when the United States was continuing to pressure China to revalue its currency, the renminbi. As noted by economist Nouriel Roubini, "We are in a world where everyone wants a weak currency," a marketplace in which all countries are looking to stimulate their domestic economies through exceptionally low interest rates and corresponding weak currency values— *a global race to the bottom.*[1]

Ironically, as illustrated in Exhibit 9.2, it appears that the intervention was largely unsuccessful. When the Bank of Japan started buying dollars in an appreciating yen market—the so-called "leaning into the wind" or "one-way intervention" strategy—it was hoping to either stop the appreciation, change the direction of the spot rate movement, or both. In either pursuit, it appears to have failed. As one analyst noted, it was essentially a short-term fix to a long-term problem. Although the yen spiked downward (more yen per dollar) for a few days, it returned once again to an appreciating path within a week. Exhibit 9.3 uses the traditional framework of supply and demand to illustrate what Japan was attempting to do through its intervention.

Japan's frequent interventions have been the subject of much study. In an August 2005 study by the IMF, it was noted that between 1991 and 2005, the Bank of Japan had intervened on 340 days, while the U.S. Federal Reserve intervened on 22 days and the European Central Bank intervened on only 4 days (since its inception in 1998). Although the IMF has never found Japanese intervention to be officially "currency manipulation," an analysis by Takatoshi Ito in 2004 concluded that there was on average a one-yen-per-dollar change in market rates, roughly 1%, as a result of Japanese intervention over time.

> *There is no historical case in which [yen] selling intervention succeeded in immediately stopping the preexisting long-term uptrend in the Japanese yen.*
>
> —Tohru Sasaki, Currency Strategist, JPMorgan.

EXHIBIT 9.3 Intervention and the Japanese Yen: Driving the Yen Down

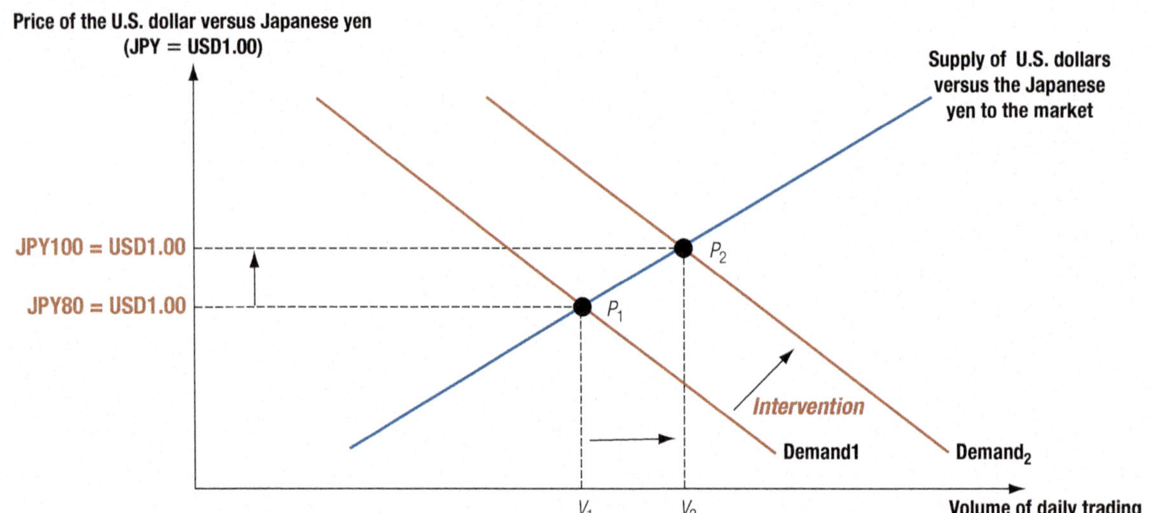

Intervention by the Bank of Japan involves the Bank entering the foreign exchange market to demand dollars—to buy U.S. dollars in exchange for Japanese yen. If the Bank's timing and magnitude of intervention are sufficient, it can shift the demand for USD outward, driving the price of the dollar up and the value of the yen down (now taking more yen to purchase one dollar).

[1] "Currency Intervention's Mixed Record of Success," Russell Hotten, *BBC News*, September 16, 2010.

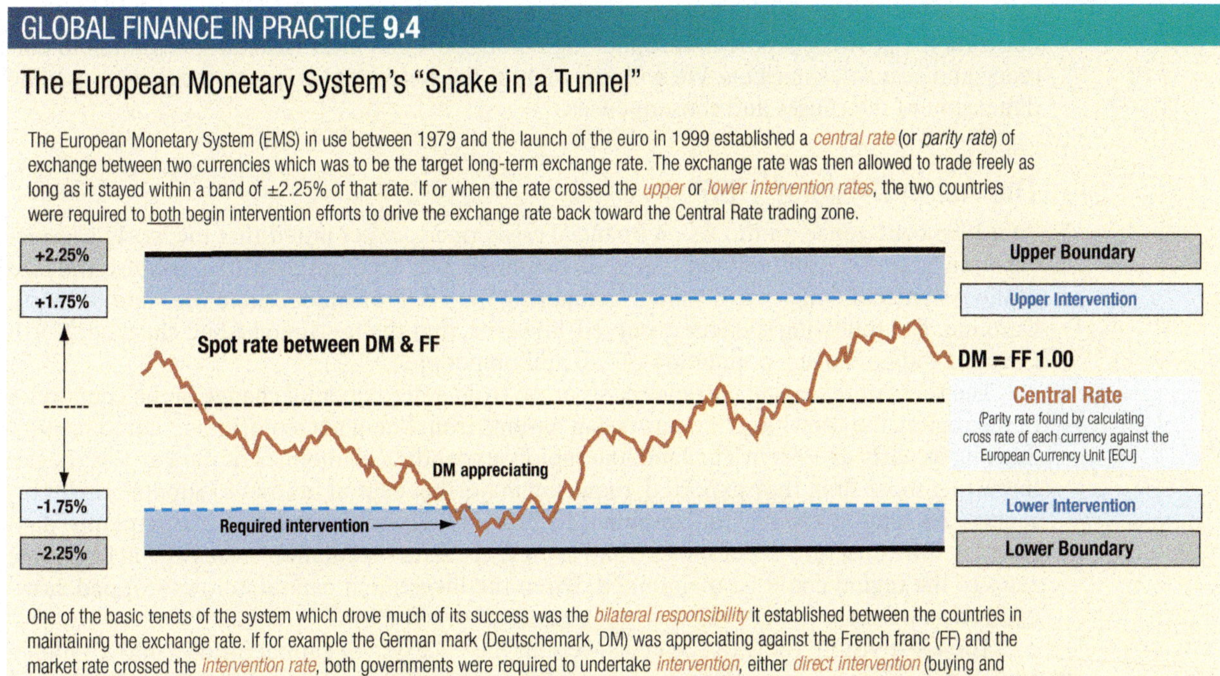

GLOBAL FINANCE IN PRACTICE **9.4**

The European Monetary System's "Snake in a Tunnel"

The European Monetary System (EMS) in use between 1979 and the launch of the euro in 1999 established a *central rate* (or *parity rate*) of exchange between two currencies which was to be the target long-term exchange rate. The exchange rate was then allowed to trade freely as long as it stayed within a band of ±2.25% of that rate. If or when the rate crossed the *upper* or *lower intervention rates*, the two countries were required to both begin intervention efforts to drive the exchange rate back toward the Central Rate trading zone.

One of the basic tenets of the system which drove much of its success was the *bilateral responsibility* it established between the countries in maintaining the exchange rate. If for example the German mark (Deutschemark, DM) was appreciating against the French franc (FF) and the market rate crossed the *intervention rate*, both governments were required to undertake *intervention*, either *direct intervention* (buying and selling their currencies in the market) or *indirect intervention* (such as changing interest rates) or both to maintain trading about the central rate.

Organizations of economic union and integration present extreme examples of currency market intervention. As described in Chapter 2, the launch of the euro in 1999 followed two decades of economic, monetary, and currency coordination and intervention. This system, the European Monetary System (EMS), used an elaborate system of bilateral responsibility, in which both country's governments were committed to maintaining the parity exchange rates. Their commitment extended to both types of intervention, direct and indirect. *Global Finance in Practice 9.4* describes the EMS system, the so-called "snake in a tunnel."

9.3 Disequilibrium: Exchange Rates in Emerging Markets

Although the three different schools of thought on exchange rate determination described earlier in Exhibit 9.1 make understanding exchange rates appear to be straightforward, that is rarely the case. The large and liquid capital and currency markets follow many of the principles outlined so far relatively well in the medium to long term. The smaller and less liquid markets, however, frequently demonstrate behaviors that seemingly contradict theory. The problem lies not in the theory, but in the relevance of the assumptions underlying the theory. An analysis of the emerging market crises illustrates a number of these seeming contradictions.

After a number of years of relative global economic tranquility, beginning in the second half of the 1990s, a series of currency crises shook all emerging markets. The Asian crisis of July 1997 and the fall of the Argentine peso in 2002 demonstrate an array of emerging market economic failures, each with its own complex causes and unknown outlooks. These crises also illustrate the growing problem of capital flight and short-run international speculation in currency and securities markets. We will use each of the individual crises to focus on a specific dimension of the causes and consequences.

The Asian Crisis of 1997

At a 1998 conference on the Asian financial crisis, one speaker noted that the world's preoccupation with the economic problems of Indonesia was incomprehensible because the size of the Asian economies was so small, comparing the GDP of Indonesia to the state of North Carolina. The following speaker observed, however, that the last time he had checked, North Carolina did not have a population of 220 million people.

The roots of the Asian currency crisis arose from a fundamental change in the economics of the region, the transition of many Asian nations from being net exporters to net importers. Starting as early as 1990 in Thailand, the rapidly expanding economies of the Far East began importing more than they exported, requiring major net capital inflows to support their currencies. As long as the capital continued to flow in—capital for manufacturing plants, dam projects, infrastructure development, and even real estate speculation—the pegged exchange rates of the region could be maintained. When the investment capital inflows stopped, however, crisis was inevitable.

The most visible roots of the crisis were in the excesses of capital inflows into Thailand. With rapid economic growth and rising profits forming the backdrop, Thai firms, banks, and finance companies had ready access to capital on the international markets, finding U.S. dollar debt cheap offshore. Thai banks continued to raise capital internationally, extending credit to a variety of domestic investments and enterprises beyond what the Thai economy could support. As capital flows into the Thai market hit record rates, financial flows poured into investments of all kinds. As the investment "bubble" expanded, some participants raised questions about the economy's ability to repay the rising debt. The baht came under attack.

Crisis. In May and June 1997, the Thai government repeatedly intervened in the foreign exchange markets directly (using up much of its foreign exchange reserves) and indirectly (by raising interest rates). A second round of speculative attacks in late June and early July proved too much for the Thai authorities. On July 2, 1997, the Thai central bank finally allowed the baht to float (or sink in this case). The baht fell 17% against the U.S. dollar and more than 12% against the Japanese yen in a matter of hours. By November, the baht had fallen from 25 to 40 baht per dollar, a fall of about 38%, as illustrated in Exhibit 9.4.

In Asia's own version of the tequila effect, a number of neighboring Asian nations, some with and some without similar characteristics to Thailand, came under speculative attack by currency traders and capital markets. The Philippine peso, the Malaysian ringgit, and the Indonesian rupiah all fell in the months following the July baht devaluation. In late October 1997, Taiwan caught the markets off balance with a surprise competitive devaluation of 15%. The Taiwanese devaluation seemed only to renew the momentum of the crisis. Although the Hong Kong dollar survived (at great expense to its foreign exchange reserves), the Korean won (KRW) was not so lucky. In November 1997, the historically stable won also fell victim, falling from 900 Korean won per dollar to more than 1100. The only currency that had not fallen besides the Hong Kong dollar was the Chinese renminbi, which was not freely convertible at the time.

Causal Complexities. The Asian economic crisis—for it was more than just a currency collapse—had many roots besides traditional balance of payments difficulties. Although the causes of crisis were a bit different in each country, all countries shared three common contributors: corporate socialism, corporate governance cronyism, and banking instability.

EXHIBIT 9.4 The Thai Baht and the Asian Crisis

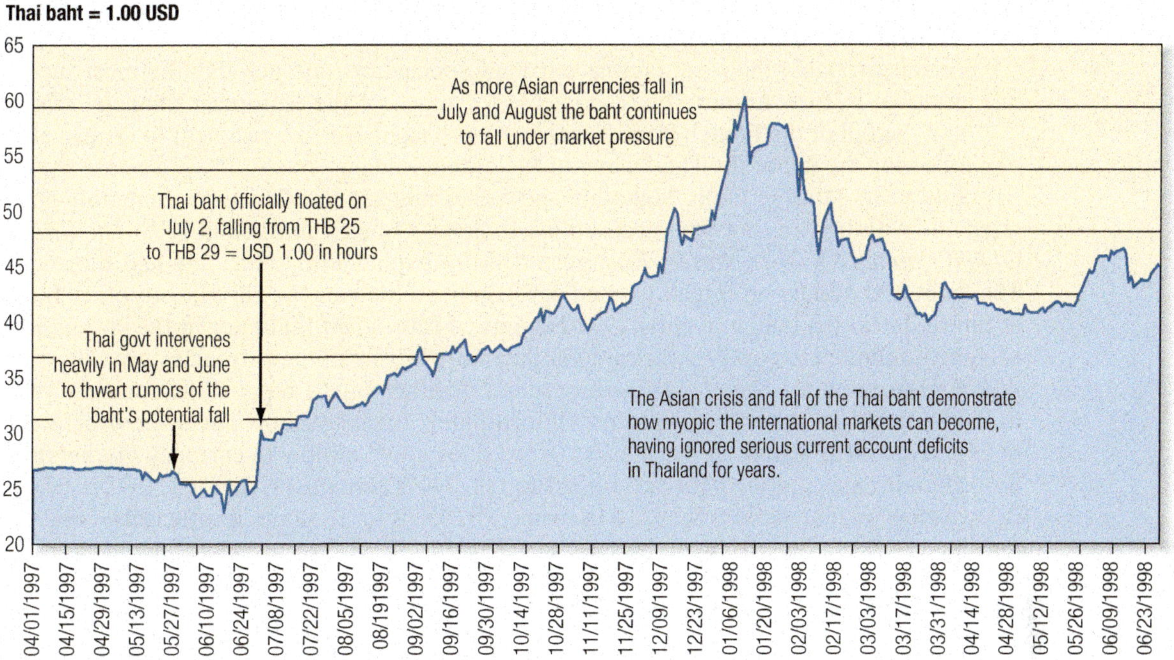

Thai baht = 1.00 USD

As more Asian currencies fall in July and August the baht continues to fall under market pressure

Thai baht officially floated on July 2, falling from THB 25 to THB 29 = USD 1.00 in hours

Thai govt intervenes heavily in May and June to thwart rumors of the baht's potential fall

The Asian crisis and fall of the Thai baht demonstrate how myopic the international markets can become, having ignored serious current account deficits in Thailand for years.

- **Corporate socialism.** The rapidly growing export-led countries of Asia had known only stability. Because of the influence of government and politics in the business arena, even in the event of failure, it was believed that government would not allow firms to fail, workers to lose their jobs, or banks to close. Practices that had persisted for decades without challenge, such as lifetime employment, were now no longer sustainable.
- **Corporate governance cronyism.** Many firms operating within the Far Eastern business environments were largely controlled either by families or by groups related to the governing party or body of the country. This concept, *cronyism*, means that the interests of minority stockholders and creditors are often secondary at best to the primary motivations of corporate management.
- **Banking instability.** The banking sector had fallen behind. Bank regulatory structures and markets had been deregulated nearly without exception across the globe. The central role played by banks in the conduct of business had largely been ignored. As firms across Asia collapsed, government coffers were emptied and banks failed. Without banks, the "plumbing" of business conduct was shut down.

In the aftermath of the Asian crisis, the international speculator and philanthropist George Soros was accused of being the instigator of the crisis. As described in *Global Finance in Practice 9.4*, Soros was likely only the messenger.

The Role of Soros. In the weeks following the start of the Asian crisis in July 1997, officials from a number of countries, including Thailand and Malaysia, blamed the international financier George Soros for causing the crisis. Particularly vocal was Prime Minister of Malaysia Dr. Mahathir Mohamad, who repeatedly implied that Soros had a political agenda associated with Burma's prospect of joining the Association of Southeast Asian Nations (ASEAN).

Mahathir noted in a number of public speeches that Soros might have been making a political statement and not just speculating against currency values. Mahathir argued that the poor people of Malaysia, Thailand, the Philippines, and Indonesia would pay a great price for Soros's attacks on Asian currencies.

Soros is probably the most famous currency speculator (and possibly the most successful) in global history. Admittedly responsible for much of the European financial crisis of 1992 and the fall of the French franc in 1993, he once again was the recipient of critical attention following the fall of the Thai baht and Malaysian ringgit.

Nine years later, in 2006, Mahathir and Soros met for the first time. Mahathir apologized and withdrew his previous accusations. In Soros's book published in 1998, *The Crisis of Global Capitalism: Open Society Endangered*, Soros explained that his fund had shorted the Thai baht and Malaysian ringgit (signed agreements to deliver the currency to other buyers at future dates) beginning in early 1997. He argued this meant that later in the spring, when his fund attempted to cover their positions, they were buyers of the currencies, not sellers, and therefore were on the "good side" and were in effect helping to support the currency values as the fund moved to realize its profits. Unfortunately the large short positions formed early in 1997 were clear signals in the market (word does move rapidly in currency markets) that Soros Funds expected the baht and ringgit to fall. *The Economist* (August 2, 1997, p. 57) had its own view on blame: "For Thailand to blame Mr. Soros for its plight is rather like condemning an undertaker for burying a suicide."

The Argentine Crisis of 2002

> *Now, most Argentines are blaming corrupt politicians and foreign devils for their ills. But few are looking inward, at mainstream societal concepts such as* viveza criolla, *an Argentine cultural quirk that applauds anyone sly enough to get away with a fast one. It is one reason behind massive tax evasion here: One of every three Argentines does so—and many like to brag about it.*
>
> —Anthony Faiola, "Once-Haughty Nation's Swagger Loses Its Currency," *The Washington Post*, March 13, 2002.

Argentina's economic ups and downs have historically been tied to the health of the Argentine peso. South America's southernmost resident—which oftentimes considered itself more European than Latin American—had been wracked by hyperinflation, international indebtedness, and economic collapse in the 1980s. By 1991, the people of Argentina had had enough. Economic reform was a common goal of the Argentine people. They were not interested in quick fixes but lasting change and a stable future. They nearly got it.

In 1991, the Argentine peso had been pegged to the U.S. dollar at a one-to-one rate of exchange. The policy was a radical departure from traditional methods of fixing the rate of a currency's value. Argentina adopted a currency board, a structure—rather than merely a commitment—to limit the growth of money in the economy. Under a currency board, the central bank may increase the money supply in the banking system only with increases in its holdings of hard currency reserves. The reserves were, in this case, U.S. dollars. By removing the ability of government to expand the rate of growth of the money supply, Argentina believed it was eliminating the source of inflation that had devastated its standard of living. It was both a recipe for conservative and prudent financial management and a decision to eliminate the power of politicians, elected and unelected, to exercise judgment, both good and bad. It was an automatic and unbendable rule.

This "cure" was a restrictive monetary policy that slowed economic growth. The country's unemployment rate rose to double-digit levels in 1994 and stayed there. The real GDP growth rate settled into recession in late 1998, and the economy continued to shrink through 2000. Argentine banks allowed depositors to hold their money in either pesos or dollars. This was intended to provide a market-based discipline to the banking and political systems and to demonstrate the government's unwavering commitment to maintaining the peso's value parity with the dollar. Although intended to build confidence in the system, in the end it proved disastrous to the Argentine banking system.

Economic Crisis. The 1998 recession proved to be unending. Three and a half years later, Argentina was still in recession. By 2001, crisis conditions had revealed three very important underlying problems with Argentina's economy: (1) the Argentine peso was overvalued, (2) the currency board regime had eliminated monetary policy alternatives for macroeconomic policy, and (3) the Argentine government budget deficit was out of control. Inflation had not been eliminated, and the world's markets were watching.

Most of the major economies of South America now slid into recession. With slowing economic activity, imports fell. Most South American currencies now fell against the U.S. dollar, but because the Argentine peso remained pegged to the dollar, Argentine exports grew increasingly overpriced. The sluggish economic growth in Argentina warranted expansionary economic policies, but the currency board's basic premise was that the money supply to the financial system could not be expanded any further or faster than the ability of the economy to capture dollar reserves—eliminating monetary policy.

Government spending was not slowing, however. As the unemployment rate grew higher, as poverty and social unrest grew—both in Buenos Aires, the civil center of Argentina, and in the outer provinces—the government was faced with pressure to close the economic and social gaps. Government spending continued to increase, but tax receipts did not. Argentina turned to the international markets to aid in financing its deficit spending. The total foreign debt of the country began rising dramatically. Only a number of IMF capital injections prevented the total foreign debt of the country from skyrocketing. By the end of the 1990s, however, total foreign debt had doubled, and the economy's earning power had not.

As economic conditions continued to deteriorate, banks suffered increasing runs. Depositors, fearing that the peso would be devalued, lined up to withdraw their money—both Argentine peso and U.S. dollar cash balances. Pesos were converted to dollars, once again adding fuel to the growing fire of currency crisis. The government, fearing that the increasing financial drain on banks would cause their collapse, closed the banks. Consumers, unable to withdraw more than $250 per week, were instructed to use debit cards and credit cards to make purchases and to conduct the everyday transactions required by society.

Devaluation. On Sunday, January 6, 2002, in the first act of his presidency, President Eduardo Duhalde devalued the peso from 1.00 Argentine peso per U.S. dollar to 1.40. But the economic pain continued. Two weeks after the devaluation, the banks were still closed. On February 3, 2002, the Argentine government announced that the peso would be floated, as shown in Exhibit 9.5. The government would no longer attempt to fix or manage its value to any specific level, allowing the market to find or set the exchange rate.

The lessons to be drawn from the Argentine story are somewhat complex. From the very beginning, Argentina and the IMF both knew the currency board system was a risky strategy, but given Argentina's long and disastrous experience with exchange rates, the strategy was one that had been deemed worth taking. In the end, however, despite best efforts, the use of such a radically strict exchange rate system, in which government gave up nearly all control over its sovereign monetary system, proved unsustainable.

EXHIBIT 9.5 The Collapse of the Argentine Peso

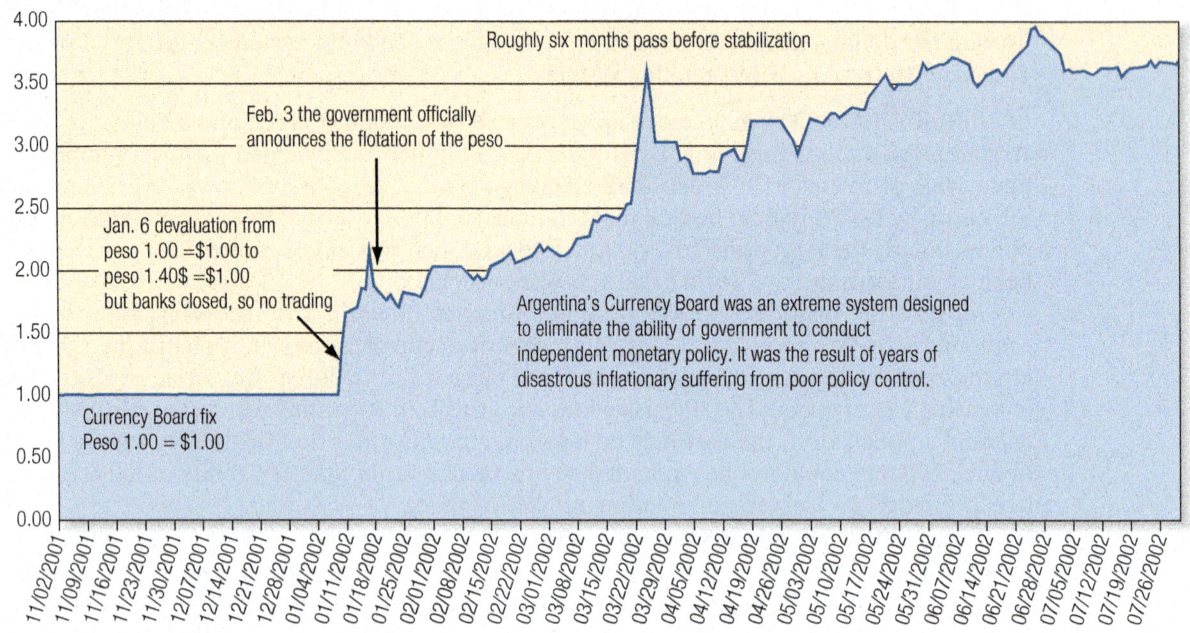

9.4 Currency Forecasting in Practice

There are numerous foreign exchange forecasting services, many of which are provided by banks and independent consultants. In addition, some multinational firms have their own in-house forecasting capabilities. Predictions can be based on econometric models, technical analysis, intuition, and a certain measure of gall.

Exhibit 9.6 summarizes the various forecasting periods, regimes, and most widely followed methodologies. Whether any of the forecasting services are worth their cost depends both on the motive for forecasting as well as the required accuracy. For example, long-run forecasts may be motivated by a multinational firm's desire to initiate a foreign investment in Japan or perhaps to raise long-term funds in Japanese yen. Or a portfolio manager may be considering diversifying for the long term in Japanese securities. The longer the time horizon of the forecast, the more inaccurate, but also the less critical the forecast is likely to be.

Short-term forecasts are typically motivated by a desire to hedge a receivable, payable, or dividend for a period of perhaps three months. Short-term forecasts rely less on long-run economic fundamentals and more on technical factors in the marketplace, government intervention, news, and the passing whims of traders and investors. Accuracy of the forecast is critical, since most of the exchange rate changes are relatively small even though the day-to-day volatility may be high.

Forecasting services normally undertake fundamental economic analysis for long-term forecasts, and some base their short-term forecasts on the same basic model. Others base their short-term forecasts on technical analysis similar to that conducted in security analysis. They attempt to correlate exchange rate changes with various other variables, regardless of whether there is any economic rationale for the correlation.

EXHIBIT 9.6 Exchange Rate Forecasting in Practice

Forecast Period	Regime	Recommended Forecast Methods
Short Run	Fixed-Rate	1. Assume the fixed-rate is maintained 2. Are there indications of stress on the fixed-rate? 3. Are there capital controls or black market exchanges? 4. Are there indicators of government's capability to maintain the fixed-rate? 5. Are there changes in foreign currency reserves?
	Floating-Rate	1. Technical methods which capture trend 2. Forward rates as forecasts (< 30 days assume random walk; 30-90 days use forward) 3. For periods of 90-360 days combine trend with fundamental analysis 4. Fundamental analysis of inflationary concerns 5. Government declarations and agreements regarding exchange rate goals 6. Cooperative agreements with other countries
Long Run	Fixed-Rate	1. Fundamental analysis 2. Balance of payments management 3. Ability to control domestic inflation 4. Ability to generate hard currency reserves to use for intervention purposes 5. Ability to run trade account surpluses
	Floating-Rate	1. Focus on inflationary fundamentals and purchasing power parity 2. Indicators of general economic health such as economic growth and stability 3. Technical analysis of long-term trends (possibility of long-term technical 'waves') 4. Government positions on relative international competitiveness and boundaries

The chances of these forecasts being consistently useful or profitable depend on whether one believes the foreign exchange market is efficient. The more efficient the market is, the more likely it is that exchange rates are "random walks," with past price behavior providing no clues to the future. The less efficient the foreign exchange market is, the better the chance that forecasters may get lucky and find a key relationship that holds, at least for the short run. If the relationship is consistent, however, others will soon discover it and the market will become efficient again with respect to that piece of information.

Technical Analysis

Technical analysts, traditionally referred to as *chartists*, focus on price and volume data to determine past trends that are expected to continue into the future. The single most important element of technical analysis is that future exchange rates are based on the current exchange rate. Exchange rate movements, similar to equity price movements, can be subdivided into three time horizons: (1) day-to-day movement, which is seemingly random; (2) short-term movements, ranging from several days to trends lasting several months; and (3) long-term movements, characterized by up and down long-term trends. Long-term technical analysis has gained new popularity as a result of recent research into the possibility that long-term "waves" in currency movements exist under floating exchange rates.

The longer the time horizon of the forecast, the more inaccurate the forecast is likely to be. Whereas forecasting for the long run must depend on economic fundamentals of exchange rate determination, many of the forecast needs of the firm are short to medium term in their time horizon and can be addressed with less theoretical approaches. These technical analyses based on time—*time series techniques*—infer no theory or causality but simply predict future values from the recent past. Forecasters freely mix fundamental theories—the three approaches listed previously in Exhibit 9.1—and technical analysis, presumably

EXHIBIT 9.7 JP Morgan Chase Forecast of the U.S. Dollar–Euro

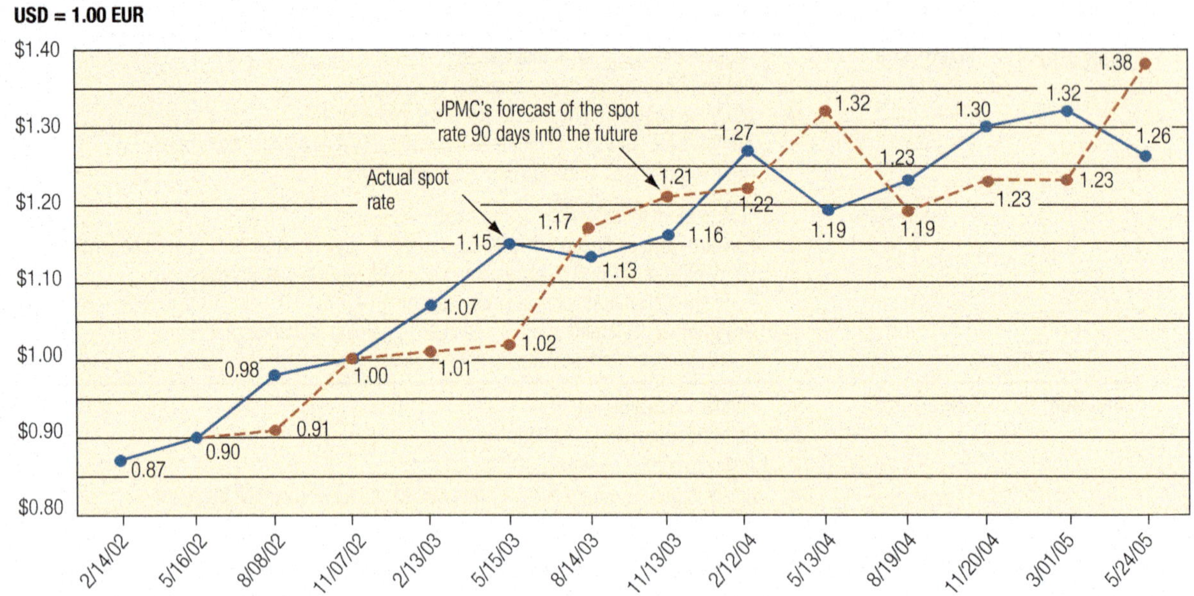

because forecasting is like playing horseshoes—*getting close counts*. Exhibit 9.7 provides a short analysis of how accurate one prestigious forecaster was over a three-year period.

There are many different foreign exchange forecasting services and service providers. JPMorgan Chase (JPMC) is one of the most prestigious and widely used. A review of JPMC's forecasting accuracy for the U.S. dollar–euro spot exchange rate for the 2002–2005 period, in 90-day increments, is presented in the exhibit.[2] The graph shows the actual spot exchange rate for the period and JPMC's forecast for the spot exchange rate for the same period.

There is good news, and there is bad news. The good news is that JPMC hit the actual spot rate dead-on in both May and November 2002. The bad news is that after that, it missed. Somewhat worrisome is when the forecast got the direction wrong. For example, in February 2004, JPMC had forecast the spot rate to move from the current rate of $1.27 = €1.00 to $1.32 = €1.00, but in fact, the dollar had appreciated dramatically in the following three-month period to close at $1.19. This was in fact a massive difference. The lesson learned is probably that regardless of how professional and prestigious a forecaster may be and how accurate it may have been in the past, forecasting the future—by anyone for anything—is challenging to say the least.

Cross-Rate Consistency in Forecasting

International financial managers must often forecast their home currency exchange rates for the set of countries in which the firm operates, not only to decide whether to hedge or to make an investment but also as part of preparing multi-country operating budgets in the home country's currency. These are the operating budgets against which the performance of foreign subsidiary managers will be judged. *Checking cross-rate consistency*—the reasonableness of the cross rates implicit in individual forecasts—acts as a reality check.

[2] This analysis uses exchange rate data as published in the print edition of *The Economist*, appearing quarterly. The source of the exchange rate forecasts, as noted in *The Economist*, is JPMorgan Chase.

Forecasting: What to Think?

Obviously, with the variety of theories and practices, forecasting exchange rates into the future is a daunting task. Here is a synthesis of our thoughts and experience:

- It appears, from decades of theoretical and empirical studies, that exchange rates do adhere to fundamental principles and theories outlined in the previous sections. Fundamentals do apply in the long term. There is, therefore, something of a *fundamental equilibrium path* for a currency's value.
- It also seems that in the short term, a variety of random events, institutional frictions, and technical factors may cause currency values to deviate significantly from their long-term fundamental path. This is sometimes referred to as noise. Clearly, therefore, we might expect deviations from the long-term path not only to occur but also to occur with some regularity and relative longevity.

Exhibit 9.8 illustrates this synthesis of forecasting thought. The long-term equilibrium path of the currency—although relatively well defined in retrospect—is not always apparent in the short term. The exchange rate itself may deviate in something of a cycle or wave about the long-term path.

If market participants agree on the general long-term path and possess *stabilizing expectations*, the currency's value will periodically return to the long-term path. It is critical, however, that when the currency's value rises above the long-term path, most market participants see it as being overvalued and respond by selling the currency—causing its price to fall. Similarly, when the currency's value falls below the long-term path, market participants respond by buying the currency—driving its value up. This is what is meant by stabilizing expectations: Market participants continually respond to deviations from the long-term path by buying or selling to drive the currency back to the long-term path.

EXHIBIT 9.8 Short-Term Noise versus Long-Term Trends

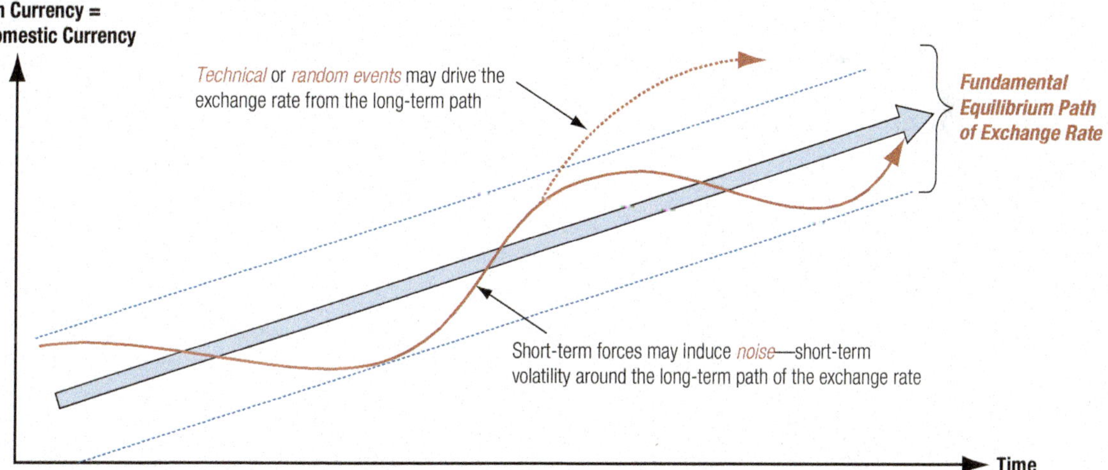

If market participants have *stabilizing expectations*, when forces drive the currency's value below the long-term fundamental equilibrium path, they will buy the currency driving its value back toward the fundamental equilibrium path. If market participants have *destabilizing expectations*, and forces drive the currency's value away from the fundamental path, participants may not move immediately or in significant volume to push the currency's value back toward the fundamental equilibrium path for an extended period of time (or possibly establish a new long-term fundamental path).

If, for some reason, the market becomes unstable, as illustrated by the dotted deviation path in Exhibit 9.8, the exchange rate may move significantly away from the long-term path for longer periods of time. Causes of these destabilizing markets—weak infrastructure (such as the banking system) and political or social events that dictate economic behaviors—are often the actions of speculators and inefficient markets.

Exchange Rate Dynamics: Making Sense of Market Movements

Although the various theories surrounding exchange rate determination are clear and sound, it may appear on a day-to-day basis that the currency markets do not pay much attention to the theories—they don't read the books! The difficulty is in understanding which fundamentals are driving markets at which points in time.

One example of this relative confusion over exchange rate dynamics is the phenomenon known as *overshooting*. Assume that the current spot rate between the dollar and the euro, as illustrated in Exhibit 9.9, is S_0. The U.S. Federal Reserve announces an expansionary monetary policy that cuts U.S. dollar interest rates. If euro-denominated interest rates remain unchanged, the new spot rate expected by the exchange markets based on interest differentials is S_1. This immediate change in the exchange rate is typical of how the markets react to news, distinct economic and political events that are observable. The immediate change in the value of the dollar-euro is therefore based on interest differentials.

As time passes, however, the price impacts of the monetary policy change start working their way through the economy. As price changes occur over the medium to long term, purchasing power parity forces drive the market dynamics, and the spot rate moves from S_1 toward S_2. Although both S_1 and S_2 rates are determined by the market, they reflect the dominance of different theoretical principles. As a result, the initial lower value of the dollar of S_1 is described as overshooting the longer-term equilibrium value of S_2.

This is, of course, only one possible series of events and market reactions. Currency markets are subject to new news every hour of every day, making it very difficult to forecast exchange rate movements in short periods of time. In the longer term, as shown in Exhibit 9.9, the markets do customarily return to the fundamentals of exchange rate determination.

EXHIBIT 9.9 Exchange Rate Dynamics: Overshooting

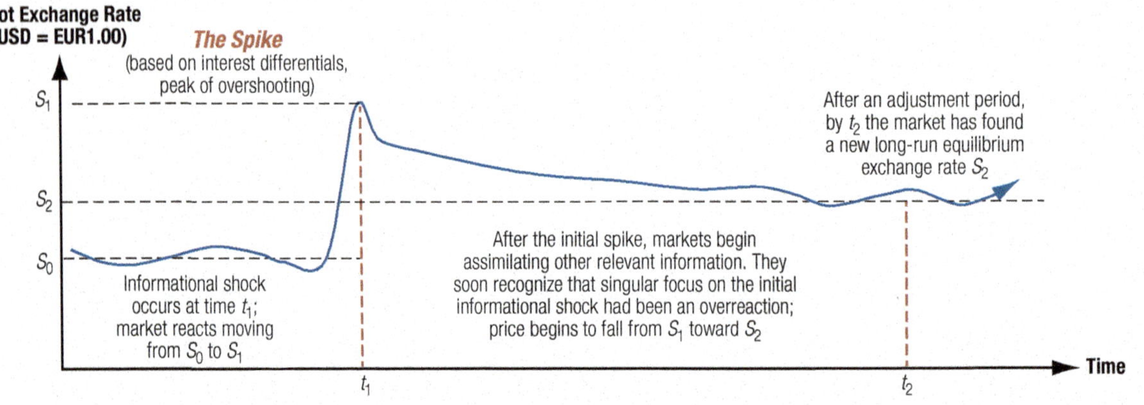

Summary Points

- There are three major theoretical approaches to explaining the economic determinants of exchange rates: parity conditions, balance of payments, and the monetary and asset market approach.
- The recurrence of exchange rate crises demonstrates not only how sensitive currency values continue to be to economic fundamentals but also how vulnerable many emerging market currencies are.
- Foreign exchange market intervention may be conducted via direct intervention, buying and selling the country's own currency, or indirect intervention, by changing the motivations and rules for capital to move into or out of a country and its currency.
- Many emerging market currencies periodically experience fundamental exchange rate disequilibrium. In the past, the most frequent cause of disequilibrium was hyperinflation, but today the most frequently experienced challenge is the large and rapid inflow and outflow of non-current account capital.
- Exchange rate forecasting is part of global business. All businesses of all kinds must form some expectation of what the future holds.
- Short-term forecasting of exchange rates, in practice, focuses on current spot rates if fixed and on trends and forward rates if floating. Longer-term forecasting requires a return to the basic analysis of exchange rate fundamentals such as balance of payments relative inflation and interest rates, and the long-run properties of purchasing power parity.
- In the short term, a variety of random events, institutional frictions, and technical factors may cause currency values to deviate significantly from their long-term fundamental path. In the long term, it does appear that exchange rates follow a fundamental equilibrium path, one consistent with the fundamental theories of exchange rate determination.

MINI-CASE

Is China a Currency Manipulator?[3]

> *Washington—The Omnibus Trade and Competitiveness Act of 1988 requires the Secretary of the Treasury to analyze the exchange rate policies of other countries. Under Section 3004 of the Act, the Secretary must "consider whether countries manipulate the rate of exchange between their currency and the United States dollar for purposes of preventing effective balance of payments adjustments or gaining unfair competitive advantage in international trade." Secretary Mnuchin, under the auspices of President Trump, has today determined that China is a Currency Manipulator.*
>
> —"Treasury Designates China as a Currency Manipulator," Press Release, U.S. Department of the Treasury, August 5, 2019.

The *Economist* magazine termed it "name calling," but many other analysts described the labeling of China as a "currency manipulator" a part of ongoing trade negotiations. It was in many ways not a surprise as U.S. President Donald Trump had been accusing China of currency manipulation for years. But this was the first time the U.S. government had labeled a trading partner as a currency manipulator in 25 years—the last case also being China.[4] It was unclear what actions—if any—the U.S. would take as a result of this designation.

U.S. grounds were laid out sequentially in its press release. China confirmed that it controlled the value of the Chinese renminbi. China had extensive foreign exchange reserves. China acknowledged active management of its currency in the recent past. China, as a member of the G20, had committed to not using competitive devaluation to gain advantages in international trade. China's currency had fallen in value versus the U.S. dollar in recent days and weeks. What the Treasury department's press release didn't say was that a full one-half of the current U.S. trade deficit was with one country—China.

U.S. Law

> *"We called them on manipulation and they brought their numbers back and they brought them back rapidly and they were able to do that because they manipulate," Trump said. "It's called monetary manipulation. Not good."*
>
> —President Donald Trump, "New IMF report doesn't back Trump's currency manipulation charge against China," Doug Palmer, *Politico,* August 19, 2019.

U.S. law was a bit confusing on the topic of currency manipulation. The Trump administration had cited the 1988

[3] This case was prepared by Professor Michael H. Moffett for the purpose of classroom discussion only.

[4] The U.S. had only ever labeled three countries as currency manipulators: China (1992–1994), Japan (1988), and Taiwan (1988).

Omnibus Foreign Trade and Competitiveness Act in its finding. Under the 1988 act, the Treasury department was to annually, in consultation with the International Monetary Fund (IMF), evaluate whether countries were manipulating their currencies against the dollar to distort balance of payments or to gain competitive advantage in trade (cheapen their products for export). The latter argument seemed to be implied by the Treasury press release.

A more recent U.S. trade law, the 2015 Trade Enforcement Act, was much more specific. It laid out three very specific criteria to be used in the determination of a trade partner manipulating their currency's trading value: (1) a bilateral trade surplus with the U.S. of at least \$20 billion; (2) an overall current account surplus exceeding 2% of GDP; and (3) direct intervention, government purchases of dollars in the foreign exchange market, in six of the last 12 months, exceeding 2% of GDP. (The Treasury department has discretion in setting the specific quantitative levels for each criteria; it had most recently set these.) A recent Treasury department report had concluded that China currently met only one of these three criteria—the first—as shown in Exhibit A. Also shown is China's official currency intervention as a percent age of GDP; although large in the past, it was negligible in 2019.

There was little doubt that China enjoyed a massive trade surplus with the U.S., \$380 billion in the third quarter of 2019. Theoretically, an undervalued currency would contribute to the creation of that, making Chinese exports to the U.S. relatively cheap and U.S. imports to China relatively expensive.

Currency manipulation, under both IMF and U.S. law and policy, was narrowly defined. Manipulation was only seen as resulting from direct intervention—the buying and selling of foreign currencies using foreign exchange reserves. Indirect intervention, such as the alteration of interest rates, had frequently been discussed as potential manipulation. By the IMF's most recent discussion on the topic in 2013 had come to no conclusion.

If the U.S. actually imposed tariffs in retaliation for what it believed to be currency manipulation, it would be considered in direct conflict with World Trade Organization (WTO) rules. That, argued trade negotiators, would likely prompt retaliatory actions by other countries.

IMF on Currency Manipulation

The IMF was established as part of the Bretton Woods Agreement in 1944 to promote stability in the international monetary system. Currency manipulation was a real concern at the time, as a multitude of countries had pursued policies of competitive devaluation in the 1930s (long argued as one of the many contributing factors to World War II).

EXHIBIT A China's Trade Surplus with the U.S. and Currency Intervention

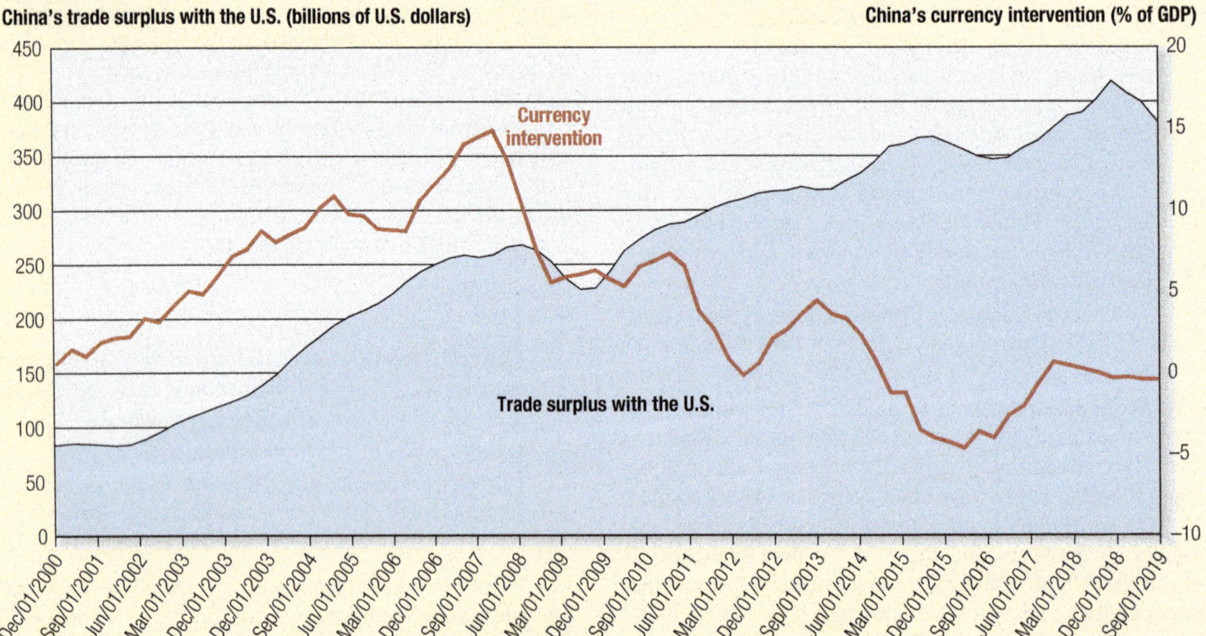

Source: Constructed by author. Quarterly data from the Council of Foreign Relations currency manipulator tracker.https://www.cfr.org/article/tracking-currency-manipulation.

When a country joined the IMF, it agreed to not use devaluation of its currency to gain trade advantages. In the 80 years since its birth, the IMF had never found a country guilty of currency manipulation.

Although there had been many instances in which currency manipulation was suspected, the IMF had found it extremely difficult to prove intent. In one glaring example of the IMF's unwillingness to push the point, in 2007 it had noted publicly that China was running a current-account surplus of 10% of GDP while simultaneously purchasing more than $2 billion a day in foreign currency-denominated assets. But it was still not considered to be officially manipulating its currency value.[5]

The IMF had recently completed a review of the Chinese economy as part of its regular monitoring of economic activity, termed Article IV, including currency issues.[6]

> **Exchange rate.** *The bilateral RMB/USD rate depreciated relatively rapidly from mid-June to early August 2018, when measures to counter depreciation pressure – the 20 percent reserve requirement for FX derivatives (a capital flow management measure [CFM]) and the countercyclical adjustment factor (CCAF) in the daily trading band's central parity formation – were reintroduced. Despite the RMB/USD depreciation, the RMB was broadly stable against the basket and depreciated in real effective terms by about 2½ percent since the last Article IV. Estimates suggest little FX intervention by the PBC. At about US$3.2 trillion, China's foreign currency reserves remain more than adequate to allow a continued transition to a floating exchange rate.*

In short, the IMF had not found China to be devaluing its currency. In fact, it noted that the government had taken active measures the previous year to "counter depreciation pressure" as well as finding little evidence that the People's Bank of China (PBC) had been conducting significant intervention.

The previous month the IMF, in a separate report, had found the U.S. dollar to be overvalued by 6% to 12%, not a significant amount. The report had also noted that direct foreign-exchange intervention had been playing an ever-smaller role in determining currency values in recent years. Economic analysts believed it was expansionary fiscal policy by the U.S. likely driving the overvaluation.

Why Now?

In an additional element of irony, the recent fall in the value of the Chinese renminbi was likely in response to new tariffs imposed by the Trump administration. Only a few days prior to Treasury's announcement, the administration had announced the imposition of a 10% tariff on more than $300 billion of U.S. imports from China. This was only the latest salvo in the deteriorating trade relationship between Washington and Beijing.

The tariff announcement immediately sent the renminbi's value down on world markets as Chinese economic prospects were seen as dimming in a growing trade war. On August 6, the renminbi had crossed what some analysts call "the line in the sand," the psychological and political barrier of 7 renminbi per dollar, as seen in Exhibit B.

Trade analysts believed that China would likely argue that it was not its responsibility to stabilize the renminbi's value when it was the actions of the U.S. government driving the change in value, and that was likely the case. Since the PBC did actively manage the renminbi's value, regularly and officially, the fall in its value to an 11-year low was allowed.

As complicated as U.S. trade law was, understanding China's currency management system was just as perplexing. As the official keeper of the renminbi, the PBC set a daily "midpoint" in trading value based on the closing value from the previous day. It then had the discretion to allow the renminbi to trade onshore plus or minus 2% from that fix. (The offshore market for the renminbi was mostly run out of Hong Kong and was not subject to direct control.) It regularly intervened to ensure the new fix. Although this procedure limited daily movement, it allowed a significant discretion in its movement over time. And there was a second more mysterious dimension to potential politically driven intervention. China's commercial banks, theoretically independent from the PBC, made frequent purchases of U.S. dollar–denominated assets and securities, like U.S. Treasury bonds. This clearly drove the demand for dollars up.

Outcome

In January 2020, five months later and two days before renewed trade negotiations were scheduled to begin between the U.S. and China, the U.S. Secretary of the Treasury announced that it was dropping the designation of China as a currency manipulator. He noted that "China has made enforceable commitments to refrain from competitive devaluation, while promoting transparency and accountability." China made no public explanation of any change in its currency policy. And for the record, the renminbi's value spent much of 2020 over the unofficial line in the sand.

[5] "America Considers Retaliating against Currency Manipulation," *The Economist*, July 27, 2019.

[6] "People's Republic of China: 2019 Article IV Consultation," Press Release; Staff Report and Stat Statement by the Executive Director for China, IMF Country Report No. 19/266, International Monetary Fund, August 2019, p. 6.

EXHIBIT B Chinese Renminbi–U.S. Dollar Exchange Rate (CNY = USD 1.00)

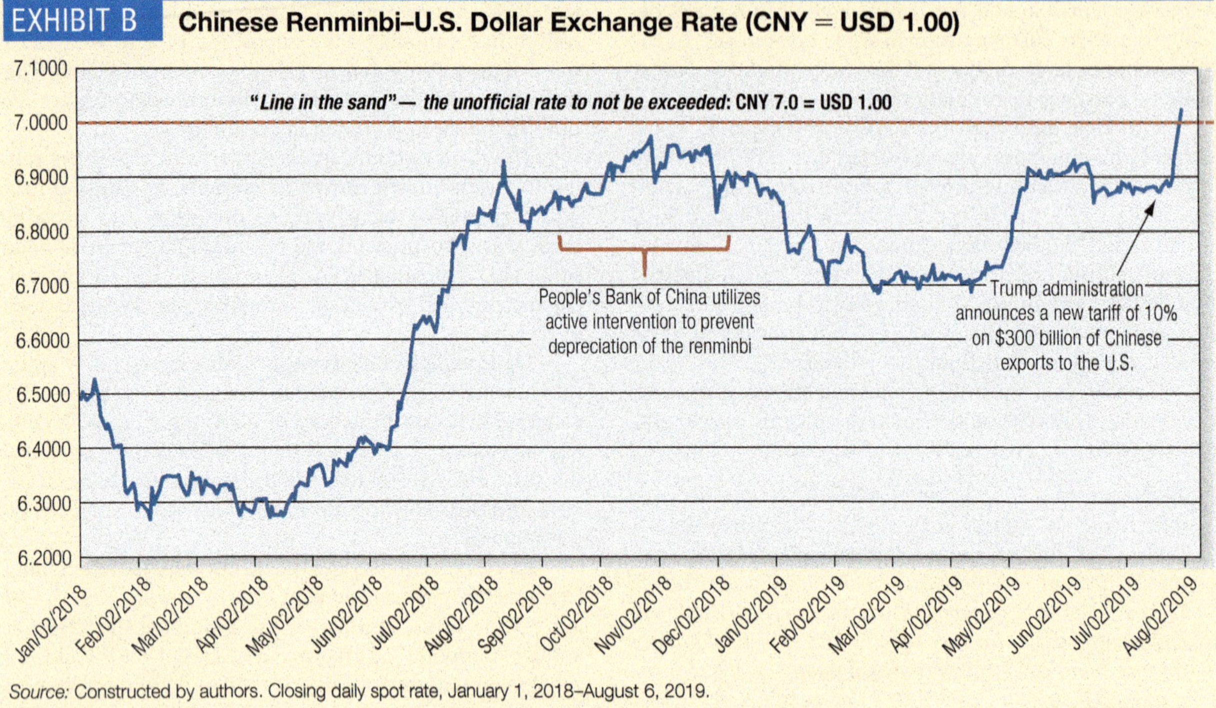

Source: Constructed by authors. Closing daily spot rate, January 1, 2018–August 6, 2019.

MINI-CASE QUESTIONS

1. What is your opinion of the three separate criteria used by the U.S. in the determination of currency manipulation?
2. Why has the IMF seemingly been so ineffective in policing currency manipulation?
3. Do you believe that the narrow definition of currency manipulation used by the IMF and the U.S. is adequate?
4. In your opinion, was China a currency manipulator?

P.S. For those interested in tracking potential currency manipulators in the eyes of the U.S., the Council on Foreign Relations has a real-time tracker of major U.S. trading partners. The tracker evaluates all major trading partners quarterly on the basis of whether they meet the three individual criteria under the 2015 Trade Enforcement Act.

https://www.cfr.org/article/tracking-currency-manipulation

Questions

9.1 Exchange Rate Determination. What are the three basic theoretical approaches to exchange rate determination?

9.2 Purchasing Power Parity Inadequacy. The most widely accepted theory of foreign exchange rate determination is purchasing power parity, yet it has proven to be quite poor at forecasting future spot exchange rates. Why?

9.3 Data and the Balance of Payments Approach. Statistics on a country's balance of payments are often used by the business press and by business itself for predicting exchange rates, but the academic profession is highly critical of the practice. Why?

9.4 Supply and Demand. Which of the three major theoretical approaches seems to put the most weight on the supply and demand for currency? What is its primary weakness?

9.5 Asset Market Approach to Forecasting. Explain how the asset market approach can be used to forecast spot exchange rates. How does the asset market approach differ from the balance of payments approach (listed in Exhibit 9.1 and detailed in Chapter 3) to forecasting?

9.6 Technical Analysis. Explain how technical analysis can be used to forecast spot exchange rates.

9.7 Intervention. What is foreign currency intervention? How is it accomplished?

9.8 Intervention Motivation. Why do governments and central banks intervene in the foreign exchange markets? If markets are efficient, why not let them determine the value of a currency?

9.9 Direct Intervention Usefulness. When is direct intervention likely to be the most successful? And when is it likely to be the least successful?

9.10 Intervention Downside. What is the downside of both direct and indirect intervention?

9.11 Capital Controls. Are capital controls really a method of currency market intervention or more of a denial of activity? How does this fit with the concept of the impossible trinity discussed previously in Chapters 2 and 6?

9.12 Asian Crisis of 1997 and Disequilibrium. What was the primary disequilibrium at work in Asia in 1997 that likely caused the Asian financial crisis? Do you think it could have been avoided?

9.13 Fundamental Equilibrium. What is meant by the term *fundamental equilibrium path* for a currency value? What is *noise*?

9.14 Argentina's Failure. What was the basis of the Argentine Currency Board, and why did it fail in 2002?

9.15 Term Forecasting. What are the major differences between short-term and long-term forecasts for a fixed exchange rate versus a floating exchange rate?

9.16 Exchange Rate Dynamics. What is meant by the term *overshooting*? What causes it, and how is it corrected?

9.17 Foreign Currency Speculation. The emerging market crises of 1997–2002 were worsened because of rampant speculation. Do speculators cause such crises, or do they simply respond to market signals of weakness? How can a government manage foreign exchange speculation?

9.18 Cross-Rate Consistency in Forecasting. Explain the meaning of *cross-rate consistency* as used by MNEs. How do MNEs use a check of cross-rate consistency in practice?

9.19 Stabilizing versus Destabilizing Expectations. Define *stabilizing* and *destabilizing expectations*, and describe how they play a role in the long-term determination of exchange rates.

9.20 Currency Forecasting Services. Many multinational firms use forecasting services regularly. If forecasting is essentially "foretelling the future" and that is theoretically impossible, why would these firms spend money on these services?

Problems

9.1 Naira's Nightmare. On Friday, June 17, 2016, the Central Bank of Nigeria (CBN) abandoned the Nigerian naira's (NGN or N) fixed exchange rate and allowed the currency to float. Previously fixed against the U.S. dollar at NGN196.50 = USD1.00, the naira closed at NGN 279.50 = USD1.00 on Monday, June 20, the first day of trading following the float. The naira quickly floated (sunk) to NGN 324.50 by August 18. Similarly, the naira fell from NGN 221.2001 = EUR1.00 to NGN 316.7294 = EUR1.00 on June 20 and NGN 347.7721 on August 18.

a. What was the percentage change in the value of the Nigerian naira versus the dollar the first trading day?

b. What was the percentage change in the value of the naira versus the dollar by August 18, 2016?

c. What was the percentage change in the value of the Nigerian naira versus the euro the first trading day?

d. What was the percentage change in the value of the naira versus the euro by August 18, 2016?

9.2 Bangkok Broken. The Thai baht (THB) was devalued by the Thai government from THB25 = USD1.00 to THB29 = USD1.00 on July 2, 1997. What was the percentage devaluation of the baht?

9.3 Reais Crisis. The value of the Brazilian reais (BRL or R$) was BRL 1.80 to 1.00 USD on Thursday, January 24, 2008. It then plunged in value to BRL 2.39 to 1.00 USD on January 26, 2009. What was the percentage change in its value?

9.4 Ecuadorian Sucre. The Ecuadorian sucre (S) suffered from hyperinflationary forces throughout 1999. Its value moved from S5,000 = $1.00 to S25,000 = $1.00. What was the percentage change in its value?

9.5 Argentine Anguish. As illustrated in the graph (on the next page), the Argentine peso moved from its fixed exchange rate of Ps1.00 = $1.00 to over Ps2.00 = $1.00 in a matter of days in early January 2002. After a brief period of high volatility, the peso's value appeared to settle down into a range varying between 2.0 and 2.5 pesos per dollar. If you were forecasting the Argentine peso further into the future, to March 30, 2002, how would you use the information in the graphic—the value of the peso freely floating in the weeks following devaluation—to forecast its future value?

9.6 Canadian Dollar/USD Dollar. The Canadian dollar's value against the U.S. dollar has seen some significant changes over recent history. Use the graph of the C$ to US$ exchange rate on the next page

Problem 9.6

Canadian dollars (CAD) = 1.00 U.S. dollar (USD) January 1980–January 2015 (monthly average)

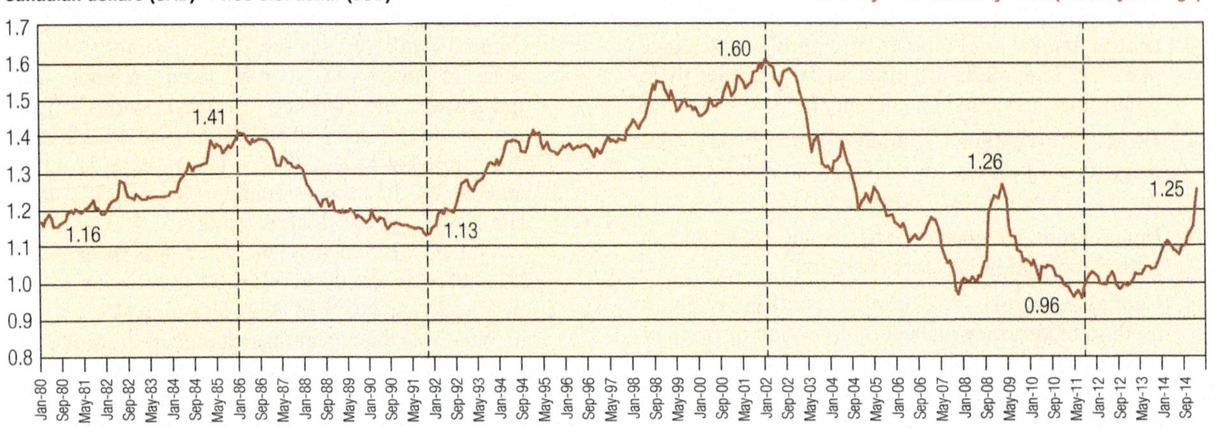

Problem 9.5

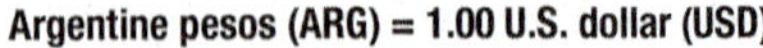

Argentine pesos (ARG) = 1.00 U.S. dollar (USD) **Daily:** Dec 17, 2001–Feb 28, 2002

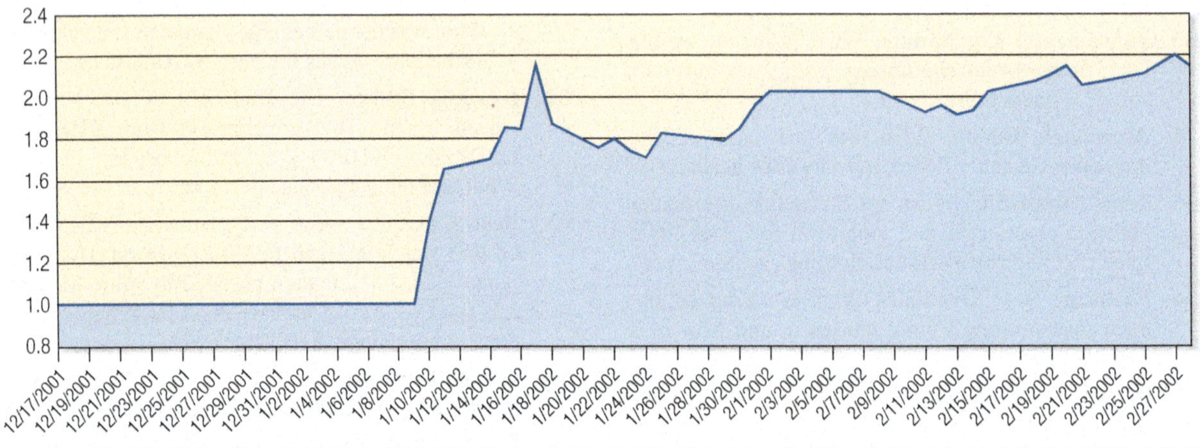

for the 30-year period between 1980 and end-of-year 2010 to estimate the percentage change in the Canadian dollar's value (affectionately known as the "loonie") versus the dollar for the following periods.

a. January 1980–January 1986
b. January 1986–October 1991
c. October 1991–December 2001
d. October 2001–April 2011
e. April 2011–January 2015

9.7 Istanbul's Issues. The Turkish lira (TL) was officially devalued by the Turkish government in February 2001 during a severe political and economic crisis. The Turkish government announced on February 21 that the lira would be devalued by 20%. The spot exchange rate on February 20 was TL68,000 = $1.00.

a. What was the exchange rate after devaluation?
b. What was percentage change after falling to TL100,000 = $1.00?

Russo-Swiss Cross—2015

Switzerland has long served as a cornerstone of banking conservatism and a safe port in a world of currency storms. Swiss banks have long been used by investors from all over the world as financially secure institutions that would preserve depositors' wealth with confidentiality. A large part of the security offered is the Swiss franc itself. Russian citizens of wealth have used Swiss banks heavily in recent years as a place where they can shelter their capital from politics, both inside Russia and the outside (EU and U.S.) world. But beginning in the fall of 2014, the Russian ruble's value began to slide against the Swiss franc, threatening their wealth. Use the following exhibit to answer Problems 9.8–9.10.

Problem 9.8–9.10

Russian Ruble Tumbles against Swiss Franc (RUB = 1.00 CHF, Nov 2014–Jan 2015)

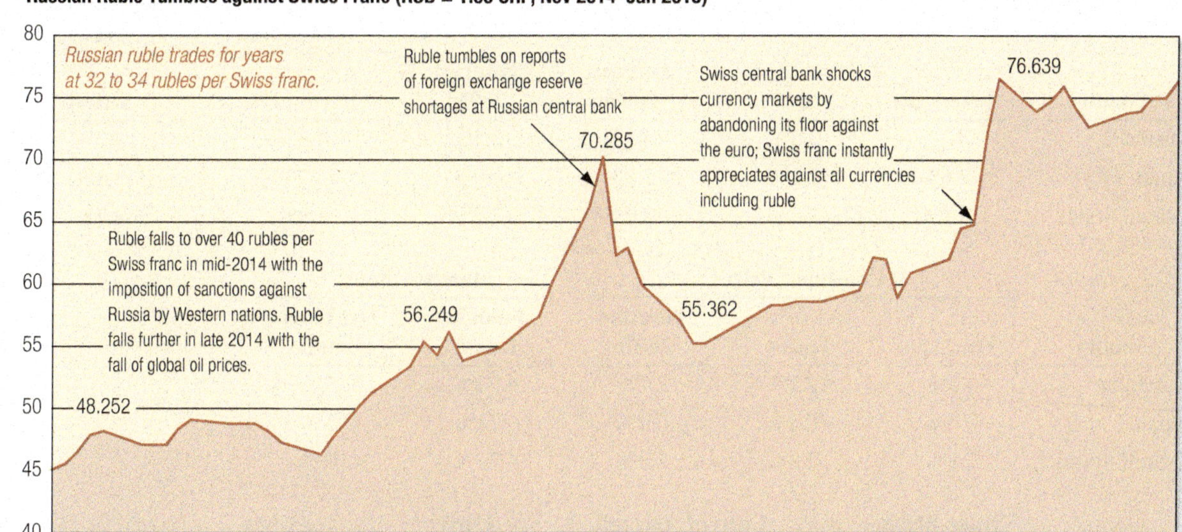

9.8 Mikhail's Portfolio. Mikhail Khodorkovsky was one of the infamous Russian oligarchs, accumulating billions of dollars in wealth in the mid-1990s with the fall of the Soviet Union. But in 2003 he had been imprisoned by the Russian state for a decade. Upon his release from prison in 2013 he had taken up residence in Switzerland—with his money. In November 2014 Mikhail held a portfolio of USD 200 million and CHF 150 million in Swiss banks, in addition to accounts in Russia still holding RUB 1.2 billion. Using the exchange rate table, answer the following:

a. What is the value of Mikhail's portfolio as measured in Russian rubles?
b. What is the value of Mikhail's portfolio as measured in Swiss francs?
c. What is the value of Mikhail's portfolio as measured in U.S. dollars?
d. Which currency demonstrated the greatest fluctuations in total value over the six dates?

9.9 Trepak—The Russian Dance. Calculate the percentage change in the value of the ruble for the three different cross rates shown in the table for the six dates. Did the ruble fall further against the U.S. dollar or the Swiss franc?

9.10 BP and Rosneft 2015. BP (UK) and Rosneft (Russia) had severed a long-term joint venture in 2013, with Rosneft buying BP out with $55 billion in cash and a 20% interest (equity interest) in Rosneft itself. Rosneft financed a large part of the buyout by borrowing heavily. The following year, in July 2014, BP received a dividend on its ownership interest in Rosneft of RUB 24 billion. But Rosneft's performance had been declining, as was the Russian ruble. The winter of 2014–2015 in Europe was a relatively mild one, and Europe's purchases of Rosneft's natural gas had fallen as had the price of natural gas. Rosneft's total sales were down, and the ruble had clearly fallen dramatically (see table). And to add debt to injury, Rosneft was due to make a payment of USD 19.5 billion in 2015 on its debt from the BP buyout.

a. Assuming a spot rate of RUB34.78 = USD1.00 in July 2014, how much was the dividend paid to BP in U.S. dollars?
b. If Rosneft were to pay the same dividend to BP in July 2015, and the spot rate at that time was RUB75 = USD1.00, what would BP receive in U.S. dollars?
c. If the combination of Western sanctions against Russia and lower global oil prices truly sent the Russian economy into recession, and the spot rate was RUB75=USD1.00 in July 2015, what might BP's dividend be in July 2015?

9.11 Current Spot Rates. What are the current spot exchange rates for the following cross rates?

a. Japanese yen to U.S. dollar exchange rate
b. Japanese yen to Australian dollar exchange rate
c. Australian dollar to U.S. dollar exchange rate

Forecasting the Pan-Pacific Pyramid: Use the following data in answering problems 9.11–9.16.

	Gross Domestic Product				Industrial Production	Unemployment Rate
Country	Latest Qtr	Qtr*	Forecast 2007e	Forecast 2008e	Recent Qtr	Latest
Australia	4.3%	3.8%	4.1%	3.5%	4.6%	4.2%
Japan	1.6%	–1.2%	2.0%	1.9%	4.3%	3.8%
United States	1.9%	3.8%	2.0%	2.2%	1.9%	4.7%

	Consumer Prices			Interest Rates	
Country	Year Ago	Latest	Forecast 2007e	3-month Latest	1-yr Govt Latest
Australia	4.0%	2.1%	2.4%	6.90%	6.23%
Japan	0.9%	–0.2%	0.0%	0.73%	1.65%
United States	2.1%	2.8%	2.8%	4.72%	4.54%

	Trade Balance	Current Account		Current Units (per US$)	
Country	Last 12 mos (billion $)	Last 12 mos (billion $)	Forecast 07 (% of GDP)	Oct 17th	Year Ago
Australia	–13.0	–$47.0	–5.7%	1.12	1.33
Japan	98.1	$197.5	4.6%	117	119
United States	–810.7	–$793.2	–5.6%	1.00	1.00

Source: Data abstracted from *The Economist*, October 20, 2007, print edition. Unless otherwise noted, percentages are percentage changes over one year. Rec Qtr = recent quarter. Values for 2007e are estimates or forecasts.

9.12 Purchasing Power Parity Forecasts. Assuming purchasing power parity, and assuming that the forecasted change in consumer prices is a good proxy of predicted inflation, forecast the following cross rates:

a. Japanese yen to U.S. dollar in one year
b. Japanese yen to Australian dollar in one year
c. Australian dollar to U.S. dollar in one year

9.13 International Fischer Forecasts. Assuming International Fisher—one version of purchasing power parity—applies to the coming year, forecast the following future spot exchange rates using the government bond rates for the respective country currencies:

a. Japanese yen to U.S. dollar in one year
b. Japanese yen to Australian dollar in one year
c. Australian dollar to U.S. dollar in one year

9.14 Implied Real Interest Rates. If the nominal interest rate is the government bond rate, and the current change in consumer prices is used as expected inflation, calculate the implied "real" rates of interest by currency.

a. Australian dollar "real" rate
b. Japanese yen "real" rate
c. U.S. dollar "real" rate

9.15 Forward Rates. Using the spot rates and three-month interest rates in the table, calculate the 90-day forward rates for:

a. Japanese yen to U.S. dollar exchange rate
b. Japanese yen to Australian dollar exchange rate
c. Australian dollar to U.S. dollar exchange rate

9.16 Real Economic Activity and Misery. Calculate the country's *Misery Index* (unemployment + inflation) and then use it like an interest differential to forecast the future spot exchange rate, one year into the future.

a. Japanese yen to U.S. dollar exchange rate in one year
b. Japanese yen to Australian dollar exchange rate in one year
c. Australian dollar to U.S. dollar exchange rate in one year

9.17 The Rising Sun and Europe. The Japanese yen–euro cross rate is one of the more significant currency values for global trade and commerce. The following graph shows this cross rate from when the euro was launched in January 1999 through January of 2015. Estimate the change in the value of the yen over the following four trend periods.

a. Jan 1999–Sept 2000
b. Sept 2000–Sept 2008
c. Sept 2008–Sept 2012
d. Sept 2012–Jan 2015

Problem 9.17

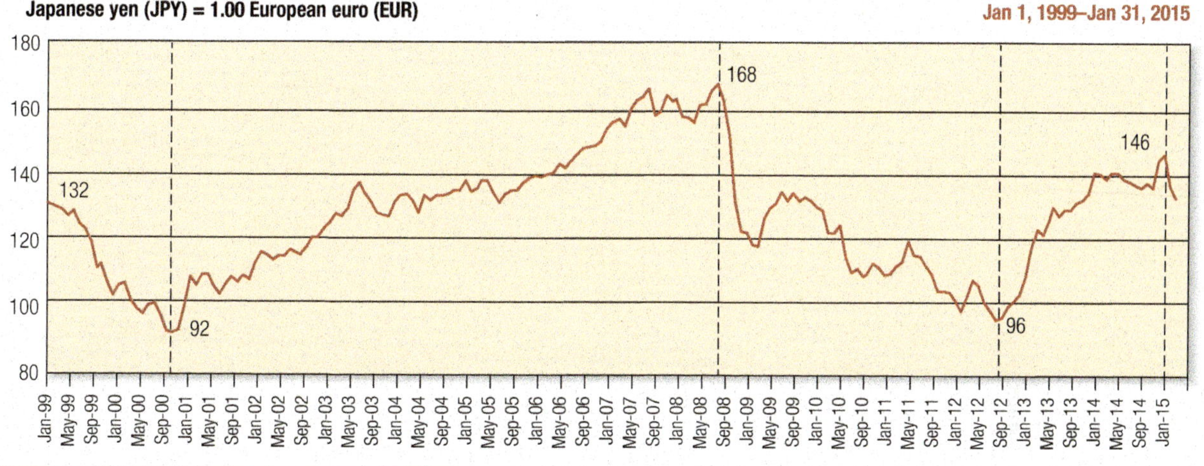

PART 3

Foreign Exchange Exposure

10

Transaction Exposure

There are two times in a man's life when he should not speculate: when he can't afford it and when he can.

—"Following the Equator, Pudd'nhead Wilson's New Calendar," Mark Twain.

LEARNING OBJECTIVES

- 10.1 Examine the three major foreign exchange exposures experienced by firms
- 10.2 Explore why firms hedge foreign exchange exposure
- 10.3 Examine how transaction exposure is defined and measured
- 10.4 Describe how one company may hedge its transaction exposures
- 10.5 Detail how foreign exchange risk management is conducted by firms today

Foreign exchange exposure is a measure of the potential for a firm's profitability, net cash flow, and market value to change because of a change in exchange rates. An important task of the financial manager is to measure foreign exchange exposure and to manage it so as to maximize the profitability, net cash flow, and market value of the firm. This chapter provides an in-depth discussion of *transaction exposure*, the exposure that generally receives the most attention by corporate financial management. The following chapters focus on *translation exposure* (Chapter 11) and *operating exposure* (Chapter 12). The chapter concludes with the mini-case *GraysonChung's FX Exposure*, examining a U.S.-based firm's hedging of Mexican peso and Japanese yen transaction exposures.

10.1 Types of Foreign Exchange Exposure

What happens to a firm when foreign exchange rates change? There are two distinct categories of foreign exchange exposure for the firm: those that are based in accounting and those that arise from economic competitiveness. Accounting exposures, specifically described as *transaction exposure* and *translation exposure*, arise from contracts and accounts being denominated in foreign currency. The *economic exposure*, which we will describe as *operating exposure*, is the potential change in the value of the firm from its changing global competitiveness as determined by exchange rates.

Exhibit 10.1 shows schematically the three main types of foreign exchange exposure: *transaction, translation*, and *operating*:

- *Transaction exposure* measures changes in the value of contractual obligations incurred between the time in which they are created and booked, and when they are settled due to a change in exchange rates. Thus, it deals with changes in expected cash flows resulting from existing contractual obligations, so-called on balance sheet obligations.

EXHIBIT 10.1 The Foreign Exchange Exposures of the Firm

Realized Exposures

Transaction Exposure
Changes in the recorded value of identifiable transactions of the firm like receivables and payables. Results in *realized* foreign exchange gains and losses in income and taxes.

Short-term to medium-term to long-term change

Economic/Operating Exposure
Changes in the expected future cash flows of the firm from unexpected changes in exchange rates. The firm's future cash flows are changed from *realized* changes in its own sales, earnings, and cash flows, as well as changes in competitor responses to exchange rates over time.

Time

Unrealized Exposures

Translation Exposure
Changes in the periodic consolidated value of the firm; results in no change in cash flow or global tax liabilities—*unrealized*—changes only the consolidated financial results reported to the market (if publicly traded). Often labeled *Accounting Exposure.*

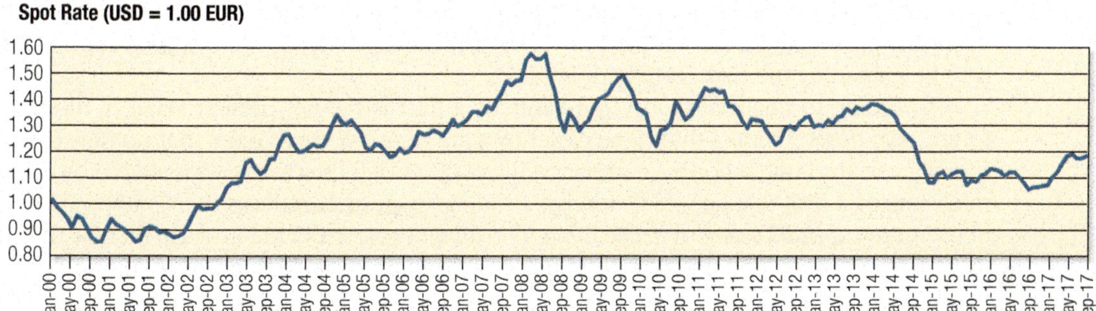

- *Translation exposure* is the potential for accounting-derived changes in owner's equity or consolidated income to occur because of the need to "translate" foreign currency financial statements of foreign subsidiaries into a single reporting currency to prepare worldwide consolidated financial statements.
- *Operating exposure*—also commonly called *economic exposure* or *competitive exposure*—measures the change in the present value of the firm resulting from any change in future operating cash flows of the firm caused by an unexpected change in exchange rates. The change in value depends on the effect of the exchange rate change on future sales volume, prices, and costs.

Transaction exposure and operating exposure both exist because of unexpected changes in future cash flows. However, while transaction exposure is concerned with future cash flows already contracted for, operating exposure focuses on expected (not yet contracted for) future cash flows that might change because a change in exchange rates has altered international competitiveness.

The three foreign exposures impact the financial statements of the multinational firm in very different ways. Transaction exposures, as noted in Exhibit 10.1, are realized—they may increase or decrease the cash flows of the firm (impacting the statement of cash flows) and its reported profitability (impacting the income statement). Translation exposure, the second accounting-based foreign exchange exposure, may impact the firm's reported consolidated income and equity. This impact, however, is purely accounting in nature and does not alter the firm's cash flows. The third and final foreign exchange exposure, operating exposure, represents risks to the firm's future sales, costs, earnings, cash flows, and asset values, all of which are beyond the current operating period. They may indeed impact the future of the firm—and its financial results—but not in the current period.

10.2 Why Hedge?

Multinational firms, as first described in Chapter 1, consist of a multitude of cash flows that are sensitive to changes in exchange rates, interest rates, and commodity prices. This chapter focuses on how the MNE's outstanding obligations, many of which are contractual in nature, are altered by changes in exchange rates. We begin by exploring the question of whether exchange rate risk should or should not be managed.

Hedging Defined

Many firms attempt to manage their foreign exchange exposure through *hedging*. Hedging requires a firm to take a position—an asset, a contract, or a derivative—the value of which will rise or fall in a manner that counters the fall or rise in value of an existing position—the exposure. Hedging protects the owner of the existing asset from loss. However, it also eliminates any gain from an increase in the value of the asset hedged. The question remains: What is to be gained by the firm from hedging?

According to financial theory, the value of a firm is the net present value of all expected future cash flows. The fact that these cash flows are *expected* emphasizes that nothing about the future is certain. If the reporting currency value of many of these cash flows is altered by exchange rate changes, a firm that hedges its foreign exchange exposures reduces the variance in the value of its future expected cash flows. The *foreign exchange exposure* of the firm can then be defined as the variance in expected cash flows arising from unexpected changes in exchange rates.

Exhibit 10.2 illustrates the distribution of expected net cash flows of the individual firm. Hedging these cash flows narrows the distribution of the cash flows about the mean of the distribution. Currency hedging reduces risk. Reduction of risk is not, however, the same as

EXHIBIT 10.2 Hedging's Impact on the Expected Cash Flows of the Firm

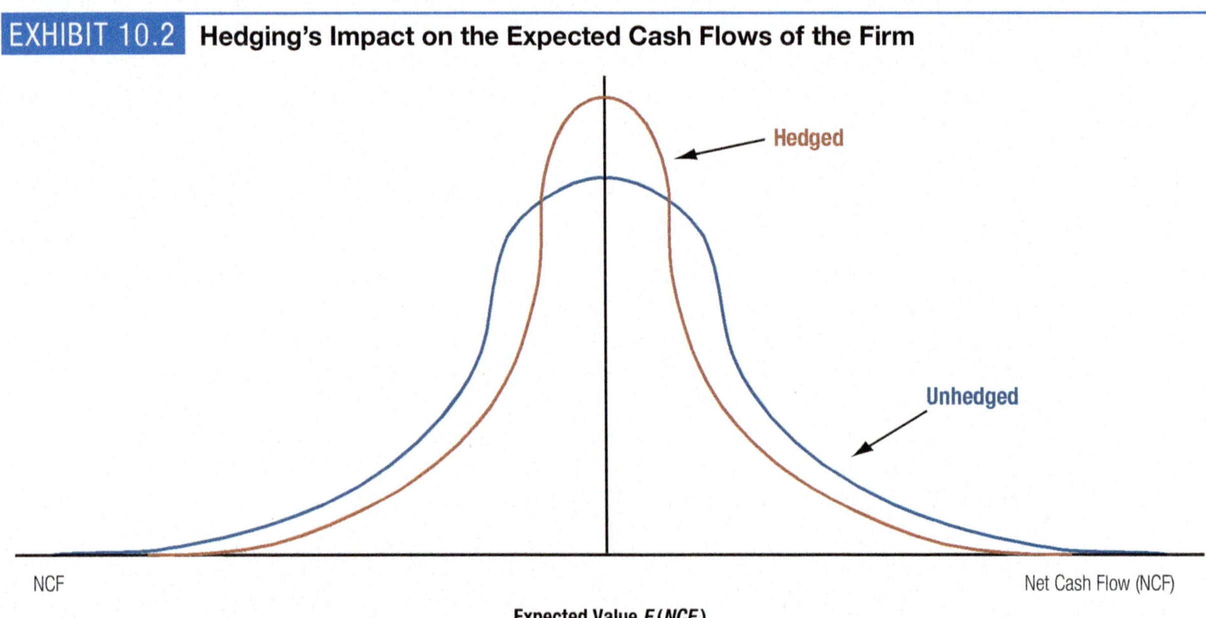

Hedging reduces the variability of expected cash flows about the mean of the distribution. This reduction of distribution variance is a reduction of risk. An added question is whether the mean of the two distributions is the same. If hedging "costs," the distribution of the hedged distribution may shift slightly to the left of the mean of the unhedged distribution.

adding value or return. The value of the firm depicted in Exhibit 10.2 would be increased only if hedging actually shifted the mean of the distribution to the right. In fact, if hedging is not "free," meaning the firm must expend resources to hedge, then hedging will add value only if the rightward shift is sufficiently large to compensate for the cost of hedging.

The Pros and Cons of Hedging

Is a reduction in the variability of cash flows sufficient reason for currency risk management?

Pros. Proponents of hedging cite the following arguments:

- Reduction in risk of future cash flows improves the planning capability of the firm. If the firm can more accurately predict future cash flows, it may be able to undertake specific investments or activities that it might not otherwise consider.
- Reduction of risk in future cash flows reduces the likelihood that the firm's cash flows will fall below a level sufficient to make debt service payments required for continued operation. This minimum level of cash flows, often referred to as the point of *financial distress*, lies to the left of the center of the distribution of expected cash flows. Hedging reduces the likelihood that the firm's cash flows will fall to this level.
- Management has a comparative advantage over the individual shareholder in knowing the actual currency risk of the firm. Regardless of the level of disclosure provided by the firm to the public, management always possesses an advantage in the depth and breadth of knowledge concerning the real risks.
- Markets are usually in disequilibrium because of structural and institutional imperfections, as well as unexpected external shocks (such as an oil crisis or war). Management is in a better position than shareholders to recognize disequilibrium conditions and to take advantage of single opportunities to enhance firm's value through *selective hedging*—hedging only exceptional exposures or the occasional use of hedging when management has a definite expectation of the direction of exchange rates.

Cons. Opponents of hedging commonly make the following arguments:

- Shareholders are more capable of diversifying currency risk than is the management of the firm. If stockholders do not wish to accept the currency risk of any specific firm, they can diversify their portfolios to manage the risk in a way that satisfies their individual preferences and risk tolerance.
- Currency hedging does not increase the expected cash flows of the firm. Currency risk management does, however, consume firm resources and so reduces cash flow. The impact on value is a combination of the reduction of cash flow (which lowers value) and the reduction in variance (which increases value).
- Management often conducts hedging activities that benefit management at the expense of the shareholders. The field of finance called *agency theory* frequently argues that management is generally more risk-averse than are shareholders.
- Managers cannot outguess the market. If and when markets are in equilibrium with respect to parity conditions, the expected net present value of hedging should be zero.
- Management's motivation to reduce variability is sometimes for accounting reasons. Management may believe that it will be criticized more severely for incurring foreign exchange losses than for incurring even higher cash costs by hedging. Foreign exchange losses appear in the income statement as a highly visible separate line item or as a footnote, but the higher costs of protection through hedging are buried in operating or interest expenses.

GLOBAL FINANCE IN PRACTICE **10.1**

Hedging and the German Automobile Industry

The leading automakers in Germany have long been some of the world's biggest advocates of currency hedging. Companies like BMW, Mercedes, Porsche—and Porsche's owner Volkswagen—have aggressively hedged their foreign currency earnings for years in response to their structural exposure: while they manufacture in the eurozone, they increasingly rely on sales in dollar, yen, or other foreign (non-euro) currency markets.

How individual companies hedge, however, differs dramatically. Some companies, like BMW, state clearly that they "hedge to protect earnings" but that they do not speculate. Others, like Porsche and Volkswagen in the past, have sometimes generated more than 40% of their earnings from their "hedges."

Hedges that earn money continue to pose difficulties for regulators, auditors, and investors worldwide. How a hedge is defined, and whether a hedge should only "cost" but not "profit," has delayed the implementation of many new regulatory efforts in the United States and Europe in the post-2008 financial crisis era. If a publicly traded company—for example, an automaker—can consistently earn profits from hedging, is its core competency automobile manufacturing and assembly or hedging/speculating on exchange rate movements?

- Efficient market theorists believe that investors can see through the "accounting veil" and therefore have already factored the foreign exchange effect into a firm's market valuation. Hedging would only add cost.

Every individual firm in the end decides whether it wishes to hedge, for what purpose, and how. But as illustrated by *Global Finance in Practice 10.1*, this often results in even more questions and more doubts.

10.3 Transaction Exposure

Transaction exposure measures gains or losses that arise from the settlement of existing financial obligations whose terms are stated in a foreign currency. Industry refers to most of these types of exposures as *balance sheet exposures*. The types of transaction exposure experienced by a multinational firm arise from a variety of business activities:

- Purchasing or selling goods or services when prices and settlement are stated in foreign currencies
- Borrowing or lending funds when repayment is to be made in a foreign currency
- Acquiring assets or incurring liabilities of any kind denominated in a foreign currency

Purchasing and Selling

The most common example of transaction exposure arises when a firm makes a sale and receives a promise of payment from the buyer (a receivable) or purchases an input and promises to pay in the future (a payable), and that transaction is denominated in a foreign currency. (Technically speaking, these types of sales or purchases are referred to as a *sale on open account* or a *purchase on open account* because goods are shipped and delivered before payment is due.) Exhibit 10.3 demonstrates how a sale by a firm creates a receivable exposure, how that exposure evolves over its life span, and how it can be decomposed into its component exposures—*quotation, backlog*, and *billing*.

A transaction exposure is theoretically created at the first moment the seller quotes a price in foreign currency terms to a potential buyer, at time t_1. The quote can be either verbal, as in a telephone quote, or as a written bid or a printed price list. This is *quotation exposure*.

EXHIBIT 10.3 **The Life Span of a Transaction Exposure**

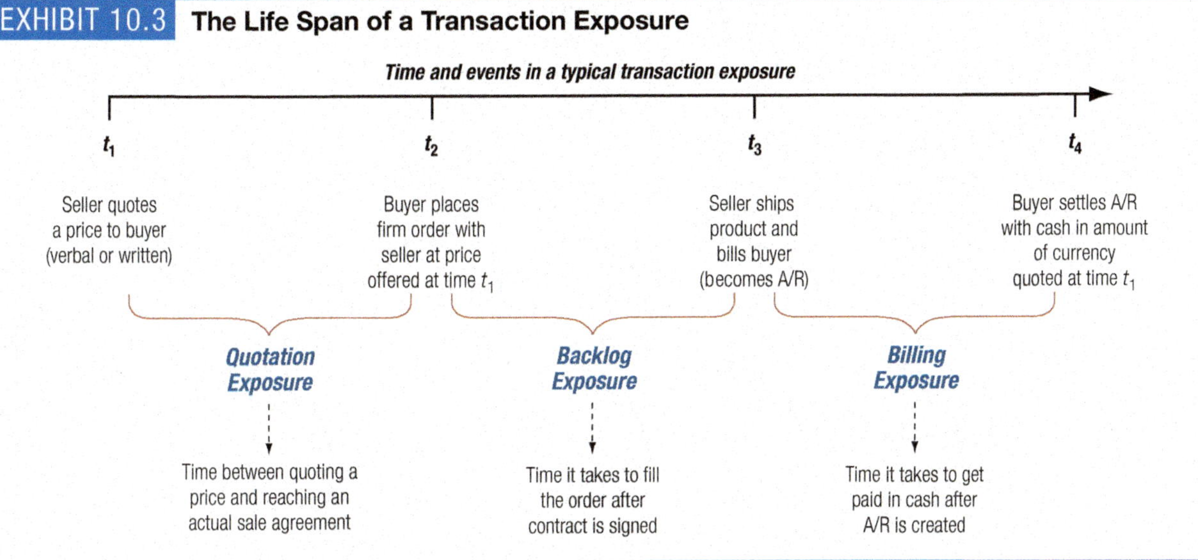

When the order is placed at time t_2, the potential exposure created at the time of the quotation is converted into an actual exposure. This is called *backlog exposure* because the product has been contracted for but not yet shipped or delivered. Backlog exposure lasts until the goods are shipped and billed at t_3, at which time it becomes *billing exposure*, which persists until payment is received by the seller at time t_4.

Many firms, however, do not recognize the creation of the exposure as a transaction exposure until time t_3. This is because many different business and contractual changes often occur during the quotation period, including contract cancellation, and the seller still has control over the product.

Suppose that Ganado Corporation, a U.S. firm, sells merchandise on open account to a Belgian buyer for €1,800,000, with payment to be made in 60 days. The spot exchange rate on the date of the sale is \$1.1200 = €1.00, and the seller expects to exchange the euros for €1,800,000 × \$1.12 = \$2,016,000 when payment is received. The \$2,016,000 is the value of the sale that is posted to the firm's books. Accounting practices stipulate that the foreign currency transaction be listed at the spot exchange rate in effect on the date of the transaction.

Transaction exposure arises because of the risk that Ganado will receive something other than the \$2,016,000 expected and booked. For example, if the euro weakens to \$1.1000 = €1.00 when payment is received, the U.S. seller will receive only €1,800,000 × \$1.100 or \$1,980,000, some \$36,000 less than what was expected at the time of sale.

Transaction settlement: €1,800,000 × \$1.1000 = €1.00	=	\$1,980,000
Transaction booked: €1,800,000 × \$1.1200 = €1.00	=	\$2,016,000
Foreign exchange gain (loss) on sale	=	(\$36,000)

If the euro should strengthen to \$1.3000 = €1.00, however, Ganado receives \$2,340,000, an increase of \$324,000 over the amount expected. Thus, Ganado's exposure is the chance of either a loss or a gain on the resulting dollar settlement versus the amount at which the sale was booked.

This U.S. seller might have avoided transaction exposure by invoicing the Belgian buyer in dollars. Of course, if the U.S. firm attempted to sell only in dollars, it might not have obtained the sale in the first place. Even if the Belgian buyer agrees to pay in dollars, transaction exposure is not eliminated. Instead, the exposure is transferred to the Belgian buyer, whose dollar account payable has an unknown cost 60 days in the future.

Borrowing and Lending

A second form of transaction exposure arises when funds are borrowed or loaned, and the amount involved is denominated in a foreign currency. For example, in 1994, PepsiCo's largest bottler outside the United States was the Mexican company, Grupo Embotellador de Mexico (Gemex). In mid-December 1994, Gemex had U.S. dollar debt of $264 million. At that time, Mexico's new peso ("Ps") was traded at Ps3.45 = $1.00, a pegged rate that had been maintained with minor variations since January 1, 1993, when the new currency unit had been created. On December 22, 1994, the peso was allowed to float because of economic and political events within Mexico, and in one day it sank to Ps4.65 = $1.00. For most of the following January it traded in a range near Ps5.50 = $1.00.

Dollar debt in mid-December 1994: $264,000,000 × Ps3.45 = $1.00	=	Ps910,800,000
Dollar debt in mid-January 1995: $264,000,000 × Ps5.50 = $1.00	=	Ps1,452,000,000
Dollar debt increase measured in Mexican pesos	=	Ps541,200,000

The number of pesos needed to repay the dollar debt increased by 59%! In U.S. dollar terms, the drop in the value of the peso meant that Gemex needed the peso-equivalent of an additional $98,400,000 to repay its debt.

Other Causes of Transaction Exposure

When a firm enters into a forward exchange contract, it is deliberately creating a transaction exposure. This risk is usually incurred to hedge an existing transaction exposure. For example, a U.S. firm might want to offset an existing obligation to purchase ¥100 million to pay for an import from Japan in 90 days. One way to offset this payment is to purchase ¥100 million in the forward market today for delivery in 90 days. In this manner any change in value of the Japanese yen relative to the dollar is neutralized. Thus, the potential transaction loss (or gain) on the account payable is offset by the transaction gain (or loss) on the forward contract. But regardless of whether the firm actually does make its yen payment in 90 days, the firm is obligated, by contract with its forward exchange contract provider (typically a bank), to settle the forward exchange contract. The contract is therefore itself a transaction exposure.

10.4 Transaction Exposure Management

Foreign exchange transaction exposure can be managed by *contractual hedges* or *operating hedges*. *Contractual hedges*, also called *financial hedges*, employ forward, money, futures, and options markets. *Operating hedges* utilize operating cash flows—cash flows originating from the operating activities of the firm—and include risk-sharing agreements and payments strategies using leads and lags. *Financial hedges* utilize financing cash flows—cash flows originating from the financing activities of the firm—and include specific types of debt and foreign currency derivatives, such as swaps. Operating and financing hedges are described in greater detail in Chapter 12.

The term *natural hedge* refers to an offsetting operating cash flow, a payable arising from the conduct of business. A *financial hedge* refers to either an offsetting debt obligation (such as a loan) or some type of financial derivative such as an interest rate swap. Care should be taken to distinguish hedges in the same way finance distinguishes cash flows, operating from financing. The following case illustrates how contractual hedging techniques may be used to protect against transaction exposure.

Ganado's Transaction Exposure

Maria Gonzalez is the chief financial officer of Ganado. She has just concluded negotiations for the sale of a turbine generator to Regency, a British firm, for £1,000,000. This single sale is quite large in relation to Ganado's present business. Ganado has no other current foreign customers, so the currency risk of this sale is of particular concern. The sale is made in March with payment due three months later in June. Exhibit 10.4 summarizes the financial and market information Maria has collected for the analysis of her currency exposure problem. The unknown—the transaction exposure—is the actual realized value of the receivable in U.S. dollars at the end of 90 days.

Ganado operates on relatively narrow margins. Although Maria and Ganado would be very happy if the pound appreciated versus the dollar, concerns center on the possibility that the pound will fall. Because this deal was deemed desirable both for financial and strategic reasons, Ganado priced and budgeted this contract with a very slim minimum acceptable margin at a sales price of $1,700,000. The budget rate, the lowest acceptable dollar per pound exchange rate, was therefore established at $1.70 = £1.00. Any exchange rate below this budget rate would result in Ganado realizing no profit on the deal.

Four alternatives are available to Ganado to manage this transaction exposure: (1) remain unhedged, (2) hedge in the forward market, (3) hedge in the money market, or (4) hedge in the options market.

EXHIBIT 10.4 Ganado's Transaction Exposure

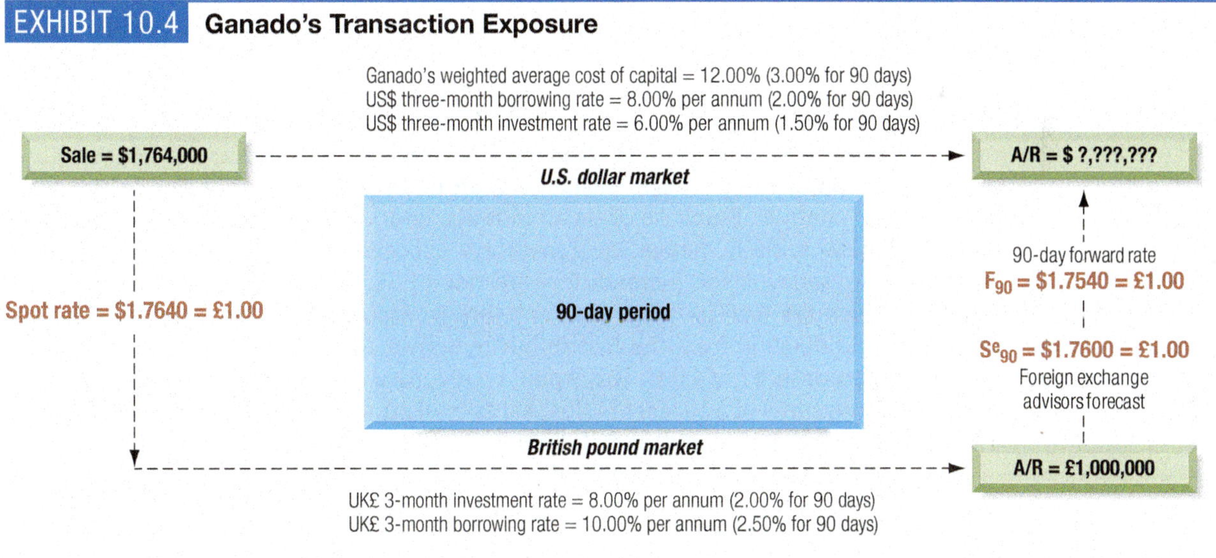

Unhedged Position

Maria may decide to accept the transaction risk. If she believes the foreign exchange advisor, she expects to receive £1,000,000 × \$1.76 = \$1,760,000 in three months. However, that amount is at risk. If the pound should fall to, say, \$1.65 = £1.00, she will receive only \$1,650,000. Exchange risk is not one-sided, however; if the transaction is left uncovered and the pound strengthens even more than forecast, Ganado will receive considerably more than \$1,760,000.

The essence of an unhedged approach is as follows:

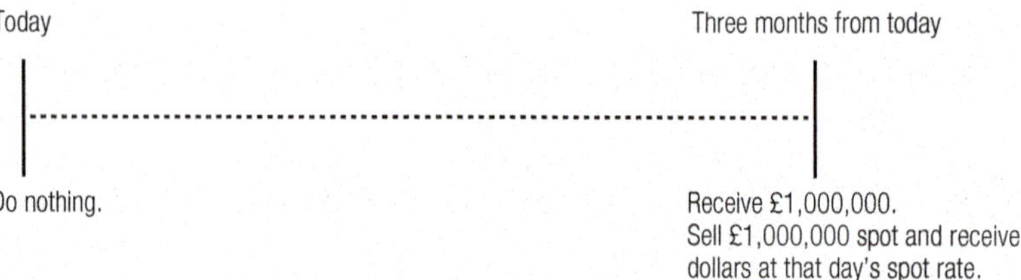

Forward Hedge

A forward hedge involves a forward (or futures) contract and a source of funds to fulfill that contract. The forward contract is entered into at the time the transaction exposure is created. In Ganado's case, that would be in March, when the sale to Regency was booked as an account receivable.

When a foreign currency denominated sale such as this is made, it is booked at the spot rate of exchange existing on the booking date. In this case, the spot rate on the date of sale was \$1.7640 = £1.00, so the receivable was booked as \$1,764,000. Funds to fulfill the forward contract will be available in June, when Regency pays £1,000,000 to Ganado. If funds to fulfill the forward contract are on hand or are due because of a business operation, the hedge is considered covered, perfect, or square because no residual foreign exchange risk exists. Funds on hand or to be received are matched by funds to be paid.

In some situations, funds to fulfill the forward exchange contract are not already available or due to be received later but must be purchased in the spot market at some future date. Such a hedge is *open* or *uncovered.* It involves considerable risk because the hedger must take a chance on purchasing foreign exchange at an uncertain future spot rate in order to fulfill the forward contract. Purchase of such funds at a later date is referred to as covering.

Should Ganado wish to hedge its transaction exposure with a forward, it will sell £1,000,000 forward today at the 3-month forward rate of \$1.7540 = £1.00. This is a *covered transaction* in which the firm no longer has any foreign exchange risk. In three months the firm will receive £1,000,000 from the British buyer, deliver that sum to the bank against its forward sale, and receive \$1,754,000. This would be recorded on Ganado's income statement as a foreign exchange loss of \$10,000 (\$1,764,000 as booked, \$1,754,000 as settled).

The essence of a forward hedge is as follows:

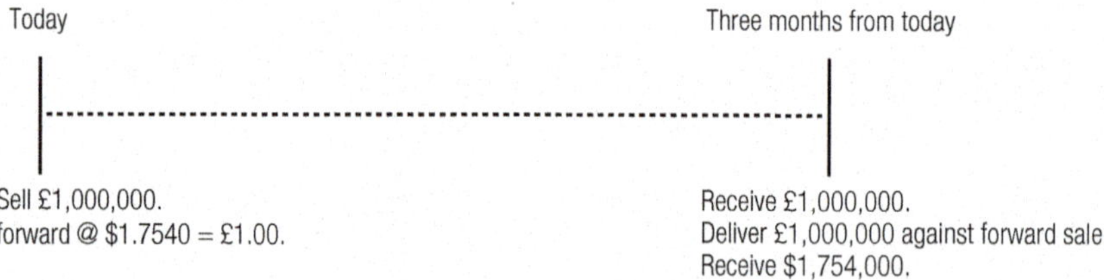

If Maria's forecast of future rates was identical to that implicit in the forward quotation, that is, $1.7540 = £1.00, then expected receipts would be the same whether or not the firm hedges. However, realized receipts under the unhedged alternative could vary considerably from the certain receipts when the transaction is hedged. Never underestimate the value of predictability of outcomes (and 90 nights of sound sleep).

Money Market Hedge (Balance Sheet Hedge)

Like a forward market hedge, a *money market hedge* (also commonly called a *balance sheet hedge*) also involves a contract and a source of funds to fulfill that contract. In this instance, the contract is a loan agreement. The firm seeking to construct a money market hedge borrows in one currency and exchanges the proceeds for another currency. Funds to fulfill the contract, to repay the loan, are generated from business operations. In this case, the account receivable generates the funds to repay the loan.

A money market hedge can cover a single transaction, such as Ganado's £1,000,000 receivable, or repeated transactions. Hedging repeated transactions is called *matching*. It requires the firm to match the expected foreign currency cash inflows and outflows by currency and maturity. For example, if Ganado had numerous sales denominated in pounds to British customers over a long period of time, then it would have somewhat predictable UK pound cash inflows. The appropriate money market hedge technique in that case would be to borrow UK pounds in an amount matching the typical size and maturity of expected pound inflows. Then, if the pound depreciated or appreciated, the foreign exchange effect on cash inflows in pounds would be offset by the effect on cash outflows in pounds from repaying the pound loan plus interest.

The structure of a money market hedge resembles that of a forward hedge. The difference is that the cost of the money market hedge is determined by different interest rates than the interest rates used in the formation of the forward rate. The difference in interest rates facing a private firm borrowing in two separate country markets may be different from the difference in risk-free government bill rates or eurocurrency interest rates in these same markets. In efficient markets interest rate parity should ensure that these costs are nearly the same, but not all markets are efficient at all times.

To hedge in the money market, Maria will borrow pounds in London at once, immediately convert the borrowed pounds into dollars, and repay the pound loan in three months with the proceeds from the sale of the generator. She will need to borrow just enough to repay both the principal and interest with the sale proceeds. The borrowing interest rate will be 10% per annum, or 2.5% for three months. Therefore, the amount to borrow now for repayment in three months is £975,610:

$$\frac{£1{,}000{,}000}{1 + 0.025} = £975{,}610$$

Maria would borrow £975,610 now and in three months repay that amount plus £24,390 of interest with the account receivable. Ganado would exchange the £975,610 loan proceeds for dollars at the current spot exchange rate of $1.7640 = £1.00, receiving $1,720,976 at once.

The money market hedge, if selected by Ganado, creates a pound-denominated liability—the pound loan—to offset the pound-denominated asset—the account receivable. The money market hedge works as a hedge by matching assets and liabilities according to their currency of denomination. Using a simple T-account illustrating Ganado's balance sheet, the loan in British pounds is seen to offset the pound-denominated account receivable:

Assets		Liabilities & Net Worth	
Account receivable	£1,000,000	Bank loan (principal)	£975,610
		Interest payable	24,390
	£1,000,000		£1,000,000

The loan acts as a *balance sheet hedge* against the pound-denominated account receivable and is based on a money market loan (90-day loan).

Forward and Money Market Hedges Compared

To compare the forward hedge with the money market hedge, one must analyze how Ganado's loan proceeds will be utilized for the next three months. Remember that the loan proceeds are received today, but the forward contract proceeds are received in three months. For comparison purposes, one must calculate either the future value of the loan proceeds or the present value of the forward contract proceeds. Since the primary uncertainty here is the dollar value in three months, we will use future value in this case.

As both the forward contract proceeds and the loan proceeds are relatively certain, it is possible to make a clear choice between the two alternatives based on the one that yields the higher dollar receipts. This result, in turn, depends on the assumed rate of investment or use of the loan proceeds.

At least three logical choices exist for an assumed investment rate for the loan proceeds for the next three months. First, if Ganado is cash rich, the loan proceeds might be invested in U.S. dollar money market instruments that yield 6% per annum. Second, Maria might simply use the pound loan proceeds to pay down dollar loans that currently cost Ganado 8% per annum. Third, Maria might invest the loan proceeds in the general operations of the firm, in which case the cost of capital of 12% per annum would be the appropriate rate. The field of finance generally uses the company's cost of capital (the *weighted average cost of capital* or WACC) to move capital forward and backward in time. We will therefore use the WACC of 12% (3% for the 90-day period here) to calculate the future value of proceeds under the money market hedge:

$$\$1{,}720{,}976 \times 1.03 = \$1{,}772{,}605$$

A break-even rate can now be calculated between the forward hedge and the money market hedge. Assume that r is the unknown 3-month investment rate (expressed as a decimal) that would equalize the proceeds from the forward and money market hedges. We have:

$$\begin{aligned}(\text{Loan proceeds}) \times (1 + \text{rate}) &= (\text{forward proceeds})\\ \$1{,}720{,}976 \times (1 + \text{rate}) &= \$1{,}754{,}000\\ \text{rate} &= 0.0192\end{aligned}$$

We now convert this three-month (90 days) investment rate to an annual whole percentage equivalent, assuming a 360-day financial year, as follows:

$$0.0192 \times \frac{360}{90} \times 100 = 7.68\%$$

In other words, if Maria Gonzalez can invest the loan proceeds at a rate higher than 7.68% per annum, she would prefer the money market hedge. If she can only invest at a rate lower than 7.68%, she would prefer the forward hedge.

The essence of a money market hedge is as follows:

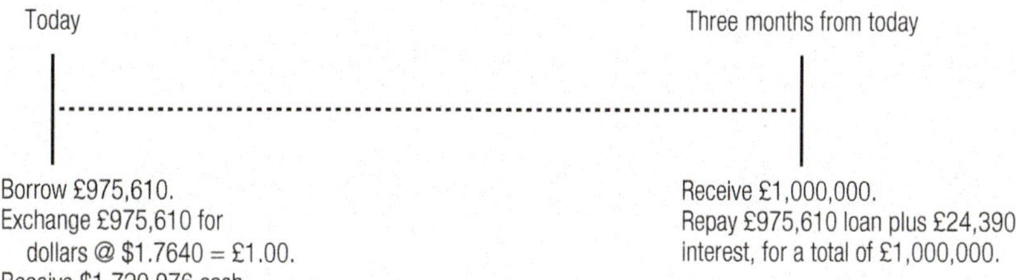

The money market hedge therefore results in cash received up-front (at the start of the period), which can then be carried forward in time for comparison with the other hedging alternatives.

Options Market Hedge

Maria Gonzalez could also cover her £1,000,000 exposure by purchasing a put option. This technique, an *option hedge*, allows her to speculate on the upside potential for appreciation of the pound while limiting downside risk to a known amount. Maria could purchase from her bank a 3-month put option on £1,000,000 at an at-the-money (ATM) strike price of $1.75 = £1.00 with a premium cost of 1.50%. The total cost of the option is calculated as follows:

$$\text{Size of option} \times \text{premium} \times \text{spot rate} = \text{total cost of option}$$

$$£1{,}000{,}000 \times 0.015 \times \$1.7640 = \$26{,}460$$

Because we are using future value to compare the various hedging alternatives, it is necessary to project the premium cost of the option forward three months. We will use the cost of capital of 12% per annum or 3% per quarter. Therefore the premium cost of the put option as of June would be $26,460 × 1.03 = $27,254. This is equal to $0.0273 per pound ($27,254 ÷ £1,000,000).

When the £1,000,000 is received in June, the value in dollars depends on the spot rate at that time. The upside potential is unlimited, the same as in the unhedged alternative. At any exchange rate above $1.75 = £1.00, Ganado would allow its option to expire unexercised and would exchange the pounds for dollars at the spot rate. If the expected rate of $1.76 materializes, Ganado would exchange the £1,000,000 in the spot market for $1,760,000. Net proceeds would be $1,760,000 minus the $27,254 cost of the option, or $1,732,746.

In contrast to the unhedged alternative, downside risk is limited with an option. If the pound depreciates below $1.75 = £1.00, Maria would exercise her option to sell (put) £1,000,000 at $1.75 = £1.00, receiving $1,750,000 gross, but $1,722,746 net of the $27,254 cost of the option. Although this downside result is worse than the downside of either the forward or money market hedges, the upside potential is unlimited.

The essence of the at-the-money (ATM) put option market hedge is as follows:

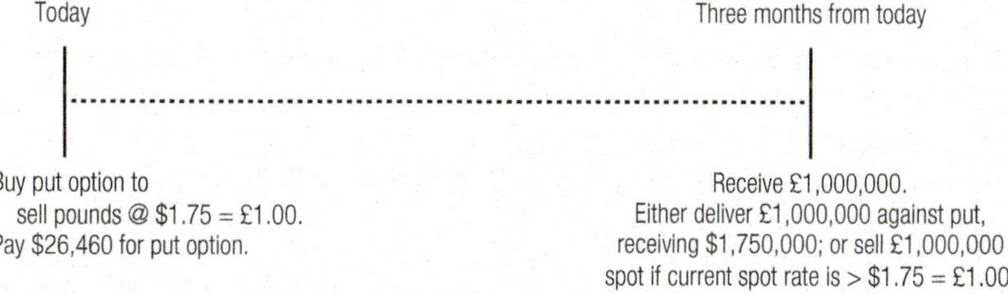

We can calculate a trading range for the pound that defines the break-even points for the option compared with the other strategies. The upper bound of the range is determined by comparison with the forward rate. The pound must appreciate enough above the $1.7540 forward rate to cover the $0.0273 per £ cost of the option. Therefore, the break-even upside spot price of the pound must be $1.7540 + $0.0273 = $1.7813. If the spot pound appreciates above $1.7813, proceeds under the option strategy will be greater than under the forward hedge. If the spot pound ends up below $1.7813, the forward hedge would have been superior in retrospect.

The lower bound of the range is determined by the unhedged strategy. If the spot price falls below $1.75 = £1.00, Maria will exercise her put and sell the proceeds at $1.75. The net proceeds will be $1.75 less than the $0.0273 cost of the option, or $1.7227 = £1.00. If the spot rate falls below $1.7227, the net proceeds from exercising the option will be greater than the net proceeds from selling the unhedged pounds in the spot market. At any spot rate above $1.7227, the spot proceeds from remaining unhedged will be greater.

Foreign currency options have a variety of hedging uses. A put option is useful to construction firms and exporters when they must submit a fixed price bid in a foreign currency without knowing until some later date whether their bid is successful. Similarly, a call option is useful to hedge a bid for a foreign firm if a potential future foreign currency payment may be required. In either case, if the bid is rejected, the loss is limited to the cost of the option.

Hedging Alternatives Compared

Exhibit 10.5 shows the value of Ganado's £1,000,000 account receivable over a range of possible ending spot exchange rates and hedging alternatives. This exhibit makes it clear that the firm's view of likely exchange rate changes aids in the hedging choice as follows:

- If the exchange rate is expected to move against Ganado, to the left of $1.76 = £1.00, the money market hedge is clearly the preferred alternative with a guaranteed value of $1,772,605.
- If the exchange rate is expected to move in Ganado's favor, to the right of $1.76, then the preferred alternative is less clear-cut, lying between remaining unhedged, the money market hedge, or the put.

Remaining unhedged is most likely an unacceptable choice. If Maria's expectations regarding the future spot rate prove to be wrong, and the spot rate falls below $1.70 = £1.00, she will not reach her budget rate. The put option offers a unique alternative. If the exchange rate moves in Ganado's favor, the put option offers nearly the same upside potential as the unhedged alternative except for the up-front costs. If, however, the exchange rate moves against Ganado, the put option limits the downside risk to $1,722,746.

So how should Maria Gonzalez choose among the alternative hedging strategies? She must select on the basis of two decision criteria: (1) the risk tolerance of Ganado, as expressed in its stated policies; and (2) her own view or expectation of the direction and distance the exchange rate will move over the coming period.

Ganado's *risk tolerance* is a combination of management's philosophy toward transaction exposure and the specific goals of treasury activities. Many firms believe that currency risk is simply a part of doing business internationally and, therefore, begin their analysis from an unhedged baseline. Other firms, however, view currency risk as unacceptable and either begin their analysis from a full forward contract cover baseline or simply mandate that all transaction exposures be fully covered by forward contracts regardless of the value of other hedging alternatives. The treasury in most firms operates as a cost or service center for the firm. On the other hand, if the treasury operates as a profit center, it might tolerate taking more risk.

EXHIBIT 10.5 Ganado's A/R Transaction Exposure Hedging Alternatives

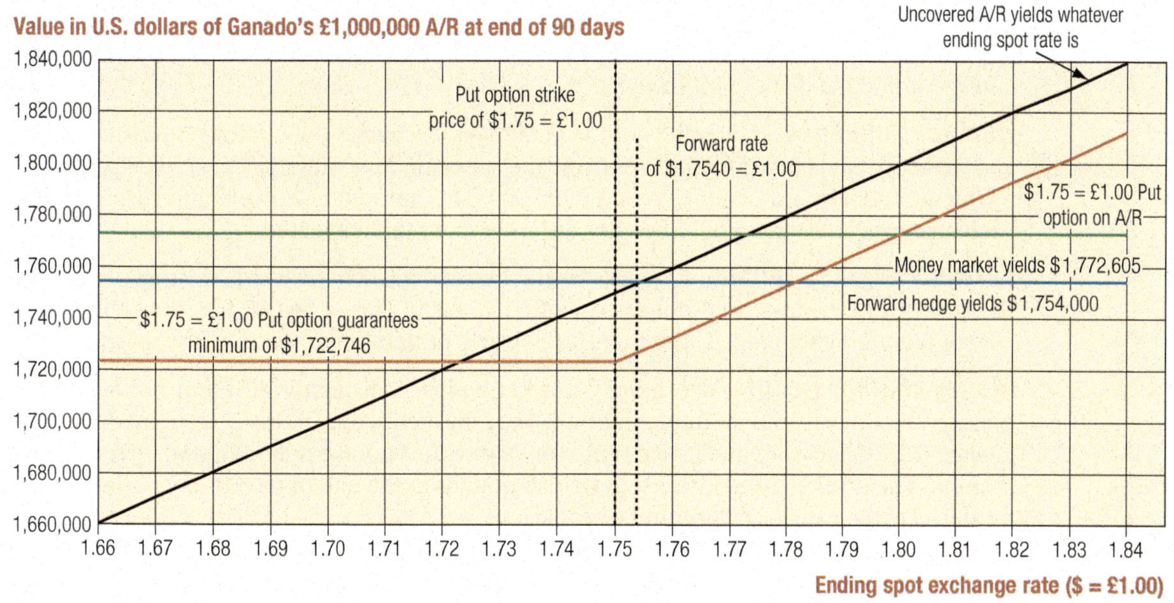

The final choice between hedges—if Maria Gonzalez does expect the pound to appreciate—combines the firm's risk tolerance, its view, and its confidence in its view. Transaction exposure management with contractual hedges requires managerial judgment. *Global Finance in Practice 10.2* describes how hedging choices may also be influenced by profitability concerns and forward premiums.

GLOBAL FINANCE IN PRACTICE 10.2

Forward Rates and the Cost of Hedging

Some multinational firms measure the cost of hedging as the "total cash flow expenses of the hedge" as a percentage of the initial booked foreign currency transaction. They define the "total cash flow expense of the hedge" as any cash expenses for purchase (e.g., option premium paid up-front, including the time value of money) plus any difference in the final cash flow settlement versus the booked transaction.

If a firm were using forwards, there is no up-front cost, so the total cash flow expense is simply the difference between the forward settlement and the booked transaction (using this definition of hedging expense). This is the forward premium. But the size of the forward premium has sometimes motivated firms to avoid using forwards.

Assume a U.S.-based firm has a GBP1 million one-year receivable. The current spot rate is USD1.6000 = GBP1.00. If U.S. dollar and British pound interest rates were 2.00% and 4.00%, respectively, the forward rate would be USD1.5692. This is a forward premium of 1.923% (the pound is selling forward at a 1.923% discount versus the dollar), and in this firm's view, the cost of hedging the transaction is then 1.923%.

However, if British pound interest rates were significantly higher, say 8.00%, then the one year forward rate would be USD1.5111, a forward premium of –5.556%. Some multinationals see using a forward in this case, in which more than 5.5% of the transaction's settlement is "lost" to hedging as too expensive. The definition of "too expensive" must be based on the philosophy of the individual firm, its risk tolerance for currency risk, and the profitability of the business and industry itself. Fundamentals of financial theory, however, would argue that the two cases are not truly different. Yet, in global business today, depending on how pricing is conducted, a loss of 5.56% on the sale settlement could destroy much of the net margin on the sale.

Hedging an Account Payable

The management of an account payable, where the firm would be required to make a foreign currency payment at a future date, is similar but not identical to the management of an account receivable. If Ganado had a £1,000,000 account payable due in 90 days, the hedging choices would include the following.

Remain Unhedged. Ganado could wait 90 days, exchange dollars for pounds at that time, and make its payment. If Ganado expects the spot rate in 90 days to be $1.7600 = £1.00, the payment would be expected to cost $1,760,000. This amount is, however, uncertain; the spot exchange rate in 90 days could be very different from that expected.

Forward Market Hedge. Ganado could buy £1,000,000 forward, locking in a rate of $1.7540 = £1.00 and a total dollar cost of $1,754,000. This is $6,000 less than the expected cost of remaining unhedged, and therefore clearly preferable to the first alternative.

Money Market Hedge. The money market hedge is distinctly different for a payable as opposed to a receivable. To implement a money market hedge in this case, Ganado would exchange U.S. dollars spot and invest them for 90 days in a pound-denominated interest-bearing account. The principal and interest in British pounds at the end of the 90-day period would be used to pay the £1,000,000 account payable.

In order to ensure that the principal and interest exactly equal the £1,000,000 due in 90 days, Ganado would discount the £1,000,000 by the pound investment interest rate of 8% for 90 days in order to determine the pounds needed today:

$$\frac{£1,000,000}{\left[1 + \left(.08 \times \frac{90}{360}\right)\right]} = £980,392.16$$

This £980,392.16 needed today would require $1,729,411.77 at the current spot rate of $1.7640 = £1.00:

$$£980,392.16 \times \$1.7640 = \$1,729,411.77.$$

Finally, in order to compare the money market hedge outcome with the other hedging alternatives, the $1,729,411.77 cost today must be carried forward 90 days to the same future date as the other hedge choices. If the current dollar cost is carried forward at Ganado's WACC of 12%, the total cost of the money market hedge is the $1,781,294.12. This is higher than the forward hedge and therefore unattractive.

$$\$1,729,411.77 \times \left[1 + \left(.12 \times \frac{90}{360}\right)\right] = \$1,781,294.12$$

Option Hedge. Ganado could cover its £1,000,000 account payable by purchasing a call option on £1,000,000. A June call option on British pounds with a near at-the-money strike price of $1.75 = £1.00 would cost 1.5% (premium) or £1,000,000 × 0.015 × $1.7640 = $26,460.

This premium, regardless of whether the call option is exercised, will be paid up front. Its value, carried forward 90 days at the WACC of 12%, would raise its end of period cost to $27,254. If the spot rate in 90 days is less than $1.75 = £1.00, the option would be allowed to expire and the £1,000,000 for the payable would be purchased on the spot market. The total cost of the call option hedge, if the option is not exercised, is theoretically smaller than any other alternative (with the exception of remaining unhedged because the option premium is still paid and lost). If the spot rate in 90 days exceeds $1.75 = £1.00, the call option would be exercised.

The total cost of the call option hedge, if exercised, is as follows:

Exercise call option (£1,000,000 × $1.75 = £1.00)	=	$1,750,000
Call option premium (carried forward 90 days)	=	27,254
Total maximum expense of call-hedged payable	=	$1,777,254

Strategy Choice. The four hedging methods of managing a £1,000,000 account payable for Ganado are summarized in Exhibit 10.6. The costs of the forward hedge and money market hedge are certain. The cost using the call option hedge is calculated as a maximum, and the cost of remaining unhedged is highly uncertain.

As with Ganado's account receivable, the final hedging choice depends on Maria's exchange rate expectations and her willingness to bear risk. The forward hedge provides the lowest cost of making the account payable payment; that is certain. If the dollar strengthens against the pound, ending up at a spot rate less than $1.75 = £1.00, the call option could potentially be the lowest cost hedge. Given an expected spot rate of $1.76 = £1.00, however, the forward hedge appears to be the preferred alternative.

10.5 Transaction Exposure Management in Practice

In theory there is no difference between theory and practice. In practice there is.

—Yogi Berra.

There are as many different approaches to transaction exposure management as there are firms. A variety of surveys of corporate risk management practices in recent years in the United States, the United Kingdom, Finland, Australia, and Germany indicate no real consensus exists regarding the single best approach. The following is our attempt to summarize

EXHIBIT 10.6 Ganado's A/P Transaction Exposure Hedging Alternatives

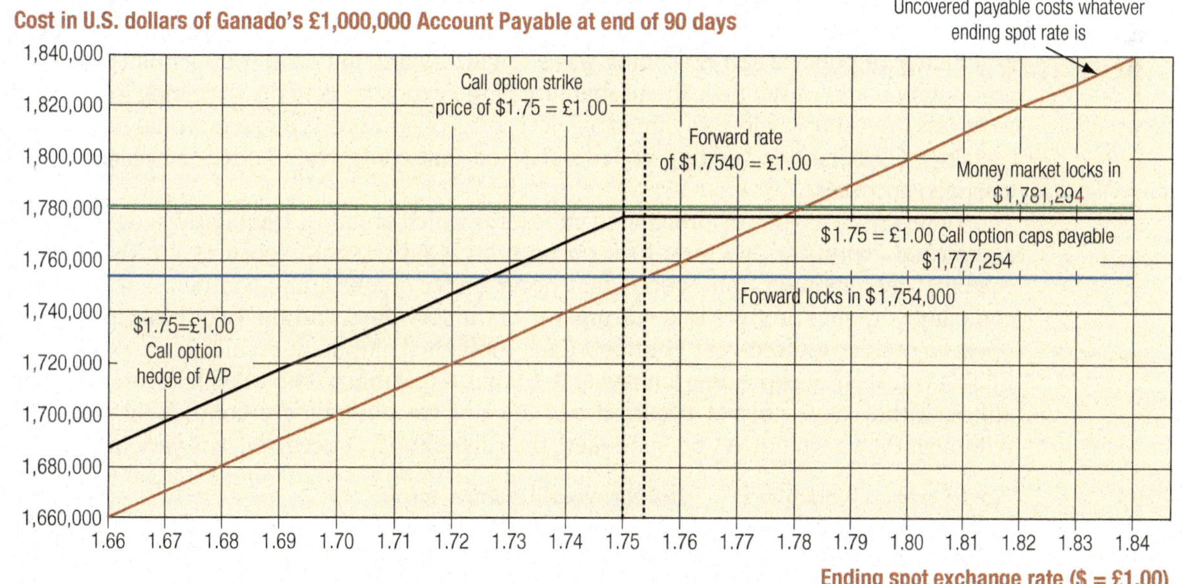

survey findings on which goals, which exposures, and which methods and hedges are most frequently used in corporate transaction exposure management.

Which Goals

The treasury function of most private firms, the group typically responsible for transaction exposure management, is usually considered a *cost center* or *shared service center*. Treasury is seldom a *profit center*; it is not expected to add profit to the firm's bottom line by taking on risk. This is not to say, however, that it is not expected to add value to the firm. Currency risk managers are expected to err on the conservative side when managing the firm's money. At the same time most multinationals do not expect their treasury groups to beat the market or predict exchange rate movements. What they often hope to do is some combination of smoothing financial results, protecting or insuring corporate cash flows (particularly against corporate budgets) and gaining increasing predictability over future cash flows.

The single most frequent corporate treasury goal in foreign exchange hedging is to minimize exchange rate-induced volatility in earnings. Investors in publicly traded firms prefer predictable and stable earnings and of course seek growth in earnings. If a hedging program can "smooth out the bumps" in earnings, then many firms attempt to do just that. This focus on earnings, however, is a function of ownership. Surveys of corporate hedging practices regularly show that publicly traded firms,[1] firms that must regularly report corporate earnings, hedge much more frequently and over longer future periods than private firms.[2]

If earnings smoothing or protection is the goal, that typically forms or determines a time horizon for exposure management. Many exposure programs will combine nearly mandatory hedging of existing exposures (most frequently within a quarter) but manage a large book of exposures and hedges which extend out at least 12 months into the future.

Which Transaction Exposures

Transaction exposure management in practice increasingly combines *existing exposures* (on balance sheet) with *anticipated exposures* (sometimes termed *forecasted transactions*, or those not yet booked but highly likely in occurrence). What is clearly changing is the willingness of more and more firms to actively hedge anticipated exposures.

In the past, many firms prohibited the hedging of any exposures not yet on balance sheet as a matter of policy. Their reasoning was straightforward: until the transaction exists on the accounting books of the firm, the probability of the exposure actually occurring is considered to be less than 100%, while any financial derivative purchased as a hedge would have a 100% certainty. Conservative hedging policies dictated that contractual hedges be placed only on existing exposures.

There are two types of anticipated exposures which are most frequently hedged by firms: *contractual exposures* and *intra-firm transactions*. Contractual exposures are those foreign currency denominated transactions that occur under a continuing contract. For example, a company may ship product to a customer every ninety days, and the two firms are currently operating under a three-year contract. Each individual shipment results in an explicit identifiable transaction exposure (a receivable to one, a payable to the other). Future shipments, although they have not yet occurred and are not yet booked, are contractual obligations. Although they have not yet been booked, their likelihood of occurrence is very high.

[1] See for example Wells Fargo's *2020 Risk Management Practices Survey*.

[2] Another important distinction between companies actively hedging foreign exchange exposures is company size; private firms surveyed are typically much smaller in total revenue than publicly traded firms surveyed. The larger the firm, the more likely the firm is to have risk managers in-house with the expertise and devoted resources to foreign exchange transaction exposure management.

GLOBAL FINANCE IN PRACTICE 10.3

Why Intra-Company Hedging Makes Sense

A common hedging debate is whether two units of the same company, when processing payments in different currencies among themselves, should hedge. The basic argument is that assuming one unit is transacting in its home currency and the other in a "foreign" currency, then hedging makes no sense because one unit's gain is the other unit's loss—net zero impact.

This argument is misleading on at least two different levels. First, hedging a foreign currency transaction exposure protects the firm against unpredictable events, like insurance. A unit making an obligated payment in foreign currency could see its cost of settlement increase dramatically if the foreign currency appreciated against the firm's own currency cash flows. This added cost would not be offset by the intra-company counterparty; the counterparty would not enjoy any foreign exchange gain as it has sold in its own currency. Secondly, multinational tax planning and management requires not only positioning of profitability but also predictability of profitability. Foreign exchange gains and losses can destroy cash flow forecasts and tax planning.

Intra-firm transactions, trade between units of the same company (either between subsidiaries or between a subsidiary and the parent company), also generate anticipated exposures. Although data is sparse in this sector, it has been estimated that more than 80% of all international commercial transactions off the West Coast of the U.S. is between units of the same companies, not between different companies—for example, shipments of components between Toyota of Japan and its U.S. subsidiary. The growth of global supply chains and integrated corporate planning has made these intra-company shipments a very predictable and stable activity, but one that inevitably results in the creation of a currency exposure for one or the other operating unit. Hedging of these exposures is for some firms now becoming routine. *Global Finance in Practice 10.3* examines intra-company hedging in more depth.

What Levels of Exposure Cover

Many multinationals follow rather rigid transaction exposure hedging policies which mandate proportional hedging (what proportion or percentage of the exposure is hedged) of collected exposures. This requires the identification of exposures by currency, maturity, and then selective hedging by cover percentage and hedging instrument.

For example, a U.S.-based business may accumulate all short and long positions against the Japanese yen arising over a one-week period. The net positions are then grouped by maturities (e.g., less than 30 days, 30 to 90 days, more than 90 days). The company will then, weekly, hedge this net exposure position by maturity given market conditions, expectations, and any company specific attitudes toward financial derivatives. These policies generally require contractual hedges on a percentage of existing transaction exposures (e.g., 90% coverage of all exposures of 30 days or less, a minimum of 50% cover for exposures of 30 to 90 days in maturity, and selective cover of exposures greater than 90 days). As the maturity of the exposures lengthens, the required forward-cover percentage decreases.

The choice of which financial derivative or structure used for hedging will then be determined by a combination of the market conditions, financial derivative alternatives, and general corporate comfort with the different hedging structures and derivatives. There are a few common sets of practices.

Which Hedging Instruments and Structures

Exhibit 10.7 summarizes the results of a recent hedging practice survey conducted by Wells Fargo covering both hedging practices and hedging instruments. Firms surveyed indicated that they hedged roughly 70% of all trade and finance-related exposures (on balance sheet) as well as 59% of forecasted exposures. Their hedging of their net investment and net income

EXHIBIT 10.7 **Transaction Exposure in Practice**

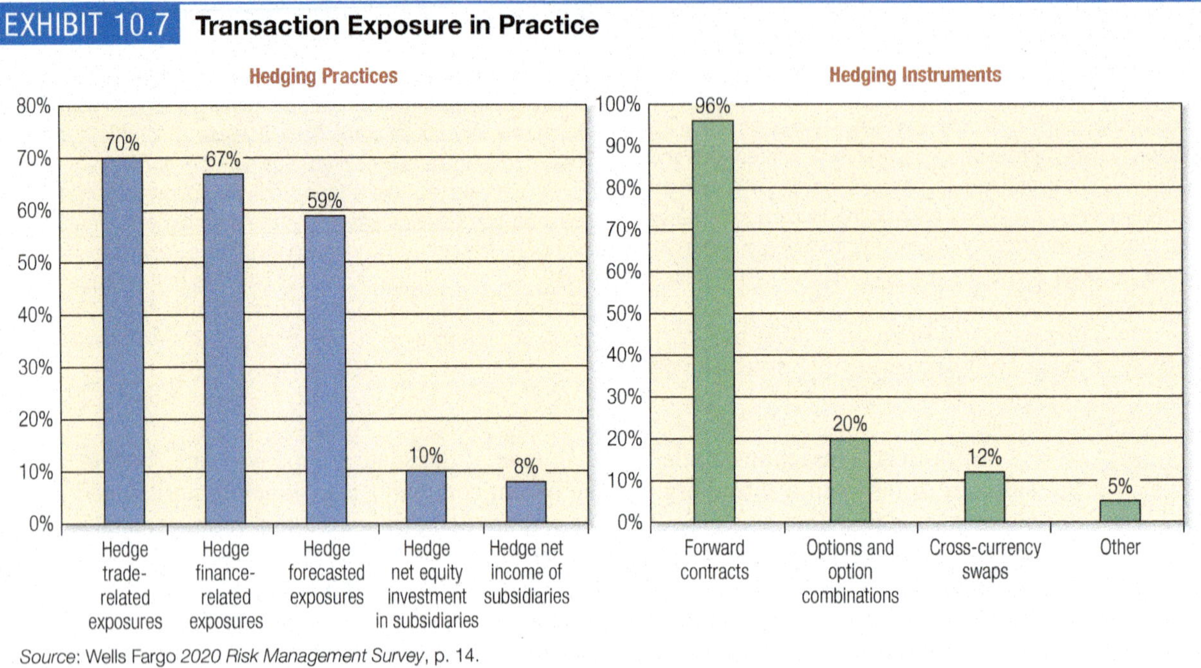

Source: Wells Fargo *2020 Risk Management Survey*, p. 14.

in their foreign subsidiaries (detailed in Chapter 11) was much lower at 10% and 8%, respectively. In terms of which hedging instruments were used, forward contracts were used by 96% of the respondents, with options and option combinations (detailed in the appendix to this chapter) used by only 20% of the firms. Cross-currency swaps were used by 12% of the firms.

As might be expected, transaction exposure management programs are generally divided along an "option line," those that use options and those that do not. There are a variety of reasons typically cited for not using purchased options—their cost, their complexity, and the fact that they only bound exposures. Even firms that are frequent users of currency options occasionally are confronted with unusual market conditions making them impractical. In 2009, in the midst of the global financial crisis, option premiums skyrocketed in expense as option volatilities rose to the mid-20s. Firms that do not use currency options rely almost exclusively on forward contracts and money market hedges.

With forward contracts being so widely used, a number of forward contract rules are often noted and used by companies hedging transaction exposures:

1. When market conditions indicate that the use of a forward contract will lock in a forward exchange gain (relative to the booked sale or payable), 100% required coverage is common.
2. When market conditions indicate that the forward premium (or discount) is quite small (1% to 2%), a high level of forward cover is required or encouraged.

In the end, forwards are used by nearly all firms all of the time.

Summary Points

- MNEs encounter three types of currency exposure: transaction exposure, translation exposure, and operating exposure.
- Transaction exposure measures gains or losses that arise from the settlement of financial obligations whose terms are stated in a foreign currency.
- Considerable theoretical debate exists as to whether firms should hedge currency risk. Theoretically, hedging reduces the variability of the cash flows to the firm. It does not increase the cash flows to the firm. In fact, the costs of hedging may potentially lower them.
- Transaction exposure can be managed by contractual techniques and certain operating strategies. Contractual hedging techniques include forward, futures, money market, and option hedges.
- The choice of which contractual hedge to use depends on the individual firm's currency risk tolerance and its expectation of the probable movement of exchange rates over the transaction exposure period.
- Risk management in practice requires a firm's treasury to identify its goals, choose and identify which currency exposures to manage, and then select what types of hedging instruments or structures to utilize.

MINI-CASE

GraysonChung's FX Exposure[3]

The business schools reward difficult complex behavior more than simple behavior, but simple behavior is more effective.

—Warren Buffett, Berkshire Hathaway.

GraysonChung (NASDAQ: GYCG) was a small publicly traded San Diego–based manufacturer of polishing and grinding equipment. The company's chemical mechanical polishing (CMP) systems were widely used in the semiconductor industry, where they were critically important for removing unevenness on wafer surfaces arising during production. Company sales for the most recent year were just over $700 million.

In July 2018's review of the most recently closed quarterly results (Exhibit A), GraysonChung's board wanted to review the company's foreign exchange management practices. The company's major analyst, Bill Kidd of Deutsche Securities, had raised questions about it. Management knew it was an issue; the questions had arisen before. GraysonChung's current practice—inherited from its founders—was not to hedge, believing that foreign exchange risk was part of the risk associated with international business.

At first glance, it was a bit difficult to see why the board was concerned. Earnings per share (EPS) had risen over the first two quarters of 2018 (making it five consecutive quarters of growing earnings), and that was despite a slight fall in sales in Q2. The second quarter had seen earnings rise to $13 million. But investors were spooked by the way the company's earnings had bounced with foreign exchange gains and losses.

Currency Exposure

The chairman of GraysonChung's board had opened the Q2 review meeting with the senior leadership team by asking what percentage of the company's sales were international. As illustrated in Exhibit B, that was 44%. The board member then used that number to argue that the company should be hedging all international sales because they represented a significant currency risk to the firm's earnings.

The task of revisiting the hedging question fell to GraysonChung's corporate treasurer, Josué Soto. Soto had explained to the board that although 44% of the company's sales were international, a large portion of those sales were invoiced in U.S. dollars, not foreign currency. Those sales might pose specific cross-border risks, but currency exchange was not one of them. Soto went on to explain that the firm's actual foreign exchange exposures arose from both sales and purchasing. In fact, a full 64% of the company's cost of sales were denominated in foreign currency.

Back in his office, Soto reviewed GraysonChung's foreign exchange gains and losses for Q1 of 2018 as seen in Exhibit C. GraysonChung was an international company, not a multinational company. It had no foreign subsidiaries, but it did source heavily from two suppliers in Mexico and sell to a single major Japanese customer. In FX jargon, the company was *long* Japanese yen (JPY)—it would be receiving yen in the future—and *short* Mexican pesos (MXN)—it would be paying pesos in the future.

In Q1 the company had booked three separate sales to its Japanese buyer, each for roughly ¥1.0 billion yen. Each sale (receivable) was booked by GraysonChung at the spot rate on that date per GAAP. GraysonChung's

[3] This case was prepared by Professor Michael H. Moffett for the purpose of classroom discussion only.

EXHIBIT A GraysonChung's Statement of Income

(millions)	2018 Q1		2018 Q2	
Revenues	$186.3	100.0%	$181.9	100.0%
Cost of sales (COS)	($129.9)	–69.7%	($128.5)	–70.6%
Gross profit	$56.4	30.3%	$53.4	29.4%
Marketing and selling	($13.5)	–7.2%	($14.5)	–8.0%
G&A expenses	($16.3)	–8.7%	($16.2)	–8.9%
Operating profit	$26.7	14.3%	$22.7	12.5%
Depreciation expense	($6.3)	–3.4%	($6.3)	–3.5%
Earnings before interest & tax	$20.4	10.9%	$16.4	9.0%
Foreign exchange gains (losses)	($0.9)	–0.5%	$4.6	2.5%
Interest expense	($2.6)	–1.4%	($3.5)	–1.9%
Earnings before taxes	$16.9	9.0%	$17.5	9.6%
Taxes (26%)	($4.4)	–2.4%	($4.6)	–2.5%
Net income	$12.5	6.7%	$13.0	7.1%
Shares outstanding	$40.0		$40.0	
Earnings per share (EPS)	$0.3		$0.3	

EXHIBIT B GraysonChung's International Transactions

	2018 Q1		2018 Q2	
Revenue				
Domestic sales	$105.02	56.4%	$101.8	56.0%
International sales	81.3	43.6%	80.1	44.0%
	$186.33	100.0%	$181.9	100.0%
International sales				
Denominated in USD	$53.63	66.0%	$52.7	65.8%
Denominated in JPY	27.7	34.0%	27.4	34.2%
	$81.31	100.0%	$80.1	100.0%
Cost of sales				
Denominated in USD	$48.00	37.0%	$46.2	36.0%
Denominated in MXN	81.9	63.0%	82.3	64.0%
	$129.90	100.0%	$128.5	100.0%

credit terms were 30 days, and its Japanese customer had been good as gold at paying on time. These sales totaled $27.68 million. Each of the receivables was settled in 30 days as scheduled, but at spot exchange rates that had—in two cases out of three—been in GraysonChung's favor. The net FX settlement resulted in a gain of $0.63 million.

On the payables side, GraysonChung had sourced from two different Mexican suppliers for many years, one in Monterey and one in San Luis Potosi. The San Luis Potosi required payment in U.S. dollars. The Monterey manufacturer, however, required invoicing and payment in Mexican pesos (MXN). This was unusual for U.S.–Mexican commercial transactions but required by the Monterey company. In Q1 GraysonChung had booked four purchases from the Monterey supplier for $20 million each. All were settled as required in 30 days. Those peso

EXHIBIT C GraysonChung's Foreign Exchange Gains & Losses, 2018 Quarter 1 (millions)

			Booked		Settled in 30 Days at Spot		
Transaction	**Receivable (JPY)**	**Date**	**Book Rate (JPY=USD1.00)**	**Booked (USD)**	**Settle Rate (JPY=USD1.00)**	**Settled (USD)**	**FX Gain (Loss)**
AR1	1,020	Jan 5	113.17	$9.01	107.66	$9.479.47	$0.46
AR2	1,004	Jan 19	108.75	$9.23	106.47	$9.43	$0.20
AR3	1,002	Feb 16	106.18	$9.44	106.50	$9.41	($0.03)
				$27.68		$28.31	$0.63
			Booked		**Settled in 30 Days at Spot**		
Transaction	**Payable (MXN)**	**Date**	**Book Rate (MXN=USD1.00)**	**Booked (USD)**	**Settle Rate (MXN=USD1.00)**	**Settled (USD)**	**FX Gain (Loss)**
AP1	390	Jan 5	19.488	$20.01	18.148	$21.49	($1.48)
AP2	388	Jan 2	18.811	$20.63	18.512	$20.96	($0.33)
AP3	382	Jan 16	18.690	$20.44	18.876	$20.24	$0.20
AP4	388	Jan 30	18.634	$20.82	18.708	$20.74	$0.08
				$81.90		$83.43	($1.53)
Net FX Gain (Loss)							($0.90)

EXHIBIT D GraysonChung's Foreign Exchange Gains and Losses, 2018 Quarter 2 (millions)

			Booked		Settled in 30 Days at Spot		
Transaction	**Receivable (JPY)**	**Date**	**Book Rate (JPY=USD1.00)**	**Booked (USD)**	**Settle Rate (JPY=USD1.00)**	**Settled (USD)**	**FX Gain (Loss)**
AR1	1,000	April 11	106.83	$9.36	109.34	$9.15	($0.21)
AR2	990	April 30	109.34	$9.05	110.30	$8.98	($0.08)
AR3	994	May 17	110.74	$8.98	110.75	$8.98	($0.00)
				$27.39		$27.10	($0.29)
			Booked		**Settled in 30 Days at Spot**		
Transaction	**Payable (MXN)**	**Date**	**Book Rate (MXN=USD1.00)**	**Booked (USD)**	**Settle Rate (MXN=USD1.00)**	**Settled (USD)**	**FX Gain (Loss)**
AP1	388	April 3	18.199	$21.32	19.083	$20.33	$0.99
AP2	386	April 17	17.983	$21.46	19.700	$19.59	$1.87
AP3	380	May 1	18.847	$20.16	19.963	$19.04	$1.13
AP4	382	May 15	19.748	$19.34	20.698	$18.46	$0.89
				$82.29		$77.42	$4.87
Net FX Gain (Loss)							$4.58

payables had resulted in an FX loss of $1.53 million. The net FX position for Q1 had been a net loss of $0.9 million ($0.63 − $1.53), the value shown in Exhibit A for foreign exchange gains/losses.

When Soto reviewed the FX results for Q2, however, he saw some very different—better—results. Q2 bookings and settlements are shown in Exhibit D. Although suffering FX losses of $0.29 million on its Japanese yen sales, the Mexican peso purchasing—due to a sliding peso—had generated a $4.87 million gain. The FX net gain in the second quarter of $4.58 million ($4.87 − $0.29) had added significantly to GraysonChung's EPS.

Although second quarter results had clearly been boosted by FX results, GraysonChung's analyst was concerned. In the company's second quarter earnings call, Bill Kidd had questioned management over the company's lack of currency hedging.

> *"Your investors signed up for CMP business-line risks, not currency risks. Don't you owe it to them to protect earnings against these unpredictable currency swings? Currency hedging is not that expensive. Have you considered it?"*

Exchange Rate Trends

The question had prompted GraysonChung's board to ask Soto to review company policy. Soto's first step was to take a look at how GraysonChung's two most influential foreign currencies had trended over time. When he looked at how the peso and yen had moved against the dollar over the past eight years, as seen in Exhibit E, he saw distinct trends. Both currencies had weakened versus the U.S. dollar. This was clearly good for GraysonChung's Mexican purchases; being short a weakening currency was always a good thing.

But Soto had to admit that was not the case with the Japanese yen. The yen was important to GraysonChung as it impacted a sizeable portion of revenues and therefore cash inflows. Clearly the yen had trended weaker against the dollar over the past decade. To add complexity, the yen had become quite "jumpy" in the past two years. Maybe it was indeed time to reconsider the company's currency hedging policy.

Hedging

Soto had joined GraysonChung's treasury in 2011, being promoted to treasurer in 2014. Long before he came on board, the company had suffered a series of what were referred to as the "derivative disasters." Soto's predecessor had utilized both forward exchange contracts and foreign currency options to manage currency exposures. But after a continuing series of quarters in which all hedges resulted in significant foreign exchange losses, the company's CFO had instructed corporate treasury to cease all hedging activities, arguing that its hedging appeared to be more like speculation than hedging—at least the way it was being done. That experience had resulted in a corporate policy of no foreign exchange hedging moving forward.

Soto knew if he were to renew foreign currency hedging activities, even on the initiative of the board, he would have to start slowly and very conservatively. That would likely translate into hedging only booked exposures (on-balance sheet receivables and payables, not anticipated transactions) and maybe only the Japanese yen. He might also have to consider hedging less than 100% of the

EXHIBIT E Japanese Yen and Mexican Peso Spot Rates, 2010–2018

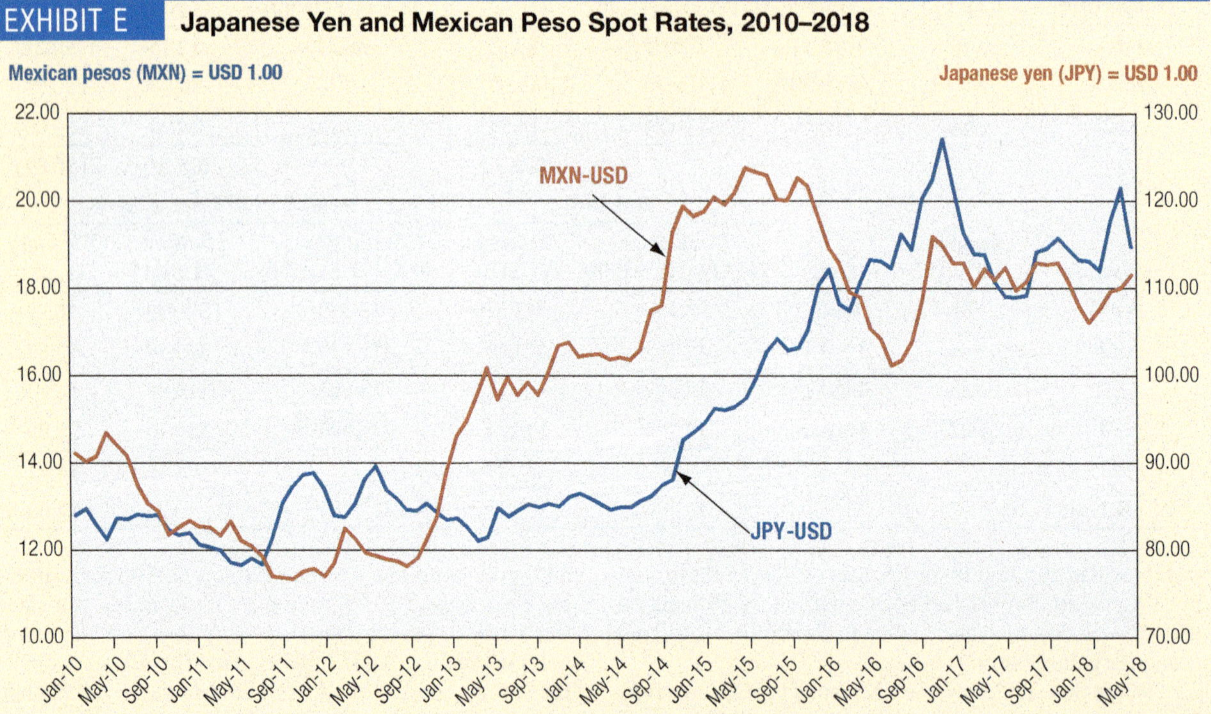

EXHIBIT F 30-Day Forward Rates and Ending Spot Rates on the JPY and MXN

Date	Spot (JPY=USD1.00)	LIBOR 1-month JPY	LIBOR 1-month USD	30-Day Forward (JPY=USD1.00)	30-Day Spot (JPY=USD1.00)
Jan 5	113.17	–0.02950%	1.5525%	**113.02**	107.66
Jan 19	108.75	–0.03830%	1.5630%	**108.61**	106.47
Feb 16	106.18	–0.04670%	1.5938%	**106.04**	106.50
Apr 11	106.83	–0.04750%	1.8956%	**106.66**	109.34
Apr 30	109.34	–0.04780%	1.9093%	**109.16**	110.30
May 17	110.74	–0.04380%	1.9478%	**110.56**	110.75

Date	Spot (MXN=USD1.00)	LIBOR 1-month MXN	LIBOR 1-month USD	30-Day Forward (MXN=USD1.00)	30-Day Spot (MXN=USD1.00)
Jan 2	19.488	8.000%	1.5618%	**19.592**	18.148
Jan 16	18.811	8.000%	1.5561%	**18.912**	18.512
Jan 30	18.690	8.000%	1.5747%	**18.790**	18.876
Feb 13	18.634	8.000%	1.5875%	**18.733**	18.708
April 3	18.199	8.000%	1.8775%	**18.292**	19.083
April 17	17.983	8.000%	1.8956%	**18.074**	19.700
May 1	18.847	8.000%	1.9088%	**18.943**	19.963
May 15	19.748	8.000%	1.9388%	**19.848**	20.698

individual exposures in case individual transactions were changed after booking.

Soto decided the next step was to do a little back-testing of hedging for GraysonChung's results. He quickly pulled together a set of exchange rate and interest rate quotes corresponding to GraysonChung's currency transactions (receivables and payables) for the first two quarters of 2018 in order to calculate some forward rates. (Soto did not want to contact any of his partner banks yet, as any calls requesting FX information would prompt a deluge of sales calls and efforts from their FX services departments.) He would calculate the 30-day forward rates corresponding to the foreign currency receivable and payable transactions over the first two quarters of 2018 using the usual forward rate formula (where the interest rates were the 30-day LIBOR rates per currency in annual terms).

He immediately ran into an anticipated problem. Getting Japanese yen LIBOR rates was not a problem. (The U.S. Federal Reserve Bank of St. Louis was a good online resource.) The yen LIBOR market was a very active and very liquid market, particularly given its ready use by private organizations and institutions in the yen-carry trade. The rates themselves were indeed quite bizarre, negative interest, as a result of the Japanese equivalent of "quantitative easing" being conducted by the Bank of Japan over recent three years.

Getting interbank interest rates on the Mexican peso was more challenging. The peso interbank market was administered by the Banco de Mexico and quite thin in terms of activity. Due to a recent resurgence of inflationary fears and a weakening peso, the central bank had driven interest rates up. After some searching Soto found a few quotes of 8.000% per annum for both overnight and one-month interbank rates in pesos, rates that were fixed by the central bank. He would make do with that for now, knowing that if he called a few banks for forward rates on the peso he would get some pretty ugly numbers. He also collected the ending spot rates corresponding to the 30-day settlements. Soto's final data table for calculating forward rates is shown in Exhibit F.[4]

Soto leaned back in his chair and stared at the ceiling fan. But what about currency options? Wouldn't they at least give the company an upside potential, if exchange rates occasionally moved in their favor? Again, given that

[4] One alternative available to Soto which he preferred to ignore was the trading in Mexican peso futures on the Chicago Mercantile Exchange. Although futures were extremely liquid, GraysonChung, like most corporates, had no interest in using futures for hedging given the daily margin calls and marked-to-market valuation fluctuations that would result.

EXHIBIT G Japanese Yen Put Option Pricing

Date	Spot (JPY= USD1.00)	LIBOR 1-month JPY	LIBOR 1-month USD	30-Day Forward (JPY= USD1.00)	30-Day Volatility (JPY-USD options)	Put on JPY Strike Rate (JPY= USD1.00)	Put Option Premium (US$ per JPY)	Put Option Notional JPY (millions)	Cost of Put Option
Jan 5	113.17	–0.02950%	1.5525%	113.02	7.650%	113.02	____	1,020	____
Jan 19	108.75	–0.03830%	1.5630%	108.61	7.810%	108.61	____	1,004	____
Feb 16	106.18	–0.04670%	1.5938%	106.04	9.413%	106.04	____	1,002	____
Apr 11	106.83	–0.04750%	1.8956%	106.66	7.545%	106.66	____	1,000	____
Apr 30	109.34	–0.04780%	1.9093%	109.16	7.250%	109.16	____	990	____
May 17	110.74	–0.04380%	1.9478%	110.56	7.298%	110.56	____	994	____

the company would not likely accept a new active currency hedging program and the wide use of currency options (at least initially, he might consider using options only on cash inflows, the Japanese yen receivables). The yen had been moving in less of a trend against the dollar, so maybe there was an opportunity to do better than forwards with the selective use of put options on yen receivables.

Soto's next task was to collect put option prices on the yen for the backdated period as well, Q1 and Q2 of 2018. He had a lot of what he already needed—spot rates, interest rates on the two currencies, calculated forward rates—but he still would need option volatilities. He checked his data terminal and was able to pull implied volatilities for 30-day yen options for the first part of the year. After some deliberation, Soto concluded that he would be as conservative as possible and only consider forward-at-the-money strike rates for his pricing and back-testing. His put option worksheet is shown in Exhibit G.

Soto had some work to do. He would first look at how the company's financial results would have looked if it had used forwards to cover all exposures in Q1 and Q2 of 2018. He wanted to look at just hedging the receivables—the yen first and then both the foreign currency exposures second. The option analysis would be a bit more involved. He had to first price the puts, estimate how much the company would be spending in option premiums, and then perform the backdated analysis to see if the options would have saved the company some money while providing exposure protection.

MINI-CASE QUESTIONS

1. What would GraysonChung's financial results have been in the first two quarters of 2018 if it had fully covered with forward contracts all Japanese yen exposures?
2. What would GraysonChung's financial results have been in the first two quarters of 2018 if it had fully covered with forward contracts all Japanese yen and Mexican peso exposures?
3. Complete the Japanese yen put option pricing worksheet (Exhibit G). What would GraysonChung's financial results have been in the first two quarters of 2018 if it had fully covered Japanese yen receivables with put options on the yen and covered all Mexican peso payables with forwards?
4. If you were Josué Soto, on the basis of your back-testing hedging analysis, what would you recommend to the company's CFO and Board?

Questions

10.1 Foreign Exchange Exposure. Define the three types of foreign exchange exposure.

10.2 Currency Exposure and Contracting. Which of the three currency exposures relate to cash flows already contracted for, and which of the exposures do not?

10.3 Currency Risk. Define currency risk.

10.4 Hedging. What is a hedge? How does that differ from speculation?

10.5 Value of the Firm. What—according to financial theory—is the value of a firm?

10.6 Cash Flow Variability. How does currency hedging theoretically change the expected cash flows of the firm?

10.7 Arguments for Currency Hedging. Describe four arguments in favor of a firm pursuing an active currency risk management program.

10.8 Arguments against Currency Hedging. Describe six arguments against a firm pursuing an active currency risk management program.

10.9 Transaction Exposure. What are the four main types of transactions from which transaction exposure arises?

10.10 Life Span of a Transaction Exposure. Diagram the life span of an exposure arising from selling a product on open account. On the diagram define and show quotation, backlog, and billing exposures.

10.11 Unperformed Contracts. Which contract is more likely not to be performed, a payment due from a customer in foreign currency (a currency exposure) or a forward contract with a bank to exchange the foreign currency for the firm's domestic currency at a contracted rate (the currency hedge)?

10.12 Cash Balances. Why do foreign currency cash balances not cause transaction exposure?

10.13 Contractual Currency Hedges. What are the four main contractual instruments used to hedge transaction exposure?

10.14 Money Market Hedges. How does a money market hedge differ for an account receivable versus that of an account payable? Is it really a meaningful difference?

10.15 Balance Sheet Hedging. What is the difference between a balance sheet hedge, a financing hedge, and a money market hedge?

10.16 Forward versus Money Market Hedging. Theoretically, shouldn't forward contract hedges and money market hedges have the same identical outcome? Don't they both use the same three specific inputs—the initial spot rate, the domestic cost of funds, and the foreign cost of funds?

10.17 Foreign Currency Option Premia. Why do many firms object to paying for foreign currency option hedges? Do firms pay for forward contract hedges? How do forwards and options differ if at all?

10.18 Decision Criteria. Ultimately, a treasurer must choose among alternative strategies to manage transaction exposure. Explain the two main decision criteria that must be used.

10.19 Risk Management Hedging Practices. According to surveys of corporate practices, which currency exposures do most firms regularly hedge?

10.20 Hedging Booked Exposures. Why do many firms only allow hedging of existing exposures and not allow the hedging of anticipated exposures?

Problems

10.1 Gray Wolf. Gray Wolf, Ltd., a Canadian manufacturer of raincoats, does not selectively hedge its transaction exposure. Instead, if the date of the transaction is known with certainty, all foreign currency-denominated cash flows must utilize the following mandatory forward cover formula:

Mandatory Forward Cover	**0-90 days**	**91-180 days**	**180 days**
Paying the points forward	75%	60%	50%
Receiving the points forward	100%	90%	50%

Gray Wolf expects to receive multiple payments in Danish kroner over the next year. DKr3,000,000 is due in 90 days, DKr2,000,000 is due in 180 days, and DKr1,000,000 is due in one year. Using the following spot and forward exchange rates, what would be the amount of forward cover required by company policy for each period?

	Dkr = C$1.00
Spot rate	4.70
3-month forward rate	4.71
6-month forward rate	4.72
12-month forward rate	4.74

10.2 Kaanapali Travel. Kaanapali Travel, a Honolulu, Hawaii–based 100% privately owned travel company, has signed an agreement to acquire a 50% ownership share of Taichung Travel, a Taiwan-based privately owned travel agency specializing in servicing inbound customers from the U.S. and Canada. The acquisition price is 7 million Taiwan dollars (TWD7,000,000) payable in cash in three months. Thomas Carson, Kaanapali's owner, believes the Taiwan dollar will either remain stable or decline slightly over the next three months. At the present spot rate of TWD33.40 = USD1.00, the amount of cash required is only $200,000, but even this relatively modest amount will need to be borrowed personally by Thomas Carson. Taiwanese interest-bearing deposits by non-residents are regulated by the government, and are currently set at 1.5% per year. He has a credit line with Bank of Hawaii for USD200,000 with a current borrowing interest rate of 8% per year. He does not believe that he can calculate a credible weighted average cost of capital since he has no stock outstanding and his competitors are all also privately held. Since the acquisition would use up all his available credit, he wonders if he should hedge this transaction exposure. He has the following quotes from the Bank of Hawaii:

Spot rate (TWD = USD1.00)	33.40
3-month forward rate (TWD = USD1.00)	32.40
3-month Taiwan dollar deposit rate	1.500%
3-month dollar borrowing rate	6.500%
3-month call option on TWD	not available

Analyze the costs and risks of each alternative, and then make a recommendation as to which alternative Thomas Carson should choose.

10.3 **Elan Pharmaceuticals.** Elan Pharmaceuticals, a U.S.-based multinational pharmaceutical company, is evaluating an export sale of its cholesterol-reduction drug with a prospective Indonesian distributor. The purchase would be for 1,650 million Indonesian rupiah (Rp), which at the current spot exchange rate of Rp9,450 = $1.00, translates into nearly $175,000. Although not a big sale by company standards, company policy dictates that sales must be settled for at least a minimum gross margin, in this case, a cash settlement of $168,000. The current 90-day forward rate is Rp9,950 = $1.00. Although this rate appeared unattractive, Elan had to contact several major banks before even finding a forward quote on the rupiah. The consensus of currency forecasters at the moment, however, is that the rupiah will hold relatively steady, possibly rising to Rp9,400 = $1.00 over the coming 90 to 120 days. Analyze the prospective sale and make a hedging recommendation.

10.4 **Embraer of Brazil.** Embraer of Brazil is one of the two leading global manufacturers of regional jets. (Bombardier of Canada is the other.) Regional jets are smaller than the traditional civilian airliners produced by Airbus and Boeing, seating between 50 and 100 people on average. Embraer has concluded an agreement with a regional U.S. airline to produce and deliver four aircraft one year from now for USD80 million.

Although Embraer will be paid in U.S. dollars, it also possesses a currency exposure of inputs—it must pay foreign suppliers USD20 million for inputs one year from now (but they will be delivering the subcomponents throughout the year). The current spot rate on the Brazilian real (BRL) is BRL1.8240 = USD1.00, but it has been steadily appreciating against the U.S. dollar over the past three years. Forward contracts are difficult to acquire and are considered expensive. Citibank Brasil has not explicitly provided Embraer a forward rate quote but has stated that it will probably be pricing a forward off the current 4.00% U.S. dollar eurocurrency rate and the 10.50% Brazilian government bond rate. Advise Embraer on its currency exposure.

10.5 **BioTron Medical, Inc.** Brent Bush, CFO of medical device distributor BioTron Medical, Inc., was approached by a Japanese customer, Numata, with a proposal to pay cash (in yen) for its typical orders of ¥12,500,000 every other month if it were given a 4.5% discount. Numata's current terms are 30 days with no discounts. Using the following quotes and estimated cost of capital for Numata, Bush will compare the proposal with covering yen payments with forward contracts. Should Brent Bush accept Numata's proposal?

Spot rate:	¥111.40 = $1.00
30-day forward rate:	¥111.00 = $1.00
90-day forward rate:	¥110.40 = $1.00
180-day forward rate:	¥109.20 = $1.00
Numata's WACC	8.850%
BioTron's WACC	9.200%

10.6 **Najafi Group.** Najafi Group, U.S.-based manufacturer of industrial equipment, just purchased a Korean company that produces plastic nuts and bolts for heavy equipment. The purchase price was 7,500 million Korean won (KRW). KRW1,000 million has already been paid, and the remaining KRW6,500 million is due in six months. The current spot rate is KRW1,110 = USD$1.00, and the 6-month forward rate is KRW1,175 = USD1.00. The 6-month Korean won interest rate is 16% per annum, the 6-month U.S. dollar rate is 4% per annum. Najafi can invest at these interest rates, or borrow at 2% per annum above those rates. A 6-month call option on won with a KRW1,200 = USD1.00 strike rate has a 3.0% premium, while the 6-month put option at the same strike rate has a 2.4% premium. Najafi's weighted average cost of capital is 10%. Compare alternate ways that Najafi might deal with its foreign exchange exposure. What do you recommend, and why?

10.7 **Siam Cement.** Siam Cement, the Bangkok-based cement manufacturer, suffered enormous losses with the coming of the Asian crisis in 1997. The company had been pursuing a very aggressive growth strategy in the mid-1990s, taking on massive quantities of foreign-currency-denominated debt (primarily U.S. dollars). When the Thai baht (B) was devalued from its pegged rate of THB25.0 = USD1.00 in July 1997, Siam's interest payments alone were over USD900 million on its outstanding dollar debt (with an average interest rate of 8.40%

on its U.S. dollar debt at that time). Assuming Siam Cement took out USD50 million in debt in June 1997 at 8.40% interest and had to repay it in one year when the spot exchange rate had stabilized at THB42.0 = USD1.00, what was the foreign exchange loss incurred on the transaction?

10.8 P&G India. Procter and Gamble's affiliate in India, P&G India, procures much of its toiletries product line from a Japanese company. Because of the shortage of working capital in India, payment terms by Indian importers are typically 180 days or longer. P&G India wishes to hedge an 8.5 million Japanese yen (JPY) payable. Although options are not available on the Indian rupee (INR), forward rates are available against the yen. Additionally, a common practice in India is for companies like P&G India to work with a currency agent who will, in this case, lock in the current spot exchange rate in exchange for a 4.85% fee. Using the following exchange rate and interest rate data, recommend a hedging strategy. (All rates of interest are stated on a per annum basis.)

Spot rate	JPY120.60 = USD1.00
Spot rate	INR47.75 = USD1.00
180-day forward rate	JPY2.400 = INR1.00
Expected spot in 180 days	JPY2.600 = INR1.00
180-day Indian rupee investing rate	8.000%
180-day Japanese yen investing rate	1.500%
Currency agent's exchange rate	4.850%
P&G India's cost of capital	12.000%

10.9 Vatten. Vatten is a U.S.-based company that manufactures, sells, and installs water purification equipment. On April 11, the company sold a system to the City of Nagasaki, Japan, for installation in Nagasaki's famous Glover Gardens (where Puccini's Madame Butterfly waited for the return of Lt. Pinkerton). The sale was priced in yen at ¥20,000,000, with payment due in three months.

Spot exchange rate:	¥118.255 = $1.00 (closing mid-rates)
1-month forward rate:	¥117.760 = $1.00, a 5.04% per annum premium
3-month forward:	¥116.830 = $1.00, a 4.88% per annum premium
1-year forward:	¥112.450 = $1.00, a 5.16% per annum premium

Money Rates	United States	Japan	Differential
One month	4.8750%	0.09375%	4.78125%
Three months	4.9375%	0.09375%	4.84375%
Twelve months	5.1875%	0.31250%	4.87500%

Note that the interest rate differentials vary slightly from the forward discounts on the yen because of time differences for the quotes. The spot ¥118.255 = $1.00, for example, is a mid-point range. On April 11, the spot yen traded in London from ¥118.30 to ¥117.550. Vatten's Japanese competitors are currently borrowing yen from Japanese banks at a spread of two percentage points above the Japanese money rate. Vatten's weighted average cost of capital is 16%, and the company wishes to protect the dollar value of this receivable.

Three-month options are available from Kyushu Bank: call option on ¥20,000,000 at exercise price of ¥118.00 = $1.00: a 1% premium or a put option on ¥20,000,000, at exercise price of ¥118.00 = $1.00: a 3% premium.

a. What are the costs and benefits of alternative hedges? Which would you recommend, and why?

b. What is the break-even reinvestment rate when comparing forward and money market alternatives?

10.10 Mattel Toys. Mattel is a U.S.-based company whose sales are roughly two-thirds in dollars (Asia and the Americas) and one-third in euros (Europe). In September, Mattel delivers a large shipment of toys (primarily Barbies and Hot Wheels) to a major distributor in Antwerp. The receivable, €30 million, is due in 90 days, standard terms for the toy industry in Europe. Mattel's treasury team has collected the following currency and market quotes. The company's foreign exchange advisors believe the euro will be at about $1.4200 = €1.00 in 90 days. Mattel's management does not use currency options in currency risk management activities. Advise Mattel on which hedging alternative is probably preferable.

Current spot rate ($ = €1.00)	$1.4158
Credit Suisse 90-day forward rate ($ = €1.00)	$1.4172
Barclays 90-day forward rate ($ = €1.00)	$1.4195
Mattel Toys WACC ($)	9.600%
90-day eurodollar interest rate	4.000%
90-day euro interest rate	3.885%
90-day eurodollar borrowing rate	5.000%
90-day euro borrowing rate	5.000%

10.11 Chronos Time Pieces. Chronos Time Pieces of Boston exports watches to many countries, selling in local currencies to stores and distributors. Chronos prides itself on being financially conservative. At least 70% of each individual transaction exposure is hedged, mostly in the forward market, but occasionally with options. Chronos' foreign exchange policy is such that the 70% hedge may be increased up to a 120% hedge if devaluation or depreciation appears imminent. Chronos has just shipped to its major North American distributor. It has issued a 90-day invoice to its buyer for €1,560,000. The current spot rate is $1.2224 = €1.00, and the 90-day forward rate is $1.2270 = €1.00. Chronos's treasurer, Manny Hernandez, has a very good track record in predicting exchange rate movements. He currently believes the euro will weaken against the dollar in the coming 90 to 120 days, possibly to around $1.16 = €1.00.

a. Evaluate the hedging alternatives for Chronos if Manny is right (Case 1: $1.16 = €1.00) and if Manny is wrong (Case 2: $1.26 = €1.00). What do you recommend?

b. What does it mean to hedge 120% of a transaction exposure?

c. What would be considered the most conservative transaction exposure management policy by a firm? How does Chronos compare?

10.12 Farah Jeans. Farah Jeans of San Antonio, Texas, is completing a new assembly plant near Guatemala City. A final construction payment of Q8,400,000 is due in six months. ("Q" is the symbol for Guatemalan quetzals.) Farah uses 20% per annum as its weighted average cost of capital. Today's foreign exchange and interest rate quotations are as follows:

Construction payment due in 6 months (A/P, quetzals)	8,400,000
Present spot rate (quetzals = $1.00)	7.0000
6-month forward rate (quetzals = $1.00)	7.1000
Guatemalan 6-month interest rate (per annum)	14.000%
U.S. dollar 6-month interest rate (per annum)	6.000%
Farah's weighted average cost of capital (WACC)	20.000%

Farah's treasury manager, concerned about the Guatemalan economy, wonders if Farah should be hedging its foreign exchange risk. The manager's own forecast is as follows:

Expected spot rate in six months (quetzals = $1.00):	
Highest expected rate (reflecting a significant devaluation)	8.0000
Expected rate	7.3000
Lowest expected rate (reflecting a strengthening of the quetzal)	6.4000

What realistic alternatives are available to Farah for making payments? Which method would you select and why?

10.13 RadioEdison Manufacturing. Carla Surz is the director of finance for RadioEdison Manufacturing, a U.S.-based manufacturer of handheld computer systems for inventory management. RadioEdison's system combines a low-cost active radio frequency identification (RFID) tag that is attached to inventory items (the tag emits an extremely low-grade radio frequency) with custom-designed hardware and software that tracks the low-grade emissions for inventory control. RadioEdison has completed the sale of an inventory management system to a British firm, Pegg Metropolitan (UK), for a total payment of £1,000,000. The exchange rates that follow were available to Burton on the dates shown, corresponding to the events of this specific export sale. Assume each month is 30 days.

a. What will be the amount of foreign exchange gain (loss) upon settlement?

b. If Carla hedges the exposure with a forward contract, what will be the net foreign exchange gain (loss) on settlement?

Problem 10.13 RadioEdison Manufacturing

Date	Event	Spot Rate ($ = £1.00)	Forward Rate ($ = £1.00)	Days Forward
February 1	Price quotation for Pegg	1.7850	1.7771	210
March 1	Contract signed for sale	1.7465	1.7381	180
	Contract amount, pounds	£1,000,000		
June 1	Product shipped to Pegg	1.7689	1.7602	90
August 1	Product received by Pegg	1.7840	1.7811	30
September 1	Pegg makes payment	1.7290	–	–

10.14 Micca Metals, Inc. Micca Metals, Inc. is a specialty materials and metals company located in Detroit, Michigan. The company specializes in specific precious metals and materials that are used in a variety of pigment applications in many industries including cosmetics, appliances, and a variety of high tinsel metal fabricating equipment. Micca just purchased a shipment of phosphates from Morocco for 6,000,000 dirhams, payable in six months.

Six-month call options on 6,000,000 dirhams at an exercise price of 10.00 dirhams per dollar are available from Bank Al-Maghrub at a premium of 2%. Six-month put options on 6,000,000 dirhams at an exercise price of 10.00 dirhams per dollar are available at a premium of 3%. Compare and contrast alternative ways that Micca might hedge its foreign exchange transaction exposure. What is your recommendation?

Assumption	**Value**
Shipment of phosphates from Morocco, Moroccan dirhams	6,000,000
Micca's cost of capital (WACC)	14.000%
Spot exchange rate, dirhams = $1.00	10.00
S-month forward rate, dirhams = $1.00	10.40

10.15 Maria Gonzalez and Ganado. Ganado—the U.S.-based company discussed in this chapter—has concluded another large sale of telecommunications equipment to Regency (UK). Total payment of £3,000,000 is due in 90 days. Maria Gonzalez has also learned that Ganado will only be able to borrow in the UK at 14% per annum (due to credit concerns of the British banks). Given the following exchange rates and interest rates, what transaction exposure hedge is now in Ganado's best interest?

Assumption	**Value**
90-day A/R in pounds	£3,000,000.00
Spot rate, US$ per pound ($ = £1.00)	$1.7620
90-day forward rate, US$ per pound ($ = £1.00)	$1.7550
3-month U.S. dollar investment rate	6.000%
3-month U.S. dollar borrowing rate	8.000%
3-month U.K. investment interest rate	8.000%
3-month U.K. borrowing interest rate	14.000%
Ganado's WACC	12.000%
Expected spot rate in 90 days ($/£)	$1.7850

Put options on the British pound:	**Strike rate ($ = £1.00)**	**Premium**
	$1.75	1.500%
	$1.71	1.000%

10.16 Larkin Hydraulics. On May 1, Larkin Hydraulics, a wholly owned subsidiary of Caterpillar (U.S.), sold a 12-megawatt compression turbine to Rebecke-Terwilleger Company of the Netherlands for €4,000,000, payable as €2,000,000 on August 1 and €2,000,000 on November 1. Larkin derived its price quote of €4,000,000 on April 1 by dividing its normal U.S. dollar sales price of $4.320,000 by the then current spot rate of $1.0800 = €1.00.

By the time the order was received and booked on May 1, the euro had strengthened to $1.1000 = €1.00, so the sale was in fact worth €4,000,000 × $1.1000 = $4,400,000. Larkin had already gained an extra $80,000 from favorable exchange rate movements. Nevertheless, Larkin's director of finance now wondered if the firm should hedge against a reversal of the recent trend of the euro. Four approaches were possible:

1. Hedge in the forward market: The 3-month forward exchange quote was $1.1060 = €1.00 and the 6-month forward quote was $1.1130 = €1.00.
2. Hedge in the money market: Larkin could borrow euros from the Frankfurt branch of its U.S. bank at 8.00% per annum.
3. Hedge with foreign currency options: August put options were available at strike price of $1.1000 = €1.00 for a premium of 2.0% per contract, and November put options were available at $1.1000 = €1.00 for a premium of 1.2%. August call options at $1.1000 = €1.00 could be purchased for a premium of 3.0%, and November call options at $1.1000 = €1.00 were available at a 2.6% premium.
4. Do nothing: Larkin could wait until the sales proceeds were received in August and November, hope the recent strengthening of the euro would continue, and sell the euros received for dollars in the spot market.

Larkin estimates the cost of equity capital to be 12% per annum. As a small firm, Larkin Hydraulics is unable to raise funds with long-term debt. U.S. T-bills yield 3.6% per annum. What should Larkin do?

10.17 Navarro. Navarro was a U.S.-based multinational company which manufactured and distributed specialty materials for sound-proofing construction. It had recently established a new European subsidiary in Barcelona, Spain, and was now in the process of establishing operating rules for transactions between the U.S. parent company and the Barcelona subsidiary. Ignacio Lopez was International Treasurer for

Navarro and was leading the effort at establishing commercial policies for the new subsidiary.

Navarro's first shipment of product to Spain was upcoming. The first shipment would carry an intra-company invoice amount of $500,000. The company was now trying to decide whether to invoice the Spanish subsidiary in U.S. dollars or European euros and, in turn, whether the resulting transaction exposure should be hedged. Ignacio's idea was to take a recent historical period of exchange rate quotes and movements and simulate the invoicing and hedging alternatives available to Navarro to try and characterize the choices.

Ignacio looked at the 90-day period which had ended the previous Friday. (Standard intra-company payment terms for transcontinental transactions was 90 days.) The quarter had opened with a spot rate of $1.0640 = €1.00, with the 90-day forward rate quoted at $1.0615 = €1.00 the same day. The quarter had closed with a spot rate of $1.0980 = €1.00.

a. Which unit would have suffered the gain (loss) on currency exchange if intra-company sales were invoiced in U.S. dollars ($), assuming both completely unhedged and fully hedged?

b. Which unit would have suffered the gain (loss) on currency exchange if intra-company sales were invoiced in euros (€), assuming both completely unhedged and fully hedged?

10.18 KAL and Boeing. Korean Airlines (KAL) has just signed a contract with Boeing to purchase two new 747-400s for a total of USD60 million, with payment in two equal tranches. The first tranche of USD30,000,000 has just been paid. The next USD30,000,000 is due three months from today. KAL currently has excess cash of 25 billion Korean won (KRW) in a Seoul bank, and it is from these funds that KAL plans to make its next payment.

The current spot rate is won KRW800 = USD1.00, and permission has been obtained for a forward rate (90 days), won KRW794 = USD1.00. The 90-day eurodollar interest rate is 6.000%, while the 90-day Korean won deposit rate (there is no euro–won rate) is 5.000%. KAL can borrow in Korea at 6.250% and can probably borrow in the U.S. dollar market at 9.375%.

A three-month call option in dollars in the over-the-counter market for a strike price of won KRW790 = USD1.00 sells at a premium of 2.9%, payable at the time the option is purchased. A 90-day put option on dollars, also at a strike price of won KRW790, sells at a premium of 1.9% (assuming a 12% volatility). KAL's foreign exchange advisory service forecasts the spot rate in three months to be KRW792 = USD1.00.

How should KAL plan to make the payment to Boeing if KAL's goal is to maximize the amount of won cash left in the bank at the end of the three month period? Make a recommendation and defend it.

CHAPTER 10 APPENDIX A

Complex Option Hedges

Ganado, the same U.S.-based firm used throughout the chapter, still possesses a long £1 million exposure—an account receivable—to be settled in 90 days. Exhibit 10A.1 summarizes the assumptions, exposure, and traditional option alternatives to be used throughout this appendix. The firm believes that the exchange rate will move in its favor over the 90-day period (the British pound will appreciate versus the U.S. dollar). Despite having this directional view or currency expectation, the firm wishes downside protection in the event the pound were to depreciate instead.

The exposure management zones that are of most interest to the firm are the two opposing triangles formed by the uncovered and forward rate profiles. The firm would like to retain all potential area in the upper-right triangle but minimize its own potential exposure to the bottom-left triangle. The put option's "kinked profile" is consistent with what the firm wishes if it believes the pound will appreciate.

The firm could consider any number of different put option strike prices, depending on what minimum assured value—degree of self-insurance—the firm is willing to accept. Exhibit 10A.1 illustrates two different put option alternatives: a forward-ATM put of strike price $1.4700 = £1.00 and a forward-OTM put with strike price $1.4400 = £1.00. Because foreign

EXHIBIT 10A.1 Ganado's A/R Exposure and Put Option Hedges

		Put Option	Strike Rate	Premium
Spot rate	$1.4790 = £1			
90-day forward rate	$1.4700 = £1			
90-day euro-$ interest rate	3.250%	Forward ATM	$1.47	$0.0318 per £
90-day euro-£ interest rate	5.720%	Out-of-the-money put	$1.44	$0.0188 per £
90-day $/£ volatility	11.000%			

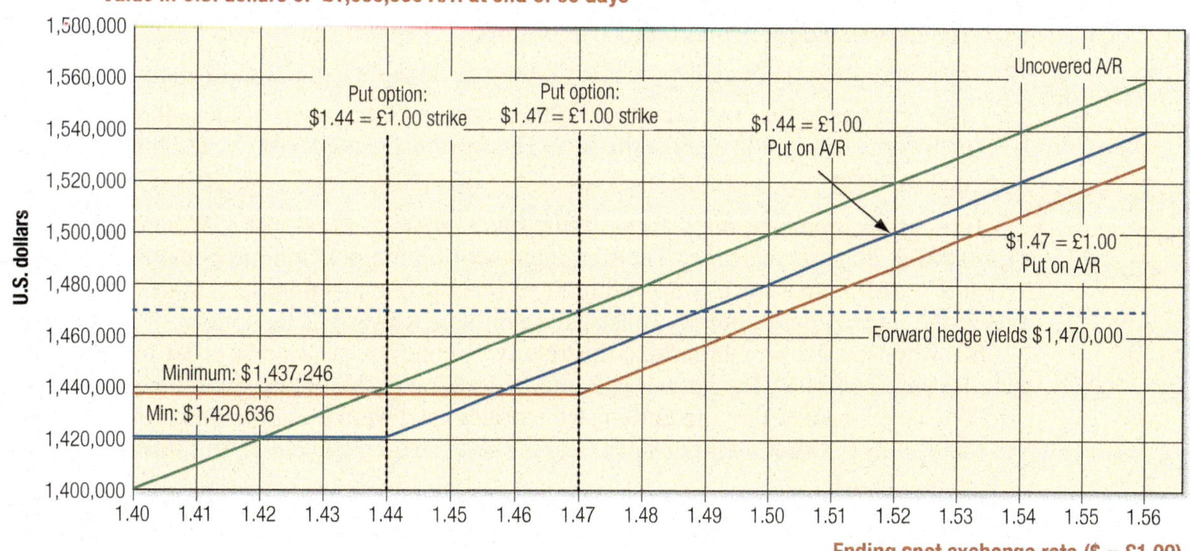

currency options are actually priced about the forward rate (see Chapter 8), not the spot rate, the correct specification of whether an option, put or call, is ITM, ATM, or OTM is in reference to the same maturity forward rate. The forward-OTM put provides protection at lower cost but also at a lower level of protection.

The Synthetic Forward

At a forward rate of $1.4700 = £1.00, the proceeds of the forward contract in 90 days will yield $1,470,000. A second alternative for the firm would be to construct a *synthetic forward* using options. The synthetic forward requires the firm to combine two options, of equal size and maturity, both with strike rates at the forward rate:

1. Buy a put option on £ bought at a strike price of $1.4700 = £1.00, paying a premium of $0.0318 per £
2. Sell a call option on £ at a strike price of $1.4700 = £1.00, earning a premium of $0.0318 per £

The purchase of the put option requires a premium payment, and the sale of the call option earns the firm a premium payment. If both options are struck at the forward rate (*forward-ATM*), the premiums should be identical and the net premium payment have a value of zero.

Exhibit 10A.2 illustrates the uncovered position, the basic forward rate hedge, and the individual profiles of the put and call options for the possible construction of a synthetic forward. The outcome of the combined position is easily confirmed by simply tracing what would happen at all exchange rates to the left of $1.4700 = £1.00 and what would happen to the right of $1.4700.

At all exchange rates to the left of $1.4700 = £1.00:

1. The firm would receive £1,000,000 in 90 days.
2. The call option on pounds sold by the firm would expire out-of-the-money.
3. The firm would exercise the put option on pounds to sell the pounds received at $1.4700.

At all exchange rates to the right of $1.4700 = £1.00:

1. The firm would receive £1,000,000 in 90 days.
2. The put option on pounds purchased by the firm would expire out-of-the-money.
3. The firm would turn over the £1,000,000 received to the buyer of the call, who now exercises the call option against the firm. The firm receives $1.4700 = £1.00 from the call option buyer.

Thus, at all exchange rates above or below $1.4700 = £1.00, the U.S.-based firm nets $1,470,000 in domestic currency. The combined spot-option position has behaved identically to that of a forward contract. A firm with the exact opposite position, a £1,000,000 payable 90 days in the future, could similarly construct a synthetic forward using options.[5]

But why would a firm undertake this relatively complex position in order to simply create a forward contract? The answer is found by looking at the option premiums earned and paid. We have assumed that the option strike prices used were precisely forward-ATM rates, and the resulting option premiums paid and earned were exactly equal. But this need not be

[5] A U.S.-based firm possessing a future foreign currency denominated payment of £1 million could construct a synthetic forward hedge by (1) buying a call option on £1 million at a strike price of $1.4700/£ and (2) selling a put option on £1 million at the same strike price of $1.4700/£, when 1.47 is the forward rate.

EXHIBIT 10A.2 Ganado's Synthetic Forward A/R Exposure Hedge

Spot rate	$1.4790 = £1.00
90-day forward rate	$1.4700 = £1.00
90-day euro-$ interest rate	3.250%
90-day euro-£ interest rate	5.720%
90-day $/£ volatility	11.000%

Option	Strike Rate	Premium
Sell a forward ATM call option	$1.47	$0.0318 per £
Buy a forward ATM put option	$1.47	$0.0318 per £

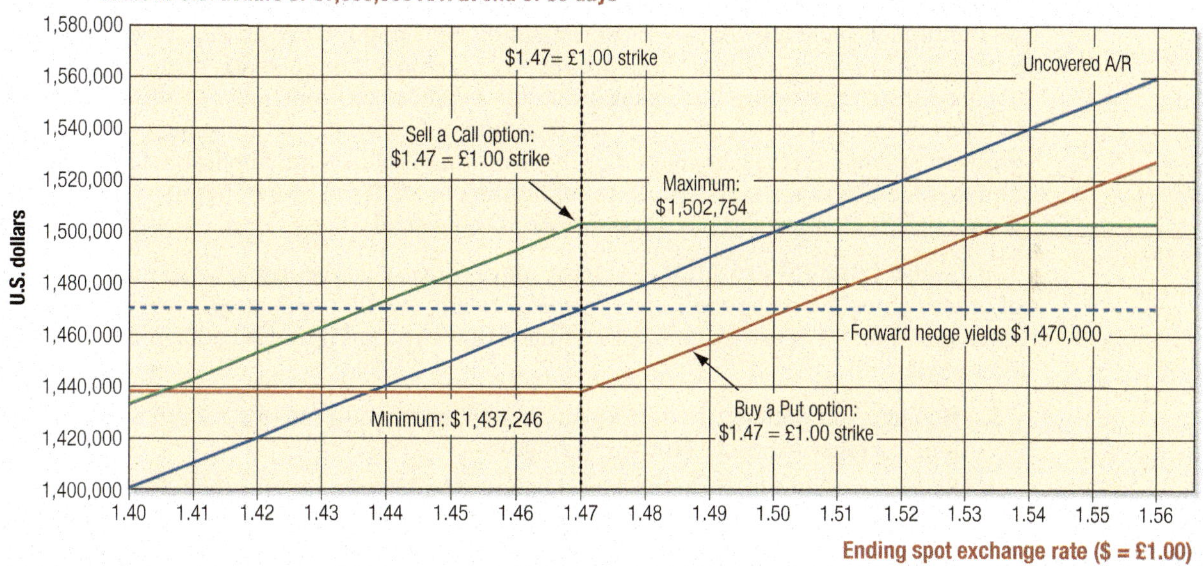

the case. If the option strike prices (remember that they must be identical for both options, bought and sold) are not precisely on the forward-ATM, the two premiums may differ by a slight amount. The net premium position may then end up as a net premium earning or a net premium payment. If positive, this amount would be added to the proceeds from the receivable to result in a higher total dollar value received than through the use of a traditional forward contract. A second possibility is that the firm, by querying a number of different financial service providers offering options, finds attractive pricing which "beats" the forward. Although this means that theoretically the options market is out of equilibrium, it happens quite frequently.

Second-Generation Currency Risk Management Products

Second-generation risk management products are constructed from the two basic derivatives used throughout this book text: the forward and the option. We will subdivide them into two groups: (1) the zero-premium option products, which focus on pricing in and around the forward rate and (2) the exotic option products (for want of a better name), which focus on alternative pricing targets. Although all of the following derivatives are sold as financial products by risk management firms, we will present each as the construction of the position from common building blocks, or LEGO®s, as they have been termed, used in traditional currency risk management, forwards, and options. As a group, they are collectively referred to as *complex options*.

Zero-Premium Option Products The primary problem with the use of options for risk management in the eyes of the firms is the up-front premium payment. Although the premium payment is only a portion of the total payoff profile of the hedge, many firms view the expenditure of substantial funds for the purchase of a financial derivative as prohibitively expensive. In comparison, the forward contract that eliminates currency risk requires no out-of-pocket expenditure by the firm (and requires no real specification of expectations regarding exchange rate movements).

Zero-premium option products (or financially engineered derivative combinations) are designed to require no out-of-pocket premium payment at the initiation of the hedge. This set of products includes what are most frequently labeled the *range forward* or *collar* and the *participating forward*. Both of these products (1) are priced on the basis of the forward rate, (2) are constructed to provide a zero-premium payment up front, and (3) allow the hedger to take advantage of expectations of the direction of exchange rate movements. For the case problem at hand, this means that all of the following products are applicable to an expectation that the U.S. dollar will depreciate versus the pound. If the hedger has no such view, they should turn back now (and buy a forward or nothing at all)!

The Range Forward or Collar The basic *range forward* has been marketed under a variety of other names, including the *collar, flexible forward, cylinder option, option fence* or simply *fence, mini-max*, or *zero-cost tunnel*. Regardless of which alias it trades under, it is constructed via two steps:

1. Buying a put option with a strike rate below the forward rate for the full amount of the long currency exposure (100% coverage)
2. Selling a call option with a strike rate above the forward rate for the full amount of the long currency exposure (100% coverage), with the same maturity as the purchased put

The hedger chooses one side of the "range" or spread, normally the downside (put strike rate), which then dictates the strike rate at which the call option will be sold. The call option must be chosen at an equal distance from the forward rate as the put option strike price from the forward rate. The distance from the forward rate for the two strike prices should be calculated in percentage, as in ± 3% from the forward rate.

If the hedger believes there is a significant possibility that the currency will move in the firm's favor, and by a sizable degree, the put-floor rate may be set relatively low in order for the ceiling to be higher or further out from the forward rate and still enjoy a zero net premium. How far down the downside protection is set is a difficult issue for the firm to determine. Often the firm's treasurer will determine at what bottom exchange rate the firm would be able to recover the minimum necessary margin on the business underlying the cash flow exposure, sometimes called the *budget rate*.

Exhibit 10A.3 illustrates the final outcome of a range forward constructed by buying a put with strike price $1.4500 = £1.00, paying a premium of $0.0226 per £, with selling a call option with strike price $1.4900 = £1.00, earning a premium of $0.0231 per £. The hedger has bounded the range over which the firm's A/R value moves as an uncovered position, with a put option floor and a sold call option ceiling. Although the put and call option premiums are in this case not identical, they are close enough to result in a near-zero net premium (a premium expense of $500 in this case):

$$\text{Net premium} = (\$0.0226 - \$0.0231) \times £1{,}000{,}000 = -\$500$$

The benefits of the combined position are readily observable, given that the put option premium alone amounts to $22,600. If the strike rates of the options are selected independently of the desire for an exact zero-net premium up-front (still bracketing the forward rate), it is termed an *option collar* or *cylinder option*.

EXHIBIT 10A.3 Ganado's Forward A/R Exposure Hedge

Spot rate	\$1.4790 = £1.00
90-day forward rate	\$1.4700 = £1.00
90-day euro-\$ interest rate	3.250%
90-day euro-£ interest rate	5.720%
90-day \$/£ volatility	11.000%

Option	Strike Rate	Premium
Buy an out-of-the-money put	\$1.45	\$0.0226 per £
Sell an out-of-the-money call	\$1.49	\$0.0231 per £

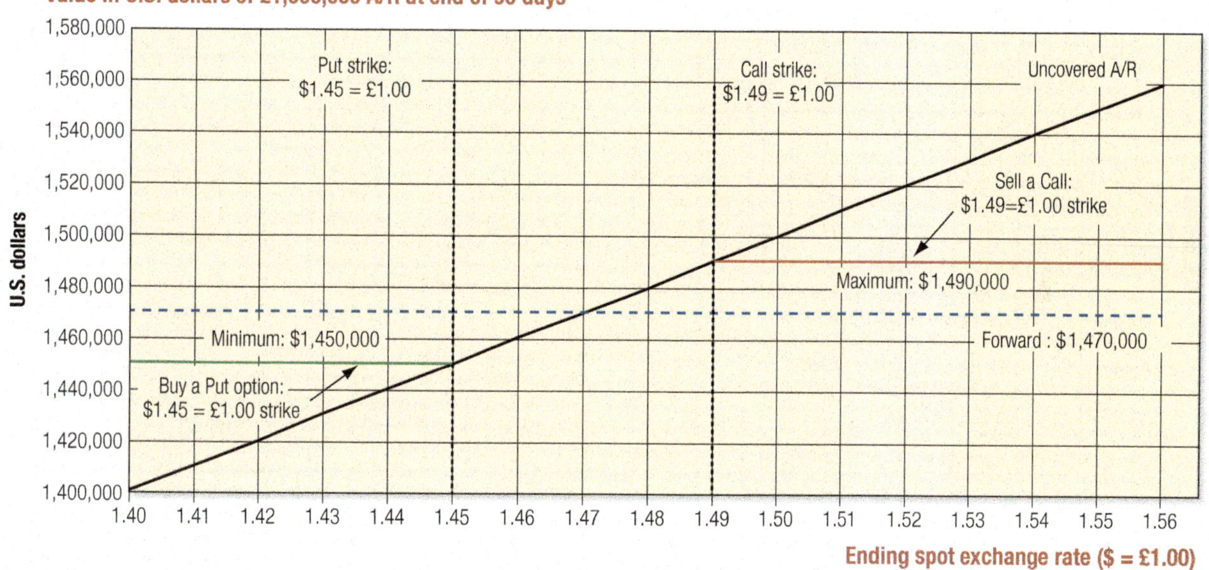

The Participating Forward The *participating forward*, also called a *zero-cost ratio option* and *forward participation agreement*, is an option combination that allows the hedger to share—or *participate*—in potential upside movements while providing option-based downside protection, all at a zero net premium. The participating forward is constructed via two steps:

1. Buying a put option with a strike price below the forward rate for the full amount of the long currency exposure (100% coverage)
2. Selling a call option with a strike price that is the same as the put option for a portion of the total currency exposure (less than 100% coverage)

Similar to the range forward, the buyer of a participating forward will choose the put option strike rate first. Because the call option strike rate is the same as the put, all that remains is to determine the participation rate, the proportion of the exposure sold as a call option.

Exhibit 10A.4 illustrates the construction of a participating forward for the chapter problem. The firm first chooses the put option protection level, in this case \$1.4500 = £1.00, with a premium of \$0.0226 per £. A call option sold with the same strike rate of \$1.4500 = £1.00 would earn the firm \$0.0425 per £. The call premium is substantially higher than the put premium because the call option is already in-the-money (ITM). The firm's objective is to sell a call option only on the number of pounds needed to fund the purchase of the put option. The total put option premium is:

$$\text{Total put premium} = \$0.0226 \times £1{,}000{,}000 = \$22{,}600$$

EXHIBIT 10A.4 Ganado's Participating Forward A/R Exposure Hedge

Instrument	Strike Rate	Premium	Notional Principal
Buy a put	\$1.45 = £1.00	\$0.0226 per £	£1,000,000
Sell a call	\$1.45= £1.00	\$0.0425 per £	£531,765

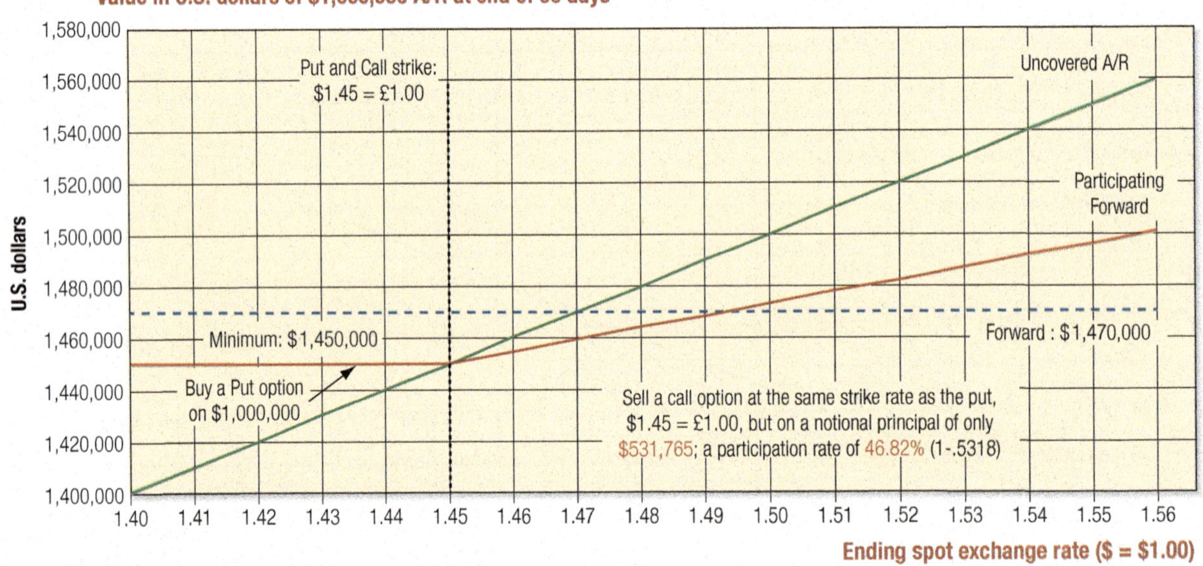

which is then used to determine the size of the call option that is needed to exactly offset the purchase of the put:

$$\$22{,}600 = \$0.0425 \text{ per £} \times \text{call principal}$$

Solving for the call principal:

$$\text{Call principal} = \frac{\$22{,}600}{\$0.0425 \text{ per £}} = \text{£}531{,}765$$

The firm must therefore sell a call option on £531,765 with a strike rate of \$1.4500=£1.00 to cover the purchase of the put option. This mismatch in option principals is what gives the participating forward its unique shape. The ratio of option premiums, as well as the ratio of option principals, is termed the percent cover:

$$\text{Percent cover} = \frac{\$0.026 \text{ per £}}{\$0.0425 \text{ per £}} = \frac{\text{£}531{,}765}{\text{£}1{,}000{,}00} = 0.5318 \approx 53.18\%$$

The *participation rate* is the residual percentage of the exposure that is not covered by the sale of the call option. For example, if the percent cover is 53.18%, the participation rate would be 1−the percent cover, or 46.82%. This means that for all favorable exchange rate movements (those above \$1.4500 = £1.00), the hedger would "participate" or enjoy 46.8% of the differential. However, like all option-based hedges, downside exposure is bounded by the put option strike rate.

The expectations of the buyer are similar to the range forward; only the degree of foreign currency bullishness is greater. For the participating forward to be superior in outcome to the range forward, it is necessary for the exchange rate to move further in the favorable direction.

Ratio Spreads One of the older methods of obtaining a zero-premium option combination, and one of the most dangerous from a hedger's perspective, is the ratio spread. This structure leaves the hedger with a large uncovered exposure.

Let us assume that Ganado decides that it wishes to establish a floor level of protection by purchasing a \$1.4700 = £1.00 put option (forward-ATM) at a cost of \$0.0318 per £ (total cost of \$31,800). This is a substantial outlay of up-front capital for the option premium, and the firm's risk management division has no budget funding for this magnitude of expenditures. The firm, feeling strongly that the dollar will depreciate against the pound, decides to "finance" the purchase of the put with the sale of an OTM call option. The firm reviews market conditions and considers a number of call option strike prices that are significantly OTM, strike prices of \$1.5200 = £1.00, \$1.5400 = £1.00, or further out.

It is decided that the \$1.5400 = £1.00 call option, with a premium of \$0.0089 per £, is to be written and sold to earn the premium and finance the put purchase. However, because the premium on the OTM call is so much smaller than the forward-ATM put premium, the size of the call option written must be larger. The firm determines the amount of the call by solving the simple problem of premium equivalency as follows:

$$\text{Cost of put premium} = \text{Earnings call premium}$$

Substituting in the put and call option premiums yields:

$$\$0.0318 \text{ per £} \times £1{,}000{,}000 = \$0.0089 \text{ per £} \times £ \text{ call}$$

Solving for the size of the call option to be written as follows:

$$\frac{\$31{,}800}{\$0.0089 \text{ per £}} = £3{,}573{,}034$$

The reason that this strategy is called a *ratio spread* is that the final position, call option size to put option size, is a ratio greater than 1 (in this case, £3,573,034 ÷ £1,000,000, or a ratio of about 3.57).

The risk to the firm in the use of a ratio spread is, however, dramatic. Although unlikely, it is possible that the spot rate could move far enough by the end of the period to put the call options written in-the-money. That would mean in our example that the firm would have written an uncovered call on £2,573,034, the call option notional principal less the exposure (£3,573,034 − £1,000,000). The loss potential in covering this position is unlimited.

An alternative form of the ratio spread is the *calendar spread*. The calendar spread would combine the 90-day put option with the sale of an OTM call option with a maturity that is longer—for example, 120 or 180 days. The longer maturity of the call option written earns the firm larger premium earnings requiring a smaller "ratio." As a number of firms using this strategy have learned the hard way, however, if the expectations of the hedger prove incorrect, and the spot rate moves past the strike price of the call option written, the firm is faced with delivering a foreign currency that it does not have. In this example, if the spot rate moved above \$1.5400 = £1.00, the firm would have to cover a position of £2,573,034.

The Average Rate Option These options are normally classified as "path-dependent" currency options because their values depend on averages of spot rates over some pre-specified period of time. Here we describe two examples of path-dependent options, the *average rate option* and the *average strike option*:

1. *Average rate option (ARO)*, also known as an *Asian option*, sets the option strike rate up front and is exercised at maturity if the average spot rate over the period (as observed by scheduled sampling) is less than the preset option strike rate.
2. *Average strike option (ASO)* establishes the option strike rate as the average of the spot rate experienced over the option's life and is exercised if the strike rate is greater than the end of period spot rate.

Like the *knock-out option*, the *average rate option* is difficult to depict because its value depends not on the ending spot rate, but rather the path the spot rate takes over its specified life span. For example, an average rate option with strike price $1.4700 = £1.00 would have a premium of only $0.0186 per £. The average rate would be calculated by weekly observations (12 full weeks, the first observation occurring 13 days from purchase) of the spot rate. Numerous different averages or paths of spot rate movement obviously exist. A few different scenarios aid in understanding how the ARO differs in valuation.

1. The spot rate moves very little over the first 70 to 80 days of the period, with a sudden movement in the spot rate below $1.4700 = £1.00 in the days prior to expiration. Although the final spot rate is below $1.4700 = £1.00, the average for the period is above $1.4700, so the option cannot be exercised. The receivable is exchanged at the spot rate (below $1.4700 = £1.00) and the cost of the option premium is still incurred.
2. The dollar slowly and steadily depreciates versus the pound, the rate rising from $1.4790 = £1.00 to $1.48, $1.49, and on up. At the end of the 90 days the option expires out of the money, the receivable is exchanged at the favorable spot rate, and the firm has enjoyed average rate option protection at substantially lower premium expense.

A variation on the average rate is the *lookback option*, with strike and without strike. A *lookback option* with strike is a European-style option with a preset strike rate that on maturity is valued versus the highest or lowest spot rate reached over the option life. A lookback option without strike is typically a European-style option that sets the strike rate at maturity as the lowest exchange rate achieved over the period for a call option, or the highest exchange rate experienced over the period for a put option, and is exercised on the basis of this strike rate versus the ending spot rate.

A variety of different types of average rate currency option products are sold by financial institutions, each having a distinct payoff structure. Because of the intricacy of the path-dependent option's value, care must be taken in the use of these instruments. As is always the case with more and more complex financial derivatives, *caveat emptor*.

CHAPTER 10 APPENDIX B

The Optimal Hedge Ratio and Hedge Effectiveness

There are a number of other theoretical dimensions to currency hedging which are not often considered in actual industry practice, including the *optimal hedge ratio, hedge symmetry, hedge effectiveness*, and *hedge timing*.

Hedge Ratio

A *transaction exposure* is the uncertainty in the value of an asset—for example, a specific amount of foreign currency—that may be recognized or realized at a future point in time. In our example in this chapter, Ganado expected to receive £1,000,000 in 90 days but does not know for certain what that £1,000,000 will be worth in U.S. dollars at that time (the spot exchange rate in 90 days).

The objective of *currency hedging* is to minimize the change in the value of the exposed asset or cash flow from a change in exchange rates. *Hedging* is accomplished by combining the *exposed asset* with a *hedge asset* to create a two asset portfolio in which the two assets react in relatively equal but opposite directions to an exchange rate change. Once formed, the most common objective of hedging is to construct a hedge which will result in a total change in value of the two asset portfolio (Δ Portfolio Value)—if perfect—of zero.

$$\Delta \text{ Portfolio Value} = \Delta \text{ Spot} + \Delta \text{ Hedge} = 0$$

A traditional forward hedge forms a two asset portfolio, combining the spot exposure with forward cover. The value of the two asset portfolio is then the sum of the foreign currency amount at the current spot rate (the exposure), with the hedge amount sold forward at the forward rate.

$$\begin{aligned}\text{Two Asset Portfolio} &= [(\text{Exposure} - \text{Hedge amount}) \times \text{Spot}] + \\ &\quad [\text{Hedge amount} \times \text{Forward rate}]\end{aligned}$$

For example, if Ganado hedged 100% of its £1,000,000 account receivable with a forward contract at time $t = 90$ (90 days till settlement), assuming a spot rate of \$1.7640 = £1.00 and a 90-day forward rate of \$1.7540 = £1.00, this two asset portfolio would be:

$$V_t = [(\pounds1{,}000{,}000 - \pounds1{,}000{,}000) \times \$1.7640] + [\pounds1{,}000{,}000 \times \$1.7540] = \$1{,}754{,}000$$

Note that when there is a full forward cover, there is no uncovered exposure remaining. The variance in the terminal value of this two asset portfolio with respect to the spot exchange rate over the following 90-day period is zero. Its value is set and certain. Also note that if the spot rate and the forward rate were exactly equal (which they are not here), the total position would be termed a *perfect hedge*.

If, however, Maria Gonzalez at Ganado decided to *selectively hedge* the exposure, covering less than 100% of the exposure, the value of the two asset portfolio would change with the spot exchange rate. The change in value could be either up or down. In this case, Maria Gonzalez would need to follow a methodology for determining what proportion, β, of the exposure, X_t, to cover (so $\beta - X_t$ is the amount of the exposure covered). Now the two asset portfolio is written:

$$V_t = [(X_t - \beta X_t) \times S_t] + [\beta X_t \times F_t]$$

where the hedge ratio, β, is defined

$$\beta = \frac{\text{Value of currency hedge}}{\text{Value of currency exposure}}$$

If the entire exposure was covered as in Ganado's example above, that is a *hedge ratio* of 1.0 or 100%. The hedge ratio, β, is the percentage of an individual exposure's nominal amount covered by a financial instrument such as a forward contract or currency option.

Hedge Symmetry. Some hedges can be constructed to result in no change in value to any and all exchange rate changes. The hedge is constructed so that whatever spot value is lost as a result of adverse exchange rate movements (Δ Spot), that value is replaced by an equal but opposite change in the value of the hedge asset, (Δ Hedge). The commonly used 100% forward contract cover is such a hedge. For example, in the case of Ganado, if the entire £1 million account receivable is sold forward, Ganado is assured of the same dollar proceeds at the end of the 90-day period regardless of which direction the exchange rate moves over the exposure period.

But changes in the underlying spot exchange rate need not only result in losses; gains from exchange rate changes are equally possible. In the case of Ganado, if the dollar were to weaken against the pound over the 90-day period, the dollar value of the account receivable would go up. Ganado may choose to construct a hedge, which would minimize the losses in the combined two asset portfolio (minimize negative Δ Value), but to allow positive changes in value (positive Δ Value) from exchange rate changes. A hedge constructed using a foreign currency option would be pursuing this alternative hedging objective. For Ganado, this would be the purchase of a put option on the pound to protect against value losses but allow Ganado to possibly reap value increases in the event the exchange rate moved in its favor.

Hedge Effectiveness. The effectiveness of a hedge is determined to what degree the change in spot asset's value is correlated with the equal but opposite change in the hedge asset's value to a change in the underlying spot exchange rate. In currency markets, spot and futures rates are nearly—but not precisely perfectly—correlated. This less-than-perfect correlation is termed *basis risk*.

Hedge Timing. The hedger must also determine the timing of the hedge objective. Does the hedger wish to protect the value of the exposed asset only at the time of its maturity or settlement or at various points in time over the life of the exposure? For example, in the case of Ganado, the various hedging alternatives explored in the problem analysis—the forward, money market, purchased option hedges—all were constructed and evaluated for the dollar value of the combined hedge portfolio only at the *end* of the 90-day period. In some cases, however, Ganado might wish to protect the value of the exposed asset prior to maturity—for example, at the end of a financial reporting period prior to the actual maturity of the exposure.

11

Translation Exposure

What gets measured gets managed.

—Anonymous.

LEARNING OBJECTIVES

11.1 Describe how the consolidation of a multinational firm's foreign entities creates translation exposure

11.2 Examine the two major methods of translation, including their theoretical and practical differences

11.3 Understand how translation can potentially alter the value of a firm

11.4 Explore how to manage translation exposure, including how one company uses swaps to do so

As you learned in Chapter 10, there are two distinct categories of foreign exchange exposure: those based in accounting and those based in economic competitiveness. The two accounting exposures are *transaction exposure*, covered in Chapter 10, and *translation exposure*. Translation exposure is the subject of this chapter.

Transaction exposure results from a firm having foreign currency-denominated contracts and commitments. *Translation exposure* arises because financial statements of foreign subsidiaries—which are stated in foreign currency—must be restated in the parent's reporting currency so that the firm can prepare consolidated financial statements. Foreign subsidiaries of U.S. companies, for example, must restate foreign currency-denominated financial statements into U.S. dollars so that the foreign values can be added to the parent's U.S. dollar-denominated balance sheet and income statement. This accounting process is called *translation. Translation exposure* is the potential for a change, positively or negatively, in the parent company's net worth and/or net income resulting from a change in exchange rates since the last translation.

The main purpose of translation is to prepare consolidated financial statements for use by investors, creditors, and governments. However, management also uses the translated statements to assess the performance of foreign subsidiaries. While such assessment by management might be performed using the local currency statements, restatement of all subsidiary statements into a single currency, the currency of the parent company, facilitates management comparison and performance evaluation. Translation, therefore, has both financial and managerial implications for the multinational. The chapter concludes with the mini-case *Electrolux of Sweden's Currency Management*, demonstrating how one major multinational firm structures and manages its currency exposures globally, combining transaction and translation exposure.

11.1 Overview of Translation

Consolidation accounting is the process of combining the financial results of all subsidiary companies into the combined financial results of the parent company. Consolidated financial results are important to, and used by, investors, creditors, governments, and other corporate stakeholders to assess the risks, returns, and prospects of these entities. Our purpose here, however, is not to discuss or detail consolidation accounting, but rather the currency risk to the multinational firm that arises from the currency translation of foreign currency-denominated financial statements of its foreign subsidiaries.

Concepts and Definitions

We will use our example multinational firm Ganado Corporation, shown in Exhibit 11.1, to demonstrate the precise definition of key translation terms. Before we do, let us describe Ganado Corporation in more detail.

- **Ganado Corporation.** Ganado Corporation is a U.S.-based multinational company. It is publicly traded on a U.S. stock exchange. It is required by law to report consolidated financial results according to U.S. GAAP in U.S. dollars—the dollar is its *reporting currency*.

EXHIBIT 11.1 **Consolidation and Translation of Financial Results for Ganado**

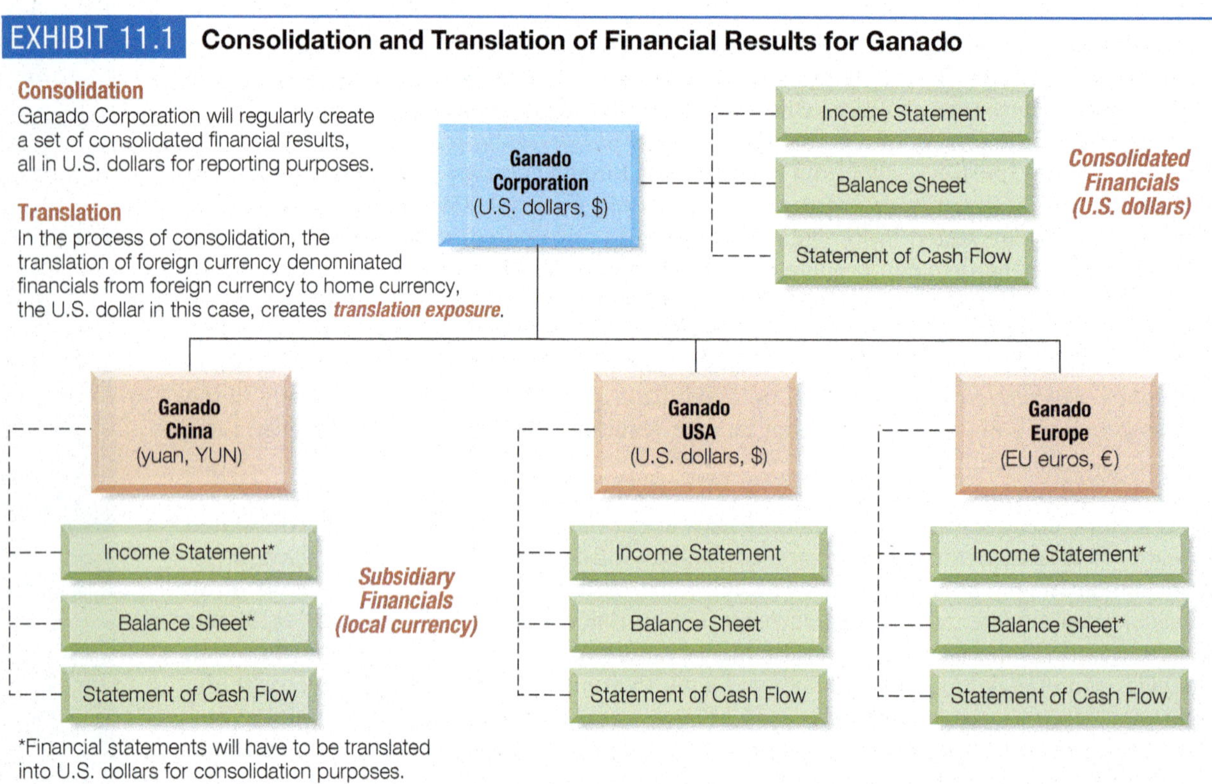

- **Ganado China.** Ganado China is a wholly owned foreign subsidiary of Ganado Corporation. As a Chinese business, it maintains its financial statements in Chinese yuan. Ganado China's business is based on importing subcomponents from the U.S., priced in U.S. dollars, and completing final assembly in China, after which it prices its products in Chinese yuan based on the converted U.S. dollar cost structure.
- **Ganado U.S.** This is the wholly owned domestic subsidiary of Ganado Corporation. As a U.S. subsidiary and business, it maintains all its financial statements in U.S. dollars. Like many U.S.-based businesses, it does on occasion purchase from and sell to other international businesses. Some of these purchases or sales are denominated in foreign currency. For those transactions, any change in the value of the transaction as a result of currency changes between the date of booking and settlement is recorded as a foreign exchange gain or loss. This was covered in detail in Chapter 10.
- **Ganado Europe.** Ganado Europe is a wholly owned foreign subsidiary of Ganado Corporation. As a European business (located in Germany), it maintains its financial statement in euros. Ganado Europe's business is distinctly separate from Ganado Corporation, as it purchases, sells, and prices in the European marketplace.

Given Ganado Corporation's structure and operations, we now set the stage for understanding translation practices in the United States with the following set of critical definitions.

Reporting Currency. The *reporting currency* is the currency that the reporting entity uses to prepare its financial statements and for consolidated reporting. In the case of Ganado, this is the U.S. dollar. Any other currency used by an entity of this same multinational firm in its financial statements is a *foreign currency*. For Ganado, this would include the Chinese yuan and the euro.

Foreign Entity. Any distinct or separable business that prepares its financial statements in any currency other than the reporting currency of the parent company is considered a *foreign entity*. A reporting entity must identify those foreign entities that maintain their statements in foreign currency for translation purposes. For Ganado Corporation—the *reporting entity*—this means that Ganado China and Ganado Europe are foreign entities. Since Ganado U.S. is a U.S.-based business, and maintains its financial statements in the company's reporting currency, the U.S. dollar, it is not a foreign entity, and its financial statements do not require translation.

Distinct and Separable Operation. This is a characterization of the relationship of the foreign subsidiary with that of the parent company. If the foreign subsidiary operates as an extension of the parent company's operations (e.g., a foreign distributor of the parent company's products—products manufactured by the parent company at home), it is classified as an *integrated foreign entity*. If the foreign subsidiary operates completely separately from the parent company (e.g., a company acquired by the parent company in a different business than the parent company, with little intracompany transactions), it is classified as a *distinct* or *separable operation*. For Ganado Corporation, Ganado Europe is considered a distinct and separable operation, while Ganado China is considered an integrated foreign entity for translation purposes.

Functional Currency. The *functional currency* is the currency of the primary economic environment in which a distinct entity operates. The functional currency of a foreign entity may or may not be the same as the currency of the country of operation. For example, the functional currency of Ganado's Chinese subsidiary is actually the U.S. dollar, not the Chinese yuan. This is the case since the Chinese subsidiary purchases the majority of its inputs priced and denominated in U.S. dollars, as well as selling products whose prices are based on U.S. dollar prices.

Foreign Currency Financial Statements. All incorporated businesses will possess all three traditional financial statements—the income statement, balance sheet, and statement of cash flows. However, only two of these statements need to be translated for consolidation purposes: the income statement and the balance sheet. (Statements of cash flow are not translated from the foreign subsidiaries. The consolidated statement of cash flow is constructed from the consolidated statement of income and consolidated balance sheet.) Consolidation will then require the translation of these foreign currency financial statements into the reporting currency of the parent company.

Remeasurement and Translation

Consolidated reporting and the preparation of financial statements of a multinational firm into the reporting currency is conducted along two distinctly separate procedures—and they have their own very specific terminology. The method applicable to an individual foreign entity is based on the characterization of the foreign entity and its financial statements.

Foreign Currency Measurement (Remeasurement). If a foreign entity's functional currency is the reporting currency (the currency of the parent company used for consolidated reporting purposes), the process for preparing the financial statements is termed *remeasurement*. This is the process by which a foreign entity expresses transactions whose terms are denominated in a foreign currency in its functional currency.

For example, Ganado China was described as having the U.S. dollar as its functional currency, the same currency as Ganado Corporation's reporting currency. Any transactions whose terms are denominated in a currency other than the U.S. dollar, such as the Chinese yuan, must be *remeasured* for consolidation purposes. Any changes arising from remeasurement are included in the consolidated net income of the company. They are therefore treated as foreign exchange gains and losses like transaction exposures described in Chapter 10.

Foreign Currency Translation. If a foreign entity's financial statements are maintained in a functional currency, and that functional currency is different from the reporting currency of the parent company, the process for preparation of the financial statements is termed *translation*. In our example, Ganado Europe's functional currency is the euro. It will then follow the practice of translation to prepare its financial statements in the reporting currency, the U.S. dollar. Any changes arising from translation are included in an equity account, *cumulative translation adjustment* (CTA), a component of other comprehensive income.

The real significance of translation exposure today for multinational firms is the way in which changes arising from the translation are included. Since remeasurement changes are included in consolidated net income—earnings and earnings per share—they may alter these widely reported and watched financial results of publicly traded companies. Changes arising from translation, however, affecting consolidated equity via the CTA account, are rarely noted in the business press. Measurement of performance inside the multinational is, however, sometimes altered by translation, as discussed in *Global Finance in Practice 11.1*

GLOBAL FINANCE IN PRACTICE **11.1**

Functional Currency and Management Performance

Multinational financial management, as is the case with all areas of business management, is influenced by the various measures used to evaluate and reward leadership in the organization. This has in specific cases included translation—specifically the choice of functional currency of a foreign subsidiary.

A number of years ago, a U.S.-based multinational electronics firm (to remain nameless) acquired an electronics firm in Germany. Initially the German business was totally unrelated to the U.S. firm in terms of operations and cash flows. In addition, the currency dominating both cash inflows and outflows was the local currency, the euro. The *functional currency* designation was therefore the euro, and the *current rate method of translation* was applied.

Over time the German business unit was structurally altered and integrated with the U.S. parent company. The German unit increasingly sourced inputs from the U.S. in U.S. dollars. At the same time, the German business unit's sales were expanded to Eastern Europe and the Middle East, with increasing currency cash inflows shifting from the euro to the dollar. The company's auditors recommended that the functional currency be changed from the euro to the U.S. dollar.

When the management team of the German business unit analyzed how their performance would be measured by the change in functional currency, their performance as measured was weaker, and the result could potentially lower their raises or bonuses. Corporate allowed the functional currency to remain the euro for two years despite the objections of the company's auditors. Finally, in the third year, the auditor threatened to not sign off on the company's financials unless the designation was changed. The auditor won.

11.2 Translation Methods

Two basic methods for translation are employed worldwide: the *current rate method* and the *temporal method.* Regardless of which method is employed, a translation method must designate at what exchange rate individual balance sheet and income statement items are remeasured and also where any imbalance is to be recorded, either in current income or in an equity reserve account in the balance sheet.

Current Rate Method

The *current rate method* of translation—known simply as "translation" in U.S. accounting and translation practices—is the most prevalent in the world today. Under this method, all financial statement line items are translated at the "current" exchange rate with few exceptions.

- **Assets and Liabilities.** All assets and liabilities are translated at the current rate of exchange; that is, at the rate of exchange in effect on the date of the balance sheet.
- **Income Statement Items.** All items, including depreciation and cost of goods sold, are translated either at the actual exchange rate on the dates the various revenues, expenses, gains, and losses were incurred or at an appropriately weighted average exchange rate for the period.
- **Distributions.** Dividends paid are translated at the exchange rate in effect on the date of payment.
- **Equity Items.** Common stock and paid-in capital accounts are translated at historical rates. Year-end retained earnings consist of the original year-beginning retained earnings plus any income/(loss) for the year.

Gains or losses caused by translation adjustments are not included in the calculation of consolidated net income. Rather, translation gains or losses are reported separately and accumulated in a separate equity reserve account (on the consolidated balance sheet) with a title such as "cumulative translation adjustment" (CTA), but it depends on the country.

If a foreign subsidiary is later sold or liquidated, translation gains or losses of past years accumulated in the CTA account are reported as one component of the total gain or loss on sale or liquidation. The total gain or loss is reported as part of the net income or loss for the period in which the sale or liquidation occurs.

Temporal Method

Under the *temporal method*, specific assets and liabilities are translated at exchange rates consistent with the timing of those item's creation. The temporal method assumes that a number of individual line item assets, such as inventory and net plant and equipment, are restated regularly to reflect market value. If these items were not restated but were instead carried at historical cost, the temporal method becomes the monetary/nonmonetary method of translation, a form of translation that is still used by a number of countries today. Line items assumed under the temporal method to be restated regularly include the following:

- **Monetary assets and monetary liabilities.** Monetary assets (primarily cash, marketable securities, accounts receivable, and long-term receivables) and monetary liabilities (primarily current liabilities and long-term debt) are translated at current exchange rates. Nonmonetary assets and liabilities (primarily inventory and fixed assets) are translated at historical rates.
- **Income statement items.** These are translated at the average exchange rate for the period, except for items such as depreciation and cost of goods sold that are directly associated with nonmonetary assets or liabilities. These accounts are translated at their historical rate.
- **Distributions.** Dividends paid are translated at the exchange rate in effect on the date of payment.
- **Equity items.** Common stock and paid-in capital accounts are translated at historical rates. Year-end retained earnings consist of the original year-beginning retained earnings plus or minus any income or loss for the year, plus or minus any imbalance from translation.

Under the temporal method, gains or losses resulting from remeasurement are carried directly to current consolidated income, and not to equity reserves. Hence, foreign exchange gains and losses arising from remeasurement may introduce volatility to consolidated earnings.

U.S. Translation Procedures

The United States differentiates foreign subsidiaries based on functional currency. The primary principles of U.S. translation are summarized as follows:

- If the financial statements of the foreign subsidiary of a U.S. company are maintained in U.S. dollars, then translation is not required.
- If the financial statements of the foreign subsidiary are maintained in the local currency and the local currency is the functional currency, then they are translated using the current rate method.
- If the financial statements of the foreign subsidiary are maintained in the local currency and the U.S. dollar is the functional currency, then they are remeasured using the temporal method.
- If the financial statements of foreign subsidiaries are maintained in the local currency and neither the local currency nor the U.S. dollar is the functional currency, then the statements must first be remeasured into the functional currency by the temporal method and then translated into dollars using the current rate method.

EXHIBIT 11.2 **Flow Chart for U.S. Translation Practices**

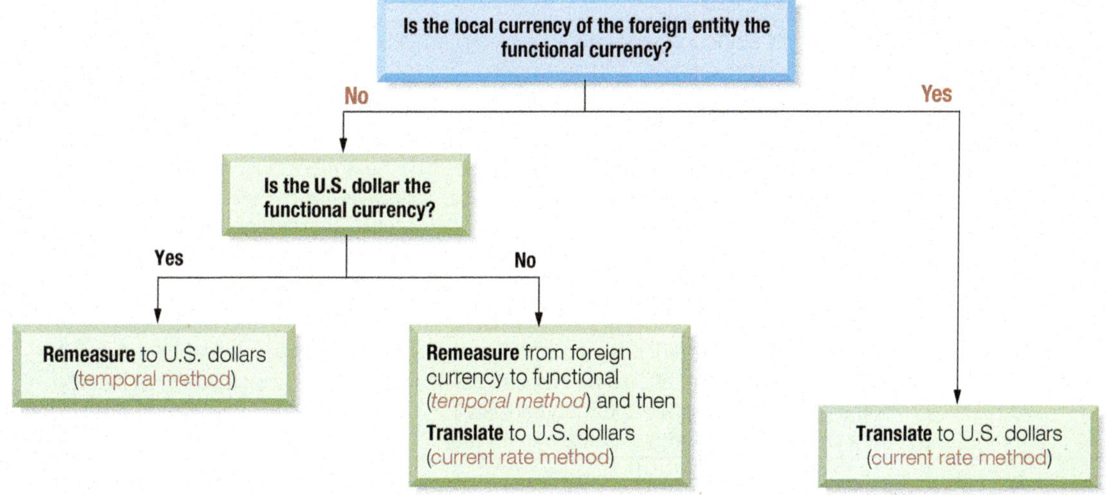

U.S. translation practices in the form of a decision-based flow chart are summarized in Exhibit 11.2. A final note, however, is important. The selection of the functional currency is determined by the economic realities of the subsidiary's operations and is not a discretionary management decision on preferred procedures or elective outcomes. Since many U.S.-based multinationals have numerous foreign subsidiaries, some dollar-functional and some foreign currency-functional, currency gains and losses may be passing through both current consolidated income and/or accruing in equity reserves.[1]

International Translation Practices

The accounting guidance for foreign currency reporting and translation issues in the U.S. is found in Financial Accounting Standards Board (FASB) Accounting Standards Codification (ASC) Topic 830, *Foreign Currency Matters*. A large part of the rest of the world, however—more than 100 countries—uses International Financial Reporting Standards (IFRS).

The accounting guidance for foreign currency translation under IFRS is contained in Standard (IAS) 21, *The Effects of Changes in Foreign Exchange Rates*, and IAS 29, *Financial Reporting in Hyperinflation Countries*. The good news is they are quite similar in most aspects of foreign currency translation.

There are, however, a number of differences that bear noting. The first difference is purely vocabulary. Whereas the U.S. categorizes foreign entities as either *integrated* or *distinct/separable*, international standards use *integrated* or *self-sustaining*. Their definitions remain the same. An *integrated foreign entity* is one that operates as an extension of the parent company, with cash flows and general business lines that are highly interrelated with those of the parent. A *self-sustaining foreign entity* is one that operates in the local economic environment independent of the parent company.

[1] Note that 2020 surveys of U.S.-based multinationals indicate that roughly 65% of their foreign subsidiaries are local currency functional, 12% are dollar functional (currency of parent), and 23% are a mixture of the two.

EXHIBIT 11.3 Differences between U.S. GAAP and IFRS Regarding Translation

Issue	International Financial Reported Standards (IFRS)	U.S. Generally Accepted Accounting Principles (GAAP)
Article for guidance	IAS 21 and IAS 29	ASC 830
Determination of Functional Currency	International standards establishes a hierarchy of indicators (primary and secondary) for determination of functional currency.	U.S. practices require analysis of a multitude of factors to determine the functional currency. These indicators are not ranked in any kind of a hierarchical structure.
Hyperinflationary Economies	Even if the entity's host country economy qualifies as hyperinflationary, the functional currency is retained.	If the entity's host country economy qualifies as hyperinflationary, financial statements are remeasured as if the parent company's reporting currency was the functional currency.
	Any financial amounts that are not already measured at the current rate of exchange at the end of the period should be indexed using a general price index and then translated into the reporting currency at the current rate.	Any exchange rate differences calculated through remeasurement are therefore included in consolidated net income.

Exhibit 11.3 provides a short summary of the two major differences between U.S. GAAP based translation and IFRS translation that are of more significance: (1) determination of functional currency and (2) treatment in economies and currencies suffering hyperinflation. The U.S. requires that a variety of indicators—cash flow, sales price, sales market, expense, financing, and intercompany transactions and arrangements—"be considered both individually and collectively when determining the functional currency." This can on occasion result in differences of opinion both inside and outside firms regarding the functional currency for a specific foreign entity. This is not the case under IFRS, as it establishes a hierarchy of indicators that are clearly more deterministic.

The second significant difference is how to treat and translate the financial statements of a foreign entity resident in a country suffering *hyperinflation*. U.S. translation practices require that remeasurement be used in cases of a highly inflationary environment—a country where cumulative inflation has been 100% or more over a three-year period. The logic behind the U.S. practice is that a currency suffering such a high rate of inflation is not stable enough to operate as a true functional currency. As described in Exhibit 11.3, IFRS standards largely allow the use of the traditional functional currency definition even in what it terms *hyperinflationary instances*. The U.S. directive, which preceded the formation of IFRS standards by many years, reflected the concerns of the time (the early 1980s) when inflation was prevalent even in the largest of industrial economies. This is not the case today.

11.3 Ganado Corporation's Translation Exposure

Using Ganado Corporation as detailed in Exhibit 11.1, we now explore the intricacies of translation exposure arising from the preparation of the functional currency versions of the income statements and balance sheets of Ganado's foreign entities.

Translation Exposure: Income

Ganado Corporation's sales and earnings, by operating unit for 2018 and 2019, are described in Exhibit 11.4. For 2019, the company generated $300 million in sales in its U.S. unit, $158.4 million in its European subsidiary (€120 million at $1.32 = €1.00), and $89.6 million

EXHIBIT 11.4 Ganado Corporation, Selected Financial Results, 2018–2019

	Sales (millions, local currency)			Average Exchange Rate ($ = €1.00 and Rmb = €1.00)			Sales (millions of $)		
	2018	2019	% Change	2018	2019	% Change	2018	2019	% Change
United States	$280	$300	7.1%	—	—	—	$280.0	$300.0	7.1%
Europe	€ 118	€ 120	1.7%	1.4000	1.3200	–5.71%	$165.2	$158.4	–4.1%
China	Rmb600	Rmb600	0.0%	6.8300	6.7000	1.94%	$87.8	$89.6	1.9%
Total							$533.0	$548.0	2.8%

	Earnings (millions, local currency)			Average Exchange Rate ($ = €1.00 and Rmb = $1.00)			Earnings (millions of $)		
	2018	2019	% Change	2018	2019	% Change	2018	2019	% Change
United States	$28.2	$28.6	1.4%	—	—	—	$28.2	$28.6	1.4%
Europe	€ 10.4	€ 10.5	1.0%	1.4000	1.3200	–5.71%	$14.6	$13.9	–4.8%
China	Rmb71.4	Rmb71.4	0.0%	6.8300	6.7000	1.94%	$10.5	$10.7	1.9%
Total							$53.2	$53.1	–0.2%

Note: Column totals for sales and earnings differ due to rounding.

in its Chinese subsidiary (Rmb600 million at Rmb6.70 = $1.00). Total global sales for 2019 were $548.0 million. This constituted sales growth of 2.8% over 2018.

The company's earnings (profits) fell in 2019, dropping to $53.1 million from $53.2 million in 2018. Although not a large drop, Wall Street would not react favorably to a fall in consolidated earnings.

A closer look at the sales and earnings by country, however, yields some interesting insights. Sales and earnings in the U.S. unit rose, sales growing 7.1% and earnings growing 1.4%. Since the U.S. unit makes up more than half of the company's total sales and profits, this is very important. The Chinese subsidiary's sales and earnings were identical in 2018 and 2019 when measured in local currency, Chinese renminbi. The renminbi, however, was revalued against the U.S. dollar by the Chinese government, from Rmb6.83 = $1.00 to Rmb6.70 = $1.00. The result was an increase in the dollar value of both Chinese sales and profits.

The European subsidiary's financial results are even more striking. In euros, sales and earnings in Europe grew from 2018 to 2019. Sales grew 1.7% while earnings increased 1.0%. But the euro depreciated against the dollar, falling from $1.40 = €1.00 to $1.32 = €1.00. This depreciation of 5.7% resulted in the financial results of European operations falling in dollar terms. As a result, Ganado's consolidated earnings (in U.S. dollars) fell in 2019. One can imagine the discussion and debate within Ganado, and among the analysts who follow the firm, over the fall in earnings reported to Wall Street.

Translation Exposure: Balance Sheet

Let us continue the example of Ganado, focusing here on the balance sheet of its European subsidiary. We previously described Ganado Europe as being self-sustaining and therefore subject to the current rate method. However, in this section we illustrate translation by both the temporal method and the current rate method in order to show the arbitrary nature of a translation gain or loss. The functional currency of Ganado Europe is the euro, and the reporting currency of its parent, Ganado Corporation, is the U.S. dollar.

Our analysis assumes that plant and equipment and long-term debt were acquired and that common stock was issued by Ganado Europe sometime in the past when the exchange rate was $1.2760 = €1.00. Inventory currently on hand was purchased or manufactured during the immediately prior quarter when the average exchange rate was \$1.2180 = €1.00. At the close of business on Monday, December 31, 2019, the current spot exchange rate was \$1.2000 = €1.00. When business reopened on January 3, 2020, after the New Year holiday, the euro had dropped in value versus the dollar to \$1.0000 = €1.00.

Current Rate Method. Exhibit 11.5 illustrates translation loss using the current rate method. Assets and liabilities on the pre-depreciation balance sheet are translated at the current exchange rate of \$1.2000 = €1.00. Capital stock is translated at the historical rate of \$1.2760 = €1.00, and retained earnings are translated at a composite rate that is equivalent to having each past year's addition to retained earnings translated at the exchange rate in effect that year. The sum of retained earnings and the CTA account must "balance" the liabilities and net worth section of the balance sheet with the asset side. For this example, we have assumed the two amounts used for the December 31 balance sheet. As shown in Exhibit 11.5, the "just before depreciation" dollar translation reports an accumulated translation loss from prior periods of \$136,800. This balance is the cumulative gain or loss from translating euro statements into dollars in prior years.

After the depreciation, Ganado Corporation translates assets and liabilities at the new exchange rate of \$1.0000 = €1.00. Equity accounts, including retained earnings, are translated just as they were before depreciation, and as a result, the cumulative translation loss increases to \$1,736,800. The increase of \$1,600,000 in this account (from a cumulative loss of \$136,800 to a new cumulative loss of \$1,736,800) is the translation loss measured by the current rate method.

This translation loss is a decrease in equity, measured in the parent's reporting currency, of "net exposed assets." An exposed asset is an asset whose value drops with the depreciation

EXHIBIT 11.5 Ganado Europe's Translation Loss after Depreciation of the Euro: Current Rate Method

		December 31, 2019		January 2, 2020	
Assets	**In Euros (€)**	**Exchange Rate (\$ = €1.00)**	**Translated Accounts (\$)**	**Exchange Rate (\$ = €1.00)**	**Translated Accounts (\$)**
Cash	1,600,000	1.2000	\$ 1,920,000	1.0000	\$ 1,600,000
Accounts receivable	3,200,000	1.2000	3,840,000	1.0000	3,200,000
Inventory	2,400,000	1.2000	2,880,000	1.0000	2,400,000
Net plant & equipment	4,800,000	1.2000	5,760,000	1.0000	4,800,000
Total	12,000,000		\$ 14,400,000		\$ 12,000,000
Liabilities & Net Worth					
Accounts payable	800,000	1.2000	\$ 960,000	1.0000	\$ 800,000
Short-term bank debt	1,600,000	1.2000	1,920,000	1.0000	1,600,000
Long-term debt	1,600,000	1.2000	1,920,000	1.0000	1,600,000
Common stock	1,800,000	1.2760	2,296,800	1.2760	2,296,800
Retained earnings	6,200,000	1.2000 (a)	7,440,000	1.2000 (b)	7,440,000
Translation adjustment (CTA)	—		\$ (136,800)		\$ (1,736,800)
Total	12,000,000		\$ 14,400,000		\$ 12,000,000

(a) Dollar retained earnings before depreciation are the cumulative sum of additions to retained earnings of all prior years, translated at exchange rates in each year.

(b) Translated into dollars at the same rate as before depreciation of the euro.

of the functional currency and rises with an appreciation of that currency. Net exposed assets in this context are exposed assets minus exposed liabilities. Net exposed assets are positive ("long") if exposed assets exceed exposed liabilities. They are negative ("short") if exposed assets are less than exposed liabilities.

Temporal Method. Translation of the same accounts under the temporal method shows the arbitrary nature of any gain or loss from translation. This is illustrated in Exhibit 11.6. Monetary assets and monetary liabilities in the pre-depreciation euro balance sheet are translated at the current rate of exchange, but other assets and the equity accounts are translated at their historic rates. For Ganado Europe, the historical rate for inventory differs from that for net plant and equipment because inventory was acquired more recently.

Under the temporal method, translation losses are not accumulated in a separate equity account. Instead, they are passed directly through each quarter's income statement. Thus, in the dollar balance sheet, translated before depreciation, retained earnings were the cumulative result of earnings from all prior years, translated at historical rates in effect each year, plus translation gains or losses from all prior years. In Exhibit 11.6, no translation loss appears in the pre-depreciation dollar balance sheet because any losses would have been closed to retained earnings.

The effect of the depreciation is to create an immediate translation loss of $160,000. This amount is shown as a separate line item in Exhibit 11.6 to focus attention on it for this example. Under the temporal method, this translation loss of $160,000 would pass through the income statement, reducing reported net income and reducing retained earnings. Ending retained

EXHIBIT 11.6 Ganado Europe's Translation Loss after Depreciation of the Euro: Temporal Method

		December 31, 2019		January 2, 2020	
Assets	**In Euros (€)**	**Exchange Rate ($ = €1.00)**	**Translated Accounts ($)**	**Exchange Rate ($ = €1.00)**	**Translated Accounts ($)**
Cash	1,600,000	1.2000	$ 1,920,000	1.0000	$ 1,600,000
Accounts receivable	3,200,000	1.2000	3,840,000	1.0000	3,200,000
Inventory	2,400,000	1.2180	2,923,200	1.2180	2,923,200
Net plant & equipment	4,800,000	1.2760	6,124,800	1.2760	6,124,800
Total	12,000,000		$ 14,808,000		$ 13,848,000
Liabilities & Net Worth					
Accounts payable	800,000	1.2000	$ 960,000	1.0000	$ 800,000
Short-term bank debt	1,600,000	1.2000	1,920,000	1.0000	1,600,000
Long-term debt	1,600,000	1.2000	1,920,000	1.0000	1,600,000
Common stock	1,800,000	1.2760	2,296,800	1.2760	2,296,800
Retained earnings	6,200,000	1.2437 (a)	7,711,200	1.2437 (b)	7,711,200
Translation gain (loss)	–				$ (160,000)(c)
Total	12,000,000		$ 14,808,000		$ 13,848,000

(a) Dollar retained earnings before depreciation are the cumulative sum of additions to retained earnings of all prior years, translated at exchange rates in each year. The result of those multiple calculations is shown here. The effective exchange rate is $1.243742 = €1.00 to produce $7,711,200.

(b) Translated into dollars at the same rate as before depreciation of the euro.

(c) Under the temporal method, the translation loss of $160,000 would be closed into retained earnings through the income statement rather than left as a separate line item as shown here. Ending retained earnings would actually be $7,711,200 − $160,000 = $7,551,200.

GLOBAL FINANCE IN PRACTICE 11.2

The Value of the Foreign Subsidiary

Since the value of a multinational enterprise is, at minimum, the sum of the parts, maintaining and growing the value of the subsidiary are critical, including value changes arising from exchange rate changes. Changes in the value of a subsidiary as a result of a change in an exchange rate can be decomposed into those changes specific to the income and the assets of the subsidiary.

$$\Delta \text{ in Value of Subsidiary} = \Delta \text{ in Value of Assets} + \Delta \text{ in Value of Earnings}$$

Subsidiary Earnings.

The earnings of the subsidiary, once remeasured into the home currency of the parent company, contribute directly to the consolidated income of the firm. An exchange rate change results in fluctuations in the value of the subsidiary's income to the global corporation. If the individual subsidiary in question constitutes a relatively significant or material component of consolidated income, the multinational firm's reported income (and earnings per share [EPS]) may be seen to change purely as a result of translation.

Subsidiary Assets

Changes in the reporting currency value of the net assets of the subsidiary are passed into consolidated income or equity. If the foreign subsidiary of a U.S. multinational was designated as "dollar functional," remeasurement results in a transaction exposure, which is passed through current consolidated income. If the foreign subsidiary was designated as "local currency functional," translation results in a translation adjustment and is reported in consolidated equity as a translation adjustment. It does not alter reported consolidated net income.

earnings would, in fact, be $7,711,200 minus $160,000, or $7,551,200. Whether gains and losses pass through the income statement under the temporal method depends upon the country.

In the case of Ganado, the translation gain or loss is larger under the current rate method because inventory and net property, plant, and equipment, as well as all monetary assets, are deemed exposed. When net exposed assets are larger, gains or losses from translation are also larger. If management expects a foreign currency to depreciate, it could minimize translation exposure by reducing net exposed assets. If management anticipates an appreciation of the foreign currency, it should increase net exposed assets to benefit from a gain. Depending on the accounting method, management might select different assets and liabilities for reduction or increase. Thus, "real" decisions about investing and financing might be dictated by which accounting technique is used, when, in fact, accounting impacts should be neutral. And as illustrated in *Global Finance in Practice 11.2*, transaction/translation exposures may become intertwined in subsidiary valuation.

11.4 Managing Translation Exposure

Covering P&L translation risk is more complex to hedge and therefore not done by corporates to the same extent as transactional risk," says Francois Masquelier, chairman of the Association of Corporate Treasurers of Luxembourg. "Of course, reported earnings can have positive or negative effects depending on what the currency does vis-à-vis your functional currency. If you have losses in the US then it can reduce those losses (when USD is weaker versus EUR), but if you have profit it can reduce that contribution to the earnings before interest, tax, depreciation and amortization and therefore your net profit.

—"Translation Risk Hits Corporate Earnings," *FX Week*, May 9, 2014.

Translation exposure poses risks to both consolidated income and consolidated equity. Although many multinationals regularly manage the risks arising from balance sheets—*net equity investment* in subsidiaries—a number of firms have also hedged the risks to their consolidated income arising from subsidiary earnings. We begin our discussion with subsidiary earnings.

Subsidiary Earnings

Multinational companies that generate large proportions of their profits offshore are particularly exposed to the currency risks associated with translation of subsidiary earnings. As demonstrated previously with Ganado's global results of sales and earnings in Exhibit 11.4, translation can result in volatility in earnings, which for publicly traded companies is a problem for share prices.

In principle, many investors both understand and accept the income risks of a multinational company generating earnings in a multitude of non-reporting currencies. It may in fact be desirable by the investor and therefore part of the multinational firm's attraction. Multinationals that carry significant subsidiary earnings exposure—for example, a firm like Toyota (Japan), which regularly generates more than 80% of its profits offshore—are very clear and detailed at "stripping" currency impacts out of investor presentations on periodic results. (This is what was shown previously in Exhibit 11.4 where the change in an individual subsidiary's sales and earnings is separated from the change in the relevant exchange rate.) The combination of transparency and acceptance has dominated, with few firms attempting to manage translation exposure of subsidiary earnings.

A few companies—for example, Coca-Cola and Goodyear, to name two—have in the past hedged subsidiary profits with financial derivatives.[2] This requires forecasting subsidiary earnings far enough out into the future—for example, 12 to 18 months—to provide material protection. But earnings result from the interplay of a multitude of individual exposures and transactions, making forecasting earnings difficult to say the least. Many firms do frequently hedge dividends declared from the subsidiary to the parent company when declared in a foreign currency. This reduces the non-hedged earnings significantly on their own.

The final drawback to hedging subsidiary earnings is accounting treatment. Under current financial accounting standards, the hedging of foreign subsidiary earnings does not qualify for *hedge accounting*. (Hedge accounting is detailed in *Global Finance in Practice 11.3*.) The primary objection to their qualification is, as we pointed out previously, the difficulty in forecasting their probable values. This means that financial derivatives like forward contracts and currency options, purchased as hedges for subsidiary earnings, must be re-valued ("marked-to-market") on a regular reporting basis, independent of the exposure itself. This means that the periodic valuation of the financial derivatives (the hedges) ends up impacting reporting earnings more often than the underlying exposure (the foreign subsidiary earnings). If a firm is attempting to hedge subsidiary earnings a year into the future, hedging could give rise to more earnings volatility rather than less.

Net Equity Investment

The main technique to minimize translation exposure is called a *balance sheet hedge*. At times, some firms have attempted to hedge translation exposure in the forward market. Such action amounts to speculating in the forward market in the hope that a cash profit will be realized to offset the noncash loss from translation. Success depends on a precise prediction of future exchange rates, for such a hedge will be effective over a range of possible future spot rates. In addition, the profit from the forward "hedge" (i.e., speculation) is taxable, but the translation loss does not reduce taxable income.

A *balance sheet hedge* requires an equal amount of exposed foreign currency assets and liabilities on a firm's consolidated balance sheet. If this can be achieved for each foreign currency,

[2] Surveys of corporate hedging practices typically find only 10% to 15% of firms surveyed actively hedge net investment risk or foreign earnings.

GLOBAL FINANCE IN PRACTICE 11.3

Foreign Currency Hedge Accounting

One of the primary objectives of foreign currency hedging is to reduce losses or fluctuations in company earnings or cash flows caused by fluctuations in foreign exchange rates. Frequently this is achieved through the use of financial derivatives. Accounting practices, however, do not always match this objective. The primary problem is *mark-to-market* (MTM) accounting, in which the value of the exposure and the value of the financial derivative hedging the exposure are valued at the end of a reporting period—prior to the maturity of the exposure/hedge. Depending on the exposure and the financial derivative, their MTM valuation may introduce more volatility, not less, to reported earnings.

The purpose of hedge accounting is to associate the exposure and the hedge so that fluctuations in value in one offset the fluctuations in value of the other—to treat them as one. Accounting standards have established hedge accounting for three different categories of foreign exchange hedges:

1. **Cash Flow Hedge.** A cash flow hedge may be designated for a highly probable forecasted transaction, a firm commitment (a transaction not yet recorded on the balance sheet), foreign currency cash flows of a recognized asset or liability, or a forecasted intercompany transaction. Hedge accounting allows the recording of fluctuations in the value of the financial derivative in a company's equity account, not impacting earnings, by deferring recognition until the transaction occurs.
2. **Fair Value Hedge.** A fair value hedge may be designated for a firm commitment (not recorded) or foreign currency cash flows of a recognized asset or liability. Hedge accounting allows marking-to-market an asset or liability (that which is being hedged), matching it to the fluctuation in value of the financial derivative hedge, neutralizing the impact on earnings.
3. **Net Investment Hedge.** A net investment hedge may be designated for the net investment in a foreign subsidiary or operation. Hedge accounting allows matching the fluctuation in earnings arising from the translation loss with the fluctuation in value arising from the hedge, whether it be a financial derivative or a debt instrument.

There are, of course, a number of very specific requirements that must be met in order to use hedge accounting, including proper designation as a firm commitment, a highly probable forecasted transaction, and hedge effectiveness. A firm commitment is a binding agreement for the exchange of a specified quantity of resources at a specified price on a specified future date (or dates). A forecasted transaction is an uncommitted but highly probable future transaction. Hedge effectiveness is the requirement that the hedge will offset between 80% and 125% of the fluctuation in the value of the exposure.

net translation exposure will be zero. A change in exchange rates will change the value of exposed liabilities in an equal amount but in a direction opposite to the change in value of exposed assets. If a firm translates by the temporal method, a zero net exposed position is called "monetary balance." Complete monetary balance cannot be achieved under the current rate method because total assets would have to be matched by an equal amount of debt, but the equity section of the balance sheet must still be translated at historic exchange rates.

The cost of a balance sheet hedge depends on relative borrowing costs. If foreign currency borrowing costs, after adjusting for foreign exchange risk, are higher than parent currency borrowing costs, the balance sheet hedge is costly, and vice versa. Normal operations, however, already require decisions about the magnitude and currency denomination of specific balance sheet accounts. Thus, balance sheet hedges are a compromise in which the denomination of balance sheet accounts is altered, perhaps at a cost in terms of interest expense or operating efficiency, in order to achieve some degree of foreign exchange protection.

To achieve a balance sheet hedge, Ganado Corporation must either (1) reduce exposed euro assets without simultaneously reducing euro liabilities or (2) increase euro liabilities without simultaneously increasing euro assets. One way to achieve this is to exchange existing euro cash for dollars. If Ganado Europe does not have large euro cash balances, it can borrow euros and exchange the borrowed euros for dollars. Another subsidiary could also borrow euros and exchange them for dollars. That is, the essence of the hedge is for the parent or any of its subsidiaries to create euro debt and exchange the proceeds for dollars.

Current Rate Method. Under the current rate method, Ganado should borrow as much as €8 million. The initial effect of this first step is to increase both an exposed asset (cash) and an exposed liability (notes payable) on the balance sheet of Ganado Europe, with no immediate effect on net exposed assets. The required follow-up step can take two forms: (1) Ganado Europe could exchange the acquired euros for U.S. dollars and hold those dollars itself, or (2) it could transfer the borrowed euros to Ganado Corporation, perhaps as a euro dividend or as repayment of intracompany debt. Ganado Corporation could then exchange the euros for dollars.

An alternative would be for Ganado Corporation or a sister subsidiary to borrow the euros, thus keeping the euro debt entirely off Ganado's books. However, the second step is still essential to eliminate euro exposure; the borrowing entity must exchange the euros for dollars or other unexposed assets. Any such borrowing should be coordinated with all other euro borrowings to avoid the possibility that one subsidiary is borrowing euros to reduce translation exposure at the same time as another subsidiary is repaying euro debt. (Note that euros can be "borrowed" by simply delaying repayment of existing euro debt; the goal is to increase euro debt, not to borrow in a literal sense.)

Temporal Method. If translation is by the temporal method, the much smaller amount of only €800,000 need be borrowed. As before, Ganado Europe could use the proceeds of the loan to acquire U.S. dollars. However, Ganado Europe could also use the proceeds to acquire inventory or fixed assets in Europe. Under the temporal method, these assets are not regarded as exposed and do not drop in dollar value when the euro depreciates.

When Is a Balance Sheet Hedge Justified?

If a firm's subsidiary is using the local currency as the functional currency, the following circumstances could justify the use of a balance sheet hedge:

- The foreign subsidiary is about to be liquidated, so that value of its CTA would be realized.
- The firm has debt covenants or bank agreements that require the firm's debt/equity ratios to be maintained within specific limits.
- Management is evaluated based on certain income statement and balance sheet measures that are affected by translation losses or gains.
- The foreign subsidiary is operating in a hyperinflationary environment.

If a firm is using the parent's home currency as the functional currency of the foreign subsidiary, all transaction gains/losses are passed through to the income statement. Hedging this consolidated income to reduce its variability may be important to investors and bond rating agencies. In the end, translation exposure is a topic of great concern and involves complex choices for all multinational firms, including whether to hedge it at all and, if so, how to hedge it.

Using Cross-Currency Swaps to Hedge Translation: The Case of McDonald's

McDonald's Corporation (NYSE: MCD) is one of the world's most recognized and valuable brands. But as McDonald's has grown and expanded globally, so have the investment risks associated with its investment in more than 100 countries. Like most multinational firms, it considers its equity investment in foreign affiliates capital at risk—risk of loss, nationalization, and currency valuation. McDonald's has been quite innovative in its hedging of these combined currency risks over time, finding new ways to construct old solutions—such as *Hoover Hedges*—but doing so with cross-currency swaps.

Hoover Hedges. When a parent company like McDonald's creates and invests in a foreign subsidiary, it creates an asset, its foreign investment in a foreign subsidiary, which corresponds to the equity investment on the balance sheet of the foreign subsidiary. But the equity investment in the foreign subsidiary is now in local currency, the currency of the foreign business environment. If this is the predominant currency of this subsidiary's business, it is the *functional currency* of the subsidiary. Then, as the exchange rate between two currencies changes, the parent company's equity investment is subject to foreign exchange risk.

Many multinationals hedge this equity investment exposure with what is described as a balance sheet hedge. Since the parent company possesses a long-term asset in the foreign currency, the company tries to hedge this asset by creating a matching long-term liability in the same currency. A long-term loan in the currency of the foreign subsidiary is frequently used. The loan itself is often structured as a bullet repayment loan, in which interest payments are made over time but the entire principal is due in a single final payment—*bullet*—at maturity. In this way, the principal on the long-term loan acts as a match to the long-term equity investment.

These hedges are referred to as *Hoover Hedges* following the court case of Hoover Company versus the U.S. Internal Revenue Service. The primary issue in the case was whether the gains and losses from short sales in foreign currency that the Hoover Company used as hedges were to be considered to be, for tax purposes, ordinary losses, business expenses, or capital losses and gains. Although borrowing in the local currency is frequently used, there are a number of other potential hedges of equity investments, including short sales and the use of traditional foreign currency derivatives like forward contracts and currency options.

McDonald's Business Forms. McDonald's has structured its business in a variety of different ways depending on the marketplace. In the U.S., the company has utilized a franchising structure, where it awards a franchise to a private investor. That investor then has exclusive rights to the sale and distribution of McDonald's products and services within the designated franchise zone. McDonald's corporation owns the land and building, but the franchisee is responsible for the investment in all equipment and furnishings required for the restaurant under the franchise agreement—"from the paint in," as they describe it. This structure allows McDonald's to expand with a lower level of capital investment (the franchisee is investing a significant portion) and at the same time create a financial incentive for the franchisee to remain focused on and committed to the restaurant's success and profitability. In return, McDonald's earns a royalty from the franchise's sales, typically 5% to 5.5% of sales.

Alternatively, in markets where the company wishes to have more direct control and is willing to make substantially larger capital investments itself, McDonald's uses the more common form of direct ownership. Although having to put up all the capital needed for the establishment of these restaurants, it gains more direct control over operations. Much of McDonald's international expansion has been structured under this more common direct ownership approach, but at the risk of substantial amounts of capital, as the company seeks to gain a major presence in a growing number of countries.

The British Subsidiary and Currency Exposure. In the United Kingdom, McDonald's owns the majority of its restaurants. These investments create three different British pound-denominated currency exposures for the parent company (detailed in Exhibit 11.7).

1. The British subsidiary has equity capital, which is a British pound-denominated asset of the parent company.

EXHIBIT 11.7 McDonald's Cross-Currency Swap Strategy for the UK

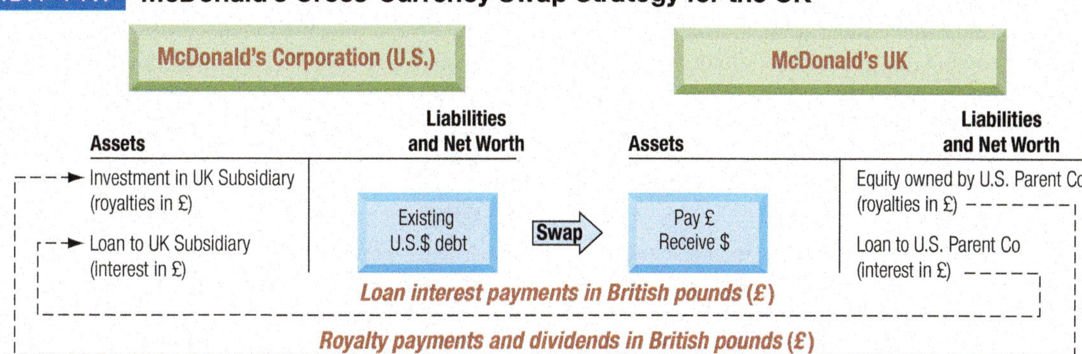

Because the British subsidiary makes all payments to the U.S. parent company in British pounds, McDonald's U.S. is long British pounds. By entering into a swap to *pay pounds* (£) and *receive dollars* ($), the swap creates an outflow of £ serviced by the $ inflows. But the cross-currency swap has one additional major feature useful to McDonald's: the cross-currency swap has a large principal which is outstanding (bullet repayment) which acts as *a counterweight*—a *match*—to the long-term investment in the UK subsidiary.

2. The parent company provides intracompany debt in the form of a four-year loan. The loan is denominated in British pounds, and carries a fixed rate of interest.
3. The British subsidiary pays a fixed percentage of gross sales in royalties to the parent company. This too is pound-denominated.

An additional technical detail further complicates the situation. When the parent company makes an intracompany loan to the British subsidiary, it must designate—according to U.S. accounting and tax law practices—whether the loan is "permanently invested" in that country. Although on the surface it seems illogical to consider four years "permanent," the loan itself could simply be continually rolled over by the parent company and never actually be repaid.

If the loan is not designated "permanent," the foreign exchange gains and losses related to the loan flow directly to the parent company's income statement, according to U.S. accounting practices, which is the primary standard for U.S. foreign currency reporting. If, however, the loan is designated as permanent, then the foreign exchange gains and losses related to the intracompany loan flow only to the cumulative translation adjustment account (CTA), a segment of consolidated equity on the company's consolidated balance sheet. To date, McDonald's has chosen to designate these loans as permanent. The functional currency of the British subsidiary for consolidation purposes is the local currency, the British pound.

Cross-Currency Swap Hedging. McDonald's has in the past hedged its rather complex British pound exposure by entering into a U.S. dollar–British pound sterling cross-currency swap. The swaps may be of differing longer and longer maturities and are agreements to receive dollars and pay pounds. Like all cross-currency swaps, the agreement requires McDonald's (U.S.) to make regular pound-denominated interest payments and a bullet principal repayment (notional principal) at the end of the swap agreement.

The cross-currency swap serves as a hedge of both the regular royalty and interest payments in British pounds made to the U.S. parent, and the outstanding swap notional principal in British pounds serves as a hedge of the equity investment by McDonald's U.S. in the British subsidiary. According to accounting practice, a company may elect to take the interest associated with a foreign currency-denominated loan and carry that directly to the parent company's consolidated income. This has been done in the past, and McDonald's benefited from the inclusion.

Summary Points

- Translation exposure results from translating foreign currency-denominated statements of foreign subsidiaries into the parent's reporting currency to prepare consolidated financial statements.
- A foreign subsidiary's functional currency is the dominant currency used by that foreign subsidiary in its day-to-day operations.
- Technical aspects of translation include questions about when to recognize gains or losses, the distinction between functional and reporting currency, and the treatment of subsidiaries in hyperinflation countries.
- Translation gains and losses can be quite different from operating gains and losses, not only in magnitude but also in direction. Management may need to determine which is of greater significance prior to deciding which exposure is to be managed first.
- The main technique for managing translation exposure is a balance sheet hedge. This calls for having an equal amount of exposed foreign currency assets and liabilities.
- Even if management chooses to follow an active policy of hedging translation exposure, it is nearly impossible to offset both transaction and translation exposure simultaneously. If forced to choose, most managers will protect against transaction losses because they impact consolidated earnings.

MINI-CASE

Electrolux of Sweden's Currency Management[3]

> *If you were to create a company that's emblematic of the global economy, it might look a lot like Electrolux. It's based in Sweden, but holds its board meetings in English, the world's common language. Top managers come from countries that include Brazil, Jamaica and Germany.*
>
> —"Straberg's Strategy: Cutting Costs Led Electrolux to Memphis," *The Commercial Appeal*, Sept 18, 2011.

Electrolux of Sweden was one of the world's premier appliance manufacturers. But it operated in an industry that was intensely competitive, the result of which was historically slim profit margins. Given this focus on managing costs and operational excellence, currency losses could potentially be devastating to profitability and shareholder value. Electrolux had established a highly structured currency exposure management program to protect those valued but slim profit margins.

Electrolux

AB Electrolux (OMB: ELUX B; ADR: ELUXY), headquartered in Stockholm, Sweden, started life as a kerosene lamp company called AB Lux in 1901. In 1919, in a new combination of companies, its name was changed to Elektrolux and eventually Electrolux. By 2016 it was selling products in 150 countries.

As illustrated in Exhibit A, Electrolux's financial results had been extremely steady over the past 16 years. Although sales had been lower every year since 2001, they had stabilized and showed glimmers of growth in recent years. Despite the intense competition and race to reduce costs globally, Electrolux had made a profit in every year, averaging about 2.13% return on sales over the period (net income/sales). Even in the midst of the global financial crisis of 2008 and 2009, the company had remained profitable.

Although the second largest appliance maker in the world behind Whirlpool (U.S.), Electrolux had long struggled with manufacturing costs, particularly labor costs. In the late 1990s it had closed manufacturing facilities across Western Europe (including its home country of Sweden), shifting significant production first to lower-labor-cost Eastern Europe and eventually to mainland China. In the process it had reduced global headcount by 12,000. In a series of renewed cuts the company had shed another 30,000 jobs worldwide between 2002 and 2014, moving from just 20% of its production in low-cost countries to more than 60%. In 2016 Electrolux employed 55,400 people worldwide.

Structure of Global Operations

Electrolux divided its product portfolio into three parts: (1) major appliances, making up 88% of global sales in 2016; (2) small appliances, 7% of sales; and (3) professional products, 5% of sales. Major appliances was obviously the core of the business and was in turn structured into four major geographic segments for global operations: Europe, Middle East, and Asia (EMEA); North America; Latin America; and Asia/Pacific.

[3] This case was prepared by Professor Michael H. Moffett for the purpose of classroom discussion only, and not to indicate either effective or ineffective management.

EXHIBIT A **Electrolux Global Sales and Profitability**

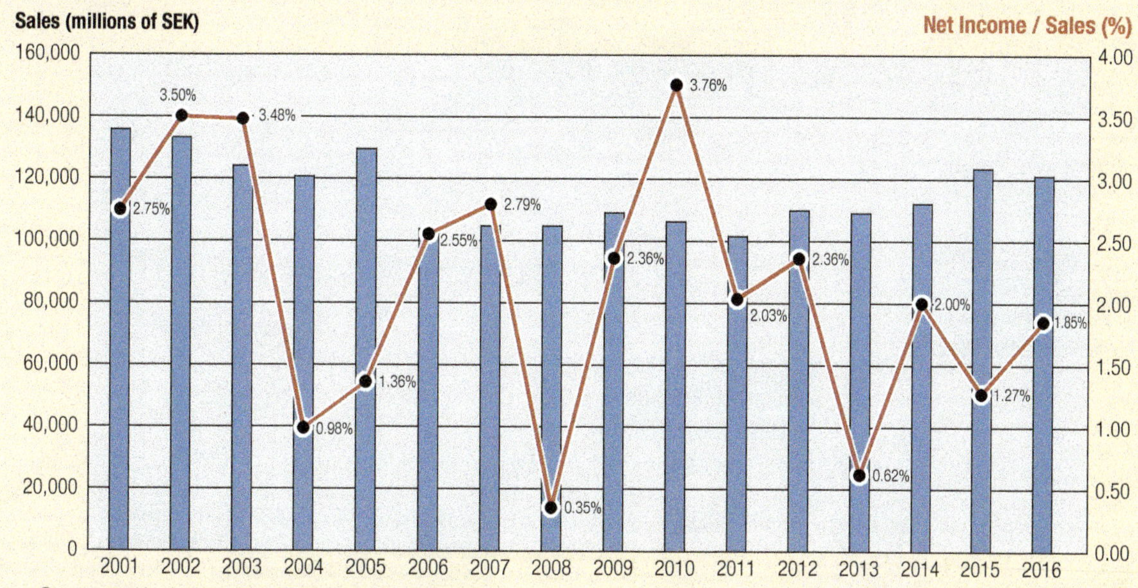

Source: Constructed by authors from Electrolux Annual Reports.

EXHIBIT B **Electrolux's Business Sales and Operating Incomes, 2016**

Electrolux Business	Net sales	Percentage of Total	Operating Income	Percent of Total	Operating Margin
Major Appliances: EMEA	37,844	31.3%	2,546	40.6%	6.7%
Major Appliances: North America	43,402	35.8%	2,671	2.2%	6.2%
Major Appliances: Latin America	15,419	12.7%	–68	–0.1%	–0.4%
Major Appliances: Asia/Pacific	9,380	7.7%	626	0.5%	6.7%
Small Appliances	8,183	6.8%	238	0.2%	2.9%
Professional Products	6,865	5.7%	954	0.8%	13.9%
Other	0	0.0%	–693	–0.6%	
	121,093	100.0%	6,274	5.2%	5.2%

Source: *Electrolux Annual Report 2016*, p. 140.

As illustrated by Exhibit B, despite being a global company, Electrolux made most of its profits in two major regions —North America and the EMEA. Although Asia/Pacific had a healthy operating margin similar to NA and the EMEA, the smaller level of sales in the region prevented its profits from having the same weight. Latin America, despite showing significant sales, was currently operating at a loss.

Global Operations and Currency Exposure

A company's global currency exposure is a combination of the structure of its manufacturing and sales—operations and how it conducts its operations—management. Electrolux had a rather unique combination that presented two very specific currency exposure challenges.

First, although the company was Swedish by incorporation and financing reporting, few actual currency transactions involved the home currency, the Swedish krona (SEK). This made nearly all other currencies "foreign currencies." Secondly, the growing use of Chinese manufacturing was shifting the company's net currency exposure. The majority of purchases of Chinese manufactured goods, from both Electrolux operations and other manufacturers, were denominated in U.S. dollars (USD), not Chinese renminbi (CNY). Only North American operations had significant purchases from China in Chinese renminbi (CNY). These two forces combined in different

EXHIBIT C Mapping a Company's Currency Exposure: Electrolux of Sweden

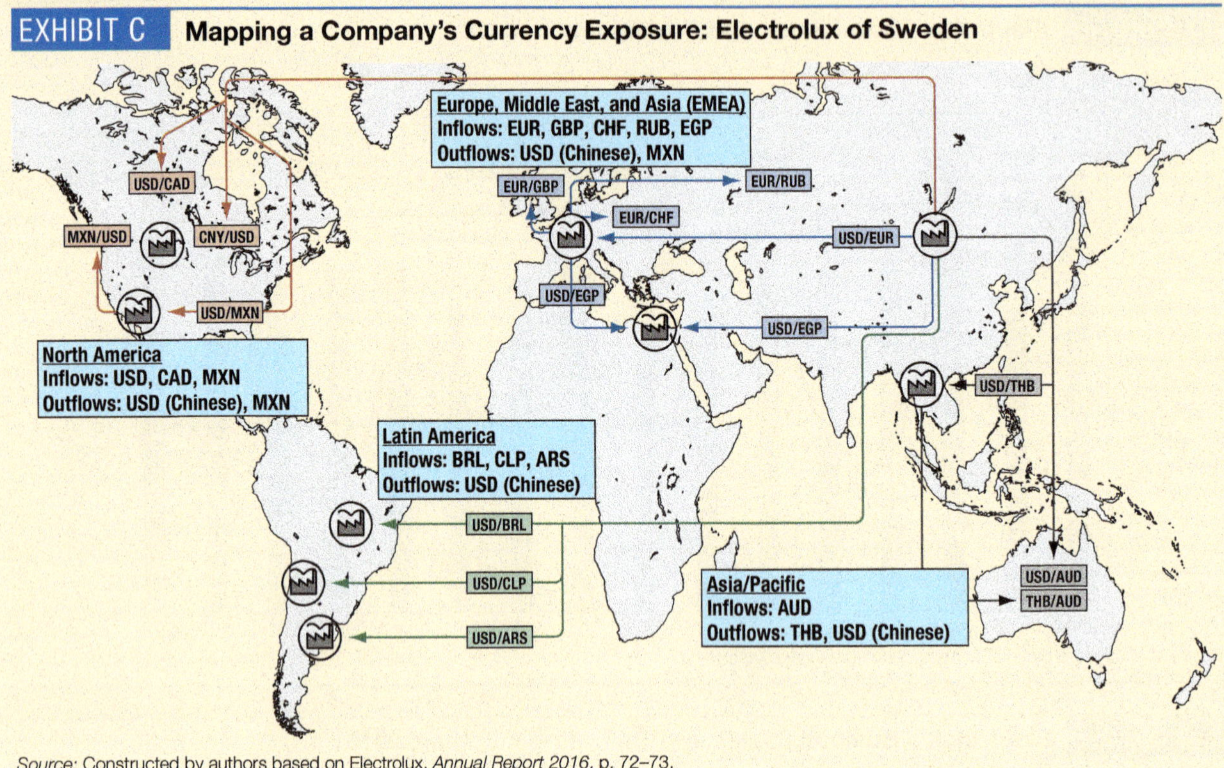

Source: Constructed by authors based on Electrolux, *Annual Report 2016*, p. 72–73.

ways to structure Electrolux's global currency transaction flows, a described in Exhibit C 's global currency map for the company.

Europe, Middle East, and Asia (EMEA). Electrolux had a large and historical base in Europe—both Western Europe and Eastern Europe. Sales in the EMEA region resulted in currency earnings in U.S. dollars (USD), European euros (EUR), Egyptian pounds (EGP), Russian rubles (RUB), Swiss francs (CHF), and British pounds (GBP). Historically, most of EMEA sales were sourced from within the area, meaning material and sourcing expenses were primarily denominated in euros. However, in the pursuit of lower and lower costs for competitiveness, more and more of the sourcing was shifting to mainland China, increasing the expenses in U.S. dollars (USD). The result was the EMEA annually experienced a net short position in the dollar and euro, with net long positions in all other EMEA sales currencies.

North America. Electrolux's North American operations were more complex. Sales in the U.S. and Canada generated long positions in local currency (USD and CAD). Sourcing, however, was from multiple facilities globally, in addition to local currency expenses and procurement. Foreign currency sourcing regularly generates short positions in Chinese renminbi (CNY), Thai baht (THB), and Mexican pesos (MXN).

Latin America. The company has manufacturing and sales activities in Argentina (ARS), Brazil (BRL), and Chile (CLP). Sales and expenses in these countries generate net long currency positions in each of these three host country currencies. Foreign sourcing costs are dominated by the USD as a result of purchasing from mainland China, with small amounts of specialty purchases from Europe in EUR.

Asia/Pacific. Composed primarily of Australian sales (long AUD), with sourcing of materials and components from Thailand, China, and Europe. This sourcing creates net short positions in the Thai baht (THB), U.S. dollar (USD), and euro (EUR).

Exhibit D provides a quantitative verification of these operating region currency exposures. This measurement provided a baseline analysis for the management of Electrolux's operating exposure. The resulting net exposures as estimated by Corporate Treasury are then transferred to the regional or country business unit. This shifts the currency gains or

EXHIBIT D Electrolux's Forecast of Global Net Currency Exposures for 2017 (millions of SEK)

Region	USD	EUR	CNY	THB	MXN	ARS	EGP	RUB	CLP	CHF	CAD	BRL	AUD	GBP
North America	2,000	(300)	(2,737)	(100)	(400)						2,036			
Europe	(3,175)	(3,728)					700	800		1,557				3,247
Asia/Pacific	(4,400)	(240)		(1,043)									2,829	
Latin America	(2,400)	(200)				200			1.179			1.895		
Net exposure	(7,975)	(4,468)	(2,737)	(1,143)	(400)	200	700	800	1.179	1,557	2,036	1.895	2,829	3,247

Source: Constructed by authors from *Electrolux Annual Report*, 2015 and 2016. Some values are approximations.

EXHIBIT E Electrolux's Forecasted Transaction Flows and Hedges for 2015 (millions of SEK)

Currency Position	USD	EUR	CNY	EGP	CLP	CHF	CAD	BRL	AUD	GBP	Other	Total
Inflow of currency	9,667	4,859	–	955	1,349	2,094	3,691	4,892	2,271	3,090	18,407	51,275
Outflow of currency	(21,023)	(8,608)	(2,618)	(162)	(310)	(733)	(1,358)	(23)	(182)	(634)	(15,624)	(51,275)
Gross transaction flow	(11,356)	(3,749)	(2,618)	793	1,039	1,361	2,333	4,869	2,089	2,456	2,783	–
Hedge positions	1,298	1,691	2,086	793	(198)	(519)	(858)	(457)	(899)	(963)	(489)	–
Net transaction flow	(10,058)	(2,058)	(532)	1,586	841	842	1,475	4,412	1,190	1,493	2,294	–

Source: Constructed by authors from *Electrolux Annual Report*, 2015. Electrolux categorizes inflows as *long positions*, outflows as short *positions*. Transaction flows for ARS, MXN, RUB, and THB are included within Other.

losses, after hedging, to the units actually generating the exposures. The company expects local business unit leadership to work to accommodate those currency gains and losses through cost reductions and price adjustments—as possible.

Currency Management

> *Foreign-exchange risk refers to the adverse effects of changes in foreign-exchange rates on the Group's income and equity. In order to manage such effects, the Group covers these risks within the framework of the Financial Policy. The Group's overall currency exposure is managed centrally.*
>
> —*Electrolux Annual Report*, 2016, p. 70.

Risk management at Electrolux included three major areas: *operational risks* (such as market risk, pricing, customer risk, commodity prices, restructuring), *financial risks* (financing, interest rates, pension commitments, and foreign exchange), and *other risks* (regulatory and reputational risks).

Electrolux, like many multinationals, manages the global currency exposure of the company centrally. Monthly, using data provided by all of its operating units, Corporate Treasury constructs a forecast of all transaction currency cash flows for the coming 12-month period. This allows the company to compile a net inflow and outflow estimate for the coming year for major currencies. The 2016 forecast and subsequent hedging positions are summarized in Exhibit E.[4]

Exhibit E indicates that Electrolux forecasted a net short position (outflows to exceed inflows) in the U.S. dollar, European euro, Chinese renminbi, and Thai baht for the coming year. Corporate Treasury then selectively hedged these short positions, with all four currency positions still net short after hedging. These residual exposures are the company's estimate of its currency exposure.

Electrolux's *Financial Policy*, the official corporate management process used in currency management, has recently changed. In 2015, the policy required the hedging of 100% of exposures maturing within two months and

[4]Electrolux net transaction and hedge positions are for shown for 2016; the company did not disclose the forecast transaction hedge positions for 2017 in its 2016 financial statements.

EXHIBIT F Sensitivity Analysis of Major Currencies

A change up or down by 10% in the value of each currency versus the SEK has the following simulated impacts on consolidated earnings.

Currency versus SEK	Symbol	Change	Profit (Loss) Impact, 2016	Profit (Loss) Impact, 2015
Australian dollar	AUD	–10%	–319	–308
British pound	GBP	–10%	–313	–319
Canadian dollar	CAD	–10%	–228	–273
Brazilian real	BRL	–10%	–213	–258
Swiss franc	CHF	–10%	–165	–166
Chilean peso	CLP	–10%	120	–114
Thai baht	THB	–10%	99	110
Chinese renminbi	CNY	–10%	244	296
European euro	EUR	–10%	321	241
U.S. dollar	USD	–10%	6608	1041

Source: Electrolux Annual Report, 2016, p. 106.

70% of exposures maturing within six months. This policy created what Electrolux considered the "hedging horizon of between three and eight months of forecast flows."

In January 2016 the company adopted a new policy (for immediate implementation), that restricted hedging to invoiced exposures only. This was a significant change. It meant that although a unit, say Australia, regularly purchased components and materials from China (in USD) and Thailand (in THB), if those purchases had not yet been invoiced (although the likelihood of the purchase is likely more than 80% or 90%), those anticipated exposures could not be hedged using financial derivatives.[5]

Restricting the use of financial derivatives does not, however, mean the exposures were not to be managed. Electrolux required all the operating units to manage, through their regional treasury centers if appropriate, through natural hedges (offsetting payments in the subject currency), price adjustments, or cost reductions.

As part of the company's currency management program, Corporate Treasury regularly conducts sensitivity analyses on all currency exposures, simulating a 10% change in a specific currency pair's impact on consolidated profits (global earnings). For example, a –10% change in the USD-SEK cross rate was estimated to have a SEK 1,083 benefit in 2014 and a SEK 1,014 impact in 2015. Exhibit F presents the analysis for 2016. Sensitivity analyses such as these were used on a regular basis to isolate which currencies were of the most potential risk to corporate profitability.

Electrolux's actual net transaction exposure by currency does not change dramatically over time. The structure of sales and manufacturing dictate the net exposure positions, and only strategic operating changes—like shifting more and more sourcing to China—has the ability to alter net exposure. It is also obvious that although there are 14 currency positions detailed in Exhibit C, the net exposures in the USD and EUR are clearly largest and most likely dominant. It is the hedging and management of these major world currencies that dominate Corporate Treasury's mindset. The company has learned over time that Electrolux's consolidated financial performance benefits from a weakening of the USD and the EUR and a strengthening of major net positive currency exposures associated with the BRL, GBP, CAD, and AUD.

Translation Exposure

Electrolux reports in Swedish krona, while nearly all of its financial results—earnings, assets, and cash flows—are generated in non-SEK currencies. This means that translation exposure is a continuing challenge for the company as well. Because most of the company's actual earnings—consolidated income and therefore the driver of earnings per share (EPS)—are generated out of the USD and EUR currencies, those two are the focus of most translation management activities.

Electrolux follows traditional translation practices as described in its *2016 Annual Report* (p. 103):

[5] There is one currency exception to the global currency management program: the CNY-USD position. Because of the complexity of moving money in and out of China and the difficulties in securing effective hedges on the Chinese renminbi, Electrolux Corporate Treasury allows a longer currency hedging outlook for the CNY-USD cross rate.

- Foreign currency transactions are translated into the functional currency using the exchange rate prevailing at the date of each transaction.
- Monetary assets and liabilities denominated in foreign currencies are valued at year-end exchange rates and any exchange-rate differences are included in income for the period, except when deferred in other comprehensive income for the effective part of qualifying net investment hedges.
- The consolidated financial statements are presented in Swedish krona (SEK), which is the Parent Company's functional and presentation currency.
- The balance sheets of foreign subsidiaries are translated into SEK at year-end closing rates. The income statements have been translated at the average rates for the year. Translation differences thus arising have been included in other comprehensive income.

What may be of some surprise is that although nearly 100% of the company's consolidated earnings are subject to exchange rate risk from translation of income statements of foreign subsidiaries into SEK, the company does not hedge this exposure.

MINI-CASE QUESTIONS

1. Which currency exposure—transaction, translation, or operating—is Electrolux hedging under its 2015 financial policy? Which under its 2016 financial policy?
2. Why is Electrolux continually experiencing such a large short currency position in U.S. dollars? What could change this in the coming years?
3. Electrolux acknowledges that its consolidated earnings are impacted by translation exposure but explicitly states that it does not hedge this exposure. Why do you think the company's rationale is for this decision?

Questions

11.1 Translation. What does the word *translation* mean? Why is translation exposure called an accounting exposure?

11.2 Causation. What activity gives rise to translation exposure?

11.3 Converting Financial Assets. In the context of preparing consolidated financial statements, are the terms *translate* and *convert* synonyms?

11.4 Subsidiary Characterization. What is the difference between a self-sustaining foreign entity and an integrated foreign entity?

11.5 Functional Currency. What is a functional currency? What do you think a "nonfunctional currency" would be?

11.6 Functional Currency Designation. Can or should a company change the functional currency designation of a foreign subsidiary from year to year? If so, when would this be justified?

11.7 Translation Methods. What are the two basic methods for translation used globally?

11.8 Current versus Historical. One of the major differences between translation methods is which balance sheet components are translated at which exchange rates, current or historical. Why would accounting practices ever use historical exchange rates?

11.9 Translating Assets. What are the major differences in translating assets between the current rate method and the temporal method?

11.10 Translating Liabilities. What are the major differences in translating liabilities between the current rate method and the temporal method?

11.11 Earnings or Equity. Where do you think most companies would prefer currency translation imbalances or adjustments to go—earnings or consolidated equity? Why?

11.12 Translation Exposure Management. What are the primary options firms have to manage translation exposure?

11.13 Accounting or Cash Flow. A U.S.-based multinational company generates more than 80% of its profits (earnings) outside the U.S., in the euro zone and Japan, and both the euro and the yen fall significantly in value versus the dollar as occurred in the second half of 2014. Is the impact on the firm only accounting, does it alter cash flow, or both?

11.14 Balance Sheet Hedge Justification. When is a balance sheet hedge justified?

11.15 Realization and Recognition. When would a multinational firm, if ever, realize and recognize the cumulative translation losses recorded over time associated with a subsidiary?

11.16 Tax Obligations. How does translation alter the global tax liabilities of a firm? If a multinational firm's consolidated earnings increase as a result of consolidation and translation, what is the impact on tax liabilities?

11.17 Hyperinflation. What is hyperinflation, and what are the consequences for translating foreign financial statements in countries experiencing hyperinflation?

11.18 Transaction versus Translation Losses. What are the main differences between losses from transaction exposure and translation exposure?

Problems

11.1 Ganado Europe (A). Using facts in the chapter for Ganado Europe, assume the exchange rate on January 2, 2020, in Exhibit 11.5 dropped in value from $1.2000 = €1.00 to $0.9000 = €1.00 (rather than to $1.0000 = €1.00). Recalculate Ganado Europe's translated balance sheet for January 2, 2020, with the new exchange rate using the current rate method.

a. What is the amount of translation gain or loss?
b. Where should the translation gain or loss appear in the financial statements?

11.2 Ganado Europe (B). Using facts in the chapter for Ganado Europe, assume as in Problem 11.1 that the exchange rate on January 2, 2020, in Exhibit 11.5 dropped from $1.2000 = €1.00 to $0.9000 = €1.00 (rather than to $1.0000/€). Recalculate Ganado Europe's translated balance sheet for January 2, 2020, with the new exchange rate using the temporal rate method.

a. What is the amount of translation gain or loss?
b. Where should it appear in the financial statements?
c. Why does the translation loss or gain under the temporal method differ from the loss or gain under the current rate method?

11.3 Ganado Europe (C). Using facts in the chapter for Ganado Europe, assume the exchange rate on January 2, 2020, in Exhibit 11.5 appreciated from $1.2000 = €1.00 to $1.500 = €1.00. Calculate Ganado Europe's translated balance sheet for January 2, 2020, with the new exchange rate using the current rate method.

a. What is the amount of translation gain or loss?
b. Where should it appear in the financial statements?

11.4 Ganado Europe (D). Using facts in the chapter for Ganado Europe, assume that the exchange rate on January 2, 2020, in Exhibit 11.5 appreciated from $1.2000 = €1.00 to $1.5000 = €1.00. Calculate Ganado Europe's translated balance sheet for January 2, 2020, with the new exchange rate using the temporal method.

a. What is the amount of translation gain or loss?
b. Where should it appear in the financial statements?

11.5 Tristan Narvaja, S.A. (A). Tristan Narvaja, S.A., is the Uruguayan subsidiary of a U.S. manufacturing company. Its balance sheet for January 1 follows. The January 1 exchange rate between the U.S. dollar and the peso Uruguayo ($U) is $U20 = $1.00. Determine Tristan Narvaja's contribution to the translation exposure of its parent on January 1, using the current rate method.

Balance Sheet (thousands of pesos Uruguayo, $U)

Assets		**Liabilities & Net Worth**	
Cash	$U 60,000	Current liabilities	$U 30,000
Accounts receivable	120,000	Long-term debt	90,000
Inventory	120,000	Capital stock	300,000
Net plant and equipment	240,000	Retained earnings	120,000
	$U 540,000		$U 540,000

11.6 Tristan Narvaja, S.A. (B). Using the same balance sheet as in Problem 11.5, calculate Tristan Narvaja's contribution to its parent's translation loss if the exchange rate on December 31 is $U22 = $1.00. Assume all peso accounts remain as they were at the beginning of the year.

11.7 Tristan Narvaja, S.A. (C). Calculate Tristan Narvaja's contribution to its parent's translation gain or loss using the current rate method if the exchange rate on December 31 is $U12 = $1.00. Assume all peso accounts remain as they were at the beginning of the year.

11.8 Bangkok Instruments, Ltd. (A). Bangkok Instruments, Ltd., the Thai subsidiary of a U.S. corporation, is a seismic instrument manufacturer. Bangkok Instruments manufactures the instruments primarily for the oil and gas industry globally, though with recent commodity price increases of all kinds, including copper, its business has begun to grow rapidly. Sales are primarily to multinational companies based in the U.S. and Europe. Bangkok Instruments' balance sheet in thousands of Thai bahts (B) as of March 31 is as follows:

Bangkok Instruments, Ltd.
Balance Sheet, March 1, thousands of Thai bahts

Assets		Liabilities and Net Worth	
Cash	B 24,000	Accounts payable	B 18,000
Accounts receivable	36,000	Bank loans	60,000
Inventory	48,000	Common stock	18,000
Net plant & equipment	60,000	Retained earnings	72,000
	B 168,000		B 168,000

Exchange rates for translating Bangkok Instrument's balance sheet into U.S. dollars are:

B 40.00 = $1.00	April 1 exchange rate after 25% devaluation.
B 30.00 = $1.00	March 31 exchange rate, before 25% devaluation. All inventory was acquired at this rate.
B 20.00 = $1.00	Historic exchange rate at which plant and equipment were acquired.

11.9 Bangkok Instruments, Ltd. (B). Using the original data provided for Bangkok Instruments, assume that the Thai baht appreciated in value from B30.00 = $1.00 to B25.00 = $1.00 between March 31 and April 1. Assuming no change in balance sheet accounts between those two days, calculate the gain or loss from translation by both the current rate method and the temporal method. Explain the translation gain or loss in terms of changes in the value of exposed accounts.

11.10 Cairo Ingot, Ltd. Cairo Ingot, Ltd., is the Egyptian subsidiary of Trans-Mediterranean Aluminum, a British multinational enterprise that fashions automobile engine blocks from aluminum. Trans-Mediterranean's home reporting currency is the British pound. Cairo Ingot's December 31 balance sheet is shown in the following table. At the date of this balance sheet, the exchange rate between Egyptian pounds and British pounds sterling was £E5.50 = UK£1.00.

Assets		Liabilities & Net Worth	
Cash	£E 16,500,000	Accounts payable	£E 24,750,000
Accounts receivable	33,000,000	Long-term debt	49,500,000
Inventory	49,500,000	Invested capital	90,750,000
Net plant and equipment	66,000,000		
	£E 165,000,000		£E 165,000,000

What is Cairo Ingot's contribution to the translation exposure of Trans-Mediterranean on December 31, using the current rate method? Calculate the translation exposure loss to Trans-Mediterranean if the exchange rate at the end of the following quarter is £E6.00 = UK£1.00. Assume all balance sheet accounts are the same at the end of the quarter as they were at the beginning.

12 Operating Exposure

Coyote is always waiting. And Coyote is always hungry.

—Navajo folk saying.

LEARNING OBJECTIVES

12.1 Examine how operating exposure arises in a multinational firm through unexpected changes in corporate cash flows

12.2 Analyze how to measure operating exposure's impact on a business unit through the sequence of volume, price, cost, and other key variable changes

12.3 Evaluate strategic alternatives to managing operating exposure

12.4 Detail the proactive policies firms use in managing operating exposure

This chapter examines the economic exposure of a firm over time, what we term *operating exposure. Operating exposure*, also referred to as *competitive exposure* or *strategic exposure*, measures changes in present value of a firm resulting from changes in future operating cash flows caused by unexpected changes in exchange rates. Operating exposure analysis assesses the impact of changing exchange rates on a firm's operations over months and years and on its competitive position vis-à-vis other firms. The goal is to identify strategic moves or operating techniques the firm might wish to adopt to enhance its value in the face of unexpected exchange rate changes.

Operating exposure and *transaction exposure* are related in that they both deal with future cash flows. They differ in terms of the cash flows that management considers and why those cash flows change when exchange rates change. We begin by revisiting our firm, Ganado Corporation, and how its structure dictates its likely operating exposure. The chapter continues with a series of strategies and structures used in the management of operating exposure and concludes with the mini-case *Brexit and Rolls-Royce*, which provides a timely debate over how a country's political decisions impact the operating exposure of its multinational companies.

12.1 A Multinational's Operating Exposure

The structure and operations of a multinational company determine the nature of its *operating exposure*. Ganado Corporation's basic structure and currencies of operation are described in Exhibit 12.1. As a U.S.-based publicly traded company, ultimately all financial metrics and values have to be consolidated and expressed in U.S. dollars. That accounting exposure of the firm—*translation exposure*—was described in Chapter 10. Operationally, however, the functional currencies of the individual subsidiaries, in combination, determine the overall operating exposure of the firm in total.

The operating exposure of any individual business or business unit is the net of cash inflows and outflows by currency and how that compares to other companies competing in the same markets. Accounts receivable are the cash flow proceeds from sales, and accounts payable are all ongoing operating costs associated with the purchase of labor, materials, and other

EXHIBIT 12.1 Ganado Corporation: Structure and Operations

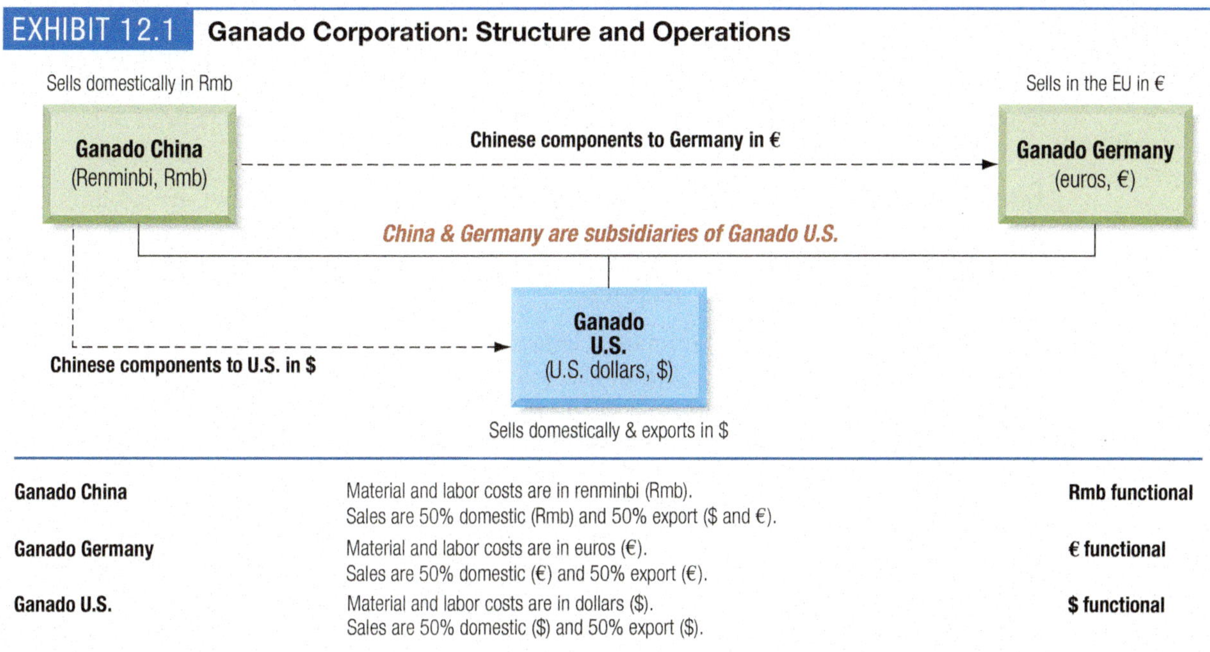

Ganado China	Material and labor costs are in renminbi (Rmb). Sales are 50% domestic (Rmb) and 50% export ($ and €).	**Rmb functional**
Ganado Germany	Material and labor costs are in euros (€). Sales are 50% domestic (€) and 50% export (€).	**€ functional**
Ganado U.S.	Material and labor costs are in dollars ($). Sales are 50% domestic ($) and 50% export ($).	**$ functional**

inputs. The net result—in general—is, in essence, the lifeblood of any business and the source of value created by the firm over time. For example, Ganado Germany sells locally and it also exports, but all sales are invoiced in euros. All operating cash inflows are therefore in its home currency, the euro. On the cost side, labor costs and many of its material input purchases are local and in euros. Ganado Germany also purchases components from Ganado China, but those too are invoiced in euros. Ganado Germany is clearly euro-functional, with all cash inflows and outflows in euros. Ganado U.S. is similar in structure to Ganado Germany. All cash inflows from sales, domestic and international, are in U.S. dollars. All costs, including labor and materials, sourced domestically and internationally, are invoiced in U.S. dollars. This includes purchases from Ganado China. Ganado U.S. is, therefore, obviously dollar functional.

Ganado China is more complex. Cash outflows, including labor and materials, are all domestic and paid in Chinese renminbi. Cash inflows, however, are generated across three different currencies as the company sells locally in renminbi, as well as exporting to both Germany in euros and the U.S. in dollars. On net, although having some cash inflows in both dollars and euros, the dominant currency is the renminbi.

Static versus Dynamic Operating Exposure

Measuring the operating exposure of a firm like Ganado requires forecasting and analyzing all the firm's future individual transaction exposures together with the future exposures of all the firm's competitors and potential competitors worldwide. Exchange rate changes in the short term affect current and immediate contracts, generally termed *transactions*. But over the longer term, as prices change and competitors react, the more fundamental economic and competitive drivers of the business may alter all cash flows of all units.

Consider Ganado Corporation's three operating subsidiaries—one each in the U.S., China, and Europe. Assume the dollar starts falling against the euro. At the same time, the Chinese government continues the gradual revaluation of the renminbi. The operating exposure of each individual business unit then needs to be examined statically (transaction exposures) and dynamically (future business transactions not yet contracted for).

Ganado China. Sales in U.S. dollars will result in fewer renminbi proceeds in the immediate period. Sales in euros may stay roughly the same in renminbi proceeds depending on the movement of the Rmb against the euro. General profitability will fall in the short run. In the longer term, depending on markets and competition, it may need to raise the price of exports, even to its U.S. parent company.

Ganado Germany. Since this business unit's cash inflows and outflows are all in euros, there is no immediate transaction exposure or change. It may suffer some rising input costs in the future if Ganado China does indeed push through price increases of component sales. Profitability is unaffected in the short term.

Ganado U.S. Like Ganado Germany, Ganado U.S. has all local currency cash inflows and outflows. A fall in the value of the dollar will have no immediate impact (transaction exposure) but cash flow may change over the medium to long term because input costs from China may rise over time as the Chinese subsidiary tries to regain prior profit margins. But, like Germany, short-term profitability is unaffected.

The net result for Ganado is possibly a fall in the total profitability of the firm in the short term, primarily from the fall in profits of the Chinese subsidiary—that is, the short-term transaction/operating exposure impact. The fall in the dollar in the short term, however, is likely to have a positive impact on translation exposure, as profits and earnings in renminbi and euros translate into more dollars. Wall Street prefers returns sooner rather than later.

Operating and Financing Cash Flows

The cash flows of the MNE can be divided into *operating cash flows* and *financing cash flows*.

- *Operating cash flows* for Ganado arise from intercompany (between unrelated companies) and intracompany (between units of the same company) receivables and payables, such as rent and lease payments for the use of facilities and equipment, royalty and license fees for the use of technology and intellectual property, and assorted management fees for services provided.
- *Financing cash flows* are payments for the use of intercompany and intracompany loans (principal and interest) and stockholder equity (new equity investments and dividends).

Each of these cash flows can occur at different time intervals, in different amounts, and in different currencies of denomination, and each has a different predictability of occurrence. We summarize cash flow possibilities in Exhibit 12.2 for Ganado China and Ganado U.S.

Expected versus Unexpected Changes in Cash Flow

Operating exposure is far more important for the long-run viability of a business than changes caused by transaction or translation exposure. However, operating exposure is inevitably subjective because it depends on estimates of future cash flow changes over an arbitrary time horizon. Thus, it springs not from the accounting process but rather from operating analysis.

Planning for operating exposure is a total management responsibility and relies upon the interaction of strategies in finance, marketing, purchasing, and production. An expected change in foreign exchange rates is not included in the definition of operating exposure because both management and investors should have factored this information into their evaluation of anticipated operating results and market value. An "expected change" arises from differing perspectives as follows:

EXHIBIT 12.2 Financial and Operating Cash Flows between Parent and Subsidiary

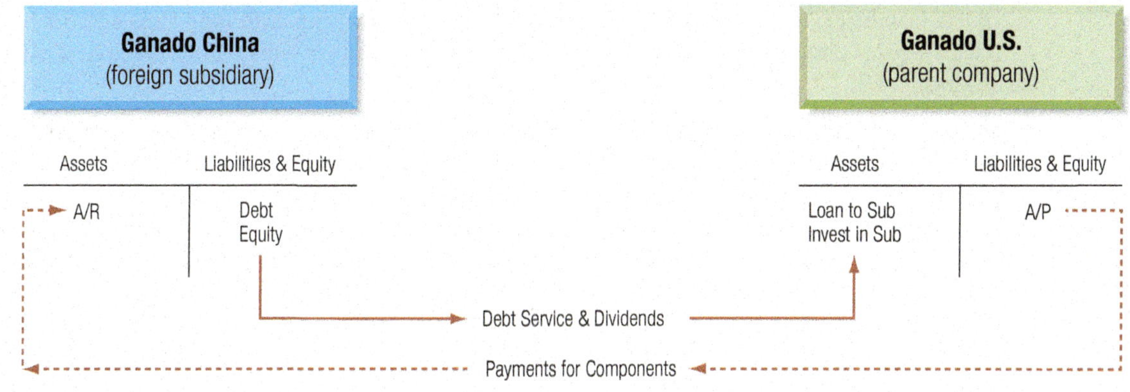

- From a management perspective, budgeted financial statements already reflect information about the effect of an expected change in exchange rates.
- From a debt service perspective, expected cash flow to amortize debt should already reflect the international Fisher effect. The level of expected interest and principal repayment should be a function of expected exchange rates rather than existing spot rates.
- From an investor's perspective, if the foreign exchange market is efficient, information about expected changes in exchange rates should be widely known and reflected in market value. This is illustrated in *Global Finance in Practice 12.1*. Only unexpected changes in exchange rates or an inefficient foreign exchange market should cause market value changes.
- From a broader macroeconomic perspective, operating exposure is not just the sensitivity of a firm's future cash flows to unexpected changes in foreign exchange rates but also its sensitivity to other key macroeconomic variables. This factor has been labeled as macroeconomic uncertainty.

GLOBAL FINANCE IN PRACTICE 12.1

Expecting the Devaluation—Ford and Venezuela

Key to the understanding of operating exposure is that expected change in foreign exchange rates is not included in the firm's operating exposure. The assumption is that the market has already taken this value change into account. But is that assumption a sound one?

Consider the case of Ford Motor Company. In December 2013, Ford was very open and public about what it expected to happen to the Venezuelan currency—further devaluation—and what that would mean for Ford's financial results. In filings with the Securities and Exchange Commission (SEC), Ford reported that it had $802 million in investments in Venezuela, that it expected the Venezuelan bolivar to fall from 6.3 to the dollar to 12, and that it could suffer a $350 million financial loss as a result. The company was speaking from some experience. Earlier in the year, it had lost $186 million when Venezuela devalued the bolivar to 6.3 from 4.3 per dollar.

12.2 Measuring Operating Exposure

So what would be the likely impact(s) of an unexpected change in exchange rates on the operating cash flows of a firm? To explore this question we decompose the possible impacts into intervals (as measured in the short run, medium run, and long run) and economic cases—price changes, volume changes, and structural changes. This taxonomy is described in Exhibit 12.3.

Short Run. The first interval impact is on expected cash flows within the one-year operating budget. The gain or loss depends on the currency of denomination of expected cash flows. These are both existing transaction exposures and anticipated exposures. The currency of denomination cannot be changed for existing obligations, or even for implied obligations, such as purchase or sales commitments. Apart from real or implied obligations, in the short run it is difficult to change sales prices or renegotiate factor costs. Therefore, realized cash flows will differ from those expected in the budget. However, as time passes, prices and costs can be changed to reflect the new competitive realities caused by a change in exchange rates.

Medium Run: Equilibrium. The second interval impact is on expected medium-run cash flows, such as those expressed in two- to five-year budgets, assuming parity conditions hold among foreign exchange rates, national inflation rates, and national interest rates. Under equilibrium conditions, the firm should be able to adjust prices and factor costs over time to maintain the expected level of cash flows. In this case, the currency of denomination of expected cash flows is not as important as the countries in which cash flows originate. National monetary, fiscal, and balance of payments policies determine whether equilibrium conditions will exist and whether firms will be allowed to adjust prices and costs.

If equilibrium exists continuously and a firm is free to adjust its prices and costs to maintain its expected competitive position, its operating exposure may be zero. Its expected cash flows would be realized and therefore its market value unchanged since the exchange rate change was anticipated. However, it is also possible that equilibrium conditions exist but the firm is unwilling or unable to adjust operations to the new competitive environment. In such a case, the firm will experience operating exposure because its realized cash flows will differ from expected cash flows. As a result, its market value may also be altered. This debate often confronts firms with a simple but perplexing challenge as described in *Global Finance in Practice 12.2*.

Medium Run: Disequilibrium. The third interval impact is on expected medium-run cash flows assuming disequilibrium conditions. In this case, the firm may not be able to adjust

EXHIBIT 12.3 Operating Exposure's Phases of Adjustment and Response

Phase	Time	Price Changes	Volume Changes	Structural Changes
Short Run	Less than 1 year	Prices are fixed through contracts	Volumes are contracted	No competitive market changes
Medium Run: Equilibrium	2 to 5 years	Complete pass-through of exchange rate changes	Volumes begin a partial response to prices	Existing competitors begin partial responses
Medium Run: Disequilibrium	2 to 5 years	Partial pass-through of exchange rate changes	Volumes begin a partial response to prices	Existing competitors begin partial responses
Long Run	More than 5 years	Completely flexible	Completely flexible	Threat of new entrants and changing competitor responses

GLOBAL FINANCE IN PRACTICE **12.2**

The Misunderstood Equation

One of the simplest and yet most misunderstood equations in global business is the foreign currency price. Assume you are a U.S.-based manufacturer who is now about to make its first export sale to Japan. The Japanese customer's procurement office requires pricing and invoicing in Japanese yen. It does this in order to compare prices of its purchases across different potential suppliers, both domestic and foreign. The U.S. firm therefore uses its U.S. dollar price as the base for setting its Japanese yen price, multiplying the dollar price by the spot exchange rate.

$$\text{Price}^{\$} \times \text{Spot}^{¥=\$1.00} = \text{Price}^{¥}$$

In its simplest form, the equation is therefore a sequence of steps,1-2-3, price in dollars, spot rate, and resulting price in Japanese yen. The initial price quote to the Japanese customer is acceptable and a sale is concluded. But then tomorrow brings a change in the spot exchange rate. If over the coming months the value of the dollar rises versus the Japanese yen (requiring more yen per dollar) and the U.S. manufacturer sets a new price in Japanese yen, the yen price the Japanese importer sees is rising. It may now see a domestic manufacturer of the same product as being cheaper than that of the U.S. firm.

The result is the never-ending debate for so many exporters, which price in the above equation should be "set" first? The price to the foreign customer in foreign currency or the price the manufacturer sells at home? This would mean reversing the application of the formula to 3-2-1. And the result may mean a very different profit margin on foreign versus domestic sales.

prices and costs to reflect the new competitive realities caused by a change in exchange rates. The primary problem may be the reactions of existing competitors. The firm's realized cash flows will differ from its expected cash flows. The firm's market value may change because of the unanticipated results.

Long Run. The fourth interval impact is on expected long-run cash flows, meaning those beyond five years. At this strategic level, a firm's cash flows will be influenced by the reactions of both existing competitors and potential competitors—possible new entrants—to exchange rate changes under disequilibrium conditions. In fact, all firms that are subject to international competition, whether they are purely domestic or multinational, are exposed to foreign exchange operating exposure in the long run whenever foreign exchange markets are not continuously in equilibrium.

Quantifying the stages of operating exposure described here is extremely difficult for multinational companies. It is in fact a two-stage problem. The first is forecasting the company's own operating cash flows into the future from possible exchange rate changes. That is possible but requires a significant amount of assumptions of what values change by what amount at what point in time. (The appendix to this chapter provides a sample of how that might be done for Ganado Germany.) The second stage challenge is estimating how competitors will respond to exchange rate changes—their pricing, volume, cost, sourcing, etc.—reactions to the unexpected exchange rate changes. That is an exercise few multinational enterprises have found fruitful.

12.3 Strategic Management of Operating Exposure

The objective of managing both operating and transaction exposure is to anticipate and influence the effect of unexpected changes in exchange rates on a firm's future cash flows rather than merely hoping for the best. To meet this objective, management can change the firm's operating and financing policies or diversify the firm's operating and financing structure.

The key to managing operating exposure at the strategic level is for management to recognize a disequilibrium in parity conditions when it occurs and to be pre-positioned to react appropriately. This task can best be accomplished if a firm diversifies internationally both its operating and its financing bases. Diversifying operations means diversifying sales, location of production facilities, and raw material sources. Diversifying financing means raising funds in more than one capital market and in more than one currency.

A diversification strategy permits the firm to react either actively or passively, depending on management's risk preference, to opportunities presented by disequilibrium conditions in the foreign exchange, capital, and product markets. Such a strategy does not require management to predict disequilibrium but only to recognize it when it occurs. It does require management to consider how competitors are pre-positioned with respect to their own operating exposures. This knowledge should reveal which firms would be helped or hurt competitively by alternative disequilibrium scenarios.

Diversifying Operations

Diversification of operations is one structural strategy to pre-positioning the firm for managing operating exposure. Consider the case in which purchasing power parity is temporarily in disequilibrium. Although the disequilibrium may have been unpredictable, management can often recognize its symptoms as soon as they occur. For example, management might notice a change in comparative costs in the firm's plants located in different countries or observe shifts in sales volumes across country markets.

Recognizing a change in worldwide competitive conditions permits management to make changes in operating strategies. Management might make marginal shifts in sourcing raw materials, components, or finished products. If spare capacity exists, production runs can be lengthened in one country and reduced in another. The marketing effort can be strengthened in export markets where the firm's products have become more price competitive because of the disequilibrium condition. And in addition to recognizing the change, an added challenge is to know when the change is temporary or semi-permanent, as described in *Global Finance in Practice 12.3.*

Even if management does not actively alter normal operations when exchange rates change, the firm should experience some beneficial portfolio effects. The variability of its cash flows is probably reduced by international diversification of its production, sourcing, and sales because exchange rate changes under disequilibrium conditions are likely to increase the firm's competitiveness in some markets while reducing it in others. In that case, operating exposure would be neutralized. In contrast to the internationally diversified MNE, a purely domestic firm might be subject to the full impact of foreign exchange operating exposure even though it does not have foreign currency cash flows. For example, it could experience import competition in its domestic market from competing firms producing in countries with undervalued currencies.

A purely domestic firm does not have the option to react to an international disequilibrium condition in the same manner as an MNE. In fact, a purely domestic firm will not be positioned to even recognize that a disequilibrium exists, because it lacks comparative data from its own internal sources. By the time external data are available, it is often too late to react. Even if a domestic firm recognizes the disequilibrium, it cannot quickly shift production and sales into foreign markets in which it has had no previous presence.

Constraints exist that may limit the feasibility of diversifying production locations. The technology of a particular industry may require large economies of scale. For example, high-tech firms, such as Intel, prefer to locate in places where they have easy access to high-tech suppliers, a highly educated workforce, and one or more leading universities. Their R&D efforts are closely tied to initial production and sales activities.

GLOBAL FINANCE IN PRACTICE 12.3

The United Kingdom and Europe: Trans-Channel Currency Shifts

The United Kingdom's largest trading partner is the European Union (EU), and although the two have been heavily intertwined for many years, the UK's recent decision to exit the EU was in many ways not that surprising. The UK never joined the euro. Keeping a separate currency, the British pound, and the associated ability to define its own monetary policy and currency has been a fundamental pillar of British pride and independence. But that independence has come at a price—what might be termed trans-channel (think English Channel) currency shifts.

The past 20 years have seen at least three different currency eras of relative strength between the pound and the euro. Prior to the launch of the euro, there was a relatively "weak pound" period. But in 1996 there was a seismic shift—roughly from GBP0.80 = EUR1.00toGBP0.65—and this shift persisted for more than a decade. During this period all things British became relatively more expensive on the Continent. British export prices were decidedly less competitive, while European exports to the UK gained at the UK's expense. As has been the case so many times around the globe, this basic terms-of-trade shift altered fundamental national economies. What the next era or cycle will look like is anyone's guess. But, despite the ebb and flow of political organizations and linkages like EU membership, the economic linkages between multinational firms on both sides of the Channel are undeniable. "Trans-channel currency shift" is operating exposure management at work.

The Trans-Channel Eras of Currency Shift

British pounds (GBP) = 1.00 European euro (EUR)

With the global financial crisis of fall 2008, the pound weakened dramatically against the euro, settling around 0.85 GBP = 1.00 EUR. In 2014, however, it started to strengthen once again, but that streak was stopped with Brexit (British exit from the EU).

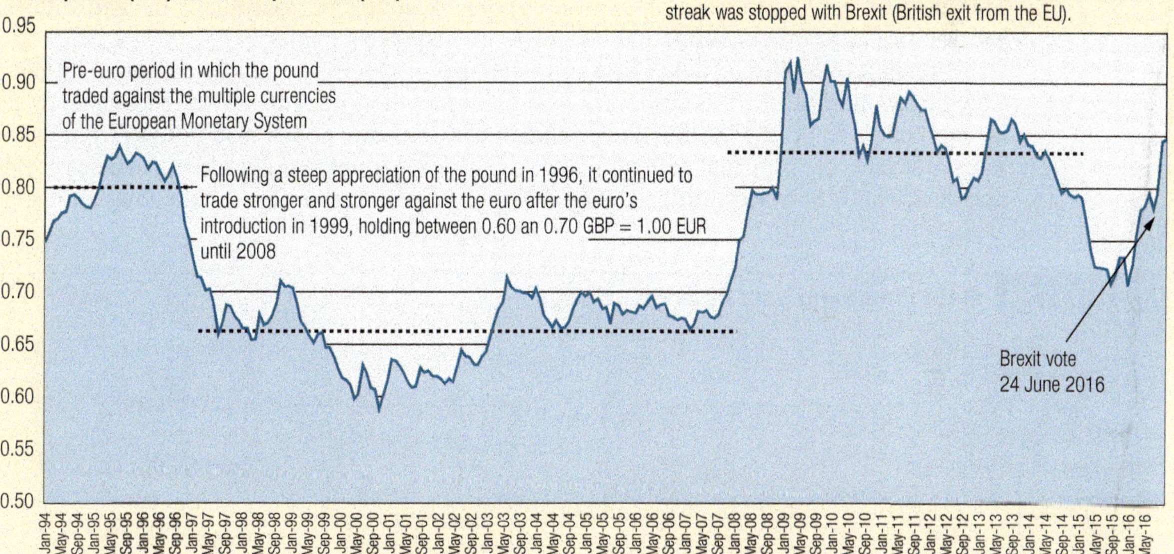

Diversifying Financing

If a firm diversifies its financing sources, it will be pre-positioned to take advantage of temporary deviations from the international Fisher effect. If interest rate differentials do not equal expected changes in exchange rates, opportunities to lower a firm's cost of capital will exist. However, to be able to switch financing sources, a firm must already be well known in the international investment community, with banking contacts firmly established. Again, this is not typically an option for a domestic firm. As we will demonstrate in Chapter 13, diversifying sources of financing, regardless of the currency of denomination, can lower a firm's cost of capital and increase its availability of capital. The ability to source capital from outside of a segmented market is especially important for firms resident in emerging markets.

12.4 Proactive Management of Operating Exposure

Operating and transaction exposures can be partially managed by adopting operating or financing policies that offset anticipated foreign exchange exposures. Five of the most commonly employed proactive policies are (1) *matching currency cash flows*, (2) *risk-sharing agreements*, (3) *back-to-back* or *parallel loans*, (4) *cross-currency swaps*, and (5) *contractual approaches*.

Matching Currency Cash Flows

One way to offset an anticipated continuous long-term exposure to a particular currency is to acquire debt denominated in that currency. Exhibit 12.4 depicts the exposure of a U.S. firm with continuing export sales to Canada. In order to compete effectively in Canadian markets, the firm invoices all export sales in Canadian dollars. This policy results in a continuing receipt of Canadian dollars month after month. If the export sales are part of a continuing supplier relationship, the long Canadian dollar position is relatively predictable and constant. This endless series of transaction exposures could of course be continually hedged with forward contracts or other contractual hedges, as discussed in Chapter 9.

But what if the firm sought out a continual use—an outflow—for its continual inflow of Canadian dollars? If the U.S. firm were to acquire part of its debt capital in the Canadian dollar markets, it could use the relatively predictable Canadian dollar cash inflows from export sales to service the principal and interest payments on Canadian dollar debt and be cash-flow matched. The U.S.-based firm has hedged an operational cash inflow by creating a financial

EXHIBIT 12.4 **Debt Financing as a Financial Hedge**

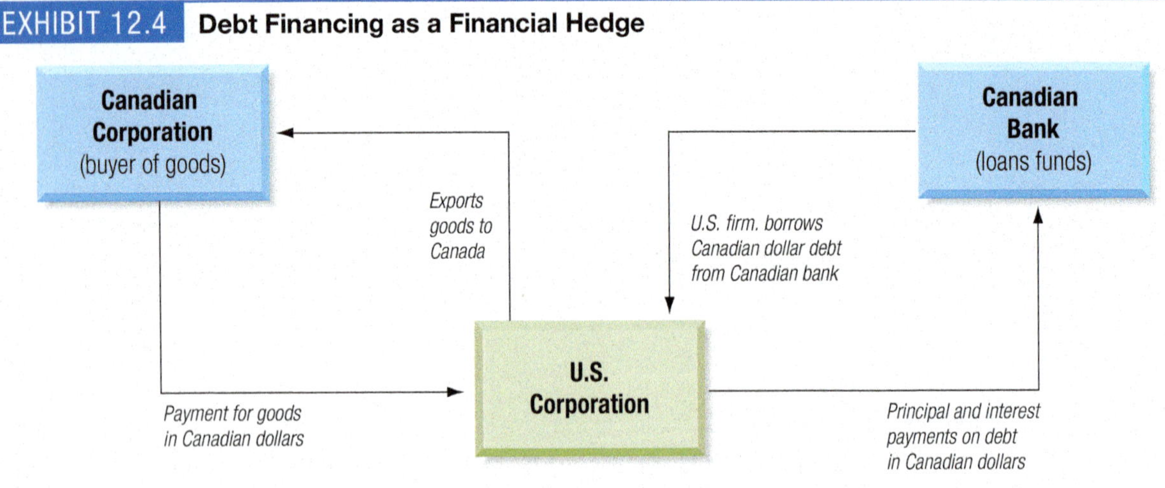

Exposure: The sale of goods by a U.S. corporation to a Canadian buyer, invoiced in Canadian dollars, creates a currency exposure—an *inflow* of Canadian dollars—for the U.S. corporation.

Hedge: The Canadian dollar debt payments act as a financial hedge by requiring debt service payments—an *outflow* in Canadian dollars—for the U.S. corporation

cash outflow, and so it does not have to actively manage the exposure with contractual financial instruments, such as forward contracts. This form of hedging, sometimes referred to as *matching*, is effective in eliminating currency exposure when the exposure cash flow is relatively constant and predictable over time.

The list of potential matching strategies is nearly endless. A second alternative would be for the U.S. firm to seek out potential suppliers of materials or components in Canada as a substitute for sourcing from U.S. or other foreign firms. The firm would then possess both an operational Canadian dollar cash inflow—a receivable—and a Canadian dollar operational cash outflow—a payable. If the cash flows were roughly the same in magnitude and timing, the strategy would be a *natural hedge*, the term *natural* referring to operating-based activities.

A third alternative, often referred to as *currency switching*, would be to pay foreign suppliers with Canadian dollars. For example, if a U.S. firm imported components from Mexico, the Mexican firms themselves might welcome payment in Canadian dollars because they are short Canadian dollars in their multinational cash flow network.

Risk-Sharing Agreements

An alternative arrangement for managing a long-term cash flow exposure between firms with a continuing buyer-supplier relationship is *risk sharing*. Risk sharing is a contractual arrangement in which the buyer and seller agree to "share" or split currency movement impacts on payments between them. If the two firms are interested in a long-term relationship based on product quality and supplier reliability, and not on the whims of the currency markets, a cooperative agreement to share the burden of currency risk may be in order.

If Ford's North American operations import automotive parts from Mazda (Japan) every month, year after year, major swings in exchange rates can benefit one party at the expense of the other. (Ford is a major stockholder of Mazda, but it does not exert control over Mazda's operations. Therefore, the risk-sharing agreement is particularly appropriate; transactions between the two are both intercompany and intracompany in nature. A risk-sharing agreement solidifies the partnership.)

One potential solution would be for Ford and Mazda to agree that all purchases by Ford will be made in Japanese yen at the current exchange rate, as long as the spot rate on the date of invoice is between, say, ¥115 = $1.00 and ¥125 = $1.00. If the exchange rate is between these values on the payment dates, Ford agrees to accept whatever transaction exposure exists (because it is paying in a foreign currency). If, however, the exchange rate falls outside this range on the payment date, Ford and Mazda will share the difference equally.

For example, Ford has an account payable of ¥25,000,000 for the month of March. If the spot rate on the date of invoice is ¥110 = $1.00, the Japanese yen would have appreciated versus the dollar, causing Ford's costs of purchasing automotive parts to rise. Since this rate falls outside the contractual range, Mazda would agree to accept a total payment in Japanese yen that would result from a difference of ¥5 per $ (i.e., ¥115 – ¥110). Ford's payment would be as follows:

$$\left[\frac{¥25{,}000{,}000}{¥115.00 - \left(\frac{¥5.00}{2}\right)}\right] = \frac{¥25{,}000{,}000}{¥112.50} = \$222{,}222.22$$

At a spot rate of ¥110 = $1.00, Ford's costs for March would be $227,272.73 without the risk-sharing agreement. With the agreement, however, Ford's payment is calculated using an exchange rate of ¥112.50 = $1.00, a payment of $222,222.22. The risk-sharing agreement constitutes a savings for Ford of $5,050.51 (this savings is a reduction in a cost increase, not a true cost reduction). Both parties therefore incur costs and benefits from exchange rate

GLOBAL FINANCE IN PRACTICE 12.4

Hedging Hogs: Risk Sharing at Harley-Davidson

Harley-Davidson (U.S.) is representative of a company with centralized manufacturing (all in the United States with costs in U.S. dollars) and global sales (predominantly in U.S. dollars, European euros, Australian dollars, and Japanese yen). Dealerships in foreign countries, therefore, purchase from Harley and sell into the local market in local currency. The foreign dealerships need to be assured of stable product costs—in local currency and at a predictable purchase price of the hogs from Harley (U.S.)—in order to offer stable and competitive prices in-country. Harley manages this problem with a risk-sharing structure similar to the following.

The risk-sharing structure is based on how the spot exchange rate moves from a predetermined central rate (exchange rate). As long as the spot rate during the period stays within the Neutral Zone, Harley is responsible for managing the currency exposures that it incurs on the corporate level. If the spot rate moves into the Sharing Zone during the period, the exchange rate used in pricing is adjusted to "share" the change equally. If the spot rate moves beyond the Sharing Zone into the Renegotiation Zone during the period, Harley will work with foreign distributors to establish a new central rate moving forward.

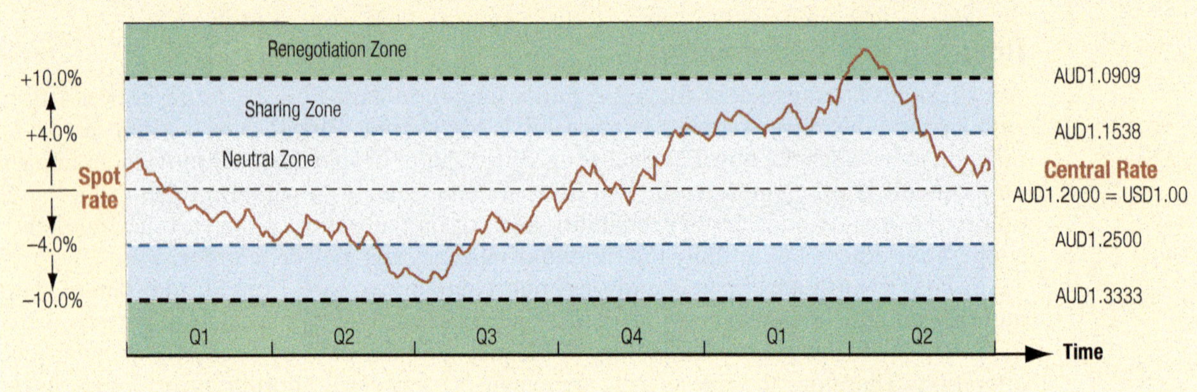

movements outside the specified band. Note that the movement could just as easily have been in Mazda's favor if the spot rate had moved to ¥130 = $1.00.

The risk-sharing arrangement is intended to smooth the impact on both parties of volatile and unpredictable exchange rate movements. Of course, a sustained appreciation of one currency versus the other would require the negotiation of a new sharing agreement, but the ultimate goal of the agreement is to alleviate currency pressures on the continuing business relationship.

Risk-sharing agreements like these have been in use for nearly 50 years on world markets. They became something of a rarity during the 1960s when exchange rates were relatively stable under the Bretton Woods Agreement. But with the return to floating exchange rates in the 1970s, firms with long-term customer-supplier relationships across borders have returned to some old ways of maintaining mutually beneficial long-term trade. *Global Finance in Practice 12.4* describes how one U.S.-based firm, Harley-Davidson, has used risk sharing.

Back-to-Back or Parallel Loans

A *back-to-back loan*, also referred to as a *parallel loan* or *credit swap*, occurs when two business firms in separate countries arrange to borrow each other's currency for a specific period of time. At an agreed terminal date, they return the borrowed currencies. The operation is conducted outside the foreign exchange markets, although spot quotations may be used as the reference point for determining the amount of funds to be swapped. Such a swap creates a covered hedge against exchange loss, since each company, on its own books, borrows the same currency it repays. Back-to-back loans are also used at a time of actual or anticipated legal limitations on the transfer of investment funds to or from either country.

The structure of a typical back-to-back loan is illustrated in Exhibit 12.5. A British parent firm that wants to invest funds in its Dutch subsidiary locates a Dutch parent firm that wants to invest funds in the United Kingdom. Avoiding the exchange markets entirely, the British parent lends pounds to the Dutch subsidiary in the United Kingdom, while the Dutch parent lends euros to the British subsidiary in the Netherlands. The two loans would be for equal values at the current spot rate and for a specified maturity. At maturity, the two separate loans would each be repaid to the original lender, again without any need to use the foreign exchange markets. Neither loan carries any foreign exchange risk, and neither loan normally needs the approval of any governmental body regulating the availability of foreign exchange for investment purposes.

Parent company guarantees are not needed on the back-to-back loans because each loan carries the right of offset in the event of default of the other loan. A further agreement can provide for maintenance of principal parity in case of changes in the spot rate between the two countries. For example, if the pound dropped by more than, say, 6% for as long as 30 days, the British parent might decide to advance additional pounds to the Dutch subsidiary to bring the principal value of the two loans back to parity. A similar provision would protect the British subsidiary if the euro should weaken. Although this parity provision might lead to changes in the amount of home currency each party must lend during the period of the agreement, it does not increase foreign exchange risk because at maturity all loans are repaid in the same currency loaned.

There are two fundamental impediments to widespread use of the back-to-back loan. First, it is difficult for a firm to find a partner, termed a *counterparty,* for the currency, amount, and timing desired. Second, a risk exists that one of the parties will fail to return the borrowed funds at the designated maturity—although this risk is minimized because each party

EXHIBIT 12.5 Back-to-Back Loans for Currency Hedging

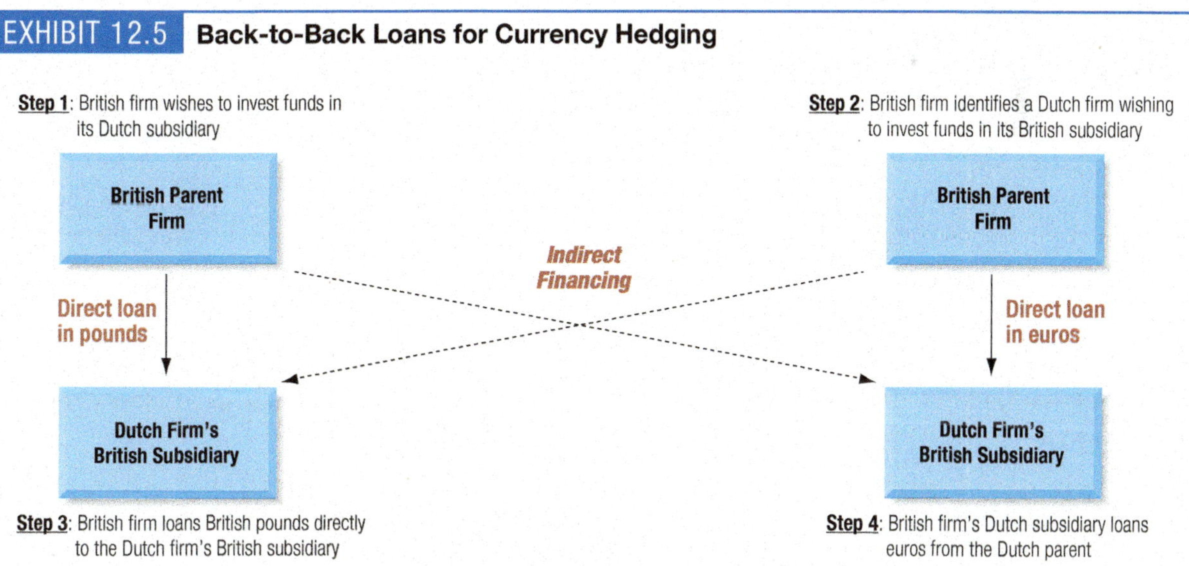

The *back-to-back loan* provides a method for parent-subsidiary cross-border financing without incurring direct currency exposure.

to the loan has, in effect, 100% collateral, albeit in a different currency. These disadvantages have led to the rapid development and wide use of the cross-currency swap.

Cross-Currency Swaps

A *cross-currency swap* resembles a back-to-back loan except that it does not appear on a firm's balance sheet. As detailed in Chapter 8, the term *swap* is used in a variety of ways in international finance, and care should be used to identify the exact use in a specific case. In a currency swap, a firm and a swap dealer (or swap bank) agree to exchange an equivalent amount of two different currencies for a specified period of time. Currency swaps can be negotiated for a wide range of maturities up to 30 years in some cases. The swap dealer or swap bank acts as a middleman in setting up the swap agreement.

A typical currency swap first requires two firms to borrow funds in markets and currencies in which they are well known. For example, a Japanese firm would typically borrow yen on a regular basis in its home market. If, however, the Japanese firm were exporting to the U.S. and earning U.S. dollars, it might wish to construct a matching cash flow hedge that would allow it to use the U.S. dollars earned to make regular debt-service payments on U.S. dollar debt. If, however, the Japanese firm is not well known in the U.S. financial markets, it may have no ready access to U.S. dollar debt.

One way in which this Japanese firm could, in effect, borrow dollars, is to participate in a cross-currency swap as seen in Exhibit 12.6. The firm could swap its yen-denominated debt service payments with another firm that has U.S. dollar-debt service payments. This swap would have the Japanese firm "paying dollars" and "receiving yen." The Japanese firm would then have dollar debt service without actually borrowing U.S. dollars. Simultaneously, a U.S. corporation would actually be entering into a cross-currency swap in the opposite direction—"paying yen" and "receiving dollars." The swap dealer takes the role of a middleman.

Swap dealers arrange most swaps on a blind basis, meaning that the initiating firm does not know who is on the other side of the swap arrangement—the counterparty. The initiating

EXHIBIT 12.6 Using Cross-Currency Swaps

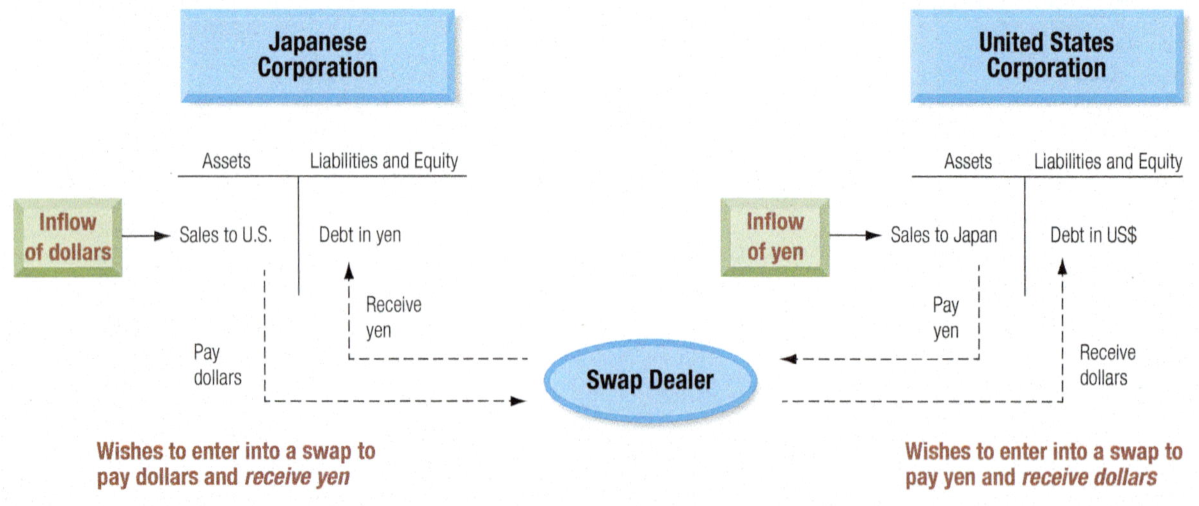

firm views the dealer or bank as its counterparty. Because swap markets are dominated by the major money center banks worldwide, the counterparty risk is considered acceptable. Because the swap dealer's business is arranging swaps, the dealer can generally arrange for the currency, amount, and timing of the desired swap. Accountants in the U.S. treat the currency swap as a foreign exchange transaction rather than as debt and they treat the obligation to reverse the swap at some later date as a forward exchange contract. (This treatment reflects a fundamental property of swaps—that they are not a source of capital, but rather an exchange of currencies and interest rates on servicing obligations.) Forward exchange contracts can be matched against assets, but they are entered in a firm's footnotes rather than as balance sheet items. The result is that both translation and operating exposures are avoided, and neither a long-term receivable nor a long-term debt is created on the balance sheet.

Contractual Approaches: Hedging the Unhedgeable

Some MNEs now attempt to hedge their operating exposure with *contractual strategies*. A number of firms like Merck (U.S.) have undertaken long-term currency option positions—hedges designed to offset lost earnings from adverse exchange rate changes. This hedging of what many of these firms refer to as strategic exposure or competitive exposure seems to fly in the face of traditional theory.

The ability of firms to hedge the "unhedgeable" is dependent upon predictability: (1) the predictability of the firm's future cash flows and (2) the predictability of the firm's competitors' responses to exchange rate changes. Although the management of many firms may believe they are capable of predicting their own cash flows, in practice, few feel capable of accurately predicting competitor response. Many firms still find timely measurement of exposure challenging. One type of predictability is that of fixed exchange rates, a debate described in *Global Finance in Practice 12.5.*

Merck is an example of a firm whose management feels capable of both. The company possesses relatively predictable long-run revenue streams due to the product-niche nature of the pharmaceuticals industry. As a U.S.-based exporter to foreign markets, markets in which sales levels by product are relatively predictable and prices are often regulated by government, Merck can accurately predict net long-term cash flows in foreign currencies 5

GLOBAL FINANCE IN PRACTICE 12.5

Do Fixed Exchange Rates Increase Corporate Currency Risk in Emerging Markets?

It has long been argued that when firms believe that the exchange rate will not change—for example, when they are operating in a country whose currency is officially fixed to a major global currency—and has been fixed for a relatively long period of time, they will conduct their business as if they have no currency exposure or risk. As one study of currency risk in India noted, "These results support the hypothesis that pegged exchange rates induce moral hazard and increase financial fragility."

Moral hazard is the concept that a party—an agent, an individual, or a firm—will take on more risk when it either knows or believes that a second party will handle, accommodate, or insure the negative repercussions of the firm's risk-taking behavior. In other words, a firm may tolerate more risks when it knows that someone else will pick up the tab. In a fixed or managed exchange rate regime, that "someone else" is represented by the central bank, which tells all those undertaking cross-currency contractual obligations and exposures that the exchange rate will not change.

Although there is still scant research on this specific practice for most emerging markets, it could prove to be a significant issue in the years to come, as many emerging markets become the object of major new international capital flows—the so-called *globalization of finance*. If commercial firms in those markets are not aware of the risk that the country itself may be taking by opening the door to international capital flows both into and out of the country and the impact those capital flows may have on the country's exchange rate, those firms may be in for a wild ride.

and 10 years into the future. Merck has a relatively undiversified operating structure, and it is highly centralized in terms of where research, development, and production costs are located. Merck's managers feel the company has no real alternatives except contractual hedging if it is to weather long-term unexpected exchange rate changes. Merck has purchased over-the-counter (OTC) long-term put options on foreign currencies versus the U.S. dollar as insurance against potential lost earnings from exchange rate changes.

A significant question remains as to the true effectiveness of hedging operating exposure with contractual hedges. The fact remains that even after feared exchange rate movements and put option position payoffs, the firm is competitively disadvantaged. The capital outlay required for the purchase of such sizeable put option positions is capital not used for the potential diversification of operations, which in the long run might have more effectively maintained the firm's global market share and international competitiveness.

Summary Points

- Operating exposure measures the change in value of the firm that results from changes in future operating cash flows caused by an unexpected change in exchange rates.
- Operating strategies for the management of operating exposure emphasize the structuring of firm operations in order to create matching streams of cash flows by currency.
- The objective of operating exposure management is to anticipate and influence the effect of unexpected changes in exchange rates on a firm's future cash flow rather than being forced into passive reaction to such changes.
- Proactive policies include matching currency cash flows, currency risk-sharing clauses, back-to-back loan structures, and cross-currency swap agreements.
- Contractual approaches (i.e., options and forwards) have occasionally been used to hedge operating exposure but are costly and possibly ineffectual.

MINI-CASE

Brexit and Rolls-Royce[1]

Rolls said it "remains committed to the UK where we are headquartered, directly employ over 23,000 talented and committed workers and where we carry out a significant majority of our research and development. The UK's decision will have no immediate impact on our day-to-day business."

—"'Business as Usual' for Rolls-Royce as It Remains on Course despite Brexit," *The Telegraph*, June 28, 2016.

The decision by the people of the United Kingdom to leave the European Union (EU)—*Brexit*—in June 2016 raised many questions over the future of many of the UK's multinational firms. One firm in the limelight was Rolls-Royce, one of the premier aerospace engine manufacturers in the world. Rolls was one of Britain's major exporters, credited with roughly 2% of the country's annual exports. Following Brexit and the sharp decline in the British pound sterling, analysts were attempting to gauge how the EU exit would alter the company's business and how the company's leadership was likely to react.

The Business and Currency Hedging

Rolls-Royce Holdings PLC is a UK-based multinational group that designs, manufactures, and distributes power systems to the aviation (civil and defense), marine, nuclear, and other industries.[2] It is listed on the London Stock Exchange (LSE: RR) and is a member of the FTSE 100 index. It is the second largest manufacturer of aircraft engines in the world, and closed 2015 with £13.725 billion in revenue and £0.084 billion in net income. In recent years nearly all of its profits have come from the aerospace sector.

[1] This case was prepared by Professor Michael H. Moffett for the purpose of classroom discussion only.

[2] Note that Rolls-Royce Automobiles is not a part of the company, having been sold off in 1973. Today the automotive unit is owned by BMW of Germany.

EXHIBIT A Currency Structure of Rolls Royce's Global Business

Rolls-Royce's business was structurally mismatched by currency. Although global sales were dominated by the U.S. dollar, costs were still largely British pound-based.

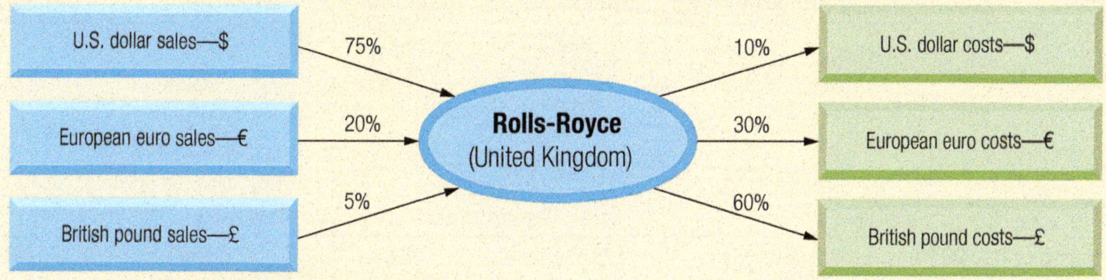

The result was a multinational company that was long U.S. dollars and short British pounds. If the U.S. dollar then appreciated versus the British pound, Rolls-Royce benefits. If, however, the dollar was to fall in value versus the pound, sales, earnings, and cash flows would fall in value as reported in British pounds.

But Rolls had a serious, long-term, structural currency problem. Although it was based in the UK, with most of its manufacturing operations in British pounds, its global sales were dominated by the U.S. dollar. This reflected the location and identities of its major customers like Boeing and Airbus. As illustrated in Exhibit A, this structural currency mismatch meant the company had a significant operating exposure problem, earning primarily U.S. dollars when paying out British pounds and euros. (Because many of the pieces, parts, and subcomponents used by Rolls were sourced from Continental Europe, the euro was a net short position for the company as well.) Since many of Rolls' sales programs were lengthy, often between three and six years in length, this long-dollar position was not only large, it was relatively predictable over time.

The Hedging Program

"Rolls-Royce operates in a number of very long cycle businesses and we therefore have a long-term hedging program to provide a degree of certainty to our cash flows going forward," Rolls-Royce spokeswoman Jane Terry said in an e-mailed statement.

—"Rolls-Royce May Rue Long-Term Hedging Decision as Pound Plunges," *Bloomberg.com*, Mar. 15, 2013.

Rolls, like most multinationals, values predictability of cash flow. In an attempt to increase the predictability of British pound proceeds from sales, given the fluctuations of exchange rates, Rolls in 2012 had started a large—more than $20 billion—long-term currency hedging program, some of it more than six years in duration. The majority of the hedge program locked-in U.S. dollar revenues at an average of $1.60 per pound, using primarily forward contracts, for six years into the future.

Exhibit B presents Rolls-Royce's currency derivatives program status as of December 31 for the previous two years. Note that the predominant value is the amount of U.S. dollars sold forward—mostly in exchange for British pounds sterling, but some also for euros and other unnamed currencies.

As is the case with unpredictable markets, the hedges had not always proved profitable when viewed in hindsight. In the summer of 2014 the pound began to fall against the dollar, a favorable movement for Rolls that the company could not fully enjoy given its lock-in hedge program. As is always the case, locking in a guaranteed rate meant that when the exchange rate moved in the company's favor, its protection would prove to be a cost, as it could not enjoy the favorable movement. Unfortunately, the pound's slide against the dollar had continued into 2016.

Publicly traded companies like Rolls must continually worry about short-term market movements while keeping long-term competitiveness in their sights. Although the company believes its long-term hedging program is in the long-term interests of the company, there will always be periods in the short-term that make the program appear to be a mistake (reflected in short-term share price movements).

Exhibit C attempts to provide some longer-term perspective to the challenge Rolls faces. The exchange rates that matter the most, the dollar and euro against the pound, show varying periods of relative strength and weakness over the past 25 years. It is apparent from Exhibit C that the pound has enjoyed a long period of relative weakness against the dollar and euro. But the recent Brexit vote seems to have pushed it down to a level not seen in the past quarter-century against the dollar, as well as approaching the historical lows versus the euro.

EXHIBIT B Derivative Financial Instruments Related to Foreign Exchange Risks

At December 31, 2015	Currencies Purchased Forward				
Currencies Sold Forward	Sterling (millions of £)	US dollars (millions of £)	Euro (millions of £)	Other (millions of £)	Total (millions of £)
Sterling	0	383	0	221	604
US dollar	18,869	0	1,552	902	21,323
Euro	2	76	0	125	203
Other	131	12	143	2	288

At December 31, 2014	Currencies Purchased Forward				
Currencies Sold Forward	Sterling (millions of £)	US dollars (millions of £)	Euro (millions of £)	Other (millions of £)	Total (millions of £)
Sterling	0	429	0	199	628
US dollar	16,659	0	2,014	938	19,611
Euro	150	61	0	185	396
Other	167	9	114	10	300

Source: Rolls-Royce Group plc, Annual Report 2015, p. 143.

EXHIBIT C Long-Term Exchange Rates of the Dollar, Euro, and Pound

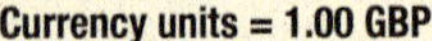

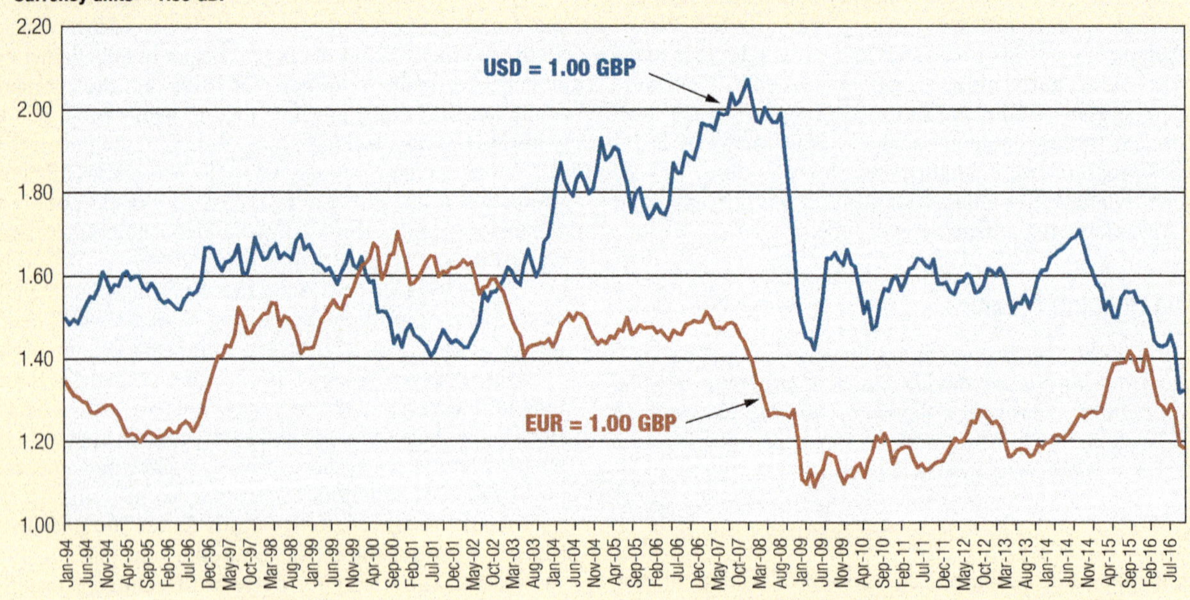

EXHIBIT D U.S. Dollars per British Pound Sterling in 2016

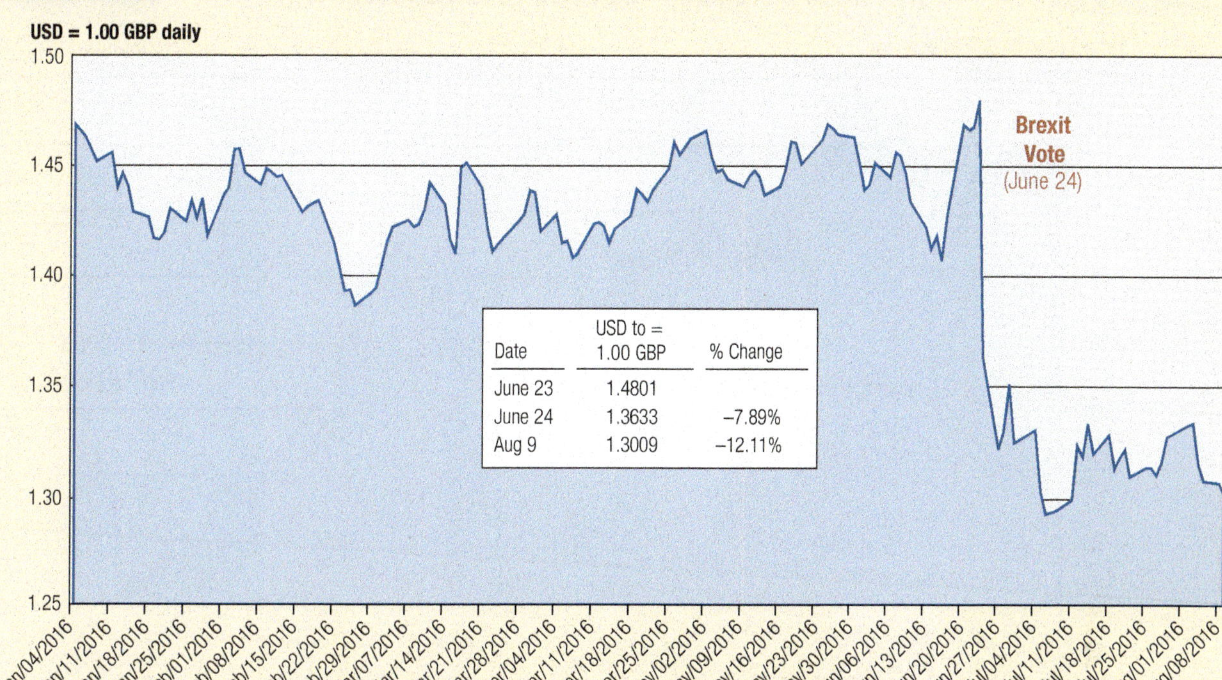

Brexit

Hey Europe, how's it going? Lost a few pounds lately?

—Note in London pub window, July 2016.

The British vote in June 2016 to exit the EU was largely based on social and political issues, not economic or financial.[3] The UK had never adopted the euro, preferring these many years to keep the pound sterling and its monetary independence. The year 2016 had been a relatively stable one for the USDGBP rate, at least up until the Brexit vote on June 24, as shown in Exhibit D. The vote had a distinctly negative impact on the value of the pound. By August the pound sterling was down more than 12% against the dollar.

But a weaker pound was essentially good news for Rolls, as shown in its share price bump following the vote and its first-half year results (see Exhibit E).

> *Rolls was of the few companies whose shares rose on the day the referendum's result was announced, with analysts pointing out that the weaker pound made the export-reliant company's products cheaper and therefore more competitive.*[4]

Posted just after the Brexit vote, Rolls's first half-year results had been in line with expectations, but expectations had been low. The slide of the pound against the dollar in late June, combined with the large forward contract hedge position, had forced the company to miss out on substantial currency gains. And that had led to the company recording a loss on its currency hedges. As one journalist explained:

> *Rolls-Royce is therefore still where it was pre-Brexit. What is actually being said here is that if Rolls-Royce didn't hedge then it would be £2 billion better off today but it did hedge so it isn't.*[5]

Rolls itself continued to try and clarify to the market the outlook for its hedging program, a program now at more than $30 billion in notional principal.[6]

> *Through our hedging activities we seek to reduce the volatility of our revenues, costs and resulting margins. Our hedging instruments are sufficiently flexible to*

[3] The *United Kingdom* is officially a country that includes England, Scotland, Wales (semi-autonomous regions of the island of Britain), and Northern Ireland, officially—*the United Kingdom of Great Britain and Northern Ireland.*

[4] "'Business as Usual' for Rolls-Royce as It Remains on Course despite Brexit; Rolls-Royce Says There Will Be No 'Immediate Impact' on It as a Result of the Referendum," Alan Tovey, *The Telegraph*, June 28, 2016.

[5] "The Mystery of Rolls-Royce's Loss from Sterling's Post-Brexit Slump," Tim Worstall, *Forbes*, July 25, 2016.

[6] *Investor Update*, Rolls-Royce Group plc, July 2016, p. 5.

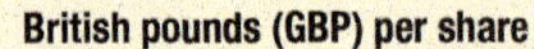

EXHIBIT E Rolls-Royce Group plc Share Price (June 2013–August 2016)

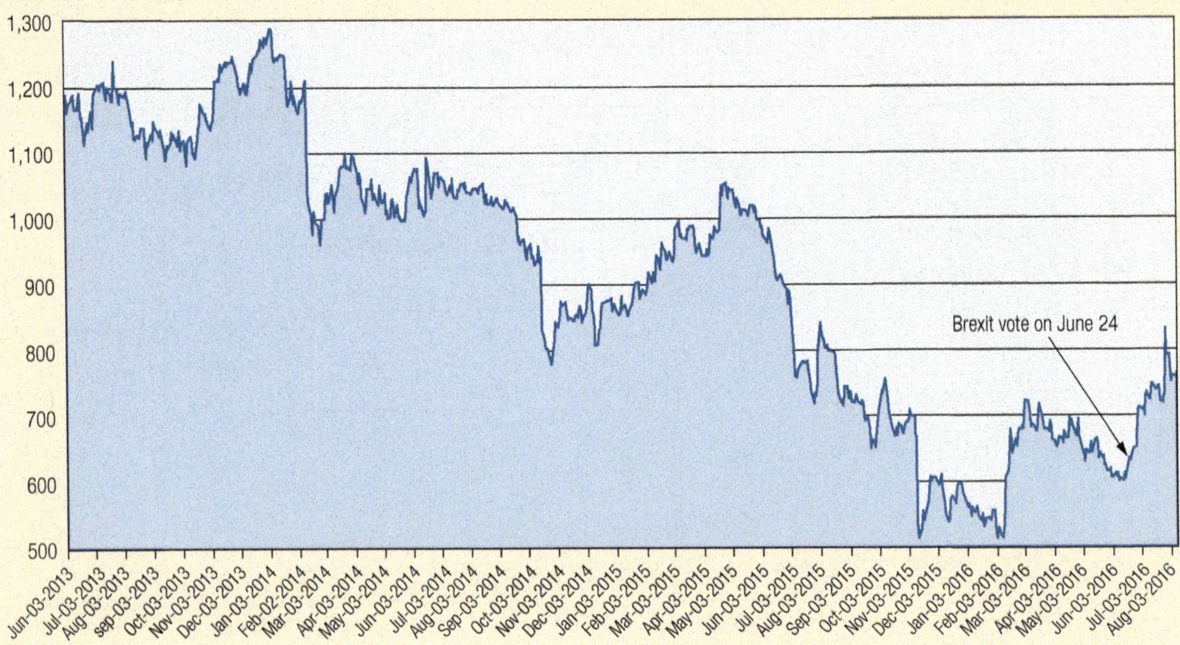

allow us to achieve near 100% cover for our transactions in the short and medium term at close to our average hedge rate which stood at around $1.59 at the end of 2015. Over the longer term, should the £/$ remain at its current lower levels we should be able to add more hedges and achieve a lower average rate. With our hedge book now over $30 billion, the impact of lower £/$ rates will be limited in the near-term.

In addition to exchange rate concerns, Brexit confronted Rolls-Royce with a number of very large long-term questions—questions about investment and strategy. Like other UK companies, Rolls was trying to decide whether to continue to invest in its operations and facilities in the UK or possibly redirect that invest to Continental Europe. No longer an EU member, UK-based companies now faced the possibility of being treated as outsiders to the Continental European markets, raising threats of trade restrictions, regulatory distinctions, and documentation requirements and delays. Rolls-Royce said it has held "high-level" talks with ministers about the areas that it is keen to resolve after the Brexit vote, while the UK boss of Airbus said he did not want to deal with thousands of pages of documents and tariffs when dealing with his colleagues in mainland Europe.[7]

MINI-CASE QUESTIONS

1. Why do you think Rolls has continued to bear this structural currency mismatch so long? Why hasn't it done what many automobile companies have done and move some of its manufacturing and assembly to the country in which the customer resides?
2. Why are Rolls-Royce's foreign currency hedges performing so poorly? Shouldn't the hedges be protecting its sales and earnings against exchange rate movements?
3. If you were a member of the leadership team at Rolls-Royce, what would you recommend the company do to manage the risks arising from Brexit?

[7] "Airbus and Rolls-Royce Say UK Must Quickly Get Beneficial EU Trade Deals; Two of Britain's Biggest Manufacturers Say Favourable Agreements Have to Be Reached Speedily to Avoid Jeopardising Investment," Graham Ruddick, *The Guardian*, July 12, 2016.

Questions

12.1 Exposure Definitions. Define *operating exposure, economic exposure*, and *competitive exposure*. Can you provide any insights into what may be behind the use of the different terms?

12.2 Operating Exposure versus Translation Exposure. What do you see as the primary difference between operating exposure and translation exposure? Would this have the same meaning to a private firm as a publicly traded firm?

12.3 Unexpected Exchange Rate Changes. Why do unexpected exchange rate changes contribute to operating exposure, but expected exchange rate changes do not?

12.4 Time Horizon. Explain the time horizons used to analyze and measure unexpected changes in exchange rates.

12.5 Static versus Dynamic. What are examples of static exposures versus dynamic exposures?

12.6 Operating versus Financing Cash Flows. According to financial theory, which is more important to the value of the firm, financing or operating cash flows?

12.7 Macroeconomic Uncertainty. Explain how the concept of macroeconomic uncertainty expands the scope of analyzing operating exposure.

12.8 Strategic Response. The objective of both operating and transaction exposure management is to anticipate and influence the effect of unexpected changes in exchange rates on a firm's future cash flows. What strategic alternative policies exist to enable management to manage these exposures?

12.9 Managing Operating Exposure. The key to managing operating exposure at the strategic level is for management to recognize a disequilibrium in parity conditions when it occurs and to be pre-positioned to react appropriately. How can this task best be accomplished?

12.10 Diversification. How can a multinational firm diversify operations? How can it diversify its financing? Do you believe these are effective ways of managing operating exposure?

12.11 Proactive Management. Operating exposures can be partially managed by adopting operating or financing policies that offset anticipated foreign exchange exposures. What are four of the most commonly employed proactive policies?

12.12 Matching Currency Exposure. Explain how matching currency cash flows can offset operating exposure.

12.13 Risk Sharing. An alternative arrangement for managing operating exposure between firms with a continuing buyer-supplier relationship is risk sharing. Explain how risk sharing works.

12.14 Back-to-Back Loans. Explain how back-to-back loans can hedge foreign exchange operating exposure. Would firms have any concerns about their partner in a back-to-back loan arrangement?

12.15 Currency Swaps. Explain how currency swaps can hedge foreign exchange operating exposure. What are the accounting advantages of currency swaps?

12.16 Hedging the Unhedgeable. How do some firms attempt to hedge their long-term operation exposure with contractual hedges? What assumptions do they make in order to justify contractual hedging of their operating exposure? How effective is such contractual hedging in your opinion?

Problems

12.1 Mauna Loa Macadamia. Mauna Loa Macadamia, a macadamia nut subsidiary of Hershey's with plantations on the slopes of its namesake volcano in Hilo, Hawaii, exports macadamia nuts worldwide. The Japanese market is its biggest export market, with average annual sales invoiced in yen to Japanese customers of ¥1,200,000,000. At the present exchange rate of ¥125 = $1.00, this is equivalent to $9,600,000. Sales are relatively equally distributed throughout the year. They show up as a ¥250,00,000 account receivable on Mauna Loa's balance sheet. Credit terms to each customer allow for 60 days before payment is due. Monthly cash collections are typically ¥100,000,000.

Mauna Loa would like to hedge its yen receipts, but it has too many customers and transactions to make it practical to sell each receivable forward. It does not want to use options because they are considered to be too expensive for this particular purpose. Therefore, they have decided to use a "matching" hedge by borrowing yen. Mauna Loa can borrow Japanese yen 4.00% per annum.

a. How much should Mauna Loa borrow in yen?
b. What should be the terms of payment on the yen loan?

12.2 Acuña Leather Goods. DeMagistris Fashion Company, based in New York City, imports leather coats from Acuña Leather Goods, a reliable and longtime supplier, based in Buenos Aires, Argentina.

Payment is in Argentine pesos. When the peso lost its parity with the U.S. dollar in January 2002, it collapsed in value to Ps4.0 = $1.00 by October 2002. The outlook was for a further decline in the peso's value. Since both DeMagistris and Acuña wanted to continue their longtime relationship, they agreed on a risk-sharing arrangement. As long as the spot rate on the date of an invoice is between Ps3.5 = $1.00 and Ps4.5 = $1.00, DeMagistris will pay based on the spot rate. If the exchange rate falls outside this range, DeMagistris will share the difference equally with Acuña Leather Goods. The risk-sharing agreement will last for six months, at which time the exchange rate limits will be reevaluated. DeMagistris contracts to import leather coats from Acuña for Ps8,000,000 or $2,000,000 at the current spot rate of Ps4.0 = $1.00 during the next six months.

a. If the exchange rate changes immediately to Ps6.0 = $1.00, what will be the dollar cost of six months of imports to DeMagistris?
b. At Ps6.0 = $1.00, what will be the peso export sales of Acuña Leather Goods to DeMagistris Fashion Company?

12.3 Richland Crane (A). Richland Crane (U.S.) exports heavy crane equipment to several Chinese dock facilities. Sales are currently 10,000 units per year at the yuan equivalent of USD24,000 each. The Chinese yuan (CNY) has been trading at CNY8.20 = USD1.00, but a Hong Kong advisory service predicts the yuan will drop in value next week to CNY9.00 = USD1.00, after which it will remain unchanged for at least a decade. Accepting this forecast as a given, Richland Crane must make a pricing decision in the face of the impending devaluation. It may either (1) maintain the same yuan price and in effect sell for fewer dollars, in which case Chinese volume will not change; or (2) maintain the same dollar price, raise the yuan price in China to offset the devaluation, and experience a 10% drop in unit volume. Direct costs are 75% of the U.S. sales price.

a. What would be the short-run (one year) impact of each pricing strategy?
b. Which do you recommend?

12.4 Richland Crane (B). Assume the same facts as in Problem 12.3. Additionally, financial management believes that if it maintains the same yuan sales price, volume will increase at 12% per annum for eight years. Dollar costs will not change. At the end of 10 years, Richland's patent expires and it will no longer export to China. After the yuan is devalued to CNY9.20 = USD1.00, no further devaluations are expected. If Richland Crane raises the yuan price so as to maintain its dollar price, volume will increase at only 1% per annum for eight years, starting from the lower initial base of 9,000 units. Again, dollar costs will not change, and at the end of eight years Richland Crane will stop exporting to China. Richland's weighted average cost of capital is 10%. Given these considerations, what should be Richland's pricing policy?

12.5 MacLoren Automotive. MacLoren Automotive manufactures British sports cars, a number of which are exported to New Zealand for payment in pounds sterling. The distributor sells the sports cars in New Zealand for New Zealand dollars. The New Zealand distributor is unable to carry all of the foreign exchange risk, and would not sell MacLoren models unless MacLoren shared some of the foreign exchange risk. MacLoren has agreed that sales for a given model year will initially be priced at a "base" spot rate between the New Zealand dollar and pound sterling set to be the spot mid-rate at the beginning of that model year. As long as the actual exchange rate is within that base rate, payment will be made in pounds sterling. That is, the New Zealand distributor assumes all foreign exchange risk. However, if the spot rate at time of shipment falls outside of this range, MacLoren will share equally (i.e., 50/50) the difference between the actual spot rate and the base rate. For the current model year the base rate is NZ$1.6400 = £1.00.

a. What are the outside ranges within which the New Zealand importer must pay at the then current spot rate?
b. If MacLoren ships 10 sports cars to the New Zealand distributor at a time when the spot exchange rate is NZ$1.7000 = £1.00, and each car has an invoice cost £32,000, what will be the cost to the distributor in New Zealand dollars? How many pounds will MacLoren receive, and how does this compare with MacLoren's expected sales receipt of £32,000 per car?
c. If MacLoren Automotive ships the same 10 cars to New Zealand at a time when the spot exchange rate is NZ$1.6500 = £1.00, how many New Zealand dollars will the distributor pay? How many pounds will MacLoren Automotive receive?
d. Does a risk-sharing agreement such as this shift the currency exposure from one party of the transaction to the other?
e. Why is such a risk-sharing agreement of benefit to MacLoren? Why is it of benefit to the New Zealand distributor?

12.6 Ganado Germany—All Domestic Competitors. Using the Ganado Germany analysis in Exhibits 12.5 and 12.6 where the euro depreciates, how would prices, costs, and volumes change if Ganado Germany was operating in a nearly purely domestic mature market with major domestic competitors?

12.7 Ganado Germany—All Foreign Competitors. Ganado Germany is now competing in a number of international (export) markets, growth markets, in which most of its competitors are foreign. Now how would you expect Ganado Germany's operating exposure to respond to the depreciation of the euro?

12.8 Rolls-Royce Turbine Engines. Rolls-Royce is struggling with its pricing strategy with a number of its major customers in Continental Europe, particularly Airbus. Since Rolls-Royce is a British company with most manufacturing of the Airbus engines in the United Kingdom, costs are predominantly denominated in British pounds. But in the period shown, 2007–2009, the pound steadily weakened against the euro. Rolls-Royce has traditionally denominated its sales contracts with Airbus in Airbus' home currency, the euro. After completing the following tables answer the questions that follow.

a. Assuming each Rolls-Royce engine marketed to Airbus is initially priced at £22.5 million, how has the price of that engine changed over the period shown when priced in euros at the current spot rate?

b. What is the cumulative percentage change in the price of the engine in euros for the three-year period?

c. If the price elasticity of demand for Rolls-Royce turbine sales to Airbus is relatively inelastic, and the price of the engine in British pounds never changes over the period, what does this price change mean for Rolls-Royce's total sales revenue on sales to Airbus of this engine?

d. Compare the prices and volumes for the first quarter of each of the three years shown (Problem 12.8 part d, on the following page). Who has benefitted the most from the exchange rate changes?

12.9 Hurte-Paroxysm Products, Inc. (A). Hurte-Paroxysm Products, Inc. (HP) of the United States, exports computer printers to Brazil, whose currency, the reais (BRL) has been trading at BRL3.40=USD1.00. Exports to Brazil are currently 50,000 printers per year at the reais-equivalent of $200 each. A rumor exists that the reais will be devalued against the dollar to BRL$4.00 within two weeks by the Brazilian government. Should the devaluation take place, the reais is expected to remain unchanged for another decade.

Accepting this forecast as given, HP faces a pricing decision that must be made before any actual devaluation: HP may either (1) maintain the same reais price and, in effect, sell for fewer dollars, in which case Brazilian volume will not change; or (2) maintain the same dollar price, raise the reais price in Brazil to compensate for the devaluation, and experience a 20% drop in volume. Direct costs in the United States are 60% of the U.S. sales price. What would be the short-run (1-year) implication of each pricing strategy? Which do you recommend?

12.10 Hurte-Paroxysm Products, Inc. (B). Assume the same facts as in Problem 12.9. HP also believes that if it maintains the same price in Brazilian reais as a permanent policy, volume will increase at 10% per annum for six years, costs will not change. At the end of six years, HP's patent expires and it will no longer export to Brazil. After the reais is devalued to BRL4.00 = USD1.00, no further devaluation is expected. If HP raises the price in reais so as to maintain its dollar price, volume will increase at only 4% per annum for six years, starting from the lower initial base of 40,000 units. Again, dollar costs will not change, and at the end of six years, HP will

Problem 12.8: Rolls-Royce Turbine Engines

Part a.

Date	1Q 2007	2Q 2007	3Q 2007	4Q 2007	1Q 2008	2Q 2008
Price (millions of pounds, £)	£22.50	£22.50	£22.50	£22.50	£22.50	£22.50
Spot rate (€=£1.00)	1.4918	1.4733	1.4696	1.4107	1.3198	1.2617
Price (millions of euros, €)	€ 33.57	______	______	______	______	______

Date	3Q 2008	4Q 2008	1Q 2009	2Q 2009	3Q 2009	4Q 2009
Price (millions of pounds, £)	£22.50	£22.50	£22.50	£22.50	£22.50	£22.50
Spot rate (€=£1.00)	1.2590	1.1924	1.1017	1.1375	1.1467	1.1066
Price (millions of euros, €)	______	______	______	______	______	______

Problem 12.8: Rolls-Royce Turbine Engines

Part d.

	1Q 2007	1Q 2008	1Q 2009	2007-2009 % Chg
Price (in millions of £)	£22.50	£22.50	£22.50	______
Spot rate (€/£)	1.4918	1.3198	1.1017	______
Price (in millions of €)	€ 33.57	______	______	______
Sales volume (engines)	200	220	240	20.0%
Total cost to Airbus (millions of €)	€ 6,713.10	______	______	______
Total revenue to RR (millions of £)	£4,500.00	______	______	______

stop exporting to Brazil. HP's weighted average cost of capital is 12%. Given these considerations, what do you recommend for HP's pricing policy? Justify your recommendation.

12.11 Truckee Tec's Yen Exposure. Truckee Tec is a privately held battery manufacturer located just outside of Reno, Nevada. The company is one of the leading manufacturers of lithium-ion batteries, specifically for the automobile market. Truckee has been in intense contract negotiations with a Japanese automaker for months. It was late December 2016, and both sides wanted to conclude a deal before the new year.

The Japanese automaker wanted a two-year supply agreement for 18,000 lithium-ion 12V battery packs per year. Battery prices had been dropping dramatically for years, but Truckee's current sales price of $1,100 per battery for the 12V model (1342OR) had held firm for months. The buyer was pushing for a lower unit price, but Truckee wanted a longer contract with higher volumes in return. After months of negotiations, the buyer agreed to increase the contract to three years, and increase annual purchases to 20,000 units. But in return, the buyer wanted a price of $990 per unit, and it wanted to pay in Japanese yen. Truckee had countered with the following proposal. Assuming 20,000 units per year at an average price of $995 per unit, and a current spot exchange rate of ¥115.00 = $1.00, the contract purchase amount per year would be:

Annual contract amount = 20,000 units

$995 per unit × ¥115 per dollar = ¥,288,500,000

The buyer accepted the counterproposal in 24 hours and a sale agreement signed and posted. The deal was done. Almost immediately the corporate treasury group at Truckee was upset about the contract. They argued that the Japanese yen had begun to plummet in value against the dollar in the past two months, so accepting payment in Japanese yen was too risky. Also, the quote had been based on a spot rate value of ¥115 = $1.00, but the rate had already moved to ¥117 = $1.00 over the past two weeks.

Truckee's corporate treasury wanted to move immediately to hedge the long-term exposure. (Internally, the group had discussed that it was technically an *anticipated transaction exposure*, not a pure *operating exposure*, since it was a single transaction—but contractual. It would continue over a three-year period, but none of it was as yet on the books.) After consulting with their bankers, they wanted to use a cross-currency swap to manage the Japanese yen risk, a swap in which Truckee would pay yen and receive dollars. Their banker offered a swap where Truckee would receive U.S. dollar LIBOR in return for paying Japanese yen at 4.500%. The swap agreement would be for three years and all payments made quarterly—to match the expected yen cash inflow from the Japanese customer.

a. Given the final contract value, what would the Japanese buyer believe they are paying per pack?
b. What is the amount of the currency exposure for Truckee Tec?
c. If the swap agreement is for a three-year loan at 4.500%, quarterly, what is the principal amount of the loan obligation (notional principal)?
d. The sales team had clearly not updated their exchange rate assumption prior to making the final contractual offer. As a result, assuming the swap was executed the same day as the closing spot rate quote, what was the actual exchange rate locked-in for the three-year period?
e. In retrospect, what do you think Truckee should have done to manage the currency risk more effectively?

PROBLEM 12.11 **Spot Rate of Exchange, JPY = 1.00 USD (daily, July 1, 2016–Dec 28, 2016)**

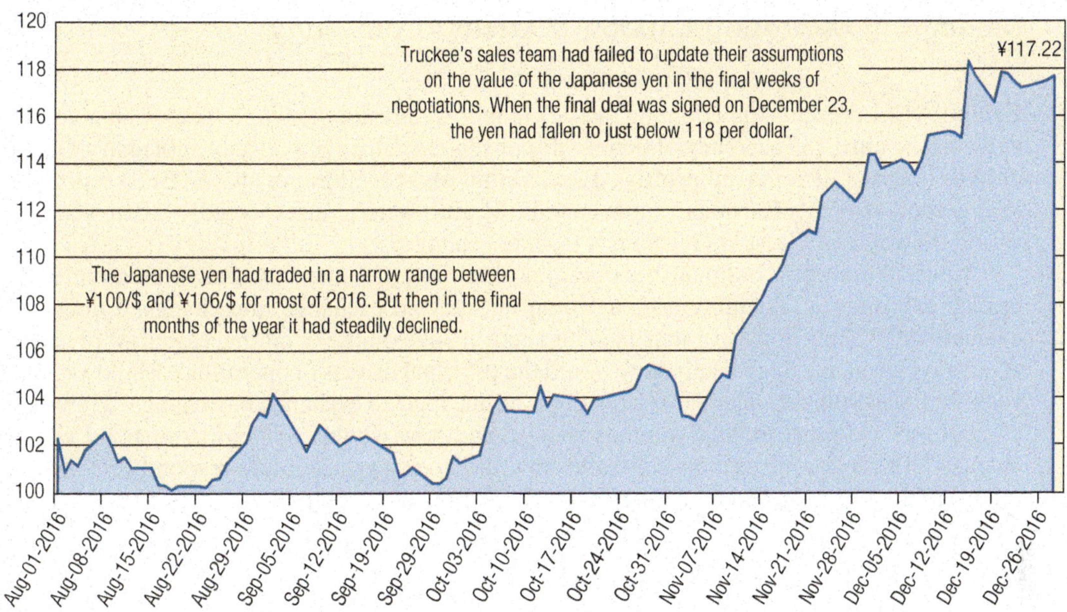

CHAPTER 12 APPENDIX

Measuring Operating Exposure: Ganado Germany

Exhibit A12.1 presents the dilemma facing Ganado as a result of an unexpected change in the value of the euro, the currency of economic consequence for the German subsidiary. Ganado derives much of its reported profits—the earnings and earnings per share (EPS) reported to Wall Street—from its European subsidiary. If the euro were to unexpectedly fall in value, how would the value of Ganado Germany's business change?

Value, in the world of finance, is operating cash flow. If Ganado wishes to measure the operating exposure of Ganado Germany to an unexpected exchange rate change, it does so by evaluating the likely impact of that exchange rate change on the operating cash flow of the firm (Ganado Germany). Specifically, how would the principal drivers of operating cash flow—prices, costs, and sales volume—change as a result of the unexpected exchange rate change? How would competitors' prices, costs, and volumes change, and how would competitors respond to those changes? The following section illustrates how those very values might respond (emphasis on might) in the short run and medium run to a fall in the value of the euro against the dollar.

The Base Case: Euro Depreciation

Ganado Germany manufactures in Germany, sells domestically, and exports; and all sales are invoiced in euros. Exhibit A12.2 summarizes the current baseline forecast for Ganado Germany income and operating cash flows for the 2021–2025 period (assume it is currently 2020). Sales volume is assumed to be a constant 1 million units per year, with a per unit sales price of €12.80 and a per unit direct cost of €9.60. The corporate income tax rate in Germany is 29.5%, and the exchange rate is \$1.20 = €1.00.

EXHIBIT A12.1 Ganado and Ganado Germany

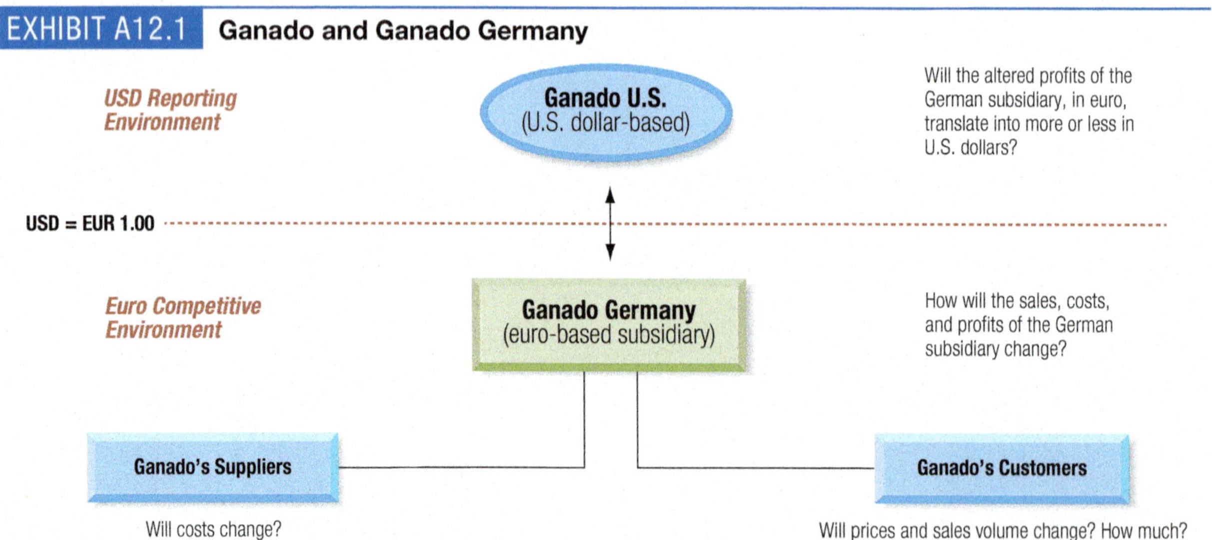

An unexpected depreciation in the value of the euro alters both the competitiveness of the subsidiary and the financial results which are consolidated with the parent company.

EXHIBIT A12.2 Ganado Germany's Valuation: Baseline Analysis

Assumptions	**2021**	**2022**	**2023**	**2024**	**2025**
Sales volume (units)	1,000,000	1,000,000	1,000,000	1,000,000	1,000,000
Sales price per unit	€ 12.80	€ 12.80	€ 12.80	€ 12.80	€ 12.80
Direct cost per unit	€ 9.60	€ 9.60	€ 9.60	€ 9.60	€ 9.60
German corporate tax rate	29.5%	29.5%	29.5%	29.5%	29.5%
Exchange rate ($ = € 1.00)	1.2000	1.2000	1.2000	1.2000	1.2000
Income-Statement	**2021**	**2022**	**2023**	**2024**	**2025**
Sales revenue	€ 12,800,000	€ 12,800,000	€ 12,800,000	€ 12,800,000	€ 12,800,000
Direct cost of goods sold	–9,600,000	–9,600,000	–9,600,000	–9,600,000	–9,600,000
Cash operating expenses (fixed)	–890,000	–890,000	–890,000	–890,000	–890,000
Depreciation	–600,000	–600,000	–600,000	–600,000	–600,000
Pretax profit	€ 1,710,000	€ 1,710,000	€ 1,710,000	€ 1,710,000	€ 1,710,000
Income tax expense	–504,450	–504,450	–504,450	–504,450	–504,450
Net income	€ 1,205,550	€ 1,205,550	€ 1,205,550	€ 1,205,550	€ 1,205,550
Cash Flows for Valuation					
Net income	€ 1,205,550	€ 1,205,550	€ 1,205,550	€ 1,205,550	€ 1,205,550
Add back depreciation	600,000	600,000	600,000	600,000	600,000
Changes in net working capital	0	0	0	0	0
Free cash flow for valuation, in euros	€ 1,805,550	€ 1,805,550	€ 1,805,550	€ 1,805,550	€ 1,805,550
Cash flow from operations, in dollars	$2,166,660	$2,166,660	$2,166,660	$2,166,660	$2,166,660
Present Value @ 15%	$7,262,980				

Notes. We assume, to simplify the analysis, that Ganado Germany has no debt and therefore no interest expenses. We also assume there are no additional capital expenditures required over the five years shown. We also assume no terminal value; Ganado is valued on its coming expected five years of cash flow only. Net working capital requirements (accounts receivable + inventory – accounts payable) require no additions in the base case due to constant sales. In subsequent scenarios it is assumed receivables are maintained at 45 days of sales, inventory at 10 days of cost of goods sold, and accounts payable at 38 days of sales.

These assumptions generate sales of €12,800,000, and €1,205,550 in net income. Adding net income to depreciation and changes in net working capital (which are zero in the base case) generates €1,805,550 or $2,166,660 in operating cash flow at $1.20 = €1.00. Ganado's management values its subsidiaries by finding the present value of these total free cash flows over the coming five-year period, in U.S. dollars, assuming a 15% discount rate. The baseline analysis finds a present value of Ganado Germany of $7,262,980. This analysis is also illustrated in the accompanying Excel spreadsheet titled *Ganado Germany Operating Exposure.xls*.

On January 1, 2021, before any commercial activity begins, the euro unexpectedly drops from $1.2000 = €1.00 to $1.0000 = €1.00. Operating exposure depends on whether an unexpected change in exchange rates causes unanticipated changes in sales volume, sales prices, or operating costs. Following a depreciation of the euro, Ganado Germany might choose to maintain its domestic sales prices constant in euro terms, or it might try to raise domestic prices because competing imports are now priced higher in Europe. The firm might choose to keep export prices constant in terms of foreign currencies, in terms of euros, or somewhere in between (partial pass-through). The strategy undertaken depends to a large measure on management's opinion about the price elasticity of demand, which would also include management's assessment of competitor response. On the cost side, Ganado Germany might raise prices because of more expensive imported raw material or components, or perhaps because all domestic prices in Germany have risen and labor is now demanding higher wages to compensate for domestic inflation.

Ganado Germany's domestic sales and costs might also be partly determined by the effect of the euro depreciation on demand. To the extent that the depreciation stimulates purchases of European goods in import-competing sectors of the economy as well as exports of German goods, by making prices of German goods initially more competitive, German national income should increase. This assumes that the favorable effect of a euro depreciation on comparative prices is not immediately offset by higher domestic inflation. Thus, Ganado Germany might be able to sell more goods domestically because of price and income effects and internationally because of price effects.

To illustrate the effect of various post-depreciation scenarios on Ganado Germany's operating exposure, consider four simple cases.

Case 1: Euro depreciation (all variables remain constant)
Case 2: Increase in sales volume (other variables remain constant)
Case 3: Increase in sales price (other variables remain constant)
Case 4: Sales price, cost, and volume increase

To calculate the changes in value under each of the scenarios, we will use a five-year horizon for any change in cash flow induced by the change in the dollar-euro exchange rate.

Case 1: Euro Depreciation—All Variables Remain Constant

Assume that in the coming five years no changes occur in sales volume, sales price, or operating costs. Profits for the coming year in euros will be as expected, and cash flow from operations will still be €1,805,550. There is no change in net working capital (receivables plus inventory minus payables) because all results in euros remain the same. The exchange rate change, however, means that operating cash flows measured in U.S. dollars decline to $1,805,550. The present value of this series of operating cash flows is $6,052,483, a fall in Ganado Germany's value—when measured in U.S. dollars—of $1,210,497.

Case 2: Volume Increases—Other Variables Remain Constant

Assume that, following the depreciation in the euro, sales within Europe increase by 40% to 1,400,000 units (assume all other variables remain constant). The depreciation has now made German-made telecom components more competitive with imports. Additionally, export volume increases because German-made components are now cheaper in countries whose currencies have not weakened. The sales price is kept constant in euro terms because management of Ganado Germany has not observed any change in local German operating costs and because it sees an opportunity to increase market share.

Ganado Germany's net income rises to €2,107,950, and operating cash flows the first year rise to €2,504,553 after a one-time increase in net working capital of €203,397 (using a portion of the increased cash flows). Operating cash flow is €2,707,950 per year for the following four years. The present value of Ganado Germany has risen by $1,637,621 over baseline to $8,900,601.

Case 3: Sales Price Increases—Other Variables Remain Constant

Assume the euro sales price is raised from €12.80 to €15.36 per unit to maintain the same U.S. dollar-equivalent price (the change offsets the depreciation of the euro) and that all other variables remain constant.

	Before	**After**
Price in euro	€12.80	€15.36
Exchange rate	$1.20 = €1.00	$1.00 = €1.00
Price in US$	$15.36	$15.36

Also assume that volume remains constant (the baseline 1,000,000 units) in spite of this price increase; that is, customers expect to pay the same dollar-equivalent price, and local costs do not change.

Ganado Germany is now better off following the depreciation than it was before because the sales price, which is pegged to the international price level, increased. And volume did not drop. Net income rises to €3,010,350 per year, with operating cash flow rising to €3,561,254 in 2021 (after a working capital increase of €49,096) and €3,610,350 per year in the following four years. Ganado Germany has now increased in value to $12,059,761.

Case 4: Price, Cost, and Volume Increases

The final case we examine, illustrated in Exhibit A12.3, is a combination of possible outcomes. Price increases by 10% to €14.08, direct cost per unit increases by 5% to €10.00, and volume rises by 10% to 1,100,000 units. Revenues rise by more than costs, and net income for Ganado Germany rises to €2,113,590. Operating cash flow rises to €2,623,683 in 2014 (after net working capital [NWC] increases) and is €2,713,590 for each of the following four years. Ganado Germany's present value is now $9,018,195.

Other Possibilities

If any portion of sales revenues was incurred in other currencies, the situation would be different. Ganado Germany might leave the foreign sales price unchanged, in effect raising the euro-equivalent price. Alternatively, it might leave the euro-equivalent price unchanged, thus lowering the foreign sales price in an attempt to gain volume. Of course, it could also position itself between these two extremes. Depending on elasticities and the proportion of foreign to domestic sales, total sales revenue might rise or fall.

If some or all raw material or components were imported and paid for in hard currencies (global currencies known to hold their value, such as the euro, dollar, and yen), then euro operating costs would increase after the depreciation of the euro. Another possibility is that local (not imported) euro costs would rise after a euro depreciation.

Measurement of Loss

Exhibit A12.4 summarizes the change in Ganado Germany's value across our small set of simple cases given an instantaneous and permanent change in the value of the euro from $1.20 to $1.00. These cases estimate Ganado Germany's operating exposure by measuring the change in the subsidiary's value as measured by the present value of its operating cash flows over the coming five-year period.

In Case 1, in which the euro depreciates (all variables remain constant), Ganado's German subsidiary's value falls by the percent change in the exchange rate. In Case 2, in which volume increased by 40% as a result of increasing price competitiveness, the German subsidiary's value increased 22.5%. In Case 3, in which the change in the exchange rate was completely passed through to a higher sales price, the result is a massive 66% increase in subsidiary value. The final case, Case 4, combines increases in all three of the income drivers. The resulting change in subsidiary valuation of 24.2% may be creeping toward a "realistic outcome," but there is obviously an infinite number of possibilities, which the subsidiary's management team should be able to narrow.

The added complication is anticipating how competitors will respond to the same exchange rate change. That will depend on a multitude of factors including their own operating structure. In the end, although the measurement of operating exposure is indeed difficult, it is not impossible in progressive financial management—and it may be worth the time and effort.

EXHIBIT A12.3 Ganado Germany Case 4: Sales Price, Volume, and Costs Increase

Assumptions	2021	2022	2023	2024	2025
Sales volume (units)	1,100,000	1,100,000	1,100,000	1,100,000	1,100,000
Sales price per unit	€ 14.08	€ 14.08	€ 14.08	€ 14.08	€ 14.08
Direct cost per unit	€ 10.00	€ 10.00	€ 10.00	€ 10.00	€ 10.00
German corporate tax rate	29.5%	29.5%	29.5%	29.5%	29.5%
Exchange rate ($ = €1.00)	1.0000	1.0000	1.0000	1.0000	1.0000

Income Statement	2021	2022	2023	2024	2025
Sales revenue	€ 15,488,000	€ 15,488,000	€ 15,488,000	€ 15,488,000	€ 15,488,000
Direct cost of goods sold	−11,000,000	−11,000,000	−11,000,000	−11,000,000	−11,000,000
Cash operating expenses (fixed)	−890,000	−890,000	−890,000	−890,000	−890,000
Depreciation	−600,000	−600,000	−600,000	−600,000	−600,000
Pretax profit	€ 2,998,000	€ 2,998,000	€ 2,998,000	€ 2,998,000	€ 2,998,000
Income tax expense	−884,410	−884,410	−884,410	−884,410	−884,410
Net income	€ 2,113,590	€ 2,113,590	€ 2,113,590	€ 2,113,590	€ 2,113,590

Cash Flows for Valuation					
Net income	€ 2,113,590	€ 2,113,590	€ 2,113,590	€ 2,113,590	€ 2,113,590
Add back depreciation	600,000	600,000	600,000	600,000	600,000
Changes in net working capital	−89,907	0	0	0	0
Free cash flow for valuation, in euros	€ 2,623,683	€ 2,713,590	€ 2,713,590	€ 2,713,590	€ 2,713,590
Cash flow from operations, in dollars	$2,623,683	$2,713,590	$2,713,590	$2,713,590	$2,713,590
Present Value @ 15%	$9,018,195				

EXHIBIT A12.4 Summary of Ganado Germany Value Changes to Depreciation of the Euro

Case	Exchange Rate	Price	Volume	Cost	Valuation	Change in Value	Percentage Change in Value
Baseline	$1.20 = €1.00	€ 12.80	1,000,000	€ 9.60	$7,262,980	–	
1: No variable changes	$1.00 = €1.00	€ 12.80	1,000,000	€ 9.60	$6,052,483	($1,210,497)	−16.7%
2: Volume increases	$1.00 = €1.00	€ 12.80	1,400,000	€ 9.60	$8,900,601	$1,637,621	22.5%
3: Sales price increases	$1.00 = €1.00	€ 15.60	1,000,000	€ 9.60	$12,059,761	$4,796,781	66.0%
4: Price, cost, volume increase	$1.00 = €1.00	€ 14.08	1,100,000	€ 10.00	$9,018,195	$1,755,215	24.2%

PART 4

Financing the Global Firm

13

Global Cost and Availability of Capital

Capital must be propelled by self-interest; it cannot be enticed by benevolence.

—Walter Bagehot, 1826–1877.

LEARNING OBJECTIVES

13.1 Explore the evolution of how corporate strategy and financial globalization may align

13.2 Examine how international portfolio theory and diversification alter the global cost of capital

13.3 Describe how international portfolio investors impact the cost of capital

13.4 Compare the weighted average cost of capital for an MNE with its domestic counterpart

13.5 Analyze the illustrative and seminal case of Novo Industri A/S's strategy to internationalize its cost and availability to capital

How can firms tap global capital markets for the purpose of minimizing their cost of capital and maximizing capital's availability? Why should they do so? Is global capital cheaper? This chapter explores these questions, concluding with the mini-case *The Recapitalization of Saudi Aramco*, which explores the international refinancing of the world's most profitable company.

13.1 Financial Globalization and Strategy

Global integration of capital markets has given many firms access to new and cheaper sources of funds, beyond the sources available in their home markets. These firms can then accept more long-term projects and invest more in capital improvements and expansion. If a firm is located in a country with illiquid and/or *segmented capital markets*, it can achieve this lower global cost and greater availability of capital through a properly designed and implemented strategy. The dimensions of the cost and availability of capital are presented in Exhibit 13.1.

A firm that must source its long-term debt and equity in a highly illiquid domestic securities market will probably have a relatively high cost of capital and will face limited availability of such capital, which in turn will lower its competitiveness both internationally and vis-à-vis foreign firms entering its home market. This category of firms includes both firms resident in emerging countries, where the capital market remains undeveloped and firms too small to gain access to their own national securities markets. Many family-owned firms find themselves in this category because they choose not to utilize securities markets to source their long-term capital needs.

EXHIBIT 13.1 **Dimensions of the Cost and Availability of Capital Strategy**

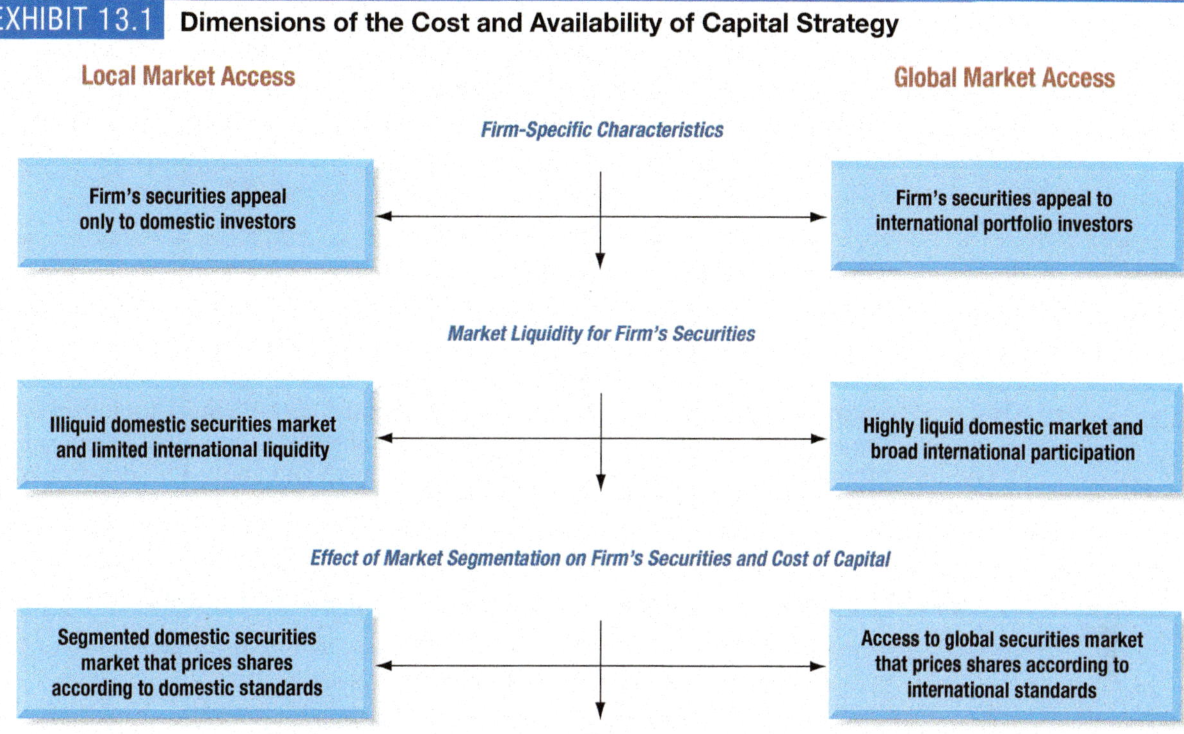

Firms resident in industrial countries with small capital markets often source their long-term debt and equity at home in these partially liquid domestic securities markets. The firms' cost and availability of capital are better than those of firms in countries with illiquid capital markets. However, if these firms can tap the highly liquid global markets, they can also strengthen their competitive advantage in sourcing capital.

Firms resident in countries with segmented capital markets must devise a strategy to escape dependence on that market for their long-term debt and equity needs. A national capital market is *segmented* if the required rate of return on securities in that market differs from the required rate of return on securities of comparable expected return and risk traded in other securities markets. Capital markets become segmented because of such factors as excessive regulatory control, perceived political risk, anticipated foreign exchange risk, lack of transparency, asymmetric availability of information, cronyism, insider trading, and many other market imperfections. Firms constrained by any of these conditions must develop a strategy to escape their own limited capital markets and source some of their long-term capital abroad. Segmented markets can arise a variety of ways, however, as described in *Global Finance in Practice 13.1* on the impact of Brexit.

Cost of Capital

A domestic firm normally finds its cost of capital by evaluating where and from whom it will raise its capital. The cost will obviously differ based on the mix of investors interested in the firm, investors willing and able to buy its equity shares, and the debt available to the firm, raised from the domestic bank and debt market.

The firm calculates its *weighted average cost of capital* (WACC) by combining the cost of equity with the cost of debt in proportion to the relative weight of each in the firm's optimal long-term financial structure. More specifically,

$$k_{\text{WACC}} = k_e \frac{E}{V} + k_d(1 - t)\frac{D}{V}$$

where k_{WACC} = weighted average after-tax cost of capital
k_e = risk-adjusted cost of equity
k_d = before-tax cost of debt
t = marginal tax rate
E = market value of the firm's equity
D = market value of the firm's debt
V = market value of the firm's securities $(D + E)$

Cost of Equity

The most widely accepted and used method of calculating the cost of equity for a firm today is the *capital asset pricing model* (*CAPM*). CAPM defines the cost of equity to be the sum of a risk-free interest component and a firm-specific spread, over and above that risk-free component, as seen in the following formula:

$$k_e = k_{rf} + \beta_j (k_m - k_{rf})$$

where k_e = expected (required) rate of return on equity
k_{rf} = rate of interest on risk-free bonds (Treasury bonds, for example)
β_j = coefficient of *systematic risk* for the firm (*beta*)
k_m = expected (required) rate of return on the market portfolio of stocks

GLOBAL FINANCE IN PRACTICE 13.1

Brexit and the Cost of Capital

The decision for the United Kingdom to leave the European Union is resulting in more and more companies having a higher cost of capital on both sides of the Channel. A restructuring of the banking sectors in both regions involves direct costs as well as more segmented markets, all at a time when global interest rates—dollar, pound, and euro—are expected to start rising as the post-COVID stimulus programs fall further and further into the past.

Impacts on Banks. Banks in the UK are already incurring sizeable restructuring costs. A number of London banks have been moving quickly to move large portions of their operations and jobs to the Continent in an effort to retain clients and market share. London banks are estimating that restructuring costs alone may range between $200 million and $400 million. The costs of capital for banks themselves are expected to rise at least 4%, and many are looking to increase their capital bases by more than 30% as they establish European banks to retain Continental clients.

Impacts on Borrowers. One of the unintended results is a multitude of banks are reducing their lines of credit and increasing their fees to many of the small to medium-sized enterprises. Companies with annual revenue of up to €10 million are defined as *small businesses*, and firms with revenue between €10 and €50 million are *medium-sized* according to the European Union. This segment of borrowers is particularly sensitive to these changes as many of these firms use only one bank for the majority of their financial services. Without alternative banks, offering either alternative services or competitive rates, they are starting to feel the impacts of reduced services and increased costs. As a result of rising bank fees and fewer alternatives, borrowers have experienced rising costs of debt.

How this will ultimately impact business activity is hard to say, but early signs from these segments are not encouraging. Some experts, including Professor Aswath Damodaran of New York University's Stern School of Business, have been encouraging companies to focus on the three drivers of business valuation—cash flows, growth rates, and discount rates—and not fall victim to pessimism. He has characterized Brexit as a "garden variety crisis" that most businesses should endure. A number of firms, however, have cut back on new investment projects. Rising capital costs make fewer prospective investments financially viable. A number of borrowers have noted that their firms will intentionally now work to increase their cash balances—a form of precautionary source of funds—as they fear reduced access to affordable debt.

The key component of CAPM is *beta* (β_j), the measure of systematic risk. *Systematic risk* is a measure of how the firm's returns vary with those of the market in which it trades. *Beta* is calculated as a function of the total variability of expected returns of the firm's stock relative to the market index and the degree to which the variability of expected returns of the firm is correlated to the expected returns on the market index. More formally,

$$\beta_j = \frac{\rho_{jm}\,\sigma_j}{\sigma_m}$$

$$\begin{aligned} \text{where } \beta_j \ (\textit{beta}) &= \text{measure of systematic risk for security } j \\ \rho \ (\text{rho}) &= \text{correlation between security } j \text{ and the market} \\ \sigma_j \ (\text{sigma}) &= \text{standard deviation of the return on firm } j \\ \sigma_m \ (\text{sigma}) &= \text{standard deviation of the market return} \end{aligned}$$

Beta will have a value of less than 1.0 if the firm's returns are less volatile than the market, 1.0 if the firm's returns are the same as the market, and greater than 1.0 if its returns are more volatile—or risky—than the market. CAPM analysis assumes that the required return estimated is an indication of what more is necessary to keep an investor's capital invested in the equity considered. If the equity's return does not reach the expected return, CAPM assumes that individual investors will liquidate their holdings.

CAPM's biggest challenge is that, for a *beta* to be most useful, it should be an indicator of the future rather than a report of the past. A prospective investor is interested in how the individual firm's returns will vary in the coming periods. Unfortunately, since the future is not known, the *beta* used in any firm's estimate of equity cost is based on evidence from the recent past.

Cost of Debt

Firms acquire debt in either the form of loans from commercial banks—the most common form of debt—or as securities sold to the debt markets, such as instruments like notes and bonds. The normal procedure for measuring the cost of debt requires a forecast of interest rates for the next few years, the proportions of various classes of debt the firm expects to use, and the corporate income tax rate. The interest costs of the different debt components are then averaged according to their proportion in the debt structure. This before-tax average, k_d, is then adjusted for corporate income taxes by multiplying it by the expression $(1 - \text{tax rate})$, to obtain $k_d\,(1 - t)$, the after-tax cost of debt.

The weighted average cost of capital is normally used as the risk-adjusted discount rate whenever a firm's new projects are in the same general risk class as its existing projects. On the other hand, a project-specific required rate of return should be used as the discount rate if a new project differs from existing projects in business or financial risk.

13.2 International Portfolio Theory and Diversification

The potential benefits to companies from raising capital on global markets are based on international portfolio theory and the benefits of international diversification. We briefly review these principles before examining the costs and capacities for raising capital in the global market.

Portfolio Risk Reduction

The risk of a portfolio is measured by the ratio of the variance of the portfolio's return relative to the variance of the market return. This is the *beta* of the portfolio. As an investor increases the number of securities in a portfolio, the portfolio's risk declines rapidly at first and then

EXHIBIT 13.2 **Market Liquidity, Segmentation, and the Marginal Cost of Capital**

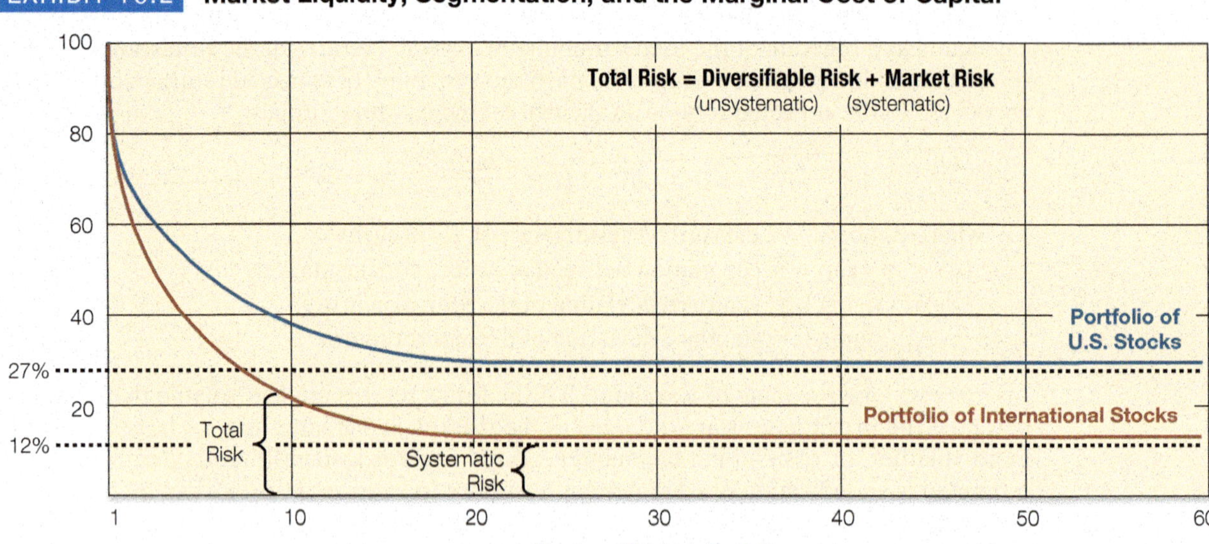

When the portfolio is diversified, the variance of the portfolio's return relative to the variance of the market's return (*beta*) is reduced to the level of systematic risk—the risk of the market itself. When the portfolio is diversified internationally, the portfolio's beta is lowered.

asymptotically approaches the level of systematic risk of the market. The total risk of any portfolio is therefore composed of systematic risk (the market) and unsystematic risk (the individual securities). Increasing the number of securities in the portfolio reduces the unsystematic risk component but leaves the systematic risk component unchanged. A fully diversified domestic portfolio would have a *beta* of 1.0. This is standard-domestic financial theory.

Exhibit 13.2 illustrates the incremental gains of diversifying both domestically and internationally. The lower line in Exhibit 13.2 (portfolio of international stocks) represents a portfolio in which foreign securities have been added. It has the same overall risk shape as the U.S. stock portfolio, but it has a lower portfolio *beta*. This means that the international portfolio's market risk is lower than that of a domestic portfolio. This situation arises because the returns on the foreign stocks are not perfectly correlated with U.S. stocks.

Foreign Exchange Risk

The foreign exchange risks of a portfolio, whether it is a securities portfolio or the general portfolio of activities of the MNE, are reduced through international diversification. The construction of internationally diversified portfolios is both the same as and different from creating a traditional domestic portfolio. Internationally diversified portfolios are the same in principle because the investor is attempting to combine assets that are less than perfectly correlated, reducing the total risk of the portfolio. In addition, by adding assets from outside the home market—assets that previously were not available to be averaged into the portfolio's expected returns and risks—the investor is tapping into a larger pool of potential investments.

But international portfolio construction is also different in that when the investor acquires assets or securities from outside the investor's host-country market, the investor may also be acquiring a *foreign currency-denominated asset*.[1] Thus, the investor has actually

[1]This is not always the case. For example, many U.S.-based investors routinely purchase and hold Eurodollar bonds on the secondary market only (illegal during primary issuance), which would not pose currency risk to the U.S.-based investor for they are denominated in the investor's home currency.

acquired two additional assets—the currency of denomination and the asset subsequently purchased with the currency—one asset in principle, but two in expected returns and risks.

A numerical example can illustrate the difficulties associated with international portfolio diversification and currency risk. A U.S.-based investor takes $1,000,000 on January 1 and invests in shares traded on the Tokyo Stock Exchange (TSE). The spot exchange rate on January 1 is ¥130.00 = $1.00. The $1 million therefore yields ¥130,000,000. The investor uses ¥130,000,000 to acquire shares on the Tokyo Stock Exchange at ¥20,000 per share, acquiring 6,500 shares, and holds the shares for one year.

At the end of one year, the investor sells the 6,500 shares at the market price, which is now ¥25,000 per share; the shares have risen ¥5,000 per share in price. The 6,500 shares at ¥25,000 per share yield proceeds of ¥162,500,000.

The Japanese yen are then exchanged back into the investor's home currency, the U.S. dollar, at the spot rate of ¥125.00 = $1.00 now in effect. This results in total U.S. dollar proceeds of $13. billion. The total return on the investment is then

$$\frac{\text{US\$ } 1{,}300{,}000 - \text{US\$ } 1{,}000{,}000}{\text{US\$ } 1{,}000{,}000} = 30.00\%$$

The total U.S. dollar return is actually a combination of the return on the Japanese yen (which in this case was positive) and the return on the shares listed on the Tokyo Stock Exchange (which was also positive). This value is expressed by isolating the percentage change in the share price (r_{shares}) in combination with the percentage change in the currency value $R^{¥=\$1.0}$:

$$R^{\$} = [(1 + r^{¥=\$1.00})(1 + r^{\text{shares, ¥}})] - 1$$

In this case, the value of the Japanese yen, in the eyes of a U.S.-based investor, rose 4.00% (from ¥130 = $1.00 to ¥125 = $1.00), while the shares traded on the Tokyo Stock Exchange rose 25.00%. The total investment return in U.S. dollars is therefore:

$$R^{\$} = [(1 + .0400)(1 + .2500)] - 1 = .3000 \text{ or } 30.00\%$$

Obviously, the risk associated with international diversification, when it includes currency risk, is inherently more complex than that of domestic investments. You should also see, however, that the presence of currency risk may alter the correlations associated with securities in different countries and currencies, providing new portfolio composition and diversification possibilities. In conclusion:

- Benefits of international diversification induce investors to demand foreign securities (the so-called *buy-side*).
- If adding a foreign security to an investor's portfolio aids in the reduction of risk for a given level of return, or if it increases the expected return for a given level of risk, then the security adds value to the portfolio.
- A security that adds value is demanded by investors. Given the limits of the potential supply of securities, increased demand will bid up the price of the security, resulting in a lower cost of capital for the firm. The firm issuing the security, the *sell-side*, is therefore able to raise capital at a lower cost.

International CAPM (ICAPM)

The traditional form of CAPM, the domestic CAPM discussed earlier, assumes the firm's equity trades in a purely domestic market. The *beta* and *market risk premium* ($k_m - k_{rf}$) used in the cost of equity calculation, therefore, are based on a purely domestic market of securities and choices. But what if globalization has opened up the global markets, integrating them and allowing investors to choose among stocks of a global portfolio?

International CAPM (ICAPM) assumes that there is a global market in which the firm's equity trades, and estimates of the firm's *beta*, β_j^g and the market risk premium, $(k_m^g - k_{rfg})$, must then reflect this global portfolio.

$$k_e^{\text{global}} = k_{rf}^g + \beta_j^g(k_m^g - k_{rf}^g)$$

The value of the risk-free rate, k_{rfg}, may not change (so that $k_{rf}^g = k_{rf}$), as a U.S. Treasury note may be the risk-free rate for a U.S.-based investor regardless of the domestic or international portfolio. The market return, k_m^g, will change, reflecting average expected global market returns for the coming periods. The firm's *beta*, β_j^g, will most assuredly change as it now will reflect the expected variations against a greater global portfolio. How that *beta* will change, however, depends.

Sample Calculation: Ganado's Cost of Capital

Maria Gonzalez, Ganado's chief financial officer, wants to calculate the company's weighted average cost of capital in both forms, the traditional CAPM and also ICAPM.

Maria assumes the risk-free rate of interest (k_{rf}) as 4%, using the U.S. government 10-year Treasury bond rate. The expected rate of return of the market portfolio (k_m) is assumed to be 9%, the expected rate of return on the market portfolio held by a well-diversified domestic investor. Ganado's estimate of its own systematic risk—its *beta*—against the domestic portfolio is 1.2. Ganado's cost of equity is then

$$k_e = k_{rf} + \beta(k_m - k_{rf}) = 4.00\% + 1.2(9.00\% - 4.00\%) = 10.00\%$$

Ganado's cost of debt (k_d), the before-tax cost of debt estimated by observing the current yield on Ganado's outstanding bonds combined with bank debt, is 8%. Using 35% as the corporate income tax rate for the United States, Ganado's after-tax cost of debt is then

$$k_d(1 - t) = 8.00(1 - 0.35) = 8.00(0.65) = 5.20\%$$

Ganado's long-term capital structure is 60% equity (E/V) and 40% debt (D/V), where V is Ganado's total market value. Ganado's weighted average cost of capital k_{wacc} is then

$$k_{\text{WACC}} = k_e\frac{E}{V} + k_d(1 - t)\frac{D}{V} = 10.00\%(.60) + 5.20\%(.40) = 8.08\%$$

This is Ganado's cost of capital using the traditional domestic CAPM estimate of the cost of equity. But Maria wonders if this is the proper approach for Ganado. As Ganado has globalized its business activities, the investor base that owns Ganado's shares has also globally diversified. Ganado's shares are now listed in London and Tokyo, in addition to their home listing on the New York Stock Exchange. Over 40% of Ganado's stock is now held by foreign portfolio investors, as part of their globally diversified portfolios, while Ganado's U.S. investors also typically hold globally diversified portfolios.

A second calculation of Ganado's cost of equity, this time using the ICAPM, yields different results. Ganado's *beta*, when calculated against a larger global equity market index, which includes these foreign markets and their investors, is a lower 0.90. The expected market return for a larger globally integrated equity market is a lower value as well, 8.00%. The ICAPM cost of equity is a much lower value of 7.60%.

$$k_e^{\text{global}} = k_{rf}^g + \beta_j^g(k_m^g - k_{rf}^g) = 4.00\% + 0.90\ (8.00\% - 4.00\%) = 7.60\%$$

Maria now recalculates Ganado's WACC using the ICAPM estimate of equity costs, assuming the same debt and equity proportions and the same cost of current debt. Ganado's WACC is now estimated at a lower cost of 6.64%.

$$k_{WACC}^{ICAPM} = k_e^{global}\frac{E}{V} + k_d(1 - t)\frac{D}{V} = 7.60\%(.60) + 5.20\%(.40) = 6.64\%.$$

Maria believes that this is a more appropriate estimate of Ganado's cost of capital. It is fully competitive with Ganado's main rivals in the telecommunications hardware industry segment worldwide, which are mainly headquartered in the United States, the United Kingdom, Canada, Finland, Sweden, Germany, Japan, and the Netherlands. The key to Ganado's favorable global cost and availability of capital going forward is its ability to attract and hold the international portfolio investors that own its stock.

ICAPM Considerations

In theory, the primary distinction in the estimation of the cost of equity for an individual firm using an internationalized version of the CAPM is the definition of the "market" and a recalculation of the firm's *beta* for that market. The three basic components of the CAPM model must then be reconsidered.

Nestlé, the Swiss-based multinational firm that produces and distributes a variety of confectionary products, serves as an excellent example of how the international investor may view the global cost of capital differently from a domestic investor, and what that means for Nestlé's estimate of its own cost of equity.[2] The numerical example for Nestlé is summarized in Exhibit 13.3.

In the case of Nestlé, a prospective Swiss investor might assume a risk-free return in Swiss francs of 3.3%—the rate of return on an index of Swiss government bond issues. That same Swiss investor might also assume an expected market return in Swiss francs of 10.2%—an average return on a portfolio of Swiss equities, the *Financial Times Swiss index*. Assuming a risk-free rate of 3.30%, an expected market return of 10.2%, and a $\beta_{Nestlé}$ of 0.885, a Swiss investor would expect Nestlé to yield 9.4065% for the coming year.

$$k_{Nestlé} = k_{RF} + \beta_{Nestlé}(k_M - k_{RF}) = 3.3 + 0.885(10.2 - 3.3) = 9.4065\%$$

But what if Swiss investors held internationally diversified portfolios instead? Both the expected market return and the *beta* estimate for Nestlé itself would be defined and determined differently. For the same period as before, a global portfolio index such as the *Financial*

EXHIBIT 13.3 The Cost of Equity for Nestlé of Switzerland

Nestlé's estimate of its cost of equity will depend upon whether a Swiss investor is thought to hold a domestic portfolio of equity securities or a global portfolio.

Domestic Portfolio for Swiss Investor	Global Portfolio for Swiss Investor
$k_{RF} = 3.3\%$ (Swiss bond index yield)	$k_{RF} = 3.3\%$ (Swiss bond index yield)
$k_M = 10.2\%$ (Swiss market portfolio in SF)	$k_M = 13.7\%$ (Financial Times Global index in SF)
$\beta_{Nestlé} = 0.885$ (Nestlé versus Swiss market portfolio)	$\beta_{Nestlé} = 0.585$ (Nestlé versus FTA-Swiss index)

$$k_{Nestlé} = k_{RF} + \beta_{Nestlé}(k_M - k_{RF})$$

Domestic	Global
Required return on Nestlé:	Required return on Nestlé:
$k_e^{Nestlé} = 9.4065\%$	$k_e^{Nestlé} = 9.3840\%$

Source: All values are taken from Rene Stulz, "The Cost of Capital in Internationally Integrated Markets: The Case of Nestlé," *European Financial Management*, Volume 1, Number 1, March 1995, 11–22.

[2]Stulz, René, "The Cost of Capital in Internationally Integrated Markets: The Case of Nestlé," *European Financial Management*, Vol. 1, No. 1, March 1995, pp. 11–22.

Times index in Swiss francs (FTA-Swiss) would show a market return of 13.7% (as opposed to the domestic Swiss index return of 10.2%). In addition, a *beta* for Nestlé estimated on Nestlé's returns versus the global portfolio index would be much smaller, 0.585 (as opposed to the 0.885 found previously). An internationally diversified Swiss investor would expect the following return on Nestlé:

$$k_{\text{Nestlé}} = k_{RF} + \beta_{\text{Nestlé}}(k_M - k_{RF}) = 3.3 + 0.585(13.7 - 3.3) = 9.3840\%$$

Admittedly, this is not a lot of difference in the end. However, given the magnitude of change in both the values of the market return average and the *beta* for the firm, it is obvious that the result could easily have varied by several hundred basis points. The proper construction of the investor's portfolio and the proper portrayal of the investor's perceptions of risk and opportunity cost are clearly important to identifying the global cost of a company's equity capital. In the end, it all depends on the specific case—the firm, the country-market, and the global portfolio. We follow the practice here of describing the internationally diversified portfolio as the global portfolio rather than the world portfolio. The distinction is important. The world portfolio is an index of all securities in the world. However, even with continued deregulation and increasing financial integration, a number of securities markets remain restricted in their access. Those securities actually available to an investor are the global portfolio.

There are many different formulations for calculating the international cost of capital. The problems with both formulation and data expand dramatically as the analysis is extended to rapidly developing markets. Harvey (2005) provides a starting point on this issue if you wish to expand your reading and research.[3]

Global Betas

International portfolio theory typically concludes that adding international securities to a domestic portfolio will reduce the portfolio's risk. Although this idea is fundamental to much of international financial theory, it still depends on individual firms in individual markets. Nestlé's *beta* went down when calculated using a global portfolio of equities, but that may not always be the case. Depending on the firm, its business line, the country it calls home, and the industry—domestically and globally—in which it competes, the *global beta* may go up or down.

One company often noted by researchers is Petrobras, the national oil company of Brazil. Although government controlled, the company is publicly traded. Its shares are listed in São Paulo and New York. It operates in a global oil market in which prices and values are set in U.S. dollars. As a result, its domestic or home *beta* has been estimated at 1.3, but its *global beta* higher, at 1.7. This is only one example of many. Although it seems obvious to some that the returns to the individual firm should become less correlated to those of the market as the market is redefined ever larger, it turns out to be more of a case of empirical analysis, not preconceived notions of correlation and covariance.

Equity Risk Premiums

In practice, calculating a firm's equity risk premium is much more controversial. Although the capital asset pricing model (CAPM has now become widely accepted in global business as the preferred method of calculating the cost of equity for a firm, there is rising debate over what numerical values should be used in its application, especially the *equity risk premium*.

[3] Campbell R. Harvey, "12 Ways to Calculate the International Cost of Capital," Duke University, unpublished, October 14, 2005.

EXHIBIT 13.4 **The Equity Risk Premium across Global Markets (Implied Premium)**

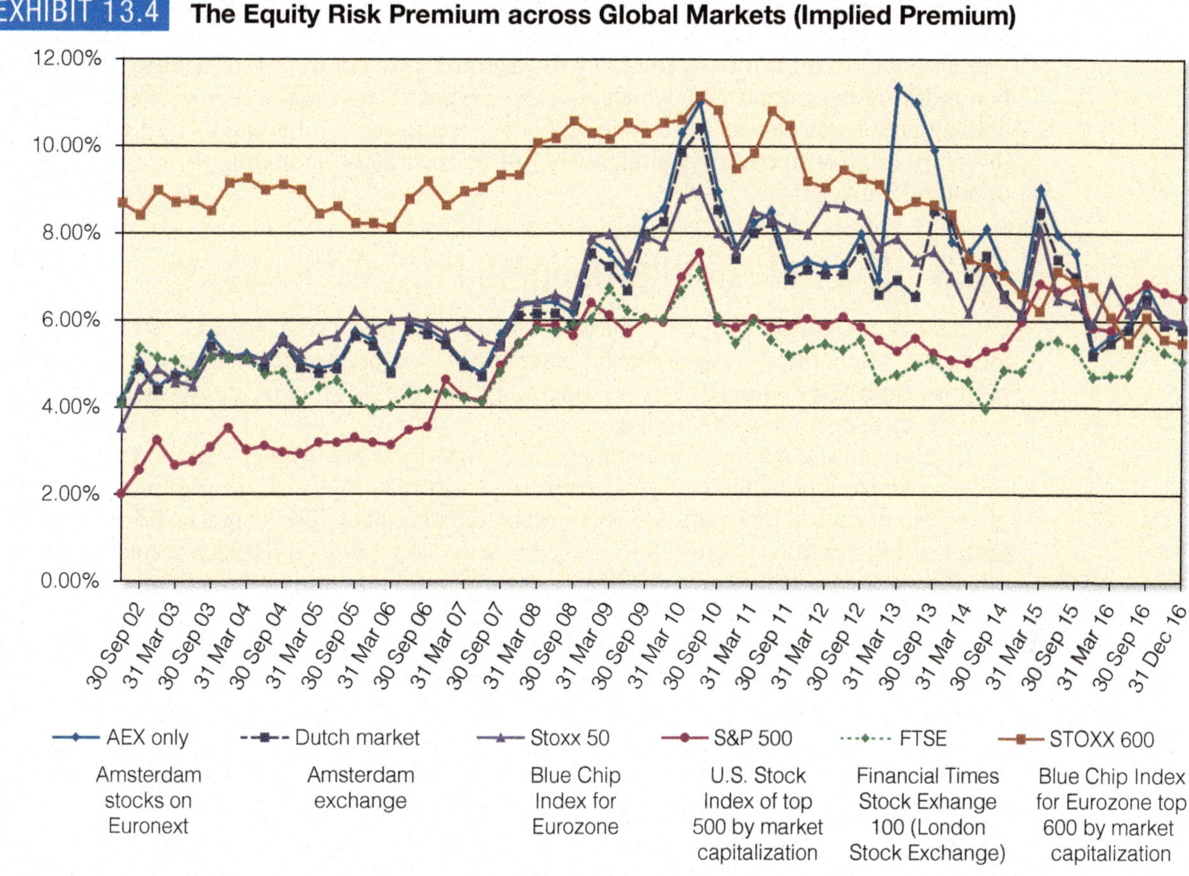

Source: Equity Market Risk Premium—Research Summary, KPMG, January 13, 2017, p. 7. KPMG derives the implied equity market risk premium by deducting the risk-free rate from the implied discount rate as yielded by the various equity market indexes.

The equity risk premium is the average annual return of the market expected by investors over and above riskless debt, the term $(k_m - k_{rf})$.

The field of finance does agree that a cost of equity calculation should be *forward looking*, meaning that the inputs to the equation should represent what is expected to happen over the relevant future time horizon. As is typically the case, however, practitioners use historical evidence as the basis for their forward-looking projections. One large study estimated the equity risk premium in 16 different developed countries for the 1900–2002 period.[4] The study found significant differences in equity returns over bill and bond returns (proxies for the risk-free rate) over time by country. For example, Italy had the highest equity risk premium, 10.3%, followed by Germany with 9.4% and Japan at 9.3%. Denmark had the lowest at 3.8%.

Equity risk premiums will also differ across country markets, as interest rate and interest rate-related returns (like risk-free rates of return) differ by currency. Exhibit 13.4 makes this readily apparent, as the equity market risk premium is both relatively stable over the recent five-year period by country but does vary by country. This study by KPMG is updated regularly, and curiously, they tend to recommend a single value for highly industrialized markets

[4]Elroy Dimson, Paul Marsh, and Mike Stanton, "Global Evidence on the Equity Risk Premium," *Journal of Applied Corporate Finance*, Volume 15, No. 4, Fall 2003, p. 31.

and not individual values like those shown in Exhibit 13.4. In the most recent report KPMG has increased its single equity market risk premium recommendation to 6.75%.[5]

How important is it for a company to accurately predict its cost of equity? The corporation must annually determine which potential investments it will accept and reject due to its limited capital resources. If the company is not accurately estimating its cost of equity, and therefore its general cost of capital, it will not be accurately estimating the net present value of potential investments.

13.3 The Role of International Portfolio Investors

Gradual deregulation of equity markets during the past three decades not only elicited increased competition from domestic players but also opened up markets to foreign competitors. International portfolio investment and the cross-listing of equity shares on foreign markets have become commonplace.

Both domestic and international portfolio managers are *asset allocators*. Their objective is to maximize a portfolio's rate of return for a given level of risk or to minimize risk for a given rate of return. International portfolio managers can choose from a larger pool of assets than portfolio managers limited to domestic-only asset allocations. As a result, internationally diversified portfolios often have a higher expected rate of return, and they nearly always have a lower level of portfolio risk, since national securities markets are imperfectly correlated with one another.

Portfolio asset allocation can be accomplished along many dimensions depending on the investment objective of the portfolio manager. For example, portfolios can be diversified according to the type of securities. They can be composed of stocks only or bonds only or a combination of both. They also can be diversified by industry or by size of capitalization (small-cap, mid-cap, and large-cap stock portfolios).

For our purposes, the most relevant dimensions are diversification by country, geographic region, stage of development, or a combination of these (global). An example of diversification by country is the Korea Fund. It was at one time the only vehicle allowing foreign investors to hold South Korean securities, but foreign ownership restrictions have more recently been liberalized. A typical regional diversification would be one of the many Asian funds. These performed exceptionally well until the "bubble" burst in Japan and Southeast Asia during the second half of the 1990s. Portfolios composed of emerging market securities are examples of diversification by stage of development. They are composed of securities from different countries, geographic regions, and stage of development. And as illustrated in *Global Finance in Practice 13.2*, corporate governance may contribute to these issues of equity and stage of development.

The Link between Cost and Availability of Capital

Ganado's weighted average cost of capital (WACC) was calculated assuming that equity and debt capital would always be available at the same required rate of return even if Ganado's capital budget expands. This is a reasonable assumption considering Ganado's excellent access through the New York Stock Exchange to international portfolio investors in global capital markets. It is a bad assumption, however, for firms resident in illiquid or segmented capital markets, small domestic firms, and family-owned firms resident in any capital market. We will now examine how market liquidity and market segmentation can affect a firm's cost of capital.

[5] *Equity Market Risk Premium, Research Summary*, KPMG, March 31, 2020, p. 9.

GLOBAL FINANCE IN PRACTICE 13.2

Emerging Market Growth Companies—IPOs and Corporate Governance

The Organisation for Economic Co-operation and Development (OECD) has recently been exploring the relationship between an emerging market company's perceived corporate governance practices and its access to capital—its ability to successfully raise equity through an initial public offering (IPO). So-called growth companies, companies pursuing relatively rapid growth in both sales and employment, require significant external capital. These organizations are thought to play a critical role in economic development, but only if they can escape what the OECD terms a "static state" of a moderate size.

Escaping the "static state" requires external capital, both debt and equity, although the OECD places specific emphasis on equity as the true facilitator of development. Emphasis is placed on capital that is both patient—willing to support research, development, and innovation over time— and limited in its burden on the firm. The preference for equity is based on its limited cash flow obligations (unlike debt, which must be regularly serviced), allowing the firms to undertake forward-looking investments.

But that same equity requires investor confidence in the corporate governance practices of the firms. Gaining access to equity requires meeting and surpassing investor expectations regarding corporate governance practices. The OECD's own Principles of Corporate Governance (detailed previously in Chapter 4) are thought to be one of the pillars of building that investor confidence framework.

The global capital markets, however, are not yet there. Roughly half of all equity raised globally via IPO since the global financial crisis of 2008 has been raised by companies from emerging markets. But these same companies are still closely held, often controlled by a single dominant owner, a structure that does not support the best in corporate governance.

Improving Market Liquidity. Although no consensus exists about the definition of market liquidity, we can observe market liquidity by noting the degree to which a firm can issue a new security without depressing the existing market price. In the domestic case, an underlying assumption is that total availability of capital to a firm at any time is determined by supply and demand in the domestic capital markets.

A firm should always expand its capital budget by raising funds in the same proportion as its optimal financial structure. As its budget expands in absolute terms, however, its marginal cost of capital will eventually increase. In other words, a firm can only tap the capital market for some limited amount in the short run before suppliers of capital balk at providing further funds, even if the same optimal financial structure is preserved. In the long run, this may not be a limitation, depending on market liquidity.

In the multinational case, a firm is able to improve market liquidity by raising funds in the euromarkets (money, bond, and equity), by selling security issues abroad, and by tapping local capital markets through foreign subsidiaries. Such activities should logically expand the capacity of an MNE to raise funds in the short run over what might have been raised if the firm were limited to its home capital market. This situation assumes that the firm preserves its optimal financial structure.

Market Segmentation. If all capital markets are fully integrated, securities of comparable expected return and risk should have the same required rate of return in each national market after adjusting for foreign exchange risk and political risk. This definition applies to both equity and debt, although it often happens that one or the other may be more integrated than its counterpart.

Capital market segmentation is a financial market imperfection caused mainly by government constraints, institutional practices, and investor perceptions. The most significant imperfections include asymmetric information between domestic and foreign investors, lack of transparency, high transaction costs, foreign exchange risks, political risks, corporate governance differences, and a variety of regulatory barriers.

Market imperfections do not necessarily imply that national securities markets are inefficient. A national securities market can be efficient in a domestic context and yet segmented in an international context. According to finance theory, a market is efficient if security prices in that market reflect all available relevant information and adjust quickly to any new relevant information. Therefore, the price of an individual security reflects its "intrinsic value," and any price fluctuations will be "random walks" around this value. Market efficiency assumes that transaction costs are low, that many participants are in the market, and that these participants have sufficient financial strength to move security prices. Empirical tests of market efficiency show that most major national markets are reasonably efficient.

An efficient national securities market might very well correctly price all securities traded in that market on the basis of information available to the investors who participate in that market. However, if that market is segmented, foreign investors will not be participants. Availability of capital depends on whether a firm can gain liquidity for its debt and equity securities and a price for those securities based on international rather than national standards. In practice, this means that the firm must define a strategy to attract international portfolio investors and thereby escape the constraints of its own illiquid or segmented national market.

The Effect of Market Liquidity and Segmentation. The degree to which capital markets are illiquid or segmented has an important influence on a firm's marginal cost of capital and thus on its weighted average cost of capital. The marginal cost of capital is the weighted average cost of the next currency unit raised. This is illustrated in Exhibit 13.5, which shows the transition from a domestic to a global marginal cost of capital.

Exhibit 13.5 shows that the MNE has a given marginal return on capital at different budget levels, represented in the line MRR. This demand is determined by ranking potential projects according to net present value or internal rate of return. The rate of return to suppliers of capital and the cost of capital to users of capital is shown on the vertical axis. If the firm is limited to raising funds in its domestic market, the line MCC_D shows the marginal domestic

EXHIBIT 13.5 **Market Liquidity, Segmentation, and the Marginal Cost of Capital**

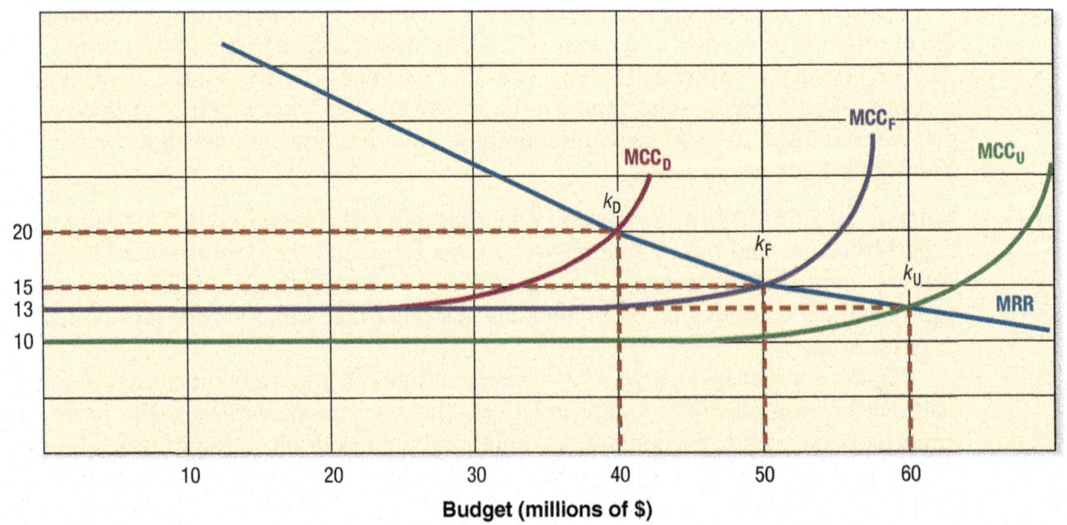

cost of capital (vertical axis) at various budget levels (horizontal axis). Remember that the firm continues to maintain the same debt ratio as it expands its budget so that financial risk does not change. The optimal budget in the domestic case is $40 million, where the marginal return on capital (MRR) just equals the marginal cost of capital (MCC_D). At this budget the marginal domestic cost of capital, k_D, would be equal to 20%.

If the MNE has access to additional sources of capital outside an illiquid domestic capital market, the marginal cost of capital should shift to the right (the line MCC_F). In other words, foreign markets can be tapped for long-term funds at times when the domestic market is saturated because of heavy use by other borrowers or equity issuers or when it is unable to absorb another issue of the MNE in the short run. Exhibit 13.5 shows that by a tap of foreign capital markets the firm has reduced its marginal international cost of capital to 15%, even while it raises an additional $10 million. This statement assumes that about $20 million is raised abroad, since only about $30 million could be raised domestically at a 15% marginal cost of capital.

If the MNE is located in a capital market that is both illiquid and segmented, the line MCC_U represents the decreased marginal cost of capital if it gains access to other equity markets. As a result of the combined effects of greater availability of capital and international pricing of the firm's securities, the marginal cost of capital, k_u, declines to 13% and the optimal capital budget climbs to $60 million.

Most of the tests of market segmentation suffer from the usual problem for models—namely, the need to abstract from reality in order to have a testable model. In our opinion, a realistic test would be to observe what happens to a single security's price when, after it has been traded only in a domestic market, it is "discovered" by foreign investors, and is then traded in a foreign market. Arbitrage should keep the market price equal in both markets. However, if during the transition we observe a significant change in the security's price, uncorrelated with price movements in either of the underlying securities markets, we can infer that the domestic market was segmented.

Unfortunately, few case studies have been documented in which a firm has escaped from a segmented capital market. In practice, escape usually means being listed on a foreign stock market such as New York or London and/or selling securities in foreign capital markets. We will explore one firm's escape from a segmented market with a discussion of Novo later in the chapter.

Globalization of Securities Markets

During the 1980s, numerous Nordic and other European firms cross-listed on major foreign exchanges, such as London and New York. They placed equity and debt issues in major securities markets. In most cases, they were successful in lowering their cost of capital and increasing its availability.

During the 1990s, national restrictions on cross-border portfolio investment were gradually eased under pressure from the OECD, a consortium of most of the world's most industrialized countries. Liberalization of European securities markets was accelerated because of the European Union's efforts to develop a single market without barriers. Emerging nation markets followed suit, as did the former Eastern Bloc countries after the breakup of the Soviet Union. Emerging national markets are often motivated by the need to source foreign capital to finance large-scale privatization.

Today, market segmentation has been significantly reduced, although the liquidity of individual national markets remains limited. Most observers believe that for better or for worse, we have achieved a global market for securities. The good news is that many firms have been assisted to become MNEs because they now have access to a global cost and

GLOBAL FINANCE IN PRACTICE 13.3

Culture, Religion, Law, and Financial Behavior

The field of finance has only begun to understand how aspects of human behavior, including national culture, ethnic culture, legal structure, and religious influence, affect financial management and investing. Research studies have often found it difficult to differentiate correlation from causation, as companies operating in specific countries follow the rule of law in each country, law that may reflect predominant religious beliefs (e.g., Islamic law and its implications for the paying of interest, altering both the banking activities and investment behaviors of people and companies) or may reflect nonreligious cultural characteristics.

There are, however, a few common observations across a number of studies. One such conclusion is that companies operating in countries with strong religious affiliations demonstrate a negative correlation with corporate risk-taking; that is, they were often observed to avoid higher-risk investments although those investments were expected to generate positive net present values to the firms.[6] In something of a consistency of behavior and law, other studies have found that the laws and regulations affording protection of investor rights were associated to differing degrees by predominant religion. Stulz and Williamson (2003) found that predominantly Protestant countries protected investor rights significantly more than predominantly Catholic countries.[7] This same study, however, found that the more open the economy to international trade the less the influence religious affiliation had on investor protections. Alderman et al., (2017) state that *"From a business perspective, this suggests that business leaders and investors should be aware of how their own religiously-inspired biases and preferences, and those of the people they employ or seek to do business with, may impact their financial decisions."*[8]

Other research studies have sought to identify risk-taking and time-based behaviors by national cultures. One such study, funded by Credit Suisse, concluded that Eastern Europeans are some of the most risk-averse investors in the world, that the U.S. investment environment is characterized by a high degree of individualism, which is in turn focused on quick profits compared to Nordic countries which demonstrate a high degree of patience. That same study came to a rather striking conclusion on how human behavior influences investing:

> *Traditional finance, based on the hypothesis of efficient markets and the optimization of statistical figures such as means and variances, suggests that investing has a lot to do with mathematics. However, behavioral finance has put the spotlight back on people. People make mistakes—even in investment decisions, which results in inefficiencies at the market level. Based on behavioral finance, investment is 80% psychology.9*

If financial management and investing is indeed about people, then we have much to learn about the linkages between culture, law, religion, and human psychology.

availability of capital. The bad news is that the correlation among securities markets has increased, thereby reducing, but not eliminating, the benefits of international portfolio diversification. Globalization of securities markets has also led to more volatility and speculative behavior, as shown by the financial crisis in the U.S. in 2008–2009 and the European sovereign debt crisis in 2009–2010. But regardless of market integration, there is growing evidence, as studied in the field of behavioral finance described in *Global Finance in Practice 13.3*, that investors and their associated cultures still differ dramatically in their willingness to accept risk in pursuit of return.

[6]See for example "Religious Culture and Corporate Risk Taking," Zhi-qiang Liu and Nan Ma, *Advances in Economics, Business and Management Research*, volume 106, 2019; and "Religious Activity, Risk Taking Preferences and Financial Behaviour: Empirical Evidence from German Survey Data," Anja Köbrich Leon and Christian Pfeifer, Working Paper Series in Economics, No. 269, Leuphana Universität Lüneburg, Institut für Volkswirtschaftslehre, Lüneburg, 2013.

[7]"Culture, Openness, and Finance," Rene M. Stulz and Rohan Williamson, *Journal of Financial Economics*, 70, 2003, 313–349.

[8]"How Religious Beliefs Influence Financial Decision-Making: Implications for Business Leaders," Jillian Alderman, Joetta Forsyth, and Richard Walton, *Graziado Business Review*, Volume 20 Issue 3, 2017.

[9]"Behavioral Finance: The Psychology of Investing," by Thorsten Hens and Anna Meier, a white paper from Behavioral Finance Solutions GmbH, the University of Zurich and Credit Suisse, Private Banking North America, undated, p. 41.

13.4 The Cost of Capital for MNEs Compared to Domestic Firms

Is the weighted average cost of capital for MNEs higher or lower than for their domestic counterparts? Mathematically, this should require nothing more than a comparison of the various components of the corporate cost of capital—the relative after-tax cost of debt, the optimal debt ratio, and the relative cost of equity. But the cost and availability of capital differs dramatically by company and country, as we explore in the following section.

Availability of Capital

Earlier in this chapter, we saw that international availability of capital to MNEs, or to other large firms that can attract international portfolio investors, may allow them to lower their cost of equity and debt compared with most domestic firms. In addition, international availability permits an MNE to maintain its desired debt ratio, even when significant amounts of new funds must be raised. In other words, an MNE's marginal cost of capital is constant for considerable ranges of its capital budget. This statement is not true for most domestic firms. They must either rely on internally generated funds or borrow in the short and medium term from commercial banks.

Financial Structure, Systematic Risk, and the Cost of Capital for MNEs

Theoretically, MNEs should be in a better position than their domestic counterparts to support higher debt ratios because their cash flows are diversified internationally. The probability of a firm's covering fixed charges under varying conditions in product, financial, and foreign exchange markets should improve if the variability of its cash flows is minimized.

By diversifying cash flows internationally, the MNE might be able to achieve the same kind of reduction in cash flow variability that portfolio investors receive from diversifying their security holdings internationally. The same argument applies to cash flow diversification—that returns are not perfectly correlated between countries. For example, in 2000, Japan was in recession, but the U.S. was experiencing rapid growth. We might have expected returns, on either a cash flow or an earnings basis, to be depressed in Japan and favorable in the U.S. An MNE with operations located in both these countries could rely on its strong U.S. cash inflow to cover debt obligations, even if its Japanese subsidiary produced weak net cash inflows.

Interestingly, despite the theoretical elegance of this hypothesis, empirical studies have come to the opposite conclusion. Despite the favorable effect of international diversification of cash flows, bankruptcy risk was only about the same for MNEs as for domestic firms. However, MNEs faced higher agency costs, political risk, foreign exchange risk, and asymmetric information. These have been identified as the factors leading to lower debt ratios and even a higher cost of long-term debt for MNEs. Domestic firms rely much more heavily on short-term and intermediate-term debt, which lie at the low-cost end of the yield curve.

Even more surprising, one study found that MNEs have a higher level of systematic risk than their domestic counterparts.[10] The same factors caused this phenomenon as caused the lower debt ratios for MNEs. The study concluded that the increased standard deviation of cash flows from internationalization more than offset the lower correlation from diversification. As we stated earlier, the systematic risk term, β_j, is defined

$$\beta_j = \frac{\rho_{jm}\,\sigma_j}{\sigma_m}$$

[10]David M. Reeb, Chuck C. Y. Kwok, and H. Young Baek, "Systematic Risk of the Multinational Corporation," *Journal of International Business Studies*, Second Quarter 1998, pp. 263–279.

where ρ_{jm} is the correlation coefficient between security j and the market, σ_j is the standard deviation of the return on firm j, and σ_m is the standard deviation of the market return. The MNE's systematic risk could increase if the decrease in the correlation coefficient, ρ_{jm}, due to international diversification, is more than offset by an increase in the standard deviation, σ_j, due to the aforementioned risk factors. This conclusion is consistent with the observation that many MNEs use a higher hurdle rate to discount expected foreign project cash flows. In essence, they are accepting projects they consider to be riskier than domestic projects, thus potentially skewing upward their perceived systematic risk. At the least, MNEs need to earn a higher rate of return than their domestic equivalents in order to maintain their market value.

Other studies have found that internationalization actually allows emerging market MNEs to carry a higher level of debt and to lower their systematic risk. This occurs because the emerging market MNEs are investing in more stable economies abroad, a strategy that lowers their operating, financial, foreign exchange, and political risks. The reduction in risk more than offsets increased agency costs and allows the firms to enjoy higher leverage and lower systematic risk than their U.S.-based MNE counterparts.

The Paradox: Is the Cost of Capital Higher for MNEs?

This is our *paradox*: The MNE is supposed to have a lower marginal cost of capital (MCC) than a domestic firm because of the MNE's access to a global cost and availability of capital, but empirical studies do not support this. Empirical studies have indicated that the MNE's cost of capital is actually higher than for a comparable domestic firm because of agency costs, foreign exchange risk, political risk, asymmetric information, and other complexities of foreign operations.

To illustrate one possible explanation, Exhibit 13.6 shows the marginal cost of capital (MCC) and a set of possible capital project (MRR) schedules for a multinational enterprise (MNE) and its domestic counterpart (Domestic). Note that the multinational has a much larger set of possible capital projects but also suffers—initially—from a higher marginal cost of capital than its domestic counterpart.

The domestic counterpart's optimal capital budget is found at the intersection of its marginal cost of capital (MCC_{DC}) and its set of possible capital projects (MRR_{DC}), point A in Exhibit 13.6. This means that the domestic firm's optimal capital budget is $120 million at a marginal cost of 10%. At these lower budget levels, the marginal cost of capital of the multinational is higher than the marginal cost of capital of its domestic counterpart. This is consistent with the findings of recent empirical studies.

The multinational enterprise's optimal capital budget is found at the intersection of its marginal cost of capital (MCC_{MNE}) and its greater set of possible capital projects (MRR_{MNE}), point C in Exhibit 13.6. The multinational's optimal capital budget is, therefore, $380 million at a marginal cost of 12%. At these higher budget levels, the multinational firm's cost of capital is much lower than that of its domestic counterpart. It is also likely that the multinational's weighted average cost of capital is also lower than its domestic counterpart, as predicted earlier in this chapter.

Generalizing these conclusions is, however, a bit difficult. Where points A and B actually occur for multinational firms and their domestic counterparts, whether they occur on the "flat spots" of MCC or at points at which MCC is rising, is a question for empirical research. Given that the global business and financial environment is both diverse and complex, the actual optimal capital budgets for firms will likely reflect unique opportunities and circumstances.

Empirical studies show that neither mature domestic firms nor MNEs are typically willing to assume the higher agency costs or bankruptcy risk associated with higher MCCs and capital budgets. In fact, most mature firms demonstrate some degree of corporate wealth-maximizing behavior. They are somewhat risk averse and tend to avoid returning to the market to raise fresh equity. They prefer to limit their capital budgets to what can be financed with free cash

EXHIBIT 13.6 Cost of Capital for MNE and Domestic Counterpart Compared

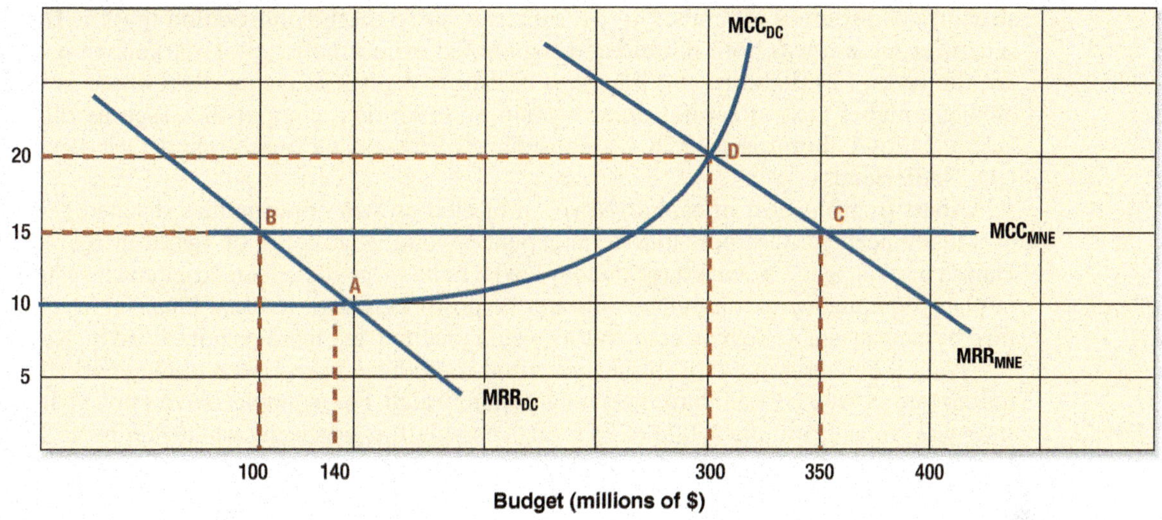

flows. Indeed, they have a so-called *pecking order* that determines the priority of which sources of funds they will tap and in what order. This behavior motivates shareholders to monitor management more closely. They tie management's compensation to stock performance and may also require other types of contractual arrangements that are part of agency costs.

In conclusion, if both multinational and domestic firms do actually limit their capital budgets to what can be financed without increasing their MCC, this supports empirical findings that MNEs have higher weighted average costs of capital, as illustrated in Exhibit 13.7. If the domestic firm has such good growth opportunities that it chooses to undertake growth despite an increasing marginal cost of capital, this would drive the cost of capital up for the domestic firm relative to the cost of capital of the MNE.

EXHIBIT 13.7 Do MNEs Have a Higher Cost of Capital Than Their Domestic Counterparts?

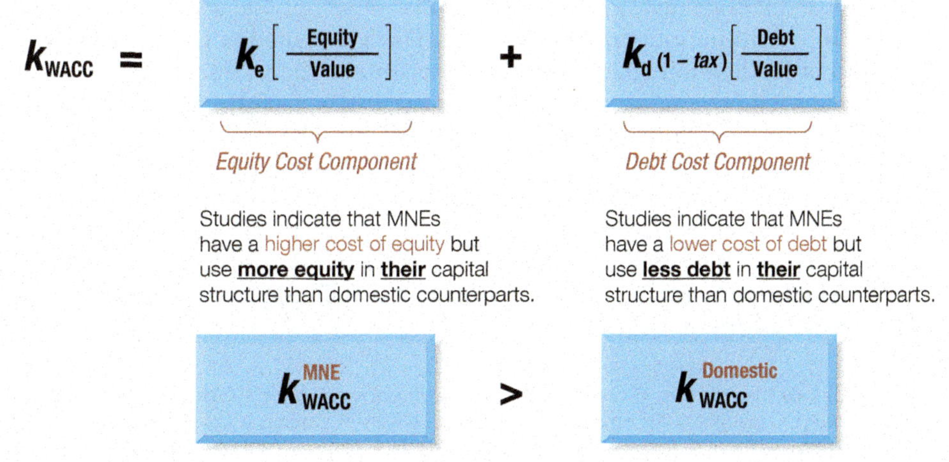

13.5 Illustrative Case: Novo Industri A/S (Novo)

Novo[11] is a Danish multinational firm that produces industrial enzymes and pharmaceuticals (mostly insulin). In 1977, Novo's management decided to "internationalize" its capital structure and sources of funds. This decision was based on the observation that the Danish securities market was both illiquid and segmented from other capital markets. In particular, the lack of availability and high cost of equity capital in Denmark resulted in Novo having a higher cost of capital than its main multinational competitors, such as Eli Lilly (U.S.), Miles Laboratories (U.S.—a subsidiary of Bayer, Germany), and Gist Brocades (the Netherlands).

Apart from the cost of capital, Novo's projected growth opportunities signaled it would eventually need to raise new long-term capital beyond what could be raised in the illiquid Danish market. Since Novo is a technology leader in its specialties, planned capital investments in plant, equipment, and research could not be postponed until internal financing from cash flow became available. Novo's competitors would preempt any markets not served by Novo.

Even if an equity issue of the size required could have been raised in Denmark, the required rate of return would have been unacceptably high. For example, Novo's price/earnings ratio was typically around 5; that of its foreign competitors was well over 10. Yet Novo's business and financial risk appeared to be about equal to that of its competitors. A price/earnings ratio of five appeared appropriate for Novo only within a domestic Danish context when compared with other domestic firms of comparable business risk.

If Denmark's securities markets were integrated with world markets, one would expect foreign investors to rush in and buy "undervalued" Danish securities. In that case, firms like Novo would enjoy an international cost of capital comparable to that of its foreign competitors. Strangely enough, no Danish governmental restrictions existed that would have prevented foreign investors from holding Danish securities. Therefore, one must look for investor perception as the main cause of market segmentation in Denmark at that time.

Market Segmentation

At least six characteristics of the Danish equity market were responsible for market segmentation: (1) asymmetric information base of Danish and foreign investors, (2) taxation, (3) alternative sets of feasible portfolios, (4) financial risk, (5) foreign exchange risk, and (6) political risk.

Asymmetric Information. Certain institutional characteristics of Denmark caused Danish and foreign investors to lack information about one another's equity securities. The most important information barrier was a Danish regulation that prohibited Danish investors from holding foreign private-sector securities. Therefore, Danish investors had no incentive to follow developments in foreign securities markets or to factor such information into their evaluation of Danish securities. As a result, Danish securities might have been priced correctly in the efficient market sense relative to one another, considering the Danish information base, but priced incorrectly considering the combined foreign and Danish information base. Another detrimental effect of this regulation was that foreign securities firms did not locate offices or personnel in Denmark, since they had no product to sell there. Lack of a physical presence in Denmark reduced the ability of foreign security analysts to follow Danish securities.

[11]*Internationalizing the Cost of Capital in Theory and Practice: The Novo Experience and National Policy Implications*. Copyright © 2001 by Arthur Stonehill and Kåre B. Dullum (Copenhagen: Nyt Nordisk Forlag Arnold Busck, 1982; and New York: Wiley, 1982). Reprinted by the permission of Arthur Stonehill.

A second information barrier was that there were too few Danish security analysts following Danish securities. Only one professional Danish securities analysis service was published (Børsinformation), and that was in the Danish language. A few Danish institutional investors employed in-house analysts, but their findings were not available to the public. Almost no foreign security analysts followed Danish securities because they had no product to sell and the Danish market was too small (small-country bias).

Other information barriers included language and accounting principles. Naturally, financial information was normally published in the Danish language using Danish accounting principles. A few firms, such as Novo, published English versions, but almost none used U.S. or British accounting principles or attempted to show any reconciliation with such principles.

Taxation. Danish taxation policy had all but eliminated investment in common stock by individuals. Until a tax law change in July 1981, capital gains on shares held for over two years were taxed at a 50% rate. Shares held for less than two years or, for "speculative" purposes, were taxed at personal income tax rates, with the top marginal rate being 75%. In contrast, capital gains on bonds were tax-free. This situation resulted in bonds being issued at deep discounts because the redemption at par at maturity was considered a capital gain. Thus, most individual investors held bonds rather than stocks. This factor reduced the liquidity of the stock market and increased the required rate of return on stocks if they were to compete with bonds.

Feasible Portfolios. Because of the prohibition on foreign security ownership, Danish investors had a very limited set of securities from which to choose a portfolio. In practice, Danish institutional portfolios were composed of Danish stocks, government bonds, and mortgage bonds. Since Danish stock price movements are closely correlated with each other, Danish portfolios possessed a rather high level of systematic risk. In addition, government policy had been to provide a relatively high real rate of return on government bonds after adjusting for inflation. The net result of taxation policies on individuals and attractive real yields on government bonds was that required rates of return on stocks were relatively high by international standards.

From a portfolio perspective, Danish stocks provided an opportunity for foreign investors to diversify internationally. If Danish stock price movements were not closely correlated with world stock price movements, inclusion of Danish stocks in foreign portfolios would reduce those portfolios' systematic risk. Furthermore, foreign investors were not subject to the high Danish income tax rates due to protections provided by tax treaties that typically limit foreign investor tax rates to 15% on dividends and capital gains. As a result of the international diversification potential, foreign investors might have required a lower rate of return on Danish stocks than the rate required by Danish investors, other things being equal. However, other things were not equal because foreign investors perceived Danish stocks to carry more financial, foreign exchange, and political risk than their own domestic securities.

Financial, Foreign Exchange, and Political Risks. Financial leverage utilized by Danish firms was relatively high by U.S. and UK standards but not abnormal for Scandinavia, Germany, Italy, or Japan. In addition, most of the debt was short term with variable interest rates. The way in which foreign investors viewed financial risk in Danish firms depended on what norms they followed in their home countries. We know from Novo's experience in tapping the eurobond market in 1978, that Morgan Grenfell, Novo's British investment banker, advised Novo to maintain a debt ratio (debt/total capitalization) closer to 50% rather than the traditional Danish 65% to 70%.

Foreign investors in Danish securities are subject to foreign exchange risk. Whether this factor is a plus or minus depends on the investor's home currency, perceptions about the future strength of the Danish krone, and its impact on a firm's operating exposure. Through personal contacts with foreign investors and bankers, Novo's management did not believe foreign exchange risk was a factor in Novo's stock price because its operations were perceived as being well diversified internationally. Over 90% of its sales were to customers located outside Denmark.

With respect to political risk, Denmark was perceived as a stable Western democracy but with the potential to cause periodic problems for foreign investors. In particular, Denmark's national debt was regarded as too high for comfort, although this judgment had not yet shown up in the form of risk premiums on Denmark's eurocurrency syndicated loans.

The Road to Globalization

Although Novo's management in 1977 wished to escape from the shackles of Denmark's segmented and illiquid capital market, many barriers had to be overcome. It is worthwhile to explore some of these obstacles because they typify the barriers faced by other firms from segmented markets that wish to internationalize their capital sources.

Closing the Information Gap. Novo had been a family-owned firm from its founding in the 1920s by the two Pedersen brothers. Then in 1974, it went public and listed its "B" shares on the Copenhagen Stock Exchange. The "A" shares were held by the Novo Foundation, and these shares were sufficient to maintain voting control. However, Novo was essentially unknown in investment circles outside of Denmark. To overcome this disparity in the information base, Novo increased the level of its financial and technical disclosure in both Danish and English versions.

The information gap was further closed when Morgan Grenfell successfully organized a syndicate to underwrite and sell a $20 million convertible eurobond issue for Novo in 1978. In connection with this offering, Novo listed its shares on the London Stock Exchange to facilitate conversion and to gain visibility. These twin actions were the key to dissolving the information barrier, and of course, they also raised a large amount of long-term capital on favorable terms, which would have been unavailable in Denmark.

Despite the favorable impact of the eurobond issue on availability of capital, Novo's cost of capital actually increased when Danish investors reacted negatively to the potential dilution effect of the conversion right. During 1979, Novo's share price declined from around Dkr300 per share to around Dkr220 per share.

The Biotechnology Boom. During 1979, a fortuitous event occurred. Biotechnology began to attract the interest of the U.S. investment community, with several sensationally oversubscribed stock issues by such start-up firms as Genentech and Cetus. Thanks to the aforementioned domestic information gap, Danish investors were unaware of these events and continued to value Novo at a low price/earnings ratio of 5, compared with over 10 for its established competitors and 30 or more for these new potential competitors.

In order to profile itself as a biotechnology firm with a proven track record, Novo organized a seminar in New York City on April 30, 1980. Soon after the seminar a few sophisticated individual U.S. investors began buying Novo's shares and convertibles through the London Stock Exchange. Danish investors were only too happy to supply this foreign demand. Therefore, despite relatively strong demand from U.S. and British investors, Novo's share price increased only gradually, climbing back to the Dkr300 level by midsummer.

However, during the following months, foreign interest began to snowball, and by the end of 1980 Novo's stock price had reached the Dkr600 level. Moreover, foreign investors had increased their proportion of share ownership from virtually nothing to around 30%.

Novo's price/earnings ratio had risen to around 16, which was now in line with that of its international competitors but not with the Danish market. At this point one must conclude that Novo had succeeded in internationalizing its cost of capital. Other Danish securities remained locked in a segmented capital market.

Directed Share Issue in the United States. During the first half of 1981, under the guidance of Goldman Sachs and with the assistance of Morgan Grenfell and Copenhagen Handelsbank, Novo prepared a prospectus for SEC registration of a U.S. share offering and eventual listing on the New York Stock Exchange. The main barriers encountered in this effort, which would have general applicability, were connected with preparing financial statements that could be reconciled with U.S. accounting principles and the higher level of disclosure required by the SEC. In particular, industry segment reporting was a problem from both a disclosure perspective and an accounting perspective because the accounting data were not available internally in that format. As it turned out, the investment barriers in the U.S. were relatively tractable, although expensive and time-consuming to overcome.

The more serious barriers were caused by a variety of institutional and governmental regulations in Denmark. The latter were never designed so that firms could issue shares at market value, since Danish firms typically issued stock at par value with preemptive rights. By this time, however, Novo's share price, driven by continued foreign buying, was so high that virtually nobody in Denmark thought it was worth the price that foreigners were willing to pay. In fact, prior to the time of the share issue in July 1981, Novo's share price had risen to over Dkr1500 before settling down to a level around Dkr1400. Foreign ownership had increased to over 50% of Novo's shares outstanding!

Stock Market Reactions. One final piece of evidence on market segmentation can be gleaned from the way Danish and foreign investors reacted to the announcement of the proposed $61 million U.S. share issue on May 29, 1981. Novo's share price dropped 156 points the next trading day in Copenhagen, equal to about 10% of its market value. As soon as trading started in New York, the stock price immediately recovered all of its loss. The Copenhagen reaction was typical for an illiquid market. Investors worried about the dilution effect of the new share issue because it would increase the number of shares outstanding by about 8%. They did not believe that Novo could invest the new funds at a rate of return that would not dilute future earnings per share. They also feared that the U.S. shares would eventually flow back to Copenhagen if biotechnology lost its glitter.

The U.S. reaction to the announcement of the new share issue was consistent with what one would expect in a liquid and integrated market. U.S. investors viewed the new issue as creating additional demand for the shares as Novo became more visible due to the selling efforts of a large aggressive syndicate. Furthermore, the marketing effort was directed at institutional investors who were previously underrepresented among Novo's U.S. investors. They had been underrepresented because U.S. institutional investors want to be assured of a liquid market in a stock in order to be able to get out, if desired, without depressing the share price. The wide distribution effected by the new issue, plus SEC registration and a New York Stock Exchange listing, all added up to more liquidity and a global cost of capital.

Effect on Novo's Weighted Average Cost of Capital. During most of 1981 and the years thereafter, Novo's share price was driven by international portfolio investors transacting on the New York, London, and Copenhagen stock exchanges. This reduced Novo's weighted average cost of capital and lowered its marginal cost of capital. Novo's systematic risk was reduced from its previous level, which was determined by nondiversified (internationally) Danish institutional investors and the Novo Foundation. However, its appropriate debt ratio level was also reduced to match the standards expected by international portfolio investors trading in the U.S., UK, and other important markets. In essence, the U.S. dollar became Novo's functional currency when being evaluated by international investors. Theoretically, its revised cost of capital should have become a new reference hurdle rate when evaluating new capital investments anywhere.

Other firms that follow Novo's strategy are also likely to have their weighted average cost of capital become a function of the requirements of international portfolio investors. Firms resident in some of the emerging market countries have already experienced "dollarization" of trade and financing for working capital. This phenomenon might be extended to long-term financing and the weighted average cost of capital.

The Novo experience can be a model for other firms wishing to escape from segmented and illiquid home equity markets. In particular, MNEs based in emerging markets often face barriers and lack of visibility similar to what Novo faced. They could benefit by following Novo's proactive strategy employed to attract international portfolio investors. However, a word of caution is advised. Novo had an excellent operating track record and a very strong worldwide market niche in two important industry sectors, insulin and industrial enzymes. This record continues to attract investors in Denmark and abroad. Other companies aspiring to achieve similar results would also need to have a favorable track record to attract foreign investors.

Globalization of Securities Markets. During the 1980s, numerous other Nordic and other European firms followed Novo's example. They cross-listed on major foreign exchanges such as London and New York. They placed equity and debt issues in major securities markets. In most cases, they were successful in lowering their WACC and increasing its availability.

During the 1980s and 1990s, national restrictions on cross-border portfolio investment were gradually eased under pressure from the OECD. Liberalization of European securities markets was accelerated because of the European Union's efforts to develop a single European market without barriers. Emerging nation markets followed suit, as did the former Eastern Bloc countries after the breakup of the Soviet Union. Emerging national markets have often been motivated by the need to source foreign capital to finance large-scale privatization.

Now, market segmentation has been significantly reduced, although the liquidity of individual national markets remains limited. Most observers believe that for better or for worse, we have achieved a global market for securities. The good news is that many firms have been assisted to become MNEs because they now have access to a global cost and availability of capital. The bad news is that the correlation among securities markets has increased, thereby reducing, but not eliminating, the benefits of international portfolio diversification. Globalization of securities markets has also led to more volatility and speculative behavior as shown by the emerging market crises of the 1995–2001 period.

Summary Points

- Gaining access to global capital markets should allow a firm to lower its cost of capital. This can be achieved by increasing the market liquidity of its shares and escaping segmentation of its home capital market.
- The cost and availability of capital is directly linked to the degree of market liquidity and segmentation.
- Firms having access to markets with high liquidity and a low level of segmentation should have a lower cost of capital and greater ability to raise new capital.
- A firm is able to increase its market liquidity by raising debt in the euromarket and by tapping local capital markets through foreign subsidiaries. Increased market liquidity causes the marginal cost of capital line to flatten out on the right. This results in the firm being able to raise more capital at a lower marginal cost.
- A national capital market is segmented if the required rate of return on securities in that market differs from the required rate of return on securities of comparable expected return and risk that are traded on other national securities markets.
- Capital market segmentation is a financial market imperfection caused by government constraints and

investor perceptions. Segmentation results in a higher cost of capital and less availability of capital.

- If a firm is resident in a segmented capital market, it can still escape from this market by sourcing its debt and equity abroad. The result should be a lower marginal cost of capital, improved liquidity for its shares, and a larger capital budget.
- Whether MNEs have a lower cost of capital than their domestic counterparts depends on their optimal financial structures, systematic risk, availability of capital, and the optimal capital budget.

MINI-CASE

The Recapitalization of Saudi Aramco[12]

Saudi Aramco was not only the world's most profitable company, but had achieved that status with little debt. The order book for its prospective $40 billion bond sale would certainly build.

Saudi Aramco's potential initial public offering (IPO) had been the subject of endless public debate. The Saudi Arabian Oil Company (Saudi Aramco) was the national oil and gas company of the Kingdom of Saudi Arabia. Headquartered in Dhahran, Saudi Arabia, it was the largest single oil producer in the world. But competing in one of the world's most capital-intensive industries, it would require massive amounts of new capital in the coming years to maintain its competitive edge. Internally, the company had been planning and preparing for its eventual entry into the global capital markets for years, and it had a plan. Debt first, then equity.

Saudi Sovereign Debt

Saudi Arabia set the stage with its own entrance onto the world's capital stage in 2016. Under the leadership of Deputy Crown Prince Mohammed bin Salman, or "MbS," Saudi Arabia wished to embark on a new future that was independent of its traditional lifeblood: oil. The nation's new economic strategy was to move its economy toward a market orientation and away from state dominance. Diversification away from oil and oil exports was deemed critical for its future, and that would require a more diversified industrial state. Infrastructure projects were canceled and public earnings and employment cut. Part of that plan was to restructure the funding of the country by taking on debt. The plan was extremely aggressive; Saudi Arabia wished to move its debt-to-GDP ratio from its current 0% level to 25% to 30% by 2020. That might mean raising over $120 billion in debt in the coming years.

In what many termed "the year of the sovereign mega-bond," Saudi Arabia successfully launched the largest single sovereign debt issue in history—the October 2016 issue of $17.5 billion. As illustrated in Exhibit A, it closely followed the record sovereign issues by Qatar and Argentina. Global markets were clearly receptive to emerging market debt. Argentina's record offering in April had been the country's first entry into global markets since its default in 2002 and only two years since its very public spat with the so-called vulture funds.

Timing was also on Saudi Arabia's side. Most of the major industrial country economies were in a period of near-zero (or near-negative) interest rates. Fixed income investors were in search of higher yields, and emerging market sovereign debt offered that. Saudi Arabia was rated A+ by Fitch and A1 by Moody's. Those A ratings, combined with its G20 economic stature, made it the crown jewel among emerging market issuers. Despite the country suffering from an extended period of low oil prices, the issue had been over-subscribed and, as a result, expanded from $15 billion to $17.5 billion. Pricing had been aggressive. The total issue was impressive: $5.5 billion in 5-year notes at 2.375%, $5.5 billion in 10-year bonds at 3.250%, $6.5 billion in 30-year bonds at 4.500%. The 30-year amount, the largest, was particularly unusual as most emerging market investors preferred shorter maturities. A number of potential buyers stayed away from the issue because they believed the market was treating Saudi Arabia more like a developed economy given the low interest rates. It was, by all metrics, an extremely successful first debt issuance by the kingdom.

Over the next two and a half years Saudi Arabia continued to issue debt. Even the global uproar over the killing of the Saudi journalist Jamal Khashoggi in October 2018 did not interrupt the flow of new issues to the market. With another issue in January 2019 of $7.5 billion (over-subscribed with $27 billion in orders), the Kingdom had now raised nearly $60 billion in debt on the international capital markets.

EXHIBIT A Record Emerging Market Debt Issues (billions of U.S. dollars)

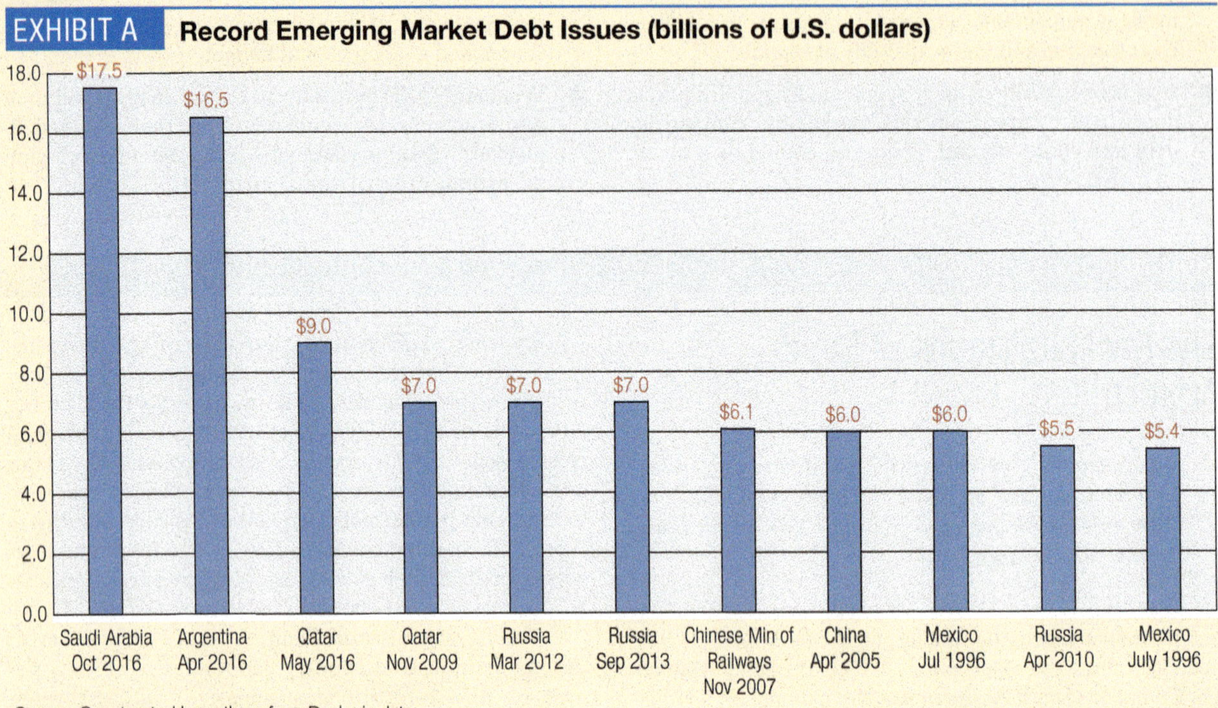

Source: Constructed by authors from Dealogic data.

Aramco Acquires Sabic

The next stage in the recapitalization of Saudi Arabia occurred in March 2019 when it was announced that Saudi Aramco would acquire a 70% interest in Saudi Basic Industries Corp (Sabic) described in Exhibit B. The interest Aramco was buying was that held by the Saudi Arabian sovereign wealth fund, the Saudi Public Investment Fund (SPIF).[13] (The remainder of Sabic's ownership, 30%, was publicly traded on the Saudi Arabian stock exchange.) The money would therefore go to SPIF. SPIF was the

EXHIBIT B Saudi Aramco's Purchase of 70% of Sabic

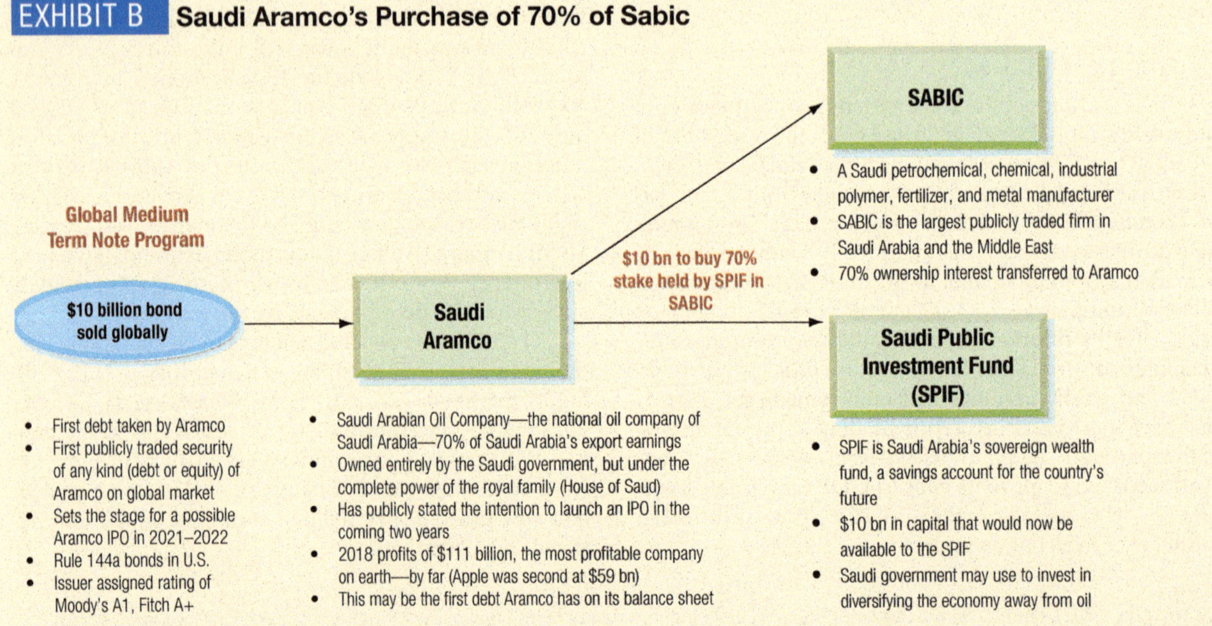

[13] Aramco agreed to pay 123.40 Saudi riyals a share, a price that was actually below the stock's closing price the previous day. Saudi officials explained that since the transaction had been discussed publicly for many months, the purchase price had already been integrated into the market price of Sabic shares.

organization behind much of the economic revitalization program now called Vision 2030. It, along with partners like SoftBank Group and Blackstone Group, had become one of the world's largest tech investors.

Saudi Aramco would need to raise capital in order to make the purchase. Senior government and corporate officials embarked on an exploration of how much appetite the global financial markets might have for debt issued by Aramco. After meetings in London and New York and additional stops in the Far East, their plans were scaled back, settling on a $10 billion global note program. Now Aramco would need to provide detailed descriptions and disclosures related to its ownership, operations, and financial results, something the company had long avoided. These were critical if its notes and bonds were to be purchased and traded in the world's financial markets.

Aramco issued its base prospectus for the global medium note program on April 1, 2019.[14] One of the key areas of interest to potential investors was the relationship between Saudi Aramco, the primary organizational unit of the hydrocarbon industry (oil and gas), and the Saudi Arabian government, described on p. 8:

> *The Kingdom's public finances are highly connected to the hydrocarbon industry. The hydrocarbon industry is the single largest contributor to the Kingdom's economy. The oil sector accounted for 44.0% and 43.0% of the Kingdom's real GDP in the years ended 31 December 2016 and 2017, respectively. Furthermore, the oil sector accounted for 64.2% and 63.0% of the Government's total revenues in the years ended 31 December 2016 and 2017, respectively. The Government is expected to continue to rely on royalties, taxes and other income from the hydrocarbon industry for a significant portion of its revenue.*

Saudi Arabia was clearly dependent on Saudi Aramco for economic activity in general and for generating the government's funding in particular. Interestingly, the government of Saudi Arabia was officially not guaranteeing the bonds. What was of some concern to prospective investors was that Aramco was not truly an independent company and that the Kingdom could potentially change the rules of engagement between the two at a moment's notice.

The prospectus was also illuminating in its description of the relationship among the state, Islam, and its ruler the King (prospectus p.132).

> *The Kingdom is a monarchy with a political system rooted in the traditions and culture of Islam. It was established by the late King Abdul Aziz bin Abdul Rahman bin Faisal Al Saud (the "Founder") in 1932, with the issuance of Royal Decree No. 2716, dated 17/5/1351 in the Hijri calendar (corresponding to 23 September 1932). The Custodian of the Two Holy Mosques, King Salman bin Abdulaziz bin Abdul Rahman bin Faisal bin Turki bin Abdullah bin Mohammed bin Saud, is both the Kingdom's Head of State and Head of Government, and has been so since 23 January 2015.*
>
> *The Basic Law of the Kingdom (the "Basic Law") was promulgated under Royal Order No. A/90, dated 27/8/1412 in the Hijri calendar (corresponding to 1 March 1992) and provides that the Holy Quran and Sunnah (i.e., the traditions of the Prophet Mohammad (PBUH)) form the primary sources of law in the Kingdom. The Basic Law sets out the framework for government and provides for the powers and authorities of the executive, administrative, and judicial authorities of the Kingdom, under the ultimate authority of the King.*

The power of the King, MbS, was absolute.

The financial results of the company, presented publicly for the first time, were impressive. Selected results are shown in Exhibit C. Aramco had closed 2018 with total revenue of $315 billion and profits of more than $111 billion. The Saudi Arabian Oil Company was the most profitable company on earth. (The most profitable publicly traded company in the world, Apple, had made $59 billion in profit in 2018, a little more than half of what Aramco generated.) The company's 35% return on revenue was more akin to a tech company like Apple than an oil and gas company operating in a low oil price environment.

The company clearly had little debt. In fact it was negative net debt (total interest-bearing debt less cash and cash equivalents). Aramco's role as a cash generator for the country was also clear. In 2018 the company had paid a dividend of $59 billion to its owner (Saudi Arabia), simultaneously paying taxes of $101 billion.

Debt Pricing

The pricing for the Aramco bonds became the subject of intense debate. Traditionally, a corporate issuer would pay a premium above the price the sovereign itself would pay for foreign currency debt (in this case, U.S. dollar-denominated debt). That premium would be based on the corporate's credit quality. Aramco had been awarded the same credit rating, A, as Saudi Arabia itself. The credit rating agency policies limited a corporate to that of its sovereign. In this case many argued that Saudi Arabia and Saudi Aramco were one and the same. Others noted that Aramco

[14]A *prospectus* in the field of finance discloses information that is deemed relevant to the ability of potential investors to assess the company's assets, liabilities, financial condition, and prospects for profitability. It typically includes a description of the business and all risk factors related to the execution of the business as well as detailed descriptions of the organization's financial results and senior management composition and compensation.

EXHIBIT C Selected Financial Results

Billions of U.S. dollars	2017	2018
Total revenues	224.1	315.2
Operating income	155.4	212.9
Net income	75.9	111.1
Net income/revenue	33.9%	35.2%
Total assets	294.0	359.0
Total debt	20.7	27.0
Cash and cash equivalents	21.7	48.8
Net debt	(1.0)	(21.8)
Operating cash flow	89.0	121.0
Investing cash flow	(31.6)	(35.0)
Financing cash flow	(58.8)	(48.5)
Net change	(1.4)	37.5
Distributions to government	(50.1)	–
Dividends	–	(58.0)
Taxes paid	(79.0)	(101.0)

Source: Saudi Arabian Oil Company.

had interests globally, and its operations and cash flows arising from outside the legal boundaries of Saudi Arabia itself might make the company of higher credit worth than the country itself, possibly entitling it to a negative premium. This was also a debut issue; Aramco had never "been to the ball before," in the words of one analyst.

One of the prime characteristics of this obligation was obviously that it was foreign currency. Borrowing billions of U.S. dollars would require repaying billions of U.S. dollars. Most sovereign borrowers had the ability to dictate and direct their exporters to turn over hard currencies like the dollar, alleviating the stress of foreign currency debt service, if their export sectors remained healthy. In the case of Aramco, nearly its entire business was based on exporting oil to a global market where not only were all transactions denominated in dollars, the product itself—oil—was priced in dollars.

The issue would have five tranches based on maturity: 3-year, 5-year, 10-year, 20-year, and 30-year pieces. The longer maturities were exceptionally rare for emerging market issuers. Saudi Arabia, bearing a single A rating, paid about 160 basis points over U.S. treasury's. Aramco, also single A, might then pay a 40 to 50 basis point spread over sovereign obligations.

As the debate over possible rates continued, the discussion focused on whether the markets would end up treating Aramco as any other major oil company, a state-owned oil company, or a sovereign like its owner. Its investment bankers believed its best prospects were portraying the company as one of the world's leading oil firms—like BP or Shell—and not as a state-owned enterprise. This was the focal point of their presentations in the various road shows for the issue.

Exhibit D provides one speculative summary. Aramco's pricing was expected to fall in line with other major multinational oil companies, paying only the slimmest of margins over Saudi Arabia's own debt costs. As the early days in April passed, the investment banks responsible for selling the securities upon issue continued to build their order books, a compilation of the level of interest in the issue by customers. And the book was growing—from the targeted $10 billion to $20 billion, $40 billion, $60 billion, and, in the day prior to issue, over $100 billion.

> *Saudi Aramco, the world's largest oil producer, has begun offering bonds. For some three decades, Aramco has operated in a financial shroud of secrecy. Recently, Aramco opened its books to tap the international capital market. Saudi Aramco received more than $100 billion in orders for its debut international bond due Tuesday, according to people familiar with the sale, as investors shrugged off concerns about the kingdom's human-rights record in order to access the world's most profitable company.*[15]

[15]Rory Jones, Summer Said, and Avantika Chilkoti, "Saudi Aramco's Debut International Bond Gets $100 Billion Orders, Investor Interest Will Be an Important Bellwether for the Oil Giant's Initial Public Offering," *Wall Street Journal*, April 9, 2019.

13.10 Cargill's Cost of Capital. Cargill is generally considered to be the largest privately held company in the world. Headquartered in Minneapolis, Minnesota, the company has been averaging sales of over $113 billion per year over the past five-year period. Although the company does not have publicly traded shares, it is still extremely important for it to calculate its weighted average cost of capital properly in order to make rational decisions on new investment proposals. Assuming a risk-free rate of 4.50%, an effective tax rate of 48%, and a market risk premium of 5.50%, estimate the weighted average cost of capital first for companies A and B, and then make a "guesstimate" of what you believe a comparable WACC would be for Cargill.

	Company A	Company B	Cargill
Company sales	$10.5 billion	$45 billion	$113 billion
Company's *beta*	0.83	0.68	??
Credit rating	AA	A	AA
Weighted average cost of debt	6.885%	7.125%	6.820%
Debt to total capital	34%	41%	28%
International sales/sales	11%	34%	54%

13.11 The Tombs. You have joined your friends at the local watering hole, The Tombs, for your weekly debate on international finance. The topic this week is whether the cost of equity can ever be cheaper than the cost of debt. The group has chosen Brazil in the mid-1990s as the subject of the debate. One of the group members has torn a table of data out of a book (shown below), which becomes the subject of the analysis. Larry argues, "It's all about expected versus delivered. You can talk about what equity investors expect, but they often find that what is delivered for years at a time is so small—even sometimes negative—that in effect, the cost of equity is cheaper than the cost of debt."

Moe interrupts, "But you're missing the point. The cost of capital is what the investor requires in compensation for the risk taken going into the investment. If he doesn't end up getting it, and that was happening here, then he pulls his capital out and walks."

Curly is the theoretician. "Ladies, this is not about empirical results; it is about the fundamental concept of risk-adjusted returns. An investor in equities knows he will reap returns only after all compensation has been made to debt providers. He is therefore always subject to a higher level of risk to his return than with debt instruments, and as the capital asset pricing model states, equity investors set their expected returns as a risk-adjusted factor over and above the returns to risk-free instruments."

At this point, Larry and Moe simply stare at Curly—pause—and order more beer. Using the Brazilian data presented, comment on this week's debate at The Tombs.

Brazilian Economic Performance	**1995**	**1996**	**1997**	**1998**	**1999**
Inflation rate (IPC)	23.20%	10.00%	4.80%	1.00%	10.50%
Bank lending rate	53.10%	27.10%	24.70%	29.20%	30.70%
Exchange rate (BRL=USD1.00)	0.972	1.039	1.117	1.207	1.700
Equity returns (São Paulo Bovespa)	16.0%	28.0%	30.2%	33.5%	151.9%

Genedak-Hogan

Use the following table to answer Problems 13.12 through 13.14.

Genedak-Hogan (G-H) is an American conglomerate that is actively debating the impacts of international diversification of its operations on its capital structure and cost of capital. The firm is planning on reducing consolidated debt after diversification.

Assumptions	Symbol	Before Diversification	After Diversification
Correlation between G-H and the market	ρ_{jm}	0.88	0.76
Standard deviation of G-H's returns	σ_j	28.0%	26.0%
Standard deviation of market's returns	σ_m	18.0%	18.0%
Risk-free rate of interest	k_{rf}	3.0%	3.0%
Additional equity risk premium for internationalization	RPM	0.0%	3.0%
Estimate of G-H's cost of debt in U.S. market	k_d	7.2%	7.0%
Market risk premium	$k_m - k_{rf}$	5.5%	5.5%
Corporate tax rate	t	35.0%	35.0%
Proportion of debt	D/V	38%	32%
Proportion of equity	E/V	62%	68%

13.12 Genedak-Hogan Cost of Equity. Senior management at Genedak-Hogan is actively debating the implications of diversification on its cost of equity. All agree that the company's returns will be less correlated with the reference market return in the future, the financial advisors believe that the market will assess an additional 3.0% risk premium for "going international" to the basic CAPM cost of equity. Calculate Genedak-Hogan's cost of equity before and after international diversification of its operations, with and without the hypothetical additional risk premium, and comment on the discussion.

13.13 Genedak-Hogan's WACC. Calculate the weighted average cost of capital for Genedak-Hogan before and after international diversification.

a. Did the reduction in debt costs reduce the firm's weighted average cost of capital? How would you describe the impact of international diversification on its costs of capital?
b. Adding the hypothetical risk premium to the cost of equity introduced in Problem 13.8 (an added 3.0% to the cost of equity because of international diversification), what is the firm's WACC?

13.14 Genedak-Hogan's WACC and Effective Tax Rate. Many MNEs have greater ability to control and reduce their effective tax rates when expanding international operations. If Genedak-Hogan were able to reduce its consolidated effective tax rate from 35% to 32%, what would be the impact on its WACC?

14

Funding the Multinational Firm

Do what you will, the capital is at hazard. All that can be required of a trustee to invest, is, that he shall conduct himself faithfully and exercise a sound discretion. He is to observe how men of prudence, discretion, and intelligence manage their own affairs, not in regard to speculation, but in regard to the permanent disposition of their funds, considering the probable income, as well as the probable safety of the capital to be invested.

—*Prudent Man Rule,* Justice Samuel Putnam, 1830.

LEARNING OBJECTIVES

14.1 Design a strategy to source capital equity globally

14.2 Examine the differences in the optimal financial structure of the multinational firm compared to that of the domestic firm

14.3 Describe the various financial instruments that can be used to source equity in the global equity markets

14.4 Understand the role of depositary receipts in raising equity

14.5 Analyze the unique role private placement enjoys in raising global capital

14.6 Explore the different structures that can be used to source debt globally

14.7 Detail the alternative methods of structuring and funding foreign subsidiaries

Chapter 13 analyzed why gaining access to global capital markets should or could lower a firm's cost of capital, increase its access to capital, and improve the liquidity of its shares by overcoming market segmentation. A firm pursuing this lofty goal, particularly a firm from a segmented or emerging market, must first design a financial strategy that will attract international investors. This involves choosing among alternative paths to access global capital markets.

This chapter focuses on firms that wish to globalize their cost and availability of capital, many that reside in less liquid, segmented, or emerging markets. Firms resident in large and highly industrialized countries already have access to their own domestic, liquid, and unsegmented markets. Although they too source equity and debt abroad, it is unlikely to have as significant an impact on their cost and availability of capital. In fact, for these firms, sourcing funds abroad is often motivated solely by the need to fund large foreign acquisitions rather than to fund existing operations.

This chapter begins with the design of a financial strategy to source both equity and debt globally. It then analyzes the optimal financial structure for a multinational enterprise (MNE) and its subsidiaries, one that minimizes its cost of capital. We then explore the alternative paths that a firm may follow in raising capital in global markets, and the alternative strategies and tactics for funding foreign subsidiaries. The chapter concludes with the mini-case *CEMEX's Debt Dilemma*, which examines the financing crisis experienced by one major multinational following an overly aggressive debt-funded acquisition.

14.1 Designing a Strategy to Source Capital Globally

Designing a capital sourcing strategy requires management to agree upon a long-run financial objective and then choose among the various alternative paths to get there. Exhibit 14.1 is a visual presentation of alternative paths to the ultimate objective of attaining a global cost and availability of capital.

Alternative Paths to Globalize the Cost and Availability of Capital

Normally, the choice of paths and implementation is aided by an early appointment of an investment bank as official advisor to the firm. Investment bankers are in touch with potential foreign investors and their current requirements. They can also help navigate the various institutional requirements and barriers that must be satisfied. Their services include advising if, when, and where a cross-listing should be initiated. They usually prepare the required prospectus if an equity or debt issue is desired, help price the issue, and maintain an aftermarket to prevent the share price from falling below its initial price.

EXHIBIT 14.1 Alternative Paths to Globalizing the Cost and Availability of Capital

Individual firms may take many different paths to globalizing their cost and availability of capital, all passing through debt to equity (listings then issuance). One of the many paths is shown here.

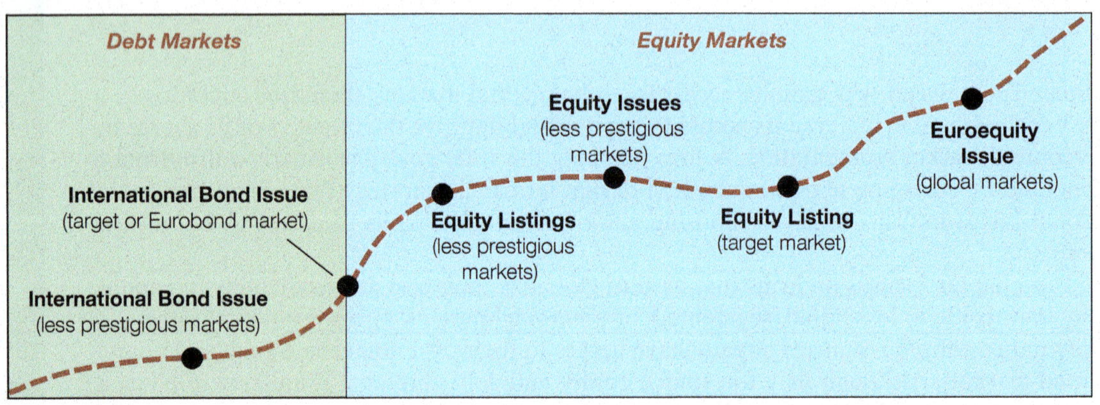

Source: Constructed by authors based on the principles described in *Corporate Strategies in Internationalizing the cost of Capital,* Oxelheim, Stonehill, Randøy, Vikkula, Dullum, and Modèn, Copenhagen Business School Press, 1998.

Most firms raise their initial capital in their own domestic market as illustrated by the lower left starting point in Exhibit 14.1. Next, they are tempted to skip all the intermediate steps along the pathway to an equity issue in a target market or a euroequity issue in global markets. This is the time when a good investment bank advisor will offer a "reality check." Most firms that have only raised capital in their own domestic market are not sufficiently well known to attract foreign investors. This was the lesson learned by Novo in Chapter 13—to start with a eurobond issue and gradually penetrate the global marketplace—in essence, a market penetration strategy.

14.2 Optimal Financial Structure

After many years of debate, finance theorists now agree that there is an optimal financial structure for a firm, and practically, they agree on how it is determined. The great debate between the so-called *traditionalists* and the Modigliani and Miller school of thought has ended in compromise:

> *When taxes and bankruptcy costs are considered, a firm has an optimal financial structure determined by that particular mix of debt and equity that minimizes the firm's cost of capital for a given level of business risk.*

If the business risk of new projects differs from the risk of existing projects, the optimal mix of debt and equity would change to recognize trade-offs between business and financial risks.

Exhibit 14.2 illustrates how the cost of capital varies with the amount of debt employed. As the debt ratio, defined as total debt divided by total assets at market values, increases, the after-tax weighted average cost of capital (k_{WACC}) decreases because of the heavier weight of low-cost debt [k_d (1 − t)] compared to high-cost equity (k_e). The low cost of debt is partly due to the tax deductibility of interest, (1 − t).

EXHIBIT 14.2 The Cost of Capital and Financial Structure

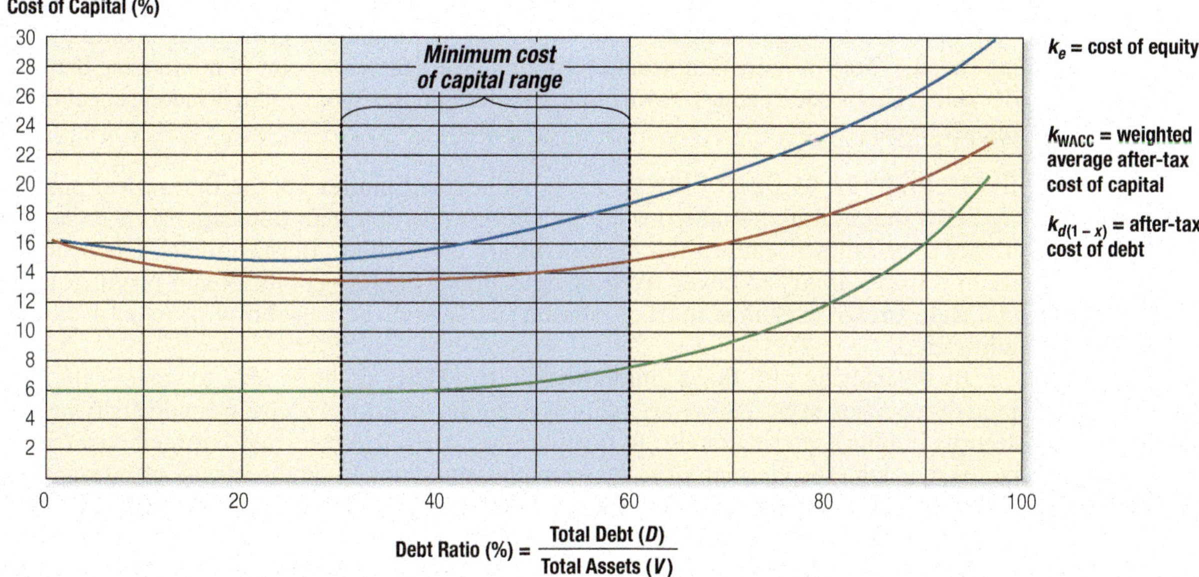

Partly offsetting the favorable effect of more debt is an increase in the cost of equity (k_e) because investors perceive greater financial risk. Nevertheless, the weighted average cost of capital (k_{WACC}) continues to decline as the debt ratio increases, until financial risk becomes so serious that investors and management alike perceive a real danger of insolvency. This result causes a sharp increase in the cost of new debt and equity, thereby increasing the WACC. The low point on the resulting U-shaped cost of capital curve, just below 14% in Exhibit 14.2, defines the debt ratio range in which the cost of capital is minimized.

Most theorists believe that the low point is actually a rather broad flat area encompassing a wide range of debt ratios (say, 30% to 50% in Exhibit 14.2), where there is little difference in the cost of capital. They also generally agree that, at least in major industrial countries, the range of the flat area and the location of a particular firm's debt ratio within that range are determined by such variables as (1) the industry in which it competes, (2) volatility of its sales and operating income, and (3) the collateral value of its assets.

Optimal Financial Structure and the Multinational

The domestic theory of optimal financial structures needs to be modified by four more variables in order to accommodate the case of the multinational enterprise. These variables are (1) availability of capital, (2) diversification of cash flows, (3) foreign exchange risk, and (4) expectations of international portfolio investors.

Availability of Capital. Chapter 13 demonstrated that access to capital in global markets allows an MNE to lower its cost of equity and debt compared with most domestic firms. It also permits an MNE to maintain its desired debt ratio, even when significant amounts of new funds must be raised. In other words, a multinational firm's marginal cost of capital is constant for considerable ranges of its capital budget. This statement is not true for most small domestic firms because they do not have access to the national equity or debt markets. They must either rely on internally generated funds or borrow for the short and medium terms from commercial banks.

Multinational firms domiciled in countries that have illiquid capital markets are in almost the same situation as small domestic firms unless they have gained a global cost and availability of capital. They must rely on internally generated funds and bank borrowing. If they need to raise significant amounts of new funds to finance growth opportunities, they may need to borrow more than would be optimal from the viewpoint of minimizing their cost of capital. This is equivalent to saying that their marginal cost of capital is increasing at higher budget levels.

Diversification of Cash Flows. As explained in Chapter 13, the theoretical possibility exists that multinational firms are in a better position than domestic firms to support higher debt ratios because their cash flows are diversified internationally. The probability of a firm's ability to cover fixed charges under varying conditions in product, financial, and foreign exchange markets should increase if the variability of its cash flows is minimized.

By diversifying cash flows internationally, the MNE might be able to achieve the same kind of reduction in cash flow variability as portfolio investors receive from diversifying their security holdings internationally. Returns are not perfectly correlated between countries. In contrast, a domestic German firm, for example, would not enjoy the benefit of international cash flow diversification. Instead, it would need to rely entirely on its own net cash inflow from domestic operations. Perceived financial risk for the German firm would be greater than for a multinational firm because the variability of its German domestic cash flows could not be offset by positive cash flows elsewhere in the world.

As discussed in Chapter 13, the diversification argument has been challenged by empirical research findings that MNEs in the United States actually have lower debt ratios than their domestic counterparts. The agency costs of debt were higher for the MNEs, as were political risks, foreign exchange risks, and asymmetric information.

Foreign Exchange Risk and the Cost of Debt. When a firm issues foreign currency denominated debt, its effective cost equals the after-tax cost of repaying the principal and interest in terms of the firm's own currency. This amount includes the nominal cost of principal and interest in foreign currency terms, adjusted for any foreign exchange gains or losses.

For example, if a U.S.-based firm borrows 1,500,000 Swiss francs (CHF) for one year at 5.00% interest and during the year the Swiss franc appreciates from an initial rate of CHF1.5000 = USD1.00 to CHF1.4400 = USD1.00, what is the dollar cost of this debt (k_d^{USD})? The dollar proceeds of the initial borrowing are calculated at the current spot rate of CHF1.5000 = USD1.00:

$$\frac{\text{CHF}\,1{,}500{,}000}{\text{CHF}\,1.5000} = \text{USD}\,1{,}000{,}000$$

At the end of one year, the U.S.-based firm is responsible for repaying the CHF1,500,000 principal plus 5.00% interest, or a total of CHF1,575,000. This repayment, however, must be made at an ending spot rate of :

$$\frac{\text{CHF}\,1{,}500{,}000 \times 1.05}{\text{CHF}\,1.4400} = \text{USD}\,1{,}093{,}750$$

The dollar cost of the loan's repayment is not the nominal 5.00% paid in Swiss franc interest, but 9.375%:

$$\frac{\text{USD}\,1{,}093{,}750}{\text{USD}\,1{,}000{,}000} - 1 = 0.09375 \approx 9.375\%$$

The dollar cost is higher than expected due to appreciation of the Swiss franc against the U.S. dollar. This total home-currency cost is actually the result of the combined percentage cost of debt and percent change in the foreign currency's value. We can find the total cost of borrowing Swiss francs by a U.S. dollar-based firm, k_d^{USD}, by multiplying one plus the Swiss franc interest expense, k_d^{CHF}, by one plus the percentage change in the CHF to USD exchange rate, s:

$$k_d^{USD} = [(1 + k_d^{CHF})] \times (1 + s)] - 1$$

where $k_d^{CHF} = 5.00\%$ and $s = 4.1667\%$. The percentage change in the value of the Swiss franc versus the U.S. dollar, when the home currency is the U.S. dollar, is

$$\frac{S_1 - S_2}{S_2} \times 100 = \frac{\text{CHF}\,1.500 - \text{CHF}\,1.4400}{\text{CHF}\,1.4400} \times 100 = +4.1667\%$$

The total expense, combining the nominal interest rate and the percentage change in the exchange rate, is

$$k_d^{USD} = [(1 + .0500) \times (1 + .041667)] - 1 = .09375 \approx 9.375\%$$

The total percentage cost of capital is 9.375%, not simply the foreign currency interest payment of 5%. The after-tax cost of this Swiss franc denominated debt, when the U.S. income tax rate is 34%, is

$$k_d^{USD}(1 - t) = 9.375\% \times 0.66 = 6.1875\%$$

The firm would report the added 4.1667% cost of this debt in terms of U.S. dollars as a foreign exchange transaction loss, and it would be deductible for tax purposes.

Expectations of International Portfolio Investors. Chapter 13 highlighted the fact that the key to gaining a global cost and availability of capital is attracting and retaining international portfolio investors. Those investors' expectations for a firm's debt ratio and overall financial structures are based on global norms that have developed over the past 30 years. Because a large proportion of international portfolio investors are based in the most liquid and unsegmented capital markets, such as the United States and the United Kingdom, their expectations tend to predominate and override individual national norms. Therefore, regardless of other factors, if a firm wants to raise capital in global markets, it must adopt global norms that are close to the U.S. and UK norms. Debt ratios up to 60% appear to be acceptable. Higher debt ratios are more difficult to sell to international portfolio investors.

14.3 Raising Equity Globally

> *We have entirely lost the idea that any undertaking likely to pay, and seen to be likely, can perish for want of money.*
>
> —Walter Bagehot, *Lombard Street: A Description of the Money Market*, Scribner, Armstrong & Co., New York, 1874.

Once a multinational firm has established its financial strategy and considered its desired and target capital structure, it then proceeds to raise capital outside its domestic market—both debt and equity—using a variety of capital-raising paths and instruments.

Exhibit 14.3 describes three key critical elements to understanding the issues that any firm must confront when seeking to raise equity capital. Although the business press does not often make a clear distinction, there is a fundamental distinction between an *equity issuance* and an *equity listing*. A firm seeking to raise equity capital is ultimately in search of an *issuance*—the IPO or SPO described in Exhibit 14.3. This generates cash proceeds to be used for funding and executing the business. But often issuances must be preceded by *listings*, in which the shares are traded on an exchange and, therefore, in a specific country market, gaining name recognition and visibility and hopefully preparing the market for an issuance.

That said, an issuance need not be public. A firm, public or private, can place an issue with private investors, a *private placement*. (Note that private placement may refer to either equity or debt.) Private placements can take a variety of different forms, and the intent of investors may be *passive* (e.g., Rule 144A investors) or *active* (e.g., private equity, where the investor intends to control and change the firm). What the holder of a private placement does not enjoy is an open and liquid market for exchange of the issue.

Publicly traded companies, in addition to raising equity capital, are also in pursuit of greater market visibility and reaching ever-larger potential investor audiences. The expectation is that the growing investor audience will result in higher share prices over time—increasing the returns to owners. Privately held companies are more singular in their objective: to raise greater quantities of equity at the lowest possible cost—privately. As discussed in Chapter 4, ownership trends in the industrialized markets have tended toward more private ownership, while many multinational firms from emerging market countries have shown growing interest in going public.

Exhibit 14.4 provides an overview of the four major equity alternatives available to multinational firms today. A firm wishing to raise equity capital outside of its home market may take a public pathway or a private one. The public pathway includes a directed public share issue or a euroequity issue. An alternative, and one that has been used with greater frequency over the past decade, is a private pathway—private placements, private equity, or a private share sale under strategic alliance.

EXHIBIT 14.3 Equity Avenues, Activities, and Attributes

Equity Issuance

- *Initial public offering (IPO)*: The initial sale of shares to the public of a private company. IPOs raise capital and typically use underwriters.
- *Seasoned public offering (SPO)*: A subsequent sale of additional shares in the publicly traded company, raising additional equity capital.
- *Euroequity*: The initial sale of shares in two or more markets and countries simultaneously.
- *Directed issue*: The sale of shares by a publicly traded company to a specific target investor or market, public or private, often in a different country.

Equity Listing

- Shares of a publicly traded firm are listed for purchase or sale on an exchange. An investment banking firm is typically retained to make a market in the shares.
- *Cross-listing* is the listing of a company's shares on an exchange in a different country market. It is intended to expand the potential market for the firm's shares to a larger universe of investors.
- *Depositary receipt (DR)*: A certificate of ownership in the shares of a company issued by a bank, representing a claim on underlying foreign securities. In the United States, they are termed *American Depositary Receipts* (ADRs), and when sold globally, *Global Depositary Receipts* (GDRs).

Private Placement

- The sale of a security (equity or debt) to a private investor. The private investors are typically institutions such as pension funds, insurance companies, or high net-worth private entities.
- *Rule 144A private placement sales are sales* of securities to *qualified institutional buyers* (QIBs) in the U.S. without SEC registration. QIBs are nonbank firms that own and invest in $100 million or more on a discretionary basis.
- *Private equity*: Equity investments in firm by large limited partnerships, institutional investors, or wealthy private investors with the intention of taking the subject firms private, revitalizing their businesses, and then selling them publicly or privately in 1 to 5 years.

Initial Public Offering (IPO)

A private firm initiates public ownership of the company through an *initial public offering* (IPO). Most IPOs begin with the organization of an underwriting and syndication group comprised of investment banking service providers. This group then assists the company in preparing the regulatory filings and disclosures required, depending on the country and stock exchange the firm is using. The firm will, in the months preceding the IPO date, publish a *prospectus*. The *prospectus* provides a description of the company's history, business, operating

EXHIBIT 14.4 Equity Alternatives in the Global Market

Initial Public Offering (IPO)

- Shares of a private company sold to the public market for the first time
- Seasoned offering—additional shares issued later
- Depositary receipts—foreign corporate issuance

Euroequity Issue

- An IPO on two or more exchanges, in two or more countries, at the same time
- Generic term for international securities issues originating and being sold anywhere in the world

Directed Public/Private Issue

- Shares sold to a specific market or exchange
- Shares sold to a specific set of private interests

Private Placement

- Private placement of public shares or private interest
- Private equity
- Strategic partner/alliance

and financing results; associated business, financial, or political risks; and business plan for the future, all to aid prospective buyers in their assessment of the firm.

The initial issuance of shares by a company typically represents somewhere between 15% and 25% of the ownership in the firm (although a number in recent years have been as little as 6% to 8%). The company may follow the IPO with additional share sales called *seasoned offerings* or *follow-on offerings* (FOs) in which more of the firm's ownership is sold in the public market. The total shares or proportion of shares traded in the public market is often referred to as the *public float* or *free float*. *Global Finance in Practice 14.1* details the recent IPO of the world's most profitable company, the Saudi Arabian Oil Company.

Once a firm has gone public, it is open to a considerably higher level of public scrutiny. This scrutiny arises from the detailed public disclosures and financial filings it must make periodically as required by government security regulators and individual stock exchanges. This continuous disclosure is not trivial in either cost or competitive implications. Public firm financial disclosures can be seen as divulging a tremendous amount of information that

GLOBAL FINANCE IN PRACTICE **14.1**

Saudi Aramco's IPO Valuation

When the Saudi Arabian Oil Company (Saudi Aramco) was approaching the date of its initial public offering (IPO) in 2019, there was substantial debate over what value to attribute to the company and its shares. There were a number of risk factors that the market was uncertain of. As a state-owned enterprise, would it focus on profitability? As the primary cash and revenue generator for the entire state—the Kingdom of Saudi Arabia—would it be free to pursue a corporate strategy separate from simply supporting the state? How would the recent execution of the Saudi journalist Jamal Khashoggi be interpreted by the market? Would the company focus on profitability or, as the lead member of Organization of the Petroleum Exporting Countries (OPEC), pursuing global oil influence? These questions and more roiled the debate.

Two different traditional equity valuation methods, *price-to-earnings* (PEs) and *dividend yield*, were looked to as guidance given the confusion, but they provided substantially different values. Aramco's value was also considered a highly politically sensitive matter, as Crown Prince Mohammed bin Salman of Saudi Arabia—known worldwide as "MbS"—believed that Aramco should be valued above $2 trillion. With a planned issue of 5% of the company, the Kingdom expected to raise $100 billion in the IPO, four times what the largest IPO in history, Alibaba, had raised in 2014. Many believed that if it did not look like that $2 trillion valuation would be met, MbS might cancel the IPO at the very last moment.

Price-to-Earnings. Saudi Aramco's earnings in 2018 of $111 billion made it the most profitable company in the world. In that same year, the average PE ratio for the five largest publicly traded oil and gas firms (BP, Chevron, ExxonMobil, RoyalDutchShell, and Total) was 18.8. But those same companies had a forward PE, a PE ratio based on the consensus of their future earnings, of only 13.8. Forward PEs often were lower for oil and gas firms due to uncertainty over the future price of oil, the main driver of their profits and market valuation but outside management control. Using a PE multiple of 18.8 gave Aramco a value of $2.1 trillion ($111 billion × 18.8 = $2.1 trillion), but the lower forward PE yielded only $1.5 trillion.

Dividend Yield. A second valuation method, *dividend yield*, provided a different outlook for the company for one very important reason: Saudi Aramco and the Saudi Arabian government had promised in the company's prospectus to pay an annual dividend of $75 billion (yes, billion) each and every year. The average dividend yield for the oil and gas majors, the international oil companies or IOCs, was 5.4% per annum, but the average for the major national oil companies (NOCs) was 5.0%.

Assuming that same 5% for Saudi Aramco and a $75 billion dividend, the company's value would be estimated to be $1.5 trillion ($75 billion ÷ 5% = $1.5 trillion). The problem was that although the $75 billion appeared to be a very large dividend commitment, it was still not large enough to constitute a 5% dividend yield for a $2 trillion valuation. That would require a dividend of $100 billion. Promising a dividend of that size each and every year, with no guarantees on what oil prices would do and therefore what corporate cash flows Aramco might yield, was likely asking too much.

Consensus Builds. In the last days prior to the IPO, the major investment banks and institutional investors across the world converged on a value for Saudi Aramco of $1.7 trillion: enormous, above the lower 5% dividend yield, but short of the $2.0 trillion value MbS sought.

In the end, Saudi Arabia decided to proceed with the IPO, but with a reduced offering of 1.5% of the company, not the 5.0% previously discussed. The market's valuation of Saudi Aramco on the day of the IPO was $1.7 trillion, yielding the Kingdom proceeds of just over $26 billion on the 1.5225% offering. (The 1.5% was increased by 15% at the last moment.)

customers, suppliers, partners, and competitors may use in their relationship with the firm. Private firms have a distinct competitive advantage in this arena. An added distinction about the publicly traded firm's shares is that they only raise capital for the firm upon issuance. Although the daily rise and fall of share prices drive the returns to the owners of those shares, that daily price movement does not change the capital of the company.

Euroequity Issue

A *euroequity* or *euroequity issue* is an initial public offering on multiple exchanges in multiple countries at the same time. Almost all euroequity issues are underwritten by international syndicates. The term *euro* in this context does not imply that the issuers or investors are located in Europe, nor does it mean the shares are denominated in euros. It is a generic term for international securities issues originating and being sold anywhere in the world. The euroequity seeks to raise more capital in its issuance by reaching as many different investors as possible. Two examples of high-profile euroequity issues would be those of British Telecommunications and the famous Italian luxury goods producer Gucci.

The largest and most spectacular issues have been made in conjunction with a wave of privatizations of state-owned enterprises (SOEs). The Thatcher government in the United Kingdom created the model when it privatized British Telecom in December 1984. That issue was so large that it was necessary and desirable to sell *tranches* to foreign investors in addition to the sale to domestic investors. (A *tranche* is an allocation of shares, typically to underwriters that are expected to sell to investors in their designated geographic markets.) The objective is both to raise the funds and to ensure post-issue worldwide liquidity.

Euroequity privatization issues have been particularly popular with international portfolio investors because most of the firms are very large with excellent credit ratings and profitable quasi-government monopolies at the time of privatization. The British privatization model has been so successful that numerous others have followed, like the Deutsche Telecom initial public offering of $13 billion in 1996.

State-owned enterprises (SOEs—government-owned firms from emerging markets—have successfully implemented large-scale privatization programs with these foreign tranches. Telefonos de Mexico, the giant Mexican telephone company, completed a $2 billion euroequity issue in 1991 and has continued to have an extremely liquid listing on the NYSE. One of the largest euroequity offerings by a firm resident in an illiquid market was the 1993 sale of $3 billion in shares by YPF Sociedad Annima, Argentina's state-owned oil company. About 75% of its shares were placed in tranches outside Argentina, with 46% in the U.S. alone.

Directed Public/Private Issue

A *directed public issue* or *directed private issue* is defined as one that is targeted at investors in a single country and underwritten in whole or in part by investment institutions from that country. The issue may or may not be denominated in the currency of the target market and is typically combined with a cross-listing on a stock exchange in the target market. A directed issue might be motivated by a need to fund acquisitions or major capital investments in a target foreign market. This is an especially important source of equity for firms that reside in smaller capital markets and that have outgrown that market.

Nycomed, a small but well-respected Norwegian pharmaceutical firm, was an example of this type of motivation for a directed issue combined with cross-listing. The firm's commercial strategy for growth was to leverage its sophisticated knowledge of certain market niches and technologies within the pharmaceutical field by acquiring other promising firms—primarily firms in Europe and the United States—that possessed relevant technologies, personnel, or market niches. The acquisitions were paid for partly with cash and partly with shares.

GLOBAL FINANCE IN PRACTICE 14.2

Global Equity Listings

The number of companies listed on public stock exchanges has remained fairly stationary for the last decade. Older markets like the U.S. and UK peaked in the 1990s. Indian listings doubled in the mid-1990s but have remained relatively the same for 25 years. Chinese listings have continued to grow steadily since 2000. It is the growth in public shares in newer markets, those included in "Rest of World," that now dominate the number of public listings. It is important to note, however, that the number of listed companies is not the same as the market values of these companies. Market values of publicly traded companies are typically described by stock exchange, with the New York Stock Exchange (NYSE) largest, followed by NASDAQ (U.S.), Shanghai Stock Exchange, Shenzhen Stock Exchange, and Euronext.

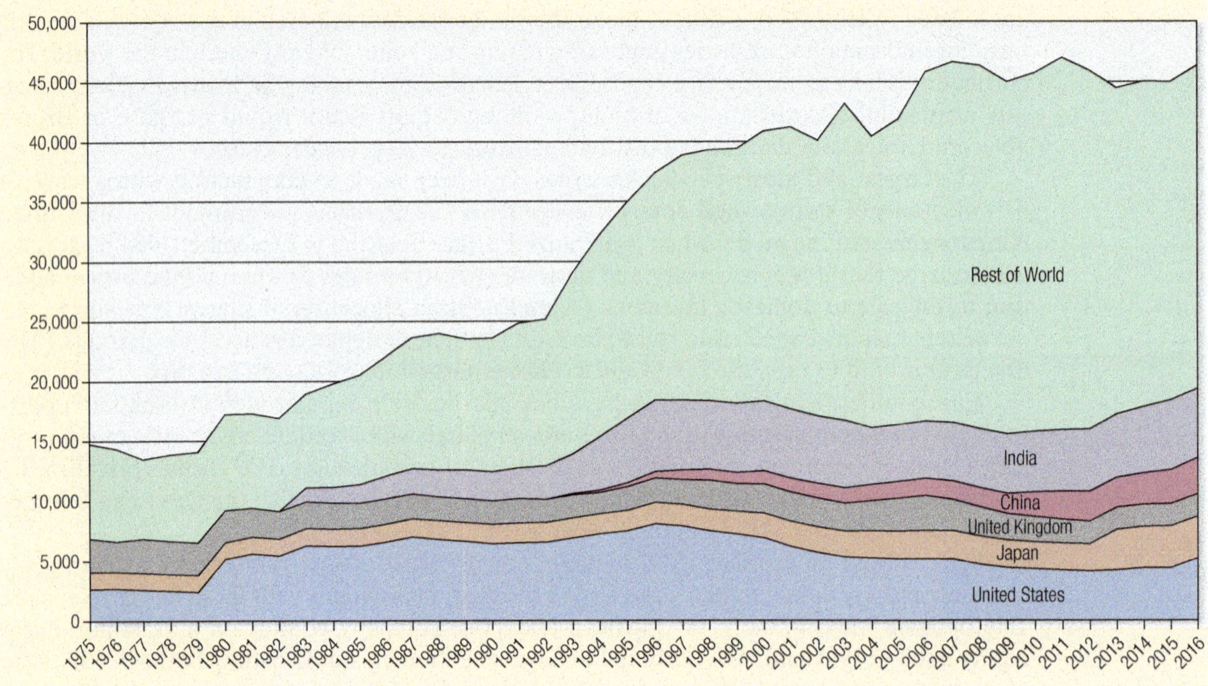

The company funded its acquisition strategy by selling two directed issues abroad. In 1989 it cross-listed on the London Stock Exchange (LSE) and raised $100 million in equity from foreign investors. Nycomed followed its LSE listing and issuance with a cross-listing and issuance on the NYSE, raising another $75 million from U.S. investors. *Global Finance in Practice 14.2* provides an overview of the number of public listings globally.

14.4 Depositary Receipts

Depositary receipts (DRs) are negotiable certificates issued by a bank to represent the underlying shares of stock that are held in trust at a foreign custodian bank. *Global depositary receipts* (GDRs) refer to certificates traded outside the U.S., and *American depositary receipts* (ADRs) refer to certificates traded in the U.S. and denominated in U.S. dollars. For a company that is incorporated outside the U.S. and wants to be listed on a U.S. exchange, the primary way of doing so is through an ADR program. For a company incorporated anywhere in the world that wants to be listed in any foreign market, this is done via a GDR program.

ADRs are sold, registered, and transferred in the U.S. in the same manner as any share of stock, with each ADR representing either a multiple or portion of the underlying foreign share. This multiple/portion allows ADRs to carry a price per share appropriate for the U.S. market (typically under $20 per share), even if the price of the foreign share is inappropriate when converted to U.S. dollars directly. A number of ADRs, like the ADR of Telefonos de Mexico (TelMex) of Mexico, have been some of the most active shares on U.S. exchanges for many years.

The first ADR program was created for a British company, Selfridges Provincial Stores Limited, a famous British retailer, in 1927. Created by J. P. Morgan, the shares were listed on the New York Curb Exchange, which in later years was transformed into the American Stock Exchange. As with many financial innovations, depositary receipts were created to defeat a regulatory restriction. In this case, the British government had prohibited British companies from registering their shares on foreign markets without British transfer agents. Depositary receipts, in essence, create a synthetic share abroad and therefore do not require actual registration of shares outside the home country—in the original case, Britain.

ADR Mechanics

Exhibit 14.5 illustrates the issuance process of a DR program, in this case a U.S.-based investor purchasing shares in a publicly traded Brazilian company—an American depositary receipt or ADR program:

1. The U.S. investor instructs a broker to make a purchase of shares in the publicly traded Brazilian company.
2. The U.S. broker contacts a local broker in Brazil (either through the broker's international offices or directly), placing the order.
3. The Brazilian broker purchases the desired ordinary shares and delivers them to a custodian bank in Brazil.
4. The U.S. broker converts the U.S. dollars received from the investor into Brazilian reais to pay the Brazilian broker for the shares purchased.
5. On the same day that the shares are delivered to the Brazilian custodian bank, the custodian notifies the U.S. depositary bank of their deposit.
6. Upon notification, the U.S. depositary bank issues and delivers DRs for the Brazilian company shares to the U.S. broker.
7. The U.S. broker then delivers the DRs to the U.S. investor.

The DRs are now held and tradable like any other common stock in the U.S. Once DRs are listed on U.S. exchanges, investors may buy or sell them the same as any equity. Exhibit 14.5 also describes the alternative process mechanics of a sale or cancellation of ADRs.

Once ADRs are created, they are tradable in the U.S. market like any other U.S. security. ADRs can be sold to other U.S. investors by simply transferring them from the existing ADR holder (the seller) to another DR holder (the buyer). This is termed *intra-market trading*. This transaction would be settled in the same manner as any other U.S. transaction, with settlement in U.S. dollars on the third business day after the trade date and typically using the depository trust company (DTC). Intra-market trading accounts for nearly 95% of all DR trading today.

ADRs can be exchanged for the underlying foreign shares, or vice versa, so arbitrage keeps foreign and U.S. prices of any given share the same after adjusting for transfer costs. For example, investor demand in one market will cause a price rise there, which will cause an

EXHIBIT 14.5 **The Structural Execution of ADRs**

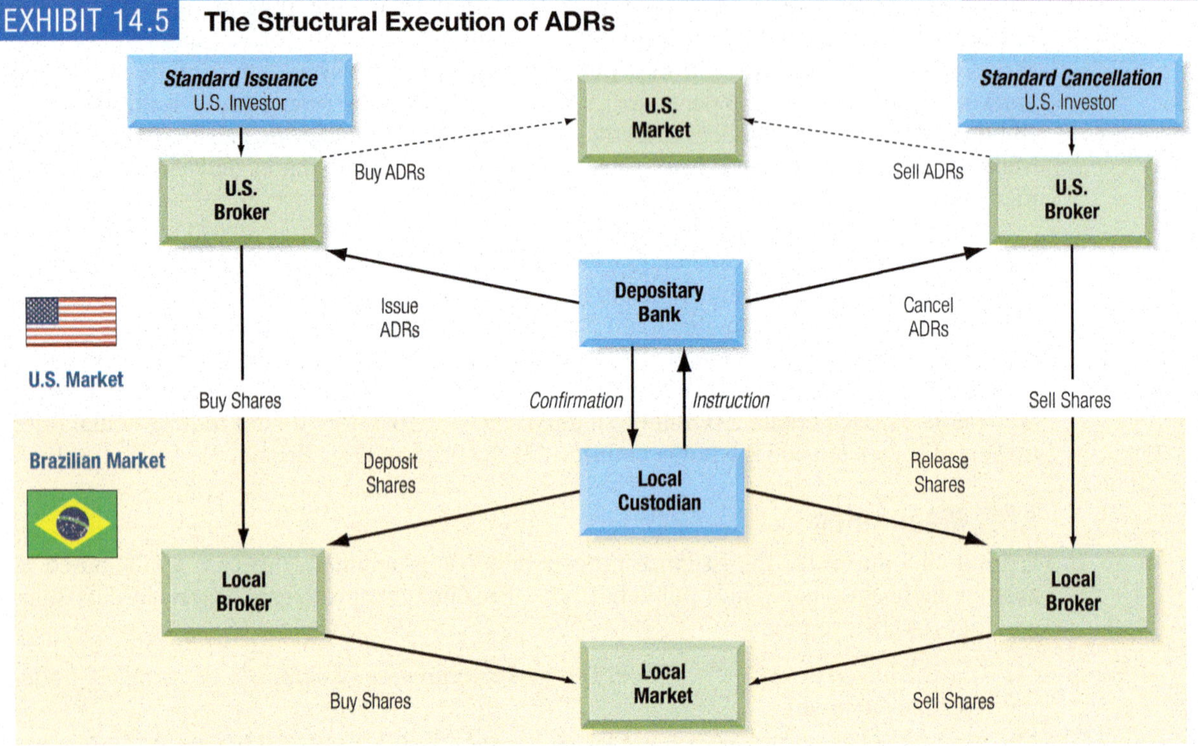

Source: Based on ***Depositary Receipts Reference Guide***, JPMorgan, 2005, p. 33.

arbitrage rise in the price on the other market even when investors there are not as bullish on the stock.

ADRs convey certain technical advantages to U.S. shareholders. Dividends paid by a foreign firm are passed to its custodial bank and then to the bank that issued the ADR. The issuing bank exchanges the foreign currency dividends for U.S. dollars and sends the dollar dividend to the ADR holders. ADRs are in registered form rather than in bearer form. Transfer of ownership occurs in the U.S. in accordance with U.S. laws and procedures. Normally, trading costs are lower than when buying or selling the underlying shares in their home market, and settlement is faster.

ADR Program Structures

The previous section described the mechanics of issuing a DR (an ADR in this case) on a Brazilian company's shares resulting from the desire of a U.S.-based investor to buy shares in a Brazilian company. But DR programs can also be viewed from the perspective of the Brazilian company—as part of its financial strategy to reach investors in the United States.

ADR programs differ in whether they are sponsored and in their certification level. Sponsored ADRs are created at the request of a foreign firm wanting its shares listed or traded in the United States. The firm applies to the U.S. SEC and a U.S. bank for registration and issuance of ADRs. The foreign firm pays all costs of creating such sponsored ADRs. If a foreign firm does not seek to have its shares listed in the United States but if U.S. investors are interested, a U.S. securities firm may initiate creation of the ADRs—an *unsponsored* ADR program. *Unsponsored* ADRs are still required by the SEC to obtain approval of the firms whose shares are to be listed. *Unsponsored* programs represent a relatively small portion of all DR programs.

The second dimension of ADR differentiation is certification level, described in detail in Exhibit 14.6. The three general levels of commitment are distinguished by degree of disclosure, listing alternatives, whether they may be used to raise capital (issue new shares), and the time typically taken to implement the programs. (SEC Rule 144A programs are described in detail later in this chapter.)

- Level I programs (over-the-counter or pink sheets) are the easiest and fastest programs to execute. A Level I program allows the foreign securities to be purchased and held by U.S. investors without being registered with the SEC. It is the least costly approach but might have a minimal impact on liquidity.
- Level II applies to firms that want to list existing shares on a U.S. stock exchange. They must meet the full registration requirements of the SEC and the rules of the specific exchange. This also means reconciling their financial accounts with those used under U.S. GAAP, raising the cost considerably.
- Level III applies to the sale of a new equity issued in the U.S. raising equity capital. It requires full registration with the SEC and an elaborate stock prospectus. This is the most expensive alternative but is the most fruitful for foreign firms wishing to raise capital in the world's largest capital markets.

DR Markets Today: Who, What, and Where

The rapid growth in emerging markets in recent years has been partly a result of the ability of companies from these countries to both list their shares and issue new shares on global equity markets. Their desire to access greater pools of affordable capital, as well as the desire for many of their owners to monetize existing value, has led to an influx of emerging market companies into the DR market.

EXHIBIT 14.6 American Depositary Receipt (ADR) Programs by Level

Type	Description	Degree of Disclosure	Listing Alternatives	Ability to Raise Capital	Implementation Timetable
Level I	Over-the-Counter ADR Program	None: home country standards apply	Over-the-counter (OTC)	---------------	6 weeks
Level I GDR	Rule 144A/ Reg. S GDR Program	None	Not listed	Yes, available only to QIBs	3 weeks
Level II	U.S.-Listed ADR Program	Detailed Sarbanes Oxley	U.S. stock exchange listings	---------------	13 weeks
Level II GDR	Rule 144A/ Reg. S GDR Program	None	DIFX	None	2 weeks
Level III	U.S.-Listed ADR Program	Rigorous Sarbanes Oxley	U.S. stock exchange listings	Yes, public offering	14 weeks
Level III GDR	Rule 144A/ Reg. S GDR Program	EU Prospectus Directive and/or US Rule 144A	London, Luxembourg, U.S. Portal	Yes, available to QIBs	2 weeks

The Who. The *Who* of global DR programs today is a mix of major multinationals from all over the world, but in recent years participation has shifted back toward industrial country companies. For example, in 2013 the largest issues came from established multinationals like BP, Vodafone, Royal Dutch Shell, and Nestlé but also included Lukoil and Gazprom of Russia and Taiwan Semiconductor Manufacturing of Taiwan. In the most recent years, there has been a growing influx of Chinese- and Indian-based companies. In 2014, the market enjoyed a boom from primarily Chinese-based issuers, but the IPO surge was short-lived as 2015 returned to relatively normal levels.

Global Registered Shares (GRSs)

A *global registered share* (GRS) is a share of equity that is traded across borders and markets without conversion, where one share on the home exchange equals one share on the foreign exchange. The identical share is listed on different stock exchanges but is listed in the currency of each exchange. GRSs can theoretically be traded "with the sun"—following markets as they open and close around the globe and around the clock. The shares are traded electronically, eliminating the specialized forms and depositaries required by share issuances like DRs.

The differences between GRSs and GDRs can be seen in the following example. Assume a German multinational has shares listed on the Frankfurt Stock Exchange and those shares are currently trading at €4.00 per share. If the spot rate is \$1.20 = €1.00, those same shares would be listed on the NYSE at \$4.80 per share.

$$€4.00 \times \$1.20 = \$4.80$$

This would be a standard GRS. But \$4.80 per share is an extremely low share price for the NYSE and the U.S. equity market.

If, however, the German firm's shares were listed in New York as ADRs, they would be converted to a value that was strategically priced for the target market—the United States. Strategic pricing in the U.S. means having share prices that are generally between \$10 and \$20 per share, a price range long thought to maximize buyer interest and liquidity. The ADR would then be constructed so that each ADR represented four shares in the company on the home market, or

$$\$4.80 \times 4 = \$19.20 \text{ per share}$$

Does this distinction matter? Clearly, the GRS is much more similar to ordinary shares than depositary receipts, and it allows easier comparison and analysis. But if target pricing is important in key markets like that of the U.S., then the ADR offers a better opportunity for a foreign firm to gain traction in the U.S.

Proponents of GRSs over ADRs make two fundamental arguments, both based on pure forces of globalization:

1. Investors and markets alike will continue to grow in their desire for securities, which are increasingly identical across markets—taking on the characteristics of commodity—like securities, changing only by the currency of denomination of the local exchange.
2. Regulations governing security trading across country markets will continue to converge toward a common set of global principles, eliminating the need for securities customized for local market attributes or requirements.

Other potential distinctions include the possibility of retaining all voting rights (GRSs do, by definition, while some ADRs may not) and the general principle that ADRs are designed for one singular cultural and legal environment—the U.S. At least to date, the GRS has not replaced the ADR or GDR.

14.5 Private Placement

Raising equity through private placement is increasingly common across the globe. Publicly traded and private firms alike raise private equity capital on occasion. A private placement is the sale of a security to a small set of qualified institutional buyers. The investors are traditionally insurance companies and investment companies. Since the securities are not registered for sale to the public, investors have typically followed a "buy and hold" policy. In the case of debt, terms are often custom designed on a negotiated basis. Private placement markets now exist in most countries.

SEC Rule 144A

In 1990, the SEC approved Rule 144A. It permits *qualified institutional buyers* (QIBs) to trade privately placed securities without the previous holding period restrictions and without requiring SEC registration. A QIB is an entity (excluding financial institutions, like banks or savings and loans) that owns and invests on a discretionary basis $100 million in securities of non-affiliates. Banks and savings and loans must meet this test but also must have a minimum net worth of $25 million.

The SEC estimates that about 4,000 QIBs exist, mainly investment advisors, investment companies, insurance companies, pension funds, and charitable institutions. Subsequently the SEC modified its regulations to permit foreign issuers to tap the U.S. private placement market through an SEC Rule 144A issue, also without SEC registration. A trading system called PORTAL was established to support the distribution of issues and to create a liquid secondary market for issues.

Since SEC registration has been identified as the main barrier to foreign firms wishing to raise funds in the United States, SEC Rule 144A placements are proving attractive to foreign issuers of both equity and debt securities. Atlas Copco, the Swedish multinational engineering firm, was the first foreign firm to take advantage of SEC Rule 144A. It raised $49 million in the United States through an ADR equity placement as part of its larger $214 million euro-equity issue in 1990. Since then, several billion dollars have been raised each year by foreign issuers with private equity placements in the United States.

Private Equity Funds

Private equity funds are usually limited partnerships of institutional and wealthy investors, such as college endowment funds, that raise capital in the most liquid capital markets. They are best known for buying control of publicly owned firms, taking them private, improving management, and then reselling them after several years (the average holding period has grown to five to seven years). They are resold in a variety of ways including selling the firms to other firms, selling to other private equity funds, or taking them public once again. The private equity funds are frequently very large but may also utilize a large amount of debt to fund their takeovers. These "alternatives," as they are called, demand fees of 2% of assets plus 20% of profits.

Many mature family-owned firms resident in emerging markets are unlikely to qualify for a global cost and availability of capital even if they follow the strategy suggested in this chapter. Although they might be consistently profitable and growing, they are still too small, too invisible to foreign investors, lacking in managerial depth, and unable to fund the up-front costs of a globalization strategy. For these firms, private equity funds may be a solution.

Private equity funds differ from traditional venture capital funds. The latter usually operate mainly in highly developed countries. They typically invest in startup firms with the goal of exiting the investment with an initial public offering (IPO) placed in those same highly liquid markets. Very little venture capital is available in emerging markets, partly because it would be difficult to exit with an IPO in an illiquid market. The same exiting problem faces the private equity funds, but they appear to have a longer time horizon. They invest in already mature and profitable companies. They are content with growing companies through better management and mergers with other firms.

Foreign Equity Listing and Issuance

According to the alternative equity pathways in the global market illustrated in Exhibit 14.1, a firm needs to choose one or more stock markets on which to cross-list its shares and sell new equity. Just where to go depends mainly on the firm's specific motives and the willingness of the host stock market to accept the firm. By cross-listing and selling its shares on a foreign exchange, a firm typically tries to accomplish one or more of the following objectives:

- Improve the liquidity of its shares and support a liquid secondary market for new equity issues in foreign markets
- Increase its share price by overcoming mis-pricing in a segmented and illiquid home capital market
- Increase the firm's visibility and acceptance to its customers, suppliers, creditors, and host governments
- Establish a liquid secondary market for shares used to acquire other firms in the host market and to compensate local management and employees of foreign subsidiaries

A recent example of this last motivation, to establish a liquid secondary market, is Kosmos Energy. Following the company's IPO in the United States in May 2011 (NYSE: KOS), the company listed its shares on the Ghanaian Stock Exchange. Ghana was the country in which the oil company had made its major discoveries and generated nearly all of its income.

14.6 Raising Debt Globally

The ability of firms to raise debt globally—outside their home country markets—goes back centuries. Most debt obligations carry specific maturities, explicit repayment schedules, and defined fixed/floating interest obligations, all factors that make their sale across borders and currencies of significantly lower risk to the investor than that seen in equities in the previous section.

The international debt markets offer the borrower a broader variety of maturities, repayment structures, and currencies of denomination than those limited options often available in their home country. The markets and their many different instruments vary by source of funding, pricing structure, maturity, and subordination or linkage to other debt and equity instruments.

International Debt Instruments

Exhibit 14.7 provides an overview of the three basic forms of international debt: *bank loans* (including syndicated bank loans), *euronotes*, and *international bonds*. These three debt pools have proven to be a major advancement over the relatively segmented national debt markets of the past, and they have provided multinational companies and sovereign governments alike with a set of choices of markets and instruments previously enjoyed only by the few major deep and developed capital markets of the industrial countries.

EXHIBIT 14.7 International Debt Markets and Instruments

Bank Loans and Syndications
(floating-rate, short to medium term)

- **International Bank Loans**
  - Similar to traditional bank loans
  - Typically called *eurodollar* credits and *eurocredits*
  - Enjoys a narrow interest rate spread of 1% or less between deposit and loan rates
- **Eurocredits**
  - Bank loans extended to MNEs, sovereign governments, and international institutions in a currency different from that of the lender
  - Typically maturities of 6 months or less, priced at LIBOR plus a spread
- **Syndicated Credits**
  - Large loans spread over a number of lenders led by a lead bank
  - Pricing is typically at LIBOR plus a spread

Euronote Market
(short to medium term)

- **Euronotes and Euronote Facilities**
  - Issues with underwriters
  - Short-term obligations that proved to be valuable replacements of syndicated credits
- **Eurocommercial Paper (ECP)**
  - Issued to the market (nonunderwritten facilities)
  - Short-term debt obligation of an MNE or bank
  - Typical maturities of 1, 3, and 6 months
- **Euro Medium-Term Notes (EMTNs)**
  - Nonunderwritten facilities
  - Bridges the maturity gap between ECP and longer-term obligations like bonds
  - Followed the forms of U.S. shelf registrations
  - Same attributes as bonds

International Bond Market
(fixed and floating-rate, mid to long term)

- **Eurobonds**
  - Underwritten by an international syndicate of banks and sold exclusively in countries other than the country in whose currency the issue is denominated
  - Straight fixed-rate issue
  - Floating-rate note (FRN)
  - Equity-related issue
- **Foreign Bond**
  - Underwritten by a syndicate of financial institutions from a single country, typically denominated in the currency of that country
  - Essentially a foreign issuer in a national bond market
  - Same attributes as traditional bonds
  - *Yankee bonds* (foreign issue in the U.S.), *Samurai bonds* (foreign issue in Japan), *Bulldogs* (foreign issue in the UK), etc.

Unique Characteristics of Eurobond Markets

Although the eurobond market evolved at about the same time as the eurodollar market, the two markets exist for different reasons, and each could exist independently of the other. The eurobond market owes its existence to several unique factors: the absence of regulatory interference, less stringent disclosure practices, favorable tax treatment, and ratings.

Absence of Regulatory Interference. National governments often impose tight controls on foreign issuers of securities denominated in the local currency and sold within their national boundaries. However, governments in general have less stringent limitations for securities denominated in foreign currencies and sold within their markets to holders of those foreign currencies. In effect, eurobond sales fall outside the regulatory domain of any single nation.

Less Stringent Disclosure. Disclosure requirements in the eurobond market are much less stringent than those of the U.S. Securities and Exchange Commission (SEC for sales within the United States. U.S. firms and non-U.S. firms alike often find that the registration costs of a eurobond offering are less than those of a domestic issue and that less time is needed to bring a new issue to market via SEC registration. However, the SEC has relaxed disclosure requirements for certain private placements (Rule 144A), which has improved the attractiveness of the U.S. domestic bond and equity markets.

Favorable Tax Treatment. Eurobonds offer tax anonymity and flexibility. Interest paid on eurobonds is generally not subject to an income withholding tax. As one might expect, eurobond interest is not always reported to tax authorities. Eurobonds are usually issued in bearer form, meaning that the name and country of residence of the owner is not on the certificate. To receive interest, the bearer cuts an interest coupon from the bond and turns it in at a banking institution listed on the issue as a paying agent. It follows, then, that bearer bond status is often tied to tax avoidance.

Ratings. Rating agencies, such as Moody's and Standard and Poor's (S&P), provide ratings for selected international bonds for a fee. Moody's rates international bonds at the request of the issuer and limits its evaluation to the issuer's ability to repay the issue in the currency of denomination. Based on supporting financial statements and other material obtained from the issuer, the rating agency makes a preliminary rating and informs the issuer, who then has an opportunity to comment. After Moody's determines its final rating, the issuer may decide not to have the rating published. Consequently, a disproportionately large number of published international ratings fall into the highest rating categories.

Purchasers of eurobonds do not generally rely only on bond-rating services or on detailed analyses of financial statements. The general reputation of the issuing corporation and its underwriters has been a major factor in obtaining favorable terms. For this reason, larger and better-known MNEs, state enterprises, and sovereign governments are able to obtain the lowest interest rates. Firms whose names are better known to the general public are often believed to have an advantage over equally qualified firms whose products are less widely known.

Access to debt capital is obviously impacted by everything from the legal and tax environments to basic societal norms. Indeed, even religion plays a part in the use and availability of debt capital. *Global Finance in Practice 14.3* illustrates one area rarely seen by Westerners, Islamic finance.

GLOBAL FINANCE IN PRACTICE 14.3

Islamic Finance

Muslims, the followers of Islam, now make up roughly one-fourth of the world's population. The countries of the world that are predominantly Islamic create roughly 10% of global GDP and comprise a large share of the emerging marketplace. Islamic law speaks to many dimensions of its practitioners' individual and organizational behaviors, including business. Islamic finance, the specific area of our interest, imposes a number of restrictions on Muslims, which have a dramatic impact on the funding and structure of Islamic businesses.

The Islamic form of finance is as old as the religion of Islam itself. The basis for all Islamic finance lies in the principles of the Sharia, or Islamic Law, which is taken from the Qur'an. Observance of these principles precipitates restrictions on business and finance practices as follows:

- Making money from money is not permissible.
- Earning interest is prohibited.
- Profit and loss should be shared.
- Speculation (gambling) is prohibited.
- Investments should support only halal activities.

For the conduct of business, the key to understanding the Sharia prohibition on earning interest is to understand that profitability from traditional Western investments arises from the returns associated with carrying risk. For example, a traditional Western bank may extend a loan to a business. It is agreed that the bank will receive its principal and interest in return regardless of the ultimate profitability of the business (the borrower). In fact, the debt is paid off before returns to equity occur. Similarly, an individual who deposits money in a Western bank will receive an interest earning on their deposit regardless of the profitability of the bank and of the bank's associated investments.

Under Sharia law, however, an Islamic bank cannot pay interest to depositors. Therefore, the depositors in an Islamic bank are, in effect, shareholders (much like credit unions in the West), and the returns they receive are a function of the profitability of the bank's investments. Their returns cannot be fixed or guaranteed because that would break the principle of profit and loss being shared.

Recently, however, a number of Islamic banking institutions have opened in Europe and North America. A Muslim now can enter into a sequence of purchases that allows him to purchase a home without departing from Islamic principles. The buyer selects the property, which is then purchased by an Islamic bank. The bank in turn resells the house to the prospective buyer at a higher price. The buyer is allowed to pay off the purchase over a series of years. Although the difference in purchase prices is, by Western thinking, implicit interest, this structure does conform to Sharia law. Unfortunately, in both the United States and the United Kingdom, unlike interest, the difference in purchase price is not a tax-deductible expense for the homeowner.

14.7 Financing Foreign Subsidiaries

Assuming that the multinational enterprise seeks to minimize the cost of capital for a given level of business risk and capital budget is the objective for the consolidated enterprise, then the financial structure of each subsidiary is relevant only to the extent that it affects this overall goal. In other words, an individual subsidiary does not theoretically have an independent cost of capital, and therefore its financial structure is not based on the objective of minimizing its cost of capital. But if that is the case, what is it based on?

The answer to this question is a complex combination of theory and practice. In theory, a foreign subsidiary is a foreign investment and as such carries with it the same risks as any cross-border investment. And as we noted, its financial structure is relevant only to the extent that it affects, on the margin, the multinational's consolidated cost of capital. In practice, a foreign subsidiary is a business operating in a completely separate economic environment, one with its own set of legal, financial, currency, tax, and institutional practices—local norms. The financing of each foreign subsidiary may, in the end, be unique.

Internal and External Subsidiary Financing

The foreign subsidiary of a multinational enterprise is funded from sources that are from both internal sources and external sources. *Internal financing* includes all potential sources of funds arising from the MNE itself—the parent company, other subsidiaries and affiliates, and funds generated over time from the subsidiary itself. *External financing* is composed of both debt, from any source that is not the MNE itself, and equity from potential partners, local or global. In addition to this internal/external dimension of financing, traditional financial structuring choices between equity and debt are also important.

EXHIBIT 14.8 **Internal Financing of the Foreign Subsidiary**

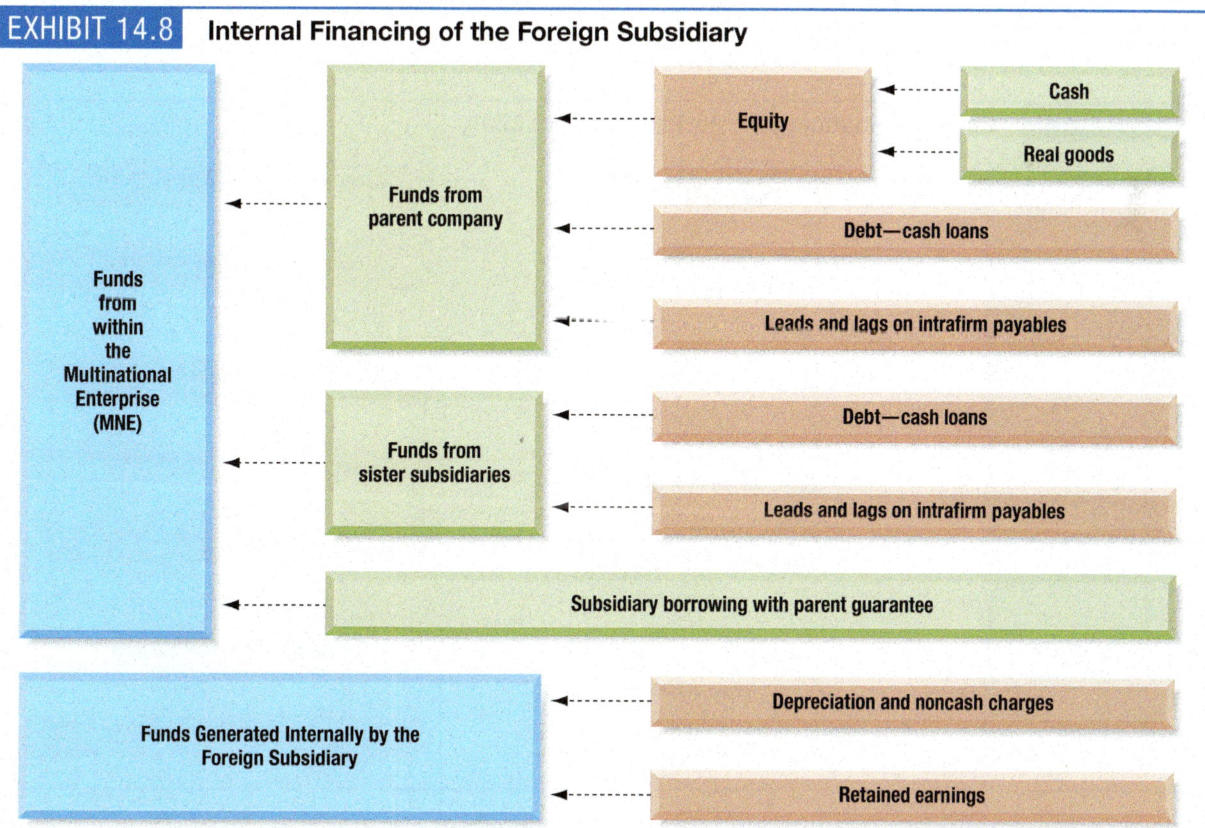

In general, although a minimum amount of equity capital from the parent company is required initially, multinationals often strive to minimize their amount of equity in foreign subsidiaries in order to reduce capital risk. As illustrated in Exhibit 14.8, which shows the internal financing sources for the foreign subsidiary, equity investment can take the form of either cash or kind (real goods such as machinery, equipment, inventory, technology, or trademarks, and others). If additional equity is needed over time, the multinational may choose to retain earnings in the subsidiary.

While debt is the preferred form of subsidiary financing, access to local host country debt is limited in the early stages of a foreign subsidiary's life. Without a history of proven operational and debt service capability, the foreign subsidiary may need to acquire its debt from the parent company or from unrelated parties with a parental guarantee (after operations have been initiated). Once the operational and financial capabilities of the subsidiaries are established, it may then enjoy preferred access to debt locally.

External sources of financing available for foreign subsidiaries, as illustrated in Exhibit 14.9, fall into three categories: (1) debt from the parent's country, (2) debt from countries outside the parent's country, and (3) local or global equity. Debt acquired from external parties in the parent's country reflects the lenders' familiarity with and confidence in the parent company itself, although the parent is in this case not providing explicit guarantees for the repayment of the debt. Local currency debt is particularly valuable to the foreign subsidiary that has substantial local currency cash inflows arising from its business activities. In the case of some emerging markets, however, local currency debt is in short supply for all borrowers, local or foreign.

Host Country Norms and Debt. Financial structure norms for firms vary widely from one country to another but vary less for firms domiciled in the same country. This statement is the conclusion of a long line of empirical studies that have investigated the question

EXHIBIT 14.9 **External Financing of the Foreign Subsidiary**

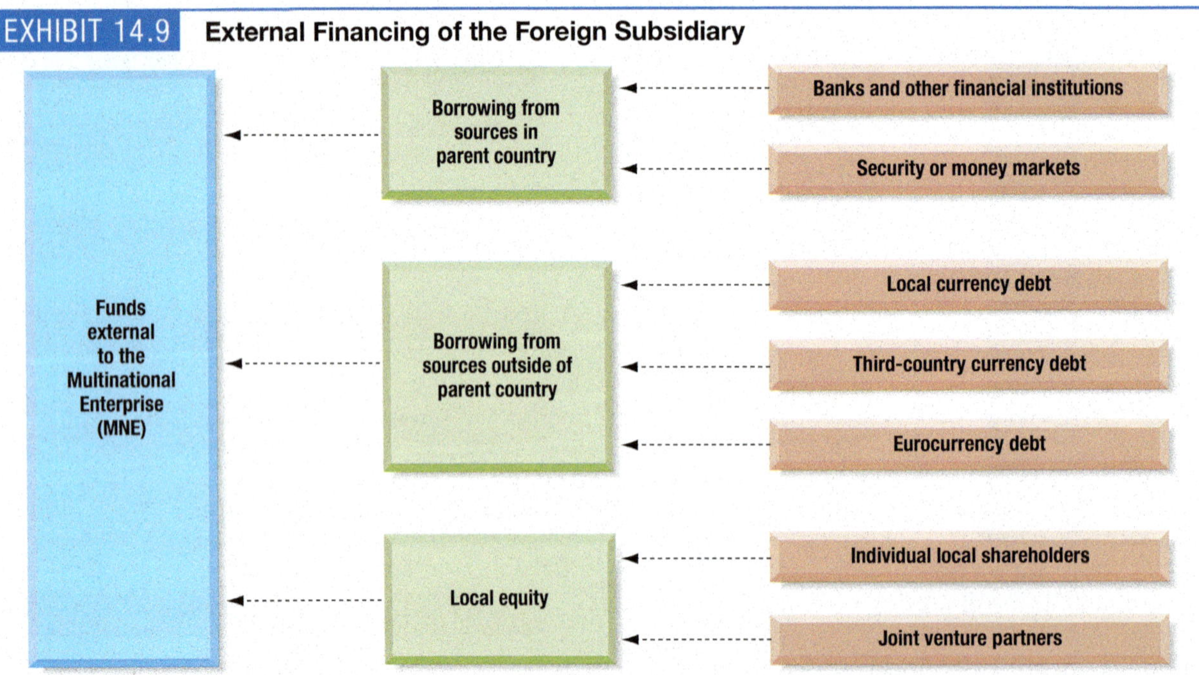

of what factors drive financial structure. Most of these international studies concluded that country-specific environmental variables are key determinants of debt ratios. These variables include historical development, taxation, corporate governance, bank influence, a viable corporate bond market, attitude toward risk, government regulation, availability of capital, and agency costs, to name a few.

But to what degree should local debt ratio norms be taken into consideration when determining the desired debt ratio for a foreign subsidiary? For definition purposes the debt considered here should include only funds borrowed from sources outside the MNE. This debt would include local and foreign currency loans as well as eurocurrency loans. The reason for this definition is that parent loans to foreign subsidiaries are often regarded as equivalent to equity investment by host countries. A parent loan is usually subordinated to other debt and does not create the same threat of insolvency as an external loan.

Host country governments would, in the extreme, prefer all inward investment be financed with equity. And they would also prefer that all profits generated by the subsidiary be reinvested in the country, not returned to the parent company via an intracompany dividend. Intracompany dividends are often considered *elective payments*—a choice not to reinvest in the country. Multinationals, however, would in the extreme prefer to fund foreign subsidiaries with debt. The resulting debt service obligations, both principal and interest, would serve as a contractual structure for remittance of cash flow returns to the multinational parent over time while minimizing their own equity capital at risk.

Foreign Exchange Concerns. Although it depends on the nature of the subsidiary's business, foreign exchange risk can be a burden on a startup subsidiary. Debt obligations in a foreign currency or intracompany purchases for products and services denominated in a foreign currency can place an undue burden of foreign exchange risk management on a startup. If the subsidiary has debt service obligations to the parent company, a startup subsidiary would prefer to make debt service payments in local currency. Local debt, if accessible, is therefore preferred.

Tax Concerns. MNE efforts to minimize tax obligations in high-tax environments (the subject of the next chapter) has led many firms to maximize the debt obligations of the foreign subsidiary—to hopefully leverage the tax deductibility of interest payments. Host country governments are well aware of this principal and have long instituted maximum levels of debt in subsidiary financial structures (limiting what they will allow as deductible toward tax liabilities). Regardless, minimization of tax obligations remains a primary consideration for all subsidiary financing.

Subsidiary Financing over Time

The financial structure and financing of any individual subsidiary will, therefore, reflect the MNE's own business, its own structure, and the local norms of the markets in which the subsidiaries are operating. But a foreign subsidiary, like any business, will have changing financing needs over time. Exhibit 14.10 illustrates how a foreign subsidiary's financing needs, concerns, and sources change as it passes through three fundamental stages of its business life cycle—startup, growth, and maturing.

Startup Stage. As a startup, the business will need sufficient funding to commence and sustain operations. Although it may have access to some debt, debt provided by its parent company, the subsidiary's financing is largely equity during this stage. Even with access to parent-provided debt, debt is largely minimized to prevent imposing cash flow burdens on the startup business. Operational capability will be largely cash-flow based; it does not have to be solely profitable on its own as a subsidiary, but it does need to pay its bills.

EXHIBIT 14.10 Foreign Subsidiary Funding over Time

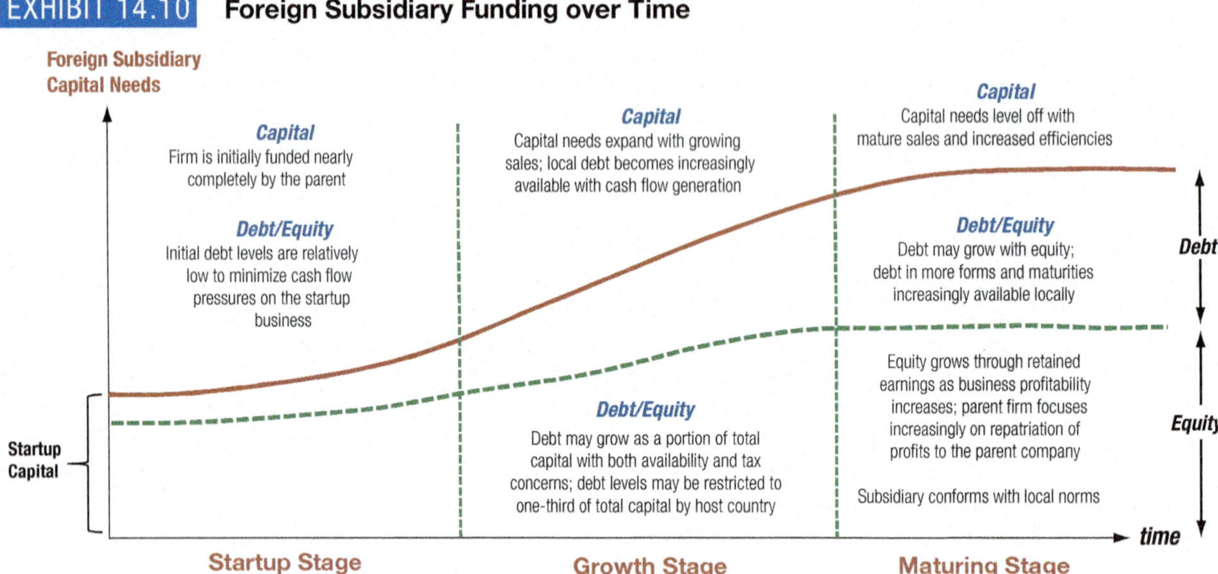

A hypothetically "typical foreign subsidiary" will need increasing capital over time as it grows. Assuming stable market conditions and increased profitability, the subsidiary may use more and more local debt in its financial structure within limits established by local norms.

Growth Stage. As the subsidiary's business grows, its capital needs may grow rapidly, depending on the nature of its business. A manufacturing business will likely be relatively capital intensive, and growing sales will require growth in working capital that will in turn require financing. For a services business with relatively low capital requirements, growth may not require significant new financing. Management will typically increase its use of debt at this stage, and as the subsidiary demonstrates increasing cash flow from operations, it may find local debt increasingly attractive and available. Although there are clear tax advantages of using increasing quantities of debt, host country authorities will be sensitive to excessive use of debt (excessive being traditionally defined as debt exceeding one-third of total capital).

Maturing Stage. In the third and final stage of a subsidiary's life cycle, business growth slows, and the need for additional financing slows with it. The subsidiary, however, may change the composition of its financial structure as sustained profits allow both retained earnings for equity capital and for repatriated earnings to the parent company (representing explicit cash flow returns to the parent). The subsidiary's debt structure may now include a multitude of maturities, rate structures, and currency of denomination as it gains access to more and more sources of debt in both the local market and global market.

In the end, the multinational enterprise is nothing more than the sum of its parts. Its parts are its business units worldwide, and the task of multinational financial management involves the structuring, funding, and managing of all capital and cash flows crossing borders. Subsidiary financing is a core element of that body.

Summary Points

- Designing a capital sourcing strategy requires management to design a long-run financial strategy. The firm must then choose among the various alternative paths to achieve its goals, including where to cross-list its shares, where to issue new equity, and in what form.
- A multinational firm's marginal cost of capital is constant for considerable ranges of its capital budget. This statement is not true for most small domestic firms.
- By diversifying cash flows internationally, the MNE may be able to achieve the same kind of reduction in cash flow variability that portfolio investors receive from diversifying their portfolios internationally.
- When a firm issues foreign currency-denominated debt, its effective cost equals the after-tax cost of repaying the principal and interest in terms of the firm's own currency. This amount includes the nominal cost of principal and interest in foreign currency terms, adjusted for any foreign exchange gains or losses.
- There is a variety of different equity pathways that firms may choose between when pursuing global sources of equity, including euroequity issues, direct foreign issuances, depositary receipt programs, and private placements.
- Depositary receipt programs, either American or global, provide an extremely effective way for firms from outside the established industrial country markets to improve the liquidity of their existing shares or issue new shares.
- Private placement is a growing segment of the market, allowing firms from emerging markets to raise capital in the largest of capital markets with limited disclosure and cost.
- The international debt markets offer the borrower a variety of different maturities, repayment structures, and currencies of denomination. The markets and their many different instruments vary by source of funding, pricing structure, maturity, and subordination or linkage to other debt and equity instruments.
- Eurocurrency markets serve two valuable purposes: (1) eurocurrency deposits are an efficient and convenient money market device for holding excess corporate liquidity, and (2) the euro-currency market is a major source of short-term bank loans to finance corporate working capital needs, including the financing of imports and exports.
- The financial structure of an MNE's foreign subsidiaries may vary significantly from that of the consolidated firm, often a result of following host country norms combined with internal and external-financing choices.

MINI-CASE

Cemex's Debt Dilemma[1]

> *"The combination of CEMEX and Rinker will create value for shareholders as well as customers, particularly in growth regions in the United States. . . . We intend to regain our financial flexibility as soon as possible and return to our steady state capital structure within two years."*
>
> —Lorenzo H. Zambrano, chairman and CEO, CEMEX.

On April 9, 2007, the board of The Rinker Group Ltd. (Australia) approved a revised offer of US$15.85 per share after CEMEX S.A.B. de C.V. (NYSE: CX)—CEMEX—raised its offer. With the backing of management, CEMEX obtained the needed 90% of shareholders' approval on July 10, 2007, to close the acquisition. CEMEX funded the acquisition nearly exclusively with short-term debt.

The Rinker Deal

In the months that followed, many analysts debated whether CEMEX had overpaid for Rinker. The final acquisition price of US$15.85 was high by market standards and constituted a 54% premium over Rinker's pre-acquisition closing price of US$10.30.

Strategic Fit

CEMEX believed the deal made sense because the acquisition expanded its diversity and strength in the aggregates and ready-mix concrete components of the concrete value chain. It also increased CEMEX's market share in several of the key growth markets in the U.S., namely Florida and Arizona, as well as added segments in Australia and China. The combining of CEMEX and Rinker operations in the U.S. market would also offer significant cost synergies. (CEMEX had expanded its estimate to more than US$400 million in potential cost synergies in 2008.)

[1] This case was prepared by Professor Michael H. Moffett for the purpose of classroom discussion only, and not to indicate either effective or ineffective management.

EXHIBIT A CEMEX's Explanation of the Rinker Acquisition

We complement the organic growth of our business with strategic acquisitions and capital investments. As a leading industry consolidator, we take a disciplined approach to capital allocation. We evaluate potential acquisitions in light of three investment criteria:

1. The acquisition should provide a return on our investment that is well in excess of our weighted cost of capital.
2. The acquisition should allow us to maintain our financial strength and investment-grade credit quality.
3. Factors that we can influence, in particular the application of our management and turnaround expertise, should principally drive the potential for increasing the acquisition's value.

Our recent acquisition of Rinker meets all of these criteria and is consistent with our business strategy. First, the acquisition will provide a return on our investment that is well in excess of our cost of capital. It also is immediately accretive to our free cash flow. Second, the acquisition allows us to maintain our financial strength and investment-grade credit quality. The transaction enhances our earnings quality, lowers our weighted average cost of capital (WACC) from 7.9% to 6.8%, and will yield our target return on capital employed of 10% over the medium term. Third, the acquisition leverages our management expertise, integration skills, and global operations network.

Source: CEMEX Annual Report, 2007, p. 20.

As described in Exhibit A, CEMEX defended the Rinker deal as meeting all of the company's corporate objectives demanded of all acquisitions.

CEMEX was a seasoned professional when it came to financing acquisitions. The company had paid down its *net debt* (debt less cash) from US$10.4 billion to just US$5.1 billion in the two years leading up to the Rinker purchase. The acquisition would be financed entirely with debt and would require CEMEX to assume US$1.3 billion of Rinker's existing debt obligations. Lorenzo Zambrano pledged to reduce CEMEX's total net debt to under 2.7 times its EBITDA within two years.

CEMEX's Acquisition Process

CEMEX took on US$14 billion in new debt in the third quarter of 2007 to finance Rinker. As illustrated in Exhibit B, this increased CEMEX's Debt-to-EBITDA ratio, a metric of indebtedness used by the company's bankers to track the firm's debt-carrying capacity.

At the time CEMEX first considered making an offer for Rinker, in mid-2006, it expected growth in the core earnings of its existing and acquired businesses. But even as it pursued the acquisition in the fall of 2006 and spring of 2007, expectations for the core business were regularly

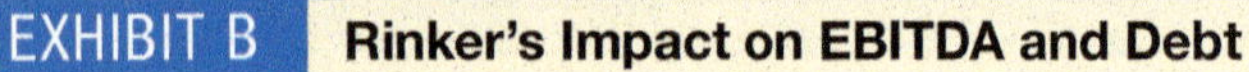

EXHIBIT B Rinker's Impact on EBITDA and Debt

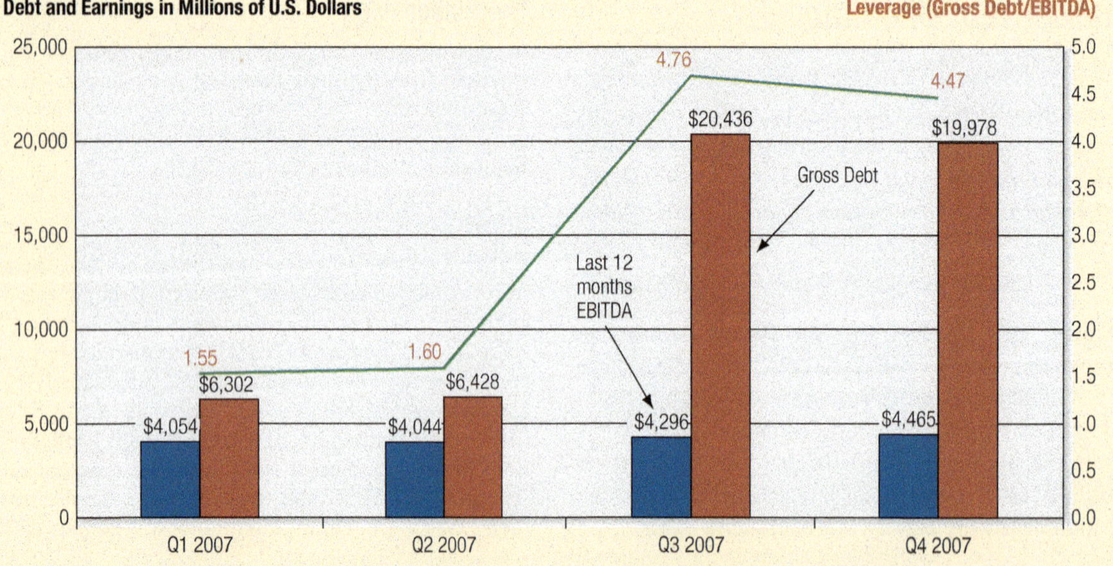

Source: Constructed by author based on data provided by CEMEX SAB de CV (ADR), RBC Capital Markets, October 4, 2011, p. 13.

revised downward. The continuing construction slump only worsened. In the summer of 2007, as the Rinker deal closed, CEMEX's earnings continued to slide. The following spring of 2008 saw growing anxiousness for the business outlook:[2] Although CEMEX's 2008 sales in the U.S. had started slowly, the company still expected to close 2008 with an EBITDA of US$5.6 billion in 2008, 22% higher than 2007's US$4.6 billion.

September 2008 Financial Crisis

What is now commonly called the *global financial crisis* exploded in the U.S. in September 2008. On September 6, 2008, the two government-sponsored mortgage associations, Fannie Mae and Freddie Mac, were put into government conservatorship. On September 15, Lehman Brothers filed for Chapter 11 bankruptcy. The next day, September 16, the U.S. government seized control of American International Group (AIG), one of the world's largest insurers. In the months that followed, businesses of all kinds plummeted. In December arrangements were made for the U.S. government to take over General Motors (GM) to avoid its collapse.

CEMEX's sales began to plummet in the third-quarter of 2008. Spain was down 26%, Mexico down 10%, the U.S. was estimated down more than 25%. Housing starts in the U.S. were now roughly one-fourth what they were two years previous. The company now experienced trouble refinancing its debt, an integral part of Zambrano's proven acquisition and integration plan:[3]

> *He largely eschewed long-term financing from capital markets in favor of shorter-term bank loans. These he would refinance a year or two following a takeover after showing lenders how well the deal was working out. The assumption was that debt markets would always be open to a business as professionally run as CEMEX.*
>
> *Now CEMEX is staring at a mountain of $16.4 billion to almost $20 billion of debt, depending on the accounting principles used, at least twice the company's stock-market value. Facing weak housing sectors in its three core markets—the U.S., Spain, and Mexico—the company is hard put to generate enough cash soon to whittle that debt much. Its annual cash flow equals about 17% of its debt, below its historic average of 30%.*

As sales and earnings declined at CEMEX and everywhere across most markets, banks began freezing up, not being willing to extend, roll over, or refinance debt. Banks stopped answering the phone, regardless of whether the caller was CEMEX, Yahoo, or Walmart. As one treasurer noted, "They don't want to say no to new financing, but they can't say yes." By December 2008, more than three months into the financial crisis, CEMEX was in crisis mode. The company began slashing its workforce and spending.

As illustrated in Exhibit C, housing starts continued to plummet. One of the most immediate and drastic of the impacts of the financial crisis was the fall of the Mexican peso and the rise of the U.S. dollar. Given the multitude of currencies CEMEX operated in and the varying sources of its debt, earnings fell further. In early December the company announced that it was unwinding its failed currency hedging program at a cost of a US$711 million. As noted, CEMEX was now facing repayment of US$5.5 billion in debt in 2009.

CEMEX and the company's creditors relied on the company's core earnings—EBITDA—to generate the cash flows to service debt. Unfortunately, expectations over CEMEX's future EBITDA were being consistently revised downward. At the time that CEMEX had initiated its hostile takeover of Rinker, in October 2006, its EBITDA was forecast to hit US$5.071 billion for 2007. In the end, actual 2007 results were only US$4.590 billion. But it was actual EBITDA for 2008 that would pose the biggest problem. Although forecast to hit US$4.600 billion, actual 2008 results were only US$3.565 billion. This was essentially the same as that for 2005, a full three years before the acquisition of Rinker. Current forecasts, made in October 2008 amid the financial crisis, were now expecting earnings to continue to fall.

Credit Quality and Corporate Cash Flow

The Rinker acquisition immediately altered CEMEX's credit profile with its lenders and posed serious challenges to the company's ability to service its debt obligations.

Debt-Carrying Capacity

CEMEX entered 2008 with an *investment grade* credit rating (S&P's BBB status). But at BBB, the company could not suffer a downgrade without being classified as *speculative grade*. Corporate credit ratings are based on a variety of factors including industry, product, or service characteristics (predominantly the ability to differentiate themselves from other competitors and gain pricing power), cyclicality of business, and debt levels. Unfortunately CEMEX was in a highly cyclical industry (construction), was producing what many considered a commodity, and had recently taken on substantial debt.

One of the most widely used measures of a firm's ability to service debt was the Net-Debt-to-EBITDA ratio. This ra-

[2]"CEMEX: Adjusting Our Target Due to a Continued Difficult Environment—Downgrading to Hold," Santander, Mexico City, March 27, 2008.

[3]Joel Millman, "Hard Times for Cement Man," *The Wall Street Journal*, December 11, 2008.

EXHIBIT C CEMEX and Housing Starts: 2000–2009

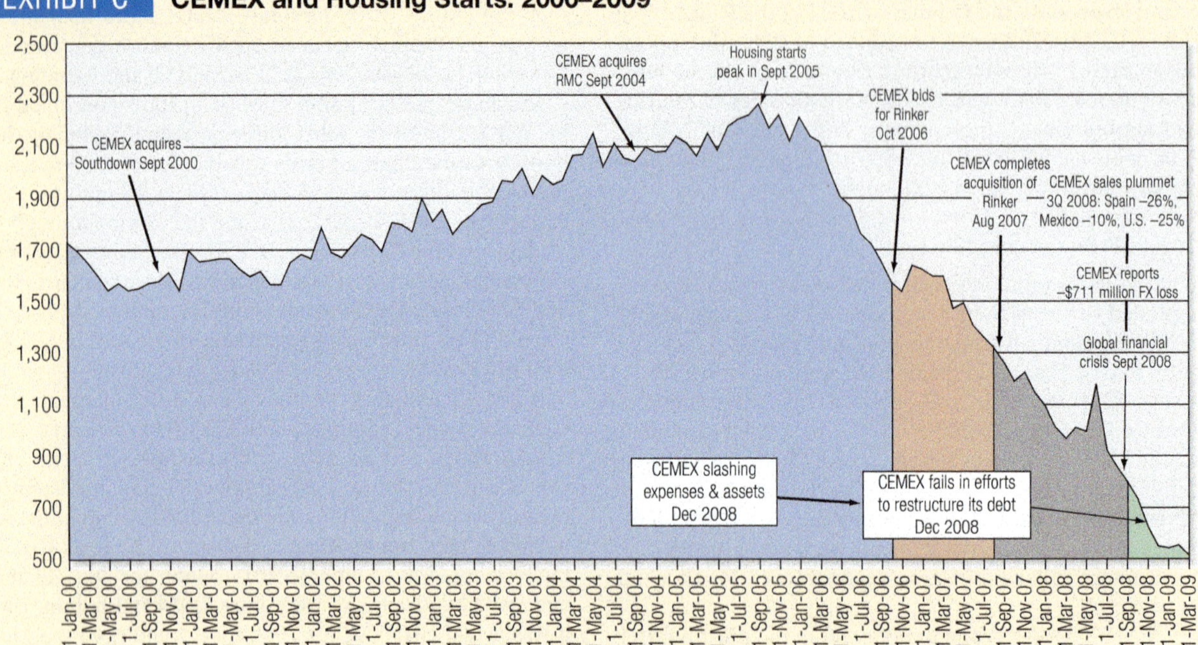

Source: "New Privately Owned Housing Units Authorized by Building Permits in Permit-Issuing Places," U.S. Census Bureau, seasonally adjusted annual rate.

tio combined the total level of *net debt* (outstanding interest-bearing debt less cash) as measured against the core earnings of the firm—EBITDA. As is the case with most financial ratios, there is no one correct value, although smaller is better. CEMEX officially considered a ratio of 2.5 *steady state*.

Prior to the Rinker acquisition, CEMEX had closed 2006 with low levels of debt and a relatively large cash balance, establishing a low Net-Debt-to-EBITDA ratio of 1.44 (all values in billions of U.S. dollars):

$$\frac{\text{Net-Debt}}{\text{EBITDA}} = \frac{\text{Short-Term Debt} + \text{Long-Term Debt} - \text{Cash}}{\text{EBITDA}}$$

$$= \frac{\$1.251 + \$6.289 - \$1.579}{\$4.137} = 1.44$$

The key driver was clear—EBITDA. The greater the core earnings of the firm, and therefore the core cash flow generated, the greater the ability to carry and adequately service more debt. Banks used this same relationship as the basis for estimating the *debt-carrying capacity* of a firm, the amount of debt the business's cash flows could support. This was found by reversing the calculation and solving for debt:

$$\text{Debt capacity} = \text{EBITDA Multiplier} \times \text{EBITDA}$$

EBITDA (credit) multipliers are highly time and industry specific. For manufacturing firms in 2006–2007, an average EBITDA multiplier of 4.0 was deemed appropriate. CEMEX, however, was in the rapidly declining housing and construction sector. Many banks now wished to limit the multiplier to 2.5 or 3.0.

For CEMEX in 2006, with EBITDA of US$4.137 billion and assuming a baseline EBITDA multiplier of 4.0, the company was deemed to have a debt-carrying capacity of US$16.5 billion. Since this was far above its 2006 net debt of US$5.961 billion, its credit rating remained BBB. But with CEMEX's acquisition of Rinker in 2007, things changed dramatically. CEMEX closed 2007 with an EBITDA of US$4.591 billion, better than 2006 but nothing close to what had been forecast when the company had initiated its hostile takeover of Rinker. With US$14 billion of new debt, the company closed 2007 with net debt of US$19.1 billion, above what the banks considered appropriate.

The financial crisis of 2008 sent the housing and construction sectors downward at an ever-increasing rate.

CEMEX's earnings plummeted, hindering its ability to pay down debt as planned. CEMEX's current debt covenants required the company to keep the Net-Debt-to-EBDITA ratio below 2.5. Rinker pushed the Net-Debt-to-EBITDA ratio well over 2.5, but CEMEX was granted a temporary waiver of the covenant by its banks until August 2008. But August came and went without significant improvement.

Credit Rating Downgrade

Zambrano, in response to the growing concerns of creditors, stockholders, and analysts, converted much of the short-term debt to long-term and committed to achieving a Net-Debt-to-EBITDA ratio of 2.7 or lower by the middle of 2009.[4] This added to the complexity of the company's cash flow planning for 2009, as it would have required the company to allocate more of its *free cash flow* (operating cash flow − capex) to debt repayment. Few believed that 2.7 was achievable.

Now at the end of 2008, two of the three major credit rating agencies—Moody's and Fitch—downgraded CEMEX to *speculative grade*, with S&P expected to soon follow. The lowest *investment grade rating* is Baa3 (Moody's) and BBB- (S&P and Fitch). The next rating downward is *speculative grade*, Ba1 (Moody's) and BB + (S&P and Fitch).

Credit rating downgrades had two immediate impacts on corporate borrowers: (1) reduced capital availability to borrowers, as many lenders either reduced their loan offerings or eliminated them; and 2) increased cost in the form of higher interest rates, often accompanied with elimination of fixed rate offers. These forces were amplified when the downgrade was from *investment grade* to *speculative grade.*

Much of CEMEX's existing debt had been floating rate debt, typically priced in U.S. dollars at six-month LIBOR plus a *credit spread*. The *credit spread* reflected CEMEX's perceived credit risk and quality. If CEMEX was indeed downgraded, the spread could increase, but even with that, it might be only 50 basis points (one-half of 1%). One of the more fortunate characteristics of the current financial crisis was that the U.S. Federal Reserve had pumped so much money into the system, interest rates collapsed. Now, at end of year 2008, six-month LIBOR was trading at 2.2165%.

Cash Flow Planning

As anyone facing growing debt obligations knows, the first and foremost priority is *cash flow*: Will the organization have the *cash flow* to service the debt as scheduled? As 2008 came to a close, a review of CEMEX's cash flows for the current year revealed indications of growing financial distress.

In 2008 the company had generated a small net income of US$167 million. Exhibit D illustrates the company's cash flows for 2008. Unfortunately, the dominant sources of cash and operating cash flow in 2008 were depreciation and a reduction in *net working capital* (receivables and inventories less payables). The company still managed US$1.727 billion in capital expenditure.[5] It had also paid down US$1.040 billion in debt and distributed US$0.476 billion in dividends to its stockholders. It partially funded

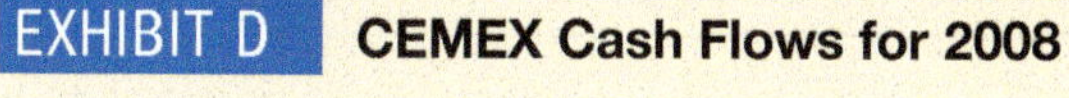
EXHIBIT D **CEMEX Cash Flows for 2008**

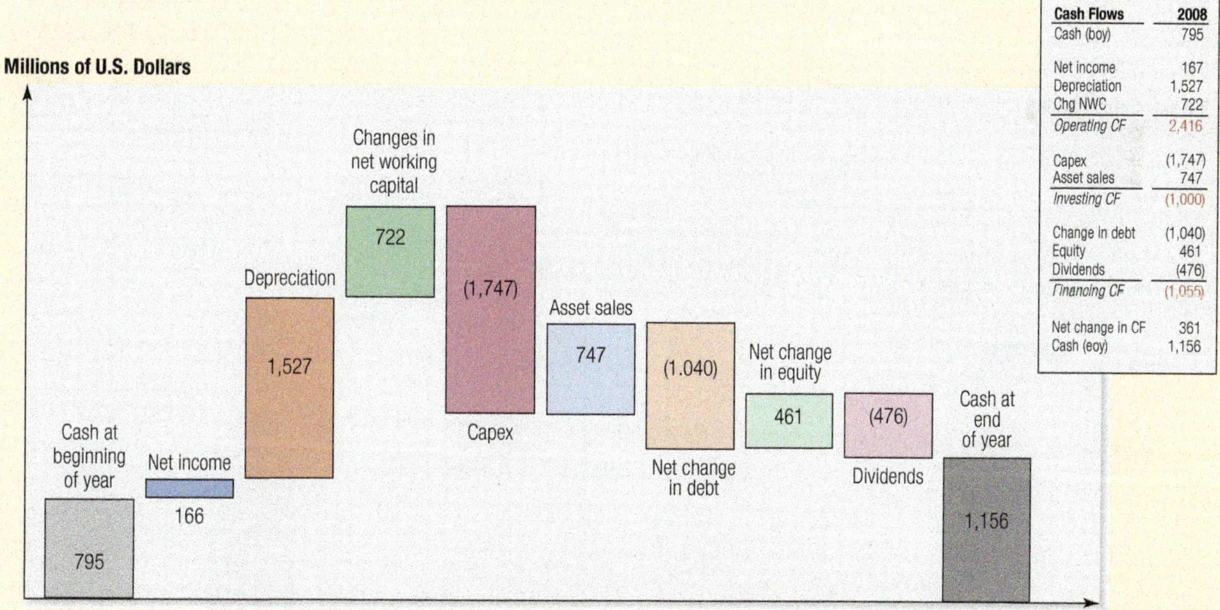

Cash Flows	2008
Cash (boy)	795
Net income	167
Depreciation	1,527
Chg NWC	722
Operating CF	2,416
Capex	(1,747)
Asset sales	747
Investing CF	(1,000)
Change in debt	(1,040)
Equity	461
Dividends	(476)
Financing CF	(1,055)
Net change in CF	361
Cash (eoy)	1,156

[4]"CEMEX Announces Increased Synergies from Rinker Integration," CEMEX Press Release, March 5, 2008.

[5]CEMEX separated capex into two categories, maintenance capex ("investments incurred with the purpose of ensuring the company's operational continuity") and expansion capex. Expansion investments were considered discretionary.

these actions by selling US$0.747 billion in assets and issuing US$0.461 billion in new shares. From end to end, the company's cash balance improved to US$1.156 billion. But 2009 posed new cash flow challenges.

A Financial Plan for 2009

CEMEX was scheduled to repay US$5.5 billion in debt by the end of 2009, US$3 billion of which was due at the end of the calendar year in December. If all values in 2008 were repeated in 2009 (those values shown in Exhibit D but debt repayment was US$5.5 billion as scheduled for 2009, CEMEX was in serious trouble, as illustrated in Exhibit E).

Elements and Alternatives

CEMEX needed a financial plan for 2009 that would allow it to continue to operate and appease its creditors. This meant restructuring the cash flows shown in Exhibit E to survive the year—to end it with a positive cash balance. If that was not possible, it would have to determine what amount of debt repayment was not possible in 2009 and work diligently with its creditors to *refinance* that debt—restructure the obligations so that the amount of repayment due in 2009 was reduced, with the maturity of some part of the total obligation maturing in later years. A successful refinancing plan would be one that found a balance in allowing the company to continue to operate and to continue to service its debt obligations—simultaneously.

CEMEX's first task was to review every cash flow element shown in Exhibits D and E, from net income to dividends, to forecast their value and explore how they might be managed in 2009 to stay solvent.

Net Income. As illustrated previously core earnings (EBITDA) had repeatedly been revised downward for the future. Even with drastic cuts in expenses, 2009 was not expected to be much better than 2008's net income of US$166 million.

Depreciation. Depreciation reflected scheduled deductions from previous year investments. Depreciation had been rising only gradually over time, so 2009 would not be much different. It had averaged US$1.2 billion over recent years but had risen to US$1.5 billion in 2008.

Changes in Net Working Capital (NWC). Net working capital was not a large component of CEMEX's cash flows. The fall in sales in 2008 had contributed to a reduction in NWC and therefore a net cash inflow to the firm, but it was not expected to contribute regularly unless sales continued to fall.

EXHIBIT E **CEMEX Cash Flows in 2009 . . . *if* . . .**

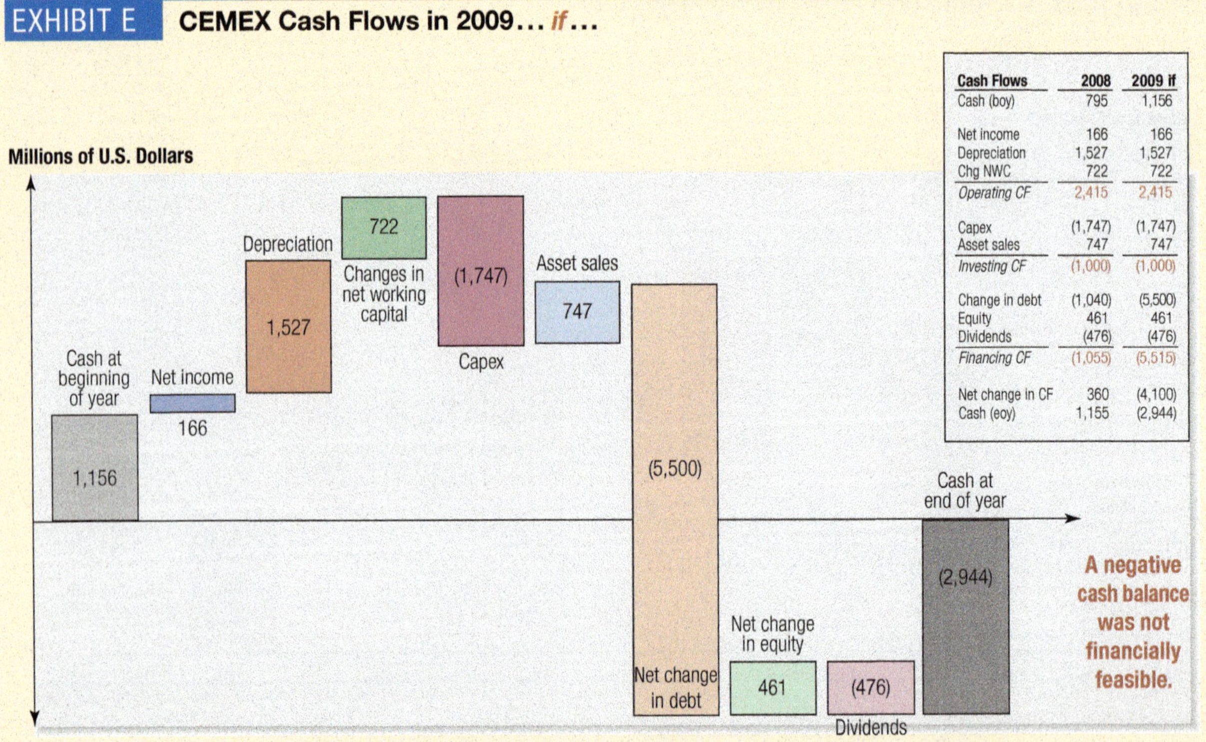

Cash Flows	2008	2009 if
Cash (boy)	795	1,156
Net income	166	166
Depreciation	1,527	1,527
Chg NWC	722	722
Operating CF	2,415	2,415
Capex	(1,747)	(1,747)
Asset sales	747	747
Investing CF	(1,000)	(1,000)
Change in debt	(1,040)	(5,500)
Equity	461	461
Dividends	(476)	(476)
Financing CF	(1,055)	(5,515)
Net change in CF	360	(4,100)
Cash (eoy)	1,155	(2,944)

Capex. There would be no *expansionary capex* in 2009, although anyone with capital would find it a time of plentiful and attractive buying opportunities. *Maintenance capital expenditures*, however, were required to sustain the business. Internally, leadership at CEMEX estimated that the company could get by investing between US$700 million and US$800 million per year for the next year or two.

Asset Sales. Divestment of assets was a common activity by most firms as part of their ongoing business activities. But the sale of assets to raise cash in times of cash shortages meant sacrificing part of the firm's future to survive the present.

CEMEX had already divested a number of units, selling operations in Hungary and Austria to Austria's Strabag (Europe's largest firm) for US$480 million (€310 million). The transaction was still awaiting approval by European Union (EU) authorities. In August 2008, the Venezuelan government had expropriated all of CEMEX's operations in the country. CEMEX had not been alone, as both Holcim and Lafarge, two of its largest global competitors, had also suffered the same fate. But as opposed to CEMEX, they had already agreed upon a settlement price with the Venezuelan government. CEMEX had argued with Venezuela that its operations were worth at least US$1.6 billion, but analysts believed the company would do well to receive US$1 billion. In early December, CEMEX agreed to sell its Canary Islands operations to Spain's Cimpor Inversiones for US$226.8 million (€162 million). It was also still waiting for final regulatory approvals to close the sale.

Additional asset sales in 2009 were possible, but the challenge was receiving *fair market value* for construction material assets during a global recession. This was the worst possible time for selling construction assets. One asset on the potential chopping block was the company's Australian operations, the ready-mix business acquired as part of the Rinker deal. It had never been the true target of the acquisition, and its sale might yield US$400 to US$500 million.

Dividends and Equity Issuance. CEMEX's dividend in 2008 absorbed US$476 million in cash flow, down from over US$608 million in 2007. (The dividend had been cut in the first quarter of the year.) Reducing or eliminating the dividend was always a possibility, but clearly a very unpopular one with shareholders. One alternative in discussion was to replace the *cash dividend* with an *equity share dividend*, where shareholders would receive some proportional additional shares in the company instead of cash.

New equity issuance was also a possibility. CEMEX had consistently issued between US$400 and US$500 million in new equity every year, a common practice in firms of its size growing rapidly. Most of these issuances had been in the form of *rights issues*, where existing shareholders were given the choice of buying new issuances before the public market, allowing them to retain their proportional ownership interest if they desired. Like asset sales, this was not good timing for new equity issuance. Economic conditions were down, construction materials sales were down, and CEMEX's sales and profits were down.

Creditor Interests

Creditors have three basic concerns when working with borrowers experiencing difficult times:

1. **Keep the loan in performing status.** Banks do not want to classify an outstanding loan as *non-performing* and then proceed, as required by law, to start writing down the loan's value. Whatever the debt covenants and repayment requirements, the bank needs to be able to classify the loan as *performing*.
2. **Continue to earn a market rate of interest.** Banks, like all businesses, must earn a risk-adjusted return on their business activities. If a borrower's credit quality has declined, meaning they are now considered riskier, interest payments on the loans should be adjusted to reflect this as would be the case if the borrower went directly to the market now to raise funds.
3. **Have a realistic plan for full repayment.** Banks need to be able to believe in the future business and cash flow prospects of the borrower. Has the borrower put together a strategy and financial plan that seems reasonable and provides adequate cash flow generating potential to repay the debt?

Whatever CEMEX formulated as a financial plan for 2009, it would have to meet creditors' needs.

CEMEX needed a plan for 2009. Hard choices would have to be made, and if the company did not make them soon, the markets—and creditors—might do it for them. Regardless of specific actions taken, one was clearly needed immediately—the renegotiation of the US$5.5 billion due to mature in 2009. It was time to start talking with the bankers.

MINI-CASE QUESTIONS

1. Why do you think CEMEX overpaid for Rinker? What was the result of this overpayment?
2. How had the decline in both CEMEX's and Rinker's operations' EBITDAs altered the debt-carrying capacity of CEMEX?
3. What combination of actions—what plan—would you recommend CEMEX undertake to meet the company's debt service obligations for 2009?

Questions

14.1 **Equity Sourcing Strategy.** Why does the strategic path to sourcing equity start with debt?

14.2 **Optimal Financial Structure.** If the cost of debt is less than the cost of equity, why doesn't the firm's cost of capital continue to decrease with the use of more and more debt?

14.3 **Multinationals and Cash Flow Diversification.** How does the multinational's ability to diversify its cash flows alter its ability to use greater amounts of debt?

14.4 **Foreign Currency Denominated Debt.** How does borrowing in a foreign currency change the risk associated with debt?

14.5 **Three Keys to Global Equity.** What are the three key elements related to raising equity capital in the global marketplace?

14.6 **Global Equity Alternatives.** What are the alternative structures available for raising equity capital on the global market?

14.7 **Directed Public Issues.** What is a directed public issue? What is the purpose of this kind of an international equity issuance?

14.8 **Depositary Receipts.** What is a depositary receipt? What are equity shares listed and issued in foreign equity markets in this form?

14.9 **GDRs, ADRs, and GRSs.** What are the differences among a GDR, ADR, and GRS? How are these differences significant?

14.10 **Sponsored and Unsponsored.** ADRs and GDRs can be sponsored or unsponsored. What does it mean, and will it matter to the investors purchasing the shares?

14.11 **ADR Levels.** Distinguish between the three levels of commitment for ADRs traded in the United States.

14.12 **IPOs and FOs.** What is the significance of IPOs versus FOs?

14.13 **Foreign Equity Listing and Issuance.** Give five reasons why a firm might cross-list and sell its shares on a very liquid stock exchange.

14.14 **Cross-Listing Abroad.** What are the main reasons causing firms to cross-list abroad?

14.15 **Barriers to Cross-Listing.** What are the main barriers to cross-listing abroad?

14.16 **Private Placement.** What is a private placement? What are the comparative pros and cons of private placement versus a public issue?

14.17 **Private Equity.** What is private equity, and how do private equity funds differ from traditional venture capital firms?

14.18 **Bank Loans versus Securitized Debt.** What is the advantage of securitized debt instruments sold on a market versus bank borrowing for multinational corporations?

14.19 **International Debt Instruments.** What are the primary alternative instruments available for raising debt on the international marketplace?

14.20 **Eurobond versus Foreign Bonds.** What is the difference between a eurobond and a foreign bond, and why do two types of international bonds exist?

14.21 **Funding Foreign Subsidiaries.** What are the primary methods of funding foreign subsidiaries, and how do host government concerns affect those choices?

14.22 **Local Norms.** Should foreign subsidiaries of multinational firms conform to the capital structure norms of the host country or to the norms of their parent's country?

14.23 **Internal Financing of Foreign Subsidiaries.** What is the difference between "internal" financing and "external" financing for a subsidiary?

14.24 **External Financing of Foreign Subsidiaries.** What are the primary alternatives for the external financing of a foreign subsidiary?

Problems

14.1 **Lafayette Group (U.S.).** The Lafayette Group, a private equity firm headquartered in Boston, borrows £5,000,000 for one year at 7.375% interest.

a. What is the dollar cost of this debt if the pound depreciates from $2.0260 = £1.00 to $1.9460 = £1.00 over the year?

b. What is the dollar cost of this debt if the pound appreciates from $2.0260 = £1.00 to $2.1640 = £1.00 over the year?

14.2 **Swissie Debt Costs.** The chapter demonstrated that a firm borrowing in a foreign currency could potentially end up paying a very different effective rate of interest than what it expected. Using the same baseline values of a debt principal of CHF1.5 million, a one-year period, an initial spot rate of CHF1.5000 = $1.00, a 5.000% cost of debt, and a 34% tax rate, what is the effective cost of debt for one year for a U.S. dollar-based company if the exchange rate at the end of the period was:

a. CHF1.5000 = $1.00?

b. CHF1.4400 = $1.00?

c. CHF1.3860 = $1.00?

d. CHF1.6240 = $1.00?

14.3 **McDougan Associates (USA).** McDougan Associates, a U.S.-based investment partnership, borrows €80,000,000 at a time when the exchange rate is \$1.3460 = €1.00. The entire principal is to be repaid in three years, and interest is 6.250% per annum, paid annually in euros. The euro is expected to depreciate vis-à-vis the dollar at 3% per annum. What is the effective cost of this loan for McDougan?

14.4 Morning Star Air (China). Morning Star Air, headquartered in Kunming, China, needs US\$25,000,000 for one year to finance working capital. The airline has two alternatives for borrowing:

a. Borrow US\$25,000,000 in eurodollars in London at 7.250% per annum.
b. Borrow HK\$195,000,000 in Hong Kong at 7.00% per annum and exchange these Hong Kong dollars at the present exchange rate of HK\$7.8 = US\$1.00 for U.S. dollars.

At what ending exchange rate would Morning Star Air be indifferent between borrowing U.S. dollars and borrowing Hong Kong dollars?

14.5 Pantheon Capital, S.A. If Pantheon Capital, S.A. is raising funds via a medium-term euronote with the following characteristics, how much in dollars will Pantheon receive for each \$1,000 note sold?

Coupon rate: 8.00% payable semiannually on June 30 and December 31
Date of issuance: February 28, 2011
Maturity: August 31, 2013

14.6 Westminster Insurance Company. Westminster Insurance Company plans to sell \$2,000,000 of eurocommercial paper with a 60-day maturity and discounted to yield 4.60% per annum. What will be the immediate proceeds to Westminster Insurance?

14.7 Styrene Polymers (U.S.). Styrene Polymers, Inc., a U.S. medical plastics manufacturer, has the following debt components in its consolidated capital section. Styrene's finance staff estimates their cost of equity to be 20%. Current exchange rates are also listed below. Income taxes are 30% around the world after allowing for credits. Calculate Styrene's weighted average cost of capital. Are any assumptions implicit in your calculation? Please see the table at the bottom of the page.

14.8 Petrol Ibérico. Petrol Ibérico, a European gas company, is borrowing US\$650 million via a syndicated eurocredit for six years at 80 basis points over LIBOR. LIBOR for the loan will be reset every six months. The funds will be provided by a syndicate of eight leading investment bankers, which will charge up-front fees totaling 1.2% of the principal amount. What is the effective interest cost for the first year if LIBOR is 4.00% for the first six months and 4.20% for the second six months?

14.9 Adamantine Architectonics. Adamantine Architectonics consists of a U.S. parent and wholly owned subsidiaries in Malaysia (A-Malaysia) and Mexico (A-Mexico). Selected portions of their non-consolidated balance sheets, translated into U.S. dollars, are shown in the table on the following page. What are the debt and equity proportions in Adamantine's consolidated balance sheet?

Problem 14.7

Styrene Polymer's Capital Structure

Component	U.S. Dollar Amount	Percent of Total	Pre-Tax Cost (%)	Post-Tax Cost (%)	Weighted Component Cost (%)
25-year U.S. dollar bonds	\$ 10,000,000	____%	6.000%	____%	____%
5-year U.S. dollar euronotes	4,000,000	____%	4.000%	____%	____%
10-year euro bonds	____	____%	5.000%	____%	____%
20-year yen bonds	____	____%	2.000%	____%	____%
Shareholders' equity	50,000,000	____%	20.000%	____%	____%
Total	____	100%		WACC =	____%

Assumption	Value
Tax rate	30.00%
10-year euro bonds (euros)	6,000,000
20-year yen bonds (yen)	750,000,000
Spot rate (\$ = €1.00)	1.2400
Spot rate (\$ = £1.00)	1.8600
Spot rate (¥ = \$1.00)	109.00

Problem 14.9

Assumptions	Value	Assumptions	Value
A-Malaysia (in ringgits):		A-Mexico (in pesos):	
Long-term debt	11,400,000	Long-term debt	20,000,000
Shareholders' equity	15,200,000	Shareholders' equity	60,000,000
Adamantine Architectonics (non-consolidated)			
Investment in subsidiaries (U.S. dollars):		Parent long-term debt	12,000,000
in A-Malaysia	4,000,000	Common stock	5,000,000
in A-Mexico	6,000,000	Retained earnings	20,000,000
Current exchange rates:			
Malaysian ringgit per dollar (RM = $1.00)	3.80		
Mexican pesos per dollar (Ps = $1.00)	10.00		

Petrobras of Brazil: Estimating Its Weighted Average Cost of Capital (WACC)

Petróleo Brasileiro S.A. or Petrobras is the national oil company of Brazil. It is publicly traded, but the government of Brazil holds the controlling share. It is the largest company in the Southern Hemisphere by market capitalization and the largest in all of Latin America. As an oil company, the primary product of its production has a price set on global markets—the price of oil—and much of its business is conducted in the global currency of oil, the U.S. dollar. The following problems examine a variety of different financial institutions' attempts to estimate the company's cost of capital.

14.10 JPMorgan. JPMorgan's Latin American Equity Research department produced the following WACC calculation for Petrobras of Brazil versus Lukoil of Russia. Evaluate the methodology and assumptions used in the calculation. Assume a 28% tax rate for both companies.

	Petrobras	Lukoil
Risk-free rate	4.8%	4.8%
Sovereign risk	7.0%	3.0%
Equity risk premium	4.5%	5.7%
Market cost of equity	16.3%	13.5%
Beta (relevered)	0.87	1.04
Cost of debt	8.4%	6.8%
Debt/capital ratio	0.333	0.475
WACC	14.7%	12.3%

14.11 UNIBANCO. UNIBANCO estimated the weighted average cost of capital for Petrobras to be 13.2% in Brazilian reais. Evaluate the methodology and assumptions used in the calculation.

Risk-free rate	4.5%	Cost of debt (after-tax)	5.7%
Beta	0.99	Tax rate	34%
Market premium	6.0%	Debt/total capital	40%
Country risk premium	5.5%	WACC (R$)	13.2%
Cost of equity (US$)	15.9%		

14.12 Citigroup SmithBarney (Dollar). Citigroup regularly performs a U.S. dollar-based discount cash flow (DCF) valuation of Petrobras in its coverage. That DCF analysis requires the use of a discount rate on which they base the company's weighted average cost of capital. Evaluate the methodology and assumptions used in the estimates of Petrobras WACC (see the following table, continued on next page).

Problem 14.12

	July 28, 2005		March 8, 2005	
Capital Cost Components	**2003A**	**2004E**	**2003A**	**2004E**
Risk-free rate	9.400%	9.400%	9.000%	9.000%
Levered *beta*	1.07	1.09	1.08	1.10
Risk premium	5.500%	5.500%	5.500%	5.500%
Cost of equity	15.285%	15.395%	14.940%	15.050%
Cost of debt	8.400%	8.400%	9.000%	9.000%

	July 28, 2005		March 8, 2005	
Capital Cost Components	**2003A**	**2004E**	**2003A**	**2004E**
Tax rate	28.500%	27.100%	28.500%	27.100%
Cost of debt, after-tax	6.006%	6.124%	6.435%	6.561%
Debt/capital ratio	32.700%	32.400%	32.700%	32.400%
Equity/capital ratio	67.300%	67.600%	67.300%	67.600%
WACC	12.20%	12.30%	12.10%	12.30%

14.13 Citigroup SmithBarney (Reais). Citigroup SmithBarney calculated a WACC for Petrobras denominated in Brazilian reais (R$). Evaluate the methodology and assumptions used in this cost of capital calculation.

Risk-free rate (Brazilian C-Bond)	9.90%
Petrobras levered *beta*	1.40
Market risk premium	5.50%
Cost of equity	17.60%
Cost of debt	10.00%
Brazilian corporate tax rate	34.00%
Long-term debt ratio (% of capital)	50.60%
WACC (R$)	12.00%

14.14 BBVA Investment Bank. BBVA utilized a rather innovative approach to deal with both country and currency risk in their report on Petrobras. Evaluate the methodology and assumptions used in this cost of capital calculation.

14.15 Petrobras WACC Comparison. The various estimates of the cost of capital for Petrobras of Brazil appear to be very different, but are they? Reorganize your answers to Problems 4.11 through 4.15 into those costs of capital in U.S. dollars versus Brazilian reais. Use the estimates for 2004 as the basis of comparison.

14.16 Grupo Modelo S.A.B. de C.V. Grupo Modelo, a brewery out of Mexico that exports such well-known varieties as Corona, Modelo, and Pacifico, is Mexican by incorporation. However, the company evaluates all business results, including financing costs, in U.S. dollars. The company needs to borrow $10 million or the foreign currency equivalent for four years. For all issues, interest is payable once per year, at the end of the year. Available alternatives are as follows:

a. Sell Japanese yen bonds at par yielding 3% per annum. The current exchange rate is ¥106/$, and the yen is expected to strengthen against the dollar by 2% per annum.
b. Sell euro-denominated bonds at par yielding 7% per annum. The current exchange rate is $1.1960/€, and the euro is expected to weaken against the dollar by 2% per annum.
c. Sell U.S. dollar bonds at par yielding 5% per annum.
d. Which course of action do you recommend Grupo Modelo take and why?

15 Multinational Tax Management

Over and over again courts have said that there is nothing sinister in so arranging one's affairs as to keep taxes as low as possible. Everybody does so, rich and poor, and all do right, for nobody owes any public duty to pay more than the law demands: taxes are enforced extractions, not voluntary contributions. To demand more in the name of morals is mere cant.

—Judge Learned Hand, *Commissioner v. Newman*, 159 F.2d 848 (CA-2, 1947).

LEARNING OBJECTIVES

15.1 Explore the tax principles and practice employed by governments around the globe

15.2 Examine how multinational firms, including U.S. firms, manage their global tax liabilities

15.3 Evaluate the relative tax competitiveness of country tax environments

15.4 Describe the U.S. tax law changes that went into effect in January 2018

Multinational companies have many choices as to where they invest, how they structure their multinational operations, and how they financially manage their global businesses. Multinational tax management is a key component in all three areas. Business, and specifically capital, is more mobile and more digital than ever. As a result, countries "compete" with other countries to attract corporate investment. A competitive tax code is one important dimension to a country's competitiveness. But to reassert a principle introduced in Chapter 1, each country's tax regime is different.

Tax planning and management for multinational operations is an extremely complex but vitally important aspect of international business. To plan effectively, multinational firms must understand not only the intricacies of their own operations worldwide but also the different structures and interpretations of tax liabilities across countries. That said, the primary objective of multinational tax planning is very clear: to minimize the firm's worldwide tax burden and, to minimize total taxes paid globally.

This objective, however, must not be pursued without full recognition that decision-making within the firm must always be based on the economic fundamentals of the firm's line of business and not on convoluted policies undertaken purely for the reduction of tax liability. As evident from previous chapters, taxes impact corporate net income and cash flow through their influence on foreign investment decisions, financial structure, cost of capital, foreign exchange management, and financial control.

This chapter provides an overview of how taxes are applied to multinational firms and how those firms manage their global tax liabilities. The first section acquaints the reader with the principles and practices of taxation in its various forms across the world. The second part examines how a multinational firm manages its global tax liabilities, specifically the

U.S.-based multinational. Although our intention is not to make this chapter U.S.-centric, we do need to illustrate how fundamentally different U.S. taxation of multinational corporations is. The third section explores how countries are now competing among themselves to attract global business and investment using taxes. The fourth and final section describes the multitude of U.S. tax law changes that went into effect in 2018. The chapter concludes with the mini-case *The Google Tax*, which explores the controversies surround multinational digital service providers and diverting of profits to low-tax countries, a challenge partially solved by the recent move by the G7 to support a global minimum tax.

15.1 Tax Principles and Practices

The sections that follow explain the most important aspects of the international tax environments and specific features that affect MNEs. Before we explain the specifics of multinational taxation in practice, however, it is necessary to introduce two fundamental tax principles: *tax morality* and *tax neutrality*.

Tax Morality

The MNE faces not only a morass of foreign taxes but also an ethical question. In many countries, taxpayers—corporate or individual—do not voluntarily comply with the tax laws. The decision to comply with tax laws (or not) is termed *tax morality*. Smaller domestic firms and individuals are the chief violators. The MNE must decide whether to follow a practice of full disclosure to tax authorities or adopt the philosophy of "when in Rome, do as the Romans do." Given the local prominence of most foreign subsidiaries, most MNEs follow the full disclosure practice. Some firms, however, believe that their competitive position would be eroded if they did not avoid taxes to the same extent as their domestic competitors. There is obviously no prescriptive answer to the problem, since business ethics are partly a function of cultural heritage and historical development.

A number of global business forces in recent years have combined to increase corporate concerns over tax morality. The growth of the digital economy, the increasing value of intellectual property, and the growing aggressiveness of multinational companies to lower their global tax liabilities have combined to create a debate as to whether multinationals should be more than "compliant." Advocates of corporate social responsibility (detailed previously in Chapter 4) believe MNEs have social or national responsibilities and should be more patriotic or socially responsible to "pay their fair share in taxes." Companies like Google and Apple, although fulfilling all legal requirements of tax law, are increasingly criticized for their aggressive tax minimization strategies. The result in some cases is damage to corporate reputations.

Tax Neutrality

When a government decides to levy a tax, it must consider not only the potential revenue from the tax and how efficiently it can be collected but also the effect the proposed tax can have on private economic behavior. The ideal tax should not only raise revenue efficiently but also have as few negative effects on economic behavior as possible. Some theorists argue that the ideal tax should be completely neutral in its effect on private decisions and completely equitable among taxpayers. This is *tax neutrality*. However, other theorists claim that national policy objectives such as balance of payments or investment in developing countries should be encouraged through an active tax incentive policy, as opposed to requiring taxes to be neutral and equitable. Most tax systems compromise between these two viewpoints.

One way to view neutrality is to require that the burden of taxation on each dollar, euro, pound, or yen of profit earned in home-country operations by an MNE be equal to the burden of taxation on each currency-equivalent of profit earned by the same firm in its foreign operations. This is called *domestic tax neutrality*. A second way to view neutrality is to require that the tax burden on each foreign subsidiary of the firm be equal to the tax burden on its competitors in the same country. This is called *foreign tax neutrality*. The latter interpretation is often supported by MNEs because it focuses more on the competitiveness of the individual firm in individual country markets.

Tax neutrality is not to be confused with tax equity. In theory, an equitable tax is one that imposes the same total tax burden on all taxpayers who are similarly situated and located in the same tax jurisdiction. In the case of foreign investment income, the U.S. Treasury argues that since the U.S. uses the nationality principle to claim tax jurisdiction, U.S.-owned foreign subsidiaries are in the same tax jurisdiction as U.S. domestic subsidiaries. Therefore, a dollar earned in foreign operations should be taxed at the same rate and paid at the same time as a dollar earned in domestic operations.

National Tax Environments

Despite the fundamental objectives of national tax authorities, it is widely agreed that taxes do affect economic decisions made by MNEs. Tax treaties between nations and differential tax structures, rates, and practices all result in a less than level playing field for the MNEs competing on world markets. Different countries use different categorizations of income (e.g., distributed versus undistributed profits) and different tax rates and have radically different tax regimes, all of which drive different global tax management strategies by multinational firms.

Nations structure their tax systems along two basic approaches: the worldwide approach or the territorial approach. Both approaches are attempts to determine which firms, foreign or domestic by incorporation, or which incomes, foreign or domestic in origin, are subject to the taxation of host-country tax authorities.

Worldwide Approach. The *worldwide approach*, also referred to as the *residential approach*, levies taxes on the income earned by firms that are incorporated in the host country, regardless of where the income was earned (domestically or abroad). An MNE earning income both at home and abroad would therefore find its worldwide income taxed by its host-country tax authorities.

The U.S. was a longtime user of the worldwide approach, taxing the income earned by firms based in the U.S. regardless of whether the income earned by the firm was domestically sourced or foreign sourced. Historically, ordinary foreign-sourced income was taxed only as remitted to the parent firm. As with all questions of tax, however, numerous conditions and exceptions exist. The primary problem is that this does not address the income earned by foreign firms operating within the United States. Countries using the worldwide approach then apply the principle of territorial taxation to foreign firms within their legal jurisdiction, taxing all income earned by foreign firms in their country.

Territorial Approach. The *territorial approach*, also termed *source approach*, focuses on the income earned by firms within the legal jurisdiction of the host country, not on the country of firm incorporation. Countries like Germany, which follow the territorial approach, apply taxes equally to foreign or domestic firms on income earned within the country, but in principle not on income earned outside the country. The territorial approach, like the worldwide approach, results in a major gap in coverage if resident firms earn income outside the country but are not taxed by the country in which the profits are earned (operations in a so-called tax haven). In this case, tax authorities extend tax coverage to income earned abroad if it is not currently covered by foreign tax jurisdictions. Once again, a mix of the two tax approaches is necessary for full coverage of income.

Most of the countries within the Organisation for Economic Co-operation and Development (OECD) currently utilize a territorial tax system. There are only a few countries that still use the worldwide approach—Chile, Israel, Korea, and Mexico. The United States, as a result of tax law changes in 2017, moved from worldwide toward territorial (more on that later). The predominance of territorial systems has grown rapidly, as more than half of these same OECD countries used worldwide systems only 10 years ago. In 2009 alone, both Japan and the United Kingdom switched from worldwide to territorial systems. And as we will detail later in this chapter, the countries continuing to use worldwide taxation are considered to have the relatively least competitive tax regimes—for attracting and hosting global business.

Tax Deferral. If the worldwide approach to international taxation were followed to the letter, it would end the tax-deferral privilege for many MNEs. Foreign subsidiaries of MNEs pay host-country corporate income taxes, but many parent countries defer claiming additional income taxes on that foreign-source income until it is remitted to the parent firm—this is called *tax deferral*. For example, U.S. corporate income taxes on some types of foreign-source income of U.S.-owned subsidiaries incorporated abroad are deferred until the earnings are remitted to the U.S. parent. However, the ability to defer corporate income taxes is highly restricted and has been the subject of many of the tax law changes in the past three decades.

Tax Treaties

A network of bilateral tax treaties, many of which are modeled after one proposed by the OECD, provides a means of reducing double taxation. Tax treaties normally define whether taxes are to be imposed on income earned in one country by the nationals of another and, if so, how. Tax treaties are bilateral, with the two signatories specifying what rates are applicable to which types of income between the two countries.

Individual bilateral tax jurisdictions as specified through tax treaties are particularly important for firms that are primarily exporting to another country rather than doing business in that country via a "permanent establishment" (for example, a manufacturing plant). A firm that only exports would not want any of its other worldwide income to be taxed by the importing country. Tax treaties define what is a "permanent establishment" and what constitutes a limited presence for tax purposes. Tax treaties also typically result in reduced withholding tax rates between the two signatory countries.

Controlled Foreign Corporations

One long-standing challenge faced by U.S. tax authorities (and other countries utilizing territorial tax regimes) was that U.S. tax liabilities on foreign source income enjoyed deferral (postponement) until the profits were remitted to the U.S. The problem was that many multinationals restructured the ownership of their foreign subsidiaries, creating subsidiary holding companies in low-tax countries or tax havens. This allowed the profits to be remitted or positioned in a low-tax environment without those profits being remitted to the U.S.

That rule was amended in 1962 for controlled foreign corporations by the creation of special *Subpart F income*. A *controlled foreign corporation* (CFC) is any foreign corporation in which U.S. shareholders, including corporate parents, own more than 50% of the combined voting power or total value.[1] The U.S. parent company therefore "controls" or dictates remittance decisions of the foreign subsidiary. The revision was designed to prevent the use

[1]A *U.S. shareholder* is a U.S. person owning 10% or more of the voting power of a controlled foreign corporation. A U.S. person is a citizen or resident of the United States, a domestic partnership, a domestic corporation, or any non-foreign trust or estate. The required percentages are based on constructive ownership, under which an individual is deemed to own shares registered in the names of other family members, trusts, and so on.

of constructed companies in tax havens as a means of deferring U.S. taxes and to encourage greater repatriation of foreign incomes. The Tax Reform Act of 1986 retained the concept of *Subpart F income* but made a number of changes that expanded categories of income subject to taxation, reduced exceptions, and raised or lowered thresholds.

Under these definitions, a more-than-50%-owned subsidiary of a U.S. corporation would be a controlled foreign corporation (CFC), and the U.S. parent would be taxed on certain undistributed income—Subpart F income—of that CFC. Subpart F income, which is subject to immediate U.S. taxation even when it is not remitted, is income of a type otherwise easily shifted offshore to avoid current taxation. It includes (1) passive income received by the foreign corporation such as dividends, interest, rents, royalties, net foreign currency gains, net commodities gains, and income from the sale of non-income-producing property; (2) income from the insurance of U.S. risks; (3) financial service income; (4) shipping income; (5) oil-related income; and (6) certain related-party sales and service income.

Exhibit 15.1 illustrates the mechanics of how a U.S. corporation attempting to use a financial subsidiary in the British Virgin Islands (one which has no economic function other than to own for tax purposes) would be treated under Subpart F income principles. CFC rules vary across countries, including the definition of what constitutes "control." Where the U.S. defines a foreign company having 50% U.S. ownership to be a CFC, others, for example Australia, consider a foreign company that is 50% controlled by four or fewer Australian residents or 40% controlled by a single Australian resident to be a CFC.

Tax Types

Taxes are classified as *direct taxes* if they are applied directly to income or *indirect taxes* if they are based on some other measurable performance characteristic of the firm.

Direct Taxes. Many governments rely on direct taxes—income taxes, both personal and corporate—for their primary sources of revenue. Corporate income tax rates differ widely across the globe, as illustrated in Exhibit 15.2, and may take a variety of different forms. Some countries, for example, impose different corporate tax rates on distributed income (often

EXHIBIT 15.1 U.S. Taxation of Foreign Source Income and Subpart F

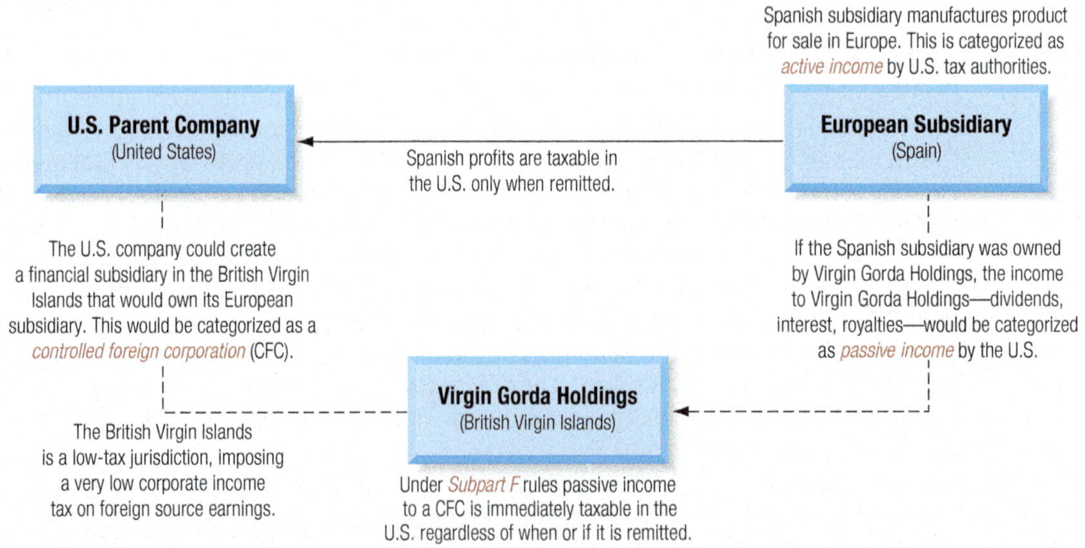

EXHIBIT 15.2 Corporate Tax Rates for Selected Countries—2017

Country	Corporate Tax Rate	Country	Corporate Tax Rate	Country	Corporate Tax Rate
Afghanistan	20%	Ecuador	22%	Lithuania	15%
Albania	15%	Egypt	22.5%	Luxembourg	27.80%
Algeria	26%	El Salvador	30%	Macau	12%
Angola	30%	Estonia	20%	Macedonia	10%
Argentina	35%	Fiji	20%	Malawi	30%
Armenia	20%	Finland	20%	Malaysia	24%
Aruba	25%	France	33.33%	Malta	35%
Australia	30%	Gabon	30%	Mauritius	15%
Austria	25%	Gambia	31%	Mexico	30%
Bahamas	0%	Georgia	15%	Moldova	12%
Bahrain	0%	Ghana	25%	Monaco	33.33%
Bangladesh	25%	Germany	29.79%	Montenegro	9%
Barbados	25%	Gibraltar	10%	Morocco	31%
Belarus	18%	Greece	29%	Mozambique	32%
Belgium	33.99%	Guatemala	25%	Myanmar	25%
Bermuda	0%	Guernsey	0%	Namibia	32%
Bolivia	25%	Honduras	25%	Netherlands	25%
Bonaire, St Eustatius, Saba	25%	Hong Kong	16.5%	New Zealand	28%
Bosnia and Herzegovina	10%	Hungary	9%	Nigeria	30%
Botswana	22%	Iceland	20%	Norway	24%
Brazil	34%	India	30%	Oman	15%
Bulgaria	10%	Iraq	25%	Pakistan	31%
Burundi	30%	Ireland	12.5%	Panama	25%
Cameroon	33%	Isle of Man	0%	Papua New Guinea	30%
Cambodia	20%	Israel	24%	Paraguay	10%
Canada	26.5%	Italy	24%	Peru	29.5%
Cayman Islands	0%	Jamaica	25%	Philippines	30%
Chile	25.5%	Japan	30.86%	Poland	19%
China	25%	Jersey	20%	Portugal	21%
Colombia	34%	Jordan	20%	Qatar	10%
Costa Rica	30%	Kazakhstan	20%	Romania	16%
Croatia	20%	Kenya	30%	Russia	20%
Curacao	22%	Kuwait	15%	Samoa	27%
Cyprus	12.5%	Latvia	15%	Saudi Arabia	20%
Czech Republic	19%	Lebanon	24%	Senegal	30%
Denmark	22%	Libya	20%	Serbia	15%
Dominican Republic	27%	Liechtenstein	12.5%	Sierra Leone	30%

(Continued)

Country	Corporate Tax Rate	Country	Corporate Tax Rate	Country	Corporate Tax Rate
Singapore	17%	Switzerland	17.77%	United Arab Emirates	55%
Slovak Republic	21%	Syria	28%	UK	19%
Slovenia	19%	Taiwan	17%	U.S.	40%
South Africa	28%	Tanzania	30%	Uruguay	25%
South Korea, Republic	22%	Thailand	20%	Vanuatu	0%
Spain	25%	Trinidad & Tobago	25%	Venezuela	34%
Sri Lanka	28%	Tunisia	25%	Vietnam	20%
St Maarten	34.5%	Turkey	20%	Yemen	20%
Sudan	36%	Uganda	30%	Zambia	35%
Sweden	22%	Ukraine	18%	Zimbabwe	25%

Source: KPMG corporate tax rate table, accessed by authors January 9, 2018. https://home.kpmg.com/xx/en/home/services/tax/tax-tools-and-resources/tax-rates-online/corporate-tax-rates-table.html.

lower) versus undistributed income (often higher) in an attempt to motivate companies to distribute greater portions of their income to their owners (who would then pay personal income taxes on those earnings).

Statutory income tax rates—the specific legal income tax rates that companies are expected to pay prior to possible deductions and adjustments—have been declining for more than a decade. That decline, however, now seems to have leveled off. Many governments are now expanding the use of indirect taxes.

These differences reflect a rapidly changing global tax environment. Corporate income taxes have been falling rapidly and widely over the past two decades. On average, the non-OECD countries have relatively lower rates on average. The highly industrialized world, for better or worse, has been reluctant to reduce corporate income tax rates as aggressively as many emerging market nations.

Corporate income tax rates, like any burden on the profitability of commercial enterprise, have become a competitive element used by many countries to promote inward investment from abroad. And if corporate tax rates are indeed an element of competition, as illustrated in Exhibit 15.3, the U.S. was clearly losing this competitive battle until the 2017–2018 tax law change. In 2017 the U.S. had the highest corporate tax rate among the 30 OECD countries shown. (The U.S. rate of 40% results from state and local taxes added to the 35% statutory corporate income tax rate.) With the new U.S. tax rate beginning in 2018 of 21%, it is now one of the lowest tax rate countries.

Another form of direct taxes comes in the form of *withholding taxes. Passive income* (such as dividends, interest, and royalties) earned by a resident of one country within the tax jurisdiction of a second country is normally subject to a withholding tax in the second country. The reason for the institution of withholding taxes is actually quite simple: governments recognize that most international investors will not file a tax return in each country in which they earn income. The government, therefore, wishes to ensure that a minimum tax payment is received. As the term implies, taxes are withheld by the corporation from the payment made to the investor, and those withheld taxes are then turned over to tax authorities. They are the subject of most bilateral tax treaties and generally range between 0% and 25%.

EXHIBIT 15.3 Comparative OECD Corporate Tax Rates

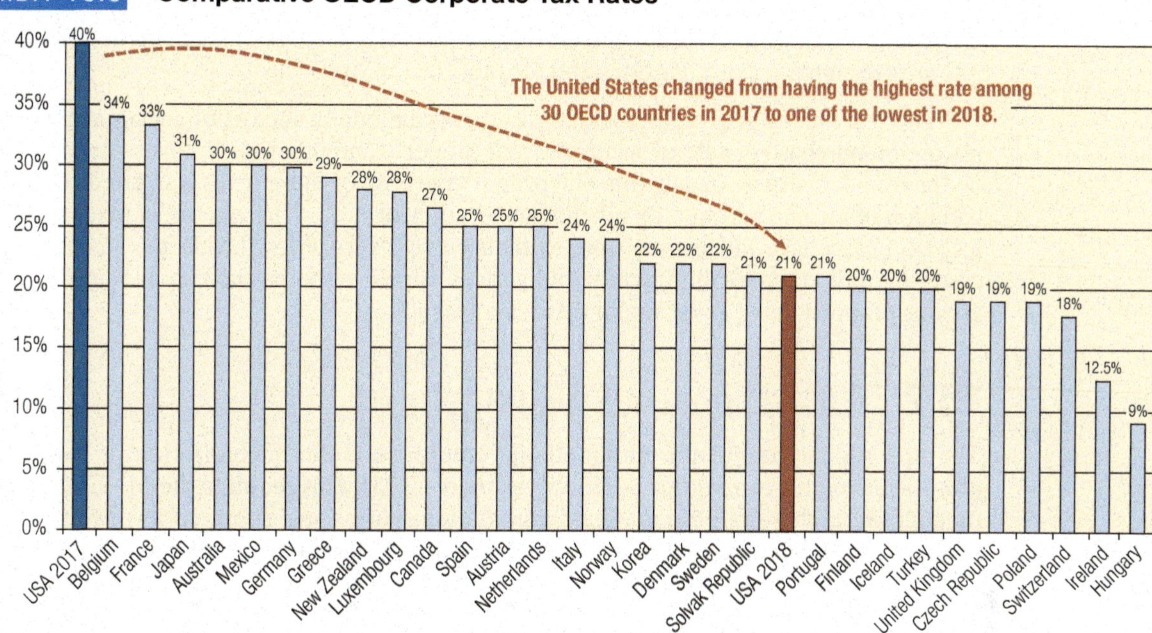

Source: Data drawn from KPMG Corporate tax rate table, January 9, 2018.

Indirect Taxes. Indirect taxes take a variety of different forms and include *value-added tax, goods and service tax, consumption tax, excise duties*, and *custom duties*.

One type of indirect tax that has achieved great prominence is the *value-added tax (VAT)*. The *value-added tax* is a type of national sales tax collected at each stage of production or upon the sale of consumption goods in proportion to the value added during that stage. In general, production goods, such as plant and equipment, have not been subject to the value-added tax. Certain necessities such as medicines and other health-related expenses, education, and religious activities are usually exempt or taxed at lower rates.

The *value-added tax* has been adopted as the main source of revenue from indirect taxation by all members of the European Union (EU), most non-EU countries in Europe, a number of Latin American countries, Canada, and scattered other countries. The U.S. remains one of the few countries that does not impose a VAT, although most states do impose sales taxes. The use of value-added taxes is currently expanding rapidly.

There are a multitude of other indirect taxes, which vary in importance from country to country, including goods and service tax, consumption tax, and a variety of excise taxes.

- *Goods and service tax* (GST) is a value-added tax applied to the sales of most goods and services. In Australia, for example, GST is levied on transactions in the production process but then refunded to all parties in the chain of production other than the final consumer.
- *Consumption taxes* are taxes charged to individuals when they spend money on goods and services. Like GST, it is a tax imposed at the point in time when money is spent rather than earned. Sales taxes in the U.S. are a form of consumption tax. They are usually charged as a percentage of the sale price.
- *Excise taxes* are taxes levied on individual items—*targeted items*—and are often charged as a set money amount on the individual item. Often referred to as *user fees,* excise taxes

on gasoline, cigarettes, trucking, and airline travel are quite common internationally. They may be charged to generate funds to support the underlying activity such as airport operations or highway maintenance. They are also often charged to act as a deterrent to use as taxes imposed on cigarettes and alcohol.

There are many other indirect taxes used internationally, such as financial turnover taxes, tax on the purchase or sale of securities, and property and inheritance taxes—taxes imposed on the transfer of asset ownership. The primary purpose of these taxes is either a social redistribution of income and wealth, revenue generation, or both. Whereas direct taxes (corporate income taxes) have fallen over time to their current record low levels, the same is not the case with indirect taxes. Indirect tax obligations appear to be on the rise and are making up greater proportions of government revenues globally.

15.2 Multinational Tax Management

The operational goal of the multinational enterprise is the maximization of consolidated after-tax income—*earnings* or *earnings per share* (EPS). This requires the MNE to minimize its effective global tax burden. Since multinational firms, incorporated in a worldwide tax country like the United States, are taxed on their worldwide income—and not just their income in-country (territorial taxation)—they will devise and pursue tax structures and strategies to minimize tax payments across all countries in which they operate. This section will focus on these tax management strategies and focuses specifically on strategies employed by U.S. multinational firms.

The following tax structures and strategies are not illegal, but rather may be considered extremely aggressive efforts to reduce tax liabilities—*tax avoidance*. Whereas illegal activities are termed *tax evasion, tax avoidance* is used to describe extremely aggressive strategies and structures used by business to reduce taxes far below what most governments expect. This latter category would include the use of offshore tax havens. The question that remains, however, is whether the MNEs are also pursuing the nonfinancial interests or responsibilities of the firm equitably or ethically.

A number of different strategies, structures, and practices are used for tax avoidance. Most methods are premised on shifting taxable profits to low tax environments while minimizing taxable income in higher tax jurisdictions. We will focus our discussion on five international tax management practices: *allocation of debt, foreign tax credits, transfer pricing, cross-crediting*, and *check-the-box*.

Allocation of Debt and Earnings Stripping

A multinational firm may allocate debt differently across its various foreign subsidiaries to reduce tax liabilities in high tax environments. Units in high tax environments may be assigned very high debt obligations in an attempt to maximize the interest deductibility provisions offered in that country. This is termed *earnings stripping*. This tax tactic is typically limited by host government requirements for minimum equity capitalizations or interest deductibility limits—so-called *thin capitalization* rules.

The U.S. defines *thin capitalization* as anything above a 3:1 debt-to-equity ratio, with net interest exceeding 50% of adjusted taxable income (taxable income plus interest plus depreciation). Interest expenses that exceed 50% paid to a related corporation are not deductible toward U.S. taxes. Unfortunately, this rule has also limited the ability of multinationals to use debt over equity in many cases unrelated to tax.

Foreign Tax Credits and Deferral

To prevent double taxation of the same income, most countries grant a *foreign tax credit* for income taxes paid to the host country. Countries differ on how they calculate the foreign tax credit and what kinds of limitations they place on the total amount claimed. Normally foreign tax credits are also available for withholding taxes paid to other countries on dividends, royalties, interest, and other income remitted to the parent. The value-added tax and other sales taxes are not eligible for a foreign tax credit but are typically deductible from pre-tax income as an expense.

A *tax credit* is a direct reduction of taxes that would otherwise be due and payable. It differs from a *deductible expense*, which is an expense used to reduce taxable income before the tax rate is applied. A \$100 tax credit reduces taxes payable by the full \$100, whereas a \$100 deductible expense reduces taxable income by \$100 and taxes payable by $\$100 \times t$, where t is the tax rate. Tax credits are more valuable on a dollar-for-dollar basis than are deductible expenses.

If there were no credits for foreign taxes paid, sequential taxation by the host government and then by the home government would result in a very high cumulative tax rate. For example, assume the wholly owned foreign subsidiary of an MNE earns \$10,000 before local income taxes and pays a dividend equal to all of its after-tax income. The host-country income tax rate is 30%, and the home country of the parent tax rate is 35%, assuming no withholding taxes. Total taxation with and without tax credits is shown in Exhibit 15.4.

If tax credits are not allowed, sequential levying of both a 30% host-country tax and then a 35% home-country tax on the income that remains results in an effective 54.5% tax (as a percentage of the original before-tax income). Such a high cumulative rate would make many MNEs uncompetitive with local firms. The effect of allowing tax credits is to limit total taxation on the original before-tax income to no more than the highest single rate among jurisdictions.

In the case depicted in Exhibit 15.4, the effective overall tax rate of 35% with foreign tax credits is equivalent to the higher tax rate of the home country (and is the tax rate payable if the income had been earned at home—domestically sourced income). The \$500 of additional home-country tax under the tax credit system in Exhibit 15.4 is the amount needed to bring total taxation (\$3,000 already paid plus the additional \$500) up to but not beyond 35% of the original \$10,000 of before-tax foreign income.

The problem, however, is that if this company repatriates the profits of its foreign businesses to the parent company, it owes more taxes. Period. If it leaves those profits in that foreign country, it enjoys what is referred to as *deferral*—it is able to defer incurring additional parent-country taxes on the foreign-source income until it does repatriate those earnings. As shown in *Global Finance in Practice 15.1*, this has motivated some countries, like the U.S., to periodically provide tax incentives for repatriating profits.

EXHIBIT 15.4 Foreign Tax Credits and the Effective Overall Tax Rate

	Without Foreign Tax Credits	With Foreign Tax Credits
Before-tax foreign income	\$10,000	\$10,000
Less foreign tax @ 30%	(3,000)	(3,000)
Available to parent and paid as dividend	\$7,000	\$7,000
Less additional parent-country tax at 35%	(2,450)	–
Less incremental tax (after credits)	–	(500)
Profit after all taxes	\$4,550	\$6,500
Total taxes, both jurisdictions	\$5,450	\$3,500
Effective overall tax rate (total taxes paid ÷ foreign income)	54.5%	35.0%

GLOBAL FINANCE IN PRACTICE 15.1

Offshore Profits and Dividend Repatriation

U.S.-based multinationals have more than one trillion dollars in un-repatriated profits offshore. Repatriating those profits, given the relatively higher effective corporate income tax rate in the U.S., would trigger significant additional tax charges in the U.S., as was seen in January 2018. But before that, in an effort to facilitate repatriation of those profits in 2004, the U.S. government passed the Homeland Investment Act of 2004. The act provided a window of opportunity in 2005 in which profits could be repatriated with only an additional tax obligation of 5.25%.

The temporary tax law change clearly had the desired impact of stimulating the repatriation of profits, as illustrated in the exhibit. Dividend repatriations skyrocketed in 2005 to over $360 billion from $60 billion the previous year. After the temporary tax revision expired, dividend repatriation fell, returning to the levels seen in the years prior to the tax holiday.

U.S. Dividend Repatriations, 1994–2010 (billions of U.S. dollars)

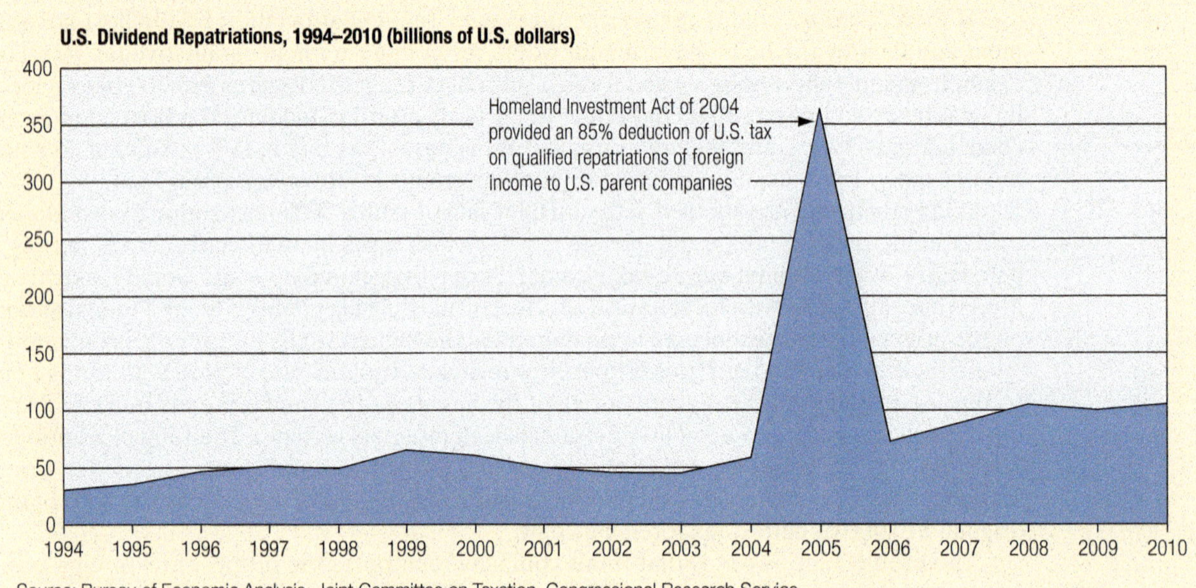

Source: Bureau of Economic Analysis, Joint Committee on Taxation, Congressional Research Service.

Transfer Pricing

The pricing of goods, services, and technology transferred to a foreign subsidiary from an affiliated company—transfer pricing—is the first and foremost method of transferring funds out of a foreign subsidiary. These costs enter directly into the cost of goods sold component of the subsidiary's income statement. This is a particularly sensitive problem for MNEs. Even purely domestic firms find it difficult to reach agreement on the best method for setting prices on transactions between related units. In the multinational case, managers must balance conflicting considerations. These include fund positioning and income taxes.

Fund Positioning Effect. A parent firm wishing to transfer funds out of a particular country can charge higher prices on goods sold to its subsidiary in that country—to the degree that government regulations allow. Payments made by the subsidiary for imports from its parent or from another foreign subsidiary transfer funds out of the subsidiary. A multinational firm can therefore charge a higher transfer price to accumulate funds in the selling country and to lower the funds (profits) remaining in the purchasing country subsidiary. The financing of foreign subsidiaries may also be altered through transfer pricing and fund repositioning. If the parent company lowers transfer prices on goods sold to a subsidiary (again to the degree that government regulations allow), funds are accumulated in the subsidiary. This is effectively a funds transfer from the parent company to the subsidiary.

Income Tax Effect. A major consideration in setting a transfer price is the *income tax effect.* The firm's global profits can be influenced when transfer prices are set to minimize taxable income in a country with a high income tax rate and to maximize taxable income in a country with a low income tax rate. A parent wishing to reduce the taxable profits of a subsidiary in a high-tax environment may set transfer prices at a higher point to increase the costs of the subsidiary, thereby reducing taxable income.

The income tax effect is illustrated in the hypothetical example presented in Exhibit 15.5. Ganado Europe is operating in a relatively high-tax environment, assuming German corporate income taxes of 45%. Ganado U.S. is in a significantly lower tax environment, assuming a U.S. corporate income tax rate of 35%, motivating Ganado to charge Ganado Europe a higher transfer price on goods produced in the U.S. and sold to Ganado Europe.

If Ganado Corporation adopts a high-markup policy by "selling" its merchandise at an intracompany sales price of $1,700,000, the same $800,000 of pre-tax consolidated income is allocated more heavily to low-tax Ganado U.S. and less heavily to high-tax Ganado Europe. (Note that it is Ganado Corporation, the corporate parent, that must adopt a transfer pricing policy that directly alters the profitability of each of the individual subsidiaries, not the

EXHIBIT 15.5 Transfer Price Impact on Ganado Europe's Net Income

Thousands of U.S. Dollars		Ganado U.S. (a Subsidiary)			Ganado Europe (a Subsidiary)	Europe and U.S. Combined
Low-Markup Policy						
Sales		$1,400	→		$2,000	$2,000
Less cost of goods sold		(1,000)	*Ganado U.S. sales price becomes cost of goods sold for Ganado Europe*		(1,400)	(1,000)
Gross profit		$ 400			$ 600	$1,000
Less operating expenses		(100)			(100)	(200)
Taxable income		$ 300			$ 500	$ 800
Less income taxes	35%	(105)		45%	(225)	(330)
Net income		$ 195			$ 275	$ 470
High-Markup Policy						
Sales		$1,700	→		$2,000	$2,000
Less cost of goods sold		(1,000)	*Ganado U.S. sales price becomes cost of goods sold for Ganado Europe*		(1,700)	(1,000)
Gross profit		$ 700			$ 300	$1,000
Less operating expenses		(100)			(100)	(200)
Taxable income		$ 600			$ 200	$ 800
Less income taxes	35%	(210)		45%	(90)	(300)
Net income		$ 390			$ 110	$ 500

subsidiary itself.) As a consequence, total taxes drop by $30,000, and consolidated net income increases by $30,000 to $500,000, all while total sales remain constant.

Ganado would naturally prefer the high-markup policy for sales from the United States to Europe. Needless to say, government tax authorities are aware of the potential income distortion from transfer price manipulation. A variety of regulations exist on the reasonableness of transfer prices, including fees and royalties as well as prices set for merchandise. Government taxing authorities obviously have the right to reject transfer prices deemed inappropriate.

U.S. IRS regulations provide three methods to establish arm's length prices: *comparable uncontrolled prices, resale prices*, and *cost-plus calculations*. All three of these methods are recommended for use in member countries by the OECD Committee on Fiscal Affairs and in some cases a combination of all three.

Section 482 of the U.S. Internal Revenue Code is typical of laws covering transfer prices. Under this authority, the IRS can reallocate gross income, deductions, credits, or allowances between related corporations in order to prevent tax evasion or to more clearly reflect a proper allocation of income. The burden of proof is on the taxpaying firm to show that the IRS has been arbitrary or unreasonable in reallocating income. This "guilty until proved innocent" approach means that MNEs must keep good documentation of the logic and costs behind their transfer prices. The "correct price" according to the guidelines is the one that reflects an *arm's length price*—a sale of the same goods or service to a comparable unrelated customer.

Managerial Incentives and Evaluation. When a firm is organized with decentralized profit centers, transfer pricing between centers can disrupt evaluation of managerial performance. This problem is not unique to MNEs; it is also a controversial issue in the "centralization versus decentralization" debate in domestic circles. In the domestic case, however, a modicum of coordination at the corporate level can alleviate some of the distortion that occurs when any profit center suboptimizes its profit for the corporate good. Also, in most domestic cases, the company can file a single (for that country) consolidated tax return, so the issue of cost allocation between affiliates is not critical from a tax-payment point of view.

For the multinational, coordination is often hindered by less-efficient channels of communication, the need to consider the unique variables that influence international pricing, and separate taxation. Even with the best of intent, a manager in one country finds it difficult to know what is best for the firm as a whole when buying at a negotiated price from related companies in another country. If corporate headquarters establish transfer prices and sourcing alternatives, one of the main advantages of a decentralized profit center system disappears: local management loses the incentive to act for its own benefit.

Exhibit 15.5 illustrated a transfer pricing example where an increase in the transfer price led to a worldwide income gain: Ganado Corporation's income rose by $195,000 (from $195,000 to $390,000) while Ganado Europe's income fell by only $165,000 (from $275,000 to $110,000) for a net gain of $30,000. Should the managers of the European subsidiary lose their bonuses (or their jobs) because of their "subpar" performance? Bonuses are usually determined by a company-wide formula based in part on the profitability of individual subsidiaries, but in this case, Ganado Europe "sacrificed" for the greater good of the whole.

Strategic transfer pricing manipulation can create measurement challenges. Transferring profit from high-tax Ganado Europe to low-tax Ganado Corporation in the U.S. affects a multitude of cash flows and performance metrics for one or both companies:

- Import tariffs paid to individual countries
- Measurements of foreign exchange exposure
- Liquidity tests, such as the current ratio, receivables turnover, and inventory turnover
- Operating efficiency as measured by the ratio of gross profit to either sales or to total assets
- Income tax payments to individual countries
- Profitability as measured by the ratio of net income to either sales or capital invested
- Dividend payout ratio as net income changes
- Internal growth rate as measured by the ratio of retained earnings to existing ownership equity

Effect on Joint-Venture Partners. Joint ventures pose a special problem in transfer pricing because serving the interest of local stockholders by maximizing local profit may be suboptimal from the overall viewpoint of the MNE. Often, the conflicting interests are irreconcilable. Indeed, the local joint-venture partner could be viewed as a potential "Trojan horse" if they complain to local authorities about the transfer pricing policy.

Cross-Crediting

One of the most valuable management methods available to companies in a worldwide tax system like that of the United States is the ability to *cross-credit* foreign tax credits with foreign tax deficits in the same period. Say a U.S. multinational remits profits from two different countries—one in a high-tax environment (relative to the U.S.) and the other in low-tax environment (relative to the U.S.). If the income is from one of the two major "baskets" of foreign source income (active or passive), the excess foreign tax credits from one can be cross-credited against the foreign tax deficits of the other.

Exhibit 15.6 summarizes how our U.S.-based multinational, Ganado, may manage dividend remittances from two of its foreign subsidiaries using cross-crediting. Ganado's dividend remittances from its two foreign subsidiaries create two different and offsetting tax credit positions.

- Because corporate income tax rates in Germany (40%) are higher than those in the United States (35%), dividends remitted to the U.S. parent from Ganado Germany result in *excess foreign tax credits*. Any applicable withholding taxes on dividends between Germany and the U.S. only increase the amount of the excess credit.
- Because corporate income tax rates in Brazil (25%) are lower than those in the United States (35%), dividends remitted to the U.S. parent from Ganado Brazil result in *deficit foreign tax credits*. If Brazil applies withholding taxes to the dividends remittances to the United States, this will reduce the size of the deficit but not eliminate it.

Ganado's management would like to manage the two dividend remittances in order to match the deficits with the credits. The most straightforward method of doing this would be to adjust the amount of dividend distributed from each foreign subsidiary so that, after all applicable income and withholding taxes have been applied, Ganado's excess foreign tax credits from Ganado Germany exactly match the excess foreign tax deficits from Ganado Brazil. There are several other methods of managing the global tax liabilities of Ganado. These include so-called repositioning of funds, by which firms strive to structure global operations to record their profits in a low-tax environment, as shown in the mini-case on *The Google Tax* at the end of this chapter.

EXHIBIT 15.6 **Ganado's Cross-Crediting of Foreign Tax Credits**

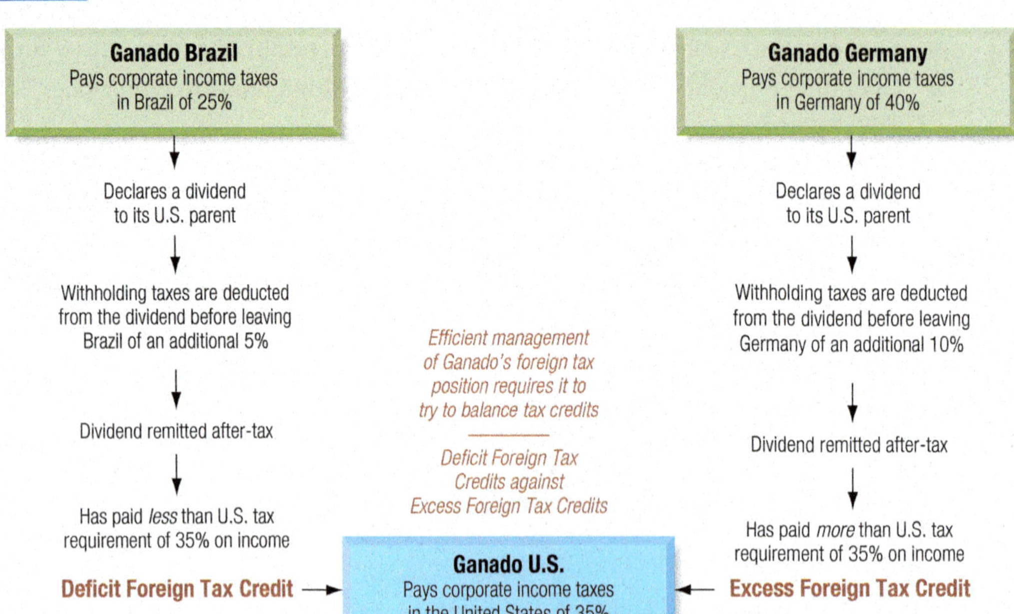

Note: Ganado pays taxes to the U.S. government separately on domestic-source income and foreign-source income.

Check-the-Box and Hybrid Entities

The U.S. Treasury's attempt to stop the repositioning of profits by U.S.-based multinationals in low-tax jurisdictions took a major step backward in 1997 when Treasury introduced what is called *check-the-box* subsidiary characterization. In an attempt to allow simplification of taxation, the U.S. Treasury changed its required filing practices to allow multinational firms to categorize subsidiaries for taxation purposes by simply "checking the box" on a single form.

One of the box choices offered, a *disregarded entity*, allowed the unit to "disappear" for tax purposes, as its results would be consolidated with those of its parent company. These combined units are termed *hybrid entities*. In the end, it allowed U.S. multinationals that have tiered ownership of offshore units to once again begin repositioning profits in low-tax environments and gain essentially permanent deferral for those earnings. In 2007, the U.S. Treasury codified this process in what is now referred to as the look-through-rules on this tax treatment of disregarded entities.

Tax Havens and International Offshore Financial Centers

Many MNEs have foreign subsidiaries that act as tax havens for corporate funds awaiting reinvestment or repatriation. Tax-haven subsidiaries, categorically referred to as *international offshore financial centers*, are partially a result of tax-deferral features on earned foreign income allowed by some of the parent countries. Exhibit 15.7 provides a map of most of the world's major offshore financial centers.

EXHIBIT 15.7 **International Offshore Financial Centers**

Tax-haven subsidiaries are typically established in a country that can meet the following requirements:

- A low tax on foreign investment or sales income earned by resident corporations and a low dividend withholding tax on dividends paid to the parent firm.
- A stable currency that allows easy conversion of funds into and out of the local currency. This requirement can be met by permitting and facilitating the use of eurocurrencies.
- The facilities to support financial services; for example, good communications, professional qualified office workers, and reputable banking services.
- A stable government that encourages the establishment of foreign-owned financial and service facilities within its borders.

The typical tax-haven subsidiary owns the common stock of its related operating foreign subsidiaries. There might be several tax-haven subsidiaries scattered around the world. The tax-haven subsidiary's equity is typically 100% owned by the parent firm. All transfers of funds might go through the tax-haven subsidiaries, including dividends and equity financing. Thus, the parent country's tax on foreign-source income, which might normally be paid when a dividend is declared by a foreign subsidiary, could continue to be deferred until the tax-haven subsidiary itself pays a dividend to the parent firm. This event can be postponed indefinitely if foreign operations continue to grow and require new internal financing from the tax-haven subsidiary. Thus, MNEs are able to operate a corporate pool of funds for foreign operations without having to repatriate foreign earnings through the parent country's tax machine.

For U.S. MNEs, the tax-deferral privilege enjoyed by foreign subsidiaries (it is considered a privilege because they do not pay tax on the foreign income until they remit dividends back to the parent company) was not originally a tax loophole. On the contrary, it was granted by the U.S. government to allow U.S. firms to expand overseas and to place those firms on even footing with foreign competitors, which also enjoy similar types of tax deferral and export subsidies of one type or another.

Unfortunately, some firms distorted the original intent of tax deferral into tax evasion. Transfer prices on goods and services bought from or sold to foreign affiliates were artificially rigged to leave all the income from the transaction in the tax-haven subsidiary. This manipulation was accomplished by routing the legal title to the goods or services through the tax-haven subsidiary, even though physically the goods or services never entered the tax-haven country. One purpose of the U.S. Internal Revenue Act of 1962 was to eliminate the tax advantages of these "paper" foreign corporations without destroying the tax-deferral privilege for those foreign subsidiaries that were established for business and economic motives rather than tax motives. A number of tax law changes in the 1990s gave new life to these offshore financial centers.

Basis Erosion and Profit Shifting (BEPS)

The increasingly aggressive structures and strategies used by multinational firms all over the world to avoid or delay paying taxes has led to a call by the finance ministers of the G20 in conjunction with the OECD to create an action plan to stop *basis erosion and profit shifting* (BEPS). This is not an effort to stop illegal activity—for most of the repositioning of profits and reduction in tax liabilities in total is legal—but to explore new initiatives to change tax laws and practices globally to reassert taxing powers.

The debate that has raged in recent years about Amazon, Apple, Microsoft, and many other multinational companies is that they are generating massive profits around the world and often paying few corporate income taxes—anywhere to anyone. All the while many other multinationals continue to pay effective tax rates in the high 20s to low 30s (percentage of consolidated pre-tax income). If that is indeed the case, it is not a level playing field, and one that many traditional manufacturers who cannot move their products and property digitally around the globe feel is biased against them.

Corporate Inversion

These expropriations aren't illegal. But they're sure immoral.

—Senator Charles E. Grassley, U.S. Senate Committee on Finance, 2002.

In a *corporate inversion*, a company changes its country of incorporation. The purpose is to reduce effective global tax liabilities by reincorporating in a lower-tax jurisdiction, typically a country using a territorial tax regime. Although the company's operations may be completely unchanged and its corporate headquarters may remain in the original country of incorporation, it will now have a new corporate home, and its old country of incorporation will now be only one of many countries in which the firm operates foreign subsidiaries.

The typical transaction is one in which a U.S. corporation and its foreign subsidiary in another country, like Bermuda, exchange ownership shares. As a result of the exchange, the U.S. company becomes the U.S. subsidiary of a Bermudian corporation. There is no change in the control of the corporation, only its place of incorporation. This is colloquially referred to as a "naked inversion." Such inversions enjoyed a short period of popularity in the late 1990s and early 2000s (Ingersoll Rand, Tyco, Foster Wheeler, and others successfully reincorporated outside the U.S.), but after one particularly tumultuous attempt—that of Stanley Works in 2002, which was not completed—the U.S. passed the American Jobs Creation Act (AJCA) of 2004, which altered the rules governing inversions in two important ways:

1. If the new foreign parent corporation is still 80% or more owned and controlled by the former parent company's stockholders, the company would continue to be treated as a domestic or U.S. incorporated company. This means that it would continue to be taxed on its worldwide income, and its U.S. "subsidiary" would be treated as its effective parent company. This is referred to as the *80% rule*.
2. If the new foreign parent corporation is still at least 60% controlled by former parent company shareholders but less than 80%, the new company is not allowed any tax credits on gains (toll taxes) on the legal transfer of assets from the old company to the new. This made many naked inversions financially unattractive, even when there was a substantial change in ownership structure.

Today there are three basic types of corporate inversions in use: the *substantial business presence, merger with a larger foreign firm*, and *merger with a smaller foreign firm*.

Substantial Business Presence. Elements of the AJCA addressing corporate inversions are specifically structured to stop corporate inversions undertaken purely for tax reduction purposes. The act, however, does not hinder inversions when the reincorporation takes place in a country in which the company does indeed have a "substantial business presence," defined as the company having 25% of its assets, income, and employees in the country to which it is moving. This will, therefore, rarely include a traditional tax haven.

Merger with a Larger Foreign Firm. The second major form of inversion is when a U.S. company is merged with a large foreign firm and the new combined entity is incorporated in the foreign country. The added stipulation is that the previous U.S. ownership must have a minority position (less than 50% ownership) in the new combined entity. One high-profile example of this was the combination of two major deep-water oil drilling firms, Pride (U.S.) with Ensco (UK) in 2011.

Merger with a Smaller Foreign Firm. The third form of corporate inversion is when a U.S. corporation merges with a smaller foreign firm, often one incorporated in Ireland, the UK, or Luxembourg. The control of the newly created company remains with the previous U.S. stockholders, so it does not fulfill the 80% rule. However, because the new corporate home is still often a low-tax jurisdiction, the ability of the U.S. to impose worldwide tax principles to the new firm is limited. Combining Easton (U.S.) and Cooper Industries (Ireland) in 2012, thereby creating a new Irish corporation, is one such example.

The rapid evolution of corporate inversions for U.S.-based multinationals over the past 20 years has heightened the awareness of the relatively high U.S. corporate tax rates, including its worldwide regime, and corporate concerns over global competitiveness. That more inversions are resulting in movements of newly merged incorporations to other major developed countries like Ireland and not to tax havens like Bermuda, the Cayman Islands, or the Bahamas has increased tensions over worldwide treaty shopping and political debate over a corporate race to the bottom of the corporate tax environment. The merger between Applied Materials (U.S.) and Tokyo Electron (Japan) in 2013, in which the two merged and reincorporated in the Netherlands, is one such complex example. The debate came to a head in late 2015 when the U.S. government moved aggressively to halt the $150 billion merger of Pfizer (U.S.) and Allergan (Ireland), imposing new rules that made it impossible for Pfizer to be considered a foreign company after the merger.

As long as there are taxes there will be tax reduction strategies. The mini-case at the end of this chapter examines the famous or infamous Google tax structure employed for many years. *Global Finance in Practice 15.2* describes yet another aggressive tax strategy, this one based on intra-company loans and cash balances.

GLOBAL FINANCE IN PRACTICE 15.2

HP's Offshore Cash and Staggered Loan Program

The U.S. worldwide corporate tax regime has motivated a number of aggressive structures and strategies to avoid paying additional U.S. taxes on foreign source income. U.S. tax law has traditionally allowed deferral of U.S. tax liabilities on foreign source income until it is repatriated to the U.S. This often resulted in large growing cash balances offshore, as the profits of foreign subsidiaries are held offshore.

One early strategy utilized by U.S. multinationals was to have a company's own foreign subsidiaries loan the parent company—in the U.S.—money. Initially these were extremely long maturities with very favorable interest rates. U.S. tax authorities concluded that these were, in effect, dividends. Section 956 of the U.S. Tax Code expressly prohibited these long-term loans being considered loans for tax purposes. They were re-designated as dividends, with associated U.S. tax liabilities, as if repatriated.

Hewlett-Packard Company (U.S.) was one of these U.S. multinationals with accumulating cash offshore, cash that was badly needed to fund U.S. operations. HP's cash was held in two specific subsidiaries, HP's Belgium Coordination Center (BCC), a clearing bank for all European operations, and Compaq Cayman Holding Corporation (CCHC), a financial subsidiary in the Cayman Islands used for collecting offshore profits from rest of world operations. (CCHC was acquired when HP acquired Compaq Computer in 2001.) Both were classified as *controlled foreign corporations*, or CFCs.

For more than a decade HP pursued an aggressive "staggered loan program" using these offshore cash balances. One foreign subsidiary, say CCHC (Cayman Islands), would loan HP U.S. billions of dollars in funds for a 45-day period. On that loan's maturity date, BCC (Belgium Center) would make a similar loan to HP U.S., the proceeds of which were to repay the other loan. As seen here, this resulted in a continuous simulated long-term alternating loan of offshore profits to HP without paying additional U.S. taxes. As long as the two financial subsidiaries and their loan programs were held separate and the loans were initiated and repaid before the end of the CFC's quarterly reporting period, they were considered conforming by HP's auditor and U.S. tax authorities. (HP had set the fiscal quarters for the two CFCs to be overlapping in order to conform.) During this period the staggered loan program provided nearly all of the debt financing required by all of HP's U.S. operations.

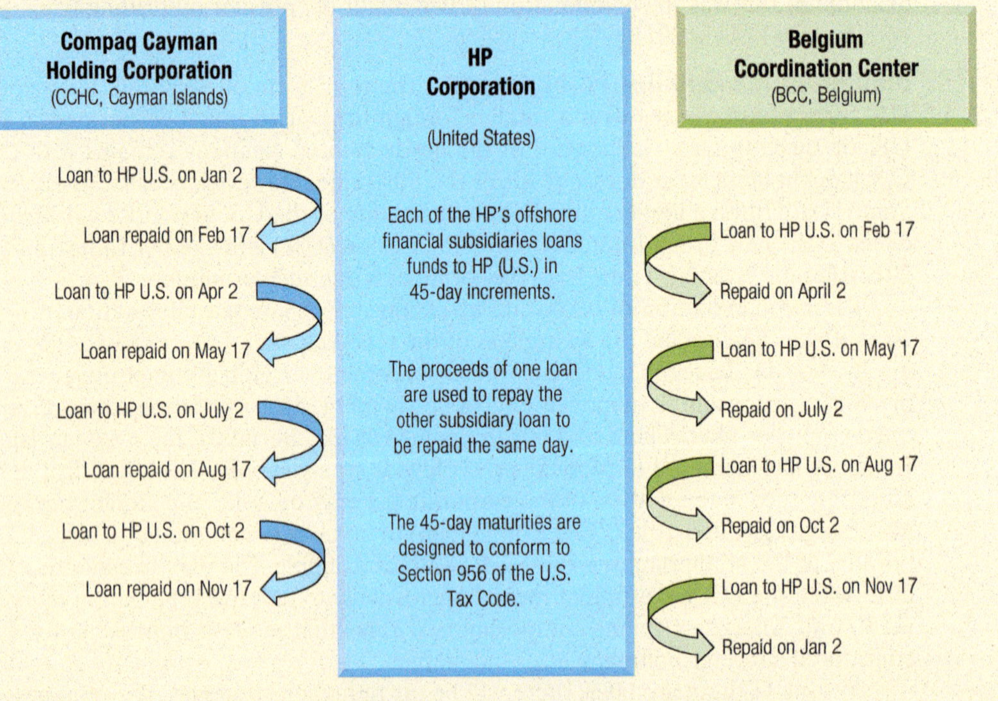

15.3 Global Tax Competitiveness

There are three distinct forces changing the global tax environment today for multinational firms. The first force is the rapid expansion of the global digital economy, requiring a redefinition of how and where a taxable event occurs. The second force is aggressive actions taken by many governments globally to increase their individual tax competitiveness to attract foreign investment. Third, and finally, many of these same governments are scrambling to replace or increase their tax *takes* from the same multinational business taxes affected by the first two forces.

The Digital Economy

Concerns over tax morality have recently become more multinational in context as the digital economy has pushed the boundaries of tax laws and tax authorities. Digital commerce has challenged the traditional definition of where—in what tax environment—a taxable transaction takes place. A traditional manufacturing activity is physically defined, and where the production and value creation process take place is observable. Digital services, however, are less easily defined.

Google's business in Great Britain serves as one example. Google's primary operations in Great Britain are located in Ireland, a low-tax environment, but much of its business is made up of customers in England, a relatively higher tax environment. A Google "consultant" will visit potential customers in London and aid in their understanding of Google's services. The customer will then go online, connecting with Google's operations in Ireland, to purchase desired services. The services are purchased from an Irish business, subject to Irish taxes. Through this structure Google generated hundreds of millions of dollars in business in England while generating few English tax liabilities—much to the chagrin of English tax authorities. As a result, many tax authorities are redefining the location of a taxable transaction from the country of the supplier to the country of the buyer. On January 1, 2015, the European Union implemented new value-added tax rules for business-to-customer (B2C) business services to make services taxable in the country of residence of the customer.

Country Tax Competitiveness

> *My advice to this committee is straightforward: lower the corporate rate as much as you can, make the tax base as broad as you can, and move to a territorial system as quickly as you can.*
>
> —Mike Duke, Walmart CFO, Testimony to Senate Finance Committee, July 26, 2011.

The global economy today is characterized by mobility and competitiveness. And in an economy when "healthy" corporate profits may be only 8% or 9% of sales and country corporate tax rates vary between 12% and 40% of earnings before tax, "tax shopping" is a very real practice. Governments worldwide are very aware that they compete for global investment on many grounds—availability of skilled labor, labor cost, infrastructure, regulatory requirements, to name a few—and they also know that a competitive tax code can be critically important. As a result, countries with few exceptions have continued to reduce corporate tax rates for more than three decades. Yet differences remain, and as illustrated by Exhibit 15.8, a territorial tax regime (e.g., Chile or Mexico) is clearly a burden.

Governments and Tax Sources

Governments do not tax people and companies out of spite—they need the money. Tax revenues are the primary source of revenue and cash flow for governments globally to fund their activities. And needless to say, there is never enough to go around.

EXHIBIT 15.8 Competitive International Tax Scores, OECD

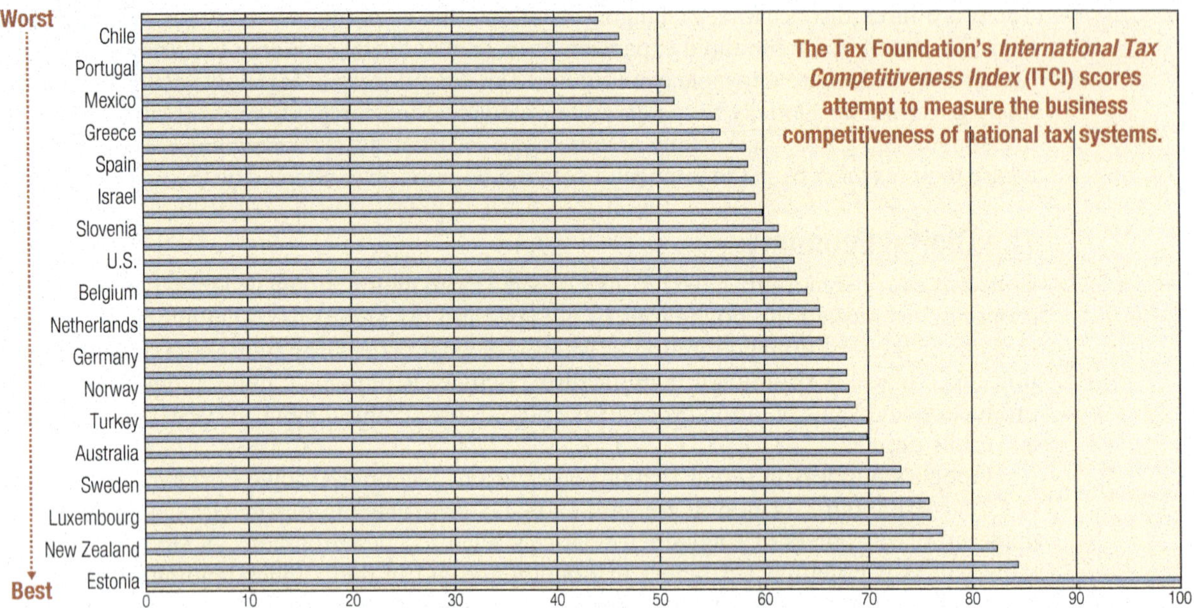

Source: Data drawn from ***International Tax Competitiveness Index*** 2020, Tax Foundation, p.3. Scores shown are the overall ranking, including individual index scores on corporate, consumption, property, individual, and international.

But different countries generate their tax revenues very differently. For example, the United States depends on individual income taxes for a very large part of its tax proceeds, while many less-developed countries do not impose personal income taxes (primarily because of the difficulty of reporting and collection—some countries do not have an effective census of their people).

Exhibit 15.9 provides a comparison of the U.S. and the average sources of tax revenue for the OECD countries. Whereas the U.S. depends on individual taxes for 37.7% of its tax revenues, the OECD averages only 24.5% and depends heavily on consumption taxes (VAT) for 32.8% of tax revenues. In both cases, however, corporate taxes—the focus of this chapter—surprisingly serve as only a minor source of tax revenue for both entities. Global tax analysts and authorities, however, all agree that in the years ahead, most of the world will move toward increased use of indirect taxes, like consumption taxes.

15.4 U.S. Tax Law Change in 2017–2018

Highlights include... Fundamental changes to the taxation of multinational entities, including a shift from the current system of worldwide taxation with deferral to a hybrid territorial system, featuring a participation exemption regime with current taxation of certain foreign income, a minimum tax on low-taxed foreign earnings, and new measures to deter base erosion and promote U.S. production.

—"New Tax Law (H.R.1)—Initial Observations," December 22, 2017, kpmg.com, p. 1.

EXHIBIT 15.9 Sources of Tax Revenue for Selected OECD Countries

Tax Source	Australia	Canada	Chile	Denmark	Japan	Mexico	U.S.	OECD Avg
Individual taxes	41.0%	36.3%	7.3%	54.0%	18.9%	19.7%	39.3%	24.0%
Corporate taxes	16.8%	10.5%	21.3%	5.3%	12.9%	16.9%	8.4%	8.8%
Social insurance taxes	0.0%	15.1%	7.2%	0.1%	39.7%	20.6%	24.1%	26.2%
Property taxes	10.1%	11.7%	4.2%	3.7%	8.5%	2.1%	10.8%	5.6%
Consumption taxes	26.9%	23.0%	55.3%	30.2%	19.8%	35.8%	17.4%	32.4%
Other taxes	5.2%	3.4%	4.7%	6.7%	0.2%	4.9%	0.0%	3.0%
Total taxes	100.0%	100.0%	100.0%	100.0%	100.0%	100.0%	100.0%	100.0%

Source: Data drawn from *Sources of Government Revenue across the OECD, 2017*, Tax Foundation, August 2017, p. 7.

On December 22, 2017, H.R. 1, formerly known as the *Tax Cuts and Jobs Act of 2017*, became law in the United States. The act constituted the most significant change in U.S. corporate taxation since 1986. The changes impact any company subject to U.S. taxation, including foreign companies operating in the U.S. as well as U.S.-based multinationals operating worldwide. The changes moved the U.S. toward a territorial taxation country.

Although the changes in U.S. tax laws went into effect on January 1, 2018, it will take a number of years to really see the total impact of these changes on U.S. multinational enterprises. By all indications, the impacts will be seismic in scope.

U.S. Taxation of Corporate Income

The act of 2017 has a multitude of provisions, but the following are likely of most significance to all U.S. companies.

- **Corporate Income Tax Rate.** The U.S. corporate income tax rate is reduced to 21%. On an effective basis, including state and local tax averages in the U.S., to 25.8% (2018) from 38.9% (years previous). This 25.8% effective rate is the most relevant when comparing to tax liabilities in other countries.
- **Corporate Interest Deductibility.** The new tax structure limits the net interest deduction toward tax liabilities to 30% of EBITDA through the year 2022.[2] After 2022, it reverts to 30% of EBIT. This means that more heavily indebted companies may lose a portion of their interest tax deductions.
- **Transition Tax.** U.S. multinationals that have unrepatriated profits in cash or marketable securities sitting outside the United States may repatriate those profits at a gross tax rate of 15.5% in the 2018 tax year. If those profits have been invested in non-cash assets, they will be deemed remitted at a tax rate of 8%.[3] This tax is based on *deemed repatriation*, meaning that regardless of whether the actual profits are remitted to the U.S. parent company, U.S. taxes are due on those past-year foreign profits.

[2]This applies to companies operating in the U.S., whether U.S.-based or U.S. subsidiaries of foreign corporations, above $25 million in gross receipts (gross revenue) as measured over a three-year period. The provision does allow carry-forward credits for current year exclusions of net interest deductions.

[3]This tax liability on previous year unremitted earnings may be paid over an eight-year period, with 8% of the tax paid in each of the first five years, 15% in the sixth year, 20% in the seventh year, and 25% in the eighth year.

- **Full Depreciation.** For the 2018–2022 period, the new tax code allows companies to deduct the entire cost of equipment purchases from their taxable income. This means that instead of spreading out the depreciation on a capital investment for tax purposes over a multiyear period (e.g., three years), the company may deduct the entire cost in the current period. This, however, applies only to tax liabilities (tax accounting) and does not affect reported taxes and earnings (financial accounting).

Taxation of Foreign Source Income

The taxation of foreign subsidiary earnings that has for many years been deferred until repatriated is now changed to what is now described as a *participation exemption system*. An additional set of new provisions are aimed at anti-basis erosion.

- **Deduction for Dividends Received (DDR).** All dividends declared by the foreign subsidiaries of U.S. companies to their U.S. parent companies will receive a 100% dividend deduction—the so-called *Deduction for Dividends Received* (DDR).[4] This dividend deduction is what is meant by the phrase "participation exemption." This means that foreign source earnings declared as dividends to the U.S. parent will not be taxed beyond those taxes paid in their host foreign country. No tax credits or deficits are created from this remitted income. This is the provision that has led many to describe the U.S. as moving toward a more territorial tax regime.
- **Undeclared Foreign Earnings.** Those earnings in foreign subsidiaries that are not declared as dividends to their U.S. parents in the period in which they are earned will be taxed as deemed dividends in the current period. Their current U.S. tax liabilities will be based on a gross-up procedure similar to that used previously, where taxes deemed paid in the host country plus any additional withholding taxes are credited against the new lower theoretical U.S. tax statutory rate of 21%. Given that the global average effective tax rate is under 23%, this means that in effect little additional U.S. tax will be due.
- **Foreign-Derived Intangible Income (FDII).** Companies operating in the U.S. that derive income from the sale of property (including licenses, leases, patents, etc.) to foreign persons for use *outside* the U.S. or for services *performed outside* the U.S. are generating FDII. Although complex, the basic tax rate applicable to FDII is 10.5% of the aggregate adjusted basis of the subject U.S. assets.
- **Global Intangible Low-Taxed Income (GILTI).** A newly created category of foreign income, GILTI effectively sets a minimum current tax on current foreign income earned by a U.S. corporation operating anywhere in the world. Specifically targeting U.S. foreign subsidiaries subject to Sub-Part F income, hybrid entities, or subsidiaries just operating in extremely low-tax environments, GILTI establishes a minimum tax rate on them.[5]

The tax liability is based on the "net deemed tangible income return" of the foreign unit. In principle, what it means is that any income by the unit that exceeds a 10% rate of return on the tangible assets of the business is subject to an additional minimum tax.[6] This means that income earned by intangible assets like intellectual property and patents that is held

[4]This applied to all foreign entities in which a U.S. company owns a deemed 10% interest or more. Although the new tax law highlights this 10% interest rule repeatedly, the vast majority of foreign affiliates of U.S.-based companies are more than 90% owned or are wholly owned foreign subsidiaries.

[5]This is also referred to as a base erosion minimum tax or *base erosion anti-abuse tax* (BEAT).

[6]The tangible assets of the foreign business for U.S. tax purposes have their own acronym, QBAI, or *qualified business asset investment.*

by these foreign businesses would become fully taxable. Since these business units typically have few tangible assets, any income above 10% rate of return on these small tangible asset bases (likely nearly the whole of the returns of the unit) is currently taxable in the U.S. under GILTI.

The effective tax rate is intricate. Starting with the corporate income tax rate of 21% and assuming most of this income would also be classified as FDII, the effective tax rate on GILTI income would be 10.5%. Since tax credits on GILTI income are limited to 80% of any taxes actually paid by the business to host country authorities, the effective tax rate on GILTI income rises to 13.125%. (Yeah, we know.)

As we noted previously, it is far too early to see how these many complex U.S. tax law changes will alter multinational financial management practices. The changes are clearly targeted at ending the practice of holding foreign profits offshore, shifting intellectual property (intangible assets) ownership to low-tax environments, and avoiding taxation of offshore profits in general through hybrid entities. Time will tell to what degree those goals will be achieved.

Summary Points

- Nations structure their tax systems along one of two basic approaches: the worldwide approach or the territorial approach. Both approaches are attempts to determine which firms and which incomes, foreign or domestic by incorporation and origin, are subject to the taxation of host-country tax authorities.
- Tax treaties normally define whether taxes are to be imposed on income earned in one country by the nationals of another and, if so, how. Tax treaties are bilateral, with the two signatories specifying what rates are applicable to which types of income between the two countries.
- Transfer pricing is the pricing of goods, services, and technology between related companies. High or low transfer prices have an effect on income taxes, funds positioning, managerial incentives and evaluation, and joint-venture partners.
- The U.S. differentiates foreign source income from domestic source income. Each is taxed separately, and tax deficits/credits in one category may not be used against deficits/credits in the other category.
- If a U.S.-based MNE receives income from a foreign country that imposes higher corporate income taxes than does the United States, total creditable taxes will exceed U.S. taxes on that foreign income, resulting in excess foreign tax credits.
- MNEs have foreign subsidiaries that act as tax havens for corporate funds awaiting reinvestment or repatriation. Tax havens are typically located in countries that have a low corporate tax rate, a stable currency, facilities to support financial services, and a stable government.
- Many U.S.-based companies have used corporate inversions in an effort to reduce their effective tax rates by reincorporating offshore in lower tax environments. An alternative to a corporate inversion is acquiring a firm incorporated within one of these low-tax environments and then adopting its incorporation for the new combined company.
- Governments today compete globally for the business and investment of multinational companies using different tax structures and strategies.
- Three forces are driving changes in corporate tax rates globally: (1) the rapid expansion of the digital economy; (2) actions taken by many governments globally to increase their individual tax competitiveness to attract foreign investment; and (3) the scramble by many of these same governments to increase their tax takes from the same multinational business taxes affected by the first two forces.
- The tax law changes enacted by the U.S. at the end of 2017 will have a dramatic impact on the multinational tax management strategies and structures for U.S.-based companies. Although it is too early to tell in much depth, it appears the long period in which U.S. multinationals could avoid paying U.S. taxes on large quantities of foreign profits left outside the U.S. are over.

MINI-CASE

The Google Tax[7]

"It's called capitalism. We are proudly capitalistic. I'm not confused about this. We pay lots of taxes; we pay them in the legally prescribed ways," he said. "I am very proud of the structure that we set up. We did it based on the incentives that the governments offered us to operate."

—Eric Schmidt, chairman, Google, 2012.

Google, a subsidiary of Alphabet, Inc., a U.S.-based multinational company, was the dominant Internet search engine. Known for encouraging all employees to "Do no evil" in the company code of conduct, it has been the subject of intense scrutiny over its global tax strategy for more than a decade. Google's ability to structure its global operations and reported profits to position them (others describe it as "reposition" or "divert" or "avoid") in low-tax environments was well known and in many circles not appreciated. But as Google's Chairman Schmidt noted at the time, the company was simply following the law and tax requirements laid out by various national authorities. This practice is known as "legal avoidance."[8]

But government tax authorities are not willing to stand by and allow Google and others like it, including Apple and Diageo, to generate hundreds of millions of dollars of sales and profits in some countries, tax-free. They are moving to change both how taxes are calculated by residence and eliminate the multitude of loopholes and structures that the many different national tax authorities have inadvertently created through national focus and lack of international cooperation. They are in search of a "Google tax."

Digital Basics

While the digital economy does not create Base Erosion and Profit Shifting (BEPS) issues, it "exacerbates the existing ones." Digital goods are highly mobile or intangible, physical presence of a company in the market country is often not needed in the digital sector, rendering it substantially different from traditional brick-and-mortar businesses. New digital business models (subscription, access or advertisement models) and new technologies such as robotics or 3D printing are not confined by national boundaries and can easily escape their tax liabilities by channeling their royalty payments towards a tax haven.

—"Tax Challenges in the Digital Economy," Study *for the* Taxe 2 Committee, European Parliament, June 2016.

One way to understand the tax problem governments face is to explore two elements of any digitally based business—its intellectual property and how it delivers its services. Intellectual property can be sold and licensed. But that sale and license can be to different incorporated subsidiaries of the same company. And at what price or at what royalty rate is this intellectual property sold or licensed? In Google's case, at very high prices and very high rates.

The second element is how and where the service is provided and delivered. Google's business in Great Britain serves as an example of this debate, as it has been the subject of much discourse.[9] Google's primary operations in Great Britain are located in Ireland (Google Ireland, Ltd). But most of Google's customers are in England. A Google consultant will visit potential customers in London and aid in their understanding of Google's services. Google describes these employees as "marketing leaders" and not salespeople. The customer will then go online, connecting with Google's operations in Ireland, to purchase desired services. The services are purchased from an Irish business, subject to Irish taxes. Through this digital delivery structure Google generated hundreds of millions of dollars in business in England while generating few English tax liabilities—much to the chagrin of English tax authorities.[10]

To avoid UK corporation tax, Google relies on the deeply unconvincing argument that its sales to UK clients take place in Ireland, despite clear evidence that the vast majority of sales activity takes place in the UK.

—"Tax Avoidance–Google," House of Commons Committee of Public Accounts, June 10, 2013, p. 3.

In hearings held in the House of Commons in 2013, Matt Brittin, Google's vice president for Northern and Central Europe, explained that Google's employees in England were not salespeople or conducting sales activities: "Nobody (in the UK) is selling." At this time, Google UK, Ltd employed 1,300 people in London, of whom 720 were providing marketing services, not sales.[11]

[8]Jane G. Gravelle, "Tax Havens: International Tax Avoidance and Evasion," Congressional Research Service, R40623, January 15, 2015.

[9]See "Tax Avoidance–Google," House of Commons Committee of Public Accounts, June 10, 2013; and Tom Bergin, "Special Report: How Google UK Clouds Its Tax Liabilities," *Reuters*, April 30, 2013.

[10]According to a Reuters research analysis Google, for the 2006–2011 period, generated $18 billion in revenues from the UK and paid just $16 million in taxes.

[11]Ireland is not the only regional sales-tax structure used by Google. In south Asia, Google uses Singapore and its tax regime and series of bilateral tax treaties in the same way it uses Ireland. For example, Google has significant sales of digital services in Indonesia, but only has a representative office in-country, booking all sales in Singapore.

Google's Revenues and Internet Users

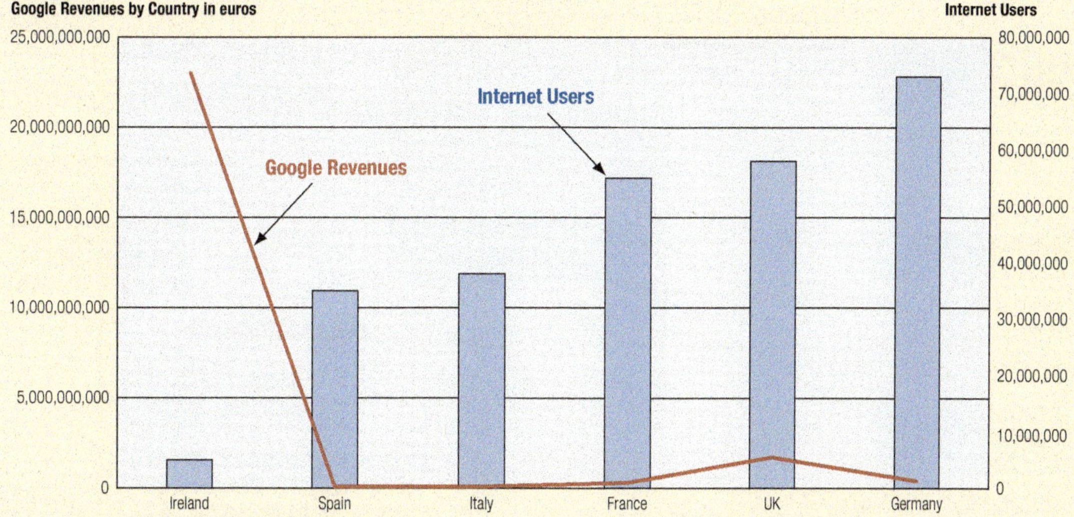

Source: Constructed by authors from data presented in "EU Tax Revenue Loss from Google and Facebook," by Paul Tang and Henri Bussink, Pvd A Europe, September 2017.

Exhibit A is one illustration of this potential digital distortion between revenues and likely customers. This analysis compares where Google's sales are booked in Europe versus the number of Internet users in those same countries. This same research study presented similar results for how Facebook conducts its business in Europe, also booking all sales in Ireland.

Double Irish Dutch Sandwich

Google's critical offshore tax strategy, the *Double Irish Dutch Sandwich*, is based on using two different Irish subsidiaries to execute ownership and sales, as illustrated in Exhibit B. All of the ownership of its intellectual property is assigned to one Irish subsidiary, while all of its European sales are assigned to another Irish subsidiary. Both enjoy Ireland's lower corporate income tax rate, lower than rates in other European countries like the United Kingdom or France. Google's Irish subsidiaries also benefit from a quirk in Irish tax law that stipulates that companies controlled from a foreign tax environment, including from a tax haven like Bermuda, only pay tax in that foreign country, not Ireland..

Key to Google's tax structure is the subject of *permanent establishment* (PE). Tax rules allow firms such as Google to fix a tax base in a low-tax country like Ireland while generating lots of business in a country where tax rates are higher, like the United Kingdom. Companies in principle are taxed not on "where they do business" but on "where they finalize their business deals with customers"—the country or jurisdiction where the final contract is signed. In the case of Google, that means most sales throughout the European Union are finalized in Ireland, where the corporate income tax rate is only 12.5%. If Google's employees in the United Kingdom were actually conducting sales activities, UK offices would have been interpreted under tax law as a permanent establishment. It is estimated that 75% of the top 50 U.S. software, Internet, and computer hardware companies use similar PE structures that help them avoid taxes.

In 2015 a new twist on the use of permanent establishment designations (or lack thereof) was unveiled in the multinational tax reporting of Pfizer, the pharmaceutical giant. U.S. tax rules say companies must include the potential U.S. tax cost of foreign earnings in their consolidated earnings, but most multinationals avoid this by designating the foreign earnings as "permanently" or indefinitely reinvested overseas, gaining deferral on the taxes and postponing recognizing additional tax obligations.

Companies that can't or don't declare their offshore profits to be permanently or indefinitely reinvested abroad record a deferred tax expense. They appear to be paying higher taxes now because the effective tax rate includes both current-year and deferred taxes. But the deferred taxes are just that—not yet paid. Pfizer reported that in 2014 it had a 25.5% global tax rate. If it had reported earnings the same way as most U.S. multinationals and not included deferred tax expense, its actual global tax rate would have been 7.5%.

EXHIBIT B Google's Double Irish Dutch Sandwich

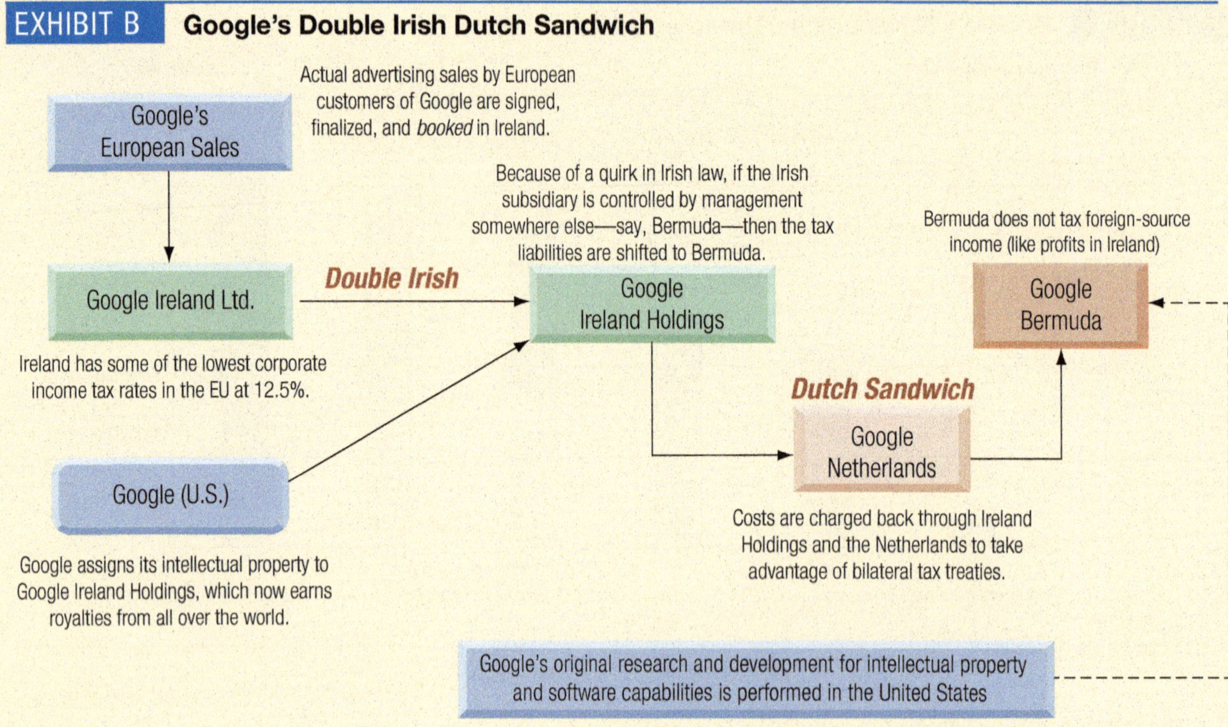

The Google Tax

While some have raised concerns about where Google pays taxes, Google's overall global tax rate has been over 23 percent for the past 10 years, in line with the 23.7 percent average statutory rate across the member countries of the Organisation for Economic Co-operation and Development (OECD).

—Karan Bhatia, vice president, Government Affairs & Public Policy, Google, blogpost, June 27, 2019.

Frustration has been growing with tax authorities all over the world with Google and other digitally based businesses like it for years.[12] That frustration has resulted in a number of new tax laws focusing on eliminating or undermining the permanent establishment principle, allowing tax authorities to tax companies on the basis of whether it appears they are intentionally repositioning or diverting profits. Australia passed one such structure, the Multinational Anti-Avoidance Law (MAAL), the United Kingdom another, the diverted profits tax (DPT). Both have been called the "Google tax."

In 2015 pressure mounted to such a degree that Ireland revoked the ability of companies to execute the Double-Irish. Although companies would have till 2020 to unwind their structures, the famed Double-Irish was bound for the scrap heap. Google itself announced in an Irish filing on New Year's Even 2019 that 2019 would be the last year it used the tax structure.

There has not, however, been international consensus on the best way to move forward on the taxation of digital services. In 2019 President Emmanuel Macron of France signed into law France's own digital services tax (DST), much to the displeasure of the United States. The DST imposed a 3% levy on gross revenues generated from providing two types of digital services "in France," digital interface services and targeted advertising services. The U.S. opened a Section 301 investigation that such a law was targeting U.S. digital services providers, and in July 2020 imposed retaliatory tariffs.[13] Those tariffs, scheduled to go into effect in January 2021 were suspended under the Biden administration.[14]

[12]Amazon, Apple, Facebook, Google, Microsoft, and Netflix—the Silicon Six—are frequently criticized as a group for their aggressive tax strategies.

[13]"Report on France's Digital Services Tax Prepared in the Investigation under Section 301 of the Trade Act of 1974," Office of the United States Trade Representative, Ambassador Robert E. Lighthizer, December 2, 2019.

[14]Interestingly, the announcement by the U.S. Trade Representative noted one reason for the suspension was ongoing investigations of similar DSTs adopted or under consideration in 10 other jurisdictions.

EXHIBIT C Apple's No Different

Although Apple produces products and not just services like Google, its global value chain and tax strategy are very similar.

- Approximately 99% of Apple's R&D is conducted in Cupertino, California, where it has its corporate headquarters.
- All microprocesessor used in all Apple products, a major core element of Apple product value, are manufactured in Austin, Texas.
- Apple then uses contract manufacturers, mostly in China, to produce their products.
- Those products are then shipped directly to Apple distributors in the Americas, Europe, and Singapore.
- All of Apple's global sales outside the U.S. are booked through (Apple Sales International), an Apple subsidiary in Ireland. Since it receives much higher prices on product than it pays for the goods, large profits are positioned in ASI.
- ASI then pays its profits as dividends to another Irish company, its own parent company, in a Double Irish.

But eliminating that one structure did not solve the fundamental problem of profit positioning globally. As long as there are differences in corporate taxation across countries, there will be multinational companies attempting to devise schemes or structures—legally—to take advantage of those differences. One of the most promising developments was the G7 agreement in June 2021 to pursue the implementation of a global minimum tax rate of 15%. (Ireland grudgingly supported it in the end.) Narrowing differences in corporate tax rates to something along the lines of 15% to 30% would help reduce profit and tax distortions greatly.

But this solution solves only one of the principle problems, strategies to reposition profits. It does not solve the problem with where the taxes are paid in digital commerce. Google has repeatedly noted that it supports changes to international tax rules so that digital transaction are paid where the products are consumed, not produced.

Many tax authorities are redefining the location of a taxable transaction from the country of the supplier to the country of the buyer. This may prove to be the most likely (but contentious) path to a solution on a global basis.

MINI-CASE QUESTIONS

1. What makes taxation of digital commerce so different and complicated?
2. Why has it been legal for companies like Apple and Google to structure their global operations to position where profits are recorded for tax purposes?
3. Many tax analysts have always considered the Double Irish Dutch Sandwich the result of a series of very special circumstances. Why is that?
4. What is the most likely future direction of digital business taxation?

Questions

15.1 Primary Objective. What is the primary objective of multinational tax planning?

15.2 Tax Morality. What is meant by the term *tax morality*? If, for example, your company has a subsidiary in Russia, where some believe tax evasion is a fine art, should you comply with Russian tax laws or violate the laws, as do your local competitors?

15.3 Tax Neutrality. What is tax neutrality? What is the difference between domestic neutrality and foreign neutrality?

15.4 Worldwide versus Territorial. What is the difference between the worldwide and territorial approaches to taxation?

15.5 Direct or Indirect. What is the difference between a direct tax and an indirect tax?

15.6 Tax Deferral. What is meant by tax deferral in the U.S. system of taxation? What is the deferral privilege?

15.7 Value-Added Tax. What is a value-added tax, and how does it differ from an income tax?

15.8 Withholding Tax. What is a withholding tax and why do governments impose them?

15.9 Tax Treaty. What is usually included within a tax treaty?

15.10 Active versus Passive. What do the terms *active* and *passive* mean in the context of U.S. taxation of foreign source income?

15.11 Tax Types. Taxes are classified based on whether they are applied directly to income—direct taxes—or to some other measurable performance characteristic of the firm—indirect taxes. Classify each of the following as a "direct tax," an "indirect tax," or something else:

a. Corporate income tax paid by a Japanese subsidiary on its operating income
b. Royalties paid to Saudi Arabia for oil extracted and shipped to world markets
c. Interest received by a U.S. parent on bank deposits held in London
d. Interest received by a U.S. parent on a loan to a subsidiary in Mexico
e. Principal repayment received by U.S. parent from Belgium on a loan to a wholly owned subsidiary in Belgium
f. Excise tax paid on cigarettes manufactured and sold within the U.S.
g. Property taxes paid on the corporate headquarters building in Seattle
h. A direct contribution to the International Committee of the Red Cross for refugee relief
i. Deferred income tax, shown as a deduction on the U.S. parent's consolidated income tax
j. Withholding taxes withheld by Germany on dividends paid to a United Kingdom parent corporation

15.12 Foreign Tax Credit. What is a foreign tax credit? Why do countries give credit for taxes paid on foreign source income?

15.13 Earnings Stripping. What is earnings stripping, and what are some examples of how multinational firms pursue earnings stripping?

15.14 Controlled Foreign Corporation. What is a controlled foreign corporation, and what is its significance in global tax management?

15.15 Transfer Pricing. What is a transfer price, and can a government regulate transfer prices? What difficulties and motives does a parent multinational firm face in setting transfer prices?

15.16 Fund Positioning. What is fund positioning?

15.17 Income Tax Effect. What is the income tax effect, and how may a multinational firm alter transfer prices as a result of the income tax effect?

15.18 Correct Pricing. What is Section 482 of the U.S. Internal Revenue Code, and what guidelines does it recommend when setting transfer prices?

15.19 Cross-Crediting. Define cross-crediting, and explain why it may or may not be consistent with a worldwide tax regime.

15.20 Check-the-Box. Explain how the check-the-box regulatory change altered the effectiveness of Subpart F income regulations.

15.21 Measuring Managerial Performance. What role does transfer pricing have within multinational companies when measuring management performance? How can transfer pricing practices within a firm conflict with performance measurement?

15.22 Tax Haven Subsidiary. What is a tax haven? Is it the same thing as an international offshore financial center? What is the purpose of a multinational creating and operating a financial subsidiary in a tax haven?

15.23 Corporate Inversion. What is a corporate inversion, and why do many U.S. corporations want to pursue it even when it is highly criticized by public and private parties alike?

15.24 Digital Commerce. How is cross-border digital commerce challenging the traditional ways in which multinational companies are taxed?

15.25 Tax Competitiveness. What does it mean for a country—or its government—to compete for business on the basis of taxation?

Problems

15.1 Avon's Foreign-Source Income. Avon is a U.S.-based direct seller of a wide array of products. Avon markets leading beauty, fashion, and home products in more than 100 countries. As part of the training in its corporate treasury offices, it has its interns build a spreadsheet analysis of the following hypothetical subsidiary earnings/distribution analysis. Use the spreadsheet presented in Exhibit 15.6 for your basic structure.

Baseline Values	Case 1	Case 2
a. Foreign corporate income tax rates	28%	45%
b. U.S. corporate income tax rate	35%	35%
c. Foreign dividend withholding tax rate	15%	0%
d. U.S. ownership in foreign firm	100%	100%
e. Dividend payout rate of foreign firm	100%	100%

a. What is the total tax payment, foreign and domestic combined, for this income?
b. What is the effective tax rate paid on this income by the U.S.-based parent company?
c. What would be the total tax payment and effective tax rate if the foreign corporate tax rate

was 45% and there were no withholding taxes on dividends?

15.2 Pacific Jewel Airlines (Hong Kong). Pacific Jewel Airlines is a U.S.-based air-freight firm with a wholly owned subsidiary in Hong Kong. The subsidiary, Jewel Hong Kong, has just completed a long-term planning report for the parent company in San Francisco, in which it has estimated the following expected earnings and payout rates for the years 2011–2014.

Jewel Hong Kong Income Items (millions US$)

	2011	2012	2013	2014
Earnings before interest and taxes (EBIT)	8,000	10,000	12,000	14,000
Less interest expenses	(800)	(1,000)	(1,200)	(1,400)
Earnings before taxes (EBT)	7,200	9,000	10,800	12,600

The current Hong Kong corporate tax rate on this category of income is 16.5%. Hong Kong imposes no withholding taxes on dividends remitted to U.S. investors (per the Hong Kong–U.S. bilateral tax treaty). The U.S. corporate income tax rate is 35%. The parent company wants to repatriate 75% of net income as dividends annually.

a. Calculate the net income available for distribution by the Hong Kong subsidiary for the years 2011–2014.
b. What is the amount of the dividend expected to be remitted to the U.S. parent each year?
c. After gross-up for U.S. tax liability purposes, what is the total dividend after tax (all Hong Kong and U.S. taxes) expected each year?
d. What is the effective tax rate on this foreign sourced income per year?

15.3 Kraftstoff of Germany. Kraftstoff is a German-based company that manufactures electronic fuel-injection carburetor assemblies for several large automobile companies in Germany, including Mercedes, BMW, and Opel. The firm, like many firms in Germany today, is revising its financial policies in line with the increasing degree of disclosure required by firms if they wish to list their shares publicly in or out of Germany. The company's earnings before tax (EBT) are €483,500,000.

Kraftstoff's primary problem is that the German corporate income tax code applies a different income tax rate to income depending on whether it is retained (45%) or distributed to stockholders (30%).

a. If Kraftstoff planned to distribute 50% of its net income, what would be its total net income and total corporate tax bills?
b. If Kraftstoff was attempting to choose between a 40% and 60% payout rate to stockholders, what arguments and values would management use in order to convince stockholders which of the two payouts is in everyone's best interest?

15.4 Gamboa's Tax Averaging. Gamboa, Incorporated is a relatively new U.S.-based retailer of specialty fruits and vegetables. The firm is vertically integrated with fruit- and vegetable-sourcing subsidiaries in Central America and distribution outlets throughout the southeastern and northeastern regions of the U.S. Gamboa's two Central American subsidiaries are in Belize and Costa Rica. Maria Gamboa, the daughter of the firm's founder, is being groomed to take over the firm's financial management in the near future. Like many firms of Gamboa's size, it has not possessed a very high degree of sophistication in financial management simply out of time and cost considerations.

Maria, however, has recently finished her MBA and is now attempting to put some specialized knowledge of U.S. taxation practices to work to save Gamboa money. Her first concern is tax averaging for foreign tax liabilities arising from the two Central American subsidiaries. Costa Rican operations are slightly more profitable than Belize, which is particularly good since Costa Rica is a relatively low-tax country. Costa Rican corporate taxes are a flat 30%, and there are no withholding taxes imposed on dividends paid by foreign firms with operations there. Belize has a higher corporate income tax rate, 40%, and imposes a 10% withholding tax on all dividends distributed to foreign investors. The current U.S. corporate income tax rate is 35%.

	Belize	Costa Rica
Earnings before taxes	$1,000,000	$1,500,000
Corporate income tax rate	40%	30%
Dividend withholding tax rate	10%	0%

a. If Maria Gamboa assumes a 50% payout rate from each subsidiary, what are the additional taxes due on foreign-sourced income from Belize and Costa Rica individually? How much in additional U.S. taxes would be due if Maria averaged the tax credits/liabilities of the two units?

b. With the same payout rate from the Belize subsidiary of 50%, how should Maria change the payout rate of the Costa Rican subsidiary in order to most efficiently manage her total foreign tax bill?
c. What is the minimum effective tax rate that Maria can achieve on her foreign-sourced income?

Chinglish Dirk

Use the following company case to answer Problems 15.5 through 15.7. Chinglish Dirk Company (Hong Kong) exports razor blades to its wholly owned parent company, Torrington Edge (Great Britain). Hong Kong tax rates are 16%, and British tax rates are 30%. Chinglish calculates its profit per container as follows (all values in British pounds).

Constructing Transfer (Sales) Price per Unit	Chinglish Dirk (British pounds)	Torrington Edge (British pounds)
Direct costs	£10,000	£16,100
Overhead	4,000	1,000
Total costs	£14,000	£17,100
Desired markup	2,100	2,565
Transfer price (sales price)	£16,100	£19,665
Income Statement		
Sales price	£16,100,000	£19,665,000
Less total costs	(14,000,000)	(17,100,000)
Taxable income	£2,100,000	£2,565,000
Less taxes	(336,000)	(769,500)
Profit, after-tax	£1,764,000	£1,795,500

15.5 Chinglish Dirk (A). Corporate management of Torrington Edge is considering repositioning profits within the multinational company. What happens to the profits of Chinglish Dirk and Torrington Edge, and the consolidated results of both, if the markup at Chinglish was increased to 20% and the markup at Torrington was reduced to 10%? What is the impact of this repositioning on consolidated tax payments?

15.6 Chinglish Dirk (B). Encouraged by the results from the previous problem's analysis, corporate management of Torrington Edge wishes to continue to reposition profit in Hong Kong. It is, however, facing two constraints. First, the final sales price in Great Britain must be £20,000 or less to remain competitive. Secondly, the British tax authorities—in working with Torrington Edge's cost accounting staff—has established a maximum transfer price allowed (from Hong Kong) of £17,800. What combination of markups do you recommend for Torrington Edge to institute? What is the impact of this repositioning on consolidated profits on after-tax and total tax payments?

15.7 Chinglish Dirk (C). Not to leave any potential tax repositioning opportunities unexplored, Torrington Edge wants to combine the components of Problem 15.6 with a redistribution of overhead costs. If overhead costs could be reallocated between the two units but still total £5,000 per unit and maintain a minimum of £1,750 per unit in Hong Kong, what is the impact of this repositioning on consolidated profits after-tax and total tax payments?

16

International Trade Finance

What the wise man does in the beginning, the fool does in the end.

—Niccolò Machiavelli

LEARNING OBJECTIVES

16.1 Discover the key elements of an import or export business transaction that define the trade relationship

16.2 Explore how the three key documents in import/export combine to finance both the transaction and to manage its risks

16.3 Describe the variety of government programs to help finance exports

16.4 Examine the major trade financing alternatives

16.5 Evaluate the use of a specialized technique, forfaiting, for medium- to long-term trade financing

The purpose of this chapter is to explain how international trade—exports and imports—is financed. The topic is of direct practical relevance both to domestic firms—that simply import and export—and to multinational firms—that trade with related and unrelated entities. The chapter opens with an exploration of the basic flows (goods, money, and documents) between importer and exporter and a discussion of the trade dilemma. The dilemma, that exporters want to be paid before they export and importers do not want to pay until they receive the goods, is at the center of trade finance. The second section then describes the three key trade documents—the *letter of credit, draft,* and *bill of lading* —and how they are used to manage the various risks of international import and export. The third section of the chapter describes government export financing programs, followed by a fourth section examining the alternative trade financing vehicles and instruments. The fifth and final section explores the use of forfaiting for the financing of medium- to long-term receivables. The mini-case at the end of the chapter, *Crosswell International and Brazil,* illustrates how an export requires the integration of management, marketing, and finance.

16.1 The Trade Relationship

As we saw in Chapter 1, the first significant global activity by a domestic firm is importing and exporting goods and services. The purpose of this chapter is to analyze the international trade phase for a domestic firm, when it begins to import goods and services from foreign suppliers and to export to foreign buyers. In the case of our firm in Chapter 1, this trade phase began with suppliers from Mexico and buyers from Canada.

Trade financing shares a number of common characteristics with the traditional value chain activities conducted by all firms. All companies must search out suppliers for the many goods and services required as inputs for their own goods production or service provision processes. The firm's Purchasing and Procurement Department must determine whether each potential supplier is capable of producing the product to required quality specifications and in a timely and reliable manner and whether the supplier will work with the firm in the ongoing process of product and process improvement for continued competitiveness. All must be at an acceptable price and payment terms. This same series of issues applies to potential customers, as their continued business is equally critical to any company's operations and success.

The Fundamental Dilemma

International trade must work around a fundamental dilemma. Imagine an importer and an exporter who would like to do business with one another. Because of the distance between the two, it is not possible to simultaneously hand over goods with one hand and accept payment with the other. Trade therefore uses a three-channel movement to execute trades. Exhibit 16.1 provides an overview of the three movements between an importer and an exporter: the flow of goods, the flow of funds, and the flow of documents. The first two, goods and funds, are obviously the objective of the trade relationship. The flow of documents, however, is composed of a series of different arrangements, contracts, loans, or commitments which assure the two parties of contractual fulfillment.

Understanding the interests of the relationship between the exporter and the importer is critical to understanding the methods for import-export financing utilized in industry. If we assume for the moment the primacy of the exporter (standing in the shoes of the exporter), we can see three basic trade relationships based on affiliation and information.

1. **Affiliated parties.** This is another unit, another subsidiary, of the same company as the exporter. As siblings, knowledge and trust is at the highest level. This export relationship may not require a contract and may or may not require protection.
2. **Unaffiliated known party.** This is another company, unrelated but known to the exporter. That knowledge is the foundation for trust in terms of paying for the goods in a timely manner. This will require a contract and possibly some type of protection against nonpayment.
3. **Unaffiliated unknown party.** This is another company that is not only unaffiliated, but one with no previous dealings with the exporter. The company may in fact be completely unknown to the exporter. This will require a contract as well as some form of protection against nonpayment.

EXHIBIT 16.1 Trade Financing: The Flow of Goods, Funds, and Documents

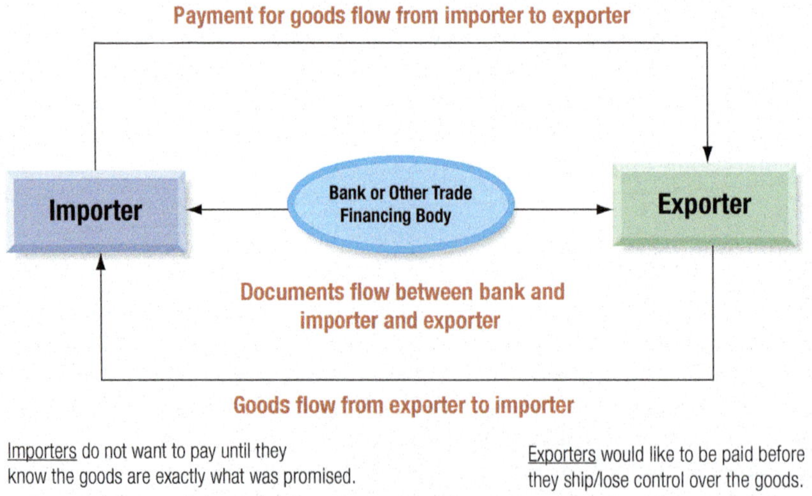

A foreign importer, which is a subsidiary business unit of the exporter, would be an affiliated party (and transactions between the two would be referred to as *intrafirm trade*). Because both businesses are part of the same MNE, the most common practice would be to conduct the trade transaction without a contract or protection against nonpayment. This is, however, not always the case. In a variety of international business situations it may still be in the exporter's best interest to detail the conditions for the business transaction and to possibly protect against any political or country-based interruption to the completion of the trade transaction. (This is particularly useful for gaining passage through ports or other logistical facilities.)

A foreign importer with which the exporter has previously conducted business successfully would be considered *unaffiliated known*. In this case, the two parties may still enter into a detailed sales contract, but specific terms and shipments or provisions of services may be significantly looser in definition. Depending on the depth of the relationship, the exporter may seek some third-party protection against noncompletion or conduct the business on an open account basis.

A foreign importer with which the exporter has not previously conducted business would be considered *unaffiliated unknown*. In this case, the two parties would need to enter into a detailed sales contract, outlining the specific responsibilities and expectations of the business agreement. The exporter would also need to seek out protection against the possibility that the importer would not make payment in full in a timely fashion.

Payment Risk

Exhibit 16.2 provides an array of different possibilities for an importer and exporter to manage payment risk. For the exporter, the safest and most secure arrangement would be for complete payment beforehand, *cash-in-advance*. That, in turn, is exactly what the importer does not want to do, having no ability to stop or withhold payment if the merchandise is not as promised. A compromise zone does exist between the extreme ends, including *letters of credit* or simple documentary collections. As we will describe in later sections, this requires contractual provisions for turning the goods over from exporter to importer and for payment.

EXHIBIT 16.2 Payment Risk: The Trade Dilemma

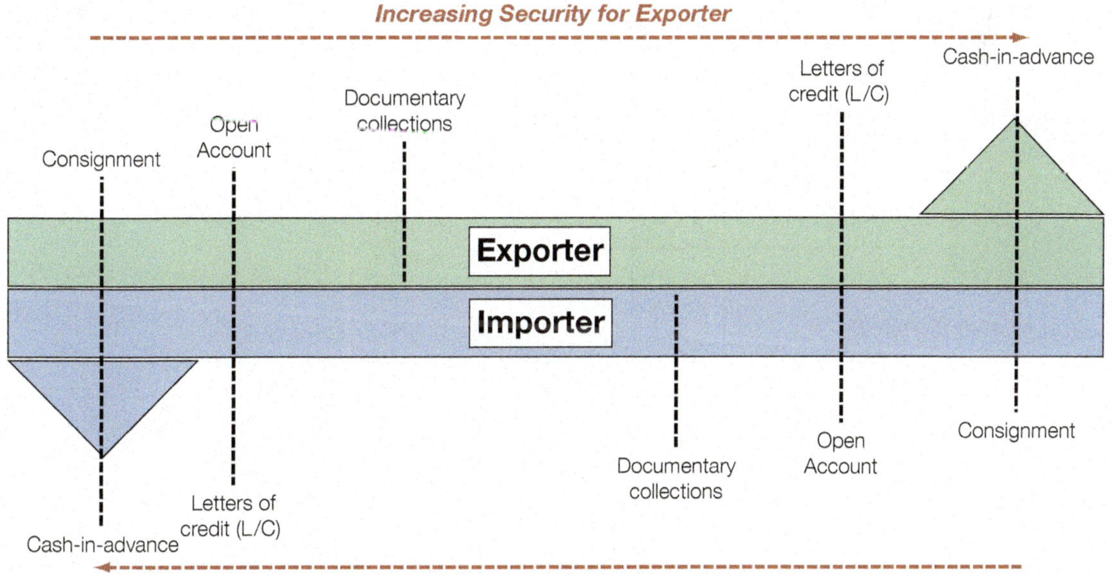

Source: Trade Finance Guide, U.S. Department of Commerce, 2012, p 3.

For the exporter, selling on *open account*, meaning no contract assuring payment, and *consignment*, getting paid only when the importer actually sells the merchandise and realizes cash settlement, are by far highly risky alternatives.

There is of course an unlimited number of different forms of possible transactions. Something as simple as an advance payment of, say, 10% can alter the trust factor completely. Regardless, it is always important to remember that the exporter has capital at risk having already invested in the manufacture of the merchandise. As a result, the exporter will try to retain control over the merchandise as long as possible until it is satisfied of getting paid.

The fundamental dilemma of being reluctant to trust a stranger in a foreign land can be resolved by using a highly respected bank as intermediary, as illustrated in Exhibit 16.3. In a greatly simplified view of this intermediary role, the importer obtains the bank's promise to pay on its behalf, knowing that the exporter will trust the bank. The bank's promise to pay is called a *letter of credit* (L/C). The exporter ships the merchandise to the importer's country. Title to the merchandise is given to the bank on a document called a bill of lading (B/L). The exporter asks the bank to pay for the goods, and the bank does so. The document requesting payment is called a *sight draft*. The bank, having paid for the goods, now passes title to the importer, whom the bank trusts. At that time or later, depending on their agreement, the importer reimburses the bank.

Financial managers of MNEs must understand these three basic documents because their firms will often trade with unaffiliated parties and also because the system of documentation provides a source of short-term capital that can be drawn upon even when shipments are to sister subsidiaries.

Benefits of the Documentary System

The three key documents and their interaction are discussed in detail later in this chapter. They constitute a system developed and modified over centuries to protect both importer and exporter from the risk of noncompletion and from foreign exchange risk as well as to provide a means of financing.

Protection against Risk of Noncompletion. As stated previously, once importer and exporter agree on terms, the seller usually prefers to maintain legal title to the goods until paid or at least until assured of payment. The buyer, however, will be reluctant to pay before receiving the goods or at least before receiving title to them. Each wants assurance that the

EXHIBIT 16.3 The Bank as an Export/Import Intermediary

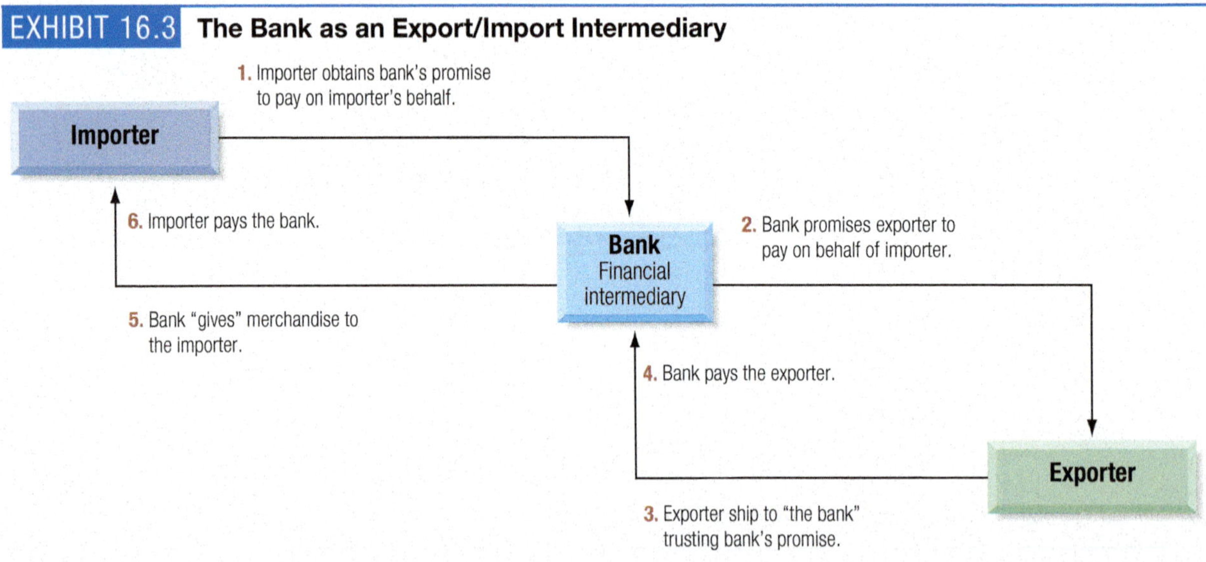

other party will complete its portion of the transaction. The letter of credit, bill of lading, and sight draft are part of a system carefully constructed to determine who bears the financial loss if one of the parties defaults at any time.

Protection against Foreign Exchange Risk. In international trade, foreign exchange risk arises from transaction exposure. If the transaction requires payment in the exporter's currency, the importer carries the foreign exchange risk. If the transaction calls for payment in the importer's currency, the exporter has the foreign exchange risk.

Transaction exposure can be hedged by the techniques described in Chapter 10, but in order to hedge, the exposed party must be certain that payment of a specified amount will be made on or near a particular date. The three key documents described in this chapter ensure both amount and time of payment and thus lay the groundwork for effective hedging.

The risk of noncompletion and foreign exchange risk are most important when the international trade is episodic, with no outstanding agreement for recurring shipments and no sustained relationship between buyer and seller. When the import/export relationship is of a recurring nature, as in the case of manufactured goods shipped weekly or monthly to a final assembly or retail outlet in another country, and when the relationship is between countries whose currencies are considered strong, the exporter may well bill the importer on open account after a normal credit check.

Financing the Trade. Most international trade involves a time lag during which funds are tied up while the merchandise is in transit. Once the risks of noncompletion and of exchange rate changes are disposed of, banks are willing to finance goods in transit. A bank can finance goods in transit, as well as goods held for sale, based on the key documents without exposing itself to questions about the quality of merchandise or aspects of shipment.

Noncompletion Risks

In order to understand the risks associated with international trade transactions, it is helpful to understand the sequence of events in any such transaction. Exhibit 16.4 illustrates, in principle, the series of events associated with a single export transaction.

From a financial management perspective, the two primary risks associated with an international trade transaction are currency risk (discussed previously in Chapter 10) and risk

EXHIBIT 16.4 The Trade Transaction Time Line

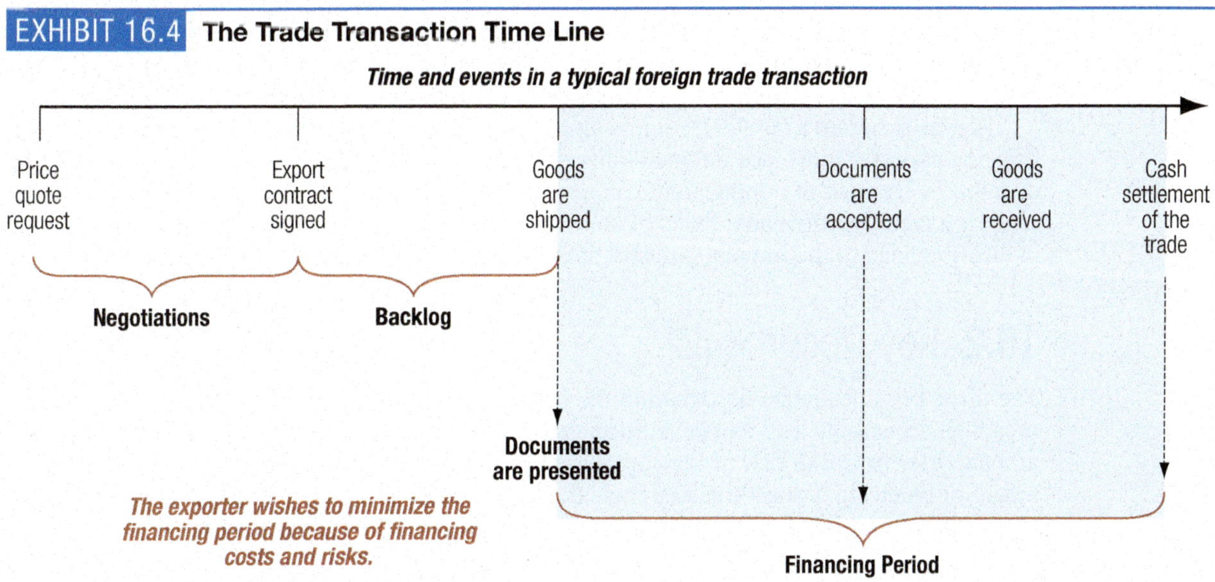

GLOBAL FINANCE IN PRACTICE 16.1

Trade Finance Gains and Losses from the Global Pandemic

Roughly 80% of all international trade requires some form of trade financing. That means that somewhere around $15 trillion of trade transactions, contracts and agreements between importers and exporters, need some form of external or third-party financing in order to happen each year. And of that $15 trillion, roughly 80% of that is funded by 10 banks in London, New York, and Singapore, which make very slim margins on the business. The average trade transaction requires the exchange of 36 documents and 240 copies, all executed under the intensity of a magnifying glass for detail and accuracy. And as noted by *The Economist*, trade finance is "notoriously paper-based." Yet despite looking like the largest low-hanging fruit in the "waiting-to-be-digitized" fintech world, trade finance has been very slow to change. Until now.

It took a pandemic. The 2020 global pandemic shut down a large part of the global economy, and that meant international trade. That trade that did continue found itself operating in a world where 30% of the people, their documents, and their approvals had disappeared. Settling transactions suddenly took longer as documents moved more and more slowly. Exporters were waiting longer and longer for cash settlement during a period in which they needed the money to pay their own bills and hopefully stay afloat. Banks saw rising default rates, causing them to add even more care to the paper-based and detail-based credit analysis needed between importer and exporter. And those rising failure rates and declining bank interest caused fees and financing costs to rise.

Then something changed. Innovation finally stepped in in the form of supply chain finance (SCF). Import facilitators, freight forwarders, and trade finance banks, all moved to cut steps and documents out of the trade finance process, automating more and more along the way. Banks improved their risk-taking ability to assess credit quality of importers, earning larger fees along the way. Fewer documents, fewer steps, faster payment. It seems that old dogs can learn new tricks.

of noncompletion. Exhibit 16.5 illustrates the traditional business problem of credit management: the exporter quotes a price, finalizes a contract, and ships the goods, losing physical control over the goods based on trust of the buyer or the promise of a bank to pay based on documents presented. The risk of default on the part of the importer—risk of noncompletion—is present as soon as the financing period begins, as depicted in Exhibit 16.4.

In many cases, the initial task of analyzing the creditworthiness of foreign customers is similar to procedures for analyzing domestic customers. If the exporter has had no experience with a foreign customer but the customer is a large, well-known firm in its home country, the exporter may simply ask for a bank credit report on that firm. The exporter may also talk to other firms that have had dealings with the foreign customer. If these investigations show the foreign customer (and country) to be completely trustworthy, the exporter would likely ship to them on open account, with a credit limit, just as they would for a domestic customer. This is the least costly method of handling exports because there are no heavy documentation or bank charges.

However, before a regular trading relationship has been established with a new or unknown firm, the exporter must face the possibility of nonpayment for its exports or noncompletion of its imports. The risk of nonpayment can be eliminated through the use of a letter of credit issued by a creditworthy bank. Risks of noncompletion skyrocketed during the global pandemic inducing change to this ancient industry, as described in *Global Finance in Practice 16.1*.

16.2 Key Documents

The three key documents described in the following pages—the letter of credit, draft, and bill of lading—constitute a system developed and modified over centuries to protect both importer and exporter from the risk of noncompletion of the trade transaction as well as to provide a means of financing. These three key trade documents are part of a carefully constructed system to determine who bears the financial loss if one of the parties defaults at any time.

EXHIBIT 16.5 **Parties to a Letter of Credit (L/C)**

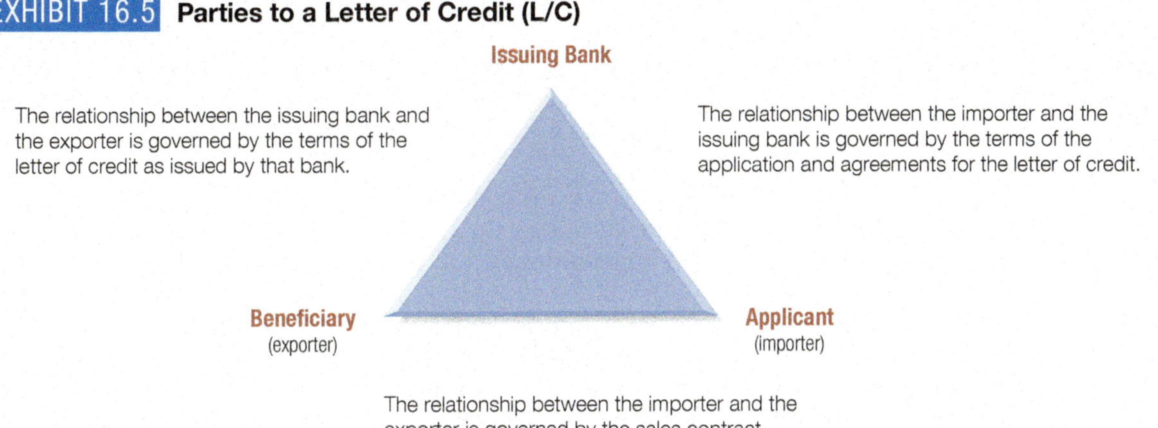

Letter of Credit (L/C)

A *letter of credit* (L/C) is a document issued by a bank at the request of an importer (the applicant/buyer) by which the bank promises to pay an exporter (the beneficiary of the letter) upon presentation of documents specified in the L/C. An L/C reduces the risk of noncompletion because the bank agrees to pay against documents rather than actual merchandise. The relationship between the three parties can be seen in Exhibit 16.5.

Parties to a Letter of Credit (L/C). A beneficiary (exporter) and an applicant (importer) agree on a transaction and the importer then applies to its local bank for the issuance of an L/C. The importer's bank issues an L/C and cuts a sales contract based on its assessment of the importer's creditworthiness, or the bank might require a cash deposit or other collateral from the importer in advance. The importer's bank will want to know the type of transaction, the amount of money involved, and what documents must accompany the draft that will be drawn against the L/C.

If the importer's bank is satisfied with the credit standing of the applicant, it will issue an L/C guaranteeing to pay for the merchandise if shipped in accordance with the instructions and conditions contained in the L/C.

The essence of an L/C is the promise of the issuing bank to pay against specified documents that must accompany any draft drawn against the credit. The L/C is not a guarantee of the underlying commercial transaction. Indeed, the L/C is a separate transaction from any sales or other contracts on which it might be based. To constitute a true L/C transaction, the following elements must be present with respect to the issuing bank:

1. The issuing bank must receive a fee or other valid business consideration for issuing the L/C.
2. The bank's L/C must contain a specified expiration date or a definite maturity.
3. The bank's commitment must have a stated maximum amount of money.
4. The bank's obligation to pay must arise only on the presentation of specific documents, and the bank must not be called on to determine disputed questions of fact or law.
5. The bank's customer must have an unqualified obligation to reimburse the bank on the same condition as the bank has paid.

Commercial letters of credit are also classified based on whether they are revocable and confirmed.

Irrevocable versus Revocable L/C. An irrevocable L/C obligates the issuing bank to honor drafts drawn in compliance with the credit and can be neither canceled nor modified without the consent of all parties, including in particular the beneficiary (exporter). A revocable L/C can be canceled or amended at any time before payment; it is intended to serve as a means of arranging payment but not as a guarantee of payment.

Confirmed versus Unconfirmed L/C. A confirmed L/C is issued by one bank and can be confirmed by another bank, in which case the confirming bank can honor drafts drawn in compliance with the L/C. An unconfirmed L/C is the obligation only of the issuing bank.

An exporter is likely to want a foreign bank's L/C confirmed by a domestic bank when the exporter has doubts about the foreign bank's ability to pay. Such doubts can arise when the exporter is unsure of the financial standing of the foreign bank or if political or economic conditions in the foreign country are unstable. The essence of an L/C is shown in Exhibit 16.6.

Most commercial letters of credit are documentary, meaning that certain documents must be included with drafts drawn under their terms. Required documents usually include a bill of lading (discussed in more detail later in the chapter), a commercial invoice, and any of the following: consular invoice, insurance certificate or policy, and packing list.

Advantages and Disadvantages of L/Cs. The primary advantage of an L/C is that it reduces risk; the exporter can sell against a bank's promise to pay rather than against the promise of a commercial firm. The exporter is also in a more secure position as to the availability of foreign exchange to pay for the sale, since banks are more likely to be aware of foreign exchange conditions and rules than is the importing firm itself. If the importing

EXHIBIT 16.6 Essence of a Letter of Credit (L/C)

Bank of the East, Ltd.
[Name of Issuing Bank]

Date: September 28, 2021
L/C Number 123456

Bank of the East, Ltd. Hereby issues this irrevocable documentary Letter of Credit to Jones Company [name of exporter] for USD5,000,000, payable 90 days after sight by a draft drawn against Bank of the East, Ltd., in accordance with Letter of Credit number 123456.

The draft is to be accompanied by the following documents:
1. Commercial invoice in triplicate
2. Packing list
3. Clean on board order bill of lading
4. Insurance documents, paid for by buyer

At maturity Bank of the East, Ltd. Will pay the face amount of the draft to the bearer of the draft.

Authorized Signature

country should change its foreign exchange rules during the course of a transaction, the government is likely to allow already outstanding bank letters of credit to be honored for fear of throwing its own domestic banks into international disrepute. Of course, if the L/C is confirmed by a bank in the exporter's country, the exporter avoids any problem of blocked foreign exchange.

An exporter may find that an order backed by an irrevocable L/C will facilitate obtaining pre-export financing in the home country. If the exporter's reputation for delivery is good, a local bank may lend funds to process and prepare the merchandise for shipment. Once the merchandise is shipped in compliance with the terms and conditions of the L/C, payment for the business transaction is made and funds will be generated to repay the pre-export loan.

Another advantage of an L/C to the importer is that the importer need not pay out funds until the documents have arrived at a local port or airfield and unless all conditions stated in the L/C have been fulfilled. The main disadvantages of L/Cs are the fees charged by the importer's bank for issuing its L/C and the possibility that the L/C reduces the importer's borrowing line of credit with its bank. It may, in fact, be a competitive disadvantage for the exporter to demand automatically an L/C from an importer, especially if the importer has a good credit record and there is no concern regarding the economic or political conditions of the importer's country. In balance, though, the value of the L/C has been well established since the beginning of commerce, as detailed in *Global Finance in Practice 16.2.*

Draft

A *draft*, sometimes called a *bill of exchange* (B/E), is the instrument normally used in international commerce to effect payment. A draft is simply an order written by an exporter (seller) instructing an importer (buyer) or its agent to pay a specified amount of money at a specified time. Thus, it is the exporter's formal demand for payment from the importer.

GLOBAL FINANCE IN PRACTICE 16.2

Florence—The Birthplace of Trade Financing

Merchant banking for international trade largely began in a landlocked city, Florence, Italy. In the late thirteenth and early fourteenth centuries as commerce grew throughout Europe and the Mediterranean, banking began to develop in both Venice and Florence. It was a time in which commerce was still in its infancy, with the Catholic Church prohibiting many aspects of commerce, including the loaning of money in return for interest usury. Although usury has come to mean the illegal activity of charging excessive rates of interest, the term originally referred to charging interest of any kind.

The florin is a small gold coin first minted in Florence in 1252. Named after the city, the florin flourished as a means of transacting trade across Europe in the following century. Merchants conducted their trade on a bench—a *banco*—which gave rise to the term for the safe place in which to keep one's money.

But the coins were heavy, and if a merchant were traveling from one city or country to another to conduct trade, the weight was substantial, as was the chance of being robbed. So the merchants created the first financial derivative, a draft on the banco—a letter of exchange—which could be carried from one city to another and was recognized as a credit for florins on account at their home banco. Payment was guaranteed within three months. Of course, with the creation of banks came the first failures—bankruptcies.

From the very beginning, whether it was the loaning of money, the validity of a letter of exchange, or even the value of a currency, all were instruments or activities that involved risk, or *risque* in the Italian of the time.

The person or business initiating the draft is known as the maker (also known as the drawer or originator). Normally, maker is the exporter who sells and ships the merchandise. The party to whom the draft is addressed is the drawee. The drawee is asked to honor the draft, that is, to pay the amount requested according to the stated terms. In commercial transactions, the drawee is either the buyer, in which case the draft is called a trade draft, or the buyer's bank, in which case the draft is called a bank draft. Bank drafts are usually drawn according to the terms of an L/C. A draft may be drawn as a bearer instrument, or it may designate a person to whom payment is to be made. This person, known as the payee, may be the drawer itself or it may be some other party such as the drawer's bank.

Negotiable Instruments. If properly drawn, drafts can become negotiable instruments. As such, they provide a convenient instrument for financing the international movement of the merchandise. To become a negotiable instrument, a draft must conform to the following requirements—Uniform Commercial Code, Section 3104(1):

1. It must be in writing and signed by the maker or drawer.
2. It must contain an unconditional promise or order to pay a definite sum of money.
3. It must be payable on demand or at a fixed or determinable future date.
4. It must be payable to order or to bearer.

If a draft is drawn in conformity with the above requirements, a person receiving it with proper endorsements becomes a "holder in due course." This is a privileged legal status that enables the holder to receive payment despite any personal disagreements between drawee and maker because of controversy over the underlying transaction. If the drawee dishonors the draft, payment must be made to any holder in due course by any prior endorser or by the maker. This clear definition of the rights of parties who hold a negotiable instrument as a holder in due course has contributed significantly to the widespread acceptance of various forms of drafts, including personal checks.

Types of Drafts. Drafts are of two types: *sight drafts* and *time drafts*. A *sight draft* is payable on presentation to the drawee; the drawee must pay at once or dishonor the draft. A *time draft*, also called a *usance draft*, allows a delay in payment. It is presented to the drawee, who accepts it by writing or stamping a notice of acceptance on its face. Once accepted, the time draft becomes a promise to pay by the accepting party (the buyer). When a time draft is drawn on and accepted by a bank, it becomes a bankers' acceptance; when drawn on and accepted by a business firm, it becomes a trade acceptance (T/A).

The time period of a draft is referred to as its *tenor*. To qualify as a negotiable instrument, and so be attractive to a holder in due course, a draft must be payable on a fixed or determinable future date. For example, "60 days after sight" is a fixed date, which is established precisely at the time the draft is accepted. However, payment "on arrival of goods" is not determinable since the date of arrival cannot be known in advance. Indeed, there is no assurance that the goods will arrive at all.

Bankers' Acceptances. When a draft is accepted by a bank, it becomes a bankers' acceptance. As such it is the unconditional promise of that bank to make payment on the draft when it matures. In quality, the bankers' acceptance is practically identical to a marketable bank certificate of deposit (CD). The holder of a bankers' acceptance need not wait until maturity to liquidate the investment but may sell the acceptance in the money market, where constant trading in such instruments occurs. The amount of the discount depends entirely on the credit rating of the bank that signs the acceptance or another bank that reconfirmed the bankers' acceptance for a fee. The total cost or all-in cost of using a bankers' acceptance compared to other short-term financing instruments is analyzed later in this chapter.

Bill of Lading (B/L)

The third key document for financing international trade is the *bill of lading* (B/L). The bill of lading is issued to the exporter by a common carrier transporting the merchandise. It serves three purposes: as a *receipt*, a *contract*, and a *document of title*.

As a *receipt*, the bill of lading indicates that the carrier has received the merchandise described on the face of the document. The carrier is not responsible for ascertaining that the containers hold what is alleged to be their contents, so descriptions of merchandise on bills of lading are usually short and simple. If shipping charges are paid in advance, the bill of lading will usually be stamped "freight paid" or "freight prepaid." If merchandise is shipped collect—a less common procedure internationally than domestically—the carrier maintains a lien on the goods until freight is paid.

As a *contract*, the bill of lading indicates the obligation of the carrier to provide certain transportation in return for certain charges. Common carriers cannot disclaim responsibility for their negligence by inserting special clauses in a bill of lading. The bill of lading may specify alternative ports in the event that delivery cannot be made to the designated port, or it may specify that the goods will be returned to the exporter at the exporter's expense.

As a *document of title*, the bill of lading is used to obtain payment or a written promise of payment before the merchandise is released to the importer. The bill of lading can also function as collateral, against which funds may be advanced to the exporter by its local bank prior to or during shipment and before final payment by the importer.

The bill of lading is typically made payable to the order of the exporter, who thus retains title to the goods after they have been handed to the carrier. Title to the merchandise remains with the exporter until payment is received, at which time the exporter endorses the bill of lading (which is negotiable) in blank (making it a bearer instrument) or to the party making the payment, usually a bank. The most common procedure would be for payment to be advanced against a documentary draft accompanied by the endorsed order bill of lading.

After paying the draft, the exporter's bank forwards the documents through bank clearing channels to the bank of the importer. The importer's bank, in turn, releases the documents to the importer after payment (sight drafts); after acceptance (time drafts addressed to the importer and marked D/A); or after payment terms have been agreed upon (drafts drawn on the importer's bank under provisions of an L/C).

Documentation in a Typical Trade Transaction

Although a trade transaction could conceivably be handled in many ways, we shall now turn to a hypothetical example that illustrates the interaction of the various documents. Assume that an exporter in the U.S. receives an order from a Canadian buyer. For the exporter, this will be an export financed under an L/C requiring a bill of lading, with the exporter collecting via a time draft that was accepted by the Canadian buyer's bank. Such a transaction proceeds as follows, illustrated in Exhibit 16.7.

1. The Canadian buyer—the Importer in Exhibit 16.7—places an order with the Exporter in Exhibit 16.7, asking if the exporter is willing to ship under an L/C.
2. The exporter agrees to ship under an L/C and specifies relevant information such as prices and terms.
3. The Canadian buyer applies to its bank, North Bank in Exhibit 16.7, for an L/C to be issued in favor of the exporter for the merchandise it wishes to buy.
4. North Bank issues the L/C in favor of the exporter and sends it to the exporter's bank, South Bank in Exhibit 16.7.
5. South Bank advises the exporter of the opening of an L/C in the exporter's favor. South Bank may or may not confirm the L/C to add its own guarantee to the document.
6. The exporter ships the goods to the Canadian buyer.
7. The exporter prepares a time draft and presents it to its bank, South Bank. The draft is drawn (i.e., addressed to) North Bank in accordance with North Bank's L/C and accompanied by other documents as required, including the bill of lading. The exporter endorses the bill of lading in blank (making it a bearer instrument) so that title to the goods goes with the holder of the documents—the holder being South Bank at this point in the transaction.
8. South Bank presents the draft and documents to North Bank for acceptance. North Bank accepts the draft by stamping and signing it (making it a bankers' acceptance), takes

EXHIBIT 16.7 Steps in a Typical Trade Transaction

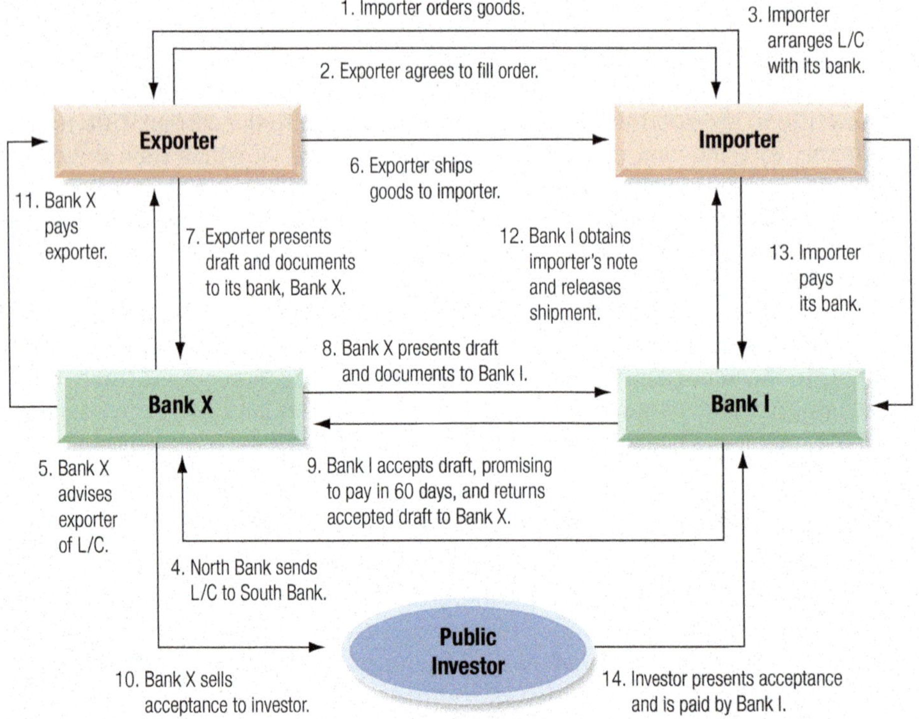

possession of the documents, and promises to pay the now-accepted draft at maturity—say, 60 days.

9. North Bank returns the accepted draft to South Bank. Alternatively, South Bank might ask North Bank to accept and discount the draft. Should this occur, North Bank would remit the cash less a discount fee rather than return the accepted draft to South Bank.
10. South Bank, having received back the accepted draft, now a bankers' acceptance, may choose between several alternatives. South Bank may sell the acceptance in the open market at a discount to an investor, typically a corporation or financial institution with excess cash it wants to invest for a short period of time. South Bank may also hold the acceptance in its own portfolio.
11. If South Bank discounts the acceptance with North Bank (mentioned in Step 9) or discounts it in the local money market, South Bank will transfer the proceeds less any fees and discount to the exporter. Another possibility would be for the exporter itself to take possession of the acceptance, hold it for 60 days, and present it for collection. Normally, however, exporters prefer to receive the discounted cash value of the acceptance at once rather than wait for the acceptance to mature and receive a slightly greater amount of cash at a later date.
12. North Bank notifies the Canadian buyer of the arrival of the documents. The Canadian buyer signs a note or makes some other agreed upon plan to pay North Bank for the merchandise in 60 days. North Bank releases the underlying documents so that the Canadian buyer can obtain physical possession of the shipment at once.
13. After 60 days, North Bank receives funds from the Canadian buyer to pay the maturing acceptance.
14. On the same day, the 60th day after acceptance, the holder of the matured acceptance presents it for payment and receives its face value. The holder may present it directly to North Bank or return it to South Bank and have South Bank collect it through normal banking channels.

Although this is a typical transaction involving an L/C, few international trade transactions are probably ever truly typical. Business, and more specifically international business, requires flexibility and creativity by management at all times. The mini-case at the end of this chapter presents an application of the mechanics of a real business situation. The result is a classic challenge to management: When and on what basis should typical procedures be compromised in order to accomplish strategic goals?

16.3 Government Programs to Help Finance Exports

Governments of most export-oriented industrialized countries have special financial institutions that provide some form of subsidized credit to their own national exporters. These export finance institutions offer terms that are better than those generally available from the private sector. Thus, domestic taxpayers are subsidizing sales to foreign buyers in order to create employment and maintain a technological edge. The most important institutions usually offer export credit insurance and an export-import bank for export financing.

Export Credit Insurance

The exporter who insists on cash or an L/C payment for foreign shipments is likely to lose orders to competitors from other countries that provide more favorable credit terms.

Better credit terms are often made possible by means of export credit insurance, which provides assurance to the exporter or the exporter's bank that, should the foreign customer default on payment, the insurance company will pay for a major portion of the loss. Because of the availability of export credit insurance, commercial banks are willing to provide medium- to long-term financing (five to seven years) for exports. Importers prefer that the exporter purchase export credit insurance to pay for nonperformance risk by the importer. In this way, the importer does not need to pay to have an L/C issued and does not reduce its credit line.

Competition between nations to increase exports by lengthening the period for which credit transactions can be insured may lead to a credit war and to unsound credit decisions. To prevent such an unhealthy development, a number of leading trading nations joined together in 1934 to create the Berne Union (officially, the *Union d'Assureurs des Credits Internationaux*) for the purpose of establishing a voluntary international understanding on export credit terms. The Berne Union recommends maximum credit terms for many items including, for example, heavy capital goods (five years), light capital goods (three years), and consumer durable goods (one year).

In the United States, export credit insurance is provided by the Foreign Credit Insurance Association (FCIA). This is an unincorporated association of private commercial insurance companies operating in cooperation with the Export-Import Bank (discussed in the next section). The FCIA provides policies protecting U.S. exporters against the risk of nonpayment by foreign debtors as a result of commercial and political risks. Losses due to commercial risk are those that result from the insolvency or protracted payment default of the buyer. Political losses arise from actions of governments beyond the control of buyer or seller.

Export-Import Bank and Export Financing

The Export-Import Bank (Eximbank) is an independent agency of the U.S. government, established in 1934 to stimulate and facilitate the foreign trade of the U.S. Interestingly, the Eximbank was originally created primarily to facilitate exports to the Soviet Union. In 1945, the Eximbank was re-chartered "to aid in financing and to facilitate exports and imports and the exchange of commodities between the United States and any foreign country or the agencies or nationals thereof."[1]

The Eximbank facilitates the financing of U.S. exports through various loan guarantee and insurance programs. The Eximbank guarantees repayment of medium-term (181 days to five years) and long-term (five years to ten years) export loans extended by U.S. banks to foreign borrowers. The Eximbank's medium- and long-term, direct-lending operation is based on participation with private sources of funds. Essentially, the Eximbank lends dollars to borrowers outside the United States for the purchase of U.S. goods and services. Proceeds of such loans are paid to U.S. suppliers. The loans themselves are repaid with interest in dollars to the Eximbank. The Eximbank requires private participation in these direct loans in order to (1) ensure that it complements rather than competes with private sources of export financing, (2) spread its resources more broadly, and (3) ensure that private financial institutions will continue to provide export credit.

The Eximbank also guarantees lease transactions; finances the costs involved in the preparation by U.S. firms of engineering, planning, and feasibility studies for non-U.S. clients on large capital projects; and supplies counseling for exporters, banks, or others needing help in finding financing for U.S. goods.

[1] The Charter of the Export-Import Bank of the United States, P.L. 114-94 codified at 12 U.S.C. §635 et seq.

16.4 Trade Financing Alternatives

In order to finance international trade receivables, firms use the same financing instruments that they use for domestic trade receivables, plus a few specialized instruments that are only available for financing international trade. Exhibit 16.8 identifies the main short-term financing instruments and their costs.

Bankers' Acceptances

Bankers' acceptances, described earlier in this chapter, can be used to finance both domestic and international trade receivables. Exhibit 16.8 shows that bankers' acceptances earn a yield comparable to other money market instruments, especially marketable bank certificates of deposit. However, the all-in cost to a firm of creating and discounting a bankers' acceptance also depends upon the commission charged by the bank that accepts the firm's draft.

The first owner of the bankers' acceptance created from an international trade transaction will be the exporter, who receives the accepted draft back after the bank has stamped it "accepted." The exporter may hold the acceptance until maturity and then collect. On an acceptance of, say, $100,000 for three months the exporter would receive the face amount less the bank's acceptance commission of 1.5% per annum:

Face amount of the acceptance	$100,000
Less 1.5% per annum commission for three months	– 375 (.015 × 3/12 × $100,000)
Amount received by exporter in three months	$ 99,625

Alternatively, the exporter may "discount"—that is, sell at a reduced price—the acceptance to its bank in order to receive funds at once. The exporter will then receive the face amount of the acceptance less both the acceptance fee and the going market rate of discount for bankers' acceptances. If the discount rate were 1.14% per annum as shown in Exhibit 16.8, the exporter would receive the following:

Face amount of the acceptance	$100,000
Less 1.5% per annum commission for three months	– 375 (.015 × 3/12 × $100,000)
Less 1.14% per annum discount rate for three months	– 285 (.0114 × 3/12 × $100,000)
Amount received by exporter at once	$ 99,340

EXHIBIT 16.8 Instruments for Financing Short-Term Trade Receivables

Instrument	Cost or Yield for 3-month Maturity
Bankers acceptances*	1.14% yield annualized
Trade acceptances*	1.17% yield annualized
Factoring	Variable rate but much higher cost than bank credit lines
Securitization	Variable rate but competitive with bank credit lines
Bank credit lines	LIBOR or Prime plus points (fewer points if covered by export credit insurance)
Commercial paper*	1.15% yield annualized

* These instruments compete with 3-month marketable bank time certificates of deposit that yield 1.17%.

Therefore, the annualized all-in cost of financing this bankers' acceptance is as follows:

$$\frac{\text{Commission} + \text{discount}}{\text{Proceeds}} \times \frac{360}{90} = \frac{\$375 + \$285}{\$99{,}340} \times \frac{360}{90} = .0266 \text{ or } 2.66\%$$

The discounting bank may hold the acceptance in its own portfolio, earning for itself the 1.14% per annum discount rate, or the acceptance may be resold in the acceptance market to portfolio investors. Investors buying bankers' acceptances provide the funds that finance the transaction.

Trade Acceptances

Trade acceptances are similar to bankers' acceptances except that the accepting entity is a commercial firm, like General Motors Acceptance Corporation (GMAC), rather than a bank. The cost of a trade acceptance depends on the credit rating of the accepting firm plus the commission it charges. Like bankers' acceptances, trade acceptances are sold at a discount to banks and other investors at a rate that is competitive with other money market instruments (see Exhibit 16.8).

Factoring

Specialized firms, known as *factors*, purchase receivables at a discount on either a non-recourse or recourse basis. Non-recourse means that the factor assumes the credit, political, and foreign exchange risk of the receivables it purchases. Recourse means that the factor can give back receivables that are not collectable. Since the factor must bear the cost and risk of assessing the creditworthiness of each receivable, the cost of factoring is usually quite high. It is more than borrowing at the prime rate plus points.

The all-in cost of factoring non-recourse receivables is similar in structure to acceptances. The factor charges a commission to cover the non-recourse risk, typically 1.5%–2.5%, plus interest deducted as a discount from the initial proceeds. On the other hand, the firm selling the non-recourse receivables avoids the cost of determining the creditworthiness of its customers.

It also does not have to show debt borrowed to finance these receivables on its balance sheet. Furthermore, the firm avoids both foreign exchange and political risk on these non-recourse receivables. *Global Finance in Practice 16.3* provides an example of the costs.

GLOBAL FINANCE IN PRACTICE **16.3**

Factoring in Practice

A U.S.-based manufacturer that suffered significant losses during first the global credit crisis and the following global recession is now cash-short. Sales, profits, and cash flows have fallen. The company is now struggling to service its high levels of debt. It does, however, have a number of new sales agreements. It is considering factoring one of its biggest new sales, a sale for $5 million to a Japanese company. The receivable is due in 90 days. After contacting a factoring agent, it is quoted the numbers shown.

If the company wishes to factor its receivable it will net $4.55 million, 91% of the face amount. Although this may at first sight appear expensive, the firm would net the proceeds in cash up-front, not having to wait 90 days for payment. And it would not be responsible for collecting on the receivable. If the firm were able to "factor in" the cost of factoring in the initial sale, all the better. Alternatively, the firm might offer a discount for cash paid in the first 10 days after shipment.

Face amount of receivable	$5,000,000
Non-recourse fee (1.5%)	–75,000
Factoring fee (2.5% per month × 3 months)	–375,000
Net proceeds on sale (received now)	$4,550,000

Securitization

The securitization of export receivables for financing trade is an attractive supplement to bankers' acceptance financing and factoring. A firm can securitize its export receivables by selling them to a legal entity established to create marketable securities based on a package of individual export receivables. An advantage of this technique is to remove the export receivables from the exporter's balance sheet because they have been sold without recourse.

Receivables are normally sold at a discount. The size of the discount depends on four factors:

1. The historic collection risk of the exporter
2. The cost of credit insurance
3. The cost of securing the desirable cash flow stream to the investors
4. The size of the financing and services fees

Securitization is more cost-effective if there is a large value of transactions with a known credit history and default probability. A large exporter could establish its own securitization entity. While the initial setup cost is high, the entity can be used on an ongoing basis. Alternatively, smaller exporters could use a common securitization entity provided by a financial institution, thereby saving the expensive setup costs.

Bank Credit Lines

A firm's bank credit line can typically be used to finance, up to a fixed upper limit, say 80%, of accounts receivable. Export receivables can be eligible for inclusion in bank credit line financing. However, credit information on foreign customers may be more difficult to collect and assess. If a firm covers its export receivables with export credit insurance, it can greatly reduce the credit risk of those receivables. This insurance enables the bank credit line to cover more export receivables and lower the interest rate for that coverage. Of course, any foreign exchange risk must be handled by the transaction exposure techniques described in Chapter 10.

The cost of using a bank credit line is usually the prime rate of interest plus points to reflect a particular firm's credit risk. As usual, 100 points is equal to 1%. In the U.S., borrowers are also expected to maintain a compensating deposit balance at the lending institution. In Europe and many other places, lending is done on an overdraft basis. An overdraft agreement allows a firm to overdraw its bank account up to the limit of its credit line. Interest at prime plus points is based only on the amount of overdraft borrowed. In either case, the all-in cost of bank borrowing using a credit line is higher than acceptance financing, as shown in Exhibit 16.8.

Commercial Paper

A firm can issue commercial paper—unsecured promissory notes—to fund its short-term financing needs, including both domestic and export receivables. However, it is only the large, well-known firms with favorable credit ratings that have access to either the domestic or euro commercial paper market. As shown in Exhibit 16.8, commercial paper interest rates lie at the low end of the yield curve.

16.5 Forfaiting

Forfaiting is a specialized technique to eliminate the risk of nonpayment by importers in instances where the importing firm and/or its government is perceived by the exporter to be too risky for open account credit. The name of the technique comes from the French *à forfait*, a term that implies "to forfeit or surrender a right."

Role of the Forfaiter

The essence of forfaiting is the non-recourse sale by an exporter of bank-guaranteed promissory notes, bills of exchange, or similar documents received from an importer in another country. The exporter receives cash at the time of the transaction by selling the notes or bills at a discount from their face value to a specialized finance firm, called a *forfaiter*. The forfaiter arranges the entire operation prior to the execution of the transaction. Although the exporting firm is responsible for the quality of delivered goods, it receives a clear and unconditional cash payment at the time of the transaction. All political and commercial risk of nonpayment by the importer is carried by the guaranteeing bank. Small exporters, who trust their clients to pay, find the forfaiting technique invaluable because it eases cash flow problems.

During the Soviet era, expertise in the technique was centered in German and Austrian banks, which used forfaiting to finance sales of capital equipment to eastern European, "Soviet Bloc" countries. British, Scandinavian, Italian, Spanish, and French exporters have now adopted the technique, but U.S. and Canadian exporters are reported to be slow to use forfaiting, possibly because they are suspicious of its simplicity and lack of complex documentation. Nevertheless, some American firms now specialize in the technique, and the Association of Forfaiters in the Americas (AFIA) has more than 20 members. Major export destinations financed via the forfaiting technique are Asia, Eastern Europe, the Middle East, and Latin America.

A Typical Forfaiting Transaction

A typical forfaiting transaction involves five parties and seven steps, as shown in Exhibit 16.9.

EXHIBIT 16.9 Typical Forfaiting Transaction

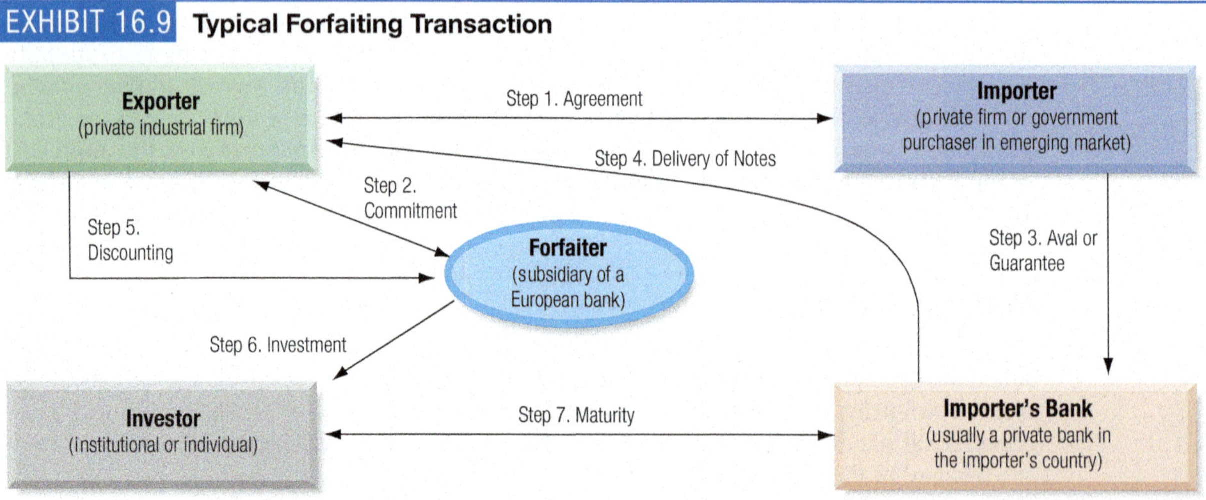

Step 1. Agreement. Importer and exporter agree on a series of imports to be paid for over a period of time, typically three to five years. However, periods as long as 10 years and as short as 180 days have been financed using the technique. The normal minimum size for a transaction is $100,000. The importer agrees to make periodic payments, often against progress on delivery or completion of a project.

Step 2. Commitment. The forfaiter promises to finance the transaction at a fixed discount rate, with payment to be made when the exporter delivers to the forfaiter the appropriate promissory notes or other specified paper. The agreed-upon discount rate is based on the cost of funds in the euromarket, usually on LIBOR for the average life of the transaction, plus a margin over LIBOR to reflect the perceived risk in the deal.

This risk premium is influenced by the size and tenor of the deal, country risk, and the quality of the guarantor institution. On a five-year deal, for example, with 10 semiannual payments, the rate used would be based on the 2.25-year LIBOR rate. This discount rate is normally added to the invoice value of the transaction so that the cost of financing is ultimately borne by the importer. The forfaiter charges an additional commitment fee of from 0.5% per annum to as high as 6.0% per annum from the date of its commitment to finance until receipt of the actual discount paper issued in accordance with the finance contract. This fee is also normally added to the invoice cost and passed on to the importer.

Step 3. Aval or Guarantee. The importer obligates itself to pay for its purchases by issuing a series of promissory notes, usually maturing every six or twelve months, against progress on delivery or completion of the project. These promissory notes are first delivered to the importer's bank where they are endorsed (that is, guaranteed) by that bank. In Europe, this unconditional guarantee is referred to as an aval, which translates into English as "backing."

At this point, the importer's bank becomes the primary obligor in the eyes of all subsequent holders of the notes. The bank's aval or guarantee must be irrevocable, unconditional, divisible, and assignable. Because U.S. banks do not issue avals, U.S. transactions are guaranteed by a standby letter of credit (L/C), which is functionally similar to an aval but more cumbersome. For example, L/Cs can normally be transferred only once.

Step 4. Delivery of Notes. The now-endorsed promissory notes are delivered to the exporter.

Step 5. Discounting. The exporter endorses the notes "without recourse" and discounts them with the forfaiter receiving the agreed-upon proceeds. Proceeds are usually received two days after the documents are presented. By endorsing the notes "without recourse," the exporter frees itself from any liability for future payment on the notes and thus receives the discounted proceeds without having to worry about any further payment difficulties.

Step 6. Investment. The forfaiting bank either holds the notes until full maturity as an investment or endorses and re-discounts them in the international money market. Such subsequent sale by the forfaiter is usually without recourse. The major rediscount markets are in London and Switzerland, plus New York for notes issued in conjunction with Latin American business.

Step 7. Maturity. At maturity, the investor holding the notes presents them for collection to the importer or to the importer's bank. The promise of the importer's bank is what gives the documents their value.

In effect, the forfaiter functions as both a money market firm (e.g., a lender of short-term financing) and a specialist in packaging financial deals involving country risk. As a money market firm, the forfaiter divides the discounted notes into appropriately sized packages and resells them to various investors having different maturity preferences. As a country risk specialist, the forfaiter assesses the risk that the notes will eventually be paid by the importer or the importer's bank and puts together a deal that satisfies the needs of both exporter and importer.

Success of the forfaiting technique springs from the belief that the aval—the guarantee of a commercial bank—can be depended upon. Although commercial banks are the normal and preferred guarantors, guarantees by government banks or government ministries of finance are accepted in some cases. On occasion, large commercial enterprises have been accepted as debtors without a bank guarantee. An additional aspect of the technique is that the endorsing bank's aval is perceived to be an "off balance sheet" obligation—the debt is presumably not considered by others in assessing the financial structure of the commercial banks.

Summary Points

- International trade takes place between three categories of relationships: unaffiliated unknown parties, unaffiliated known parties, and affiliated parties.
- International trade transactions between affiliated parties typically do not require contractual arrangements or external financing. Trade transactions between unaffiliated parties typically require contracts and some type of external financing, such as that available through letters of credit.
- The basic procedure of financing international trade rests on the interrelationship between three key documents: the letter of credit (L/C), the bill of lading, and the draft.
- In the L/C, the bank substitutes its credit for that of the importer and promises to pay if certain documents are submitted to the bank. The exporter may now rely on the promise of the bank rather than on the promise of the importer.
- The exporter typically ships with a bill of lading, attaches the bill of lading to a draft that orders payment from the importer's bank, and presents these documents, plus any of a number of additional documents, through its own bank to the importer's bank.
- If the documents are in order, the importer's bank either pays the draft (a sight draft) or accepts the draft (a time draft). In the latter case, the bank promises to pay in the future. At this step, the importer's bank acquires title to the merchandise through the bill of lading and releases the merchandise to the importer.
- The total costs to an exporter of entering a foreign market include the transaction costs of the trade financing, the import and export duties and tariffs applied by exporting and importing nations, and the costs of foreign market penetration.
- Trade financing uses the same financing instruments as does domestic receivables financing, plus some specialized instruments that are only available for financing international trade. A popular instrument for short-term financing is a bankers' acceptance.
- Other short-term financing instruments with a domestic counterpart are trade acceptances, factoring, securitization, bank credit lines (usually covered by export credit insurance), and commercial paper

MINI-CASE

Crosswell International and Brazil[2]

Crosswell International is a U.S.-based manufacturer and distributor of health care products, including children's diapers. Crosswell has been approached by Leonardo Sousa, the president of Material Hospitalar, a distributor of health care products throughout Brazil. Sousa is interested in distributing Crosswell's major diaper product, Precious Diapers, but only if an acceptable arrangement regarding pricing and payment terms can be reached.

Exporting to Brazil

Crosswell's manager for export operations, Geoff Mathieux, followed up the preliminary discussions by putting together an estimate of export costs and pricing for discussion purposes with Sousa. Crosswell needs to know all of the costs and pricing assumptions for the entire supply and value chain as it reaches the consumer. Mathieux believes it critical that any arrangement that Crosswell enters into results in a price to consumers in the Brazilian marketplace that is both fair to all parties involved and competitive, given the market niche Crosswell hopes to penetrate. This first cut on pricing Precious Diapers into Brazil is presented in Exhibit A.

Crosswell proposes to sell the basic diaper line to the Brazilian distributor for $34.00 per case, FAS (free alongside ship) Miami docks. This means that the seller, Crosswell, agrees to cover all costs associated with getting the diapers to the Miami docks. The costs of loading the diapers onto the ship, of the actual shipping (freight), and of the associated documents is $4.32 per case. The running subtotal, $38.32 per case, is termed CFR (cost and freight). Finally, the insurance expenses related to the potential loss of the goods while in transit to final port of destination, export insurance, are $0.86 per case. The total CIF (cost, insurance, and freight) is $39.18 per case, or 97.95 Brazilian real per case, assuming an exchange rate of 2.50 Brazilian real (R$) per U.S. dollar ($). In summary, the CIF cost of R$97.95 is the price charged by the exporter to the importer on arrival in Brazil, and is calculated as follows:

$$\begin{aligned} CIF &= FAS + freight + export\ insurance \\ &= (\$34.00 + \$4.32 + \$0.86) \times R\$2.50 \\ &= R\$97.95 \end{aligned}$$

The actual cost to the distributor in getting the diapers through the port and customs warehouses must also be calculated in terms of what Leonardo Sousa's costs are in reality. The various fees and taxes detailed in Exhibit A raise the fully landed cost of the Precious Diapers to R$107.63 per case. The distributor would now bear storage and inventory costs totaling R$8.33 per case, which would bring the costs to R$115.96. The distributor then adds a margin for distribution services of 20% (R$23.19), raising the price as sold to the final retailer to R$139.15 per case.

Finally, the retailer (a supermarket or other retailer of consumer health care products) would include its expenses, taxes, and markup to reach the final shelf price to the customer of R$245.48 per case. This final retail price estimate now allows both Crosswell and Material Hospitalar to evaluate the price competitiveness of the Precious Ultra-Thin Diaper in the Brazilian marketplace and provides a basis for further negotiations between the two parties.

The Precious Ultra-Thin Diaper will be shipped via container. Each container will hold 968 cases of diapers. The costs and prices in Exhibit A are calculated on a per case basis, although some costs and fees are assessed by container. Mathieux provides the export price quotation shown in Exhibit A, an outline of a potential representation agreement (for Sousa to represent Crosswell's product lines in the Brazilian marketplace), and payment and credit terms to Leonardo Sousa. Crosswell's payment and credit terms are that Sousa either pay in full in cash in advance or remit a confirmed irrevocable documentary L/C with a time draft specifying a tenor of 60 days.

Crosswell also requests from Sousa financial statements, banking references, foreign commercial references, descriptions of regional sales forces, and sales forecasts for the Precious Diaper line. These last requests allow Crosswell to assess Material Hospitalar's ability to be a dependable, creditworthy, and capable long-term partner and representative of the firm in the Brazilian marketplace. The discussions that follow focus on finding acceptable common ground between the two parties and on working to increase the competitiveness of the Precious Diaper product line in the Brazilian marketplace

Crosswell's Proposal

The proposed sale by Crosswell to Material Hospitalar, at least in the initial shipment, is for 10 containers of 968 cases of diapers at $39.18 per case, CIF Brazil, payable in U.S. dollars. This is a total invoice amount of $379,262.40. Payment terms are that a confirmed L/C will be required of Material Hospitalar on a U.S. bank. The payment will be based on a time draft of 60 days, presentation to the

[2] This case was prepared by Doug Mathieux and Geoff Mathieux under the direction of Professors Michael H. Moffett and James L. Mills for the purpose of classroom discussion, and not to indicate either effective or ineffective management.

EXHIBIT A Export Pricing for the Precious Diaper Line to Brazil

The *Precious Ultra-Thin Diaper* will be shipped via container. Each container will hold 968 cases of diapers. The costs and prices below are calculated on a per case basis, although some costs and fees are assessed per container.

Exports Costs and Pricing to Brazil	Per Case	Rates and Calculation
FAS price per case, Miami	$34.00	
Freight, loading and documentation	4.32	$4,180 per container/968 = $4.32
CFR price per case, Brazilian port (Santos)	$38.32	
Export insurance	0.86	2.25% of CIF
CIF to Brazilian port	$39.18	
CIF to Brazilian port, in Brazilian real	R$97.95	2.50 Real/US$ × $39.18
Brazilian Importation Costs		
Import duties	1.96	2.00% of CIF
Merchant marine renovation fee	2.70	25.00% of freight
Port storage fees	1.27	1.30% of CIF
Port handling fees	0.01	R$12 per container
Additional handling fees	0.26	20.00% of storage and handling
Customs brokerage fees	1.96	2.00% of CIF
Import license fee	0.05	R$50 per container
Local transportation charges	1.47	1.50% of CIF
Total cost to distributor in real	R$107.63	
Distributor's Costs and Pricing		
Storage cost	1.47	1.50% of CIF × months
Cost of financing diaper inventory	6.86	7.00% of CIF × months
Distributor's margin	23.19	20.00% of Price + storage + financing
Price to retailer in real	R$139.15	
Brazilian Retailer Costs and Pricing		
Industrial product tax (IPT)	20.87	15.00% of price to retailer
Mercantile circulation services tax (MCS)	28.80	18.00% of price + PIT
Retailer costs and markup	56.65	30.00% of price + PIT + MCS
Price to consumer in real	R$245.48	

Diaper Prices to Consumers	Diapers per Case	Price per Diaper
Small size	352	R$0.70
Medium size	256	R$0.96
Large size	192	R$1.28

bank for acceptance with other documents on the date of shipment. Both the exporter and the exporter's bank will expect payment from the importer or the importer's bank 60 days from this date of shipment.

What Should Crosswell Expect?

Assuming Material Hospitalar acquires the L/C and it is confirmed by Crosswell's bank in the United States, Crosswell will ship the goods after the initial agreement—say, 15 days—as illustrated in Exhibit B. Simultaneous with the shipment, when Crosswell has lost physical control over the goods, Crosswell will present the bill of lading (acquired at the time of shipment) with the other needed documents to its bank requesting payment. Because the export is under a confirmed L/C, assuming all documents are in order, Crosswell's bank will give Crosswell two choices:

1. Wait the full time period of the time draft of 60 days and receive the entire payment in full ($379,262.40).
2. Receive the discounted value of this amount today. The discounted amount, assuming U.S. dollar interest rate of 6.00% per annum (1.00% per 60 days):

$$\frac{\$379{,}262.40}{(1 + 0.01)} = \frac{\$379{,}262.40}{1.01} = \$375{,}507.33$$

EXHIBIT B Export Payment Terms on Crosswell's Export to Brazil

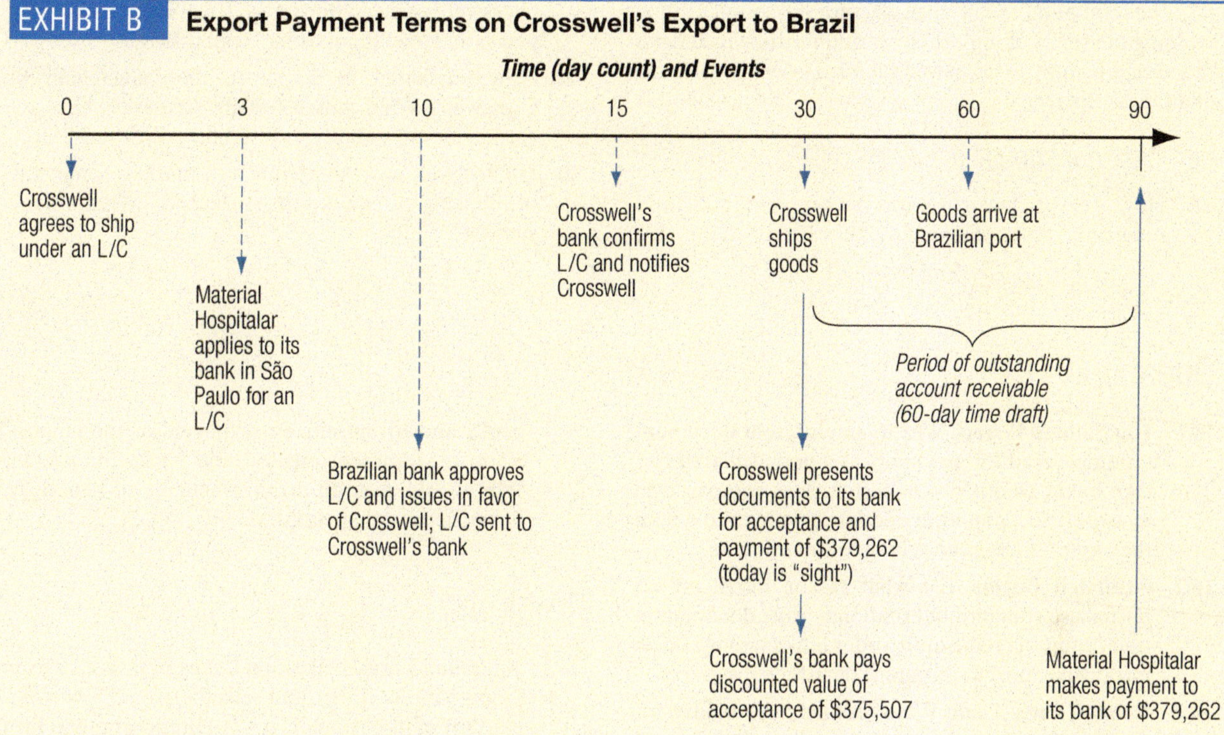

Because the invoice is denominated in U.S. dollars, Crosswell need not worry about currency value changes (currency risk). And because its bank has confirmed the L/C, it is protected against changes or deteriorations in Material Hospitalar's ability to pay on the future date.

What Should Material Hospitalar Expect?

Material Hospitalar will receive the goods on or before day 60. It will then move the goods through its distribution system to retailers. Depending on the payment terms between Material Hospitalar and its buyers (retailers), it could either receive cash or terms for payment for the goods. Because Material Hospitalar purchased the goods via the 60-day time draft and an L/C from its Brazilian bank, total payment of $379,262.40 is due on day 90 (shipment and presentation of documents was on 30 + 60 day time draft) to the Brazilian bank. Material Hospitalar, because it is a Brazilian-based company and has agreed to make payment in U.S. dollars (foreign currency), carries the currency risk of the transaction.

Crosswell/Material Hospitalar's Concern

The concern the two companies hold, however, is that the total price to the consumer in Brazil, R$245.48 per case, or R$0.70/diaper (small size), is too high. The major competitors in the Brazilian market for premium quality diapers, Kenko do Brasil (Japan), Johnson and Johnson (U.S.), and Procter and Gamble (U.S.), are cheaper (see Exhibit C).

EXHIBIT C Competitive Diaper Prices in the Brazilian Market (in Brazilian real)

		Price per Diaper by Size		
Company (Country)	**Brand**	**Small**	**Medium**	**Large**
Kenko (Japan)	Monica Plus	0.68	0.85	1.18
Procter & Gamble (USA)	Pampers Uni	0.65	0.80	1.08
Johnson & Johnson (USA)	Sempre Seca Plus	0.65	0.80	1.08
Crosswell (USA)	Precious	0.70	0.96	1.40

The competitors all manufacture in-country, thus avoiding the series of import duties and tariffs, which have added significantly to Crosswell's landed prices in the Brazilian marketplace.

MINI-CASE QUESTIONS

1. How are pricing, currency of denomination, and financing interrelated in the value-chain for Crosswell's penetration of the Brazilian market? Can you summarize them using Exhibit B?
2. How important is Sousa to the value-chain of Crosswell? What worries might Crosswell have regarding Sousa's ability to fulfill his obligations?
3. If Crosswell is to penetrate the market, some way of reducing its prices will be required. What do you suggest?

Questions

16.1 Unaffiliated Buyers. Why might different documentation be used for an export to a non-affiliated foreign buyer who is a new customer as compared to an export to a non-affiliated foreign buyer to whom the exporter has been selling for many years?

16.2 Affiliated Buyers. For what reason might an exporter use standard international trade documentation (letter of credit, draft, order bill of lading) on an intrafirm export to its parent or sister subsidiary?

16.3 Related Party Trade. What reasons can you give for the observation that intrafirm trade is now greater than trade between non-affiliated exporters and importers?

16.4 Documents. Explain the difference between a letter of credit (L/C) and a draft. How are they linked?

16.5 Risks. What is the major difference between "currency risk" and "risk of noncompletion?" How are these risks handled in a typical international trade transaction?

16.6 Letter of Credit. Identify each party to a letter of credit (L/C) and indicate its responsibility.

16.7 Confirmed Letter of Credit. Why would an exporter insist on a confirmed letter of credit?

16.8 Documenting an Export of Hard Drives. List the steps involved in the export of computer hard disk drives from Penang, Malaysia, to San Jose, California, using an unconfirmed letter of credit authorizing payment on sight.

16.9 Documenting an Export of Lumber from Portland to Yokohama. List the steps involved in the export of lumber from Portland, Oregon, to Yokohama, Japan, using a confirmed letter of credit, payment to be made in 120 days.

16.10 Governmentally Supplied Credit. Various governments have established agencies to insure against nonpayment for exports and/or to provide export credit. This shifts credit risk away from private banks and to the citizen taxpayers of the country whose government created and backs the agency. Why would such an arrangement be of benefit to the citizens of that country?

Problems

16.1 Nakatomi Lexus. Nakatomi Lexus buys its cars from Lexus Motors (U.S.), and sells them to U.S. customers. One of its customers is EcoHire, a car rental firm that buys cars from Nakatomi Lexus at a wholesale price. Final payment is due to Nakatomi Lexus in six months. EcoHire has bought USD800,000 worth of cars from Nakatomi, with a cash down payment of USD160,000 and the balance due in six months without any interest charged as a sales incentive. Nakatomi Lexus will have the EcoHire receivable accepted by Alliance Acceptance for a 2% fee, and then sell it at a 3% per annum discount to Wells Fargo Bank.

a. What is the annualized percentage all-in cost to Nakatomi Lexus?
b. What are Nakatomi's net cash proceeds, including the cash down payment?

16.2 Victory Cycles (A). Victory Cycles (U.S.) exports large-engine motorcycles (greater than 700cc) to Australia and invoices its customers in U.S. dollars. Sydney Wholesale Imports has purchased $3,000,000 of merchandise from Victory, with payment due in six months. The payment will be made with a bankers' acceptance issued by Charter Bank of Sydney at a fee of 1.75% per annum. Victory has a weighted average cost of capital of 10%. If Victory holds this acceptance to maturity, what is its annualized percentage all-in cost?

16.3 Victory Cycles (B). Assuming the facts in Problem 16.3, Bank of America is now willing to buy Victory's bankers' acceptance for a discount of

6% per annum. What would be Victory's annualized percentage all-in cost of financing its $3 million Australian receivable?

16.4 San Mateo Servers (A). San Mateo Servers (U.S.) has sold Internet servers to Telecom España for EUR700,000. Payment is due in three months and will be made with a trade acceptance from Telecom España Acceptance. The acceptance fee is 1.0% per annum of the face amount of the note. This acceptance will be sold at a 4% per annum discount. What is the annualized percentage all-in cost in euros of this method of trade financing?

16.5 San Mateo Servers (B). Assume that San Mateo Servers prefers to receive U.S. dollars rather than euros for the trade transaction described in Problem 16.4. It is considering two alternatives: (1) sell the acceptance for euros at once and convert the euros immediately to U.S. dollars at the spot rate of exchange of USD1.000 = €1.00 or (2) hold the euro acceptance until maturity but at the start sell the expected euro proceeds forward for dollars at the 3-month forward rate of USD1.02 = EUR1.00.

a. What are the U.S. dollar net proceeds received at once from the discounted trade acceptance in alternative 1?
b. What are the U.S. dollar net proceeds received in three months in alternative 2?
c. What is the break-even investment rate that would equalize the net U.S. dollar proceeds from both alternatives?
d. Which alternative should Nikken Microsystems choose?

16.6 Forfaiting at Umaru Oil (Nigeria). Umaru Oil of Nigeria has purchased $1,000,000 of oil drilling equipment from Gunslinger Drilling of Houston, Texas. Umaru Oil must pay for this purchase over the next five years at a rate of $200,000 per year due on March 1 of each year. Bank of Zurich, a Swiss forfaiter, has agreed to buy the five notes of $200,000 each at a discount. The discount rate would be approximately 8% per annum based on the expected 3-year LIBOR rate plus 200 basis points, paid by Umaru Oil. Bank of Zurich would also charge Umaru Oil an additional commitment fee of 2% per annum from the date of its commitment to finance until receipt of the actual discounted notes issued in accordance with the financing contract. The $200,000 promissory notes will come due on March 1 in successive years. The promissory notes issued by Umaru Oil will be endorsed by their bank, Lagos City Bank, for a 1% fee and delivered to Gunslinger Drilling. At this point, Gunslinger Drilling will endorse the notes without recourse and discount them with the forfaiter, Bank of Zurich, receiving the full $200,000 principal amount. Bank of Zurich will sell the notes by re-discounting them to investors in the international money market without recourse. At maturity, the investors holding the notes will present them for collection at Lagos City Bank. If Lagos City Bank defaults on payment, the investors will collect on the notes from Bank of Zurich.

a. What is the annualized percentage all-in cost to Umaru Oil of financing the first $200,000 note due March 1, 2011?
b. What might motivate Umaru Oil to use this relatively expensive alternative for financing?

16.7 MiraWest Enterprises (A). MiraWest Enterprises has sold a combination of films and DVDs to Hong Kong Media Incorporated for US$100,000, with payment due in six months. MiraWest has the following alternatives for financing this receivable: (1) Use its bank credit line. Interest would be at the prime rate of 5% plus 150 basis points per annum. (2) Use its bank credit line but purchase export credit insurance for a 1% fee. Because of the reduced risk, the bank interest rate would be reduced to 5% per annum without any points. In both cases MiraWest would need to maintain a compensating balance of 20% of the loan's face amount, and no interest will be paid on the compensating balance by the bank.

a. What are the annualized percentage all-in costs of each alternative?
b. What are the advantages and disadvantages of each alternative?
c. Which alternative would you recommend?

16.8 MiraWest Enterprises (B). MiraWest Enterprises has been approached by a factor that offers to purchase the Hong Kong Media Imports receivable at a 16% per annum discount plus a 2% charge for a non-recourse clause.

a. What is the annualized percentage all-in cost of this factoring alternative?
b. What are the advantages and disadvantages of the factoring alternative compared to the alternatives in Problem 16.7?

16.9 BlackComb Sports (A). BlackComb Sports (BlackComb) is considering bidding to sell $100,000 of ski equipment to Phang Family Enterprises of Seoul, Korea. Payment would be due in six months. Since BlackComb cannot find good credit information on Phang, BlackComb wants to protect its credit risk. It is considering the following financing solution.

Phang's bank issues a letter of credit on behalf of Phang and agrees to accept BlackComb's draft for $100,000 due in six months. The acceptance fee would cost BlackComb $500, plus reduce Phang's available credit line by $100,000. The bankers' acceptance note of $100,000 would be sold at a 2% per annum discount in the money market. What is the annualized percentage all-in cost to BlackComb of this bankers' acceptance financing?

16.10 BlackComb Sports (B). BlackComb could also buy export credit insurance from FCIA for a 1.5% premium. It finances the $100,000 receivable from Phang from its credit line at 6% per annum interest. No compensating bank balance would be required.

a. What is BlackComb's annualized percentage all-in cost of financing?
b. What are Phang's costs?
c. What are the advantages and disadvantages of this alternative compared to the bankers' acceptance financing in Problem 16.9? Which alternative would you recommend?

16.11 Inca Breweries of Peru. Inca Breweries of Lima, Peru, has received an order for 10,000 cartons of beer from Alicante Importers of Alicante, Spain. The beer will be exported to Spain under the terms of a letter of credit issued by a Madrid bank on behalf of Alicante Importers. The letter of credit specifies that the face value of the shipment, $720,000 U.S. dollars, will be paid 90 days after the Madrid bank accepts a draft drawn by Inca Breweries in accordance with the terms of the letter of credit.

The current discount rate on 3-month bankers' acceptance is 8% per annum, and Inca Breweries estimates its weighted average cost of capital to be 20% per annum. The commission for selling a bankers' acceptance in the discount market is 1.2% of the face amount.

a. What is the difference, in present value terms, between holding the acceptance to maturity versus selling the banker's acceptance today in the money market?
b. What would you recommend Inca Breweries do?

16.12 Talishan Shoe Company (A). Talishan Shoe Company of Durham, North Carolina, has received an order for 50,000 cartons of athletic shoes from Southampton Footware, Ltd., of England, payment to be in British pounds sterling. The shoes will be shipped to Southampton Footware under the terms of a letter of credit issued by a London bank on behalf of Southampton Footware. The letter of credit specifies that the face value of the shipment, £400,000, will be paid 120 days after the London bank accepts a draft drawn by Southampton Footware in accordance with the terms of the letter of credit. The current discount rate in London on 120-day bankers' acceptances is 12% per annum, and Southampton Footware estimates its weighted average cost of capital to be 18% per annum. The commission for selling a bankers' acceptance in the discount market is 2.0% of the face amount.

a. Would Talishan Shoe Company gain by holding the acceptance to maturity, as compared to discounting the bankers' acceptance at once?
b. Does Talishan Shoe Company incur any other risks in this transaction?

16.13 Talishan Shoe Company (B). Assume that Great Britain charges an import duty of 10% on shoes imported into the United Kingdom. Talishan Shoe Company, in Problem 16.12, discovers that it can manufacture shoes in Ireland and import them into Britain free of any import duty. What factors should Talishan consider in deciding to continue to export shoes from North Carolina versus manufacture them in Ireland?

PART

5

Foreign Investments and Investment Analysis

17

Foreign Direct Investment and Political Risk

In this world, shipmates, Sin that pays its way can travel freely, and without passport; whereas Virtue, if a pauper, is stopped at all frontiers.

—Herman Melville, Chapter 9, The Sermon, in *Moby Dick*, 1851

LEARNING OBJECTIVES

17.1 Demonstrate how key competitive advantages support a strategy to sustain direct foreign investment

17.2 Explore the decision process of the multinational in its choices of markets and structural choices for market entry

17.3 Define and classify the political risks faced by multinational firms when investing abroad

17.4 Examine the financial impacts of political risk on the multinational firm

17.5 Discuss the many different methods employed by multinationals to mitigate political risks

A multinational firm investing in other countries is executing its corporate strategy with foreign direct investment (FDI). This chapter first explores the theoretical foundations of the decision to undertake FDI. This is followed by an exploration of how the multinational may choose a country or market and then what form of entry it chooses to utilize. In each of these we focus on the financial risks and returns associated with these decisions. The third section of the chapter introduces, defines, and provides a classification scheme for political risk. The fourth section examines the potential financial impacts of political risk, with the fifth and final section providing an overview of the multitude of mitigation strategies used by multinationals when confronting these political risks. The chapter concludes with the mini-case *Argentina and the Vulture Funds*, an exploration of a unique series of legal and political risks in global financial markets and the sovereign borrowers who depend on them.

17.1 The Foreign Direct Investment Decision

The strategic decision to undertake foreign direct investment (FDI) by a multinational firm is an expansion of its global strategy. The *OLI Paradigm* helps to explain the decision by a multinational firm to undertake FDI.[1] The OLI Paradigm creates an overall framework to explain why multinational enterprises choose *foreign direct investment* (FDI) rather than choosing to serve foreign markets through alternative modes, such as licensing or exporting.

[1] Peter J. Buckley, and Mark Casson, *The Future of the Multinational Enterprise*, London: McMillan, 1976; and John H. Dunning, "Trade Location of Economic Activity and the MNE: A Search for an Eclectic Approach," in *The International Allocation of Economic Activity*, Bertil Ohlin, Per-Ove Hesselborn, and Per Magnus Wijkman, eds., New York: Holmes and Meier, 1977, pp. 395–418.

The OLI Paradigm states that a firm must first have some competitive advantage in its home market —"O" for ownership advantages—that can be transferred abroad if the firm is to be successful in foreign direct investment. Second, the firm must be attracted by specific characteristics of the foreign market—"L" for location advantages—that will allow it to exploit its competitive advantages in that market. Third, the firm will maintain its competitive position by attempting to control the entire value chain in its industry—"I" for internationalization advantages. The satisfaction of these three conditions can lead the MNE to select foreign direct investment over licensing or outsourcing.

Ownership Advantages. As described earlier, a firm must have competitive advantages in its home market. These advantages must be firm specific, not easily copied, and in a form that allows them to be transferred to foreign subsidiaries. For example, economies of scale and financial strength are not necessarily firm specific because they can be achieved by many other firms. Certain kinds of technology can be purchased, licensed, or copied. Even differentiated products can lose their advantage to slightly altered versions, given enough marketing effort and the right price.

Location Advantages. These factors are typically market imperfections or genuine comparative advantages that attract FDI to particular locations. These factors might include a low-cost but productive labor force, unique sources of raw materials, a large domestic market, defensive investments to counter other competitors, or centers of technological excellence.

Internationalization Advantages. According to the OLI Paradigm, the key ingredient for maintaining a firm specific competitive advantage is possession of proprietary information and control of the human capital that can generate new information through expertise in research. Needless to say, once again, large research-intensive firms are most likely to fit this description. Minimizing transactions costs is a key element in a successful internationalization strategy. Wholly owned FDI reduces the agency costs that arise from asymmetric information, lack of trust, and the need to monitor foreign partners, suppliers, and financial institutions. Self-financing eliminates the need to observe specific debt covenants on foreign subsidiaries that are financed locally or by joint venture partners. If a multinational firm has a low global cost and high availability of capital, why share it with joint venture partners, distributors, licensees, and local banks, all of which probably have a higher cost of capital?

The Financial Strategy. Financial strategies are directly related to the OLI Paradigm in explaining FDI, as shown in Exhibit 17.1. The MNE's financial managers can proactively formulate financial strategies in advance. These include strategies necessary to gain an advantage from lower global cost and greater availability of capital. Other proactive financial strategies include negotiating financial subsidies and/or reduced taxation to increase free cash flows, reducing financial agency costs through FDI, and reducing operating and transaction exposure through FDI.

Reactive financial strategies, as illustrated in Exhibit 17.1, depend on discovering market imperfections. For example, the MNE can exploit misaligned exchange rates and stock prices. It also needs to react to capital controls that prevent the free movement of funds and react to opportunities to minimize worldwide taxation.

17.2 Structural Choices for Foreign Market Entry

A multinational firm's decision to invest abroad is followed by choices of which markets and how to enter them—through which business forms and structures. Ultimately, the choice of both target markets and entry structures will establish what types of political risk (the subject of the following section of this chapter) the firm then faces.

EXHIBIT 17.1 Finance Factors and the OLI Paradigm

	Proactive Financial Strategies	Reactive Financial Strategies
Ownership Advantages	• Competitive sourcing of capital globally • Strategic cross-listing • Accounting and disclosure transparency • Maintaining financial relationships • Maintaining competitive credit rating	
Location Advantages	• Competitive sourcing of capital globally • Maintaining competitive credit rating • Negotiating tax and financial subsidies	• Exploiting exchange rates • Exploiting stock prices • Reacting to capital controls • Minimizing taxation
Internationalization Advantages	• Maintaining competitive credit rating • Reducing agency costs through FDI	• Minimizing taxation

Source: Constructed by authors based on "On the Treatment of Finance-Specific Factors within the OLI Paradigm," by Lars Oxelheim. Arthur Stonehill, and Trond Randoy, *International Business Review* 10, 2001, pp. 381–398.

Selecting Target Markets

The decision about where to invest abroad for the first time is influenced by behavioral factors. A firm learns from its first few investments abroad, and the lessons learned influence subsequent investments. Theoretically, the MNE will search worldwide for market imperfections and comparative advantage until it finds a country in which it expects to enjoy a competitive advantage large enough to generate an acceptable risk-adjusted rate of return on new investments.

In practice, firms follow a sequential pattern in their search for target markets. This logical pattern of rational thought lies behind two behavioral theories of FDI described next, the behavioral approach and the international network theory.

The Behavioral Approach to FDI. The behavioral approach to analyzing the FDI decision is typified by the so-called Swedish School of economists.[2] The Swedish School has rather successfully explained not just the initial decision to invest abroad but also later decisions to reinvest elsewhere and to change the structure of a firm's international involvement over time.

Based on the internationalization process of a sample of Swedish MNEs, economists observed that these firms tended to invest first in countries that were not too far distant in psychic terms. Countries having close psychic distance were defined as those with a cultural, legal, and institutional environment similar to Sweden's, such as Norway, Denmark, Finland, Germany, and the United Kingdom. Initial investments were modest in size, minimizing the risk of an uncertain foreign environment. As Swedish firms learned from their

[2]John Johansen, and F. Wiedersheim-Paul, "The Internationalization of the Firm: Four Swedish Case Studies," *Journal of Management Studies*, Vol. 12, No. 3, 1975; and John Johansen and Jan Erik Vahlne, "The Internationalization of the Firm: A Model of Knowledge Development and Increasing Foreign Market Commitments," *Journal of International Business Studies*, Vol. 8, No. 1, 1977.

initial investments, they became willing to take greater risks with respect to both the psychic distance of the countries and the size of the investments.

MNEs in a Network Perspective. As the Swedish MNEs grew and matured, so did the nature of their international involvement, what is often termed the *network perspective*. Today, each MNE is perceived as being a member of an international network, with nodes based in each of the foreign subsidiaries, as well as the parent firm itself. Centralized (hierarchical) control has given way to decentralized (heterarchical) control. Foreign subsidiaries compete with each other and with the parent for expanded resource commitments, thus influencing the strategy and reinvestment decisions.

Many of these MNEs have become political coalitions with competing internal and external networks. Each subsidiary is embedded in its host country's network of suppliers and customers. It is also a member of a worldwide network based on its industry. Finally, it is a member of an organizational network under the control of the parent firm. Complicating matters still further is the possibility that the parent itself may have evolved into a transnational firm, one owned by a coalition of investors located in different countries.

Choosing Entry Structures

The multinational investor has a number of different alternatives for penetrating a foreign market. In principle, the greater the depth of market penetration desired with greater expected returns, the greater the investment required with higher potential risks. The globalization process includes a sequence of decisions regarding where production is to occur and who is to own and control assets, both production facilities and intellectual property. Exhibit 17.2 provides a road map to explain this FDI sequence. Again, our interest and focus throughout the section is on the specific financial and financial management dimensions of the business.

EXHIBIT 17.2 **The Foreign Direct Investment Sequence**

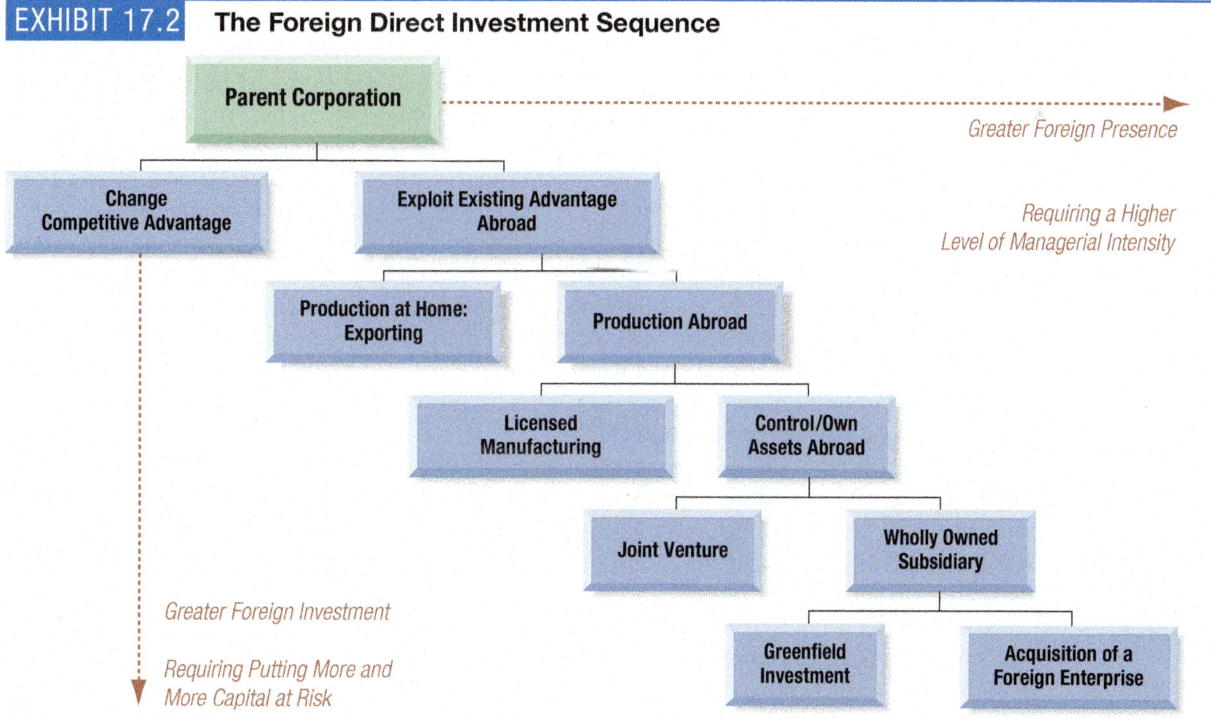

The first and most fundamental of choices is that between choosing to change the firm's competitive advantage or to pursue a foreign market expansion of its existing competitive advantage. Our subject here is the latter, the selection of the preferred entry structure abroad in concert with the firm's existing competitive advantage. The choice to change competitive advantage is the subject for courses in global strategy.

Exporting versus Production Abroad. There are several advantages to limiting a firm's activities to exports. Exporting has none of the unique risks facing FDI, joint ventures, strategic alliances, and licensing. Political risks are minimal. Agency costs, such as monitoring and evaluating foreign units, are avoided. The amount of front-end investment is typically lower than in other modes of foreign involvement. Foreign exchange risks remain, however. The fact that a significant share of exports (and imports) is executed between MNEs and their foreign subsidiaries and affiliates further reduces the risk of exports compared to other modes of involvement.

There are also disadvantages of limiting a firm's activities to exports. The firm's ability to leverage its competencies, its product and services sales reach, is more limited than if it invested directly. The firm also risks losing markets to imitators and global competitors that might be more cost efficient in production abroad, as well as having deeper distribution. Allowing competitors to gain strength, competency, and reach in foreign markets may expose the firm in its own home market. Defensive FDI is often motivated by the need to prevent this kind of predatory behavior as well as to preempt foreign markets from competitors.

Licensing and Management Contracts. Licensing is a popular method for domestic firms to profit from foreign markets without the need to commit sizeable funds. Since the foreign producer is typically wholly owned locally, political risk is minimized. In recent years, a number of host countries have demanded that MNEs sell their services in pieces ("unbundled form") rather than only through FDI. Such countries would like their local firms to purchase managerial expertise and knowledge of product and factor markets through management contracts and purchase technology through licensing agreements.

The main disadvantage of licensing is that license fees are likely to be lower than FDI profits, although the return on the marginal investment might be higher. Licensing income is often much steadier as an income stream, as licensing fees are normally calculated as a percentage of sales (the top line, typically large and relatively stable) versus FDI profits based on business returns (the bottom line, which can be negative). Other disadvantages to licensing include possible loss of control, specifically quality control; the potential to create a new competitor at home and abroad; and the possibility that the technology will be stolen.

MNEs have not typically used licensing of independent firms. On the contrary, most licensing arrangements have been with their own foreign subsidiaries or joint ventures. The returns to licensing, license fees, are a way to spread the corporate research and development cost among all operating units and a means of repatriating profits in a form more acceptable to some host countries than dividends.

Management contracts are similar to licensing insofar as they provide for some cash flow from a foreign source without significant foreign investment or exposure. Management contracts probably lessen political risk because repatriation of managers is easy. International consulting and engineering firms traditionally conduct their foreign business based on a management contract.

Whether licensing and management contracts are cost-effective compared to FDI depends on the price host countries will pay for the unbundled services. If the price were high enough, many firms would prefer to take advantage of market imperfections in an unbundled way, particularly in view of the lower political, foreign exchange, and business risks. Because we observe MNEs continuing to prefer FDI, we must assume that the price for selling unbundled services is still too low, as managerial expertise is often dependent on a delicate mix of organizational support factors that cannot be transferred abroad efficiently.

Joint Venture versus Wholly Owned Subsidiary. A joint venture (JV) is a business entity with shared ownership, sharing both risks and returns in the business. A foreign business unit that is partially owned by the parent company is typically termed a foreign affiliate. A foreign business unit that is 50% or more owned (and therefore controlled) by the parent company is typically designated a foreign subsidiary. A JV would therefore typically be described as a foreign affiliate, but not a foreign subsidiary.

There are three primary motivations for using a JV to share control, ownership, and expected returns: (1) a requirement for entry into the host country; (2) joining with a partner that brings unique and valued qualities or capabilities to the business; and (3) as a way to mitigate the political, business, and capital risks associated with the investment.

Developing countries see FDI as a major contributor to economic and income development. But these nation-building benefits are potentially more rapidly and effectively captured if the JV includes a domestic partner (from the host country). Domestic partners often have substantially less experience and capital to contribute to the JV yet bring extensive and rare knowledge of doing business in their home country (including business and political relationships) and the ability to contribute more mid-level managers of competence. This last element, the ability to contribute skilled management on multiple levels to the JV business, is invaluable in many cases.

Many FDI investments require unique combinations of skills, technology, and competencies that many firms, even multinational firms, do not possess on their own. A JV partner, domestic or foreign, that brings those skills to the partnership may make the difference between success and failure.

The third motivation for using a JV structure, risk mitigation, is particularly valuable in infrastructure and natural resource development projects in emerging economies. First, the capital requirements for such projects are of such a scale, they may constitute a "bet the ranch" proposition for any one firm on its own. Secondly, many host country governments find it politically appealing that the JV represents a multilateral investment in their country. Without playing favorites, the host country in many cases gains additional bargaining strength in and amongst the partners themselves.

Most joint ventures, despite the "sharing" elements that make them desirable to begin with, still often establish one partner as the operator for efficiency of leadership and control. The desire for singular control, however, is also why JVs are still not as common as wholly owned subsidiaries. MNEs fear interference by the partner in certain critical decision areas. Indeed, what is optimal from the viewpoint of the local venture may be suboptimal for the multinational operation as a whole. The most important potential conflicts or difficulties are these:

- Local and foreign partners may have divergent views about the need for cash dividends or about the desirability of growth financed from retained earnings versus new financing.
- Transfer pricing on products or components, bought from or sold to related companies, creates a potential for conflict of interest.
- Ability of a firm to rationalize production on a worldwide basis can be jeopardized if such rationalization would act to the disadvantage of local joint venture partners.
- Financial disclosure of local results might be necessary with locally traded shares or a local partner, whereas if the firm is wholly owned from abroad such disclosure is not needed.

- Valuation of equity shares is difficult. How much should the local partner pay for its share? What is the value of contributed technology, or of contributed land in a country where all land is state owned?
- It is highly unlikely that foreign and host country partners have similar opportunity costs of capital, expectations about the required rate of return, or perceptions of appropriate premiums for business, foreign exchange, and political risks.
- Insofar as the venture is a component of the portfolio of each investor, its contribution to portfolio return and variance may be quite different for each.

In the end, depending on the size and capital required for project development, the typical joint venture lasts only five to seven years. JVs between a multinational partner and a domestic partner do, however, have a history of longer effective business lives. *Global Finance in Practice 17.1* describes one of the oldest operating joint ventures in Russia by a U.S. firm, GM-AvtoVAZ.

GLOBAL FINANCE IN PRACTICE 17.1

Financial Structure of a Russian Joint Venture

The General Motors (U.S.) and AvtoVAZ (Russia) joint venture serves as a classic example of a successful joint venture's financing over time. The JV was originally created in 2001 as a joint venture between three parties—General Motors Corporation, AvtoVAZ OAO of Russia, and the European Bank for Reconstruction and Development (EBRD)—to produce a new, higher-quality, co-branded vehicle—the Chevrolet Niva.

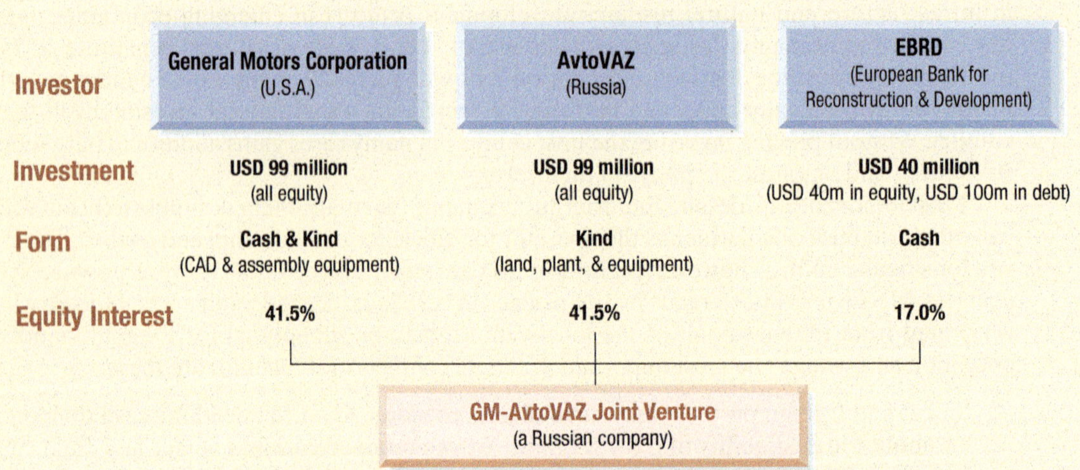

- JV equity interests were determined by percentage of total equity contribution. JV capital structure totaled $338 million, $238 million in equity and $100 million in debt. JV commenced operations in 2002 and was successful at generating healthy operating cash flows over time.
- JV eventually repaid its debt obligations to EBRD, replacing that debt with local debt. In 2012 EBRD sold its equity interest in the JV to its partners, who then became equal owners.
- As opposed to the average JV which lasts between 5 and 7 years, the GM-AvtoVAZ JV did not stop operating until 2019 when AvtoVAZ became the sole owner.

Greenfield Investments and Foreign Acquisitions. A wholly owned foreign investment maximizes both the risks and potential returns to the multinational parent company. Whether it is a greenfield investment, a project built from the ground up anew (hence, from a green field), or via an acquisition, the purchase of an existing business in-country, the MNE would maximize its effective control over its investment future (at least to the level that host country authorities will allow). The disadvantages, however, may be substantial, and the multinational parent would likely miss out on the many benefits enjoyed by having a domestic partner as described above.

Strategic Alliances. A final mode of foreign investment that can apply to a number of the forms described in Exhibit 17.2 is the strategic alliance. A strategic alliance may take a variety of different forms depending on its primary objective. Common forms include joint marketing and servicing agreements, cross-ownership swaps, and more comprehensive partnerships and joint ventures.

A first level of cooperation might be in the form of a joint marketing and servicing agreement in which each partner represents the other in certain markets. This is a very common form used by companies with consumer product industries, in which different firms or partners have different regional or national presence advantages. In some cases, however, this form of cooperation has often been criticized as resembling the industrial cartels prevalent in several industrial markets in the 1920s and 1930s. Because they reduce competition, these agreements—if deemed a cartel—have been banned by international agreements and by many national laws.

A second level of alliance is when two firms exchange a share of ownership with one another. This form of strategic alliance can serve the purpose of being a takeover defense, particularly if the prime purpose is for a firm to place some of its stock in stable and friendly hands. If that is all that occurs, then it is in reality just another form of portfolio investment.

A third level of strategic alliance is more comprehensive. In addition to exchanging stock, the partners establish a separate joint venture (or a number of joint ventures) to develop and manufacture a product or service. Numerous examples of these alliances can be found in the automotive, electronics, telecommunications, and aircraft industries. Such alliances are particularly suited to capital-intensive and high-technology industries where the cost of research and development is high and timely introduction of improvements is important.

Foreign investment, however, is not always a purely enterprise-based concept. As described in *Global Finance in Practice 17.2,* the largest global investment in terms of total capital has been that under the auspices of the Chinese Belt and Road Initiative (BRI).

17.3 Political Risk: Definition and Classification

Political risk is the possibility that political events in a particular country or involving that country through international law will influence the economic well-being of a firm operating in that country. Multinational firms need to anticipate and manage political risk. In order to do that, the firm must understand the differing types of risks and their likelihood of occurrence.

The political risks facing a multinational firm can be categorized as *firm-specific* or *country-specific*, both occurring within a global context—global-specific risks—as described

GLOBAL FINANCE IN PRACTICE 17.2

The Chinese Belt and Road Initiative (BRI) and Debt-Trap Diplomacy

The Belt and Road Initiative (BRI), formally launched by the Chinese government, is the largest agglomeration of global investments in the developing world in history. Under the auspices of the People's Republic of China (PRC), this collection of Chinese organizations has negotiated the development of infrastructure projects in more than 60 countries. The BRI has two parts, the *belt*—which theoretically recreates the old Silk Road land trade route, and the *road*—a patchwork water route across oceans.

The BRI has focused on infrastructure projects including dams, roads, ports, power plants, airports, and hospitals. These projects clearly increase Chinese national and corporate interests across the developing world. But the true scope of Chinese capital in this space is difficult to measure and complex in form. Despite essentially all BRI projects being state-sponsored, there is no ready disclosure of the investments and loans across countries. Adding to that complexity is that each project is unique in scope and scale, requiring differing forms of capital commitments and arrangements. Yet the BRI continues to be highly controversial, labeled everything from "man's largest concerted effort for global cooperative economic development" to China using "debt-trap diplomacy" to entrap developing countries with debt, leaving them with little choice but to follow China's political directives.

The debt-trap criticism has been the subject of much debate. Host countries have enjoyed massive capital projects and investments sponsored and supported by Chinese capital and capabilities but are often saddled with legacies of debt obligations and operating entanglements far into the future.

The BRI Project Development Path

BRI projects follow a fundamentally distinct and different development process than traditional infrastructure projects. This difference, detailed in the exhibit, arises from the dominant role of the Chinese government, its banks, and its engineering, procurement, and construction (EPC) firms, in project development. Because the BRI's activities are largely infrastructure investments, they are not investments—in principle—for profit. These types of projects are developed for the public good rather than private gain since they are traditionally investments made by governments or multilateral development organizations like the World Bank. Projects are typically identified by a government itself or in consultation with a multilateral development bank. Once approved, they are funded largely through development bank loans.

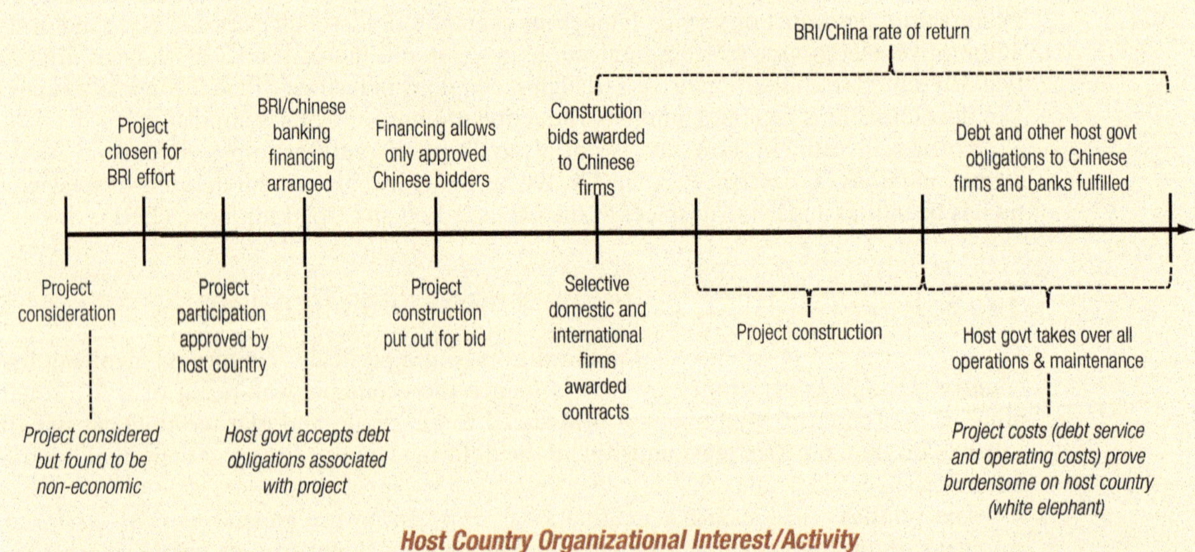

Source: Constructed by authors.

EXHIBIT 17.3 Classification of Political Risks

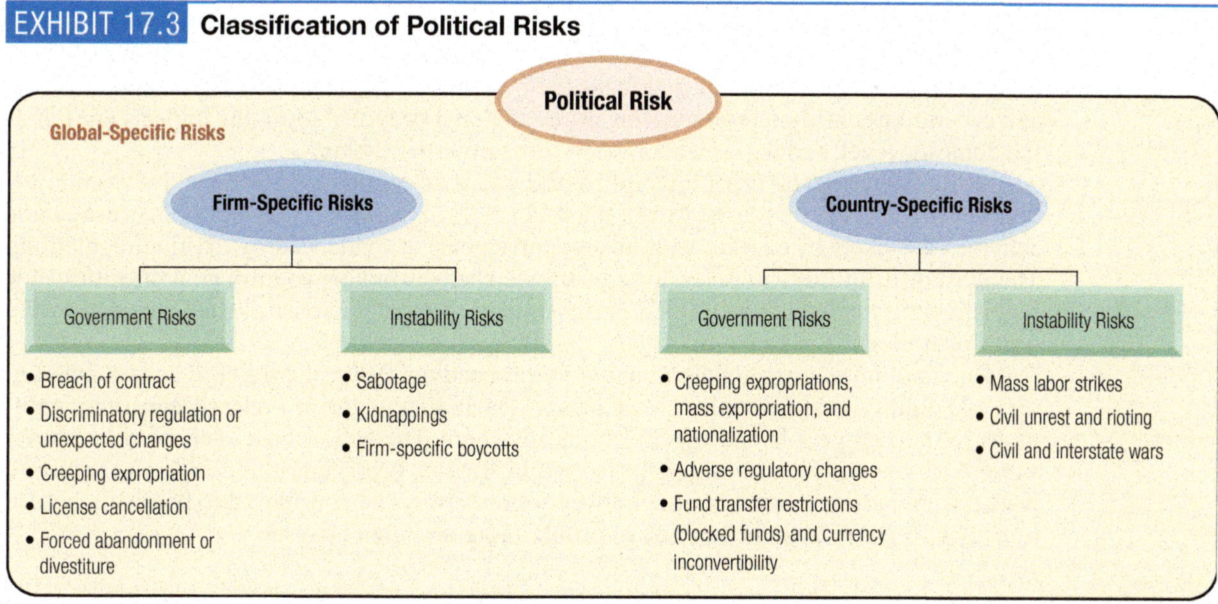

in Exhibit 17.3. Also note that as opposed to the traditional theoretical definition of risk in finance, where it is often defined statistically such as the standard deviation of returns over time, our definitions and classification of political risks are one-sided. Political risks are always seen as negative in their impact on the operations and prospects of the multinational firm.

Firm-Specific Risks. *Firm-specific risks*, also known as *micro risks*, are those that affect the multinational at the project or corporate level. These firm-specific risks can be further subdivided into those risks arising from the national government and its possible intervention in legal contracts, government risks, and the possible impacts of other external interests like sabotage or boycotts, instability risks. The most frequently experienced government risks are breach of contract, regulatory changes, and *expropriation* (particularly creeping expropriation, explained further below).

All nations, highly industrialized and emerging markets alike, experience regulatory changes over time. That is inevitable and is to be expected by a multinational firm operating in a national environment. But when those regulatory changes single out the MNE's activities, treating it differently compared to similar firms in the domestic market, the multinational is clearly suffering discriminatory treatment. As will be described in detail later in this chapter, multinational firms actively work to mitigate these risks, in both prevention and treatment.

Country-Specific Risks. *Country-specific risks*, also known as *macro risks*, are those that affect the MNE at the project or corporate level but originate at the country level. As was the case with firm-specific risks, these two can be further subdivided into government risks and instability risks.

The most frequently seen government risks are expropriation (nationalization when experienced on a country level), regulatory changes, and fund transfer restrictions (blocked funds). Instability risks on a country level include mass labor movements or strikes, civil unrest, and near war-like conditions. Examples of these are, unfortunately, too long and too easy to list.

Global-Specific Risks. Global specific risks are those that can impact both domestic and multinational enterprises at the project or corporate level but originate at the global level. Examples are terrorism, the anti-globalization movement, environmental concerns, poverty, and cyberattacks. Although originating at the regional or global level, the impacts are felt at the domestic level, and that is where we will focus our discussion.

At the macro level, firms attempt to assess a host country's political stability and attitude toward foreign investors. At the micro level, firms analyze whether their firm-specific activities are likely to conflict with host country goals as evidenced by existing regulations. The most difficult task, however, is to anticipate changes in host country goal priorities, new regulations to implement reordered priorities, and the likely impact of such changes on the firm's operations.

One final note bears highlighting before proceeding. Political risks such as war, civil unrest, and politically motivated acts of violence—including terrorism—clearly constitute enormous risks to all people and organizations anywhere. The seriousness of these risks always supersedes our subset of business-based political risks. Protecting the health and safety of workers, no matter citizenship or employer, should always be considered to be the highest of priorities. Regardless of the sanctity of profits, there are higher causes.

17.4 Financial Impacts of Political Risk

The financial impacts on the multinational firm of political change in foreign countries covers the full gamut of business finance—from earnings to operating cash flow to asset ownership. On a purely elemental level, these risks change both how multinational firms operate in a host country and, more importantly, their willingness to continue to invest—or, in the extreme, invest at all. This section focuses on the various micro or firm-based political risks directly linked to the conduct of business, by a business, in a host country.

Exhibit 17.4 provides a brief overview of these financial impacts ranging from low to high in financial severity. Although expropriation—the taking of private assets for public purposes by the state—has historically been the most "feared" of political risks, it is still relatively infrequent. The more common form today is the creeping expropriation, where a government imposes a variety of the various forms of commercial interference described in Categories 1 and 2, eventually culminating in an effective expropriation. It is, in fact, the multitude of policies and regulations in the first two categories of political risks that have the most common and often somewhat insidious impact on financial performance.

The specific financial costs and losses associated with a variety of the causes in Exhibit 17.4, however, are not always so neat. A breach of contract for a multinational construction management firm developing infrastructure facilities in Mozambique, a Category 1 risk, could prove more costly than any specific state seizure of the multinational's property or assets, a Category 3 risk. As we dig deeper into the variety of risks, it will become increasingly obvious how they are often intertwined in incidence.

Category 1: Losses in Operating Profitability

The most common political risks that multinationals face are changes in the various regulations, restrictions, and requirements for operating in the host country. The two most often cited causes of financial harm according to MNEs are breach of contract and adverse regulatory changes.

Financial harm typically comes in the form of lost business and sales opportunities, discriminatory treatment—being treated differently than other domestic or foreign

EXHIBIT 17.4 **Categorizing Potential Finance Losses and Political Risk**

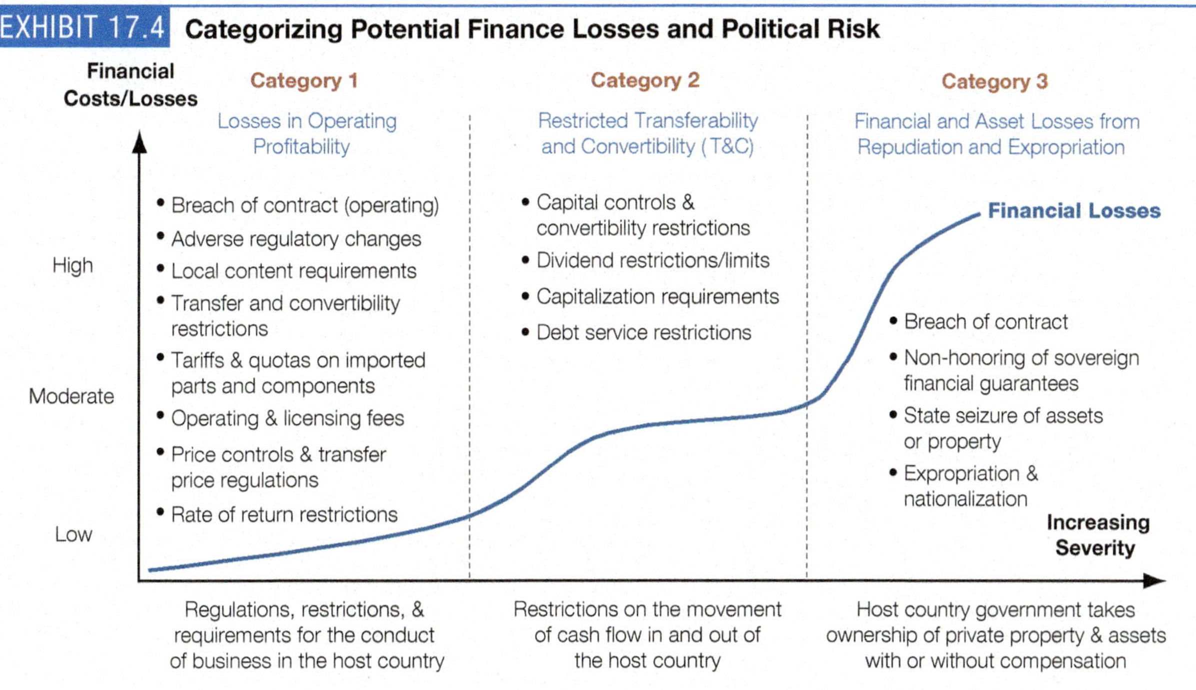

competitors—required staffing or procurement practices in the host country, and broken promises as a whole. Since most multinational firms see political risk arising primarily in emerging markets or low-income countries, the risks tend to align with or accompany specific sectors, such as infrastructure development and major natural resource development projects. Both sectors, infrastructure construction and natural resource development, are now suffering disruptive change following years of privatization. These businesses are often public-private collaborations, a characteristic common in the developing world where the state has historically owned industries and assets, but less so in the industrial country markets that many multinationals call home.

Adverse Regulatory Change. Adverse regulatory change, also termed *regulatory risk*, refers to changes in host country regulations that alter operating conditions of investments. As noted, we refer to "adverse" changes, as few multinationals enjoy changes that reduce cost or operating requirements once the investment has been made and the investor has lost much of its negotiating strength. There are few limits to the nature of these regulation changes, though many in the past decade have fallen in the environmental, human health, and local content/sourcing areas.

Breach of Contract. Breach of contract refers to losses arising from a government or state-owned enterprise breaking or breaching of a business contract with the foreign private investor.

A frequently cited cause of harm is either a change in host country law or a failure to comply with principles of the rule of law. And as opposed to projects and investments in the 1960s or 1970s, host government entities today are often quite sophisticated in their ability to navigate these legal changes and environments. They are also no longer in the weaker negotiating position common 50 years ago. Today host country governments are well aware of their ability to demand balanced contracts that share both the risks and returns of business ventures.

A short list of deal-specific issues leading to breach of contract would include the following: (1) how the contract was awarded, bid or no-bid; (2) what contractual payment structure is used, cost-plus, fixed price, or other; and (3) whether the contract is still relevant, the *obsolescing bargain principle*. Political risk studies in recent years have found that the probability of a material contract breach increases rapidly with contract and business maturity. The *obsolescing bargain premise* is that with time, business and social and political forces change, undermining the relevancy of the contract and business. Other forces also contribute to this obsolescence, including the deterioration of foundational relationships (the "connections" that gave rise to the contract) and shifts in negotiating strength (host countries gain relative bargaining strength after the foreign investor has put bricks and mortar and capital on the ground).

Local Content Requirements. Host governments may require foreign firms to purchase raw material and components locally as a way to maximize value-added benefits and to increase local employment. From the viewpoint of the foreign firm trying to adapt to host country goals, local sourcing reduces political risk, albeit at a trade-off with other factors. Local strikes or other turmoil may shut down the operation and such issues as quality control, high local prices, and unreliable delivery schedules become important. Often, through local sourcing, the MNE lowers political risk only by increasing its financial and commercial risk.

Category 2: Transfer and Convertibility Risk

Transfer and convertibility risk, often abbreviated in industry to *T&C risk*, is the risk that a host country will restrict the ability of the multinational firm to move money in or out of the country—transfer risk—and possibly restrict its ability to exchange local currency for foreign currency—convertibility risk—in an expeditious manner. This restriction of access and exchange is referred to as blocked funds. T&C risk can be extremely costly for some multinationals, as delayed payments may result in financial charges, penalties, exchange rate losses, and, in some cases, insolvency. Financial impacts need not be confined to the foreign subsidiary itself, as in some cases sister affiliates or even the parent company may be in critical need for expected cash flow transfers.

In theory, these limitations do not necessarily discriminate against foreign-owned firms because they apply to everyone; in practice, however, foreign firms have more at stake because of their foreign ownership. Depending on the size of a foreign exchange shortage, the host government might simply require approval of all transfers of funds abroad, thus reserving the right to set a priority on the use of scarce foreign exchange. In very severe cases, the government might make its currency nonconvertible into other currencies, thereby fully blocking transfers of funds abroad. In between these positions are policies that restrict the size and timing of dividends, debt amortization, royalties, and service fees.

Many countries have been known to restrict convertibility in an effort to stop capital flight and the depletion of foreign exchange reserves (when attempting to maintain a fixed exchange rate regime in the face of pessimistic expectations). Both Argentina and Venezuela are examples of countries that have in recent years allowed conversion of local currency to hard currency, typically to the U.S. dollar, but only to approved parties for specific transactions (e.g., a toy importer requesting approval for payment to a Chinese exporter for a specific purchase, an invoice for a toy purchase). These approvals rarely include multinational firms operating in-country. Sovereign debt obligations, often requiring payment in a hard currency earned only through export, also sometimes drive governments to withhold access by private investors to foreign exchange.

Category 3: Expropriation and Nationalization

Government hardly could go on if to some extent values incident to property could not be diminished without paying for every such change in the general law. As long recognized some values are enjoyed under an implied limitation and must yield to the police power. But obviously the implied limitation must have its limits or the contract and due process clauses are gone. One fact for consideration in determining such limits is the extent of the diminution. When it reaches a certain magnitude, in most if not in all cases there must be an exercise of eminent domain and compensation to sustain the act.

—Justice Oliver Wendell Holmes, *Pennsylvania Coal Co. v. Mahon et al.*, No. 549, Decided December 11, 1922 [260 U.S. 393].

The most extreme form of political risk is expropriation, the seizure of the multinational company's business, assets, or license to operate in the country by the government—the public taking of private assets. Technically, if the seizure or transfer of ownership is made on a statewide or industry-wide basis and not a singular or specific firm, the action is termed *nationalization* (the "evil twin" of expropriation).

The state, any state, has the sovereign right under international law to take property held by private entities, domestic or foreign, through expropriation for economic, political, or social reasons. (The taking of domestic property is referred to as *eminent domain*.) But in order to be "lawful" under international law, the expropriation needs to meet four criteria:[3]

1. Property has to be taken for a public purpose
2. On a nondiscriminatory basis
3. In accordance with due process of law
4. Accompanied by compensation

Direct versus Indirect. Direct expropriation is the transfer of title or outright seizure of property. This was the customary form of expropriation seen in the early twentieth century in countries like Russia and Mexico. Property was seen as purely physical in nature and included land, buildings, capital equipment, and other physical assets in addition to any ongoing business activity. Worldwide attention to and criticism of these unilateral actions were severe.

In the era beginning after World War II, partially in response to widespread criticism of direct expropriation, some nations began using a variety of other measures of commercial interference (many of those described in the previous categories) that incrementally and cumulatively begin to permanently destroy the economic value of the investment. These measures typically revolve around the ability of the investor to manage or control the business or property in a meaningful manner and are collectively termed *indirect expropriation*. At the same time the definition of property was expanded from physical to include "non-corporal" or intangible property, specifically rights held by the investor that possess monetary value.

An additional form of indirect expropriation is creeping expropriation, when a variety of seemingly small or individual restrictions and interventions are considered in sum. This includes increased regulations, confiscatory taxes, limits on the repatriation of currency, changes in exchange rates, and forced renegotiation of licenses or contracts. This has led to considerable debate in both the courts and boardrooms around the globe as nations have argued that these individual actions do not constitute "takings" yet multinationals argue that considered in total they are effective seizures. In some instances the largest loss in value to

[3] *Expropriation: UNCTAD Series on Issues in International Investment Agreements II*, United Nations Conference on Trade and Development, New York and Geneva, 2012, p. 1.

the multinational investor is when the host government imposes so many restrictions or costs upon the venture without expropriation that the investment is a loss without compensation.

There is also a vaguely defined third category of material interference by the state that is based on the state's right to regulate in the public interest. Nations argue that when they intervene in this manner, in their sovereign role of policing, they are not required to compensate investors for their losses. Of course in the eyes of many multinational investors, these are still forms of indirect expropriation.

Compensation. A "lawful expropriation" must be accompanied by compensation. Most international investment agreements require compensation that meets three conditions: prompt—paid without delay, adequate—a value with a reasonable relationship with a market value of the investment, and effective—paid in a convertible or freely useable currency.

What is adequate or appropriate compensation is a highly contentious debate depending on the case and whether the party is the company or country. There are three basic valuation approaches used globally for determining compensation that any student of finance will recognize: (1) market valuation, (2) net book valuation, and (3) net present value of discounted cash flow valuation. Although different treaties and agreements use differing terminologies of what compensation is to be paid—"fair value" or "just" or "appropriate" or "what a willing buyer would pay to a willing seller"—many governments frequently pay less than what most valuations call for.

The largest arbitration award resulting from an illegal expropriation of assets of all time is that of OAO Yukos Oil Company, the Russian oil and gas company seized by the Russian Federation in 2007. In 2014 a tribunal awarded the former shareholders of Yukos, which was at the time of expropriation the largest oil company in Russia, more than $50 billion. Interestingly, this was the amount after it had been reduced by 25% as a result of the tribunal's assessment that the claimants themselves (the stockholders) also had "unclean hands." *Global Finance in Practice 17.3* provides a number of examples of how one of the world's largest and most global of industries, oil and gas development, has been the subject of frequent expropriations, particularly in Latin America. Note also how host governments have employed a number of interference instruments and strategies of their own to execute a creeping expropriation in some cases.

17.5 Political Risk Mitigation

Despite more than two decades of high-speed globalization, all indications are that political risk is rising. That challenge combined with multinational firms that grow more risk-averse every day has fueled efforts of political risk mitigation. More multinational enterprises than ever before actively monitor political risk threats in an effort to protect their people, their assets, and their business brand/reputation. They are also taking more proactive steps earlier in the foreign direct investment process to reduce and manage their own exposure. Here we explore seven of the most common political risk mitigation techniques: stakeholder engagement, use of domestic partners, international investment agreements, gradual investing, blocked funds management, dispute resolution, and political risk insurance.

Stakeholder Engagement

Prior and early engagement with key FDI stakeholders—host governments, key political leaders, and impacted communities—is often seen as "an ounce of prevention." The most frequently cited risk mitigation strategy by multinationals, developing and nurturing relationships with key host country stakeholders, is seen as a way to both prevent individual firm exposure

GLOBAL FINANCE IN PRACTICE 17.3

Selective Examples of Expropriation in the Global Oil and Gas Industry

The global oil and gas industry has been the subject of a multitude of expropriations over time owing to its truly global structure (companies must go where the oil and gas is regardless of political, economic, or social infrastructure and development). But even within that global industry, Latin American countries have led the way in expropriation and nationalization. A few recent examples highlight the linkage between seizure of assets and the rights or "license to operate" parameters in the industry.

Argentina. On April 16, 2012, President Cristina Fernández de Kirchner of Argentina introduced a bill to begin the renationalization of YPF (Repsol of Spain), the nation's largest energy firm. The national government would take 51% controlling interest with the remaining 49% passing to the provincial governments. Several years later the government of Argentina paid Repsol of Spain $5 billion in compensation.

Bolivia. Bolivia may have been the first country in Latin America to expropriate a major oil company when *disappropriating* the assets and operations of Standard Oil of New Jersey (U.S.), the predecessor to today's ExxonMobil, in 1937. For that taking the government eventually paid Standard Oil $1,729,375. *Misappropriating*, the term used in Bolivia for expropriation or nationalization, is based on the concept that the people of Bolivia are "taking back" a right or ownership that had previously been allocated. Bolivia, under the leadership of newly elected President Evo Morales, issued Supreme Decree No. 28701 on May 1, 2006, requiring oil producers to relinquish control of their operations to the state oil and gas company, Yacimientos Petroliferos Fiscales Bolivianos (YPFB). Bolivia had originally created YPFB expressly to take over Standard Oil's assets and operations.

Ecuador. Ecuador has imposed a deadline for oil companies to accept new subcontracting agreements, which would cancel existing joint venture agreements. The new agreements would also prevent oil companies from making appeals to the International Center for the Settlement of Disputes (ICSID). Ecuador also created a 50% tax on "extraordinary profits" based on crude oil prices. Ecuador expropriated Occidental Petroleum's interest in the Block 15 Field, previously awarded, in 2006.

Mexico. In what may have been the most infamous of all, President Lázaro Cárdenas announced the expropriation of all oil resources and facilities by the state, expropriating the U.S. and Anglo-Dutch (Mexican Eagle Petroleum Company) oil companies on March 18, 1938. The government of Mexico eventually created Petróleos de Mexico (Pemex) to be the sole oil and gas company for the country.

Venezuela. Venezuela, led by President Hugo Chavez, issued Decree No. 5.200 in February 2007, requiring all operating companies in Venezuela's Orinoco Belt to agree to new contracts with the state oil company, Petróleos de Venezuela SA (PDVSA). They were informed that if they did not agree to new terms, they faced expropriation. Eventually, that is exactly what the government did—expropriating the operating properties of two major foreign oil and gas companies, ExxonMobil and ConocoPhillips, both U.S. companies.

ExxonMobil, having been the subject of expropriation before (both around the world and in Venezuela) responded with a series of aggressive legal actions to freeze the assets of PDVSA outside Venezuela—specifically in the U.S. In January 2012, nearly five years later, a tribunal with the World Bank's International Centre for Settlement of Investment Disputes (ICSID) awarded ExxonMobil $1.6 billion in compensation, far below the $10 billion the company had sought. Even the greatly reduced value would prove difficult to collect as Venezuela withdrew from the ICSID in 2012 and once again neared financial collapse in 2018.

and to serve as an early warning device for trouble. Possibly the most critical of stakeholders is the host country government. Recent studies have shown that greater government involvement is associated with the business venture's high likelihood to survive a breach event.

Use of Domestic Partners

Either as a result of true public policy or preferential domestic politics, all host country governments would prefer that new capital projects and business developments in country be undertaken by domestic companies. If, however, the business initiative is coming via a foreign multinational, if that firm partners with in-country interests, the goals of the country are partially met. Domestic partners, once having a formal business interest in the project, act as both a champion and a potential "shield" in potentially preventing government from implementing additional interference in the conduct of the business.

Many governments have in the past required a domestic equity partner—requiring in effect a joint venture with a domestic company—as an explicit requirement for entry. This was the case in all pillar industries in mainland China in the 1980s and 1990s. A specific intention is that by working in collaboration, much of the multinational firm's experience, knowledge, and technology will also pass to the domestic partner.

International Investment Agreements

The best way to mitigate political risk is to anticipate the risks, negotiate a priori agreement with host country authorities—international investment agreements (IIAs)—and, in addition, be prepared. Different cultures apply different ethics to the question of honoring contracts, especially when they were negotiated with a previous administration. Nevertheless, prenegotiation of all conceivable areas of conflict provides a better basis for a successful future for both parties than does overlooking the possibility that divergent objectives will evolve over time.

Prenegotiation often includes negotiating IIAs, buying investment insurance and guarantees, and designing risk-reducing operating strategies to be used after the foreign investment decision has been made. An IIA spells out specific rights and responsibilities of both the foreign firm and the host government. In many cases the operating presence of specific multinationals not only is desired by the country but may be actively "recruited" or requested by the government to bid for entry. All parties have alternatives and so bargaining is appropriate.

Today most IIAs begin with a standard clause to assert the four criteria defined previously in regard to expropriation:

> *Neither of the Contracting Parties shall take, either directly or indirectly, measures of expropriation, nationalization or any other measures having the same nature or the same effect against investments of investors of the other Contracting Party, unless the measures are taken in the public benefit, on a non-discriminatory basis, and under due process of law, and provided that provisions be made for effective and adequate compensation.*
>
> —Agreement between Swiss Confederation and Republic of Chile on the promotion and reciprocal protection of Investments, UNCTAD, 1999.

These criteria and similar legal clauses have been widely used for the past century in an attempt to find some balance between investor protection and state sovereignty. Other standard components of an IIA include the following financial and management issues:

- The basis on which dividends, management fees, royalties, and loan repayments may be remitted
- The basis for setting transfer prices
- The right to export to third-country markets
- Obligations to fund, build, or support social infrastructure such as schools and hospitals
- Methods of taxation, including the rate, type, and means by which the rate base is determined
- Access to host country capital markets, particularly for long-term borrowing
- Permission for 100% foreign ownership versus required local ownership (joint venture) participation
- Price controls, if any, applicable to sales in the host country markets
- Requirements for local sourcing versus import of raw materials and components
- Permission to use expatriate managerial and technical personnel with limited intervention or charges

- Provision for arbitration of disputes
- Provision for planned divestment, should such be required, describing an exit or windup process

Although political changes can and may render existing agreements null and void on occasion, a carefully negotiated IIA prior to entry has been shown to consistently increase the probability of a longer and healthier business venture. *Global Finance in Practice 17.4* describes how international sanctions against Iran have largely taken all choices away from multinational enterprises of all countries.

Gradual Investing

A multinational firm entering a problematic country may choose to follow a "prudent investment" policy. This is often applicable to a country that either has a history of significant intervention in the activities of foreign investors, for example a history of expropriation, or has a current governance regime that does not instill confidence in the investor's ability to operate for any term without intervention. A prudent investment policy invests capital in stages, often starting with only core activities on a smaller scale than what the long-term investment objective calls for. The multinational will then, assuming limited interference, rely primarily upon retained earnings from the business itself for additional capital and expansion.

This gradual investment approach is, however, often not well received by host countries, and in the case of the business being a joint venture with a domestic private or public institution (such as a state owned enterprise), this can lead to significant friction between the partners over time. The mini-case at the end of this chapter illustrates one example in which gradual investment proved a double-edged sword in protecting the rights and investment of the foreign firm.

GLOBAL FINANCE IN PRACTICE 17.4

U.S. Financial Sanctions On Iran

Sanctions are used by nations and multilateral organizations for a variety of purposes. Economic, political, and military sanctions are by far the most serious, although sports sanctions and environmental sanctions have gained substantial notoriety in recent years. Trade sanctions, the imposition of tariffs, quotas, or other commercial trade restrictions are considered a subcategory of economic sanctions. The primary motivations for sanctions are to force adherence to international law and to contain perceived threats to peace in a region. That motivation is specific to the United Nations Security Council's condemnation of actions of a specific member nation.

A series of successive U.S. administrations have used economic sanctions to try to alter Iran's purported support of regional armed factions and conflicts as well as its development of missiles and nuclear arms. U.S. sanctions against Iran are classified as secondary sanctions, applying to any organization attempting to conduct business with Iran. Although U.S. sanctions in some form have been in effect against Iran since its seizure of the U.S. embassy in Tehran in 1979, in October 2020 the U.S. imposed new sanctions that specifically targeted Iran's financial sector.

These most recent sanctions prohibit all U.S. financial institutions from conducting business with 18 Iranian banks and also impose penalties on any businesses or financial institutions from third-party countries for conducting any business with them. Previously the U.S. had focused its financial sanctions on the Iranian Central Bank and any third-party banks conducting business with it. The Iranian Central Bank maintains accounts with banks and central banks all over the world, partly for the settlement of international financial and exchange rate settlements but also for settlement of payments for Iranian oil exports. U.S. sanctions against the Iranian Central Bank were intended to shut down most Iranian oil exports.

The 2020 sanctions are believed to effectively cut off most of the Iranian economy from the international financial system. European nations have opposed the U.S. "blanket sanction" against financial activities, as a number of European and European Union members continue to maintain an open relationship with Iran.

Blocked Funds Management

Multinational firms can react to the potential for blocked funds at three stages:

1. Prior to investing, a firm can analyze the effect of blocked funds on expected return on investment, the desired local financial structure, and optimal links with subsidiaries.
2. During operations, a firm can attempt to move funds through a variety of repositioning techniques.
3. Funds that cannot be moved must be reinvested in the local country in a manner that avoids deterioration in their real value because of inflation or local currency depreciation.

The first management alternative, including the likelihood of blocked funds in the capital budgeting process, results in a lower expected net present value and would often eliminate the proposal as an acceptable investment. If after inclusion the project is still considered acceptable, preinvestment analysis allows the potential to minimize the impact of blocked funds by financing strategies such as use of local borrowing (in-country) instead of parent equity, swap agreements (back-to-back loans are one example), and other techniques to reduce local currency exposure.

The second management alternative is the use of any number of techniques to move blocked funds after operations begin. This includes fronting loans and the creation of unrelated exports. A fronting loan is a parent-to-subsidiary loan channeled through a financial intermediary, usually a large international bank. Fronting loans differ from "parallel" or "back-to-back" loans discussed in Chapter 12. The latter are offsetting loans between commercial businesses arranged outside the banking system. Fronting loans are sometimes referred to as link financing. In a fronting loan, the "lending" parent or subsidiary deposits funds in, say, a London bank, and that bank loans the same amount to the borrowing subsidiary in the host country. From the London bank's point of view, the loan is risk-free because the bank has 100% collateral in the form of the parent's deposit. In effect, the bank "fronts" for the parent—hence the name.

Another approach to blocked funds that benefits both the subsidiary and host country is the creation of unrelated exports. Because the main reason for stringent exchange controls is usually a host country's persistent inability to earn hard currencies, anything a multinational firm can do to create new exports from the host country is considered helpful and provides a potential means to transfer funds out. Some new exports can often be created from present productive capacity with little or no additional investment, especially if they are in product lines related to existing operations. Other new exports may require reinvestment or new funds, although if the funds reinvested consist of those already blocked, little is lost in the way of opportunity costs.

If funds are indeed blocked from transfer into foreign exchange, they are by definition "reinvested." Under such a situation, the firm must find local opportunities that will maximize the rate of return for a given acceptable level of risk. If blockage is expected to be temporary, the most obvious alternative is to invest in local money market instruments.

Unfortunately, in many countries, such instruments are not available in sufficient quantity or with adequate liquidity. In some cases, government Treasury bills, bank deposits, and other short-term instruments have yields that are kept artificially low relative to local rates of inflation or probable changes in exchange rates. Thus, the firm often loses real value during the period of blockage. Investment in additional production facilities may in some cases be the only alternative. Often, this investment is what the host country is seeking by its exchange controls, even if exchange controls is counterproductive to additional foreign investment.

Dispute Resolution

A multinational firm knows, prior to investing in any specific country, that it will bear the risk that its contracts or agreements will not be enforceable by the host country court and judicial system. A common mitigation strategy is therefore to require all disputes to go to international arbitration. There are a number of established bodies solely for this purpose—the American Arbitration Association, the International Chamber of Commerce, the London Court of International Arbitration, to name a few.

International arbitration is also facilitated as a result of more than 100 countries being signatories to the 1958 New York Convention on the Recognition of Foreign Arbitral Awards, a program run by the United Nations Commission on International Trade Law (UNICTRAL). A second approach of value to multinationals is to contractually require all disputes to be resolved according to the rules of the International Center of the Settlement of Disputes (ICSID). About 130 countries have signed the ICSID Convention on the Settlement of Investment Disputes between States and Nationals of Other States. One key outcome of either of these strategies is that signatory countries agree to enforce arbitration awards. Therefore a monetary judgment awarded via international arbitration may be more likely to be collected.

Political Risk Insurance

Political risk insurance, as it sounds, is insurance acquired by the multinational to serve as some financial protection against losses arising from select forms of political risk. Governmental and private insurers offer policies designed to manage political risks, including the risk of expropriation and nationalization. Many countries have governmental or quasi-governmental entities that provide political risk insurance for companies from that country when investing internationally.

Providers. Most political risk insurance is provided—*written*—by members of the Berne Union, the International Union of Credit & Investment Insurers, an international organization of export credit agencies made up of multilateral trade groups and private insurers. Founded in 1934, its first meetings were held in Berne, Switzerland; it is estimated that 10% of all world trade is covered by Berne Union members. Those members are both public and private. For example, the Multilateral Investment Guarantee Agency (MIGA), an agency of the World Bank Group, "promotes foreign direct investment by providing political risk insurance and credit enhancement to investors and lenders against losses caused by noncommercial risks."

An additional benefit of MIGA is that recent studies indicate that the greater the participation of an international financial institution (IFI) like the World Bank, such as credit provisions, project guarantees, or equity participation, the greater the likelihood of project or business success. There are a multitude of other country-based insurance providers:

- Australia: Export Finance and Insurance Corporation (EXIC)
- Canada: Export Development Canada (EDC)
- France: Compagnie Franc arise d'Assurance pour le Commerce Extevieure (COFACE)
- Germany: German State Export Guarantee Scheme, managed by HERMES
- Japan: Nippon Export and Investment Insurance (NEXI)
- United States: Overseas Private Investment Corporation (OPIC)
- United Kingdom: Export Credits Guarantee Department (ECGD)

There are also several semi-governmental organizations that offer political risk insurance like the U.S. Export/Import Bank as well as private insurers like Chubb and Zurich.

Multinational Use. MNEs can also sometimes transfer political risk to a host country public agency through an investment insurance and guarantee program. Many developed countries have such programs to protect investments by their nationals in developing countries.

For example, in the United States, the investment insurance and guarantee program is managed by the government-owned Overseas Private Investment Corporation (OPIC). An OPIC's purpose is to mobilize and facilitate the participation of U.S. private capital and skills in the economic and social progress of less-developed friendly countries and areas, thereby complementing the developmental assistance of the United States. An OPIC offers insurance coverage for four separate types of political risk, which have their own specific definitions for insurance purposes including: (1) business income coverage from asset damage resulting from political violence; (2) inconvertibility of profits, royalties, fees, or other income into U.S. dollars; (3) expropriation; and (4) losses of physical property values resulting from war, revolution, insurrection, and civil strife. Depending on the nature of the project, OPIC will insure up to $400 million of an individual project.

Foreign direct investment and political risk are inevitably intertwined, but with considerable preparation and planning, the multinational may be able to navigate often very difficult and contentious political environments. And as illustrated in *Global Finance in Practice 17.5*, the relationship between the multinational enterprise and a host country need not always be adversarial.

GLOBAL FINANCE IN PRACTICE **17.5**

Structuring Incentives in Foreign Direct Investments

Cementos Mexicanos (Cemex) is one of the leading firms in the world in its industry. It has made dozens of acquisitions in a multitude of countries. So when it constructed its bid for PT Semen Gresik of Indonesia in 1998, it knew what it was getting into. The Indonesian government was under pressure to privatize, largely by the International Monetary Fund (IMF), following the Asian Crisis. PT Semen Gresik was a crown jewel, a large, new, state-of-the-art set of cement manufacturing facilities.

The Indonesian government owned 65%, with the other 35% free float (traded on the Jakarta Stock Exchange). At first the government said it would sell 35% of the total to the highest bidder, but after management and workers alike took to the streets to oppose the sale, the government backed down to selling only 14%. Now Cemex could, at best, gain a minority interest of 49%.

So when Cemex constructed its final bid, it put together a set of pieces that were intended to provide a series of incentives for the government of Indonesia to work with the company in expanding the business post-sale. The bid had five elements:

1. Share price bid. A bid of $1.38/share for 35% of Semen Gresik held by the Indonesian government. Given a current share price of Rp 9,150 ($0.63/share at Rp14,500 = $1.00), this represented nearly a 100% premium.
2. An announced intention to purchase additional shares on the open market. Originally this had been stated at 16% to bring its total ownership to 51% (35% + 16%), but that had changed.
3. Inclusion of a five-year put option to the Indonesian government to sell its remaining shares to Cemex at a base price of $1.38/share plus an 8.2% annual premium.
4. A one-off payment of $130 million to the Indonesian government in 2006 if Semen Gresik's performance, as measured by earnings before interest and taxes (EBIT), surpassed specific hurdles in the coming years.
5. A contribution of approximately $50 million to the ongoing port facilities upgrade and capacity expansion of Semen Gresik.

Of course this was a lot more intricate than what the Indonesian government had envisioned as a "bid." Years later, the author had a chance to discuss the bidding strategy with the chief negotiator for the Cemex team, Mr. Javier Boffarull. The first component constituted a minimum bid—a price, and one with a significant premium. The second element was a clear message to the Indonesian government of Cemex's commitment and intentions—to gain greater interest and possibly control. The third element, the put option, was to make it very clear that if in the future the government needed to liquidate more shares for capital, it had a minimum guaranteed income already on the table. Fourth, the one-off payment, was an incentive for the government to not take any actions post-sale that would prevent Cemex from expanding the profitability of the business. This was a lesson Cemex had learned the hard way in a number of acquisitions in a number of countries over the years. Cemex also knew

GLOBAL FINANCE IN PRACTICE 17.5 *(Continued)*

from experience that regardless of what percentage ownership it gained, 25%, 49%, 65%, it would never have complete control of a company so large and so important to Indonesia. The fifth and final element, a major capital contribution toward infrastructure and expansion, was an added enticement for the government itself to continue to invest in the industry itself.

By including all five elements in the bid, Cemex gave the Indonesian government every opportunity—before the sale—to state any opposition to the plan. The Indonesian government did not have any opposition—Cemex won the bid and gained its minority interest. As the saying goes, it is sometimes more useful to use carrots rather than sticks.

Summary Points

- The strategic decision to undertake foreign direct investment (FDI) by a multinational firm is an expansion of its global strategy.
- The OLI Paradigm is an attempt to create an overall framework to explain why multinational enterprises (MNEs) choose FDI rather than choosing to serve foreign markets through alternative modes, such as licensing, joint ventures, strategic alliances, management contracts, and exporting.
- A multinational firm's decision to invest abroad is followed by choosing markets to enter and choosing the business forms and structures by which to enter those markets. Ultimately, the choice of both target markets and entry structures will establish what types of political risk and exposure the firm then faces.
- The financial risks borne by multinational firms in entering foreign markets are separable into three categories: operating results, transfer risk, and expropriation risks.
- Political risks can be defined on three levels: firm-specific, country-specific, or global-specific.
- The seven most common political risk mitigation techniques are stakeholder engagement, use of domestic partners, international investment agreements, gradual investing, blocked funds management, dispute resolution, and political risk insurance.

MINI-CASE

Argentina and the Vulture Funds[4]

Argentina's default on its foreign-currency-denominated sovereign debt in 2001 had proved to be a never-ending nightmare. Now, in June 2014, 13 years after the default, the U.S. Supreme Court had confirmed a lower-court ruling that would force Argentina to consider defaulting on its international debt obligations once again. But the story was a tangled one, which included investors all over the world, international financial law, courts in New York State and the European Union, and a battle between hedge funds and so-called *vulture funds*—funds that purchased distressed sovereign debt at low prices and then pursued full repayment through litigation. Time was running out.

The Default

Argentina's currency and economy had nearly collapsed in 1999. The rising sovereign debt obligations of the Argentine government, debt denominated in U.S. dollars and European euros, could not be serviced by the faltering economy. In late December 2001, Argentina officially defaulted on its foreign debt: $81.8 billion in private debt, $6.3 billion to the Paris Club, and $9.5 billion to the International Monetary Fund (IMF).

The debt had been originally issued in 1994 and registered under New York State governing law. New York law was specifically chosen because Argentina had become known as a *serial defaulter*. The bonds were issued under a specific structure, a Fiscal Agency Agreement (hence FAA Bonds), which would require all debt service to be made through escrow accounts in New York.

The normal process following default is for the debtor to enter into talks with its creditors to restructure its debt obligations. Reaching consensus on sovereign debt restructuring, however, can be difficult because there is no international statutory regime for sovereign default similar to domestic bankruptcy codes. This leaves three options: (1) a collective solution, (2) a voluntary exchange of old debt for restructured obligations, or (3) litigation.

[4] This case was prepared by Professor Michael H. Moffett for the purpose of classroom discussion only.

The first option, the collective solution, is usually accomplished via the use of *collective action* clauses (CCAs) that impose similar reorganization terms on all creditors once a specific percentage of creditors, 75% to 90%, have agreed to the restructuring terms. These CCAs prevent a small number of creditors—*holdouts*—from blocking restructuring. Unfortunately, the Argentine bonds did not have collective action clauses.

Given the absence of a collective action clause, Argentina was left with the second option, a voluntary exchange of old debt for new debt. Debt restructuring itself normally includes four key elements: (1) a reduction in the principal of the obligation, (2) a reduction in the interest rate, (3) an extension of the obligation's maturity, and (4) capitalization of missed interest payments. The total result is a reduction in the net present value of the debt obligation, the so-called haircut, which may range anywhere from a reduction of 30% to 70%.

A second common clause included within sovereign debt, the *pari passu* clause (Latin for "equal steps" and read as "equal among equals"), calls for all creditors to be treated equally, ensuring that private or individual deals are not made in preference to some creditors over others. Argentina's sovereign debt did include a *pari passu* clause (Argentine Fiscal Agency Agreement (1994), Clause 1c):

> *The Securities will constitute... direct, unconditional, unsecured and unsubordinated obligations of the Republic and shall at all times rank pari passu and without any preference among themselves. The payment obligations of the Republic under the Securities shall at all times rank at least equally with all its other present and future unsecured and unsubordinated External Indebtedness (as defined in this Agreement).*

Restructuring

Following the December 2001 default, Argentina initiated restructuring discussions with its creditors. From the very beginning, it took a hard line. Nearly every dimension of the proposed restructuring was in debate, but the 70% haircut Argentina proposed was the single biggest problem. What followed, as shown in Exhibit A, was a long and twisted path toward debt resolution. It is important to note that many buyers of these bonds in the secondary markets were not original investors—they were intentionally buying defaulted debt. After three years of contentious talks and two unsuccessful proposals, Argentina moved forward with a unilateral reorganization offer to all creditors in early 2005. In preparation for the offer, Argentina passed the *Lock Law, Ley cerrojo*. The Lock Law prohibited Argentina from making any arrangement to pay the unexchanged bonds:

> *The national State shall be prohibited from conducting any type of in-court, out-of-court or private settlement with respect to the FAA [Fiscal Agency Agreement] bonds.*
>
> —U.S. District Court Southern District of New York.

EXHIBIT A Argentine Sovereign Bond Price and Default (due Nov 2002/defaulted)

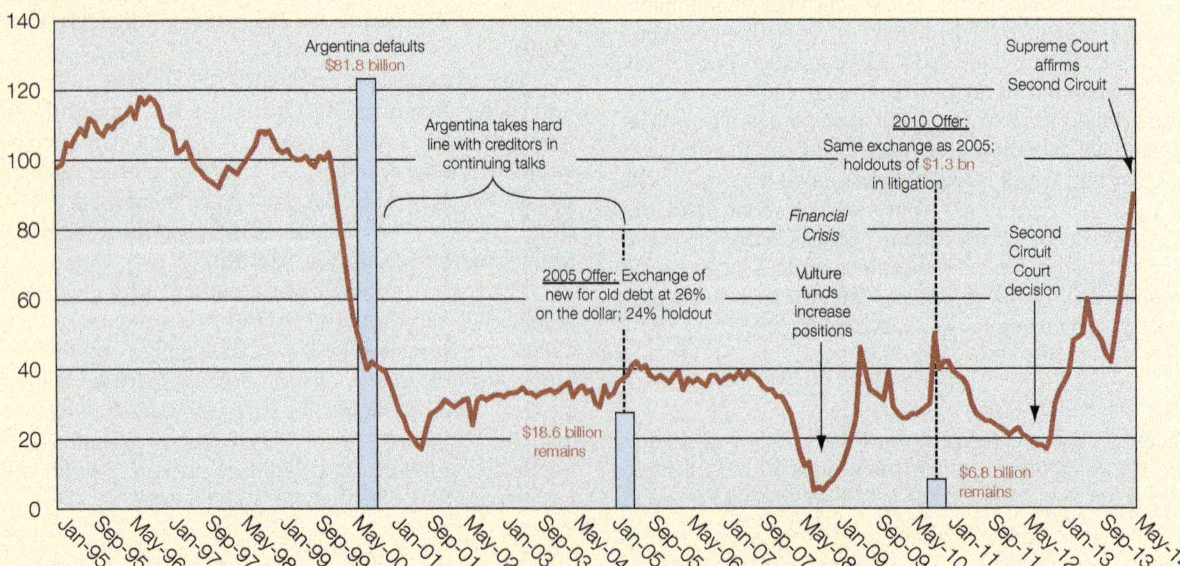

The Lock Law was meant to provide additional incentive for all creditors to exchange old debt for new debt—immediately. Characterized as a "take it or leave it" offer, creditors were offered 26% to 30% of the net present value of the original face value of bond obligations, and as a result of the Lock Law, it was a one-time only offer. The offer was accepted by 75% of Argentina's creditors, reducing outstanding private debt from $81.8 billion to $18.6 billion. The offer was executed by exchanging the original bonds for new Argentina bonds.

The following year Argentina repaid the $9.5 billion in debt owed to the IMF. In 2010, in an attempt to eliminate the remaining outstanding private debt, Argentina temporarily suspended the Lock Law to allow the same bond exchange terms to be offered once again to private debt holders. This second offer reduced the outstanding private debt principal to $8.6 billion. A full 92% of all original creditors had now exchanged the original debt for the reduced value new debt instruments. But a number of holdouts still refused the exchange and instead pursued litigation.

In the prospectus associated with the 2005 and 2010 exchange offers (Exhibit B summarizes both offers), Argentina made it very clear that it did not intend to ever make further payments on the original FAA bonds:

> *[FAA Bonds] that are in default and that are not tendered may remain in default indefinitely... Argentina does not expect to resume payments on any [FAA Bonds] that remain outstanding following the expiration of the exchange offer... there can be no assurance that [holders of unexchanged FAA Bonds] will receive any future payments or be able to collect through litigation...*
>
> —United States District Court Southern District of New York.

Dueling Hedge Funds

Distressed sovereign debt is not a rarity, and so it is not surprising that a number of hedge funds have made the buying and selling of publicly traded distressed debt a business line. There was, however, a fundamental difference between hedge fund investing in corporate distressed debt and sovereign distressed debt. A fund purchasing a substantial portion of distressed corporate debt may become integrally involved in turning around the company; that was not the case with distressed sovereign debt.

Gramercy. One sovereign debt investor of note was Gramercy. In Gramercy's promotion of its distressed debt fund shown in Exhibit C, it highlighted its investments in the debt of Argentina. Note that the stated target return greatly exceeds the yield to maturity (the rate of return expected by a prospective investor at issuance who holds the security to maturity). The higher target return is based on the highly discounted purchase price of the securities relative to the price at which Gramercy hopes/expects to sell the securities at a future date. Gramercy reportedly held $400 million in Argentine bonds in 2012 and still in 2014.

In addition to its purchase of distressed sovereign debt, Gramercy also aggressively protected its investments on the downside through the use of credit default swaps (CDSs). The CDS is a derivative contract that derives its value from the credit quality and performance of any specific asset. A CDS allows an investor to bet on whether a specific security will either fail to pay on time or fail to pay at all. In some cases, CDSs provide insurance against the possibility that a borrower might not pay. In other instances, CDSs allow a speculator to bet against an increasingly risky security. In contrast to traditional insurance where an owner of an asset purchases insurance for that asset, an investor in CDSs need not own the asset (like your neighbor purchasing fire insurance on your house).

EXHIBIT B The Terms of the 2010 Argentina Bond Exchange

Bond Characteristic	Retail Investors	Institutional Investors
Bond Type	Par Bond (pays face value)	Discount Bond (66.3% reduction from face value)
Amount	Up to $2.0 billion	Up to $16.3 billion
Maturity Date	Dec-38	31-Dec-33
Annual Interest Rate	2.5%-5.25% increasing over time	8.28%
Past Due Interest (PDI)	cash payment	Separate 2017 global bonds @ 8.75%
Bank Commission	0.40%	0.40%

Source: Securities and Exchange Commission, Amendment #5 to Argentina 18-K, April 19, 2010, and Prospectus Directive, April 27, 2010, pp. 11, 33–42, 106–112.

EXHIBIT C **Gramercy's Holdings of Argentine Debt**

Security	Maturity	Yield to Maturity	Average Entry Price	Target Exit Price	Target Return
Argentina Par 2.5% (USD)	Dec 2038	11.82%	$32.67	$59.00	88.25%
Argentina Bonar 7% (USD)	Apr 2017	14.42%	$66.20	$100.00	61.63%
Argentina Discount 8.28% (USD)	Dec 2033	12.81%	$65.79	$107.50	75.99%

Source: Abstracted from "Gramercy Distressed Opportunity Fund II," September 2012, Current Investments, p. 12.

Gramercy's chief investment officer was Robert Koenigsberger, formerly the manager of the sovereign debt restructuring team at Lehman Brothers. Koenigsberger had acted as an advisor to Argentina in its arguments in U.S. and European courts. It was, in fact, Gramercy that had persuaded Argentina to reopen the 2005 restructuring negotiations in 2010.

As Gramercy championed the 2010 restructuring offering, it argued that the markets were mispricing Argentine debt on the basis of government debt as percentage of GDP. Argentina's credit default swap (CDS) spread was a full 700 basis points—7.00%—above U.S. Treasuries, although Argentina's debt/GDP ratio was a moderate 46.4%. At the same time, Brazil had a CDS spread of 119 basis points with a 61.7% debt/GDP ratio, and Turkey had a CDS spread of 150 basis point with a 49.0% debt/GDP ratio. If Gramercy was correct and if the market "corrected its error," the prices of the Argentine bonds would rise dramatically.

Elliot. A second hedge fund, Elliot Management Corp, had waged war on Argentina and its debt for years. Elliot, led by Paul Singer, a 68-year-old billionaire and a high-profile supporter of the U.S. Republican Party, was one of the chief litigants against Argentina. Singer had been called the father of vulture funds and in recent years had used this same investment strategy in Peru, the Democratic Republic of Congo, and Panama.

Elliot's fund, NML Capital Ltd., had first invested in Argentine bonds before the 2001 default but had purchased most of its holdings as late as 2008, in the midst of the global financial crisis, at rock-bottom prices. (One story reported that Elliot paid $48.7 million for $832 million in bonds—$0.06 on the dollar.) Elliott now claimed it was due $2.5 billion. As the lead holdout, Elliot had refused the offered exchange in both 2005 and 2010. Elliot was known for hard-knuckle tactics, actually having detained an Argentine naval training vessel, the *ARA Libertad*, in a Ghanaian port for more than two months in an attempt to attach collateral.

NML Ltd. v. Republic of Argentina

Because the distressed debt was under the jurisdiction of New York State law, specifically the Fiscal Agency Agreement (FAA), the case was eventually heard in U.S. District Court. The FAA stipulated that the repayments on the bonds were to be made by Argentina through a trustee based in New York, giving U.S. courts jurisdiction. On October 25, 2012, Judge Thomas P. Griesa for the U.S. District Court for the Southern District of New York, in *NML Capital, Ltd. v. Republic of Argentina*, found in favor of the plaintiff:

> *[T]he judgements of the district court (1) granting summary judgment to plaintiffs on their claims for breach of the Equal Treatment Provision and (2) ordering Argentina to make "Ratable Payments" to plaintiffs concurrent with or in advance of its payments to holders of the 2005 and 2010 restructured debt are affirmed.*

The impact of the court's decision was dramatic. Argentina immediately announced that it would not honor the court's decision. One month later Argentina lost its appeal, with Judge Griesa instructing Argentina to move forward quickly to comply with the Court's judgment. Again, Argentina refused to comply. Fitch, one of the three major global sovereign credit rating services, then downgraded Argentina's credit rating (long-term foreign currency) from B to CC, noting that "a default by Argentina isprobable."

The markets closely followed the case. As illustrated by Exhibit D, the value of the outstanding Argentine exchange bonds plummeted in the days and months following the rulings. For example, the Argentine 2017 Global Bond (exchange bond from 2005) carrying an 8.75% coupon fell 9.9% in the one day following the court judgment and fell a cumulative 24% by the following week. In subsequent hearings Judge Griesa cautioned Argentina on altering the payment processes on the bonds. This was in response to Argentina's newest strategy to circumvent the U.S. courts by processing payments to the exchanged bondholders through financial institutions outside the United States. The FAA bonds and their governing law expressly required processing through New York financial institutions.

On appeal Argentina argued that the District Court had misconstrued the *pari passu* clause, but the Second Circuit court was not persuaded. The court noted that the combination of the issuance and service on the exchange

EXHIBIT D District Court Ruling Impact on Exchange Bond Values

	Republic Global Bond (Exchange), 8.75%, 2017			Republic Global Bond (Exchange 2005), 8.28%, 2033		
Date	**Price**	**Change**	**Spread vs. U.S. Treasury**	**Price**	**Change**	**Chg in Spread vs. U.S. Treasury**
October 25, 2012	$100.053		3.04%	$80.428		
October 26, 2012	$90.157	−9.9%		$72.125	−10.3%	1.5%
November 2, 2012	$76.483	−23.6%	7.79%	$61.278	−23.8%	3.74%

Source: Petition for a Writ of Certiorari, Supreme Court of the United States, No. 13, *Exchange Bondholder Group v. NNL Capital., Ltd.*, February 21, 2014.

bonds, without making equal payments to the holdouts and simultaneously stating under the Lock Law that the holdouts would not ever be paid, was in effect ranking or subordinating the original debt. The court went on to note the particularly critical role the *pari passu* clause plays:

> *When sovereigns default they do not enter bankruptcy proceedings where the legal rank of debt determines the order in which creditors will be paid. Instead, sovereigns can choose for themselves the order in which creditors will be paid. In this context, the [Pari Passu Clause] prevents Argentina as payor from discriminating against the FAA bonds in favor of other unsubordinated, foreign bonds.*

To its credit, Argentina had made substantial efforts at repairing its relationship with the outside world. By late May, it had committed to repaying the $9.7 billion owed to the Paris Club and had agreed to pay Repsol of Spain $5 billion in Argentine bonds for its seizure of Repsol's Argentine subsidiary earlier in 2013.

On Monday, June 25, 2014, Argentina deposited $832 million in a New York bank in preparation for payment of interest on its exchange bonds. This would be in direct conflict with the ruling of the courts. According to Argentina's economic minister: "Complying with a ruling doesn't exempt us from honouring our obligations. Argentina will meet its obligations, will pay its debt, will honour its promises." A full-page official communique was placed in the *Financial Times* explaining the country's position. But the court order prevented the banks from dispensing payments on the restructured debt unless holdout creditors were also paid. Argentina argued that because it had deposited the money in the transfer accounts for payment, the bondholders had been paid. The courts disagreed.

What Now?

Argentina's response to the latest U.S. court rulings was outrage. Within days, Argentina announced a plan to swap existing bonds governed by U.S. law for debt issued under Argentine law. Although unprecedented in sovereign debt markets, the move had been anticipated by market analysts. If investors were willing to undertake the exchange, they would receive some of the highest interest yields in the world—foregoing default—but they would give up all legal rights and protection provided under U.S. law.

Judge Griesa released a statement that any attempt by Argentina to proceed with payments on its restructured debt, without settling with holdouts first, was illegal. Argentina continued to argue that this was impossible. According to the Argentine finance minister, if Argentina settled with the holdouts, the exchange bondholders could possibly sue for equal treatment—the *RUFO (Rights Upon Future Offer) clause*—and total claims could reach $120 billion. The RUFO clause, contained in all of the exchange bonds issued in 2005 and 2010, guaranteed exchange bondholders the same rights and payments that might possibly be provided the holdout bondholders. Given the renewed currency crises the country was suffering, Argentina's hard currency reserves were estimated at only $30 billion, inadequate to settle potential RUFO claims.

On June 30, 2014, Argentina failed to make payments on its outstanding exchange bonds. The country now had a single 30-day grace period before entering into selective default. In early July, representatives of the Argentine Finance Ministry and the Elliot Group met to see if they could find an acceptable solution.

MINI-CASE QUESTIONS

1. What role is played by legal clauses such as the collective action clause and the *pari passu* clause in sovereign debt issuances?
2. What is the difference between a typical hedge fund investing in sovereign debt (even distressed sovereign debt) and the so-called vulture funds?
3. If you were appointed as a mediator by the court to find a solution, what options or alternatives would you suggest for resolving this crisis?

Questions

17.1 **Evolving into Multinationalism.** As a firm evolves from purely domestic into a true multinational enterprise (MNE), it must consider (1) its competitive advantages, (2) its production location, (3) the type of control it wants to have over any foreign operations, and (4) how much monetary capital to invest abroad. Explain how each of these considerations is important to the success of foreign operations.

17.2 **Market Imperfections.** MNEs strive to take advantage of market imperfections in national markets for products, factors of production, and financial assets. Large international firms are better able to exploit such imperfections. What are their main competitive advantages?

17.3 **Competitive Advantage.** In deciding whether to invest abroad, management must first determine whether the firm has a sustainable competitive advantage that enables it to compete effectively in the home market. What are the necessary characteristics of this competitive advantage?

17.4 **Economies of Scale and Scope.** Explain briefly how economies of scale and scope can be developed in production, marketing, finance, research and development, transportation, and purchasing.

17.5 **Competitiveness of the Home Market.** A strongly competitive home market can sharpen a firm's competitive advantage relative to firms located in less competitive markets. Explain what is meant by the "competitive advantage of nations."

17.6 **OLI Paradigm.** The OLI Paradigm is an attempt to create an overall framework to explain why MNEs choose foreign direct investment (FDI) rather than serve foreign markets through alternative modes. Explain what is meant by the "O," the "L," and the "I" of the paradigm.

17.7 **Financial Links to OLI.** Financial strategies are directly related to the OLI Paradigm.

a. Explain how proactive financial strategies are related to OLI.
b. Explain how reactive financial strategies are related to OLI.

17.8 **Where to Invest.** The decision about where to invest abroad is influenced by behavioral factors.

a. Explain the behavioral approach to FDI.
b. Explain the international network theory explanation of FDI.

17.9 **Exporting versus Producing Abroad.** What are the advantages and disadvantages of limiting a firm's activities to exporting compared to producing abroad?

17.10 **Licensing and Management Contracts versus Producing Abroad.** What are the advantages and disadvantages of licensing and management contracts compared to producing abroad?

17.11 **Joint Venture versus Wholly Owned Production Subsidiary.** What are the advantages and disadvantages of forming a joint venture to serve a foreign market compared to serving that market with a wholly owned production subsidiary?

17.12 **Greenfield Investment versus Acquisition.** What are the advantages and disadvantages of serving a foreign market through a greenfield FDI compared to an acquisition of a local firm in the target market?

17.13 **Cross-Border Strategic Alliance.** The term *cross-border strategic alliance* conveys different meanings to different observers. What are the meanings?

17.14 **Political Risk.** How is political risk defined, and how does political risk associated with business differ from a more general political risk to all social activities? What is the difference between firm-specific risk and country-specific risk?

17.15 **Potential Financial Losses Political Risk.** How do the major categories of potential financial losses to multinational companies associated with political risk differ across financial form—profitability, cash flow, and asset ownership?

17.16 **Common Forms.** Define the following types of political risk:

a. Adverse regulatory change
b. Breach of contract
c. Expropriation

17.17 **Lawful Expropriation.** What criteria have to be met for a government's seizure of a company's business to be considered "lawful" by international law?

17.18 **Expropriation Distinctions.** Answer the following:

a. What is the difference between expropriation and creeping expropriation?
b. What is the difference between direct and indirect expropriation?

17.19 **Lawful Compensation.** Lawful expropriation must be accompanied by lawful compensation. What criteria have to be met to fulfill this requirement?

17.20 **Political Risk Mitigation.** What are the seven most common political risk mitigation strategies employed by MNEs?

17.21 **Government Stakeholder Engagement.** Have studies found that more or less government involvement in a prospective project is helpful in the success of the business?

17.22 International Investment Agreement. An international investment agreement spells out specific rights and responsibilities of both the foreign firm and the host government. What are the main financial policies that should be included in an investment agreement?

17.23 Investment Insurance. What is investment insurance, and what organizations provide such coverage?

17.24 OPIC. Answer the following questions about OPIC:

a. What is OPIC?

b. What types of political risks can OPIC insure against?

17.25 Gradual Investing. What are the primary pros and cons of using a gradual investing strategy to mitigate political risk?

17.26 Dispute Resolution. What are some of the characteristics of a well-designed dispute resolution process?

17.27 Blocked Funds. Explain the strategies used by an MNE to counter blocked funds.

18 Multinational Capital Budgeting and Cross-Border Acquisitions

Cecil Graham: What is a cynic?
Lord Darlington: A man who knows the price of everything, and the value of nothing.
Cecil Graham: And a sentimentalist, my dear Darlington, is a man who sees an absurd value in everything and doesn't know the market price of any single thing.
—Oscar Wilde, *Lady Windermere's Fan*, February 1892.

LEARNING OBJECTIVES

18.1 Explore the complexities of budgeting for a foreign project

18.2 Illustrate multinational capital budgeting with the case of Cemex entering Indonesia

18.3 Describe the use of real option analysis

18.4 Examine the use of project finance to fund and evaluate large global projects

18.5 Introduce the principles of cross-border mergers and acquisitions

This chapter describes in detail the issues and principles related to investment in real productive assets in foreign countries, generally referred to as *multinational capital budgeting*. The chapter first describes the complexities of budgeting for a foreign project. Second, we describe the insights gained by valuing a project from both the project's viewpoint and the parent's viewpoint using an illustrative case involving an investment by Cemex of Mexico in Indonesia. The illustrative case is followed by an exploration of the use of *real option analysis* for a foreign project. Next, the use of *project financing* today is discussed, and the final section describes the stages involved in affecting cross-border acquisitions. The chapter concludes with the mini-case *Mittal's Hostile Acquisition of Arcelor*, one of the most famous cross-border acquisitions in European history.

Although the original decision to undertake an investment in a particular foreign country may be determined by a mix of strategic, behavioral, and economic factors, the specific project should be justified—as should all reinvestment decisions—by traditional financial analysis. For example, a production efficiency opportunity may exist for a U.S. firm to invest abroad, but the type of plant, mix of labor and capital, kinds of equipment, method of financing, and other project variables must be analyzed with traditional discounted cash flow analysis. The firm must also consider the impact of the proposed foreign project on consolidated earnings, cash flows from subsidiaries in other countries, and the market value of the parent firm. Multinational capital budgeting for a foreign project uses the same theoretical framework as domestic capital budgeting—with a few very important differences. The basic steps are as follows:

- Identify the initial capital invested or put at risk.
- Estimate cash flows to be derived from the project over time, including an estimate of the terminal or salvage value of the investment.
- Identify the appropriate discount rate for determining the present value of the expected cash flows.
- Apply traditional capital budgeting decision criteria such as net present value (NPV) and internal rate of return (IRR) to determine the acceptability of or priority ranking of potential projects.

18.1 Complexities of Budgeting for a Foreign Project

Capital budgeting for a foreign project is considerably more complex than the domestic case. Two broad categories of factors contribute to this greater complexity, cash flows and managerial expectations.

Cash Flows

- Parent cash flows must be distinguished from project cash flows. Each of these two types of flows contributes to a different view of value.
- Parent cash flows often depend on the form of financing. Thus, we cannot clearly separate cash flows from financing decisions, as we can in domestic capital budgeting.
- Additional cash flows generated by a new investment in one foreign subsidiary may be in part or in whole taken away from another subsidiary, with the net result that the project is favorable from a single subsidiary's point of view but contributes nothing to worldwide cash flows.
- The parent must explicitly recognize remittance of funds because of differing tax systems, legal and political constraints on the movement of funds, local business norms, and differences in the way financial markets and institutions function.
- An array of nonfinancial payments can generate cash flows from subsidiaries to the parent, including payment of license fees and payments for imports from the parent.

Management Expectations

- Managers must anticipate differing rates of national inflation because of their potential to cause changes in competitive position, and thus changes in cash flows over a period of time.
- Managers must keep the possibility of unanticipated foreign exchange rate changes in mind because of possible direct effects on the value of local cash flows as well as indirect effects on the competitive position of the foreign subsidiary.
- Use of segmented national capital markets may create an opportunity for financial gains or may lead to additional financial costs.
- Use of host-government subsidized loans complicates both capital structure and the parent's ability to determine an appropriate weighted average cost of capital for discounting purposes.

- Managers must evaluate political risk because political events can drastically reduce the value or availability of expected cash flows.
- Terminal value is more difficult to estimate because potential purchasers from the host, parent, or third countries or from the private or public sector may have widely divergent perspectives on the value to them of acquiring the project.

Since the same theoretical capital budgeting framework is used to choose among competing foreign and domestic projects, it is critical that we have a common standard. Thus, all foreign complexities must be quantified as modifications to either expected cash flow or the rate of discount. Although in practice many firms make such modifications arbitrarily, readily available information, theoretical deduction, or just plain common sense can be used to make less arbitrary and more reasonable choices.

Project versus Parent Valuation

Consider a foreign direct investment like that illustrated in Exhibit 18.1. A U.S. multinational invests capital in a foreign project in a foreign country, the results of which—if they occur—are generated over time. Similar to any investment, domestically or internationally, the return on the investment is based on the outcomes to the parent company. Given that the initial investment is in the parent's own or home currency, the U.S. dollar in this case, then those returns over time need to be denominated in that same currency for evaluation purposes.

A strong theoretical argument exists in favor of analyzing any foreign project from the viewpoint of the parent. Cash flows to the parent are ultimately the basis for dividends to stockholders, reinvestment elsewhere in the world, repayment of corporate-wide debt, and other purposes that affect the firm's many interest groups. However, since most of a project's cash flows to its parent or sister subsidiaries are financial cash flows rather than operating cash flows, the parent viewpoint violates a cardinal concept of capital budgeting, namely, that financial cash flows should not be mixed with operating cash flows. Often the difference is not important because the two are almost identical, but in some instances a sharp divergence in these cash flows will exist. For example, funds that are permanently blocked from repatriation, or "forcibly reinvested," are not available for dividends to the stockholders or for repayment of parent debt. Therefore, shareholders will not perceive the blocked earnings as

EXHIBIT 18.1 Multinational Capital Budgeting: Project and Parent Viewpoints

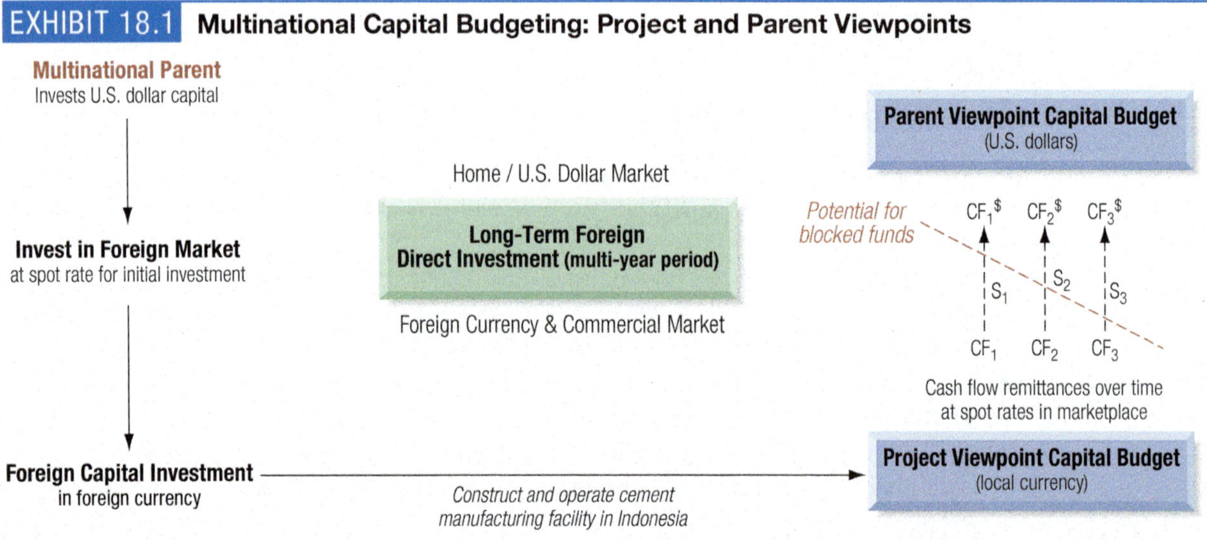

contributing to the value of the firm, and creditors will not count on them in calculating interest coverage ratios and other metrics of debt service capability.

Evaluation of a project from the local viewpoint—the *project viewpoint*—serves a number of useful purposes as well. In evaluating a foreign project's performance relative to the potential of a competing project in the same host country, we must pay attention to the project's local return. Almost any project should at least be able to earn a cash return equal to the yield available on host government bonds with a maturity equal to the project's economic life if a free market exists for such bonds. Host-government bonds ordinarily reflect the local risk-free rate of return, including a premium equal to the expected rate of inflation. If a project cannot earn more than such a bond yield, the parent firm should buy host government bonds rather than invest in a riskier project.

Multinational firms should invest only if they can earn a risk-adjusted return greater than locally based competitors can earn on the same project (and of course above their cost of capital). If they are unable to earn superior returns on foreign projects, their stockholders would be better off buying shares in local firms, where possible, and letting those companies carry out the local projects. Apart from these theoretical arguments, surveys over the past 40 years show that in practice MNEs continue to evaluate foreign investments from both the parent and project viewpoint. The attention paid to project returns in various surveys may reflect an emphasis on maximizing reported earnings per share as a corporate financial goal of publicly traded companies. It is not clear that privately held firms place the same emphasis on consolidated results, given that few public investors ever see their financial results. Consolidation practices, including translation, as described in Chapter 11, remeasure foreign project cash flows, earnings, and assets as if they are "returned" to the parent company. And as long as foreign earnings are not blocked, they can be consolidated with the earnings of both the remaining subsidiaries and the parent.[1] Even in the case of temporarily blocked funds, some of the most mature MNEs do not necessarily eliminate a project from financial consideration. They take a very long-run view of world business opportunities.

If blocked funds can be reinvested in the country and earn a rate of return at least equal to what they would have earned when repatriated to the parent company, the impacts on the firm's capital investments—its capital budgeting income—are roughly equal. This assumes that the forced reinvestment in the country and in the business will yield higher returns from that investment. Since large multinationals hold a portfolio of domestic and foreign projects, corporate liquidity is not impaired if a few projects have blocked funds; alternate sources of funds are available to meet all planned uses of funds. Furthermore, a long-run historical perspective on blocked funds lends support to the belief that funds are almost never permanently blocked. However, waiting for the release of such funds can be frustrating, and sometimes the blocked funds lose value while blocked because of inflation or unexpected exchange rate deterioration, even though they have been reinvested in the host country to protect at least part of their value in real terms.

In conclusion, most firms appear to evaluate foreign projects from both parent and project viewpoints. The parent's viewpoint gives results closer to the traditional meaning of net present value in capital budgeting theoretically but, as we will demonstrate, possibly not in practice. Project valuation provides a closer approximation of the effect on consolidated earnings per share, an effect that all surveys indicate is of major concern to practicing managers. To illustrate the foreign complexities of multinational capital budgeting, we now analyze a hypothetical market-seeking foreign direct investment by Cemex in Indonesia.

[1] U.S. firms must consolidate foreign subsidiaries that are over 50% owned. If a firm is owned between 20% and 49% by a parent, it is called an *affiliate*. *Affiliates* are consolidate with the parent owner on a *pro rata* basis. Subsidiaries less than 20% owned are normally carried as unconsolidated investments.

18.2 Illustrative Case: Cemex Enters Indonesia[2]

Cementos Mexicanos, Cemex, is considering the construction of a cement manufacturing facility on the Indonesian island of Sumatra. The project, Semen Indonesia (the Indonesian word for "cement" is *semen*), would be a wholly owned greenfield investment with a total installed capacity of 20 million metric tonnes per year (mmt/y). Although that is large by Asian production standards, Cemex believes that its latest cement manufacturing technology would be most efficiently utilized with a production facility of this scale.

Cemex has three driving reasons for the project: (1) the firm wishes to enter the Southeast Asian market, a new market for Cemex; (2) the prospects for Asian infrastructure development and growth appear very good over the longer term; and (3) Indonesia has become an attractive produce-for-export site as a result of the depreciation of the Indonesian rupiah (Rp) in recent years.

Cemex, the world's third-largest cement manufacturer, is an MNE headquartered in an emerging market but competing in a global arena. The firm competes in the global marketplace for both market share and capital. The international cement market, like markets in other commodities such as oil, is a dollar-based market. For this reason, and for comparisons against its major competitors in both Germany and Switzerland, Cemex considers the U.S. dollar to be its functional currency.

Cemex's shares are listed in both Mexico City and New York (OTC: CMXSY). The firm has successfully raised capital—both debt and equity—outside Mexico in U.S. dollars. Its investor base is increasingly global, with the U.S. share turnover rising rapidly as a percentage of total trading. As a result, its cost and availability of capital are internationalized and dominated by U.S. dollar investors. Ultimately, the Semen Indonesia project will be evaluated—in both cash flows and capital cost—in U.S. dollars.

Overview

The first step in analyzing Cemex's potential investment in Indonesia is to construct a set of pro forma financial statements for Semen Indonesia, all in Indonesian rupiah. The next step is to create two capital budgets, the project viewpoint and parent viewpoint. Semen Indonesia will take only one year to build the plant, with actual operations commencing in year 1. The Indonesian government has only recently deregulated the heavier industries to allow foreign ownership.

All of the following analysis is conducted assuming that purchasing power parity (PPP) holds for the rupiah-to-dollar exchange rate for the life of the Indonesian project. This is a standard financial assumption made by Cemex for its foreign investments. Thus, if we assume an initial spot rate of Rp10,000 = $1.00 and Indonesian and U.S. inflation rates of 30% and 3% per annum, respectively, for the life of the project, forecasted spot exchange rates follow the usual PPP calculation. For example, the forecasted exchange rate for year 1 of the project would be as follows:

$$\text{Spot rate (one 1 year now)} = [\text{Rp10,000 per\$}] \times \frac{1 + .30}{1 + .03} = \text{Rp12,621 per\$}$$

The financial statements shown in Exhibits 18.2 through 18.5 are based on these assumptions.

Capital Investment. Although the cost of building new cement manufacturing capacity anywhere in the industrial countries is now estimated at roughly $150/tonne of installed

[2] Cemex is a real company. However, the greenfield investment, Semen Indonesia, described here is hypothetical.

capacity, Cemex believed that it could build a state-of-the-art production and shipment facility in Sumatra at roughly $110/tonne (see Exhibit 18.2). Assuming a 20 mmt/y capacity and a year 0 average exchange rate of Rp10,000 = $1.00, this cost will constitute an investment of Rp22 trillion ($2.2 billion). This figure includes an investment of Rp17.6 trillion in plant and equipment, giving rise to an annual depreciation charge of Rp1.76 trillion if we assume a 10-year straight-line depreciation schedule. The relatively short depreciation schedule is one of the policies of the Indonesian tax authorities meant to attract foreign investment.

EXHIBIT 18.2 Investment and Financing of the Semen Indonesia Project (in 000s)

INVESMENT		FINANCING	
Average exchange rate, Rp = $1.00	10,000	Equity	11,000,000,000
Cost of installed capacity ($/tonne)	$110	Debt:	11,000,000,000
Installed capacity	20,000	Rupiah debt	2,750,000,000
Investment in US$	$2,200,000	US$ debt in rupiah	8,250,000,000
Investment in rupiah	22,000,000,000	Total	22,000,000,000
Percentage of investment in plant & equip	80%	Note: US$ debt principal	$825,000
Plant and equipment (000s Rp)	17,600,000,000		
Depreciation of capital equipment (years)	10.00		
Annual depreciation (millions)	(1,760,000)		
Costs of Capital: Cemex (Mexico)			
Risk-free rate	6.000%	Cemex beta	1.50
Credit premium	2.000%	Equity risk premium	7.000%
Cost of debt	8.000%	Cost of equity	16.500%
Corporate income tax rate	35.000%	Percent equity	60.0%
Cost of debt after-tax	5.200%	**WACC**	**11.980%**
Percent debt	40.0%		
Cost of Capital: Semen Indonesia (Indonesia)			
Risk-free rate	33.000%	Semen Indonesia beta	1.000
Credit premium	2.000%	Equity risk premium	6.000%
Cost of rupiah debt	35.000%	Cost of equity	40.000%
Indonesia corporate income tax rate	30.000%	Percent equity	50.0%
Cost of US$ debt, after-tax	5.200%	**WACC**	**33.257%**
Cost of US$ debt, (rupiah equivalent)	38.835%		
Cost of US$ debt, after-tax (rupiah eq)	27.184%		
Percent debt	50.0%		

The cost of the US$ loan is stated in rupiah terms assuming purchasing power parity and U.S. dollar and Indonesian inflation rates of 3% and 30% per annum, respectively, throughout the subject period.

Semen Indonesia (Rp)	Amount	Financing Proportion	Cost	After-tax Cost	Component Cost
Rupiah loan	2,750,000,000	12.5%	35.000%	24.500%	3.063%
Cemex loan	8,250,000,000	37.5%	38.835%	27.184%	10.194%
Total debt	11,000,000,000	50.0%			
Equity	11,000,000,000	50.0%	40.000%	40.000%	20.000%
Total financing	22,000,000,000	100.0%		**WACC**	**33.257%**

Financing. This massive investment would be financed with 50% equity, all from Cemex, and 50% debt—75% from Cemex and 25% from a bank consortium arranged by the Indonesian government. Cemex's own U.S. dollar-based weighted average cost of capital (WACC) was currently estimated at 11.98%. The WACC for the project itself on a local Indonesian level in rupiah terms was estimated at 33.257%. The details of this calculation are discussed later in this chapter.

The cost of the U.S. dollar–denominated loan is stated in rupiah terms assuming purchasing power parity and U.S. dollar and Indonesian inflation rates of 3% and 30% per annum, respectively, throughout the subject period. The explicit debt structures, including repayment schedules, are presented in Exhibit 18.3. The loan arranged by the Indonesian government, part of the government's economic development incentive program, is an eight-year loan, in rupiah, at 35% annual interest, fully amortizing. The interest payments are fully deductible against corporate tax liabilities.

EXHIBIT 18.3 Semen Indonesia's Debt Service Schedules and Foreign Exchange Gains/Losses

Spot rate (Rp=$1.00)	**10,000**	**12,621**	**15,930**	**20,106**	**25,376**	**32,028**
Project Year	**0**	**1**	**2**	**3**	**4**	**5**
Indonesian loan @ 35% for 8 years (millions of rupiah)						
Loan principal	2,750,000					
Interest payment		(962,500)	(928,921)	(883,590)	(822,393)	(739,777)
Principal payment		(95,939)	(129,518)	(174,849)	(236,046)	(318,662)
Total payment		(1,058,439)	(1,058,439)	(1,058,439)	(1,058,439)	(1,058,439)
Cemex loan @ 10% for five years (millions of U.S. dollars)						
Loan principal	825					
Interest payment		($82.50)	($68.99)	($54.12)	($37.77)	($19.78)
Principal payment		($135.13)	($148.65)	($163.51)	($179.86)	($197.85)
Total payment		($217.63)	($217.63)	($217.63)	($217.63)	($217.63)
Cemex loan converted to Rp at scheduled and current spot rates (millions of Rp):						
Scheduled at Rp10,000/$:						
Interest payment		(825,000)	(689,867)	(541,221)	(377,710)	(197,848)
Principal payment		(1,351,329)	(1,486,462)	(1,635,108)	(1,798,619)	(1,978,481)
Total payment		(2,176,329)	(2,176,329)	(2,176,329)	(2,176,329)	(2,176,329)
Actual (at current spot rate):						
Interest payment		(1,041,262)	(1,098,949)	(1,088,160)	(958,480)	(633,669)
Principal payment		(1,705,561)	(2,367,915)	(3,287,494)	(4,564,190)	(6,336,691)
Total payment		(2,746,823)	(3,466,864)	(4,375,654)	(5,522,670)	(6,970,360)
Cash flows in Rp on Cemex loan (millions of Rp):						
Total actual cash flows	8,250,000	(2,746,823)	(3,466,864)	(4,375,654)	(5,522,670)	(6,970,360)
IRR of cash flows	**38.835%**					
Foreign exchange gains (losses) on Cemex loan (millions of Rp):						
Foreign exchange gains (losses) on interest		(216,262)	(409,082)	(546,940)	(580,770)	(435,821)
Foreign exchange gains (losses) on principal		(354,232)	(881,453)	(1,652,385)	(2,765,571)	(4,358,210)
Total foreign exchange losses on debt		(570,494)	(1,290,535)	(2,199,325)	(3,346,341)	(4,794,031)

The loan by Cemex to the Indonesian subsidiary is denominated in U.S. dollars. Therefore, the loan will have to be repaid in U.S. dollars, not rupiah. At the time of the loan agreement, the spot exchange rate is Rp10,000 = $1.00. This is the assumption used in calculating the "scheduled" repaying of principal and interest in rupiah. The rupiah, however, is expected to depreciate in line with purchasing power parity. As it is repaid, the "actual" exchange rate will therefore give rise to a foreign exchange loss as it takes more and more rupiah to acquire U.S. dollars for debt service, both principal and interest. The foreign exchange losses on this debt service will be recognized on the Indonesian income statement.

The majority of the debt, however, is being provided by the parent company, Cemex. After raising the capital from its financing subsidiary, Cemex will re-lend the capital to Semen Indonesia. The loan is denominated in U.S. dollars, five years maturity, with an annual interest rate of 10%. Because the debt will have to be repaid from the rupiah earnings of the Indonesian enterprise, the pro forma financial statements are constructed so that the expected costs of servicing the dollar debt are included in the firm's pro forma income statement. The dollar loan, if the rupiah follows the purchasing power parity forecast, will have an effective interest expense in rupiah terms of 38.835% before taxes. We find this rate by determining the internal rate of return of repaying the dollar loan in full in rupiah (see Exhibit 18.3).

The loan by Cemex to the Indonesian subsidiary is denominated in U.S. dollars. Therefore, the loan will have to be repaid in U.S. dollars, not rupiah. At the time of the loan agreement, the spot exchange rate is Rp10,000 = $1.00. This is the assumption used in calculating the "scheduled" repaying of principal and interest in rupiah. The rupiah, however, is expected to depreciate in line with purchasing power parity. As it is repaid, the "actual" exchange rate will therefore give rise to a foreign exchange loss as it takes more and more rupiah to acquire U.S. dollars for debt service, both principal and interest. The foreign exchange losses on this debt service will be recognized on the Indonesian income statement.

Revenues. Given the current existing cement manufacturing in Indonesia and its currently depressed state as a result of the Asian crisis, all sales are based on export. The 20 mmt/y facility is expected to operate at only 40% capacity (producing 8 million metric tonnes). Cement produced will be sold in the export market at $58/tonne (delivered). Note also that, at least for the conservative baseline analysis, we assume no increase in the price received over time.

Costs. The cash costs of cement manufacturing (labor, materials, power, and so forth) are estimated at Rp115,000 per tonne for year 1, rising at about the rate of inflation, 30% per year. Additional production costs of Rp20,000 per tonne for year 1 are also assumed to rise at the rate of inflation. As a result of all production being exported, loading costs of $2.00/tonne shipping of $2.00/tonne and shipping of $10.00/tonne must also be included. Note that these costs are originally stated in U.S. dollars, and for the purposes of Semen Indonesia's income statement, they must be converted to rupiah terms. This is the case because both ship loading and shipping costs are international services governed by contracts denominated in dollars. As a result, they are expected to rise over time only at the U.S. dollar rate of inflation (3%).

Semen Indonesia's pro forma income statement is illustrated in Exhibit 18.4. This is the typical financial statement measurement of the profitability of any business, whether domestic or international. The baseline analysis assumes a capacity utilization rate of only 40% (year 1), 50% (year 2), and 60% in the following years. Management believes this is necessary since existing in-country cement manufacturers are averaging only 40% of capacity at this time.

Additional expenses in the pro forma financial analysis include license fees paid by the subsidiary to the parent company of 2.0% of sales, and general and administrative expenses for Indonesian operations of 8.0% per year (and growing an additional 1% per year). Foreign exchange gains and losses are those related to the servicing of the U.S. dollar-denominated debt provided by the parent and are drawn from the bottom of Exhibit 18.3. In summary, the subsidiary operation is expected to begin turning an accounting profit in its fourth year of operations, with profits rising as capacity utilization increases over time.

The loan by Cemex to the Indonesian subsidiary is denominated in U.S. dollars. Therefore, the loan will be repaid in U.S. dollars, not rupiah. At the time of the loan agreement, the spot exchange rate is Rp10,000 = $1.00. This is the assumption used in calculating the "scheduled" repaying of principal and interest in rupiah. The rupiah, however, is expected to depreciate in line with purchasing power parity. As it is repaid, the "actual" exchange rate will

EXHIBIT 18.4 Semen Indonesia's Pro Forma Income Statement (millions of rupiah)

Exchange rate (Rp=$1.00)	10,000	12,621	15,930	20,106	25,376	32,028
Project Year	**0**	**1**	**2**	**3**	**4**	**5**
Sales volume		8.00	10.00	12.00	12.00	12.00
Sales price (US$)		58.00	58.00	58.00	58.00	58.00
Sales price (Rp)		732,039	923,933	1,166,128	1,471,813	1,857,627
Total revenue		5,856,311	9,239,325	13,993,541	17,661,751	22,291,530
Less cash costs		(920,000)	(1,495,000)	(2,332,200)	(3,031,860)	(3,941,418)
Less other production costs		(160,000)	(260,000)	(405,600)	(527,280)	(685,464)
Less loading costs		(201,942)	(328,155)	(511,922)	(665,499)	(865,149)
Less shipping costs		(1,009,709)	(1,640,777)	(2,559,612)	(3,327,495)	(4,325,744)
Total production costs		(2,291,650)	(3,723,932)	(5,809,334)	(7,552,134)	(9,817,774)
Gross profit		3,564,660	5,515,393	8,184,207	10,109,617	12,473,756
Gross margin		*60.9%*	*59.7%*	*58.5%*	*57.2%*	*56.0%*
Less license fees		(117,126)	(184,787)	(279,871)	(353,235)	(445,831)
Less general & administrative		(468,505)	(831,539)	(1,399,354)	(1,942,793)	(2,674,984)
EBITDA		2,979,029	4,499,067	6,504,982	7,813,589	9,352,941
Less depreciation & amortization		(1,760,000)	(1,760,000)	(1,760,000)	(1,760,000)	(1,760,000)
EBIT		1,219,029	2,739,067	4,744,982	6,053,589	7,592,941
Less interest on Cemex debt		(825,000)	(689,867)	(541,221)	(377,710)	(197,848)
Foreign exchange losses on debt		(570,494)	(1,290,535)	(2,199,325)	(3,346,341)	(4,794,031)
Less interest on local debt		(962,500)	(928,921)	(883,590)	(822,393)	(739,777)
EBT		(1,138,965)	(170,256)	1,120,846	1,507,145	1,861,285
Less income taxes (30%)		-	-	-	(395,631)	(558,386)
Net income		(1,138,965)	(170,256)	1,120,846	1,111,514	1,302,900
Net income (millions of US$)		(90)	(11)	56	44	41
Return on sales		*-19.4%*	*-1.8%*	*8.0%*	*6.3%*	*5.8%*
Dividends distributed		-	-	560,423	555,757	651,450
Retained		(1,138,965)	(170,256)	560,423	555,757	651,450

EBITDA = earnings before interest, taxes, depreciation, and amortization EBIT = earnings before interest and taxes EBT = earnings before taxes
Tax credits resulting from current period losses are carried forward toward next year's tax liabilities. Dividends are not distributed in the first year of operations as a result of losses and are distributed at a 50% rate in years 3–5.
All calculations are exact but may appear not to add due to reported decimal places. The tax payment for year 3 is zero and year 4 is less than 30% as a result of tax loss carry-forwards from previous years.

therefore give rise to a foreign exchange loss as it takes more and more rupiah to acquire U.S. dollars for debt service, both principal and interest. The foreign exchange losses on this debt service will be recognized on the Indonesian income statement.

Tax credits resulting from current period losses are carried forward toward next year's tax liabilities. As a result of losses, no dividends are distributed in the first year of operations; in years 0–3, dividends are distributed at a 50% rate.

Project Viewpoint Capital Budget

The capital budget for the Semen Indonesia project from a *project viewpoint* is shown in Exhibit 18.5. We find the net cash flow, free cash flow as it is often labeled, by summing (1) EBITDA (earnings before interest, taxes, depreciation, and amortization), (2) recalculated taxes, (3) changes in net working capital (the sum of the net additions to receivables, inventories, and payables necessary to support sales growth), and (4) capital investment.

Note that EBIT, not EBT, is used in the capital budget, which contains both depreciation and interest expense. Depreciation and amortization are noncash expenses of the firm and therefore contribute positive cash flow. Because the capital budget creates cash flows that will be discounted to present value with a discount rate and the discount rate includes the cost of debt—interest—we do not wish to subtract interest twice. Therefore, taxes are recalculated on the basis of EBIT.[3] The firm's cost of capital used in discounting also includes the deductibility of debt interest in its calculation.

The initial investment of Rp22 trillion is the total capital invested to support these earnings. Although receivables average 50 to 55 days sales outstanding (DSO) and inventories average 65 to 70 DSO, payables and trade credit are also relatively long at 114 DSO in the Indonesian cement industry. Semen Indonesia expects to add approximately 15 net DSO to its investment with sales growth. The remaining elements to complete the project viewpoint's capital budget are the terminal value (discussed below) and the discount rate of 33.257% (the firm's weighted average cost of capital).

The *terminal value* (TV) of the project represents the continuing value of the cement manufacturing facility in the years after year 5, the last year of the detailed pro forma financial analysis shown in Exhibit 18.5. This value, like all asset values according to financial theory, is the present value of all future free cash flows that the asset is expected to yield. We calculate the TV as the present value of a perpetual *net operating cash flow* (NOCF) generated in the fifth year by Semen Indonesia, the growth rate assumed for that net operating cash flow (g), and the firm's weighted average cost of capital (k_{WACC}):

$$\text{Terminal value} = \frac{\text{NOCF}_5(1+g)}{K_{\text{wacc}} - g} = \frac{7{,}075{,}059(1+0)}{.33257 - 0} = \text{Rp}21{,}274{,}102$$

or Rp21,274,102 trillion. The assumption that $g = 0$, that is, that net operating cash flows will not grow past year 5, is probably not true, but it is a prudent assumption for Cemex to make when estimating future cash flows. (If Semen Indonesia's business was to continue to grow in line with the Indonesian economy, g may well be 1% or 2%.) The results of the capital budget from the project viewpoint indicate a negative *net present value* (NPV) and an *internal rate of return* (IRR) of only 19.1% compared to the 33.257% cost of capital. These are the returns the project would yield to a local or Indonesian investor in Indonesian rupiah. The project, from this viewpoint, is not acceptable.

[3] This highlights the distinction between an income statement and a capital budget. The project's income statement shows losses the first two years of operations as a result of interest expenses and forecast foreign exchange losses, so it is not expected to pay taxes. But the capital budget, constructed on the basis of EBIT, before these financing and foreign exchange expenses, calculates a positive tax payment.

EXHIBIT 18.5 Semen Indonesia Capital Budget: Project Viewpoint (millions of rupiah)

Exchange rate (Rp = $1.00)	**10,000**	**12,621**	**15,930**	**20,106**	**25,376**	**32,028**
Project Year	**0**	**1**	**2**	**3**	**4**	**5**
EBIT		1,219,029	2,739,067	4,744,982	6,053,589	7,592,941
Less recalculated taxes @ 30%		(365,709)	(821,720)	(1,423,495)	(1,816,077)	(2,277,882)
Add back depreciation		1,760,000	1,760,000	1,760,000	1,760,000	1,760,000
Net operating cash flow		2,613,320	3,677,347	5,081,487	5,997,512	7,075,059
Less changes to NWC		(240,670)	(139,028)	(195,379)	(150,748)	(190,265)
Initial investment	(22,000,000)					
Terminal value						21,274,102
Free cash flow (FCF)	(22,000,000)	2,372,650	3,538,319	4,886,109	5,846,764	28,158,896
NPV @ 33.257%	**(7,606,313)**					
IRR	**19.1%**					

NWC = net working capital. NPV = net present value. Discount rate is Semen Indonesia's WACC of 33.257%. IRR = internal rate of return, the rate of discount yielding an NPV of exactly zero. Values in exhibit are exact and are rounded to the nearest million.

Note that net working capital (NWC) is not included in the terminal value. This is an item of considerable debate. Traditional capital budgeting typically recaptures NWC as part of the final year cash flows, others argue that the project is continuing and will not recapture working capital as if the project were shutdown. In business, however, if the business were sold, NWC would be separately estimated and included (as if part of terminal value).

Parent Viewpoint Capital Budget

The first step to the creation of the *parent viewpoint capital budget* is to collect all incremental earnings to Cemex from its prospective investment in Indonesia. As described in the section preceding this illustrative case, *Project versus Parent Valuation*, a foreign investor's assessment of a project's returns depends on the actual cash flows that are returned to it in its own currency via actual potential cash flow channels. For Cemex, this means that the investment must be analyzed in terms of the actual likely U.S. dollar cash inflows and outflows associated with the investment over the life of the project, after-tax, discounted at its appropriate cost of capital.

The parent viewpoint capital budget is constructed in two steps:

1. First, we isolate the individual cash flows, cash flows by channel, adjusted for any withholding taxes imposed by the Indonesian government and converted to U.S. dollars. (Statutory withholding taxes on international transfers are set by bilateral tax treaties, but individual firms may negotiate lower rates with governmental tax authorities. In the case of Semen Indonesia, withholding taxes will be imposed by the Indonesian government of 15% on dividend payments, 10% on interest payments, and 5% on licensing fees.) Mexico does not tax repatriated earnings since they have already been taxed in Indonesia. (The U.S. does levy a contingent tax on repatriated earnings of foreign source income.)
2. The second step, the actual parent viewpoint capital budget, combines these U.S. dollar after-tax cash flows with the initial investment to determine the net present value of the proposed Semen Indonesia subsidiary in the eyes (and pocketbook) of Cemex. This is illustrated in Exhibit 18.6, which shows all incremental earnings to Cemex from the prospective investment project. A specific peculiarity of this parent viewpoint capital budget is that only the capital invested into the project by Cemex itself, $1,925 million, is included in the initial investment (the $1,100 million in equity and the $825 million loan).

EXHIBIT 18.6 Semen Indonesia's Remittance of Income to Parent Company (millions of rupiah and U.S. dollars)

Exchange rate (Rp = $1.00)	10,000	12,621	15,930	20,106	25,376	32,028
Project Year	**0**	**1**	**2**	**3**	**4**	**5**
Dividend Remittance						
Dividends paid (Rp)		–	–	560,423	555,757	651,450
Less Indonesian withholding taxes		–	–	(84,063)	(83,364)	(97,717)
Net dividend remitted (Rp)		–	–	476,360	472,393	553,732
Net dividend remitted (US$)		–	–	23.69	18.62	17.29
License Fees Remittance						
License fees remitted (Rp)		117,126	184,787	279,871	353,235	445,831
Less Indonesian withholding taxes		(5,856)	(9,239)	(13,994)	(17,662)	(22,292)
Net license fees remitted (Rp)		111,270	175,547	265,877	335,573	423,539
Net license fees remitted (US$)		8.82	11.02	13.22	13.22	13.22
Debt Service Remittance						
Promised interest paid (US$)		82.50	68.99	54.12	37.77	19.78
Less Indonesian withholding tax @ 10%		(8.25)	(6.90)	(5.41)	(3.78)	(1.98)
Net interest remitted (US$)		74.25	62.09	48.71	33.99	17.81
Principal payments remitted (US$)		135.13	148.65	163.51	179.86	197.85
Total principal and interest remitted		$209.38	$210.73	$212.22	$213.86	$215.65
Capital Budget: Parent Viewpoint (millions of U.S. dollars)						
Dividends		$0.0	$0.0	$23.7	$18.6	$17.3
License fees		8.8	11.0	13.2	13.2	13.2
Debt service		209.4	210.7	212.2	213.9	215.7
Total earnings		$218.2	$221.8	$249.1	$245.7	$246.2
Initial investment	(1,925.0)					
Terminal value						664.2
Net cash flows	($1,925.0)	$218.2	$221.8	$249.1	$245.7	$910.4
NPV @ 17.98%	**(903.9)**					
IRR	**−1.12%**					

NPV calculated using a company-determined discount rate of WACC + foreign investment premium, or 11.98% + 6.00% = 17.98%.

The Indonesian debt of Rp2.75 billion ($275 million) is not included in the Cemex parent viewpoint capital budget.

Finally, all cash flow estimates are now constructed to form the parent viewpoint's capital budget, detailed in the bottom of Exhibit 18.6. The cash flows generated by Semen Indonesia from its Indonesian operations, dividends, license fees, debt service, and terminal value are now valued in U.S. dollar terms after-tax.

In order to evaluate the project's cash flows that are returned to the parent company, Cemex must discount these at the corporate cost of capital. Remembering that Cemex considers its functional currency to be the U.S. dollar, it calculates its cost of capital in U.S. dollars. As described in Chapter 12, the customary weighted average cost of capital formula is as follows:

$$k_{\text{WACC}} = k_e \frac{E}{V} + k_d (1 - t) \frac{D}{V}$$

where k_e is the risk-adjusted cost of equity, k_d is the before-tax cost of debt, t is the marginal tax rate, E is the market value of the firm's equity, D is the market value of the firm's debt, and V is the total market value of the firm's securities $(E + D)$.

Cemex's cost of equity is calculated using the capital asset pricing model (CAPM):

$$k_e = k_{rf} + (k_m - k_{rf})\beta_{\text{Cemex}} = 6.00\% + (13.00\% - 6.00\%)\,1.5 = 16.50\%$$

This assumes the risk-adjusted cost of equity (k_e) is based on the risk-free rate of interest (k_{rf}), as measured by the U.S. Treasury intermediate bond yield of 6.00%, the expected rate of return in U.S. equity markets (k_m) is 13.00%, and the measure of Cemex's individual risk relative to the market (β_{Cemex}) is 1.5. The result is a cost of equity—required rate of return on equity investment in Cemex—of 16.50%.

The investment will be funded internally by the parent company, roughly in the same debt-to-equity proportions as the consolidated firm, 40% debt (D/V) and 60% equity (E/V). The current cost of debt for Cemex is 8.00%, and the effective tax rate is 35%. The cost of equity, when combined with the other components, results in a weighted average cost of capital for Cemex of

$$k_{\text{WACC}} = k_e\frac{E}{V} + k_d(1 - t)\frac{D}{V} = (16.50\%)(.60) + (8.00\%)(1 - .35)(.40) = 11.98\%$$

Cemex customarily uses this weighted average cost of capital of 11.98% to discount prospective investment cash flows for project ranking purposes. The Indonesian investment poses a variety of risks, however, which the typical domestic investment does not.

If Cemex were undertaking an investment of the same relative degree of risk as the firm itself, a simple discount rate of 11.980% might be adequate. Cemex, however, generally requires new investments to yield an additional 3% over the cost of capital for domestic investments, and 6% more for international projects (these are company-required spreads and will differ dramatically across companies). The discount rate for Semen Indonesia's cash flows repatriated to Cemex will therefore be discounted at 11.98% + 6.00%, or 17.98%. The project's baseline analysis indicates a negative NPV with an IRR of −1.12%, which means that it is an unacceptable investment from the parent's viewpoint.

Most corporations require that new investments more than cover the cost of the capital employed in their undertaking. It is therefore not unusual for the firm to require a hurdle rate of 3% to 6% above its cost of capital in order to identify potential investments that will literally add value to stockholder wealth. An NPV of zero means the investment is "acceptable," but NPV values that exceed zero are literally the present value of wealth to be added to the value of the firm and its shareholders. For foreign projects, as discussed previously, we must adjust for agency costs and foreign exchange risks and costs.

Sensitivity Analysis: Project Viewpoint

So far, the project investigation team has used a set of "most likely" assumptions to forecast rates of return. It is now time to subject the most likely outcome to sensitivity analyses. The same probabilistic techniques are available to test the sensitivity of results to political and foreign exchange risks as are used to test sensitivity to business and financial risks. Many decision makers feel more uncomfortable about the necessity to guess probabilities for unfamiliar political and foreign exchange events than they do about guessing their own more familiar business or financial risks. Therefore, it is more common to test sensitivity to political and foreign exchange risk by simulating what would happen to net present value and earnings under a variety of "what if" scenarios.

Political Risk. What if Indonesia imposes controls on the payment of dividends or license fees to Cemex? The impact of blocked funds on the rate of return from Cemex's perspective would depend on when the blockage occurs, what reinvestment opportunities exist for the blocked funds in Indonesia, and when the blocked funds would eventually be released to Cemex. We could simulate various scenarios for blocked funds and rerun the cash flow analysis in Exhibit 18.6 to estimate the effect on Cemex's rate of return.

What if Indonesia expropriates Semen Indonesia? The effect of expropriation would depend on the following factors:

1. When the expropriation occurs, in terms of number of years after the business began operation
2. How much compensation the Indonesian government will pay and how long after expropriation the payment will be made
3. How much debt is still outstanding to Indonesian lenders and whether the parent, Cemex, will have to pay this debt because of its parental guarantee
4. The tax consequences of the expropriation
5. Whether the future cash flows are forgone

Many expropriations eventually result in some form of compensation to the former owners. This compensation can come from a negotiated settlement with the host government or from payment of political risk insurance by the parent government. Negotiating a settlement takes time, and the eventual compensation is sometimes paid in installments over a further period of time. Thus, the present value of the compensation is often much lower than its nominal value. Furthermore, most settlements are based on book value of the firm at the time of expropriation rather than the firm's market value.

The tax consequences of expropriation would depend on the timing and amount of capital loss recognized by Mexico. This loss would usually be based on the uncompensated book value of the Indonesian investment. The problem is that there is often some doubt as to when a write-off is appropriate for tax purposes, particularly if negotiations for a settlement drag on. In some ways, a nice clear expropriation without hope of compensation, such as occurred in Cuba in the early 1960s, is preferred to a slow "bleeding death" in protracted negotiations. The former leads to an earlier use of the tax shield and a one-shot write-off against earnings, whereas the latter tends to depress earnings for years, as legal and other costs continue and no tax shelter is achieved.

Foreign Exchange Risk. The project investigation team assumed that the Indonesian rupiah would depreciate versus the U.S. dollar at the PPP "rate" (approximately 20.767% per year in the baseline analysis). What if the rate of rupiah depreciation is greater? Although more rapid rupiah depreciation would make the expected cash flows to Cemex worth less in dollars, operating exposure analysis would be necessary to determine whether the cheaper rupiah made Semen Indonesia more competitive. For example, since Semen Indonesia's exports to Taiwan are denominated in U.S. dollars, a weakening of the rupiah versus the dollar could result in greater rupiah earnings from those export sales. This serves to somewhat offset the imported components that Semen Indonesia purchases from the parent company that are also denominated in U.S. dollars. Semen Indonesia is representative of firms today that have both cash inflows and outflows denominated in foreign currencies, providing a partial natural hedge against currency movements.

What if the rupiah appreciates against the dollar? The same kind of economic exposure analysis is needed. In this particular case, we might guess that the effect would be positive on both local sales in Indonesia and the value in dollars of dividends and license fees paid to Cemex by Semen Indonesia. Note, however, that an appreciation of the rupiah might lead to more competition within Indonesia from firms in other countries with now lower cost structures, lessening Semen Indonesia's sales. Sometimes foreign exchange risk and political risks were inseparable, as was the case of Venezuela in 2015 as examined in *Global Finance in Practice 18.1.*

GLOBAL FINANCE IN PRACTICE 18.1

Venezuelan Currency and Capital Controls Force Devaluation of Business

The Venezuelan government's restrictions on access to hard currency have now lasted more than 12 years, and foreign corporate interests have had enough. Throughout 2014 and into 2015 many international investors in Venezuela struggled to run and value their businesses.

Air Canada suspended all flights to Venezuela in March 2014, citing concern over its ability to ensure passenger safety in light of ongoing civil protest in the country. Air Canada was also due millions of dollars in back payments for services rendered. International airlines in total claimed that they were owed more than $2 billion in back payments. Other companies like Avon and Merck wrote down their investments in Venezuela as a result of the continuing fall in the market value of the Venezuelan bolivar. Manufacturing companies like GM continued to struggle to even operate, as restricted access to hard currency prevented them from purchasing critical inputs and components for their products. Factories stopped; layoffs followed.

In February 2015, the Venezuelan government announced yet another "new" currency exchange rate system. The new system, however, was very similar to the existing three-tiered system in effect. The new system was constructed as follows: (1) the official exchange rate of 6.3 bolivars to the U.S. dollar (but outside of food and medical purchases, few companies had access to this rate); (2) a second or middle-tier rate, called SICAD 1, offered to select companies, of 12 bolivars to the U.S. dollar; and (3) a third tier rate, SICAD 2, theoretically open to all who needed it, hovering around 52 bolivars to the U.S. dollar. Finally, since the third-tier rate was not in reality open to all who needed it, many Venezuelans were forced into what would be a "fourth tier," the black-market rate, where the currency was trading at 190 bolivars per dollar.

Regardless of the next exchange rate system or next devaluation, multinational firms from all over the world continued to write down their Venezuelan investments. This included Coca-Cola (U.S.), Telefónica (Spain), and drug maker Bayer (Germany). So what was the value of investing or doing business in Venezuela?

Other Sensitivity Variables. The project rate of return to Cemex would also be sensitive to a change in the assumed terminal value, the capacity utilization rate, the size of the license fee paid by Semen Indonesia, the size of the initial project cost, the amount of working capital financed locally, and the tax rates in Indonesia and Mexico. Since some of these variables are within the control of Cemex, it is still possible that the Semen Indonesia project could be improved in its value to the firm and become acceptable.

Sensitivity Analysis: Parent Viewpoint

When a foreign project is analyzed from the parent's point of view, the additional risk that stems from its "foreign" location can be measured in two ways, adjusting the discount rates or adjusting the cash flows.

Adjusting Discount Rates. The first method is to treat all foreign risk as a single problem, by adjusting the discount rate applicable to foreign projects relative to the rate used for domestic projects to reflect the greater foreign exchange risk, political risk, agency costs, asymmetric information, and other uncertainties perceived in foreign operations. However, adjusting the discount rate applied to a foreign project's cash flow to reflect these uncertainties does not penalize net present value in proportion either to the actual amount at risk or to possible variations in the nature of that risk over time. Combining all risks into a single discount rate may thus cause us to discard much information about the uncertainties of the future.

In the case of foreign exchange risk, changes in exchange rates have a potential effect on future cash flows because of operating exposure. The direction of the effect, however, can either decrease or increase net cash inflows, depending on where the products are sold and where inputs are sourced. To increase the discount rate applicable to a foreign project on the assumption that the foreign currency might depreciate more than expected is to ignore the possible favorable effect of a foreign currency depreciation on the project's competitive position. Increased sales volume might more than offset a lower value of the local currency. Such an increase in the discount rate also ignores the possibility that the foreign currency may appreciate (two-sided risk).

Adjusting Cash Flows. In the second method, we incorporate foreign risks in adjustments to forecasted cash flows of the project. The discount rate for the foreign project is risk-adjusted only for overall business and financial risk, in the same manner as for domestic projects. Simulation-based assessment utilizes scenario development to estimate cash flows to the parent arising from the project over time under different alternative economic futures.

Certainty regarding the quantity and timing of cash flows in a prospective foreign investment is, to quote Shakespeare, "the stuff that dreams are made of." Due to the complexity of economic forces at work in major investment projects, it is paramount that the analyst understands the subjectivity of the forecast cash flows. Humility in analysis is a valuable trait.

Shortcomings of Each Method. In many cases, however, neither adjusting the discount rate nor adjusting cash flows is optimal. For example, political uncertainties are a threat to the entire investment, not just the annual cash flows. Potential loss depends partly on the terminal value of the unrecovered parent investment, which will vary depending on how the project was financed, whether political risk insurance was obtained, and what investment horizon is contemplated. Furthermore, if the political climate were expected to be unfavorable in the near future, any investment would probably be unacceptable. Political uncertainty usually relates to possible adverse events that might occur in the more distant future, but that cannot be foreseen at the present. Adjusting the discount rate for political risk thus penalizes early cash flows too heavily while not penalizing distant cash flows enough.

Repercussions to the Investor. Apart from anticipated political and foreign exchange risks, MNEs sometimes worry that taking on foreign projects may increase the firm's overall cost of capital because of investors' perceptions of foreign risk. This worry seemed reasonable if a firm had significant investments in Iraq, Iran, Russia, Serbia, or Afghanistan in recent years. However, the argument loses persuasiveness when applied to diversified foreign investments with a heavy balance in the industrial countries of Canada, Western Europe, Australia, Latin America, and Asia where, in fact, the bulk of foreign direct investment is located. These countries have a reputation for treating foreign investments by consistent standards, and empirical evidence confirms that a foreign presence in these countries may not increase the cost of capital. In fact, some studies indicate that required returns on foreign projects may even be lower than those for domestic projects.

MNE Practices. Surveys of MNEs over the past 35 years have shown that about half of them adjust the discount rate and half adjust the cash flows. One recent survey indicated a rising use of adjusting discount rates over adjusting cash flows. However, the survey also indicated an increasing use of multifactor methods—discount rate adjustment, cash flow adjustment, real options analysis, and qualitative criteria—in evaluating foreign investments.[4]

Portfolio Risk Measurement

The field of finance has distinguished two different definitions of risk: (1) the risk of the individual security (standard deviation of expected return) and (2) the risk of the individual security as a component of a portfolio (*beta*). A foreign investment undertaken in order to

[4] Tom Keck, Eric Levengood, and Al Longield, "Using Discounted Cash Flow Analysis in an International Setting: A Survey of Issues in Modeling the Cost of Capital," *Journal of Applied Corporate Finance*, Volume 11, No. 3, Fall 1998, pp. 82–99.

enter a local or regional market—*market seeking*—will have returns that are more or less correlated with those of the local market. A portfolio-based assessment of the investment's prospects would then seem appropriate. A foreign investment undertaken for *resource-seeking* or *production-seeking* purposes may have returns related to those of the parent company or business units located somewhere else in the world and have little to do with local markets.

Cemex's proposed investment in Semen Indonesia is both market-seeking and production-seeking (for export). The decision about which approach is to be used by the MNE in evaluating prospective foreign investments may be the single most important analytical decision it makes. An investment's acceptability may change dramatically across criteria.

For comparisons within the local host country, we should overlook a project's actual financing or parent-influenced debt capacity, since these would probably be different for local investors than they are for a multinational owner. In addition, the risks of the project to local investors might differ from those perceived by a foreign multinational owner because of the opportunities an MNE has to take advantage of market imperfections. Moreover, the local project may be only one out of an internationally diversified portfolio of projects for the multinational owner; if undertaken by local investors, it might have to stand alone without international diversification. Since diversification reduces risk, the MNE can require a lower rate of return than is required by local investors.

Thus, the discount rate used locally must be a hypothetical rate based on a judgment as to what independent local investors would probably demand were they to own the business. Consequently, application of the local discount rate to local cash flows provides only a rough measure of the value of the project as a stand-alone local venture rather than an absolute valuation.

18.3 Real Option Analysis

The discounted cash flow (DCF) approach used in the valuation of Semen Indonesia—and capital budgeting and valuation in general—has long had its critics. Investments that have long lives, cash flow returns in later years, or higher levels of risk than those typical of the firm's current business activities are often rejected by traditional DCF financial analysis. More importantly, when MNEs evaluate competitive projects, traditional discounted cash flow analysis is typically unable to capture the strategic options that an individual investment option may offer. This has led to the development of real option analysis. Real option analysis is the application of option theory to capital budgeting decisions.

Real options present a different way of thinking about investment values. At its core, it is a cross between decision-tree analysis and pure option-based valuation. It is particularly useful when analyzing investment projects that will follow very different value paths at decision points in time where management decisions are made regarding project pursuit. This wide range of potential outcomes is at the heart of real option theory. These wide ranges of value are volatilities, the basic element of option pricing theory described previously.

Real option valuation also allows us to analyze a number of managerial decisions, which in practice characterize many major capital investment projects:

- The option to defer
- The option to abandon
- The option to alter capacity
- The option to start up or shut down (switching)

Real option analysis treats cash flows in terms of future value in a positive sense, whereas DCF treats future cash flows negatively (on a discounted basis). Real option analysis is a particularly powerful device when addressing potential investment projects with extremely long life spans or investments that do not commence until future dates. Real option analysis acknowledges the way information is gathered over time to support decision-making. Management learns from both active (searching it out) and passive (observing market conditions) knowledge-gathering and then uses this knowledge to make better decisions.

18.4 Project Financing

One of the more unique structures used in international finance is *project finance*, which refers to the arrangement of financing for long-term capital projects, which are large in scale, long in life, and generally high in risk. This is a very general definition, however, because there are many different forms and structures that fall under this generic heading.

Project finance is not new. Examples of project finance go back centuries and include many famous early international businesses such as the Dutch East India Company and the British East India Company. These entrepreneurial importers financed their trade ventures to Asia on a voyage-by-voyage basis, with each voyage's financing being like venture capital—investors would be repaid when the shipper returned and the fruits of the Asian marketplace were sold at the docks to Mediterranean and European merchants. If all went well, the individual shareholders of the voyage were paid in full.

Project finance is used widely today in the development of large-scale infrastructure projects in China, India, and many other emerging markets. Although each individual project has unique characteristics, most are highly leveraged transactions, with debt making up more than 60% of the total financing. Equity is a small component of project financing for two reasons: first, the simple scale of the investment project often precludes a single investor or even a collection of private investors from being able to fund it; second, many of these projects involve subjects traditionally funded by governments—such as electrical power generation, dam building, highway construction, energy exploration, production, and distribution.

This level of debt, however, places an enormous burden on cash flow for debt service. Therefore, project financing usually requires a number of additional levels of risk reduction. The lenders involved in these investments must feel secure that they will be repaid; bankers are not by nature entrepreneurs and do not enjoy entrepreneurial returns from project finance. Project finance has a number of basic properties that are critical to its success.

Separability of the Project from Its Investors

The project is established as an individual legal entity, separate from the legal and financial responsibilities of its individual investors. This not only serves to protect the assets of equity investors but also provides a controlled platform upon which creditors can evaluate the risks associated with the singular project and the ability of the project's cash flows to service debt and can rest assured that the debt service payments will be automatically allocated by and from the project itself (and not from a decision by management within an MNE).

Long-Lived and Capital-Intensive Singular Projects

Not only must the individual project be separable and large in proportion to the financial resources of its owners, but also its business line must be singular in its construction, operation, and size (capacity). The size is set at inception and is seldom, if ever, changed over the project's life. A prime example of this would be an oil pipeline, such as the 1,768-kilometer-long Baku-Tbilisi-Ceyhan (BTC) pipeline extending between Baku, Azerbaijan, and Ceyhan, Turkey. The BTC's size, its length and capacity, were established with its construction and would obviously not change over its life span (at least not without a major reconstruction effort).

Cash Flow Predictability from Third-Party Commitments

An oil field or electric power plant produces a homogeneous commodity product that can produce predictable cash flows if third-party commitments to take and pay can be established. In addition to revenue predictability, nonfinancial costs of production need to be controlled over time, usually through long-term supplier contracts with price adjustment clauses based on inflation. The predictability of net cash inflows to long-term contracts eliminates much of the individual project's business risk, allowing the financial structure to be heavily debt-financed and still be safe from financial distress.

The predictability of the project's revenue stream is essential in securing project financing. Typical contract provisions that are intended to ensure adequate cash flow normally include the following clauses: quantity and quality of the project's output; a pricing formula that enhances the predictability of adequate margin to cover operating costs and debt service payments; and a clear statement of the circumstances that permit significant changes in the contract, such as force majeure or adverse business conditions.

Finite Projects with Finite Lives

Even with a longer-term investment, it is critical that the project have a definite ending point at which all debt and equity have been repaid. Because the project is a stand-alone investment in which its cash flows go directly to the servicing of its capital structure and not to reinvestment for growth or other investment alternatives, investors of all kinds need assurances that the project's returns will be attained in a finite period. There is no capital appreciation, only cash flow.

Examples of project finance include some of the largest individual investments undertaken in the past three decades, such as British Petroleum's financing of its interest in the North Sea and the Trans-Alaska Pipeline. The Trans-Alaska Pipeline was a joint venture among Standard Oil of Ohio, Atlantic Richfield, Exxon, British Petroleum, Mobil Oil, Philips Petroleum, Union Oil, and Amerada Hess. Each of these projects was at or above $1 billion and represented capital expenditures that no single firm would or could attempt to finance. Yet, through a joint venture arrangement, the higher-than-normal risk absorbed by the capital employed could be managed.

18.5 Cross-Border Mergers and Acquisitions

The drivers of mergers and acquisitions (M&A) activity, summarized in Exhibit 18.7, are both macro in scope—the global competitive environment—and micro in scope—the variety of industry and firm-level forces and actions driving individual firm value. The primary forces of change in the global competitive environment—technological change, regulatory change, and capital market change—create new business opportunities for MNEs, which they pursue aggressively.

But the global competitive environment is really just the playing field, the ground upon which the individual players compete. MNEs undertake cross-border mergers and acquisitions for a variety of reasons. As shown in Exhibit 18.7, the drivers are strategic responses by MNEs to defend and enhance their global competitiveness.

As opposed to greenfield investment, a cross-border acquisition has a number of significant advantages. First and foremost, it is quicker. Greenfield investment frequently requires extended periods of physical construction and organizational development. By acquiring an existing firm, the MNE shortens the time required to gain a presence and facilitate competitive entry into the market. Second, acquisition may be a cost-effective way of gaining competitive

EXHIBIT 18.7 **Driving Forces behind Cross-Border Acquisitions**

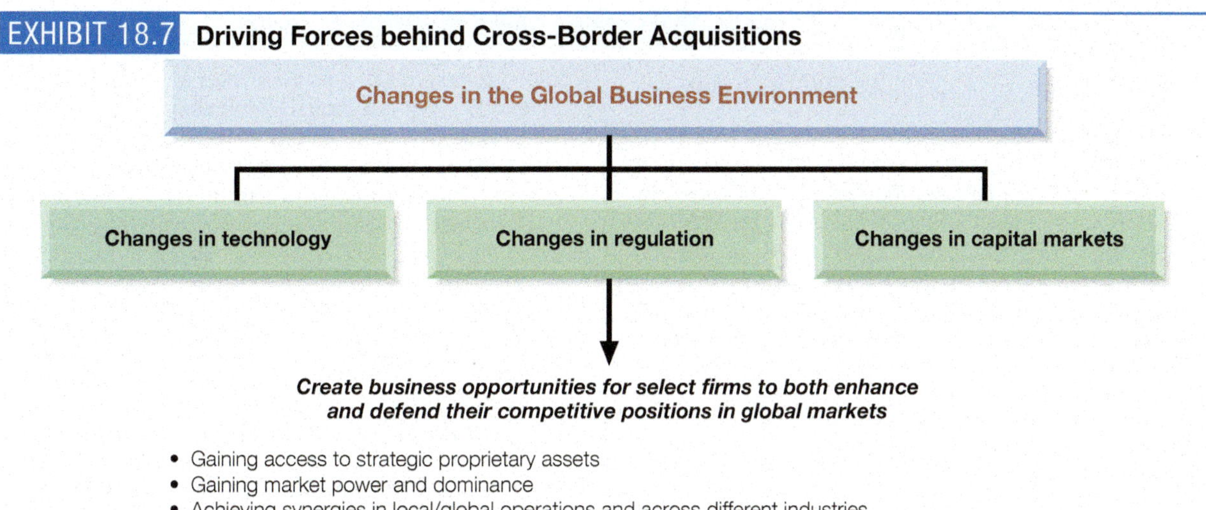

- Gaining access to strategic proprietary assets
- Gaining market power and dominance
- Achieving synergies in local/global operations and across different industries
- Becoming larger and then reaping the benefits of size in competition and negotiation
- Diversifying and spreading their risks wider
- Exploiting financial opportunities they may possess and others desire

advantages, such as technology, brand names valued in the target market, and logistical and distribution advantages, while simultaneously eliminating a local competitor. Third, specific to cross-border acquisitions, international economic, political, and foreign exchange conditions may result in market imperfections, allowing target firms to be undervalued.

Cross-border acquisitions are not, however, without their pitfalls. As with all acquisitions—domestic or cross-border—there are problems of paying too much or suffering excessive financing costs. Melding corporate cultures can be traumatic. Managing the post-acquisition process is frequently characterized by downsizing to gain economies of scale and scope in overhead functions. This results in nonproductive impacts on the firm as individuals attempt to save their own jobs. Internationally, additional difficulties arise from host governments intervening in pricing, financing, employment guarantees, market segmentation, and general nationalism and favoritism. In fact, the ability to successfully complete cross-border acquisitions may itself be a test of competency of the MNE when entering emerging markets. *Global Finance in Practice 18.2* illustrates a number of these potential acquisition challenges.

The Cross-Border Acquisition Process

Although the field of finance has sometimes viewed acquisition as mainly an issue of valuation, it is a much more complex and rich process than simply determining what price to pay. As depicted in Exhibit 18.8, the process begins with the strategic drivers discussed in the previous section.

The process of acquiring an enterprise anywhere in the world has three common elements: (1) identification and valuation of the target, (2) completion of the ownership change—the tender, and (3) management of the post-acquisition transition.

Stage 1: Identification and Valuation. Identification of potential acquisition targets requires a well-defined corporate strategy and focus. The identification of the target market typically precedes the identification of the target firm. Entering a highly developed market

GLOBAL FINANCE IN PRACTICE 18.2

Values Change: GE Appliances and Electrolux

GE math. Consider: Let's assume GE mispriced Appliances when it tried to sell it six years ago (a safe assumption, since it didn't sell). So, let's say the Appliances business was worth not $8 billion back then, but rather just half that—$4 billion. Add the $1 billion spent spiffing up the business, and divide the resulting $5 billion value into the best-case price GE is expected to get for the unit today: $2.5 billion. That works out to a 50% loss for GE shareholders.

—"Is General Electric Company About to Make Its Biggest Mistake Ever?," *The Motley Fool*, July 19, 2014.

General Electric (GE) first tried to sell its appliance business in 2008. GE had placed an $8 billion price tag on the century-old business, but amid a financial crisis, there were no takers. Six years later, it tried again. This time Electrolux of Sweden, one of the world's largest appliance makers, was very interested. After months of negotiations, the two parties agreed in July 2014 upon a sale price of $3.3 billion—a dramatic drop from the previous price GE had asked.

Completion of the sale was expected in 2015, after receiving the approval of the U.S. Justice Department regarding antitrust concerns (combining GE's and Electrolux's market shares in some product lines could yield a potential market share of 40%). But the Justice Department did not like the growing consolidation in the U.S. appliance market, and it pushed Electrolux to promise to sell off a number of segments to prevent anti-competitive impacts. In September 2015, Electrolux refused to offer any business sales or compromises to the agreed-upon acquisition. Finally, in December 2015, after continued objections by the U.S. Department of Justice, Electrolux and GE canceled the sale. GE did receive a $175 million agreement termination payment from Electrolux that the two parties had included in the original sales agreement.

GE renewed its search for a buyer of the appliance unit immediately, and rumors of a potential sale to Haier (China) rapidly grew. Haier had only a very small, specialized product line in the U.S., so gaining GE Appliances would make it an instant player in the large U.S. market. On January 15, 2016, less than two months after the Electrolux agreement was terminated, GE announced that it was selling its appliance unit to Haier for $5.4 billion, an enormous improvement over the previous $3.3 billion agreement with Electrolux. This new deal was with a company that had a relatively small presence in the U.S. market and that clearly would not enjoy the cost synergies that Electrolux had expected to leverage. Value is indeed in the eyes of the beholder.

EXHIBIT 18.8 The Cross-Border Acquisition Process

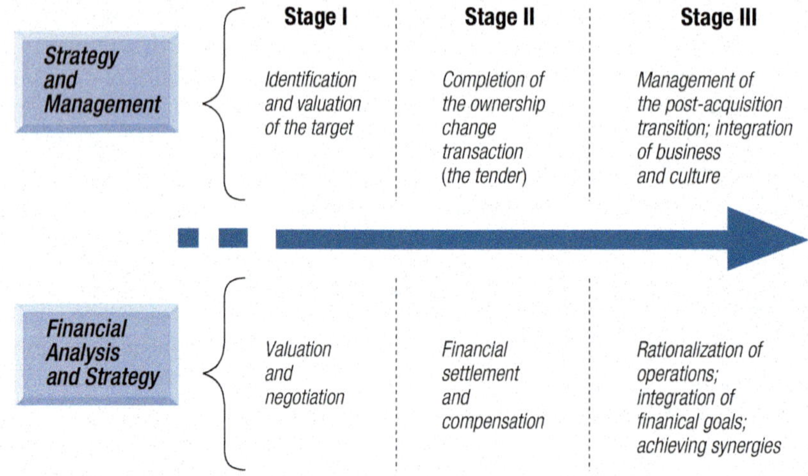

offers the widest choice of publicly traded firms with relatively well-defined markets and publicly disclosed financial and operational data. In this case, the tender offer is made publicly, although target company management may openly recommend that its shareholders reject the offer. If enough shareholders take the offer, the acquiring company may gain sufficient ownership influence or control to change management.

During this rather confrontational process, it is up to the board of the target company to continue to take actions consistent with protecting the rights of shareholders. The board may need to provide rather strong oversight of management during this process to ensure that the acts of management are consistent with protecting and building shareholder value.

Once identification has been completed, the process of valuing the target begins. A variety of valuation techniques are widely used in global business today, each with its own merits. In addition to the fundamental methodologies of discounted cash flow (DCF) and multiples (earnings and cash flows), there are also industry-specific measures that focus on the most significant elements of value in business lines. The completion of various alternative valuations for the target firm aids not only in gaining a more complete picture of what price must be paid to complete the transaction but also in determining whether the price is attractive.

Stage 2: Completion of the Ownership Change. Once an acquisition target has been identified and valued, the process of gaining approval from management and ownership of the target, getting approvals from government regulatory bodies, and finally determining method of compensation—the complete execution of the acquisition strategy—can be time-consuming and complex.

Gaining the approval of the target company has been the highlight of some of the most famous acquisitions in business history. The critical distinction here is whether the acquisition is supported by the target company's management. Although there is probably no "typical transaction," many acquisitions flow relatively smoothly through a friendly process. The acquiring firm will approach the managers of the target company and attempt to convince them of the business logic of the acquisition. (Gaining their support is sometimes difficult, but assuring target company managers that they will not be replaced is often quite convincing!) If the target's management is supportive, management may then recommend to stockholders that they accept the offer of the acquiring company. One problem that occasionally surfaces at this stage is that influential shareholders may object to the offer, either in principle or based on price, and may therefore feel that management is not taking appropriate steps to protect and build shareholder value.

The process takes on a very different dynamic when the acquisition is not supported by the target company management—the so-called *hostile takeover*. The acquiring company may choose to pursue the acquisition without the target's support and instead go directly to the target shareholders. In this case, the tender offer is made publicly, although target company management may openly recommend that its shareholders reject the offer. If enough shareholders take the offer, the acquiring company may gain sufficient ownership influence or control to change management. During this rather confrontational process, it is up to the board of the target company to continue to take actions consistent with protecting the rights of shareholders. As in Stage 1, the board may need to provide strong oversight of management during this process to ensure that the acts of management are consistent with protecting and building shareholder value. Regulatory approval alone may prove to be a major hurdle in the execution of the deal.

An acquisition may be subject to significant regulatory approval if it involves a company in an industry considered fundamental to national security or if there is concern over major concentration and anti-competitive results from consolidation.

The proposed acquisition of Honeywell International (itself the result of a merger of Honeywell U.S. and Allied-Signal U.S.) by General Electric (U.S.) in 2001 was something of a watershed event in the field of regulatory approval. General Electric's acquisition of Honeywell had been approved by management, ownership, and U.S. regulatory bodies when it then sought approval within the European Union. Jack Welch, the charismatic chief executive officer and president of GE, did not anticipate the degree of opposition that the merger would face from EU authorities. After a continuing series of demands by the EU that specific businesses within the combined companies be sold off to reduce anti-competitive effects, Welch withdrew the request for acquisition approval, arguing that the liquidations would destroy most of the value-enhancing benefits of the acquisition. The acquisition was canceled. This case may have far-reaching effects on cross-border M&A for years to come, as the power of regulatory authorities within strong economic zones like the EU to block the combination of two MNEs may foretell a change in regulatory strength and breadth.

The last act within this second stage of cross-border acquisition, compensation settlement, is the payment to shareholders of the target company. Shareholders of the target company are typically paid either in shares of the acquiring company or in cash. If a share exchange occurs, the exchange is generally defined by some ratio of acquiring company shares to target company shares (say, two shares of acquirer in exchange for three shares of target), and the stockholder is typically not taxed—the shares of ownership are simply replaced by other shares in a nontaxable transaction.

If cash is paid to the target company shareholder, it is the same as if the shareholder sold the shares on the open market, resulting in a capital gain or loss (a gain, it is hoped, in the case of an acquisition) with tax liabilities. Because of the tax ramifications, shareholders are typically more receptive to share exchanges so that they may choose whether and when tax liabilities will arise.

A variety of factors go into the determination of the type of settlement. The availability of cash, the size of the acquisition, the friendliness of the takeover, and the relative valuations of both acquiring firm and target firm affect the decision. One of the most destructive forces that sometimes arises at this stage is regulatory delay and its impact on the share prices of the two firms. If regulatory body approval drags out over time, the possibility of a drop in share price increases and can change the attractiveness of the share swap.

Stage 3: Post-Acquisition Transition Management. Although the headlines and flash of investment banking activities are typically focused on the valuation and bidding process in an acquisition transaction, post-transaction management is probably the most critical of the three stages in determining an acquisition's success or failure. An acquiring firm can pay too little or too much, but if the post transaction is not managed effectively, the entire return on the investment is squandered. Post-acquisition management is the stage in which the motivations for the transaction must be realized. The goals of acquisition—such as more effective management, synergies arising from the new combination, or the injection of capital at a cost and availability previously out of the reach of the acquisition target—must be effectively implemented after the transaction. The biggest problem, however, is nearly always melding corporate cultures.

The clash of corporate cultures and personalities poses both the biggest risk and the biggest potential gain from cross-border mergers and acquisitions. Although not readily measurable as are price/earnings ratios or share price premiums, in the end, the value is either gained or lost in the hearts and minds of the stakeholders.

Currency Risks in Cross-Border Acquisitions

The pursuit and execution of a cross-border acquisition poses a number of challenging foreign currency risks and exposures for an MNE. As illustrated by Exhibit 18.9, the nature of the currency exposure related to any specific cross-border acquisition evolves as the bidding and negotiating process itself evolves across the bidding, financing, transaction (settlement), and operational stages. The assorted risks, in both the timing and information related to the various stages of a cross-border acquisition, make the management of the currency exposures difficult. As illustrated in Exhibit 18.9, the uncertainty related to the multitude of stages declines over time as stages are completed and contracts and agreements reached.

EXHIBIT 18.9 **Currency Risks in Cross-Border Acquisitions**

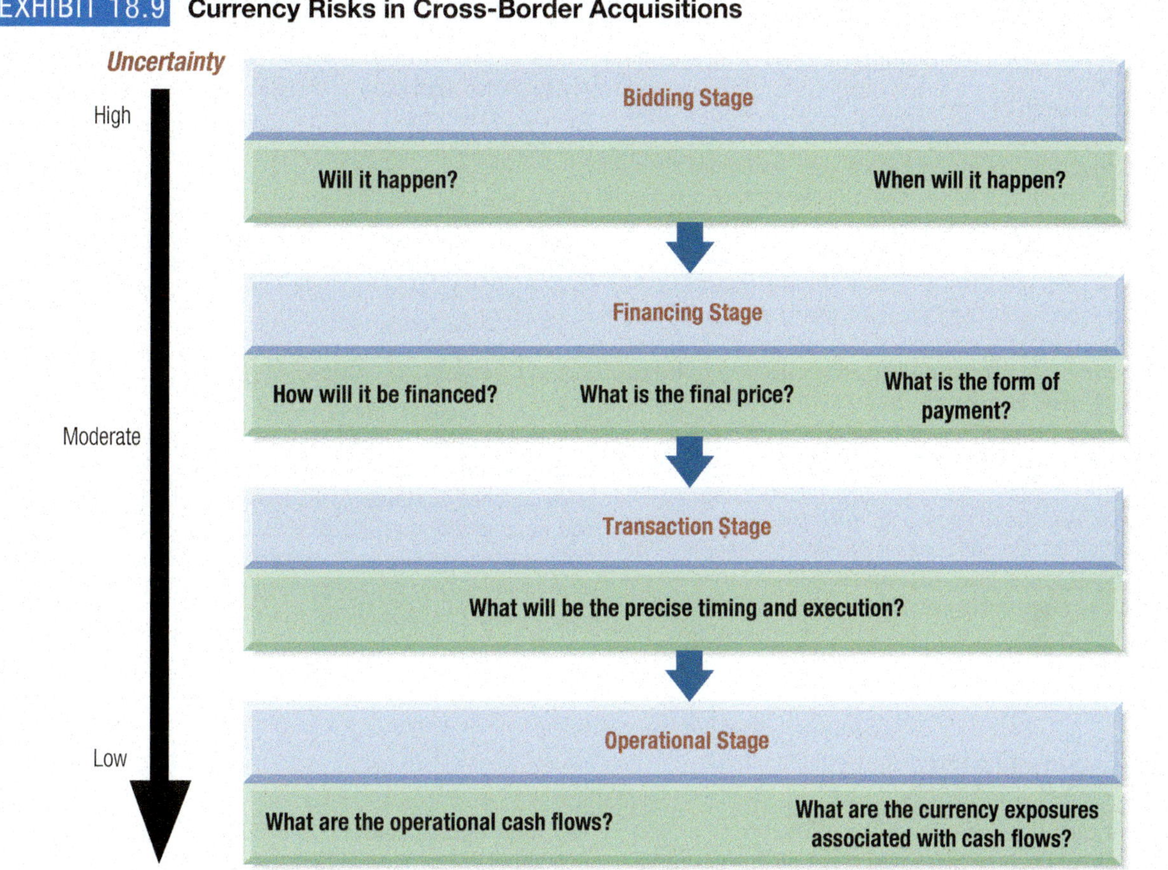

The initial bid, if denominated in a foreign currency, creates a contingent foreign currency exposure for the bidder. This contingent exposure grows in certainty of occurrence over time as negotiations continue, regulatory requests and approvals are gained, and competitive bidders emerge. Although a variety of hedging strategies might be employed, the use of a purchased currency call option is the simplest. The option's notional principal would be for the estimated purchase price, but the maturity, for the sake of conservatism, might possibly be significantly longer than probably needed to allow for extended bidding, regulatory, and negotiation delays.

Once the bidder has successfully won the acquisition, the exposure evolves from a contingent exposure to a transaction exposure. Although a variety of uncertainties remain as to the exact timing of the transaction settlement, the certainty over the occurrence of the currency exposure is largely eliminated. Some combination of forward contracts and purchased currency options may then be used to manage the currency risks associated with the completion of the cross-border acquisition.

Once consummated, the currency risks and exposures of the cross-border acquisition, now a property and foreign subsidiary of the MNE, changes from being a transaction-based cash flow exposure to the MNE to part of its multinational structure and therefore part of its operating exposure from that time forward. Time, as is always the case involving currency exposure management in multinational business, is the greatest challenge to the MNE, as illustrated by *Global Finance in Practice 18.3.*

GLOBAL FINANCE IN PRACTICE 18.3

Statoil of Norway's Acquisition of Esso of Sweden

Statoil's acquisition of Svenska Esso (Exxon's wholly owned subsidiary in Sweden) in 1986 was one of the more uniquely challenging cross-border acquisitions ever completed. First, Statoil was the national oil company of Norway and therefore a government-owned and operated business bidding for a private company in another country. Second, if completed, the acquisition's proposed financing would increase the financial obligations of Svenska Esso (debt levels and debt service), reducing the company's tax liabilities to Sweden. The proposed cross-border transaction was characterized as a value transfer from the Swedish government to the Norwegian government.

As a result of the extended period of bidding, negotiation, and regulatory approvals, the currency risk of the transaction was both large and extensive. Statoil, being a Norwegian oil company, was a Norwegian krone (NOK)-based company with the U.S. dollar as its functional currency as a result of the global oil industry being dollar-denominated. Svenska Esso, although Swedish by incorporation, was the wholly owned subsidiary of a U.S.-based MNE, Exxon, and the final bid and cash settlement on the sale were therefore U.S. dollar-denominated.

On March 26, 1985, Statoil and Exxon agreed upon the sale of Svenska Esso for USD260 million, or NOK2.47 billion at the current exchange rate of NOK9.50 = USD1.00. (This was by far the weakest the Norwegian krone had ever been against the dollar; many analysts believed the dollar to be significantly overvalued at the time.) The sale could not be consummated without the approval of the Swedish government. That approval process—eventually requiring the approval of Swedish Prime Minister Olaf Palme—took nine months. Because Statoil considered the U.S. dollar as its true operating currency, it chose not to hedge the purchase price currency exposure. At the time of settlement, the krone had appreciated to NOK7.65 = USD1.00, for a final acquisition cost in Norwegian kroner of NOK1.989 billion. Statoil saved nearly 20% on the purchase price, NOK0.481 billion, as a result of not hedging.

Summary Points

- Parent cash flows must be distinguished from project cash flows. Each of these two types of flows contributes to a different view of value.
- Parent cash flows often depend on the form of financing. Thus, cash flows cannot be clearly separated from financing decisions, as is done in domestic capital budgeting.
- Remittance of funds to the parent must be explicitly recognized because of differing tax systems, legal and political constraints on the movement of funds, local business norms, and differences in how financial markets and institutions function.
- When a foreign project is analyzed from the project's point of view, risk analysis focuses on the use of sensitivities as well as consideration of foreign exchange and political risks associated with the project's execution over time.
- When a foreign project is analyzed from the parent's point of view, the additional risk that stems from its "foreign" location can be measured in at least two ways, adjusting the discount rates or adjusting the cash flows.
- Real option analysis is a different way of thinking about investment values. At its core, it is a cross between decision-tree analysis and pure option-based valuation. Real option analysis allows us to evaluate options, such as whether to defer, abandon, alter the size or capacity of, or start up or shut down a project.
- Project finance is used widely today in the development of large-scale infrastructure projects in many emerging markets. Although each individual project has unique characteristics, most are highly leveraged transactions, with debt making up more than 60% of the total financing.
- The process of acquiring an enterprise anywhere in the world has three common elements: (1) identification and valuation of the target, (2) completion of the ownership change transaction (the tender), and (3) the management of the post-acquisition transition.
- Cross-border mergers, acquisitions, and strategic alliances all face similar challenges: they must value the target enterprise on the basis of its projected performance in its market. This process of enterprise valuation combines elements of strategy, management, and finance.

MINI-CASE

Mittal's Hostile Acquisition of Arcelor[5]

Therefore, the [Arcelor] Board of Directors has resolved that it:

1. *unanimously rejects Mittal Steel's unsolicited proposal which it considers hostile,*
2. *recommends to Arcelor's shareholders not to tender their shares into the proposed offer, if and when submitted,*
3. *mandates the Management Board to present to the Board of Directors all actions and options that are in the best interests of all stakeholders.*

—"Arcelor Board of Directors Unanimously Rejects Mittal's Hostile Proposal," press release, Luxembourg, January 29, 2006.

The European Union (EU) rarely saw hostile corporate takeovers. The structure of corporate ownership and governance across most of Europe made gaining control—without the cooperation of the target firm—exceedingly difficult. Despite the challenge, Mittal Steel, the world's largest steel producer, was determined to acquire Arcelor, the world's second-largest steel maker.

Global Steel Consolidation

[There is] a strong relationship in the value created by an industry and its degree of consolidation. The steel industry is very fragmented, much more fragmented than some key suppliers like iron ore companies. And much more fragmented than some key customers, automotive companies for example. It's very important for us to be much more consolidated in the future, not just on a regional basis but also on an intercontinental basis.

—Guy Dollé, CEO, Arcelor.[6]

The global steel industry in 2006 was surprisingly unconcentrated. Mittal Steel and Arcelor were the two largest steel manufacturers in the world, Mittal moving into the number-one position in 2005. Together the two companies produced 110 million tons of steel in 2005, a remarkably small 10% of global production.

But consolidation was underway. Arcelor (Luxembourg) itself was the result of a merger of three major steel companies from within the EU in 2002—Aceralia of Spain, Usinor of France, and Arbed of Luxembourg. That merger made it the largest steel maker in the world. And Arcelor had also exemplified one of the key drivers for consolidation—the capture of cost synergies. In its first three years of operation Arcelor reduced global headcount from 100,000 to under 90,000. Other cost synergies of consolidation included overhead, procurement, operations, and a variety of marketing and logistic functions.

Mittal Steel (Netherlands) too was the result of consolidation. The company's founder, Lakshmi Mittal, born in India, started working in his family's steel business in Indonesia when he was only 21 years old. The company grew steadily through opportunistic acquisitions of previously state-owned and operated steel makers in need of new investment and technology. The opportunities were recessions, and Mittal seized every opening to acquire. Markets included Canada, Mexico, Trinidad and Tobago, and Eastern Europe.

Lakshmi Mittal favored aggressive growth. He had combined two of his firms, one private (LNM Holdings) and one public (Ispat), into a single publicly listed firm, Ispat International. In the process, he gained much attention when he paid himself a £1 billion pound dividend. In 2005 he acquired a major North American steel company in bankruptcy, ISG. The newly formed firm, Mittal Steel, became the largest steel maker in the world, making Mittal the world's third-richest person behind Bill Gates and Warren Buffett.

In 2005, both Arcelor and Nucor (U.S.) began bidding to acquire the Canadian steelmaker Dofasco. Dofasco was an attractive target: a major producer in the North American market and a non-union workforce, carrying little debt. The bidding started at $43 a share and increased, with Nucor withdrawing after the entry of ThyssenKrupp (Germany) into the fray. These were unsolicited offers, *hostile* offers, as Dofasco was not interested in being acquired and would not cooperate with either bidder. Dofasco's stance changed when Arcelor's offer reached $56. Fearing that Arcelor's offer might be too enticing for shareholders to turn down, Dofasco aligned itself with ThyssenKrupp in a *friendly* offer. Both firms continued to raise their bids until Arcelor's bid of $71. Market analysts believed Arcelor would suffer the "winner's curse"—it had won by paying more than the company was worth.

Mittal Bids for Arcelor

This is a great opportunity for us to take the steel industry to the next level. Our customers are becoming global; our suppliers are becoming global; everyone is looking for a stronger global player.

—Lakshmi Mittal, London, January 27, 2006.

[6] "Guy Dollé: Learning to Be a Team Player," CNN.com, June 6, 2005.

EXHIBIT A Arcelor and Mittal Steel

2005 (billions)	Arcelor	Mittal Steel
Revenue	€32,963	€23,749
Net Income	€3,873	€3,204
Margin	11.7%	13.5%
Total Assets	€35,864	€28,591
Short-Term Debt	€658	€122
Long-Term Debt	€4,215	€6,732
Cash	€4,645	€1,730
Net Debt	€228	€5,124
Operating Cash Flow	€4,464	€3,270
Capital Expenditure	€2,070	€997
Free Cash Flow	€2,394	€2,273
Price/Earnings Ratio	3.32	5.52

Source: Corporate annual reports for 2005 (restated); Bloomberg.

On Friday, January 27, 2006, Mittal Steel shocked global markets with an unsolicited offer to acquire Arcelor, the largest steel company in Europe and the second-largest steel maker in the world. Mittal offered Arcelor shareholders four Mittal shares plus €35.25 in cash for every five shares of Arcelor. The offer valued each Arcelor share at €28.21, a 27% premium over Arcelor's closing share price of €22.20 the day before.

Mittal Steel was registered in the Netherlands with headquarters in both London and Rotterdam. Mittal's core sales were in basic steel products generating volume growth at relatively low margins. Although publicly traded in Amsterdam and New York, the company was controlled by the Mittal family with its 88% interest. Lakshmi was CEO and chairman, his son managing director and CFO. Mittal had a major presence in America, Central Europe, Eastern Europe, Africa, Kazakhstan, and a share of Western Europe.

Arcelor was headquartered in Luxembourg City. Its current CEO was Guy Dollé, with Joseph Kinsch as chairman. Employing 110,000, Arcelor specialized in high-margin, high-grade steel products for the construction and automobile industries. The company's major markets were Western Europe and America, with a small presence in Eastern Europe and Asia. The company was listed on stock exchanges in Brussels, Luxembourg, Paris, and Madrid. Exhibit A provides a brief overview of the two firms' financials.

Lakshmi Mittal first approached Guy Dollé of Arcelor at a private dinner at Mittal's mansion in London on January 13 at the suggestion of Lakshmi's son. Mittal suggested looking into combining the two companies. According to Dollé, "There was no discussion, there was no offer. There was a discussion of four minutes at the end of an aperitif. A company worth up to €40 billion in revenues deserves more than a four-minute conversation."[7] Dollé did relay to Mittal that, in his opinion, 75% to 80% of all mergers fail because of cultural differences. Two weeks later Mittal called Dollé to inform him Mittal would be announcing a public tender offer for Arcelor.

> *What makes this deal unique is that this is the steel sector. Until very recently, this business was protected by the governments and no one thought that companies could make hostile takeover offers on this scale, despite the fact that the sector was in the process of consolidation.*
>
> —"Forging a Steel Giant: Mittal's Bid for Arcelor," *Knowledge at Wharton,* February 8, 2006.

Lakshmi Mittal and his son Aditya, Mittal's CFO, believed that combining the world's two largest steel manufacturers would create a world leader and a European

[7] Gow, David, "Sparks Fly as Arcelor Attacks Mittal Steel Bid," *The Guardian*, January 30, 2006.

champion (a message they pushed with all European government leaders in the weeks following the offer). Mittal saw great opportunities for cost synergies, potentially reducing combined operating costs by more than $1 billion.

The Mittal team's experience with acquisitions allowed it to anticipate deal barriers. The most common political barrier was job losses; Mittal promised to deliver all cost reductions without plant closures or job losses in Arcelor's plants. The second-most common hurdle was regulatory concern over growing monopoly power. Mittal believed the two companies had little overlap in products or markets. There was one possible problem: Arcelor's acquisition of Dofasco. So on the same day he announced Mittal's bid for Arcelor, he offered to sell Dofasco to ThyssenKrupp at the last price Thyssen had bid, $68 per share.

EU Takeover Law

The market for corporate control has always operated under different sets of rules across countries. The U.S. and the UK have long enjoyed very open and unrestricted markets, in which creeping acquisitions and hostile takeovers are commonplace. These are markets in which the ownership of publicly traded companies is relatively wide, with few individual investors or organizations holding large and influential shares of the companies. Shareholders in these markets may be described more as investors than owners, as their primary interest is in their financial returns.

Continental Europe is characterized by companies that are heavily led by concentrated power—singular owners, families, groups linked through shareholder agreements, or even pyramid structures of indirect influence. Governments keep a watchful eye on acquisitions and restructurings that might possibly reduce employment or competition. Concentrated ownership and nationalistic tendencies made creeping acquisitions and hostile takeovers rare. Concentrated ownership also meant that owners valued control, something that shareholders in the U.S. or UK placed less value on as they generally held less influence.

The EU had struggled to foster an active cross-border market for corporate control for years. A new effort resulted in the *EU Takeover Directive of 2004*. The directive was intended to harmonize EU takeover law and kick-start consolidation of EU companies in pursuit of greater internal efficiency and external competitiveness. Modeled after the UK's takeover code, it suffered massive change and dilution in its path to adoption. In the end, it contained three provisions fundamental to takeover laws globally: (1) equal treatment of shareholders, particularly minority shareholders; (2) access to information to allow informed decisions on bids; and (3) restrictions and prohibitions on market manipulation.

The final EU framework focused on the mandatory bid rule. The EU believed it would ensure fair and equitable treatment for all shareholders in the event of a change in control. The directive failed, however, to gain EU-wide agreement on two other principles, the *board neutrality rule* and the *breakthrough rules*. The *board neutrality rule* prohibits the supervisory board of a target firm from taking any "frustrating actions" against a potential acquirer once a bid has been announced. (The rule does allow boards to seek out alternative bids.) In theory it requires the target board to remain neutral. The *breakthrough rules* prohibit clauses in corporate articles of association that restrict the ability of target company shareholders from tendering their shares or voting at shareholder meetings.

Those EU members that did not have existing takeover codes were now to adopt the principles of the EU Takeover Directive. France and Belgium already had codes; Luxembourg—Arcelor's home—did not. Luxembourg had until the end of May to adopt its own version of the EU directive.

Arcelor—and Europe—Fights Back

It's not an Indian company per se, it's a company of Indians, in particular by Mr Mittal's family; most of the positions on the management committee are held by Indians, and the company's specialty; when it makes an acquisition, is generally to send in a dozen or so Indians to improve plant operations.

—Guy Dollé, CEO, Arcelor

Arcelor's immediate reaction to Mittal's bid was a clear *no*, as seen in Arcelor's press release (page 1). Within days the hostile bid, or "unsolicited offer" as Lakshmi Mittal preferred to call it, sparked pan-European debate. With 80% of Arcelor's shares in free float, Mittal had a very good chance of convincing at least 50% of Arcelor's shareholders to back the deal at an attractive price.

As opposed to Lakshmi Mittal's low-key, unassuming personality, Guy Dollé was known to be both emotional and unpredictable. In Dollé's first interview following the announcement he described Mittal Steel as a "company full of Indians" seeking to buy Arcelor with *monnaie de singe*, a French term for monopoly money, small change, or peanuts as in "monkey money."[8] He went on to characterize Mittal as a crude maker of commodity steel, plebeian *eau de cologne* compared to Arcelor's aristocratic perfume.

If this raid succeeds, it will bring down one of the rare edifices of industrial Europe, proving that no position is secure any longer in a world of global competition.

—Le Monde, January 29, 2006.

[8] Mittal Steel did indeed depend on a strong engineering core recruited from India that was willing to work hard for lower wages. Management, however, was not all from India. Of Mittal's 17 regional managers, nine held Indian passports. Mittal Steel had no operations in India.

Dollé saw the proposed combination as an impossible force fit of two very different business cultures. He described Arcelor as the "embodiment of the European social model," as opposed to "the Indians" being like "the Airbus of the steel industry." The French minister of finance believed that Arcelor should have a "European character" although acknowledging that steel was not one of France's protected strategic industries despite Arcelor employing 30,000 people in France.[9] Dollé believed Mittal to be out of step with European governance practices. Under Mittal's proposal, since Lakshmi Mittal's shares held two votes per share, he would maintain control of the combined company with more than 50% of the ownership rights and 64% of the voting rights. But Arcelor was a Luxembourg company, a country prohibiting dual voting shares.

> *It is not about the money. . . . No, we want to remain a strategic partner in a European company with a European social dimension, in a European environment and a European concept of governance, with its headquarters in Luxembourg.*
>
> —Luxembourg Prime Minister Jean-Claude Juncker, January 30, 2006.

Governments Respond. Within hours of the unsolicited bid, governments responded. The French minister of finance explained directly to Lakshmi Mittal that "this is not how things are done in continental Europe." He did not believe that Mittal respected what the French call *la grammaire des affaires*—normal business practices. A large part of that grammar was a detailed explanation of the takeover—before the bid. The Luxembourg, French, and Belgian governments could also be seen as walking a fine line between the past, in which hostile acquisitions were not tolerated, and the present, an integrated set of countries that espoused the benefits of globalization but still struggled to free up the movement of capital and opportunity.

France, Belgium, Spain, and Luxembourg were hosts to most of Arcelor's operations but had limited powers to stop the hostile acquisition. The primary barrier to EC approval would be on competition grounds. Technically, the proposal would have to be approved by the European Commission (EC) before Mittal could offer it to shareholders. The EC committed to evaluating the proposal only on the basis of competition.

There were five key events in the coming months instrumental to the takeover approval: (1) earnings releases for both companies—February 15; (2) the EC's ruling on the bid—probably in April; (3) Arcelor's annual shareholder general meeting, including the reelection of the board—April 28; and (4) Luxembourg's adoption of a takeover code—by May 20. Arcelor believed it would have the upper hand in each.

Arcelor's Defense Strategy. Arcelor began gathering a massive defense team. The team proposed a *value-based defense*, one based on how the two businesses could not thrive under one roof. The company's consultants proposed a *regulatory arbitrage defense*, to leverage the many regulators across countries that needed to approve the deal. Arcelor's legal counsel, however, cautioned Arcelor's leadership that it could not take any direct action to stop the takeover attempt; that would be seen as management acting against the interests of shareholders.

Corporate Governance. Unlike most European multinationals, 88% of Arcelor's shares were in *free float*, traded on the open market. The two single largest shareholders were the Luxembourg government with 5.6% and the Aristrain family of Spain with 3.6%. Given that part of the Mittal offer was in shares, Mittal's record in growing share prices came into question. Mittal had grown rapidly through acquisitions, generating returns for Mittal family members but minor returns for shareholders. Arcelor's own share price performance was similarly underwhelming. In fact, Mittal's offer had caused the largest increase in the share price in years. Arcelor was also tight with dividends; shareholders were described as "cash-starved."

Arcelor was widely held, Mittal was not. Mittal used a two-tier voting structure of A and B class shares. A shares, those held by the public, had one vote per share. B shares, 67% of which were held by the Mittal family, had 10 votes per share. The Mittal family controlled 98% of the votes. Lakshmi Mittal was told he would have to give ground on governance and control. He now countered with new promises: the headquarters of the merged group would be kept in Luxembourg, and there would be no layoffs.

Arcelor believed the company was protected by its corporate charter requiring offers to be all cash. But when the legal team examined the code, they discovered a very important condition. If a predator had accumulated 30% of Arcelor's shares in a creeping acquisition, then it was required to make an all-cash offer. But Mittal had not accumulated any significant shareholdings in Arcelor.

Luxembourg allowed companies to undertake defensive measures like poison pills without the approval of shareholders. A spokesman for the EC did not find it surprising or significant: "We don't believe this really changes anything on the ground. Already there is a certain leeway to use national laws for poison pill defenses."[10] Nationalist concerns had always been strong in Europe, even across EU members. For example, France had identified certain industries as being "strategic assets" including yogurt-making.

[9]David Gow, "Sparks Fly as Arcelor Attacks Mittal Steel Bid," *The Guardian*, January 30, 2006.

[10]James Kanter, "Arcelor: Looking to the Law to Repel Mittal," *The New York Times*, February 7, 2006.

On February 15, Arcelor released its earnings for 2005, all of which was good news. Total turnover was up 8% to €32.6 billion, but group profits were up 68% to €3.85 billion. In a surprising move, the company doubled the dividend, from €0.65 to €1.25 per share. The next day Mittal reported 2005 results, showing large gains in turnover, from $22 billion to $28 billion, but a decrease of 28% in profits, to $3.36 billion.

Arcelor Goes on the Defensive. On April 4, Arcelor announced a new series of defensive actions.

- First, it transferred control of the recently acquired Dofasco of Canada to a newly formed Dutch foundation, Strategic Steel Stichting. The *stichting* trust, a unique organizational creation under Dutch law, would control any ownership changes for five years. Its three-member Arcelor-appointed board held sole discretion over any ownership changes.[11] Mittal's plan to sell Dofasco to ThyssenKrupp of Germany to avoid antitrust issues in the U.S. now appeared moot.
- Secondly, Arcelor increased its dividend—again. With Arcelor's high free float, it knew that the acquisition premium offered by Mittal would be attractive. Arcelor announced it would increase its dividend from €1.25/share to €1.85/share for 2006, an 85% increase.
- Third, the company committed to returning more cash flow to shareholders via a proposed share buyback program totaling €6.6 billion. This would theoretically increase Arcelor's share price and simultaneously reduce the number of shares and votes outstanding. This would require shareholder approval.

By late April, it appeared that management's actions were gaining traction with shareholders. On April 28, shareholders voted to retain Arcelor's current board. This was not overly surprising since fewer than 35% of its shareholders attended or sent representatives to shareholder meetings. Arcelor was confident in its ability to manage its shareholders. But then the tide started turning.

On May 4, Luxembourg adopted its new takeover law, choosing to take a very pro-open approach to takeovers, wishing to retain its image as an open financial center rather than a restrictive, protectionist, anti-takeover duchy. Arcelor would gain no protection from the directive. The EC's analysis of the combination yielded only minor objections, allowing Mittal to proceed with its offer. The next day the U.S. SEC found that the Dofasco stichting structure was not an issue as far as it was concerned.

On May 18, Mittal formally launched its takeover bid. The bid would remain open for 35 working days, until June 29. The following day Mittal increased its bid, offering shareholders a choice—either one share in the new combined company plus €11.10 in cash for each Arcelor share or €37.74 in cash for each Arcelor share. The offer constituted a 70% premium over Arcelor's closing share price the day before the first Mittal offer on January 27. The offer value was now €22.7billion. Lakshmi Mittal also agreed to lower his interest in the combined company to less than 50%. Belgium now openly supported the Mittal bid, while both Luxembourg and France said that it was up to Arcelor's shareholders to decide. Arcelor still had one tool at its disposal: the right to issue an additional 30% in shares to the market without shareholder approval.

The Russian White Knight. On May 26, Arcelor unexpectedly announced that it would merge with the largest steel and mining firm in Russia, OAO Severstal. The company was controlled by Alexei Mordashov, a Russian *oligarch*, a Russian businessman who gained power and wealth during the post-Soviet privatization of the 1990s.[12] His political ties were strong; he had already consulted with Russian President Putin.

Under the Severstal proposal, Arcelor would purchase the 90% share in Severstal held by Mordashov, who would use that money (plus additional debt) to take a 32% share of Arcelor. He could not acquire additional shares for a minimum of four years. This prevented the deal from triggering Luxembourg's definition of a corporate takeover. And he was restricted for five years from selling any of his shares. Severstal would have six of the 18 board seats and included a €140 million breakup fee to Mordashov if the deal failed. Arcelor's CEO and chairman would both keep their jobs under the merger agreement.

Arcelor's board formally rejected Mittal's revised offer on June 11. The following day Arcelor's board recommended to shareholders that they accept the Severstal merger proposal. Arcelor's press release stated:

> *"[H]aving consulted Morgan Stanley on the financial aspects of Mittal Steel's revised offer, the board has unanimously concluded that Mittal Steel's current offer is inadequate as it continues to undervalue Arcelor; the Severstal transaction is a more attractive alternative from a strategic, financial and social point of view."*

Arcelor's planned share buyback plan now became much more significant. Arcelor would buy back 150 million

[11] A *stichting* (foundation in English) is a Dutch special purpose legal entity with limited liability but possessing no share capital. The structure separated ownership and control. During the World War II Dutch companies transferred ownership to stichtings based in the Netherlands Antilles (Caribbean) in an effort to protect them from German occupiers.

[12] Mordashov often used an analogy to characterize his meteoric rise to power. "I was at the rear of the camel train heading across the desert when the train turned on itself and I found myself at the front."

of its own shares from current shareholders (the open market) at €44 each, a substantial premium over Arcelor's current share price of €33. Mordashov's share of Arcelor would, as a result, rise to 38%. This would be above the 33.3% mandatory bid threshold under Luxembourg law. Luxembourg quickly waived its mandatory bid rule on the Severstal merger.

Arcelor scheduled the shareholder vote on Severstal for June 19. The vote would be unusual. Instead of asking shareholders to approve the merger, shareholders would have to explicitly vote no on the deal to stop the deal, a *veto-vote*. Arcelor shareholders found the Severstal proposal difficult to understand, suggesting that it was an "anti-Mittal" strategy and not a strategy for growth. Severstal now revised its offer to reduce its share in Arcelor from 32% to 25%. Mordashov promised not to go over 33% in the future without making a tender offer for the entire firm.

Shareholders had until July 5 to tender their shares to Mittal Steel. The shareholder vote on Severstal was rescheduled from June 19 to June 30. A Luxembourg court then declared Arcelor's share buyback plan illegal, canceling the buyback vote on June 21. Shareholders would vote on the Mittal offer on June 26.

The Deal

Arcelor and Mittal continued their discussions, now in earnest, as shareholder and governmental pressures increased. Mittal, in a final push to secure an agreement, increased its offer to €40.37 per share. Mittal's final accepted offer was a combination of cash and shares: 13 Mittal shares + €150.60 in cash in exchange for 12 Arcelor shares, or €40.37 per share. Mittal's share price at that time was €25.68. On June 25 an agreement was announced. Arcelor's board would recommend shareholders approve the Mittal offer.

MINI-CASE QUESTIONS

1. What is the core value proposition that Mittal Steel believes justifies this large, complex, hostile acquisition? Will it be worth it? To whom?
2. What are the public arguments and possible private reasons that Arcelor opposes the combination?
3. Arcelor's defensive actions were extensive. Detail the theory and execution of the multitude of defensive tactics used by Arcelor.
4. Ultimately, which entity do you believe has the power in today's global marketplace to govern a cross-border acquisition like Mittal's acquisition of Arcelor?

Questions

18.1 Capital Budgeting Theoretical Framework. Capital budgeting for a foreign project uses the same theoretical framework as domestic capital budgeting. What are the basic steps in domestic capital budgeting?

18.2 Foreign Complexities. Capital budgeting for a foreign project is considerably more complex than the domestic case. What are the factors that add complexity?

18.3 Project versus Parent Valuation. Why should a foreign project be evaluated both from a project and parent viewpoint?

18.4 Viewpoint and Net Present Value. Which viewpoint, project or parent, gives results closer to the traditional meaning of net present value (NPV) in capital budgeting?

18.5 Viewpoint and Consolidated Earnings. Which viewpoint gives results closer to the effect on consolidated earnings per share?

18.6 Operating and Financing Cash Flows. Capital projects provide both operating cash flows and financial cash flows. Why are operating cash flows preferred for domestic capital budgeting but financial cash flows given major consideration in international projects?

18.7 Risk-Adjusted Return. Should the anticipated internal rate of return (IRR) for a proposed foreign project be compared to (a) alternative home country proposals, (b) returns earned by local companies in the same industry and/or risk class, or (c) both? Justify your answer.

18.8 Blocked Cash Flows. In the evaluation of a potential foreign investment, how should a multinational firm evaluate cash flows in the host foreign country that are blocked from being repatriated to the firm's home country?

18.9 Host Country Inflation. How should an MNE factor host country inflation into its evaluation of an investment proposal?

18.10 Cost of Equity. A foreign subsidiary does not have an independent cost of capital. However, in order to estimate the discount rate for a comparable host-country firm, the analyst should try to calculate a hypothetical cost of capital. How is this done?

18.11 Viewpoint Cash Flows. What are the differences in the cash flows used in a project point of view analysis and a parent point of view analysis?

18.12 Foreign Exchange Risk and Capital Budgeting. How is foreign exchange risk sensitivity factored into the capital budgeting analysis of a foreign project?

18.13 Expropriation Risk. How is expropriation risk factored into the capital budgeting analysis of a foreign project?

18.14 Real Option Analysis. What is real option analysis? How is it a better method of making investment decisions than traditional capital budgeting analysis?

18.15 Mergers and Acquisitions Business Drivers. What are the primary driving forces that motivate cross-border mergers and acquisitions?

18.16 Three Stages of Cross-Border Acquisitions. What are the three stages of a cross-border acquisition? What are the core financial elements integral to each stage?

18.17 Currency Risks in Cross-Border Acquisitions. What are the currency risks that arise in the process of making a cross-border acquisition?

18.18 Contingent Currency Exposure. What are the largest contingent currency exposures that arise in the process of pursuing and executing a cross-border acquisition?

Problems

18.1 Finisterra, S.A. Finisterra, S.A., located in the state of Baja California, Mexico, manufactures frozen Mexican food, which enjoys a large following in the U.S. states of California and Arizona to the north. In order to be closer to its U.S. market, Finisterra is considering moving some of its manufacturing operations to southern California. Operations in California would begin in year 1 and have the following attributes.

Assumptions	Value
Sales price per unit, year 1 (US$)	$5.00
Sales price increase, per year	3.00%
Initial sales volume, year 1, units	1,000,000
Sales volume increase, per year	10.00%
Production costs per unit, year 1	$ 4.00
Production cost per unit increase, per year	4.00%
General and administrative expenses, per year	$100,000
Depreciation expenses, per year	$ 80,000
Spot exchange rate (Peso=US$1.00)	Year 0: 8.00 Year 1: 9.00 Year 2: 10.00 Year 3: 11.00
Finisterra's WACC (pesos)	16.00%
Terminal value discount rate 20.00%	20.00%

The operations in California will pay 80% of its accounting profit to Finisterra as an annual cash dividend. Mexican taxes are calculated on grossed up dividends from foreign countries, with a credit for host-country taxes already paid. What is the maximum U.S. dollar price Finisterra should offer in year 1 for the investment?

18.2 Schism Systems. Schism Systems Inc. manufactures design components for personal computers. Until the present, manufacturing has been subcontracted to other companies, but for reasons of quality control Schism has decided to manufacture itself in Asia. Analysis has narrowed the choice to two possibilities, Penang, Malaysia, and Manila, the Philippines.

At the moment only the summary of expected, after-tax, cash flows displayed below is available. Although most operating outflows would be in Malaysian ringgit or Philippine pesos, some additional U.S. dollar cash outflows (expenses) would be necessary, also shown in the table. The Malaysia ringgit currently trades at MYR4.20 = USD1.00 and the Philippine peso trades at PHP50.00 = USD1.00. Schism expects the Malaysian ringgit to appreciate 2.0% per year against the dollar, and the Philippine peso to depreciate 5.0% per year against the dollar. If the weighted average cost of capital for Schism Systems is 14.0%, which project looks most promising on the basis of present value?

Problem 18.2: Schism Cash Flow Estimates

Schism in Penang (after-tax)	2022	2023	2024	2025	2026	2027
Net ringgit cash flows	(MYR 26,000)	MYR 8,000	MYR 6,800	MYR 7,400	MYR 9,200	MYR 10,000
Dollar cash outflows	USD 0	(USD 100)	(USD 120)	(USD 150)	(USD 150)	USD 0
Schism in Manila (after-tax)						
Net peso cash flows	(PHP 560,000)	PHP 190,000	PHP 180,000	PHP 200,000	PHP 210,000	PHP 200,000
Dollar cash outflows	USD 0	(USD 100)	(USD 200)	(USD 300)	(USD 400)	USD 0

18.3 Grenouille Properties. Grenouille Properties (U.S.) expects to receive cash dividends from a French joint venture over the coming three years. The first dividend, to be paid one year from now on December 31, is expected to be €720,000. The dividend is then expected to grow 10.0% per year over the following two years. The current exchange rate is $1.1940 = €1.00. Grenouille's weighted average cost of capital is 12%.

a. What is the present value of the expected euro dividend stream if the euro is expected to appreciate 4.00% per annum against the dollar?
b. What is the present value of the expected dividend stream if the euro were to depreciate 3.00% per annum against the dollar?

18.4 Natural Mosaic. Natural Mosaic Company (U.S.) is considering investing INR50,000,000 in India to create a wholly owned tile manufacturing plant to export to the European market. After five years, the subsidiary would be sold to Indian investors for INR100,000,000. A pro forma income statement for the Indian operation predicts the generation of INR7,000,000 of annual cash flow, is listed in the following table.

Sales revenue	INR30,000,000
Less cash operating expenses	(17,000,000)
Gross income	13,000,000
Less depreciation expenses	(1,000,000)
Earnings before interest and taxes	12,000,000
Less Indian taxes at 50%	(6,000,000)
Net income	6,000,000
Add back depreciation	1,000,000
Annual cash flow	INR7,000,000

The initial investment will be made on December 31, 2021, and cash flows will occur on December 31 of each succeeding year. Annual cash dividends to Natural Mosaic from India will equal 75% of accounting income. The U.S. corporate tax rate is 21% and the Indian corporate tax rate is 25%. Because the Indian tax rate is greater than the U.S. tax rate, annual dividends paid to Natural Mosaic will not be subject to additional taxes in the United States. There are no capital gains taxes on the final sale. Natural Mosaic uses a weighted average cost of capital of 14% on domestic investments but will add six percentage points for the Indian investment because of perceived greater risk. Natural Mosaic forecasts the Indian rupee to U.S. dollar exchange rate for December 31 on the next six years are listed as follows.

INR = USD1.00		INR = USD1.00	
2021	76	2024	88
2022	80	2025	92
2023	84	2026	96

What is the net present value and internal rate of return on this investment?

18.5 Carambola de Honduras. Slinger Wayne, a U.S.-based private equity firm, is trying to determine what it should pay for a tool manufacturing firm in Honduras named Carambola. Slinger Wayne estimates that Carambola will generate a free cash flow of 13 million Honduran lempiras (Lp) next year (2022) and that this free cash flow will continue to grow at a constant rate of 8.0% per annum indefinitely.

A private equity firm like Slinger Wayne, however, is not interested in owning a company for long, and plans to sell Carambola at the end of three years for approximately 10 times Carambola's free cash flow in that year. The current spot exchange rate is, Lp23.90=$1.00, but the Honduran inflation rate is expected to remain at a relatively high rate of 16.0% per annum compared to the U.S. dollar inflation rate of only 2.0% per annum. Slinger Wayne expects to earn at least a 20% annual rate of return on international investments like Carambola.

a. What is Carambola worth if the Honduran lempira were to remain fixed over the three-year investment period?
b. What is Carambola worth if the Honduran lempira were to change in value over time according to purchasing power parity?

18.6 Wenceslas Refining Company. Privately owned Wenceslas Refining Company is considering investing in the Czech Republic so as to have a refinery source closer to its European customers. The original investment in Czech korunas (CZK) would amount to CZK250 million, or USD11,627,907 at the current exchange rate of CZK21.50 = USD1.00, all in fixed assets, which will be depreciated over 10 years by the straight-line method. An additional CZK100,000,000 will be needed for working capital. Wenceslas does not believe it can forecast exchange rates so assumes they will remain fixed at the current spot rate over the entire period.

For capital budgeting purposes Wenceslas assumes sale as a going concern at the end of the third year at a price, after all taxes, equal to the net book value of fixed assets alone (not including working capital). All free cash flow, basically net income, will be repatriated to the United States as a dividend each year. In evaluating the venture, the U.S. dollar forecasts are shown in the following table.

Problem 18.6: Wenceslas Refining

Assumptions	0	1	2	3
Original investment (Czech korunas, CZK)	CZK 250,000,000			
Spot exchange rate CZK = USD1.00	CZK 21.50	CZK 21.50	CZK 21.50	CZK 21.50
Unit demand		700,000	900,000	1,000,000
Unit sales price		USD 32.00	USD 33.00	USD 34.00
Fixed cash operating expenses		USD 1,000,000	USD 1,030,000	USD 1,060,000
Depreciation		USD 500,000	USD 500,000	USD 500,000
Investment in working capital (CZK)	CZK 100,000,000			

Variable manufacturing costs are expected to be 50% of sales. No additional funds need be invested in the U.S. subsidiary during the period under consideration. The Czech Republic imposes no restrictions on repatriation of any funds of any sort. The Czech corporate tax rate is 19% and the United States rate is 21%. Both countries allow a tax credit for taxes paid in other countries. Wenceslas uses 12% as its cost of capital, and its objective is to maximize present value.

Is the investment attractive to Wenceslas Refining?

Hermosa Beach Components (U.S.)

Use the following information and assumptions to answer Problems 18.7–18.10.

Hermosa Beach Components, Inc., of California exports 24,000 sets of low-density light bulbs per year to Argentina under an import license that expires in five years. In Argentina, the bulbs are sold for the Argentine peso equivalent of $60 per set. Direct manufacturing costs in the United States and shipping together amount to $40 per set. The market for this type of bulb in Argentina is stable, neither growing nor shrinking, and Hermosa holds the major portion of the market.

The Argentine government has invited Hermosa to open a manufacturing plant so imported bulbs can be replaced by local production. If Hermosa makes the investment, it will operate the plant for five years and then sell the building and equipment to Argentine investors at net book value at the time of sale plus the value of any net working capital. (Net working capital is the amount of current assets less any portion financed by local debt.) Hermosa will be allowed to repatriate all net income and depreciation funds to the United States each year. Hermosa traditionally evaluates all foreign investments in U.S. dollar terms.

- **Investment.** Hermosa's anticipated cash outlay in U.S. dollars in 2012 would be as follows:

Building and equipment	$1,000,000
Net working capital	$1,000,000
Total investment	$2,000,000

All investment outlays will be made in 2012, and all operating cash flows will occur at the end of years 2013 through 2017.

- **Depreciation and Investment Recovery.** Building and equipment will be depreciated over five years on a straight-line basis. At the end of the fifth year, the $1,000,000 of net working capital may also be repatriated to the United States, as may the remaining net book value of the plant.
- **Sales Price of Bulbs.** Locally manufactured bulbs will be sold for the Argentine peso equivalent of $60 per set.
- **Operating Expenses per Set of Bulbs.** Material purchases are as follows:

Materials purchased in Argentina (U.S. dollar equivalent)	$20 per set
Materials imported from Hermosa Beach (U.S.)	10 per set
Total variable costs	$30 per set

- **Transfer Prices.** The $10 transfer price per set for raw material sold by the parent consists of $5 of direct and indirect costs incurred in the United States on their manufacture, creating $5 of pre-tax profit to Hermosa Beach.

- **Taxes.** The corporate income tax rate is 28% in both Argentina and the United States (combined federal and state/province). There are no capital gains taxes on the future sale of the Argentine subsidiary, either in Argentina or the United States.
- **Discount Rate.** Hermosa Components uses a 15% discount rate to evaluate all domestic and foreign projects.

18.7 Hermosa Components: Baseline Analysis. Evaluate the proposed investment in Argentina by Hermosa Components (U.S.). Hermosa's management wishes the baseline analysis to be performed in U.S. dollars (and implicitly also assumes the exchange rate remains fixed throughout the life of the project). Create a project viewpoint capital budget and a parent viewpoint capital budget. What do you conclude from your analysis?

18.8 Hermosa Components: Revenue Growth Scenario. As a result of their analysis in Problem 18.7, Hermosa wishes to explore the implications of being able to grow sales volume by 4% per year. Argentine inflation is expected to average 5% per year, so sales price and material cost increases of 7% and 6% per year, respectively, are thought reasonable. Although material costs in Argentina are expected to rise, U.S.-based costs are not expected to change over the five-year period. Evaluate this scenario for both the project and parent viewpoints. Is the project under this revenue growth scenario acceptable?

18.9 Hermosa Components: Revenue Growth and Sales Price Scenario. In addition to the assumptions employed in Problem 18.8, Hermosa now wishes to evaluate the prospect of being able to sell the Argentine subsidiary at the end of year 5 at a multiple of the business's earnings in that year. Hermosa believes that a multiple of six is a conservative estimate of the market value of the firm at that time. Evaluate the project and parent viewpoint capital budgets.

18.10 Hermosa Components: Revenue Growth, Sales Price, and Currency Risk Scenario. Melinda Deane, a new analyst at Hermosa and a recent MBA graduate, believes that it is a fundamental error to evaluate the Argentine project's prospective earnings and cash flows in dollars, rather than first estimating their Argentine peso (Ps) value and then converting cash flow returns to the United States in dollars. She believes the correct method is to use the end-of-year spot rate in 2012 of Ps3.50 = $1.00 and assume it will change in relation to purchasing power. (She is assuming U.S. inflation to be 1% per annum and Argentine inflation to be 5% per annum.) She also believes that Hermosa should use a risk-adjusted discount rate in Argentina which reflects Argentine capital costs (20% is her estimate) and a risk-adjusted discount rate for the parent viewpoint capital budget (18%) on the assumption that international projects in a risky currency environment should require a higher expected return than other lower-risk projects. How do these assumptions and changes alter Hermosa's perspective on the proposed investment?

Answers to Selected End-of-Chapter Problems

Chapter 1: Multinational Financial Management: Challenges and Opportunities

1.6 a. $0.9444
b. ¥94.44

1.16 a. $16.83
b. $12.72

Chapter 2: The International Monetary System

2.7 -41.82%

2.11 1.1398

2.16 $40,257.65

Chapter 3: The Balance of Payments

Questions	2010	2011	2012	2013	2014	2015	2016	2017	2018	2019	2020
3.1 What is Australia's balance on goods? (goods exports – goods imports)	11.335	22.744	–8.276	7.311	2.190	–19.013	–5.795	10.503	20.943	48.014	39.940
3.2 What is Australia's balance on services? (services credit – services debit)	–5.150	–10.181	–13.167	–14.731	–11.274	–8.762	–4.442	–3.300	–3.849	–1.045	10.035
3.3 What is Australian's balance on goods and services? (balance on goods + balance on services)	6.186	12.563	–21.443	–7.421	–9.084	–27.775	–10.238	7.202	17.094	46.969	49.975
3.4 What is Australian's current account balance? (the sum of the four balances listed above, goods, services, income and current transfers)	–44.714	–44.431	–64.483	–47.872	–43.398	–56.959	–41.035	–35.952	–29.786	8.033	33.829

Chapter 4: Financial Goals and Corporate Governance

4.1 a. 25.000%
 b. 33.333%
 c. Dividend yield = 8.333%, capital gains = 25.00%, total shareholder return = 33.333%

4.2 a. 64.23%
 b. 4.19%
 c. 71.12%

Chapter 5: The Foreign Exchange Market

5.3 a. 1.0238
 b. AUD 1,024

5.7 a. Profit of 26,143.79
 b. Loss of (26,086.96)

Chapter 6: International Parity Conditions

6.2 a. 1.0941
 b. 1.1155, and 948.19.

6.9 A CIA profit potential of -0.042% tells Takeshi he should borrow Japanese yen and invest in the higher yielding currency, the U.S. dollar, to earn a CIA profit of 55,000.

Chapter 7: Foreign Currency Futures and Options

7.1 a. Yize should buy a call on Singapore dollars
 b. $0.65046
 c. Gross profit = $0.05000 Net profit = $0.04954
 d. Gross profit = $0.15000 Net profit = $0.14954

7.5 a. ($49,080.00)
 b. $38,920.00
 c. ($9,080.00)

Chapter 8: Interest Rate Derivatives and Swaps

	3-month	**6-month**
8.3 a. Discount on sale	$6.07	$23.26
b. Simple yield	0.0607%	0.2331%
c. Annualized yield	0.2432%	0.4668%

8.5 a. 15-year mortgage: $1,662
 30-year mortgage: $1,261
 b. $1,957

c. 15-year mortgage: ($12,000)
30-year mortgage: ($12,000)

Chapter 9: Exchange Rate Determination and Forecasting

9.2 -13.79%

9.4 -80.00%

Chapter 10: Transaction Exposure

10.2 Do nothing: Could be anything
Forward: $216,049.38
Money market: $212,190.81
Forward is preferable choice if bank allows an expanded line

10.7 Foreign exchange loss of $921,400,000

Chapter 11: Translation Exposure

11.1 a. Translation loss is ($2,400,000)
b. Loss is accumulated on the consolidated balance sheet in the CTA account, and does not pass through consolidated income if the subsidiary is foreign currency functional

11.5 Net exposure is $U420,000, and a translation exposure to the U.S. parent of $21,000

Chapter 12: Operating Exposure

12.1 a. $9,984,000
b. To be paid out of monthly cash flow

12.4 Alternative 1: Keep same Chinese sale price. Cum PV = USD 262,919,509
Alternative 2: Raise Chinese sale price. Cum PV = USD 296,903,613

Chapter 13: The Global Cost and Availability of Capital

13.6 Domestic: 7.0210%
Global: 4.7945%

13.7 a. 6.550%
b. 5.950%

Chapter 14: Raising Equity and Debt Globally

14.4 7.7818

14.8 4.960%

Chapter 15: Multinational Tax Management

15.1 a. $1,319,200
 b. 38.8%
 c. $1,530,000 and 45.0%

15.4 a. No additional US taxes are due
 b. Costa Rica payout should be 73.33% for a total effective tax rate of 35.0%
 c. 35.0%

Chapter 16: International Trade Finance

16.1 a. 5.128%
 b. $196,000.00

16.2 Amount received is $2,973,750, at an all-in-cost of 11.765%

Chapter 17: Foreign Direct Investment and Political Risk

No quantitative problems in this chapter.

Chapter 18: Multinational Capital Budgeting and Cross Border Acquisitions

18.1 Cumulative PV = Ps28,442,771 or $3,555,346

18.5 a. $4,899,930
 b. $3,459,790

Glossary

Absolute advantage. The ability of an individual party or country to produce more of a product or service with the same inputs as another party. It is therefore possible for a country to have no absolute advantage in any international trade activity. *See also* Comparative advantage.

Absolute purchasing power parity. The theory that the exact rate of exchange between two currencies is found by equalizing the purchasing power of the two currencies.

Accounting exposure. Another name for translation exposure. *See* Translation exposure.

ADR. *See* American Depositary Receipt.

Affiliate. *See* Foreign affiliate.

Affiliated. In business, a close association between two companies. Usually implies a partial but not controlling equity or ownership position by one in the other.

Affiliated party. A related party, as in a branch or subsidiary of a multinational enterprise.

Agency theory. The costs and risks of aligning interests between shareholders of the firm and their agents, management, in the conduct of firm business and strategy. Also referred to as the *agency problem* or *agency issue*.

All-in cost (AIC). The total cost, including interest rate and fees, associated with a loan or debt obligation.

American Depositary Receipt (ADR). A certificate of ownership, issued by a U.S. bank, representing a claim on underlying foreign securities. ADRs may be traded in lieu of trading in the actual underlying shares.

American option. An option that can be exercised at any time up to and including the expiration date.

American terms. Foreign exchange quotations for the U.S. dollar, expressed as the number of U.S. dollars per unit of non-U.S. currency.

Anchor currency. *See* Reserve currency.

Angel investor. An investor who provides capital for small business startups.

Anticipated exposure. A foreign exchange exposure that is believed by management to have a very high likelihood of occurring, but is not yet contractual, and is therefore not yet certain.

Appreciation. In the context of exchange rate changes, a rise in the foreign exchange value of a currency that is pegged to other currencies or to gold. Also called revaluation.

Arbitrage. A trading strategy based on the purchase of a commodity, including foreign exchange, in one market at one price while simultaneously selling it in another market at a more advantageous price, in order to obtain a risk-free profit on the price differential.

Arbitrager. An individual or company that practices arbitrage.

Arm's length price. The price at which a willing buyer and a willing, unrelated seller freely agree to carry out a transaction. In effect, a free market price. Applied by tax authorities in judging the appropriateness of transfer prices between related companies.

Ask. The price at which a dealer is willing to sell foreign exchange, securities, or commodities. Also called offer price.

Asset market approach. A strategy that determines whether foreigners are willing to hold claims in monetary form, depending on an extensive set of investment considerations or drivers.

At-the-money (ATM). An option whose exercise price is the same as the spot price of the underlying currency.

Aval. An endorsement by a third party, acting as guarantor, for the full amount of a debt. The third party (guarantor) commits to cover the payment of the amount of the credit title and its interest in the event the original debtor does not fulfill his or her obligation.

Backlog exposure. The period of time between contract initiation and fulfillment through delivery of services or shipping of goods.

Back-to-back loan. A loan in which two companies in separate countries borrow each other's currency for a specific period of time and repay the other's currency at an agreed maturity. Sometimes the two loans are channeled through an intermediate bank. Back-to-back financing is also called link financing. Also known as a *parallel loan* or a *credit swap*.

Balance of payments (BOP). A financial statement summarizing the flow of goods, services, and investment funds between residents of a given country and residents of the rest of the world.

Balance of trade (BOT). An entry in the balance of payments measuring the difference between the monetary value of merchandise exports and merchandise imports.

Balance on goods and services. A sub-balance within the Current Account of a nation's balance of payments, indicating the net position in the export and import of both goods manufacturing and services trade.

Balance sheet hedge. *See* Money market hedge.

Bank draft. A check for payment drawing upon a bank's own account; a check whose payment is guaranteed by a bank.

Bank for International Settlements (BIS). A bank in Basel, Switzerland, that functions as a bank for European central banks.

Bankers' acceptance. An unconditional promise by a bank to make payment on a draft when it matures. This comes in the form of the bank's endorsement (acceptance) of a draft drawn against that bank in accordance with the terms of a letter of credit issued by the bank.

Barter. International trade conducted by the direct exchange of physical goods, rather than by separate purchases and sales at prices and exchange rates set by a free market.

Base currency. The *base* or *unit currency* is the USD in a currency quotation, such as USD1.0750 = EUR1.00.

Basic balance. In a country's balance of payments, the net of exports and imports of goods and services, unilateral transfers, and long-term capital flows.

Basis erosion and profit shifting (BEPS). The reallocation of corporate profits to lower-tax environments, away from higher-tax environments that are arguably their proper state.

Basis point. One one-hundredth of one percentage point, often used in quotations of spreads between interest rates or to describe changes in yields in securities.

Basis risk. A type of interest rate risk in which the interest rate base is mismatched.

Bearer bond. Corporate or governmental debt in bond form that is not registered to any owner. Possession of the bond implies ownership, and interest is obtained by clipping a coupon attached to the bond. The advantage of the bearer form is easy transfer at the time of a sale, easy use as collateral for a debt, and what some cynics call taxpayer anonymity, meaning that governments find it hard to trace interest payments in order to collect income taxes. Bearer bonds are common in Europe but are seldom issued any more in the United States. The alternate form to a bearer bond is a registered bond.

Beta. Second letter of the Greek alphabet, used as a statistical measure of risk in the Capital Asset Pricing Model. Beta is the covariance between returns on a given asset and returns on the market portfolio, divided by the variance of returns on the market portfolio.

Bid. The price that a dealer is willing to pay to purchase foreign exchange or a security. Also referred to as the *bid rate*.

Bid-ask spread. The difference between a bid and an ask quotation.

Bill of exchange (B/E). A written order requesting one party (such as an importer) to pay a specified amount of money at a specified time to the writer of the bill. Also called a draft. *See* Sight draft.

Bill of lading (B/L). A contract between a common carrier and a shipper to transport goods to a named destination. The bill of lading is also a receipt for the goods. Bills of lading are usually negotiable, meaning they are made to the order of a particular party and can be endorsed to transfer title to another party.

Billing exposure. The time it takes to get paid in cash after the issuance of an account receivable (A/R).

Black market. An illegal foreign exchange market.

Blocked funds. Funds in one country's currency that may not be exchanged freely for foreign currencies because of exchange controls.

Branch. A foreign operation not incorporated in the host country, in contrast to a subsidiary.

Bretton Woods Agreement. An agreement negotiated at a 1944 international conference and in effect from 1945 to 1971 that established the international monetary system. The conference was held in Bretton Woods, New Hampshire, United States.

BRIC. A frequently used acronym for the four largest emerging market countries—Brazil, Russia, India, and China.

Bulldog. British pound-denominated bond issued within the United Kingdom by a foreign borrower.

Cable. The U.S. dollar per British pound cross rate.

Call. An option with the right, but not the obligation, to buy foreign exchange or another financial contract at a specified price within a specified time. *See also* Foreign currency option.

Capital account. A section of the balance of payments accounts. Under the revised format of the International Monetary Fund, the capital account measures capital transfers and the acquisition and disposal of nonproduced, nonfinancial assets. Under traditional definitions, still used by many countries, the capital account measures public and private international lending and investment. Most of the traditional definition of the capital account is now incorporated into IMF statements as the financial account.

Capital Asset Pricing Model (CAPM). A theoretical model that relates the return on an asset to its risk, where risk is the contribution of the asset to the volatility of a portfolio. Risk and return are presumed to be determined in competitive and efficient financial markets.

Capital budgeting. The analytical approach used to determine whether investment in long-lived assets or projects is viable. *See also* Multinational capital budgeting.

Capital control. Restrictions, requirements, taxes or prohibitions on the movements of capital across borders as imposed and enforced by governments.

Capital flight. Movement of funds out of a country because of political risk.

Capital gain. A profit or loss arising from the sale of an asset of any kind such as a stock, bond, business, or real estate.

Capital lifecycle. The changing capital needs, in both form, maturity, and amount, which a firm experiences from inception through maturity.

Capital markets. The financial markets of various countries in which various types of long-term debt and/or ownership securities, or claims on those securities, are purchased and sold.

Capital mobility. The degree to which private capital moves freely from country to country in search of the most promising investment opportunities.

Carry trade. The strategy of borrowing in a low interest rate currency to fund investing in higher yielding currencies. Also termed *currency carry trade*, the strategy is speculative in that currency risk is present and not managed or hedged.

Cash rates. Forward exchange rate contracts of one year or less in maturity. If longer than one year, forward contracts are often called *swap rates*.

Caveat emptor. Latin for "buyer beware."

Certificate of Deposit (CD). A negotiable receipt issued by a bank for funds deposited for a certain period of time. CDs can be purchased or sold prior to their maturity in a secondary market, making them an interest-earning marketable security.

CFR (cost and freight). *See* Cost and freight (CFR).

CIF (cost, insurance, and freight). *See* Cost, insurance, and freight (CIF).

Classical gold standard. *See* Gold standard.

Clearinghouse. An institution through which financial obligations are cleared by the process of settling the obligations of various members.

Clearinghouse Interbank Payments System (CHIPS). A New York-based computerized clearing system used by banks to settle interbank foreign exchange obligations (mostly U.S. dollars) between members.

Collateral. *See* margin.

Collective action clause (CCA). A contractual clause in a bond or other debt agreement allowing a supermajority of bondholders to agree to a debt restructuring that is legally binding on all bondholders.

Commercial risk. In banking, the likelihood that a foreign debtor will be unable to repay its debts because of business events, as distinct from political ones.

Comparative advantage. A theory that everyone gains if each nation specializes in the production of those goods that it produces relatively most efficiently and imports those goods that other countries produce relatively most efficiently. The theory supports free trade arguments.

Competitive exposure. *See* Operating exposure.

Consolidated financial statement. A corporate financial statement in which accounts of a parent company and its subsidiaries are added together to produce a statement which reports the status of the worldwide enterprise as if it were a single corporation. Internal obligations are eliminated in consolidated statements.

Consolidation. In the context of accounting for multinational corporations, the process of preparing a single reporting currency financial statement, which combines financial statements of subsidiaries that are in fact measured in different currencies.

Contagion. The spread of a crisis in one country to its neighboring countries and other countries with similar characteristics—at least in the eyes of cross-border investors.

Contingent foreign currency exposure. The final determination of the exposure is contingent upon another firm's decision, such as a decision to invest or the winning of a business or construction bid.

Contingent Value Right (CVR). A right given to shareholders of an acquired company (or company facing acquisition) that promises them to receive additional cash or shares if a specified event occurs. CVRs are similar to options because they carry an expiration date related to the time in which the contingent event must occur.

Continuous Linked Settlements (CLS). A U.S. financial institution that provides foreign exchange settlement services to members.

Contractual hedge. A foreign currency hedging agreement or contract, typically using a financial derivative such as a forward contract or foreign currency option.

Controlled foreign corporation (CFC). A foreign corporation in which U.S. shareholders own more than 50% of the combined voting power or total value. Under U.S. tax law, U.S. shareholders may be liable for taxes on undistributed earnings of the controlled foreign corporation.

Convertible currency. A currency that can be exchanged freely for any other currency without government restrictions.

Corporate governance. The relationship among stakeholders used to determine and control the strategic direction and performance of an organization.

Corporate inversion. The reincorporation of a company from a low-tax country environment from a high-tax country environment. Nearly exclusively applies to the United States.

Corporate social responsibility (CSR). A form of corporate self-regulation to pursue business in a legal, ethical manner, and consistent with a series of social norms such as environmental and social sustainability.

Correspondent bank. A bank that holds deposits for and provides services to another bank, located in another geographic area, on a reciprocal basis.

Cost and freight (CFR). Price, as quoted by an exporter, that includes the cost of transportation to the named port of destination.

Cost, insurance, and freight (CIF). Exporter's quoted price including the cost of packaging, freight or carriage, insurance premium, and other charges paid in respect of the goods from the time of loading in the country of export to their arrival at the named port of destination or place of transshipment.

Cost of capital. The cost, expressed as a percentage and on a weighted average basis, of raising equity and debt at current market rates. More commonly referred to as the *weighted average cost of capital*, or WACC.

Counterparty. The opposite party in a double transaction, such as a swap or back-to-back loan, which involves an exchange of financial instruments or obligations now and a reversal of that same transaction at an agreed-upon later date.

Counterparty risk. The potential exposure any individual firm bears that the second party to any financial contract may be unable to fulfill its obligations under the contract's specifications.

Country risk. In banking, the likelihood that unexpected events within a host country will influence a client's or a government's ability to repay a loan. Country risk is often divided into sovereign (political) risk and foreign exchange (currency) risk. *See also* Country-specific risk.

Country-specific risk. Political risk that affects the MNE at the country level, such as transfer risk (blocked funds) and cultural and institutional risks.

Covered interest arbitrage (CIA). The process whereby an investor earns a risk-free profit by

(1) borrowing funds in one currency, (2) exchanging those funds in the spot market for a foreign currency, (3) investing the foreign currency at interest rates in a foreign country, (4) selling forward, at the time of original investment, the investment proceeds to be received at maturity, (5) using the proceeds of the forward sale to repay the original loan, and (6) sustaining a remaining profit balance.

Covered transaction. A foreign currency exposure which has been hedged or "covered."

Covering. A transaction in the forward foreign exchange market or money market that protects the value of future cash flows. Covering is another term for hedging. *See* Hedging.

Crawling peg. A foreign exchange rate system in which the exchange rate is adjusted very frequently to reflect prevailing rate of inflation.

Credit risk. The possibility that a borrower's credit worth, at the time of renewing a credit, is reclassified by the lender.

Credit spread. The added interest cost assessed a borrower to compensate the lender or investor for the assessed credit risk of the borrower. The spread is typically based upon the credit rating of the borrower. Also termed *credit risk premium*.

Credit swap. *See* Back-to-back loan.

Cross-border acquisition. A purchase in which one firm acquires another firm located in a different country.

Cross-currency interest rate swap. *See* Currency swap.

Cross-currency swap. *See* Currency swap.

Cross-listing. The listing of shares of common stock on two or more stock exchanges.

Cross rate. An exchange rate between two currencies derived by dividing each currency's exchange rate with a third currency. Colloquially, it is often used to refer to a specific currency pair such as the euro/yen cross rate, as the yen/dollar and dollar/euro are the more common currency quotations.

Crowdfunding. The practice of funding a startup business or enterprise of some kind by raising money in small amounts from a large number of people, typically via the Internet.

Cryptocurrency. A currency created and exchanged using the secure information processes and principles of cryptography. One of the first and most well-known cryptocurrencies is Bitcoin.

Cumulative translation adjustment (CTA) account. An entry in a translated balance sheet in which gains and/or losses from translation have been accumulated over a period of years.

Currency Adjustment Clause (CAC). A contractual arrangement to share or split changes in exchange rates between two parties. Commonly used in long-term supplier contracts.

Currency board. A currency board exists when a country's central bank commits to back its money supply entirely with foreign reserves at all times.

Currency contract period. The period immediately following a change in the value of a currency in which existing contracts do not allow any change in prices—yet.

Currency risk. The variance in expected cash flows arising from unexpected changes in exchange rates.

Currency swap. A transaction in which two counterparties exchange specific amounts of two different currencies at the outset, and then repay over time according to an agreed-upon contract that reflects interest payments and possibly amortization of principal. In a currency swap, the cash flows are similar to those in a spot and forward foreign exchange transaction. *See also* Swap.

Currency switching. Where a firm uses foreign exchange received in the course of business to settle obligations to a third party, often located in a third country.

Current account. In the balance of payments, the net flow of goods, services, and unilateral transfers (such as gifts) between a country and all foreign countries.

Current rate method. A method of translating the financial statements of foreign subsidiaries into the parent's reporting currency. All assets and liabilities are translated at the current exchange rate.

D/A. Documents against acceptance. D/A is an international trade term.

Deductible expense. A business expense that is recognized by tax officials as deductible toward the firm's income tax liabilities.

Degree of pass-through. *See* Exchange rate pass-through.

Delta. The change in an option's price divided by the change in the price of the underlying instrument. Hedging strategies are based on delta ratios.

Depositary receipt (DR). *See* American Depositary Receipt (ADR).

Depreciation. A market-driven change in the value of a currency that results in reduced value or purchasing power.

Derivative. *See* Financial derivative.

Devaluation. The action of a government or central bank authority to drop the spot foreign exchange value of a currency that is pegged to another currency or to gold.

Dim Sum Bond Market. The market for Chinese renminbi (yuan) denominated securities as issued in Hong Kong.

Direct intervention. The purchase or the sale of a country's home currency by its own fiscal or monetary authority in order to influence the value of the domestic currency.

Direct investment. *See* Foreign direct investment (FDI).

Direct quote. The price of a unit of foreign exchange expressed in the home country's currency. The term has meaning only when the home country is specified.

Direct tax. A tax paid directly to the government by the person on whom it is imposed.

Directed issue. *See* Directed public share issue.

Directed public share issue. An issue that is targeted at investors in a single country and underwritten in whole or in part by investment institutions from that country.

Discount. In the foreign exchange market, the amount by which a currency is cheaper for future delivery than for spot (immediate) delivery. The opposite of discount is premium.

Dividend yield. The current period dividend distribution as a percentage of the beginning of period share price.

Dollarization. The use of the U.S. dollar as the official currency of a country.

Draft. An unconditional written order requesting one party (such as an importer) to pay a specified amount of money at a specified time to the order of the writer of the draft. Also called a bill of exchange. Personal checks are one type of draft.

Dutch Disease. A term invented by the *Economist* magazine, referring to the process of a country's currency appreciating in value as a result of the discovery and development of a natural resource like natural gas or oil. The result of the currency appreciation is to make other exports from the country less competitive in the export market. The Dutch reference was the *Economist*'s use of the term to explain what happened to the Dutch florin after the discovery of natural gas in the Netherlands in 1959.

Earnings stripping. *See* Basis erosion and profit shifting (BEPS).

Economic exposure. Another name for operating exposure. *See* Operating exposure.

Effective tax rate. Actual taxes paid as a percentage of actual income before tax.

Efficient market. A market in which all relevant information is already reflected in market prices. The term is most frequently applied to foreign exchange markets and securities markets.

Equity issuance. The issuance to the public market of shares of ownership in a publicly traded company.

Equity listing. The listing of a company's shares on a public stock exchange.

Equity risk premium. The average annual return of the market expected by investors over and above riskless debt.

Euro. A single new currency unit adopted by the 11 participating members of the European Union's European Monetary System in January 1999, replacing their individual currencies.

Eurobank. A bank, or bank department, that bids for time deposits and makes loans in currencies other than that of the country where the bank is located.

Eurobond. A bond originally offered outside the country in whose currency it is denominated. For example, a dollar-denominated bond originally offered for sale to investors outside the United States.

Eurocommercial paper (ECP). Short-term notes (30, 60, 90, 120, 180, 270, and 360 days) sold in international money markets.

Eurocredit. Bank loans to MNEs, sovereign governments, international institutions, and banks denominated in eurocurrencies and extended by banks in countries other than the country in whose currency the loan is denominated.

Eurocurrency. A currency deposited in a bank located in a country other than the country issuing the currency.

Eurodollar. A U.S. dollar deposited in a bank outside the United States. A eurodollar is a type of eurocurrency. Also termed a *Eurodollar deposit*.

Euroequity. A new equity issue that is underwritten and distributed in multiple foreign equity markets, sometimes simultaneously with distribution in the domestic market.

Euronote market. Short- to medium-term debt instruments sold in the eurocurrency market.

European Central Bank (ECB). Conducts monetary policy of the European Monetary Union. Its goal is to safeguard the stability of the euro and minimize inflation.

European Currency Unit (ECU). A composite currency created by the European Monetary System prior to the euro, which was designed to function as a reserve currency numeraire. The ECU was used as the numeraire for denominating a number of financial instruments and obligations.

European Monetary System (EMS). A system of exchange rate and monetary system linkages first established in 1979 between 15 European countries. The EMS laid the groundwork for the eventual creation of the euro. The EMS has continued to expand its membership over time.

European option. An option that can be exercised only on the day on which it expires.

European terms. Foreign exchange quotations for the U.S. dollar, expressed as the number of non-U.S. currency units per U.S. dollar.

European Union (EU). The official name of the former European Economic Community (EEC) as of January 1, 1994.

Eurozone. The countries that officially use the euro as their currency.

Exchange rate. *See* foreign exchange rate.

Exchange Rate Mechanism (ERM). The means by which members of the EMS formerly maintained their currency exchange rates within an agreed-upon range with respect to the other member currencies.

Exchange rate pass-through. The degree to which the prices of imported and exported goods change as a result of exchange rate changes.

Exercise price. Same as the *strike price*; the agreed upon rate of exchange within an option contract to buy or sell the underlying asset.

Export credit insurance. Provides assurance to the exporter or the exporter's bank that, should the foreign customer default on payment, the insurance company will pay for a major portion of the loss. *See also* Foreign Credit Insurance Association (FCIA).

Export-Import Bank (Eximbank). A U.S. government agency created to finance and otherwise facilitate imports and exports.

Exposed asset. An asset whose value is subject to change as a result of the translation of its value from local currency financial statements to home currency financial statements as a result of financial statement consolidation. The change in value typically results from moving from historical to current exchange rates for translation and remeasurement.

Expropriation. Official government seizure of private property, recognized by international law as the right of any sovereign state provided expropriated owners are given prompt compensation and fair market value in convertible currencies.

Factoring. Specialized firms, known as factors, purchase receivables at a discount on either a nonrecourse or recourse basis.

Fair value. The estimated true market value of an item or asset.

FAS (free alongside ship). An international trade term in which the seller's quoted price for goods includes all costs of delivery of the goods alongside a vessel at the port of embarkation.

FIBOR. Frankfurt interbank offered rate.

Financial account. A section of the balance of payments accounts. Under the revised format of the International Monetary Fund, the financial account measures long-term financial flows including direct foreign investment, portfolio investments, and other long-term movements. Under the traditional definition, which is still used by many countries, items in the financial account were included in the capital account.

Financial derivative. A financial instrument, such as a futures contract or option, whose value is derived from an underlying asset like a stock or currency.

Financing cash flow. Cash flows originating from financing activities of the firm, including interest payments and dividend distributions.

Firm-specific risk. Political risk that affects the MNE at the project or corporate level. Governance risk due to goal conflict between an MNE and its host government is the main political firm-specific risk.

Fisher Effect. A theory that nominal interest rates in two or more countries should be equal to the required real rate of return to investors plus compensation for the expected amount of inflation in each country.

Fixed exchange rates. Foreign exchange rates tied to the currency of a major country (such as the United States), to gold, or to a basket of currencies such as Special Drawing Rights.

Flexible exchange rates. The opposite of fixed exchange rates. The foreign exchange rate is adjusted periodically by the country's monetary authorities in accordance with their judgment and/or an external set of economic indicators.

Floating exchange rates. Foreign exchange rates determined by demand and supply in an open market that is presumably free of government interference.

Floating-rate note (FRN). Medium-term securities with interest rates pegged to LIBOR and adjusted quarterly or semiannually.

Follow-on offering (FO). Additional offerings of equity shares post-IPO.

Forced delistings. The requirement by a stock exchange for a publicly traded share on that exchange to be delisted from active trading, typically from failure to maintain a minimum level of market capitalization.

Foreign affiliate. A foreign business unit that is less than 50% owned by the parent company.

Foreign bond. A bond issued by a foreign corporation or government for sale in the domestic capital market of another country and denominated in the currency of that country.

Foreign Credit Insurance Association (FCIA). An unincorporated association of private commercial insurance companies, in cooperation with the Export-Import Bank of the United States, that provides export credit insurance to U.S. firms.

Foreign currency. Any currency other than that used officially for contracts and transactions in the domestic economy.

Foreign currency exchange rate. Same as *foreign exchange rate.*

Foreign currency intervention. Any activity or policy initiative by a government or central bank with the intent of changing a currency value on the open market. They may include *direct intervention*, where the central bank may buy or sell its own currency, or *indirect intervention*, in which it may change interest rates in order to change the attractiveness of domestic currency obligations in the eyes of foreign investors.

Foreign currency option. A financial contract or derivative which guarantees the holder the right to buy or sell a specific amount of foreign currency at a specific rate by a stated expiration or maturity date.

Foreign currency translation. *See* Translation.

Foreign direct investment (FDI). Purchase of physical assets, such as plant and equipment, in a foreign country, to be managed by the parent corporation. FDI is distinguished from foreign portfolio investment.

Foreign exchange broker. An individual or firm that arranges foreign exchange transactions between two parties but is not itself a principal in the trade. Foreign exchange brokers earn a commission for their efforts.

Foreign exchange dealer (or trader). An individual or firm that buys foreign exchange from one party (at a bid price), and then sells it (at an ask price) to another party. The dealer is a principal in two transactions and profits via the spread between the bid and ask prices.

Foreign exchange intervention. The active entry into the foreign exchange market by buying and selling a currency by an official authority in order to manage or fix the currency's value relative to other traded currencies.

Foreign exchange rate. The price of one country's currency in terms of another currency, or in terms of a commodity such as gold or silver. Also termed *foreign currency exchange rate. See also* Exchange rate.

Foreign exchange risk. The likelihood that an unexpected change in exchange rates will alter the home currency value of foreign currency cash payments expected from a foreign source. Also, the likelihood that an unexpected change in exchange rates will alter the amount of home currency needed to repay a debt denominated in a foreign currency.

Foreign subsidiary. A foreign operation incorporated in the host country and owned 50% or more by a parent corporation. Foreign operations that are not incorporated are called branches.

Foreign tax credit. The amount by which a domestic firm may reduce (credit) domestic income taxes for income tax payments to a foreign government.

Foreign tax neutrality. The principle that tax obligations or tax burdens are the same on taxable earnings, regardless of where the earnings were generated, in domestic or foreign markets.

Forfaiting (forfeiting). A technique for arranging nonrecourse medium-term export financing, used most frequently to finance imports into Eastern Europe. A third party, usually a specialized financial institution, guaranteeing the financing.

Forward-ATM. The strike rate or exercise price of a foreign exchange derivative set equivalent to the forward exchange rate.

Forward contract. An agreement to exchange currencies of different countries at a specified future date and at a specified forward rate.

Forward discount. The difference between spot and forward rates, expressed as an annual percentage, also known as the *forward premium*.

Forward exchange rate (Forward rate). An exchange rate quoted for settlement at some future date. The rate used in a forward transaction.

Forward-forward swap. The exchange of two different maturities of forward exchange contracts.

Forward hedge. The use of a forward exchange contract to hedge or protect the value of a foreign currency denominated transaction.

Forward premium. *See* Forward discount.

Forward rate. *See* Forward exchange rate.

Forward rate agreement (FRA). An interbank-traded contract to buy or sell interest rate payments on a notional principal.

Forward transaction. An agreed-upon foreign exchange transaction to be settled at a specified future date, often one, two, or three months after the transaction date.

Free alongside ship (FAS). *See* FAS (free alongside ship).

Free cash flow. Operating cash flow less capital expenditures (capex).

Free float. The portion of publicly traded shares of a corporation that are held by public investors as opposed to locked-in stock held by promoters (underwriters), company officers, controlling-interest investors, or government.

Fronting loan. A parent-to-subsidiary loan that is channeled through a financial intermediary such as a large international bank in order to reduce political risk. Presumably government authorities are less likely to prevent a foreign subsidiary repaying an established bank than repaying the subsidiary's corporate parent.

Functional currency. In the context of translating financial statements, the currency of the primary economic environment in which a foreign subsidiary operates and in which it generates cash flows.

Futures, or futures contracts. *See* Interest rate futures.

Gamma. A measure of the sensitivity of an option's delta ratio to small unit changes in the price of the underlying security.

Generally Accepted Accounting Principles (GAAP). Approved accounting principles for U.S. firms, defined by the Financial Accounting Standards Board (FASB).

Global depositary receipt (GDR). Similar to American Depositary Receipts (ADRs), it is a bank certificate issued in multiple countries for shares in a foreign company. Actual company shares are held by a foreign branch of an international bank. The shares are traded as domestic shares, but are offered for sale globally by sponsoring banks.

Global registered shares (GRS). Similar to ordinary shares, global registered shares have the added benefit of being tradable on equity exchanges around the globe in a variety of currencies.

Global reserve currency. *See* Reserve currency.

Global-specific risks. Political risks that originate at the global level, such as terrorism, the antiglobalization movement, environmental concerns, poverty, and cyber attacks.

Gold standard or Gold-exchange standard. A monetary system in which currencies are defined in terms of their gold content, and payment imbalances between countries are settled in gold.

Greenfield investment. An initial investment in a new foreign subsidiary with no predecessor operation in that location. This is in contrast to a new subsidiary created by the purchase of an already existing operation. An investment that starts, conceptually if not literally, with an undeveloped "green field."

Haircut. The percentage of the market value of a financial asset recognized as the collateral value or redeemed value of the asset.

Hard currency. A freely convertible currency that is not expected to depreciate in value in the foreseeable future.

Hedging. Purchasing a contract (including forward foreign exchange) or tangible good that will rise in value and offset a drop in value of another contract or tangible good. Hedges are undertaken to reduce risk by protecting an owner from loss.

Herstatt risk. The risk arising from foreign exchange trades between banks operating in different countries and different time zones. Also termed *settlement risk*.

Historical exchange rate. In accounting, the exchange rate in effect when an asset or liability was acquired.

Home currency. The currency of a company's incorporation; the currency for financial reporting purposes.

Hoover Hedges. Hedges constructed to protect the value of a long-term investment or loan in a foreign currency.

Hot money. Money that moves internationally from one currency and/or country to another in response to interest rate differences, and moves away immediately when the interest advantage disappears.

Hurdle rate. The required rate of return by a firm on a potential new investment in order to approve accepting the investment. The rate is typically based on the company's current cost of capital, including debt and equity. In some cases the firm will require some premium or additional margin on certain investments above and beyond its cost of capital in the calculation of the hurdle rate (e.g., cost of capital + premium = hurdle rate).

Hyperinflation countries. Countries with a very high rate of inflation. Under United States FASB 52, these are defined as countries where the cumulative three-year inflation amounts to 100% or more.

Impossible trinity. An ideal currency would have exchange rate stability, full financial integration, and monetary independence.

In-the-money (ITM). Circumstance in which an option is profitable, excluding the cost of the premium, if exercised immediately.

Indication. A quotation, typically in the form of a bid rate and ask rate, for a currency or other financial asset.

Indirect intervention. Actions taken by central banks or other monetary authorities to influence the supply and demand for a country's own currency. The most common form of indirect intervention is the alteration of interest rates.

Indirect quote. The price of a unit of a home country's currency expressed in terms of a foreign country's currency.

Initial public offering (IPO). The initial sale of shares of ownership of a company to the general public. The issuing firm raises capital for the conduct of its business and return to its original owners through the IPO.

Integrated foreign entity. An entity that operates as an extension of the parent company, with cash flows and general business lines that are highly interrelated with those of the parent.

Interest rate futures. Exchange-traded agreements calling for future delivery of a standard amount of any good, e.g., foreign exchange, at a fixed time, place, and price.

Interest rate parity (IRP). A theory that the differences in national interest rates for securities of similar risk and maturity should be equal to but opposite in sign (positive or negative) to the forward exchange rate discount or premium for the foreign currency.

Interest rate risk. The risk to the organization arising from interest-bearing debt obligations, either fixed or floating rate obligations. It is typically used to refer to the changing interest rates which a company may incur by borrowing at floating rates of interest.

Interest rate swap. A transaction in which two counterparties exchange interest payment streams of different character (such as floating vs. fixed), based on an underlying notional principal amount.

Internal rate of return (IRR). A capital budgeting approach in which a discount rate is found that matches the present value of expected future cash inflows with the present value of outflows.

International Bank for Reconstruction and Development (IBRD or World Bank). International development bank owned by member nations that makes development loans to member countries.

International CAPM (ICAPM). A strategy in which the primary distinction in the estimation of the cost of equity for an individual firm using an internationalized version of the domestic capital asset pricing model is the definition of the "market" and a recalculation of the firm's beta for that market.

International Fisher effect. A theory that the spot exchange rate should change by an amount equal to the difference in interest rates between two countries.

International Monetary Fund (IMF). An international organization created in 1944 to promote exchange rate stability and provide temporary financing for countries experiencing balance of payments difficulties.

International Monetary Market (IMM). A branch of the Chicago Mercantile Exchange that specializes in trading currency and financial futures contracts.

International monetary system. The structure within which foreign exchange rates are determined, international trade and capital flows are accommodated, and balance of payments adjustments made.

International parity conditions. In the context of international finance, a set of basic economic relationships that provide for equilibrium between spot and forward foreign exchange rates, interest rates, and inflation rates.

International Swaps and Derivatives Association (ISDA). A New York City trade association for over-the-counter (OTC) derivatives. The ISDA maintains the documentation used in most of the financial services trading of financial derivatives used globally.

Intrafirm trade. Trade in goods and services between incorporated units of the same multinational business or enterprise.

Intrinsic value. The financial gain if an option is exercised immediately.

Investment agreement. An agreement that spells out specific rights and responsibilities of both the investing foreign firm and the host government. Also termed an *international investment agreement.*

Investment grade. A credit rating, typically assigned by Moody's, Standard & Poor's, or Fitch, symbolizing the assured ability of a borrower to repay in a timely manner regardless of business or market conditions. Denoted as BBB- (or equivalent by credit rating agency) or higher.

Islamic finance. Banking or financing activity that is consistent with the principles of *sharia* and Islamic economics.

J-curve. The adjustment path of a country's trade balance following a devaluation or significant depreciation of the country's currency. The path first worsens as a result of existing contracts before improving as a result of more competitive pricing conditions.

Joint venture (JV). A business venture that is owned by two or more entities, often from different countries.

Lag. In the context of leads and lags, payment of a financial obligation later than is expected or required.

Lambda. A measure of the sensitivity of an option premium to a unit change in volatility.

Law of one price. The concept that if an identical product or service can be sold in two different markets, and no restrictions exist on the sale or transportation costs of moving the product between markets, the product's price should be the same in both markets.

Lead. In the context of *leads and lags*, the payment of a financial obligation earlier than is expected or required.

Legal tender. A medium of payment allowed by law or recognized by a legal system to be valid for meeting a financial obligation.

Letter of credit (L/C). An instrument issued by a bank, in which the bank promises to pay a beneficiary upon presentation of documents specified in the letter.

Link financing. *See* Back-to-back loan or Fronting loan.

Liquid. The ability to exchange an asset for cash at or near its fair market value.

London Interbank Offered Rate (LIBOR). The deposit rate applicable to interbank loans in London. LIBOR is used as the reference rate for many international interest rate transactions.

Long position. A position in which foreign currency assets exceed foreign currency liabilities. The opposite of a long position is a short position.

Maastricht Treaty. A treaty among the 12 European Union countries that specified a plan and timetable for the introduction of a single European currency, to be called the euro.

Macro risk. *See* Country-specific risk.

Macroeconomic uncertainty. Operating exposure's sensitivity to key macroeconomic variables, such as exchange rates, interest rates, and inflation rates.

Managed float. A country allows its currency to trade within a given band of exchange rates.

Margin. A deposit made as security for a financial transaction otherwise financed on credit.

Marked-to-market. The condition in which the value of a futures contract is assigned to market value daily, and all changes in value are paid in cash daily. The value of the contract is revalued using the closing price for the day. The amount to be paid is called the variation margin.

Market capitalization. The total market value of a publicly traded company, calculated as the total number of shares outstanding multiplied by the market-determined price per share.

Market liquidity. The degree to which a firm can issue a new security without depressing the existing market price, as well as the degree to which a change in price of its securities elicits a substantial order flow.

Matching currency cash flows. The strategy of offsetting anticipated continuous long exposure to a particular currency by acquiring debt denominated in that currency.

Merchant bank. A bank that specializes in helping corporations and governments finance by any of a variety of market and/or traditional techniques. European merchant banks are sometimes differentiated from clearing banks, which tend to focus on bank deposits and clearing balances for the majority of the population.

MIBOR. Madrid interbank offered rate.

Micro risk. *See* Firm-specific risk.

Monetary assets or liabilities. Assets in the form of cash or claims to cash (such as accounts receivable), or liabilities payable in cash. Monetary assets minus monetary liabilities are called net monetary assets.

Monetary/nonmonetary method. A method of translating the financial statements of foreign subsidiaries into the parent's reporting currency. All monetary accounts are translated at the current rate, and all nonmonetary accounts are translated at their historical rates. Sometimes called temporal method in the United States.

Money laundering. The process of depositing or inserting illegally generated money or cash into the financial system.

Money market hedge. The use of foreign currency borrowing to reduce transaction or accounting foreign exchange exposure.

Money markets. The financial markets in various countries in which various types of short-term debt instruments, including bank loans, are purchased and sold.

Moral hazard. When an individual or organization takes on more risk than it would normally as a result of the existence or support of a secondary insuring or protecting authority or organization.

Multinational capital budgeting. The financial analysis of foreign investment projects requiring the use of discounted cash flow analysis. Also termed *international capital budgeting* and *capital budgeting of foreign projects*.

Multinational enterprise (MNE). A firm that has operating subsidiaries, branches, or affiliates located in foreign countries.

National approach (to taxes). *See* Worldwide approach (to taxes).

Natural hedge. The use or existence of an offsetting or matching cash flow from firm operating activities to hedge a currency exposure.

Negotiable instrument. A written draft or promissory note, signed by the maker or drawer, that contains an unconditional promise or order to pay a definite sum of money on demand or at a determinable future date, and is payable to order or to bearer. A holder of a negotiable instrument is entitled to payment despite any personal disagreements between the drawee and maker.

Net international investment position (NIIP). The net difference between a country's external financial assets and liabilities as defined by nationality of ownership. A country's external debt includes both its government debt and private debt, and similarly its public and privately held legal residents.

Net operating cash flow (NOCF). The cash generated by the normal operations of the business. It is considered a measure of the value created by the business. It is calculated as the sum of net income, depreciation, and changes in net working capital.

Net present value (NPV). A capital budgeting approach in which the present value of expected future cash inflows is subtracted from the present value of outflows.

Net working capital (NWC). Accounts receivable plus inventories less accounts payable.

Netting. The process of netting intracompany payments in order to reduce the size and frequency of cash and currency exchanges.

Nominal exchange rate. The actual foreign exchange quotation, in contrast to *real exchange rate*, which is adjusted for changes in purchasing power. May be constructed as an index.

Nondeliverable forward (NDF). A forward or futures contract on currencies, settled on the basis of the differential between the contracted forward rate and occurring spot rate, but settled in the currency of the traders. For example, a forward contract on the Chinese yuan that is settled in dollars, not yuan.

North American Free Trade Agreement (NAFTA). A treaty allowing free trade and investment between Canada, the United States, and Mexico.

Notional principal. The size of a derivative contract, in total currency value, as used in futures contracts, forward contracts, option contracts, or swap agreements.

NPV. *See* Net present value (NPV).

Offer. *See* Ask.

Offer rate. The price of sale or ask as in *bid-ask* and *bid-offer*.

Official reserves account. Total reserves held by official monetary authorities within the country, such as gold, SDRs, and major currencies.

OLI Paradigm. An attempt to create an overall framework to explain why MNEs choose foreign direct investment rather than serve foreign markets through alternative modes such as licensing, joint ventures, strategic alliances, management contracts, and exporting.

Open account. A sale where goods are shipped and delivered before payment is due or made. Payment is typically made anywhere between 30 and 90 days later, depending on industry and national practices.

Operating cash flows. The primary cash flows generated by a business from the conduct of trade, typically composed of earnings, depreciation and amortization, and changes in net working capital.

Operating exposure. The potential for a change in expected cash flows, and thus in value, of a foreign subsidiary as a result of an unexpected change in exchange rates. Also called economic exposure.

Option. *See* Foreign currency option.

Option collar. The simultaneous purchase of a put option and sale of a call option, or vice versa, resulting in a form of hybrid option.

Order bill of lading. A shipping document through which possession and title to the shipment reside with the owner of the bill.

Out-of-the-money (OTM). An option that would not be profitable, excluding the cost of the premium, if exercised immediately.

Outright forward. *See* Forward rate.

Outright forward transaction. *See* Forward transaction.

Overseas Private Investment Corporation (OPIC). A U.S. government-owned insurance company that insures U.S. corporations against various political risks.

Overshooting. A behavior in financial markets in which a major market adjustment in price changes "overshoots" or surpasses the likely value it will settle at after a longer adjustment period. A market movement akin to an "overreaction."

Over-the-counter (OTC) market. A market for share of stock, options (including foreign currency options), or other financial contracts conducted via electronic connections between dealers. The over-the-counter market has no physical location or address, and is thus differentiated from organized exchanges that have a physical location where trading takes place.

Panda Bond. The issuance of a yuan-denominated bond in the Chinese market by a foreign borrower.

Parallel loan. Another name for a back-to-back loan, in which two companies in separate countries borrow each other's currency for a specific period of time and repay the other's currency at an agreed maturity. *See also* Back-to-back loan.

Participating forward. A complex option position which combines a bought put and a sold call option at the same strike price to create a net zero position. Also called zero-cost option and forward participation agreement.

Pass-through or Pass-through period. The time it takes for an exchange rate change to be reflected in market prices of products or services.

Phi. The expected change in an option premium caused by a small change in the foreign interest rate (interest rate for the foreign currency).

PIBOR. Paris interbank offered rate.

Pip. Percentage in point, in reference to an exchange rate fluctuation.

Plain vanilla swap. An interest rate swap agreement to exchange fixed interest payments for floating interest payments, all in the same currency.

Points. The smallest units of price change quoted, given a conventional number of digits in which a quotation is stated.

Political risk. The possibility that political events in a particular country will influence the economic well-being of firms in that country.

Portfolio investment. Purchase of foreign stocks and bonds, in contrast to foreign direct investment.

Premium. In a foreign exchange market, the amount by which a currency is more expensive for future delivery than for spot (immediate) delivery. The opposite of premium is discount.

Price currency. The quote currency in a currency price quotation. The euro (EUR) is the price currency in a typical exchange rate quotation on the dollar-euro such as USD1.0750 = EUR1.00.

Price elasticity of demand. From economic theory, the percentage change in the quantity demanded as a result of a one percent change in the product price.

Principal agent problem. *See* Agency theory.

Private equity (PE). Asset ownership in a business that is not publicly traded. Private equity investments are typically made by private equity firms or private equity funds.

Private placement. The sale of a security issue to a small set of qualified institutional buyers.

Project finance. A financial structure used in the financing for long-term capital projects, which are large in scale, long in life, and generally high in risk. Under a project financing, the project alone is liable for all debt-financing service, and not the corporate or project sponsors.

Project financing. Arrangement of financing for long-term capital projects, large in scale, long in life, and generally high in risk.

Prospectus. A document disclosing the prospective risks and returns associated with the proposed public sale of a security. The prospectus commonly includes material information such as a description of the company's business, financial statements, biographies of officers and directors, detailed information about their compensation, any litigation that is pending, a list of material properties, and any other material information.

Protectionism. A political attitude or policy intended to inhibit or prohibit the import of foreign goods and services. The opposite of free trade policies.

Psychic distance. Firms tend to invest first in countries with a similar cultural, legal, and institutional environment.

Public debt. The debt obligation of a governmental body or sovereign authority.

Purchasing power parity (PPP). A theory that the price of internationally traded commodities should be the same in every country, and hence the exchange rate between the two currencies should be the ratio of prices in the two countries.

Put. An option to sell foreign exchange or financial contracts. *See also* Foreign currency option.

Qualified institutional buyer (QIB). An entity (except a bank or a savings and loan) that owns and invests on a discretionary basis a minimum of $100 million in securities of non-affiliates.

Quota. A limit, mandatory or voluntary, set on the import of a product.

Quotation. In foreign exchange trading, the pair of prices (bid and ask) at which a dealer is willing to buy or sell foreign exchange.

Quotation exposure. The period of time in which a seller has quoted a fixed price in a foreign currency to a potential buyer, but the buyer has yet to agree.

Quote currency. *See* Price currency.

Range forward. A complex option position that combines the purchase of a put option and the sale of a call option with strike prices equidistant from the forward rate. Also called *flexible forward*, *cylinder option*, *option fence*, *mini-max*, and *zero-cost tunnel*.

Real option analysis. The application of option theory to capital budgeting decisions.

Reference rate. The rate of interest used in a standardized quotation, loan agreement, or financial derivative valuation.

Relative purchasing power parity. A theory that if the spot exchange rate between two countries starts in equilibrium, any change in the differential rate of inflation between them tends to be offset over the long run by an equal but opposite change in the spot exchange rate.

Remittance. A transfer of money or currency from one party to another in payment or gift or saving.

Renminbi (RMB). The alternative official name (the yuan, CNY) of the currency of the People's Republic of China.

Reporting currency. In the context of translating financial statements, the currency in which a parent firm prepares its own financial statements. Usually this is the parent's home currency.

Repositioning of funds. The movement of funds from one currency or country to another. An MNE faces a variety of political, tax, foreign exchange, and liquidity constraints that limit its ability to move funds easily and without cost.

Repricing risk. The risk of changes in interest rates charged or earned at the time a financial contract's rate is reset.

Reserve currency. A currency used by a government or central banking authority as a resource asset or currency to be used in market interventions to alter the market value of the domestic currency.

Residential approach. The levy of taxes against the worldwide income earned by a business by home country tax authorities regardless of where or in which country the income was earned.

Revaluation. A rise in the foreign exchange value of a currency that is pegged to other currencies or to gold. Also called *appreciation.*

Rho. The expected change in an option premium caused by a small change in the domestic interest rate (interest rate for the home currency).

Risk. The likelihood that an actual outcome will differ from an expected outcome. The actual outcome could be better or worse than expected (two-sided risk), although in common practice risk is more often used only in the context of an adverse outcome (one-sided risk). Risk can exist for any number of uncertain future situations, including future spot rates or the results of political events.

Risk-free rate of interest. The return on an asset assumed to possess no possibility of failure to pay. Typically a debt security issued by a government like a U.S. Treasury bill, note, or bond.

Risk-sharing. A contractual arrangement in which the buyer and seller agree to share or split currency movement impacts on payments between them.

Roll-over risk. *See* Credit risk.

Rules of the Game. The basis of exchange rate determination under the international gold standard during most of the 19th and early 20th centuries. All countries agreed informally to follow the rule of buying and selling their currency at a fixed and predetermined price against gold.

Samurai bond. Yen-denominated bond issued within Japan by a foreign borrower.

Sarbanes-Oxley Act. An act passed in 2002 to regulate corporate governance in the United States.

Seasoned offering. *See* Follow-on offering (FO).

SEC Rule 144A. Permits qualified institutional buyers to trade privately placed securities without requiring SEC registration.

Section 482. The set of U.S. Treasury regulations governing transfer prices.

Securitization. The replacement of nonmarketable loans (such as direct bank loans) with negotiable securities (such as publicly traded marketable notes and bonds), so that the risk can be spread widely among many investors, each of whom can add or subtract the amount of risk carried by buying or selling the marketable security.

Seigniorage. The net revenues or proceeds garnered by a government from the printing of its money.

Selective hedging. Hedging only exceptional exposures or the occasional use of hedging when management has a definite expectation of the direction of exchange rates.

Self-sustaining foreign entity. One that operates in the local economic environment independent of the parent company.

Selling short (shorting). The sale of an asset which the seller does not (yet) own. The premise is that the seller believes he will be able to purchase the asset for contract fulfillment at a lower price before sale contract expiration.

Shareholder. An individual or institution that holds legal ownership to a share or stock in a publicly traded company.

Shareholder wealth maximization (SWM). The corporate goal of maximizing the total value of the shareholders' investment in the company.

Short position. *See* Long position.

SIBOR. Singapore interbank offered rate.

Sight draft. A bill of exchange (B/E) that is due on demand; i.e., when presented to the bank. *See also* Bill of exchange (B/E).

Source approach. Another name for the *territorial approach to taxation.*

Sovereign credit risk. The risk that a host government may unilaterally repudiate its foreign obligations or may prevent local firms from honoring their foreign obligations. Sovereign risk is often regarded as a subset of political risk.

Sovereign debt. The debt obligation or a sovereign or governmental authority or body.

Sovereign spread. The credit spread paid by a sovereign borrower on a major foreign currency-denominated debt obligation. For example, the credit spread paid by the Venezuelan government to borrow U.S. dollars over and above a similar maturity issuance by the U.S. Treasury.

Special Drawing Right (SDR). An international reserve asset, defined by the International Monetary Fund as the value of a weighted basket of five currencies.

Speculation. An attempt to make a profit by trading on expectations about future prices.

Speculative grade. A credit quality that is below BBB, below investment grade. The designation implies a possibility of borrower default in the event of unfavorable economic or business conditions.

Spot rate. The price at which foreign exchange can be purchased (its bid) or sold (its ask) in a spot transaction. *See* Spot transaction.

Spot transaction. A foreign exchange transaction to be settled (paid for) on the second following business day.

Spread. The difference between the bid (buying) quote and the ask (selling) quote.

Stakeholder capitalism model (SCM). Another name for corporate wealth maximization.

State-owned enterprise (SOE). Any organization or business which is owned (in-whole or in-part) and controlled by government, typically created to conduct commercial business activities.

Statutory tax rate. The legally imposed tax rate.

Strategic alliance. A formal relationship, short of a merger or acquisition, between two companies, formed for the purpose of gaining synergies because in some aspect the two companies complement each other.

Strategic exposure. *See* Operating exposure.

Strike price. The agreed upon rate of exchange within an option contract. *See also* Exercise price.

Subpart F income. A type of foreign income, as defined in the U.S. tax code, which under certain conditions is taxed immediately in the United States even though it has not been repatriated to the United States. It is income of a type that is otherwise easily shifted offshore to avoid current taxation.

Swap or Swap transaction. In general it is the simultaneous purchase and sale of foreign exchange or securities, with the purchase executed at once and the sale back to the same party carried out at an agreed-upon price to be completed at a specified future date. Swaps include interest rate swaps, currency swaps, and credit swaps.

Swap rate. A forward foreign exchange quotation expressed in terms of the number of points by which the forward rate differs from the spot rate.

SWIFT. The Society for Worldwide Interbank Financial Telecommunication (SWIFT). The SWIFT system, initiated in 1973, is a network that allows financial institutions all over the world to send and receive information about financial transactions in a secure, standardized, and reliable manner. The SWIFT network sends payment orders, but does not facilitate the actual transfer of funds (settlement). Nearly all cross-border foreign exchange transactions are executed via SWIFT today.

Syndicated loan. A large loan made by a group of banks to a large multinational firm or government. Syndicated loans allow the participating banks to maintain diversification by not lending too much to a single borrower. Also termed a Syndicated bank credit.

Synthetic forward. A complex option position which combines the purchase of a put option and the sale of a call option, or vice versa, both at the forward rate. Theoretically, the combined position should have a net-zero premium.

Systematic risk. In portfolio theory, the risk of the market itself, i.e., risk that cannot be diversified away.

Tariff. A duty or tax on imports that can be levied as a percentage of cost or as a specific amount per unit of import.

Tax deferral. Foreign subsidiaries of MNEs pay host country corporate income taxes, but many parent countries, including the United States, defer claiming additional taxes on that foreign source income until it is remitted to the parent firm.

Tax exposure. The potential for tax liability on a given income stream or on the value of an asset. Usually used in the context of a multinational firm being able to minimize its tax liabilities by locating some portion of operations in a country where the tax liability is minimized.

Tax haven. A country with either no or very low tax rates that uses its tax structure to attract foreign investment or international financial dealings.

Tax morality. The consideration of conduct by an MNE to decide whether to follow a practice of full disclosure to local tax authorities or adopt the philosophy, "When in Rome, do as the Romans do."

Tax neutrality. In domestic tax, the requirement that the burden of taxation on earnings in home country operations by an MNE be equal to the burden of taxation on each currency equivalent of profit earned by the same firm in its foreign operations. Foreign tax neutrality requires that the tax burden on each foreign subsidiary of the firm be equal to the tax burden on its competitors in the same country.

Tax treaties. A network of bilateral treaties that provide a means of reducing double taxation.

Technical analysis. The focus on price and volume data to determine past trends that are expected to continue into the future. Analysts believe that future exchange rates are based on the current exchange rate.

TED Spread. Treasury Eurodollar Spread. The difference, in basis points, between the 3-month interest rate swap index or the 3-month LIBOR interest rate, and the 90-day U.S. Treasury bill rate. It is sometimes used as an indicator of credit crisis or fear over bank credit quality.

Temporal method. In the United States, term for a codification of a translation method essentially similar to the monetary/nonmonetary method.

Tender. To offer for sale or purchase.

Tenor. The length of time of a contract or debt obligation; loan repayment period.

Tequila effect. Term used to describe how the Mexican peso crisis of December 1994 quickly spread to other Latin American currency and equity markets through the contagion effect.

Terminal value (TV). The continuing value of a project or investment beyond the period shown in detail. It represents the present value at a future point in time of all future cash flows assuming a stable perpetual growth rate.

Terms of trade. The weighted average exchange ratio between a nation's export prices and its import prices, used to measure gains from trade. Gains from trade refers to increases in total consumption resulting from production specialization and international trade.

Territorial approach (to taxes). Also called *territorial taxation*. Taxation of income earned by firms within the legal jurisdiction of the host country, not on the country of the firm's incorporation.

Theory of comparative advantage. Based on the concept of *absolute advantage*, in which each country specializes in the production of those goods for which it is uniquely suited, the theory of comparative advantage states that exchange between these countries will result in all parties or countries being better off through specialization and exchange than by attempting to produce all at home.

Theta. The expected change in an option premium caused by a small change in the time to expiration.

Thin capitalization. When a company's capital structure is deemed to be excessively based on debt rather than equity. It is typically used to reduce domestic tax liabilities through interest-based deductions.

Time draft. A draft that allows a delay in payment. It is presented to the drawee, who accepts it by writing a notice of acceptance on its face. Once accepted, the time draft becomes a promise to pay by the accepting party. *See also* Bankers' acceptance.

Trade acceptance (T/A). An international trade term. A bill of exchange drawn directly upon and accepted by an importer or purchaser, rather than a bank, and due at a specified future time.

Tranche. An allocation of shares, typically to underwriters that are expected to sell to investors in their designated geographic markets.

Transaction exposure. The potential for a change in the value of outstanding financial obligations entered into prior to a change in exchange rates but not due to be settled until after the exchange rates change.

Transfer pricing. The setting of prices to be charged by one unit (such as a foreign subsidiary) of a multi-unit corporation to another unit (such as the parent corporation) for goods or services sold between such related units.

Translation. The remeasurement of a financial statement from one currency to another.

Translation exposure. The potential for an accounting-derived change in owners' equity resulting from exchange rate changes and the need to restate financial statements of foreign subsidiaries in the single currency of the parent corporation. *See also* Accounting exposure.

Transnational firm. A company owned by a coalition of investors located in different countries.

Transparency. The degree to which an investor can discern the true activities and value drivers of a company from the disclosures and financial results reported.

Triangular arbitrage. An arbitrage activity of exchanging currency A for currency B for currency C back to currency A to exploit slight disequilibrium in exchange rates.

Triffin Dilemma (or Triffin Paradox). The potential conflict in objectives which may arise between domestic monetary policy and currency policy when a country's currency is used as a reserve currency.

Trilemma of international finance. The difficult but required choice which a government must make between three conflicting international financial system goals: (1) a fixed exchange rate; (2) independent monetary policy; and (3) free mobility of capital.

Turnover tax. A tax based on turnover or sales, and is similar in structure to a VAT, in which taxes may be assessed on intermediate stages of a good's production.

Unaffiliated. An independent third-party. May also be further characterized by whether the third-party is known or unknown.

Uncovered interest arbitrage (UIA). The process by which investors borrow in countries and currencies exhibiting relatively low interest rates and convert the proceeds into currencies that offer much higher interest rates. The transaction is "uncovered" because the investor does not sell the higher yielding currency proceeds forward.

Unit currency. *See* Base currency.

Unsystematic risk. In a portfolio, the amount of risk that can be eliminated by diversification.

Usance draft. *See* Time draft.

Valley of Death. The period in capital raising for a startup firm between seed capital and more formal forms such as angel financing and venture capital. So-named because many business startups fail in this stage as a result of not finding funding sources.

Value-added tax. A type of national sales tax collected at each stage of production or sale of consumption goods and levied in proportion to the value added during that stage.

Value date. The date when value is given (i.e., funds are deposited) for foreign exchange transactions between banks.

Value firm. A reference to a larger, older, more mature business that typically demonstrates little movement in its share price.

Venture capitalist (VC). An investor or fund that provides capital and funding to early-stage business startups. The startups are typically considered of high potential growth and possibility as a result of unique intellectual property or technology.

Volatility. In connection with options, the standard deviation of daily spot price movement.

Vulture funds. Investment funds which specialize in acquiring debt that is in default and then pursuing legal means to obtain either collateral or full payment via legal means.

Weighted average cost of capital (WACC). The sum of the proportionally weighted costs of different sources of capital, used as the minimum acceptable target return on new investments.

Wire transfer. Electronic transfer of funds.

Working capital management. The management of the net working capital requirements (A/R plus inventories less A/P) of the firm.

World Bank. *See* International Bank for Reconstruction and Development.

Worldwide approach (to taxes). The principle that taxes are levied on the income earned by firms that are incorporated in a host country, regardless of where the income was earned.

Yankee bond. Dollar-denominated bond issued within the United States by a foreign borrower.

Yield to maturity. The rate of interest (discount) that equates future cash flows of a bond, both interest and principal, with the present market price. Yield to maturity is thus the time-adjusted rate of return earned by a bond investor.

Yuan (CNY). The official currency of the People's Republic of China, also termed the renminbi.

Index

F

G

N

O

P

Q

R

S

Currencies of the World

Country	Currency	ISO-4217 Code	Symbol
Afghanistan	Afghan afghani	AFN	
Albania	Albanian lek	ALL	
Algeria	Algerian dinar	DZD	
American Samoa	*see* U.S.		
Andorra	*see* Spain and France		
Angola	Angolan kwanza	AOA	
Anguilla	East Caribbean dollar	XCD	EC$
Antigua and Barbuda	East Caribbean dollar	XCD	EC$
Argentina	Argentine peso	ARS	
Armenia	Armenian dram	AMD	
Aruba	Aruban florin	AWG	*f*
Australia	Australian dollar	AUD	$
Austria	European euro	EUR	€
Azerbaijan	Azerbaijani manat	AZN	
Bahamas	Bahamian dollar	BSD	B$
Bahrain	Bahraini dinar	BHD	
Bangladesh	Bangladeshi taka	BDT	
Barbados	Barbadian dollar	BBD	Bds$
Belarus	Belarusian ruble	BYR	Br
Belgium	European euro	EUR	€
Belize	Belize dollar	BZD	BZ$
Benin	West African CFA franc	XOF	CFA
Bermuda	Bermudian dollar	BMD	BD$
Bhutan	Bhutanese ngultrum	BTN	Nu.
Bolivia	Bolivian boliviano	BOB	Bs.
Bosnia-Herzegovina	Bosnia and Herzegovina konvertibilna marka	BAM	KM
Botswana	Botswana pula	BWP	P
Brazil	Brazilian real	BRL	R$
British Indian Ocean Territory	*see* UK		
Brunei	Brunei dollar	BND	B$
Bulgaria	Bulgarian lev	BGN	
Burkina Faso	West African CFA franc	XOF	CFA
Burma	*see* Myanmar		
Burundi	Burundi franc	BIF	FBu
Cambodia	Cambodian riel	KHR	
Cameroon	Central African CFA franc	XAF	CFA
Canada	Canadian dollar	CAD	$
Canton and Enderbury Islands	*see* Kiribati		
Cape Verde	Cape Verdean escudo	CVE	Esc
Cayman Islands	Cayman Islands dollar	KYD	KY$
Central African Republic	Central African CFA franc	XAF	CFA
Chad	Central African CFA franc	XAF	CFA
Chile	Chilean peso	CLP	$

Country	Currency	ISO-4217 Code	Symbol
China	Chinese renminbi	CNY	¥
Christmas Island	*see* Australia		
Cocos (Keeling) Islands	*see* Australia		
Colombia	Colombian peso	COP	Col$
Comoros	Comorian franc	KMF	
Congo	Central African CFA franc	XAF	CFA
Congo, Democratic Republic	Congolese franc	CDF	F
Cook Islands	*see* New Zealand		
Costa Rica	Costa Rican colon	CRC	₡
Côte d'Ivoire	West African CFA franc	XOF	CFA
Croatia	Croatian kuna	HRK	kn
Cuba	Cuban peso	CUC	$
Cyprus	European euro	EUR	€
Czech Republic	Czech koruna	CZK	Kč
Denmark	Danish krone	DKK	Kr
Djibouti	Djiboutian franc	DJF	Fdj
Dominica	East Caribbean dollar	XCD	EC$
Dominican Republic	Dominican peso	DOP	RD$
Dronning Maud Land	*see* Norway		
East Timor	*see* Timor-Leste		
Ecuador	uses the U.S. Dollar		
Egypt	Egyptian pound	EGP	£
El Salvador	uses the U.S. Dollar		
Equatorial Guinea	Central African CFA franc	GQE	CFA
Eritrea	Eritrean nakfa	ERN	Nfa
Estonia	Estonian kroon	EEK	KR
Ethiopia	Ethiopian birr	ETB	Br
Faeroe Islands (Føroyar)	*see* Denmark		
Falkland Islands	Falkland Islands pound	FKP	£
Fiji	Fijian dollar	FJD	FJ$
Finland	European euro	EUR	€
France	European euro	EUR	€
French Guiana	*see* France		
French Polynesia	CFP franc	XPF	F
Gabon	Central African CFA franc	XAF	CFA
Gambia	Gambian dalasi	GMD	D
Georgia	Georgian lari	GEL	
Germany	European euro	EUR	€
Ghana	Ghanaian cedi	GHS	
Gibraltar	Gibraltar pound	GIP	£
Great Britain	*see* UK		
Greece	European euro	EUR	€
Greenland	*see* Denmark		

Currencies of the World (continued)

Country	Currency	ISO-4217 Code	Symbol
Grenada	East Caribbean dollar	XCD	EC$
Guadeloupe	*see* France		
Guam	*see* U.S.		
Guatemala	Guatemalan quetzal	GTQ	Q
Guernsey	*see* UK		
Guinea-Bissau	West African CFA franc	XOF	CFA
Guinea	Guinean franc	GNF	FG
Guyana	Guyanese dollar	GYD	GY$
Haiti	Haitian gourde	HTG	G
Heard and McDonald Islands	*see* Australia		
Honduras	Honduran lempira	HNL	L
Hong Kong	Hong Kong dollar	HKD	HK$
Hungary	Hungarian forint	HUF	Ft
Iceland	Icelandic króna	ISK	kr
India	Indian rupee	INR	₹
Indonesia	Indonesian rupiah	IDR	Rp
International Monetary Fund	Special Drawing Rights	XDR	SDR
Iran	Iranian rial	IRR	
Iraq	Iraqi dinar	IQD	
Ireland	European euro	EUR	€
Isle of Man	*see* UK		
Israel	Israeli new sheqel	ILS	
Italy	European euro	EUR	€
Ivory Coast	*see* Côte d'Ivoire		
Jamaica	Jamaican dollar	JMD	J$
Japan	Japanese yen	JPY	¥
Jersey	*see* UK		
Johnston Island	*see* U.S.		
Jordan	Jordanian dinar	JOD	
Kampuchea	*see* Cambodia		
Kazakhstan	Kazakhstani tenge	KZT	T
Kenya	Kenyan shilling	KES	KSh
Kiribati	*see* Australia		
Korea, North	North Korean won	KPW	W
Korea, South	South Korean won	KRW	W
Kuwait	Kuwaiti dinar	KWD	
Kyrgyzstan	Kyrgyzstani som	KGS	
Laos	Lao kip	LAK	KN
Latvia	Latvian lats	LVL	Ls
Lebanon	Lebanese lira	LBP	
Lesotho	Lesotho loti	LSL	M
Liberia	Liberian dollar	LRD	L$
Libya	Libyan dinar	LYD	LD

Country	Currency	ISO-4217 Code	Symbol
Liechtenstein	uses the Swiss Franc		
Lithuania	Lithuanian litas	LTL	Lt
Luxembourg	European euro	EUR	€
Macau	Macanese pataca	MOP	P
Macedonia (Former Yug. Rep.)	Macedonian denar	MKD	
Madagascar	Malagasy ariary	MGA	FMG
Malawi	Malawian kwacha	MWK	MK
Malaysia	Malaysian ringgit	MYR	RM
Maldives	Maldivian rufiyaa	MVR	Rf
Mali	West African CFA franc	XOF	CFA
Malta	European Euro	EUR	€
Martinique	*see* France		
Mauritania	Mauritanian ouguiya	MRO	UM
Mauritius	Mauritian rupee	MUR	Rs
Mayotte	*see* France		
Micronesia	U.S.		
Midway Islands	*see* U.S.		
Mexico	Mexican peso	MXN	$
Moldova	Moldovan leu	MDL	
Monaco	*see* France		
Mongolia	Mongolian tugrik	MNT	₮
Montenegro	*see* Italy		
Montserrat	East Caribbean dollar	XCD	EC$
Morocco	Moroccan dirham	MAD	
Mozambique	Mozambican metical	MZM	MTn
Myanmar	Myanma kyat	MMK	K
Nauru	*see* Australia		
Namibia	Namibian dollar	NAD	N$
Nepal	Nepalese rupee	NPR	NRs
Netherlands Antilles	Netherlands Antillean gulden	ANG	NA*f*
Netherlands	European euro	EUR	€
New Caledonia	CFP franc	XPF	F
New Zealand	New Zealand dollar	NZD	NZ$
Nicaragua	Nicaraguan córdoba	NIO	C$
Niger	West African CFA franc	XOF	CFA
Nigeria	Nigerian naira	NGN	₦
Niue	*see* New Zealand		
Norfolk Island	*see* Australia		
Northern Mariana Islands	*see* U.S.		
Norway	Norwegian krone	NOK	kr
Oman	Omani rial	OMR	
Pakistan	Pakistani rupee	PKR	Rs.
Palau	*see* U.S.		

Currencies of the World (continued)

Country	Currency	ISO-4217 Code	Symbol
Panama	Panamanian balboa	PAB	B/
Panama Canal Zone	*see* U.S.		
Papua New Guinea	Papua New Guinean kina	PGK	K
Paraguay	Paraguayan guarani	PYG	
Peru	Peruvian nuevo sol	PEN	S/.
Philippines	Philippine peso	PHP	₱
Pitcairn Island	*see* New Zealand		
Poland	Polish zloty	PLN	
Portugal	European euro	EUR	€
Puerto Rico	*see* U.S.		
Qatar	Qatari riyal	QAR	QR
Reunion	*see* France		
Romania	Romanian leu	RON	L
Russia	Russian ruble	RUB	R
Rwanda	Rwandan franc	RWF	RF
Samoa (Western)	*see* Western Samoa		
Samoa (America)	*see* U.S.		
San Marino	*see* Italy		
São Tomé and Príncipe	São Tomé and Príncipe dobra	STD	Db
Saudi Arabia	Saudi riyal	SAR	SR
Sénégal	West African CFA franc	XOF	CFA
Serbia	Serbian dinar	RSD	din.
Seychelles	Seychellois rupee	SCR	SR
Sierra Leone	Sierra Leonean leone	SLL	Le
Singapore	Singapore dollar	SGD	S$
Slovakia	European Euro	EUR	€
Slovenia	European euro	EUR	€
Solomon Islands	Solomon Islands dollar	SBD	SI$
Somalia	Somali shilling	SOS	Sh.
South Africa	South African rand	ZAR	R
Spain	European euro	EUR	€
Sri Lanka	Sri Lankan rupee	LKR	Rs
St. Helena	Saint Helena pound	SHP	£
St. Kitts and Nevis	East Caribbean dollar	XCD	EC$
St. Lucia	East Caribbean dollar	XCD	EC$
St. Vincent and the Grenadines	East Caribbean dollar	XCD	EC$
Sudan	Sudanese pound	SDG	
Suriname	Surinamese dollar	SRD	$
Svalbard and Jan Mayen Islands	*see* Norway		

Country	Currency	ISO-4217 Code	Symbol
Swaziland	Swazi lilangeni	SZL	E
Sweden	Swedish krona	SEK	kr
Switzerland	Swiss franc	CHF	Fr.
Syria	Syrian pound	SYP	
Tahiti	*see* French Polynesia		
Taiwan	New Taiwan dollar	TWD	NT$
Tajikistan	Tajikistani somoni	TJS	
Tanzania	Tanzanian shilling	TZS	
Thailand	Thai baht	THB	฿
Timor-Leste	uses the U.S. dollar		
Togo	West African CFA franc	XOF	CFA
Trinidad and Tobago	Trinidad and Tobago dollar	TTD	TT$
Tunisia	Tunisian dinar	TND	DT
Turkey	Turkish new lira	TRY	YTL
Turkmenistan	Turkmen manat	TMM	m
Turks and Caicos Islands	*see* U.S.		
Tuvalu	*see* Australia		
Uganda	Ugandan shilling	UGX	USh
Ukraine	Ukrainian hryvnia	UAH	
United Arab Emirates	UAE dirham	AED	
UK	British pound	GBP	£
U.S.	U.S. dollar	USD	US$
Upper Volta	*see* Burkina Faso		
Uruguay	Uruguayan peso	UYU	$U
Uzbekistan	Uzbekistani som	UZS	
Vanuatu	Vanuatu vatu	VUV	VT
Vatican	*see* Italy		
Venezuela	Venezuelan bolivar	VEB	Bs
Vietnam	Vietnamese dong	VND	₫
Virgin Islands	*see* U.S.		
Wake Island	*see* U.S.		
Wallis and Futuna Islands	CFP franc	XPF	F
Western Sahara	*see* Spain, Mauritania, and Morocco		
Western Samoa	Samoan tala	WST	WS$
Yemen	Yemeni rial	YER	
Zaïre	*see* Congo, Democratic Republic		
Zambia	Zambian kwacha	ZMK	ZK
Zimbabwe	Zimbabwean dollar	ZWD	Z$